Applications of Feminist Legal Theory to Women's Lives

SEX, VIOLENCE, WORK, AND REPRODUCTION

In the series

Women in the Political Economy
edited by Ronnie J. Steinberg

Applications of Feminist Legal Theory to Women's Lives

 SEX, VIOLENCE, WORK, AND REPRODUCTION

Edited by

D. KELLY WEISBERG

TEMPLE UNIVERSITY PRESS

Philadelphia

To Aaron and Sarah

Temple University Press, Philadelphia 19122
Copyright © 1996 by Temple University
All rights reserved
Published 1996
Printed in the United States of America

♾ The paper used in this publication meets the requirements of the American National Standard for Information Sciences—Permanence of Paper for Printed Library Materials, ANSI Z39.48–1984

Text design by Bruce Gore

Library of Congress Cataloging-in-Publication Data

Applications of feminist legal theory to women's lives : sex, violence, work, and reproduction / edited by D. Kelly Weisberg.
    p. cm. — (Women in the political economy)
   Companion volume to: Feminist legal theory. 1993.
   Includes index.
   ISBN 1-56639-423-6 (cloth : alk. paper). — ISBN 1-56639-424-4 (paper : alk. paper)
   1. Feminist jurisprudence. 2. Sex and law. 3. Women—Legal status, laws, etc. 4. Feminist theory. 5. Feminist criticism.
I. Weisberg, D. Kelly. II. Feminist legal theory. III. Series.
K349.A67 1996
340'.082—dc20   96-11491

CONTENTS

PART IV: REPRODUCTION

6. MOTHERHOOD AND REPRODUCTIVE CONTROL

A. *Motherhood*

B. *Abortion*

PREFACE

THIS BOOK is the second of two volumes of collected essays on feminist legal theory. The underlying theme explores the relationship between law, gender, and equality. The book applies notions and theories of equality to contexts of both sexuality (prostitution and pornography) and violence (rape and battering), while recognizing that these contexts are not analytically distinct because male violence against women pervades both.

Although issues of sexuality and violence galvanize public and scholarly attention, other important issues emerge on the feminist agenda. For this reason, the book also addresses employment (particularly, the work-family conflict, sex segregation, comparable worth, and sexual harassment) and reproductive freedom and control (abortion, new reproductive technologies, and adoption).

The debate over the meaning of equality is central to feminist legal theory. The first volume of this collection, *Feminist Legal Theory: Foundations,* explores fundamental theoretical issues of equality, including the meaning of equality; different models of and approaches to equality; the limitations of equality theory, including the difficulty of accommodating differences within equality analysis; the implications of woman's self-definition for women's equality (in terms of race and gender essentialism, for example); the contribution of feminist methodology; and the relevance of various theories (classic liberalism, Marxism, legal positivism, and critical legal studies, among others) to the struggle for equality.

This second volume continues the exploration of these issues as applied to substantive contexts. It examines, for example, whether specific practices (such as pornography, prostitution, and surrogacy) contribute to women's subordination or, conversely, to their empowerment; whether taking into account women's biological differences (in the contexts of battered women, rape, sexual harassment, reproductive freedom and control) contributes to women's equality or inequality; and whether women's barriers in the workplace stem from biological differences or, conversely, from discrimination.

Despite their many differences of opinion, feminist legal theorists are united by a central belief that society is patriarchal, shaped and dominated by men. Thus, feminist legal theory consists, on the one hand, of an analysis and critique of the role of law in perpetuating women's position in patriarchal society. On the other hand, feminist legal theory contains a transformative element in its exploration of methods of eliminating patriarchy.

The essays in this volume illustrate these dual objectives. They analyze the nature and extent of women's subordination in various legal contexts. In addition, they criticize existing law with an eye toward effectuating reform to improve women's status. In many areas of the law, as the reader will discover, feminist criticisms have contributed significantly to legal reforms. In other areas, feminist criticisms merely reflect the distance we have yet to travel.

A note about editing and style is necessary . The essays herein are edited works. Of necessity, many of these articles have been greatly shortened in both their text and their footnotes. Footnotes have had to be renumbered. Many subheads have been eliminated; paragraphs have occasionally been combined. Because of the editing process, some of the richness of argument and research inevitably is lost. Readers who wish a more in-depth discussion are urged to consult the original works.

Further, the footnote style of the articles in this collection by and large reflects the accepted usage of the discipline of the respective authors. While this collection was in process, the style manual for legal scholarship (*A Uniform System of Citation*) changed. Largely in response to feminist complaints, the manual now dictates citation of authors by full first names, in order not to camouflage female identity. Nonetheless, since several articles originally appeared prior to that change, the citation style of some articles reflects the earlier accepted usage.

The publication of a book is always the product of many individuals. First, I am grateful to the authors of the essays for their significant contributions to this field. Second, I would like to thank several colleagues who gave me such good counsel during the process of bringing this book to fruition—especially Lucinda Finley, Martha Chamallas, Carol Sanger, Pat Cain, and Joe Singer, as well as the anonymous reviewers.

I also want to express my gratitude to Michael Ames of Temple University Press for his superb editorial skills, moral support, and good humor throughout this lengthy endeavor. Without his foresight in 1989, perceiving the need for a book in a very young field, this two-volume collection would never have seen the light of day.

I also express appreciation to Fran Nowve who accomplished the herculean task of typing the manuscript with good grace and consummate skill. Several research assistants (especially Melissa Burke, Diane Eisenberg, Cheryl Feiner, Jenny Gutman, Kelly Happe, Lauren Knutsen, and Sonia Martin) provided valuable help. Without their cite checking, literature reviews, and administrative assistance (especially indexing and proofing), this book would not have been possible. And, as always, Laura Perritore of the Hastings Law Library provided conscientious and invaluable assistance. Last, but certainly not least, I am profoundly grateful to my family—my husband, son, and daughter—for their willingness to share my attention.

❖ PART I

SEXUALITY

Section 1

Pornography

Introduction

THE ANTIPORNOGRAPHY MOVEMENT has ignited one of the most heated controversies in feminist legal theory today. Feminist scholarship about pornography dates to the 1970s.[1] During that period, writers Robin Morgan, Susan Brownmiller, and Andrea Dworkin[2] introduced the view that pornography represents an ideology that influences social attitudes.

Robin Morgan, for example, linked pornography and rape. "Pornography is the theory, and rape the practice," she wrote.[3] Similarly, Susan Brownmiller, in *Against Our Will: Men, Women and Rape,* identified pornography as one of two major institutions (along with prostitution) that contribute to rape.[4] Calling for a ban on pornography, she wrote that pornography, like rape, is "designed to dehumanize women, to reduce the female to an object of sexual access, not to free sensuality from moralistic or parental inhibition."[5] In addition, Andrea Dworkin in *Woman Hating* exposed several societal practices and beliefs, including pornography, as forms of "woman hating."[6]

During the same era, feminists also began addressing pornography as a political issue.[7] In 1970 Robin Morgan and a group of women staged a sit-in at Grove Press, claiming that the press had "earned millions off the basic theme of humiliating, degrading, and dehumanizing women through sadomasochistic literature, pornographic films, and oppressive and exploitative practices."[8] In Los Angeles in 1976, feminists staged a demonstration and held a press conference to protest a billboard of a chained and bruised woman, captioned "I'm black and blue from the Rolling Stones and I love it." In Rochester, New York, women vandalized a cinema showing a film in which a woman was reputedly tortured and murdered for sexual titillation. In San Francisco in 1978, Women Against Violence in Pornography and Media organized a national conference and staged a "Take Back the Night" march through the city's red-light district. Finally, in New York City in 1979, a newly formed organization (Women Against Pornography) offered biweekly antipornography tours of Times Square.[9]

Although feminist concern about pornography was intensifying, feminists were not united in their views. By the end of the 1970s, significant divisions had emerged. Articles and books criticized the antipornography position.[10] As Freedman and Thorne describe:

> This latest political split within the women's movement, like all such splits, has been painful for participants and observers alike. It is especially unsettling for a movement that has flourished on an ideal of female unity and a dream of a common sexual politics. At times many of us have wished that the debate would simply fade away, or magically resolve itself, without our having to take personal stock of our confusion about sexuality, violence, pornography, and power. But when feelings run so high, on so central a political concern, there is, we sense, more than mere factionalism, personality conflict, or a natural process of organizational subdivision at stake. The debates and their intensity signal important issues that come at a critical moment in the history of our movement.[11]

Feminists directed subsequent scholarship, in the 1980s, toward political reform.[12] One form targeted the findings of two government commissions on pornography: the Commission on Obscenity and Pornography created in 1967 by President Lyndon Johnson and chaired by constitutional scholar William Lockhart; and the U.S. Attorney General's Commission on Pornography (named the Meese commission after Attorney General Edwin Meese), which was established in 1985.[13] Both commissions studied the nature, extent, and impact on society of pornography and made recommendations. Whereas the Lockhart commission found no empirical evidence linking pornography with criminal behavior,[14] and consequently recommended repeal of legislation prohibiting its sale, exhibition, or distribution to consenting adults, the Meese commission recommended increased prosecution and the enactment of more restrictive legislation.[15] Feminists from both the antipornography and the anticensorship positions criticized the commissions' findings.[16]

Feminist political action targeted the legislative process as well. Catharine MacKinnon[17] and Andrea Dworkin[18] in particular were leading reformers, creating a novel legal theory to regulate pornography. Together, they drafted an antipornography ordinance that provided the basis for legislative efforts in Minneapolis and Indianapolis.[19] The ordinance became the focus of intense philosophical and legal controversy involving issues of women's sexuality, feminist theory and practice, and constitutional law.

In addition, the Feminist Anti-Censorship Task Force (FACT) was formed in 1984 in New York by feminist activists and scholars to oppose the MacKinnon-Dworkin ordinance.[20] Attorney Nan Hunter, founding member of FACT and director of the American Civil Liberties Union Lesbian and Gay Rights Project, was one of the foremost critics of the antipornography position.[21] Her beliefs are reflected here in an essay (coauthored with Sylvia Law) which takes the form of an *amicus curiae* brief. Both liberal and libertarian feminists join in the FACT brief.[22]

The MacKinnon-Dworkin ordinance is premised on the idea that pornography constitutes a form of discrimination against women and a violation of their civil rights. The ordinance distinguishes between sexually explicit materials that subordinate or degrade women and those that do not, providing a civil remedy for injuries caused only by the former. The ordinance defines pornography as

> the graphic sexually explicit subordination of women, whether in pictures or in words, that also includes one or more of the following: women are presented as sexual objects who enjoy pain or humiliation; or . . . being raped; or . . . are presented as . . . tied up or cut up or mutilated or bruised or . . . dismembered; or . . . as being penetrated by objects or animals; or . . . women are presented as sexual objects for domination, conquest, . . . possession, or use, or through . . . positions of servility or submission or display.[23]

The ordinance is based on the following beliefs (beliefs expressed in legislative findings that were accepted in the *Hudnut* case, discussed below): pornography has a significant negative impact on women's lives, through the creation and maintenance of inequality between the sexes; promotion of bigotry, contempt, and aggression; and the undermining of women's rights to speech and action.

The ordinance provides that pornography is civilly actionable as a form of sexual discrimination when any of the following can be proven: (1) coercion into pornography; (2) forcing pornography on a person; (3) assaulting or physically attacking someone due to pornography; or (4) defaming a person through the use of their name, image, or likeness in pornography. Finally, the ordinance makes the production, sale, exhibition, and distribution of pornography a wrong that gives rise to injunctive relief by those who establish that they were specifically harmed by pornography.

MacKinnon and Dworkin first proposed the ordinance as an amendment to the Minneapolis city code.[24] After hearings in 1983, the Minneapolis City Council passed the legislation; however, the mayor vetoed it. Despite its redrafting and reenactment in 1984, the mayor vetoed the legislation once again.

Feminists were more successful in Indianapolis, where the city council passed a version of the ordinance in April 1984,[25] which was signed into law by Mayor William H. Hudnut. Soon, however, media trade groups and civil libertarians challenged the ordinance on First Amendment grounds. In November 1984, in American Booksellers Ass'n, Inc. v. Hudnut,[26] a federal district court granted plaintiffs' motion for summary judgment and declared the ordinance unconstitutional on grounds that it was vague, overbroad, and a prior restraint on speech. The court reasoned that the ordinance could survive attack only if the state's interest in prohibiting sex discrimination was so compelling as to outweigh the protected interest of free speech; the court ruled, as a matter of law, that the state's interest was not. In addition, the district court rejected defendants' argument that the interest of protecting women from sex-based discrimination was analogous to the state interest (previously recognized by the Supreme Court)[27] in protecting children from pornography.

On appeal, the Seventh Circuit Court of Appeals, in an opinion reprinted here (subsequently summarily affirmed by the U.S. Supreme Court),[28] affirmed the district court's holding. Although accepting "the premises of this legislation" ". . .[that the depictions] tend to perpetuate [women's] subordination," the court nonetheless found that the ordinance violated the First Amendment because it constituted impermissible viewpoint-based regulation.[29]

Liberal Feminism

The subject of pornography has fragmented feminists into several camps. These factions include those who oppose censorship (liberal and libertarian feminists) and those who oppose pornography (radical feminists).[30]

Liberal feminists, although united with other feminists in their opposition to restraints on sexual freedom, part company with most other feminists on the issue of pornography. Their commitment to certain liberal values, such as individual dignity and autonomy, equality, and self-fulfillment, leads them to believe it is wrong to restrict pornography.[31] They adopt the liberal view of the state as a politically neutral institution whose function is to guarantee equal opportunity for self-fulfillment, to protect persons and property from unnecessary governmental interference.

Liberals distinguish between the private sphere of the family and the public sphere—a distinction that has implications for pornography.[32] Classic liberals are united in their opposition to state intervention in the private sphere.[33] As Jaggar notes:

> The liberal commitment to liberty and the inviolability of private life places liberal feminists among most other feminists in their opposition to restraints on contraception, abortion, homosexuality, etc. The same commitment, however, separates liberal feminists from most other feminists on the issue of pornography. . . . Pornography presents a special problem for liberal feminists because of liberalism's historic commitment to freedom of expression and the right to privacy. Liberal feminists may be "personally" or "privately" revolted or titillated by pornography, but they have no "political" grounds for opposing it unless it can be shown to have a direct causal connection with the violation of women's rights.[34]

Liberal feminists' criticisms, many of which are voiced in the following essays by Hunter and Law, Strossen, and Meyer, include the views that censorship would (1) ban some overtly feminist works; (2) discriminate against the least popular segments of society (including feminists and lesbians); (3) perpetuate paternalistic and demeaning gender stereotypes; (4) disempower women by emphasizing their victimization; (5) deprive women of employment opportunities in the sex industry; and (6) distract attention from more meaningful approaches to combating violence and discrimination against women.

Because liberal feminists do not believe that pornography is harmful,[35] they oppose regulation. They fear that increased regulation will have negative effects on individual freedom in general. As liberal feminist Wendy Kaminer, a member of Women Against Pornography, writes:

> Legislative or judicial control of pornography is simply not possible without breaking down the legal principles and procedures that are essential to our right to speak. . . . We must continue to organize against pornography . . . but we must not ask the government to take up our struggle for us. The power it will assume to do so will be far more dangerous to us all than the 'power' of pornography.[36]

Increasingly, however, some feminists are critical of liberals' anticensorship position, as the essays here illustrate.

Libertarian Feminism

The term *libertarian feminist* was coined by Ann Ferguson[37] to characterize a variant, sexual/radical view in the liberal tradition.[38] Whereas some liberals conceive of rights as positive entitlements, with the state playing an active role to ensure those rights,[39] other liberals conceive of rights as negative freedom: the right to be free from governmental constraints. Therefore they oppose state regulation. In this latter group are laissez-faire economists, who oppose economic regulation, and libertarians, who oppose regulation in private matters as well (such as speech and sexual behavior). Laissez-faire economists and libertarians, although both descendants of classic liberalism, are sometimes thought of as conservative because of their position on economic issues and, paradoxically, as liberal in their support of pornography.

Libertarians criticize radical feminists for conflating sex and violence.[40] They accuse radical feminists of attempting to return to a repressive moral code that stifles female sexuality.[41] Whereas radical feminists criticize libertarians as reinforcing male violence, libertarian feminists criticize radical feminists for overemphasizing victimization.[42] Moreover, libertarian feminists find that radical feminist explanations of pornography's effects on men (male motivation as an unreflective behavioral response) are overly simplistic.[43] Underscoring women's sexual repression rather than their victimization, libertarian feminists emphasize the liberating potential of pornography for women.[44]

Radical Feminism

Radical feminism is a perspective that adopts as its central concern the subordination of women. Sexuality is the source of that subordination. According to this school of thought, women must organize against patriarchy as a class, in Marxist terms, in order to achieve social change by transforming the sexual practices that contribute to their subordination.[45]

Ferguson characterizes the pornography debate as a polarization between radical and libertarian feminist views about sexual morality.[46] Radical feminists oppose pornography because it reinforces the power relations that perpetuate male dominance.[47] Radical feminists perceive all forms of sexuality, including pornography, as based on power inequality.

Radical feminists question the idea of consent as freely given between equals. For these feminists, the social conditions of male dominance and gender inequality render consent problematic because women may perceive no alternatives. Not only are women confronted with pornographic images in private and in public, but they may be compelled to replicate such acts to please their partners.[48] Radical feminist Kathleen Barry, who defines pornography as the practice of "cultural sadism," elaborates:

> In cultural sadism, the question of woman's will is a spurious one. Women exist as objects and as such will be taken if they don't give themselves. While a woman may choose to participate in the practices of cultural sadism, that choice implies neither freedom nor sexual liberation.[49]

Both Dworkin and MacKinnon believe that pornography objectifies, degrades, and dehumanizes women. MacKinnon identifies the harms as those affecting the participants in the production of pornography, the victims of sex crimes prompted by pornography, and society, through social conditioning that fosters discrimination and other unlawful behavior.[50] Barry similarly characterizes pornography as an ideology that regards sexual violence as normative and pleasurable for women—a belief that is diffused into both mainstream culture and sexual behavior.[51]

Radical feminism has recently come under attack with the publication of Richard Posner's *Sex and Reason*.[52] Posner believes that pornography satisfies a basic sociobiological urge analogous to eating: the achievement of sexual pleasure. Men demand pornography, according to Posner, because of their sexual differences from women: their stronger biological sex drive and the greater importance of visual stimulation to their sexual arousal.[53] Based on these beliefs, Posner disagrees that pornography constitutes a form of, or contributes to, sex discrimination.

> Many feminists believe that even if pornography does not actually incite men to rape, it makes them devalue women and thereby contributes to sexual harassment and other forms of sex discrimination and oppression, large and small. This is possible, but it is a suggestion in considerable tension with the aphrodisiacal thrust of pornography. The audience for pornography is interested in sexual stimulation, not in sexual politics. Pornography does present women as sexual objects, but in moments of sexual excitement even egalitarian men conceive of women in this way.[54]

Posner questions whether the prohibition of pornography would result in improving men's regard for women.

It might make a difference how steady a diet of pornography a given man consumed. It seems to me that only a man truly immersed in the stuff would find his ideas about the proper status of women altered; and we must consider whether a man prone to such immersion is, as it were, redeemable for feminism by being denied the bath he seeks.[55]

Posner attempts to refute further the link between pornography and women's subordination by pointing to the example of Scandinavia, where access to pornography is accompanied by an enhanced status of women. He also notes that misogynistic attitudes fail to explain homosexual pornography or conservatives' participation in the antipornography campaign.[56]

Feminists have severely criticized Posner's theory of human sexuality.[57] Carol Sanger, for example, alleges that Posner reasons about sex from a masculine perspective. "What sex is, what counts as 'aspects of sexuality' susceptible to economic analysis, how the benefits and costs of sex are measured . . . are organized and informed from the perspective of industrial-strength masculinity."[58] Robin West, another of Posner's critics, charges that Posner's explanation excuses misogynist practices by attributing them to an unalterable biological condition.[59] She criticizes the view that objectification, according to Posner, is "simply a rational reproductive strategy, not emblematic of men's control of women's sexuality in any sort of objectionable way."[60]

Catharine MacKinnon has also criticized Posner's sociobiological views. She charges that Posner "slights[s] the social determinants of sexuality."[61] This leads him to fail to comprehend the important *social* reality of male dominance. Regarding the subject of pornography, specifically, MacKinnon criticizes Posner's biological explanation of the male response to pornographic materials. She charges that this view ignores the socially conditioned nature of that response, as well as the negative consequences of that response for women and society. She writes:

> [Posner's] objectification of women through visual cues as the essence of heterosexual excitement is pornography by another name. Male dominance, in other words, is essential. Sex inequality in society is not what Judge Posner sets out to explain because, as a system of social force, he does not seem to know it is there. It is remarkable that one can still attribute what is, in fact, male dominance to the genes and be taken as making a serious contribution to policy and scholarship.[62]

Although radical feminists are united in their condemnation of pornography, they are divided in their views about the appropriateness of legal action. Some radical feminists concentrate their efforts outside of the legal arena, opting for anarchistic, violent methods, such as the destruction of pornographic literature and records and of businesses engaged in pornography.[63] Many radical feminists believe that legal reforms are ineffectual and that society will be transformed only through methods that illuminate the power of male dominance. One radical feminist elaborates:

> We simply cannot look to the government to rid us of pornography; legally there are no "final solutions." The feminist movement against pornography

must remain an antidefamation movement involved in education, consciousness-raising, and the development of private strategies against the industry.[64]

In contrast, radical feminists MacKinnon and Dworkin believe that the law can be an effective tool in combatting pornography. Under their civil rights approach, pornography is analogized to discrimination in employment, housing, and access to public accommodations.[65] MacKinnon proposes an additional legal tool to combat pornography. In *Only Words*,[66] she suggests that, even if pornography is protected by the First Amendment, it nonetheless offends a competing constitutional value of equality protected by the Fourteenth Amendment. She argues that the latter value should prevail.[67] This would lead

> to a new model for freedom of expression in which the free speech position no longer supports social dominance, as it does now; in which free speech does not most readily protect the activities of Nazis, Klansmen, and pornographers, while doing nothing for their victims as it does now.[68]

Although MacKinnon's views have come under attack by some liberal scholars who weigh the balance differently, her views have been gaining acceptance in some circles, as discussed herein.[69]

Marxist Feminism

Influenced significantly by Sigmund Freud, modern Marxists (such as Wilhelm Reich, Erich Fromm, Herbert Marcuse, and Juliet Mitchell)[70] have explored the connections between sexuality and the political economy. However, Marxists generally have neglected the issue of pornography,[71] in part because classic Marxist political theory (including Marx's own writings) ignores issues of sexuality. Even Engels's *The Origin of the Family*, the most detailed early account of women's roles in Marxism, fails to address pornography.[72]

Another reason for the neglect, according to Soble, is the Marxist emphasis on economic considerations.

> Marxists have not found pornography interesting because they have always felt the importance of concentrating on the relations of production of capitalism, because they (for example, Reich) assumed that the poor lonely soul who consumes pornography was a manifestation of the psychologically destructive effects of capitalism and would not exist in communist society, and because they thought that such a shining example of bourgeois decadence as pornography would simply wither away in the transitions first to socialism and then to communism. Marxists writing about sexuality failed to realize that their own theories might provide a justification for nonsexist pornography.[73]

Jaggar contrasts Marxists' neglect with the views of radical feminists.

> Questions of sex, gender and procreation are virtually ignored by liberal and Marxist political theory: where the sexual division of labor *is* examined, it is primarily in connection with so-called economic production, not in connection with sexuality, childbearing or childrearing. The radical feminist conception of human nature, by contrast, makes possible systematic reflection on the political significance of human reproductive biology. It provides the conceptual foundation for bringing sexual, childbearing and childrearing practices into the domain of politics.[74]

Among modern Marxists, Wilhelm Reich's discussion of pornography under capitalism is especially provocative.[75] In his synthesis of Marxism and Freudian psychoanalytic theory, Reich expresses his belief that sexual pathology (including homosexuality, masturbation, rape, prostitution, and pornography) arises because the structure of capitalism, with its social norms and economic necessity, prevents the individual from attaining satisfying sexual relations.[76]

Nonfeminists and feminists alike have criticized Reich's model of sexuality. Michel Foucault, one of Reich's foremost critics, argues that sexuality, rather than a biological given, is a product of history.[77] Feminist Martha Vicinus criticizes the Reichian framework by arguing that the model applies only to male sexuality.[78] "The male bias of the energy-control model reflects both the gender of the major theoreticians and the unchanging assumptions of a male-dominated society."[79]

One modern Marxist provides a defense of pornography. Soble argues that man's desire for pornography is not a reflection of man's power over women. In stark contrast to radical feminist views, Soble posits that man's interest in pornography reflects man's powerlessness, constituting a defense mechanism to women's unwillingness to accommodate male sexual desires. Soble concludes by suggesting that political and societal changes (the elimination of class and gender distinctions) could result in "nonsexist pornography."[80]

Marxists generally do not support the feminist campaign against pornography. Jaggar explains, "[Marxists] may fear that restrictions on pornography would simply increase the power of the state to control freedom of expression—a power that would ultimately be used against the political expression of socialists."[81] Marxist feminists also argue that protective legislation constitutes a form of legal paternalism that "inevitably has discriminatory effects."[82]

Socialist Feminism

Socialist feminism consists of a confluence of Marxist, radical, and psychoanalytic schools of feminist theory. It stems from Marxist feminists' dissatisfaction with Marxism's neglect of gender. Prominent socialist feminists in the women's movement include Juliet Mitchell,[83] Iris Young,[84] Heidi Hartmann,[85] and Alison Jaggar.[86]

Despite an emphasis on sexuality and procreation,[87] socialist feminism has developed a limited analysis of pornography.[88] Among socialist feminists, Jaggar's and Ferguson's theories have special relevance. Jaggar identifies alienation as the concept capable of unifying the feminist perspectives of Marxist, radical, psychoanalytic, and liberal feminist thought. She distinguishes the different explanations of women's oppression thus:

> Liberal feminists . . . believe that women are oppressed insofar as they suffer unjust discrimination; traditional Marxists believe that women are oppressed in their exclusion from public production; radical feminists see women's oppression as consisting primarily in the universal male control of women's sexual and procreative capacities; while socialist feminists characterize women's oppression in terms of a revised version of the Marxist theory of alienation.[89]

Jaggar categorizes woman's alienation under the categories of sexuality, motherhood, and intellectuality. Under patriarchal capitalism, she describes, women are socially constructed as sexual objects to satisfy man's desires. Woman's body becomes an object for men and for the woman herself. Just as the wage worker is alienated from the product of his labor, woman becomes alienated from her body. She becomes alienated from her sexuality by not being "free to express [her] sexual preferences" and by not being able to discover what her sexual preferences are.[90] According to Jaggar, an understanding of these aspects of women's oppression is essential for the elimination of that oppression in social institutions and cultural structures.

Their critique of sexuality has implications for socialist feminists' views of pornography. Highly critical of the mass marketing of sex under capitalism, socialist feminists regard pornography as reinforcing patriarchal institutions.[91] Despite pornography's potential to liberate women, socialist feminists are quick to point out that pornography ultimately reinforces sexist values.[92]

Socialist feminism, according to some thinkers,[93] may offer the most promising framework for addressing the polarization between radical feminists and libertarian feminists, because socialist feminism attempts to integrate insights of perspectives. Ferguson, for example, suggests that the radical versus libertarian feminist debate can be resolved through a third perspective which she terms "a (not the) socialist feminist perspective."[94] Such a perspective might alert people to the contradictions inherent in pornography and encourage the adoption of a "transitional" feminist sexual morality.[95] A feminist morality should be pluralist, Ferguson suggests, with respect to those sexual practices (such as sadomasochism, pornography, and prostitution) that are merely suspected of leading to dominant/subordinate relationships. Thus feminists would be free to express their sexuality without fear of moral condemnation from other feminists.

What is the role of the law in addressing pornography according to socialist feminism? Berger, Searles, and Cottle contend:

> Although socialist feminists, like Marxists, are generally cautious of special protection legislation for women, many would support nonlegal strategies vis-a-vis

pornography such as educational and consciousness-raising efforts and civil disobedience against the purveyors of misogynist pornographic imagery. More importantly, socialist feminists emphasize strategies not directly related to pornography but designed to improve the condition of women in other areas.[96]

Berger cites, for example, the work of Varda Burstyn[97] for her advocacy of "positive strategies" to address pornography by means of economic and social programs for women; reproductive and erotic rights for women and sexual minorities; and legal protection and improved working conditions for sex-industry workers.[98] Other scholars suggest additional, nonlegal approaches to pornography, such as sex education[99] and rape prevention techniques,[100] in order to convey information about sexuality and to counter gender role stereotypes. Some nonlegal approaches would regulate the media, through either "cooperative consultation" or "pressure confrontation" tactics.[101] According to socialist feminists, Berger concludes, the problems associated with pornography "are symptomatic of other societal forces that cannot be transformed by a political strategy that focuses on pornography itself."[102] Some of these strategies are explored in the essays that follow.

The Debate Continues

The antipornography/anticensorship debate continues. Although the MacKinnon-Dworkin ordinance was declared unconstitutional in *Hudnut,* the litigation did not end the debate. Its legacy was renewed interest in legal strategies to address pornography.

Several tactics have been suggested. One of the foremost is increased enforcement of existing law. Robel[103] advocates a multidimensional legal approach: reliance on Title VII to address pornography in the workplace; use of existing tort actions of intentional and negligent infliction of emotional distress; limiting the scope of existing laws addressing "display" of pornographic materials to proscribe only pictorial representations; the extension of existing tort law for invasion of privacy, imposing liability for the unauthorized use of sexual materials; and increased enforcement of obscenity law to eliminate the production, sale, and distribution of at least hard core pornographic material.[104] Jacobs also advocates enforcement of existing law.[105] In particular, she targets existing laws against rape and prostitution to remedy harm to actresses; enforcement of nuisance and zoning laws; utilization of tort suits by models and other victims; and taxation of materials.

On the other hand, several scholars propose legislative reform. One approach advocates legislation to combat the production and distribution of pornography while retaining Dworkin and MacKinnon's recognition of pornography as a form of sex discrimination. Cass Sunstein, for example, suggests that violent pornography can be regulated in conformity with traditional First Amendment doctrine by narrowly defining the matters to be regulated.[106] He advocates regulation that would address material that is (1) sexually explicit; (2) depicts women as enjoying or deserving some form of physical abuse; and (3) has the purpose and effect of sexual stimulation.[107] His focus on violent material emphasizes the nexus between pornography and sexual violence against women.[108]

He also believes that antipornography legislation might be regulated so that it protects passages in longer works or does not apply if the material on the whole generates little harm. Consistent with the standard enunciated in Miller v. California,[109] (explained below), Sunstein suggests that antipornography legislation could be limited to material devoid of serious social value, excluding from its scope works with literary, artistic, or other social value. Finally, regulation of pornography might be limited to visual materials, such as motion pictures and photography, that pose more harm than written materials.[110]

As support for such an approach, Sunstein distinguishes pornography from other protected speech. According to Sunstein, under current doctrine, speech that lies at the "periphery of constitutional concern"[111] may be regulated on a lesser showing of government interest than pure political speech, for example. Sunstein believes that some pornographic materials lie at this periphery. These "low-value" pornographic materials are analytically unlike protected speech, which promotes deliberation on public or private issues.

Sunstein also argues that pornography regulation does not constitute impermissible viewpoint-based regulation. Although acknowledging that First Amendment protection insulates the individual from government "antipathy to viewpoint,"[112] Sunstein argues that antipornography law aimed at preventing harm to women is not viewpoint based in the same way as other regulation. Pornography regulation does not, for example, "interfere with speech that appeals to deliberative processes but instead with speech that aims at something else altogether."[113]

Another commentator similarly proposes narrow legal reforms. Downs[114] argues against establishing a new category of violent pornography. He suggests amending the constitutional standard to determine whether material is obscene. Specifically, he proposes adding a fourth prong to the existing three-part test.[115] In Miller v. California, the Supreme Court held that only "obscene" material could be regulated and defined the term as material that (1) the average person, applying community standards, would find, taken as a whole, appeals to the prurient interest; (2) depicts sexual conduct in a patently offensive way; and (3) taken as a whole, lacks serious literary, artistic, political, or scientific value. Downs advocates adding another prong regulating the form of pornography that most concerns feminists.[116] He explains:

> Portrayals of murder, dismemberment, brutality or violence in the context of obscene acts (that is, those which depict ultimate sexual acts, lewdly displayed naked bodies, or excess of sexual detail) would be subject to the designation of "violent obscenity."[117]

Downs suggests that his approach merely modifies existing obscenity law by supplementing *Miller*.

MacKinnon and Dworkin continue to advocate, although with limited success, the legislative approach challenged in *Hudnut.* Feminist groups, with MacKinnon and Dworkin's support, lobbied on behalf of similar legislation (House Bill 5194) before the Massachusetts legislature.[118] In contrast to the Indianapolis ordinance, the proposed Massachusetts legislation exempts libraries and academic institutions and limits the trafficking provisions to visual materials. Although the subject of contentious hearings, the legislation failed to emerge from committee and was not refiled. Similar legislation was enacted in Washington state and subsequently declared unconstitutional by a federal district court.[119] In addition, legislation imposing civil liability against pornographers was enacted in Illinois,[120] although it has not yet been challenged.

Legislation also was introduced on the federal level. The Pornography Victims' Compensation Act (PVCA) of 1992 was proposed to enable victims of sexual crimes to hold producers, distributors, and sellers of obscene material and child pornography civilly liable if their product constitutes a "substantial cause" of the ensuing criminal conduct.[121] Unlike the civil rights approach advocated by MacKinnon and Dworkin, the PVCA was based in tort law. The effectiveness of the proposed act was limited by the requirements that, before a civil suit may be brought, the perpetrator must be found guilty of a sexual assault and in addition must be found guilty under criminal obscenity or child pornography laws.[122] An additional problem was the establishment of the causal nexus, that the exposure to pornography precipitated the sexual crime.[123]

Feminist opposition to the proposed federal legislation coalesced with the formation of the Feminists for Free Expression (FFE).[124] The FFE formulated its anticensorship position in a letter signed by over two hundred women, which they sent to Senator Joseph Biden, chair of the Senate Judiciary Committee. The proposed legislation was not enacted and has not been reintroduced.

Current supporters of the antipornography position may have their hopes bolstered by recent developments. MacKinnon's and Dworkin's views on pornography influenced the Supreme Court of Canada. In Butler v. Her Majesty the Queen,[125] reprinted here, the Canadian Court unanimously ruled that, although a federal obscenity law infringed on freedom of expression protected by the Canadian Charter of Rights and Freedoms,[126] the state may nonetheless ban pornography that is harmful to women. Adopting the view that such material is distinguishable from traditionally protected speech, the Court accepted two arguments central to radical feminism: pornography harms women and contributes to their inequality.

Although *Butler* signifies a victory for radical feminism, it is worth noting the reasons for Canada's receptivity to the radical feminist argument. *Butler* rests in part on an analogy to hate speech, which the Canadian Supreme Court has regulated on the theory that such speech presents harm to society.[127] American federal courts have been particularly unreceptive to this theory.[128] Moreover, the Canadian Charter of Rights and Freedoms includes a more expansive guarantee of equality than our Equal Protection Clause.[129]

Antipornography advocates may be bolstered by another legal victory which relies on increased enforcement of existing laws to regulate pornography in the workplace. In Robinson v. Jacksonville Shipyards,[130] a federal judge ruled that a male employee sexually harassed a female welder by posting graphic sexual posters and calendars. The court expanded sexual harassment law by concluding that the posting of pornography creates a hostile work environment, thereby constituting sexual discrimination under Title VII.[131]

Finally, a major legal victory stemming from the antipornography campaign is the enactment in 1994 of the Violence of Women Act (VAWA).[132] The VAWA, based on the notion that violence against women is sexual discrimination, creates a statutory right to be free from crimes of gender-motivated violence. Title III of the VAWA establishes a new federal civil rights-based remedy for victims of gender-motivated offenses. It enables victims to obtain relief (similar to that available to victims of race-based violence) in the form of compensatory and punitive damages as well as injunctive and declaratory relief.[133]

The feminist debate about pornography in the essays herein explores equality concerns by illuminating the relationship between pornography and women's subordination and exploring the appropriate role of law in achieving equality. In the first essay to follow, Andrea Dworkin examines, in the radical feminist tradition, the manner in which pornography subordinates women.

On a more theoretical note, in "Not a Moral Issue," Catharine MacKinnon refutes the First Amendment defense of pornography. This defense, she argues, is based on the public-private dichotomy that is not a meaningful distinction for women. She suggests also that civil libertarians' protection leads to the stifling of women's voices and institutionalization of inequality. In a subsequent essay, "Francis Biddle's Sister," MacKinnon examines the specific harms of pornography that led her to formulate, with Andrea Dworkin, the Minneapolis ordinance.

Thomas Emerson (MacKinnon's former professor) refutes several of MacKinnon's arguments. According to this classic liberal position, freedom of expression is essential to the democratic process. Like the classic exchange between MacKinnon and Emerson, Rae Langton rebuts Ronald Dworkin's defense of pornography.[134] In an essay elsewhere,[135] Dworkin argues that liberal theory dictates that consumers of pornography have rights that must defeat prohibitive policy. Langton dismantles Dworkin's objections by showing that prohibition of pornography is consistent with Dworkin's liberalism and indeed that the approach he utilizes to support affirmative action[136] dictates that pornography be restricted.

Nan Hunter and Sylvia Law, as well as Nadine Strossen,[137] present liberal and libertarian arguments against censorship. Like other scholars represented here, Hunter and Law point out the constitutional infirmities of the MacKinnon-Dworkin ordinance. Echoing many of the same criticisms, Strossen makes the additional charge that censorship would harm women who make a living in the sex industry and would strengthen the religious right. Concurring with Hunter and Law, Strossen argues that censorship distracts from the causes of gender inequality and misogynistic violence.

Continuing Strossen's refrain, Carlin Meyer suggests that more substantial changes are necessary to address the ills of pornography. In particular, she theorizes that sports and militarism are more pervasive factors that contribute to gender inequality by engendering stereotypical beliefs.

Concluding this section, Robin West explores women's sexuality from a new perspective. West suggests that both liberal and radical feminist legal criticism are flawed by their interpretations of women's humanity and emphasis on autonomy. West contends that only by focusing on women's hedonic lives will any real change in women's status be effected. West's phenomenological critique sheds new light on the relationship between pornography and women's subordination.

Notes

1. The women's movement was slow to address pornography for several reasons. At first, political and economic issues dominated the feminist agenda. Diana Russell suggests additional reasons: feminists were disenchanted by the politics (conservative, homophobic, antisex, and profamily) of the antipornography forces; they feared that association with this movement would result in being labeled unliberated; they denied or were unconvinced about the misogyny in pornography; and they failed to recognize the link between the various forms of sexual violence. D. Russell, Pornography and the Women's Liberation Movement, in L. Lederer ed., Take Back the Night: Women on Pornography 301–306 (Morrow, 1980). Soble offers an alternative explanation, theorizing that feminists only gradually recognized the threat of the male backlash to the women's movement (the backlash taking the form of a "pornography explosion"). A. Soble, Pornography: Marxism, Feminism, and the Future of Sexuality 85–87 (Yale Univ. Press, 1986). On the backlash, see generally S. Faludi, Backlash: The Undeclared War Against American Women (Crown, 1991).

2. S. Brownmiller, Against Our Will: Men, Women and Rape (Simon & Schuster, 1975); A. Dworkin, Woman Hating (Dutton, 1974); R. Morgan, Theory and Practice: Pornography and Rape, in Going Too Far (Random House, 1977, 1st ed. 1968); Morgan, How to Run the Pornographers Out of Town (and Preserve the First Amendment), Ms. Magazine, November 1978, at 55. For other early feminist writing on pornography, see Steinem, Erotica and Pornography: A Clear and Present Difference, Ms. Magazine, November 1978, at 53; S. Griffin, Pornography and Silence: Culture's Revenge Against Nature (Harper & Row, 1981); Lederer, *supra* note 1.

3. Morgan, Theory and Practice, *supra* note 2, at 169.

4. Brownmiller, *supra* note 2, at 290. In a subsequent article, Brownmiller elaborated that pornography represents hatred of women with the intent to humiliate, degrade and dehumanize. Maintaining that pornography has nothing to do with political rights, she wrote: "[It has] everything to do with the creation of a cultural climate in which a rapist feels he is merely giving in to a normal urge." S. Brownmiller, Let's Put Pornography Back in the Closet, in Lederer, Take Back the Night, *supra* note 1, at 254.

5. Brownmiller, s*upra* note 2, at 394.

6. Dworkin, Woman Hating, *supra* note 2. This early work foreshadowed A. Dworkin, Pornography: Men Possessing Women (Perigee, 1981).

7. Several of these events are discussed in Lederer, *supra* note 1, at 15.

8. Cited in Brest & Vandenberg, Politics, Feminism, and the Constitution: The Anti-Pornography Movement in Minneapolis, 39 Stan. L. Rev. 607, 611 (1987).

9. Lederer, *supra* note 1, at 1.

10. Early feminist defenses of pornography include SAMOIS ed., Coming to Power: Writings and Graphics on Lesbian S/M (Alyson Publications, 1982); Garry, Pornography and Respect for Women, 4 Soc. Theory & Prac. 395 (1978); Califia, A Thorny Issue Splits the Movement, The Advocate, Oct. 30, 1980; Webster, Pornography and Pleasure, 12 Heresies 49 (1981). For the anticensorship position, see K. Ellis, B. O'Dair & A. Talmer eds., Caught Looking (Caught Looking Inc., 1986); and V. Burstyn ed., Women Against Censorship (Douglas & McIntyre, 1985). Another illustration of the schism surfaced at a conference on sexuality at Barnard College of Columbia University on the theme of "pleasure and danger." A group of antipornography feminists called for a boycott of speakers who, they believed, promoted nonfeminist views on sexuality and sexual practice. For essays stemming from this conference, see C. Vance ed., Pleasure and Danger: Exploring Female Sexuality (Routledge & Kegan Paul, 1984). See also C. Vance, More Pleasure, More Danger: A Decade After the Barnard Sexuality Conference, in Pleasure and Danger: Exploring Female Sexuality, 2d ed. (Routledge & Kegan Paul, 1992). Similarly, when radical feminist Andrea Dworkin spoke at the New York hearings on pornography, anticensorship feminists criticized her for not representing the views of all women. See Van Gelder, Pornography Goes to Washington: What Can Reagan, Meese, the Radical Right, and Feminists Possibly Have to Say to Each Other About Porn? Ms. Magazine, June 1986, at 52, 54.

11. Freedman & Thorne, Introduction to the Feminist Sexuality Debates, 10 Signs 102, 104 (1984).

12. Hess and Ferree attribute women's increasing politicization to their awareness of pornography as yet another manifestation of male violence against women. B. Hess & M. Ferree, Analyzing Gender: A Handbook of Social Science Research 146 (Sage, 1987).

13. Similar commissions were established in Canada (the Special Committee on Pornography and Prostitution, called the Fraser committee) and Great Britain (the Home Office Departmental Committee on Obscenity and Film Censorship, named the Williams committee after its chairperson, Cambridge University Professor Bernard Williams). See generally G. Hawkins & F. Zimring, Pornography in a Free Society (Harvard Univ. Press, 1988) (discussing the work of several government commissions).

14. See U.S. Commission on Obscenity and Pornography, Report of the Commission on Obscenity and Pornography 27 (Washington, D.C.: U.S. Government Printing Office, 1970).

15. See Attorney General's Commission on Pornography, U.S. Dept. of Justice, Final Report (Washington, D.C.: U.S. Government Printing Office, 1986).

16. See, e.g., West, The Feminist Anti-Conservative Anti-Pornography Alliance and the 1986 Attorney General's Commission on Pornography Report, 4 Am. Bar Fdn. Res. J. 681 (1987); Meese Commission Exposed (National Coalition Against Censorship, 1986) (commentary by Harriet Pilpel, Betty Friedan, and others). Also, compare P. Bart & M. Jozsa, Dirty Books, Dirty Films and Dirty Data, in Lederer, *supra* note 1, at 204, and K. Barry, Female Sexual Slavery 199–214 (Prentice-Hall, 1979) (both antipornography), with McCormack, Machismo in Media Research: A Critical Review of Research on Violence and Pornography, 25 Soc. Probs. 544 (1978) (anticensorship).

17. MacKinnon, at that time a professor at the University of Minnesota Law School, specialized in constitutional law and sex discrimination. She is currently a professor at the University of Michigan School of Law. In addition to MacKinnon's essay included herein, see also A. Dworkin & C. MacKinnon, Pornography and Civil Rights: A New Day for Women's Equality (Organizing Against Pornography, 734 E. Lake St., Minneapolis, 1988); C. MacKinnon, Only Words (Harvard Univ. Press, 1993); Francis Biddle's Sister: Pornography, Civil Rights, and Speech, in Feminism Unmodified: Discourses on Life and Law 163–197 (Harvard Univ. Press, 1987); Pornography: On Morality and Politics, in Toward a Feminist Theory of the State 195–214 (Harvard Univ. Press, 1989); Pornography as Defamation and Discrimination, 71 B.U. L. Rev. 793 (1991); Pornography as Sex Discrimination, 4 Law & Ineq. J. 38 (1986); Pornography, Civil Rights and Speech, 20 Harv. C.R.-C.L. L. Rev. 1 (1985); Pornography Left and Right, 30 Harv. C.R.-C.L. L. Rev. 143 (1995); Sexuality, Pornography and Method: Pleasure Under Patriarchy, 99 Ethics 316 (1989).

18. Dworkin, an adjunct professor on the same law faculty as MacKinnon, and coteacher of a seminar on pornography, is a feminist author and orator. For her early writings, see Woman Hating, *supra* note 2; Our Blood: Prophecies and Discourses on Sexual Politics (Harper & Row, 1976); Pornography: Men Possessing Women, *supra* note 6; and Right-Wing Women (Coward, McCann, 1983).

19. For additional historical background on the antipornography ordinance, see Brest & Vandenberg, *supra* note 8; Dworkin, Against the Male Flood: Censorship, Pornography, and Equality, herein.

20. FACT chapters sprang up to oppose the ordinance as it was introduced in Long Island; Madison, Wisconsin; San Francisco; Los Angeles; and Cambridge, Massachusetts. On FACT, see generally Hawkins & Zimring, *supra* note 13, at 167; F. Osanka & S. Johann, Sourcebook on Pornography 268–269, 288–290 (Lexington Books, 1989).

21. Osanka & Johann, *supra* note 20, at 268. For another critique of the MacKinnon-Dworkin ordinance by FACT members, see L. Duggan, N. Hunter & C. Vance, False Promises: Feminist Antipornography Legislation in the U.S., in Burstyn, *supra* note 10.

22. Feminists from diverse philosophical orientations joined in the FACT brief. Although classification of feminists is sometimes problematic, those who might be labeled liberal feminist supporters include Sylvia Law, Susan Estrich, Betty Friedan, Sue Deller Ross, Nadine Strossen, and Wendy Williams. Nan Hunter might be categorized as a libertarian feminist. Radical feminists Adrienne Rich and Kate Millett also joined in the FACT brief. For additional supporters, see Strossen, A Feminist Critique of "The" Feminist Critique of Pornography, 79 Va. L. Rev. 1099, 1109 n.32 (1993).

23. Indianapolis, Ind., City Council Gen'l Ordinance No. 24, Ch. 16 (amended May 1, 1984) as cited in American Booksellers Ass'n, Inc. v. Hudnut, 598 F. Supp. 1316, 1318 (1984).

24. Minneapolis, Minn., Ordinance Amending tit. 7, chs. 139, 141.

25. Indianapolis, Ind., City Council Gen'l Ordinance No. 24, Ch. 16 (amended May 1, 1984).

26. 598 F. Supp. 1316 (S.D. Ind. 1984), *aff'd,* 771 F.2d 323 (7th Cir. 1985), *aff'd,* 475 U.S. 1001 (1986).

27. In New York v. Ferber, 458 U.S. 747 (1982), the Supreme Court upheld, based on the state's interest in child protection, an ordinance banning the distribution of child pornography that was not legally obscene.

28. Three members of the Court (Chief Justice Burger and Justices Rehnquist and O'Connor) would have set the case for oral argument, suggesting they might have voted to uphold the statute. See American Booksellers Ass'n, Inc., v. Hudnut, 475 U.S. 1001 (1986).

29. American Booksellers Ass'n, Inc. v. Hudnut, 771 F.2d 323, 328 (7th Cir. 1985).

30. The review that follows relies heavily on a number of excellent sources, especially R. Berger, P. Searles & C. Cottle, Feminism and Pornography (Praeger, 1991); L. Clark, Liberalism and Pornography, in D. Copp & S. Wendell eds., Pornography and Censorship 45 (Prometheus, 1983); D. Downs, The New Politics of Pornography (Univ. of Chicago Press, 1989); Ferguson, Sex War: The Debate Between Radical and Libertarian Feminists, 10 Signs 106 (1984); A. Jaggar, Feminist Politics and Human Nature (Rowman & Allanheld, 1983); A. Snitow, Retrenchment Versus Transformation: The Politics of the Antipornography Movement, in Burstyn, *supra* note 10; Soble, *supra* note 1; Vance, Pleasure and Danger, *supra* note 10; Vance & Snitow, Toward a Conversation About Sex in Feminism: A Modest Proposal, 10 Signs 126 (1984).

31. See generally Jaggar, *supra* note 30, at 174.

32. Berger, Searles & Cottle, *supra* note 30, at 53.

33. Rosemarie Tong notes that not all contemporary liberals oppose governmental intervention. She distinguishes contemporary "welfare liberals" from classic liberals, noting that the former advocate government intervention, as in the form of government income transfer programs (AFDC, Social Security, etc). R. Tong, Feminist Thought: A Comprehensive Introduction 12 (Westview Press, 1989).

34. Jaggar, *supra* note 30, at 180.

35. See, e.g., Clark, *supra* note 30, at 54.

36. Cited in Brest & Vandenberg, *supra* note 8, at 616.

37. Ferguson, *supra* note 30, at 106.

38. Prominent libertarian feminist works include Califia, Feminism and Sadomaschism, 12 Heresies 30 (1981); L. Duggan, N. Hunter & C. Vance, False Promises: Feminist Antipornography Legislation in the U.S., in Burstyn ed., Women Against Censorship, *supra* note 10; Rubin, English & Hollibaugh, Talking Sex: A Conversation on Sexuality and Feminism, 11 Socialist Rev. 43 (1981); A. Snitow, C. Stansell & S. Thompson eds., Powers of Desire: The Politics of Sexuality 245 (Monthly Review Press, 1983); Vance, *supra* note 10; Vance & Snitow, *supra* note 30.

39. This discussion of the differences between the philosophical positions within liberalism and their ramifications for feminist thought relies on the excellent discussion in P. England, Comparable Worth: Theories and Evidence 257–264 (Aldine, 1992).

40. See, e.g., Vance & Snitow, *supra* note 30, at 128, 130.

41. Ferguson, *supra* note 30, at 109, 110.

42. See, e.g., Duggan, Hunter & Vance, *supra* note 38, at 145.

43. Vance & Snitow, *supra* note 30, at 131.

44. Ferguson, *supra* note 30, at 109.

45. Jaggar, *supra* note 30, at 100, 105.

46. Ferguson, *supra* note 30.

47. For prominent radical feminist works criticizing pornography, see Barry, Female Sexual Slavery, *supra* note 16; Brownmiller, *supra* note 2; Dworkin, Pornography: Men Possessing Women, *supra* note 6; Dworkin, Against the Male Flood, herein; Griffin, *supra* note 2; Lederer, *supra* note 1; and MacKinnon's works cited *supra* note 17. Not all radical feminists agree with MacKinnon and Dworkin. See, e.g., Ellis, O'Dair & Talmer, Caught Looking, *supra* note 10, at 6 (criticizing MacKinnon's and

Dworkin's views as "a dangerous oversimplification that is ultimately harmful to women").

48. Radical feminists argue that consent is absent in women's exposure to pornography. Berger, Searles & Cottle, *supra* note 30, at 36.

49. Barry, *supra* note 16, at 212.

50. MacKinnon, Pornography, Civil Rights and Speech, *supra* note 17, at 32–60. See also MacKinnon, Francis Biddle's Sister, *supra* note 17, at 179–191.

51. Barry, *supra* note 16, at 177.

52. Although Posner devotes a chapter of *Sex and Reason* to pornography, he discusses the feminist debate only briefly. See R. Posner, Sex and Reason 371–372 (Harvard Univ. Press, 1992).

53. *Id.* at 352, 354.

54. *Id.* at 371.

55. *Id.*

56. *Id.*

57. For feminist criticism of *Sex and Reason,* see Bartlett, Rumpelstiltskin, 25 Conn. L. Rev. 473 (1993); Fineman, The Hermeneutics of Reason: A Commentary on Sex and Reason, 25 Conn. L. Rev. 503 (1993); Hadfield, Flirting with Science: Richard Posner on the Bioeconomics of Sexual Man, 106 Harv. L. Rev. 479 (1992); MacKinnon, Pornography Left and Right, 30 Harv. C.R-C.L. L. Rev. 143 (1995); Sanger, He's Gotta Have It, 66 S. Cal. L. Rev. 1221 (1993); West, Sex, Reason, and a Taste for the Absurd, 81 Georgetown L.J. 2413 (1993). For Posner's response to some of these criticisms, see Posner, The Radical Feminist Critique of *Sex and Reason,* 25 Conn. L. Rev. 515 (1993), and the surreply, Hadfield, Not the "Radical" Feminist Critique of Sex and Reason, 25 Conn. L. Rev. 533 (1993).

58. Sanger, *supra* note 57, at 1223.

59. West, *supra* note 57, at 2441.

60. *Id.*

61. MacKinnon, *supra* note 57, at 153.

62. *Id.* at 156–157.

63. Jaggar, *supra* note 30, at 283, 286.

64. W. Kaminer, Pornography and the First Amendment: Prior Restraints and Private Action, in Lederer, *supra* note 1, at 247 (cited in Jaggar, *supra* note 30, at 286).

65. L. Robel, Pornography and Existing Law: What the Law Can Do, in S. Gubar & J. Hoff eds., For Adult Users Only: The Dilemma of Violent Pornography 179 (Univ. Indiana Press, 1989).

66. MacKinnon, Only Words, *supra* note 17. The three essays in the book were originally lectures.

67. *Id.* at 85.

68. *Id.* at 109.

69. See, e.g., Dworkin, Women and Pornography, N.Y. Rev. Books, Oct. 21, 1993, at 36, 40. See also MacKinnon, Pornography: An Exchange, N.Y. Rev. Books, Mar. 3, 1994, at 47–48 (MacKinnon's reply); Dworkin, Reply, N.Y. Rev. Books, Mar. 3, 1994, at 48 (Dworkin's surreply). Dworkin warns:

> If we abandon our traditional understanding of equality for a different one that allows a majority to define some people as too corrupt or offensive or radical to join in the informal moral life of the nation, we will have begun a process

that ends, as it has in so many other parts of the world, in making equality something to be feared rather than celebrated, a mocking, "correct" euphemism for tyranny.

Dworkin, Women and Pornography, *supra* this note, at 42. For additional authorities reflecting the liberal position, see Strossen, *supra* note 22, at 1108 n.27. For another proponent of this position, see Posner, Only Words: Book Review, New Republic, Oct. 18, 1993, at 31 (criticizing MacKinnon's views based on a defense of civil liberties).

70. See, e.g., E. Fromm, Escape from Freedom (Farrar & Rinehart, 1941); H. Marcuse, One Dimensional Man: Studies in the Ideology of Advanced Industrial Society (Beacon, 1964); J. Mitchell, Psychoanalysis and Feminism: Freud, Reich, Lang and Women (Vintage, 1974); J. Mitchell, Woman's Estate (Pantheon, 1971); W. Reich, The Sexual Revolution: Toward a Self-Governing Character Structure (Farrar, Straus & Giroux, 1945).

71. Soble, *supra* note 1, at 2, 4.

72. F. Engels, The Origin of the Family, Private Property and the State (International Publishers, 1972). Engels's work, however, does touch on prostitution. For a discussion of his views, see *infra* pp. 191–192.

73. Soble, *supra* note 1, at 5.

74. Jaggar, *supra* note 30, at 106.

75. Of Reich it has been said: "No psychoanalytic writer has done more to explain what a liberated sexuality might be and what the contrast between an unliberated and liberated sexuality consists in than Wilhelm Reich." A. MacIntyre, Herbert Marcuse: An Exposition and a Polemic 51 (Viking Press, 1970).

76. See, e.g., Reich, *supra* note 70.

77. Foucault notes: "Sexuality must not be thought of as a kind of natural given which power tries to hold in check. . . . It is the name that can be given to a historical construct . . . what is involved is the production of sexuality rather than the repression of sex." M. Foucault, The History of Sexuality 105, 114 (Vintage, 1980).

78. Vicinus, Sexuality and Power, 8 Feminist Stud. 133 (1982).

79. *Id.* at 136 (cited in Soble, *supra* note 1, at 21).

80. Soble, *supra* note 1, at 132.

81. Jaggar, *supra* note 30, at 238.

82. Berger, Searles & Cottle, *supra* note 30, at 60 (citing Rafter & Natalizia, Marxist Feminism: Implications for Criminal Justice, 27 Crime & Delinq. 81 (1981)).

83. Mitchell, Woman's Estate, *supra* note 70; Mitchell, Psychoanalysis and Feminism, *supra* note 70.

84. Young, Socialist Feminism and the Limits of Dual Systems Theory, 10 Socialist Rev. 174 (1980).

85. H. Hartmann, The Unhappy Marriage of Marxism and Feminism: Towards a More Progressive Union, in L. Sargent ed., Women and Revolution: A Discussion of the Unhappy Marriage of Marxism and Feminism 1 (South End Press, 1981); Hartmann & Markusen, Contemporary Marxist Theory and Practice: A Feminist Critique, 12 Rev. Radical Pol. Econ. 87 (1980).

86. Jaggar, *supra* note 30.

87. *Id.* at 128.

88. Berger, Searles & Cottle, *supra* note 30.

89. Jaggar, *supra* note 30, at 308.

90. *Id.* at 309.

91. Berger, Searles & Cottle, *supra* note 30, at 62.

92. Burstyn, Beyond Despair: Positive Strategies, in Women Against Censorship, *supra* note 10, at 157.

93. Berger, Searles & Cottle, *supra* note 30, at 63.

94. Ferguson, *supra* note 30, at 108. See also her essay The Sex Debate Within the Women's Movement: A Socialist-Feminist View, Against the Current, Sept.–Oct. 1983, at 10.

95. Ferguson, *supra* note 30, at 111.

96. Berger, Searles & Cottle, *supra* note 30, at 65–66.

97. Burstyn, *supra* note 10.

98. Cited in Berger, Searles & Cottle, *supra* note 30, at 66.

99. *Id.* at 137 (citing Malamuth, The Mass Media and Aggression Against Women: Research Findings and Prevention, in A. Burgess ed., Rape and Sexual Assault: A Research Handbook 403, 405 (Garland, 1985)).

100. *Id.* at 137 (citing Searles & Berger, The Feminist Self-Defense Movement: A Case Study, 1 Gender & Soc'y 61 (1987)).

101. *Id.* at 134 (citing Malamuth, *supra* note 99, at 403–404); Cottle, *supra* note 30, at 134. Berger points out "many feminists undoubtedly would find the cooperative approach ("negotiating with the enemy") problematic since it might seem to imply approval of or license for particular enterprises. Some would prefer more confrontational strategies in addition to or instead of cooperative ones." *Id.* at 136. Hawkins and Zimring also advocate industry regulation to improve the film rating scheme by providing better notice to viewers. Hawkins & Zimring, *supra* note 13, at 207.

102. Berger, Searles & Cottle, *supra* note 30, at 66.

103. Robel, *supra* note 65, at 178.

104. *Id.* at 183–189.

105. Jacobs, Patterns of Violence: A Feminist Perspective on the Regulation of Pornography, 7 Harv. Women's L.J. 5 (1984).

106. Sunstein, Pornography and the First Amendment, 1986 Duke L.J. 589. See also Sunstein, Neutrality in Constitutional Law (with Special Reference to Pornography, Abortion, and Surrogacy), 92 Colum. L. Rev. 1 (1992); Sunstein, Notes on Pornography and the First Amendment, 4 Law & Ineq. J. 28 (1986).

107. Sunstein, Pornography and the First Amendment, *supra* note 106, at 592.

108. Sunstein, Neutrality, *supra* note 106, at 23.

109. 413 U.S. 15 (1973).

110. Sunstein, Notes, *supra* note 106, at 36.

111. Sunstein, Neutrality, *supra* note 106, at 21–22; Sunstein, Notes, *supra* note 106, at 29.

112. Sunstein, Notes, *supra* note 106, at 32.

113. *Id.*

114. Downs, *supra* note 30, at 174–194.

115. 413 U.S. 15 (1973).

116. Downs, *supra* note 30, at 195–198.

117. *Id.* at 195.

118. An Act to Protect the Civil Rights of Women and Children, Mass. H.B. 5194, 177th Gen. Ct., Reg. Sess. (1992), available in LEXIS, Legis Library, Mabill File. See also Elson, Passions over Pornography, Time, Mar. 30, 1992, at 52.

119. Strossen, *supra* note 22, at 1105 n.18 (citing the unreported case of Village Books et al. v. City of Bellingham, C88-147OD (W.D. Wash.)).

120. Ill. Ann. Stat. ch. 720, para. 5/12–18.1 (Smith-Hurd 1993). See generally Morrison Torrey, The Resurrection of the Anti-Pornography Ordinance, 2 Tex. J. Women & L. 113, 120 (1993).

121. Pornography Victims' Compensation Act, S. 1521, 102d Cong., 2d Sess. (1992). On the history of the legislation, see Joan Kennedy Taylor, Does Sexual Speech Harm Women? The Split Within Feminism, 5 Stan. L. & Pol'y Rev. 49, 50 (1994); Torrey, *supra* note 120, at 116 n.17. See generally Daniel A. Cohen, Compensating Pornography's Victims: A First Amendment Analysis, 29 Val. U. L. Rev. 285 (1994); Sheila J. Winkelman, Making a Woman's Safety More Important than Peep Shows: A Review of the Pornography Victim's Compensation Act, 44 Wash. U. J. Urb. & Contemp. L. 237 (1993).

122. Torrey, *supra* note 120, at 117.

123. Taylor, *supra* note 121, at 51; Torrey, *supra* note 120, at 116.

124. Taylor, *supra* note 121, at 51.

125. Butler v. Her Majesty the Queen, [1992] 1 S.C.R. 452. The Canadian Special Committee on Pornography and Prostitution was also influenced by MacKinnon and Dworkin's views. Hawkins and Zimring point out that four of seven members "viewed with sympathy the feminist argument that pornography was 'an evil which limits the full human rights and dignity of women.' It also made some proposals for legislation reflecting that view." Hawkins & Zimring, *supra* note 13, at 153.

126. Can. Const. (Constitution Act, 1982) pt. I (Canadian Charter of Rights and Freedoms), §2(b).

127. Her Majesty the Queen v. Keegstra, [1990] 3 S.C.R. 697.

128. See, e.g., R.A.V. v. City of St. Paul, 505 U.S. 377 (1992) (holding that a municipal "hate speech" ordinance that prohibited bias-motivated criminal conduct was facially invalid under the First Amendment). See generally Kagan, Regulation of Pornography and Hate Speech After *R.A.V.,* 60 U. Chi. L. Rev. 873 (1993); Matsuda, Public Response to Racist Speech: Considering the Victim's Story, 87 Mich. L. Rev. 2320 (1989); Scales, Feminist Legal Method: Not So Scary, 2 UCLA Women's L.J. 1 (1992).

129. Can. Const. (Constitution Act, 1982) pt. I (Canadian Charter of Rights and Freedoms), 1.

130. Robinson v. Jacksonville Shipyards, Inc., 760 F. Supp. 1486 (M.D. Fla. 1991).

131. *Id.* at 1522–1527. See generally Note, Pornography, Equality, and a Discrimination-Free Workplace: A Comparative Perspective, 106 Harv. L. Rev. 1075 (1993).

132. The Violence Against Women Act of 1994, Pub. L. No. 103–322, 108 Stat. 1796 (codified in scattered sections of 8 U.S.C., 18 U.S.C. & 42 U.S.C.) At least one commentator has suggested that the Act might be utilized as a weapon against violent pornography. See, e.g., W.H. Hallock, Note, The Violence Against Women Act: Civil Rights for Sexual Assault Victims, 68 Ind. L.J. 577, 608 (1993).

133. The VAWA also has 4 other titles. Title I, Safe Streets for Women, provides increased protection against sexual assault, specifically allocating funds to increase the safety of women in public parks and transit systems; Title II, Safe Homes for Women, addresses domestic violence through the creation of a federal remedy for interstate crimes of abuse, increased funding, and the provision for interstate enforcement of protection orders; Title IV, Safe Campuses, funds programs to improve the safety of women on college campuses; and, Title V, Equal Justice for Women in the Courts, allocates funding for consciousness raising of state and federal judges on the issue of gender bias.

134. For another feminist criticism of liberalism's position on pornography, see Clark, *supra* note 30.

135. Ronald Dworkin (not to be confused with Andrea Dworkin) is Professor of Jurisprudence and Fellow of University College, Oxford, and also on the faculty at New York University. Dworkin expressed his views in Do We Have a Right to Pornography?, 1 Oxford J. Legal Stud. 177 (1981).

136. See R. Dworkin, Reverse Discrimination, in Taking Rights Seriously 223 (Harvard Univ. Press, 1977).

137. Nadine Strossen, professor and currently president, American Civil Liberties Union, joined the FACT brief (reprinted here) that was coauthored by Hunter and Law. See also N. Strossen, Defending Pornography: Free Speech, Sex, and the Fight for Women's Rights (Scribner, 1995). For a book review comparing Strossen's book and MacKinnon's Only Words, see Margaret McIntyre, Sex Panic or False Alarm? The Latest Round in the Feminist Debate Over Pornography, 6 UCLA Women's L.J. 189 (1995).

Against the Male Flood: Censorship, Pornography, and Equality

ANDREA DWORKIN

III. Pornography

IN THE UNITED STATES, it is an $8-billion trade in sexual exploitation.

It is women turned into subhumans, beaver, pussy, body parts, genitals exposed, buttocks, breasts, mouths opened and throats penetrated, covered in semen, pissed on, shitted on, hung from light fixtures, tortured, maimed, bleeding, disemboweled, killed.

It is some creature called female, used.

It is scissors poised at the vagina and objects stuck in it, a smile on the woman's face, her tongue hanging out.

It is a woman being fucked by dogs, horses, snakes.

It is every torture in every prison cell in the world, done to women and sold as sexual entertainment.

It is rape and gang rape and anal rape and throat rape: and it is the woman raped, asking for more.

It is the woman in the picture to whom it is really happening and the women against whom the picture is used, to make them do what the woman in the picture is doing.

It is the power men have over women turned into sexual acts men do to women, because pornography is the power and the act.

It is the conditioning of erection and orgasm in men to the powerlessness of women: our inferiority, humiliation, pain, torment; to us as objects, things, or commodities for use in sex as servants.

It sexualizes inequality and in doing so creates discrimination as a sex-based practice.

It permeates the political condition of women in society by being the substance of our inequality however located—in jobs, in education, in marriage, *in life.*

It is women, kept a sexual underclass, kept available for rape and battery and incest and prostitution.

It is what we are under male domination; it is what we are for under male domination. It is the heretofore hidden (from us) system of subordination that women have been told is just life.

Under male supremacy, it is the synonym for what being a woman is.

It is access to our bodies as a birthright to men: the grant, the gift, the permission, the license, the proof, the promise, the method, how-to; it is us accessible, no matter what the law pretends to say, no matter what we pretend to say.

It is physical injury and physical humiliation and physical pain: to the women against whom it is used after it is made; to the women used to make it.

As words alone, or words and pictures, moving or still, it creates systematic harm to women in the form of discrimination and physical hurt. It creates harm inevitably by its nature because of what it is and what it does. The harm will occur as long as it is made and used. The name of the next victim is unknown, but everything else is known.

Because of it—because it is the subordination of women perfectly achieved—the abuse done to us by any human standard is perceived as using us for what we are by nature: women are whores; women want to be raped; she provoked it; women like to be hurt; she says no but means yes because she wants to be taken against her will which is not really her will because what she wants underneath is to have anything done to her that violates or humiliates or hurts her; she wants it, because she is a woman, no matter what it is, because she is a woman; that is how women are, what women are, what women are for. This view is institutionally expressed in law. So much for equal protection.

If it were being done to human beings, it would be reckoned an atrocity. It is being done to women. It is reckoned fun, pleasure, entertainment, sex, somebody's (no something's) civil liberty no less. . . .

V. Subordination

In an amendment to the Human Rights Ordinance of the City of Minneapolis written by Catharine A. MacKinnon and myself, pornography is defined as the graphic, sexually explicit subordination of women whether in pictures or in words that also includes one or more of the following: women are presented dehumanized as sexual objects, things or commodities; or women are presented as sexual objects who enjoy pain or humiliation; or women are presented as sexual objects who experience sexual pleasure in being raped; or women are presented as sexual objects tied up or cut up or mutilated or bruised or physically hurt; or women are presented in postures of sexual submission; or women's body parts are exhibited, such that women are reduced to those parts; or women are presented in scenarios of degradation, injury, abasement, torture, shown as filthy or inferior, bleeding, bruised, or hurt in a context that makes these conditions sexual.

This statutory definition is an objectively accurate definition of what pornography is, based on an analysis of the material produced by the $8-billion-a-year industry, and also on extensive study of the whole range of pornography extant from other eras and other cultures. Given the fact that women's oppression has an ahistorical character—a sameness across time and cultures expressed in rape, battery, incest, and prostitution—it is no surprise that pornography, a central phenomenon in that oppression, has precisely that quality of sameness. It does not significantly change in what it is, what it does, what is in it, or how it works, whether it is, for instance, classical or feudal or modern, Western or Asian; whether the method of manufacture is words, photographs, or video. What is changed is the public availability of pornography and the numbers of live women used in it because of new technologies: not its nature. Many people note what seems to them a qualitative change in pornography—that it has gotten more violent, even grotesquely violent, over the last two decades. The change is only in what is publicly visible: not in the range or preponderance of violent pornography (e.g., the place of rape in pornography stays constant and central, no matter where, when, or how the pornography is produced); not in the character, quality, or content of what the pornographers actually produce; not in the harm caused; not in the valuation of women in it, or the metaphysical definition of what women are; not in the sexual abuse promoted, including rape, battery, and incest; not in the centrality of its role in subordinating women. Until recently, pornography operated in private, where most abuse of women takes place.

The oppression of women occurs through sexual subordination. It is the use of sex as the medium of oppression that makes the subordination of women so distinct from racism or prejudice against a group based on religion or national origin. Social inequality is created in many different ways. In my view, the radical responsibility is to isolate the material means of creating the inequality so that material remedies can be found for it.

This is particularly difficult with respect to women's inequality because that inequality is achieved through sex. Sex as desired by the class that dominates women is held by that class to be elemental, urgent, necessary, even if or even though it appears to *require* the repudiation of any claim women might have to full human standing. In the subordination of women, inequality itself is sexualized: made into the experience of sexual pleasure, essential to sexual desire. Pornography is the material means of sexualizing inequality; and that is why pornography is a central practice in the subordination of women.

Subordination itself is a broad, deep, systematic dynamic discernible in any persecution based on race or sex. Social subordination has four main parts. First, there is *hierarchy,* a group on top and a group on the bottom. For women, this hierarchy is experienced both socially and sexually, publicly and privately. Women are physically integrated into the society in which we are held to be inferior, and our low status is both put in place and maintained in the sexual usage of us by men; and so women's experience of hierarchy is incredibly intimate and wounding.

Second, subordination is *objectification.* Objectification occurs when a human being, through social means, is made less than human, turned into a thing or commodity, bought and sold. When objectification occurs, a person is depersonalized, so that no individuality or integrity is available socially or in what is an extremely circumscribed privacy (because those who dominate determine its boundaries). Objectification is an injury right at the heart of discrimination: those who can be used as if they are not fully human in social terms; their humanity is hurt by being diminished.

Third, subordination is *submission*. A person is at the bottom of a hierarchy because of a condition of birth, a person on the bottom is dehumanized, an object or commodity; inevitably, the situation of that person requires obedience and compliance. That diminished person is expected to be submissive; there is no longer any right to self-determination, because there is no basis in equality for any such right to exist. In a condition of inferiority and objectification, submission is usually essential for survival. Oppressed groups are known for their abilities to anticipate the orders and desires of those who have power over them, to comply with an obsequiousness that is then used by the dominant group to justify its own dominance: the master, not able to imagine a human like himself in such degrading servility, thinks the servility is proof that the hierarchy is natural and that the objectification simply amounts to seeing these lesser creatures for what they are. The submission forced on inferior, objectified groups precisely by hierarchy and objectification is taken to be the proof of inherent inferiority and subhuman capacities.

Fourth, subordination is *violence.* The violence is systematic, endemic enough to be unremarkable and normative, usually taken as an implicit right of the one committing the violence. In my view, hierarchy, objectification, and submission are the preconditions for systematic social violence against any group targeted because of a condition of birth. If violence against a group is both socially pervasive and socially normal, then hierarchy, objectification, and submission are already solidly in place.

The role of violence in subordinating women has one special characteristic congruent with sex as the instrumentality of subordination: the violence is supposed to be sex for the woman too—what women want and like as part of our sexual nature; it is supposed to give women pleasure (as in rape); it is supposed to mean love to a woman from her point of view (as in battery). The violence against women is seen to be done not just in accord with something compliant in women, but in response to something active in and basic to women's nature.

Pornography uses each component of social subordination. Its particular medium is sex. Hierarchy, objectification, submission, and violence all become alive with sexual energy and sexual meaning. A hierarchy, for instance, can have a static quality; but pornography, by sexualizing it, makes it dynamic, almost carnivorous, so that men keep imposing it for the sake of their own sexual pleasure—for the sexual pleasure it gives them to impose it. In pornography, each element of subordination is conveyed through the sexually explicit usage of women: pornography in fact is what women are and what women are for and how women are used in a society premised on the inferiority of women. It is a metaphysics of women's subjugation: our existence delineated in a definition of our nature; our status in society predetermined by the uses to which we are put. The woman's body is what is materially subordinated. Sex is the material means through which the subordination is accomplished. Pornography is the institution of male dominance that sexualizes hierarchy, objectification, submission, and violence. As such, pornography creates inequality, not as artifact but as a system of social reality; it creates the necessity for and the actual behaviors that constitute sex inequality.

VI. Speech

Subordination can be so deep that those who are hurt by it are utterly silent. Subordination can create a silence quieter than death. The women flattened out on the page are deathly still, except for *hurt me. Hurt me* is not women's speech. It is the speech imposed on women by pimps to cover the awful, condemning silence. The Three Marias of Portugal went to jail for writing this: "Let no one tell me that silence gives consent, because whoever is silent dissents."[1] The women say the pimp's words: the language is another element of the rape; the language is part of the humiliation; the language is part of the forced sex. Real silence might signify dissent, for those reared to understand its sad discourse. The pimps cannot tolerate literal silence—it is too eloquent as testimony—so they force the words out of the woman's mouth. The women say pimp's words: which is worse than silence. The silence of the women not in the picture, outside the pages, hurt but silent, is staggering in how deep and wide it goes. It is a silence over centuries: an exile into speechlessness. One is shut up by the inferiority and the abuse. One is shut up by the threat and the injury. In her memoir of the Stalin period, Hope Against Hope, Nadezha Mandelstam wrote that screaming

> is a man's way of leaving a trace, of telling people how he lived and died. By his screams he asserts his right to live, sends a message to the outside world demanding help and calling for resistance. If nothing else is left, one must scream. Silence is the real crime against humanity.[2]

Screaming is a man's way of leaving a trace. The scream of a man is never misunderstood as a scream of pleasure by passersby or politicians or historians, nor by the tormentor. A man's scream is a call for resistance. A man's scream asserts his right to live, sends a message; he leaves a trace. A woman's scream is the sound of her female will and her female pleasure in doing what the pornographers say she is for. Her scream is a sound of celebration to those who overhear. Woman's way of leaving a trace is the silence, centuries' worth: the entirely inhuman silence that surely one day will be noticed, someone will say that something is wrong, some sound is missing, some voice is lost; the entirely inhuman silence that will be a clue to human hope denied, a shard of evidence that a crime has occurred, the crime that created the silence; the entirely inhuman silence that is a cold, cold condemnation of hurt sustained in speechlessness, a cold, cold condemnation of what those who speak have done to those who do not.

But there is more than the *hurt me* forced out of us, and the silence in which it lies. The pornographers actually use our bodies as their language. Our bodies are the building blocks of their sentences. What they do to us [is] called speech. . . .

Protecting what they "say" means protecting what they do to us, how they do it. It means protecting their sadism on our bodies, because that is how they write: not like a writer at all; like a torturer. Protecting what they "say" means protecting sexual exploitation, because they cannot "say" anything without diminishing, hurting, or destroying us. Their rights of speech express their rights over us. Their rights of speech require our inferiority: and that we be powerless in relation to them. Their rights of speech mean that hurt me is accepted as the real speech of women, not speech forced on us as part of the sex forced on us but originating with us because we are what the pornographers "say" we are.

If what we want to say is not *hurt me,* we have the real social power only to use silence as eloquent dissent. Silence is what women have instead of speech. Silence is our dissent during rape unless the rapist, like the pornographer, prefers hurt me, in which case we have no dissent. Silence is our moving, persuasive dissent during battery unless the batterer, like the pornographer, prefers hurt me. Silence is a fine dissent during incest and for all the long years after.

Silence is not speech. We have silence, not speech. We fight rape, battery, incest, and prostitution with it. We lose. But someday someone will notice: that people called women were buried in a long silence that meant dissent and that the pornographers—with needles set in like the teeth of a harrow—chattered on.

VII. Equality

To get that word, male, out of the Constitution, cost the women of this country fifty-two years of pauseless campaign; 56 state referendum campaigns; 480 legislative campaigns to get state suffrage amendments submitted; 47 state constitutional convention campaigns; 277 state party convention campaigns; 30 national party convention campaigns to get suffrage planks in the party platforms; 19 campaigns with 19 successive Congresses to get the federal amendment submitted, and the final ratification campaign.

Millions of dollars were raised, mostly in small sums, and spent with economic care. Hundreds of women gave the accumulated possibilities of an entire lifetime, thousands gave years of their lives, hundreds of thousands gave constant interest and such aid as they could. It was a continuous and seemingly endless chain of activity. Young suffragists who helped forge the last links of that chain were not born when it began. Old suffragists who helped forge the first links were dead when it ended.

—Carrie Chapman Catt

Feminists have wanted equality. Radicals and reformists have different ideas of what equality would be, but it has been the wisdom of feminism to value equality as a political goal with social integrity and complex meaning. The Jacobins also wanted equality, and the French Revolution was fought to accomplish it. Conservatism as a modern political movement actually developed to resist social and political movements for equality, beginning with the egalitarian imperatives of the French Revolution.

Women have had to prove human status, before having any claim to equality. But equality has been impossible to achieve, perhaps because, really, women have not been able to prove human status. The burden of proof is on the victim.

Not one inch of change has been easy or cheap. We have fought so hard and so long for so little. The vote did not change the status of women. The changes in women's lives that we can see on the surface do not change the status of women. By the year 2000, women are expected to be one hundred percent of this nation's poor. We are raped, battered, and prostituted: these acts against us are in the fabric of social life. As children, we are raped, physically abused, and prostituted. The country enjoys the injuries done to us, and spends $8 billion a year on the pleasure of watching us being hurt (exploitation as well as torture constituting substantive harm). The subordination gets deeper: we keep getting pushed down further. Rape is an entertainment. The contempt for us in that fact is immeasurable; yet we live under the weight of it. Discrimination is a euphemism for what happens to us.

It has plagued us to try to understand why the status of women does not change. Those who hate the politics of equality say they know: we are biologically destined for rape; God made us to be submissive unto our husbands. We change, but our status does not change. Laws change, but our status stays fixed. We move into the marketplace, only to face there classic sexual exploitation, now called sexual harassment. Rape, battery, prostitution, and incest stay the same in that they keep happening to us as part of what life is: even though we name the crimes against us as such and try to keep the victims from being destroyed by what we cannot stop from happening to them. And the silence stays in place too, however much we try to dislodge it with our truths. We say what has happened to us, but newspapers, governments, the culture that excludes us as fully human participants, wipe us out, wipe out our speech: by refusing to hear it. We are the tree falling in the desert. Should it matter: they are the desert.

The cost of trying to shatter the silence is astonishing to those who do it: the women, raped, battered, prostituted, who have something to say and say it. They stand there, even as they are erased. Governments turn from them; courts ignore them; this country disavows and dispossesses them. Men ridicule, threaten or hurt them. Women jeopardized by them—silence being safer than speech—betray them. It is ugly to watch the complacent destroy the brave. It is horrible to watch power win.

Still, equality is what we want, and we are going to get it. What we understand about it now is that it cannot be proclaimed; it must be created. It has to take the place of subordination in human experience: physically replace it. Equality does not co-exist with subordination, as if it were a little pocket located somewhere within it. Equality has to win. Subordination has to lose. The subordination of women has not even been knocked loose, and equality has not materially advanced, at least in part because the pornography has been creating sexualized inequality in hiding, in private, where the abuses occur on a massive scale.

Equality for women requires material remedies for pornography, whether pornography is central to the inequality of women or only one cause of it. Pornography's antagonism to civil equality, integrity, and self-determination for women is absolute; and it is effective in making that antagonism socially real and socially determining.

The law that Catharine A. MacKinnon and I wrote making pornography a violation of women's civil rights recognizes the injury that pornography does: how it hurts women's rights of citizenship through sexual exploitation and sexual torture both.

The civil rights law empowers women by allowing women to civilly sue those who hurt us through pornography by trafficking in it, coercing people into it, forcing it on people, and assaulting people directly because of a specific piece of it.

The civil rights law does not force the pornography back underground. There is no prior restraint or police power to make arrests, which would then result in a revivified black market. This respects the reach of the first amendment, but it also keeps the pornography from getting sexier—hidden, forbidden, dirty, happily back in the land of the obscene, sexy slime oozing on great books. Wanting to cover the pornography up, hide it, is the first response to those who need pornography to the civil rights law. If pornography is hidden, it is still accessible to men as a male right of access to women; its injuries to the status of women are safe and secure in those hidden rooms, behind those opaque covers; the abuses of women are sustained as a private right supported by public policy. The civil rights law puts a flood of light on the pornography, what it is, how it is used, what it does, those who are hurt by it.

The civil rights law changes the power relationship between the pornographers and women: it stops the pornographers from producing discrimination with the total impunity they now enjoy, and gives women a legal standing resembling equality from which to repudiate the subordination itself. The secret-police power of the pornographers suddenly has to confront a modest amount of due process.

The civil rights law undermines the subordination of women in society by confronting the pornography, which is the systematic sexualization of that subordination. Pornography is inequality. The civil rights law would allow women to advance equality by removing this concrete discrimination and hurting economically those who make, sell, distribute, or exhibit it. The pornography, being power, has a right to exist that we are not allowed to challenge under this system of law. After it hurts us by being what it is and doing what it does, the civil rights law would allow us to hurt it back. Women, not being power, do not have a right to exist equal to the right the pornography has. If we did, the pornographers would be precluded from exercising their rights at the expense of ours, and since they cannot exercise them any other way, they would be precluded period. We come to the legal system beggars: though in the public dialogue around the passage of this civil rights law we have the satisfaction of being regarded as thieves.

The civil rights law is women's speech. It defines an injury to us from our point of view. It is premised on a repudiation of sexual subordination which is born of our experience of it. It breaks the silence. It is a sentence that can hold its own against the male flood. It is a sentence on which we can build a paragraph, then a page.

It is my view, learned largely from Catharine MacKinnon, that women have a right to be effective. The pornographers, of course, do not think so, nor do other male supremacists; and it is hard for women to think so. We have been told to educate people on the evils of pornography: before the development of this civil rights law, we were told just to keep quiet about pornography altogether; but now that we have a law we want to use, we are encouraged to educate and stop there. Law educates. This law educates. It allows women to do something. In hurting the pornography back, we gain ground in making equality more likely, more possible—someday it will be real. We have a means to fight the pornographers' trade in women. We have a means to get at the torture and the terror. We have a means with which to challenge the pornography's efficacy in making exploitation and inferiority the bedrock of women's social status. The civil rights law introduces into the public consciousness an analysis: of what pornography is, what sexual subordination is, what equality might be. The civil rights law introduces a new legal standard: these things are not done to citizens of this country. The civil rights law introduces a new political standard: these things are not done to human beings. The civil rights law provides a new mode of action for women through which we can pursue equality and because of which our speech will have social meaning. The civil rights law gives us back what the pornographers have taken from us: hope rooted in real possibility.

Notes

1. M.I. Barreno, M.T. Horta & M. Velho da Costa, The Three Marias: New Portuguese Letters 291 (H.R. Lane trans. 1976).
2. N. Mandelstam, Hope Against Hope 24–43 (M. Hayward trans. 1978).

◈ *Not a Moral Issue*

CATHARINE A. MACKINNON

> Pornosec, the subsection of the Fiction Department which turned out
> cheap pornography for distribution among the proles . . . nicknamed
> Muck House by the people who worked in it . . . produce[d] booklets
> in sealed packets with titles like "Spanking Stories" or "One Night in a
> Girls' School," to be bought furtively by proletarian youths who were
> under the impression that they were buying something illegal.
>
> George Orwell, Nineteen Eighty-Four 108–109 (1949)

A CRITIQUE OF pornography[1] is to feminism what its defense is to male supremacy. Central to the institutionalization of male dominance, pornography cannot be reformed or suppressed or banned. It can only be changed. The legal doctrine of obscenity, the state's closest approximation to addressing the pornography question, has made the First Amendment into a barrier to this process. This is partly because the pornographers' lawyers have persuasively presented First Amendment absolutism,[2] their advocacy position, as a legal fact, which it never has been. But they have gotten away with this (to the extent they have) in part because the abstractness of obscenity as a concept, situated within an equally abstract approach to freedom of speech embodied in First Amendment doctrine, has made the indistinguishability of the pornographers' speech from everyone else's speech, their freedom from our freedom, appear credible, appealing, necessary, inevitable, *principled*. To expose the absence of a critique of gender in this area of law is to expose both the enforced silence of women and the limits of liberalism.

This brief preliminary commentary focuses on the obscenity standard in order to explore some of the larger implications of a feminist critique of pornography for First Amendment theory. This is the argument. Obscenity law is concerned with morality, specifically morals from the male point of view, meaning the standpoint of male domi-

---

This speech was originally delivered to the Morality Colloquim, University of Minnesota, February 23, 1983. . . . The title of this article is a play on "Not a Love Story," a 1983 anti-pornography film by the Canadian Film Board.

nance. The feminist critique of pornography is a politics, specifically politics from women's point of view, meaning the standpoint of the subordination of women to men.[3] Morality here means good and evil; politics means power and powerlessness. Obscenity is a moral idea; pornography is a political practice. Obscenity is abstract; pornography is concrete. The two concepts represent two entirely different things. Nudity, explicitness, excess of candor, arousal or excitement, prurience, unnaturalness—these qualities bother obscenity law when sex is depicted or portrayed. Abortion, birth control information, and treatments for "restoring sexual virility" (whose, do you suppose?) have also been included. Sex forced on real women so that it can be sold at a profit to be forced on other real women; women's bodies trussed and maimed and raped and made into things to be hurt and obtained and accessed and this presented as the nature of women; the coercion that is visible and the coercion that has become invisible—this and more bothers feminists about pornography. Obscenity as such probably does little harm;[4] pornography causes attitudes and behaviors of violence and discrimination that define the treatment and status of half of the population.[5] To make the legal and philosophical consequences of this distinction clear, I will describe the feminist critique of pornography, then criticize the law of obscenity in terms of it, then discuss the criticism that pornography "dehumanizes" women to distinguish the male morality of liberalism and obscenity law from a feminist political critique of pornography.[6]

This inquiry is part of a larger project that attempts to account for gender inequality in the socially constructed relationship between power—the political—on the one hand and the knowledge of truth and reality—the epistemological—on the other.[7] For example, the candid description Justice Stewart once offered of his obscenity standard, "I know it when I see it,"[8] becomes even more revealing than it is usually understood to be, if taken as a statement that connects epistemology with power. If I ask, from the point of view of women's experience, does he know what I know when I see what I see, I find that I doubt it, given what's on the newsstands. How does his point of view keep what is there, there? To liberal critics, his admission exposed the obscenity standard's relativity, its partiality, its insufficient abstractness. Not to be emptily universal, to leave your concreteness showing, is a sin among men. Their problem with Justice Stewart's formulation is that it implies that anything, capriciously, could be suppressed. They are only right by half. My problem is more the other half: the meaning of what his view permits, which, as it turns out, is anything but capricious. In fact, it is entirely systematic and determinate. To me, his statement is precisely descriptively accurate; its candor is why it has drawn so much criticism.[9] Justice Stewart got in so much trouble because he said out loud what is actually done all the time; in so doing, he both *did it* and gave it the stature of doctrine, even if only dictum. That is, the obscenity standard—in this it is not unique—is built on what the male standpoint sees. My point is: *so is pornography*. In this way the law of obscenity reproduces the pornographic point of view on women on the level of Constitutional jurisprudence.

Pornography, in the feminist view, is a form of forced sex, a practice of sexual politics, an institution of gender inequality. In this perspective, pornography is not harmless fantasy or a corrupt and confused misrepresentation of an otherwise natural and healthy sexuality. Along with the rape and prostitution in which it participates, pornography institutionalizes the sexuality of male supremacy, which fuses the erotization of dominance and submission with the social construction of male and female. Gender is sexual. Pornography constitutes the meaning of that sexuality. Men treat women as who they see women as being. Pornography constructs who that is. Men's power over women means that the way men see women defines who women can be. Pornography is that way.

In pornography, women desire dispossession and cruelty. Men, permitted to put words (and other things) in women's mouths, create scenes in which women desperately want to be bound, battered and tortured, humiliated, and killed. Or, merely taken and used. This is erotic to the male point of view. Subjection itself, with self-determination ecstatically relinquished, is the content of women's sexual desire and desirability. Women are there to be violated and possessed, men to violate and possess them, either on screen or by camera or pen, on behalf of the viewer.

One can be for or against this pornography without getting beyond liberalism. The critical yet formally liberal view of Susan Griffin, for example, conceptualizes eroticism as natural and healthy but corrupted and confused by "the pornographic mind."[10] Pornography distorts Eros, which preexists and persists, despite male culture's pornographic "revenge" upon it. Eros is, unaccountably, *still there.* Pornography mis-takes it, mis-images it, mis-represents it. There is no critique of *reality* here, only objections to how it is seen; no critique of that reality that pornography imposes on women's real lives, those lives that are so seamlessly *consistent* with the pornography that pornography can be credibly defended by saying it is only a mirror of reality.

Contrast this view with the feminist analysis of Andrea Dworkin, in which sexuality itself is a social construct, gendered to the ground. Male dominance here is not an artificial overlay upon an underlying inalterable substratum of uncorrupted essential sexual being. Sexuality free of male dominance will require *change* not reconceptualization, transcendence, or excavation. Pornography is not imagery in some relation to a reality elsewhere constructed. It is not a distortion, reflection, projection, expression, fantasy, representation or symbol either. It is sexual reality. Dworkin's *Pornography: Men Possessing Women* presents a sexual theory of gender inequality of which pornography is a core constitutive practice. The way pornography produces its meaning constructs and defines men and women as such. Gender is what gender means. It has no basis in anything other than the social reality its hegemony constructs. The process that gives sexuality its male supremacist meaning is therefore the process through which gender inequality becomes socially real.

In this analysis, the liberal defense of pornography as human sexual liberation, as de-repression—whether by feminists, lawyers, or neo-Freudians[11]—is a defense not only of force and sexual terrorism, but of the subordination of women. Sexual liberation in the liberal sense frees male sexual aggression in the feminist sense. What looks like love and romance in the liberal view looks a lot like hatred and torture in the feminist view. Pleasure and eroticism became violation. Desire appears as lust for dominance and submission. The vulnerability of women's projected sexual availability—

that acting we are allowed: asking to be acted upon—is victimization. Play conforms to scripted roles, fantasy expresses ideology—is not exempt from it—and admiration of natural physical beauty becomes objectification.

The experience of the (overwhelmingly) male audiences who consume pornography is therefore not fantasy or simulation or catharsis[12] but sexual reality: the level of reality on which sex itself largely operates. To understand this, one does not have to notice that pornography models are real women to whom something real is being done,[13] nor does one have to inquire into the systematic infliction of pornographic sexuality upon women,[14] although its helps. The aesthetic of pornography itself, the *way* it provides what those who consume it want, is itself the evidence. When uncensored explicit—i.e., the most pornographic—pornography tells all, all means what a distanced detached observer would report about who did what to whom. This is the turn-on. Why does observing sex objectively presented cause the male viewer to experience his own sexuality? Because his eroticism is, socially, a watched thing.

If objectivity is the epistemological stance of which objectification is the social process,[15] the way a perceptual posture is embodied as a social form of power, the most sexually potent depictions and descriptions *would* be the most objective blow-by-blow re-presentations. Pornography participates in its audience's eroticism because it creates an accessible sexual object, the possession and consumption of which *is* male sexuality, to be consumed and possessed as which *is* female sexuality. In this sense, sex in life is no less mediated than it is in art. Men *have sex* with their *image* of a woman. Escalating explicitness, "exceeding the bounds of candor," is the aesthetic of pornography not because the materials depict objectified sex but because they create the experience of a sexuality that is itself objectified. It is not that life and art imitate each other; in sexuality, they *are* each other.

The law of obscenity, the state's primary approach to its version of the pornography question, has literally nothing in common with this feminist critique. Their obscenity is not our pornography. One commentator has said, "Obscenity is not suppressed primarily for the protection of others. Much of it is suppressed for the purity of the 'community.' Obscenity, at bottom, is not a crime. Obscenity is a sin."[16] This is, on one level, literally accurate. Men are turned on by obscenity, including its suppression, the same way they are by sin. Animated by morality from the male standpoint, in which violation—of women and rules—is eroticized, obscenity law can be seen to proceed according to the interest of male power, robed in gender-neutral good and evil.

Morality in its specifically liberal form (although, as with most dimensions of male dominance, the distinction between left and right is more formal than substantive) revolves around a set of parallel distinctions that can be consistently traced through obscenity law. Even though the approach this law takes to the problem it envisions has shifted over time, its fundamental norms remain consistent: public is opposed to private, in parallel with ethics and morality, and factual is opposed to valued determinations. Under male supremacy, these distinctions are gender-based: female is private, moral, valued, subjective; male is public, ethical, factual, objective. If such gendered concepts are constructs of the male experience, imposed from the male standpoint on society as a whole, liberal morality expresses male supremacist politics. That is, discourse conducted in terms of good and evil that does not expose the gendered foundations of these concepts proceeds oblivious to—and serves to disguise—the position of power that underlies, and is furthered by, that discourse.

For example, obscenity law proposes to control what and how sex can be publicly shown. In practice, its standard centers upon the same features feminism identifies as key to male sexuality: the erect penis and penetration.[17] Historically, obscenity law was vexed by restricting such portrayals while protecting great literature. (Nobody considered protecting women.) Having solved this by exempting works of perceived value from obscenity restrictions, the subsequent relaxation—some might say collapse—of obscenity restrictions in the last decade reveals a significant shift. The old private rules have become the new public rules. The old law governing pornography was that it would be publicly repudiated while being privately consumed and actualized: do anything to women with impunity in private behind a veil of public denial and civility. Now pornography is publicly celebrated. This victory for Freudian derepression theory probably did not alter the actual treatment of women all that much. Women were sex and still are sex. Greater efforts of brutality have become necessary to eroticize the taboo—each taboo being a hierarchy in disguise—since the frontier of the taboo keeps vanishing as one crosses it. Put another way, more and more violence has become necessary to keep the progressively desensitized consumer aroused to the illusion that sex is (and he is) daring and dangerous. Making sex with the powerless "not allowed" is a way of defining "getting it" as an act of power, an assertion of hierarchy. In addition, pornography has become ubiquitous. Sexual terrorism has become democratized. Crucially, pornography has become truly available to women for the first time in history. Show me an atrocity to women, I'll show it to you eroticized in the pornography. This central mechanism of sexual subordination, this means of systematizing the definition of women as a sexual class, has now become available to its victims for scrutiny and analysis as an open public system, not just as a private secret abuse.[18] Hopefully, this was a mistake.

Reexamining the law of obscenity in light of the feminist critique of pornography that has become possible, it becomes clear that male morality sees as good that which maintains its power and sees as evil that which undermines or qualifies it or questions its absoluteness. Differences in the law over time—such as the liberalization of obscenity doctrine—reflect either changes in the group of men in power or shifts in their perceptions of the best strategy for maintaining male supremacy—probably some of both. But it must be made to work. The outcome, descriptively analyzed, is that obscenity law prohibits what it sees as immoral, which from a feminist standpoint tends to be relatively harmless, while protecting what it sees as moral, which from a feminist standpoint is often that which is damaging to women. So it, too, is a politics, only covertly so. What male morality finds evil, meaning threatening to its power, feminist politics tends to find comparatively harmless. What feminist politics identifies as central in our subordination—the erotization of dominance and submission—male morality will tend to find comparatively harmless or defends as affirmatively valuable, hence protected speech.

In 1973, obscenity under law came to mean "that which 'the average person applying contemporary community standards' would find that, . . . taken as a whole, appeals to the prurient interest . . . [which] depicts or describes, in a patently offensive way, sexual conduct specifically defined by the applicable state law; and [which], taken as a whole, lacks serious literary, artistic, political, or scientific value."[19] Feminism doubts whether the average person, gender neutral, exists; has more questions about the content and process of definition of community standards than deviations from them; wonders why prurience counts but powerlessness doesn't; why sensibilities are better protected from offense than women are from exploitation; defines sexuality, hence its violation and expropriation, more broadly than does any state law and wonders why a body of law that can't in practice tell rape from intercourse should be entrusted with telling pornography from anything less. The law of obscenity says that intercourse on streetcorners is not legitimized by the fact that the persons are "simultaneously engaged in a valid political dialogue."[20] But, in a feminist light, one sees that the requirement that a work be considered "as a whole" legitimizes something very like that on the level of publications like *Playboy*. Experimental evidence is beginning to support what victims have long known: legitimate settings diminish the injury perceived as done to the women whose trivialization and objectification it contextualizes.[21] Besides, if a woman is subjected, why should it matter that the work has other value?[22] Perhaps what redeems a work's value among men *enhances* its injury to women. Existing standards of literature, art, science, and politics are, in feminist light, remarkably consonant with pornography's mode, meaning, and message. Finally and foremost, a feminist approach reveals that although the content and dynamic of pornography are about women—about the sexuality of women, about women as sexuality—in the same way that the vast majority of "obscenities" refer specifically to women's bodies, our invisibility has been such that the law of obscenity has *never even considered pornography a women's issue.*[23]

To appeal to "prurient interest" means, I believe, to give a man an erection. Men are scared to make it possible for some men to tell other men what they can and cannot have sexual access to because men have power. If you don't let them have theirs, they might not let you have yours. This is why the *indefinability* of pornography, "all the one man's this is another man's that,"[24] is so central to pornography's *definition*. It is not because they are such great liberals, but because some men might be able to do to them whatever they can do to those other men, and this is more why the liberal principle is what it is. Because the fought-over are invisible in this, it obscures the fact that the fight over a definition of obscenity is a fight among men over the best means to guarantee male power as a system. The question is, whose sexual practices threaten this system that can afford to be sacrificed to its maintenance for the rest? Public sexual access by men to anything other than women is less likely to be protected speech. This is not to say that male sexual access to anything—children, other men, women with women, objects, animals—is not the real system. The issue is *how public* that system will be, which the obscenity laws, their definition and patterns of enforcement, have a major role in regulating that. The bind of the "prurient interest" standard here is that, to find it as a fact, someone has to admit that they are sexually aroused by the materials, but male sexual arousal signals the importance of protecting them. They put themselves in this bind and then wonder why they cannot agree. Sometimes I think that what is ultimately found obscene is what does *not* turn on the Supreme Court, or what revolts them more, which is rare, since revulsion is eroticized; sometimes I think that what is obscene is what turns on those men that the men in power think they can afford to ignore; sometimes I think that part of it is that what looks obscene to them is what makes them see themselves as potential targets of male sexual aggression, even if only momentarily; sometimes I think that the real issue is how male sexuality is presented, so that anything can be done to a woman, but obscenity is that sex that makes male sexuality look bad.[25]

The difficulties courts have in framing workable standards to separate "prurient" from other sexual interest, commercial exploitation from art or advertising, sexual speech from sexual conduct, and obscenity from great literature make the feminist point. These lines have proven elusive in law because they do not exist in life. Commercial sex resembles art because both exploit women's sexuality. The liberal's slippery slope is the feminist totality. Whatever obscenity may do, pornography converges with more conventionally acceptable depictions and descriptions just as rape converges with intercourse because both express the same power relation. Just as it is difficult to distinguish literature or art against a background, a standard, of objectification, it is difficult to discern sexual freedom against a background, a standard, of sexual coercion. This does not mean it cannot be done. It means that legal standards will be practically unenforceable, will reproduce this problem rather than solve it, until they address its fundamental issue—gender inequality—directly.

To define the pornographic as the "patently offensive" further misconstrues its harm. Pornography is not bad manners or poor choice of audience; obscenity is. Pornography is also not an idea; obscenity is. The legal fiction whereby the obscene is "not speech" has deceived few; it *has* effectively avoided the need to adjudicate pornography's social etiology. But obscenity law got one thing right: pornography is more act-like than thought-like. The fact that pornography, in a feminist view furthers the idea of the sexual inferiority of women, a political idea, does not make the pornography itself a political idea. That one can express the idea a practice embodies does not make that practice into an idea. Pornography is not an idea any more than segregation is an idea, although both institutionalize the idea of the inferiority of one group to another. The law considers obscenity deviant, anti-social. If it causes harm, it causes anti-social acts, acts against the social order.[26] In a feminist perspective, pornography is the essence of a sexist social order, its quintessential social act.

If pornography is an act of male supremacy, its harm is the harm of male supremacy made difficult to see because of its pervasiveness, potency, and success in making the world a pornographic place. Specifically, the harm cannot be discerned from the objective standpoint because it *is* so much of "what is." Women live in the world pornography creates. We live its lie as reality. As Naomi Scheman has said, "Lies are what we have lived, not just what we have told, and no story about correspondence to what is real will enable us to distinguish the truth from the lie."[27] So the issue is not whether pornography is harmful, but how the harm of pornography is to become visible. As compared with what? To the extent pornography succeeds in constructing social reality, it becomes *invisible as harm.* Any perceptions of the success, therefore the harm, of pornography, I will argue, is precluded by liberalism and so has been defined out of the customary approach taken to, and dominant values underlying, the First Amendment.

The theory of the First Amendment under which most pornography is protected from governmental restriction proceeds from liberal assumptions[28] that do not apply to the situation of women. First Amendment theory, like virtually all liberal legal theory, presumes the validity of the distinction between public and private: the "role of law [is] to mark and guard the line between the sphere of social power, organized in the form of the state, and the area of private right."[29] On this basis, courts distinguish between obscenity in public (which can be regulated, even if some attempts founder, seemingly in part *because* the presentations are public)[30] and the private possession of obscenity in the home.[31] The problem is that not only the public but also the private *is* a "sphere of social power" of sexism. On paper and in life pornography is thrust upon unwilling women in their homes.[32] The distinction between public and private does not cut the same for women as for men.[33] It is men's right to inflict pornography upon women in private that is protected.

The liberal theory underlying First Amendment law further believes that free speech, including pornography, helps discover truth. Censorship restricts society to partial truths. So why are we now—with more pornography available than ever before—buried in all these lies? *Laissez faire* might be an adequate theory of the social preconditions for knowledge in a nonhierarchical society. But in a society of gender inequality, the speech of the powerful impresses its view upon the world, concealing the truth of powerlessness under that despairing acquiescence that provides the appearance of consent and makes protest inaudible as well as rare. Pornography can invent women because it has the power to make its vision into reality, which then passes, objectively, for truth. So while the First Amendment supports pornography, believing that consensus and progress are facilitated by allowing all views, however divergent and unorthodox, it fails to notice that pornography (like the racism, in which I include anti-Semitism, of the Nazis and the Klan) is not at all divergent or unorthodox. It is the ruling ideology. Feminism, the dissenting view, is suppressed by pornography. Thus, while defenders of pornography argue that allowing all speech, including pornography, frees the mind to fulfill itself, pornography freely enslaves women's minds and bodies inseparably, normalizing the terror that enforces silence from women's point of view.

To liberals, speech must never be sacrificed for other social goals. But liberalism has never understood that the free speech of men silences the free speech of women. It is the same social goal, just other *people*. This is what a real inequality, a real conflict, a real disparity in social power looks like. The law of the First Amendment comprehends that freedom of expression, in the abstract, is a system, but it fails to comprehend that sexism (and racism), *in the concrete,* are also systems. That pornography chills women's expression is difficult to demonstrate empirically because silence is not eloquent. Yet on no more of the same kind of evidence, the argument that suppressing pornography might chill legitimate speech had supported its protection.

First Amendment logic, like nearly all legal reasoning, has difficulty grasping harm that is not linearly caused in the "John hit Mary" sense. The idea is that words or pictures can be harmful only if they produce harm in a form that is considered an action. Words work in the province of attitudes, actions in the realm of behavior. Words cannot constitute harm in themselves—never mind libel, invasion of privacy, blackmail, bribery, conspiracy or most sexual harassment. But which is saying "kill" to a trained guard dog, a word or an act? Which is its training? How about a sign that reads "Whites only"? Is that the idea or the practice of segregation? Is a woman raped by an attitude or a behavior? Which is sexual arousal? Notice that the specific idea of causality used in obscenity law dates from around the time that it was first "proved" that it is impossible to prove that pornography causes harm.[34] Instead of the more complex causality implicit in the above examples, the view became that pornography must cause harm the way negligence causes car accidents or its effects are not cognizable as harm. The trouble with this individuated, atomistic, linear, isolated, tort-like—in a word, positivistic—conception of injury is that the way pornography targets and defines women for abuse and discrimination does not work like this. It does hurt individuals, not *as* individuals in a one-at-a-time sense, but a members of the group "women." Harm is caused to one individual woman rather than another essentially the way one number rather than another is caused in roulette. But on a group basis, as women, the selection process is absolutely selective and systematic. Its causality is essentially collective and totalistic and contextual. To reassert atomistic linear causality as a *sine qua non* of injury—you cannot be harmed unless you are harmed through this etiology—is to refuse to respond to the true nature of this specific kind of harm. Such refusals call for explanation. Morton Horowitz says that the issue of causality in tort law is "one of the pivotal ideas in a system of legal thought that sought to separate private law from politics and to insulate the legal system from the threat of redistribution."[35] Perhaps causality in the pornography issue is an attempt to privatize the injury pornography does to women in order to insulate the same system from the threat of gender equality, also a form of redistribution.

Women are known to be brutally coerced into pornographic performances.[36] But so far it is only with children, usually male children, that courts consider that the speech of pornographers was once someone else's *life.*[37] Courts and commissions and legislatures and researchers have searched and re-searched, largely in vain, for the injury of pornography in the mind of the (male) consumer or in "society," or in empirical correlations between variations in levels of "anti-social" acts and liberalization in obscenity laws.[38] Speech can be regulated "in the interests of unwilling viewers, captive audiences, young children, and beleaguered neighborhoods,"[39] but the normal level of sexual force—force that is not seen as force because it is inflicted on women and called sex—has never been a policy issue. Until the last few years experimental research never approached the question of whether pornographic stimuli might support *sexual* aggression against women[40] or whether violence might be sexually stimulating or have sexual sequelae.[41] Only in the last few months have laboratory researches begun to learn the consequences for women of so-called consensual sexual depictions that show normal dominance and submission.[42] We still don't have this kind of data on the impact of female-only nudity or of depictions of specific acts like penetration or even of mutual sex in a social context of gender inequality.

The most basic assumption underlying First Amendment adjudication is that, socially, speech is free. The First Amendment says, "Congress shall not abridge *the freedom of speech.*" Free speech exists. The problem for government is to avoid constraining that which, if unconstrained by government, *is* free. This tends to presuppose that whole segments of the population are not systematically silenced *socially*, prior to government action. The place of pornography in the inequality of the sexes makes such presupposition untenable and makes any approach to *our* freedom of expression so based worse than useless. For women, the urgent issue of freedom of speech is not primarily their avoidance of state intervention as such, but finding an affirmative means to get access to speech for those to whom it has been denied.

Beyond offensiveness or prurience, to say that pornography is "dehumanizing" is an attempt to articulate harm. But "human being" is a social concept with many possible meanings. Here I will criticize some liberal moral meanings of personhood through a feminist political analysis of what pornography does to women, showing how the inadequacy of the liberal dehumanization critique reflects the inadequacy of its concept of person. In a feminist perspective, pornography dehumanizes women in a culturally specific and empirically descriptive—not liberal moral—sense. Pornography dispossesses women of the power of which, in the same act, it possesses men: the power of sexual, hence gender, definition. Perhaps a human being, for gender purposes, is someone who controls the social definition of sexuality.

A person, in one Kantian view, is a free and rational agent whose existence is an end in itself, as opposed to instrumental.[43] In pornography, women exist to the *end* of male pleasure. Kant sees human as characterized by universal abstract rationality, with no component of individual or group differences, and as a "bundle or rights."[44] Pornography purports to define what a woman *is*. It does this on a group basis, including when it raises individual qualities to sexual stereotypes, as in the strategy of *Playboy*'s "Playmate of the Month." I also think that pornography derives much of its sexual power, as well as part of its justification, from the implicit assumption that the Kantian notion of person actually describes the condition of women in this society. According to that assumption, if we are there, we are freely and rationally there, when the fact is that women—in pornography and in part because of pornography—have no such rights.

Other views of the person include one of Wittgenstein's, who says that the best picture of the human soul is the human body.[45] I guess this depends upon what picture of the human body you have in mind. Marx's work offers various concepts of personhood deducible from his critique of various forms of productive organization. A person is defined by whatever material conditions the society values; in a bourgeois society, a person might be a property owner.[46] The problem here is that women *are* the property that constitutes the personhood, the masculinity, of men under capitalism. Thinking further in Marxian theoretical terms, I have wondered whether women in pornography are more properly conceived as fetishes or objects. Does pornography more attribute life-likeness to that which is dead—as in fetishism—or make death-like that which is alive—as in objectification? I guess it depends upon whether, socially speaking, women are more alive than dead.

In Hume's concept of a person as a bundle or collection of sense perceptions, such that the feeling of self-identity over time is a persistent illusion,[47] we finally have a view of the human that coincides with the view of women in pornography. That is, the empiricist view of person is the pornographic view of women. No critique of dominance or subjection, certainly not of objectification, can be grounded in a vision of reality in which all sense perceptions are just sense perceptions. This is one way an objectivist epistemology supports the unequal holding and wielding of power in a society in which the persistent illusion of selfhood of one half of the population is materially supported and maintained at the expense of the other half. What I'm saying is that those who are socially allowed a self are also allowed the luxury of postulating its illusoriness and having that called a philosophical position. Whatever self they ineluctably have, they don't lose by saying it is an illusion. Even if it is not particularly explanatory such male ideology, if taken as such, is often highly descriptive. Thus Hume defines the human in the same terms feminism uses to define women's dehumanization: for women in pornography, the self is, precisely, a persistent illusion.

Contemporary ordinary language philosopher Bernard Williams says "person" ordinarily means things like valuing self-respect and feeling pain.[48] How self is defined, what respect attaches to, stimuli of pleasure and to an extent stimuli and thresholds of pain, are cultural variables. Women in pornography are turned on by being put down and feel pain as pleasure. We want it; we beg for it; we get it. To argue that this is dehumanizing need not mean to take respect as an ahistorical absolute or to treat the social meaning of pain as invariant or uniformly negative. Rather, it is to argue that it is the acceptance of the social definition of these values—the acceptance of self-respect and the avoidance of pain as values—that permits the erotization of their negative—debasement and torture—in pornography. It is only to the extent that each of these values is *accepted as human* that their negation becomes a quality of, and is eroticized in and as, woman. Only when self-respect is accepted as human does debasement become sexy and female; only when the avoidance of pain is accepted as human does torture become sexy and female. In this way, women's sexuality as expressed in pornography precisely negates her status as human. But there is more: exactly what is defined as degrading to a human being, *however* that is socially defined, is exactly what is sexually arousing to the male point of view in pornography, just as the one to whom it is done is the girl regardless of sex. In this way, it is specifically women whom pornography identifies with and by sexuality, as the erotic is equated with the dehumanizing.

To define the pornographic as that which is violent, not sexual, as liberal moral analyses tend to, is to trivialize and evade the essence of this critique, while seeming to express it. As with rape, where the issue is not the presence or absence of force but what sex *is* as distinct from coercion,[49] the question for pornography is what eroticism *is* as distinct from the subordination of women. This is not a rhetorical question. Under male dominance, whatever sexually arouses a man is sex. In pornography the violence *is* the sex. The inequality is the sex. Pornography does not work sexually without hierarchy. If there is no inequality, no violation, no dominance, no force, there is no sexual arousal. Obscenity law does the pornographers a real favor by clouding this, pornography's central dynamic, under the coy gender-neutral abstraction of "prurient interest." Obscenity law also adds the attraction of state prohibition, a tool of dominance, to whatever the law of obscenity is seen to encompass.

Calling rape and pornography violent, not sexual, the banner of much anti-rape and anti-pornography organizing,[50] is an attempt to protest that women do not find rape pleasurable or pornography stimulating while avoiding claiming this rejection as *women's* point of view. The concession to the objective stance, the attempt to achieve credibility by covering up the specificity of one's viewpoint, not only abstracts from our experience, it lies about it. Women and men know men find rape sexual and pornography erotic. It therefore *is*. We also know that sexuality is commonly violent without being any the less sexual. To deny this sets up the situation so that when women are aroused by sexual violation, meaning we experience it *as* our sexuality, the feminist analysis is seen to be contradicted. But it is not contradicted, it is *proved*. The male supremacist definition of female sexuality as lust for self-annihilation has won. It would be surprising, feminist analysis would be wrong, and sexism would be trivial, if this were merely exceptional (One might ask at this point, not why some women embrace explicit sado-masochism, but why any women do not.) To reject forced sex in the name of women's point of view requires an account of women's experience of being violated by the same acts both sexes have learned as natural and fulfilling and erotic, when no critique, no alternatives, and few transgressions have been permitted.

The depersonalization critique, with the "violence not sex" critique, exposes pornography's double standard, but does not attack the masculinity of the standards for personhood and for sex that pornography sets. The critiques are thus useful, to some extent deconstructive, but beg the deeper questions of the place of pornography in sexuality and of sexuality in the construction of women's definition and status, because they act as if women can be "persons" by interpretation, as if the concept is not, in every socially real way, defined by and in terms of and reserved for men and as if sexuality is not itself a construct of male power. To do this is to act as if pornography did not exist or were impotent. Deeper than the personhood question or the violence question is the question of the mechanism of social causation by which pornography *constructs* women and sex, defines what "women" means and what sexuality is, in terms of each other.

The law of obscenity at times says that sexual expression is only talk, therefore cannot be intrinsically harmful. Yet somehow pornographic talk is vital to protect. If pornography is a practice of the ideology of gender inequality, and gender *is an ideology,* if pornography is sex and gender is sexual, the question of the relation between pornography and life is nothing less than the question of the dynamic of the subordination of women to men. If "objectification . . . is never trivial,"[52] girls *are* ruined by books.[53] To comprehend this process will require an entirely new theory of social causality—of ideology in life, of the dynamic of mind and body in social power—that connects point of view with politics. The development of such an analysis has been stymied equally by fear of repressive state use of any critique of any form of expression, by the power of pornography to create women in its image of use, and by the power of pornographers to create a climate hostile to inquiry into their power and profits.

I said all that in order to say this: the law of obscenity has the same surface theme and the same underlying theme as pornography itself. Superficially both involve morality: rules made and transgressed for purposes of sexual arousal. Actually, both are about power, about the equation between the erotic and the control of women by men: *women* made and transgressed for purpose of sexual arousal. It seems essential to the kick of pornography that it be to some degree against the rules, but it is never truly unavailable or truly illegitimate. Thus obscenity law, like the law of rape, preserves the value of, without restricting the ability to get, that which it purports to both devalue and to prohibit. Obscenity law helps keep pornography sexy by putting state power—force, hierarchy—behind its purported prohibition on what men can have sexual access to. The law of obscenity is to pornography as pornography is to sex: a map that purports to be a mirror, a legitimization and authorization and set of directions and guiding controls that project themselves onto social reality while claiming merely to reflect the image of what is already there. Pornography presents itself as fantasy or illusion or idea, which can be good or bad as it is accurate or inaccurate, while it actually, *hence accurately,* distributes power. Liberal morality cannot deal with illusions that *constitute* reality because its theory of reality, lacking a substantive critique of the distribution of social power, cannot get behind the empirical world, truth by correspondence. On the surface, both pornography and the law of obscenity are about sex. In fact, it is the status of women that is at stake.

Notes

Many of the ideas in this essay were developed and refined in close collaboration with Andrea Dworkin. It is difficult at times to distinguish the contribution of each of us to a body of work that—through shared teaching, writing, speaking, organizing, and political action on every level—has been created together. I have tried to credit specific contributions that I am aware are distinctly hers. This text is mine; she does not necessarily agree with everything in it.

1. This speech as a whole is intended to communicate what I mean by pornography. The key work on the subject is Andrea Dworkin, Pornography: Men Possessing Women (1981). No definition can convey the meaning of a word as well as its use in context can. However, what Andrea Dworkin and I mean by pornography is rather well captured in our legal definition: "Pornography is the graphic sexually explicit subordination of women, whether in pictures or in words, that also includes one or more of the following: (i) women are presented dehumanized as sexual objects, things or commodities; or (ii) women are presented as sexual objects who enjoy pain or humiliation; or (iii) women are presented as sexual objects who experience sexual pleasure in being raped; or (iv) women are presented as sexual objects tied up or cut up or mutilated or bruised or physically hurt; or (v) women are presented in postures in sexual submission, servility or display; or (vi) women's body parts—including but not limited to vaginas, breasts, and buttocks—are exhibited, such that women are reduced to those parts; or (vii) women are presented as whores by nature; or (viii) women are presented as being penetrated by objects or animals; or (ix) women are presented in scenarios of degradation, injury, torture, shown as filthy or inferior, bleeding, bruised, or hurt in a context that makes these conditions sexual." Pornography also includes "the use of men, children or transexuals in the place of women." Pornography, thus defined, is discrimination on the basis of sex and; as such, a civil rights violation. This definition is a slightly modified version of the one passed by the Minneapolis City Council on December 30, 1983. Minneapolis, Minn, Ordinance amending tit. 7., chs. 139 and 141, Minneapolis Code of Ordinances Relating to Civil Rights (Dec. 30, 1983). . . .

2. Justice Black, at times joined by Justice Douglas, took the position that the Bill of Rights, including the First Amendment, was "absolute." Hugo Black, The Bill of Rights, 35 N.Y.U. L. Rev. 865, 867 (1960); Edmund Cahn, Justice Black and First Amendment "Absolutes": A Public Interview, 37 N.Y.U. L. Rev. 549 (1962). For a discussion, see Harry Kalven, Upon Rereading Mr. Justice Black on the First Amendment, 14 UCLA L. Rev. 428 (1967). . . .

3. The sense in which I mean women's perspective as different from men's is like that of Virginia Woolf's reference to "the difference of view, the difference of standard" in her George Eliot, 1 Collected Essays 204 (1966). Neither of us uses the notion of a gender difference to refer to something biological or natural or transcendental or existential. Perspective parallels standards because the social experience of gender is confined by gender. See Catharine A. MacKinnon, Sexual Harassment of Working Women 107–141 (1979), and the articles mentioned in note 7, *infra*; Virginia Woolf, Three Guineas (1938); see also Andrea Dworkin, The Root Cause, in Our Blood: Essays and Discourses on Sexual Politics 96 (1976). I do not refer to the gender difference here descriptively, leaving its roots and implications unspecified, so they could be biological, existential, transcendental, in any sense inherent, or social but necessary. I mean "point of view" as a view, hence a standard, that is imposed on women by force of sex inequality, which is a political condition. "Male," which is an adjective here, is a social and political concept, not a biological attribute; it is a status socially conferred upon a person because of a condition of birth. As I use "male," it has nothing whatever to do with inherency, preexistence, nature, inevitability, or body as such. Because it is in the interest of men to be male in the system we live under (male being powerful as well as human), they seldom question its rewards or even see it as a status at all.

4. The Report of the Commission on Obscenity and Pornography (1970) (majority report). The accuracy of the commission's findings is called into question by: (1) widespread criticism of the commission's methodology from a variety of perspectives, e.g., L. Sunderland, Obscenity—The Court, the Congress and the President's Commission (1975); Edward Donnerstein, Pornography Commission Revisited: Aggression—Erotica and Violence against Women, 39 J. Personality & Soc. Psychol. 269 (1980); Ann Garry, Pornography and Respect for Women; 4 Soc. Theory & Prac. 395 (Summer 1978); Irene Diamond, Pornography and Repression, 5 Signs 686 (1980); Victor Cline, Another View: Pornography Effects, the State of the Art, in V. B. Cline ed., Where Do You Draw the Line? (1974); Pauline Bart & Margaret Jozsa, Dirty Books, Dirty Films, and Dirty Data, in Laura Lederer ed., Take Back the Night: Women on Pornography 204 (1982); (2) the commission's tendency to minimize the significance of its own findings, e.g., those by Donald Mosher on the differential effects of exposure by gender; and (3) the design of the commission's research. The commission did not focus on questions about gender, did its best to eliminate "violence" from its materials (so as not to overlap with the Violence Commission), and propounded unscientific theories such as Puritan guilt to explain women's negative responses to the materials.

Further, scientific causality is unnecessary to legally validate an obscenity regulation: "But, it is argued, there is no scientific data which conclusively demonstrate that exposure to obscene materials adversely affects men and women or their society. It is [urged] that, absent such a demonstration, any kind of state regulation is 'impermissible.' *We reject this argument.* It is not for us to resolve empirical uncertainties underlying state legislation, save in the exceptional case where that legislation plainly impinges upon rights protected by the Constitution itself. . . . Although there is no conclusive proof of a connection between antisocial behavior and obscene material, the legislature of Georgia could quite reasonably determine that such a connection does or might exist." Paris Adult Theatre I v. Slaton, 413 U.S. 49, 60–61 (1973) (Burger, J., for the majority) (emphasis added); see also Roth v. U.S., 354 U.S. 476, 501 (1957).

5. Some of the harm of pornography to women, as defined in note 1 above, and as discussed in this talk, has been documented in empirical studies. Recent studies have found that exposure to pornography increases the willingness of normal men to aggress against women under laboratory conditions; makes both women and men substantially less able to perceive accounts of rape as accounts of rape; makes normal men more closely resemble convicted rapists psychologically; increases attitudinal measures that are known to correlate with rape, such as hostility toward women, propensity to rape, condoning rape, and predictions that one would rape or force sex on a woman if one knew one would not get caught; and produces other attitude changes in men, such as increasing the extent of their trivialization, dehumanization, and objectification of women. Diana E. H. Russell, Pornography and Violence: What Does the New Research Say?, in Lederer, *supra* note 4, at 216; Neil M. Malamuth & Edward Donnerstein eds., Pornography and Sexual Aggression (1984); Dolph Zillman, The Connection between Sex and Aggression (1984); J. V. P. Check, N. Malamuth, & R. Stille, Hostility to Women Scale (1983) (unpublished manuscript); Edward Donnerstein, Pornography: Its Effects on Violence against Women, in Malamuth & Donnerstein eds., Pornography and Sexual Aggression (1984); Neil M. Malamuth & J. V. P. Check, The Effects of Mass Media Exposure on Acceptance of Violence against Women: A Field Experiment, 15 J. Res. Personality 436 (1981); Neil M. Malamuth, Rape Proclivities among Males, 37 J. Soc. Issues 138 (1981); Neil M. Malamuth & Barry Spinner, A

Longitudinal Content Analysis of Sexual Violence in the Best-Selling Erotic Magazines, 16 J. Sex Res. 226 (1980); Mosher, Sex Callousness Towards Women, in 8 Technical Report of the Commission on Obscenity and Pornography 313 (1971); Dolph Zillman & J. Bryant, Effects of Massive Exposure to Pornography, in Malamuth & Donnerstein eds., Pornography and Sexual Aggression (1984).

6. The following are illustrative, not exhaustive, of the body of work I term the "feminist critique of pornography." Andrea Dworkin, *supra* note 1; Dorchen Leidholdt, Where Pornography Meets Fascism, Win, Mar. 15, 1983, at 18; George Steiner, Night Words, in D. Holbrook ed., The Case Against Pornography 227 (1973); Susan Brownmiller, Against Our Will: Men, Women and Rape 394 (1975); Robin Morgan, Pornography and Rape: Theory and Practice, in Robin Morgan ed., Going Too Far 165 (1977); Kathleen Barry, Female Sexual Slavery (1979); R. R. Linden, D. R. Pagano, D. E. H. Russell, & S. L. Star eds., Against Sado-Masochism: A Radical Feminist Analysis (1982), especially chapters by Ti-Grace Atkinson, Judy Butler, Andrea Dworkin, Alice Walker, John Stoltenberg, Audre Lorde, and Susan Leigh Star; Alice Walker, Coming Apart, in Lederer, Take Back the Night, *supra* note 4, and other articles in that volume with the exception of the legal ones; Gore Vidal, Women's Liberation Meets the Miller-Mailer-Manson Man, in Homage to Daniel Shays: Collected Essays 1952–1972, 389 (1972); Linda Lovelace & Michael McGrady, Ordeal (1980). Works basic to the perspective taken here are Kate Millett, Sexual Politics (1969), and Florence Rush, The Best-Kept Secret: Sexual Abuse of Children (1980). Violent Pornography: Degradation of Women versus Right of Free Speech, 8 N.Y.U. Rev. L. & Soc. Change 181 (1978) contains both feminist and nonfeminist arguments.

7. For more extensive discussions of this subject, see my prior work, especially Feminism, Marxism, Method and the State: An Agenda for Theory, 7 Signs 515 (1982) [hereinafter cited as Signs I]; Feminism, Marxism, Method and the State: Toward Feminist Jurisprudence, 8 Signs 636 (1983) [hereinafter cited as Signs II] [both reprinted in D. Weisberg ed., Feminist Legal Theory: Foundations (Temple Univ. Press, 1993)].

8. Jacobellis v. Ohio, 378 U.S. 184, 197 (1964) (Stewart, J., concurring).

9. Justice Stewart has been said to have complained that this single line was more quoted and remembered than anything else he ever said.

10. Susan Griffin, Pornography and Silence: Culture's Revenge Against Nature 2–4, 251–265 (1981).

11. The position that pornography is sex—that whatever you think of sex you think of pornography—underlies nearly every treatment of the subject. In particular, nearly every nonfeminist treatment proceeds on the implicit or explicit assumption, argument, criticism, or suspicion that pornography is sexually liberating in some way, a position unifying an otherwise diverse literature. See, e.g., D. H. Lawrence, Pornography and Obscenity, in his Sex, Literature and Censorship 64 (1959); Hugh Hefner, The Playboy Philosophy, Playboy, Dec. 1962, at 73, and Playboy, February 1963, at 43; Henry Miller, Obscenity and the Law of Reflection, in his Remember to Remember 274, 286 (1947); Deirdre English, The Politics of Porn: Can Feminists Walk the Line?, Mother Jones, Apr. 1980, at 20; Jean Bethke Elshtain, The Victim Syndrome: A Troupling Turn in Feminism, The Progressive, June 1982, at 42. . . .

12. The "fantasy" and "catharsis" hypotheses, together, assert that pornography cathects sexuality on the level of fantasy fulfillment. The work of Edward Donnerstein, particularly, shows that the opposite is true. The more pornography is viewed, the *more* pornography—and the more brutal pornography—is both wanted and required for sexual arousal. What occurs is not catharis, but desensitization, requiring progressively

more potent stimulation. See works cited *supra* note 5; Murray Straus, Leveling, Civility, and Violence in the Family," 36 J. Marriage & Fam. 13 (1974).

13. Lovelace & McGrady, *supra* note 6, provides an account by one coerced pornography model. See also Andrea Dworkin, Pornography's "Exquisite Volunteers," Ms., Mar. 1981, at 65.

14. However, for one such inquiry, see Russell, *supra* note 5, at 228: a random sample of 930 San Francisco households found that 10 percent of women had at least once "been upset by anyone trying to get you to do what they'd seen in pornographic pictures, movies or books." Obviously, this figure could only include those who knew that the pornography was the source of the sex, so this finding is conservative. See also Diana E. H. Russell, Rape in Marriage 27–41 (1983) (discussing the data base). The hearings Andrea Dworkin and I held for the Minneapolis City Council on the ordinance cited *supra* note 1 produced many accounts of the use of pornography to force sex on women and children. Public Hearings on Ordinances to Add Pornography as Discrimination Against Women, Committee on Government Operations, City Council, Minneapolis, Minn., Dec. 12–13, 1983 [hereinafter cited as Hearings].

15. See Signs I; see also Susan Sontag, The Pornographic Imagination, 34 Partisan Rev. 181 (1977).

16. Louis Henkin, Morals and the Constitution: The Sin of Obscenity, 63 Colum. L. Rev. 391, 395 (1963).

17. A reading of case law supports the reports in Robert Woodward and Scott Armstrong, The Brethren 194 (1979), to the effect that this is a "bottom line" criterion for at least some justices. The interesting question becomes why the tactics of male supremacy would change from keeping the penis hidden, covertly glorified, to having it everywhere on display, overtly glorified. This suggests at least that a major shift from private terrorism to public terrorism has occurred. What used to be perceived as a danger to male power, the exposure of the penis, has now become a strategy in maintaining it.

18. Those termed "fathers" and "sons" in Dworkin's article [Why So-Called Radical Men Love and Need Pornography, in Lederer, *supra* note 4, at 141], we came to call "the old boys," whose strategy for male dominance involves keeping pornography and the abuse of women private, and "the new boys," whose strategy for male dominance involves making pornography and the abuse of women public. In my view, Freud and the popularization of his derepression hypothesis figure centrally in "the new boys'" approach and success. To conclude, as some have, that women have benefitted from the public availability of pornography and hence should be grateful for and have a stake in its continuing availability is to say that the merits of open condoned oppression relative to covert condoned oppression warrant its continuation. This reasoning obscures the possibility of *ending* the oppression. The benefit of pornography's open availability, it seems to me, is that women can know who and what we are dealing with in order to end it. How, is the question.

19. Miller v. California, 413 U.S. 15, 24 (1973).

20. Paris Adult Theatre I v. Slaton, 413 U.S. 49, 67 (1973). See also Miller v. California, 413 U.S. 15, 25 n. 7 ("A quotation from Voltaire in the flyleaf of a book will not constitutionally redeem an otherwise obscene publication," quoting Kois v. Wisconsin, 408 U.S. 229, 231 [1972]).

21. Malamuth & Spinner, *supra* note 5 (". . . the portrayal of sexual aggression within such 'legitimate' magazines as Playboy and Penthouse may have a greater impact than similar portrayals in hard-core pornography"); Neil M. Malamuth & Edward Donnerstein, The Effects of Aggressive-Pornographic Mass Media Stimuli, 15 Advances Experimental Soc. Psychol. 103, 130 (1982).

22. Some courts, under the obscenity rubric, seem to have understood that the quality of artistry does not undo the damage. People v. Mature Enterprises, 343 N.Y.S.2d 911, 925 n.14 (N.Y. Sup. 1973) ("This court will not adopt a rule of law which states that obscenity is suppressible but that well-written or technically well produced obscenity is not," quoting, in part, People v. Fritch, 13 N.Y.2d 119, 126, 243 N.Y.S.2d 1, 7, 192 N.E.2d 713 [1963]). More to the point of my argument here is Justice O'Connor's observation that "[t]he compelling interests identified in today's opinion . . . suggests that the Constitution might in fact permit New York to ban knowing distribution of works depicting minors engaged in explicit sexual conduct, regardless of the social value of the depictions. For example, a 12-year-old child photographed while masturbating surely suffers the same psychological harm whether the community labels the photograph 'edifying' or 'tasteless.' The audience's appreciation of the depiction is simply irrelevant to New York's asserted interest in protecting children from psychological, emotional, and mental harm." New York v. Ferber, 458 U.S. 747, 774–775 (1982) (concurring). Put another way, how does it make a harmed child *not harmed* that what was produced by harming him is great art?

23. Women typically get mentioned in obscenity law only in the phrase, "women and men," used as synonym for "people." At the same time, exactly who the victim of pornography is, has long been a great mystery. The few references to "exploitation" in obscenity litigation do not evoke a woman victim. For example, one reference to "a system of commercial exploitation of people with sadomasochistic sexual aberrations" concerned the customers of women dominatrixes, all of whom were men. State v. Von Cleef, 102 N.J. Super. 104, 245 A.2d 495, 505 (1968). The children at issue in *Ferber* were boys. Similarly, Justice Frankfurter invoked the "sordid exploitation of man's nature and impulses" in discussing his conception of pornography in Kingsley Pictures Corp. v. Regents, 360 U.S. 684, 692 (1958).

24. See, e.g., Miller v. California, 413 U.S. at 40–41 (Douglas, J., dissenting) ("What shocks me may be sustenance for my neighbors") U.S. v. 12 200-Ft. Reels of Super 8mm Film, 413 U.S. 123, 137 (1972) (Douglas J., dissenting) ("[W]hat may be trash to me may be prized by others"); Cohen v. California, 403 U.S. 15, 25 (1970) (Harlan, J.) ("One man's vulgarity is another's lyric"); Winters v. New York, 333 U.S. 507, 510 (1947) ("What is one man's amusement, teaches another's doctrine"); Lawrence, *supra* note 11, at 195 ("What is Pornography to one man is the laughter of genius to another"); Ginsberg v. United States, 383 U.S. 463, 489 (1966) (Douglas J., dissenting) ("Some like Chopin, others like 'rock and roll'"). As one man, the pimp who forced Linda Lovelace into pornography, said to another: "I don't tell you how to write your column. Don't tell me how to treat my broads." (Quoted in Gloria Steinem, The Real Linda Lovelace, in Outrageous Acts and Everyday Rebellions 243, 252 [1983].)

25. None of this is intended as a comment about the personal sexuality or principles of any judicial individual; it is rather a series of analytic observations that emerge from a feminist attempt to interpret the deep social structure of a vast body of case law on the basis of a critique of gender. Further research should systematically analyze the contents of the pornography involved in the cases. For instance, with respect to the last hypothesis in the text above, is it just chance that the first film to be found obscene by a state supreme court depicts male masturbation? Landau v. Fording, 245 C.A.2d 820, 54 Cal. Rptr. 177 (1966). Given the ubiquity of the infantilization of women and the sexualization of little girls, would *Ferber* have been decided the same way if it had shown twelve-year-old girls masturbating? Did works like *Lady Chatterley's Lover* and *Tropic of Cancer* get in trouble because male sexuality is depicted in a way that men think is dangerous for women and children to see?

26. E.g., The Report of the Commission on Obscenity and Pornography, *supra* note 4, at 1, charges the Commission to study "[t]he effect of obscenity and pornography upon the public and particularly minors and its relation to crime and other antisocial behavior."

27. N. Scheman, Making it All Up (transcript of speech), Jan. 1982, at 7.

28. This body of work is usually taken to be diverse. Thomas I. Emerson, Toward a General Theory of the First Amendment (1966); Emerson, The System of Freedom of Expression (1970); Alexander Meiklejohn, Free Speech and Its Relation to Self-Government (1948); Whitney v. California, 274 U.S. 357, 375 (1927) (Brandeis, J., concurring, joined by Holmes, J.); T. Scanlon, A Theory of Free Expression, 1 Phil. & Pub. Aff. 204 (1972); John Hart Ely, Flag Desecration: A Case Study in the Roles of Categorization and Balancing in First Amendment Analysis, 88 Harv. L. Rev. 1482 (1975); Zechariah Chafee, Free Speech in the United States 245 (1948). This literature is ably summarized and anatomized by Ed Baker, who proposes an interpretative theory that goes far toward responding to my objections here, without really altering the basic assumptions I criticize. See C. E. Baker, Scope of the First Amendment Freedom of Speech, 25 UCLA L. Rev. 964 (1978), and The Process of Change and the Liberty Theory of the First Amendment, 55 S. Cal. L. Rev. 293 (1982).

29. Emerson, Toward a General Theory of the First Amendment, *supra* note 28, at 28.

30. See Erznoznik v. City of Jacksonville, 422 U.S. 205 (1975); Breard v. Alexandria, 341 U.S. 622, 641–645 (1951); Kovacs v. Cooper, 336 U.S. 77, 87–89 (1949).

31. Stanley v. Georgia, 394 U.S. 557 (1969).

32. See Walker, Coming Apart, in Lederer, *supra* note 4, at 85; Russell, *supra* note 5; *Hearings* (Minneapolis) *supra* note 14. Cf. Paris Adult Theatre I v Slaton, 413 U.S. 49, 71 (1973) (Douglas, J., dissenting) ("[In] a life that has not been short, I have yet to be trapped into seeing or reading something that would offend me"). He probably hadn't.

33. See MacKinnon, Privacy v. Equality, in Feminism Unmodified, for a fuller discussion of this point.

34. The essentially scientific notion of causality did not *first* appear in this law at this time, however. See, e.g., U.S. v. Roth, 237 F.2d 796, 812–817, (2d Cir. 1956) (Frank, J., concurring) ("According to Judge Bok, an obscenity statute may be validly enforced when there is proof of a causal relation between a particular book and undesirable conduct. Almost surely, such proof cannot ever be adduced." *Id.,* 826 n.70).

Werner Heisenberg, criticizing old ideas of atomic physics, in light of Einstein's theory of relativity , states the conditions that must exist for a causal relation to make sense: "To coordinate a definite cause to a definite effect has sense only when both can be observed without introducing a foreign element disturbing their interrelation. The law of causality, because of its very nature, can only be defined for isolated systems." Werner Heisenberg, The Physical Principles of the Quantum Theory 63 (1930). Among the influences that disturb the isolation of systems are observers. Underlying the adoption of a causality standard in obscenity law is a rather hasty analogy between the regularities of physical and social systems, an analogy which has seldom been explicitly justified or even updated as the physical sciences have questioned their epistemological foundations. This kind of scientific causality may not be readily susceptible to measurement in social systems for the simple reason that social systems are not isolated systems; experimental research (which is where it *has* been shown that pornography causes harm) can only minimize the influence of what will always be "foreign elements." Pornography and harm may not be two definite events anyway; perhaps pornography *is* a harm. Moreover, if the effects of pornography are systematic, they may not be isolable from the system in which they exist. This would not mean that no harm exists. Rather, it would mean that because the harm is so pervasive, it cannot be sufficiently isolated to be *perceived* as existing according to this causal model. In other words, if pornography is seen as harmful only if it causes harm by this model, and if it exists socially only in ways that cannot be isolated from society itself, its harm will not be perceived to exist. I think this describes the conceptual situation in which we find ourselves.

35. Morton Horowitz, The Doctrine of Objective Causation, in David Kairys ed., The Politics of Law 201 (1982). The pervasiveness of the objectification of women has been treated as a reason why pandering should not be Constitutionally restricted: "The advertisements of our best magazines are chock-full of thighs, ankles, calves, bosoms, eyes, and hair, to draw the potential buyer's attention to lotions, tires, food, liquor, clothing, autos, and even insurance policies." Ginsberg v. U.S., 383 U.S. 463, 482 (1966) (Douglas J., dissenting). Justice Douglas thereby illustrated, apparently without noticing, that *somebody* knows that associating sex, that is, women's bodies, with things causes people to *act* on that association.

36. See Lovelace & McGrady, *supra* note 6.

37. Two boys masturbating with no showing of explicit force demonstrates the harm of child pornography in New York v. Ferber, 458 U.S. 747 (1982), while shoving money up a woman's vagina, among other acts, raises serious questions of "regulation of 'conduct' having a communicative element" in live sex adjudications, California v. LaRue, 409 U.S. 109, 113 (1972) (live sex can be regulated by a state in connection with serving alcoholic beverages). "Snuff" films, in which a woman is actually murdered to produce a film for sexual entertainment, are known to exist. People v. Douglas and Hernandez, Felony Complaint No. NF8300382, Municipal Court, North Judicial District, Orange County, Calif., Aug. 5, 1983, alleges the murder of two young girls to make a pornographic film. Hernandez turned state's evidence; Douglas was convicted of first-degree murder in November 1984. No snuff film was found. (Conversation with Tony Rackackaus, district attorney, Sept. 3, 1986.)

38. Both Griffin, *supra* note 10, and the oldest Anglo-Saxon obscenity cases locate the harm of pornography in the mind of the consumer. See, e.g., Regina v. Hicklin, 3 L.R.-Q.B. 360, 371 (1868) ("tendency . . . to deprave and corrupt those whose minds are open to such immoral influences and into whose hands a publication of this sort may fall"). The data of John Court and Berl Kutchinsky, both correlational, reach contrary conclusions on the relation of pornography's availability to crime statistics. Kutchinsky, Towards an Explanation of the Decrease in Registered Sex Crimes in Copenhagen, 7 Technical Report of the Commission on Obscenity and Pornography 263 (1971); Kutchinsky, The Effect of Easy Availability of Pornography on the Incidence of Sex Crimes: The Danish Experience, 29 J. Soc. Issues 163 (1973); cf. Court, Pornography and Sex Crimes: A Re-Evaluation in the Light of Recent Trends around the World, 5 Int'l J. Criminology & Penology 129 (1977). More recent investigations into correlations focused on rape in the United States have reached still other conclusions. Larry Baron and Murray Straus have found a strong correlation between state-to-state variations in the rate of reported rape and the aggregate circulation rate of popular men's sex magazines, including *Playboy* and *Hustler.* "Sexual Stratification, Pornography, and Rape," Family Research Laboratory and Department of Sociology, University of New Hampshire, Durham, N.H., Nov. 18, 1983 (manuscript). The authors conclude that "the findings suggest that the combination of a society which is

characterized by a struggle to secure equal rights for women, by a high readership of sex magazines which depict women in ways which may legitimize violence, and by a context in which there is a high level of non-sexual violence, constitutes a mix of societal characteristics which precipitate rape" at 16. See also Report of the Committee on Obscenity and Film Censorship (the Williams Report) (1981), and the opinions of Justice Harlan on the injury to "society" as a permissible basis for legislative judgments in this area. Roth v. U.S., 354 U.S. 476, 501–502 (1957) (concurring in companion case, Alberts v. California).

39. Laurence Tribe, American Constitutional Law 662 (1978).

40. I am conceiving rape as *sexual* aggression. On the connection between pornography and rape, see Neil M. Malamuth, Rape Proclivity among Men, 37 J. Soc. Issues 138 (1981); Neil M. Malamuth, Rape Fantasies as a Function of Exposure to Violent Sexual Stimuli, 10 Archives Sexual Behav. 33 (1981); Scott Haber & Seymour Feshbach, Testing Hypotheses Regarding Rape: Exposure to Sexual Violence, Sex Differences, and the "Normality" of Rapists, 14 J. Res. Personality 121 (1980); Maggie Heim & Seymour Feshbach, Sexual Responsiveness of College Students to Rape Depictions: Inhibitory and Disinhibitory Effects, 38 J. Personality & Soc. Psychol. 399 (1980). See also works by Malamuth, *supra* note 5. Of course, there are difficulties in measuring rape as a direct consequence of laboratory experiments, difficulties that have led researchers to substitute other measures of willingness to aggress, such as electric shocks.

41. Apparently, it may be impossible to make a film for experimental purposes that portrays violence or aggression by a man against a woman that a substantial number of male experimental subjects do not perceive as sexual. See Hearings, *supra* note 14, at 31 (testimony of Edward Donnerstein).

42. See works of Zillman, *supra* note 5.

43. Immanuel Kant, Fundamental Principles of the Metaphysics of Morals (T. Abbott trans. 1969); Arthur Danto, Persons in P. Edwards ed., 6 Encyclopedia Phil. 10 (1967); Margaret Radin, Property and Personhood, 34 Stan. L. Rev. 957 (1982).

44. See Kant, *supra* note 43; Danto, *supra* note 43; Radin, *supra* note 43. See also the "original position" of John Rawls, A Theory of Justice (1971), and Rawls, Kantian Constructivism in Moral Theory, 9 J. Phil. 515, 533–535 (1980).

45. Ludwig Wittgenstein, Philosophical Investigations 178 (G. Anscombe trans., 3d ed. 1958).

46. Karl Marx's critique of capitalist society is epitomized in Capital chap. 1 (1867). His concept of the "fetishism of commodities" in which "relations between men [assume], in their eyes, the fantastic form of a relation between things" (emphasis added) is presented in the 1970 edition at 72.

47. David Hume, Of Personal Identity, in A Treatise of Human Nature bk. I, pt. IV, §VI (1888).

48. Bernard Williams, Are Persons Bodies? Personal Identity and Individualization, *and,* Bodily Continuity and Personal Identity, in his Problems of the Self 1, 64 (1973). Bernard Williams was principal author of the "Williams Report," *supra* note 38, Britain's equivalent of the U.S. Commission on Obscenity and Pornography, in which none of his values of "persons" were noticed lacking in, or women deprived of them by, pornography.

49. See Signs I and II.

50. Brownmiller, *supra* note 6, is widely considered to present the view that rape is an act of violence, not sex. Women Against Pornography, a New York–based antipornography group, has argued that pornography is violence against women, not sex.

This has been almost universally taken as *the* feminist position on the issue. For an indication of possible change, see 4 NCASA News 19–21 (May 1984).

51. This, again, does not mean that it is an *idea.* A new theory of ideology, prefigured in Dworkin, *supra* note 1, will be needed to conceptualize the role of pornography in constructing the condition of women.

52. Dworkin, *supra* note 1, at 115.

53. "Echoing Macaulay, 'Jimmy' Walker remarked that he had never heard of a woman seduced by a book." U.S. v. Roth, 237 F.2d 796, 812 (1956) (appendix to concurrence of Frank, J.). What is classically called seduction, I expect feminists might interpret as rape or forced sex.

❖ Francis Biddle's Sister: Pornography, Civil Rights, and Speech

Catharine A. MacKinnon

. . .

AT THE REQUEST of the city of Minneapolis, Andrea Dworkin and I conceived and designed a local human rights ordinance in accordance with our approach to the pornography issue. We define pornography as a practice of sex discrimination, a violation of women's civil rights, the opposite of sexual equality. Its point is to hold those who profit from and benefit from that injury accountable to those who are injured. It means that women's injury—our damage, our pain, our enforced inferiority—should outweigh their pleasure and their profits, or sex equality is meaningless.

We define pornography as the graphic sexually explicit subordination of women through pictures or words that also includes women dehumanized as sexual objects, things, or commodities; enjoying pain or humiliation or rape; being tied up, cut up, mutilated, bruised, or physically hurt; in postures of sexual submission or servility or display; reduced to body parts, penetrated by objects or animals, or presented in scenarios of degradation, injury, torture; shown as filthy or inferior; bleeding, bruised, or hurt in a context that makes these conditions sexual. Erotica, defined by distinction as not this, might be sexually explicit materials premised on equality. We also provide that the use of men, children, or transsexuals in the place of women is pornography. The definition is substantive in that it is sex-specific, but it covers everyone in a sex-specific way, so is gender neutral in overall design.

There is a buried issue within sex discrimination law about what sex, meaning gender, is. If sex is a *difference*, social or biological, one looks to see if a challenged practice occurs along the same lines; if it does, or if it is done to both sexes, the practice is not discrimination, not inequality. If, by contrast, sex has been a matter of *dominance*, the issue is not the gender difference but the difference gender makes. In this more substantive, less abstract approach, the concern with inequality is whether a practice *subordinates* on the basis of sex. The first approach implies that marginal correction is needed; the second requires social change. Equality, in the first view, centers on abstract symmetry between equivalent categories; the asymmetry that occurs when categories are not equivalent is not inequality, it is treating unlikes differently. In the second approach, inequality centers on the substantive, cumulative disadvantagement of social hierarchy. Equality for the first is nondifferentiation; for the second, nonsubordination. Although it is consonant with both approaches, our antipornography statute emerges largely from an analysis of the problem under the second approach.

To define pornography as a practice of sex discrimination combines a mode of portrayal that has a legal history—the sexually explicit—with an active term that is central to the inequality of the sexes—subordination. Among other things, subordination means to be in a position of inferiority or loss of power, or to be demeaned or denigrated. To be someone's subordinate is the opposite of being their equal. The definition does not include all sexually explicit depictions *of* the subordination of women. That is not what it says. It says, this which *does* that: the sexually explicit that subordinates women. To these active terms to capture what the pornography *does*, the definition adds a list of what it must also contain. This list, from our analysis, is an exhaustive description of what must be in the pornography for it to do what it does behaviorally. Each item in the definition is supported by experimental, testimonial, social, and clinical evidence. We made a legislative choice to be exhaustive and specific and concrete rather than conceptual and general, to minimize problems of chilling effect, making it hard to guess wrong, thus making self-censorship less likely, but encouraging (to use a phrase from discrimination law) voluntary compliance, knowing that if something turns up that is not on the list, the law will not be expansively interpreted.

The list in the definition, by itself, would be a content regulation. But together with the first part, the definition is not simply a content regulation. It is a medium-message combination that resembles many other such exceptions to First Amendment guarantees.

To focus what our law is, I will say what it is not. It is not a prior restraint. It does not go to possession. It does not turn on offensiveness. It is not a ban, unless relief for a proven injury is a "ban" on doing that injury again. Its principal enforcement mechanism is the civil rights commission, although it contains an option for direct access to court as well as de novo judicial review of administrative determinations, to ensure that no case will escape full judicial scrutiny and full due process. I will also not discuss various threshold issues, such as the sources of municipal authority, preemption, or abstention, or even issues of overbreadth or vagueness, nor will I defend the ordinance from views that never have been law, such as First Amendment absolutism. I will discuss the merits: how pornography by this definition is a harm, specifically how it is a harm of gender inequality, and how that harm outweighs any social interest in its protection by recognized First Amendment standards.[1]

This law aspires to guarantee women's rights consistent with the First Amendment by making visible a conflict of rights between the equality guaranteed to all women and what, in some legal sense, is now the freedom of the pornographers to make and sell, and their consumers to have access to, the materials this ordinance defines. Judicial resolution of this conflict, if the judges do for women what they have done for others, is likely to entail a balancing of the rights of women arguing that our lives and opportunities, including our freedom of speech and action, are constrained by—and in many cases flatly precluded by, in, and through—pornography, against those who argue that the pornography is harmless, or harmful only in part but not in the whole of the definition; or that it is more important to preserve the pornography than it is to prevent or remedy whatever harm it does.

In predicting how a court would balance these interests, it is important to understand that this ordinance cannot now be said to be either conclusively legal or illegal under existing law or precedent,[2] although I think the weight of authority is on our side. This ordinance enunciates a new form of the previously recognized governmental interest in sex equality. Many laws make sex equality a governmental interest. Our law is designed to further the equality of the sexes, to help make sex equality real. Pornography is a practice of discrimination on the basis of sex, on one level because of its role in creating and maintaining sex as a basis for discrimination. It harms many women one at a time and helps keep all women in an inferior status by defining our subordination as our sexuality and equating that with our gender. It is also sex discrimination because its victims, including men, are selected for victimization on the basis of their gender. But for their sex, they would not be so treated.

The harm of pornography, broadly speaking, is the harm of the civil inequality of the sexes made invisible as harm because it has become accepted as the sex difference. Consider this analogy with race: if you see Black people as different, there is no harm to segregation; it is merely a recognition of that difference. To neutral principles, separate but equal was equal. The injury of racial separation to Blacks arises "solely because [they] choose to put that construction upon it."[3] Epistemologically translated: how you see it is not the way it is. Similarly, if you see women as just different, even or especially if you don't know that you do, subordination will not look like subordination at all, much less like harm. It will merely look like an appropriate recognition of the sex difference.

Pornography does treat the sexes differently, so the case for sex differentiation can be made here. But men as a group do not tend to be (although some individuals may be) treated the way women are treated in pornography. As a social group, men are not hurt by pornography the way women as a social group are. Their social status is not defined as *less* by it. So the major argument does not turn on mistaken differentiation, particularly since the treatment of women according to pornography's dictates makes it all too often accurate. The salient quality of a distinction between the top and the bottom in a hierarchy is not difference, although top is certainly different from bottom; it is power. So the major argument is: subordinate but equal is not equal.

Particularly since this is a new legal theory, a new law, and "new" facts, perhaps the situation of women it newly exposes deserves to be considered on its own terms. Why do the problems of 53 percent of the population have to look like somebody else's problems before they can be recognized as existing? Then, too, they can't be addressed if they do look like other people's problems, about which something might have to be done if something is done about these. This construction of the situation truly deserves inquiry. Limiting the justification for this law to the situation of the sexes would serve to limit the precedential value of a favorable ruling.

Its particularity to one side, the *approach* to the injury is supported by a whole array of prior decisions that have justified exceptions to First Amendment guarantees when something that matters is seen to be directly at stake. What unites many cases in which speech interests are raised and implicated but not, on balance, protected, is harm, harm that counts. In some existing exceptions, the definitions are much more open-ended than ours. In some the sanctions are more severe, or potentially more so. For instance, ours is a civil law; most others, although not all, are criminal. Almost no other exceptions show as many people directly affected. Evidence of harm in other cases tends to be vastly less concrete and more conjectural, which is not to say that there is necessarily less of it.[4] None of the previous cases addresses a problem of this scope or magnitude—for instance, an eight-billion-dollar-a-year industry. Nor do other cases address an abuse that has such widespread legitimacy. Courts have seen harm in other cases. The question is, will they see it here, especially given that the pornographers got there first. I will confine myself here to arguing from cases on harm to people, on the supposition that, the pornographers notwithstanding, women are not flags.[5]

I will discuss the four injuries we make actionable with as much evidence as time permits. I want to hear the voices of the women and men who spoke at our hearing.

· · ·

The first victims of pornography are the ones in it. To date, it has only been with children, and male children at that, that the Supreme Court has understood that before the pornography became the pornographer's speech, it was somebody's life. This is particularly true in visual media, where it takes a real person doing each act to make what you see. This is the double meaning in a statement one ex-prostitute made at our hearing: "[E]very single thing you see in pornography is happening to a real woman right now."[6] Linda Marchiano, in her book *Ordeal*,[7] recounts being coerced as "Linda Lovelace" into performing for *Deep Throat,* a fabulously profitable film, by being abducted, systematically beaten, kept prisoner, watched every minute, threatened with her life and the lives of her family if she left, tortured, and kept under constant psychological intimidation and duress. Not all pornography models are, to our knowledge, coerced so expressly, but the fact that some are not does not mean that those who are, aren't. It only means that coercion into pornography cannot be said to be biologically female. The further fact that prostitution and modeling are structurally women's best economic options should give pause to those who would consider women's presence there a true act of free choice. In the case of other inequalities, it is sometimes understood that people do degrading work out of a lack of options caused by, say poverty. The work is not seen as *not* degrading "for them" because they do it. With women, it just proves that this is what we are really for, this is our true nature. I will leave you wondering, with me, why it is that when a woman spreads her legs for a camera, she is assumed to be exercising free will. Woman's freedom is rather substantively defined here. And as you think about the assumption of consent that follows women into pornography, look closely sometime for the skinned knees, the bruises,

the welts from the whippings, the scratches, the gashes. Many of them are not simulated. One relatively soft-core pornography model said, "I knew the pose was right
when it hurt."[8] It certainly seems important to the audiences that the events in the
pornography be real. For this reason pornography becomes a motive for murder, as in
"snuff" films, in which someone is tortured to death to make a sex film. They exist.[9]

Coerced pornography models encounter devastating problems of lack of credibility because of a cycle of forced acts in which coercion into pornography is central. For
example, children are typically forced to perform the acts in the pornography that is
forced on them; photographs are taken of these rapes, and the photographs are used
to coerce the children into prostitution or into staying in prostitution. They are told
that if they try to leave, the pictures will be shown to the authorities, their parents, their
teachers (whoever is *not* coercing them at the time), and no one will believe them. This
gets them into prostitution and keeps them there. Understand, the documentation of
the harm as it is being done is taken as evidence that no harm was done. In part, the
victim's desire for the abuse is attributed to the victim's nature from the fact of the
abuse: she's a natural-born whore; see, there she is chained to a bed. Too, the victims
are often forced to act as though they are enjoying the abuse. One pornographer said
to a woman he abducted and was photographing while bound: "Smile or I'll kill you. I
can get lots of money for pictures of women who smile when they're tied up like you."[10]
When women say they were forced, they are not believed, in part because, as Linda
Marchiano says, "What people remember is the smile on my face."[11]

Pornography defines what a woman is through conditioning the male sexual response to that definition, to the unilateral sexuality pornography is part of and provides. Its power can be illustrated by considering the credibility problems Linda
Marchiano encounters when she says that the presentation of her in *Deep Throat* is not
true, in the sense that she does not and did not feel or enjoy what the character she
was forced to portray felt and enjoyed. Most concretely, before "Linda Lovelace" was
seen performing deep throat, no one had ever seen it being done in that way, largely
because it cannot be done without hypnosis to repress the natural gag response. *Yet it
was believed.* Men proceeded to demand it of women, causing the distress of many and
the death of some. Yet when Linda Marchiano now tells that it took kidnapping and
death threats and hypnosis to put here there, that is found *difficult to believe.*

The point is not only that when women can be coerced with impunity the results,
when mass-produced, set standards that are devastating and dangerous for all women.
The point is also that the assumptions the law of the First Amendment makes about
adults—that adults are autonomous, self-defining, freely acting, *equal* individuals—are
exactly those qualities that pornography systematically denies and undermines for
women. Some of the same reasons children are granted some specific legal avenues for
redress—relative lack of power, inability to command respect for their consent and
self-determination, in some cases less physical strength or lowered legitimacy in using
it, specific credibility problems, and lack of access to resources for meaningful self-expression—also hold true for the social position of women compared to men. It is therefore vicious to suggest, as many have, that women like Linda Marchiano should rem-

edy their situations through the exercise of more speech. Pornography makes their speech impossible, and where possible, worthless. Pornography makes women into objects. Objects do not speak. When they do, they are by then regarded as objects, not as humans, which is what it means to have no credibility. Besides, it is unclear how Ms. Marchiano's speech is supposed to redress her injury, except by producing this legal remedy, since no amount of saying anything remedies what is being *done* to her in theaters and on home videos all over the world, where she is repeatedly raped for public entertainment and private profit.

What would justice look like for these women?[12] Linda Marchiano said, "Virtually every time someone watches that film, they are watching me being raped."[13] Nancy Holmes, who was forced to perform for pornography by her father and who, like many such victims, has been searching for the film for years, says,

> You wonder who might have seen the film. In some back-alley adult book shop someone has dropped a quarter and maybe it might be you they are looking at. You would not ordinarily mix company with this person under these circumstances . . . [b]ut in some back alley, in someone's dark mind you are worth 25 cents. Someone has just paid 25 cents to see you being brutally raped and beaten. And some total stranger gets to gain sadistic and voyeuristic pleasure from your pain. It costs you your sanity and years of suffering and psychological turmoil. It cost him only a quarter, and he gained tremendous pleasure. It robbed you of your childhood; it gave him satisfaction.[14]

Now think about this freedom and her powerlessness, and think about what it means to call that "just the construction she chooses to put upon it."

As part of the relief for people who can prove this was done to them, our law provides an injunction to remove these materials from public view. The best authority we have for this is the *Ferber* case which permits criminal prohibitions on child pornography.[15] That case recognized that child pornography need not be obscene to be child abuse. The Court found such pornography harmful in part because it constituted "a permanent record of children's participation and the harm to the child is exacerbated by circulation."[16] This was a film, by the way, largely of two boys masturbating. The sensitivities of obscenity law, the Court noted, were inapt because "a work which, taken on the whole, contains value may nevertheless embody the hardest core of child pornography."[17] Whether a work appeals to the prurient interest is not the same as whether a child is physically or psychologically harmed to make it.

Both of these reasons apply to coerced women. Women are not children, but coerced women are effectively deprived of power over the expressive products of their coercion. Coerced pornography should meet the test that "the evil to be restricted . . . overwhelmingly outweighs the expressive interests, if any, at stake."[18] Unless one wishes to retain the incentive structure that has introduced a profit motive into rape, pornography made this way should be able to be eliminated.[19]

. . .

We also make it actionable to force pornography on a person in employment, education, in a home, or in any public place. Persons who are forced cannot, under this part of the law, reach the pornography, but they can reach the perpetrator or institution that does the forcing. In our hearings we heard the ways in which pornography is forced on people. It is used to show children how to perform sex acts, to duplicate exactly these so-called natural childish acts; on men's jobs, it is used to intimidate women into leaving; in women's jobs, to have or set up a sexual encounter; it is used to show prostitutes or wives what a "natural woman" is supposed to do. In therapy, it is seen as aiding in transference, meaning submitting to the therapist; in medical school, it desensitizes doctors so that when patients say they are masturbating with a chicken or wondering if intercourse with a cow will give them exotic diseases, the doctor does not react. In language classes, it becomes material to be worked over meticulously for translation. It is used to terrorize children in homes, so they will keep still about its use in the rape of their mothers and sisters: look at this; if you tell, here's what I'll do to you. Sometimes it ends there; some children "only" have the pornography forced on them. Some of them later develop psychological difficulties that are identical to those of children who had the *acts* forced on them. Do a thought-act distinction on that one.

Women who live in neighborhoods where pornography is concentrated, much of it through state and local legal action called "zoning," report similar effects on a broad scale.[20] Because prostitutes know what others seem to have a lot staked on denying, which is that pornography makes men want the real thing, they sometimes locate around it. This means that any woman there may be considered a prostitute, which is dangerous enough if you are one, but becomes particularly dangerous if you are not. The threat of sexual harassment is constant. The presence of the pornography conditions women's physical environment. Women have no place to go to avoid it, no place to avert their eyes *to*. Certainly not home, where the presence of pornography is so sanctified we don't even challenge it in this law. One woman who as a child was a victim of incest and now lives in a community saturated with pornography, relates a Skokie-type injury. She relives the incest every time she walks by the pornography she cannot avoid. "[L]ooking at the women in those pictures, I saw myself at 14, at 15, at 16. I felt the weight of that man's body, the pain, the disgust . . . I don't need studies and statistics to tell me that there is a relationship between pornography and real violence against women. My body remembers."[21] Now recall that more than a third of all women are victims of child sexual abuse; about the same proportion are victims of domestic battery; just under half are victims of rape or attempted rape. I am not saying that every such presence of the pornography is legally force, but what does it mean for targeted survivors to live in a society in which the rehearsal and celebration and ritual reenactment of our victimization is enjoyed, is an entertainment industry, is arguably a constitutional right?

. . .

Specific pornography does directly cause some assaults. Some rapes *are* performed by men with paperback books in their pockets. One young woman testified in our hearings about walking through a forest at thirteen and coming across a group of armed hunters reading pornography. As they looked up and saw her, one said, "There is a live one."[22] They gang-raped her at gunpoint for several hours. One Native American woman told us about being gang-raped in a reenactment of a video game on her. "[T]hat's what they screamed in my face as they threw me to the ground. 'This is more fun than Custer's Last Stand.' They held me down and as one was running the tip of his knife across my face and throat he said, 'Do you want to play Custer's Last Stand? It's great, you lose but you don't care, do you? You like a little pain, don't you, squaw? . . . Maybe we will tie you to a tree and start a fire around you."[23]

Received wisdom seems to be that because there is so little difference between convicted rapists and the rest of the male population in levels and patterns of exposure, response to, and consumption of pornography, the role of pornography in rape is insignificant. A more parsimonious explanation of this data is that knowing patterns of exposure to, response to, or consumption of pornography will not tell you who will be reported, apprehended, and convicted for rape. But the commonalities such data reveal between convicted rapists and other men are certainly consistent with the fact that only a tiny fraction of rapes ever come to the attention of authorities. It does not make sense to assume that pornography has no role in rape simply because little about its use or effects distinguishes convicted rapists from other men, when we know that a lot of those other men *do* rape women; they just never get caught. In other words, the significance of pornography in acts of forced sex is one thing if sex offenders are considered deviants and another if they are considered relatively nonexceptional except for the fact of their apprehension and incarceration. Professionals who work with that tiny percentage of men who get reported and convicted for such offenses, a group made special only by our ability to assume that they once had sex by force in a way that someone (in addition to their victim) eventually regarded as serious, made the following observations about the population they work with. "Pornography is the permission and direction and rehearsal for sexual violence."[24] "[P]ornography is often used by sex offenders as a stimulus to their sexually acting out." It is the "tools of sexual assault,"[25] "a way in which they practice" their crimes, "like a loaded gun,"[26] "like drinking salt water,"[27] "the chemical of sexual addiction."[28] They hypothesize that pornography leads some men to abusiveness out of fear of loss of the control that has come to mean masculinity when real women won't accept sex on the one-sided terms that pornography gives and from which they have learned what sex is. Because pornography is reinforcing, and leads to sexual release, it "leads men to want the experience which they have in photographic fantasy to happen in 'real' life."[29] "They live vicariously through the pictures. Eventually, that is not satisfying enough and they end up acting out sexually."[30] "[S]exual fantasy represents the hope for reality."[31] These professionals are referring to what others are fond of terming "just an idea."

Although police have known it for years, reported cases are increasingly noting the causal role of pornography in some sexual abuse. In a recent Minnesota case, a four-teen-year-old girl on a bicycle was stopped with a knife and forced into a car. Her hands were tied with a belt, she was pushed to the floor and covered with a blanket. The knife was then used to cut off her clothes, and fingers and a knife were inserted into her vagina. Then the man had her dress, drove her to a gravel pit, ordered her to stick a safety pin into the nipple of her left breast, and forced her to ask him to hit her. After hitting her, he forced her to commit fellatio and to submit to anal penetration, and made her use a cigarette to burn herself on her breast and near her pubic area. Then he defecated and urinated on her face, forced her to ingest some of the excrement and urine and made her urinate into a cup and drink it. He took a string from her blouse and choked her to the point of unconsciousness, leaving burn marks on her neck, and after cutting her with with his knife in a couple of places, drove her back to where he had gotten her and let her go. The books that were found with this man were: *"Violent Stories of Kinky Humiliation," "Violent Stories of Dominance and Submission"*—you think feminists made up these words?— *"Bizarre Sex Crimes, Shamed Victims,"* and *"Water Sports Fetish, Enemas and Golden Showers."* The Minnesota Supreme Court said "It appears that in committing these various acts, the defendant was giving life to some stories he had read in various pornographic books."[32]

. . .

To reach the magnitude of this problem on the scale it exists, our law makes trafficking in pornography—production, sale, exhibition, or distribution—actionable. Under the obscenity rubric, much legal and psychological scholarship has centered on a search for the elusive link between harm and pornography defined as obscenity.[33] Although they were not very clear on what obscenity was, it was its harm they truly could not find. They looked high and low—in the mind of the male consumer, in society or in its "moral fabric," in correlations between variations in levels of antisocial acts and liberalization of obscenity laws. The only harm they have found has been harm to "the social interest in order and mortality."[34] Until recently, no one looked very persistently for harm to women, particularly harm to women through men. The rather obvious fact that the sexes *relate* has been overlooked in the inquiry into the male consumer and his mind. The pornography doesn't just drop out of the sky, go into his head, and stop there. Specifically, men rape, batter, prostitute, molest, and sexually harass women. Under conditions of inequality, they also hire, fire, promote, and grade women, decide how much or whether we are worth paying and for what, define and approve and disapprove of women in ways that count, that determine our lives.

If women are not just born to be sexually used, the fact that we are seen and treated as though that is what we are born for becomes something in need of explanation. If we see that men relate to women in a pattern of who they see women as being, and that forms a pattern of inequality, it becomes important to ask where that view came from or, minimally, how it is perpetuated or escalated. Asking this requires asking different questions about pornography than the ones obscenity law made salient.

Now I'm going to talk about causality in its narrowest sense. Recent experimental research on pornography[35] shows that the materials covered by our definition cause measurable harm to women through increasing men's attitudes and behaviors of discrimination in both violent and nonviolent forms. Exposure to some of the pornography in our definition increases the immediately subsequent willingness of normal men to aggress against women under laboratory conditions.[36] It makes normal men more closely resemble convicted rapists attitudinally, although as a group they don't look all that different from them to start with.[37] Exposure to pornography also significantly increases attitudinal measures known to correlate with rape and self-reports of aggressive acts, measures such as hostility toward women, propensity to rape, condoning rape, and predicting that one would rape or force sex on a woman if one know one would not get caught.[38] On this latter measure, by the way, about a third of all men predict that they would rape, and half would force sex on a woman.[39]

As to that pornography covered by our definition in which normal research subjects seldom perceive violence, long-term exposure still makes them see women as more worthless, trivial, nonhuman, and objectlike,[40] that is, the way those who are discriminated against are seen by those who discriminate against them. Crucially, all pornography by our definition acts dynamically over time to diminish the consumer's ability to distinguish sex from violence. The materials work behaviorally to diminish the capacity of men (but not women) to perceive that an account of rape is an account of rape. The so-called sex-only materials, those in which subjects perceive no force, also increase perceptions that a rape victim is worthless and decrease the perception that she was harmed. The overall direction of current research suggests that the more expressly violent materials accomplish with less exposure what the less overtly violent— that is, the so-called sex-only materials—accomplish over the longer term. Women are rendered fit for use and targeted for abuse. The only thing that the research cannot document is which individual women will be next on the list. (This cannot be documented experimentally because of ethics constraints on the researchers—constraints that do not operate in life.) Although the targeting is systematic on the basis of sex, for individuals it is random. They are selected on a roulette basis. Pornography can no longer be said to be just a mirror. It does not just reflect the world or some people's perceptions. It *moves* them. It increases attitudes that are lived out, circumscribing the status of half the population.

What the experimental data predict will happen actually does happen in women's real lives. You know, it's fairly frustrating that women have known for some time that these things do happen. As Ed Donnerstein, an experimental researcher in this area, often puts it, "We just quantify the obvious."[41] It is women, primarily, to whom the research results have been the obvious, because we live them. But not until a laboratory study predicts that these things *will* happen do people begin to believe you when you say they *did* happen to you. There is no—*not any*—inconsistency between the patterns the laboratory studies predict and the data on what actually happens to real women. Show me an abuse of women in society, I'll show it to you made sex in the pornography. If you want to know who is being hurt in this society, go see what is being done and to whom in pornography and then go look for them other places in the world. You will find them being hurt in just that way. We did in our hearings.

In our hearings women spoke, to my knowledge for the first time in history in public, about the damage pornography does to them. We learned that pornography is used to break women, to train women to sexual submission, to season women, to terrorize women, and to silence their dissent. It is this that has previously been termed "having no effect." The way men inflict on women the sex they experience through the pornography gives women no choice about seeing the pornography or doing the sex. Asked if anyone ever tried to inflict unwanted sex acts on them that they knew came from pornography, 10 percent of women in a recent random study said yes. Among married women, 24 percent said yes.[42] That is a lot of women. A lot more don't know. Some of those who do testified in Minneapolis. One wife said of her ex-husband, "He would read from the pornography like a textbook, like a journal. In fact when he asked me to be bound, when he finally convinced me to do it, he read in the magazine how to tie the knots."[43] Another woman said of her boyfriend, "[H]e went to this party, saw pornography, got an erection, got me . . . to inflict his erection on. . . . There is a direct causal relationship there."[44] One woman, who said her husband had rape and bondage magazines all over the house, discovered two suitcases full of Barbie dolls with rope tied on their arms and legs and with tape across their mouths.[45] Now think about the silence of women. She said, "He used to tie me up and he tried those things on me." A therapist in private practice reported:

> Presently or recently I have worked with clients who have been sodomized by broom handles, forced to have sex with over 20 dogs in the back seat of their car, tied up and then electrocuted on their genitals. These are children, [all] in the ages of 14 to 18, all of whom [have been directly affected by pornography,] [e]ither where the perpetrator has read the manuals and manuscripts at night and used these as recipe books by day or had the pornography present at the time of the sexual violence.

One woman, testifying that all the women in the group of ex-prostitutes were brought into prostitution as children through pornography, characterized their collective experience: "[I]n my experience there was not one situation where a client was not using pornography while he was using me or that he had not just watched pornography or that it was verbally referred to and directed me to pornography." "Men," she continued "witness the abuse of women in pornography constantly and if they can't engage in that behavior with their wives, girl friends or children, they force a whore to do it."[48]

Men also testified about how pornography hurts them. One young gay man who had seen *Playboy* and *Penthouse* as a child said of such heterosexual pornography: "It was one of the places I learned about sex and it showed me that sex was violence. What I saw there was a specific relationship between men and women . . . [T]he woman was to be used, objectified, humiliated and hurt; the man was in a superior position, a position to be violent. In pornography I learned that what it meant to be sexual with a man or to be loved by a man was to accept his violence."[49] For this reason, when he was battered by his first lover, which he described as "one of the most profoundly destructive experiences of my life," he accepted it.

Pornography also hurts men's capacity to relate to women. One young man spoke about this in a way that connects pornography—not the prohibition on pornography—with fascism. He spoke of his struggle to repudiate the thrill of dominance, of his difficulty finding connection with a woman to whom he is close. He said: "My point is that if women in a society filled by pornography must be wary for their physical selves, a man, even a man of good intentions, must be wary for his mind . . . I do not want to be a mechanical, goose-stepping follower of the Playboy bunny, because that is what I think it is . . . [T]hese are the experiments a master race perpetuates on those slated for extinction." The woman he lives with is Jewish. There was a very brutal rape near their house. She was afraid; she tried to joke. It didn't work. "She was still afraid. And just as a well-meaning German was afraid in 1933, I am also very much afraid."[50]

Pornography stimulates and reinforces, it does not cathect or mirror, the connection between one-sided freely available sexual access to women and masculine sexual excitement and sexual satisfaction. The catharsis hypothesis is fantasy. The fantasy theory is fantasy. Reality is: pornography conditions male orgasm to female subordination. It tells men what sex means, what a real woman is, and codes them together in a way that is behaviorally reinforcing. This is a real five-dollar sentence, but I'm going to say it anyway: pornography is a set of hermeneutical equivalences that work on the epistemological level. Substantively, pornography defines the meaning of what a woman is seen to be by connecting access to her sexuality with masculinity through orgasm. What pornography means *is* what it does.

So far, opposition to our ordinance centers on the trafficking provision. This means not only that it is difficult to comprehend a group injury in a liberal culture—that what it *means* to be a woman is defined by this and that it is an injury for all women, even if not for all women equally. It is not only that the pornography has got to be accessible, which is the bottom line of virtually every objection to this law. It is also that power, as I said, is when you say something, it is taken for reality. If you talk about rape, it will be agreed that rape is awful. But rape is a conclusion. If a victim describes the facts of a rape, maybe she was asking for it or enjoyed it or at least consented to it, or the man might have thought she did, or maybe she had had sex before. It is now agreed that there is something wrong with sexual harassment. But describe what happened to you, and it may be trivial or personal or paranoid, or maybe you should have worn a bra that day. People are against discrimination. But describe the situation of a real woman, and they are not so sure she wasn't just unqualified. In law, all these disjunctions between women's perspective on our injuries and the standards we have to meet go under dignified legal rubrics like burden of proof, credibility, defenses, elements of the crime, and so on. These standards all contain a definition of what a woman is in terms of what sex is and the low value placed on us through it. They reduce injuries done to us to authentic expressions of who we are. Our silence is written all over them. So is the pornography.

We have as yet encountered comparatively little objection to the coercion, force, or assault provisions of our ordinance. I think that's partly because the people who make and approve laws may not yet see what they do as that. They *know* they use the pornography as we have described it in this law, and our law defines that, the reality of pornography, as a harm to women. If they suspect that they might on occasion engage in or benefit from coercion or force or assault, they may think that the victims won't be able to prove it—and they're right. Women who charge men with sexual abuse are not believed. The pornographic view of them is: they want it; they all want it. When women bring charges of sexual assault, motives such as veniality or sexual repression must be invented, because we cannot really have been hurt. Under the trafficking provision, women's lack of credibility cannot be relied upon to negate the harm. There's no woman's story to destroy, no credibility-based decision on what happened. The hearings establish the harm. The definition sets the standard. The grounds of reality definition are authoritatively shifted. Pornography is bigotry, *period*. We are now—*in* the world pornography has decisively defined—having to meet the burden of proving, once and for all, for all of the rape and torture and battery, all of the sexual harassment, all of the child sexual abuse, all of the forced prostitution, *all* of it that the pornography is part of and that is part of the pornography, that the harm *does happen* and that when it happens it looks like this. Which may be why all this evidence never seems to be enough.

. . .

It is worth considering what evidence has been enough when other harms involving other purported speech interests have been allowed to be legislated against. By comparison to our trafficking provision, analytically similar restrictions have been allowed under the First Amendment, with a legislative basis far less massive, detailed, concrete, and conclusive. Our statutory language is more ordinary, objective, and precise and covers a harm far narrower than the legislative record substantiates. Under *Miller*, obscenity was allowed to be made criminal in the name of the "danger of offending the sensibilities of unwilling recipients, or exposure to juveniles."[51] Under our law, we have direct evidence of harm, not just a conjectural danger, that unwilling women in considerable numbers are not simply offended in their sensibilities, but are violated in their persons and restricted in their options. Obscenity law also suggests that the applicable standard for legal adequacy in measuring such connections may not be statistical certainty. The Supreme Court has said that it is not their job to resolve empirical uncertainties that underlie state obscenity legislation.[52] Rather, it is for them to determine whether a legislature could reasonably have determined that a connection might exist between the prohibited material and harm of a kind in which the state has legitimate interest. Equality should be such an area. The Supreme Court recently recognized that prevention of sexual exploitation and abuse of children is, in their words, "a governmental objective of surpassing importance."[53] This might also be the case for sexual exploitation and abuse of women, although I think a civil remedy is initially more appropriate to the goal of empowering adult women than a criminal prohibition would be.

Other rubrics provide further support for the argument that this law is narrowly tailored to further a legitimate governmental interest consistent with the goals underlying the First Amendment. Exceptions to the First Amendment—you may have gathered from this—exist. The reason they exist is that the harm done by some speech outweighs its expressive value, if any. In our law a legislature recognizes that pornography, as defined and made actionable, undermines sex equality. One can say—and I have—that pornography is a causal factor in violations of women; one can also say that women will be violated so long as pornography exists; but one can also say simply that pornography violates women. Perhaps this is what the woman had in mind who testified at our hearings that for her the question is not just whether pornography causes violent acts to be perpetrated against some women. "Porn is already a violent act against women. It is our mothers, our daughters, our sisters, and our wives that are for sale for pocket change at the newsstands in this country."[54] Chaplinsky v. New Hampshire recognized the ability to restrict as "fighting words" speech which, "by [its] very utterance inflicts injury."[55] Perhaps the only reason that pornography has not been "fighting words"—in the sense of words that by their utterance tend to incite immediate breach of the peace—is that women have seldom fought back, yet.

Some concerns that are close to those of this ordinance underlie group libel laws, although the differences are equally important. In group libel law, as Justice Frankfurter's opinion in *Beauharnais* illustrates, it has been understood that an individual's treatment and alternatives in life may depend as much on the reputation of the group to which that person belongs as on their own merit.[56] Not even a partial analogy can be made to group libel doctrine without examining the point made by Justice Brandeis[57] and recently underlined by Larry Tribe:[58] would more speech, rather than less, remedy the harm? In the end, the answer may be yes, but not under the abstract system of free speech, which only enhances the power of the pornographers while doing nothing substantively to guarantee the free speech of women, for which we need civil equality. The situation in which women presently find ourselves with respect to the pornography is one in which more *pornography* is inconsistent with rectifying or even counterbalancing its damage through speech, because so long as the pornography exists in the way it does there *will not be more speech by women*. Pornography strips and devastates women of credibility, from our accounts of sexual assault to our everyday reality of sexual subordination. We are stripped of authority and reduced and devalidated and silenced. Silenced here means that the purposes of the First Amendment, premised upon conditions presumed and promoted by protecting free speech, do not pertain to women because they are not our conditions. Consider them: individual self-fulfillment[59]—how does pornography promote our individual self-fulfillment? How does sexual inequality even permit it? Even if she can form words, who listens to a woman with a penis in her mouth? Facilitating consensus—to the extent pornography does so, it does so one-sidedly by silencing protest over the injustice of sexual subordination. Participation in civic life—central to Professor Meiklejohn's theory[60]—how does pornography enhance women's participation in civic life? Anyone who cannot walk down the street or even lie down in her own bed without keeping her eyes cast down and her body clenched against assault is unlikely to have much to say about the issues of the day, still less will she become Tolstoy. Facilitating change[61]—*this law* facilitates the change that existing First Amendment theory had been used to throttle. Any system of freedom of expression that does not address a problem where the free speech of men silences the free speech of women, a real conflict between speech interests as well as between people, is not serious about securing freedom of expression in this country.

For those of you who still think pornography is only an idea, consider the possibility that obscenity law got one thing right. Pornography is more actlike than thought-like. The fact that pornography, in a feminist view, furthers the idea of the sexual in-feriority of women, which is a political idea, doesn't make the pornography itself into a political idea. One can express the idea a practice embodies. That does not make that practice into an idea. Segregation expresses the idea of the inferiority of one group to another on the basis of race. That does not make segregation an idea. A sign that says "Whites Only" is only words. Is it therefore protected by the First Amendment? Is it not an act, a practice, of segregation because what it means is inseparable from what it does? *Law* is only words.

The issue here is whether the fact that words and pictures are the central link in the cycle of abuse will immunize that entire cycle, about which we cannot do anything without doing something about the pornography. As Justice Stewart said in *Ginsberg,* "When expression occurs in a setting where the capacity to make a choice is absent, government regulation of that expression may coexist with and *even implement* First Amendment guarantees."[62] I would even go so far as to say that the pattern of evidence we have closely approaches Justice Douglas' requirement that "freedom of expression can be suppressed if, and to the extent that, it is so closely brigaded with illegal action as to be an inseparable part of it."[63] Those of you who have been trying to separate the acts from the speech—that's an act, that's an act, there's a law against that act, regu-late that act, don't tough the speech—notice here that the illegality of the acts involved doesn't mean that the speech that is "brigaded with" it *cannot* be regulated. This is when it *can* be.[64]

I take one of two penultimate points from Andrea Dworkin, who has often said that pornography is not speech for women, it is the silence of women. Remember the mouth taped, the woman gagged, "Smile, I can get a lot of money for that." The smile is not her expression, it is her silence. It is not her expression not because it didn't happen, but because it *did* happen. The screams of the women in pornography are silence, like the screams of Kitty Genovese, whose plight was misinterpreted by some onlookers as a lover's quarrel. The flat expressionless voice of the woman in the New Bedford gang rape, testifying, is silence. She was raped as men cheered and watched, as they do in and with the pornography. When women resist and men say, "Like this, you stupid bitch, here is how to do it" and shove their faces into the pornography, this "truth of sex"[65] is the silence of women. When they say, "If you love me, you'll try," the enjoyment we fake, the enjoyment we learn is silence. Women who submit because there is more dignity in it than in losing the fight over and over live in silence. Having to sleep with your pub-lisher or director to get access to what men call speech is silence. Being humiliated on the basis of your appearance, whether by approval or disapproval, because you have to look a certain way for a certain job, whether you get the job or not, is silence. The ab-sence of a woman's voice, everywhere it cannot be heard, is silence. And anyone who thinks that what women say in pornography is women's speech—the "Fuck me, do it to me, harder," all of that—has never heard the sound of a woman's voice.

The most basic assumption underlying First Amendment adjudication is that, so-cially, speech is free. The First Amendment says Congress shall not abridge the free-dom of speech. Free speech, get it, *exists.* Those who wrote the First Amendment *had* speech—they wrote the Constitution. *Their* problem was to keep it free from the only power that realistically threatened it: the federal government. They designed the First Amendment to prevent government from constraining that which, if unconstrained by government, was free, meaning *accessible to them.* At the same time, we can't tell much about the intent of the framers with regard to the question of women's speech, because I don't think we crossed their minds. It is consistent with this analysis that their posture toward freedom of speech tends to presuppose that whole segments of the population are not systematically silenced socially, prior to government action. If everyone's power were equal to theirs, if this were a nonhierarchical society, that might make sense. But the place of pornography in the inequality of the sexes makes the assumption of equal power untrue.

This is a hard question. It involves risks. Classically, opposition to censorship has involved keeping government off the backs of people. Our law is about getting some people off the backs of other people. The risks that it will be misused have to be measured against the risks of the status quo. Women will never have that dignity, security, compensation that is the promise of equality so long as the pornography exists as it does now. The situation of women suggests that the urgent issue of our freedom of speech is not primarily the avoidance of state intervention as such, but getting affirmative access to speech for those to whom it has been denied. . . .

Notes

[From the Francis Biddle Memorial Lecture, Harvard Law School, Cambridge, Massachusetts, April 5, 1984. For the author's most recent discussion of the harm of pornography, see her book *Only Words* (Harvard Univ. Press, 1994). *Ed.*]

1. See Young v. American Mini Theatres, Inc., 427 U.S. 50 (1976); Pittsburgh Press Co. v. Human Relations Comm'n, 413 U.S. 376 (1973); Konigsberg v. State Bar of California, 366 U.S. 36, 49–51 (1961).

2. After the delivery of the Biddle Lecture, an Indiana federal court declared the ordinance unconstitutional in a facial challenge brought by the "Media Coalition," an association of publishers and distributors. The ordinance is repeatedly misquoted, and the misquotations are underscored to illustrate its legal errors. Arguments not made in support of the law are invented and attributed to the city and found legally inadequate. Evidence of harm before the legislature is given no weight at all, while purportedly being undisturbed, as an absolutist approach is implicitly adopted, unlike any existing Supreme Court precedent. To the extent that existing law, such as obscenity law, overlaps with the ordinance, even it would be invalidated under this ruling. And clear law on sex equality is flatly misstated. The opinion permits a ludicrous suit by mostly legitimate trade publishers, parties whose interests are at most tenuously and remotely implicated under the ordinance, to test a law that directly and importantly would affect others, such as pornographers and their victims. The decision also seems far more permissive toward racism than would be allowed in a concrete case even under existing law, and displays blame-the-victim misogyny: "Adult women generally have the capacity to protect themselves from participating in and being personally victimized by pornography. . . ." American Booksellers v. Hudnut, 598 F. Supp. 1316, 1334 (S.D. Ind.

1984). For subsequent developments, see Catharine A. MacKinnon, The Sexual Politics of the First Amendment, in Feminism Unmodified: Discourses on Life and Law 206 (Harvard Univ. Press, 1987).

3. See Plessy v. Ferguson, 163 U.S. 537, 551 (1896); Herbert Wechsler, Toward Neutral Principles of Constitutional Law, 73 Harv. L. Rev. 1, 33 (1959).

4. The harm of obscenity recognized in Miller v. California, 413 U.S. 15 (1973), was the "danger of offending the sensibilities of unwilling recipients or of exposure to juveniles." *Id.* at 19. This statement was adduced from the Presidential Commission on Obscenity finding that it could not be concluded that obscenity causes harm. "[The] Commission cannot conclude that exposure to erotic materials is a factor in the causation of sex crime or sex delinquency." Report of the Presidential Commission on Obscenity and Pornography 27 (1970). The harm in F.C.C. v. Pacifica Found., 438 U.S. 726 (1978), was the possible overhearing of indecent speech by children, since radio intrudes into the home. *Id.* at 748–750. In United States v. Orito, 413 U.S. 139, 143 (1973), a federal ban on interstate transportation of obscene materials for private use was sustained on "a legislatively determined risk of ultimate exposure to juveniles or to the public." Throughout, exposure of juveniles to obscenity is assumed to be a risk, but the harm that exposure does per se is unspecified, not to say unsubstantiated and not in evidence. The harm recognized in New York v. Ferber, 458 U.S. 747 (1982), appears to be that done to a minor male by being seen having sex. The film depicted two boys masturbating; the Court concluded that this was "a permanent record of children's participation and the harm to the child is exacerbated by [its] circulation." *Id.* at 759. This same harm is at times characterized by the Court as "psychological," *id.* at 759 n. 10, but is otherwise unspecified and in evidence only in the form of the film. In Chaplinsky v. New Hampshire, 315 U.S. 568 (1942), the harm apparently was a combination of the offense given by the speech itself with the risk of imminent breach of the peace occasioned by its utterance. As to group libel, the harm of the racist leaflet to the group as a whole recognized in Beauharnais v. Illinois, 343 U.S. 250 (1952), was *inferred* from observed racial inequality and racial unrest. *Id.* at 258–261.

5. Flags, seen as symbols for the nation rather than mere pieces of brightly colored cloth or even as personal property, receive special solicitude by legislatures and courts, as to both the patriotic value of their protection and the expressive value of their desecration. See, e.g., Spence v. Washington, 418 U.S. 405 (1974); Street v. New York, 394 U.S. 576 (1969). I have not considered the applicability of this line of cases here, in light of my view that women in pornography are not simply symbols of all women but also *are* women. Of course, under male supremacy, each woman represents all women to one degree or another, whether in pornography or in bed or walking down the street, because of the stereotyping intrinsic to gender inequality. But that does not mean that, in a feminist perspective, each woman, including those in pornography, can be treated solely in terms of her representative or symbolic qualities, as if she is not at the same time alive and human. An underlying issue has to do with the extent to which women's bodies must be freely available as vocabulary and imagery for the expression of others, such that once they are so converted, whatever the means, women retain no rights in their use or abuse, in the face of evidence of the harm from such expropriation and exposure ranging from the individual so used to anonymous women subsequently used or treated or seen in light of their availability for such use. (Given the extent to which women now must be men's speech, one might rather be a flag.)

6. Public Hearings on Ordinances to Add Pornography as Discrimination Against Women 75, Committee on Government Operations, City Council, Minneapolis, Minn.

(Dec. 12–13, 1983) [hereinafter cited as Hearings] (testimony of a named former prostitute).

7. Linda Lovelace & Michael McGrady, Ordeal (1980).

8. Priscilla Alexander, coordinator for the National Organization for Women's Task Force on Prostitution, said she was told this by a woman pornography model. Panel on Pornography, National Association of Women and the Law, Los Angeles, Apr. 1, 1984.

9. "In the movies known as snuff films, victims sometimes are actually murdered." 130 Cong. Rec. S13192 (daily ed. Oct. 3, 1984) (statement of Senator Spector introducing the Pornography Victims Protection Act). Information the subject is understandably hard to get. See People v. Douglas, Felony Complaint No. NF 8300382 (Municipal Court, Orange County, Cal., Aug. 5, 1983); Slain Teens Needed Jobs, Tried Porn, *and* Two Accused of Murder in "Snuff" Films, Oakland Tribune, Aug. 6, 1983. See also "Not A Moral Issue" [reprinted herein, at 37]; L. Smith, The Chicken Hawks (1975) (unpublished manuscript).

10. Speech by Andrea Dworkin, in Toronto, Feb. 1984 (account told to Dworkin), reprinted in Healthsharing, Summer 1984, at 25.

11. Linda Marchiano, Panel on Pornography, Stanford University, Apr. 2, 1982.

12. This question and the paragraph that follows draw directly on Andrea Dworkin's speech, *supra* note 10.

13. I Hearings 56.

14. National Task Force on Child Pornography, Let's Protect Our Children 17 (1983).

15. 458 U.S. 747 (1982).

16. *Id.* at 759.

17. *Id.* at 761.

18. *Id.* at 763–764.

19. The harm of child pornography cannot be stopped effectively without also addressing the pornography of adult women. Adult pornography has been found commonly used "to show, teach or induce the children into the sexual activity or pornographic modeling" by child sex rings. See A. Burgess, C. Hartman, M. McCausland, & P. Powers, Response Patterns in Children and Adolescents Exploited through Sex Rings and Pornography, 141 Am. J. Psychiatry 656, 657–658 (1984). Given what is done in pornography, it is even more difficult than usual to distinguish between adults and children. Adult women are infantilized in pornography; children are dressed and used as if they were adult women. The resulting materials are then used against both, and target both for abuse relatively interchangeably. For instance, the "shaved pussy" genre, in which adult women's genitals are made to resemble those of young girls, converges with the "Lolita" or "cherry tarts" genre, in which young girls are presented resembling the pornographers' image of adult female sexuality. It also seems worth observing that a law that has the abuse disappear legally when its victims get one day older is difficult to administer effectively.

20. See II Hearings 90–100. A woman who lived in a neighborhood into which pornography had been zoned said, if you think pornography is harmless, "you move into my neighborhood and I will move into yours." Testimony of Shannon M., *id.* at 99.

21. III Hearings 112 (testimony of Mags. D.).

22. *Id.* at 43 (testimony of Rita M.).

23. II Hearings 18–19 (testimony of Carol L.).

24. *Id.* at 36 (testimony of Barbara Chester, director of the Rape and Sexual Assault Center, Hennepin County, Minn.).

25. *Id.* at 44–45 (testimony of Bill Seals, director of Sexual Assault Services, Center for Behavior Therapy, Minneapolis, Minn.).

26. *Id.* at 64 (testimony of Nancy Steele, therapist with sex offenders).

27. *Id.*

28. *Id.* at 88 (testimony of Michael Laslett, reading statement by Floyd Winecoff, psychotherapist specializing in services for men).

29. *Id.* at 86.

30. *Id.* at 44 (testimony of Bill Seals).

31. *Id.* at 59 (testimony of Gerry Kaplan, executive director of Alpha Human Services, an inpatient program for sex offenders).

32. State v. Herberg, 324 N.W.2d 346, 347 (Minn. 1982).

33. See, e.g., U.S. Commission on Obscenity and Pornography, Commission Report (1970); Commission on Obscenity and Film Censorship, Report Cmd. No. 7772 (1979) (United Kingdom).

34. Roth v. United States, 354 U.S. 476, 485 (1957) (quoting Chaplinsky v. New Hampshire, 315 U.S. 568, 572 [1942]). See also Paris Adult Theatre I v. Slaton, 413 U.S. 49, 57–58 (1973) ("[T]here are legitimate state interests at stake . . . [T]hese include the interest of the public in the quality of life").

35. Major sources are Neil M. Malamuth & Edward Donnerstein eds., Pornography and Sexual Aggression (1984); Dolph Zillman, Connections Between Sex and Aggression (1984); Edward Donnerstein & Leonard Barkowitz, Victim Reactions in Aggressive Erotic Films as a Factor in Violence against Women, 41 J. Personality & Soc. Psych. 710–724 (1981); Neil M. Malamuth & John H. Check, The Effects of Mass Media Exposure on Acceptance of Violence against Women: A Field Experiment, 15 J. Res. Personality 436–446 (1981); Neil M. Malamuth & Edward Donnerstein, The Effects of Aggressive-Pornographic Mass Media Stimuli, 15 Advances in Experimental Soc. Psych. 103 (1982); Diana Russell, Pornography and Violence: What Does the New Research Say? in L. Lederer ed., Take Back the Night 216 (1983); Dolph Zillman & Jennings Bryant, Pornography, Sexual Callousness, and the Trivialization of Rape, 32 J. Communication 16–18 (1982); I Hearings 13–45 (testimony of Edward Donnerstein); Daniel Linz, Edward Donnerstein, & Steven Penrod, Long-Term Exposure to Violent and Sexually Degrading Depictions of Women, 55 J. Personality & Soc. Psych. 758 (1988).

36. In addition to the references listed in note 35 above, see E. Donnerstein & J. Hallam, The Facilitating Effects of Erotica on Aggression Toward Females, 36 J. Personality & Soc. Psych. 1270 (1978); R. Geen, D. Stonner, & G. Shope, The Facilitation of Aggression by Aggression: Evidence against the Catharsis Hypothesis, 31 J. Personality & Soc. Psych. 721 (1975); B. S. Sapolsky & Dolph Zillman, The Effect of Soft-Core and Hard-Core Erotica on Provoked and Unprovoked Hostile Behavior, 17 J. Sex Res. 319 (1981); Dolph Zillman, J. L. Hoyt, & K. B. Day, Strength and Duration of the Effect of Aggressive, Violent, and Erotic Communications on Subsequent Aggressive Behavior, 1 Communication Res. 286 (1974). See also N. Malamuth, Factors Associated with Rape as Predictors of Laboratory Aggression against Women, 45 J. Personality & Soc. Psych. 432 (1983) (valid relation between factors associated with real-world aggression against women and laboratory aggression).

37. Neil M. Malamuth & John Check, Penile Tumescence and Perceptual Responses to Rape as a Function of Victim's Perceived Reactions, 10 J. Applied Soc. Psych. 528 (1980); Neil M. Malamuth, Scott Haber, & Seymour Feshback, Testing Hypotheses Regarding Rape: Exposure to Sexual Violence, Sex Difference, and the 'Normality' of Rapists, 14 J. Res. Personality 121 (1980). The lack of distinction between reactions

of convicted rapists and of control groups may be the reason many people have concluded that pornography does not do anything. When all the unreported, undetected, not to mention unconscious or potential, rapists in the control groups are considered, this conclusion stops being mysterious. . . .See also Gene Abel, Judith Becker, & L. Skinner, Aggressive Behavior and Sex, 3 Psychiatric Clinics of North America 133, 140 (1980) (fewer than 5 percent of rapists are psychotic while raping); N. Malamuth, Rape Proclivity among Males, 37 J Soc. Issues 4 (1981); Malamuth & Check, note 35 above; N. Malamuth, J. Heim, & S Feshbach, Sexual Responsiveness of College Students to Rape Depictions: Inhibitory and Disinhibitory Effects, 38 Soc. Psych. 399 (1980).

On the general subject of men's attitudes toward rape, see T. Beneke, Men on Rape (1982); P. Burt, Cultural Myths and Supports for Rape, 38 J. Personality & Soc. Psych. 217 (1980); S. D. Smithyman, The Undetected Rapist (Ph.D. diss., Claremont Graduate School 1978). A currently unknown number of incidents originally reported as rapes are now considered by police to be unfounded, meaning "the police established that no forcible rape offense or attempt occurred." In 1976, the last year the FBI reported its "unfounding" rate, it was 19 percent of reports. Federal Bureau of Investigation, Crime in America 16 (1976). . . .

38. See *supra* notes 35 and 37. It is perhaps worth noting that there is no experimental research to the contrary.

39. See John Briere & Neil M. Malamuth, Self-Reported Likelihood of Sexually Aggressive Behavior: Attitudinal versus Sexual Explanations, 37 J. Res. in Personality 315, 318 (1983) (58 percent of college males in survey reported some likelihood of forcing sex on a woman if they knew they would not get caught). See also Mary Koss & Cheryl J. Oros, Sexual Experiences Survey: A Research Instrument Investigating Sexual Aggression and Victimization, 50 J. Consulting & Clinical Psych. 455 (1982).

40. See I Hearings 21–38 (testimony of E. Donnerstein discussing supporting data submitted in the record). See also Zillman & Bryant, note 35 above (normal males exposed to films like "Debbie Does Dallas" see rape victims as many times more worthless than men who had not seen the films, and also saw less than half the amount of injury to the victim). In spite of this factual support, it is likely that the Indianapolis version of the ordinance would not apply to trafficking in such materials. See §16-3(8) of the Indianapolis Ordinance, which states "Defenses: It shall be a defense to a complaint under paragraph (g)(4). . .that the materials complained of are those covered only by paragraph (q)(6)."

41. Dr. Donnerstein says this in most of his talks.

42. Russell, Rape in Marriage 84, 228 (1984).

43. See II Hearings 68 (testimony of Ruth M.).

44. *Id.* at 55 (testimony of Nancy C.).

45. III Hearings 29 (testimony of Sharon Rice Vaughn, reading statement by Donna Dunn of Women's Shelter, Inc., in Rochester, Minn., which describes events reported by a woman at the shelter).

46. *Id.*

47. *Id.* at 83 (testimony of Sue Schafer).

48. II Hearings 74–75 (testimony of a named former prostitute). [See also Mimi Silbert & Ayala Pines, Pornography and Sexual Abuse of Women, 10 Sex Roles 857 (1984).]

49. I Hearings 56 (testimony of Gordon C.).

50. III Hearings 95 (testimony of Omar J.).

51. See Miller v. California, 413 U.S. 15, 19 (1973).

52. See Kaplan v. California, 413 U.S. 115, 120 (1973); Paris Adult Theatre I v. Slaton, 413 U.S. 49, 60 (1973); Roth v. United States, 354 U.S. 476, 501 (1957) (Harlan, J., concurring).

53. New York v. Ferber, 458 U.S. 742, 757 (1982).

54. III Hearings 53 (testimony of Cheryl Champion, member, Sexual Abuse Unit, Washington County, Minn., Human Services).

55. 315 U.S. 568, 572 (1941).

56. See Beauharnais v. Illinois, 343 U.S. 250, 263 (1952) ("[T]he dignity accorded him may depend as much on the reputation of the racial and religious group to which he willy-nilly belongs as on his own merits").

57. See Whitney v. California, 274 U.S. 357, 377 (1927) (Brandeis, J., concurring).

58. See Laurence Tribe, American Constitutional Law 731 (1978).

59. See T. Emerson, Toward a General Theory of the First Amendment, 72 Yale L.J. 877, 879–881 (1963); C. E. Baker, Scope of the First Amendment Freedom of Speech, 25 UCLA L. Rev. 964, 990–1005 (1978).

60. See A. Meiklejohn, Political Freedom 24–28 (1960). The importance of participation in civil life is also recognized by Emerson: "[M]an in his capacity as a member of society has a right to share in the common decisions that affect him." T. Emerson, The System of Freedom of Expression 6 (1970).

61. See T. Emerson, *supra* note 60. Emerson is entirely aware that some groups lack power in a way that the political process does not accommodate, but simply considers this a risk posed principally to "the nonbelonging individual," *id.* at 37, rather than advancing any substantive analysis of who does and does not have power and thus access to the means of speech. In the absence of such a substantive analysis, pornographers can cast themselves as outsiders when they are actually paradigmatic. See also Clark, Liberalism and Pornography, in D. Copp & S. Wendell eds., Pornography and Censorship 57 (1983).

62. Ginsberg v. New York, 390 U.S. 629, 649 (1968) (Stewart, J., concurring in result) (emphasis added).

63. Roth v. United States, 354 U.S. 476, 514 (Douglas, J., dissenting) (citing Giboney v. Empire Storage & Ice Co., 336 U.S. 490, 498 [1949]); Labor Board v. Virginia Power Co., 314 U.S. 469, 477–478 (1941). . . .

64. Rape, battery, assault, kidnaping, and prostitution are all crimes, and they are absolutely integral to pornography as we define and make it actionable. Compare with *Ferber*, 458 U.S. 747 (1982): masturbating is not a crime, nor is watching it; yet making and distributing a film of two boys masturbating is.

65. See Foucault, The West and the Truth of Sex, 20 Sub-stance 5 (1978).

Pornography and the First Amendment: A Reply to Professor MacKinnon

THOMAS I. EMERSON

PROFESSOR CATHARINE MACKINNON, in a recent article . . . , powerfully and perceptively developed her thesis that pornography is "[c]entral to the institutionalization of male dominance."[1] Pornography, she urges, is "a political practice" that "causes attitudes and behaviors of violence and discrimination which define the treatment and status of half of the population." I am not sure that I would draw the line between Eros and dehumanization at the same point as Professor MacKinnon appears to. Moreover, all the evidence is not yet in as to the actual impact of pornography, and Professor MacKinnon may overstate its role in the subordination of women.[2] . . .

My concern arises not from Professor MacKinnon's statement of the problem but from her proposal for a solution. . . . Professor MacKinnon would deal with the problem by invoking the power of the government to suppress pornography. Her specific proposals are embodied in the Minneapolis and Indianapolis Ordinances, which she and Andrea Dworkin drafted and persuaded the city councils of those cities to adopt. The Minneapolis ordinance was vetoed by the Mayor as a violation of the first amendment, but the Indianapolis ordinance was signed into law and is now the subject of litigation in the federal courts. . . .[3]

The Indianapolis Ordinance is based upon the theory that "pornography is a discriminatory practice based on sex which denies women equal opportunities in society." It creates administrative and judicial machinery empowering any woman to bring civil proceedings for . . . an injunction. . . .

The sweep of the Indianapolis Ordinance is breathtaking. It would subject to governmental ban virtually all depictions of rape, verbal or pictorial, and substantial proportion of other presentations of sexual encounters. More specifically, it would outlaw such works of literature as the *Arabian Nights,* John Cleland's *Fanny Hill,* Henry Miller's *Tropic of Cancer,* William Faulkner's *Sanctuary,* and Norman Mailer's *Ancient Evenings,* to name but a few. The ban would extend from Greek mythology and Shakespeare to the millions of copies of "romance novels" now being sold in the supermarkets. It

---

3 Yale L. & Pol'y Rev. 130 (1984).

would embrace much of the world's art, from ancient carvings to Picasso, well-known films too numerous to mention, and a large number of commercial advertising.

The scope of the Indianapolis Ordinance is not accidental. Nor could it be limited by more precise drafting without defeating the purpose of its authors. As Professor MacKinnon emphasizes, male domination has deep, pervasive and ancient roots in our society, so it is not surprising that our literature, art, entertainment and commercial practices are permeated by attitudes and behavior that create and reflect the inferior status of women. If the answer to the problem, as Professor MacKinnon describes it, is government suppression of sexual expression that contributes to female subordination, then the net of restraint has to be cast on a nearly limitless scale. . . .

I. The Ban on Pornography and Traditional First Amendment Doctrine

If we test Professor MacKinnon's proposals against traditional first amendment doctrine, there is no way that her solution of the pornography problem can be sustained. Obviously, the founding fathers, whatever restrictions they might have found constitutionally permissible with respect to sexually explicit speech, could not have intended the first amendment to allow the government to prohibit all speech that supported male domination. On Professor MacKinnon's own analysis, the very idea could not have occurred to them as members of the dominant male hierarchy. Insofar as "original intention" is a guide to constitutional interpretation, then it runs squarely counter to the position taken by the proponents of the Indianapolis Ordinance.

Nor can government suppression of pornography be justified under current first amendment doctrine. The core element in first amendment theory is that the impact of speech—whether considered good, bad or indifferent—cannot be invoked as a basis for government control of speech. Speech, or more generally expression, occupies a specially protected place in a democratic society. As Justice Holmes remarked long ago: "[I]f there is any principle of the Constitution that more imperatively calls for attachment than any other it is the principle of free thought—not free thought for those who agree with us but freedom for the thought that we hate."[4]

The reason for the supremacy of freedom of expression in our constitutional hierarchy is that it is essential to the operation of the democratic process. The values served by a system of free expression—individual self-fulfillment, advancement of knowledge, participation in self-government, and promotion of consensus by non-violent means—form the bedrock of our democratic existence.[5]

It follows that, as a general proposition, speech cannot be prohibited, curtailed or interfered with by government authorities. The state must seek to achieve its social goals by methods other than the suppression of expression. Were it otherwise, the government could readily outlaw or regulate expression that hampered the effectiveness of government operations, urged basic reform in our society, opposed government policies abroad, or cast aspersions on fellow citizens. Clearly the suppression of pornographic speech, on the ground that it causes or reflects discrimination against women, would run afoul of this basic mandate of the first amendment.

The Supreme Court has, of course, made some exceptions to the constitutional protection afforded freedom of expression. . . .

The exception that bears the closest resemblance to the proposed ban on pornography is found in the law concerning obscenity. In its obscenity decisions, the Supreme Court has ruled that the government may prohibit the dissemination of materials "which taken as a whole, appeal to the prurient interest in sex, which portray sexual conduct in a patently offensive way, and which, taken as a whole, do not have serious literary, artistic, political, or scientific value."[6] . . .

[I]t is difficult to make a rational projection as to how far the obscenity exception extends. As a practical matter, however, it is inconceivable that the Supreme Court would hold that the far broader area of "pornography" is simply outside the scope of first amendment protection. More importantly, as Professor MacKinnon points out, the social goals sought by the obscenity laws are essentially moral in nature; they do not extend to what Professor MacKinnon describes as a political process—discrimination against the female sex. The likelihood that the Supreme Court would permit the government to embark upon a venture to control speech in this area of politics, free from the restraints of the first amendment, is most remote.

A second exception to the general rule that expression is entitled to the full protection of the first amendment occurs in the case of expression by, or directed to, children [New York v. Ferber]. . . .[7] [T]he Supreme Court has made it plain that the special rules pertaining to children cannot operate to infringe the first amendment rights of adults.

Other exceptions to full protection under the first amendment are based on doctrines pertaining to libel, clear and present danger, and regulation of the time, place and manner of expression. None of these theories justifies the relaxation of the traditional guarantees of the first amendment in the case of pornographic materials. . . . In all these areas, first amendment theory requires that the exceptions be confined to narrow and concrete categories that have the least inhibiting effect upon the system of freedom of expression. Creation of a vast new exception that would remove from the protection of the first amendment all sexually explicit expression that tended to promote the subordination of women would, to the contrary, leave the system a shadow of its former self.

The nearest analogy to what is proposed in the Indianapolis Ordinance would be an official enactment prohibiting all expression that promoted or encouraged racism in our society. The laws, constitutional and statutory, that attempt to eradicate racism in our national life have never been carried to such a point. They deal with discriminatory acts, not the expression of discriminatory beliefs, opinions, ideas or attitudes. And it is hard to believe that the Supreme Court would permit their extension into such areas. One is not likely to find the Supreme Court enjoining performance of the *Merchant of Venice* or banning William B. Shockley from expounding his views on the inferiority of the Negro race. . . .

The Indianapolis Ordinance's banning of pornography not only fails to fit within any of the exceptions to protection under the first amendment, but also relies heavily upon the injunctive powers of the courts. This is a crippling form of "prior restraint" that seeks to suppress expression in advance of its publication or dissemination. . . . Few prior restraints have been upheld by the Supreme Court, and none on the scale contemplated by the Indianapolis Ordinance.

Finally, it should be noted that the attempt to avoid first amendment difficulties in the Indianapolis Ordinance by asserting that pornography "is a discriminatory practice" cannot succeed. This device, which has been hailed as a new approach to the problem, is no more than a play on words. Pornography is speech or expression, as those terms are used in first amendment theory, and like most expression has an impact upon attitudes and behavior. The question is whether, because of this impact, pornography can be proscribed. It does not help to eliminate the intermediate step in the legal analysis and declare that pornography "is" discrimination.

II. The Dynamics of Suppressing Pornography

Professor MacKinnon argues the case for the suppression of pornography at a high level of abstraction. One must also take into account the dynamics at work in implementing a program such as she contemplates. The hazards to our system of freedom of expression are manifest.

Most important is the inhibiting atmosphere inevitably created by subjecting a broad area of expression to governmental intervention. Persons engaging in any form of communication touching on sexual matters face the prospect of being hauled before a censorship board, involved in prolonged litigation, saddled with back-breaking legal fees, compelled to justify their exercise of first amendment rights to government officials, threatened with damage awards and subjected to other forms of "affirmative action" such as confiscation of earnings—all of this occurring at countless locations scattered across the country. It is true that the Indianapolis Ordinance does not provide for criminal penalties, apart from the possibility of criminal contempt. There is nothing in the legal theory underlying the Ordinance, however, that would preclude the censorship of sexual materials through the apparatus of police investigations, criminal prosecutions and prison sentences. One can hardly expect a system of freedom of expression to flourish under these conditions.

Moreover, there is a strong likelihood that the powers conferred by the Indianapolis Ordinance would be diverted to reactionary political ends. . . . It is entirely possible that the more powerful interests in our society, possessing the requisite funds, could utilize the machinery of government censorship of pornography to harass or silence unwanted points of view. One can readily imagine the Moral Majority or similar groups invoking anti-pornography laws against feminist authors who seek to make male domination "graphic" and "sexually explicit." . . . Thus, censorship of pornography, far from being a liberating force, could become a tool with which to harass feminist or other progressive movements.

Along the same lines, the suppression of pornography through governmental intervention encourages the intolerance syndrome throughout a society. Civil liberties are, as is often said, indivisible. The legal doctrines, governmental machinery and attitudes that suppress speech in one area also promote suppression in other areas. The censorship of pornography thus gives comfort to the forces of reaction and advances the cause of those who seek a closed society. The movement for gender equality has little to gain from such a climate of opinion.

One additional, overriding consideration must be faced: The elimination of pornography by governmental censorship is simply not workable, at least by any democratic process. The area of prohibition is so vast, the machinery of civil litigation so cumbersome, the hope of changing attitudes by government decree so quixotic, that nothing positive is likely to be accomplished. Rather, the results, in terms of selective enforcement, underground circulation of "violative materials," encouragement of organized crime, and the general discrediting of law enforcement, would be entirely negative. In the ensuing confusion, the original problem would remain unsolved.

III. The Rejection of Traditional First Amendment Theory

Professor MacKinnon, as I read her, rests her case not primarily on traditional first amendment theory but rather on an attack upon first amendment theory. Her position is that "[t]he theory of the first amendment under which most pornography is protected from governmental restriction proceeds from liberal assumptions which do not apply to the situation of women." . . . In my judgment, Professor MacKinnon seriously overstates the case against traditional first amendment doctrine and thereby grossly underestimates, in fact neglects altogether, the role that the system of freedom of expression can play in dealing with the issue of pornography and gender equality.

Professor MacKinnon's critique of the "liberal assumptions" underlying first amendment theory rests upon four propositions. The first is that the first amendment "presumes the validity of the distinction between public and private," the former being "the sphere of social power" and the latter "the area of private right." She contends that this distinction "does not cut the same for women as for men" because the exercise of male power that results in the subordination of women, as in the case of pornography, often takes place in the home, and that women may therefore need a higher degree of governmental, or social, intervention in the "private" than in the "public" sphere.

The private-public distinction is not one between governmental controls of conduct inside or outside the home, but one between individual right and collective power. The making of this distinction is a basic problem in any society, liberal or otherwise. The first amendment, generally speaking, places speech within the realm of individual right and action within the realm of collective power. This does preclude governmental control of pornographic speech, but it also leaves open a vast area of governmental control over male domination in the form of action. And this control can be directed against conduct inside the home as well as outside. Legislation imposing penalties for spousal rape, now being enacted in a number of states, illustrates that no liberal public-private assumptions foreclose such governmental attempts to achieve equality between the sexes.

Professor MacKinnon's second criticism of liberal first amendment theory deals with the assumption that freedom of expression "helps discover truth," promotes "consensus," facilitates "progress," and "frees the mind to fulfill itself." She argues that, although securing these values may justify freedom of expression "in a non-hierarchical society," the theory is not adequate "in a society of gender inequality." In such a society, she urges, "the speech of the powerful impresses its view upon the world," providing "the appearance of consent" but making "protest inaudible as well as rare."

There can be little doubt that, in any society, the more powerful forces will engage in a greater volume of speech, on a more pervasive scale, and with a deeper impact than the less powerful groups. A fully balanced equality of speech among all groups and individuals is probably unattainable, at least without a degree of governmental intervention that would destroy the freedom of the system. What the system does guarantee is that the unorthodox, minority, dissenting and submerged elements of the society have a constitutional right to express their views and endeavor to gain adherents. . . . It is designed precisely to give a subordinated group, such as women, a way out of their "powerlessness" by some method other than force.

It should be added that Professor MacKinnon has surely overdrawn the picture in contending that, under the first amendment today, protest against the status of women is "inaudible as well as rare." Her own work, and that of the whole feminist movement, can scarcely be so described.

Professor MacKinnon's third criticism of traditional first amendment doctrine is that it fails to recognize the harm that can be caused by speech. . . . This is not correct; first amendment theory does recognize that speech may cause harm, as well as good, and it is quite capable of recognizing the kind of harm that Professor MacKinnon describes. The theory rests upon the proposition, however, that the values served by freedom of expression are so essential to a free society that speech requires special, near absolute, protection against government interference regardless of any harm that may be caused. It also rests upon the premise, as noted above, that the government possesses sufficient powers to deal with such harms through means other than the suppression of speech. Thus, again, a vast area is open for government measures to promote gender equality. . . .

Professor MacKinnon's fourth criticism, which is closely related to the second, challenges the first amendment assumption that "socially, speech is free," and that the problem is to prevent the government from constraining it. In actuality, she contends, "whole segments of the population" are "systematically silenced *socially,* prior to government action." "For women," she concludes, "the urgent issue of freedom of speech is not primarily the avoidance of state intervention as such, but finding an affirmative means to get access to speech for those to whom it has been denied."

Insofar as the argument is that the speech of the most powerful forces in society "impresses its view upon the world," the answer is the same as above: Freedom of speech does not protect individuals or groups from being persuaded, even against their own interests, but it does guarantee that every individual or group has a right to try to persuade others. Granted the right exists, the question of actually obtaining access to the means of communication becomes a crucial one. There is nothing in the first amendment, however, that precludes "finding an affirmative means to get access" for the less powerful, and indeed the failure to do so is one of the major weaknesses in our system of freedom of expression. But that does not sanction government intervention to restrict the free speech rights of others or to take any similar form of action that would undermine the system as a whole. Nor can it be said, as a factual matter, that those who have wished to speak out for women's rights have been denied access to do so.

Taking all these factors into consideration, it would seem that proponents of equality for women in our society have more to gain from participating in the traditional system of freedom of expression than from abandoning it in favor of a form of relief that would destroy it.

Notes

1. MacKinnon, Not a Moral Issue, 2 Yale L. & Pol'y Rev. 321 (1984), reprinted herein, at 37.

2. See Affidavit of Richard Green, American Booksellers Ass'n, Inc. v. Hudnut, Cause No. IP 84–791C, slip op. (S.D.Ind. 1984). This psychiatrist concludes: "The relationship between the availability of pornography to the public and the incidence of sex crimes does not support the view that pornography leads to sexual assault. Indeed, the data suggest the reverse effect." *Id.* at 5. See also D. Copp & S. Wendell eds., Pornography and Censorship (1983). This book contains essays from a number of social scientists who have attempted to ascertain whether the wide availability of pornography has produced harmful consequences. The editors conclude that "the question cannot yet be given a definitive answer." *Id.* at 12.

3. . . . On November 19, 1984, a federal district court in Indianapolis declared the ordinance unconstitutional in American Booksellers Ass'n, Inc. v. Hudnut, 598 F. Supp. 1316 (S.D.Ind. 1984). Judge Sarah Evans Barker held that "pornography," as defined and regulated by the Ordinance, "is constitutionally protected speech under the First Amendment." *Id.* at 1337.

4. United States v. Schwimmer, 279 U.S. 644, 654–655 (1929).

5. It is for this reason that Ku Klux Klansmen may assemble peacefully to burn their crosses, that adherents of religious cults may proselytize at public airports, and that members of the American Nazi Party may march through a predominantly Jewish community. . . . For a more extensive exposition of first amendment theory, see Emerson, The System of Freedom of Expression ch. I (1970).

6. Miller v. California, 413 U.S. 15, 24 (1973).

7. 458 U.S. 747 (1982).

Whose Right? Ronald Dworkin, Women, and Pornographers

RAE LANGTON

. . . SHOULD LIBERAL THEORISTS be in favor of permitting pornography? As champions of our basic liberties, and as champions especially of free speech, liberals have found it easy to answer this question with a simple "yes." They are of course accustomed to viewing their opponents in this debate as conservatives, who want pornography prohibited because it is immoral: liberals view moralistic motives of this kind with deep (and doubtless justified) suspicion. But there are other voices in the debate, too, voices arguing that we have reason to be concerned about pornography not because it is morally suspect, but because we care about equality and the rights of women. This aspect of the debate between liberals and their opponents can begin to look like an argument about liberty and equality—freedom of speech versus women's rights—and so, apparently, it has been regarded by the courts.

Ronald Dworkin is one liberal theorist who has defended a right to pornography, addressing the topic in "Do We Have a Right to Pornography?"[1] He is, in addition, a liberal who thinks that there can be no real conflict between liberty and equality.[2] Given that the pornography issue can be seen as apparently posing just such a conflict, it is natural to wonder whether Dworkin is right. . . .

I. Theoretical Framework

In "What Rights Do We Have?" Dworkin sets out some basic elements of his political theory, and the role that rights have to play in that theory. . . . Dworkin takes as his starting point certain "postulates of political morality" that are central, he says, to a liberal conception of equality. They can be summed up in the slogan "Government must treat those whom it governs with equal concern and respect." . . .

[The] distinction between personal and external preferences is one that is crucial to the development of Dworkin's theory of rights. One simple way to see that theory . . . is

Langton, Rae: Whose Right? Ronald Dworkin, Women, and Pornographers. 19 Phil. & Pub. Aff. 311 (1990). Copyright © 1990 by Princeton University Press. Reprinted by permission of Princeton University Press.

as a response to the inadequacies of unrestricted utilitarianism when it is confronted with the demands of a liberal principle of equality.[3] In brief: Utilitarianism tells us to maximize the satisfaction of preferences; but if we do that without first disqualifying the preferences of any citizen for the assignment of goods and opportunities to citizens other than himself, the calculations may be distorted, a form of "double counting" may result, and the final outcome may be one that does not treat each citizen with equal concern and respect. Rights are a useful theoretical means of preventing this unwelcome result; rights are a means of protecting individuals from the external preferences of other individuals.

What counts as an external preference? And how do such preferences disrupt the otherwise egalitarian character of utilitarian arguments? We can, says Dworkin, distinguish two ways in which the preference of a citizen can be external, ways that correspond to the twin aspects of the equality principle. The citizen may, first, prefer that another citizen be assigned fewer goods and opportunities than others because he thinks that that *person* is simply worth less concern than others. Consider, for example, a group of citizens who believe that blacks are simply worth less concern than whites, and whose preferences manifest this prejudice. They prefer, say, that the preferences of blacks be worth half those of whites in the utilitarian calculus. If such racist preferences are taken into account, says Dworkin, the utilitarian calculus will be distorted, and blacks will suffer unjustly as a result.

Alternatively, and here we have the second kind of preference, a citizen may prefer that another citizen be assigned fewer goods and opportunities than others because he believes the person's *conception of the good life* to be worthy of less respect than the conceptions of others. Dworkin gives as examples of this second variety the moralistic preferences of people who disapprove of various practices (such as homosexuality, pornography, Communist party adherence) and prefer that no one in society pursue such practices. If such preferences are taken into account, the individuals in question (homosexuals, pornographers, communists) will suffer, not simply because in the competing demands for scarce resources some preferences must lose out, and they happen to be the unlucky ones. They suffer, rather because their own views about how to live their lives are thought to be deserving of less respect.[4] . . .

III. Dworkin on Pornography

In "Do We Have a Right to Pornography?" [w]hat might we expect Dworkin's approach to be? On the one hand, Dworkin is first and foremost a liberal theorist, and the freedom to produce and consume pornography has long been a liberal cause. But he is at the same time a writer famous for taking the principle of equality to be the starting point for sound political thinking; a writer whose sensitivity in dealing with the complex issues surrounding prejudice against an oppressed group we have already witnessed;[5] and a writer who begins his discussion of the pornography question by drawing an analogy between laws concerning pornography and laws concerning racist speech. "Should be we free to incite racial hatred?" he asks his readers in the opening paragraph—an interesting question and one whose implications seem worth pursuing.

Given this hopeful start, and given also that the feminist "armies" had already begun to mass at the time of this writing,[6] we might reasonably expect that a rights-based argument *against* pornography would merit at least some brief mention in this essay. Such hopes, as it turns out, are disappointed, and Dworkin's question in the opening paragraph is not pursued in any detail. He considers, at various points throughout the essay, a vast number of ways in which pornography might more or less plausibly be construed as a harm. The sample that follows is by no means exhaustive, but I can assure my reader that there is one construal that is conspicuous by its absence, namely, that women as a group might be harmed by pornography.

Here is the quick sample. Since most people would prefer censorship, permitting pornography harms general utility by leaving the majority of preferences unsatisfied. Pornography damages the cultural environment. It upsets and disgusts people. It limits people's ability to lead the kind of lives they would want for themselves and their children. It makes sex seem less valuable. People find discomfort in encountering blatant nudity because they detest themselves for taking an interest in the proceedings, and they are forcefully reminded of what their neighbors are like and of what their neighbors are getting away with.

To be fair, Dworkin does indeed raise the issue of whether pornography ever presents a "special danger of personal harm narrowly conceived,"[7] and although he usually takes this to be a question about people's responses when directly confronted with pornography, he, along with the Williams Committee,[8] "concedes . . . the relevance of the question whether an increase in the amount of pornography in circulation in the community is likely to produce more violence or more sexual crimes of any particular sort. . . ."[9] This is as close as Dworkin ever gets to considering whether or not it may be women who are, in the end, the ones hurt by the pornography industry. As a rule, when he raises the possibility of any link between pornography and harm to women of a concrete and familiar sort, he fails to take it seriously. Indeed, were it not for the evidence we already have of Dworkin's awareness of the subtle complexities surrounding questions of group oppression, the reader might be tempted to suppose that Dworkin's chief interest is to lampoon the idea. Imagining that pornography might lead to violence is like imagining that reading *Hamlet* might lead to violence.[10] Or, in another passage, he wonders whether pornography might be like "breakfast television": both might be found to encourage absenteeism from work, and thereby have (perish the thought!) some special and deleterious effect on the general economy."[11] [H]e thinks that questions about concrete harm are mere "academic speculation";[12] the pornography issue is itself a "relatively trivial" problem.[13] By contrast, embarrassment—that is, embarrassment on the part of the "shy pornographer" [consumer]—he describes as raising an "interesting and important question."[14] . . .

Readers may have gathered by now that Dworkin and I do not share exactly the same view about what is and what is not an important question. Embarrassment is not, all things considered, a very important question; the well-being of women is. Leaving such sympathies aside, there are of course some relevant empirical questions to be addressed here. And on certain questions of this kind Dworkin accepts the findings of the Williams Committee, namely that there is no persuasive evidence that pornography causes violent crime.[15] On other empirical questions—for example, questions about pornography's possible role in a society in which women happen to be widely oppressed—Dworkin is comfortably silent. One wonders whether he would have been as comfortable had Sweatt's* opponents cited, in support of their case, similar findings that had reached a similarly happy conclusion that there was no persuasive evidence that the practice of racial segregation causes violent crime. One does not always need conclusive evidence about crime to have cause for concern, nor is violence the only worry in situations in which there is widespread prejudice and discrimination against a particular group. . . .

. . . Why, we may be forgiven for asking, does Dworkin consider this "relatively trivial" issue to be worthy of serious attention . . . ? If we look again at the first of Dworkin's suggestions about the harm pornography brings about, we will find our answer. Most people, he says, would *prefer* censorship; if, in spite of this, we permit pornography, *general utility* will be harmed, since the majority preferences will be left unsatisfied.

This is enough to give us a fair idea of Dworkin's special interest in the question. We have the starting point for a familiar Dworkinian recipe for identifying rights, where one begins by noting that there is a good utilitarian argument for a certain policy, and that certain individuals will suffer as a result of this policy; investigates the preferences upon which the utilitarian argument is based; shows that they are external preferences; and finally concludes that the individuals concerned have rights that must defeat the policy in question. . . .

Dworkin proceeds to show how it is possible to mount an argument of principle against a prohibitive policy. Suppose, he says, that the policy of prohibiting pornography would satisfy the preferences of the majority, and that the opportunities of the consumers of pornography would be curtailed as a result. Our next step, if we are interested in finding out whether pornographers might have rights against this policy, is to consider the character of the preferences upon which the policy relies, since the right to equality demands that certain preferences be disregarded. Does the prohibitive policy rely on any external preferences? Remember that external preferences can be of two broad types: one can prefer that another person receive fewer goods and opportunities because one thinks that that person is worth less concern, or, alternatively, because one thinks that that person's conception of the good life deserves less respect. The external preferences involved in the Sweatt argument were of the former variety;

---

*Sweatt is a hypothetical character in Dworkin's "Reverse Discrimination." In that essay, Dworkin applies his general principles to racial discrimination by comparing the case of a black man (Sweatt) denied admission to the white-only law school at the University of Texas and a white man (DeFunis) denied admission to a law school at the University of Washington, with an affirmative action plan giving preference to minority applicants. Dworkin concludes that the former's rights have been violated but not the latter's because segregation conflicts with the principle of equal concern and respect and is inherently insulting, whereas the latter case does not conflict with the equality principle, is not inherently insulting, and is favored by a strong policy. *Ed.*

in the case of pornography I take it that Dworkin thinks they are of the latter. People want pornography to be prohibited chiefly because they think that it is ignoble or wrong, and that a conception of the good life that holds otherwise deserves less respect. "Moralistic" preferences of this kind must, says Dworkin, be defeated by a corresponding "right to moral independence," which he describes as "the right not to suffer disadvantage in the distribution of social goods and opportunities, including disadvantage in the liberties permitted to them by the criminal law, just on the ground that their officials or fellow citizens think that their opinions about the right way for them to lead their own lives are ignoble or wrong."[16] Insofar as the utilitarian argument hinges on moralistic preferences, the consumers of pornography have rights that trump the prohibitive policy, and our policy should be permissive.[17]

It is crucial to note that pornographers are said to have rights not because there is something special about speech per se, and pornography is speech; nor because there is something special about the private domain in which pornography is often consumed; but simply because they are vulnerable to the effects of the external preferences of others, and equality demands that such preferences be ignored. This essay provides a good illustration of Dworkin's strategy of deriving traditional liberties from the principle of equality alone. It is also worth pointing out that Dworkin claims that his own strategy, as illustrated here, does justice to deeply held liberal convictions about the value of free speech in a way that competing theoretical strategies cannot hope to do so.

IV. Pornography and Civil Rights: A Feminist Response

The purpose of this section is to review briefly a certain feminist civil rights argument about pornography, in the hope of showing how the question is transformed once it is placed in a civil rights context. . . . The reader should be aware that the argument reviewed in this section is one of a variety of feminist responses, many of which disagree with both the analysis and the course of action advocated by this one.[18]

[T]his feminist argument against pornography sets aside questions about "morality" and focuses instead on the civil status of women. The argument has been put very forcefully by Catharine MacKinnon. . . .

The distinctive feature of the MacKinnon argument is that it views pornography—as defined in the ordinance—as having implications for sexual equality: pornography is seen as a practice that contributes to the subordinate status of women, just as certain other practices (segregation among them) contribute to the subordinate status of blacks. The argument seeks to establish at least two things: one is that women do not, as a matter of fact, currently have equal status; and the other is that pornography does, as a matter of fact, contribute significantly to the continuing subordinate position of women.

The first claim is, I think, not very controversial. . . .

What is different about MacKinnon's approach . . . is that she sees sexual violence not simply as "crime" (as Dworkin seemed apt to do), but rather as a dimension to the inequality of the sexes. . . . To call such violence simply "crime" says MacKinnon, without remarking upon the interesting fact that the perpetrators are nearly always members of one class of citizens, and the victims members of another, would be to disguise its systematically discriminatory nature.

Turning now to the second claim, the feminist argument can be seen as offering a hypothesis about the explanation for this pattern of sexual abuse; part of the explanation lies in the fact that certain kinds of pornography help to form and propagate certain views about women and sexuality. Such pornography is said to work as a kind of propaganda, which both expresses a certain view about women and sexuality and perpetuates that view: it "sexualizes rape, battery, sexual harassment, prostitution and child sexual abuse; it thereby celebrates, promotes, authorizes and legitimizes them."[19] To back up this claim, a substantial amount of empirical evidence was cited by those supporting the ordinance. . . .[20] . . .

The [Hudnut] case was viewed by the district court as presenting a conflict between First Amendment guarantees of free speech and the Fourteenth Amendment right to be free from sex-based discrimination. The ordinance would survive constitutional scrutiny only if the state's interest in sex-based equality were "so compelling as to be fundamental," for "only then can it be deemed to outweigh the interest of free speech." And the court concluded, as a matter of law, that the state's interest in sex-based equality was not so compelling.

It is worth noting that the empirical findings were not disputed; in fact, when the case went to the court of appeals, Judge Frank Easterbrook went so far as to say, "We accept the premises of this legislation. Depictions of subordination tend to perpetuate subordination. The subordinate status of women in turn leads to affront and lower pay at work, insult and injury at home, battery and rape on the streets." His conclusion, however, is that "this simply demonstrates the power of pornography as speech."[21]

V. A New Start

What I want to do now is to take certain elements from the feminist case . . . and put them in the context of Dworkinian political theory. . . .

1. Prohibiting Pornography: An Argument of Principle

Let us begin by reminding ourselves of the general Dworkinian recipe for a good argument of principle. We saw this general recipe at work in both "Reverse Discrimination" and "Do We Have a Right to Pornography?": (a) Begin with what looks like a good utilitarian argument for a particular policy; (b) look at the individuals who appear to suffer as a result of the policy, and ask whether the policy violates the rights of those individuals; (c) inspect the preferences upon which the utilitarian argument is based, and show that they are external preferences; (d) conclude that the individuals concerned do have rights that are trumps against the policy in question. This is precisely the recipe I now propose to follow. . . .

A. THE UTILITARIAN ARGUMENT

In the two essays mentioned above, Dworkin's starting point was an apparent utilitarian argument in favor of a position that most liberals would eschew. In the case of Sweatt, the balance of preferences apparently comes out in favor of segregation; in the case of pornography, the balance of preferences apparently comes out in favor of prohibition.

. . . In "Do We Have a Right to Pornography?" Dworkin assumed that our preferences about pornography would come out in favor of prohibition. I am not so sure. The power of the pornography industry in sheer monetary terms bears eloquent witness to the popularity of its product. . . . Given [this], and given a general ignorance about or indifference to pornography's influence, can we be sure, as Dworkin seems to be, that a utilitarian argument would support a prohibitive policy? . . . I think it is at least possible that overall preferences would come out in favor of a permissive policy. . . .

B. THE INDIVIDUALS WHO SUFFER

Women appear to suffer as a result of this policy. . . . We are not asking, at this point, whether women suffer in any respect that would be sufficient to justify changing the policy, but only whether they suffer at all. The purpose of this step in the argument is only to establish a certain prima facie cause for complaint; the question of whether such complaint is justified is addressed only at a later stage of the argument. Sweatt and DeFunis both had cause for complaint in this sense: each might have felt deeply insulted by the admissions policy that excluded him; each was apparently disadvantaged by the policy; each way, arguably, denied opportunities that would not otherwise have been available to him. . . . In what ways does the permissive policy harm women?

[I]t is certainly the case that some women feel deeply distressed about and insulted by pornography. Dworkin would, I take it, agree that this counts as a harm, since part of his argument . . . relies on the claim that distress at the mere thought that pornography exists is indeed a kind of harm, and one that governments have a prima facie obligation to take into account. Of course, the fact that a policy causes some insult and distress is not sufficient reason for thinking that there is something wrong with the policy, when that policy is otherwise justified. "Everything depends," as Dworkin so clearly puts it in the Sweatt context, "upon whether the feeling of insult is produced by some more objective feature that would disqualify the policy even if the insult were not felt."[22] If no such feature can be found, then the felt insult "must be based on a misperception."[23] Whether the permissive policy has an "objective feature" of this kind is a question I will turn to in the next step of the argument.

However, to leave the harm at the level of "insult and distress" would be to seriously misrepresent the feminist argument I am attempting to interpret. The central point of the argument is that some pornography can work as a kind of propaganda, which constitutes a threat to women's well-being, and, more generally, a threat to women's equality. . . . Some liberal theorists seem to come close to concurring with the view that pornography of certain kinds can be like propaganda. Violent pornographic depictions of certain kinds "reenforce macho ideology," writes Joel Feinberg, and this ideology is one that has done "manifest harm" to women.[24] To avoid needless controversy, let me confine the discussion of harm to some aspects about which there seems to be a greater likelihood of achieving agreement. It is probably the case that violent and degrading pornography "reenforces macho ideology," as Feinberg puts it, and thereby perpetuates the subordinate status of women; the resulting "manifest harm" to women probably includes, but is not confined to, sexual abuse of various kinds (including sexual harassment and rape), harm to reputation, and loss of credibility.

It will be seen that what I have described above is something other than the conclusive evidence of crimes of violence that Dworkin appeared to demand of an antipornography argument. I have spoken of "probable" harm, and of harm other than violence. This talk of "probable" harm raises, of course, difficult questions about burdens of proof. Recall that we attributed to Dworkin a certain implicit principle about burdens of proof, a principle that was relevant in some important contexts, such as the civil rights context of Sweatt. One could accept that Sweatt had prima facie cause for complaint, even if he were bringing his case in the context of a broader "separate-but-equal" social policy; even if, that is, it were impossible to establish conclusively that Sweatt was disadvantaged by the segregatory policy. [T]o take such an approach would be reasonable, and would amount to a certain presumption in Sweatt's favor . . . that he probably is harmed by the policy. . . . I assume a similar burden of proof here: we are entitled to say that women are probably harmed by the permissive policy, and that although this harm is not (as far as this argument is concerned) sufficient to warrant changing the policy, it prompts us to move on to the question of whether there is real injustice. . . .

Women apparently suffer as a result of the policy of permitting violent and degrading pornography. We can now ask, Does that policy violate women's rights?

C. PREFERENCES

At this point we must look more closely at the preferences upon which the utilitarian policy might be based. There are all kinds of reasons that people might have for wanting pornography to be permitted. Many people like pornography (including violent pornography) and want to be able to consume it without restriction; some people do not like it themselves, but are happy enough for others to enjoy it; some people are afraid of the "slippery slope," and worry that allowing the state to prohibit pornography would raise the likelihood of government abuse of power. It seems likely that the preferences upon which the argument hinges will be of the very first kind, namely the preferences of the consumers of pornography for pornography itself.

What kind of preferences are these? On the face of it, they all seem to be personal. . . . Dworkin has already endorsed a version of the view that the personal is sometimes political, or, more precisely, that apparently personal preferences can have implications for political questions about rights. . . . Is the situation we are considering one in which prejudice against the disadvantaged group is strong and pervasive in society? Surely that much at least is uncontroversial.

But if so, there are further questions to be asked. If the prejudice against women did not exist, would the preferences for this kind of pornography exist? This is a complicated hypothetical question, but at least one eminent liberal theorist has offered a fairly confident answer to it. This kind of violent pornography "does not appeal at all," says Feinberg, to a male who is "not in the grip of the macho cult. In fact these pictures, stories, and films have no other function but to express and reenforce the macho ideology. 'Get your sexual kicks,' they seem to say, 'but make sure you get them by humiliating the woman, and showing her who's boss.' "[25] Feinberg thinks that the possession of "macho" values is a necessary condition for the appeal of violent pornography; he also thinks that macho values embody a view about the worth of women. If one were to accept his suggestion, one would be accepting that a preference for pornography of this kind depends upon a view about the worth of women, and hence that such preferences are, by Dworkinian standards, external preferences.

What Feinberg is suggesting here sounds interestingly similar to Dworkin's description of the associational preference of a white law student. . . . Dworkin described such a preference as "parasitic upon external preferences . . . a white student prefers the company of other whites because he has racist social and political convictions, or because he has contempt for blacks as a group."[26] If Feinberg is right, then what we have in the case of violent and degrading pornography is just the same kind of thing. To paraphrase Dworkin's words, an apparently personal preference for such pornography is really "parasitic upon external preferences . . . the consumer prefers pornography of this kind because he has macho social and political convictions, or because he has contempt for women as a group."

Feinberg's suggestion surely has some plausibility. One could, however, be somewhat more cautious. One could suppose that, while a great many such preferences depended on the possession of certain antecedent values, people were sometimes drawn to violent pornography through other motives, such as curiosity, or simple peer pressure. Such preferences might simply be personal. While there is some likelihood that many of the relevant preferences are affected by prejudice, it is possible that what one has here is a complicated situation of the kind Dworkin describes elsewhere, in which "personal and external preferences are so inextricably tied together, and so mutually dependent, that no practical test for measuring preferences will be able to discriminate the personal and external elements in any individual's overall preferences."[27]

Suppose that this is the case. Suppose it is difficult to disentangle personal preferences about pornography of this kind from external preferences, difficult to answer the hypothetical question about the dependence of the desire on the prejudice. What should we conclude in such circumstances? . . .

Women as a group have rights against the consumers of pornography and thereby have rights that are trumps against the policy of permitting pornography. The permissive policy has a certain "objective feature," to use Dworkin's phrase; it relies on external preferences, that is, preferences that are dependent on views about the worth of other people. This is enough to establish that the permissive policy is in conflict with the principle of equal concern and respect, and that women accordingly have rights against it.[28] . . .

2. Prohibiting Pornography: An Argument of Policy

In constructing a Dworkinian argument of [policy] in favor of prohibiting pornography . . . I again take my lessons from Dworkin's approach in "Reverse Discrimination," this time looking not at Sweatt but at DeFunis.

We were presented in the analysis of DeFunis with the following powerful argumentative strategy: (a) There was an *ideal* argument of policy, with equality as its goal: the practice of affirmative action was taken to be one that would lead to a more equal, and therefore more just, society (regardless of the preferences of its citizens); and (b) there was also, crucially, an *absence* of any countervailing argument of principle. DeFunis was found to have no right against the policy in question, and given that there were no further objections, that particular affirmative action policy was held to be in harmony with the principle of equal concern and respect. In order to apply this approach to the pornography question, an argument that has both of the above features will be needed.

a. The Ideal Argument

We begin, then, by offering an ideal argument of policy. We consider the policy of prohibiting violent pornography, and form the hypothesis that this policy would help us make progress toward an important goal, namely, a more equal, and therefore more just, society. Given that there is some evidence that pornography of this kind plays a role in perpetuating the subordinate status of women, in reinforcing "macho ideology," it is not altogether unreasonable to suppose that to prohibit pornography would be to remove one of the many impediments to women's equal civil status.

This empirical hypothesis is of course vulnerable. Although it cannot be said to be implausible, it may be controversial. Perhaps the policy will not work in the way we hope. Perhaps it will turn out to have some bad effects, although if Dworkin were right the consequences of the policy would not be too dire; in Dworkin's view, it "seems implausible that any important human interests are damaged by denying dirty books or films,"[29] and if it seems implausible for pornography generally, it will presumably seem even more so for the subset of pornography we are considering here. It is possible, though, that the policy will backfire, and promote, say, misogyny rather than equality. However, the fact that the hypothesis is controversial should not in itself be a bar to the policy's constitutionality, if Dworkin is right. For it is not, says Dworkin, "the business of judges . . . to overthrow decisions of other officials because the judges disagree about the efficiency of social policies."[30] If one is to condemn the policy as unjust, it must be for reasons other than its possible inefficiency. [A]re [there] such reasons?

b. ABSENCE OF ANY COUNTERVAILING ARGUMENT OF PRINCIPLE

We must ask at this point whether there is any countervailing argument of principle that would defeat the proposed policy. Do people have a *right* to pornography? Dworkin is, as we have seen, a champion of the rights of pornographers against those who seek censorship. Can his argument provide a means of trumping this argument of policy? It seems not. First of all, Dworkin's rights-based argument was directed against a utilitarian, rather than an ideal, argument of policy. Pornography was to be prohibited, not because such a policy would promote the equality of its citizens, but because most citizens were thought to *prefer* that pornography be prohibited. Given the utilitarian starting point of Dworkin's analysis in "Do We Have a Right to Pornography?" his approach there has little to say in response to an ideal argument of the kind being proposed here, an argument that does not consider the preferences of citizens at all. Pornographers may well have a "right to moral independence" of the kind Dworkin describes, namely, "the right not to suffer disadvantage in the distribution of social goods and opportunities, including disadvantage in the liberties permitted to them by the criminal law, just on the ground that their officials or fellow citizens think that their opinions about the right way for them to lead their own lives are ignoble or wrong."[31] But such a right, however admirably it may protect the liberty of pornographers from moralistic arguments, will do them no good here. This prohibitive argument of policy is no more moralistic than the argument invoked in *DeFunis*. The policy will, admittedly, somewhat restrict the liberty of the pornographer; but this does not have to be interpreted as a denial of his treatment as an equal. Policies that constrain the liberty of the pornographer conflict with the equality principle "only when the constraint is justified in some way that depends on the fact that others condemn his convictions or values."[32] The policy we are considering here depends on no such fact. It relies rather "on the independent argument that a more equal society is a better society even if its citizens prefer inequality."[33]

Although it seems that Dworkin has provided no answer to the ideal argument proposed here, it would perhaps be unfair to stop at this point. All arguments of policy, whether utilitarian or ideal, are vulnerable, according to Dworkin, to arguments of principle. While Dworkin's failure to supply a defense of a right to pornography against the feminist argument outlined above suggests that his remarks about the relevance of this argument to "recent history" were a little hasty, it should not be taken as implying that no such defense is possible. How might one go about trying to construct a rights-based argument against an ideal, rather than a utilitarian, argument?

Ideal arguments of policy can sometimes conflict with the principle of equal concern and respect. An example mentioned by Dworkin . . . is that of an argument of policy that supports the goal of achieving a culturally sophisticated community, in a situation in which no one wants such sophistication. A goal of this kind is in conflict with the "neutrality" aspect of the equality principle: a government that is committed to treating competing accounts of the good life with equal respect cannot act on the grounds that "cultural sophistication" is inherently more valuable than some other conception of the good life.

But in the context of pornography, as in the context of affirmative action, we are dealing with a goal of a rather different kind: namely, equality itself. While one can see how a goal like cultural sophistication might be vulnerable in the way that Dworkin suggests, it is harder to see how equality itself could come into conflict with the equality principle. There is, of course, an important distinction to be aware of here. As Dworkin comments, "part of the importance of DeFunis's case [is] that it forces us to acknowledge the distinction between equality as a policy and equality as a right, a distinction that political theory has virtually ignored."[34] Even policies that have equality as their goal can conflict with the principle of equal concern and respect, and in such cases it will be possible to raise an argument of principle against the policy. Dworkin has an imaginary example:

> Suppose a law school were to charge a few middle class students, selected by lot, double tuition in order to increase the scholarship fund for poor students. It would be serving a desirable policy—equality of opportunity—by means that violated the right of the students selected by lot to be treated equally with other students who could also afford the increased fees.[35]

But the policy of prohibiting pornography that we are considering here does not seem to be inequitable in this procedural way; and in the absence of any further clues as to how we are to go about identifying rights in the context of ideal arguments, we need to pursue this path no further. Given that the ideal argument does not depend on the fact that others condemn the pornographer's convictions and values, and given that it is not otherwise in conflict with the equality principle, we can conclude that a prohibitive policy is permissible. Ideal arguments of this kind, whether for affirmative action or for the prohibition of some kinds of pornography, apparently work hand in hand with the principle of equal concern and respect, relying as they do "on the independent argument that a more equal society is a better society even if its citizens prefer inequality. That argument does not deny anyone's right to be treated as an equal himself."[36]

VI. Concluding Remarks

In the preceding section I advanced two "Dworkinian" arguments in favor of prohibiting a certain kind of pornography. The first was an argument of principle that relied on the idea of equality as a right, and took the following form: To permit such pornography is to have a policy that relies crucially on external preferences; so such pornography should not be permitted. The second was an argument of policy that relied on the idea of equality as a goal, and took the following form: Prohibiting pornography of this kind would help achieve a desirable social goal, namely equality; given that there is no countervailing rights-based argument, such pornography should be prohibited.

Notice that pornography is to be prohibited, according to these two arguments, not because there is conclusive evidence that it causes violent crime, but rather because it is in conflict with equality. Conclusive evidence of a causal link to violence is not demanded, as it might be demanded by an argument that relied on a simple harm principle. It should be clear that these Dworkinian strategies have significantly altered the burden of proof, with regard to both the argument of principle and the argument of policy. With respect to the argument of principle, demanding conclusive evidence that pornography causes violent crime would be like requiring of Sweatt (in a hypothetical "separate-but-equal" social context) that he produce conclusive evidence that the "separate-but-equal" strategy harmed him. With respect to the argument of policy, demanding such evidence would be like requiring the University of Washington Law School to supply proof that *failure* to have an affirmative action policy brought about some grave harm, rather than simply expecting the administrators to have a reasonable empirical hypothesis about the probable social benefits of affirmative action, and to ensure that the policy violates no one's right to be treated as an equal. In sum, if Dworkin were demanding that a case against pornography produce conclusive evidence about violence, then he is requiring both a kind of harm and a degree of evidence that he would not demand in civil rights contexts like that of *Sweatt* and *DeFunis.* . . .

It is time now to return to the question I posed at the beginning. . . . What, exactly, has been achieved by demonstrating an apparent harmony between Dworkin's theory and the feminist view he opposes? Two responses are possible.

The first response is that what we have here is an interesting conclusion about pornography and liberalism. A prohibitive policy about violent and degrading pornography is not only consistent with, but apparently demanded by, liberal theory. Well, so much the worse for pornography. What has been shown is the depth of liberalism's commitment to equality; liberalism will approve whatever steps are necessary to protect the right to equality, and to achieve equality as a social goal, even when those steps seem restrictive, provided that no one's right to be treated as an equal is violated. Perhaps such a conclusion will prompt some reevaluation of the liberal agenda, that loose package of causes described by Dworkin in his article "Liberalism."[37] Liberals, he says, traditionally "support racial equality and approve government intervention to secure it, through constraints on both public and private discrimination."[38] However, he continues, "they oppose other forms of collective regulation of individual decision: they oppose regulation of the content of political speech . . . and they oppose regulation of sexual literature and conduct."[39] Perhaps the last of those causes is due for revision, in the light of an awareness that "sexual literature" at any rate might sometime have implications for equality. If liberalism cares just as deeply about sexual equality as it cares about racial equality, it might be led to approve whatever measures are necessary to secure it.

A second and alternative response is that what we have here is not an interesting conclusion about pornography and liberalism, but rather a conclusion about Dworkin. What I have shown is that a prohibitive policy is in harmony with *Dworkinian* liberal theory. Well, so much the worse for Dworkin. Since the conclusion about pornography is unacceptable (so this response runs), there must be something wrong with the Dworkinian premises. What has become evident here is not so much the compatibility of liberalism with restrictive policies on pornography as the weakness of Dworkin's own approach to civil liberties.

Those who are tempted to make this latter response might feel that their suspicions were confirmed if it appeared that these Dworkinian strategies could be used to undermine other liberties. Suppose we explore this possibility, confining ourselves for simplicity's sake to the right of free speech. [L]et me consider . . . a rather different kind of speech, which is not sexually explicit, which is apparently constitutionally protected, and which does nonetheless seem to be vulnerable to the above strategies. . . .

. . . Dworkin remarks in the opening paragraph of "Do We Have a Right to Pornography?" that the United Kingdom Race Relations Law "makes it a crime to advocate racial prejudice."[40] He appears to believe that in doing so, the law—which he says would be found unconstitutional in the United States—conflicts with a principle of equal concern and respect.[41] But the United Kingdom legislators might surely justify their policy by appeal to arguments of the [following kind]. To permit incitement to racial hatred would be to give weight to racist preferences of a kind that egalitarian governments have a duty to ignore, so such speech should not be permitted. Or: to prohibit such speech would be to make progress toward an important social goal, namely, equality, so such speech should be prohibited. If this were the case, then the United Kingdom policy would not conflict with a principle of equal concern and respect. It would, on the contrary, be in harmony with it.

What the Indianapolis ordinance and the United Kingdom Race Relations law appear to have in common is a concern for equality that runs very deep—so deep that the silencing of some speech is not regarded as too high a price to pay for it.[42] The Dworkin commitment to equality appears to run equally deep. Recall that Dworkin said that there could be no real conflict between liberty and equality, since if there *were* any genuine conflict between the two, it would be a contest that liberty must lose. It seems that Dworkin's prognosis about such a contest was correct. Where liberty and equality conflict in the ways I have described, it is indeed liberty that loses assuming that one regards the conflict through the lens of Dworkinian liberal theory. That theory seems unable, in such circumstances, to supply a defense of free expression, even when that expression is of a kind to which the First Amendment extends its protection. Those of us who share the concern for equality expressed in the ordinance and Race Relations law may welcome these results, happy to find in Dworkin an unexpected ally. Those of us who find the results unwelcome may conclude that Dworkin has not taken civil liberties seriously enough, and that rights to such liberties as free expression may need to be theoretically fundamental if they are to be successfully defended. Perhaps Dworkin has been hasty in dismissing as illusory all apparent conflict between liberty and equality. Perhaps, on the other hand, the apparent conflicts I have described are only that: apparent. I leave such questions to the reader's judgment.

Notes

1. Ronald Dworkin, Do We have a Right to Pornography? 1 Oxford J. Legal Stud. 177–212 (1981); reprinted in A Matter of Principle 335–372 (Harvard Univ. Press, 1985). Page references are to the reprint.

2. Ronald Dworkin, What Is Equality? Part 3: The Place of Liberty, 73 Iowa L. Rev. 9 (1987).

3. My concern in this article is almost exclusively with Dworkin's theory as it appears in Taking Rights Seriously (Harvard Univ. Press, 1977), and A Matter of Principle. Dworkin's views have undergone some changes (e.g., in "What Is Equality?" *supra* note 2), but these are not, I think, changes that substantially affect the points I want to make here. . . .

4. Dworkin, What Rights Do We Have?, in Taking Rights Seriously, *supra* note 3, at 276.

5. See, e.g., Ronald Dworkin, Reverse Discrimination, in Taking Rights Seriously, *supra* note 3, at 266–278.

6. As demonstrated, for example, in the classic collection of essays Take Back the Night: Women on Pornography (William Morrow, 1980), containing essays published earlier.

7. Dworkin, *supra* note 1, at 340.

8. [The Home Office Departmental Committee on Obscenity and Film Censorship was a British commission established in 1977 to study pornography and to make recommendations regarding legislation. The committee was named "the Williams Committee" after its chairperson, Cambridge University Professor Bernard Williams. Gordon Hawkins & Franklin Zimring, Pornography in a Free Society ix (Cambridge Univ. Press, 1988). See Home Office, Report of the Committee on Obscenity and Firm Censorship, Cmnd. 7772 (Her Majesty's Stationery Office, 1979) (hereafter Williams Report). The committee recommended that some forms of pornography (child pornography, for example) be banned but other forms be permitted. *Ed.*]

9. Dworkin, *supra* note 1, at 338.

10. *Id.* at 355.

11. *Id.* at 354.

12. *Id.* at 355.

13. *Id.* at 359.

14. *Id.* at 358. . . .

15. *Id.* . . .

16. *Id.* at 353.

17. Insofar as this permissive policy would in turn constrain the ability of other people to lead the lives of their choice, we have an argument for restriction of some form. So what Dworkin ends up with, balancing their conflicting considerations, is an endorsement of the compromise solution offered by the Williams Report, i.e., that most pornography should be permitted but restricted through measures such as zoning (*id.* at 358).

18. For a range of views other than MacKinnon's, see, e.g., Gail Chester & Julienne Dickey eds., Feminism and Censorship: The Current Debate (Bridgeport, Eng.: Prism Press, 1988); Nan D. Hunter & Sylvia A. Law, Brief Amici Curiae of Feminist Anti-Censorship Taskforce, et al., in American Booksellers Ass'n, Inc. v. Hudnut, (1985), herein, at 118; Andrea Dworkin, Pornography: Men Possessing Women (London: The Women's Press, 1981); Varda Burstyn ed., Women Against Censorship (Vancouver: Douglas and MacIntyre, 1985); Edward Donnerstein, Daniel Linz & Steven Penrod, The Question of Pornography: Research Findings and Policy Implications chaps. 7, 8 (New York: Free Press; London: Collier Macmillan, 1987).

19. MacKinnon, Francis Biddle's Sister, in Feminism Unmodified 171–172 (Harvard Univ. Press, 1987).

20. The question of what is involved in making a causal claim of this kind is an important one. No one is claiming, of course, that there is a simple link; one can agree with Feinberg that "pornography does not cause normal decent chaps, through a single exposure, to metamorphose into rapists" (Offense to Others 153 [Oxford Univ. Press, 1985]). For an interesting discussion of the notions of causality that bear on questions of this kind, see Frederick Schauer, Causation Theory and the Causes of Sexual Violence, 4 Am. B. Found. Res. J. 737 (1987). Questions about the empirical evidence are also important, and deserve more attention than I can give them here. [F]or a more comprehensive discussion of the social science evidence, see Donnerstein et al., The Question of Pornography, *supra* note 18.

21. 771 F.2d 329 (7th Cir. 1985).

22. Dworkin, *supra* note 5, at 231.

23. *Id.*

24. Feinberg, *supra* note 20, at 150–151. Feinberg, it should be noted, . . . thinks the macho ideology has done manifest harm to men as well; and although he thinks violent pornography "reenforces" that ideology, he does not think it is a major cause of it (*id.* at 153).

25. *Id.* at 151.

26. Dworkin, *supra* note 5, at 236.

27. *Id.*

28. One possible response to this argument that I do not address here is that the argument, if correct, shows that pornography of this kind presents an apparent conflict of rights, the rights of pornographers against moralists and the rights of women against pornographers. How one goes about resolving such conflicts is not clear, but one way might be to think about what a fully reconstructed utilitarian argument might look like, that is, one that laundered out external preferences of both varieties. On this subject one must, perforce, be somewhat speculative; but if we were to take preferences at all, we might begin by considering the following three varieties: (i) preferences of some women that some pornography not be permitted because they view it as deeply insulting; preferences of women for an environment in which they can pursue their goals and life plans without the threat of discrimination and sexual abuse that pornography of this kind arguably engenders; (ii) moralistic preferences of disapprovers, who want pornography prohibited because they view it as immoral; and (iii) preferences of pornographers that pornography be permitted. There may be others, but these would surely be among the most important. Dworkin considers chiefly the second and third varieties. By Dworkin's argument, the second set count as external; I accept this for the purposes of this essay. I have argued that the preferences of this third variety are also external. This would leave the laundered utilitarian calculus with only the first to consider. I take it that preferences of the first variety are personal, and while pornographers may have rights against the second variety, they would have no rights against the first. So a fully reconstructed utilitarian argument would, it seems, yield a restrictive conclusion.

29. Dworkin, *supra* note 1, at 369–370.

30. Dworkin, *supra* note 5, at 224.

31. Dworkin, *supra* note 1, at 353.

32. *Id.* at 366.

33. Dworkin, *supra* note 5, at 239.

34. *Id.* at 226.

35. *Id.*

36. *Id.* at 239.

37. Dworkin, Liberalism, in A Matter of Principle, *supra* note 1, at 181–204.

38. *Id.* at 187.

39. *Id.*

40. Cited in Dworkin, *supra* note 1, at 335.

41. In "Right to Pornography?" (*id.*) Dworkin takes freedom to advocate racial prejudice as a case of freedom to speak "unpopular or wicked thoughts," a liberty that he clearly supports (*id.* at 352) and apparently thinks would be defended along lines similar to a defense of a right to pornography.

42. As a matter of fact, members of the feminist antipornography movement in Britain have proposed (at the 1987 annual general meeting of the National Council of Civil Liberties) that "the Race Relations Act of 1976 be used as a model for legislating against pornography: making it unlawful to publish or distribute material likely to stir up sexual as well as racial hatred" (Itzin, Sex and Censorship: The Political Implications, in Feminism and Censorship, *supra* note 18, at 46).

AMERICAN BOOKSELLERS ASS'N, INC.
v. HUDNUT

771 F.2d 323 (7th Cir. 1985), *aff'd*, 475 U.S. 1001 (1986)

EASTERBROOK, Circuit Judge.

Indianapolis enacted an ordinance defining "pornography" as a practice that discriminates against women. "Pornography" is to be redressed through the administrative and judicial methods used for other discrimination. The City's definition of "pornography" is considerably different from "obscenity," which the Supreme Court has held is not protected by the First Amendment.

[In Miller v. California, 413 U.S. 15 (1973), the Supreme Court held that for a publication to be obscene, it must, taken as a whole, appeal to the prurient interest, must contain patently offensive depictions or descriptions of specified sexual conduct, and have no serious literary, artistic, political, or scientific value. Offensiveness is to be assessed under prevailing community standards. *Ed.*].

"Pornography" under the ordinance is "the graphic sexually explicit subordination of women, whether in pictures or in words, that also includes one or more of the following: (1) Women are presented as sexual objects who enjoy pain or humiliation; or (2) Women are presented as sexual objects who experience sexual pleasure in being raped; or (3) Women are presented as sexual objects tied up or cut up or mutilated or bruised or physically hurt, or as dismembered or truncated or fragmented or severed into body parts; or (4) Women are presented as being penetrated by objects or animals; or (5) Women are presented in scenarios of degradation, injury, abasement, torture, shown as filthy or inferior, bleeding, bruised, or hurt in a context that makes these conditions sexual; or (6) Women are presented as sexual objects for domination, conquest, violation, exploitation, possession, or use, or through postures or positions of servility or submission or display." Indianapolis Code §16-3(q). The statute provides that the "use of men, children, or transsexuals in the place of women in paragraphs (1) through (6) above shall also constitute pornography under this section." The ordinance as passed in April 1984 defined "sexually explicit" to mean actual or simulated intercourse or the uncovered exhibition of the genitals, buttocks or anus. An amendment in June 1984 deleted this provision, leaving the term undefined.

The Indianapolis ordinance does not refer to the prurient interest, to offensiveness, or to the standards of the community. It demands attention to particular depictions, not to the work judged as a whole. It is irrelevant under the ordinance whether the work has literary, artistic, political, or scientific value. The City and many *amici* point to these omissions as virtues. They maintain that pornography influences attitudes, and the statute is a way to alter the socialization of men and women rather than to vindicate community standards of offensiveness. And as one of the principal drafters of the ordinance has asserted, "if a woman is subjected, why should it matter that the work has other value?" Catharine A. MacKinnon, Pornography, Civil Rights, and Speech, 20 Harv. Civ. Rts.-Civ. Lib. L. Rev. 1, 21 (1985).

Civil rights groups and feminists have entered this case as *amici* on both sides. Those supporting the ordinance say that it will play an important role in reducing the tendency of men to view women as sexual objects, a tendency that leads to both unacceptable attitudes and discrimination in the workplace and violence away from it. Those opposing the ordinance point out that much radical feminist literature is explicit and depicts women in ways forbidden by the ordinance and that the ordinance would reopen old battles. It is unclear how Indianapolis would treat works from James Joyce's *Ulysses* to Homer's *Iliad;* both depict women as submissive objects for conquest and domination.

We do not try to balance the arguments for and against an ordinance such as this. The ordinance discriminates on the ground of the content of the speech. Speech treating women in the approved way—in sexual encounters "premised on equality" (MacKinnon, *supra*, at 22)—is lawful no matter how sexually explicit. Speech treating women in the disapproved way—as submissive in matters sexual or as enjoying humiliation—is unlawful no matter how significant the literary, artistic, or political qualities of the work taken as a whole. The state may not ordain preferred viewpoints in this way. The Constitution forbids the state to declare one perspective right and silence opponents.

The ordinance contains four prohibitions. People may not "traffic" in pornography, "coerce" others into performing in pornographic works, or "force" pornography on anyone. Anyone injured by someone who has seen or read pornography has a right of action against the maker or seller. . . .

[The district court held the ordinance unconstitutional, concluding that the ordinance regulates speech, rather than conduct, and that such regulation could be justified only by a compelling interest. The court determined that Indianapolis had not established the requisite interest in reducing discrimination. In addition, the court held that the ordinance was vague, overbroad and a prior restraint. 598 F.Supp. 1316 (S.D. Ind. 1984).]

The plaintiffs are a congeries of distributors and readers of books, magazines, and films. The American Booksellers Association comprises about 5,200 bookstores and chains. . . .

"If there is any fixed star in our constitutional constellation, it is that no official, high or petty, can prescribe what shall be orthodox in politics, nationalism, religion, or other matters of opinion or force citizens to confess by word or act their faith therein." West

Virginia State Board of Education v. Barnette, 319 U.S. 624, 642 (1943). Under the First Amendment the government must leave to the people the evaluation of ideas. Bald or subtle, an idea is as powerful as the audience allows it to be. A belief may be pernicious—the beliefs of Nazis led to the death of millions, those of the Klan to the repression of millions. A pernicious belief may prevail. Totalitarian governments today rule much of the planet, practicing suppression of billions and spreading dogma that may enslave others. One of the things that separates our society from theirs is our absolute right to propagate opinions that the government finds wrong or even hateful. . . .

Under the ordinance graphic sexually explicit speech is "pornography" or not depending on the perspective the author adopts. Speech that "subordinates" women and also, for example, presents women as enjoying pain, humiliation, or rape, or even simply presents women in "positions of servility or submission or display" is forbidden, no matter how great the literary or political value of the work taken as a whole. Speech that portrays women in positions of equality is lawful, no matter how graphic the sexual content. This is thought control. It establishes an "approved" view of women, of how they may react to sexual encounters, of how the sexes may relate to each other. Those who espouse the approved view may use sexual images; those who do not, may not.

Indianapolis justifies the ordinance on the ground that pornography affects thoughts. Men who see women depicted as subordinate are more likely to treat them so. Pornography is an aspect of dominance. It does not persuade people so much as change them. It works by socializing, by establishing the expected and the permissible. In this view pornography is not an idea; pornography is the injury.

There is much to this perspective. Beliefs are also facts. People often act in accordance with the images and patterns they find around them. . . . People taught from birth that black people are fit only for slavery rarely rebelled against that creed; beliefs coupled with the self-interest of the masters established a social structure that inflicted great harm while enduring for centuries. Words and images act at the level of the subconscious before they persuade at the level of the conscious. . . .

Therefore we accept the premises of this legislation. Depictions of subordination tend to perpetuate subordination. The subordinate status of women in turn leads to affront and lower pay at work, insult and injury at home, battery and rape on the streets.[1] In the language of the legislature, "[p]ornography is central in creating and maintaining sex as a basis of discrimination. Pornography is a systematic practice of exploitation and subordination based on sex which differentially harms women. The

---

[1]MacKinnon's article collects empirical work that supports this proposition. The social science studies are very difficult to interpret, however, and they conflict. Because much of the effect of speech comes through a process of socialization, it is difficult to measure incremental benefits and injuries caused by particular speech. Several psychologists have found, for example, that those who see violent, sexually explicit films tend to have more violent thoughts. But how often does this lead to actual violence? National commissions on obscenity here, in the United Kingdom, and in Canada have found that it is not possible to demonstrate a direct link between obscenity and rape or exhibitionism. . . . In saying that we accept the finding that pornography as the ordinance defines it leads to unhappy consequences, we mean only that there is evidence to this effect, that this evidence is consistent with much human experience, and that as judges we must accept the legislative resolution of such disputed empirical questions.

bigotry and contempt it produces, with the acts of aggression it fosters, harm women's opportunities for equality and rights [of all kinds]." Indianapolis Code §16-1(a)(2).

Yet this simply demonstrates the power of pornography as speech. All of these unhappy effects depend on mental intermediation. Pornography affects how people see the world, their fellows, and social relations. If pornography is what pornography does, so is other speech. . . .

Racial bigotry, anti-semitism, violence on television, reporters' biases—these and many more influence the culture and shape our socialization. None is directly answerable by more speech, unless that speech too finds its place in the popular culture. Yet all is protected as speech, however insidious. Any other answer leaves the government in control of all of the institutions of culture, the great censor and director of which thoughts are good for us.

Sexual responses often are unthinking responses, and the association of sexual arousal with the subordination of women therefore may have a substantial effect. But almost all cultural stimuli provoke unconscious responses. Religious ceremonies condition their participants. Teachers convey messages by selecting what not to cover; the implicit message about what is off limits or unthinkable may be more powerful than the messages for which they present rational argument. Television scripts contain unarticulated assumptions. People may be conditioned in subtle ways. If the fact that speech plays a role in a process of conditioning were enough to permit governmental regulation, that would be the end of freedom of speech.

It is possible to interpret the claim that the pornography is the harm in a different way. Indianapolis emphasizes the injury that models in pornographic films and pictures may suffer. The record contains materials depicting sexual torture, penetration of women by red-hot irons and the like. These concerns have nothing to do with written materials subject to the statute, and physical injury can occur with or without the "subordination" of women. [A] state may make injury in the course of producing a film unlawful independent of the viewpoint expressed in the film.

The more immediate point, however, is that the image of pain is not necessarily pain. In *Body Double*, a suspense film directed by Brian DePalma, a woman who has disrobed and presented a sexually explicit display is murdered by an intruder with a drill. The drill runs through the woman's body. The film is sexually explicit and a murder occurs—yet no one believes that the actress suffered pain or died. In *Barbarella* a character played by Jane Fonda is at times displayed in sexually explicit ways and at times shown "bleeding, bruised, [and] hurt in a context that makes these conditions sexual"—and again no one believes that Fonda was actually tortured to make the film. In *Carnal Knowledge* a woman grovels to please the sexual whims of a character played by Jack Nicholson; no one believes that there was a real sexual submission, and the Supreme Court held the film protected by the First Amendment. And this works both ways. The description of women's sexual domination of men in *Lysistrata* was not real dominance. Depictions may affect slavery, war, or sexual roles, but a book about slavery is not itself slavery, or a book about death by poison a murder.

Much of Indianapolis's argument rests on the belief that when speech is "unanswerable," and the metaphor that there is a "marketplace of ideas" does not apply, the First Amendment does not apply either. The metaphor is honored; Milton's *Areopagitica* and John Stuart Mill's *On Liberty* defend freedom of speech on the ground that the truth will prevail, and many of the most important cases under the First Amendment recite this position. The Framers undoubtedly believed it. As a general matter it is true. But the Constitution does not make the dominance of truth a necessary condition of freedom of speech. To say that it does would be to confuse an outcome of free speech with a necessary condition for the application of the amendment. . . .

The Supreme Court has rejected the position that speech must be "effectively answerable" to be protected by the Constitution. . . .

We come, finally, to the argument that pornography is "low value" speech, that it is enough like obscenity that Indianapolis may prohibit it. Some cases hold that speech far removed from politics and other subjects at the core of the Framers' concerns may be subjected to special regulation. . . .

At all events, "pornography" is not low value speech within the meaning of these cases. Indianapolis seeks to prohibit certain speech because it believes this speech influences social relations and politics on a grand scale, that it controls attitudes at home and in the legislature. This precludes a characterization of the speech as low value. True, pornography and obscenity have sex in common. But Indianapolis left out of its definition any reference to literary, artistic, political, or scientific value. The ordinance applies to graphic sexually explicit subordination in works great and small. The Court sometimes balances the value of speech against the costs of its restriction, but it does this by category of speech and not by the content of particular works. Indianapolis has created an approved point of view and so loses the support of these cases.

Any rationale we could imagine in support of this ordinance could not be limited to sex discrimination. Free speech has been on balance an ally of those seeking change. Governments that want stasis start by restricting speech. Culture is a powerful force of continuity; Indianapolis paints pornography as part of the culture of power. Change in any complex system ultimately depends on the ability of outsiders to challenge accepted views and the reigning institutions. Without a strong guarantee of freedom of speech, there is no effective right to challenge what is.

The definition of "pornography" is unconstitutional. No construction or excision of particular terms could save it. The offense of trafficking in pornography necessarily falls with the definition. We express no view on the district court's conclusions that the ordinance is vague and that it establishes a prior restraint. Neither is necessary to our judgment. We also express no view on the argument presented by several *amici* that the ordinance is itself a form of discrimination on account of sex.

Section 8 of the ordinance is a strong severability clause, and Indianapolis asks that we . . . save what we can. [W]e conclude that nothing short of rewriting could save anything.

The offense of coercion to engage in a pornographic performance, for example, has elements that might be constitutional. Without question a state may prohibit fraud, trickery, or the use of force to induce people to perform—in pornographic films or in any other films. Such a statute may be written without regard to the viewpoint depicted in the work. . . .

But the Indianapolis ordinance, unlike our hypothetical statute, is not neutral with respect to viewpoint. The ban on distribution of works containing coerced performances is limited to pornography; coercion is irrelevant if the work is not "pornography," and we have held the definition of "pornography" to be defective root and branch. A legislature might replace "pornography" in §16-3(g)(4) with "any film containing explicit sex" or some similar expression, but even the broadest severability clause does not permit a federal court to rewrite as opposed to excise. Rewriting is work for the legislature of Indianapolis.

The offense of forcing pornography on unwilling recipients is harder to assess. Many kinds of forcing (such as giving texts to students for translation) may themselves be protected speech. . . . Exposure to sex is not something the government may prevent. We therefore could not save the offense of "forcing" by redefining "pornography" as all sexually-offensive speech or some related category. The statute needs a definition of "forcing" that removes the government from the role of censor. . . .

The section creating remedies for injuries and assaults attributable to pornography also is salvageable in principle, although not by us. The First Amendment does not prohibit redress of all injuries caused by speech. Injury to reputation is redressed through the law of libel, which is constitutional subject to strict limitations. . . .

[T]he Indianapolis ordinance requires the complainant to show that the attack was "directly caused by specific pornography" (§16-3(g)(7)), and it is not beyond the realm of possibility that a state court could construe this limitation in a way that would make the statute constitutional. We are not authorized to prevent the state from trying.

Again, however, the assault statute is tied to "pornography," and we cannot find a sensible way to repair the defect without seizing power that belongs elsewhere. Indianapolis might choose to have no ordinance if it cannot be limited to viewpoint-specific harms, or it might choose to extend the scope to all speech, just as the law of libel applies to all speech. An attempt to repair this ordinance would be nothing but a blind guess.

No amount of struggle with particular words and phrases in this ordinance can leave anything in effect. . . . Affirmed.

BUTLER v. THE QUEEN

[1992] 1 S.C.R. 452

SOPINKA, J.

[The defendant, Butler, owned and operated a store selling and renting hard core pornographic videos and magazines and selling sexual paraphernalia. He was convicted of 8 counts of possession and sale of obscene materials (relating to eight different films) and acquitted on 242 counts. The Crown appealed the 242 acquittals; Butler appealed the convictions. The Court of Appeal for Manitoba dismissed Butler's appeal, and entered convictions on the remaining 242 counts. However, the Court of Appeal, disagreeing with the trial court which had ruled that the obscene articles were protected by the free expression guarantee, concluded that obscene materials were *not* protected by §2(b) of the Charter because they were materials which (1) did not convey or attempt to convey meaning and (2) consisted of undue exploitation of sex and degradation of sexuality, a form of activity which the Charter was not intended to protect.]

Criminal Code, R.S.C. 1985, c. C-46, §163 provides:

(1) Every one commits an offence who,

(a) makes, prints, publishes, distributes, circulates, or has in his possession for the purpose of publication, distribution, or circulation any obscene written matter, picture, model, phonograph record or other things whatever. . . .

(8) For the purpose of this Act, any publication a dominant characteristic of which is the undue exploitation of sex, or of sex and any one or more of the following subjects, namely, crime, horror, cruelty and violence, shall be deemed to be obscene.

The following constitutional questions are raised by this appeal: [Does §163 of the Criminal Code violate §2(b), the freedom of expression guarantee, of the Canadian Charter of Rights and Freedoms? If so, can Section 163 nonetheless be upheld under §1 of the Charter, the guarantee of equality, as a reasonable limit prescribed by law?]

. . . Before proceeding to consider the constitutional questions, it will be helpful to review the legislative history of the provision. . . . [Justice Sopinka first noted the absence of any early statutory definition. Although the judiciary later supplied a definition in R. v. Hicklin, (1868) L.R. 3 Q.B. 360, that definition was repudiated subsequently by Parliament. As a result, the Criminal Code became the exclusive definition of obscenity—

liament. As a result, the Criminal Code became the exclusive definition of obscenity—
"[i]n order for the work or material to qualify as 'obscene,' the exploitation of sex must
not only be its dominant characteristic, but such exploitation must be 'undue.'"
Sopinka then addressed the judicially developed tests of "undue exploitation."]

. . . The most important [test] is the "community standard of intolerance" test. . . .
It is the standards of the community as a whole which must be considered and not the
standards of a small segment of that community. . . . The standard to be applied is a
national one. [T]he community standards test is concerned not with what Canadians
would not tolerate being exposed to themselves, but what they would not tolerate *other*
Canadians being exposed to. . . .

[Another test is the "degradation or dehumanization" test.] There has been a growing recognition . . . that material which may be said to exploit sex in a "degrading or
dehumanizing" manner will necessarily fail the community standards test. . . . Among
other things, degrading or dehumanizing materials place women (and sometimes
men) in positions of subordination, servile submission or humiliation. They run
against the principles of equality and dignity of all human beings. In the appreciation
of whether material is degrading or dehumanizing, the appearance of consent is not
necessarily determinative. Consent cannot save materials that otherwise contain degrading or dehumanizing scenes. Sometimes the very appearance of consent makes
the depicted acts even more degrading or dehumanizing.

This type of material would, apparently, fail the community standards test not because it offends against morals but because it is perceived by public opinion to be harmful to society, particularly to women. While the accuracy of this perception is not susceptible of exact proof, there is a substantial body of opinion that holds that the portrayal
of persons being subjected to degrading or dehumanizing sexual treatment results in
harm, particularly to women and therefore to society as a whole. See R. v. Wagner, (1985)
43 C.R.(3d) 318, 336. See also Attorney General's Commission on Pornography (the
"Meese Commission"), Final Report (U.S., 1986), vol. 1, at pp. 938–1035; Metro Toronto
Task Force on Public Violence Against Women and Children, Final Report (1984), at p.
66; Report of the Joint Select Committee on Video Material (Australia, 1988), at pp.
185–230; Pornography: Report of the Ministerial Committee of Inquiry into Pornography (New Zealand, 1988), at pp. 38–45. It would be reasonable to conclude that there is
an appreciable risk of harm to society in the portrayal of such material. . . .

[A third test for determining whether the exploitation of sex is "undue," is the test
of "internal necessities," which holds that exploitation of sex is not undue if there is no
more emphasis on the theme than is required in the serious treatment of the theme
of a novel. That is, even material which by itself offends community standards will not
be considered "undue," if it is required for the serious treatment of a theme.] [Justice
Sopinka then discussed the interrelationship of these tests.]

Pornography can be usefully divided into three categories: (1) explicit sex with violence, (2) explicit sex without violence but which subjects people to treatment that is
degrading or dehumanizing, and (3) explicit sex without violence that is neither degrading nor dehumanizing. Violence in this context includes both actual physical violence and threats of physical violence. . . .

[W]ith respect to the three categories of pornography referred to above, the portrayal of sex coupled with violence will almost always constitute the undue exploitation of sex. Explicit sex which is degrading or dehumanizing may be undue if the risk of harm is substantial. Finally, explicit sex that is not violent and neither degrading nor dehumanizing is generally tolerated in our society and will not qualify as the undue exploitation of sex unless it employs children in its production. . . .

C. Does §163 violate §2(b) of the Charter?

. . . In my view, the majority of the Manitoba Court of Appeal erred in several respects. [First, the court] misinterpreted the distinction between purely physical activity and activity having expressive content. The subject-matter of the materials in this case is clearly "physical," but this does not mean that the materials do not convey or attempt to convey meaning such that they are without expressive content. . . . As Twaddle J.A. noted [Irwin Toy Ltd. v. Quebec, [1989] 1 S.C.R. 927]:

> The subject matter of the material under review . . . is sexual activity. Such activity is part of the human experience. . . . The depiction of such activity has the potential of titillating some and of informing others. How can images which have such effect be meaningless?

In my view, the content of a video movie, the content of a magazine and the imagery of a sexual gadget are all within the freedom of expression [at pp. 237–238].

Second, the majority of the Court of Appeal erred in failing to properly draw the distinction between the content of the materials and the form of expression. [The Court of Appeal had concluded that the "form" of expression was the undue exploitation of sex and the degradation of human sexuality.]

The form of activity in this case is the medium through which the meaning sought to be conveyed is expressed, namely, the film, magazine, written matter, or sexual gadget. There is nothing inherently violent in the vehicle of expression, and it accordingly does not fall outside the protected sphere of activity.

In light of our recent decision in R. v. Keegstra, [1990] 3 S.C.R. 697, the respondent, and most of the parties intervening in support of the respondent, do not take issue with the proposition that §163 of the Criminal Code violates §2(b) of the Charter. In *Keegstra,* we were unanimous in advocating a generous approach to the protection afforded by §2(b) of the Charter. Our Court confirmed the view. . .that activities cannot be excluded from the scope of the guaranteed freedom on the basis of the content or meaning being conveyed. McLauchlin J. wrote:

> As this Court has repeatedly affirmed, the content of a statement cannot deprive it of the protection accorded by §2(b), no matter how offensive it may be. The content of Mr. Keegstra's statements was offensive and demeaning in the extreme; nevertheless, on the principles affirmed by this Court, that alone would appear not to deprive them of the protection guaranteed by the Charter. [At p. 828.]
>
> . . .

In this case, both the purpose and effect of §163 is specifically to restrict the communication of certain types of materials based on their content. In my view, there is no doubt that §163 seeks to prohibit certain types of expressive activity and thereby infringes §2(b) of the Charter. . . . I would conclude that the first constitutional question should be answered in the affirmative.

D. Is §163 justified under §1 of the Charter?

[The court first discussed and dismissed a constitutional challenge that §163 was void for vagueness.]

The respondent argues that there are several pressing and substantial objectives which justify overriding the freedom to distribute obscene materials. Essentially, these objectives are the avoidance of harm resulting from antisocial attitudinal changes that exposure to obscene material causes and the public interest in maintaining a "decent society." On the other hand, the appellant argues that the objective of §163 is to have the state act as "moral custodian" in sexual matters and to impose subjective standards of morality.

The obscenity legislation and jurisprudence prior to the enactment of §163 were evidently concerned with prohibiting the "immoral influences" of obscene publications and safeguarding the morals of individuals into whose hands such works could fall. [T]his particular objective is no longer defensible in view of the Charter. To impose a certain standard of public and sexual morality, solely because it reflects the conventions of a given community, is inimical to the exercise and enjoyment of individual freedoms, which form the basis of our social contract. . . . The prevention of "dirt for dirt's sake" is not a legitimate objective which would justify the violation of one of the most fundamental freedoms enshrined in the Charter.

On the other hand, I cannot agree with the suggestion of the appellant that Parliament does not have the right to legislate on the basis of some fundamental conception of morality for the purposes of safeguarding the values which are integral to a free and democratic society. . . . In this regard, criminalizing the proliferation of materials which undermine another basic Charter right may indeed be a legitimate objective.

In my view, however, the overriding objective of §163 is not moral disapprobation but the avoidance of harm to society. In Towne Cinema [v. R., [1985] 1 S.C.R. 494], Dickson C.J. stated (at p. 507): "It is harm to society from undue exploitation that is aimed at by the section, not simply lapses in propriety or good taste."

The harm was described in the following way in the Report on Pornography by the Standing Committee on Justice and Legal Affairs (MacGuigan Report) (1978) (at p. 18:4.):

> The clear and unquestionable danger of this type of material is that it reinforces some unhealthy tendencies in Canadian society. The effect of this type of material is to reinforce male-female stereotypes to the detriment of both sexes. It attempts to make degradation, humiliation, victimization, and violence in human relationships appear normal and acceptable. A society which holds that egalitarianism, non-violence, consensualism, and mutuality are basic to any

human interaction, whether sexual or other, is clearly justified in controlling and prohibiting any medium of depiction, description or advocacy which violates these principles.

. . . This being the objective, is it pressing and substantial? Does the prevention of the harm associated with the dissemination of certain obscene materials constitute a sufficiently pressing and substantial concern to warrant a restriction on the freedom of expression? In this regard, it should be recalled that in *Keegstra, supra,* this court unanimously accepted that the prevention of the influence of hate propaganda on society at large was a legitimate objective. Dickson C.J. wrote with respect to the changes in attitudes which exposure to hate propaganda can bring about (at pp. 747–748):

> . . . the alteration of views held by the recipients of hate propaganda may occur subtly, and is not always attendant upon conscious acceptance of the communicated ideas. Even if the message of hate propaganda is outwardly rejected, there is evidence that its premise of racial or religious inferiority may persist in a recipient's mind as an idea that holds some truth, an incipient effect not to be entirely discounted. . .

> The threat to the self-dignity of target group members is thus matched by the possibility that prejudiced messages will gain some credence, with the attendant result of discrimination, and perhaps even violence, against minority groups in Canadian society.

This Court has thus recognized that the harm caused by the proliferation of materials which seriously offend the values fundamental to our society is a substantial concern which justifies restricting the otherwise full exercise of the freedom of expression. In my view, the harm sought to be avoided in the case of the dissemination of obscene materials is similar. In the words of Nemetz C.J.B.C. in R. v. Red Hot Video Ltd. (1985), 45 C.R. (3rd) 36 (B.C.C.A.), there is a growing concern that the exploitation of women and children, depicted in publications and films can, in certain circumstances, lead to "abject and servile victimization" (at pp. 43–44). As Anderson J.A. also noted in that same case, "if true equality between male and female persons is to be achieved, we cannot ignore the threat to equality resulting from exposure to audiences of certain types of violent and degrading material. Materials portraying women as a class as objects for sexual exploitation and abuse have a negative impact on 'the individual's sense of self-worth and acceptance.'". . .

Finally, it should be noted that the burgeoning pornography industry renders the concern even more pressing and substantial than when the impugned provisions were first enacted. . . . I must now determine whether the section is rationally connected and proportional to this objective [avoidance of harm to society]. . . .

The values which underlie the protection of freedom of expression relate to the search for truth, participation in the political process, and individual self-fulfilment. The Attorney-General for Ontario argues that of these, only "individual self-fulfilment," and only in its most base aspect, that of physical arousal, is engaged by pornography. On the other hand, the civil liberties groups argue that pornography forces us to question conventional notions of sexuality and thereby launches us into an inherently political discourse. In their factum, the B.C. Civil Liberties Association adopts a passage from R. West, "The Feminist-Conservative Anti-Pornography Alliance and the 1986 Attorney General's Commission on Pornography Report," 4 Am. Bar Found. Res. J. 68 (1987), at p. 696:

> Good pornography has value because it validates women's will to pleasure. It celebrates female nature. It validates a range of female sexuality that is wider and truer than that legitimated by the non-pornographic culture. Pornography (when it is good) celebrates both female pleasure and male rationality.

A proper application of the test should not suppress what West refers to as "good pornography." The objective of the impugned provision is not to inhibit the celebration of human sexuality. However, it cannot be ignored that the realities of the pornography industry are far from the picture which the B.C. Civil Liberties Association would have us paint. Shannon J., in R. v. Wagner, *supra*, described the materials more accurately when he observed (at p. 331):

> Women, particularly, are deprived of unique human character or identity and are depicted as sexual playthings, hysterically and instantly responsive to male sexual demands. They worship male genitals and their own value depends upon the quality of their genitals and breasts.

In my view, the kind of expression which is sought to be advanced does not stand on equal footing with other kinds of expression which directly engage the "core" of the freedom of expression values.

This conclusion is further buttressed by the fact that the targeted material is expression which is motivated, in the overwhelming majority of cases, by economic profit. . . .

The message of obscenity which degrades and dehumanizes is analogous to that of hate propaganda. As the Attorney-General of Ontario has argued in its factum, obscenity wields the power to wreak social damage in that a significant portion of the population is humiliated by its gross misrepresentations.

Accordingly, the rational link between §163 and the objective of Parliament relates to the actual causal relationship between obscenity and the risk of harm to society at large. On this point, it is clear that the literature of the social sciences remains subject to controversy. . . . The recent conclusions of the Fraser Report, *supra*, could not postulate any causal relationship between pornography and the commission of violent crimes, the sexual abuse of children, or the disintegration of communities and society. This is in contrast to the findings of the MacGuigan Report, *supra*.

While a direct link between obscenity and harm to society may be difficult, if not impossible, to establish, it is reasonable to presume that exposure to images bears a causal relationship to changes in attitudes and beliefs. The Meese Commission Report, *supra*, concluded in respect of sexually violent material (vol. 1, at p. 326):

. . . the available evidence strongly supports the hypothesis that substantial exposure to sexually violent materials as described here bears a causal relationship to antisocial acts of sexual violence and, for some subgroups, possibly to unlawful acts of sexual violence.

Although we rely for this conclusion on significant scientific empirical evidence, we feel it worthwhile to note the underlying logic of the conclusion. The evidence says simply that the images that people are exposed to bear a causal relationship to their behaviour. This is hardly surprising. What would be surprising would be to find otherwise, and we have not so found. We have not, of course, found that the images people are exposed to are a greater cause of sexual violence than all or even many other possible causes the investigation of which has been beyond our mandate. Nevertheless, it would be strange indeed if graphic representations of a form of behaviour, especially in a form that almost exclusively portrays such behaviour as desirable, did not have at least some effect on patterns of behaviour.

In the face of inconclusive social science evidence, the approach adopted by our court in [Irwin Toy, Ltd. v. Quebec, [1989] 1 S.C.R. 927] is instructive. In that case, the basis for the legislation was that television advertising directed at young children is per se manipulative. The court made it clear that in choosing its mode of intervention, it is sufficient that Parliament had a *reasonable basis.* . . .

Similarly, in *Keegstra,* supra, the absence of proof of a causative link between hate propaganda and hatred of an identifiable group was discounted as a determinative factor in assessing the constitutionality of the hate literature provisions of the Criminal Code. . . .

The American approach on the necessity of a causal link between obscenity and harm to society was set out by Burger C.J. in Paris Adult Theatre I v. Slaton, 413 U.S. 49, 60–61 (1972):

> Although there is no conclusive proof of a connection between antisocial behaviour and obscene material, the legislature . . . could quite reasonably determine that such a connection does or might exist.
>
> . . .

Accordingly, I am of the view that there is a sufficiently rational link between the criminal sanction, which demonstrates our community's disapproval of the dissemination of materials which potentially victimize women and which restricts the negative influence which such materials have on changes in attitudes and behaviour, and the objective. . . . In determining whether less intrusive legislation may be imagined, this court [previously has] stressed . . . that it is not necessary that the legislative scheme be the "perfect" scheme, but that it be appropriately tailored *in the context of the infringed right.* . . .

. . . Finally, I wish to address the arguments of the interveners, Canadian Civil Liberties Association and Manitoba Association for Rights and Liberties, that the objectives of this kind of legislation may be met by alternative, less intrusive measures. First, it is submitted that reasonable time, manner and place restrictions would be preferable to outright prohibition. I am of the view that this argument should be rejected. Once it has been established that the objective is the avoidance of harm caused by the degradation which many women feel as "victims" of the message of obscenity, and of the negative impact exposure to such material has on perceptions and attitudes towards women, it is untenable to argue that these harms could be avoided by placing restrictions on access to such material. Making the materials more difficult to obtain by increasing their cost and reducing their availability does not achieve the same objective. . . . The harm sought to be avoided would remain the same in either case.

It is also submitted that there are more effective techniques to promote the objectives of Parliament. For example, if pornography is seen as encouraging violence against women, there are certain activities which discourage it—counselling rape victims to charge their assailants, provision of shelter and assistance for battered women, campaigns for laws against discrimination on the grounds of sex, education to increase the sensitivity of law enforcement agencies and other governmental authorities. . . .

However, given the gravity of the harm, and the threat to the values at stake, I do not believe that the measure chosen by Parliament is equalled by the alternatives which have been suggested. [T]his is in no way intended to deny the value of other educational and counselling measures to deal with the roots and effects of negative attitudes. Rather, it is only to stress the arbitrariness and unacceptability of the claim that such measures represent the sole legitimate means of addressing the phenomenon. . . .

The final question to be answered . . . is whether the effects of the law so severely trench on a protected right that the legislative objective is outweighed by the infringement. The infringement on freedom of expression is confined to a measure designed to prohibit the distribution of sexually explicit materials accompanied by violence, and those without violence that are degrading or dehumanizing. As I have already concluded, this kind of expression lies far from the core of the guarantee of freedom of expression. It appeals only to the most base aspect of individual fulfilment, and it is primarily economically motivated.

The objective of the legislation, on the other hand, is of fundamental importance in a free and democratic society. It is aimed at avoiding harm, which Parliament has reasonably concluded will be caused directly or indirectly, to individuals, groups such as women and children, and consequently to society as a whole, by the distribution of these materials. It thus seeks to enhance respect for all members of society, and nonviolence and equality in their relations with each other.

I therefore conclude that the restriction on freedom of expression does not outweigh the importance of the legislative objective. . . .

❖ Brief Amici Curiae of Feminist Anti-Censorship Taskforce et al., in American Booksellers Association, Inc. v. Hudnut

NAN D. HUNTER AND SYLVIA A. LAW

THE DOCUMENT that follows represents both a legal brief and a political statement. It was written for two purposes: to mobilize, in a highly visible way, a broad spectrum of feminist opposition to the enactment of laws expanding state suppression of sexually explicit material; and to place before the Court of Appeals for the Seventh Circuit a cogent legal argument for the constitutional invalidity of an Indianapolis municipal ordinance that would have permitted private civil suits to ban such material, purportedly to protect women.[1] . . .

The brief was written on behalf of the Feminist Anti-Censorship Taskforce (FACT). . . . The analysis of sexuality underlying the brief flows directly from a long tradition of nineteenth-century women's rights activists who sought sexual self-determination as an essential aspect of full liberation. From the beginning, others within the early feminist movement opposed this understanding of feminism because they viewed sexuality as a realm in which women often suffered. To protect women, they sought to restrict male sexual freedom by imposing on men that standard of sexual purity already applied to women.[2]

The modern feminist movement has continued this divergence of viewpoint. Simone de Beauvoir, for example, saw the erotic as an aspect of human liberty and insisted that sexual self-determination constitutes a fundamental part of women's liberation.[3] Since 1966, women's demands have included calls for greater sexual freedom for women and an end to double standards. At the same time, the movement has fought for and won a number of reforms to curb rape and other violence directed pointedly at women. A part of the feminist antiviolence movement evolved first into a campaign aimed at depictions of violence against women in a variety of media and then into a campaign aimed at all pornographic imagery, whether violent or not.

Meanwhile, as feminist discourse on issues of sexuality became more elaborate, conservative forces also mobilized around issues of sexual imagery. An alliance of traditional moralists, the New Right, and some feminists promoted and defended the Indianapolis ordinance. . . . For conservatives, the current interest in suppression of

21 U. Mich. J.L. Ref. 69 (1987–1988).

118

pornography forms part of a larger agenda to reverse recent feminist gains through a moral crusade against abortion, lesbian and gay rights, contraceptive education and services, and women's fragile economic achievements. Conservatives and religious fundamentalists oppose pornography because it appears to depict and approve of sex outside marriage and procreation. . . .

In 1985, conservative efforts to focus attention on suppression of sexual imagery culminated in Attorney General William French Smith's establishment of a Commission on Pornography charged to find "more effective ways in which the spread of pornography could be contained."[4] Because most Americans do not share the moral view that confines sex to a solely procreative role, the Commission's mission was to modernize the assault on sexually explicit images by demonstrating that pornography causes violence. Despite the number of members chosen with a history of vehement opposition to sexually explicit material and tight control of the witness list, the Commission was unable to "prove" that pornography causes violence.

Social scientists, whose work the antipornography movement had previously utilized, refused in their testimony to draw the simple connections between pornography and violence that the Commission sought. Like FACT, these researchers urged the use of caution in the extension of artificial laboratory findings to naturalistic settings. Further, they testified that aggressive imagery and the mainstream media present more worrisome concerns than sexual imagery and X-rated channels. . . .

Perhaps the most significant and most telling aspect of the Commission's work was its inability to agree on a definition of pornography. . . .

[Also, the] Commission recommended new federal and state legislation and increased prosecution to suppress sexually explicit materials to the maximum extent constitutionally possible. Unfortunately, it failed to embrace the recommendation of the 1970 Commission on Obscenity and Pornography to commence a serious sex education effort [of] young people. [Nor did it] call for legislation to remove spousal immunity in sexual assault cases or for funding to improve law enforcement against domestic violence. . . .

The feminists of FACT have helped to transform the contemporary dialogue about pornography. . . . FACT affirms that sexuality is, for women, a source of pleasure and power, as well as a realm of danger and oppression. As a consequence, discussion of pornography and sexuality is more intricately contextualized and appropriately complex. . . .

Despite the contradictory strands in the feminist approach, the empirical and intellectual exploration of sexuality remains a central enterprise for the contemporary feminist movement.[5] Sexual ideas, images, and practices have been dominated by and oriented toward men. . . . Furthermore, feminism's core insight emphasizes that gender is socially defined. Social and sexual role acculturation largely determine gender differences; accordingly, these differences are not natural or immutable. In Simone de Beauvoir's classic words, "One is not born, but rather becomes, a woman."[6] Social ideas and material arrangements give deep meaning to masculinity and femininity. The social significance of gender is fabricated to favor men systematically through economic, political, and legal structures that rest upon and reinforce gender. Sexual desire, both powerful and pliable, forms a part of that gender system. Discovering, describing, and analyzing the complex interaction of gender and sexuality, of representation and reality, thus remains a key project of feminist theory and lives.

Introduction

The instant case involves the constitutionality of an anti-pornography ordinance enacted by the City Council of Indianapolis. . . .

Amici believe that the ordinance violates both the First Amendment guarantee of freedom of speech and the Fourteenth Amendment guarantee of equal treatment under the law. Under its trafficking provision, the ordinance would allow injunctions to issue against the distribution, sale, exhibition or production of any sexually explicit materials which fall within its definition of pornography. No showing of harm to the plaintiff (individual or class) is required as proof prior to the issuance of such an injunction. Because the trafficking provision and the definition most flagrantly violate constitutional principles, this brief concentrates its focus on those two aspects of the ordinance.

I. The Ordinance Suppresses Constitutionally Protected Speech in a Manner Particularly Detrimental to Women.

Although Appellants argue that the ordinance is designed to restrict images which legitimate violence and coercion against women, the definition of pornography in the ordinance is not limited to images of violence or of coercion, or to images produced by women who were coerced. Nor is it limited to materials which advocate or depict the torture or rape of women as a form of sexual pleasure. It extends to any sexually explicit material which an agency or court finds to be "subordinating" to a claimant acting on behalf of women and which fits within one of the descriptive categories which complete the definition of pornography.

For purposes of the trafficking cause of action, the ordinance defines pornography as the "graphic sexually explicit subordination of women, whether in pictures or in words, that also includes one or more" of the depictions described in six categories. The violent and brutal images which Appellants use as illustrative examples[7] cannot obscure the fact that the ordinance authorizes suppression of material that is sexually explicit, but in no way violent. The language of the definition mixes phrases that have clear meanings and thus ascertainable applications (e.g., "cut up or mutilated") with others which are sufficiently elastic to encompass almost any sexually explicit image that someone might find offensive (e.g., "scenarios of degradation" or "abasement"). The material that could be suppressed under the latter category is virtually limitless. . . .

The constitutionality of the ordinance depends on the assumption that state agencies and courts can develop clear legal definitions of terms like "sexually explicit subordination," "sexual object," and "scenarios of degradation" and "abasement." In truth, these terms are highly contextual and of varying meanings. Worse, many of their most commonly accepted meanings would, if applied in the context of this ordinance, reinforce rather than erode archaic and untrue stereotypes about women's sexuality.

A. HISTORICALLY THE LAW HAS INCORPORATED A SEXUAL DOUBLE STANDARD DENYING WOMEN'S INTEREST IN SEXUAL EXPRESSION.

Traditionally, laws regulating sexual activity were premised upon and reinforced a gender-based double standard which assumed:

> that women are delicate, that voluntary sexual intercourse may harm them in certain circumstances and that they may be seriously injured by words as well as deeds. The statutes also suggest that, despite the generally delicate nature of most women, there exists a class of women who are not delicate or who are not worthy of protection. [By contrast, the law's treatment of male sexuality reflected] the underlying assumption that only males have aggressive sexual desires [and] hence they must be restrained. . . . The detail and comprehensiveness of [such] laws suggest that men are considered almost crazed by sex.
>
> K. Davidson, R. Ginsburg & H. Kay, Sex-Based Discrimination 892 (1974).

The Indianapolis ordinance is squarely within the tradition of the sexual double standard. It allows little room for women to openly express certain sexual desires and resurrects the notion that sexually explicit materials are subordinating and degrading to women. Because the "trafficking" cause of action allows one woman to obtain a court order suppressing images which fall within the ordinance's definition of pornography, it implies that individual women are incapable of choosing for themselves what they consider to be enjoyable, sexually arousing material without being degraded or humiliated.

The legal system has used many vehicles to enforce the sexual double standard which protected "good" women. . . .

The common law also reinforced the image of "good" women as asexual and vulnerable by providing the husband, but not the wife, remedies for "interference" with his right to sole possession of his wife's body and services. The early writ of "ravishment" listed the wife with the husband's chattels. . . .

While denying the possibility that "good" women could be sexual, the common law dealt harshly with the "bad" women who were. Prostitution laws often penalized only the woman, and not the man, and even facially neutral laws were and are enforced primarily against women. . . .

The suppression of sexually explicit material most devastating to women was the restriction on dissemination of birth control information, common until 1971. . . . [Eisenstadt v. Baird, 405 U.S. 438 (1972).] For the previous century, the federal Comstock law, passed in 1873, had prohibited mailing, transporting or importing "obscene, lewd or lascivious" items, specifically including all devices and information pertaining to "preventing conception and producing abortion."[8] Women were jailed for distributing educational materials regarding birth control to other women because the materials were deemed sexually explicit. . . .

The Mann Act also was premised on the notion that women require special protection from sexual activity. 35 Stat. 825 (1910), 18 U.S.C. §§2421–2422. . . . As the legislative history reveals, the Act reflects the assumption that women have no will of their own and must be protected against themselves. . . .

Society's attempts to "protect" women's chastity through criminal and civil laws have resulted in restrictions on women's freedom to engage in sexual activity, to discuss it publicly, and to protect themselves from the risk of pregnancy. These disabling restrictions reinforced the gender roles which have oppressed women for centuries. The Indianapolis ordinance resonates with the traditional concept that sex itself degrades women, and its enforcement would reinvigorate those discriminatory moral standards which have limited women's equality in the past.

B. The Ordinance Is Unconstitutionally Vague Because Context Inescapably Determines the Effect of Sexual Texts and Images.

The ordinance authorizes court orders removing from public or private availability "graphic sexually explicit" words and images which "subordinate" women. A judge presented with a civil complaint filed pursuant to this law would be required to determine whether the material in question "subordinated" women. . . . In the sexual realm, perhaps more so than in any other, messages and their impact on the viewer or reader are often multiple, contradictory, layered and highly contextual.

The film *Swept Away* illustrates that serious problems of context and interpretation confound even the categories which on first reading might seem reasonably easy to apply. Made in 1975 by Italian director Lina Wertmuller, *Swept Away* tells a powerful story of dominance and submission. A rich attractive woman and a younger working class man are first shown as class antagonists during a yachting trip on which the man is a deckhand and the woman a viciously rude boss, and then as sexual antagonists when they are stranded on a Mediterranean island and the man exacts his revenge. During the second part of the film, the man rapes the woman and repeatedly assaults her. She initially resists, then falls in love with him, and he with her.

Scenes in *Swept Away* clearly present the woman character as "experienc[ing] sexual pleasure" during rape. In addition, she is humiliated, graphically and sexually, and appears to grow to enjoy it. . . . It is virtually certain that the film could be suppressed under the ordinance. . . .

Swept Away is an example of graphic, sexually explicit images and characterizations used to treat themes of power imbalance, to push at the edges of what is thought to be acceptable or desirable, and to shock. Critical and popular opinions of the film varied, ranging from admiration to repulsion. Whatever one's interpretation of the film, however, its profoundly important themes entitle it to a place in the realm of public discourse.

Context often determines meaning. Whether a specific image could be found to "subordinate" or "degrade" women may depend entirely on such factors as the purpose of the presentation; the size and nature of the audience, the surrounding messages; the expectation and attitude of the viewer; and where the presentation takes place, among others. Yet the trafficking provision allows blanket suppression of images based on highly subjective criteria which masquerade as simple, delineating definitions.

C. The Ordinance Is Unconstitutionally Vague Because Its Central Terms Have No Fixed Meaning, and the Most Common Meanings of These Terms Are Sexist and Damaging to Women.

The ordinance's definition of pornography, essential to each cause of action, is fatally flawed. It relies on words often defined in ways that reinforce a constricted and constricting view of women's sexuality. Thus *amici* fear that experimentations in feminist art which deal openly and explicitly with sexual themes will be easily targeted for suppression under this ordinance.

The central term "sexually explicit subordination" is not defined.[9] Appellants argue that "subordination" means that which "places women in positions of inferiority, loss of power, degradation and submission, among other things." . . . The core question, however, is left begging: what kinds of sexually explicit acts place a woman in an inferior status? Appellants argued in their brief to the District Court that "[t]he mere existence of pornography in society degrades and demeans all women." . . . To some observers, any graphic image of sexual acts is "degrading" to women and hence would subordinate them. To some, the required element of subordination or "position of . . . submission" might be satisfied by the image of a woman lying on her back inviting intercourse, while others might view the same image as affirming women's sexual pleasure and initiative. Some might draw the line at acts outside the bounds of marriage or with multiple partners. Others might see a simple image of the most traditional heterosexual act as subordinating in presenting the man in a physical position of superiority and the woman in a position of inferiority.

In any of these contexts, it is not clear whether the ordinance is to be interpreted with a subjective or an objective standard. If a subjective interpretation of "subordination" is contemplated, the ordinance vests in individual women a power to impose their views of politically or morally correct sexuality upon other women by calling for repression of images consistent with those views. The evaluative terms—subordination, degradation, abasement—are initially within the definitional control of the plaintiff, whose interpretation, if colorable, must be accepted by the court. An objective standard would require a court to determine whether plaintiff's reaction to the material comports with some generalized notion of which images do or do not degrade women. It would require the judiciary to impose its views of correct sexuality on a diverse community. The inevitable result would be to disapprove those images that are least conventional and privilege those that are closest to majoritarian beliefs about proper sexuality. . . .

The danger of discrimination is illustrated by the probability that some women would consider any explicit lesbian scene as subordinating, or as causing "[their] dignity [to] suffer," Appellants' brief at 36. Appellants plainly intend to include same-sex depictions, since their carefully selected trial court exhibits include such materials. Lesbians and gay men encounter massive discrimination based on prejudice related to their sexuality. The trafficking provision of the ordinance virtually invites new manifestations of this prejudice by means of civil litigation against the erotica of sexual minorities.

The six subsections of the definition applicable to a trafficking complaint provide no clarification. The term "sexual object," for example, appears frequently in the definition. . . . Yet, although "sex object" may be a phrase which has begun to enjoy widened popular usage, its precise meaning is far from clear. . . .

Appellants argue that the meaning of "subordination" and "degradation" can be determined in relation to "common usage and understanding." Appellants' brief at 33. But as we have seen, the common understanding of sexuality is one that incorporates a sexual double standard. Historically, virtually all sexually explicit literature and imagery has been thought to be degrading or abasing or humiliating, especially to women.

The interpretation of such morally charged terms has varied notoriously over time and place. . . . Words like "degradation," "abasement," and "humiliation" have been used in the past synonymously with subjective, moralistic terms. There is no reason to believe that the language in this ordinance will be magically resistant to that kind of interpretation.

The First Amendment prohibits any law regulating expression which would of necessity result in such unpredictable and arbitrary interpretations. This ordinance transgresses all three of the measures of impermissible vagueness. A person of ordinary intelligence would be at a loss to predict how any of a huge range of sexually explicit materials would be interpreted by a court. . . . Protected expression would be chilled because the makers, distributors, and exhibitors of sexually explicit works would be induced to practice self-censorship rather than risk potentially endless lawsuits under this ordinance. . . . Lastly, the absence of reasonably clear guidelines for triers of fact would open the door to arbitrary and discriminatory enforcement of the ordinance. . . .

D. SEXUALLY EXPLICIT SPEECH DOES NOT CAUSE OR INCITE VIOLENCE IN A MANNER SUFFICIENTLY DIRECT TO JUSTIFY ITS SUPPRESSION UNDER THE FIRST AMENDMENT.

To uphold this ordinance and the potential suppression of all speech which could be found to fall within its definition of pornography, this court must invent a new exception to the First Amendment. To justify that, Appellants must show that the speech to be suppressed will lead to immediate and concrete harm. . . . Only a small number of social science studies which purport to show a connection between violent pornography and negative attitudes and behavior toward women have been offered to support this position. For many reasons, their effort must fail.

Substantively, the studies relied upon do not justify the sweeping suppression authorized by the ordinance. Appellants cite the social science data in highly selective and grossly distorting ways. They fail to acknowledge that most of it is limited to studies of a narrow class of violent imagery. The ordinance, by contrast, both leaves untouched most of the images which may be said to cause negative effects and would allow the suppression of many images which have not been shown to have any harmful effect. Appellants also fail to mention that the "debriefing" phase of the cited experiments suggests that negative changes in attitudes may be corrected through further speech. They seek to create the false impression that new social science data have completely refuted the finding in 1971 by the Presidential Commission on Obscenity and Pornography that pornography was not harmful. . . .

Lastly, whatever Appellants' claims, numerous methodological problems make these studies too unreliable as predictors of real world behavior to sustain the withdrawal of constitutional protection from what is now permitted speech. . . .

Violent and misogynist images are pervasive in our culture. Nothing in the research cited by Appellants proves their hypothesis that these messages are believed in a qualitatively different way when they are communicated through the medium of sexually explicit material. . . .

In life, more than in a laboratory, a multitude of interacting factors shape behavior, including early childhood experiences, family dynamics, religious training, formal education, and one's perceived relation to governmental structures and the legal system, as well as the entire range of media stimuli.[10] It is difficult even in the laboratory to identify a single "cause" for behavior. Every study finding a negative effect under laboratory conditions from viewing an image cannot be grounds for rewriting the First Amendment.

Appellants and supporting *amici* also claim a causal connection between the availability of pornography and rape. Such a claim is implausible on its face. Acts of rape and coercion long preceded the mass distribution of pornography, and in many cultures pornography is unavailable, yet the incidence of rape, and of discrimination against women generally, is high. The converse is also true; that is, there are places where pornography is widely available, and the incidence of rape is low compared to the United States. . . .

II. The Ordinance Unconstitutionally Discriminates on the Basis of Sex and Reinforces Sexist Stereotypes.

The challenged ordinance posits a great chasm—a categorical difference—between the make-up and needs of men and women. It goes far beyond acknowledgment of the differences in life experiences which are inevitably produced by social structures of gender inequality. The ordinance presumes women as a class (and only women) are subordinated by virtually any sexually explicit image. It presumes women as a class (and only women) are incapable of making a binding agreement to participate in the creation of sexually explicit material. And it presumes men as a class (and only men) are conditioned by sexually explicit depictions to commit acts of aggression and to believe misogynist myths.

Such assumptions reinforce and perpetuate central sexist stereotypes; they weaken, rather than enhance, women's struggles to free themselves of archaic notions of gender roles. In so doing, this ordinance itself violates the equal protection clause of the

Fourteenth Amendment. In treating women as a special class, it repeats the error of earlier protectionist legislation which gave women no significant benefits and denied their equality.

A. THE DISTRICT COURT ERRED IN ACCEPTING APPELLANTS' ASSERTION THAT PORNOGRAPHY IS A DISCRIMINATORY PRACTICE BASED ON SEX.

The ordinance is predicated on a finding that:

> Pornography is a discriminatory practice based on sex which denies women equal opportunities in society. Pornography is central in creating and maintaining sex as a basis for discrimination. . . . [It harms] women's opportunities for equality of rights in employment, education, access to and use of public accommodations, and acquisition of real property; promote[s] rape, battery, child abuse, kidnapping and prostitution and inhibit[s] just enforcement of laws against such acts. . . .

Indianapolis, Ind., Code §16–1(a)(2).

The District Court accepted that finding, but held that First Amendment values outweighed the asserted interest in protecting women. . . . *Amici* dispute the City and County's "finding" that "pornography is central in creating and maintaining sex as a basis for discrimination." . . .

It is true that sex discrimination takes multiple forms, which are reflected in the media. But the finding that "pornography is central in creating and maintaining sex as a basis for discrimination" does not represent our best understanding of the complex, deep-seated and structural causes of gender inequality. In the past decade, many people have grappled with the question of causation. Feminist law professors and scholars have published and revised collections of cases and materials. K. Davidson, R. Ginsberg & H. Kay, *supra* p. 3 (1974 & 2d ed. 1981); B. Babcock, A. Freedman, E. Norton & S. Ross, Sex Discrimination and the Law: Causes and Remedies (1974 & Supp. 1978). The factors they find most significant include: the sex segregated wage labor market; systematic devaluation of work traditionally done by women; sexist concepts of marriage and family; inadequate income maintenance programs for women unable to find wage work; lack of day care services and the premise that child care is an exclusively female responsibility; barriers to reproductive freedom; and discrimination and segregation in education and athletics. Numerous feminist scholars have written major works tracing the cultural, economic, and psychosocial roots of women's oppression.[11] . . .

Amici also dispute the "finding" that pornography, as defined by the ordinance, is "a discriminatory practice . . . which denies women equal opportunities." Images and fictional text are not the same thing as subordinating conduct. The ordinance does not target discriminatory *actions* denying access to jobs, education, public accommodations, or real property. It prohibits images. Although ideas have impact, images of discrimination are not the discrimination.

Further, the ordinance is cast in a form very different from the traditional antidiscrimination principles embodied in the Constitution and federal civil rights laws. Antidiscrimination laws demand equality of treatment for men and women, blacks and whites. The ordinance, by contrast, purports to protect women. It assumes that women are subordinated by sexual images and that men act uncontrollably if exposed to them. Sexist stereotypes are thus built into its very premises, and, as we demonstrate *infra,* its effect will be to reinforce those stereotypes.

Hence, the District Court misperceived this case as one requiring the assignment of rank in a constitutional hierarchy. It is not necessary to rule that either gender equality or free speech is more important. The ordinance is fatally flawed not only because it authorizes suppression of speech protected by the First Amendment but also because it violates the constitutional guarantee of sex-based equality. . . .

C. The Ordinance Is Unconstitutional Because It Reinforces Sexist Stereotypes and Classifies on the Basis of Sex.

In recent years, the Supreme Court has firmly and repeatedly rejected gender-based classifications, such as that embodied in the ordinance. . . .

The ordinance damages individuals who do not fit the stereotypes it embodies. It delegitimates and makes socially invisible women who find sexually explicit images of women "in positions of display" or "penetrated by objects" to be erotic, liberating, or educational. These women are told that their perceptions are a product of "false consciousness" and that such images are so inherently degrading that they may be suppressed by the state. At the same time, it stamps the imprimatur of state approval on the belief that men are attack dogs triggered to violence by the sight of a sexually explicit image of a woman. It delegitimates and makes socially invisible those men who consider themselves gentle, respectful of women, or inhibited about expressing their sexuality.

Even worse, the stereotypes of the ordinance perpetuate traditional social views of sex-based difference. By defining sexually explicit images of woman as subordinating and degrading to them, the ordinance reinforces the stereotypical view that "good" women do not seek and enjoy sex. As applied, it would deny women access to sexually explicit material at a time in our history when women have just begun to acquire the social and economic power to develop our own images of sexuality. . . .

Finally, the ordinance perpetuates a stereotype of women as helpless victims, incapable of consent, and in need of protection. . . . We have learned through hard experience that gender-based classifications protecting women from their own presumed innate vulnerability reflect "an attitude of 'romantic paternalism' which, in practical effect, puts women not on a pedestal but in a cage." Frontiero v. Richardson, 411 U.S. 677, 684 (1973). . . .

Until quite recently, the law commonly provided women special protections against exploitation. [In the form of protective labor legislation.] The protectionist premise of these cases is now discredited. . . .

[T]he laws that "protected' only women from exploitation in wage labor hurt them. B. Babcock, A. Freedman, E. Norton & S. Ross, *supra* p. 25, at 48, 191–217. Many employers responded by barring women from the best paying jobs with the greatest opportunity for advancement. Further, the protective labor laws reinforced general beliefs about women's vulnerability and incompetence. Similarly here, the protection of the ordinance reinforces the idea that women are incompetent, particularly in relation to sex. . . .

Some of the proponents of the ordinance believe that it will empower women, while others support it for more traditional, patriarchal reasons. . . . But many gender-based classifications are premised on a good faith intent to help or protect women. Good intent does not justify an otherwise invidious gender-based law. . . .

D. THE SEX-BASED CLASSIFICATION AND STEREOTYPES CREATED BY THE ORDINANCE ARE NOT CAREFULLY TAILORED TO SERVE IMPORTANT STATE PURPOSES.

Appellants claim that the ordinance serves the "governmental interest in promoting sex equality." Appellants' brief at 23. Certainly preventing the violent subordination of women is the sort of compelling public purpose that might justify sex-based classification. But, as is often true of classifications justified on grounds that they protect women, the benefits actually provided are minimal. The ordinance thus also fails the requirement for a "substantial relationship" between its classification and the achievement of its asserted goal. . . .

Supporters of the ordinance describe acts of violence against women and claim that the ordinance would provide a remedy for those injuries. But the only new remedy it provides is suppression of sexually explicit materials, a wholly inadequate and misdirected response to real violence. . . . The remedy this ordinance provides for violence and sexual coercion is illusory.

Individuals who commit acts of violence must be held legally and morally accountable. The law should not displace responsibility onto imagery. *Amicus* Women Against Pornography describe as victims of pornography married women coerced to perform sexual acts depicted in pornographic works, working women harassed on the job with pornographic images, and children who have pornography forced on them during acts of child abuse. Appellants' brief at 13. Each of these examples describes victims of violence and coercion, not of images. The acts are wrong, whether or not the perpetrator refers to an image. . . . The law should punish the abuser, not the image. . . .

To resist forced sex and violence, women need the material resources to enable them to reject jobs or marriages in which they are abused or assaulted and the internal and collective strength to fight the conditions of abuse. The ordinance does nothing to enhance the concrete economic and social power of women. . . .

Suppression of sexually explicit material will not eliminate the pervasive sexist images of the mainstream culture or the discriminatory economic and social treatment that maintains women's second class status. Such suppression will not empower women to enter into sexual relationships on a voluntary, consensual basis. Empowering women requires something more than suppression of texts and images. . . .

Conclusion

Sexually explicit speech is not *per se* sexist or harmful to women. Like any mode of expression, it can be used to attack women's struggle for equal rights, but it is also a category of speech from which women have been excluded. The suppression authorized by the Indianapolis ordinance of a potentially enormous range of sexual imagery and texts reinforces the notion that women are too fragile, and men too uncontrollable, absent the aid of the censor, to be trusted to reject or enjoy sexually explicit speech for themselves. By identifying "subordination of women" as the concept that distinguishes sexually explicit material which is tolerable from that to be condemned, the ordinance incorporates a vague and asymmetric standard for censorship that can as readily be used to curtail feminist speech about sexuality, or to target the speech of sexual minorities, as to halt hateful speech about women. Worse, perpetuation of the concept of gender-determined roles in regard to sexuality strengthens one of the main obstacles to achieving real change and ending sexual violence.

Notes

1. . . . The Court of Appeals held that the Indianapolis ordinance violated the First Amendment, and the Supreme Court affirmed that ruling without issuing an opinion. American Booksellers Ass'n Inc. v. Hudnut, 771 F.2d 323 (7th Cir. 1985), *af-f'd*, 475 U.S. 1001 (1986). It appears that the Feminist Anti-Censorship Taskforce (FACT) analysis had some influence on Judge Easterbrook's approach to the constitutional issues presented. The opinion discusses concrete examples illustrating the difficulty of distinguishing images that liberate women. *Id.* at 330. It addresses the relationship between images, ideas, and behavior, and the distinction between fantasy and reality, in terms that are unusually rich and thoughtful for a judicial opinion. *Id.* The court rightly rejects the state's claim that pornography is "low value" speech, entitled to lesser constitutional protection than "serious" talk about public issues. *Id.* at 331.

2. DuBois & Gordon, Seeking Ecstasy on the Battlefield: Danger and Pleasure in Nineteenth-Century Feminist Sexual Thought, in C. Vance ed., Pleasure and Danger: Exploring Female Sexuality 31 (1984).

3. S. De Beauvoir, The Second Sex 202–203, 366–413 (H. Parshley trans., 5th printing 1968).

4. 2 Attorney General's Comm'n on Pornography, U.S. Dep't of Just. Final Report app. A, at 1957 (1986) [hereinafter Comm'n on Pornography].

5. For three excellent feminist collections, see A. Snitow, C. Stansell & S. Thompson eds., Powers of Desire: The Politics of Sexuality (1983); C. Vance, *supra* note 2; V. Burstyn ed., Women Against Censorship (1985).

6. S. De Beauvoir, *supra* note 3, at 273.

7. By the use of highly selected examples, Appellants and supporting *amici* convey the impression that the great majority of materials considered pornographic are brutal. Although most commercial pornography, like much of all media, is sexist, most is not violent. A study of pictorials and cartoons in *Playboy* and *Penthouse* between 1973 and 1977 found that, by 1977, about 5% of the pictorials were rated as sexually violent.

. . . Malamuth & Spinner, A Longitudinal Content Analysis of Sexual Violence in the Best-Selling Erotic Magazines, 16 J. Sex. Research 226, 237 (1980). . . .

8. 18 U.S.C.A. §§1461–1462 (West 1984); 19 U.S.C.A. §1305 (West 1980 & Supp. 1984). . . .

9. To define 'pornography' as that which subordinates women, and then prohibit as pornographic that which subordinates, makes the claim that pornography subordinates either circular or logically trivial.

10. See also Abramson & Hayashi, Pornography in Japan: Cross-Cultural and Theoretical Considerations, in N. Malamuth & E. Donnerstein eds., Pornography and Sexual Aggression 173 (1984). Japanese pornography contains more depictions of rape and bondage than does American pornography and is also more readily available in popular magazines and on television. Yet, Japan has a substantially lower incidence of rape than any western country and a lower incidence of violent crime generally. The authors attribute the lower crime rate to cultural factors unrelated to pornography.

11. See, e.g., R. Reiter ed., Toward an Anthropology of Women (1975); M. Rosaldo & L. Lamphere, Women, Culture and Society (1974); M. Ryan, Womanhood in America: From Colonial Times to the Present (1979); N. Chodorow, The Reproduction of Mothering: Psychoanalysis and the Sociology of Gender (1978); D. Dinnerstein, The Mermaid and the Minotaur: Sexual Arrangements and Human Malaise (1976); J. Mitchell, Woman's Estate (1972).

A Feminist Critique of "The" Feminist Critique of Pornography

NADINE STROSSEN

[THIS ESSAY] counters the Dworkin-MacKinnon pro-censorship position with an argument grounded in feminist principles and concerns. [It] elaborates upon ten major ways in which censoring "pornography"[1] would have an adverse impact upon women's rights and interests. . . .

A. Any Censorship Scheme Would Inevitably Encompass Many Works That Are Especially Valuable to Feminists

The ACLU's brief in *Hudnut* noted the adverse impact of "pornography" censorship on feminist concerns. It explained that the Dworkin-MacKinnon model law, by proscribing sexually explicit depictions of women's "subordination," outlawed not only many valuable works of art and literature in general, but also many such works that are particularly important to women and feminists:

> Ironically, much overtly feminist scholarly material designed to address the same concerns prompting the [ordinance] would fall within [its] sweeping definition of pornography. Prominent examples include Kate Millett's *The Basement,* a graphic chronicle of sexual torture; . . . works on rape, wife beating and domestic violence; court testimony and photographic evidence in rape and sexual assault cases; works like [Susan] Brownmiller's *Against Our Will: Men, Women and Rape;* and psychiatric literature describing sexual pathologies and therapeutic modalities. Indeed, *Pornography: Men Possessing Women,* a work by Andrea Dworkin, one of the ordinance's original drafters, contains . . . so many . . . passages graphically depicting the explicit sexual subordination of women that it could easily be pornographic under the ordinance.[1]

79 Va. L. Rev. 1099 (1993).

I have been told that Andrea Dworkin acknowledges that much of her own work would be censored under her model law, but that she considers this "a price worth paying" for the power to censor other works that would also be viewed as "pornography." Even assuming that Andrea Dworkin or other advocates of censoring "pornography" do in fact take this position, they certainly do not speak for all feminists on this point. Many may well believe that works such as Dworkin's, by depicting and deploring violence and discrimination against women, make invaluable contributions to redressing those problems.

The sweeping breadth of the Dworkin-MacKinnon model anti-"pornography" law is not the accidental result of poor drafting. To the contrary, their proposed law well reflects their view of the problem, and hence of its solution. In an exchange with Catharine MacKinnon, Professor Thomas Emerson made this point, as follows:

> As Professor MacKinnon emphasizes, male domination has deep, pervasive and ancient roots in our society, so it is not surprising that our literature, art, entertainment and commercial practices are permeated by attitudes and behavior that create and reflect the inferior status of women. If the answer to the problem, as Professor MacKinnon describes it, is government suppression of sexual expression that contributes to female subordination, then the net of restraint must be cast on a nearly limitless scale. Even narrowing the proscribed area to depictions of sexual activities involving violence would outlaw a large segment of the world's literature and art.[3]

B. Any Censorship Scheme Would Be Enforced in a Way That Discriminates Against the Least Popular, Least Powerful Groups in Our Society, Including Feminists and Lesbians

Vague censorship laws always rebound against the groups that hope to be "protected" by them. This is because such laws are enforced by the very power structure against which the disempowered censorship advocates seek protection. Given that the laws' vague and open-ended terms require the enforcing authorities to make subjective, discretionary judgments, it should not be surprising that these judgments are unsympathetic to the disempowered and marginalized.

The phenomenon of disempowered groups being disproportionately targeted under censorship schemes that are designed for their benefit is vividly illustrated, for example, by the enforcement record of laws against "hate speech"—i.e., speech that expresses racial, religious, sexist, and other forms of invidious discrimination. In the U.S., recently implemented campus hate speech codes consistently have been used disproportionately to punish the speech of the very racial minority groups whose interests, according to the code proponents, should have been advanced by such codes.[4] . . .

Censorship of "pornography," defined by Dworkin and MacKinnon as the sexually explicit depiction of women's "subordination," necessarily vests in government officials the power to impose on others their views about what forms of sexuality are politically or morally correct. The criteria for assessing "subordination" under the Dworkin-MacKinnon model statute accentuate the problem of vesting open-ended, discretionary power in enforcing authorities. These vague criteria are merely invitations for subjective, value-laden interpretations.[5]

Because of the inherently subjective nature of determinations as to which sexually explicit imagery is pleasurable or otherwise positive, it is antithetical to feminism to impose censorship schemes that deprive individual women (and men) of the right to make these determinations for themselves. As Feminists for Free Expression stated in its letter to the Senate Judiciary Committee opposing the Pornography Victims' Compensation Act:

> It is no goal of feminism to restrict individual choices or stamp out sexual imagery. Though some women and men may have this on their platform, they represent only themselves. Women are as varied as any citizens of a democracy; there is no agreement or feminist code as to what images are distasteful or even sexist. It is the right and responsibility of each woman to read, view or produce the sexual material she chooses without the intervention of the state "for her own good." We believe genuine feminism encourages individuals to make these choices for themselves. This is the great benefit of being feminists in a free society.[6]

Even beyond the significant danger that censoring "pornography" poses to individual sexual choices in general, such censorship poses a special threat to any sexual expression that society views as unconventional. Censors would likely target "pornography" that conveys pro-feminist or pro-lesbian themes, because of its inconsistency with "traditional family values" or conventional morality. For example, "pornography" "may convey the message that sexuality need not be tied to reproduction, men, or domesticity."[7] It may extol sex for no reason other than pleasure, sex without commitment, and sexual adventure.

Years ago, feminist writer Erica Jong predicted that the enforcement of any "pornography" censorship scheme would probably target expression by and about feminists and others who challenge prevailing cultural norms, such as gay men and lesbians: "Despite the ugliness of a lot of pornography, . . . I believe that censorship only springs back against the givers of culture—against authors, artists, and feminists, against anybody who wants to change society. Should censorship be imposed . . . feminists would be the first to suffer."[8]

Jong's predictions came to pass in Canada, after the 1992 Canadian Supreme Court decision referred to above, which empowered the government to prosecute sexually explicit expression that is "degrading" or "dehumanizing" to women. One of the first targets of the new law was a lesbian and gay bookstore, Glad Day Bookstore, and a magazine produced by lesbians for lesbians.[9] Not surprisingly, the police, prosecutors, and other government officials viewed this lesbian imagery as degrading. They did not so view violent, misogynistic imagery. Other actions on the part of Canadian authorities that hold censorship power reflect similar attitudes.[10]

Canada's gay and lesbian bookstores have been so conspicuously singled out under the new Canadian law that one of them initiated a lawsuit claiming that it had been subjected to governmental harassment.[11] After the lawsuit was instituted—and, some critics charge, specifically to blunt its allegations—Canadian officials broadened their enforcement efforts to include university bookstores and radical bookstores. [T]he Canadian Supreme Court's adoption of the Dworkin-MacKinnon approach has given government officials a broad, discretionary weapon with which they could target radical dissent, should they so choose.

The Canadian experience has proven the sadly prophetic nature of Erica Jong's warnings in a particularly ironic development. Pursuant to their new-found authority to interdict at the border material that is "degrading" or "dehumanizing" to women, Canadian customs officials have confiscated several feminist works that Canadian bookstores sought to import from the United States, including two books that were written by Andrea Dworkin herself![12] . . .

C. Censorship Is Paternalistic, Perpetuating Demeaning Stereotypes About Women, Including That Sex Is Bad for Us

Ironically, the Dworkin-MacKinnon effort to extirpate sexually explicit expression that, in their view, perpetuates demeaning stereotypes about women, itself perpetuates such demeaning stereotypes. One subordinating stereotype that is central to the feminist censorship movement is that sex is inherently degrading to women.

To emphasize that the feminist pro-censorship position rests upon traditional, stereotypical views disapproving sex and denying women's sexuality, anti-censorship feminists have characterized their own views as "pro-sex."[13] The basic contours of these opposing "anti-sex" and "pro-sex" positions—which are linked, respectively, to the pro- and anti-censorship positions—are delineated by three feminist scholars and activists as follows:

> Embedded in [the feminist pro-censorship] view are several . . . familiar themes: that sex is degrading to women, but not to men; that men are raving beasts; that sex is dangerous for women; that sexuality is male, not female; that women are victims, not sexual actors; that men inflict "it" on women; that penetration is submission; that heterosexual sexuality, rather than the institution of heterosexuality, is sexist.
>
> . . . It's ironic that a feminist position on pornography incorporates most of the myths about sexuality that feminism has struggled to displace.
>
> . . . Underlying virtually every section of the [Dworkin-MacKinnon model law] there is an assumption that sexuality is a realm of unremitting, unequaled victimization for women. . . . But this analysis is not the only feminist perspective on sexuality. Feminist theorists have also argued that the sexual terrain, however power-laden, is actively contested. Women are agents, and not merely

victims, who make decisions and act on them, and who desire, seek out and enjoy sexuality.[14]

The "anti-sex" position of the pro-censorship feminists essentially posits a mutual inconsistency between a woman's freedom and her participation in sexual relations with men. For example, both Dworkin and MacKinnon have argued that, in light of society's pervasive sexism, women cannot freely consent to sexual relations with men. Dworkin makes this point in the most dramatic and extreme terms in her book *Intercourse,* which equates *all* heterosexual intercourse with rape.[15]

In contrast to the "anti-sex," pro-censorship view that women's freedom is undermined by their sexual relations with men, the "pro-sex," anti-censorship position regards these phenomena as mutually reinforcing. . . .

The feminist pro-censorship movement inverts central tenets of the feminism of the 1960s and 1970s, which criticized the idea that sex degrades women as reflecting patriarchal, subordinating stereotypes. Like labor laws that many states passed in the early twentieth century, to "protect" women in the workplace, censorship of "pornography" also aims to shelter women from our presumed innate vulnerability. As the Supreme Court said in a 1973 decision upholding women's equality rights, such "protective" legislation reflected attitudes of "romantic paternalism" that, in practical effect, "put women, not on a pedestal, but in a cage."[16]

A feminist legal scholar and historian has shown that the misogynistic stereotypes that contemporary pro-censorship feminists perpetuate by advocating censorship (as well as other "special" treatment of women) have even deeper historical roots than the early twentieth century "protective" labor legislation. She wrote:

> When I first read Robin West's essay ["Jurisprudence and Gender"], I felt within me an undeniable resonance. Yet the "radical" theories she described did not accurately represent my own experiences or my observations of the men and women that I knew. . . .
>
> It was only after rereading certain historical works . . . that I realized why these theories seemed so elemental to me. They were eerily reminiscent of the theories of sexuality and female personality of my Roman Catholic upbringing. . . . My experience was not the recognition of a dimly perceived truth, but the imperfect recollection of lies told to me in my childhood, which I since have consciously tried to forget.[17] . . .

A recent article by Cathy Young also points out the "uncanny resemblance" between the religious right and pro-censorship feminists concerning sex, stressing that both camps see women as inevitable victims in terms of sex.[18] . . .

D. Censorship Perpetuates the Disempowering Notion That Women Are Essentially Victims

Just as the pro-censorship movement views women as inevitably being victims in sexual matters, that movement also perpetuates the stereotype that women are victims in a more general sense. For example, feminist law professor Carlin Meyer has noted the pro-censorship feminists' "general tendency to view women as actually, not merely portrayed as, submissive—as acted upon rather than acting; as objects of male will rather than subjects able to challenge or change cultural norms."[19]

As Cathy Young has observed, it is considered strategically advantageous from some perspectives to depict women as victims: "Victimhood is [p]owerful. Both feminists and antifeminists see advantages in keeping women down."[20]

On the other hand, though, growing numbers of feminists are recognizing that purveying the view of women as victims can backfire against gender equality.[21] This increasing realization was described by a female journalist as follows:

> On issues from domestic violence to pornography, feminists are rethinking their emphasis on women as victims—and looking for new legal and political approaches to enable women to force social change. Fifteen years ago, Elizabeth Schneider helped develop the legal argument that battered women who killed husbands who had abused them for years were the victims, not the aggressors. Now she worries [that] battered women are victims of their victim status. [She said:] "Courts and society have glommed onto the victim image. . . . But it's a two-edged sword. Many battered women lose custody of their children because judges see them as helpless, paralyzed victims who can't manage daily life. And if a woman seems too capable, too much in charge of her life to fit the victim image, she may not be believed."[22]

E. Censorship Distracts from Constructive Approaches to Reducing Discrimination and Violence Against Women

Like all censorship schemes, the feminist proposal to censor "pornography" diverts attention and resources from constructive, meaningful steps to address the societal problem at which the censorship is aimed—in this case, discrimination and violence against women. Feminist advocates of censoring "pornography"—along with feminist opponents of such censorship—are concerned about the very real, very disturbing societal problems of discrimination and violence against women. The focus on censoring "pornography," though, diverts attention from the root causes of discrimination and violence against women—of which violent, misogynistic "pornography" is merely one symptom—and from actual acts of discrimination and violence.

For those with a more complex analysis of the manifold causes and reflections of women's inferior societal status, the Dworkin-MacKinnon focus on "pornography" is at best myopic, and at worst blinding. As Canadian feminist Varda Burstyn has written:

> [T]here has been, among the antipornography feminists, a series of subtle shifts in ideas about the forms and causes of women's oppression. From an appreciation of the multidimensional reality of masculine dominance, vocal fem-

inists have been increasingly narrowing their focus to one dimension: . . . pornography. Women's attention has been diverted from the causes to the depictions of their oppression.[23]

The Dworkin-MacKinnon tunnel-visioned focus on "pornography" overlooks the many complex factors that contribute to sexism and violence against women in our society. . . .

Proponents of censorship in all contexts have designed their censorship regimes to advance some important societal goal. In operation, though, censorship always is at best ineffective and at worst counter-productive in terms of actually advancing that goal. The reason is that, by focusing on expressions of the problem, censorship targets symptoms rather than causes; it does not address either the problem's root causes or its actual manifestations. Consequently, censorship distracts from more constructive, more effective approaches.

1. Distraction from Real Causes of and Solutions to Gender Inequality

Many senators who supported the Pornography Victims' Compensation Act, allegedly as a means to assist women, have not supported various constructive measures that would actually counter discrimination against women, including: the Family and Medical Leave Act; government-funded day care; elimination of the damage cap on gender-based employment discrimination lawsuits; legislation to lift the "gag rule," which prohibited the provision of information about abortion at federally funded family planning clinics; and government funding for abortions for poor women, under programs that subsidize poor women's pregnancy and childbirth expenses.[24]

By asserting that "pornography" is a central cause—or even *the* central cause—of sex discrimination, pro-censorship feminists deflect energy and attention from the factors that feminist scholars and the U.S. Commission on Civil Rights have found to be the most significant causes of such discrimination: sex-segregated labor markets; systematic devaluation of work traditionally done by women; sexist concepts of marriage and family; inadequate income-maintenance programs for women unable to find wage work; lack of day care services and the premise that child care is an exclusively or largely female responsibility; barriers to reproductive freedom; and discrimination and segregation in education.

Feminist sociologist Thelma McCormack has strongly denounced "the uninformed claim that pornography is in any way a factor" in causing gender inequality.[25] She derides this view as "an insult to social scientists and the broader intellectual community for whom structural equality is the crux of social justice and [who] have laboured to develop the knowledge that would clarify and deepen our understanding of it."[26]

Professor McCormack has aptly described how those feminists who seek to censor "pornography" are mischanneling their energies. Rather than fighting the "*degradation*" of women that they see in "pornography," she urges those who want to advance women's equality to fight instead against the "*devaluation*" of women that permeates our mainstream culture. She explains: "Devaluation means that if, by some strange set of circumstances, we could eliminate all forms of pornography . . . [women] would still be under-represented politically, and would still be culturally marginalized. The prohibition of obscenity . . . accomplishes nothing in the struggle for equality because it confuses symbolic degradation with instrumental devaluation."[27]

2. Distraction from Real Causes of and Solutions to Misogynistic Violence

Just as the focus on "pornography" distracts from the real causes of gender discrimination, it also distracts from the real causes of anti-female violence. A comprehensive analysis of the literature on this issue concluded:

> Leading feminists and the U.S. Commission on Civil Rights suggest that violence against women begins with educational and economic discrimination. . . . Men learn to consider women burdens, stiflers and drags on their freedom. Women, in turn, do not have the economic independence and access to day care that would enable them to leave abusive settings. Feminists also suggest that violence begins with the infantilization of women so that men hold them in contempt and see them as easily dismissed or lampooned and ready targets for anger.[28]

By arguing that exposure to "pornography" causes violent crimes against women, pro-censorship feminists dilute the accountability of men who commit these crimes by displacing some of it onto words and images, or those who create or distribute them. . . .

The Senate Judiciary Committee's Minority Report on the Pornography Victims' Compensation Act emphasized that "pornography" censorship displaces responsibility from actual rapists and others who assault women. The committee members who opposed the PVCA explained that "the bill sends the wrong message to sex offenders. . . . Criminal defendants could use [this] to assert impaired or diminished capacity, available in many States as a defense to specific intent crimes such as rape."[29]

For the same reason, feminist law professor Nan Hunter suggests that, to convey its actual impact, the PVCA should be renamed the "Rapists' Exculpation Act."[30] As she explained, the Act's "porn-made-me-do-it" approach would severely set back the women's movement's efforts to ensure that our criminal justice system vigorously enforces laws criminalizing sexual assaults. Instead, it would again allow defenses to such crimes that are not allowed for other crimes. . . .[31] Feminist writers themselves could be held accountable for harm allegedly caused by their writings. As writer Pete Hamill explained: "The legal theory that endorses pornography-made-me-do-it, if accepted, would have no limits. Someone could claim that his family was destroyed as the result of published feminist theories attacking the family, and that feminist writers and their publishers must pay for the damage."[32]

Criminal defendants already have sought to reduce their punishments by relying on the Dworkin-MacKinnon analysis of "pornography." For example, a defendant who was convicted of a brutal rape and murder challenged the trial judge's imposition of the death penalty on the ground that the judge had failed to consider his extensive viewing of rape "pornography" and snuff films to be mitigating circumstances.[33] The defendant had argued that such viewing is akin to intoxication or mental disease or defect, rendering him unable to appreciate the criminality of his conduct. In rejecting this contention, the U.S. Court of Appeals for the Seventh Circuit stressed that such arguments would prevent the punishment of rapists and others who commit violence against women.[34]

In displacing responsibility from the men who commit violence against women onto some external factor, the current feminist censorship movement parallels an earlier feminist faction. As feminist law professor Nan Hunter notes, to single out "pornography" as women's archenemy is to:

> repeat[ ] the mistake of some of our foremothers, the leaders of the women's temperance movement who sought a ban on alcohol. Those women believed that alcohol caused much of men's violence against women, particularly domestic violence. . . . But we have learned from the work of anti-violence groups that alcohol is not the *cause* of violence against women; it is the *excuse* for it. The same is true of pornography.[35]

Those who are committed to assisting victims of misogynistic violence—rather than to treating their assailants as "victims" of "pornography"[36] advocate constructive alternative measures in place of demonizing "pornography" [such as] "government funding for services for the victims of sexual assault and abuse, as well as funding of research to discover the causes and prevention of sexual violence."[37]

3. "Blaming the Book" and "Blaming the Victim"

Censorship's "blame-the-book" attitude closely parallels a "blame-the-victim" attitude that has characterized some perceptions of female victims of sexual assault, and that until recently was enshrined in American law. While the assaulted woman herself used to be blamed for the assault if, for example, her skirt was "too short" or her sweater was "too tight," now it is the woman who poses for a sexually suggestive photograph or film who is blamed.[38]

What "blaming the book" and "blaming the victim" have in common is the creation of a scapegoat. They divert attention away from the real problem, which is the men who discriminate or commit violence against women, and they ignore the real solution, which is the imposition of measures to prevent and punish such actions.

The appeal of any censorship movement, including the one directed at "pornography," is understandable insofar as it appears to offer a simple "solution" to complex, troubling societal problems. Citizens who are concerned about such problems are attracted to measures that promise a "quick fix," and politicians likewise are inclined to endorse such popular approaches, especially because censorship is a relatively inexpensive strategy. In contrast, measures that are designed to redress the root causes of these complex societal problems are not only more complex themselves, but also less dramatic and more expensive than censorship. . . .

F. Censorship Would Harm Women Who Make a Living in the Sex Industry

The Dworkin-MacKinnon approach to sexually oriented expression would undermine the interests of women who choose to make their living in the sex industry in several respects. Most obviously, by seeking to ban major aspects of this industry, the Dworkin-MacKinnon regime would deprive women of an option that many now affirm they have freely chosen.

Moreover, as even feminist censorship advocates recognize, the practical impact of their approach would not be to prevent the production of sexually explicit expression altogether, but rather simply to drive that production underground. In consequence, the women who participate in producing sexually oriented materials would be more subject to exploitation and less amenable to legal protection. The Dworkin-MacKinnon approach also deprives women who pose for sexually explicit works of an important tool for guarding their economic and other interests because it deems women incompetent to enter into legally binding contracts regarding the production of such works.

In contrast, under a non-censorship regime, individual women, or organized groups of women, could seek improved compensation and other working conditions, to protect their health, safety, and welfare, through contractual negotiations.[39] Additionally, governmental regulation could provide these protections for sex industry workers.

For the foregoing reasons, it is not surprising that virtually all of the organized workers in sex trades have opposed schemes to censor "pornography."[40] It is also not surprising that sex industry workers widely perceive the feminist anti-"pornography" movement as censuring their occupational choices and undermining their interests both in making such choices and in improving their terms and conditions of employment.[41] . . .

G. Censorship Would Harm Women's Efforts to Develop Their Own Sexuality

As each successive wave of the women's movement has recognized, sexual liberation is an essential aspect of what has been called "women's liberation." Feminist law professor Carlin Meyer explains that the Dworkin-MacKinnon analysis strongly supports the conclusion that gender equality and sexual freedom are closely interconnected:

> If [feminist advocates of censoring "pornography"] are right that sex is central to patriarchal control of women, then freedom to explore it is crucial to women's ability to achieve change. Precisely to the extent that sexuality has historically been a crucial site of repression and oppression for women, it is critically important to women's liberation.[42]

Conversely, throughout history, opponents of women's rights have sought to limit the production and dissemination of information about women's sexuality. By censoring sexually explicit words and imagery, the Dworkin-MacKinnon movement shores up the efforts of its right-wing allies to deprive women of information important to developing their own sense of sexual and gender-role identity. On an even more basic level, such censorship schemes would deprive women of vital information concerning sexuality and health. Accordingly, feminist anthropologist Carole Vance predicted that if the Pornography Victims' Compensation Act were adopted, conservatives would utilize it to target sexuality educators, sexologists, and HIV/AIDS educators.[43]

Dr. Leonore Tiefer [professor of psychology specializing in research on sexuality], who believes that "women are in more danger from the repression of sexually explicit materials than from their expression,"[44] grounds that conclusion in large part on the fact that such materials are especially important for women's "struggl[e] to develop their own sexualities. . . . "[45] She explains:

> We need the freedom for new female sexual visions to inspire our minds and practices away from the ruts worn by centuries of religious inhibition, fear of pregnancy and disease, compulsory heterosexuality, lies and ignorance of all kinds.
> . . . Female sexuality is a joke without freely available information and ideas.[46]

Censoring "pornography" would also stultify discussions and explorations of female sexuality by women, including by female artists. As one woman artist stated: "Censorship can only accentuate the taboos that already surround women's open exploration of their sexuality. There are too many other obstacles now in place to women becoming artists or writers, or even speaking out publicly, without inviting the judicial control of censorship."[47]

H. Censorship Would Strengthen the Religious Right, Whose Patriarchal Agenda Would Curtail Women's Rights

As discussed above, the traditional, right-wing groups that have exercised much political power since 1980 have lent that strength to the feminist pro-censorship faction by using its rhetoric in an attempt to justify various censorship measures. The feminist and right-wing advocates of censoring "pornography" have a symbiotic relationship. Thus, just as the right-wing activists have reinforced the influence of the pro-censorship feminists, so too, the pro-censorship feminists have strengthened the political power of the religious right.

History teaches that such a symbiotic relationship between those who view themselves as social reformers and those with more traditional values redounds to the reformers' disadvantage. Professor Walter Kendrick concludes his powerful study of "pornography" in modern culture with the following lament about the failure of current feminist censorship advocates to heed these historical lessons:

> The most dismaying aspect of the feminist antipornography campaign is its exact resemblance to every such effort that preceded it, from . . . that of Comstock and all the Societies for the Suppression of Vice, to the modern vigilantism of Leagues and Legions of Decency. . . . If the twisted history of "pornography" shows nothing else, it shows that forgetfulness of history is the chief weapon in the armory of those who would forbid us to see and know.[48]

The Dworkin-MacKinnon faction has ignored the specific lesson from this history: that when women's rights advocates form alliances with conservatives over such issues as "pornography" or "temperance," they promote the conservatives' anti-feminist goals, relegating women to traditional sexual and gender roles.[49] Feminist historian Judith Walkowitz drew this conclusion. She wrote an award-winning book about such a misalliance between feminists and traditionalists in late nineteenth century England,[50] when both groups sought to protect young girls from prostitution. Warning contemporary feminists to be wary of repeating their foremothers' mistakes, Walkowitz stressed that the earlier feminists' efforts were ultimately taken over by a repressive coalition that passed sweeping sexual legislation that regulated women. That provides a lesson for politics today.[51]

I. By Undermining Free Speech, Censorship Would Deprive Feminists of a Powerful Tool for Advancing Women's Equality

Because free speech is a powerful tool for advancing women's equality, and because censorship consistently has been used to undermine women's rights, advocates of such rights have far more to lose than to gain from any censorship scheme. For example, free speech has proven to be an effective ally even of feminism's anti-"pornography" faction; they and others have successfully used "pornography" itself, as well as other expression, to counter misogynistic attitudes.

I have already noted one positive impact of free speech in the women's rights context: the fact that anti-"pornography" activists have effectively utilized their free speech rights—including, specifically, the right to display "pornography"—to galvanize public concern about the ongoing problems of anti-female discrimination and violence, and to heighten public awareness that some sexually oriented expression may convey misogynistic messages. To the extent that censorship would make such images less visible, the protest against sexism would be weakened. As feminist filmmaker Anna Gronau explained:

> The recent rise of violent pornography has coincided with increased power on the part of women. Censoring this material, I believe, only abets those who

seek a return to the former distribution of power, for such action will remove the public proof that violence and other wrongs against women continue to exist in society. We may, once again begin to doubt our perceptions; censorship seeks to hide the evidence of sexism, silencing those who try to confront it.[52]

The social science studies as to whether there is any causal connection between exposure to "pornography" and the commission of actual violence against real women demonstrate another positive impact of free speech protection specifically for "pornography." Extensive and widely cited experiments by Edward Donnerstein and other researchers involved intensively exposing male college students to violent, misogynistic, sexually oriented films, depicting women as welcoming rape. Shortly after this concentrated exposure, the experimental subjects temporarily revealed attitudinal changes that made them more receptive to adverse stereotyping of women, including the "rape myth" that women really want to be raped.[53] However, when the researchers followed the massive exposure to these violent, misogynistic films with debriefing sessions in which the college men were exposed to materials dispelling the rape myth,[54] the net impact of their exposure to the full range of expression (both the violent, misogynistic films and the pro-feminist material) was striking—the college men had more positive, less discriminatory, and less stereotyped attitudes toward women than they had before the experiment. Moreover, the combined exposure to misogynistic and feminist materials reduced negative attitudes even more effectively than exposure to the latter alone.[55]

The efficacy of "counterspeech" to mitigate the temporary attitudinal impact of exposure to violent "pornography" has been demonstrated by several studies.[56] In fact, the Surgeon General's Report that was specifically requested by the Meese Pornography Commission recognized that such educational strategies could effectively counteract any negative attitudinal impact that viewing violent "pornography" might temporarily have.[57]

The foregoing experience in the "pornography" context is completely consistent with a central tenet of U.S. free speech jurisprudence: that the appropriate antidote to speech with which we disagree, or which offends us, is more speech. . . .

There is a broader reason why free speech is especially precious to feminists: as Judge Sara Evans Barker stressed in *Hudnut,* and as Professor Thelma McCormack stressed [as well],[58] feminists, like all who seek social change and equality, are especially dependent on free expression. Conversely, those who seek to repress women's rights consistently have used censorship as *their* tool. This has been true from the nineteenth-century Comstock Act,[59] which banned the distribution of information about birth control, to the recently revoked "gag rule," which banned the dissemination of information about abortion at federally funded family planning clinics.[60]

Significantly, these censorship efforts often have linked the suppression of sexually oriented material with the suppression of material important to women's rights—namely, information regarding women's health and reproductive freedom. For example, the Comstock Act banned both sexually oriented material and material related to contraception or abortion. Accordingly, the writings of feminist and birth control advocate Margaret Sanger were banned under that law as "obscene." Sanger's campaign to convey accurate sexual information began in 1912 with two articles in a New York City newspaper. The first, entitled "What Every Mother Should Know," ran without incident, but the Post Office barred the second, "What Every Girl Should Know." It contained no information on birth control, but postal officials were offended by Margaret Sanger's explanation of venereal disease and her use of words such as "gonorrhea" and "syphilis." Consequently, the newspaper's next issue contained the following announcement: "What Every Girl Should Know: 'NOTHING! By order of the Post Office Department.' "[61]

The use of censorship laws aimed at sexually explicit expression to stifle information about women's sexuality, women's health, and women's reproductive choices has continued to the present day. In addition to the "gag rule's" censorship of accurate information about abortion, frequent targets of censorship efforts include such feminist health guides as *Our Bodies, Our Selves*.[62]

Ominously, Andrea Dworkin herself recently has sought to prevent the publication, distribution, and sale of a book about women's reproductive health, which was authored by two feminists, because she disagreed with one point they made.[63] Likewise, in the fall of 1992, students at the University of Michigan Law School, where Catharine MacKinnon teaches, removed an exhibit of works by seven feminist artists, five of whom were female, because Dworkin-MacKinnon followers objected to the perspectives that at least one of these works conveyed about prostitution and "pornography."[64] These episodes vividly demonstrate that Dworkin-MacKinnon style censorship laws, along with their predecessors, would likely be wielded to suppress vital information about women's health, women's reproduction, and women's sexuality.

J. Freedom for Sexually Explicit Expression Is an Essential Aspect of Human Freedom; Restricting It Undermines Human Rights More Broadly

What is at issue in the effort to defend freedom for those who choose to create, pose for, or view "pornography" is not only freedom for this particular type of expression, but also freedom of expression in general. Ultimately, though, the stakes are even higher. As compellingly explained by . . . Gary Mongiovi . . . , sexual expression is an integral aspect of human freedom more broadly. Accordingly, as he reminds us, "[a]ttempts to stifle sexual expression are part of a larger agenda directed at the suppression of human freedom and individuality more generally."[65]

Throughout history, down to the present day, the suppression of sexually explicit speech characterizes regimes that repress human rights in general. As writer Pete Hamill commented:

> Recent history teaches us that most tyrannies have a puritanical nature. The
> sexual restrictions of Stalin's Soviet Union, Hitler's Germany and Mao's China

would have gladdened the hearts of those Americans who fear sexual images and literature. Their ironfisted puritanism wasn't motivated by a need to erase sexual inequality. They wanted to smother the personal chaos that can accompany sexual freedom and subordinate it to the granite face of the state. Every tyrant knows that if he can control human sexuality, he can control life.[66]

Like all groups who seek equal rights and freedoms, women and feminists have an especially important stake in securing human rights in general. Therefore, they should be especially reluctant to hand over to government what history has proven to be an important tool for repressing human rights: the power to censor sexually explicit speech. Given the pro-censorship feminists' powerful critique of the patriarchal nature of government power,[67] it is especially ironic—and tragically misguided—that their censorship scheme would augment that very power. . . .

Notes

1. [Strossen explains that she places "pornography" in quotations throughout her essay in order to signify that she uses the term in the same sense as MacKinnon and Dwokin, i.e., sexually explicit speech that allegedly subordinates women. *Ed.*]

2. Brief Amici Curiae of the American Civil Liberties Union, the Indiana Civil Liberties Union, and the American Civil Liberties Union of Illinois 8a, American Booksellers Ass'n, Inc. v. Hudnut, 598 F. Supp. 1316 (D.Ind. 1984) (No. IP 84–791C), *aff'd*, 771 F.2d 323 (7th Cir. 1985), *aff'd*, 475 U.S. 1001 (1986).

3. Thomas I. Emerson, Pornography and the First Amendment: A Reply to Professor MacKinnon, herein, at 80, 81.

4. See Nadine Strossen, Regulating Racist Speech on Campus: A Modest Proposal?, 1990 Duke L.J. 484, 556–558.

5. . . . The problematic criteria include the following: "women are presented dehumanized as sexual objects"; "women are presented in postures or positions of sexual submission . . . or display"; "women's body parts . . . are exhibited such that women are reduced to those parts"; "women are presented in scenarios of degradation"; and "[women are] shown as . . . inferior."

6. [See letter from the Ad Hoc Committee of Feminists for Free Expression to the Members of the Senate Judiciary Committee, Feb. 14, 1992, reprinted at 79 Va. L. Rev. 1099, 1188 (1993)].

7. Nan D. Hunter & Sylvia A. Law, Brief Amici Curiae of Feminist Anti-Censorship Taskforce et al. 21 U. Mich. J.L. Ref. 69, 121 (1987–1988), reprinted herein, at 118.

8. Mary Kay Blakely, Is One Woman's Sexuality Another Woman's Pornography? Ms., Apr. 1985, at 37, 38 (quoting Erica Jong).

9. See Chris Bearchell, Gay Porn is Getting Skinned Alive, Toronto Star, Jan. 15, 1993, at A23.

10. See Lynn King, Censorship and Law Reform: Will Changing the Laws Mean a Change for the Better? in Varda Burstyn ed., Women Against Censorship 79, 80–81 (1985) (stating that the Ontario Board of Censors, while asserting the purpose of protecting women, has exercised its discretionary power "not [to] eliminat[e] misogynist images but mainly [to] ensur[e] that explicit sexuality is avoided and traditional values upheld"); *id.* at 84 (stating that the Ontario Board of Censors censored a pro-feminist

film); see also Myrna Kostash, Second Thoughts, in *id.* (stating that although Canadian customs officers found reproductions of sexually explicit art in *Penthouse Magazine* obscene, they did not make the same finding with respect to a sexually explicit cartoon in the same magazine that depicted violence against a woman).

11. See Pierre Berton, How Otto Jelinek Guards Our Morals, Toronto Star, May 29, 1993, at H3.

12. *Id.*

13. See, e.g., Barbara Ehrenreich, What Is This Thing Called Sex? The Nation, Sept. 24, 1983, at 245 (reviewing Ann Snitow, Christine Stansell & Sharon Thompson eds., Powers of Desire: The Politics of Sexuality (1983)). For collections of "pro-sex" writings, see Carole S. Vance ed., Pleasure and Danger: Exploring Female Sexuality (1984); Ann Snitow, Christine Stansell & Sharon Thompson eds., Powers of Desire: The Politics of Sexuality (1983).

14. Lisa Duggan, Nan Hunter & Carole S. Vance, False Promises: Feminist Antipornography Legislation in the U.S., in Women Against Censorship, *supra* note 10, at 142–143, 151.

15. Andrea Dworkin, Intercourse 137 (1987) (stating that "intercourse remains a means or the means of physiologically making a woman inferior"); see also Andrea Dworkin, Pornography: Men Possessing Women 23 (1981). . . .

16. Frontiero v. Richardson, 411 U.S. 677, 684 (1973) (plurality opinion). . . .

17. Jeanne L. Schroeder, Feminism Historicized: Medieval Misogynist Stereotypes in Contemporary Feminist Jurisprudence, 75 Iowa L. Rev. 1135, 1136 (1990).

18. See Cathy Young, Victimhood Is Powerful, Reason, Oct. 1992, at 18, 21.

19. Carlin Meyer, Sex, Sin, and Women's Liberation, herein, at 150.

20. Young, *supra* note 18, at 18.

21. See, e.g., Katie Roiphe, Date Rape's Other Victim, N.Y. Times Mag., June 13, 1993, at 26 (criticizing expansive definitions of rape among many feminists, as including consensual sex induced by emotional pressure, for reinforcing traditional, ultimately anti-feminist, notions about women's equality and sexuality). . . .

22. Tamar Lewin, Feminists Wonder if It Was Progress to Become "Victims," N.Y. Times, May 10, 1992, at D6. . . .

23. Varda Burstyn, Political Precedents and Moral Crusades: Women, Sex and the State, in Women Against Censorship, *supra* note 10, at 4, 25–26.

24. See Carole S. Vance, New Threat to Sexual Expression: The Pornography Victims' Compensation Act, SIECUS Report, Feb./Mar. 1992. "The legislative records of conservative Republicans, such as [PVCA] cosponsors Senators Strom Thurmond (R-SC), Mitch McConnell (R-KY) and Charles Grassley (R-IA), show minimal support for initiatives that empower women or attack inequality. Their interest in women's victimization is piqued, it seems, only when female "victims of pornography" can be used as a rationale to curtail sexually explicit speech." *Id.* at 20, 21.

25. Thelma McCormack, If Pornography Is the Theory, Is Inequality the Practice? 43 (Nov. 1992) (unpublished paper delivered at Public Forum, held in York, Canada, Refusing Censorship: Feminists and Activists Fights Back).

26. *Id.*

27. *Id.* at 26. . . .

28. Marcia Pally, Sense and Censorship: The Vanity of Bonfires 14 (1991).

29. S. Rep. No. 372, 102d Cong., 2d Sess. 34 (1992).

30. Nan D. Hunter, §1521: A Rapist's Exculpation Act? 1 (1992) (unpublished manuscript).

31. *Id.* at 14. . . .

32. Pete Hamill, Women on the Verge of a Legal Breakdown, Playboy, Jan. 1993, at 186, 188.

33. Schiro v. Clark, 963 F.2d 962, 972 (7th Cir. 1992).

34. *Id.* . . .

35. Hunter, *supra* note 30, at 10–11. . . .

36. *Id.* at 13 (stating that "perhaps the biggest beneficiaries of this 'pornography victims compensation act' will be the newest 'victims'—men who commit rape and assault").

37. Letter from Dr. Judith V. Becker, Professor of Psychiatry and Psychology, to Senator Hank Brown 1–2 (Apr. 3, 1992); see also Varda Burstyn, Beyond Despair: Positive Strategies, in Women Against Censorship, *supra* note 10, at 152 (describing noncensorship measures designed to decrease discrimination and violence against women). . . .

38. See Pally, Sense and Censorship, *supra* note 28, at 31 (stating that "according to antipornography logic, it is still the woman's fault—[i]f not the woman in the room, then the woman on the screen, calendar or wall"); see also Hunter, *supra* note 230. . . .

39. See Charles I. Nero, Free Speech or Hate Speech: Pornography and Its Means of Production, 2 Law & Sexuality 3, 6 (1992): "[M]aking pictorial pornography illegal may actually hurt the performers and models who make a living in it. British psychologist Lynne Segal notes that 'sex workers themselves have almost always objected to others' attempts to save them from such forms of "exploitation," knowing full well that the economic alternatives open to them are likely to be no less, indeed perhaps a very great deal more, exploitative.' African-American porno actress Angel Kelly made the point that making pornography illegal hurts the performers [because it] prevents the workers from demanding better wages and working conditions. Also, the [Meese Pornography Commission Report] included statements from sex workers that coercive practices most often happen in 'home-made, noncommercial' pornography." *Id.* (citations omitted).

40. Laurie Bell ed., Good Girls/Bad Girls: Feminists and Sex Trade Workers Face to Face 79–144 (1987).

41. *Id.*

42. Meyer 24, herein, at 150.

43. See Vance, New Threat to Sexual Expression, *supra* note 24, at 21.

44. Leonore Tiefer, On Censorship and Women, American Theatre, Jan. 1991, at 50.

45. *Id.*

46. *Id.*; see also Sallie Tisdale, Talk Dirty to Me: A Woman's Taste for Pornography, Harpers Mag., Feb. 1992, at 37, 39 ("For young women, porn may be important not so much because of its information about sex, but because it is about sexual parameters, the bounds of the normal, and provides not only reassurance but permission to be sexual.").

47. Anna Gronau, Women and Images: Toward a Feminist Analysis of Censorship, in Women Against Censorship, *supra* note 10, at 91, 97. . . .

48. Walter Kendrick, The Secret Museum: Pornography in Modern Culture 239 (1987).

49. See Leonore Tiefer, Freedom's Not a Dirty Word: Some Harms To Women of Restrictions on Sexually Related Expression, Address Delivered at the National Coalition Against Censorship Meeting 5–7 (May 17, 1990) (unpublished manuscript); ac-

cord Varda Burstyn, Political Precedents and Moral Crusades: Women, Sex and the State, in Women Against Censorship, *supra* note 10, at 25. . . .

50. Judith R. Walkowitz, Prostitution and Victorian Society: Women, Class and the State (1980).

51. *Id.* at 255.

52. Gronau, *supra* note 47, at 96.

53. Edward Donnerstein, Daniel Linz & Steven Penrod, The Question of Pornography: Research Findings and Policy Implications 180–185 (1987). It should be stressed that these data show at most that exposure to aggressive or violent sexually explicit images may lead to short-term attitudinal changes and provide no evidence that exposure to such images increases the probability that the viewer will actually commit harmful acts.

54. *Id.*

55. See, e.g., Neil Malamuth & Edward I. Donnerstein, The Effects of Aggressive-Pornographic Mass Media Stimuli, in 15 Advances Experimental Psychol. 103, 129 (1982); Donnerstein, *supra* note 53, at 180–185.

56. See Pally, *supra* note 28, at 34–36.

57. For example, Marcia Pally states: "Several studies have shown that presentations outlining the ways that violent sexual material can foster or reinforce incorrect beliefs or negative attitudes have been able to prevent the expected results of exposure. In other words, educating people about the possible effects of exposure, in conjunction with exposure, appears to reduce or eliminate the shifts in attitudes that are usually seen after exposure." *Id.* at 34 (citing the Report of the Surgeon General's Workshop on Pornography and Public Health 50 (1986)).

58. McCormack, *supra* note 25, at 12.

59. 18 U.S.C. §§1461, 1462 (1982) & 19 U.S.C. §1305 (1982 & Supp. II (1984)). The Act's official title was "An Act for the Suppression of Trade in, and Circulation of, [O]bscene Literature and Articles of [I]mmoral Use." 17 Stat. 598 (1873). . . .

60. Regulations of the Department of Health and Human Services, 42 C.F.R. §§59.8, 59.10 (1992) (suspended by 58 Fed. Reg. 7462 (1993); repealed by 58 Fed. Reg. 7455 (1993)). The "gag rule," imposed in 1988, was repealed by President Clinton on January 22, 1993. See 58 Fed. Reg. 7455 (1993). . . .

61. See Margaret A. Blanchard, The American Urge to Censor: Freedom of Expression Versus the Desire to Sanitize Society—From Anthony Comstock to 2 Live Crew, 33 Wm. & Mary L. Rev. 741, 766 (1992) (citing David M. Kennedy, Birth Control in America: The Career of Margaret Sanger 16 (1970)).

62. See also Salvail v. Nashua Bd. of Ed., 469 F. Supp. 1269, 1275–1276 (D.N.H. 1979) (holding that the removal of *Ms.* magazine from a high school library violated the First Amendment). Similarly, Carole Vance has predicted that if the Pornography Victims' Compensation Act were to become law, conservatives would attempt to make its major targets sexuality educators, sexologists, and HIV/AIDS educators. Vance, New Threat to Sexual Expression, *supra* note 24, at 21.

63. See Cass Clare McHugh, in Feminist Abortion Squall, Bigfoot Dworkin Stops the Press, N.Y. Observer, Oct. 26, 1992, at 1 ("That the radical anti-pornography crusader and novelist would interfere with the publishing of a book written by fellow travelers in the feminist movement—and yet not contact the authors to discuss her objections directly—strikes some women's rights advocates as, well, misogynist.").

64. See Tamar Lewin, Furor on Exhibit at Law School Splits Feminists, N.Y. Times, Nov. 13, 1992, at B16. . . .

65. Letter to the Editor, Civil Liberties, Spring/Summer 1991, at 4, from Gory Mongiovi, Ph.D., an economist who teaches at St. John's University.

66. Hamill, *supra* note 32, at 189.

67. See, e.g., Andrea Dworkin, Our Blood: Prophecies and Discourses on Sexual Politics 20 (1976): "Under patriarchy, no woman is safe to live her life, or to love, or to mother children. Under patriarchy, every woman is a victim, past, present and future. Under patriarchy, every woman's daughter is a victim, past, present, and future. Under patriarchy, every woman's son is her potential betrayer and also the inevitable rapist or exploiter of another woman." *Id.*

Sex, Sin, and Women's Liberation: Against Porn-Suppression

CARLIN MEYER

What's Porn Got to Do with It?. . .

IF PORN-SUPPRESSION reduced violence and aggression against women, thereby enhancing women's self-expression and power, it might arguably be a worthwhile effort, notwithstanding its harmful effects. Appealing as it may be to discover in pornography's vulgar phallocentrism the well-spring of male domination, porn simply is not that important.[1] Treating it as such merely deflects attention and inquiry from crucial economic, political, and social bases for sexual exploitation and inequality. The institutionalization of eroticized aggression against women takes place not merely through its depiction, but by locating and elaborating it in complex social structures. . . .

Imagery does not exist or gain persuasive power in a vacuum. Its power depends upon and is inseparable from the institutions and practices that give meaning to its depiction and generate the real-life effects of that which is depicted. Although advocates of porn-suppression call it a "practice" reflected and institutionalized in eroticized male violence against women, that violence is not an institution in the sense in which that term is normally used. . . .

Much has been written about the complex manner in which Western sexuality has been thoroughly institutionalized. The areas of religion, legal jurisprudence, science and technology, modern medicine, sports, military culture, and artistic and entertainment culture have all played a part. Each has institutionalized its viewpoints in daily practices as well as in its imagery.

Among the many institutions that eroticize aggression against women, sports and militarism surely play a far more prominent role than porn. Both became closely linked in the late nineteenth century to combating the "feminization" of American culture by stressing "manly virtues" such as competition, combativeness, physical aggression, and domination. . . .

Published originally in 72 *Texas Law Review* 1097 (1994). Copyright 1994 by the Texas Law Review Association. Reprinted by permission.

Sports: Male Bonding in Erotic Aggression

Sports has for more than a century been central to male education, entertainment, and bonding across and between generations, beginning in the earliest years and continuing throughout the lives of most males.[2] Organized in its modern form as an all-male enterprise in reaction to the late nineteenth-century fear of "feminization" and to the increasing penetration of women into previously male spheres of power, sports culture sought to inculcate in young males the values and attitudes that would prevent them from becoming "soft." "In promoting dominance and submission, in equating force and aggression with physical strength, modern sport naturalized the equation of maleness with power, thus legitimizing a challenged and faltering system of masculine domination.[3]

Beginning quite early in life, the vast majority of males engage in individual or team sports from which they "learn the dominant culture conceptions of what it means to be male."[4] . . .

And what does it teach men to value? It teaches them that winning is everything, and that to win, competitiveness and aggression are essential skills—skills that are effectively mobilized by fostering male bonding through emphasizing and vilifying its opposite, femininity. Men learn a "masculinity based upon status-seeking through successful athletic competition and through aggressive verbal sparring which is both homophobic and sexist."[5] Denigration of women and gay men is endemic; masculinity in sports depends on not being or appearing "feminine.". . .

Competitive success is the route to recognized masculine status; winning is everything, and to get to the top, aggression and violence are both necessary and acceptable. And females frequently become targets of such male ambitions through being made the objects of a variety of masculine aggressions: of sexual conquest and harassment aimed at "gaining status in the male peer group,"[6] of jokes and loudly recounted stories (whether real or fictionalized) of such "conquest[s],"[7] and of actual violence. . . .

Certainly, much sports imagery reinforces these practices. From the annual "swimsuit" edition of *Sports Illustrated,* to the blatantly sexist advertising that inevitably accompanies sports events,[8] to prime-time television's presentation of barely clothed, swaying cheerleaders at sports events, sports imagery epitomizes the view of women castigated by anti-porn feminists without displaying a single sexually explicit image. As with porn, however, the imagery's projection and reinforcement of the values it depicts is far more complex than simply direct promulgation and absorption. . . .

Yet, however complex may be the process by which sports culture affects men and women, it is surely far more significant and powerful both in constituting the relations between them, and in promoting male domination, aggression, and violence toward women than is porn.

Military Conquest of the Other: Erotic Aggression; Women as Enemies . . .

Manliness and masculinity have long been associated with military "virtues." Military culture teaches boys through toys and games,[9] through clothing, television and film, to admire and participate in a culture that glorifies violence and associates aggression against women with aggression against "the enemy." Boys learn that masculinity is personified by a culture that

> provides men with the perfect psychologic backdrop to give vent to their contempt for women. The very maleness of the military—the brute power of weaponry exclusive in their hands, the spiritual bonding of men at arms, the manly discipline of orders given and orders obeyed, the simple logic of the hierarchical command—confirms for men what they long suspect, that women are peripheral, irrelevant to the world that counts, passive spectators to the action in the center ring.[10]

Boys learn that women are not simply spectators, but fair game. Pressure in the military constantly to demonstrate masculinity through unhesitating and fearless physical aggression, its stress on unthinking adherence to authoritarian commands, and the emphasis on resolving even internal disputes through physical force and punishment, all contribute to a culture that fosters hostility to, domination of, and aggression against women. In 1990, the first Pentagon study of sexual harassment in the military concluded that more than a third of the women had been subject to abuse ranging from fondling to rape.[11] . . .

Prostitution, pornography, spousal abuse, and even rape are an integral part of military life in both Western and Eastern societies. Sex and violence are linked, both on and off the battlefield. . . . [R]ecent stories of the deliberate strategy of brutal rape by the Bosnian Serb military make the link between sex and violence in military life all too clear.[12] Off-base recreation is frequently sexual, and even military-sponsored recreation emphasizes sex.

Moreover, from time immemorial, war has been romanticized: its heroes, erotic figures; women, its spoils. Films . . . depict the way in which "the activities of breaking hearts and taking lives—that is, sexual domination and wartime aggression" are deeply intertwined, so that "[i]n fantasies of war, sexuality is manifested in violence, and violence carries an explosive sexual charge."[13] . . .

The Insignificance of Porn: Pop Culture Is More Insidious and More Prevalent than Porn . . .

Mass dissemination of the sexually explicit fare targeted by porn-suppressionists is a relatively recent phenomenon.[14] And while it may be that, as with most forms of popular culture, porn's consumption and profitability are increasing, porn is hardly as widely or frequently consumed as such mainstream material as romance novels, videos, comic books, teen magazines, or religious texts.

Surely the commonplace whispers of these other texts, which are so ordinary as to seem invisible, are more influential in fostering Western attitudes about sexuality than is the vocal vulgarity of porn. Modern society so bombards us with commercial imagery that it is part of our consciousness almost without noticing it. The female body, in particular, is the subject of this commercial imagery. Porn may be, as anti-advocates claim, an $8 billion industry,[15] but advertising generates $130 million annually, diet industry revenues have been put at $33 billion, "youth" cosmetics at $20 billion, and cosmetic surgery at $300 million.

Prime time television sitcoms, soaps, and serials . . . present women either as "selfless adjuncts to men" or as "witches, bitches, mothers and imps" whose sexuality is "potentially harmful or dangerous" or, sometimes, both.[16] Small wonder that several commentators have noted that the dominant portrayal of women in mainstream imagery differs little from that purveyed in soft-core porn.[17]

Suppression advocates argue that porn powerfully influences male attitudes toward women because it reaches boys early in life, when hormones are raging and ascension to manhood is in progress. But mainstream imagery reaches children even earlier, during the periods psychologists teach are most critical to identity and value formation. Boys and girls learn from Barbie dolls what they only years later see mimicked in porn pin-up calendars of "The Barbies"—that sexy women are unnaturally long-legged, smooth, full-breasted, and artificially free of blemishes or imperfections. They learn about brainless bimbos —a term never applied to males—from imagery ranging from television sitcoms to cartoons, comic, and Disney films long before most come into contact with porn. Boys, who constitute ninety percent of the video game audience, will have played hundreds of thousands of games in which females are altogether absent, or shown only as damsels in distress,[18] by the time they reach adolescence. Most will have read hundreds of comic books.[19] They will have had far fewer encounters with porn.

And even after they encounter porn, most boys (and girls) will spend far more time listening to popular music and watching music videos that portray a world in which "women are rarely shown other than as objects."[20] [T]hese works surely influence their vast and susceptible audiences more than *Hustler* photos, *Playboy* centerfolds, or even the most crass and violent porn. But to acknowledge the breadth of misogynistic imagery is to admit the futility of suppression as a strategy of reform. Moreover, culture rectification campaigns have been notoriously unsuccessful, as the explosion in porn, as well as rap, rock, and heavy metal music in Eastern Europe and the Russian republics attests.[21] Cultural critique makes sense; cultural suppression is not merely ineffectual, but dangerous. . .

The Insignificance of Porn: The Sounds of Silencing

. . . Those who favor suppression frequently credit porn with "silencing" women and argue that women cannot freely examine, explore, and redefine sexuality as long as its proliferation remains unchecked. Although women have been historically "silenced" in many ways, and sex and sexuality have been areas of particular inarticulateness for women, it is neither obvious that this process is deepening rather than declining, nor is there evidence that porn has contributed significantly to it.

According to porn-suppressionists, ubiquitous porn imagery silences women from full society participation by constantly reminding them that men see them as worthy only of domination and abuse and will abuse them in the ways shown in pornography.[22] Some women may indeed be inhibited from fully expressing themselves because of male aggression; they may refrain from saying what they please in relationships and workplaces where men hold power over [them]; from speaking their minds in class-rooms and on streets for fear of retribution; from acting in any way that might be in-terpreted as sexual; or even from going out alone in public, especially "after hours," thereby "inviting" abuse and rape.

However, the silencing of women by violence and threats of violence cannot be at-tributed to porn. Men are impelled to violence from anger at and fear of matriarchal rule (and of mothers' scorn and punishment); from fury at women for imposing on them a moral straitjacket while simultaneously tempting them to sin; from denigra-tion and disdain for women's purported lack of intelligence and capacity; from the desire for conquest and control—whether of the Father's possessions, the Mother's domain, or the Other, the Enemy.[23] Indeed, the very sexual taboos that, I argue, are *fostered* by porn-suppression are probably more central to silencing women than is porn.

Moreover, the roots of silencing run far deeper. Women, like other historically op-pressed groups, lack both a language on which to express their experiences, as well as the tools to make those experiences that can be expressed heard and felt. Women self-censor because of profound, culturally-fostered beliefs that their views are unimpor-tant or will receive no audience. And on issues of sex and sexuality, women are silenced by fear of reprisals—not simply physical, but ostracism, loss of jobs and friends, and the like—for transgressing the permissible.

Yet women do not seem to be as silenced as anti-porn advocates claim: Across class, race, occupation, ethnicity, and geographic locale, women are speaking out and being listened to as never before. Advocates of suppression answer that porn is proliferating precisely because women's voices have begun to emerge, and porn is part of society's way of shutting women back up.[24] Though the evidence of backlash against women's changing roles and newly emergent power is plentiful,[25] and though porn prolifera-tion is very likely part of it, it is but a minor part and has not, so far, seemed to silence women. Indeed, "it is precisely since the 1970s, and the explosion of pornography in the West, that women have been most vociferously—and successfully—*objecting* to men's violence against them."[26]

Finally, the little evidence available seems to suggest that women in cultures where sexuality and its imagery are suppressed are far more silenced in every way than women in cultures where sexual discourse, including porn, is uninhibited.[27] . . .

In sum, porn simply is not the powerful force that anti-porn advocates imagine. It may often be sexist, vulgar, violent, and horrific. The wish to be rid of it is surely understandable. But there are no easy ways to be rid of imagery that portrays women in ways we might wish women not be portrayed—nor, especially, be treated—and suppressionist quick-fix strategies do more harm than good.

Conclusion

. . . How, then, do we change the vision of women reflected and institutionalized in Western culture? First and foremost, feminism needs to reassert its grounding in a critique of social, economic, and political forces that reaches far beyond the specifically sexual constitution and treatment of men and women and focuses as much on institutionalized practices as on cultural conditioning. Without doubt, the constitution of the sexual has played, and continues to play, an important role in creating the conditions and reality of women's—and, indeed, of other outcast groups'—oppression. But the deeply gendered ways of categorizing, thinking, and acting that undergird women's unequal status go far beyond the specifically sexual.

And while what bell hooks has called the "racialized pornographic imagination"[28] permeates—indeed, dominates—the entire cultural continuum from advertising to film, it is neither peculiar to porn nor influential apart from its embodiment in laws, institutions, and social practices. Anti-porn feminists not only accord too much power to porn, but too much to the cultural realm altogether.

Yet culture is important, and feminists have not been shy about taking it on. But how best to do so? For feminist porn-suppressionists, the answer is cultural cleansing. Since women do not control the media or the other institutions that foster misogynist conceptions, the best that can be done is to join the conservative call for governmental suppression of sexist sexual depiction.

But for literally thousands of writers, artists, filmmakers, scholars, and activists who have for decades been exploring the interstices of Western culture and using available tools of critique to "[m]ak[e] a space for the transgressive image, the outlaw rebel vision,"[29] the process of transformation, of "com[ing] to voice"[30] is rather more complex and demanding and is not furthered by sexual censorship. It begins with acknowledging the difficult dilemmas involved in re-imagining and recreating Western ways of seeing and looking.

As Margaret Marshment has trenchantly shown, no matter what critical stance feminists take, we risk misinterpretation, error, or marginalization.[31] Critiques and alternative portrayals that emphasize women's strong, active, and independent natures and that highlight the fact that women possess traits traditionally valued as masculine, risk suggesting that women are "just like" men and that these traits are more important than those associated with femininity. But to emphasize traditionally female roles, traits, and values is to risk reifying gender dichotomies in the opposite direction. . . . Yet feminists cannot allow our inevitable frustration over the difficulty of avoiding "having our ideas and fantasies reduced and manipulated—even travestied—by the underlying market forces"[32] to direct us into dead-end paths, especially those of sexual suppression. Rather, feminists must bring to the fore and demand a close look at female desire and sexuality—as it has been constructed, as well as the ways in which it may be biologically delimited.

Another important task is to break through the "wall of denial consumers of images construct so as not to face that the real world of image-making is political—that politics of domination inform the way the vast majority of images we consume are constructed and marketed."[33] "Fierce critical interrogation"[34] is necessary; and it must address not merely or even mainly the marginal, but must take on the mainstream, including Hollywood film and television, music video, romance literature, and advertising. Indeed, establishing a Feminist Board of Critics to rate mainstream film, music, and television—to give awards like the Oscars (to the least) or the Golden Fleeces (to the most) sexist, racist, homophobic, or class-stereotyped films, soap operas, sitcoms, and advertisements—could extend feminist analysis beyond the academic world and, if well promoted, do far more to create public discussion of sexist depiction than censorship strategies. Instead of blanket condemnation, the Board could offer alternative ratings by a variety of feminist critics to demonstrate that differences in point of view about culture exist even among like minds.

In addition, feminists should not only encourage mainstream film and television reviews to address issues of race, class, and gender consistently, but also seek to establish columns and television roundtables of our own.

Critique should continue to be leveled at sexual practices and imagery (including porn) that foster acceptance of phallocentric norms of masculinity and present disempowering conceptions of femininity and women's roles. But feminist critique must be careful to avoid simply replicating pervasive views about the inevitability of male sexual aggression and domination, views derived from nineteenth-century sexology's view of male sexuality as defined by the overpowering and unbridled male sex drive. We need to analyze and reform this ideology and the institutions which foster it, not replicate it. "If patriarchy fuses gender and sexuality, the analytic task of feminism is to take them apart,"[35] which requires not merely a critique of imagery, but basic institutional and social reform.

Feminists should especially target the places in which ideologies of masculinity are most centrally forged and practiced, and where the association between masculinity and abuse of women is earliest and most deeply inculcated. Sports is one such realm. . . . Similarly, feminists should challenge the norms of military masculinity—in Hollywood portrayal as well as in actual practice.

Moreover, it is essential to deconstruct the way in which "romance ideology" and the forms of its institutionalization in modern marriage are or can be disempowering to women. Although the romance ideology of contemporary film and fiction is often far more varied and complex than that exemplified by its Victorian and 1950s predecessors—and much of it has been updated to reflect changes in women's status and roles—all too often plots still end with female protagonists walking into the sunset with their magically encountered perfect loves or portray sinfully sexual women threatening the stability of monogamous marriages and families. Honest debate about the relation of pleasure to peril, passion to power, aversion to arousal, fascination to repugnance, and guilt to temptation is sorely lacking.

But because sexuality remains so complex and contested a realm, one so in flux, feminists should tread softly in invoking law to achieve reform in that sphere. Legal intervention should be sparingly used to achieve narrow, concrete goals in ways that do not grant to still largely male and conservative legislatures and courts broad power to delineate "good" sex from "bad." This is not to say that women should never use the legal system to redress sexual harms, but rather that feminists should be wary of using that system as a means by which to define those harms before arriving, if not at consensus, at least at a majoritarian progressive view after a full airing of the issue in feminist fora. Legislative hearings held in alliance with anti-sex conservatives are not the places within which to determine whether, for example, to create a civil harm for street whistling. Neither are they the place to determine whether it is rape, as MacKinnon suggests, whenever a woman "has sex and feels violated."[36] Legal definitions of sexual harm should be generated based on strong feminist agreement, forged among those who share common minimum goals concerning women's sexual freedom and reproductive control.[37]

Critique must also be accompanied by presentation and praise of alternative imagery—new scripts, stories, films, television programs, recordings and the like. This creation of alternative imagery should be complemented by efforts to open up television and other media to constituencies willing to present such imagery, as well as by efforts to increase government funding for alternative media. Inducing producers and publishers to make non-sexist music, film, and stories available—especially for children—is vital. Teachers and parents need to encourage and join with children to analyze and be critical of toys, programs, and advertising, and to enlist youth and the youth culture to engage in self-critique.

Critical interrogation is necessary not only to challenge dominant viewpoints, but also to imagine a future. As Annette Kuhn has written, "[F]eminist analysis of mainstream images of women . . . may . . . teach us to recognize inconsistencies and contradictions within dominant traditions of representation, to identify points of leverage for our own intervention: cracks and fissures through which may be captured glimpses of what might in other circumstances be possible. . . ."[38]

Some argue that feminist analysis and condemnation of porn has contributed mightily to the very critique I propose.[39] My objection is not to the deconstruction of the dominant messages of porn; that work is important and was well underway before legal suppression took center stage. But with its focus on explicit (and deviant) sex, the suppression strategy directs inquiry away from the subtleties of cultural construction and feminist analysis. In the words of Carol Smart, "The aim of 'fitting' feminist ideas on pornography into a legal framework that might be 'workable' (in narrow legal terms) or politically 'acceptable,' means that many of the subtle insights and complexities of feminist analysis are necessarily lost."[40] Moreover, it has deflected inquiry into dead-end investigation of the degree to which porn images directly spawn violent acts against women and has transformed debate into questions of First Amendment doctrine—all at the expense of widening the reach of feminist insight concerning sexuality.[41] Indeed, . . . the underlying ideology of feminist porn-suppression undermines those insights, by merging with and fostering traditional, mainstream conservative ideas about sexuality.

Because the feminist porn-suppression effort is anchored in a theory which recognizes no cracks or fissures, it can imagine only instant revolutionary transformation—which is impossible as long as women lack sufficient media/cultural power—or elimination of the supposedly worst imagery. Sufficient power to accomplish the latter can perhaps be mustered by alliance with conservatives who favor general sexual repression. Unfortunately, the latter strategy fosters sexual concern of women and does little to reform patriarchal conceptions of masculinity or Western culture's ways of looking at women.

Just as societal lust, lasciviousness, and immorality could not be eliminated by the famous "bruciamenti" of 1496 in which music, books, painting, sculpture, and even lutes were burned,[42] we cannot today eradicate pornographic ways of looking and seeing by enjoining production of "bad" images. Much as we might wish it otherwise, there simply is no quick fix by which Western erotica can be reformed or reconstituted.

Notes

1. . . . I assume that a significant dent could be made in the dissemination and consumption of porn via suppression, and I ask whether it would make a similarly significant dent in gender discrimination. It is clear, however, that the suppression effort has not made and is unlikely ever to make a dent in pornography's production and dissemination.

2. In required gym classes and in extra-curricular activities, success at aggressive sports is an immediate source of attention and status for young males. As entertainment, it is central to lifetime bonding with other boys and with fathers: from viewing and playing sports; to collecting sports cards, magazines, and jokes; to citing statistics and making sports analogies. See generally Myriam Miedzian, Boys Will Be Boys: Breaking the Link Between Masculinity and Violence 177–206 (1991). . . .

3. Michael A. Messner, Power At Play: Sports and the Problem of Masculinity 15 (1992). . . .

4. *Id.* at 19.

5. *Id.* at 37.

6. *Id.* at 97. . . .

7. *Id.* at 97–98.

8. Beer ads, which frequently appear in conjunction with sporting events, are notorious for their sexism; some have even led to litigation alleging that they contribute to workplace sexual harassment. See Additional Sexual Harassment Suits Filed Against the Stroh Brewery Co., 1993 Daily Lab. Rep. (BNA), 230, at A8 (Jan. 29, 1992) (reporting on lawsuits against Stroh alleging that its advertising promotional materials featuring the "Swedish bikini team" created a hostile work environment). . . . For a critique of the Stroh Brewery cases, see Nadine Strossen, Regulating Workplace Sexual Harassment and Upholding the First Amendment—Avoiding a Collision, 37 Vill. L. Rev. 757–77 (1992) arguing that the claims against Stroh related to advertising content should fail because the ads are protected by the First Amendment).

9. See Miedzian, *supra* note 2, at 161–169 (discussing "violence toys" that encourage and direct childhood play and describing their pervasive effect on boyhood development); Divina Paredes-Japa, Waging War on Violent Toys, Newsday, Dec. 23, 1991, at 21 (reporting on the efforts by activists to educate parents about the dangers of war toys). In addition, video war games, which rarely picture women as other than damsels in distress, are common. Ninety percent of video game players are male. Miedzian, *supra* note 2, at 263.

10. Susan Brownmiller, Against Our Will: Men, Women and Rape 32 (1975). Notably, Brownmiller uses a sports metaphor. See Lynne Segal, Slow Motion: Changing Masculinities, Changing Men 18 (1990) (noting that army training often revolves around intensifying the opposition between males and females, "thereby cementing the prevalent cultural links between virility, sexuality and aggressiveness").

11. See Melanie Martindale, Sexual Harassment in the Military: 1988 xii–xiv (Sept. 1990) (unpublished report) (summarizing the results of a survey by the Department of Defense of all active members of the military).

12. See John F. Burns, Bosnia War Crime Trial Hears Serb's Confession, N.Y. Times, Mar. 14, 1993, §1, at 10. . . .

13. Tania Modleski, Feminism Without Women, Culture and Criticism in a "Postfeminist" Age 62 (1991). . . .

14. Although sexually explicit depiction has a long history in virtually every culture, pornography, like all "culture," was elite fare until relatively recently. See, e.g., Linda Williams, Hard Core: Power, Pleasure and the "Frenzy of the Visible" 28 (1989) (noting that until recently most pornographic images have been distributed only underground). . . .

Not until the 18th and 19th centuries did mass dissemination begin to occur, and today's porn "explosion" did not begin until *Playboy* began publishing in 1955. Since then, improving printing, copying, film, video, and computer technology, as well as changes in societal views of morality and decency reflected in decreased legal enforcement, have opened up the mass market in sexual representations. . . .

15. Catharine A. MacKinnon, Feminism Unmodified: Discourses on Life and Law 179 (1987).

16. Diane M. Meehan, Ladies of the Evening: Women Characters of Prime-Time Television 113, 131 (1983). . . .

17. Lisa Steele, A Capital Idea: Gendering in the Mass Media, in Varda Burstyn ed., Women Against Censorship 58 (1985) ("[I]mages of women that exist within hard and soft-core porn are but one part of th[e] process of representation—a process that is more characterized by continuity between the various sectors—that is, television programming, advertising, mass-circulation porn publications and so on—than it is by discord."). The porn-suppression effort, by treating pornography as segregable from other imagery, suggests that it is uniquely problematic; see also Daniel Linz & Neil Malamuth, Communications Concepts 5: Pornography 51 (1993) (describing a study which found that "mass media depictions that are not sexually explicit may also increase acceptance of violence against women") (citing Neil M. Malamuth & James V. P. Check, The Effects of Mass Media Exposure on Acceptance of Violence Against Women: A Field Experiment, 15 J. Res. Personality 436 (1981)).

18. Jon Katz, The War on Children's Culture, N.Y. Times, Aug. 4, 1991, §2, at 7, 15 (noting that in the popular Teen-Age Mutant Ninja Turtles cartoon, the only female character is constantly being rescued by the male heroes).

19. A recent survey showed that 84% of comics were purchased by males. Julie Stuempfig, State of the Industry: Who Buys Comic Books? in Comics Buyer's Guide 44 (1993). Comic books were themselves the targets of 1950s censors because of their (for that time) explicit sex and violence. See Note, Regulation of Comic Books, 68 Harv. L. Rev. 489, 506 (1955) (advocating the voluntary adoption of self-limiting measures by the comic book industry in order to "eliminate crime, horror, and sex comic books"). . . .

20. William A. Davis, MTV vs. the Professor: Music Service Challenges UMass Teacher's Use of Videos to Dissect Sexism, Boston Globe, May 17, 1991, at 29 (quoting University of Massachusetts professor Sut Jhally). Jhally's video made from clips of 165 rock videos suggests a view of women little different from that purveyed in much porn. . . .

21. See Nomi Morris, Eastern Europeans Wallow in a New Sexual Freedom, S.F. Chron., June 27, 1991, at A15 (describing the boom in pornography sweeping the former Communist states of Europe and Russia). . . .

22. See MacKinnon, *supra* note 15, at 140, 153, 156 ("Pornography terrorizes women into silence. . . . [P]ornography freely enslaves women's minds and bodies inseparably, normalizing the terror that enforces silence from women's point of view.").

23. See Sander L. Gilman, Difference and Pathology. Stereotypes of Sexuality, Race, and Madness 107 (1985). ("The 'white *man's* burden,' his sexuality and its control is displaced into the need to control the sexuality of the Other, the Other as sexualized female" (emphasis in original).)

24. Cf. MacKinnon, *supra* note 15, at 171–174 (arguing that pornography reinforces male dominance by depicting women as objects incapable of speech and desiring subjugation).

25. See Barbara Ehrenreich, The Hearts of Men: American Dreams and the Flight from Commitment 146–147 (1983) (commenting on the male rebellion against the feminist movement and noting that its primary impact concerns male abandonment of his duty to family); Susan Faludi, Backlash: The Undeclared War Against American Women 46–72, 454–460 (1991) (describing the origins and effects of the backlash against the feminist movement).

26. Segal, *supra* note 10, at 227. Segal points out that "in the staid and censorious fifties where there was little explicit pornography openly available, there was no public outcry against wife-beating, marital rape, [or] child abuse." *Id.* at 227–228.

27. See *id.* at 228 (noting that in many parts of the world, women's suppression is based on class, race, and patterns of dominance rather than on the availability of pornography); Kim Edwards, In Rooms of Women, in Laurence Goldstein ed., The Female Body: Figures, Styles, Speculations 142–144 (1991) (describing Muslim Malaysia as far more silencing than pornography-prone Japan).

28. bell hooks, Black Looks: Race and Representation 72 (1992).

29. *Id.* at 4.

30. *Id.* at 80.

31. Margaret Marshment, Substantial Women, in Lorraine Gamman & Margaret Marshment eds., The Female Gaze: Women as Viewers of Popular Culture 27, 27–28 (1989).

32. Maggie Anwell, Lolita Meets the Werewolf, in The Female Gaze, *supra* note 31, at 76.

33. hooks, *supra* note 28, at 5. . . .

34. *Id.*

35. Carole S. Vance & Ann B. Snitow, Toward a Conversation Abut Sex in Feminism, 10 Signs 131 (1984).

36. Katie Roiphe, Date Rape's Other Victim, N.Y. Times, June 13, 1993 (Magazine) at 30.

37. Cf. Constance L. Hays, If That Man Is Following Her, Connecticut Is Going to Follow Him, N.Y. Times, June 5, 1992, at B1 (describing stalking laws passed in several states with the organized support of entertainment figures and victim-support groups). . . .

38. Annette Kuhn, The Power of the Image: Essays on Representation and Sexuality 10 (1985).

39. "We could argue that since pornography *symbolizes* men's power over women . . . , women's attacks on it *symbolize* women's resistance to men's power over them." Segal, *supra* note 10, at 229 (emphasis in original). But, as Segal notes, symbolic resistance is one thing when it richly deconstructs imagery, and quite another when it ideologically and politically allies with conservatism in furthering "state control over all representations of sexuality." *Id.* . . .

40. Carol Smart, Feminism and the Power of Law 115 (1989).

41. See *id.* (pointing out that "feminist work on pornography becomes increasingly collapsed into traditional discussions of how sex depraves or how representations of violence cause actual violence").

42. See David Freedberg, The Power of Images: Studies in the History and Theory of Response 348 (1989).

The Difference in Women's Hedonic Lives: A Phenomenological Critique of Feminist Legal Theory

ROBIN L. WEST

WOMEN'S SUBJECTIVE, hedonic lives are different from men's. The quality of our suffering is different from that of men's, as is the nature of our joy. Furthermore, and of more direct concern to feminist lawyers, the quality of pain and pleasure enjoyed or suffered by the two genders is different: women suffer more than men. The two points are related. One reason that women suffer more than men is that women often find painful the same objective event or condition that men find pleasurable. The introduction of oxymorons in our vocabulary, wrought by feminist victories, evidences this difference in women's and men's hedonic lives. The phrases "date-rape," for example and "sexual harassment," capture these different subjective experiences of shared social realities: For the man, the office pass was sex (and pleasurable), for the woman, it was harassment (and painful); for the man the evening was a date—perhaps not pleasant, but certainly not frightening—for the woman, it was a rape and very scary indeed. Similarly, a man may experience as at worst offensive, and at best stimulating, that which a woman finds debilitating, dehumanizing or even life-threatening. Pornographic depictions of women which facilitate by legitimating the violent brutalization of our bodies are obvious examples. Finally, many men are simply oblivious—they do not experience at all—external conditions which for women are painful, frightening, stunting, torturous and pervasive—including domestic violence in the home, sexual assault on the street, and sexual harassment in the workplace and school.

Feminists generally agree—it should go without saying—that women suffer in ways which men do not, and that the gender-specific suffering that women endure is routinely ignored or trivialized in the larger (male) legal culture. Just as women's work is not recognized or compensated by the market culture, women's injuries are often not recognized or compensated *as injuries* by the legal culture. The dismissal of women's gender-specific suffering comes in various forms, but the outcome is always the same: women's suffering for one reason or another is outside the scope of legal redress. Thus, women's distinctive, gender-specific injuries are now or have in the recent past been variously dismissed as trivial (sexual harassment on the street); consensual (sexual ha-

3 Wisc. Women's L.J. 81 (1987).

rassment on the job); humorous (non-violent marital rape); participatory, subconsciously wanted, or self-induced (father/daughter incest); natural or biological, and therefore inevitable (childbirth); sporadic, and conceptually continuous with gender-neutral pain (rape, viewed as a crime of violence); deserved or private (domestic violence); non-existent (pornography); incomprehensible (unpleasant and unwanted consensual sex) or legally predetermined (marital rape, in states with the marital exemption).

It is not so clear, though, *why* women's suffering is so pervasively dismissed or trivialized by legal culture, or more importantly what to do about it. . . .

[I]t would seem that feminist legal theorists should be hard at work providing rich descriptions of women's subjective, hedonic lives, particularly the pain in those lives, and more particularly the pain in our lives which is different. And *yet we aren't.* . . . [F]eminist legal theorists, I believe, are dangerously neglecting the phenomenological, subjective, and hedonic distinctiveness of women's lives, and the relevance of this aspect of our difference to legal criticism. I can think of four possible reasons for this neglect.

The first reason is linguistic. . . . Our language is inadequate to the task. As women become more powerful, this linguistic barrier is eased: we now possess, for example, the legal and social labels that at least identify some of our experiences as injurious, such as "sexual harassment" and "date-rape." But we still lack the descriptive vocabulary necessary to convey the quality of the pain we sustain by virtue of these experiences. The second reason is psychological. Before we can convince others of the seriousness of the injuries we sustain, we must first convince ourselves, and so long as others are unconvinced, to some extent, we will be as well. . . . The third and underlying problem is political. The inadequacy of language and the problem of "false consciousness" are but reflections of what is surely the core obstacle . . . an unwilling and resisting audience. When we struggle to find the words to describe the pain (or pleasure) in our lives, and the effort is rewarded with dismissal and trivialization, the fully human response is to silence ourselves.

However, . . . the main reason . . . and the subject of this article [is] the emerging logic of feminist legal theory. . . . Unlike feminist political theorists, feminist legal theorists have followed largely derivative normative strategies.[1] That is, feminist legal theorists have adopted *non-feminist* normative models of legal criticism, and then applied those models to women's problems. . . .

[L]iberal-legal feminist theorists—true to their liberalism—want women to have more choices, and . . . *radical-legal* feminist theorists—true to their radicalism—want women to have more power. Both models direct our critical attention *outward*—liberalism to the number of choices we have, radicalism to the amount of power. Neither model . . . of feminist legal criticism . . . posits subjective happiness as the direct goal of legal reform, or subjective suffering as the direct evil to be eradicated. Neither model directs our critical attention *inward.* . . .

The cost *to women* of feminist legal theorists' endorsement of the anti-phenomenological methodology[2] and anti-hedonic norms of the models they endorse is very high. It renders liberal and radical feminist legal theorists peculiarly uncritical—*as feminists*—of the visions of the human and thus of the normative assumptions of the models for legal criticism which they have respectively embraced. The anti-phe-nomenological methodology of radicalism and liberalism rule out the only inquiry which could conceivably determine the value *to women* of the model itself, and that is whether the description of the human which each model embraces is true of women. Thus, liberal feminists fail to ask—*by virtue of the intrinsic commitments of liberalism*—whether the liberal conception of the phenomenology of choice is true of *women's* experience. As a result liberal feminist legal theorists cannot even ask the question which as feminists they should start with, and that is whether the liberalism they embrace will be of any value to women. Radical feminists fail to ask—*by virtue of the intrinsic commitments of radicalism*—whether the radical commitment to the ideal of equality resonates with *women's* felt desires. As a result, radical feminist legal theorists cannot even ask the question which as feminists they should start with, and that is whether the radical ideal of equality is desirable *for women*. It is only by focusing directly on what both models definitionally exclude—our phenomenological, hedonic experience—that we will be able to ask these questions. And it is only by asking these questions that we will determine the limits of liberal and radical models of legal criticism and reform, and it is only by understanding those limits that we will understand where a truly feminist model of legal criticism must begin. . . .

I. Liberal Feminism: Consent, Autonomy and the Giving Self

Perhaps the most widely held normative commitment of mainstream liberal legal theorists is that individuals should be free to choose their own style of life, and to exercise that freedom of choice in as many spheres as possible—economic, political and personal. . . . Individual freedom is the ideal toward which law and legal reform ought to press, and coercion or restraint on freedom is the evil.

The contribution of feminist liberal legalism has been to extend the umbrella of this normative vision to women as well as men. The liberal legal feminist insists that the depiction of the human embraced by liberal legalism—which I will sometimes refer to as the "liberal self"—is also true of women, and that therefore the relationship of the state to the individual must be the same for both women and men. [W]omen should be equally free to choose their own life plans, and women should be equally entitled to the respect from the state that that freedom requires.

The liberal feminist legal strategy for dealing with women's suffering is directly entailed by her liberalism. Women, like men, consent to that which will minimize their own suffering and maximize their own felt happiness. Therefore, the way to deal with women's suffering is to increase women's sphere of consensual freedom. What we should do with law, then, is to insure that women's sphere of consensual freedom is as large as possible, or at least as large as men's. Thus, the liberal feminist's central jurisprudential commitment tracks the liberal's: a law is a good law if it increases the freedom of women to enter into consensual transactions or if it equalizes that freedom with that enjoyed by men. A law is a bad law if it decreases that freedom.

Liberal feminist legal theory carries with it the same problems which now plague liberal legalism, but multiplied. Modern liberal legal feminists, like modern liberals generally, have failed to examine the essentially descriptive claims about the human being that underlie their normative model. The liberal claim that human beings consent to transactions in order to maximize their welfare may be false. If it is, then the liberal claim that social value is created through facilitating choice will be false as well. But furthermore, *women* may be "different" in precisely the way which would render the empirical assumptions regarding human motivation which underlie the liberal's commitment to the ethics of consent *more false for women than for men*. Thus, it may be that women generally *don't* consent to changes *so as* to increase our own pleasures or satisfy our own desires. It may be that women consent to changes so as to increase the pleasure or satisfy the desires of *others*. The descriptive account of the phenomenology of choice that underlies the liberal's conceptual defense of the moral primacy of consent may be wildly at odds with the way women phenomenologically experience the act of consent. If it is—if women "consent" to transactions not to increase our own welfare, but to increase the welfare of others—if women are "different" in this psychological way—then the liberal's ethic of consent, with its presumption of an essentially selfish human (male) actor and an essentially selfish consensual act, when even-handedly applied to both genders, will have disastrous implications for women. For if women consent to changes so as to increase the happiness of others rather than to increase our own happiness, then the ethic of consent, applied even-handedly, may indeed increase the amount of happiness in the world, but women will not be the beneficiaries.

And indeed, the liberal ethic of consent does, oftentimes, have less than happy consequences for women. The magnitude of the disservice should be obvious to anyone who can resist the staggeringly seductive liberal urge to imply an increase in subjective happiness from the objective act of consent. The rather inescapable fact is that much of the misery women endure is fully "consensual." That is, much of women's suffering is a product of a state of being which was *itself* brought into being through a transaction to which women unquestionably tendered consent. A woman's experience of marital sexuality, for example, may range from boring to irritating to invasive to intensely painful. Similarly, a female employee may experience the sexual advances of an employer as degrading. But the fact is that neither the wife nor the employee was brought to the altar in shackles or place of employment in chains. Put affirmatively, the conditions which create our misery—unwanted pregnancies, violent and abusive marriages, sexual harassment on the job —are often traceable to acts of consent. Women—somewhat uniquely—consent to their misery. An ethical standard which ties value to the act of consent by presumptively assuming that people consent to their circumstances so as to bring about their own happiness—and by so doing thereby create value—leaves these miserable consensual relationships beyond criticism. . . .

A. A Phenomenological Critique of Liberal Feminism

[M]any women, much of the time, consent to transactions, changes, or situations in the world so as to satisfy not their own desires or to maximize their own pleasure, as liberal legalism and liberal legal feminism both presume, but to maximize the pleasure and satiate the desires of others. [T]hey do so by virtue of conditions which only women experience. I will sometimes call the cluster of "other-regarding," other-pleasing motivations that rule these women's actions the "giving self," so as to distinguish it from the "liberal self": the cluster of self-regarding "rational" motivations presumed by liberal legalism. Thus my descriptive claim is that many women much of the time are giving selves rather than liberal selves. . . .

I believe that women become giving rather than liberal selves for a range of reasons—including our (biological) pregnability and our (social) training for our role as primary caretakers. [O]ne causal hypothesis, which (I think) has great explanatory force . . . is this: women's lives are dangerous, and it is the acquisitive and potentially violent nature of male sexuality which is the cause of the danger. A fully justified fear of acquisitive and violent male sexuality consequently permeates many women's—perhaps all women's —sexual and emotional self-definition. Women respond to this fear by *reconstituting* themselves in a way that controls the danger and suppresses the fear. . . .

The danger, and hence the fear, that women live with is very hard for others (men) to acknowledge or understand for two reasons. First, both the objective danger and the subjective fear are "different." The danger and the endangered fear are pervasive rather than sporadic conditions of our lives. There is a world of difference between the threat of sporadic violence (with which men are imminently familiar, from barroom brawls to wars), and hence sporadic fear, and a threat of *pervasive* violence, and hence *definitional* fear. One responds to sporadic fear and the threat of sporadic violence by changing one's behavior. One moves to a safer neighborhood, one fights back, one runs away, one cowers, or whatever, but one knows that the barroom brawl, the mugging, or the war will be over, and that when it is over, the state of normalcy—safety—will return. By contrast, one responds to pervasive fear and pervasive threat not by changing one's behavior, but by *re-defining oneself.* Women cannot eliminate the danger our sexuality poses by moving to a safer neighborhood, any more than blacks can respond to the danger their color poses by moving to a safer race. Nor will the danger cease when the war ends. We respond to the pervasive threat of violent and acquisitive male sexuality instead by changing ourselves, rather than respond to the conditions which cause it.

The danger, the violence, and the fear with which women live and which informs our self-definition are invisible, which is the second reason they are misunderstood. They are not a part of men's world, externally or internally. [M]en, unlike women, do not experience the fear of violent sexuality as a part of their self-definition. . . . Furthermore, women's definitional fear is not a part of their external world. . . . Left and liberal men do not see women shake with fear. They do not see women getting harassed on the street; when men accompany women, as all women know, harassment stops. For the same reason, they do not see women sexually harassed at work. They do not see women battered in the home. They do not see women being raped, by strangers, dates or husbands. They do not see women violated, abused and afraid. To these men, violence against women, the pain women feel as a result of it, and the fear of its recurrence, are invisible. It is not surprising that the claim that women's lives are ruled by fear is heard by these men as wildly implausible. . . .

How does a pervasive and largely invisible danger, and an equally pervasive and invisible fear, affect women's lives? Women cannot, and do not live in a state of constant fear of male sexual violence any more than workers can live in a state of constant fear of material deprivation. One way (there are others) that women control the danger—and thus suppress the fear—is by redefining themselves as "giving selves." Most simply, a woman will define herself as a "giving self" so that she will not be violated. She defines herself as a being who "gives" sex, so that she will not become a being *from whom sex is taken.* In a deep sense (too deep: she tends to forget it), this transformation is consensual: she "consents" to being a "giving self"—the dependent party in a comparatively protective relationship—for self-regarding liberal reasons; she consents in order to control the danger both inside and outside of the relationship, and in order to suppress the fear that danger engenders. Once redefined, however, and once within those institutions that support the definition, she becomes a person who gives her consent *so as to ensure the other's happiness* (not her own), so as to satiate the *other's* desires (not her own), so as to promote the *other's* well-being (not her own), and ultimately *so as to obey the other's commands.* In other words, she embraces a self-definition and a motive for acting which is the direct antithesis of the internal motivation life presupposed by liberalism. . . .

I have no interest in arguing that all women are giving selves all of the time. I want to suggest . . . that enough women have lived with enough fear and danger in their lives as to justify the inference that significant numbers of women have defined themselves in a way that undercuts the commitment to the ethical primacy of consent which underlies liberal feminist legal theory. . . .

. . . A "liberal feminism" would be truer to not only the guiding historical strengths of liberalism but also the goals of feminism if it would aim to eradicate the fear that presently dominates women's choices, rather than merely celebrating in the name of formal equality whatever choices we presently make. The stunted self-definitions which women embrace today are at least in part a reaction to fear: the fear we have learned first hand from the violence in our lives, and the fear we have been taught to harbor. Both feminism and liberalism have been at their best when they have attacked the multiple dangers that rule people's lives. If we could get rid of the danger, we could get rid of the fear; without the fear, our choices would, I have no doubt, take on great meaning. When we are free of fear, we will indeed be strengthened rather than weakened by the "voluntary transactions" which we enter. When we are free of fear we will be truly autonomous. Then our "giving selves"—if we choose to be such—will be something to admire rather than disparage. For only then will our generosity, our charity, and our communitarian instincts be true to ourselves as well as nurturant of the needs of others.

II. Radical Feminism and the Ethical Primacy of Power and Equality

Radical feminist legal theory begins with a description of women which is diametrically opposed to that embraced by liberal feminists. Liberal feminists assume a definitional *equality*—a "sameness"—between the female and male experience of consensual choice, and then argue that the legal system should respect that fundamental, empirical equality. In sharp contrast, radical feminists assume a definitional *in*equality of women—women are *definitionally* the disempowered group—and urge the legal system to eradicate that disempowerment and thereby make women what they presently are not, and that is equal. Radical feminism thus begins with a denial of the liberal feminist's starting assumption. Women and men are *not* equally autonomous individuals. Women, unlike men, live in a world with two sovereigns—the state, and men—and this is true not just some of the time but all of time. Women, unlike men, are definitionally submissive twice over; once vis-a-vis the state, and once vis-a-vis the superior power of men. A legal regime which ignores this central reality will simply perpetuate the fundamental, underlying inequality.

The cause of women's disempowerment, as well as its effect, is the expropriation of our sexuality. Women are the group, in Catharine MacKinnon's phase, "from whom sexuality is expropriated," in the same sense that workers are, definitionally, the group from whom labor is expropriated. . . . Women *as women* suffer the threat of acquisitive and potentially violent male sexuality. The threat of male violence and violent sexuality both defines the class *woman* and causes her disempowerment and the expropriation of her sexuality, just as the threat of starvation and material deprivation both defines the worker, and causes his disempowerment and the expropriation of his labor.

This much, radical feminist legal theory shares with radical feminism. . . . Where radical feminist legal theory has departed from radical feminism, I believe, is in the normative argument it draws from the insight that women are, definitionally, the group from whom sexuality is expropriated. The argument, I believe, owes more to radical legalism than to radical feminism. The argument has three steps.

First, radical feminist legal theory, like radical legalism, begins with a highly particularized although largely implicit description of the human being. People are, in short, assumed to be such that there exists a correlation between objectively equal distributions of power—including sexual power—and subjectively happy and good lives. Domination makes us evil and submission makes us miserable; substantive equality will make us both moral and happy; and both claims are true because of, and by reference to, this conception of our essential human nature. Radical legal theorists, including radical feminist legal theorists, are as committed to the equation of objective, substantive equality and subjective well being, and the view of our nature on which it rests, as the liberal legal theorist is committed to the equation of objective consent and subjective happiness.

Second, both radical legalism and radical feminist legalism draw from this depiction of the human being the normative inference that it is the imbalance of power which facilitates expropriation (of work for the radical legalist, of sex for the radical feminist legalist), rather than the expropriation itself, which is *definitionally* bad, and then the further inference that it is definitionally bad *whether or not the expropriation it facilitates is experientially felt as painful*. The strategic consequence immediately follows: radical legal reform should aim to eradicate hierarchy and thereby attain a substantively equal social world. Thus we should oppose not what makes us miserable—the violent expropriation of our work or our sexuality—but the hierarchy of power which facilitates it, for by doing so we will better target the true cause of our misery. We should support not what makes us happy, but what makes us substantively equal, because by doing so we will invariably further our true interest, even if not our felt pleasure. Thus, radical feminist legal theory shares with general radical legal thought a refusal to ground its opposition to expropriation (whether of sex or work) in the subjective suffering of the disempowered which such expropriation entails. Instead, for both groups expropriation must be opposed because it is symptomatic of the true cause of our misery—our material or sexual disempowerment, respectively—reflecting in turn our relative material or sexual inequality. The expropriation which the disempowered suffer is regarded by the radical as *bad,* but *not* because the expropriation has been shown to be painful, but instead because it is symptomatic of a larger violation of our essential nature, *and hence of our inherent ideal.*

Finally, radical feminist legal theorists share with radical legalists a methodological insistence that the correlation between objective equality and subjective well-being is foundational and definitional; it is therefore *not* something that can be discredited by counter-example. Both groups of theorists accordingly refuse to credit the *phenomenological* evidence that the essentially descriptive claims that underlie the normative commitment to substantive equality may be false.[3] Thus, to radical legalists generally, and to radical feminist legalists in particular, the extent to which the disempowered desire anything other than their own empowerment, and anything at odds with an equalitarian idea, is the extent to which the disempowered are victims of false consciousness. Phenomenological reports by the disempowered of pleasure and desire that counter the radical correlation of equality and subjective well-being thus reinforce, rather than cast in doubt, the radical's definitional assumptions. They reflect the permeating influence of our objective condition, not the limit, imposed by subjective pleasure and desire, of the normative ideal.

The striking political contribution of radical *feminist* legal theory has been to extend the umbrella of the normative argument of radical legalism to include women as well as men, and thus to address hierarchies of gender as well as hierarchies dictated by class and race. If hierarchy is bad, then hierarchies and sexual hierarchies according to sex and gender are bad; if disempowerment is a prescription for misery, then women's disempowerment is a prescription for misery; and if expropriation is bad, then expropriation of our sexuality is bad. The radical feminist legalist's commitment to gender equality stems from her empirical insistence that in the only respect which should be of concern to radical legalists, women and men are the same: women, like men, *suffer* from relative disempowerment and inequality, and will therefore benefit from empowerment and equality. . . . The legal strategy is directly entailed. . . . What we should do with law, then, if we mean to address the problem of women's suffering, is disable the objective hierarchies of gender that cause it. . . .

The inclusion of women under the radical legalist's normative umbrella is a great triumph, but it is costly: the adoption of radical legalist methodology by feminist legal theorists has also occasioned a damaging methodological divide between radical feminism and radical feminist legalism. Radical feminist legal theorists, true to their radicalism, refuse to consider whether or not the definitional implication it assumes between objective equality and subjective well-being resonates with women's desires and pleasures, and hence whether the conception of the human on which that implication is based is true of *women*. The radical feminist legal theorist—to the extent that she is a radical—will—must deny that substantive equality in any sphere could ever be less than ideal or that empowerment of women could ever work to our disadvantage. Thus, to radical feminists, that women on occasion take pleasure in their own submissiveness, is simply a manifestation of their disempowered state, not a meaningful counter-example to the posited egalitarian ideal. As with radical legalists generally, the stated definition ideal must trump the experiential counter-report.

For feminists, this radical legalist methodology should raise serious warning signals. First, we should remember that the ideal and the description of "essential human nature" on which it rests is itself drawn from a male, if "left" intellectual tradition, and is therefore *not* an ideal we should readily assume will be true of *women*. The ideal, in other words, against which we are judging our own and each others' consciousness to be "false" may be an ideal which is true of men, but not women. But second, and perhaps more fundamentally, it is feminism's most crucial insight that *our experience* must be primary—and not to be trumped by posited ideals or definitions. . . .

A. A Hedonistic Phenomenological Critique of Radical Feminist Legal Theory

Radical feminist legal theorists' failure to credit phenomenological reports of conflict between egalitarian ideals and women's subjective, hedonic, felt pleasures is generally benign. . . . Over vast areas of our lives, there is no conflict between our desires, our felt pleasures, and radical feminist ideals.

In one area of our lives, however—namely our erotic lives—there has emerged a conflict between the radical feminist legal theorists' conception of an equalitarian ideal and women's subjective desire. The radical feminist's commitment to equality, and identification of the expropriation of our sexuality as the consequence of our relative disempowerment entails the normative conclusion that sexual inequality *itself* is what is politically undesirable.[4] Thus, male dominance and female submission in sexuality *is* the evil: they express as well as *are* women's substantive inequality. But women report—with increasing frequency and as often as not in consciousness-raising sessions—that equality *in sexuality* is not what we find pleasurable or desirable. Rather, the experience of dominance and submission that go with the controlled, but fantastic, "expropriation" of our sexuality is precisely what *is* sexually desirable, exciting and pleasurable—in fantasy for many; in reality for some. This creates a conflict between theory and method as well as between stated ideal and felt pleasure: what should we *do* when the consciousness that is raised in consciousness-raising finds pleasure in what is definitionally regarded as substantively undesirable—sexual submission, domination and erotic inequality? In the words of one prominent feminist: "how can you maintain that you desire freedom and equality, when fundamentally [what you desire is to be] a slave?"[5] The conflict between felt pleasure and stated ideal has become a dilemma for radical feminism, but it has created an unprecedented debacle for our very young radical feminist legal theory, and one which threatens to be fatal.

. . . Radical feminist legal theorists—distinctively, in feminist literature—respond to the conflict between political ideal and subjective, erotic pleasure by adamantly refusing to address it, and it is that refusal more than the dilemma itself which is threatening the survival of radical feminist legal theory. In the feminist legal literature two strategies of avoidance have emerged. The first—advocated by Andrea Dworkin and Catharine Mac-Kinnon—regards the undeniable reality of the pleasure many women find in the eroticization of controlled submission as simply an example—perhaps an example *par excellence*—of the false consciousness of the oppressed.[6] The desires reflected in fantasies of erotic domination are false definitionally—they are false because the object of desire is submission, and submission is precisely what is definitionally *un*desirable. The second strategy—advocated by Sylvia Law and Nan Hunter—constitutes in essence a retreat to liberal principles. Fantasies are private and beyond political analysis; the role of law should be to expand, not shrink, the options available to women, including the option, if freely chosen, of masochistic desire, fantasy, practice and pleasure.[7]

I will examine [next] the pornography debate which these two feminist responses have generated. Here, I want to focus on what the two factions share: *both positions, at critical theoretical junctures, abandon feminist practice.* As a result both positions definitionally exclude the very issue which should be of greatest concern to feminists, and that is the meaning and the value, to women, of the pleasure we take in our fantasies of eroticized submission. The MacKinnon position that the pleasure in erotic submission is "false" because sexual submission is that which is undesirable resolves by definitional fiat what should be resolved by experiential, particularized, contextualized investigation —and that is what these fantasies of eroticized submission mean, what their value is in our lives, and what they can tell us about the desirability as well as the nature of sexual equality and power. The Law/Hunter position that fantasies are free choices which— again definitionally—must like all other choices be respected, hides the same issues, but this time in the name of liberal tolerance rather than radical equalitarianism.

This abandonment by feminist legal theorists of the phenomenological realm of pleasure and desire is a function of legalism, not true feminism. It reflects the extent to which we have embraced the ideals of legalism—whether we regard those ideals as substantive equality, liberal tolerance, privacy or individual autonomy—rather than the methodology of feminism—careful attention to phenomenological narrative. It reflects the extent to which we have allowed liberal and radical norms drawn from nonfeminist traditions to become the criteria by which we judge the narratives of our lives that emerge from consciousness-raising, *instead of the other way around*. More than any other issue, the pleasure that we obtain from the eroticization of submission poses an indissoluble conflict—or exposes an indissoluble conflict—between feminist method and feminist-legalist ideals, whether that legalism is radical or liberal. Hiding this conflict under the rug—whether in the name of liberal tolerance or radical equality—does far more harm than the conflict itself could ever dream of inflicting.

1. EQUALITARIAN IDEALS AND EROTIC SUBMISSION

. . . The contours of the conflict between stated ideal and felt pleasure, and between method and theory with which radical feminism is now grappling, I believe, are starkly brought out in [Danish radical feminist Maria Marcus's] detailed, moving, and candid account of her own profoundly ambivalent reaction to *The Story of O.*[8] . . . Written pseudonymously in the mid-fifties, it is without question the unsurpassed, modern, masochistic text. It is a stunning piece of pornography. Marcus summarizes the plot thusly:

> Chateau Roissy is owned by a secret brotherhood, and there Rene abandons his lover to the inhabitants and their regime. Briefly, this aims to turn the women who come there into utter slaves, with the aid of force, whips and rape. These means are used according to carefully arranged and familiar rituals—performed sometimes by the gentlemen, sometimes by the servants—and in the course of a few weeks O has become what they wish her to be. She has learnt to obey the rules of the mansion, which are all concerned with her three orifices—never to close her mouth; always to be dressed so that she is freely accessible, including from behind. The three orifices are the only things of hers that are of importance, so they no longer belong to her, but only to the men. She may not use her mouth to speak with (except when asked to do so) and neither is she allowed to look on a man's face—she may not raise her eyes above the level of his genitals, her lord and master. . . .[9]

Marcus quickly alludes to the very general conflict between pleasure and democratic political ideal which she perceives to be at least in part the novel's subject-matter:

> O's compulsive submissiveness goes against all the ideas we live by in Western democracies, in which every human being is born free and equal and this freedom and equality must not be suppressed. *The Story of O* says the opposite, that some people, possibly all people, are born into inequality and bondage, and can only be happy by losing their false freedom and equality and giving themselves over to submissiveness and slavery.[10]

. . . Marcus does not simply condemn O and the society that created her. She has an intensely empathic and sexual response to *The Story of O.* . . .

> When I first read *The Story of O,* it filled me with a mixture of sexual excitement, horror, anxiety—and envy. I read it many times, each time with the same feel-

ings. But gradually, as I had the good fortune to plunge to some extent into act-ing out an "Imitation of O," my envy, anyhow, lessened, because on one [sic] imitates O with overstepping a boundary into a state which is not particularly enviable. But I must still say that Pauline Reage is right—the description is cor-rect and I understand O. I understand her pride in the weals from the whip. . . . He owns me. I'm worth owning. Look what he makes me put up with. Look how strong the man who loves me is. Look I'm valuable. I *exist.* I understand that O comes to feel an inner peace, strength, dignity, security and psychic energy in this particular way, an energy that is nothing like anything else I (O) know.[11]

The Story of O, Marcus concludes, is *the* text with which radical feminists must concern themselves, and the magnitude of female readers' responsive, empathic and erotic re-sponse to the text is the issue with which radical feminism must come to grips.

Radical feminists have responded, I believe, to the conflict between pleasure and ideal posed by the undeniable female eroticization of sexual submission in three char-acteristic ways. First, some feminists claim that there is no conflict between stated ideal and felt pleasure because feminist consciousness-raising—properly understood—has revealed the falsity of these pleasures. Thus there is no contradiction between feminist methodology—consciousness raising—and feminist goal—sexual equality. What the methodology reveals is that the pleasure had in sexual submission is false. . . .

The second response (which was, until very recently, the near-standard feminist re-sponse) is simply to abandon feminist methodology. One way of maintaining the ideals of freedom and equality is by abandoning whatever methodology brought you to the conclusion that you enjoy being a sexual slave. If that methodology is feminist con-sciousness-raising, then so much the worse for consciousness-raising. Thus, in her re-sponse to Pat Califia's defense of lesbian sado-masochism (that it is (1) consensual; (2) rebellious; and (3) threatened),[12] Jayne Eagerton abandons entirely the first person narrative voice which is the distinction of consciousness-raising as moral method and adopts instead an outsider's condemnatory voice. . . .[13]

The third possible response to the conflict between the pleasure we take in erotic domination and our equalitarian ideals is to put our ideals in abeyance—maybe they are what is false—and hold true to consciousness-raising. This is the position for which I will argue. First I want to comment on the two feminist responses which I think fail. . . .

[The first response, the dismissal of the desire for erotic submission and the plea-sure obtained from it, may be criticized as at odds with the methodology of conscious-ness-raising.] [T]he judgment that women's desires for erotic submission are "false" is typically made by reference to the content of those desires, not their source. [T]he de-sire is judged false not because it is determined to be *a lie*—not truly felt to be plea-surable but only reported as such—but solely because of its content, solely because it is a desire for sexual submission. And finally . . . the discovery of the falsity of these de-sires has not typically come from the women who have them, but almost always from the women who do not. . . . This truly is a profound departure from feminist method-ology which is also truly offensive—consciousness-raising is not about the imposition of judgments of truth or falsity on the desires of others.

I do not believe that on the basis of a truly feminist consciousness-raising methodology these desires would inevitably be discovered to be false. First, they do not ring of the "giving self." The women who have desires for, construct fantasies of, and take pleasure in erotic submission are rather clearly expressing desires, fantasies and pleasures that are their own. . . .

The crux of the feminist claim that the pleasure had in fantasies and enactment of erotic submission is "false" is not that the pleasure is logically incoherent. It is that the pleasure is quite literally *false,* not contradictory: submission is felt to be pleasurable, *but it is not.* Submission is thought to be desirable, but it is not. The pleasure is *therefore* on some level a lie, either to others or oneself. And yet, if we examine the accounts of the pleasure had in erotic submission and domination for indicia of lying by any criterion other than content, the charge is singularly hard to substantiate. . . .

[The second response which is] abandonment of consciousness-raising as method and its concomitant dismissal of women's internal lives as a criterion of value in favor of an objective political agenda has at least three costs. First, it has already done and will continue to do enormous damage to our integrity. As Adrienne Rich has eloquently argued, one of women's most disabling problems is that women *lie.*[14] For a multitude of reasons, we lie to ourselves and to others. And, one thing women lie about more than any other, perhaps, is the quality and content of our own hedonic lives. We tell others we are happy when we are not; we tell others that our marriages are good when they are in fact brutal; we tell others we are sexually fulfilled when we are deprived. . . . One reason we lie, perhaps more than any other, is to fulfill the politically dictated expectations of others. . . . This lying has hurt us. We lie so often we don't know when we are doing it. We lie so often we lack the sense of internal identity necessary to the identification of a proposition's truth or falsity. We lie so often that we lack a self who lies. We just *are* lies; we inhabit falsehood. Our lives are themselves lies.

Consciousness-raising, more than any other feminist methodology, has given women a means by which to break the chain of deception in which we live. By learning to identify the falsehoods we utter, we have learned to create a self who can assert a truth. Consciousness-raising is the discovery of the power of *truth,* not just *a* truth. When we abandon consciousness-raising we run the risk of losing truth. We run a high risk of losing ourselves again. . . .

[I]f feminists abandon consciousness-raising as a method in favor of an authoritatively pronounced objective ideal, many women will be foregoing a source of sexual pleasure. This is not a trivial sacrifice. When we deny what gives us sexual pleasure, and when we thereby deny ourselves that sexual pleasure itself —when we deny both truth and pleasure—we deny not just one but two important aspects of our selves. We become, yet again, *not entitled;* this time—and let's not forget, not for the first time—not entitled to sexual pleasure. We become, once again, sexually *errant.* [God damn: Wrong *again!*] We become, if we forego the sexual pleasure we have learned to own, once again, the conveyors of sexual pleasure for others, and once again, our role will be dictated by someone else's conception of sexual right and wrong.

[I]f we give up on feminist consciousness-raising, we will be giving up a method of self-creation that has, for many women, *worked*. We have learned through consciousness-raising to trust our experiences. . . . If we now shift ground—if we now begin to test the validity of our lived experiences by reference to political ideals—we run the risk of forgetting. . . . We run the risk of forgetting the importance of learning to identify, acknowledge and act on the desires we have painstakingly learned to honor as our own. We run the risk of giving ourselves once again, this time for principle rather than protection.

So—the third response to the problem posed by women's enjoyment of erotic submission, endorsed by a small but growing number of radical feminists, is to understand rather than judge these pleasures in their historical context and in their full experiential truth. . . . Such an understanding, I believe, is essential to any dynamic future for radical feminism. First, only by such a process will we achieve any meaningful understanding of these pleasures, but we will not achieve that so long as we allow stated ideals to trump and silence felt pleasure. But second, I believe, only by understanding our felt pleasures will we achieve any meaningful understanding of our stated ideals. We cannot possibly give content to the substantive equality we seek until we understand the erotic appeal of submission. If we can identify what human needs are met through eroticized submission, perhaps we can better understand, and identify, the human needs which will be met or frustrated through political, legal and economic equality. . . .

B. Radical Feminist Legal Reform: The Pornography Debate

. . . Catharine MacKinnon asks, again and again, why feminists are defending the rights of pornographers. The question . . . is a very good one. . . . I believe that the first amendment issue for feminists is a sincerely felt feminist concern—the FACT (Feminists Against Censorship Taskforce) women, I'm sure, do genuinely fear that censorship will hurt women (as opposed to hurting pornographers) more than pornography hurts women, and they may be right. I also believe, though, that the First Amendment is not the only reason feminists are opposing the ordinance. I want to suggest another reason. . . .

The ordinance and theory behind it defines and targets pornography as the subordination of women through sexually explicit graphic or textual means. *Subordination* is (unfortunately) not defined, but nevertheless, the ordinance rests on the clear normative premise that it is bad. Furthermore, to "submit" is to consent to one's subordination. Sexual submission, then, is likewise bad. More directly, sexual submission is bad because submission itself is bad, and submission is bad because equality is good, and equality is good because people, definitionally, simply are such that equality is good. Yet many women . . . don't *feel* sexual submission as bad. [M]any women feel sexual submission as pleasurable. . . . And many women have come to this understanding of themselves and of their pleasure through consciousness-raising sessions. . . . The ordinance raises the conflict between objective ideal and subjective pleasure, and the result has been chaos.

First, a historical reminder—it was not always thus. When the anti-pornography campaign commenced in the late seventies and early eighties, there was *widespread* feminist consensus on the evil of pornography. That consensus, it now goes without saying, has dissolved. Why? One reason might be this: in the early days of the campaign feminists understood the evil of pornography to be that it causes *violence* (and more specifically sexual violence) against women. Now, anti-pornography advocates urge that the evil of pornography is not that it causes *violence* against women, but that it *subordinates* women, on the theory, no doubt, that the former is symptom, the latter is root cause. The shift from "violence" to "subordination" has splintered the movement, for, I think, primarily the reason noted above—subordination is taken to be both reflected in and caused by sexual submission and consensual, controlled, sexual submission is hedonically, for many, pleasurable.

This is the lesson I draw: we might be able to re-build a consensus on pornography by focusing our attention on the harm we want to eradicate, rather than on the classification or description of the thing we want to prohibit. . . . What we all know . . . to be undeniably painful is the expropriation of our sexuality which is motivated by *fear*—sexual submission under threat or memory of sexual compulsion—the ever-present threat of that expropriation, the fear which the threat engenders, the danger with which we consequently live, and the torture we endure when the fear proves to be horrifically well-grounded. When we "give" ourselves because we have been taught to *and the teacher is fear,* the "giving" is *not pleasurable.* . . . Both the coercive and the consensual relinquishment of control expressed in sexual relationships, which is grounded in fear, is damaging, painful, unpleasant, deadening, and not at all erotic. Relinquishment of control over one's body that is motivated by fear is damaging *whether or not the external indicia of "consent" to the relationship or transfer are present.* Pornographic literature that facilitates by legitimating *either* the violent expropriation of our sexuality or fear-induced *giving* so as not to be one from whom sexuality is taken, hurts us. . . . If pornography proximately causes that injury and the proximity is provable, it should be civilly actionable.

By contrast, the relinquishment of authority and responsibility expressed in masochistic sexual fantasy and controlled masochistic practice at least sometimes constitutes a willed sexual submission which is motivated by *trust,* not fear. When motivated by trust, that submission can be pleasurable, erotic, and therefor valuable. Erotic literature that facilitates sexual fantasies or consensual practices (or understanding of those fantasies) which express and give rise to the experience of trust, can, I think, be pleasurable, erotic, and of value regardless of the content of the fantasy or the practice.

There is no contradiction in holding both of these positions simultaneously. What they pose is a difficult causation question, but that's a far cry from being faced with a disabling *contradiction* between theory and method or ideal and pleasure. We need to know what pornography hurts us and endangers us and what pornography frees us or enlivens us. . . . This may be a very difficult factual question . . . but it does not give rise to a "contradiction." Fire too sometimes warms and sometimes burns. And—it is not, after all, *always* hard to distinguish the warm glow from the scorching blaze. We need to know whether we can differentiate and describe the sub-category of what is now over-defined as "pornography" that hurts women by encouraging, validating or legitimating the violent expropriation through fear of our sexuality. . . . If pornography hurts us in this way, then we should rid ourselves of it, but not because it embodies or expresses a pleasure we have defined as undesirable. We should be rid of it because, and to the extent that, we discover that it hurts.

I have no doubt that a lot of pornography injures us in just this way—I have no doubt that pornography can precipitate sexual violence, because it has happened to me. I know that pornography legitimates sexual coercion and cruelty. I also know that women are coerced to participate in pornography, and I know that the violence depicted in pornography is, more often than we would like to think, a recording not a simulation of real violence. I also, though, have no doubt that some pornography —as it is defined under this ordinance—is pleasurable to women and occasionally profoundly so. . . . The understanding and eradication of the sources of women's suffering is obviously an important feminist goal. But it is also—or ought to be—an important item on any feminist agenda to facilitate the exploration of women's sources of pleasure. Women take pleasure—and often, intense pleasure—in eroticized submission. Whatever causes women pleasure without causing attendant pain is something we should celebrate, not censure.

Empirically, we need to know what sub-category of the pornography as it is now defined significantly contributes to the violent expropriation of our sexuality. The pornography that should be actionable is the pornography that causes the violent expropriation of our sexuality—*that* is the injury. . . . But pornography that depicts sexual relationships of domination and submission which does not legitimate or encourage the violent, forced, coercive expropriation of sexuality—even if it depicts unquestionably hierarchical sex—regardless of content and regardless of whether we call it S&M porn, butch-fem porn, soft-core porn, romance, or erotica—may well be relatively harmless, is probably a pleasure for many, and might be liberating for a few. . . . The sexual violence that pornography may cause—not the erotic domination it may depict—should be the key to what is actionable (and whether it is actionable) for the simple reason that it is the sexual violence in our lives, not the erotic domination, which hurts us.

I think the crisis in radical feminist legal theory which the pornography debate has engendered is false, for this reason. First, it is at least possible that on this issue we can have it both ways. Many of us are debating the pornography issue without having looked at much of it. We have a "category" in mind that might not be a sensible category. If we *look* at what is presently and too broadly defined as pornography, we might discover that the pornography which hurts us . . . is not so hard to distinguish from the pornography that doesn't hurt us and which might be pleasurable. . . . For example, it may just be true—the Meese report suggests it is—that pictures are more prone to cause violence than words, and that violent pictures are more prone to cause violence than non-violent pictures. It may also be true—sales of pornography to women suggest it is —that *words* are erotic in the way described above while pictures of dominance and submission are not. *The Story of O* —unquestionably violent—is, as Marcus suggests, a "lyrical poem."[15] Whatever else it is, it is *words*.

It also, of course, may not be true. *The Story of O,* no matter how erotic as text, might be proximately causing literally untold miseries—silenced, actual, fearful, terrifying enslavements—and *no woman wants that.* If it is, then we cannot have it both ways, and as Wendy Williams has said in a different context, where we can't have it both ways we have to think carefully about which way we want to have it.[16] . . . For me, this is not a close question, although I know it may be for others. But again—this poses a choice, and even if it is a hard choice, that is a far cry from a disabling contradiction. Erotic energy—no less than clean, cheap nuclear energy —comes with a price, and the price of both energies may be too high.

Finally, we should draft an ordinance which properly targets the real injury without offending First Amendment principles; first because we will have to if we intend to actually use it, and second because those first amendment principles further more than they hinder feminist goals. We need at least some of this literature, and we need it for genuinely liberal as well as genuinely feminist reasons. First, we need to understand our ideals better than we presently do. The sexual high many women reach from controlled objectification, domination, and submission might stem from the pleasure of trust that can accompany inequality. Then again, it might not. But either way, it would be nice to *know.* There may be contained in that pleasure the kernel of a critique of our dominant ideals of individual autonomy and equality. If we really believe that the personal is political, that should not sound ludicrous. It might, of course, be both nonludicrous and wrong: all that might be contained in our pleasure is a reflection of the extent of our debasement. But we won't know one way or the other unless we think about it, and we won't think about it so long as we regard the subject as taboo. . . .

There are other reasons, though, that women in particular need this literature. Some of us need it for sexual pleasure and release, which is not an insignificant need. All women, though, need the literature if we are ever to understand ourselves. We need, for example, *The Story of O.* If we are going to give it up because it causes injuries, then we should at least understand what we're giving up. Marcia Marcus explains why:

> Germaine Greer was in Copenhagen in 1972 and a meeting was held at which she addressed and talked with Danish women. The atmosphere in the hall was high-spirited and optimistic, when suddenly a young woman cried out with desperation in her voice: "But how can we start a women's movement when I bet three-quarters of us sitting in this room are masochists?"[17]

Marcus concludes her discussion of *The Story of O* with this plea:

> I have kept back *The Story of O* for so long because I know no other book expressing so well all the contradictions involved in our image of womanhood. It features them so sharply and intensely that we cannot avoid feeling them in our bodies and deep down in our souls. What shall we do about those contradictions?
>
> O gives us a kind of answer, for she lives out what many of the rest of us have vague dreams about. Her story can teach us something about ourselves—what we must expect if we join in on male society's idea of what a woman is. It is a *fa-*

ble about women. But it will never come up with an unambiguous answer. It offers no solution, only a question mark.

So we shall have to continue concerning ourselves with *The Story of O,* and I know no book that should be more central for the feminist movement to commit itself to, among other things, to be able to answer the young woman at the meeting with Germaine Greer.[18]

Conclusion: Women's Difference, and an Alternative Standard for a Feminist Critique of Law

Although liberal and radical legalism are typically contrasted . . . it is by virtue of an assumption that liberalism and radicalism share that their respective chosen proxies for well-being—choice and power—are so at odds with women's subjective, hedonic lives. Both liberal and radical legalism share a vision of the human being—and therefore of our subjective well-being—as "autonomous." The liberal insists that choice is necessary for the "true" exercise of that autonomy—and thus is an adequate proxy for subjective well-being—while the radical insists the same for power.[19] But this strategic difference should not blind us to their commonality. Both the liberal and the radical legalist have accepted the Kantian assumption that *to be human* is to be in some sense autonomous—meaning, minimally, to be differentiated, or individuated, from the rest of social life.

Underlying and underscoring the poor fit between the proxies for subjective well-being endorsed by liberals and radicals —choice and power—and women's subjective, hedonic lives is the simple fact that women's lives—*because of our biological reproductive role*—are drastically at odds with this fundamental vision of human life. Women's lives are not autonomous, they are profoundly relational. This is at least the biological reflection, if not the biological cause, of virtually all aspects, hedonic and otherwise, of our "difference." . . . The experience of being human, for women, differentially from men, includes the counter-autonomous experience of a shared physical identity between women and fetus, as well as the counter-autonomous experience of the emotional and psychological bond between mother and infant. . . .

. . . If women's "difference" lies in the fact that our lives are relational rather than autonomous, and if autonomy is a necessary attribute of a human being, then women's difference rather abruptly implies that women are not human beings. . . .

This is not a novel insight: that women are not human as human is now conceived has in a sense always been the dominant problem for feminism. But the two characteristic ways in which modern feminist legal theorists have responded to this dilemma are both, I think, flawed. The liberal feminist's solution is to deny it. The fact that women become pregnant, give birth, and nurse infants is a difference that *does not count.* It does not make us any less "autonomous" than men.[20] For reasons which by now should be familiar, this response does not work: if the last century has taught us anything at all, it is that this liberal strategy of denial is a disservice. If we embrace a false conception of our nature we can be sure of only one thing, and that is that legal reform based on such a conception will only occasionally—and then only incidentally—benefit real instead of hypothetical women.

The radical feminist's proposal is that we seek to *become* autonomous creatures. We are indeed not "autonomous," but what that reflects is our lack of power—our social, political and legal victimization—not our essential nature. To the extent that we become autonomous by gaining power, we will *become* the beneficiaries of the legal system designed to promote the well-being of just such people.[21] This radical vision is at root deeply assimilationist—by gaining power, we become equal, as we become equal we become less "relational"—meaning less victimized—as we become less relational we become more autonomous, and as we become more autonomous we become more like "human beings"—more like men. Radical assimilation, though, has costs no less weighty (and no less familiar) than liberal denial. There is no guarantee that women can become autonomous "human beings," no guarantee that women want to, and at heart, no persuasive argument that women should.

A very new and third response . . . is that feminists should insist on women's humanity—and thus on our entitlements—and on the wrongness of the dominant conception of what it means to be a "human being." We should insist, as Christine Littleton has argued, for an equal "acceptance of our difference."[22] This third course is surely more promising . . . but without hedonistic criticism it is insufficient. . . . Our "difference" has many dimensions. If "difference" includes our differential suffering, or our differential vulnerability to sexual assault, or our differential endurance of pain, or our differentially negative self-esteem, then "acceptance" of those differences will backfire. We need more than just acceptance of our differences; we need a vocabulary in which to articulate and then evaluate them, as well as the power to reject or affirm them.

My proposal is that we address the multiple problems posed by our differences from men by adopting a critical legal method which aims directly for women's subjective well-being, rather than indirectly through a gauze of definitional presuppositions about the nature of human life which almost invariably excludes women's lives. We should aim, simply, to increase women's happiness, joy and pleasure, and to lessen women's suffering, misery and pain. As feminist legal critics we could employ this standard: a law is a good law if it makes our lives happier and less painful and a bad law if it makes us miserable, or stabilizes the conditions that cause our suffering. A shift toward this direct hedonism, I believe, would do four things for our developing feminist legal theory.

First, a move toward hedonistic criticism would free us from false conceptions of our nature. Our present "equality" discourse (whether cast in terms of equal freedom or equal power) has forced us to accept dominant visions of the "human being" whose equality we seek. By forgoing proxies for subjective well-being which are in turn derived from those visions, and insisting instead on pleasure and pain, happiness and misery, joy and sorrow, as our central normative categories, we can remain agnostic toward varying definitional conceptions of who we are.

Second, a move toward hedonistic criticism would facilitate an unclouded articulation of the equality of women's hedonic lives. When we try to squeeze descriptions of our lives into the parameters laid out for us, the results are often not just distorted, but profoundly anomalous. We are trying too hard to assimilate, in our theory as well as in our professional and personal lives.

Third, I believe, a shift toward a discourse that would focus attention on the pain in women's lives, and away from the oppression and subordination we suffer, would make us more effective. If we are ever going to make progress in alleviating women's misery—surely an important goal for feminist legalists—we must insist loudly upon the normative significance of our hedonic lives. To draw an analogy, Martin Luther King argued again and again[23] that the essence—the dominant fact—of the Negro's life is *pain,* that that fact would not change until the white liberal would come to *share* it, that he would not share it until he *felt* it, that he would not be able to feel it until he understood it, and that he would not understand it until the *Negro* succeeded in bringing the pain to the surface—until he could make its content palpable. Only then would the pain be mitigated. I believe that the same is true of women. . . . If we are ever to do anything about the pain which is women's lives—the violence, the danger, the boredom, the ennui, the non-productivity, the poverty, the fear, the numbness, the frigidity, the isolation, the low self-esteem, and the pathetic attempts to assimilate—we must first make the feel of that pain palpable, and hence shared. But we will not even attempt to do so as long as we embrace models of legal criticism that deny the relevance of subjective pain and pleasure, happiness and suffering, joy and sorrow, to the critical evaluation of law. . . .

Lastly, by forcing into the public discourse descriptions of women's subjective, hedonic lives, the conception of the "human being" assumed by that discourse—the substantive description of experienced human life which the phase "human being" denotes—might change so as to actually include women. For this reason alone, women need to develop descriptions of the quality of our hedonic lives.

There are two problems. Women's subjective, internal pain, because it is so silent and invisible—and because it is so different—is quite literally incomprehensible. [M]en do not understand, have not shared, have not heard, and have not felt, the pain. . . .

The second problem is this: women have a seemingly endless capacity to lie, both to ourselves and others, about what gives us pain and what gives us pleasure. . . .

Both problems strike me as surmountable. Women must start speaking the truth about the quality of our internal lives. The pain women feel may be unique, but women and men (I believe) are alike in this way: both women and men resist pain when it is our own, and (most) women and (most) men will sympathetically resist pain suffered by others, when that pain is meaningfully communicated. . . . But more fundamentally, women will come to recognize the truth about our inner lives only when we start to speak it. Women's inner reality simply does not fit the Kantian conception of human nature that underlies so much of our liberal and radical legalist commitments. It is only by starting with our own experiences that we will be able to develop a description of human nature which is faithful to our lived reality, rather than one which ignores it. From that set of descriptions, and only from that set of descriptions, can we construct, or reconstruct, our own political ideals, whether they be autonomy, equality, freedom, fraternity, sisterhood, or something completely other, and as yet unnamed.

Notes

1. See generally A. Jaggar, Feminist Politics and Human Nature (1983) for a discussion of the relation between liberal feminism and liberalism, radical feminism and radicalism, socialist feminism and socialism, and Marxist feminism and Marxism.

Feminists who write from a "difference" perspective, and who are generally critical of an "equality" approach to women's liberation both legal and otherwise, tend to note that the equality discourse employed by both liberal and radical feminist legal theory is "borrowed." See, e.g., Note (Prof. Christine Littleton), Toward a Redefinition of Sexual Equality, 95 Harv. L. Rev. 487 (1981); and Finley, Transcending Equality Theory: A Way Out of the Maternity and the Workplace Debate, in D. Weisberg ed., Feminist Legal Theory: Foundations 190 (Temple Univ. Press, 1993).

2. I will happily abandon this awkward phrase, if there is a better one. I mean simply that liberal and radical theory refuse to test their assumptions regarding our nature against the evidence of our phenomenal perceptions. I am not claiming that desires, motivations, or experience of pleasure and pain are not socially constructed, or that perceptions of them are in some way pure. But it does not follow that hedonic lives *don't exist,* or, just as bad, that they cannot be falsely characterized, or that they are infinitely malleable.

3. The problem is succinctly stated in the following passage:

> In order to account for women's consciousness . . . feminism must grasp that male power produces the world before it distorts it. Women's acceptance of their condition does not contradict its fundamental unacceptability if women have little choice but to become persons who freely choose women's roles. For this reason, the reality of women's oppression is, finally, neither demonstrable nor refutable empirically. Until this is confronted on the level of method, criticism of what exists can be undercut by pointing to the reality to be criticized. Women's bondage, degradation, damage, complicity, and inferiority—together with the possibility of resistance, movement, or exceptions—will operate as barriers to consciousness rather than as means of access to what women need to become conscious of in order to change.

C. MacKinnon, Feminism, Marxism, Method, and the State: An Agenda for Theory, in D. Weisberg ed., Feminist Legal Theory, *supra* note 1, at 437, 449. Consciousness-raising is itself defined restrictively, so as to minimize conflict between commitment to method and the substantive goal of equality: "In consciousness raising, often in groups, the impact of male dominance is concretely uncovered and analyzed through the collective speaking of women's experience, from the perspective of that experience". *Id.* at 440. . . .

4. For some descriptions from heterosexual women, see A. Snitow, C. Stansell & S. Thompson eds., Powers of Desire: The Politics of Sexuality (1983), *and* for some descriptions from lesbian women, see P. Califia, Sapphistry: The Book of Lesbian Sexuality (1980) and Rubin, Sexual Politics, the New Right and the Sexual Fringe, in What Color Is Your Handkerchief: A Lesbian S/M Sexuality Reader 28 (1979).

5. M. Marcus, A Taste for Pain: On Masochism and Female Sexuality 210 (1981).

6. See MacKinnon, Agenda, *supra* note 3. . . .

7. See the *Amicus* Brief filed by Nan Hunter and Sylvia Law on behalf of the Feminist Anti-Censorship Taskforce, in American Booksellers Ass'n, Inc. v. Hudnut, herein, at 118.

8. P. Reage, The Story of O (1954).

9. Marcus, *supra* note 5, at 193–194.

10. *Id.* at 204.

11. *Id.* at 207.

12. See Califia, *supra* note 4. . . .

13. D. Rhodes & S. McNeil eds., Women Against Violence Against Women 212–213 (1985).

14. A. Rich, On Lies, Secrets, and Silence: Selected Prose 1966–1978 (1979).

15. Marcus, *supra* note 5, at 200.

16. Williams, The Equality Crisis: Some Reflections on Culture, Courts, and Feminism, 7 Women's Rts. L. Rep. 175, 195 (1982).

17. Marcus, *supra* note 5, dedication page.

18. *Id.* at 208–209.

19. Liberal feminism's embrace of "pro-choice" rhetoric as the language in which to couch their advocacy of reproductive freedom is the most obvious reflection of this commitment. The claim that "a woman has the right to control her own body" similarly reflects the liberal's belief that choice is central to our physical, as well as legal claim to autonomy.

MacKinnon's belief that women's relationality reflects our victimization, not our essence, is vividly conveyed in her exchange with Gilligan in the Buffalo Symposium. See Feminist Discourse, Moral Values, and the Law—A Conversation, 34 Buffalo L. Rev. 11, 72–77, 74–76 (1985).

20. As Sylvia Law says, "An assimilationist vision that ignores differences between men and women does not help us to reconcile the ideal of equality with the reality of difference." Law, Rethinking Sex and the Constitution, 132 Penn. L. Rev. 955, 966 (1984). Law's own position, though, that only biology differentiates women from men, has more in common with the assimilationist view she attacks than it does with radical feminism. See also Scales, Towards a Feminist Jurisprudence, 56 Ind. L. J. 375 (1981).

21. Compare MacKinnon, who wants to "get the boot off of women's necks," with Dinnerstein, who wants to share the burden of child-rearing. Both view women's lack of autonomy as the obstacle to full participation in society, and accordingly as the cause of women's misery. Compare MacKinnon, Buffalo Symposium, *supra* note 19, with D. Dinnerstein, The Mermaid and the Minotaur (1976).

22. [See] Note (Littleton), *supra* note 1.

23. See, e.g., M. L. King, The Words of Martin Luther King 22 (Coretta Scott King ed., 1983).

Section 2

Prostitution

Introduction

PROSTITUTION has been a longstanding topic of concern for feminists. Prostitution, like pornography, raises fundamental issues regarding the male right of access to women's bodies and the relationships among sexuality, gender, and equality.

Historically, feminists have espoused different views about prostitution. In the eighteenth and nineteenth centuries, as Pateman explains:

> Prostitution was seen, for example, as a necessary evil that protected young women from rape and shielded marriage and the family from the ravages of men's sexual appetites; or as an unfortunate outcome of poverty and the economic constraints facing women who had to support themselves; or prostitution was seen as no worse, and as more honest, than "legal prostitution," as Mary Wollstonecraft called marriage in 1790.[1]

During the Victorian era in both England and the United States, women devoted efforts to the eradication of the "social evil," as prostitution was euphemistically termed. In the United States in the 1830s, reform groups sprang up on the East Coast to combat prostitution. One group in particular, the New England Female Moral Reform Society, founded in 1836, remained active for nearly fifty-five years and in its heyday claimed sixty-one chapters.[2] These reformers focused on the control of male sexual behavior: "[i]n order to protect their sex women had to form an alliance, a moral counterforce, that would compel men to adopt the same codes of behavior and accountability as were applied to women."[3] The Society portrayed prostitutes as innocent victims of depraved men. Their goal was "to guard our daughters, sisters, and female acquaintances from the delusive acts of corrupt and unprincipled men" and "to bring back to the paths of virtue those who have been drawn aside through the wiles of the destroyer."[4]

Although the New England Female Moral Reform Society had limited impact on the legal system,[5] its English counterpart—the Ladies National Association (LNA)—successfully challenged laws regulating prostitution. Nineteenth-century English feminists, led by middle-class reformer Josephine Butler,[6] mounted a concerted attack on prostitution. With moralistic fervor, they condemned the double standard of sexual morality which condoned male sexual promiscuity. The LNA viewed prostitution as a social problem through which men followed their animal instincts to the ruination of women.[7]

The LNA reform agenda concentrated on the repeal of the Contagious Disease Acts enacted in 1864, which required the identification and physical examination of suspected prostitutes.[8] This legislation has been called the high water mark of the double standard because its inspections were designed to protect men at the price of prostitutes' "humiliation and shame."[9] English feminists protested government attempts at licensing prostitutes that subjected prostitutes to mandatory medical examinations with crude instruments. The feminists identified with their fallen sisters and viewed such state regulation as endangering all women; any woman on the streets at night was subject to possible examination. For these feminists, "prostitution represented in the starkest form the sexual domination of women by men."[10]

The nineteenth-century British campaign was aimed not only at improving the condition of prostitutes. Josephine Butler had a broader agenda of improving the status of women.

> Hers was more than a reform campaign for equality. It was a demand for a fundamental change in values that would lead to liberty based on individual freedom and self respect. . . . On behalf of the most oppressed and exploited of women, she demanded a change in values that amounted to nothing less than a feminist revolution.[11]

In the second wave of feminism in the 1970s, prostitution surfaced again as a topic of concern. Radical feminist Kate Millett wrote an article on prostitution in one of the first feminist readers.[12] According to Millett, prostitution represents an illustration of power relations. In the theoretical framework of Millett's *Sexual Politics*,[13] relationships are equated with politics in which some persons (men) control others (women). Economic power becomes a consequence, then, of psychological domination. For social change to occur, attitudes, rather than the means of production in the Marxist sense, must be transformed. Methodologically, Millett emphasizes the necessity for incorporating the views of those most affected: the prostitutes themselves.

Radical feminist Susan Brownmiller, noted for her classic *Against Our Will: Men, Women and Rape,*[14] also focused on prostitution[15] early in the women's movement. She elucidates the link between prostitution and rape. According to Brownmiller, prostitution institutionalizes the concept of male right of access to the female body and of sex as an obligatory female service. This perception of male power and female sexuality fuels rape mentality and must be changed in order to eliminate sexual violence against women.[16]

Brownmiller's early article on prostitution includes remarks she presented at a filibuster of a New York legislative hearing on "Prostitution as a Victimless Crime,"[17] in which she argues that the woman is indeed a victim, a victim of the "male power principle."[18] In the radical feminist tradition, she questions the notion of consent. She criticizes the "myth" that the prostitute has made a free choice to sell her body.

Brownmiller holds out little hope for legal remedies, because "[t]he woman's movement will not tolerate the legalization of sexual slavery."[19] The solution for Brownmiller is equality: prostitution will not end until men see women as equals. "And men will never see women as equals until there's an end to prostitution. So it seems that we will have to work for the full equality of women and the end of prostitution side by side. One cannot occur without the other."[20] Strains of these radical feminist views are echoed in the essays that follow.

A number of factors coalesced in the 1970s to contribute to increasing scholarly and public attention on prostitution. These factors included the rise of the women's movement, the growing importance of the civil rights movement, expanding notions of the law of privacy, a new concern about victimless crimes, and frank public discussion of sexual mores.[21] The year 1973 witnessed for the first time the formation of prostitutes' rights groups. One such group, "Call Off Your Old Tired Ethics" (COYOTE), promised to work for decriminalization of prostitution and increased social acceptance of prostitutes. COYOTE prefers decriminalization to legalization, stemming from the fear that legalization would still involve government regulation.

At the same time, legal scholars[22] joined civil libertarians in criticizing prostitution primarily on the grounds that the laws (1) violate equal protection because of the lack of even-handed enforcement against the customer; (2) violate the right of privacy to control one's own body without unreasonable governmental interference; and (3) constitute a denial of due process (by criminalizing loitering and vagrancy) due to arbitrary enforcement and vagueness.

Increasingly, theoretical works on prostitution are emerging in the different schools of feminist thought.[23] These works focus on the nature of prostitution as a source of women's oppression as well as on the optimum avenues of reform. A brief discussion of these perspectives follows.

The Liberal Feminist Perspective

Classic liberal philosophy, in the tradition of John Stuart Mill, advocates the view that the state should not interfere in individuals' lives, especially in regulating private morality.[24] In accordance with this belief, Alison Jaggar notes:

> The usual liberal recommendation on prostitution, then, is that it should be treated as an ordinary business transaction, the sale of a service; in this case, of

a sexual service. Because the prostitute engages in it out of economic motivation, liberals view prostitution as quite different from a sexual act committed by physical force or under threat of force; they view prostitution as quite different, for instance, from rape. Instead, they see it as a contract like other contracts, entered into by each individual for her or his own benefit, each striking the best bargain that she or he is able. The state has exactly the same interest in the prostitution contract as in all other contracts and may therefore regulate certain aspects by law . . . hygiene, control of disease, minimum standards of service and of working conditions, misleading advertising, payment of taxes and social security, etc. It should also ensure equal opportunity. . . .[25]

This liberal position on prostitution, sometimes referred to as the "contractarian view" or the "contractarian defense of prostitution," is explored more fully below in essays by Ericsson and Pateman.

Liberal feminists note that, in the absence of coercion, prostitution is a legitimate employment for women. As Jaggar explains, this liberal conception of coercion is narrower than either radical feminist or Marxist views.[26] Radical feminists see the implicit coercion of gender relations generally; Marxists regard coercion as economic.

The movement aimed at reform of prostitution laws is not indebted solely to feminism. Two groups, reflecting the "standard liberal position on prostitution,"[27] independently advocated major legal reforms. For example, the British Wolfenden Committee in the early 1960s published a report (the Wolfenden Report)[28] exploring issues of homosexuality and prostitution. The rationale of the Wolfenden Report was that private sexual conduct should not be the subject of criminal law. In line with this view, the Wolfenden Committee recommended that prostitution be decriminalized: neither prostitutes nor their customers should be subject to penalties for engaging in acts of prostitution (although soliciting would still constitute an offense).

In the United States in the early 1970s, the American Civil Liberties Union (ACLU) also began pressing for legal reform. The ACLU argued that laws prohibiting prostitution were unconstitutional as violations of equal protection (by punishing only women prostitutes, not male customers) and of due process (by using loitering as a category for punishment, despite problems of vagueness and arbitrary enforcement).[29] The ACLU also charged that prohibitions on prostitution violate the individual's right to control her body without unreasonable interference from the state. Suggested legal reforms again included decriminalization. ACLU arguments went beyond the Wolfenden Report by suggesting that even solicitation should not be punished.[30]

Although sharing many of the same ideas as the British Wolfenden Committee and the ACLU, liberal feminists are not united in their moral views on prostitution. Some liberal feminists perceive prostitution similarly to Marxist feminists, socialist feminists, and radical feminists—as degrading to women. Other liberal feminists, however, "claim to see nothing wrong with prostitution."[31] Liberal feminists representing this latter view share some similarities with members of another school of feminism, existential feminism.

Existentialist Feminism

A dramatic change in feminist theory concerning prostitution has occurred in the last few decades. In the views of many liberal feminists and existentialist feminists alike, the prostitute is not a fallen and oppressed victim, but rather "the quintessential liberated woman."[32] Tong attributes the existentialist feminist school of thought to Simone de Beauvoir.[33] De Beauvoir's *The Second Sex*,[34] which electrified the early days of the women's liberation movement, set forth the view that woman is always the "other," passive and dependent on the man and able to live only through him. The woman is socialized to accept passivity; only the man plays an active, creative role in society.

In her discussion of prostitution, de Beauvoir points out the then-shocking view that prostitution may be empowering for the woman. The prostitute may find liberation in the money and benefits she obtains. Especially when not employed by a pimp, the prostitute exerts power over men. "The man may think he 'has' her, but his sexual possession is an illusion; it is she who has him . . . she will not be 'taken,' since she is being paid."[35]

Prostitutes adopted these existential views in the 1970s when they began organizing in the United States, England, and Australia to improve their working conditions. The prostitutes aimed to combat, generally, violence toward women and, in particular, hostility toward prostitutes. They also worked toward the decriminalization of prostitution. In an interesting similarity to Marxist feminists, prostitutes' rights groups analogized the prostitute and the worker. Although prostitutes are similar to workers in many ways, they lack trade union safeguards and other protections. In this conceptualization of prostitution as an occupation and in their suggested avenues of reform, prostitutes' rights advocates have much in common with liberal feminists.

Classical Marxism

The classical Marxist view is that the difference between a prostitute and a married woman is one of degree. In the Marxist framework, marriage constitutes the exchange of sexual and other tangible and intangible services, which a woman provides her husband in exchange for economic support. Engels, in his discussion of the bourgeois family, amplifies on this analogy:

> . . . marriage is determined by the class position of the participants, and to that extent always remains marriage of convenience. . . . [T]his marriage of convenience often enough turns into the crassest prostitution—sometimes on both sides, but much more generally on the part of the wife, who differs from the ordinary courtesan only in that she does not hire out her body, like a wage-worker, on piecework, but sells it into slavery once and for all.[36]

"Prostitution" writes Marx, "is only a *specific* expression of the *general* prostitution of the laborer. . . ."[37] Forced to work in order to survive, the wage laborer produces labor which is not one's own and thereby becomes alienated from the product of that labor, the act of production, and fellow workers. This ensuing alienation and objectification led Marx to theorize the similarity between prostitution and wage labor. Classical Marxist feminists adopt the Marx/Engels analysis of prostitution: the socioeconomic conditions under capitalism dictate that the woman remain an object and prevent her transformation into an individual in charge of her destiny.[38]

A moral component that is for the most part lacking in the liberal tradition is apparent in the Marxist view of prostitution. Prostitution, like wage labor, degrades the actor. It is dehumanizing not only for the prostitute and the wage laborer, but also for the prostitute's client and the laborer's employer.[39]

Marxists pose a remedy to the dehumanization and alienation of the prostitute (and wage laborer). Capitalism, with its resultant inequality of wealth, class system, and private property, must be eliminated. With adequate wages, women will no longer be forced to choose prostitution as a career. By eliminating the supply of prostitutes, the bourgeois demand for prostitutes will be exhausted. As Tong notes, "This is precisely why not only Engels and Marx, but most Marxist feminists insist that 'to fight prostitution is to fight the foundations of capitalist society' especially the institution of private property and the class system it generates."[40]

The Marxist solution to prostitution thus is not a legal one. Tong amplifies:

> . . . under capitalism no legal remedy can assuage the prostitute's plight, since capitalist law exists to serve the capitalist economy. Capitalists will criminalize, legalize, or decriminalize prostitution in accordance with self-interest. For example, were capitalists to legalize prostitution, they would do so not out of concern for the prostitute, but out of a desire either to fill the state's coffers with tax revenues or to line the pockets of those who would operate the legitimate "cathouses." In neither of these latter events would the condition of the prostitute herself be ameliorated.[41]

The law, according to Marxist feminists, is ineffectual to remedy women's oppression. Only the economic solution of a socialist revolution will alter society to ensure this result.

The Socialist Feminist Perspective

Socialist feminists share many views with Marxist feminists, especially a moral perspective which condemns prostitution. Socialist feminists differ in their definition of prostitution, as well as in their explanations of the nature and roots of women's oppression.

In contrast to the Marxist definition, socialist feminists define prostitution in its more common sense as an exchange of sexual services. Socialist feminists also offer a more complex view of the origins of women's oppression. Whereas classical Marxist doctrine is based on economic determinism, socialist feminists explain the origins of women's condition as social and psychological.

Socialist feminists, according to Tong, point out the flawed nature of the Marxist argument that capitalism is the source of women's sexual and economic oppression.[42] Socialist feminists are able to see that prostitution flourishes in countries that have abolished capitalism: that is, in such socialist societies as mainland China and Russia. Therefore, capitalism cannot be the root problem. Moreover, socialist feminists criticize classical Marxist feminists for their overemphasis on the role of the mode of production without regard for such important factors as women's role in reproduction, the socialization of children, and the role of sexuality in women's lives.[43] Moreover, Tong continues, socialist feminists endorse a broader conceptualization of prostitution as a socioeconomic phenomenon.[44] That is, they recognize that working-class men, as well as middle- and upper-class men, patronize prostitutes.

Like Marxist feminists, socialist feminists do not believe that the solution to women's oppression in general and to prostitution in particular is through legal channels. Neither, however, is it economic. The supply and demand of prostitutes is not merely a function of economics.[45] Tong writes that many socialist feminists would concur with the views expressed here, in the essay by Lars O. Ericsson, that

> the classical Marxist analysis . . . is bound to fail for the simple and obvious reason that the sex drive—which constitutes a necessary condition for the demand of prostitutes—is neither an economic phenomenon nor a phenomenon less basic (in fact it is more basic) than any economic factor.[46]

Socialist feminists stress far-reaching reform efforts along social, cultural, and psychological dimensions, especially in the areas of childbearing and childrearing. Only a change in these practices and attitudes will ensure women's equality.

The Radical Feminist Perspective

Radical feminists share similarities with the preceding schools of thought. Radical feminists share the moral condemnation of prostitution of both Marxist feminists and socialist feminists.[47] Like Marxist feminists, they incorporate a broadened understanding of prostitution—perhaps the broadest of all. According to this perspective, any significant interaction between men and women is a form of prostitution. As Jaggar describes:

> Contemporary radical feminists . . . perceive most social interaction between women and men as some form of prostitution. Thus, they believe that almost every man/woman encounter has sexual overtones and typically is designed to reinforce the sexual dominance of men.[48]

Radical feminists regard prostitution as an institution affecting men's relationship with women. Unlike Marxists, however, radical feminists do not focus on the similarities between prostitution and wage labor. The relevant comparison, according to radical feminists, is rape because of its incorporation of the elements of objectification and coercion. Rape and prostitution alike become examples of male power and female subordination.

[U]ltimately the moral status of prostitution is identical with that of rape. Like rape, prostitution perpetuates the oppression of women by encouraging the view that women are mere sexual objects, hence reinforcing male dominance and female inferiority.[49]

Like socialist feminists, radical feminists disagree with classical Marxists about the origins of women's oppression. Many radical feminists conclude that women's subordination derives from sexual and procreative practices. In line with this belief, radical feminists attribute the origins of prostitution to "the sex drive as it is institutionalized by society,"[50] irrespective of capitalism or socialism. According to the radical feminist view, men are socialized to have sexual desires and to feel entitled to have those desires met, whereas women are socialized to meet those desires and to internalize accepted definitions of femininity and sexual objectification. Such views, according to radical feminists, perpetuate prostitution.

Radical feminists conceptualize coercion in broad social terms rather than in the narrow economic terms of Marxism. The former "point out the total coerciveness of a social system in which the primary criterion for evaluating women, other than their fertility, is their sexual attractiveness to men."[51] They deny that women enter prostitution of their own free choice. Radical feminists reconceptualize consent as coercion by patriarchy. This radical feminist view is beginning to find its way into law in terms of an expanded statutory definition of the coercion used in prostitution.[52]

Radical feminists also share a desire with other feminists to alleviate women's oppression. One method is the elimination of prostitution. For many radical feminists, the solution is not legal: radical feminists believe that the male monopoly of economic power must be abolished. Sexual stereotypes, social attitudes, and myths about male sexuality must undergo a radical transformation. Ultimately, when men view women as equals and not as sex objects, men will no longer demand prostitutes. However, some radical feminists, such as Catharine MacKinnon (in an essay herein) and Margaret Baldwin (via statutory reforms of definition of coercion), are suggesting novel legal remedies.[53]

The diversity of perspectives about prostitution is explored by the essays here, which address fundamental questions about the nature of prostitution as a source of women's oppression; concerns about issues of autonomy, consent, liberty, and privacy; the relationship between gender, sexuality, and equality; and the appropriate role of the state in addressing the phenomenon.

In the opening essay, Judith Walkowitz criticizes early feminist reform measures for playing into the hands of a powerful moralist group that held opposing beliefs. Walkowitz concludes by warning contemporary feminists of the dangers of making alliances with conservative forces.[54]

In contrast to Walkowitz's historical analysis, Lars Ericsson provides a philosophical contractarian defense of prostitution. Ericsson considers, and dismisses, the feminist charge that prostitution reflects male subjugation. In an echo of de Beauvoir, Ericsson counters that the position of the prostitute is superior to that of the suburban housewife. He also disagrees that prostitution reflects inequality or objectifies women.

If prostitution imposes burdens, he counters, then the occupation should be regulated to eliminate such burdens. Ericsson advocates what he terms a "sound" prostitution, in which prostitutes have the same rights as others, prostitution is available to both sexes, and negative attitudes toward sexuality and women are altered.

Carole Pateman counters Ericsson's liberal contractarian defense by contending that it ignores the patriarchal dimension of society.[55] Unlike Ericsson, who treats prostitution as a natural biological urge (a view he shares with Richard Posner),[56] Pateman contends that prostitution must be placed in its social context of sexual relations. Whereas Ericsson advocates state regulation, Pateman argues that regulation fails to remedy the underlying power inequality.

Radical feminist Catharine MacKinnon reconceptualizes the debate about prostitution by exploring prostitution in terms of its denial of women's civil rights. Her novel legal approach to prostitution, analogizing prostitution to slavery, would utilize the Thirteenth Amendment in its civil application to enable prostitutes to sue pimps for sexual slavery.

Although retaining MacKinnon's emphasis on the experiences of prostitutes, Jody Freeman shifts the focus to prostitutes' rights groups. Freeman identifies the basis of the divergent beliefs of prostitutes' rights groups and radical feminists in their contrasting definitions of consent and coercion. Although critical of, yet sympathetic to, radical feminist beliefs, Freeman's solution differs from that of radical feminists. Based on her perception of prostitutes' wishes, Freeman would permit prostitution in certain cases, supplemented by increased funding for resources. Like other authors here, Freeman points out the inadequacy of resort to legal reform alone to address prostitution.

The two final essays explore the meaning of legal language about prostitution. Mary Joe Frug examines prostitution from a postmodernist perspective, emphasizing the importance of legal language in the construction of meaning about gender differences. Frug suggests that legal rules, by contributing to "terrorization," "maternalization," and "sexualization" of the female body, impede reform strategies.

Radical feminist Margaret A. Baldwin in her essay theorizes that legal discourse propounds a dichotomy that has significance for prostitutes and nonprostitutes alike. If a woman is determined to be a prostitute, she is an object of censure. As a result, victims of sexual violence (sexual abuse, rape, battering) must distance themselves from the label of "prostitute" to obtain legal redress. Baldwin thus joins Frug in recommending reform in the nature of legal discourse itself.

Notes

1. C. Pateman, The Sexual Contract 190 (Stanford Univ. Press, 1988).
2. B. Hobson, Uneasy Virtue: The Politics of Prostitution and the American Reform Tradition 53 (Basic Books, 1987). On the feminist purity campaign, see also E. DuBois & L. Gordon, Seeking Ecstasy on the Battlefield: Danger and Pleasure in Nineteenth Century Feminist Sexual Thought, in C. Vance ed., Pleasure and Danger: Exploring Female Sexuality (Pandora, 1989); J. Walkowitz, Prostitution and Victorian So-

ciety: Women, Class, and the State (Cambridge Univ. Press, 1980); J. Walkowitz, Male Vice and Female Virtue: Feminism and the Politics of Prostitution in Nineteenth-Century Britain, *infra* this chapter.

3. Hobson, *supra* note 2, at 50.

4. *Id.* at 55.

5. *Id.* at 70.

6. On the role of Josephine Butler in nineteenth century feminism, see B. Caine, Josephine Butler, in Victorian Feminists 150–195 (Oxford Univ. Press, 1992); G. Petrie, A Singular Iniquity: The Campaigns of Josephine Butler (Viking, 1971). See also K. Barry, Josephine Butler: The First Wave of Protest, in Female Sexual Slavery 12–32 (Prentice-Hall, 1979).

7. P. McHugh, Prostitution and Victorian Social Reform 21 (Croom Helm, 1980).

8. *Id.* at 16.

9. *Id.* at 17 (citing Thomas, The Double Standard, J. Hist. Ideas 20 (1955)). Butler quoted the lament of a prostitute from Kent who was subjected to this examination: "It is men, only men, from the first to the last that we have to do with! To please a man I did wrong, at first, then I was flung about from man to man. Men police lay hands on us. By men we are examined, doctored and messed on with. In the hospital it is a man again who made prayers and reads the Bible for us. We are had up before magistrates who are men, and we never get out of the hands of men until we die." *Id.* at 167–168.

10. Pateman, *supra* note 1, at 196.

11. Barry, *supra* note 6, at 16.

12. K. Millett, Prostitution: A Quartet for Female Voices, in V. Gornick & B. Moran eds., Woman in Sexist Society: Studies in Power and Powerlessness 21-69 (Basic Books, 1971).

13. K. Millett, Sexual Politics (Doubleday, 1970).

14. S. Brownmiller, Against Our Will: Men, Women and Rape (Simon & Schuster, 1975; Bantam Books, 1986). Page references are to the Bantam Books edition.

15. S. Brownmiller, Speaking Out on Prostitution, in A. Koedt and S. Firestone eds., Notes From the Third Year 72–77 (Notes From the Second Year, Inc., 1971).

16. Brownmiller, *supra* note 14, at 438–441.

17. Brownmiller, *supra* note 15.

18. *Id.* at 73.

19. *Id.* at 75.

20. *Id.* at 76.

21. Haft, Hustling for Rights, 1 Civ. Lib. Rev. 8, 9 (Winter/Spring 1974).

22. A burgeoning literature in the 1970s began exploring legal issues involved in prostitution. See, e.g., Abramson, A Note on Prostitution: Victims Without Crime—or There's No Crime but the Victim is Ideology, 17 Duquesne L. Rev. 355 (1978–1979); Jennings, The Victim as Criminal: A Consideration of California's Prostitution Law, 64 Cal. L. Rev. 1235 (1976); Rosenbleet & Pariente, The Prostitution of the Criminal Law, 11 Am. Crim. L. Rev. 373 (1973).

23. Feminist theorists categorize differently the perspectives on prostitution. Tong refers to the predominant views as classical Marxist, socialist feminist, radical feminist, and existentialist feminist. R. Tong, Women, Sex and the Law 48–55 (Rowman & Littlefield, 1984). Jaggar highlights three views which she terms liberal, classical Marxist, and radical feminist approaches. A. Jaggar, Prostitution, in A. Soble, The Philosophy of Sex: Contemporary Readings 260–274 (Rowman & Littlefield, 1991). The discussion that follows relies heavily on these two excellent works, as well as A. Jaggar, Feminist Politics and Human Nature (Rowman & Littlefield, 1988).

24. John Stuart Mill, On Liberty 17 (Cambridge Univ. Press, 1989).

25. Jaggar, Prostitution, in Soble, The Philosophy of Sex, *supra* note 23, at 262–263.

26. *Id.* at 264.

27. *Id.* at 260.

28. See The Wolfenden Report: Report of the Committee on Homosexual Offences and Prostitution, authorized American edition (Stein & Day, 1963).

29. See S. Ross, The Rights of Women: The Basic ACLU Guide to Women's Rights 176–179 (Discus Books, 1973) for a discussion of the ACLU position.

30. Jaggar, Prostitution, in Soble, The Philosophy of Sex, *supra* note 23, at 262–263.

31. *Id.* at 262.

32. Jaggar, Feminist Politics, *supra* note 23, at 53.

33. R. Tong, Feminist Thought: A Comprehensive Introduction 201 (Westview Press, 1989).

34. S. de Beauvoir, The Second Sex (Vintage Books, 1974).

35. *Id.* at 632.

36. F. Engels, The Origin of the Family, Private Property and the State, in R. Tucker ed., The Marx-Engels Reader 742 (W. W. Norton & Co., 2d ed. 1978).

37. K. Marx, Economic and Philosophic Manuscripts of 1844, in Tucker, *supra* note 36, at 82 n.7 (emphasis in the original).

38. Tong, *supra* note 23, at 49.

39. Jaggar, Prostitution, in Soble, *supra* note 23, at 268.

40. Tong, *supra* note 23, at 49.

41. *Id.* at 50. See also Jaggar, Prostitution, in Soble, *supra* note 23, at 269 ("Marx and Engels certainly do not suggest that this end may be achieved by legal prohibition.").

42. Tong, *supra* note 23, at 50–51.

43. *Id.* at 51 (citing J. Mitchell, Woman's Estate 144–151 (Pantheon Books, 1971)).

44. Tong, *supra* note 23, at 50.

45. *Id.* at 51.

46. *Id.* at 51 (citing Ericsson).

47. Prominent radical feminists who have espoused views on prostitution include Susan Brownmiller, Shulamith Firestone, Catharine MacKinnon, and Andrea Dworkin. Additional radical feminists addressing prostitution include Lindsey, Prostitution and the Law, 1 The Second Wave 6 (1972); B. Mehrhof & P. Kearon, Prostitution, in A. Koedt & S. Firestone eds., Notes from the Third Year: Women's Liberation 72 (Notes from the Second Year, Inc., 1971); MacMillan, Prostitution as Sexual Politics, 4 Quest: A Feminist Quarterly 43 (Summer 1977).

48. Jaggar, Feminist Politics, *supra* note 23, at 270.

49. *Id.* at 272.

50. Tong, *supra* note 23, at 51.

51. Jaggar, Feminist Politics, *supra* note 23, at 264.

52. See, e.g., Fla. Stat. Ann. ch. 796.09 (Harrison 1992 & Supp. 1995) (affording compensatory and punitive damages to women coerced into prostitution, coercion being defined as, *inter alia,* restraint of speech or communication with others, and exploitation of human needs for food, shelter, safety, or affection). See Baldwin, Strategies of Connection, Prostitution and Feminist Politics, 1 Mich. J. Gender & L. 65, 70–72 (1993) (discussing passage of the legislation).

53. See Baldwin, *supra* note 52, at 70–72.

54. See also J. Walkowitz, Prostitution and Victorian Society, *supra* note 2. Other feminist historians share Walkowitz's concern with the tactics of the nineteenth century feminists. See, e.g., DuBois & Gordon, *supra* note 2, at 38.

For other essays exploring the feminist response to prostitution in historical context, see G. Barker-Benfield, The Horrors of the Half-Known Life: Male Attitudes Toward Women and Sexuality in Nineteenth Century America (Harper & Row, 1976); DuBois & Gordon, *supra* note 2; J. D'Emilio & E. Freedman, Intimate Matters: A History of Sexuality in America (Harper & Row, 1988); R. Rosen, The Lost Sisterhood: Prostitution in America, 1900–1918 (Johns Hopkins Univ. Press, 1982); Freedman, Sexuality in Nineteenth Century America: Behavior, Ideology and Politics, 10 Rev. Am. His. 196–215 (1982). For an application of Walkowitz's analysis to the contemporary pornography debate, see V. Burstyn, Political Precedents and Moral Crusades: Women, Sex, and the State, in V. Burstyn ed., Women Against Censorship 4 (Salem House, 1985).

55. For another radical feminist refutation of liberal arguments, see Evelina Giobbe, Confronting the Liberal Lies About Prostitution, in D. Leidholdt & J. Raymond eds., The Sexual Liberals and the Attack on Feminism (Pergamon, 1990).

56. See R. Posner, Sex and Reason (Harvard, 1992). For feminist criticism of this view, see Carol Sanger, He's Gotta Have It, 66 S. Cal. L. Rev. 1221 (1993) (book review).

Male Vice and Female Virtue: Feminism and the Politics of Prostitution in Nineteenth-Century Britain

JUDITH R. WALKOWITZ

. . . PAST GENERATIONS of feminists attacked prostitution, pornography, white slavery, and homosexuality as manifestations of undifferentiated male lust. These campaigns were brilliant organizing drives that stimulated grass-roots organizations and mobilized women not previously brought into the political arena. The vitality of the woman's suffrage movement of the late nineteenth and early twentieth centuries cannot be understood without reference to the revivalistic quality of these anti-vice campaigns, which often ran parallel with the struggle for the vote. By demanding women's right to protect their own persons against male sexual abuse and ultimately extending their critique of sexual violence to the "private" sphere of the family, they achieved some permanent gains for women.

Nonetheless, judging by the goals stated by feminists themselves—to protect and empower women—these campaigns were often self-defeating. A libertarian defense of prostitutes found no place in the social purity struggle; all too often prostitutes were objects of purity attack. Feminists started a discourse on sex, mobilized an offensive against male vice, but they lost control of the movement as it diversified. In part this outcome was the result of certain contradictions in these feminists' attitudes; in part it reflected their impotence in their effort to reshape the world according to their own image.

In Great Britain explicitly feminist moral crusades against male vice began with a struggle against state regulation of prostitution.[1] Parliament passed the first of three statutes providing for the sanitary inspection of prostitutes in specific military depots in southern England and Ireland of 1864. Initially this first Contagious Diseases Act, as it was obliquely entitled, aroused little attention inside or outside of governmental circles. Public opposition to regulation did, however, surface in the 1870s, when a coalition of middle-class evangelicals, feminists, and radical workingmen challenged the acts as immoral and unconstitutional, and called for their repeal. The participation of middle-class women in these repeal efforts shocked many contemporary observers,

In Ann Snitow, Christine Stansell & Sharon Thompson eds., Powers of Desire: The Politics of Sexuality 419–438 (Monthly Review Press, 1983). Copyright © 1983 by Ann Snitow, Christine Stansell, and Sharon Thompson. Reprinted by permission of Monthly Review Foundation.

who regarded this female rebellion as a disturbing sign of the times. The suffrage movement was in its infancy, and respectable commentators looked on with horror and fascination as middle-class ladies mounted public platforms across the country to denounce the acts as a "sacrifice of female liberties" to the "slavery of men's lust" and to describe in minute detail the "instrumental rape" of the internal exam.[2] . . .

Under the leadership of Josephine Butler, the Ladies National Association (LNA) was founded in late 1869 as a separatist feminist organization. A "Ladies Manifesto" was issued, which denounced the acts as a blatant example of class and sex discrimination. The manifesto further argued that the acts not only deprived poor women of their constitutional rights and forced them to submit to a degrading internal examination, but also officially sanctioned a double standard of sexual morality, which justified male sexual access to a class of "fallen" women yet penalized women for engaging in the same vice as men.[3]

The campaign drew thousands of women into the political arena for the first time, by encouraging them to challenge male centers of power—such as the police, Parliament, and the medical and military establishments—that were implicated in the administration of the acts. Rallying to the defense of members of their own sex, these women opposed the sexual and political prerogatives of men. They rejected the prevailing social view of "fallen women" as pollutants of men and depicted them instead as victims of male pollution, as women who had been invaded by men's bodies, men's laws, and by that "steel penis," the speculum.[4] This entailed a powerful identification with the fate of registered prostitutes.

Mid-Victorian feminists treated prostitution as the result of the artificial constraints placed on women's social and economic activity: inadequate wages and restrictions of women's industrial employment forced some women onto the streets, where they took up the "best paid industry"—prostitution. They also saw prostitution as a paradigm for the female condition, a symbol of women's powerlessness and sexual victimization.[5] Feminists realized that the popular sentimentalization of "female influence" and motherhood only thinly masked an older contempt and distrust for women, as "The Sex," as sexual objects to be bought and sold by men.[6] The treatment of prostitutes under the acts epitomized this more pervasive and underlying misogyny. "Sirs," declared Butler, "you cannot hold us in honor so long as you drag our sisters in the mire. As you are unjust and cruel to them, you will become unjust and cruel to us."[7]

As "mothers" and "sisters," feminists asserted their right to defend prostitutes, thereby invoking two different kinds of authority relationships. A mother's right to defend "daughters" was only partially an extension and continuation of women's traditional role within the family. It was also a political device, aimed at subverting and superseding patriarchal authority: it gave mothers, not fathers, the right to control sexual access to the daughters, sanctioning an authority relationship between older middle-class women and young working-class women that was hierarchical and custodial as well as caring and protective. In other contexts, feminist repealers approached prostitutes on a more egalitarian basis, as sisters, albeit fallen ones, whose individual rights deserved to be respected and who, if they sold their bodies on the streets, had the right to do so unmolested by the police.[8]

This was the radical message of the repeal campaign. It was linked to an enlightened view of prostitution as an irregular and temporary livelihood for adult working-class women.[9] The regulation system, feminists argued, not prostitution per se, doomed inscribed women to a life of sin by publicly stigmatizing them and preventing them from finding alternative respectable employment. "Among the poor," declared Josephine Butler, the "boundary lines between the virtuous and the vicious" were "gradually and imperceptibly shaded off" so that it was "impossible to affix a distinct name and infallibly assign" prostitutes to an outcast category.[10] In fact, the young women brought under the acts lived as part of a distinct female subgroup in common lodging houses, among a heterogeneous community of the casual laboring poor. [T]heir lives were a piece with the lives of the large body of laboring women who had to eke out a precarious living in the urban job market. For these women, sexual coercion was but one form of exploitation to which they were subjected. . . .

. . . Feminist leaders used sensational stories of false entrapment or instrumental rape to appeal to all supporters of repeal—to working-class radicals and middle-class evangelicals alike. These accounts depicted registered women as innocent victims of male lust and medical and police tyranny —appropriate objects of solicitude, even for middle-class moralists who chiefly condemned the acts for making "vice" safe.[11] Furthermore, feminist propaganda was still constrained by an extremely limited vocabulary—constructed around the theme of female victimization. Defenses of prostitutes as women who were not yet "dead to shame," who still had "womanly modesty," were common.[12] By mystifying prostitution and women's move into it, this propaganda imperfectly educated the LNA rank and file on the "politics of prostitution."

A politics of motherhood also structured the cross-class alliance between feminists and radical workingmen within the repeal camp. As mothers, LNA leaders called on the sons of the people to join with them in a servile rebellion against the evil fathers, clearly presuming that their working-class allies would follow their political lead. "Our working men . . . are not unwilling to follow the gentle guidance of a grave and educated lady" or to "devote the whole influence of their vote . . . when the right chord in their hearts and consciences is touched by a delicate hand."[13] Ironically, feminists encouraged workingmen to assume a custodial role toward "their" women and frequently reminded them of their patriarchal responsibilities as defenders of the family. One LNA poster, for instance, warned "Working Men!" to "Look to the protection of your wives and daughters. They are at the mercy of the police where these Acts are in force."[14]

Propaganda of this sort aroused popular indignation against regulation, but it also buttressed a patriarchal stance and a sexual hierarchy within the organized working class that feminists had vigorously challenged in other contexts. At the same time that Butler and her friends were trying to build bridges with the organized working class, they had to struggle with their new allies over proposals to restrict female employment. . . . Despite her strong feelings against protective legislation, Butler hesitated to press the point at the annual meeting of the Trades Union Congress. "I think it might be wise for us not to raise the question of the restrictions on female labor in the Trades Congress, this year. . . . It is such a serious question for the future, that we must try to avoid that awful thing—a real breach between women and workingmen."[15] . . .

After the suspension of the acts in 1883, Butler and her circle turned their attention to the agitation against the foreign "traffic in women" and the entrapment of children into prostitution in London. When Parliament refused to pass a bill raising the age of consent and punishing traffickers in vice, Butler and Catherine Booth of the Salvation Army approached W. T. Stead of the Pall Mall Gazette for assistance. The result was the "Maiden Tribute of Modern Babylon," published in the summer of 1885.[16]

The "Maiden Tribute" was one of the most successful pieces of scandal journalism published in Britain in the nineteenth century. By using sexual scandal to sell newspapers to a middle-class and working-class readership, Stead ushered in a new era of tabloid sensationalism and cross-class prurience. New typographical and journalist techniques were introduced to sell an old story, the seduction of poor girls by vicious aristocrats, one of the most popular themes of nineteenth-century melodrama, street literature, and women's penny magazines. The "Maiden Tribute" resembled popular fiction and drama in that it contained a criticism of the vicious upper classes; but, as in the case of melodrama, this class criticism was immediately undercut by sentimental moralism, prurient details, and a focus on passive, innocent female victims and individual evil men that diverted attention away from the structural issues related to prostitution. . . . The "Maiden Tribute" episode strikingly illustrates both the mystification and its political consequences. Shifting the cultural image of the prostitute to the innocent child victim encouraged new, more repressive, political initiatives over sex.

Why then did feminist reformers endorse this crusade? Why did they ally with repressive moralists and anti-suffragists who were as anxious to clear the streets of prostitutes as to protect young girls from evil procurers and vicious aristocrats? Like the image of the instrumental violation of registered women under the Contagious Diseases Acts, the story of aristocratic corruption of virgins "generated a sense of outrage with which a wide spectrum of public opinion found itself in sympathy."[17] Feminist repealers undoubtedly believed they could manipulate this popular anger for their own purposes, first to secure the full repeal of the acts (they were finally removed from the statute books in 1886) and then to launch a sustained assault on the double standard. They were also attracted to the radical message in Stead's exposé of aristocratic vice. The disreputable performance of M.P.'s during the debates over the age of consent confirmed feminists' worst suspicions about "the vicious upper classes." During the debates, old rakes like Cavendish Bentinck treated prostitution as a necessary and inevitable evil, while others openly defended sexual access to working-class girls as a time-honored prerogative of gentlemen. . . .

Feminists felt obliged to redress the sexual wrongs done to poor girls by men of a superior class, but they registered the same repugnance and ambivalence towards incorrigible girls as they had earlier toward unrepentant prostitutes. For them as well as for more repressive moralists, the desire to protect young working-class girls masked impulses to control their sexuality, which in turn reflected their desire to impose a social code that stressed female adolescent dependency. This code was more in keeping with middle-class notions of girlhood than with the lived reality of the exposed and unsupervised daughters of the laboring poor who were on the streets. Respectable working-class parents certainly shared many of the same sentiments toward female adolescents. Despite the fact that they often sent their own daughters out to work at thirteen, they nonetheless took pains to restrict their social independence and sexual knowledge and experience.[18]

A subtheme of this feminist discussion was that females of all classes were vulnerable to male sexual violence. "There was no place of absolute safety, neither in streets, nor parks, nor railways, nor in the houses, where the procuresses were often known to enter as charwomen, nor indeed in the very churches and chapels," one speaker announced at a meeting of middle-class women.[19] Although female victimization was a sincere concern of feminists, it also served diverse political interests. Whereas feminists identified the "outlawed political condition of women"[20] as the root cause of the crimes exposed in the "Maiden Tribute," anti-feminists used the occasion to activate men into a new crusade to protect rather than emancipate women. . . .

What was the outcome of the "Maiden Tribute" affair? The public furor over the "Maiden Tribute" forced the passage of the Criminal Law Amendment Act of 1885, a particularly nasty and pernicious piece of omnibus legislation. The 1885 act raised the age of consent for girls from thirteen to sixteen, but it also gave police far greater summary jurisdiction over poor working-class women and children—a trend that Butler and her circle had always opposed. Finally, it contained a clause making indecent acts between consenting male adults a crime, thus forming the basis of legal prosecution of male homosexuals in Britain until 1967. An anti-aristocratic bias may have prompted the inclusion of this clause (reformers accepted its inclusion but did not themselves propose it), as homosexuality was associated with the corruption of working-class youth by the same upper-class profligates who, on other occasions, were thought to buy the services of young girls.[21]

Despite the public outcry against corrupt aristocrats and international traffickers, the clauses of the new bill were mainly enforced against working-class women, and regulated adult rather than youthful sexual behavior. Between 1890 and 1914, the systematic repression of lodging-house brothels was carried out in almost every major city in Great Britain. In many locales, legal repression dramatically affected the structure and organization of prostitution. Prostitutes were uprooted from their neighborhoods and forced to find lodgings in other areas of the city. Their activity became more covert and furtive. Cut off from any other sustaining relationship, they were forced to rely increasingly on pimps for emotional security as well as protection against legal authorities. Indeed, with the wide prevalence of pimps in the early twentieth century, prostitution shifted from a female- to a male-dominated trade. Further, there now existed a greater number of third parties with a strong interest in prolonging women's stay on the streets. In these and other respects, the 1885 act drove a wedge between prostitutes and the poor working-class community. It effectively destroyed the brothel as a family industry and a center of a specific female subculture, further undermined the social and economic autonomy of prostitutes; and increasingly rendered them social outcasts.[22]

But prostitutes were not the only objects of reformist attacks. In the wake of Stead's "shocking revelations," the National Vigilance Association (NVA) was formed. First organized to ensure the local enforcement of the Criminal Law Amendment Act, NVA soon turned its attention to burning obscene books, attacking music halls, theaters, and nude paintings. It condemned the works of Balzac, Zola, and Rabelais as obscene and successfully prosecuted their British distributors; it attacked birth control literature and advertisements for "female pills" (abortifacient drugs) on the same grounds. To these moral crusaders, "pornographic literature," thus broadly defined, was a vile expression of the same "undifferentiated male lust"[23] that ultimately led to homosexuality and prostitution. . . .

What was the subsequent relationship between feminism and social purity? Although prominent feminists initially filled many of the committee positions of the National Vigilance Association, this connection was short-lived for Butler and her circle, who resigned when the prurient and repressive direction of NVA became apparent. Throughout the late 1880s and 1890s, Butlerites warned their workers to "beware" of the repressive methods of the social purity societies, which were "ready to accept and endorse any amount of coercive and degrading treatment of their fellow creatures in the fatuous belief that you can oblige human beings to be moral by force."[24] But their warnings were too late. The new social purity movement had passed them by, while absorbing a goodly number of the LNA rank and file.[25] . . .

Although some feminists still maintained a national presence in the purity crusade, all in all, by the late 1880s feminists had lost considerable authority in the public discussion over sex to a coalition of male professional experts, conservative churchmen, and social purity advocates. On the other hand, social purity permanently left its imprint on the women's movement through the First World War. Both the sixteen-year campaign against state regulation and sexual scandals such as the "Maiden Tribute" ingrained the theme of the sexual wrongs perpetrated against women by men on later feminist consciousness. [T]he obsession with male vice again sidetracked early-twentieth-century feminists into another crusade against white slavery (1912), while obscuring the economic basis of prostitution. It even prompted the most progressive women of the day to advocate raising the age of consent to twenty-one. Finally, it led to repressive public policies. Commenting on the enforcement of the White Slavery Act of 1912, Sylvia Pankhurst remarked, "It is a strange thing that the latest Criminal Amendment Act, which was passed ostensibly to protect women, is being used almost exclusively to punish women."[26] As late as 1914, first-wave feminists were rediscovering that the state "protection" of young women usually led to coercive and repressive measures against those same women.

These then are the early historical links between feminism and repressive crusades against prostitution, pornography, and homosexuality. Begun as a libertarian struggle against the state sanction of male vice, the repeal campaign helped to spawn a hydra-headed assault on nonmarital, nonreproductive sexuality. The struggle against state regulation evolved into a movement that used the instruments of the state for repressive purposes. It may be misleading to interpret the effects of these later crusades solely as "blind" repressive attacks on sexuality; in many ways they clarified and identified whole new areas of sexuality. According to Michel Foucault, this elaboration of new sexualities was a strategy for exercising power in society. By ferreting out new areas of illicit sexual activity and sometimes defining them into existence, a new "technology of power" was created that facilitated control over an ever-widening circle of human activity.[27] But power is not simply immanent in society; it is deployed by specific historical agents, who have access to varying sources and levels of power.[28] The reality of a hierarchy of power severely impeded feminists' efforts to use purity crusades to defend and empower women. . . . The feminist challenge to male sexual prerogatives was a major historic development, one necessary precondition for the ideology of egalitarian heterosexual relations: but when feminists tried to use the powers of the state to protect women, particularly prostitutes who had been the original objects of their pity and concern, they usually came face to face with their own impotence.

What are the moral lessons to these moral crusades? If there is a moral lesson, it is that commercial sex as a locus of sexual violence against women is a hot and dangerous issue for feminists. In their defense of prostitutes and concern to protect women from male sexual aggression, feminists were limited by their own class bias and by their continued adherence to a separate-sphere ideology that stressed women's purity, moral supremacy, and domestic virtues. Moreover, they lacked the cultural and political power to reshape the world according to their own image. Although they tried to set the standards of sexual conduct, they did not control the instruments of state that ultimately enforced these norms. There were times, particularly during the anti-regulationist campaign, when feminists were able to dominate and structure the public discourse on sex and to arouse popular female anger at male sexual license. Yet this anger was easily subverted into repressive campaigns against male vice and sexual variation, controlled by men and conservative interests whose goals were antithetical to the values and ideals of feminism.

Yet this leaves us with a central dilemma: how to devise an effective strategy to combat sexual violence and humiliation in our society, where violent misogyny seems so deeply rooted and where the media continues to amplify the terror of male violence, as it did during the sexual scandals of the 1880s, convincing women that they are helpless victims. We must struggle to live our lives freely, without humiliation and violence. But we have to be aware of the painful contradictions of our sexual strategy, not only for the sex workers who still regard commercial sex as the "best paid industry" available to them, but also for ourselves as feminists. We must take care not to play into the hands of the New Right or the Moral Majority, who are only too delighted to cast women as victims requiring male protection and control, and who desire to turn feminist protest into a politics of repression.[29]

Notes

1. Edward Bristow, Vice and Vigilance: Purity Movements in Britain Since 1700 (Dublin, 1977); Deborah Gorham, The "Maiden Tribute of Modern Babylon" Re-examined: Child Prostitution and the Idea of Childhood in Late-Victorian England, 21 Victorian Stud. 353–369 (Spring 1978); Paul McHugh, Prostitution and Victorian Social Reform (New York: St. Martin's, 1980); Judith R. Walkowitz, Prostitution and Victorian Society: Women, Class, and the State (New York: Cambridge Univ. Press, 1980); Jeffrey Weeks, Sex, Politics, and Society chap. 5 (London: Longman, 1981).

2. Mrs. Kell of Southampton, quoted in Walkowitz, Prostitution, *supra* note 1, at 170; National League Journal (London), 1 September 1879.

3. Women's Protest, quoted in Josephine Butler, Personal Reminiscences of a Great Crusade 9, 10 (London, 1911) Keith Thomas, The Double Standard, 20 J. Hist. Ideas 195–216 (1959).

4. Thanks to Martha Vicinus and Carroll Smith-Rosenberg for these perceptions.

5. Mary Hume Rothery, A Letter Addressed to the Right Hon. W. E. Gladstone, M.P., and the Other Members of Her Majesty's Government and of Both Houses of Parliament, Touching the Contagious Diseases Acts of 1866 and 1869, and Their Proposed Extension to the Civil Population 18 (Manchester, 1870). Sally Mitchell notes the changing definition and social identity of the "fallen woman" in women's fiction, from an object of charity in the 1840s and 1850s to a reader substitute in the 1860s. See Sentiment and Suffering: Women's Recreational Reading in the 1860s, 21 Victorian Stud. 29–45 (1977).

6. Nancy F. Cott, Passionlessness: An Interpretation of Victorian Sexual Ideology, 1790–1850, 4 Signs 219–236 (1978); Thomas, *supra* note 3, at 213, 214.

7. Josephine Butler, quoted in Bristow, *supra* note 1, at 83.

8. The Royal Commission as a Court of Justice. Being an Examination of the Declaration that "The Police Are Not Chargeable with Any Abuse of Their Authority" (London, 1871).

9. *Id.*; Judith R. Walkowitz, The Making of an Outcast Group: Prostitutes and Working Women in Nineteenth-Century Plymouth and Southampton, in Martha Vicinus ed., A Widening Sphere: Changing Roles of Victorian Women 72–93 (Univ. Illinois Press, 1977).

10. Butler, Moral Reclaimability.

11. Josephine Butler, Recollections of George Butler 272–277 (Bristol, 1893); Reverend Author, quoted in Transactions of the National Association for the Promotion of Social Science 448, 449 (London, 1869).

12. Josephine Butler, quoted in Walkowitz, Prostitution, *supra* note 1, at 186.

13. Seventh Annual Report of the LNA, . . . 1876, LNA Reports, 1870–1886, Butler Collection, Fawcett Library, London (hereafter cited as LNA Reports).

14. Working Men! LNA poster displayed during the Colchester by-election of 1870, H. J. Wilson Collection, Fawcett Library, London.

15. Josephine Butler to Mary Priestman, 5 December 1876, Butler Collection.

16. The Maiden Tribute of Modern Babylon, I, II, III, IV, Pall Mall Gazette, 6, 7, 8, 10 July 1885; Gorham, Maiden Tribute, and Bristow, Vice and Vigilance, are the best secondary discussions of the scandal.

17. Gorham, *supra* note 1, at 355.

18. *Id.*, at 372, 373; Walkowitz, Prostitution, *supra* note 1, at 249. For reformers, "girlhood" was a stage in life marked by dependency but not any specific psychosexual development. Accordingly, debates over the age of consent rarely included reference to the actual sexual development of the girls they were seeking to protect. The age of consent was arbitrary; indeed, many reformers wanted to raise it to eighteen, some to twenty-one. Moreover, many of the same assumptions about protecting and controlling female adolescents ultimately led to the definition and incarceration of sexually active girls as "sex delinquents."

19. The Crusade Against the Crimes of Modern Babylon, Pall Mall Gazette, 23 July 1885.

20. Mary Priestman to the editor, Pall Mall Gazette, 23 July 1885.

21. Jeffrey Weeks, Coming Out: Homosexual Politics in Britain from the Nineteenth Century to the Present (London, Quartet, 1977), pp. 18–20.

22. See Walkowitz, Prostitution, *supra* note 1, at 210–213.

23. Weeks, *supra* note 21, at 18.

24. Josephine Butler, quoted in Jessie Higson, The Story of a Beginning 35, 36 (London, 1955).

25. For recruitment of repealers into social purity, see Walkowitz, Prostitution, *supra* note 1, at 239–243; Bristow, Vice and Vigilance, *supra* note 1, at 98, 99.

26. Protecting Women? Woman's Dreadnought, 19 December 1914.

27. Michel Foucault, The History of Sexuality, Vol. 1: An Introduction, tr. Robert Hurley (Pantheon, 1978).

28. Thanks to Jeffrey Weeks and Ellen DuBois for this perception.

29. Rosalind Petchesky, Antiabortion, Antifeminism, and the Rise of the New Right, 5 Feminist Stud. 206–246 (1980).

Charges Against Prostitution: An Attempt at a Philosophical Assessment

Lars O. Ericsson

[T]his paper [undertakes] a critical assessment of the view that prostitution is an undesirable social phenomenon that ought to be eradicated. . . .

The Feminist Charge

[Prostitution] is held to be undesirable on the ground that it constitutes an extreme instance of the inequality between the sexes. Whoredom is regarded as displaying the male oppression of the female in its most naked form. It is contended that the relation between hooker and "John" is one of object to subject—the prostitute being reified into a mere object, a thing for the male's pleasure, lust, and contempt. The customer-man pays to use the whore-woman and consequently has the upper hand. He is the dominating figure, the master. It is the whore's task to oblige, to satisfy his most "perverse" and secret desires, desires that the male is unable to reveal to his wife or girl friend. Prostitution, it is argued, reduces the woman to a piece of merchandise that anyone who can pay the price may buy. The unequal nature of prostitution is also contended to consist in the fact that it represents a way out of *misère sexuel* only for men. Instead of trying to solve the sexual problems together with his wife, the married man can resort to the services of the hustler; but the married woman lacks the same advantage, since there are not so many male heterosexual prostitutes around. I shall refer to this group of arguments as "the feminist charge."

Like the moralist and the Marxist, the feminist is of the opinion that prostitution can and ought to be eradicated. Some feminists, like the moralist, even want to criminalize prostitution. But unlike the moralist they want to criminalize both whore and customer.

The core of the feminist charge—that prostitution is unequal and disfavors the female sex—deserves to be taken seriously. For social inequality is a serious matter both morally and politically. And inequalities based on differences with regard to race, color of skin, re-

90 Ethics 335 (April 1980). © 1980 by The University of Chicago. Reprinted by permission of the University of Chicago Press.

ligious belief, sex, and the like are particularly serious. Thus, if valid, the feminist critique would constitute powerful support for the view that prostitution is undesirable.

Before I proceed to an attempt to counter the feminist charge, I would like to add a few nuancing facts to the prostitute-customer picture. . . . [1] No one denies that a majority of prostitutes are women, and no one denies that a majority of customers are men. But it is clear from the evidence that a large portion of the prostitutes, especially in metropolitan areas, are male homosexuals. There is also lesbian prostitution, though this is not (at least not yet) sufficiently widespread to be of any great social importance. And finally, there is male heterosexual prostitution, the prevalence of which is also rather limited. We may sum up by saying that, rather than constituting a dichotomy between the sexes, prostitution has the characteristic that a considerable portion of the prostitutes are men, and a small minority of the customers are women. I mention this because I think that a rational assessment should not be based on an incomplete picture of the phenomenon under assessment and I consider these data to have some relevance with respect to the feminist charge against prostitution.

There are at least two types of inequalities. In the one, the inequality consists in the fact that some *benefit* is withheld from some group or individual. A typical example: only white members of a society are allowed to vote. In the other, the inequality consists in the fact that some *burden* is placed only on some group or individual. A typical example: a feudal society in which peasants and artisans are the only ones who have to pay taxes. We may also distinguish between unequal practices which, like racial discrimination, are best dealt with through a complete *abolition* of them, and unequal practices which, like male franchise, are best dealt with by *modifying* them (in the case of male franchise, by granting the franchise to women). The one type of unequal practice is always and under all conditions undesirable: there is no remedy to the inequality of apartheid but abolition. The other type of unequal practice is also undesirable, but it has the seed of something defensible or valuable in it: the franchise is something good, although the franchise restricted to males is not. Obviously, these two pairs of categories are not mutually exclusive. On the contrary, all combinations of them are possible.

After these preliminaries, we come to the question of how prostitution is to be classified. Is harlotry an unequal practice? And if so, in what precisely does its inequality consist?

If it is conceded that in exchange for his money the customer receives a service—something that at least the sentimentalist seems most reluctant to concede—it could be argued that harlotry is unequal in the sense that some benefit is withheld from or denied women that is not withheld from or denied men. This is perhaps how the argument that hustling represents a way out only for men should be understood. However, if this is what the feminist charge amounts to, two things appear to be eminently clear. The first is that prostitution is unequal in a less serious way than, for instance, male franchise. For in the latter the benefit (opportunity to vote) which is withheld from women is withheld from them in the strong sense that it is not legally possible for the women to vote, while in the former no such legal or formal obstacle stands in their way. In fact, instead of saying that the sex services of prostitutes are withheld or denied women, it would be more appropriate to say that centuries of cultural and social conditioning makes them desist from asking for them. It is after all only recently that women have begun to define their sexuality and require that their sexual needs and desires be recognized. . . . The second point is that if, through prostitution, a benefit is "withheld" from the female sex, the best way to deal with this inequality would not be an attempt to stamp out the institution but an attempt to modify it, by making the benefit in question available to both sexes.

Could it be then that the inequality of whoredom consists in the fact that some burden is unequally placed on the two sexes and in disfavor of the female sex? . . .

[One] way of interpreting this allegation is to say that prostitution constitutes exploitation of the female sex, since harlots are being exploited by, *inter alia,* sex capitalists and customers, and a majority of harlots are women. This interpretation of the allegation merits careful study. . . .

It is of course true that not all prostitutes can be described as workers in the sex industry. Some are in point of fact more adequately described as small-scale private entrepreneurs. Others are being exploited without being exploited by sex capitalists. Those who can be regarded as workers in the sex industry—the growing number of girls working in sex clubs and similar establishments for instance—are, of course, according to Marxist theory, being exploited in the same sense as any wage worker is exploited. But exploitation in this Marxist sense, although perhaps effective as an argument against wage labor in general, is hardly effective as an argument against prostitution.

There is no doubt, however, that practically all harlots—irrespective of whether they are high-class call girls, cheap streetwalkers, or sex-club performers—are being exploited, economically, in a much more crude sense than that in which an automobile worker at General Motors is being exploited. I am thinking here of the fact that all of them—there are very few exceptions to this—have to pay usury rents in order to be able to operate. Many are literally being plundered by their landlords—sex capitalists who often specialize in letting out rooms, flats, or apartments to people in the racket. Not a few prostitutes also have to pay for "protection" to mafiosi with close connections to organized crime.

What makes all this possible? And what are the implications of the existence of conditions such as these for the question of the alleged undesirability of prostitution? With respect to the first of these questions the answer, it seems to me, is that the major culprit is society's hypocritical attitude toward harlotry and harlots. It is this hypocrisy which creates the prerequisites for the sex-capitalist exploitation of the prostitutes. Let me exemplify what I mean by society's hypocritical—and, I might add, totally inconsistent—attitude here. On the one hand, most societies, at least in the West (one deplorable exception is the United States), have followed the UN declaration which recommends that prostitution in itself should not be made illegal.[2] One would therefore expect that someone who pursues a legal activity would have the right to rent the necessary premises to advertise her services, and so on. But not so! The penal code persecutes those who rent out rooms, apartments, and other premises to prostitutes. . . . In what other legal field or branch would contradictions such as these be considered tolerable? . . . In practice, the risk of being thrown in jail of course scares away all but the unscrupulous individuals, who can charge sky-high rents (after all they take a certain risk) and who often are associated with the criminal world. . . .

The conclusion I draw from this is that the crude economic exploitation of the prostitutes is not an argument against prostitution. It rather constitutes an accusation against the laws, regulations, and attitudes which create the preconditions for that exploitation. . . .

A third way of interpreting the charge that prostitution is unequal in the sense that it places a burden on women that it does not place on men is to say that whores are being oppressed, reified, and reduced to a piece of merchandise by their male customers. To begin with the last version of this charge first, I [point out] the obvious, namely, that whores do not sell themselves. The individual hooker is not for sale, but her sexual services are. One could therefore with equal lack of propriety say of any person whose job it is to sell a certain service that he, as a result thereof, is reduced to a piece of merchandise. I cannot help suspecting that behind this talk of reduction to a piece of merchandise lies a good portion of contempt for prostitutes and the kind of services they offer for sale.

As for the version according to which the whore is reified—turned into an object, a thing—it can be understood in a similar way as the one just dealt with. But it can also be understood as the view that the customer does not look upon the prostitute as a human being but as "a piece of ass." He is not interested in her as a person. He is exclusively interested in her sexual performance. As far as I can see, this version of the charge collapses into the kind of sentimentalistic critique that I discussed [above]. Let me just add this: Since when does the fact that we, when visiting a professional, are not interested in him or her as a person, but only in his or her professional performance, constitute a ground for saying that the professional is dehumanized, turned into an object?

The "reification charge" may, however, be understood in still another way. It may be interpreted as saying that the whore is nothing but a means, a mere instrument, for the male customer's ends. This also comes rather close to the sentimentalist charge. Its Kantian character does perhaps deserve a few words of comment, however. First of all, that the customer treats the harlot as a means to his ends is only partly true. The other part of the truth is that the prostitute treats her customer as a means to *her* ends. Thus, the complete truth (if it deserves to be called that) is that prostitute and customer treat *one another* as means rather than as ends.

I have to say, however, that I do not find much substance in this Kantian-inspired talk about means and ends. The kind of relationship that exists between prostitute and customer is one that we find in most service professions. It is simply cultural blindness and sexual taboos that prevent so many of us from seeing this. . . . The means-ends talk is just a way of rationalizing a preconceived opinion.

I shall [consider] the charge that harlotry constitutes oppression of the female sex. Prostitution is here regarded as displaying male oppression of the female in its most overt and extreme form. The seriousness of this charge calls, to begin with, for a clarification of the meaning of the word "oppression." If A opposes B, I take it that B's freedom of choice and action is severely reduced, against his will, as a result of actions un-dertaken by A against B. In this case of political oppression, for example, A thwarts B's desire to form unions and political parties, prevents B from expressing his political opinions, throws B in jail if he refuses to comply, and so on.

It can hardly be disputed that prostitutes are oppressed in this sense. They would not have chosen to become hustlers if some better alternative had been open to them. They are very much aware of the fact that to be a prostitute is to be socially devalued; to be at the bottom of society. To become a hooker is to make just the reverse of a career. It should be observed, however, that none of this warrants the charge that prostitution means the oppression of the female by the male sex. The oppression just described is not an oppression on the basis of sex, as male franchise would be. The "oppressor" is rather those social conditions—present in practically all known social systems—which offer some individuals (both men and women) no better alternative than hustling.

But perhaps what the charge amounts to is that the male sex's oppression of the fe-male sex consists in the oppression of the whore by her male customer. It certainly hap-pens that customers treat prostitutes in ways which could motivate use of the term "op-pression." But this does not mean that this term typically applies to the prostitute-customer relationship. Moreover, harlots usually develop a keen eye for judging peo-ple, and that helps them to avoid many of the (latently) dangerous customers. For it is just a myth that their freedom of choice and action is reduced to a point where they have to accept customers indiscriminately. This is not even true of prostitutes in the lowest bracket, and it certainly is not true of girls in the higher ones.

It is not seldom argued from feminist quarters that the liberation of women must start with the liberation of women from exploitation of their sex. Hence the crusade against prostitution, pornography, and the use of beautiful women in commercial ad-vertising, etc. It is argued that women's lib must have as its primary goal the abolition of the (ab)use of the female sex as a commodity. As long as the female sex is up for sale just like any other commercial object, there can be no true liberation from oppression.

To the reader who has read this far it should be obvious that, at least in part, this type of reasoning rests on or is misguided by such misnomers as "the whore sells her body," "to live by selling oneself," "to buy oneself a piece of ass," etc. So I need not say any more about that. Instead I wish to make a comparison between a typical middle-class housewife in suburbia and her prostitute counterpart, the moderately successful call girl. And I ask, emotional prejudice aside, which of them needs to be "liberated" the most? Both are doing fairly well economically, but while the housewife is totally de-pendent on her husband, at least economically, the call girl in that respect stands on her own two feet. If she has a pimp, it is she, not he, who is the breadwinner in the fam-ily. Is she a traitor to her own sex? If she is (which I doubt), she is no more a traitor to her own sex that her bourgeois counterpart. For after all, Engels was basically right when he said the major difference between the two is that the one hires out her body on piecework while the other hires it out once and for all.

All this does not mean that I am unsympathetic toward the aspirations of the fem-inist movement. It rather means that I disagree with its order of priorities.

Both men and women need to be liberated from the harness of their respective sex roles. But in order to be able to do this, we must liberate ourselves from those mental fossils which prevent us from looking upon sex and sexuality with the same naturalness as upon our cravings for food and drink. And, contrary to popular belief, we may have something to learn from prostitution in this respect, namely, that coition resembles nourishment in that if it can not be obtained in any other way it can always be bought. And bought meals are not always the worst. . . .

X. Some Policy Suggestions

In . . . this essay I have had occasion to discuss the negative features of prostitution as it functions today (and has long functioned) in most societies: the great professional hazards; the economic exploitation; the antisocial tendencies of people in the racket, their frequent association with the criminal world and organized crime, and the stigma attached to their profession; etc. But in distinction to all those who hold these negative features against prostitution (as if they were intrinsic to it), I regard them as the avoidable result of values and attitudes of the society wherein prostitution occurs. And these values and attitudes are not only detrimental to prostitution, *they are also detrimental to the relations between the sexes generally.* . . .

I admit, of course, that a change in our attitudes toward prostitution must be regarded as a long-range goal that it will take a long time to realize. . . . A program for more immediate action is therefore also called for. . . .

The first and most urgent step to take is to decriminalize prostitution in those places where it is still a crime to be or to visit a whore. For, as long as harlotry is lumped together with crime there are hardly any chances of improvement. Fortunately, most societies have taken this step. But even in these societies the progress made is not seldom threatened by various groups who would like to see prostitution recriminalized.

The second step is to improve the housing situation for prostitutes. The prostitute must be given the right to rent a suitable location in her/his capacity as a prostitute. The same legal rules that prohibit a landlord from refusing a tenant *in spe* should be made to apply in the case of the prostitute. Thus, that the tenant *in spe* is a harlot should not constitute adequate ground for refusal. It should also be made impossible for a landlord to evict a person simply because she/he is a hustler. Nor should it be allowed to refuse or evict someone on the ground that other tenants do not wish to live next door to a whore. . . .

What positive effects would this have? First, it would greatly reduce the crude economic exploitation of harlots. Being able to rent a flat without pretense, they would no longer have to pay usury rents to unscrupulous landlords. Second, it would tend to diminish some of the occupational hazards, notably those related to the feeling of insecurity, of being secluded, deprived of the rights of ordinary citizens. Third, it would tend to weaken the association between prostitution and organized crime.

What negative effects, if any, would this have? As far as I can see, the major negative effect would be that certain "respectable" citizens would get their feelings of decency upset by having to live in the same house or neighborhood as a prostitute. But this negative effect is, in my opinion, outweighed by the fact that the customers will not have to walk so far to visit one.

A third urgent step is to develop a program intended to get rid of child and teenage prostitution. Minors should as far as possible be prevented from entrance into prostitution, not on moralistic but on paternalistic grounds. For in the case of minors, paternalistic measures seem justified for the same reasons as they are justified in other social matters. Do I contradict myself when I recommend this? Not at all, for from the fact that prostitution generally is inevitable it does not follow that prostitution among minors is. . . .

As for adult prostitution, I have suggested that it should be reformed rather than abolished. But the most important part of that reform does not concern prostitution and prostitutes but our *attitudes* toward them. For it seems to me impossible to come to grips with the negative aspects of harlotry without a change of our values and attitudes. Which values and attitudes? And why should they be changed? . . .

In my view, contempt for whores and contempt for women are closely related. The devaluation of the female sex is a permanent part of the Western tradition of ideas, reinforced by the Christian so-called culture. As an early example, according to Aristotle we should "look upon the female state as being as it were a deformity though one which occurs in the ordinary course of nature."[3] And according to Freud, who in many respects echoes Aristotle, woman is pictured as partial man: "She [the female child] acknowledges the fact of her castration, and with it too, the superiority of the male."[4] The influence of these and numerous other similar ideas has, with the passage of the years and often in vulgarized form, been sedimented in public opinion.

In order to see the relationship between contempt for women and contempt for harlots, another important part of the Western tradition of ideas must be added, namely, the devaluation of sexuality. Both contempt for the female sex and the devaluation of sexuality have their roots in the ancient notion that man consists of two distinct parts, body and soul, of which the second is immensely more valuable than the first. As is well known, the soul, according to Plato, does not really belong here in our material world, the world of the senses. It belongs to the spiritual world, although it temporarily takes its seat (or is imprisoned) in the body. These ideas were later developed by Aristotle and the purveyor of philosophy to the Catholic church, Thomas Aquinas. The originally Orphic distinction between body and soul was soon transformed, especially under the influence of Christian thinkers such as Saint Augustine, to a general devaluation of the body, bodily functions, and sexuality. . . .

In a culture where both the female sex and sexuality are devaluated it is only "logical" to place the prostitute—an individual who is not only a female but who also earns her living by means of her female sex by selling sexual services—at the bottom of the scale of social approval. . . .

. . . Our outlook as far as sex roles, relations between the sexes, and sexuality are concerned is still very much under the influence of time-honored, but primitive, ideas and attitudes—ideas and attitudes which have negative effects not only on prostitution and prostitutes but also on the relations between the sexes generally. I find it particularly sad that so many feminists seem unable to understand that contempt for harlotry involves contempt for the female sex.

Our attitudes toward sexual expression in general, and mercenary sex in particular, ought to be modified or abandoned partly because of the damage that they do, partly because they represent prejudices in the sense that they are rooted in false beliefs. Women are not partial men nor is the female sex a deformity. And the distinction between body and soul, with all its metaphysical and religious ramifications, apart from being philosophically highly dubious, is the source of more human misery than almost any other.

A sound prostitution is, first of all, a prostitution that is allowed to function in a social climate freed from emotional prejudice of the kind described above. Prostitution can never be rid of its most serious negative aspects (primarily the suffering the prostitutes have to endure) in a society where females are regarded as inferior to males and where man's physical nature is regarded as inferior to his spiritual nature.

A sound prostitution is, furthermore, a prostitution such that those who become prostitutes are adults who are not compelled to prostitute themselves but who freely choose to do so in the same sense of "freely" as anyone's trade or occupation may be said to be freely chosen. A sound prostitution is, in other words, a prostitution of voluntary, not compulsive, hustlers.

A sound prostitution is, third, a prostitution that is legal, and where the prostitutes are not persecuted but attributed the same rights as ordinary citizens as a recognition of the fact that they fulfill a socially valuable function by, *inter alia,* decreasing the amount of sexual misery in society.

A sound prostitution is, fourth, a prostitution such that the prostitutes are no more economically exploited than wage workers in general.

A sound prostitution is, finally, a prostitution that is equally available to both sexes.

Of these conditions I regard the first as the most fundamental. Without it being at least partially satisfied, the satisfaction of the others seems most difficult. Thus, if I were to sum up the principal view put forward [here], it would be formulated as follows: *in order to improve prostitution, we must first and foremost improve our attitudes toward it. . . .*

In conclusion, I wish to emphasize once again that I do not regard prostitution, not even a sound prostitution, as in any way *ultimately* desirable. Its desirability is conditional upon certain ubiquitous and permanent imperfections of actual human societies. In a perfectly good society, however, it would be superfluous.

Notes

1. My major source of information has here as elsewhere been Harry Benjamin and R. E. L. Masters, Prostitution and Morality (Julian Press, 1964), esp. chaps. 5, 6,

and 10. I have also consulted the reports of Jens Jersild, Boy Prostitution (Copenhagen, G. E. C. Gad., 1956) and W. M. Butts, Boy Prostitution of the Metropolis, 8 J. Clinical Psychopathology 673–681 (1947).

2. United Nations, Study on Traffic in Persons and Prostitution (New York, 1959).

3. Aristotle, The Generation of Animals, quoted in Caroline Whitbeck, Theories of Sex Difference, 5 Phil. F. 54, 56 (1973–1974).

4. Sigmund Freud, Female Sexuality, quoted in Whitbeck, *supra* note 3, at 69.

❖ Defending Prostitution: Charges Against Ericsson

CAROLE PATEMAN

ERICSSON'S contractarian defense of prostitution[1] extends the liberal ideals of individualism, equality of opportunity, and the free market to sexual life. The real problem with prostitution, Ericsson claims, is the hypocrisy, prejudice, and punitive attitudes that surround it. Once unblinkered, we can see that prostitution is merely one service occupation among others and that, with some reforms, a morally acceptable, or "sound," prostitution could exist. This defense has its appeal at a time when strict control of sexual conduct is again being strenuously advocated. However, Ericsson's argument fails to overcome the general weaknesses of abstract contractarianism, and his claim that he has rebutted the feminist charge against prostitution cannot be granted. The central feminist argument is that prostitution remains morally undesirable, no matter what reforms are made, because it is one of the most graphic examples of men's domination of women.

Ericsson's argument illustrates nicely how liberal contractarianism systematically excludes the patriarchal dimension of our society from philosophical scrutiny. He interprets feminists as arguing that prostitution is "undesirable on the ground that it constitutes an extreme instance of the inequality between the sexes," and he then interprets inequality to be a matter of the distribution of benefits and burdens. It thus appears that a remedy can be found for the withholding of a benefit (access to prostitutes) from women by extending equality of opportunity to buy and sell sexual services on the market to both sexes. Ericsson ignores the fact that men earn a good deal more than women, so the latter would still have a greater incentive to be sellers than buyers (or would be confined to the cheaper end of the market as buyers; Ericsson pays no attention to the different categories of prostitution). Moreover, Ericsson notes that three-quarters of the men who are in the market for prostitutes are married. Any change in attitudes would have to be sufficient to make it acceptable that wives could spend what they save from housekeeping money, or spend part of their own earnings, on prostitutes. Second, Ericsson dismisses as meaningless the charge that prostitution unfairly burdens women because they are oppressed as prostitutes; properly understood, prostitution is an example of a free contract between individuals in the market

93 Ethics 561 (April 1983). © 1983 by The University of Chicago. Reprinted by permission of the University of Chicago Press.

in which services are exchanged for money. Ericsson's defense does not and cannot confront the feminist objection to prostitution. Feminists do not see prostitution as unacceptable because it distributes benefits and burdens unequally; rather, to use Ericsson's language of inequality, because prostitution is grounded in the inequality of domination and subjection. The problem of domination is both denied by and hidden behind Ericsson's assertion that prostitution is a free contract or an equal exchange.

The most striking feature of Ericsson's defense is that he makes no attempt to substantiate the key claim that prostitution *is* the sale of sexual services. His assertion relies on the conventional assumption that free wage labor stands at the opposite pole from slavery. The worker freely contracts to sell labor power or services for a specified period, whereas the person of the slave is sold for an unlimited time. Ericsson comments that if a prostitute "actually did sell herself, she would no longer be a prostitute but a sexual slave". More exactly, since she has the civil and juridical status of a free individual in the capitalist market, she would be in a form of subjection that fell short of slavery. Ericsson avoids discussing whether this is indeed the position of the prostitute because he ignores the problems involved in separating the sale of services through contract from the sale of the body and the self. In capitalist societies it appears as if labor power and services are bought and sold on the market, but "labor power" and "services" are abstractions. When workers sell labor power, or professionals sell services to clients (and Ericsson regards some prostitutes as "small scale private entrepreneurs"),[2] neither the labor power nor services can in reality be separated from the person offering them for sale. Unless the "owners" of these abstractions agree to, or are compelled to, use them in certain ways, which means that the "owners" act in a specified manner, there is nothing to be sold. The employer appears to buy labor power; what he actually obtains is the right to command over workers, the right to put their capacities, their bodies, to use as he determines.

Services and labor power are inseparably connected to the body and the body is, in turn, inseparably connected to the sense of self. Ericsson writes of the prostitute as a kind of social worker, but the services of the prostitute are related in a more intimate manner to her body than those of other professionals. Sexual services, that is to say, sex and sexuality, are constitutive of the body in a way in which the counseling skills of the social worker are not (a point illustrated in a backhanded way by the ubiquitous use by men of vulgar terms for female sexual organs to refer to women themselves). Sexuality and the body are, further, integrally connected to conceptions of femininity and masculinity, and all these are constitutive of our individuality, our sense of self-identity. When sex becomes a commodity in the capitalist market so, necessarily, do bodies and selves. The prostitute cannot sell sexual services alone; what she sells is her body. To supply services contracted for, professionals must act in certain ways, or use their bodies; to use the labor power he has bought the employer has command over the worker's capacities and body; to use the prostitute's "services," her purchaser must buy her body and use her body. In prostitution, because of the relation between the commodity being marketed and the body, it is the body that is up for sale.

Critics of marriage have often claimed that wives are no different from prostitutes. Women who marry also contract away their bodies but (in principle) for life rather than for minutes or hours like the prostitute. However, a form of marriage in which the husband gains legal right of sexual use of his wife's body is only one possible form. The conjugal relation is not necessarily one of domination and subjection, and in this it differs from prostitution. Ericsson's defense is about prostitution in capitalist societies; that is, the practice through which women's bodies become commodities in the market which can be bought (contracted for) for sexual use. The questions his defense raises are why there is a demand for this commodity, exactly what the commodity is, and why it is *men* who demand it.

Ericsson cannot admit that the first two questions arise. The third he treats as unproblematic. He stands firmly in the patriarchal tradition which discusses prostitution as a problem about the women who are prostitutes, and our attitudes to them, not a problem about the men who demand to buy them. For Ericsson it is merely a contingent fact that most prostitutes are women and customers men.[3] He claims that the demand for prostitution could never disappear because of some "ubiquitous and permanent imperfections" of human existence arising from the sexual urge. In other words, prostitution is a natural feature of human life. Certainly, sexual impulses are part of our natural constitution as humans, but the sale of "sexual services" as a commodity in the capitalist market cannot be reduced to an expression of our natural biology and physiology. To compare the fulfillment of sexual urges through prostitution to other natural necessities of human survival, to argue from the fact that we need food, so it should be available, to the claim that "our sexual desires are just as basic, natural, and compelling as our appetite for food, [so] this also holds for them," is, to say the least, disingenuous. What counts as "food" varies widely, of course, in different cultures, but, at the most fundamental level of survival there is one obvious difference between sex and other human needs. Without a certain minimum of food, drink, and shelter, people die; but, to my knowledge, no one has yet died from want of sexual release. Moreover, sometimes food and drink are impossible to obtain no matter what people do, but every person has the means to find sexual release at hand.

To treat prostitution as a natural way of satisfying a basic human need, to state that "bought meals are not always the worst," neatly, if vulgarly, obscures the real, social character of contemporary sexual relations. Prostitution is not, as Ericsson claims, the same as "sex without love or mutual affection." The latter is morally acceptable *if* it is the result of mutual physical attraction that is freely expressed by both individuals. The difference between sex without love and prostitution is not the difference between cooking at home and buying food in restaurants; the difference is that between the reciprocal expression of desire and unilateral subjection to sexual acts with the consolation of payment: it is the difference for women between freedom and subjection.

To understand why men (not women) demand prostitutes, and what is demanded, prostitution has to be rescued from Ericsson's abstract contractarianism and placed in the social context of the structure of sexual relations between women and men. Since the revival of the organized feminist movement, moral and political philosophers have begun to turn their attention to sexual life, but their discussions are usually divided into a set of discrete compartments which take for granted that a clear distinction can be drawn between consensual and coercive sexual relationships. However, as an examination of consent and rape makes graphically clear,[4] throughout the whole of sexual life domination, subjection, and enforced submission are confused with consent, free association, and the reciprocal fulfillment of mutual desire. The assertion that prostitution is no more than an example of a free contract between equal individuals in the market is another illustration of the presentation of submission as freedom. Feminists have often argued that what is fundamentally at issue in relations between women and men is not sex but power. But, in the present circumstances of our sexual lives, it is not possible to separate power from sex. The expression of sexuality and what it means to be feminine and a woman, or masculine and a man, is developed within, and intricately bound up with, relations of domination and subordination.

Ericsson remarks that "the best prostitutional sex available is probably much better from the customer's point of view than average marital sex." It is far from obvious that it is either "quality" or the "need" for sex, in the commonsense view of "quality" and "sex," that explains why three-quarters of these customers are husbands. In the "permissive society" there are numerous ways in which men can find sex without payment, in addition to the access that husbands have to wives. But, except in the case of the most brutal husbands, most spouses work out a modus vivendi about all aspects of their lives, including the wife's bodily integrity. Not all husbands exercise to the full their socially and legally recognized right—which is the right of a master. There is, however, another institution which enables all men to affirm themselves as master. To be able to purchase a body in the market presupposes the existence of masters. Prostitution is the public recognition of men as sexual masters; it puts submission on sale as a commodity in the market.

The outline of an answer to the complex question of why men demand this commodity can be found in recent feminist interpretations of psychoanalytic theory. Feminist discussions of the differential development of gendered individuality suggest that the masculine sense of self is grounded in separateness, especially separation from those other (opposing) feminine selves which proclaim what masculinity is not.[5] Hegel showed theoretically in his famous dialectic of mastery and servitude that a self so conceived always attempts to gain recognition and maintain its subjective isolation through domination. When women and men are seen in their substantive individuality, and not as abstract makers of contracts, an explanation can be found for why it is *men* who demand to buy women's bodies in the market. The demand by men for prostitutes in patriarchal capitalist society is bound up with a historically and culturally distinctive form of masculine individuality. The structure of the relation between the sexes reaches into the unconscious early development of little boys and girls and out into the form of economic organization in which the capacities of individuals, and even women's bodies, become commodities to be alienated to the control and use of others.

The peculiarity of Ericsson's argument for equality of opportunity in "sound" prostitution should now be apparent. He assumes that the (sexual) selves of women and men are interchangeable. This may appear radical, but it is a purely abstract radical-ism that reduces differentiated, gendered individuality to the seemingly natural, un-differentiated, and universal figure of the "individual"—which is an implicit generaliz-ation of the masculine self. The feminist exploration of gendered individuality provides the material, sociological grounding for that familiar, liberal abstraction, the possessive, atomistic self that appears as the bearer of rights and the maker of contracts in civil society. The logic of Ericsson's sexual contractarianism also leads to two un-palatable conclusions that he is unwilling to draw. The first is that all sexual relations should take the form of universal prostitution, the buying and selling of sexual services on the market. The equal right of access to sexual use of a body (or "sexual services") can be established more economically and advantageously for the individual through universal prostitution than through (the contract of) marriage. Second, it is unneces-sary to confine the buying and selling of sexual services to adults. Ericsson is faint-hearted in his contractarianism when he excludes children from the market. Strictly, the capacity to make a contract is all that is required; surely not a capacity confined to those who are statutorily adults.

Ericsson shows how complete is his misunderstanding of feminism and the femi-nist criticism of prostitution when he complains that "so many feminists seem unable to understand that contempt for harlotry involves contempt for the female sex." Nei-ther contempt for women nor their ancient profession underlies feminist arguments; rather, they are sad and angry about what the demand for prostitution reveals of the general character of (private and public) relations between the sexes. The claim that what is really wrong with prostitution is hypocrisy and outdated attitudes to sex is the tribute that liberal permissiveness pays to political mystification.

Notes

1. L. O. Ericsson, Charges Against Prostitution: An Attempt at a Philosophical As-sessment, herein, at 208.

2. On workers as "petty entrepreneurs," their labor power or services, see R. P. Wolff, A Critique and Reinterpretation of Marx's Labor Theory of Value, 10 Phil. & Pub. Aff. 89 (1981), esp. 109–111.

3. . . . Following Ericsson, I discuss only heterosexual (genitally oriented) prosti-tution. It is not immediately clear that homosexual prostitution has the same social significance.

4. See my Women and Consent, 8 Pol. Theory 149 (1980).

5. See, esp., J. Benjamin, The Bonds of Love: Rational Violence and Erotic Domi-nation, 6 Feminist Stud. 175 (1980). Benjamin builds on N. Chodorow, The Repro-duction of Mothering: Psychoanalysis and the Sociology of Gender (Univ. California Press, 1978).

Prostitution and Civil Rights

CATHARINE A. MACKINNON

THE GAP BETWEEN the promise of civil rights and the real lives of prostitutes is an abyss which swallows up prostituted women.[1] To speak of prostitution and civil rights in one breath moves the two into one world, at once exposing and narrowing the distance between them.

Women in prostitution are denied every imaginable civil right in every imaginable and unimaginable way,[2] such that it makes sense to understand prostitution as consisting in the denial of women's humanity, no matter how humanity is defined. It is denied both through the social definition and condition of prostitutes and through the meaning of some civil rights.

The legal right to be free from torture and cruel and inhuman or degrading treatment is recognized by most nations and is internationally guaranteed. In prostitution, women are tortured through repeated rape and in all the more conventionally recognized ways. Women are prostituted precisely in order to be degraded and subjected to cruel and brutal treatment without human limits; it is the opportunity to do this that is exchanged when women are bought and sold for sex. The fact that most legal prohibitions on torture apply only to official torture, specifically torture by state actors, illustrates the degree to which the legal design of civil rights has excluded women's experience of being denied them.

Security of the person is fundamental to society. The point of prostitution is to transgress women's personal security. Every time the woman walks up to the man's car, every time the man walks into the brothel, the personhood of women—not that secure in a male dominated society to begin with—is made more insecure. Women in prostitution attempt to set limits on what can be done to them. But nothing backs them up. Pimps supposedly do, but it shows how insecure prostitutes' lives are that pimps can look like security. Nothing limits pimps, and, ultimately, anything can be done to their property for a price. As Andrea Dworkin has said, "whatever can be stolen can be sold."[3] In rape, the security of women's person is stolen; in prostitution, it is stolen and sold.

---

1 Mich. J. Gender & Law 13 (1993).

Liberty is a primary civil right. Kathleen Barry has analyzed female sexual slavery as prostitution one cannot get out of.[4] A recent study of street prostitutes in Toronto found that about ninety percent wanted to leave but could not.[5] If they are there because they cannot leave, they are sexual slaves. Need it be said: to be a slave is to be deprived of liberty, not to exercise it. To lack the ability to set limits on one's condition or to leave it is to lack consent to it. At the same time, liberty for men is often construed in sexual terms and includes liberal access to women, including prostituted ones. So while, for men, liberty entails that women be prostituted, for women, prostitution entails loss of all that liberty means.

The right to privacy is often included among civil rights. In the United States, one meaning privacy has effectively come to have is the right to dominate free of public scrutiny. The private is then defined as a place of freedom by effectively rendering consensual what women and children are forced to do out of the public eye. Prostitution is thus often referred to as occurring in private between consenting adults, as is marriage and family. The result is to extend the aura of privacy and protection from public intervention from sex to sexual abuse. In prostitution, women have no space they can call off-limits to prying eyes, prying hands, or prying other parts of the anatomy, not even inside their own skin.

Freedom from arbitrary arrest is also a civil right. Criminal prostitution laws make women into criminals for being victimized as women, so are arguably arbitrary in the first place. Then these laws are often enforced for bureaucratic, turf-protective, funding, political, or advancement reasons[6]—that is, arbitrarily, against women.

Property ownership is recognized as a civil right in many countries. Women in prostitution not only begin poor, they are systematically kept poor by pimps who take the lion's share of what they earn. They are the property of the men who buy and sell and rent them—placing the civil right, once again, in the hands of their tormenters.

Particularly in the United States, the right to freedom of speech is cherished. Prostitution as an institution silences women by brutalizing and terrorizing them so horribly that no words can form, by punishing them for telling the truth about their condition, by degrading whatever they do manage to say about virtually anything because of who they are seen as being. The pornography that is made of their violation—pimps' speech—is protected expression.[7]

One civil right is so deep it is seldom mentioned: to be recognized as a person before the law. To be a prostitute is to be a legal nonperson in the ways that matter. What for Blackstone and others was the legal nonpersonhood of wives[8] is extended for prostitutes from one man to all men as a class. Anyone can do anything to you and nothing legal will be done about it. John Stoltenberg has shown how the social definition of personhood for men is importantly premised on the prostitution of women.[9] Prostitution as a social institution gives men personhood—in this case, manhood—through depriving women of theirs.

The civil right to life is basic. The Green River murders, the serial murders of women in Los Angeles, the eleven dead African-American women who had been in prostitution and were found under piles of rags in Detroit—these acts are "gender cleansing." Snuff films are part of it. When killing women becomes a sex act, women have no right to their lives. Women in prostitution, along with women cohabiting with men, are the most exposed.

Equality is also a civil right, both equal humanity in substance and formal equality before the law. In the United States, constitutional equality encompasses equal protection of the laws under the Fourteenth Amendment and freedom from slavery or involuntary servitude under the Thirteenth Amendment. Prostitution implicates both.

The Fourteenth Amendment provides for equal protection and benefit of the law without discrimination. What little equality litigation exists in the prostitution context misses the point of their unequal treatment in a number of illuminating ways. Some older prostitution statutes, challenged as sex discriminatory on their face, made prostitution illegal only when a woman engaged in it. For example, Louisiana provided that "[p]rostitution is the practice by a female of indiscriminate sexual intercourse with males for compensation."[10] Applying the sex discrimination test at the time, the court ruled that "[d]ifferences between the sexes does bear a rational relationship to the prohibition of prostitution by females."[11] In other words, defining prostitution as something only women do is simple realism. Women really do this; mostly only women do this; it seems to have something to do with being a woman to do this; therefore, it is not sex discrimination to have a law that punishes only women for doing this.

Here, the fact that most prostitutes are women is not a sex inequality, nor does equating prostitution with being a woman tell us anything about what being a woman means. That most prostitutes are women is the reason why legally defining the problem of prostitution as a problem of women is not a sex inequality. Thus does the soft focus of gender neutrality blur sex distinctions by law and rigidly sex-divided social realities at the same time. By now, most legislatures have gender neutralized their prostitution laws—without having done anything to gender-neutralize prostitution's realities.

The cases that adjudicate equal protection challenges to sex-discriminatory enforcement of prostitution laws extend this rationale. Police usually send men to impersonate tricks in order to arrest prostitutes. Not surprisingly, many more women than men are arrested in this way.[12] The cases hold that this is not intentional sex discrimination but a good faith effort by the state to get at "the sellers of sex,"[13] "the profiteer."[14] Sometimes the tricks are even described by police as the women's "victim."[15] Courts seem to think the women make the money; in most instances, they are conduits from trick to pimp and the money is never theirs.[16] Sometimes the male police decoys wait to arrest until the sex act is about to happen—or, prostitutes complain, until after it happens.[17]

Another all-too-common practice is arresting accused prostitutes, women, while letting arrested customers, men, go with a citation or a warning.[18] This, too, has been challenged as sex discrimination, and it sure sounds like it. Yet this, courts say, is not sex discrimination because male and female prostitutes are treated alike[19] or because customers violate a different, noncomparable, law from the one under which the women are charged.[20] There are some men in prostitution, most (but not all) prostituting as women. You can tell you have walked into the world of gender neutrality when the law treats men as badly as women when they do what mostly women do, and that makes treating women badly non-sex-based. Of course, compared with customers, prostitutes also more often fail to satisfy the gender-neutral conditions of release: good money, good name, good job, good family, good record, good lawyer, good three-piece suit. . . .

Some states quarantine arrested women prostitutes but not arrested male customers. This, too, is not sex discrimination, according to the courts, because the women are more likely to communicate venereal diseases than the men are.[21] Where the women got the venereal diseases is not discussed; women are walking disease vectors from which men's health must be protected. This was before AIDS, but the reality remains—the recipient of the sperm is most likely to become infected.[22]

These cases represent the extent to which equal protection of the laws has been litigated for prostitutes.[23] The disparity between the focus of this litigation and the civil rights violations inherent in prostitution is staggering. Behind the blatant sex discrimination these cases rationalize is the vision of equality they offer prostitutes—the right to be prostituted without being disproportionately punished for it. As unprincipled as the losses in these cases are, if they had been won, this is the equality they would have won.

Criminal laws against prostitution make women into criminals for being victimized as women, yet there are no cases challenging these laws as sex discrimination on this ground. Criminal prostitution laws collaborate elaborately in women's social inequality;[24] through them, the state enforces the exploitation of prostituted women directly. When legal victimization is piled on top of social victimization, women are dug deeper and deeper into civil inferiority, their subordination and isolation legally ratified and legitimated. Disparate enforcement combines with this discriminatory design to violate prostituted women's Fourteenth Amendment right to equal protection of the laws.

This is not to argue that prostitutes have a sex equality right to engage in prostitution. Rather, prostitution subordinates and exploits and disadvantages women as women in social life, a social inequality which prostitution laws then seal with a criminal sanction.

The argument to decriminalize trafficking women has no such support. Disadvantage on the basis of sex directly supports strict enforcement of laws against pimps, who exploit women's inequality for gain,[25] and against tricks, who benefit from women's oppressed status and subordinate individual women skin on skin.

Beyond eliminating discriminatory criminal laws and enforcing appropriate ones, it is time the law did something for women in prostitution. Getting the criminal law off their backs may keep the state from reinforcing their subordinate status but it does nothing to change that status. The Thirteenth Amendment, which applies whether or not the state is involved, may help.

The Thirteenth Amendment prohibits slavery and involuntary servitude. It, and its implementing statutes, was passed to invalidate the chattel slavery of African-Americans and kindred social institutions.[26] Its language that slavery "shall [not] exist" gives support to its affirmative elimination. The Thirteenth Amendment has been applied to invalidate a range of arrangements of forced labor and exploitive servitude.[27] The slavery of African-Americans is not the first or last example of enslavement, although it has rightly been one of the most notorious. To apply the Thirteenth Amendment to prostitution is not to equate prostitution with the chattel slavery of African-Americans but to draw on common features of institutions of forcible inequality in the context of the Thirteenth Amendment's implementation.

Compared with slavery of African-Americans, prostitution is older, more pervasive across cultures, does not include as much non-sexual exploitation, and is based on sex, and sex and race combined. For Black women in the United States, the relation between prostitution and slavery is less one of analogy than of continuity with their sexual use under slavery.[28] Applying the Thirteenth Amendment to prostitution claims enslavement as a term and reality of wider application, which historically it has been. It also takes the view that the Thirteenth Amendment was intended to prohibit the forms slavery took for Black women just as much as those it took for Black men.

Thirteenth Amendment[29] standards require a showing of legal or physical force, used or threatened, to secure service, which must be "distinctly personal service . . . in which one person possesses virtually unlimited authority over another."[30] Some cases predicated servitude on psychological coercion,[31] but the Supreme Court recently held that a climate of fear alone is not enough.[32] The vulnerabilities of the victims are still relevant to determining whether physical or legal coercion or threats compel the service, rendering it "slavelike."[33] Recognized vulnerabilities have included mental retardation, being an illegal immigrant, not speaking the language, being a child, and being stranded in a foreign city without means of support.[34] Poverty has been pervasively understood as part of the setting of force.[35]

The Thirteenth Amendment has often been found violated when a person is tricked into peonage or service through fraud or deceit and is then kept unable to leave, including through contrived and manipulated indebtedness.[36] Debt is not a requirement of servitude, but it is a common incident of it. One recent case found that victims—called victims in these cases—were forced into domestic service by enticing them to travel to the United States, where they were paid little for exorbitant work hours and had their passports and return tickets withheld, while they were required to work off, as servants, the cost of their transportation.[37] Corroborating evidence has included extremely poor working conditions.[38]

Indentured servitude has long been legally prohibited in the United States, even prior to the passage of the Thirteenth Amendment.[39] In interpreting the Thirteenth Amendment in contemporary peonage contexts, courts have been far less concerned with whether the condition was voluntarily entered and far more with whether the subsequent service was involuntary.[40] That victims believe they have no viable alternative but to serve in the ways in which they are being forced has also supported a finding of coercion, and with it the conclusion that the condition is one of enslavement.[41] Involuntary servitude has embraced situations in which a person has made a difficult but rational decision to remain in bondage.[42]

If the legal standards for involuntary servitude developed outside the sexual context are applied to the facts of prostitution, the situations of most of the women in it are clearly prohibited. In prostitution, human beings are bought and sold as chattel for use in "distinctly personal service."[43] Many women and girls are sold by one pimp to another as well as from pimp to trick and for pornography. Prostitution was not formerly called "white *slavery*" for nothing.[44]

Prostitution occurs within multiple power relations of domination, degradation, and subservience[45] of the pimp and trick over the prostitute: men over women, older over younger, citizen over alien, moneyed over impoverished, violent over victimized, connected over isolated, housed over homeless, tolerated and respected over despised. All of the forms of coercion and vulnerabilities recognized under the Thirteenth Amendment are common in prostitution, and then some. No social institution exceeds it in physical violence. It is common for prostitutes to be deprived of food and sleep and money, beaten, tortured, raped, and threatened with their lives, both as acts for which the pimp is paid by other men and to keep the women in line.[46] Women in prostitution are subject to near total domination. Much of this is physical, but pimps also develop to a high art forms of nonphysical force to subjugate the women's will. Their techniques of mind control often exploit skills women have developed to survive sexual abuse, such as denial, dissociation, and multiplicity. They also manipulate women's desire for respect and self-respect.

Criminal laws against prostitution provide legal force behind its social involuntariness. Women in prostitution have no police protection because they are criminals, making pimps' protection racket both possible and necessary. In addition to being able to inflict physical abuse with impunity, pimps confiscate the women's earnings and isolate them even beyond the stigma they carry. The women then have nowhere but pimps to turn to bail them out after arrest, leaving them in debt for their fines which must be worked out in trade. Thus the law collaborates in enforcing women's involuntary servitude by turning the victim of peonage into a criminal. Such legal complicity is state action, raising a claim under the Fourteenth Amendment for sex discrimination by state law.[47]

While it is dangerous to imply that some prostitution is forced, leaving the rest of it to seem free, as a matter of fact, most if not all prostitution is ringed with force in the most conventional sense, from incest to kidnapping to forced drugging to assault to criminal law. Sex-based poverty, both prior to and during prostitution, enforces it; while poverty alone has not been recognized as making out a case of coercion, it has been recognized as making exit impossible in many cases in which coercion has been found. If all of the instances in which these factors interacted to keep a woman in prostitution were addressed, there would be little of it left.

Beyond this, the Thirteenth Amendment may prohibit prostitution as an institution. In the words of The Three Prostitutes' Collectives from Nice, "*all* prostitution is forced prostitution . . . we would not lead the 'life' if we were in a position to leave it."[48] In this perspective, prostitution as such is coerced, hence could be prohibited as servitude. At the very least, there is authority for taking the victims' inequality into account when courts assess whether deprivation of freedom of choice is proven.[49]

On a few occasions in the past, the Thirteenth Amendment has been used to prosecute pimps for prostituting women.[50] In these federal criminal cases, the prostitution was forced in order to pay a debt the women supposedly owed the pimp. In one case, the defendant procured two women from a prison by paying their fines and then forced them to repay him by prostituting at his road house.[51] In another, young Mexican women were induced to accept free transportation to jobs which did not exist and then were told they could not return home until they repaid the cost of the transportation through prostitution.[52] These women were financially trapped, sometimes physically assaulted, always threatened, and in fear. Some complied with the prostitution; some were able to resist. In these cases, the prostitution as such was not considered involuntary servitude—the coercion into doing it was. But it is implicit in these cases that prostitution is not something a woman, absent force, would choose to do.

It is worth asking whether coercion of women into sex in a Thirteenth Amendment context would be measured by the legal standards by which courts have measured the coerciveness of nonsexual exploitation of groups that include men. The coercion of women into and within prostitution has been invisible because prostitution is considered sex and sex is considered what women are for. The standards for the meaning of women's "yes" in the sexual context range from approximating a dead body's enthusiasm, to fighting back and screaming "no," to pleading with an armed rapist to use a condom.[53] This being free choice, one wonders what coercion would look like. Sex in general, particularly sex for survival, is so pervasively merged with the meaning of being a woman that whenever sex occurs, under whatever conditions, the woman tends to be defined as freely acting.

Suits for prostitution as involuntary servitude confront the notion that women—some women who are "just like that" or women in general—are in prostitution freely. No condition of freedom is prepared for by sexual abuse in childhood, permits and condones repeated rapes and beatings, and subjects its participants to a risk of premature death of forty times the national average.[54] The fact that most women in prostitution were sexually abused as children,[55] and most entered prostitution itself before they were adults,[56] undermines the patina of freedom and the glamour of liberation that is the marketing strategy apparently needed for most customers to enjoy using them. Such suits would also challenge freedom of choice as a meaningful concept for women under conditions of sex inequality. Women's precluded options in societies that discriminate on the basis of sex, including in employment, are fundamental to the prostitution context. If prostitution is a free choice, why are the women with the fewest choices the ones most often found doing it?[57]

When a battered woman sustains the abuse of one man for economic survival for twenty years, not even this legal system believes she consents to the abuse anymore. Asking why she did not leave has begun to be replaced by noticing what keeps her there.[58] Perhaps when women in prostitution sustain the abuse of thousands of men for economic survival for twenty years, this will, at some point, come to be understood as non-consensual as well. And many do not survive. They are merely kept alive until they can no longer be used. Then they are sold one last time to someone who kills them for sex, or they are OD'd in an alley or otherwise end up under those trash heaps in Detroit.

The fact that the coercion in prostitution will be difficult to establish in law when it is so overwhelmingly obvious in life is both why it would be difficult to win these cases and why it is crucial to try. It is also helpful to be trying in a legal context such as the Thirteenth Amendment that has traditionally emphasized less how one was subjected in the first place and more the barriers to leaving the subjected state.

The best thing about criminal law is that the state does it, so women do not have to. The worst thing about criminal law is that the state does not do it, so women still have to. Fortunately for women, the Thirteenth Amendment has a civil application, meaning we can use it ourselves. Under §1985(3), prostituted women could allege that they have been subjected to a conspiracy to deprive them of civil rights as women. The conspiracy is the easy part—pimps never do this alone. In a supply-side conspiracy, they prostitute women through organized crime, gangs, associations, cults, families, hotel owners, and police. There is also a demand-side conspiracy, more difficult to argue but certainly there, between pimps and tricks.

Long unresolved is whether §1985(3) applies to conspiracies on the basis of sex. In a recent case, the Supreme Court held that the group "women who seek and receive abortions" was not an adequate class for purposes of §1985(3) because it was not based on sex.[59] The court did not say that sex-based conspiracies are not actionable under §1985(3); several members of the court said that they are. Prostituted women are an even more persuasive sex-based class. How hard can it be to prove that women are prostituted as women? Not only is prostitution overwhelmingly done to women by men, every aspect of the condition has defined gender female as such and as inferior for centuries. Evelina Giobbe explains how the status and treatment of prostitutes defines all women as a sex: "[T]he prostitute symbolizes the value of women in society. She is paradigmatic of women's social, sexual, and economic subordination in that her status is the basic unit by which all women's value is measured and to which all women can be reduced."[60] As Dorchen Leidholdt puts it: "What other job is so deeply gendered that one's breasts, vagina and rectum constitute the working equipment? Is so deeply gendered that the workers are exclusively women and children and young men used like women?"[61] In addition, the fact that some men are also sold for sex helps make prostitution look less than biological, less like a sex difference. Treatment that is socially and legally damaging and stereotypical that overwhelmingly burdens one sex, but is not unique to one sex, is most readily seen as sex discrimination.

A civil action under §1985(3) would allow prostituted women to sue pimps for sexual slavery, refuting the lie that prostitution is just a job. Slavery is a lot of work, but that does not make it just a job, picking cotton being just picking cotton. The enforced inequality is the issue.

In addition to these legal tools, the law against pornography that Andrea Dworkin and I wrote gives civil rights to women in prostitution in a way that could begin to end that institution.[62] Pornography is an arm of prostitution. As Annie McCombs once put it to me, when you make pornography of a woman, you make a prostitute out of her. The pornography law we wrote is concretely grounded in the experience of prostituted women; women coerced into pornography are coerced into prostitution. It is also based on the experience of women in prostitution who are assaulted because of pornography. Beyond this, under its trafficking provision, any woman, in or out of prostitution, who can prove women are harmed through the materials could sue pornographers for trafficking women. This provision recognizes the unity of women as a class rather than dividing prostituted women from all women. The precluded options that get women into prostitution, hence pornography, affect all women, as does the fact that pornography harms all women, if not all in the same way.

Subordination on the basis of sex is key to our pornography law. Pornography is defined as graphic sexually explicit materials that subordinate women (or anyone) on the basis of sex. Women in prostitution are the first women pornography subordinates. In its prohibition on coercion into pornography, in making their subordination actionable, this law sets the first floor beneath the condition of prostituted women, offers the first civil right that limits how much they can be violated. It does not do all that they need, but it is a lot more than the nothing that they have.

This law uses the artifact nature of pornography to hold the perpetrators accountable for what they do. Before this, the pictures have been used against women: to blackmail them into prostitution and keep them there, as a technologically sophisticated way of possessing and exchanging women as a class. Under this law, the pornography becomes proof of the woman's injury as well as an instance of it.

Because pornography affects all women and connects all forms of sexual subordination, so does this law. And this law reaches the pornography. The way subordination is done in pornography is the way it is done in prostitution is the way it is done in the rest of the world: rape, battering, sexual abuse of children, sexual harassment, and murder are sold in prostitution and are the acts out of which pornography is made. Addressing pornography in this way builds a base among women for going after prostitution as a violation of equality rights.

For years I have been saying that I do not know what to do, legally, about prostitution. I still do not. State constitutions and human rights remedies could be adapted to use the argument I offer here. The Florida statute Meg Baldwin wrote and got passed is brilliant and is beginning to be used by women.[63] Recent international initiatives build on superb long-term work and support these efforts.[64] I do know that we need to put the power to act directly in women's hands more than we have.[65]

These thoughts are offered to honor Evelina Giobbe's demand for an institutional policy response to the reality of prostitution, toward the civil rights all women are entitled to.

Notes

[This speech was given at a symposium "Prostitution: From Academia to Activism," University of Michigan Law School, Oct. 31, 1972. *Ed.*]

1. This discussion focuses on prostituted women and girls as the paradigm case, remembering that boys and sometimes men are also prostituted.

2. This discussion builds upon prior presentations . . . in which the conditions of

women in prostitution were documented. See generally Evelina Giobbe, Juvenile Prostitution: Profile of Recruitment, in Ann W. Burgess ed., Child Trauma I: Issues and Research 117 (1992); Evelina Giobbe, Prostitution: Buying the Right to Rape, in Ann W. Burgess ed., Rape and Sexual Assault III: A Research Handbook 143 (1991); and citations throughout this article.

3. See Andrea Dworkin, Letters from a War Zone: Writings 1976–1986, 229 (1989).

4. See generally Kathleen Barry, Female Sexual Slavery (1979).

5. Elizabeth Fry Society of Toronto, Streetwork Outreach with Female Street Prostitutes 13 (May 1987) (Approximately 90% of the women contacted indicated they wished to stop working on the streets at some point, but felt unable or unclear about how to even begin this process.").

6. See generally People v. Superior Court of Alameda County, 562 P.2d 1315 (Cal. 1977).

7. See generally American Booksellers Ass'n v. Hudnut, 771 F.2d 323 (7th Cir. 1985), *aff'd*, 475 U.S. 1001 (1986).

8. 1 William Blackstone, Commentaries *442.

9. See generally John Stoltenberg, Male Sexuality: Why Ownership Is Sexy, 1 Mich. J. Gender & L. 59 (1993).

10. State v. DeVall, 302 So. 2d 909, 910 (La. 1974) (quoting La. Rev. Stat. Ann. §14:82 (West 1986)).

11. *DeVall*, 302 So. 2d at 913. See also City of Minneapolis v. Burchette, 240 N.W.2d 500, 505 (Minn. 1976) (arresting chiefly female violators of prostitution law is a rational way to meet the objective of controlling prostitution). This position has not changed significantly with elevated scrutiny. See, e.g., State v. Sandoval, 649 P. 2d 485, 487 (N.M. Ct. App. 1982) (ruling that there is no arbitrary enforcement of prostitution statute under state equal rights amendment); Bolser v. Washington State Liquor Control Bd., 580 P.2d 629, 633 (Wash. 1978) (holding that male and female dancers are equally covered by restrictions on topless dancing, resulting in no violation of state equal rights amendment).

12. I am told by women police officers that they loathe being decoys, although some of their work has resulted in spectacular arrests of pillars of the community. No woman should be forced to present herself as available for sexual use, whether as a prostitute or as a police officer ordered to pose as a prostitute as part of her employment.

13. United States v. Moses, 339 A.2d 46, 55 (D.C. 1975). Another reason offered for not using women police decoys is that, due to past sex discrimination, there are few or no women to use. See People v. Burton, 432 N.Y.S.2d 312, 315 (City Ct. of Buffalo 1980).

14. People v. Superior Court of Alameda County, 562 P.2d 1315, 1321 (Cal. 1977).

15. People v. Nelson, 427 N.Y.S.2d 194, 195 (City Ct. of Syracuse 1980).

16. Janice Toner, a former prostitute, argued that the money she made as a prostitute was not income to her because she was merely a conduit to her husband/pimp, who beat and threatened to kill her and their children. The Tax Court rejected the argument, although her husband was convicted of assault in a separate case. Toner v. Commissioner, 60 T.C.M. (CCH) 1016, 1019 (1990). The Court found that Toner did not show that her husband's abuse was causally connected to her earning of an income from prostitution and characterized her as an active, voluntary participant in some aspects of the prostitution business. *Id.* at 1021.

17. State v. Tookes, 699 P.2d 983, 984 (Haw. 1985) (finding no denial of due process when civilian police agent had sex with woman for money before arresting her for prostitution).

18. See Superior Court of Alameda County, 562 P.2d at 1320–1323. When both prostitute and customer are male, anecdotal evidence suggests that it is more typical to arrest both. Some cases alleging sex-differential enforcement fail for lack of showing of discriminatory intent. Others fail for lack of proof that men in comparable circumstances are treated differently. . . . [citations omitted. *Ed.*]

19. See Superior Court of Alameda County, 562 P.2d at 1323. See also Morgan v. City of Detroit, 389 F. Supp. 922, 928 (E.D. Mich. 1975).

20. One court rejected this decisively in the 1920s:

> Men caught with women in an act of prostitution are equally guilty, and should be arrested and held for trial with the women. The law is clear, and the duty of the police is to act in pursuance of the law. The practical application of the law as heretofore enforced is an unjust discrimination against women in the matter of an offense which, in its very nature, if completed, requires the participation of men. . . . As long as the law is upon the statute books, it must be impartially administered without sex discrimination.

People v. Edwards, 180 N.Y.S. 631, 635 (Ct. Gen. Sess. 1920). In 1980, the City Court of Syracuse, endorsing this reasoning, further rejected the dodge arguing that prostitute and patron are "not similarly situated" for equal protection purposes because they violate separate sections of the penal code. That court found that "the only significant difference in the proscribed behavior is that the prostitute sells sex and the patron buys it. Neither gender nor solicitation is a differentiating factor." People v. Nelson, 427 N.Y.S.2d 194, 197 (City Ct. of Syracuse 1980) (finding no evidence of intent to discriminate, therefore no discrimination shown). One court upheld a gender-neutral prostitution law from equal protection attack by pointing out that "[w]hat would be prostitution for a female would be equally prohibited and punished as lewdness for a male." State v. Price, 237 N.W.2d 813, 815 (Iowa 1976), *appeal dismissed,* 426 U.S. 916 (1976). It was apparently inconceivable that a male could be a prostitute. Most courts that have considered sex-differential enforcement challenges on equal protection grounds have relied, for rejecting them, on the distinction in statutes under which prostitutes and patrons fall. See, e.g., Matter of Dora P., 418 N.Y.S.2d 597, 604 (N.Y. App. Div. 1979) (prostitution and patronizing a prostitute are discrete crimes making differential treatment of women and men under them not discriminatory); Commonwealth v. King, 372 N.E.2d 196 (Sup. Jud. Ct. Mass. 1977) (finding that the lack of a statute against patronage does not violate equal protection rights of prostitutes). See also Garrett v. United States, 339 A.2d 372 (D.C. Ct. App. 1975) (holding that a state's failure to require corroboration in prostitution cases, although requiring it in homosexuality cases, is not unconstitutional sex discrimination because it is not based on gender). A ray of reality is provided by one recent ruling holding that women's equality rights were violated when female performers, and not male patrons, were selectively prosecuted for sexual activity at a private club. However, it was important to the ruling that the sexes were "similarly situated" because the women and the men could have been charged under the same statutory provision. See generally State v. McCollum, 464 N.W.2d 44 (Wis. Ct. App. 1990).

21. See Superior Court of Alameda County, 562 P.2d at 1323.

22. See Reynolds v. McNichols, 488 F.2d 1378, 1383 (10th Cir. 1973) (finding no equal protection violation in arresting only the prostitute when she is regarded as "the potential source" of venereal disease and the customer is not).

23. One significant departure from this line of cases, from the standpoint of equality analysis, is represented by the Seventh Circuit's invalidation of a strip-search policy for prostituted women only, which ignored "similarly situated males." This policy was found not to be validly based on gender and therefore in violation of the equal protection guarantee under current standards of scrutiny. Mary Beth G. v. City of Chicago, 723 F.2d 1263, 1273–1274 (7th Cir. 1983). See also White v. Fleming, 522 F.2d 730 (7th Cir. 1975) (finding that a statute prohibiting female, but not male, bar-employees from sitting or standing at or behind the bar violates equal protection).

24. As Margaret Baldwin has stressed to me, part of the complexity of this situation is that jail sometimes provides comparative safety for the women, and the criminal status of prostitution provides some barrier to recruitment and validation for the women's sense of violation. These concerns could be met without making women criminals.

25. For a vivid description of the inequality between pimp and prostitute, see Dorchen Leidholdt, Prostitution: A Violation of Women's Human Rights, 1 Cardozo Women's L.J. 133 (1993).

26. U.S. Const. amend. XIII, §I ("Neither slavery nor involuntary servitude, except as a punishment for crime whereof the party shall have been duly convicted, shall exist within the United States, or any place subject to their jurisdiction."). See also Robertson v. Baldwin, 165 U.S. 275, 282 (1897) (Justice Brown said that "involuntary servitude" was added to "slavery" to cover the peonage of Mexicans and the trade in Chinese labor); Butler v. Perry, 240 U.S. 328, 332 (1916) ("[T]he term involuntary servitude was intended to cover those forms of compulsory labor akin to African slavery which in practical operation would tend to produce like undesirable results."). See generally Howard D. Hamilton, The Legislative and Judicial History of the Thirteenth Amendment, 9 Nat'l B.J. 7 (1951) (an illuminating history of the early years of the Thirteenth Amendment).

27. See Bailey v. Alabama, 219 U.S. 219, 241 (1911) ("[T]he words involuntary servitude have a 'larger meaning than slavery.'") (quoting The Slaughter-House Cases, 83 U.S. (16 Wall.) 36, 69 (1872)). Also the Ninth Circuit has stated:

> [Y]esterday's slave may be today's migrant worker or domestic servant. Today's involuntary servitor is not always black; he or she may just as well be Asian, Hispanic, or a member of some other minority group. Also, the methods of subjugating people's wills have changed from blatant slavery to more subtle, if equally effective, forms of coercion.

United States v. Mussry, 726 F.2d 1448, 1451–1452 (9th Cir. 1984) (citation and footnotes omitted), *cert. denied*, 469 U.S. 855 (1984).

28. See Vednita Nelson, Prostitution: Where Racism & Sexism Intersect, 1 Mich. J. Gender & L. 81, 84, 85 (1993).

29. Prosecutions under the Thirteenth Amendment are typically brought under 18 U.S.C. §1584 (1988), which makes it a crime knowingly and willfully to hold or sell another person "to involuntary servitude," and 18 U.S.C. §241 (1988), which prohibits conspiracy to interfere with an individual's Thirteenth Amendment right to be free from "involuntary servitude."

30. Hamilton, *supra* note 26, at 7.

31. See, e.g., United States v. Ancarola, 1 F. 676, 683 (C.C.S.D.N.Y. 1880) (considering the case of an eleven-year-old Italian boy held in involuntary servitude by a

padrone due to his youth and dependence which left him incapable of choosing alternatives).

32. United States v. Kozminski, 487 U.S. 931, 949–950 (1988). For an analysis of combined psychological and economic coercion, see United States v. Shackney, 333 F.2d 475 (2d Cir. 1964).

33. *Kozminski,* 487 U.S. at 952.

34. See *id.* (mental retardation); United States v. King, 840 F.2d 1276 (6th Cir.), *cert. denied,* 488 U.S. 894 (1988) (children); United States v. Mussry, 726 F.2d 1448, 1450 (9th Cir.), *cert. denied,* 469 U.S. 855 (1984) (non–English speaking, passports withheld, paid little money for services); Bernal v. United States, 241 F. 339, 341 (5th Cir. 1917), *cert. denied,* 245 U.S. 672 (1918) (alienage, no means of support, "did not know her way about town"); Ancarold, 1 F. at 676 (child).

35. No cases of involuntary servitude involve wealthy or solvent victims. . . . [Citation omitted. *Ed.*]

36. See generally *Mussry,* 726 F.2d 1448.

37. *Id.* at 1450, 1453.

38. *Kozminski,* 487 U.S. at 952 (O'Connor, J., for the plurality); *id.,* at 956 (Brennan, J., concurring).

39. Case of Mary Clark, 1 Blackf. 122 (Ind. 1821). See generally Hamilton, *supra* note 26.

40. See, e.g., *Mussry,* 726 F.2d 1448. The later ruling by the Supreme Court in *Kozminski,* 487 U.S. 931, restricting *Mussry* doctrines does not cut back on this aspect of the courts' customary approach to this issue.

41. United States v. King, 840 F.2d 1276, 1281 (6th Cir. 1988), *cert. denied,* 488 U.S. 894 (1988) (finding a conspiracy to deprive children living in a religious commune of rights under Thirteenth Amendment, in part because of a belief by the children that they "had no viable alternative but to perform service for the defendants."). When physical force is also present, *Kozminski* poses no barrier to prosecution. *Id.* at 1281.

42. United States v. Bibbs, 564 F.2d 1165, 1168 (5th Cir. 1977), *cert. denied,* 435 U.S. 1007 (1978).

43. Hamilton, *supra* note 26, at 7.

44. This term was apparently used originally to parallel and distinguish prostitution of all women, including women of color, from slavery of Africans as such. *Traite des Noires,* trade in Blacks, referred to slavery of Blacks; in 1905, *Traite des Blanches,* trade in whites, was used at an international conference to refer to sexual sale and purchase of women and children. Marlene D. Beckman, The White Slave Traffic Act: The Historical Impact of a Criminal Law Policy on Women, 72 Geo. L.J. 1111 n.2 (1984) (citing V. Bullough, Prostitution: An Illustrated History 245 (1978)); Kathleen Barry, *supra* note 4, at 32 (1979). The British government translated the latter term as "White Slave Traffic or Trade," then shortened to white slavery. Beckman, *supra,* at 1111 n.2 (quoting Bullough, at 245). Whatever its initial intent, the appellation "had immediate appeal to racists who could and did conclude that the efforts were against in international traffic in *white* women," although women of all colors were exploited in prostitution. Barry, *supra* note 4, at 32. Kathleen Barry further observes that the 1921 substitution of the term "Traffic in Women and Children" for white slavery worked to separate international trafficking in women from local prostitution, "thereby distracting attention from the continuing enslavement of women in local prostitution." Barry, *supra* note 4, at 32–33. Recognizing prostitution as unconstitutional slavery would help restore this attention.

45. Here I draw on Akhil Amar's and Daniel Widawsky's proposed working definition of slavery. Akhil Amar & Daniel Widawsky, Child Abuse as Slavery: A Thirteenth Amendment Response to *DeShaney*, 105 Harv. L. Rev. 1359, 1365 (1992).

46. See generally Leidholdt, *supra* note 25; Barry, *supra* note 4, at 3–5; Activities for the Advancement of Women: Equality, Development and Peace, U.N. ESCOR, 1st Sess., Provisional Agenda Item 12, at 7–8, U.N. Doc. E/1983/7 (1983).

47. This raises a civil claim under 42 U.S.C. §1983 (1981) and potential criminal prosecution under 18 U.S.C. §242 (Supp. 1992).

48. Activities for the Advancement of Women: Equality, Development and Peace, *supra* note 46, at 8 (quoting testimony by three "collectives" of women prostitutes given to the Congress of Nice on September 8, 1981).

49. The Peonage Cases, 123 F. 671, 681 (M.D. Ala. 1903) (stating that the trier of fact "must consider the situation of the parties, the relative inferiority or inequality between the person contracting to perform the service and the person exercising the force or influence to compel its performance . . . .").

50. See, e.g., Pierce v. United States, 146 F.2d 84 (5th Cir. 1944), *cert. denied*, 324 U.S. 873 (1945); Bernal v. United States, 241 F. 339 (5th Cir. 1917), *cert. denied*, 245 U.S. 672 (1918). See also United States v. Harris, 534 F.2d 207, 214 (10th Cir. 1975), *cert. denied*, 429 U.S. 941 (1976) (upholding conviction for involuntary servitude in prostitution context).

51. *Pierce*, 146 F.2d at 84.

52. *Bernal*, 241 F. at 341.

53. A grand jury in Austin, Texas, failed to indict a man for rape where the victim asked him to wear a condom. Apparently, the woman's request somehow implied her consent. Ross E. Milloy, Furor Over a Decision Not to Indict in a Rape Care, N.Y. Times, Oct. 25, 1992, §1 at 30. A second grand jury did indict the man for rape and he was later convicted in a jury trial. Rapist Who Agreed to Use Condom Gets 40 Years, N.Y. Times, May 15, 1993, §1 at 6.

54. For data on rape in prostitution, see Leidholdt, *supra* note 25, at 138; Mimi H. Silbert & Ayala M. Pines, Occupational Hazards of Street Prostitutes, 8 Crim. Just. Behav. 395, 397 (1981) (70% of San Francisco street prostitutes reported rape by clients an average of 31 times); Council for Prostitution Alternatives, 1991 Annual Report 4 (48% of prostitutes were raped by pimps an average of 16 times a year, 79% by johns an average of 33 times a year). For data on beatings, see Silbert & Pines, *supra,* at 397 (65% of prostitutes beaten by customers); Council for Prostitution Alternatives, *supra,* at 4 (63% were beaten by pimps an average of 58 times a year). For data on mortality, see Pornography and Prostitution in Canada: Report of the Special Committee on Pornography and Prostitution, Vol. II, 350 (1985) (finding that in Canada the mortality rate for prostituted women is 40 times the national average); Leidholdt, *supra* note 25, at 138 n.15 (the Justice Department estimates that a third of the over 4,000 women killed by serial murderers in 1982 were prostitutes).

55. See Mimi H. Silbert & Ayala M. Pines, Entrance into Prostitution, 13 Youth & Society 471, 479 (1982) (60% of prostitutes were sexually abused in childhood); Leidholdt, *supra* note 25, at 136 n.4 (quoting Mimi Silbert, Sexual Assault of Prostitutes: Phase One 40 (1980)) (66% of subjects are sexually assaulted by father or father figure); The Council for Prostitution Alternatives, 1991 Annual Report 3 (85% of clients have histories of sexual abuse in childhood, 70% most frequently by their fathers).

56. See Cecilie Høigard & Liv Finstad, Backstreets: Prostitution, Money, and Love 76 (Katherine Hanson et al. trans., 1992) (average age of prostitutes interviewed in

Norway began at 15½ years). Compare Leidholdt, *supra* note 25, at 136 n.3 (citing Evelina Giobbe, founder of Minneapolis-based advocacy project, Women Hurt in Systems of Prostitution Engaged in Revolt [WHISPER]) (fourteen is the average age of women's entry into prostitution); Roberta Perkins, Working Girls: Prostitutes, This Life and Social Control 258 (1991) (finding in her Australian sample that almost half entered prostitution before age 20, and over 80% before age 25); Mimi H. Silbert & Ayala M. Pines, Occupational Hazards of Street Prostitutes, 8 Crim. Just. Behav. 395, 396 (1981) (68% were 16 years or younger when entered prostitution).

57. For a superb discussion of the "choice" illusion, see Leidholdt, *supra* note 25, at 136–138.

58. For an argument that domestic battery of women is involuntary servitude, see Joyce E. McConnell, Beyond Metaphor: Battered Woman, Involuntary Servitude, and the Thirteenth Amendment, 4 Yale J.L. & Feminism 207 (1992).

59. Bray v. Alexandria Women's Health Clinic, 122 L. Ed. 2d 34, 46, 47 n.2 (1993).

60. Evelina Giobbe, Confronting the Liberal Lies about Prostitution, in Dorchen Leidholdt & Janice G. Raymond eds., The Sexual Liberty and the Attack on Feminism 67, 77 (1990).

61. Leidholdt, *supra* note 25, at 138–139.

62. See Andrea Dworkin & Catharine A. Mackinnon, Pornography & Civil Rights: A New Day for Women's Equality apps. A, B, C (1988).

63. Fla. Stat. ch. 796.09 (1992) (providing a cause of action for those coerced into prostitution to sue their pimps for compensatory and punitive damages). See Margaret A. Baldwin, Strategies of Connection: Prostitution and Feminist Politics, 1 Mich. J. Gender & L. 65, 70 (1993) (reporting that several cases utilizing this statute are currently underway at the discovery stage prior to filing).

64. See Gayle Kirshenbaum, A Potential Landmark for Female Human Rights, Ms., Sept./Oct. 1991, at 13 (report on proposed U.N. Convention Against All Forms of Sexual Exploitation).

65. The proposed Sexual Exploitation convention would require states' parties to adopt legislation to "hold liable" traffickers in pornography. International Convention to Eliminate All Forms of Sexual Exploitation, Sept. 1993, Art. 6(d).

The Feminist Debate over Prostitution Reform: Prostitutes' Rights Groups, Radical Feminists, and the (Im)possibility of Consent

JODY FREEMAN

THIS ARTICLE has two purposes. The first is to identify the theoretical basis for the divergence between prostitutes' rights groups and radical feminists over prostitution reform. I will argue that the crux of the divergence is different understandings of consent and coercion. The second purpose is to argue that despite their deep differences, both groups should support decriminalization as the only acceptable short-term option. . . .

What Sex-Trade Workers Think—Not a United Front

Women who have been, or are presently, in the sex trade disagree over many contentious issues: whether their work is chosen, whether they participate in their own oppression, and whether their economic self-interest should outweigh the concern that prostitution contributes to women's subordination. Prostitutes' rights groups, such as Cast Off Your Old Tired Ethics (COYOTE)[1] and the Canadian Organization for the Rights of Prostitutes (CORP),[2] demand that prostitution be decriminalized because it is dignified, respectable work. CORP's leadership says prostitutes should be entitled to organize, advertise, pay taxes, and receive unemployment insurance. . . .

CORP actually views prostitution as superior to many other jobs since it has distinct advantages: women set their hours and wages, work where they want to, and service only customers they choose. Prostitutes' rights groups say prostitution empowers women because it enables them to earn a living in an environment they control, or would control but for state interference. . . .

The National Task Force on Prostitution (NTFP),[3] an American organization promoting prostitutes' rights, argues that despite some exceptions, prostitution amounts to a voluntary exchange of sexual services for money. The NTFP seeks to empower prostitutes to bargain with employers and improve their working conditions. The NTFP is similar to COYOTE and CORP in its support of prostitution as legitimate work, as is the English Collective of Prostitutes. . . .

The Charter for the International Committee for Prostitutes Rights (ICPR), which sponsored the first and second World Whores' Congress, calls for the decriminalization of all aspects of adult prostitution and affirms the basic human rights of prostitutes to work, immigrate, and claim unemployment and health insurance.[4] . . .

Before accepting the CORP/ICPR position as the definitive word on what prostitutes think, one should consider that women in the industry have not yet reached a consensus on whether prostitution is empowering for women. . . .

[There are] organizations that work in direct opposition to CORP, COYOTE and the NTPF. Sarah Wynter, founder and editor of Women Hurt in Systems of Prostitution Engaged in Revolt (WHISPER), argues,

> There has been a deliberate attempt to validate men's perceived need, and self-proclaimed right, to buy and sell women's bodies for sexual use. This has been accomplished, in part, by euphemizing prostitution as an occupation. Men have promoted the cultural myth that women actively seek out prostitution as a pleasurable economic alternative to low-paying, low-skilled, monotonous labor, conveniently ignoring the conditions that insure women's inequality and the pre-conditions which make women vulnerable to prostitution.[5]

Wynter maintains that prostitution is not a "valid," freely chosen occupation. She wants us "to stop defining prostitution as a victimless crime, and acknowledge it for what it is—a crime committed against women by men."[6]

Despite their disagreement over whether prostitution is a legitimate occupation, virtually all those with experience inside the industry agree that the current conditions under which prostitutes must work are intolerable. Nearly universal support exists among sex-trade workers for decriminalization as a necessary first step toward (in CORP and COYOTE's case) finally seeing prostitution as valid employment or (in WHISPER's case) finally eradicating it as a means of oppressing women. Despite their different ultimate goals, all sex-trade workers want control of their lives. As long as prostitution is criminalized, they say, they will not have it.

The "Consent is Possible Approach" (Liberal Feminism)

The assumptions about consent and coercion that inform the prostitutes' rights groups' position can be traced to traditional liberal theory, which is committed to autonomy, individualism, and minimal state interference in private choice. Liberal theory is premised on an assumption that individuals are atomistic, pre-social beings who exist independent of their community.[7] The justification for state power in the liberal paradigm is the notion of implied consent: individuals surrender a certain amount of authority to the state in order to protect the autonomy of everyone.[8] . . .

To the extent that liberal feminism is traceable to liberalism, it too accepts the notion of a pre-social autonomous individual capable of consent and choice. I understand liberal feminism to be "mainstream" feminism, the popular feminism that Zillah Eisenstein attributes to Betty Friedan.[9] In my view, members of CORP and COYOTE and those feminists that support their position are essentially liberal and only reluctantly feminist. Their vision is one of equal access to an equality defined and perpetuated by men; it is not concerned with the sexual subordination of women as a "class" and the need for structural change.

Liberal theory has traditionally advocated formal equality, without attempting to significantly restructure society or question the assumption of choice and consent that informs liberal theory. . . .

Because it assumes that people are autonomous, self-interested actors, I understand liberal feminist analysis to begin with a presumption of consent. That is, in the absence of clear evidence to the contrary, a woman who says "yes" consents, regardless of the social context, the woman's past experience, or the constraints of ascribing meaning to language. Because the liberal feminist is committed to maximizing autonomy and individual choice, she presumptively sees individual expressions of sexuality as implicitly consensual, liberating, and empowering. Commercializing sex per se does not bother her; it is up to the individual woman to decide if she wants to use her body in a way that brings her money and satisfaction, even if that means trading in sex.

Zillah Eisenstein describes liberal feminism as more sophisticated than a sum of liberalism and feminism. This is because she believes that liberal individualism is incompatible with feminist sex-class consciousness since the former depends on atomistic actors completely divorced from social influence, and the latter depends on connections amongst individuals.[10] Liberal theory is inadequate for feminist practice, according to Eisenstein, because it lacks a theory of sex-class consciousness. She argues that the challenge facing feminists is to realize the radical potential of liberal feminism which lies in devising a theory of sex-class based oppression, without abandoning the value of individuality adopted from liberalism. . . .

Eisenstein envisions all feminism, from socialist to radical to lesbian, as rooted in a notion of individuality (which she says makes it "liberal" in origin), but distinguishes individuality from liberal individualism:

> By "liberal individualism," I mean the view of the individual pictured as atomized and disconnected from the social relations that actually affect his or her choices and options; by "individuality," I refer to the capacities of the individual conceptualized as part of a social structure that can either enhance or constrain his or her individual potential for human development.[11]

I agree with Eisenstein to the extent that she rejects liberal theory as ill-suited to contemporary feminist practice and thought. Her conception of individuality has nothing to do with the liberal view of autonomy because the latter depends on a notion of individuals disconnected from the social context which creates them and which they help create. Without explicitly saying so, and by distinguishing between liberal individualism (understood as separateness from social structure) and individuality (understood as independence within a potentially limiting social structure), Eisenstein re-defines autonomy. Her version of individuality is quite different from liberalism's autonomy. . . .

If Eisenstein's purpose is to rescue liberal feminism as a viable feminist "category," I think she fails. Feminism stands in direct opposition to the central tenets of liberal theory, and the crux of the divergence is the meaning of autonomy. . . .

However, Eisenstein's endorsement of individuality is a valuable acknowledgment that a conception of autonomy is something important for feminist theory.[12] What matters to me about autonomy is that one's view of it can account for whether or not one believes consent is possible. If, as Eisenstein proposes, individuality is socially contingent, then consent must be relative and free choice always limited by social structure. The autonomy posited by liberal individualism is, by contrast, absolute and un-restrained by social influence. Herein lies the root of the disagreement over consent between liberals and radical feminists. Liberals do not envision socially structured, subjectively mediated consent, while radicals do. Radical feminists criticize the simplistic liberal assumption that "yes," or even silence, is consent. Liberals resist the language of victimization used by radical feminists to describe a complete absence of consent.

If liberal feminism realizes its radical potential to develop a sex-class theory of oppression in the way Eisenstein suggests, how will it resolve the debate between those who support the right to choose prostitution as an exercise of autonomy and those who believe prostitution subordinates women as a class? The answer depends on what autonomy would look like post-radicalization. A concept of autonomy that fits both Eisenstein's notion of individuality and a theory of sex-class oppression cannot be the same as the autonomy of liberal individualism which places individual license to do as one pleases ahead of community interests. It will inevitably be a conception of autonomy that understands and responds to group harm. Adopting such a notion of autonomy reinforces the idea that prostitutes do not exist in isolation from their social context. Adopting this view of autonomy reinforces the claim that the harm prostitution causes to women as a class matters, and that consent is socially contingent.

Prostitutes' rights groups do not acknowledge the contradiction in their politics that Eisenstein points out is inherent in liberal feminism, and they do not fit within her reformulation because they minimize the harmful impact that prostitution has on women as a class. In many cases, prostitutes' rights groups see feminism as another enemy, along with the police and government. Feminists are either self-righteous puritans or unrealistic academics. . . .

CORP and COYOTE's essentially liberal argument is that women and men should be permitted to use their bodies and express their sexuality as they see fit. Underlying this position is an assumption that choice is possible and that prostitutes are entitled to determine for themselves whether selling sex is harmful. They encourage prostitution as sexual expression, even if it is considered "deviant," because it is private, freely chosen, and harmless to those not involved in the transaction. Harm is defined restrictively so that contributing to the subordination of women as a class does not count.

Although prostitutes' rights groups are fairly clear on their analysis of harm, their position on the possibility of choice is more confusing. I think they must be saying one of two things: either that choice exists (without really analyzing to what extent that is true, and whether this choice varies among "classes" of prostitutes)[13] or that hookers have as little real choice as all women and they are trying to make the best of their situation in a world of coercion. These two statements mean very different things in terms of the presumption of consent. I understand CORP to be arguing the former: that prostitutes have and make choices and, furthermore, that other women should not criticize prostitution as harmful when they are guilty of "commercializing" sex themselves, by choice, in more subtle ways.

Prostitution is largely a response to a lack of economic alternatives. It is not surprising that women do it for the money. As Simone de Beauvoir remarks,

> It is naive to wonder what motives drive woman to prostitution. . . . The truth is that in a world where misery and unemployment prevail, there will be people to enter any profession that is open. . . . It is often asked: why does she choose it? The question is, rather: why has she not chosen it?[14]

However, despite the obvious constraints that economic need imposes on women, prostitutes' rights groups refuse to acknowledge the relativity of choice. The only situations they acknowledge as coercive are those in which the use of force is extremely obvious, such as when pimps use threats and violence to keep teenage runaways in the trade.

Even if prostitutes' rights groups would agree that a presumption of coercion is appropriate in cases where the activity in question is incompatible with individual freedom (slavery is an example), they would insist that prostitution enhances freedom. Rather than extinguish autonomy, prostitution enables it to flourish. Prostitutes may surrender themselves to the desires of others, but only for discrete periods and ideally under conditions they control. They can withdraw their services at their discretion. Their autonomy is never irretrievable. This is, of course, just one picture of prostitution, and the one portrayed by CORP to be most accurate.[15]

CORP does not seem concerned with the extent to which authentic choice depends on the context in which it is exercised. CORP's leadership argues that decriminalizing and legitimizing prostitution promotes autonomy and is also the only effective way of minimizing the coercion present in "exceptional" cases. If prostitutes are permitted to organize, form support groups, and run self-help networks, they will then be able to exert some control over the coercive elements of the sex-trade. Putting power into the hands of the women in the industry will enable them to prevent the worst abuses of the system. Obviously, the "consent is possible" approach is fuelled by the claim that prostitutes make free choices. Many feminists have challenged that claim by questioning the accuracy of the liberal version of freedom. Radical feminists have directed their attention, instead, to coercion.

The "Consent Is Not Possible" Approach

Contrary to liberal feminism, radical feminism focuses on sexuality as the mechanism of women's oppression. It has the sex-class consciousness that Eisenstein says liberalism lacks and, because it rejects the central tenets of liberalism, it does not assume that individuals exist in isolation from social context. Radical feminism has traditionally sought to expose and change the fact that we live in a male-defined, male-centered world in which women are objectified through sexuality. It seeks to displace the ubiquitous male voice with a multiplicity of female voices. It places value on subjectivity over objectivity, intuition over proof, community over individuality.[16] Consciousness-raising is its method and epistemology. Radical feminists have historically seen heterosexuality, pregnancy, and childrearing as institutions forced by men on women and used by men to reinforce male dominance.[17]

Radical feminists reject the notion that women are empowered by fulfilling male desire, and they see the desire for prostitution as male. They would likely dismiss [prostitutes' rights representatives] as having internalized male justifications for exploiting women and would treat prostitutes as victims, even if some insist that they enjoy their work and have freely chosen it.[18] Radical feminists say that prostitution is not a harmless, "private" transaction but a powerful means of creating, reinforcing, and perpetuating the objectification of women through sexuality. They do not take the criminalization of prostitution to mean that society is committed to undoing the subordination of women. Rather, it serves as proof that female sexuality is not only manufactured by men, but also legally controlled through the exercise of authority in order to keep women isolated and powerless.[19] Society's acceptance of the persistent male demand for prostitutes only reminds us that all women are thought to be accessible (for a price) and that their commodification is natural.

Carole Pateman points out that in all traditional theories of the state women have never been seen as "individuals" capable of making contracts; rather, they are the subject of them. She criticizes classic social contract theory as incomplete because it represses one of its most central elements—the sexual contract. She explains the relationship between women and contract:

> Women are not party to the original contract through which men transform their natural freedom into the security of civil freedom. Women are the subject of the contract. The (sexual) contract is the vehicle through which men transform their natural right over women into the security of civil patriarchal right.[20]

The difference between men and women is constructed through contract, she says, into the difference between freedom and subjection. She calls the liberal justification of prostitution a "contractarian defense" because it attributes "the lack of acceptance of the prostitute . . . to the hypocrisy and distorted attitudes surrounding sexual activity," without addressing the role that prostitution plays in the political subordination of women.[21]

Radical feminism understands prostitution to be a microcosm of gender hierarchy. It not only encapsulates but reinforces the objectification of women. Even an argument that prostitution has "therapeutic" potential for providing sex to those who are socially or sexually dysfunctional cannot, to the radical feminist, redeem an institution that is so central to male dominance. In the story of the sexual contract, argues Pateman, "[P]rostitution is part of the exercise of the law of male sex-right, one of the ways in which men are ensured access to women's bodies. . . ."[22] She goes on to say that male access to females, "is part of the construction of what it means to be a man, part of the contemporary expression of masculine sexuality."[23]

The liberal would criticize the radical feminist approach as patronizing. It tells women who hold a positive view of prostituting themselves that they are deluded. It denies the reality and validity of their experience. The radical approach to the prostitution debate, with its condemnation of the subordination inherent in prostitution and its emphasis on power relations at a macro level, is not helpful for prostitutes who feel that state regulation, not male-defined sexuality, is responsible for the lack of control over their lives.

Catharine MacKinnon . . . argues that sexuality defines gender through the eroticization of submission and dominance. Prostitution and pornography are central to that process. The power differential between men and women is socially and sexually constructed and so pervasive that it usually goes unnoticed. MacKinnon writes, "The perspective from the male standpoint enforces woman's definition, encircles her body, circumlocutes her speech, and describes her life. The male perspective is systemic and hegemonic."[24] The world MacKinnon sees is one in which "female" and "feminine" attributes correspond directly to what society does not value, or values only as objects, while male and masculine attributes are highly prized. MacKinnon argues that it is impossible to conceive of an alternative female sexuality until men get their feet "off our necks."[25]

Unlike liberalism, which is premised on the notion of an autonomous self, MacKinnon's analysis leads us to question whether we have a "self" at all.

> If women are socially defined such that female sexuality cannot be lived or spoken or felt or even somatically sensed apart from its enforced definition, so that it *is* its own lack, then there is no such thing as a woman as such, there are only walking embodiments of men's projected needs. For feminism, asking whether there is, socially, a female sexuality is the same as asking whether women exist.[26]

MacKinnon's analysis begins with a presumption of coercion. If we have no "self" it is difficult to imagine how we can consent to anything. The presumption of coercion forces us to confront the fact that our ability to consent is always socially constrained. . . .

The pervasiveness of coercion should be a signal that women have not participated in the definition of their own sexuality. Although it is difficult to "prove" that MacKinnon's picture of the world is true, if one looks at how women are treated in this society, there is ample evidence that the male construction of women's sexuality serves male purposes exclusively. Men manufacture pornography for a male audience and traffic in women to feed male consumption. Women are seen as sexual objects and victims. Their vulnerability to male violence makes them dependent on some men to protect them from other men. Under current conditions, women are overwhelmingly victims of male violence—not the other way around. These observations should lead one to suspect that the socially constructed view of women's sexuality may be "inauthentic" for women and that the possibility of real choice is limited at best.

A central argument in MacKinnon's critique is that women participate in their own subordination. They internalize dominance and submission as "normal" sexuality and, therefore, find accounts of oppression incompatible with their perception of their own experience. MacKinnon implies that women are not aware of what is in their own self-interest, since they perceive their needs only as a reflection of male desire.

The circularity of that argument makes it difficult to refute. If one denies being subordinated, the disagreement itself is illustrative of collaborating in one's oppression. MacKinnon's analysis is frequently criticized as a betrayal of feminist methodology because it distrusts women and discounts the possibility of consensual submission. West has critiqued the radical feminist conclusion that women suffer from false consciousness:

> The judgment of falsehood is almost always against the will as well as the opinion of the woman who has the desire [for erotic submission]. This truly is a profound departure from feminist methodology which is also truly offensive—consciousness-raising is not about the imposition of judgments of truth or falsity on the desires of others.[27]

MacKinnon herself is a glaring example of why her analysis, if taken literally, cannot be true. How does she know this? What is the epistomological value of her critique if one never knows the difference between "glimpsing freedom"[28] and living male fantasies?

At least one feminist has criticized MacKinnon for failing to provide a theory of consciousness. Ruth Colker says that a woman has no basis for knowing whether or not to agree with MacKinnon because she must distrust her own perceptions of her condition. Colker maintains that without a theory of consciousness to explain what women should believe, MacKinnon's theory is "pure assertion."[29] Whether one thinks that women can "know" their own sexuality, or at least recognize it, has to do with the degree to which one believes women can tell the difference between engaging in their own pleasure and collaborating in their oppression.[30]

MacKinnon and radical feminists, like liberal feminists, do not pay enough attention to the relativity of consent. Liberal feminism assumes without explanation that choice is possible. MacKinnon resolves the matter in an equally unsatisfying way by assuming that choice is not possible for women under current conditions of male dominance, where, "[f]orce is exercised as consent, its authority as participation."[31] In my view, the notion that consent is relative and socially contingent makes sense within a feminist framework. It fits well with the value feminists place on subjectivity and community, but MacKinnon seems not to acknowledge the possibility of consent in a world where women's sexuality is not their own. This refusal to acknowledge the possibility of consent is ironic since her vision of a truly "female" sexuality (implied by her critique of the male colonization of female sexuality) depends, in my view, on a fluid notion of consent. Admittedly, in MacKinnon's most recent work, she has explained the underlying constraints on consent more fully, but this analysis leads to the conclusion that genuine consent does not exist. She writes,

> Consent is supposed to be women's form of control over intercourse, different from but equal to the custom of male initiative. Man proposes, woman disposes. Even the ideal is not mutual. Apart from the disparate consequences of refusal, this model does not envision a situation the woman controls being placed in, or choices she frames.[32]

Consent and Consciousness

Neither radical feminism nor liberalism offers an account of the complexity of the underlying structural constraints on the meaning of consent. In liberal discourse, consent is assumed as a constant. If MacKinnon is right about the inevitability of collaborating in our own oppression, there is no hope for consent. Her critique denies the subjective ability of individuals to participate in its construction. For the radical feminist then, even saying "yes" in a given situation does not guarantee an absence of coercion. Neither does it incorporate the structure and fluidity of consent into the interaction. . . .

Proponents of critical legal theory argue that individuals determine what consent means in any given situation within the context of their own past experience and present knowledge; they mediate structure through a complex process of sifting and internalizing dominant social norms and contextual factors.[33] Consent is structural and changeable. Interpreting what consent means in a given situation is partly objective, and partly subjective. One is constrained to a certain extent by socially determined meanings (for instance, the common definition of intercourse versus rape), but interpreting one's experience of an event is always subjective. So when one consents, one is both responding to and creating the meaning of the term at a particular time in a particular context. A woman's past experience, her socialized self-image, her fears and expectations about sexuality—all of these are in play when she says yes, no, or remains silent.

Given the complexity of such an analysis of consent, I am skeptical about the liberal feminist assumption that choice is the norm and that it is absent only in extreme circumstances which we "objectively" recognize as coercion (i.e., the rapist is using a gun). The fixed nature of liberal consent fails to appreciate the importance of social context and human mediation. . . .

The liberal individualist understanding of consent is an example of how ideology affects consciousness. Much of women's misery could be thought of as voluntary. To the extent that women marry, seek employment, and engage in heterosexual sex, they expose themselves to abuse, sexual harassment, and male expectations of their sexuality, all of which are often pleasurable for men and painful for women. And yet, to some extent all of these social arrangements are consensual. Liberal theory does not reflect the fact that choice and consent mean different things for men and women and that women's "choices" usually reinforce male power. In the liberal paradigm, when subjects do not explicitly choose to submit to state authority, tacit consent is imputed to them. As Vega points out, "Freedom includes submission, and submission includes freedom. Within the liberal theory, this is . . . never considered to be a serious dilemma for the autonomous subject: he survives without hesitation."[34]. . .

The Argument for Decriminalization

Criminalization only makes life more difficult for prostitutes, minimizing their chances of leaving the trade. The way to empower women is not to punish them for being powerless. Anything that pushes prostitution further underground and makes it more dangerous also makes it more profitable to pimps. If prostitution were decriminalized it would not necessarily be unregulated. Prostitutes would still be subject to sections of the relevant criminal code pertaining to nuisance, indecency, and causing a public disturbance. They would also have to abide by municipal zoning laws.

Even though I am sympathetic to the radical presumption of coercion, CORP's argument should be given some weight not because prostitution is legitimate and fully consensual, but rather because everyone's choices are limited in this world, and prostitutes should be entitled to make the best of a bad situation. However, not all aspects of the trade should be decriminalized. As the Fraser Report suggests, procuring and living off the avails of prostitution should still be criminal where this is effected through threats and coercion.

The best short-term approach to reform entails removing prostitution from the criminal realm (subject to exceptions for pimping through coercion) so that it becomes an issue of gender equality and, at the same time, taking affirmative steps to destroy the conditions that create male consumption and drive women to the trade. We should decriminalize prostitution per se, permit small groups to operate out of their own homes, provide education and information programs for those trying to leave the trade, and devote the money presently used for criminal law enforcement to prostitute self-help networks, havens, and halfway houses.

Reform should also include provisions for vigorously prosecuting pimps who coerce women, particularly juveniles, into the trade. We should initiate training programs for women with little or no education, increase the minimum wage, finance businesses run by and for women, and design cooperative living and working arrangements for runaways and those with no place to go. Special police task forces should be devoted to prosecuting pimps but should be trained to treat prostitutes humanely. Public funds should be spent on the street and in the schools to raise awareness about equality, sexual abuse, and incest, as well as sexuality in general.

These proposals cost money and require a commitment from government and law enforcement agencies. If put into effect, they could dispel any notion that decriminalization was meant to legitimize prostitution. Rather they would be seen as the best alternative to a frustrating social problem.

Conclusion

I suspect that the law punishes prostitutes for reasons that have little to do with the interests of either prostitutes or women in general. Criminalization is clearly not informed by a conception of women as victims, because it punishes women who are already at a social and economic disadvantage. Rather, criminalization is likely intended to keep property values from dropping (as they would were brothels permitted in residential districts), prevent public nuisance, and keep children from being morally corrupted by witnessing the transaction between prostitute and customer. The jurisdictions that have licensed prostitution, Nevada for example, seem to have chosen this solution in response to primarily liberal arguments that prostitution is a valid occupation and that it is "victimless." It seems that no North American scheme has adequately addressed the role prostitution plays in the subordination of women. The best proposal I have seen thus far, and the only one that attempts to respond to feminist concerns, is the Canadian Fraser Report which recommends broad social and economic reforms coupled with decriminalization.

While we develop a theory of consciousness and wonder about consent, and while we dream of a world free of paid sex, real prostitutes face daily abuse. If radical feminists seek to eliminate prostitution, they should align themselves with liberal prostitutes' rights groups and support decriminalization, while simultaneously undermining gender hierarchy with every means at their disposal. What separates radical feminists and prostitutes' rights groups is that for the former, decriminalization is not enough. It is, however, a necessary part of a holistic approach which I believe we must embrace. This is not a concession to valueless individualism. It is an admission that the world radical feminists seek remains elusive and that a policy of reform must respond to the reality of women's lives. It is a step we must take without abandoning our aspirations for a world in which choice is more possible and consent truly authentic.

Notes

1. COYOTE was the first American prostitutes' rights group founded by Margo St. James.

2. Founded in Toronto in 1983 and headed by Valerie Scott, CORP includes both male and female sex-trade workers.

3. The NTFP and its affiliates have evolved from COYOTE and other prostitutes' rights organizations. Coyote/National Task Force on Prostitution, in Frédérique Delacoste and Priscilla Alexander eds., Sex Work 290, 291–293 (Cleis, 1987).

4. International Committee for Prostitutes' Rights, International Committee for Prostitutes' Rights World Charter and World Whores' Congress Statements, in Sex Work, *supra* note 3, at 305.

5. Sarah Wynter, Whisper: Women Hurt in Systems of Prostitution Engaged in Revolt, in Sex Work, *supra* note 3, at 266.

6. *Id.* at 270.

7. John Locke, Two Treatises of Government, 287 (Peter Laslett, ed., Cambridge Univ. Press, 2d ed. 1967). . . .

8. Thomas Hobbs, Leviathan 56 (Michael Oakeshott ed., Macmillan, 1962). . . .

9. Zillah Eisenstein, The Radical Future of Liberal Feminism 177 (Northeastern Press, 1981).

10. *Id.* at 116.

11. *Id.* at 114.

12. See Jennifer Nedelsky, Reconceiving Autonomy: Sources, Thoughts and Possibilities, 1 Yale J. L. & Fem. 7 (1989).

13. It is impossible to avoid the class implications of COYOTE's or CORP's defense of prostitution. High class callgirls with some control over their working environment and clientele obviously have a different quality of "choice." . . . Prostitution reform should not be designed with only the high class "businesswoman" hooker in mind—to think they represent the prostitution trade is to gloss over the majority of women working under conditions that are considerably less safe.

14. Simone de Beauvoir, The Second Sex 524–525 (H. M. Parshely ed. & trans., Bantam Books, 1952).

15. The other picture, described by Kathleen Barry, portrays prostitution as inherently coercive. To Barry, prostitution is synonymous with sexual slavery and the constituency that CORP seems to represent—self-possessed, college educated, and high class hookers—is really a small minority of the huge numbers of women coerced into selling sex. See K. Barry, Female Sexual Slavery 39–40 (N.Y.U. Press 1979).

16. Alison M. Jaggar, Feminist Politics and Human Nature (Rowman & Allanheld, 1983).

17. See generally, Catharine A. MacKinnon, Feminism Unmodified: Discourses on Life and Law (Harvard Univ. Press, 1987); Catharine A. MacKinnon, Feminism, Marxism, Method and the State: An Agenda for Theory, in D. Weisberg ed., Feminist Legal Theory: Foundations 437 (Temple Univ. Press, 1993).

18. Barry, Sexual Slavery, *supra* note 15, at 119–120.

19. Andrea Dworkin, Letters from a War Zone 120 (Secker & Warburg, 1988). Dworkin writes:

> Hard-working prostitutes earn enormous gross sums of money (compared to gross sums typically earned by other women), but they do not go on to become financiers or founders of universities. Instead, their money goes to men, because men control, profit from, and perpetuate female prostitution. The men their money goes to are pimps, racketeers, lawyers, police and the like, all of whom, because they are men and not women, can turn that money into more money, social status, and influence. The prostitute herself is marked with a scarlet "W"—stigmatized as whore, ostracized as whore, exiled as whore into a world circumscribed by organized crime, narcotics, and the notorious brutality of pimps. The prostitute's utterly degraded social status functions to punish her for daring to make money at all. The abuse that accrues to her prevents her from translating money into dignity or self-determination; it serves to keep her in her place, female, cunt, at the mercy of the men who profit from her flesh.

20. Carole Pateman, The Sexual Contract 6 (Stanford Univ. Press, 1988).

21. *Id.* at 200.

22. *Id.*

23. *Id.* at 199.

24. Catharine A. MacKinnon, Feminism, Marxism, Method and the State: Toward

Feminist Jurisprudence, in D. Weisberg ed., Feminist Legal Theory: Foundations 427 (Temple Univ. Press, 1993).

25. Ellen DuBois et al., Feminist Discourse, Moral Values and the Law: A Conversation (James McCormick Mitchell Lecture, 1984), 34 Buff. L. Rev. 11, 28 (1985).

26. MacKinnon, Agenda for Theory, *supra* note 17, at 447.

27. Robin West, The Difference in Women's Hedonic Lives: A Phenomenological Critique of Feminist Legal Theory, herein, at 162.

28. MacKinnon, Feminism Unmodified, *supra* note 17, at 218. "Sex feeling good may mean . . . that one has glimpsed freedom, a rare and valuable and contradictory event."

29. Conversation with Ruth Colker, Nov. 17, 1988, during Feminist Bridge Week at the University of Toronto Faculty of Law.

30. . . . See Ruth Colker, Feminism, Sexuality and Self: A Preliminary Inquiry into the Politics of Authenticity (Book Review), 68 Boston Univ. L. Rev 217 (1988). . . .

31. MacKinnon, Toward Feminist Jurisprudence, *supra* note 24, at 428. . . .

32. C. MacKinnon, Toward a Feminist Theory of the State 174 (Harvard Univ. Press, 1989).

33. Rosemary J. Coombe, Room for Manoeuver: Towards a Theory of Practice in Critical Legal Studies, Law & Soc. Inq. 69, 79–83 (1989).

34. Judith Vega, Coercion and Consent: Classic Liberal Concepts in Texts on Sexual Violence, 16 Int'l J. Soc. L. 75, 79 (1988).

◈ A Postmodern Feminist Legal Manifesto (An Unfinished Draft)

MARY JOE FRUG

THE FOLLOWING COMMENTARY is an unfinished work. Professor Frug was working on this Commentary when she was murdered on April 4, 1991. . . .

Applying Postmodern "Principles": Law and the Female Body

A. Introduction

Most feminists are committed to the position that however "natural" and common sex differences may seem, the differences between women and men are not biologically compelled; they are, rather, "socially constructed." Over the past two decades this conviction has fueled many efforts to change the ways in which law produces—or socially constructs—the differences and the hierarchies between the sexes. Feminists have reasoned, for example, that when women are uneducated for "men's work," or when they are sexually harassed in the men's work they do, they are not "naturally" more suited for "women's work"; they have been constructed to be that way. Although law is by no means the only factor that influences which jobs men and women prefer, how well they perform at work, or the intensity of their wage market commitment, outlawing employment discrimination can affect to some degree what women and men are "like" as workers. What law (at least in part) constructs, law reform projects can re-construct or alter.

Regardless of how commonplace the constructed character of sex differences may be, particular differences can seem quite deeply embedded within the sexes—so much so, in fact, that the social construction thesis is undermined. When applied to differences that seem especially entrenched—differences such as masculine aggression or feminine compassion, or differences related to the erotic and reproductive aspects of women's lives, social construction seems like a cliched, improbable, and unconvincing account of experience, an explanation for sex differences that undervalues "reality."

105 Harv. L. Rev. 1045 (1992). Copyright © 1992 by the Harvard Law Review Association.

This reaction does not necessarily provoke a return to a "natural" explanation for sex differences; but it does radically stunt the liberatory potential of the social construction thesis. One's expectations for law reform projects are reduced; law might be able to mitigate the harsh impact of these embedded traits on women's lives, but law does not seem responsible for constructing them.

The subject of [this] Part is the role of law in the production of sex differences that seem "natural." One of my objectives is to explain and challenge the essentializing impulse that places particular sex differences outside the borders of legal responsibility. Another objective is to provide an analysis of the legal role in the production of gendered identity that will invigorate the liberatory potential of the social construction thesis.

I have chosen the relationship of law to the female body as my principal focus. I am convinced that law is more cunningly disguised but just as implicated in the production of apparently intractable sex-related traits as in those that seem more legally malleable. Since the anatomical distinctions between the sexes seem not only "natural" but fundamental to identity, proposing and describing the role of law in the production of the meaning of the female body seems like the most convincing subject with which to defend my case. In the following section, I will argue that legal rules—like other cultural mechanisms—encode the female body with meanings. Legal discourse then explains and rationalizes these meanings by an appeal to the "natural" differences between the sexes, differences that the rules themselves help to produce. The formal norm of legal neutrality conceals the way in which legal rules participate in the construction of those meanings.

The proliferation of women's legal rights during the past two decades has liberated women from some of the restraining meanings of femininity. This liberation has been enhanced by the emergence of different feminisms over the past decade. These feminisms have made possible a stance of opposition toward a singular feminine identity; they have demonstrated that women stand in a multitude of places, depending on time and geographical location, on race, age, sexual preference, health, class status, religion, and other factors. Despite these significant changes, there remains a common residue of meaning that seems affixed, as if by nature, to the female body. Law participates in creating that meaning.

I will argue that there are at least three general claims that can be made about the relationship between legal rules and legal discourse and the meaning of the female body:

1. Legal rules permit and sometimes mandate the terrorization of the female body. This occurs by a combination of provisions that inadequately protect women against physical abuse and that encourage women to seek refuge against insecurity. One meaning of "female body," then, is a body that is "in terror," a body that has learned to scurry, to cringe, and to submit. Legal discourse supports that meaning.

2. Legal rules permit and sometimes mandate the maternalization of the female body. This occurs with the use of provisions that reward women for singularly

assuming responsibilities after childbirth and with those that penalize conduct—such as sexuality or labor market work—that conflicts with mothering. Maternalization also occurs through rules such as abortion restrictions that compel women to become mothers and by domestic relations rules that favor mothers over fathers as parents. Another meaning of "female body," then, is a body that is "for" maternity. Legal discourse supports that meaning.

3. Legal rules permit and sometimes mandate the sexualization of the female body. This occurs through provisions that criminalize individual sexual conduct, such as rules against commercial sex (prostitution) or same sex practices (homosexuality) and also through rules that legitimate and support institutions such as the pornography, advertising, and entertainment industries that eroticize the female body. Sexualization also occurs, paradoxically, in the application of rules such as rape and sexual harassment laws that are designed to protect women against sex-related injuries. These rules grant or deny women protection by interrogating their sexual promiscuity. The more sexually available or desiring a woman looks, the less protection these rules are likely to give her. Another meaning of "female body," then, is a body that is "for" sex with men, a body that is "desirable" and also rapable, that wants sex and wants raping. Legal discourse supports that meaning.

These groups of legal rules and discourse constitute a system that "constructs" or engenders the female body. The feminine figures the rules pose are naturalized within legal discourse by declaration—"women are (choose one) weak, nurturing, sexy"—and by a host of linguistic strategies that link women to particular images of the female body. By deploying these images, legal discourse rationalizes, explains, and renders authoritative the female body rule network. The impact of the rule network on women's reality in turn reacts back on the discourse, reinforcing the "truth" of these images.

Contractions of confidence in the thesis that sex differences are socially constructed have had a significant impact on women in law. Liberal jurists, for example, have been unwilling to extend the protection of the gender equality guarantee to anatomical distinctions between female and male bodies; these differences seem so basic to individual identity that law need not—or should not—be responsible for them. Feminist legal scholars have been unable to overcome this intransigence, partly because we ourselves sometimes find particular sex-related traits quite intransigent. Indeed, one way to understand the fracturing of law-related feminism into separate schools of thought over the past decade is by the sexual traits that are considered unsusceptible to legal transformation[1] and by the criticisms these analyses have provoked within our own ranks.[2]

The fracturing of feminist criticism has occurred partly because particular sex differences seem so powerfully fixed that feminists are as unable to resist their "naturalization" as liberal jurists. But feminists also cling to particular sex-related differences because of a strategic desire to protect the feminist legal agenda from sabotage. Many feminist critics have argued that the condition of "real" women makes it too early to be post-feminist. The social construction thesis is useful to feminists insofar as it informs and supports our efforts to improve the condition of women in law. If, or when, the social construction thesis seems about to deconstruct the basic category of woman, its usefulness to feminism is problematized. How can we build a political coalition to advance the position of women in law if the subject that drives our efforts is "indeterminate," "incoherent," or "contingent?"

I think this concern is based upon a misperception of where we are in the legal struggle against sexism. I think we are in danger of being politically immobilized by a system for the production of what sex means that makes particular sex differences seem "natural." If my assessment is right, then describing the mechanics of this system is potentially enabling rather than disempowering; it may reveal opportunities for resisting the legal role in producing the radical asymmetry between the sexes.

I also think this concern is based on a misperception about the impact of deconstruction. Skeptics tend to think, I believe, that the legal deconstruction of "woman"—in one paper or in many papers, say, written over the next decade—will entail the immediate destruction of "women" as identifiable subjects who are affected by law reform projects. Despite the healthy, self-serving respect I have for the influence of legal scholarship and for the role of law as a significant cultural factor (among many) that contributes to the production of femininity, I think "women" cannot be eliminated from our lexicon very quickly. The question this paper addresses is not whether sex differences exist—they do—or how to transcend them—we can't—but the character of their treatment in law.

B. Sexualization, Terrorization and Maternalization: The Case of Prostitution

Since most anti-prostitution rules are gender neutral, let me explain, before going any further, how I can argue that they have a particular impact on the meaning of the female body. Like other rules regulating sexual conduct, anti-prostitution rules sexualize male as well as female bodies; they indicate that sex—unlike, say, laughing, sneezing, or making eye contact—is legally regulated. Regardless of whether one is male or female, the pleasures and the virtue of sex are produced, at least in part, by legal rules.[3] The gendered lopsidedness of this meaning system—which I describe below—occurs, quite simply, because most sex workers are women. Thus, even though anti-prostitution rules could, in theory, generate parallel meanings for male and female bodies, in practice they just don't. At least they don't right now.

The legal definition of prostitution as the unlawful sale of sex occurs in statutes that criminalize specific commercial sex practices and in decisional law, such as contract cases that hold that agreements for the sale of sexual services are legally unenforceable. By characterizing certain sexual practices as illegal, these rules sexualize the female body. They invite a sexual interrogation of every female body: is it for or against prostitution?

This sexualization of the female body explains an experience many women have: an insistent concern that this outfit, this pose, this gesture may send the wrong signal—a fear of looking like a whore. Sexy talking, sexy walking, sexy dressing seem sexy, at least in part, because they are the telltale signs of a sex worker plying her trade. This sexualization also explains the shadow many women feel when having sex for unromantic reasons—to comfort themselves, to avoid a confrontation over some domestic issue, or to secure a favor—a fear of acting like a whore.[4]

This reading of the relationship between prostitution rules and the female body is aligned with but somewhat different from the radical feminist description of the relationship between prostitution and female subjectivity. Catharine MacKinnon . . . describes the relationship this way:

> [Feminist] investigations reveal . . . [that] prostitution [is] not primarily [an] abuse[] of physical force, violence, authority, or economics. [It is an] abuse[] of sex. [It] need not and do[es] not rely for [its] coerciveness upon forms of enforcement other than the sexual. . . .
>
> . . . If women are socially defined such that female sexuality cannot be lived or spoken or felt or even somatically sensed apart from its enforced definition, so that it *is* its own lack, then there is no such thing as a woman as such, there are only walking embodiments of men's projected needs.[5]

MacKinnon's description of the impact of prostitution on women suggests that the sexual experience of all women may be, like sex work, the experience of having sex solely at the command of and for the pleasure of an other. This is a more extreme interpretation of the sexualized female body than mine and not one all women share.

The feminists' point of view? Well, I would like to point out that they're missing a couple of things, because, you know, I may be dressing like the typical bimbo, whatever, but I'm in charge. You know. I'm in charge of my fantasies. I put myself in these situations with men, you know. . . . [A]ren't I in charge of my life?[6]

Although I believe Madonna's claim about herself, there are probably a number of people who don't. Anyone who looks as much like a sex worker as she does couldn't possibly be in charge of herself, they are likely to say; she is an example of exactly what MacKinnon means by a "walking embodiment[ ] of men's projected needs."[7] Without going further into the cottage industry of Madonna interpretation, it seems indisputable that Madonna's version of the female sexualized body is radically more autonomous and self-serving than MacKinnon's interpretation, and significantly less troubled and doubled than mine.

Because sex differences are semiotic—because the female body is produced and interpreted through a system of signs—all three of these interpretations of the sexualized female body may be accurate. The truth of any particular meaning would depend on the circumstances in which it was asserted. Thus, the sexualized female body that is produced and sustained by the legal regulation of prostitution may have multiple meanings. Moreover, the meaning of the sexualized female body for an individual woman is also affected by other feminine images that the legal regulation of prostitution produces.

Anti-prostitution rules terrorize the female body. The regulation of prostitution is accomplished not only by rules that expressly repress or prohibit commercialized sex.

Prostitution regulation also occurs through a network of cultural practices that endanger sex workers' lives and make their work terrifying. These practices include the random, demeaning, and sometimes brutal character of anti-prostitution law enforcement. They also include the symbiotic relationship between the illegal drug industry and sex work, the use of prostitutes in the production of certain forms of pornography, hotel compliance with sex work, inadequate police protection for crimes against sex workers, and unregulated bias against prostitutes and their children in housing, education, the health care system, and in domestic relations law. Legal rules support and facilitate these practices.

The legal terrorization of prostitutes forces many sex workers to rely on pimps for protection and security, an arrangement which in most cases is also terrorizing. Pimps control when sex workers work, what kind of sex they do for money, and how much they make for doing it; they often use sexual seduction and physical abuse to "manage" the women who work for them. The terrorization of sex workers affects women who are not sex workers by encouraging them to do whatever they can to avoid being asked if they are "for" illegal sex. Indeed, marriage can function as one of these avoidance mechanisms, in that, conventionally, marriage signals that a woman has chosen legal sex over illegal sex.

One might argue that the terrorized female body is not that much different from the sexualized female body. Both experiences of femininity often—some might say always—entail being dominated by a man. Regardless of whether a woman is terrorized or sexualized, there are social incentives to reduce the hardships of her position, either by marrying or by aligning herself with a pimp. In both cases she typically becomes emotionally, financially, physically, and sexually dependent on and subordinate to a man.

If the terrorized and sexualized female bodies can be conflated and reduced to a dominated female body, then Madonna's claim that she's in charge, like the claims other women make that they experience sexual pleasure or autonomy in their relations with men, is suspect—perhaps, even, the product of false consciousness. But I argue that the dominated female body does not fully capture the impact of anti-prostitution rules on women. This is because anti-prostitution rules also maternalize the female body, by virtue of the interrelationship between anti-prostitution rules and legal rules that encourage women to bear and rear children. The maternalized female body triangulates the relationship between law and the meanings of the female body. It proposes a choice of roles for women.

The maternalization of the female body can be explained through the operation of the first and second postmodern "principles." That is, because we construct our identities in language and because the meaning of language is contextual and contingent, the relationship between anti-prostitution rules and the meaning of the female body is also affected by other legal rules and their relationship to the female body. The legal rules that criminalize prostitution are located in a legal system in which other legal rules legalize sex—rules, for example, that establish marriage as the legal site of sex and that link marital sex to reproduction by, for example, legitimating children born in marriage. As a result of this conjuncture, anti-prostitution rules maternalize the female body. They not only interrogate women with the question of whether they are for or against prostitution; they also raise the question of whether a woman is for illegal sex or whether she is for legal, maternalized sex.

The legal system maintains a shaky line between sex workers and other women. Anti-prostitution laws are erratically enforced; eager customers and obliging hotel services collaborate in the "crimes" prostitutes commit with relative impunity, and the legal, systemic devaluation of "women's work" sometimes makes prostitution more lucrative for women than legitimate wage labor. Anti-prostitution rules formally preserve the distinction between legal and illegal sexual activity. By preventing the line between sex workers and "mothers" from disappearing altogether, anti-prostitution rules reinforce the maternalized female body that other legal rules more directly support.

The legal discourse of anti-prostitution law explicitly deploys the image of maternalized femininity in order to contrast sex workers with women who are not sex workers. This can be observed in defamation cases involving women who are incorrectly identified or depicted as whores. In authorizing compensation for such women, courts typically appeal to maternal imagery to describe the woman who has been wrongly described; they justify their decisions by contrasting the images of two female bodies against each other, the virgin and the whore—madonna and bimbo. The discourse of these decisions maternalizes the female body.[8] The maternalized female body is responsible for her children. Madonna's bambino puts her in charge.

The conjunction and displacement of these alternative meanings of the female body are rationalized in legal discourse, where they are presented as both "natural" but also necessary, for reasons associated with liberalism. A Massachusetts case involving a rape prosecution[9] and feminist controversy regarding the decriminalization of prostitution provide two examples.

Sometime after three o'clock in the morning on a December night in Malden Square, a police cruiser entered a parking lot where police officers had heard screams. "Seeing the headlights of an approaching car," Judge Liacos wrote for the Supreme Judicial Court, a woman "naked and bleeding around the mouth, jumped from the defendant's car and ran toward [the police cruiser] screaming and waving her arms."[10] She claimed that she had been raped, that the defendant had forced her to perform oral sex and to engage in intercourse twice. After the defendant was convicted on charges of rape and commission of an unnatural and lascivious act, he appealed. He claimed that he had wrongfully been denied the opportunity to inform the jury that the complainant had twice been charged with prostitution. He argued that the complainant's allegation of rape, which he denied, "may have been motivated by her desire to avoid further prosecution."[11]

The trial court had prohibited the defendant from mentioning the complainant's arrests to the jury because of the Massachusetts rape shield statute,[12] a rule that prohibits the admission of reputation evidence or of specific instances of victim's sexual conduct in a rape trial. The purpose of the rule is to encourage victims to report rapes, to eliminate victim harassment at trial, and to support the assumption that reputation evidence is "only marginally, if at all, probative of consent."[13] Reasoning that a defendant's right to argue bias "may be the last refuge of an innocent defendant," the Supreme Judicial Court lifted the shield.[14]

> We emphasize that we do not depart from the long held view that prostitution is not relevant to credibility. . . . Nor do we depart from the policy of the statute in viewing prostitution or the lack of chastity as inadmissible on the issue of consent. Where, however, such facts are relevant to a showing of bias or motive to lie, the general evidentiary rule of exclusion must give way to the constitutionally based right of effective cross-examination.[15]

This interpretation of the rape-shield statute, broadly applied, denies sex workers who dare to complain of sexual violence the presumption of innocence. Because prostitution is unlawful, this ruling simultaneously terrorizes, sexualizes, and de-maternalizes sex workers. This triple whammy is accomplished by an appeal to fairness:

> [T]he defendant is entitled to present his own theory of the encounter to the jury. . . . The relevancy of testimony depends on whether it has a "rational tendency to prove an issue in the case." . . . Under the defendant's theory he and the complainant, previously strangers to each other, were in a car late at night parked in a vacant parking lot. Having just engaged in sexual acts, they were both naked. A police car was approaching. The defendant intended to show that the complainant, having been found in a similar situation on two prior occasions, had been arrested on each occasion and charged with prostitution. We cannot say that this evidence has no rational tendency to prove that the complainant was motivated falsely to accuse the defendant of rape by a desire to avoid further prosecution.[16]

Seems perfectly reasonable. Fair. If a guy can't explain a gal's reasons for misrepresenting a situation, that bleeding mouth might compromise his credibility.

It might seem obvious, at this point, that decriminalization of prostitution would be an appropriate strategy for feminist legal activists concerned about the physical security of sex workers. However, although the feminists I've read all agree that prostitution should be decriminalized, they disagree about how decriminalization should occur. The arguments in this dispute are another example of how legal discourse reproduces and is mired in the interpretations of the female body produced by legal rules.

Should the reform of prostitution law be restricted to the repeal of rules penalizing the sale of sex, or should other legally supported structures that create, sustain and degrade sex work also be challenged? Feminists in favor of legalization—this is the postmodern position—argue that, unlike a narrowly defined decriminalization campaign, legalization might significantly improve the lives of sex workers. Legalization, for example, might extend unemployment insurance benefits to sex workers; it might allow sex workers to participate in the social security system; it might prohibit pimping; it might authorize advertising for their business.

Feminists who are against legalization—this is the radical position—envision a decriminalization project that would develop strategies for preventing women from participating in sex work, rather than strategies that would make prostitution a more comfortable line of work. Radical feminists, such as Kathleen Barry, are sympathetic to the plight of sex workers.[17] But their conviction that women are defined as women by their sexual subordination to men leads them to argue that sex workers are particularly victimized by patriarchy and that they should be extricated from their condition rather than supported in their work. These arguments against legalization are in the language of the terrorized female body.

Not all legal feminists believe that prostitutes are terrorized full time. Some feminists—I'll call this group the liberals—believe that at least some sex workers, occasionally, exercise sexual autonomy. But these feminists do not favor assimilating sex work into the wage market. They oppose legalization because they object to the kind of sexual autonomy legalization would support.[18] That is, although they support the right of women to do sex work—even at the cost of reinforcing male dominance—they resist the commodification of women's sexuality.

Sex workers themselves—who inspire the postmodern position as I develop it here—want legal support for sex that is severed from its reproduction function and from romance, affection, and long-term relationships.[19] Because "legal" sexual autonomy is conventionally extended to women only by rules that locate sexuality in marriage or by rules that allow women decisional autonomy regarding reproductive issues, arguments in support of law reforms that would legalize sex work conflict with the language of the maternalized female body. The arguments that sex workers are making to assimilate their work into the wage market appeal to a sexualized femininity that is something other than a choice between criminalized and maternalized sex or a choice between terrorized and maternalized sex. This appeal to a fresh image of the female body is based on a reorganization of the three images of femininity I described earlier; it arises within the play of these three images. Its originality suggests, to me, resistance to the dominant images.

It is significant that sex workers have "found" a different voice of feminine sexuality through the process of political organizing, through efforts to speak out against and to change the conditions of their lives. For me, the promise of postmodern legal feminism lies in the juncture of feminist politics and the genealogy of the female body in law. It is in this juncture that we can simultaneously deploy the commonalities among real women, in their historically situated, material circumstances, and at the same time challenge the conventional meanings of "woman" that sustain the subordinating conditions of women's lives.

I do not think that the sex workers' claims for legalization constitute "the" postmodern feminist legal voice. I am also unsure whether I support their position on legalization. But I believe that my analysis of the decriminalization dispute in which they are participating illustrates how postmodern legal feminism can seek and claim different voices, voices which will challenge the power of the congealed meanings of the female body that legal rules and legal discourse permit and sustain. . . .

Notes

1. For the radical feminist focus on male domination, see Andrea Dworkin, Pornography: Men Possessing Women 14–18, 53–56 (1989); Dworkin, Right-Wing

Women 78–87 (1983); Catharine A. MacKinnon, Feminism Unmodified: Discourses on Life and Law 40–45, 171–174 (1987); MacKinnon, Feminism, Marxism, Method and the State: An Agenda for Theory, in D. Weisberg ed., Feminist Legal Theory: Foundations 437 (Temple Univ. Press, 1993); and MacKinnon, Feminism, Marxism, Method and the State: Toward Feminist Jurisprudence, in D. Weisberg ed., Feminist Legal Theory: Foundations 427 (Temple Univ. Press, 1993). For the cultural feminist focus on the ethic of care, see Carol Gilligan, In a Different Voice: Psychological Theory and Women's Development 64–105 (1982); and Leslie Bender, A Lawyer's Primer on Feminist Theory and Tort, 38 J. Legal Educ. 3, 28–37 (1988) (suggesting the incorporation of Gilligan's ethic into tort law's standard of care).

2. For a race-conscious critique of liberal, radical, and cultural feminism for overlooking minority women concerns, see Kimberle Crenshaw, Demarginalizing the Intersection of Race and Sex: A Black Feminist Critique of Antidiscrimination Doctrine, Feminist Theory and Antiracist Politics, 1989 U. Chi. Legal F. 139, 140, 152–160; Angela P. Harris, Race and Essentialism in Feminist Legal Theory, 42 Stan. L. Rev. 581 (1990); and Marlee Kline, Race, Racism, and Feminist Legal Theory, 12 Harv. Women's L.J. 115 (1989) [all reprinted in Feminist Legal Theory: Foundations, Chapter 4]. For the lesbian feminist critique of heterosexist assumptions in liberal, radical, and cultural feminisms, see Audre Lorde, Sister Outsider 114–123 (1984); Adrienne Rich, Compulsory Heterosexuality and Lesbian Existence, in Ann Snitow, Christine Stansell & Sharon Thompson eds., Powers of Desire: The Politics of Sexuality 177, 178–182 (1983). For a class-conscious feminist critique of the class bias inherent in liberal, radical, and cultural feminisms, see Kristin Luker, Abortion and the Politics of Motherhood 192–215 (1984).

3. Cf. Louis Althusser, Lenin and Philosophy and Other Essays (Ben Brewster trans., 1971) (demonstrating the role of ideology and social structure in shaping personality); Michel Foucault, 1 The History of Sexuality 6–7 (Robert Hurley trans., 1978) (discussing the power-sex relationship in terms of affirmation).

4. Even sex workers who are "in the life" feel interrogated by the sexualization question; they too struggle against acting like whores. Consider, for example, one sex worker's description of the discomfort she experienced because she sexually responded to her customer during an act of prostitution. Her orgasm in those circumstances broke down a distinction she sought to maintain between her work and the sexual pleasure she obtained from her non–work-related sexual activity. See Judy Edelstein, In the Massage Parlor, in Frédérique Delacoste & Priscilla Alexander eds., Sex Work: Writings by Women in the Sex Industry 62, 62–63 (1987) [hereinafter Sex Work]. Consider also the many accounts of sex workers who feel degraded or angry about their work; this is an experience of sexual division, a fear that, in their work as whores, they are acting like whores. See, e.g., Jean Johnston, Speaking in Tongues, in Sex Work, *supra*, at 70; Sharon Kaiser, Coming Out of Denial, in Sex Work, *supra*, at 104, 104–105; Rosie Summers, Prostitution, in Sex Work, *supra*, at 113, 114–115.

5. MacKinnon, Agenda for Theory, *supra* note 1, at 447.

6. Nightline: Interview with Madonna (ABC television broadcast, Dec. 3, 1990).

7. MacKinnon, Agenda for Theory, *supra* note 1, at 447.

8. See, e.g., Veazy v. Blair, 86 Ga. App. 721, 726 (1952) (holding that a cause of action existed when the defendant had stated that "the plaintiff, a pure and chaste lady of unblemished character, was a 'public whore'"); Mullins v. Mutter, 151 S.W.2d 1047, 1048, 1051 (Ken. 1941) (upholding a large slander award when the defendant called the plaintiff a "damned whore"). In Mullins, the court noted that: "In this case plain-

tiff is an orphaned girl, bearing—so far as the record discloses—a good reputation. . . . Up to the time complained of no breath of suspicion had been leveled against her chastity. But, so emphatically repeated charges by defendant was calculated to leave a scar upon her reputation that might follow her to her grave." *Id.* at 1051.

9. See Commonwealth v. Joyce, 415 N.E.2d 181 (Mass. 1981).

10. *Id.* at 183.

11. *Id.* at 184.

12. See Mass. Gen. L. ch. 233, §21B (1991).

13. *Joyce,* 415 N.E.2d at 186.

14. *Id.*

15. *Id.* at 187 (citations omitted).

16. *Id.* (citations omitted).

17. See Kathleen Barry, Female Sexual Slavery 226–237 (1979).

18. See Margaret J. Radin, Market-Inalienability, 100 Harv. L. Rev. 1849, 1921–1925 (1987) (favoring limited decriminalization of prostitution, at least for the short term). But see Jody Freeman, The Feminist Debate Over Prostitution Reform: Prostitutes' Rights Groups, Radical Feminists, and the (Im)possibility of Consent, [reprinted herein] (arguing that "the best short-term approach to reform entails removing prostitution from the criminal realm . . . and, at the same time taking affirmative steps to destroy the conditions that create consumption and drive women to the trade").

19. Not all sex workers seek to legalize as well as decriminalize their work, but many do. See, e.g., Gail Pheterson, A Vindication of The Rights of Whores 33–34 (1989); Draft Statements from the 2nd World Whores' Congress (1986), in Sex Work, *supra* note 4, at 307, 307; International Committee for Prostitutes' Rights World Charter, in Sex Work, *supra* note 4, at 305.

Split at the Root: Prostitution and Feminist Discourses of Law Reform

Margaret A. Baldwin

. . . "Prostitution isn't like anything else. Rather, everything else is like prostitution because it is the model for women's condition."[1] . . .

This paper attempts to begin a response to [this] insight. The fundamental inquiry I pursue is how the relationship between "prostitutes" and "other women" is given meaning in the sexual abuse of women and girls, in the legal response to that abuse, and in feminist reform strategies. In the design of existing law, in the behavior of individual men, and in the leading strategies of feminist law reform, the relationship is cast in oppositional terms: whoever a "prostitute" is, "other women" are not. In substance, the distinction provides a handy means of identifying appropriate female objects of punishment and contempt. To be deemed a "prostitute," whether by the state, by a john, or by any other man for that matter, immediately targets a girl or woman for arrest, for sexual assault, for murder, or, at the very least, dismissive scorn. Victims of rape, of incest, of domestic battery, of sexual harassment, are quite familiar with this difficulty. Declared to be "whores" and "sluts" by the men who abuse them, women then confront a legal system which puts the same issue in the form of a question: was she in fact a "slut" who deserved it, as the perpetrator claims, or not-a-slut, deserving of some redress? (The outcome of this interrogation is commonly referred to as "justice.")

. . . Feminist legal reformers have long challenged the legal relegation of "other women" to the status of prostitutes, in rape law reform, in representation of battered women in court, and in anti-sexual harassment advocacy. However, as I further contend, these strategies have less undermined the dichotomy between "prostitutes" and "other women" than they have further entrenched it. The core assertion advanced by this work has been the claim that "other women" are not "really" prostitutes, after all, and, therefore, denied justice by evidentiary standards and uneducated inferences yielding the contrary conclusion. . . .

In the seeming absence of other alternatives, feminist advocates for prostitutes have attempted to establish that prostitutes, too, are "other women" in the same sense in which "other women" have employed the term to distance themselves from prostitutes. . . . I ar-

Reprinted by permission of the Yale Journal of Law and Feminism from *The Yale Journal of Law and Feminism*, Vol. 5, No. 1, pp. 47–120.

gue that "distancing" oneself from prostitution, while representing oneself as an "other woman," the political position adopted by all of these advocates, is both the sexual demand made of women *in* prostitution, and the political demand made of all women vis a vis the state. . . .

[T]he first question I would like to explore [is] the political significance of the dichotomy drawn between "prostitutes" and "other women," in life and then again in law, a dichotomy exactly founded on the assumption that "prostitution isn't like anything else."

I begin with a story.

I. A Twice Told Tale

My activist colleague, K. C. Reed, is a strong woman. She was raped by her father and then sexually abused by her grandfather from the age of two, and prostituted for over 20 years, first at age 13.[2] "She is now trying to remember her life as a way of beginning to live it in her own self. She needs to remember where she has lived, whether she did or did not attend a community college sometime in the 1970's, when and where she was in prison. This is difficult work. Her life's witnesses—family, friends, lovers, children, even the shreds of paper we rely on to remind us who we are and who we have been—number few. Many of the men are dangerous to her. Her children are far away. One of them, a daughter, is dead. K. C. believes she was murdered by a trick. Her sons are in the care of others. K. C. hopes for them but has no direct contact with them. Other family members know little. The facts have faded. The feelings were always wrapped tightly, or foregone by numbness, or dreamed in hard drugs that can make you feel a tenderness inside. Her memory is complex, kaleidoscoped, fluid. She is smart and vivid and full of devotion. She organizes on behalf of herself and other women in prostitution for support and for help in ending prostitution.

K. C. recently wrote down what happened to her during one night in prostitution when she was 15 years old. She and two other women had run away from a state hospital. They were picked up by some men and taken to a hotel room where about 25 other men had assembled. She describes how the men talked and acted, how many men penetrated her (15), in what positions, and with what objects after the penises gave out, how the men insisted that the women have sex with each other when the men wanted to watch, how the pictures were taken, how she moved to the next gang of men, the next road. She mailed her testimony to the newsletter of a feminist anti-rape organization for publication. One of the members of the board questioned whether her piece should be printed, objecting to formal deficiencies: "It just goes on and on and there's no point to it." The author's response, arguing to mimetic virtuosity, was simple. "Yes, that's right. It went on and on and there was no point to it."[3]

I have just now told you a story of my own. Mine too may seem simply an overlong account of a mere episode, and a needlessly pointed description of a fleeting, embarrassing moment of inadvertence and failed attention. In substance, in other words, an isolated incident. In form, however, my story occupies the status of creation myth in modern feminism: a story about a woman telling another woman a story about herself. As "consciousness-raising," it is feminism's tale of origin;[4] as "feminist epistemology," it is feminism's claim to coherence;[5] as "woman identification," it is the basis of our self-understanding.[6] In substance, our stories, our activism and our theoretical interventions are grounded principally in women's struggles for representational authority, in both senses of the term "representational": for the authorial power over the meaning of our experience, and for the political strength to make those meanings count for something reliably real. . . .

Yet, despite these shared commitments, K. C. Reed told a story that another woman, a feminist, could not hear. She heard words, "on and on," but not a proper "story." She heard some representational version of nagging incoherencies within the conceptual grid, the linguistic equivalent of insanity. These are the charges we conventionally associate with the suppression of women's voices within masculinist systems of meaning: less that we do not or cannot *talk* (although women's occupation of verbal space remains a controversial entitlement), than that we do not make *sense* (a conclusion further weakening our claim to verbal space). . . . The editor is a fine woman, clear-headed, smart, dedicated; she is neither cruel nor insensitive. But what K. C. had to say about one night of prostitution didn't yield meaning to her on its own terms.

I am compelled by this story, and wanted to tell it to you, for a number of reasons in addition to witnessing to the anguish of my friend. I am haunted by the fear that this story is less anecdote than synecdoche, characteristic of a profound incomprehensibility of prostitution to feminism. Certainly I need search neither long nor hard to discover myself in K. C.'s editor. . . .

One of feminism's stories, entrenched deeply in the history and political landscape of the contemporary movement, is that prostitution is indeed not "like anything else." The theme was often sounded in the early movement that prostitution is only a story, a representational overlay masking and justifying real abuse and sex-based inequality suffered by (other?) women. "Prostitution" was conceived as a symbol, a groundless stereotype, a cancerous, run-amok ideological construct; "the prostitute" was the embodied cultural sign representing the sum of depravations suffered by "all women" (real women?). . . .

The problem of prostitution to feminist reform, in consequence, comes to be posed as the problem the *idea* of prostitution poses for women's authority to tell our own, authentic stories of our own experiences. . . .

At least for women who are not publicly identified as "prostitutes," this understanding of prostitution as a false and dangerous idea [seems] supported in the experience of many women. . . . Especially on occasions of sexually exploitative and violent episodes, the characterization of women as "sluts" by assaultive men runs like a sturdy thread through women's accounts of sexual victimization. The epithet is apparently intended to humiliate, to eroticize, and to satisfy an urge for self-justification. In contemporary empirical research, the apparent irrationality of the charge threatens to render its content invisible, abstracted away in subsuming conclusions. The empirical preference too, it seems, is to perceive the allegation as "just a story," not a concrete explanatory or descriptive datum. Yet the charge is near-universally to be found, in the particular, if untheorized, event.

For example, investigators of wife beating commonly recite "jealousy" as an asserted motivation for men to beat and torture women with whom they are intimate.[7] Submerged in this conclusion are the allegations of prostitution which repeatedly emerge as the stated origin of that jealousy. In one collection of thirty-three women's accounts of their experience of being battered, nearly one third had been accused of prostitution or labelled as "whores" during the course of beatings and rapes. . . . [8] Similar recitations figure obsessively in prosecutions for men's murders of wives and girlfriends. As one defendant put the point, the victim was "just a slut" and he "had to kill her."[9] The same theme arises repeatedly in divorce actions, commonly where the husband beat and tortured his wife during the course of the marriage, and explains his behavior by reference to her whorish behavior.[10] . . .

Nor is the charge of prostitution limited to errant wives. While again little accounted for theoretically, it is by now a sad therapeutic commonplace that female victims of incest tend to identify as "prostitutes" as adult women, and to feel irrevocably separated from other, "normal" women.[11] . . . Abusers may directly label their victims as "sluts" to enforce the girls' silence, to explain their compliance, and to reinforce their sense of complicity. Those who learn of the abuse may make similar predictions, excusing the father's behavior and furnishing justification for further punishment of the girl. . . .

Similar patterns are discernible in less intimate relationships such as sexual harassment and rape. In substance, as Catharine A. MacKinnon points out, "a great many instances of sexual harassment in essence amount to solicitation for prostitution."[12] Some years later the Eighth Circuit Court of Appeal made the same connection, observing that "[a] woman invited to trade herself for a job is in effect being asked to become a prostitute."[13] . . . The same presumption of a woman's exploitative "sluttish" sexual enticement of a rapist, summed up neatly by one defendant's view that "all women were whores and sluts and they all deserved what [the victim] was getting,"[14] persists *ad nauseam*.[15] . . .

Given the enormous prevalence rates of each of these forms of sexual violence, it may be the rare woman who has not encountered a charge of prostitution or heard a justification for abusive behavior couched in related terms. As an ascriptive matter, the terms "prostitute" and "prostitution" seem to expand boundlessly, applied whenever we are punished for sexual behavior, fantasized or real, or for simply occupying the body of a woman, for which the punishment takes the form of sexualized terrorism. . . .

[M]uch feminist legal reform work against sexual violence has explicitly or implicitly advanced [strategies of] separation, distinguishing with great delicacy and equal urgency between "prostitutes" and "other women." The political rescue of "real womanhood" from conditions of prostitution, within the spheres of life believed occupied by "normal women," has been the mainstream feminist tactic advanced within many of our campaigns. These reform strategies have sought to displace these false beliefs by persuasion to counter-representations of our own devising, for example, "sexual harassment," "pornography victims," and "battered women." Each of these counter-stories . . . promotes a predictable theme about prostitution: emphatically, that we are *not* prostitutes. A mistake has been made—a grievous failure to contour the proper distinctions between the prostitution with which we are charged and our own conduct, and a consequent failure to treat us with justice. . . .

The success of these distancing strategies relies in the first instance on a threshold agreement among all concerned that we know who a prostitute *is,* "truly," permitting a tidy boundary to be drawn between ourselves and those others, with some hope of agreement on the distinction. . . . Feminist legal reformers have concurred, enthusiastically if implicitly, in these definitional judgments. Each of our counterrepresentations, our "true" stories, seeks to disidentify any particular sexual violence victim from the status of "prostitute" by distinguishing her behavior from at least one of the legal elements of prostitution.

In rape law reform, for example, feminist lawyers have long labored to establish a victim's "discriminateness," both in articulating the injury rape entails and in the representation of the victim at trial. Our most significant work focuses on the habilitation of a woman's "no" as probative of her lack of consent. This commitment in turn locates the injury of rape in the disregard of a woman's sexual selectiveness.[16] The enforcement of rape shield evidentiary rules and the articulation of women's injury through testimony of rape trauma syndrome continue this theme. Rape shield rules limit the admissibility of a woman's prior sexual history for the purpose of proving consent, at least when the defendant has not had sex with her before.[17] This representational spin control seeks to sever in a jury's mind the inferential connection it might otherwise draw between a woman's sexual "promiscuity" and her conduct on a particular occasion. Less politely, these rules of exclusion are designed to defeat the whore status her prior activity would ascribe to her.[18] The admissibility of evidence of rape trauma syndrome, cataloging the physical, psychological, and behavioral symptoms commonly consequent to sexual assault,[19] has also been advocated by feminist reformers both to corroborate a woman's testimony that she did not consent to the act, and to dispel juror misunderstanding that women "ask for it," by rendering plain the profound, complex, and enduring suffering that unwanted sex causes. . . .

Taken together, these boundary defenses form a solid wall against the imputation of prostitution to particular "other" women: she is not sexually promiscuous, does not subject herself to random treatment by strangers, and doesn't do it for cash. Beyond these defenses, is but silence. Domestic legal reform activity on prostitution is nearly nonexistent, both in feminist legislative projects[20] and feminist legal scholarships.[21] The recent legal scholarship on prostitution that exists is largely limited in vision to the rather narrow question of whether prostitution should or should not be decriminalized,[22] a discourse closely enmeshed with and perhaps as unproductive to feminist imagination as the never ending debates over the legal treatment of obscenity. . . .

Our activism in providing support services and progessive organizing has done little better than our legal initiatives. Domestic violence shelters remain in effect inaccessible to women and girls in prostitution, for reasons as precise as express policies excluding drug and alcohol dependent women from admission to shelters, as well as denying access to women who engage in illegal activities of any kind. In addition to specific policy restraints, the invisibility of prostitution to service providers limits their awareness of prostituted women's access and safety needs, the urgency of maintaining confidentiality of the identities of minor girls when sought by police and social service agencies, and the requirement of long-term support for prostituted women and girls. From my observation, once women are admitted to shelters, they often feel constrained to lie about their circumstances, reducing the possible benefits of proffered support to painful farce.[23] Her pimp becomes her husband, the cigarette burns on her thighs the consequence of a jealous outburst over her "seeing" other men, she is sexually harassed on the job, and on and on. Anti-pornography activism, which has mobilized the most visible contemporary feminist challenge to prostitution in the United States, has been largely pushed "underground," unlike pornography or prostitution.[24] Women's health agendas, to the extent that work has comprehended prostitution as a health issue at all, have limited the scope of their consideration of prostitution to the risks of AIDS transmission to and by prostitutes.[25] This emphasis obscures the significance of research indicating that chronic poor health among juvenile prostitutes is often a consequence of inadequate clothing,[26] that injuries from beatings and sexual assaults most commonly immobilize women in prostitution,[27] and the social targeting of all prostitutes for murder.[28]

Prostitution, indeed, is not like "anything else," especially anything that we might be. The most brutal rendition of this theme may be Kate Millett's account, as recounted by Alice Echols, of an episode at a radical feminist conference on prostitution in 1971:

> The place finally erupted when a member of The Feminists declared herself an "honorable woman" because she lived in a tenement, worked as a secretary, and yet refused to sell her body. As Millett noted, "the accusation, so long buried in liberal good-will and radical rhetoric—"You're selling it, I could too, but I won't"—was finally heard. Said out loud at last.[29]

The form of this claim is also familiar, if usually more delicately expressed. Women make it all the time, especially before we identify as feminists or engage in experiences of feminist consciousness-raising. *It's not me:* if they say it is, I can recite sixteen reasons and change why they are wrong.

[T]his feminist flight from prostitution seems largely reactive, driven by a tacit recognition that legal regulation of sexual violence and sex discrimination at bottom always functions as some form of judicial review of a man's conclusion that a complaining woman was, in fact, a whore, and therefore a permissible target of misogynist rage, contempt, and sexual use. The fate of a woman's claims on justice, we all seem to know somewhere, crucially depends on her success in proving that she is not, and never has been, a prostitute. As Andrea Dworkin puts the point, "The woman's effort to stay innocent, her efforts to prove innocence, her effort to prove that she was used against her will is always and unequivocally an effort to prove she is not a whore."[30]

"There is no point to it." The point, apparently, is to fix a point of departure from which to flee. With Freud's Dora, we may acknowledge the prostitute only to expel her.[31] . . .

[III. Untitled]

There is one more prostitution story I want to tell you. This is it:

> There you are, in a dump that's more or less clean, holding a towel in your hand, looking at somebody you've never seen before. The more you retreat, the more he advances; since the room is fairly cramped, you soon find yourself with your back against the wall. The guy's arms are around you, they're all over your body like slimy tentacles that grope you, strip you, and drag you down as he pulls you over the bed . . .
>
> For an instant, you escape from the nightmare: you are back in the church play-ground, playing hopscotch. It seems like yesterday. You almost feel good, and you shut your eyes to make the dream last. When you reopen them, after a split second, reality blinds you.
>
> Reality has taken the form of a cock, a real family man's wiener, a little soft but still enterprising.[32]

This is not an isolated incident. It is a commonplace observation within prostitution support and advocacy circles that dissociative strategies of distancing the act, herself, and the john are routine tactics practiced by women in prostitution, described by Kathleen Barry as constructing a "split-identity" between "that" woman performing an act of prostitution and her "other" self.[33] "Disengagement," Barry explains, "is the up-front strategy of women in prostitution."[34] Nor is this a costless tactic. The terrible psychic injury absorbed as a consequence of these survival tactics is recorded in the litany of "splitting" disturbances suffered by prostitutes. As is becoming better known, similar strategies of disengagement, of "not being there," are also commonly employed by women and girls to avoid trauma in incest and rape.[35] The term "denial," I think, but weakly and perhaps misleadingly conveys this experience. From the "inside," the feeling is less one of repression than of being released to someplace *else,* anywhere else, where it feels better, or doesn't feel at all. . . .

These disengagement strategies, though, as Barry further points out, are not only the last defenses of the used. "Disengagement" from her "real self" is the fundamental demand made of women in prostitution, the essential term of the transaction itself. What a john wants is for the woman to act the woman he wants, and for the woman to maintain a credible performance as part of the bargain. She is to act as if she *is* the role he wants her to play. Barry explains:

> [C]ustomers generally require that prostitutes act as if they are engaged with the customer emotionally, psychically, effectively by entering into a fantasy or by feigning the role of a lover. Either the prostitute is to act like a whore or she is to act like an affectionate lover. . . . In prostitution, what men expect from women is the *semblance* of emotional involvement, pleasure and consent, a *semblance that they can treat as if it is real* in the moment of the commodity exchange.[36]

This dynamic plainly exceeds in complexity the description of prostitution as "objectified sex," understood as a wholly unselfconscious, unilateral act of sexual consumption. Rather, the demand made of the woman is to demonstrate a happy complicity, to whatever role is demanded.

I would suggest that a similar demand, and similar strategy in the fact of it, drives the design of our feminist strategies in our public advocacy. The disengagement tactic step [says] whatever we are, wherever we are, it is not prostitution. It is love, or freedom, or work, or force, or fear; anything but prostitution. We can prove it by our arguments, over and over, from every possible angle that might be mustered in opposition. It is all a great mistake, and if no one else is convinced, we can at least convince ourselves. "I was never really into it." How many times a day do we turn this trick? How many years has feminism told this story, been "somewhere else" as a strategy of resisting what we are told we are?

And who are we talking to? Who is it, who cares so much, that we should care to convince? The men, it seems: the men who feel license to destroy us if we fail to convince them, the johns we hope at the risk of our lives will remember we are human beings. We are not prostitutes, and hope we can act well enough to fit the part of not being one. The law, too, we hope to convince. Our stories of "consent," of "work," of "intimacy," have been crafted with the law in mind, placating its demand that we not "really" be sluts. We deliver the goods, compliantly, now in the name of a self-determining, liberated feminism. . . .

My further intuition is that this is a structural political requirement, not only a problem of bad men, silly laws, or short-sighted feminism. My belief, also my fear, is that within the existing political and legal order, and the possibilities for change afforded some women, is embedded a profound bargain: take what you can, but it will always be at the price of abandoning prostitutes, of gaining your advantage at her expense. There is a term for women who accept bargains like that. It's called being a pimp's "bottom woman," the one who treasures his highest regard, and sometimes gets off the street herself, but only if she helps run the less lucky girls. There is also a term for the arrangement which makes this bargain compelling. It's called pimping, period. If my intuition is correct, this is the arrangement women presently have with the state, motivating the "not a prostitute" content of our legal stories as a condition of our legal citizenship. . . .

Notes

1. Evelina Giobbe, Confronting the Liberal Lies About Prostitution, in Dorchen Leidholdt & Janice Raymond, eds., The Sexual Liberals and the Attack on Feminism 67, 76 (1990).

2. K. C. Reed, There Isn't No Easy Way 1–2 (July 6, 1990) (unpublished pamphlet).

3. Thankfully, with the support of other board members, Reed's piece was ultimately published. See K. C. Reed, A Fomer Prostitute Speaks, NCASA News, Fall/Winter 1990, at 24. . . .

4. Catharine A. MacKinnon explicitly theorizes consciousness-raising in these terms. See MacKinnon, Toward a Feminist Theory of the State (1989) ("Consciousness raising is the process through which the contemporary radical feminist analysis of the situation of women has been shaped and shared," *id.* at 84). Historical accounts of contemporary feminism characteristically posit the formation of consciousness-raising groups as its constitutive event. See Sarah Evans, Personal Politics 212–232 (1980); Elizabeth Fox-Genovese, Feminism Without Illusions: A Critique of Individualism 13–15 (1991); Mary King, Freedom Song (1987); Alix Kates Schulman, Sex and Power: Sexual Bases of Radical Feminism, in Catherine Stimpson & Ethel Person eds., Women: Sex and Sexuality 21, 23–27 (1980). . . .

5. See, e.g., MacKinnon, Toward a Feminist Theory of the State, *supra* note 4, at 106–125; Nancy Hartsock, The Feminist Standpoint: Developing the Ground for a Specifically Feminist Historical Materialism, in Sandra Harding, ed., Feminism and Methodology 157 (1987); Teresa de Lauretis, Feminist Studies/Critical Studies: Issues, Terms and Contexts, in Teresa de Lauretis ed., Feminist Studies/Critical Studies 1 (1986); Dorothy Smith, Women's Perspective as a Radical Critique of Sociology, in Sandra Harding ed., Feminism & Methodology 84 (1987). . . .

6. As Teresa de Lauretis puts the point, at the bottom of feminist interpretive practices is the simple commitment to "reading, speaking, and listening to one another." De Lauretis, *supra* note 5, at 8. . . .

7. See, e.g., Lenore Walker, The Battered Woman 114–115 (1979) ("Sexual jealousy is almost universally present in the battering relationship."); Del Martin, Battered Wives 58–61 (1976); Erin Pizzey, Scream Quietly or the Neighbors Will Hear 85 (1974).

8. Gina Nicarthy, The Ones Who Got Away: Women Who Left Abusive Partners 290 (1987). . . .

9. People v. Carroll, 180 Cal. Rptr. 327 (Cal. Ct. App. 1983). . . .

10. [See, e.g., Parker v. Parker, 519 So.2d 1232 (Miss. 1988); In re the Marriage of Ruby Elizabeth Walls, 743 S.W.2d 137 (Mo. Ct. App. 1988); Rollyson v. Rollyson, 294 S.E.2d 131 (W. Va. 1982); Stillwell v. Stillwell, 357 So.2d 355 (Ala. Civ. App. 1978). . . .]

11. Judith Herman, Father-Daughter Incest 96–98 (1981); Diana Russell, The Secret Trauma: Incest in the Lives of Girls and Women 167–170 (1986). . . .

12. Catharine A. MacKinnon, Sexual Harrassment of Working Women: A Case of Sex Discrimination 159 (1979). . . .

13. Lucas v. Brown & Root, Inc., 736 F.2d 1202 (8th Cir. 1984) . . .

14. Fuget v. State, 522 A.2d 1371 (Md. App. 1987). . . .

15. Diana Scully reports that, among her sample of 114 convicted rapists, 69% of those who denied having committed a "real" rape justified their behavior "by claiming that the victim was known to be a prostitute, or a 'loose' woman, or to have had a lot of affairs, or to have had a child out of wedlock." Diana Scully, Understanding Sexual Violence: A Study of Convicted Rapists 108 (1990). . . .

16. See, e.g., Susan Estrich, Real Rape 102 (1987) ("'Consent' should be defined so that no means no."); Kristin Bumiller, Rape as a Legal Symbol: An Essay on Sexual Violence and Racism, 42 U. of Miami L. Rev. 75, 76–77 (1987) (emphasis in feminist rape reform is on taking a woman "for her word"). . . .

17. For a fine discussion of the rationale and statutory variations among state and federal rape shield rules, see Harriet Galvin, Shielding Rape Victims in the State and Federal Courts: A Proposal for the Second Decade, 70 Minn. L. Rev. 763 (1983).

18. The point is put bluntly in the Florida case law predating the enactment of the Florida shield statute. In that jurisdiction, evidence of prior sexual history was admis-

sible to prove "promiscuous intercourse with men, or common prostitution." Rice v. State, 17 So. 286, 287 (Fla. 1895). . . .

19. The term, and the symptomology it substantiates, was first developed by Ann Burgess and Lynda Holmstrom in 1974, based on their study of 146 women who entered the emergency room of Boston City Hospital alleging they had been raped. See Ann Burgess & Lynda Holmstrom, Rape Trauma Syndrome, 131 Am. J. Psychiatry 981 (1974); see also Ann Burgess & Lynda Holmstrom, Assessing Trauma in the Rape Victim, in D. Nass ed., The Rape Victim 112 (1977).

20. Much of the legislative activity on behalf of women in recent years has been inspired and guided by state gender bias commission studies. See Lynn Hecht Shafran, Gender and Justice: Florida and the Nation, 42 Fla. L. Rev. 181 (1990); Elizabeth M. Schneider, Task Force Reports on Women in the Courts: The Challenge for Legal Education, 38 J. Legal Educ. 87 (1988). Only Florida's study has included prostitution as subject matter for scrutiny, and is the only state to have enacted legislation affecting prostitution in consequence of those findings. See Fla. Stat. Ann. §796.09 (West 1991 Supp.). I initiated that process in Florida and drafted the core provisions of our new state legislation. . . .

21. But a few law review articles on the legal treatment of prostitution have appeared since 1985, a remarkably slim bibliography given the relative robustness of feminist legal inquiry generally in the same period. [See, e.g.,] Jody Freeman, The Feminist Debate over Prostitution Reform: Prostitutes' Rights Groups, Radical Feminists, and the (Im)possibility of Consent, herein, at 237; Pasqua Scibelli, Empowering Prostitutes: A Proposal for International Reform, 10 Harv. Women's L.J. 117 (1987); Nancy Erbe, Prostitutes: Victims of Men's Exploitation and Abuse, 2 Law & Inequality 609 (1984); Belinda Cooper, Prostitution: A Feminist Analysis, 11 Women's Rts. L. Rep. 98 (1989); P. R. Glazebrook, Sexist Sex Law, 44 Cambridge L.J. 42 (1985); Lori Douglass Hutchins, Pornography: The Prosecution of Pornographers Under Prostitution Statutes—A New Approach, 37 Syracuse L. Rev. 977 (1986); Beth Bergman, AIDS, Prostitution and the Use of Historical Stereotypes to Legislate Sexuality, 21 J. Marshall L. Rev. 777 (1998); Christine L. M. Boyle & Sheila Noonan, Prostitution and Pornography: Beyond Formal Equality, 10 Dalhousie L.J. 225 (1986); Lan Cao, Illegal Traffic in Women: A Civil RICO Proposal, 96 Yale L.J. 1297 (1987); Julie Pearl, The Highest Paying Customers: America's Cities and the Costs of Prostitution Control, 38 Hastings L.J. 769 (1987); Ina L. Potter, Locking Out Prostitution, 15 Hastings Const. L.Q. 181 (1987); Belinda M. Cheney, Prostitution—A Feminist Jurisprudential Perspective, 18 V.U.W. L. Rev. 239 (1988).

22. See, e.g., Deborah L. Rhode, Justice and Gender: Sex Discrimination and the Law 259 (1989) (criminalization asserted as origin of problems women in prostitution encounter); Freeman, *supra* note 21, at 77–83 (analysis of consent, legal regulation focused on question of decriminalization), Margaret J. Radin, Market Inalienability, 100 Harv. L. Rev. 1849, 1924–1925 (1987) (arguing for decriminalization combined with regulation of advertising and promotion); Scibelli, *supra* note 21 (same); Nancy Erbe's article pursues instead an analysis of the conditions of violence dominating the lives of women and girls in prostitution. See generally Erbe, *supra* note 21.

23. These comments are based on personal conversations with women in prostitution who have sought assistance from a variety of shelters. These reports are echoed in the responses of some service providers with whom I have discussed these concerns, who express fear that women in prostitution who are open about their circumstances will disturb and frighten the other women in the shelters. (It is uncontemplated that those "other women" might be prostitutes, too.)

24. In my view, the suppression of anti-pornography work is part and parcel of the denial of prostitution I am describing here. . . .

25. See Gloria Lockett, Prostitution, in Ellen White ed., Black Women's Health-book 189 (1990). . . .

26. D. Kelly Weisberg, Children of the Night: A Study of Adolescent Prostitution 116 (1985) (citing Dorothy H. Bracey, Baby-Pros: Preliminary Profiles of Juvenile Prostitutes 62–63 (1979)).

27. Eleanor Miller reports of her research on health conditions of "street women": "Health-related [concerns] . . . even more frequently mentioned as occasions for temporary withdrawal from street life than disease or pregnancy included the bruises, broken bones, cuts and abrasions that were the result of the ever-present risk of violence on the streets. The beatings and sexual assaults female street hustlers received at the hands of their 'men,' their dates, their wives-in-law, former 'women' of their 'men,' and other street people as well as the police were numerous and often brutal." Eleanor Miller, Street Woman 138 (1986).

28. See Jane Caputi, The Sexual Politics of Murder, 3 Gender & Soc. 437 (1989). . . .

29. Alice Echols, Daring to Be Bad: Radical Feminism in America 1967–1975, 194 (1989). See also Gail Pheterson, Not Repeating History, in A Vindication of the Rights of Whores 3, 18 (1989) ("Feminists who followed the anti-prostitution and anti-pornography line were often viewed by political prostitutes as naive or self-righteous agents of control and condemnation.").

30. Andrea Dworkin, Pornography: Men Possessing Women 204 (1983).

31. I am here paraphrasing Jane Gallop: "As a threatening representative of the symbolic, the economic, the extrafamilial, the maid must be both seduced (assimilated) and abandoned (expelled). . . . Dora and Freud cannot bear to identify with the governess because they think there is still someplace where one can escape the structural exchange of women. They still believe there is some mother who is not a governess." Jane Gallop, Keys to Dora, in Charles Bernheimer & Claire Kahane eds., In Dora's Case: Freud-Hysteria-Feminism 200, 216 (1989). . . .

32. Jeanne Cordelier, The Life: Memoirs of a French Hooker 69–70 (1978), quoted in Kathleen Barry, Prostitution, Sexual Violence, and Victimization: Feminist Perspectives on Women's Human Rights 7–8 (1991) (unpublished manuscript).

33. Kathleen Barry, Social Etiology of Crimes Against Women, 10 Victimology 164, 171 (1985). . . .

34. Barry, *supra* note 32, at 5. In the words of women Barry quotes: "Dia says: 'I have to be a little stoned to go through with it. I have to shove my emotions completely to the side. I get talkative and don't give a shit.' Elizabeth reports: 'You switch off your feelings, you have to do it.' Brita reports 'I've taught myself to switch off, to shove my feelings away. I don't give a damn, as long as there's money. It doesn't have anything to do with feelings.'" *Id.* at 5. Former prostitute Rosie Summers describes the sexual experiences of prostitution as "a [woman] turning off her emotions, being psychically someplace else while someone who despises her is making love to her." Rosie Summers, Prostitution, in Frédérique Delacoste & Priscilla Alexander eds., Sex Work: Writings by Women in the Sex Industry 117–118 (1987).

35. See, e.g., Women's Research Centre, Recollecting Our Lives: Women's Experiences of Childhood Sexual Abuse (1989); Elizabeth A. Stanko, Intimate Intrusions: Women's Experience of Male Violence (1985).

36. Barry, *supra* note 32, at 6–7.

❖ PART II

VIOLENCE

Section 3

Battered Women

Introduction

Feminist interest in wife beating dates back to the first wave of feminism.[1] Nineteenth-century Victorian reformers and suffragists championed women's right to be free from physical abuse by their husbands.[2] Wife beating also has longstanding roots in Anglo-American law, as explained by William Blackstone in his *Commentaries*.

> The husband also (by the old law) might give his wife moderate correction. For, as he is to answer for her misbehavior, the law thought it reasonable to entrust him with this power of restraining her, by domestic chastisement, in the same moderation that a man is allowed to correct his servants or children; for whom the master or parent is also liable in some cases to answer. But this power of correction was confined within reasonable bounds; and the husband was prohibited to use any violence to his wife, *aliter quam ad virum, ex causa regiminis et castigationis uxoris suae, licite et rationabiliter pertinent* [other than what is reasonably necessary to the discipline and correction of the wife]. The civil law gave the husband the same, or a larger, authority over his wife; allowing him, for some misdemeanors, *flagellis et fustibus acriter verberare uxorem* [to wound his wife severely with whips and fists]; for others, only *modicam castigationem adhibere* [to apply modest corrective punishment].[3]

A few nineteenth-century American cases upheld the husband's right of corporal punishment.[4] Pleck, although emphasizing that these particular appellate cases represent extreme views, nonetheless concurs that, for abused wives, "American legal justice in the Victorian age was mostly ineffectual."[5]

Scholars have explored the roots of the contemporary battered women's movement.[6] Some date its origins to the 1960s, when interest focused on child abuse.[7] One scholar points to earlier origins in the depression and World War II—a period that generated both popular support for the idea of government intervention and a general societal concern with injustice.[8] Other scholars highlight societal trends that contributed to the concern with family violence generally, such as: (1) a tendency to see family violence as a symptom of a crisis in the family; (2) attitudes toward child-centered parenthood that made coercion by family members less acceptable; (3) the development of a culture promoting self-exposure (commercial and artistic, as well as personal); and (4) a decreased emphasis on religious and moral values.[9] Still other scholars (including Susan Schechter in an essay herein) point to the anti-rape movement as an additional precursor of the battered women's movement.[10]

In the second wave of feminism, feminists turned their attention to wife beating after focusing on abortion and rape.[11] Feminist interest stemmed in part from a concern with the family.[12] Also influencing the battered women's movement were such factors as the proliferation of feminist organizations in social work, mental health, and the legal professions; a feminist emphasis on decentralized organization structure enabling adaptation to local conditions; and feminists' ability to promote cooperation between battered women's groups and their sponsors.[13]

Feminists effected far-reaching social and legal reform by establishing shelters and enacting government policy.[14] Feminists were active on both sides of the Atlantic. The first battered women's shelter ("refuge") was established in London in 1971.[15] Feminists soon established "Women's Aid" groups throughout Britain to seek funding for shelters. By 1975 feminists formed the National Women's Aid Federation to advocate legislation, shelter services, and education.[16] Parliamentary committees held hearings culminating in the passage of protective legislation.[17]

In this country, public attention focused on wife beating in the early 1970s.[18] The first shelter opened its doors in Phoenix, Arizona, in 1973,[19] and was soon followed by others.[20] References to wife beating began appearing in the media from 1974 on.[21]

The National Organization for Women (NOW) established local and national task forces.[22] A member of NOW, herself a battered wife, organized the first local task force in 1973 in Pennsylvania.[23] In October 1975, at its eighth annual meeting, NOW created a National Task Force on Battered Women/Household Violence.[24] A national network, the National Coalition Against Domestic Violence, came into being in 1978.[25]

Despite their similarities, the British and American battered women's movements differed in approach. Dobash and Dobash explain:

> When translated into action, American attention is drawn to individual rights and personal problems. This leads to an emphasis on the law and the psycho-medico professions. Legislative reform is directed at providing individuals with the vehicle for obtaining personal rights in law, while a variety of therapeutic responses are developed to deal with techniques for coping and/or personal development. . . .
>
> In Britain, the orientation to community and state responses led to greater emphasis on the work of voluntary agencies, such as Women's Aid, and on

changes in the support offered by state agencies such as housing and social work. Much less attention is paid to criminal justice and little to therapy.[26]

Feminist reform efforts spurred legislation on both the state and the federal level. The first state statutes enacted in 1976 "provided funding for shelters, improved reporting procedures, repealed intraspousal immunity from torts, and established more effective criminal court procedures."[27] Subsequent legislation increased penalties and strengthened civil protections. "By 1980, 45 states and the District of Columbia had made special legal provisions for cases of wife beating."[28] Feminists directed their efforts toward funding family violence programs by increasing marriage license fees.[29] Florida first imposed such a surcharge in 1978; 16 states soon followed.[30]

Feminists filed class actions to improve law enforcement.[31] Feminist litigators in both California and New York charged the police with an unwillingness to arrest abusers.[32] Feminist lawyers began raising self-defense claims on behalf of battered women who killed their husbands.[33]

On the federal level, despite Civil Rights Commission hearings on battering,[34] initial legislative efforts met with little success.[35] Beginning in 1977, Congress considered, but defeated, several bills, including the Domestic Violence Assistance Act in 1978 and the Domestic Violence Prevention and Services Act in 1980.[36] Commentators explain the reasons for the defeat as follows:

> [A]ttempts failed, however, due to the opposition of the Moral Majority and other political conservatives who perceived the bills as an attempt to promote radical feminist causes through improper federal intrusions into the private domestic sphere.[37]

Finally, in 1984 Congress enacted the Family Violence Prevention and Services Act[38] which furnished funds for shelters and programs. Pleck attributes the ultimate success to the linking of battering with child abuse, thereby muting conservatives' opposition.[39]

Today the impact of the battered women's movement is reflected in the proliferation of both services and legislative reform. Between 1975 and 1978, more than 170 shelters opened.[40] This number has grown to approximately 1,600 battered women's programs, including shelters, individual homes, hotlines, and advocacy projects.[41] Legislative reform continues on the state and federal levels to provide improved services and remedies.[42]

Evolution of Feminist Theories of Violence

Feminist theories about male violence toward women have undergone significant evolution.[43] The early focus was broad based, highlighting the multifaced forms of male violence.

> Linkages began to be sketched out among a variety of phenomena which had previously been theorized separated. The existence of rape was seen to be

rooted in an aggressive male sexual consumerism, for example, which also gives rise to other phenomena such as pornography and prostitution, while wife battering was seen to be linked both to the economic dependence of women on men, and to an oppressive ideology of the family.[44]

The early focus was also pragmatic, proposing recommendations for improved legal and social services to victims.[45] A theoretical stage evolved, reflecting a concern with the origins and pervasiveness of male violence.[46]

Feminist writings highlight theories of power, violence, and social control. An important contribution is the recognition of the victimization paradigm.[47] Radical feminists, including Catharine MacKinnon,[48] have been criticized for an overemphasis on women's victimization.[49] Some popular writers extend this criticism to the women's movement generally.[50] Gordon points out that this paradigm has both "dominated and crippled" feminist scholarship.[51] Several of the essays herein elaborate on this criticism.

Contemporary feminist theory continues to explore the link between battering and other forms of male control of female sexuality (such as rape, sexual harassment, and child sexual abuse). Sheffield, for example, underscores the need to broaden our understanding of the definitions and scope of sexual violence by including victims' voices; to study the common characteristics of forms of sexual violence; and to address, at a macro level, the role of violence in structuring male-female relationships.[52]

Feminists first formulated theoretical perspectives in the 1980s on gender and power in the context of wife beating.[53] They locate the sources of intimate violence on the societal level, focusing on group rather than individual explanations[54] in the belief that "the social institutions of marriage and family are special contexts that may promote, maintain, and even support men's use of physical force against women."[55] Feminist works on battering emphasize not only the relationship between gender and power, but also the historical analysis of the family as a social institution, the importance of understanding abuse from women's perspective, and the use of research to benefit women.[56]

Philosophical Perspectives

Liberal feminists played an important role in theory and practice regarding battering. Although early liberal feminists (such as the National Organization for Women) sought formal equality for women in the public sphere comprised of employment, education, and political life,[57] subsequent liberal feminists addressed the private sphere. Their concern with privacy led them to oppose restraints on pornography, contraception, abortion, and homosexuality, as well as battering.[58] When liberal feminists targeted wife beating, their strategies for social change emphasized the role of law. They advocated not only services for victims of wife beating, rape, and incest,[59] but also the passage of state and federal legislation.

In contrast to the role of liberal feminism, Marxist writings add little to the subject of violence toward women in general and wife beating in particular. Traditional Marxist analysis of women's oppression focuses on capitalism's exclusion of women from wage labor.[60] Neither Marx nor Engels expands on the discussion of marital violence. According to Marxist belief, "[m]arriage is, in fact, a relation that is remarkably similar to the feudal relation of vassalage: it provides a means for exchanging support and protection from the husband in return for services and devotion from the wife."[61] Engels's discussion of the oppression of women in the monogamous family under capitalism includes only one allusion to wife beating.[62]

Marxist feminists, like Marxists, have spent little time addressing family violence—despite the former's criticism of traditional Marxism for its inattention to family-related issues.[63] One noteworthy exception by Rafter and Natalizia[64] attributes the law's inadequate response to the patriarchal concept of women as sexual chattel. The authors conclude on a hopeful note that Marxist feminism has potential for ameliorating the position of women generally, as well as that of abuse victims, in the criminal justice system.

Socialist feminist writings, similarly, are curiously silent about wife beating. Occasional references can be found in the early work of Sheila Rowbotham. Rowbotham, like other socialist feminists,[65] believes that the family has a dual meaning in feminist theory. Not only is it a sanctuary, it is also "the repository of ghostly substitutes, emotional fictions which dissolve into cloying sentimentality or explode into thrashing, battering, remorseless violence."[66] Rowbotham makes clear that wife beating is one of many evils to which the family is subject under capitalism. According to Rowbotham, the division of labor relegates caretaking to women and is a cause of their isolation.

> If care were truly social, there would be no need for defensive homes as castles, tenderness would not be connected with submission, nor love with possession. It is not surprising that violence breaks out in the family, or that people are made victims of families, that children are devoured, and smothered and hurt and battered in families. The family under capitalism carries an intolerable weight.[67]

More recent socialist feminist writings continue the scholarly neglect. When socialist feminists Ferguson and Folbre point to areas around which to organize the feminist movement,[68] the topic of violence in the home is absent.[69] Perhaps such an omission stems from socialist feminism's predominant concern with reproduction and sexuality.

In contrast to Marxist and socialist feminists, radical feminists do address marital violence. Their primary concern is male domination, especially male control of women's sexual and procreative capacities.[70] After focusing initially on male violence in terms of rape, radical feminists broaden their focus to battering.[71]

Kate Millett, one of the first radical feminists to illuminate the link between male violence and patriarchy,[72] notes in her classic *Sexual Politics:* "Emotional response to violence against women in patriarchy is often curiously ambivalent; references to wife-beating, for example, invariably produce laughter and some embarrassment."[73] Despite Millett's awareness, however, she fails to see wife beating as important or pervasive. Instead, she concentrates on other forms of violence—"institutional" (legal) and sexual (rape).

By the end of the 1970s, prompted in part by a spate of popular and scholarly publications,[74] wife beating became a focus of the radical feminist literature. For Kathleen Barry, "wife battery" constitutes one of many forms of "female sexual slavery,"[75] along with prostitution, incest, and pornography. Similar to other radical, as well as socialist, feminists, Barry claims that the family harms its members.

> Wife battery . . . illustrate[s] how the family institutionalizes male power and authority. Exploitative and violent use of that power in the family is sanctioned and justified through inadequate laws to protect women, through poor law enforcement of existing laws, and by keeping the abuse of women . . . in the home, private, and therefore, inaccessible to scrutiny.[76]

Barry is one of the first radical feminists to criticize the legal system for its policy of non-interference in the private sphere.

Other radical feminists address battering from the vantage point of a concern with violence and sexuality.[77] MacKinnon refers to wife beating in her discussions of rape, sexual harassment, and pornography. Analogizing rape and wife beating, MacKinnon points to the law's failure to address the conditions contributing to male violence.[78] Later, analogizing the violent and sexual aspects of marital rape and wife beating,[79] MacKinnon theorizes that wife beating may be conceptualized as sexual, because it is often provoked by noncompliance with traditional roles or behavior; the practice predominates in the bedroom or kitchen; and also, "[t]he battery cycle accords with the rhythms of heterosexual sex."[80]

Additional references to wife beating may be found in other writings by MacKinnon. *Feminism Unmodified* contains mentions of "domestic battery of women,"[81] including statistics.[82] By the late 1970s, MacKinnon had adopted the popular terminology "wife beating."[83] In her classic work on sexual harassment, she analogizes such harassment to wife beating because of victims' neglect by the legal system.[84]

We also find references to wife beating in MacKinnon's writings on pornography. MacKinnon criticizes the argument that male violence (sexual harassment, rape, and spousal abuse) affects the sexes equally, charging that this assertion obscures the predominance of female victims.[85] MacKinnon also includes wife beating among the many forms of male violence that reflect women's subordination and inequality.[86]

The most detailed discussion of MacKinnon's views on wife beating may be found in her review of Ann Jones's *Women Who Kill*.[87] Given the centrality of MacKinnon's writings to feminist legal theory, MacKinnon's book review (written from the "perspective of political and legal theory")[88] furnishes a unique vantage point from which to explore her theories on battering.

In that review, MacKinnon zeroes in on a key concept regarding battered women— their "agency." Ever since Lenore Walker presented her theory of "learned helplessness"[89] to explain why women stay in abusive relationships (a theory which found its way into the law by means of the battered women's syndrome),[90] feminist and other commentators have criticized the characterization of battered women who kill as "passive."[91] MacKinnon charges that such a critique constitutes a "parody" of autonomy.

> Responding to a man who makes your life unspeakable by killing him, given that the state will judge you for it according to the same values that condoned or ignored his treatment of you for so long, is the ultimate act of self-destruction. It is suicide by means of murder, the only consolation being that you took him with you. I think it parodies autonomy to say that someone pushed to the wall who lashes out and is imprisoned for life as a consequence acted autonomously, even in the single moment of lashing out. It ignores why she needed to act and what she paid for it, neither of which she chose.[92]

MacKinnon advocates broadening the analysis to include women's acts before *and* after the act. "Such an analysis would construe their homicidal self-acting within a totality of being acted upon."[93]

MacKinnon's significant contribution is her analysis of equality theory as applied to battering. She points to internal contradictions and unresolved questions in equality theory before suggesting that equality may take on a variety of meanings when applied to battered women—"[the] highest goal, a valid ideal mistakenly applied, a complete shibboleth, and an unfair standard in an equal world."[94] She focuses on the fundamental question: Does gender specificity benefit or disadvantage women? In the context of State v. Wanrow (a case included herein that validates woman's subjective perceptions of reasonableness),[95] MacKinnon posits that the legal system's special treatment works to women's detriment.

> To the *Wanrow* court, to judge a woman's conduct in light of the "individual physical handicaps which are the product of sex discrimination" was not to apply a dual standard. Rather, to fail to consider women's heritage is "to deny the right of individual women involved to trial by the same rules which are applicable to male defendants." Equality apparently means that men are judged against a reasonable man standard, women against a reasonable woman standard. But is this two rules or one? This is more than a superficially semantic or inconsequentially symbolic concern. Double standards have often been a legal means for disadvantaging women, as well as for rationalizing women's social exclusion and denigration.[96]

She concludes, "the price of this special consideration seems to be that women not only be perceived as weak, or as rationally perceiving themselves as such, but that we actually remain so."[97]

Legal Literature

Legal commentators began addressing battering at about the same time as popular writers.[98] Early legal writing focused on the inapplicability to women of a general self-defense standard[99] and, more narrowly, on the application of the self-defense doctrine to battered women who kill their abusers.[100] Scholars criticized the criminal justice system generally,[101] emphasizing the lack of enforcement[102] as well as the insensitivity of the criminal justice process.[103] Articles focused on the potential of litigation against police departments[104] and addressed evidentiary reforms, especially the admissibility of the battered woman syndrome.[105]

Additional writing evaluates the effectiveness of civil remedies (such as restraining orders and tort actions).[106] Articles criticized criminal remedies as well (criminal charges for assault and battery).[107] Scholars broadened their focus to other legal contexts, including battering and custody decision making,[108] and to informal dispute resolution[109] to reveal that battered women frequently are disadvantaged in decision-making processes because of gender stereotypes.

Writers (such as Ruthann Robson herein) also expanded the focus to highlight victims of battering who had previously been ignored, such as lesbian partners.[110] Scholars also explored the influence of class and race,[111] pointing out that an African-American woman "finds herself in racist binds that do not affect battered white women."[112]

In an insightful exploration of the significance of the battered women's movement for feminist legal theory, Currie points out that feminists' demands early in the battered women's movement advocated the redistribution of social power.[113] The essays in this chapter illustrate attempts to grapple with the same focal concern: the relationship between gender and power. The essays provide illustrations that the battered women's movement, in Currie's words, "provides important insights for how we think about the state and feminist struggle for its reform."[114]

Susan Schechter links the origins of the battered women's movement to the anti-rape movement. She identifies radical and socialist feminist influences on the movement by their questioning the privacy of the family and setting the movement's egalitarian organizational structure. Her essay is noteworthy for its affirmation of the role of ideology in shaping social movements and the law.[115]

In "Describing and Changing: Women's Self-Defense Work and the Problem of Expert Testimony on Battering," Elizabeth Schneider, one of the foremost litigators and legal scholars in battered women's defense work,[116] explores the ramifications of the admissibility of expert testimony on the battered woman syndrome.[117] Schneider's thesis is that, although judicial acceptance of the syndrome evidence is laudatory, the admission of such testimony has negative implications for battered women's self-defense claims. Schneider makes an especially important contribution with her criticism of the victimization paradigm.[118] Her essay also explores the significance of State v. Wanrow (included here) for battered women's defense work.

Christine Littleton returns to the implications of gender stereotypes for practice and theory. Littleton identifies and explores an important stage of legal reform which she terms "transition"—the point at which significant gains have been made but work remains. The "problem of transition," as Littleton defines it, is to continue progress without sacrificing legal victories. To address this problem, Littleton identifies several strategies aimed at the abuser.

Also exploring battering from the victim's perspective,[119] Martha Mahoney illustrates the necessity for a new theory based on the underlying power struggle in relationships. Mahoney's major contribution is her recognition that the departure from violent relationships is a process. Her essay expands our knowledge of the relationship between gender and power by illuminating the range of responses and counterresponses to coercion.[120]

Current research suggests that the problem of violence in lesbian relationships is as frequent as that in heterosexual relationships.[121] The "discovery" of lesbian victims is a natural outgrowth of research on violence against women.[122] Lesbian legal theory has found a niche in feminist legal theory,[123] as lesbian perspectives emerge on pornography, prostitution, rape, and sexual harassment, as well as battering.[124] The essay by Ruthann Robson has a dual purpose: to explore the law's response to violence in lesbian relationships and to suggest the utility of lesbian legal theory for law reform.[125] Robson argues that stereotypes have limited the law's ability to combat violence. Her essay thus adds a valuable criticism of essentialism in legal theory.

In the final essay, "The Violence of Privacy," Elizabeth Schneider explores a theme central to liberal, socialist, and radical feminist perspectives: the private family as oppressive for women. As theory on battered women has evolved, Schneider speculates that a backlash jeopardizes reform.[126] Schneider concludes by urging a reconceptualization of privacy to recognize its "affirmative role" in promoting the autonomy and liberty essential to the achievement of equality.

Notes

1. The terms *wife beating* and *battered women* are used here based on the feminist view that "[gender-neutral] terms obscure the dimensions of gender and power that are fundamental to understanding wife abuse." M. Bograd, Feminist Perspectives on Wife Abuse: An Introduction, in K. Yllo & M. Bograd eds., Feminist Perspectives on Wife Abuse 13 (Sage Publications, 1988). For feminist criticisms of gender neutral terminology, see A. Baron, Feminist Legal Strategies: The Powers of Difference, in B. Hess & M. Ferree eds., Analyzing Gender: A Handbook of Social Science Research 495 (Sage Publications, 1987); R. E. Dobash & R. P. Dobash, Research as Social Action: The Struggle for Battered Women, in Feminist Perspectives, *supra* this note, at 66; E. Pleck, Domestic Tyranny: The Making of Social Policy Against Family Violence from Colonial Times to the Present 195 (Oxford Univ. Press, 1987).

2. Nineteenth-century reformers included Frances Power, an upper-class British author of a 1878 article "Wife-Torture in England," and also John Stuart Mill. See C. Bauer & L. Ritt, The Work of Frances Power Cobbe: A Victorian Indictment of Wife-Beating, in G. Russell ed., Violence in Intimate Relationships 7 (PMA Pub., 1988). On Mill's influence, see T. Davidson, Wifebeating: A Recurring Phenomenon Throughout History, in M. Roy ed., Battered Women: A Psychosociological Study of Domestic Violence 16 (Van Nostrand Reinhold, 1977) (suggesting that *The Subjection of Women* "may have been the first significant document to spark the raising of public consciousness about the plight of battered wives"). See also Pleck, Wife Beating in Nineteenth-Century America, 4 Victimology 60, 64, 68 (1979) [hereafter Wife Beating]; Pleck, Feminist Responses to "Crimes Against Women," 1868–1896, 8 Signs 451, 453 (1983)

[hereafter Feminist Responses] (discussing anti-battering campaign of liberal feminists Elizabeth Cady Stanton, Susan B. Anthony, and Sarah Grimke). On feminist historical interest in wife beating, see generally L. Gordon, Heroes of Their Own Lives: The Politics and History of Family Violence, Boston 1880–1960 (Viking, 1988); Pleck, Wife Beating, *supra* this note; Pleck, Feminist Responses, *supra* this note.

3. 1 W. Blackstone, Commentaries *442–443. Legend has it that a "rule of thumb" (the width of the weapon) regulated the force with which a husband could beat his wife. See, e.g., Davidson, Wifebeating, *supra* note 2, at 18. Recently, this theory has come into disrepute. See H. Kelly, *Rule of Thumb* and the Folklore of the Husband's Stick, 44 J. Legal Educ. 341 (1994).

4. Davidson, Wifebeating, in Battered Women, *supra* note 2, at 19 (citing Bradley v. State, 1 Miss. 156 (1 Walker 1824); State v. Oliver, 70 N.C. 44, 45 (1874)). The policy on which *Oliver* is based (nonintervention in an ongoing marriage) has been the subject of heated feminist criticism. See, e.g., Shultz, Contractual Ordering of Marriage: A New Model for State Policy, 70 Cal. L. Rev. 204, 237–238 (1982); Taub & Schneider, Women's Subordination and the Role of Law, in D. Weisberg ed., Feminist Legal Theory: Foundations 9, 11–12. (Temple Univ. Press, 1993).

5. Pleck, Wife Beating, *supra* note 2, at 62, 64. Pleck disagrees with the portrayal of wife-beating in nineteenth-century America as legal and pervasive, arguing that the practice was prohibited in most states by 1870. *Id.* at 71.

6. See, e.g., F. Davis, Moving the Mountain: The Women's Movement in America Since 1960 (Simon & Schuster, 1991); Gordon, *supra* note 2; S. Schechter, Women and Male Violence: The Visions and Struggles of the Battered Women's Movement (South End Press, 1982); Tierney, The Battered Woman Movement and the Creation of the Wife-Beating Problem, 29 Soc. Probs. 207 (1982).

7. Gordon, *supra* note 2, at 2; Pleck, Domestic Tyranny, *supra* note 1, at 198.

8. J. Blackman, Intimate Violence: A Study of Injustice 3–4 (Columbia Univ. Press, 1989).

9. Breines & Gordon, Review Essay: The New Scholarship on Family Violence 8 Signs 490, 491 (1983). For a social problems approach explaining the emergence of child abuse, see Pfohl, The "Discovery" of Child Abuse, 24 Soc. Probs. 310 (1977) (physical abuse); Weisberg, The "Discovery" of Sexual Abuse: Experts' Role in Legal Policy Formulation, 18 U.C. Davis L. Rev. 1 (1984) (sexual abuse).

10. See, e.g., Davis, *supra* note 6, at 319; A. Edwards, Male Violence in Feminist Theory: An Analysis of the Changing Conceptions of Sex/Gender Violence and Male Dominance, in J. Hanmer & M. Maynard eds., Women, Violence and Social Control: Essays in Social Theory 18 (Humanities Press Int'l, 1987); Pleck, Domestic Tyranny, *supra* note 1, at 184; Rose, Rape as a Social Problem: A Byproduct of the Feminist Movement, 25 Soc. Probs. 75 (1978).

11. Davis, *supra* note 6, at 319 (rape crisis counselors first noticed wife beating); Pleck, Domestic Tyranny, *supra* note 1, at 183 (NOW devoted early attention to childcare, employment discrimination, abortion, and the Equal Rights Amendment; radical feminists focused first on abortion, next rape, and then battering); S. Weddington, A Question of Choice 35–36 (G. P. Putnam's Sons, 1992) (dating interest in abortion to 1969). See also the essay by Susan Schechter herein. Pleck writes: "It was ironic that rape appeared as a woman's issue before wife beating, because complaints of wife abuse to the police far exceeded reports of sexual assault. Nonetheless, the issue of rape was focused on first because it fitted more closely the radical feminist emphasis

on the deliberate channeling of female sexuality into the service of male domination." Pleck, Domestic Tyranny, *supra* note 1, at 184.

12. Breines & Gordon, *supra* note 9, at 491.

13. Tierney, *supra* note 6, at 211–212.

14. Feminists and feminist organizations, of course, were not the only influences on the battered women's movement. For a discussion of the influence of mental health, social service, religious groups, and law enforcement, see *id.* at 208.

15. Davis, *supra* note 6, at 320; Dobash & Dobash, Research as Social Action, in Feminist Perspectives, *supra* note 1, at 52. On the British battered women's movement, see generally R. E. Dobash & R. P. Dobash, The Response of the British and American Movements to Violence Against Women, in Women, Violence and Social Control, *supra* note 10, at 169–179; A. Edwards, Male Violence, in Women, Violence and Social Control, *supra* note 10, at 21; E. Pizzey, Scream Quietly or the Neighbours will Hear (Harmondsworth Penguin, 1974; Enslow Pub. 1977); Pleck, Domestic Tyranny, *supra* note 1, at 188–189; Sutton, The Growth of the British Movement for Battered Women, 2 Victimology 576 (1977).

16. Dobash & Dobash, Research as Social Action, in Feminist Perspectives, *supra* note 1, at 53.

17. Discussed in Tierney, *supra* note 6, at 207. See also Dobash & Dobash, Response of the Movements, in Women, Violence and Social Control, *supra* note 10, at 173.

18. For two of the earliest books, see generally S. Steinmetz & M. Straus eds., Violence in the Family (Harper & Row, 1974); R. Gelles, The Violent Home: A Study of Physical Aggression Between Husbands and Wives (Sage, 1972). For a more popular early book, see D. Martin, Battered Wives (Glide, 1976).

19. Tierney, *supra* note 6, at 207. Other scholars point to other programs as being first. See, e.g., Davis, *supra* note 6, at 320–321 (St. Paul shelter); Dobash & Dobash, Response of the Movements, in Women, Violence and Social Control, *supra* note 10, at 170 (same). Cf. Pleck, Domestic Tyranny, *supra* note 1, at 189 (noting that the St. Paul center, although not the first, was "still the first to reflect the impact of the modern feminist movement").

20. Tierney, *supra* note 6, at 207 (citing shelters in Pasadena and San Francisco, California; Cambridge, Massachusetts; and St. Paul, Minnesota).

21. For accounts dating the proliferation of articles to the early 1970s, see Pleck, Domestic Tyranny, *supra* note 1, at 182; Tierney, *supra* note 6, at 212–213.

22. Tierney, *supra* note 6, at 208 (Ann Arbor, Michigan, chapter of NOW; New York City and other local NOW chapters formed their own task force in early 1976). *Id.*

23. Pleck, Domestic Tyranny, *supra* note 1, at 187.

24. Tierney, *supra* note 6, at 208.

25. Dobash & Dobash, Response of the Movements, in Women, Violence and Social Control, *supra* note 10, at 174. See also Davis, *supra* note 6, at 321.

26. Dobash & Dobash, Response of the Movements, in Women, Violence and Social Control, *supra* note 10, at 177.

27. Pleck, Domestic Tyranny, *supra* note 1, at 192.

28. Tierney, *supra* note 6, at 209.

29. *Id.* (referring to legislation in Ohio, Florida, Montana, California, and Pennsylvania). See also Developments in the Law: Legal Responses to Domestic Violence, 106 Harv. L. Rev. 1498, 1507 (1993).

30. Pleck, Domestic Tyranny, *supra* note 1, at 190.

31. See, e.g., Bruno v. Codd, 396 N.Y.S.2d 974 (Sup. Ct. 1977), *rev'd in part, dismissed in part,* 407 N.Y.S.2d 165 (N.Y. App. Div. 1978), *aff'd,* 393 N.E.2d 976 (N.Y. 1979); Nearing v. Weaver, 670 P.2d 137 (Or. 1983); Raguz v. Chandler, No. C-74–1064 (N.D. Ohio 1975); Scott v. Hart, No. C76–2395 (N.D. Cal. 1976). See generally Gee, Ensuring Police Protection of Battered Women: The Scott v. Hart Suit, 8 Signs 554 (1982); Woods, Litigation on Behalf of Battered Women, 5 Women's Rts. L. Rep. 7 (1978).

32. Pleck, Domestic Tyranny, *supra* note 1, at 186–187.

33. *Id.* at 187.

34. Dobash & Dobash, Response of the Movements, in Women, Violence and Social Control, *supra* note 10, at 173. On the Civil Rights Commission hearings, see Pleck, Domestic Tyranny, *supra* note 1, at 195.

35. Tierney, *supra* note 6, at 209.

36. Domestic Violence Assistance Act, H.R. 12,999, 95th Cong., 2d Sess. (1978); Domestic Violence Prevention and Services Act, H.R. 2977, 96th Cong., 2d Sess. (1980). For discussion of these early unsuccessful efforts, see Pleck, Domestic Tyranny, *supra* note 1, at 196; Tierney, *supra* note 6, at 222; Developments in the Law, *supra* note 29, at 1543.

37. Developments in the Law, *supra* note 29, at 1543. See also Pleck, Domestic Tyranny, *supra* note 1, at 196–197 (attributing defeat to conservatives' lobbying in 1980 that portrayed the legislation as a feminist attack on "motherhood, the family and Christian values").

38. Pub. L. No. 98–457, 98 Stat. 1757 (codified as amended at 42 U.S.C. §10401 (1984 & Supp. V 1993)) (amended 1992). See also Davis, *supra* note 6, at 322; Pleck, Domestic Tyranny, *supra* note 1, at 198.

39. Pleck, Domestic Tyranny, *supra* note 1, at 198.

40. Tierney, *supra* note 6, at 208.

41. Davis, *supra* note 6, at 322.

42. Many states have enacted mandatory arrest statutes that eliminate discretion on the part of law enforcement personnel. See Ruttenberg, A Feminist Critique of Mandatory Arrest: An Analysis of Race and Gender in Domestic Violence Policy, 2 Am. U. J. Gender & L. 171, 180 n. 44 (1994) (citing 22 states and the District of Columbia).

On the federal level, Congress recently passed the Violence Against Women Act (VAWA) as part of the Violent Crime Control and Law Enforcement Act of 1994, Pub. L. No. 103–322, 108 Stat. 1796 (codified as amended at 42 U.S.C. §13981 (1994)). Title II, Safe Homes for Women, addresses battering by creating a federal remedy for interstate crimes of abuse, increased funding, and the provision for interstate enforcement of protection orders. See generally Developments in the Law, *supra* note 29, at 1544–1546; Frazee, An Imperfect Remedy for Imperfect Violence: The Construction of Civil Rights in the Violence Against Women Act, 1 Mich. J. Gender & L. 163 (1993); Symposium, Violent Crime Control and the Law Enforcement Act of 1994, 20 U. Dayton L. Rev. 557 (1994).

43. See, e.g., Liddle, Feminist Contributions to an Understanding of Violence Against Women—Three Stages Forward, Two Steps Back, 26 Canad. Rev. Soc. & Anth. 759, 760 (1989) (citing A. Edwards, Male Violence, in Women, Violence and Social Control, *supra* note 10).

44. Liddle, *supra* note 43, at 760. Liddle criticizes feminist scholarship for impeding the understanding of violence by a "one-dimensional" model of human agency

(i.e., attributing dubious intentionality to perpetrators), *id.* at 762–765, and vague characterizations about the nature of violence (e.g., defining violence to include threats), *id.* at 765.

45. *Id.*

46. *Id.*

47. Gordon, Family Violence, Feminism, and Social Control, 12 Feminist Stud. 453, 455–456 (1986).

48. See, e.g., Finley, The Nature of Domination and the Nature of Women: Reflections on Feminism Unmodified, 82 Nw. U. L. Rev. 352, 378–380 (1988) (reviewing Catherine A. MacKinnon, Feminism Unmodified: Discourses on Life and Law (1987)).

49. Such criticisms are especially prominent in the pornography debate. See generally L. Baron & M. Straus, The Victim Ideology of Antipornography Feminists, in Four Theories of Rape in American Society: A State-Level Analysis 99 (Yale Univ. Press, 1989). Baron and Straus observe that some feminists criticize the victim ideology of antipornography feminists as constituting "a dramatic break" with the views of earlier radical feminists: "Previously, radical feminists had addressed such issues as sex-role stereotyping, the patriarchal nuclear family, and economic inequality, whereas antipornography feminists focus their attention on compulsory heterosexuality, sexual slavery, and images of eroticized violence. This change in political priorities is also reflected in much radical feminist theory." *Id.*

50. See, e.g., K. Roiphe, The Morning After: Sex, Fear, and Feminism on Campus (Little, Brown, 1993). See also Kathryn Abrams, Sons of Innocence and Experience: Dominance Feminism in the University, 103 Yale L.J. 1533 (1994) (book review of K. Roiphe, The Morning After, 1993).

51. Gordon, *supra* note 47, at 475–476.

52. C. Sheffield, Sexual Terrorism: The Social Control of Women, in Analyzing Gender, *supra* note 1, 171, 184–186.

53. Activists and researchers began developing feminist perspectives on wife beating in 1984 at the Second National Conference for Family Violence Researchers. Bograd, Introduction, in Feminist Perspectives, *supra* note 1, at 11.

54. *Id.* at 13.

55. *Id.* at 12.

56. *Id.* at 13–16.

57. A. Jaggar, Feminist Politics and Human Nature 178, 181–182 (Rowman & Allanheld, 1983). The National Organization for Women's Bill of Rights, adopted at the first national conference in 1967, highlighted sex discrimination in employment, child care, education, reproduction and the Equal Rights Amendment, as well as discrimination in housing and credit. See NOW Bill of Rights, reprinted in R. Morgan, Sisterhood is Powerful: An Anthology of Writings from the Women's Liberation Movement 575–577 (Vintage, 1970). NOW is generally recognized as a liberal feminist organization. Z. Eisenstein, The Radical Future of Liberal Feminism 177 (Longman, 1981).

58. Jaggar, *supra* note 57, at 180, 183.

59. *Id.* at 183, 184. They also advocated funds for childcare and the provision of abortion, especially for the poor.

60. *Id.* at 215. Jaggar explains Marxism's neglect of the topic of male violence as follows: "It may be, however, that Marxism spends little time in providing a theoretical analysis of these phenomena because it considers that the oppressiveness of these practices is less concealed than the oppression inherent in wage labor." *Id.* at 222.

61. *Id.* at 217.

62. As Jaggar notes: ". . . Engels hints that the economic dominance of the husband may be the basis of what is now called 'wife battery' or 'wife abuse.' Engels does not name this directly, but he mentions, as if it were a matter of common knowledge 'the brutality towards women that has spread since the introduction of monogamy.'" Jaggar, *supra* note 57, at 219 (citing F. Engels, The Origin of the Family, Private Property and the State 135 (International Pub., 1972, originally published 1902)).

63. See Jaggar, *supra* note 57, at 238.

64. Rafter & Natalizia, Marxist Feminism: Implications for Criminal Justice, 27 Crime & Delinq. 81 (1981).

65. See J. Donovan, Feminist Theory: The Intellectual Traditions of American Feminism 18–19 (Frederick Ungar, 1990) (socialist feminists such as Ann Foreman, Zillah Eisenstein, and Mariarosa Dalla Costa "see the domestic sphere as inherently alienating to women").

66. S. Rowbotham, Woman's Consciousness, Man's World 59 (Harmondsworth, Penguin, 1973).

67. *Id.* at 77.

68. A. Ferguson & N. Folbre, The Unhappy Marriage of Patriarchy and Capitalism, in L. Sargent ed., Women and Revolution: A Discussion of the Unhappy Marriage of Marxism and Feminism 330–331 (South End Press, 1981).

69. *Id.* at 330–332. They identify issues of childcare and reproductive rights; sexual freedom; a woman's culture which supports women and teaches feminist values; and economic support systems for women.

70. See generally Jaggar, *supra* note 57, at 266–270.

71. Pleck, Domestic Tyranny, *supra* note 1, at 184–185 (brought about by consciousness-raising groups and the experiences of rape crisis counselors). Pleck points out, "Radical feminism, most critical of the traditional family, was responsible for the subsequent rediscovery of wife beating." *Id.* at 184.

72. Edwards points out that Millett, more than other early feminist writers, saw the importance of male violence. Edwards, Male Violence, in Women, Violence and Social Control, *supra* note 10, at 18.

73. K. Millett, Sexual Politics 44–45 (Doubleday, 1970).

74. See, e.g., T. Davidson, Conjugal Crime: Understanding and Changing the Wife Beating Pattern (Hawthorn Books, 1978); Martin, *supra* note 21; Roy, *supra* note 2; Pizzey, *supra* note 15; L. Walker, The Battered Woman (Harper & Row, 1979); Walker, Battered Women and Learned Helplessness, 2 Victimology 525 (1978).

75. K. Barry, Female Sexual Slavery (Prentice-Hall, 1979).

76. *Id.* at 151.

77. Jaggar, *supra* note 57, at 269 (citing Artemis March, A Paradigm for Feminist Theory, paper delivered at the Second Sex Conference, New York, September 1979, referring to the works of such early radical feminists as Griffin, Dworkin, Brownmiller, Morgan, and Firestone). Jaggar also includes MacKinnon in this characterization. *Id.* at 270.

78. MacKinnon, Feminism, Marxism, Method, and the State: Toward Feminist Jurisprudence, in D. Weisberg ed., Feminist Legal Theory: Foundations 427, 431 (Temple Univ. Press, 1993). Also, her discussions of rape sometimes refer to "battery of wives." See, e.g., C. MacKinnon, Rape: On Coercion and Consent, herein, at 471, 476.

79. C. MacKinnon, Rape, in Feminism Unmodified: Discourses on Life and Law

178 (Harv. Univ. Press, 1987). See also MacKinnon, Sex and Violence: A Perspective, in *id.* at 92.

80. MacKinnon, Rape, in Feminism Unmodified, *supra* note 79, at 178.

81. *Id.* at 1, 41, 170.

82. *Id.* at 24.

83. C. MacKinnon, Sexual Harassment of Working Women: A Case of Sex Discrimination 160 (Yale Univ. Press, 1979).

84. She writes: "The guarantee of impunity seems to be particularly firm when incidents involve either sexuality or violence within a relationship presumed to have a sexual dimension." *Id.*

85. *Id.* at 164–166. It may be that a stage in research on social problems is the recognition that a social problem primarily affecting women also affects men. For an example of such scholarship, see Steinmetz, The Battered Husband Syndrome, 2 Victimology 499 (1977).

86. The forms also include pornography, sexual harassment and rape. MacKinnon, Francis Biddle's Sister: Pornography, Civil Rights, and Speech, herein, at 59. Pleck points out that radical feminist Andrea Dworkin (who shares a similar view with MacKinnon) was herself a battered wife. Pleck, Domestic Tyranny, *supra* note 1, at 184.

87. MacKinnon, Toward Feminist Jurisprudence, 34 Stan. L. Rev. 703, 736 (1982) (reviewing Ann Jones, Women Who Kill (1980)) [hereafter Book Review].

88. *Id.* at 736.

89. Walker, Battered Woman, *supra* note 74; Walker, Learned Helplessness, *supra* note 74.

90. For a discussion of current judicial use of the battered woman syndrome, see Dowd, Dispelling the Myths about the "Battered Woman's Defense": Towards a New Understanding, 19 Fordham Urb. L.J. 567 (1992); Note, You've Come a Long Way, Baby: The Battered Woman's Syndrome Revisited, 9 N.Y.L. Sch. J. Hum. Rts. 111 (1991). For an interesting comparative law perspective, see Byrd, Till Death Us Do Part: A Comparative Law Approach to Justifying Lethal Self-Defense by Battered Women, 2 Duke J. Comp. & Int'l Law 169 (1991) (comparing U.S. and German law regarding the excuse of self-defense for battered women).

91. See, e.g., Schneider, Describing and Changing: Women's Self-Defense Work and The Problem of Expert Testimony on Battering, herein, at 311, 322–323; Schulhofer, The Gender Question in Criminal Law, 7 Soc. Phil. & Pol'y 105 (1990). See also M. Mahoney, Victimization or Oppression? Women's Lives, Violence, and Agency, in M. Fineman ed., The Public Nature of Private Violence 59 (Routledge, 1994).

92. MacKinnon, Book Review, *supra* note 87, at 735.

93. *Id.*

94. *Id.* at 723.

95. 559 P.2d 548 (Wash. 1977).

96. MacKinnon, Book Review, *supra* note 87, at 725 (citing State v. Wanrow).

97. *Id.* at 732.

98. For early articles, see Bard & Zacker, Assaultiveness and Alcohol Use in Family Disputes: Police Perceptions, 12 Criminology 281 (1974); Parnas, Prosecutorial and Judicial Handling of Family Violence, 9 Crim. L. Bull. 733 (1973); Truninger, Marital Violence: The Legal Solutions, 23 Hastings L.J. 259 (1971). Such articles were indexed under "Domestic Relations" in the *Index to Legal Periodicals;* no entry for battering existed until the 1982 edition when entries appeared on "Domestic Violence" and "Battered Women," as did a cross-reference to "Wife Abuse." See S. Rosen ed., Index to Le-

gal Periodicals (September 1980 to August 1981) 39, 133, 454 (H. W. Wilson Co., 1982). For a rare early article, see Stedman, Right of Husband to Chastise Wife, 3 Va. L. Reg. 241 (1917) (legal history of wife beating).

99. Collins, Language, History and the Legal Process: A Profile of the "Reasonable Man," 8 Rut.-Cam. L.J. 311 (1977); Donovan & Wildman, Is the Reasonable Man Obsolete? A Critical Perspective on Self-Defense and Provocation, 14 Loy. L.A. L. Rev. 435 (1981).

100. See, e.g., Schneider & Jordan, Representation of Women Who Defend Themselves in Response to Physical or Sexual Assault, 4 Women's Rts. L. Rep. 149 (1978); Schneider, Equal Rights to Trial for Women: Sex Bias in the Law of Self-Defense, 15 Harv. Civ. C.R.-C.L. L. Rev. 624 (1980); T. Kieviet, Comment, The Battered Wife Syndrome: A Potential Defense to a Homicide Charge, 6 Pepperdine L. Rev. 213 (1978); Eisenberg & Seymour, The Self-Defense Plea and Battered Women, Trial 34 (July 1978).

101. See, e.g., Hanmer & Stanko, Stripping Away the Rhetoric of Protection: Violence to Women, Law and the State in Britain and the U.S.A., 13 Int'l J. Soc. L. 357 (1985); Waits, The Criminal Justice System's Response to Battering: Understanding the Problem, Forging the Solutions, 60 Wash. L. Rev. 267 (1985); Taub, Ex Parte Proceedings in Domestic Violence Situations: Alternative Frameworks for Constitutional Scrutiny, 9 Hofstra L. Rev. 95 (1980).

102. See, e.g., Eppler, Battered Women and the Equal Protection Clause: Will the Constitution Help Them When the Police Won't, 95 Yale L. J. 788 (1986); Pastoor, Police Training and the Effectiveness of Minnesota "Domestic Abuse" Laws, 2 Law & Ineq. J. 557 (1984) (suggestions for effectuating reform in police protection); Scutt, Going Backwards: Law Reform and Women Bashing, 9 Women's Stud. Int'l F. 49 (1986).

103. Eisenberg & Micklow, The Assaulted Wife: "Catch 22" Revisited, 3 Women's Rts. L. Rep. 138, 149–151 (1977).

104. See generally R. Tong, Women, Sex & the Law 142 (Rowman & Allanheld, 1984); Gee, supra note 31, at 566 n.38; Woods, supra note 31, at 7.

105. See generally Bunyak, Battered Wives Who Kill: Civil Liability and the Admissibility of Battered Woman's Syndrome Testimony, 4 Law & Ineq. J. 603 (1986); Crocker, The Meaning of Equality for Battered Women Who Kill Men in Self-Defense, 8 Harv. Women's L.J. 121 (1985); Kinports, Defending Battered Women's Self-Defense Claims, 67 Ore. L. Rev. 393 (1988); Mather, The Skeleton in the Closet: The Battered Woman Syndrome, Self-Defense, and Expert Testimony, 39 Mercer L. Rev. 545 (1988); Thyfault, Self-Defense: Battered Women Syndrome on Trial, 20 Cal. W. L. Rev. 485 (1984); Walker, Thyfault & Browne, Beyond the Juror's Ken: Battered Women, 7 Vt. L. Rev. 1 (1982).

106. See, e.g., Scherer, Tort Remedies for Victims of Domestic Abuse, 43 S.C. L. Rev. 543 (1992); Taub, supra note 101; Note, Why Civil Protection Orders Are Effective Remedies for Domestic Violence But Mutual Protective Orders Are Not, 67 Ind. L.J. 1039 (1992); Comment, The Battered Woman and Tort Law: A New Approach to Fighting Domestic Violence, 25 Loy. L.A. L. Rev. 1025 (1992). On civil protection orders against battering, see generally Developments in the Law, supra note 29, at 1509–1514.

107. See generally Tong, supra note 104, at 130–133 (civil remedies), 133–141 (criminal remedies); Developments in the Law, supra note 29, at 1535–1541; Note, Explaining the Legal System's Inadequate Response to the Abuse of Women: A Lack of

Coordination, 8 N.Y.L. Sch. J. Hum. Rts. 149 (1990); Note, The Case for Legal Remedies for Abused Women, 6 N.Y.U. Rev. L. & Soc. Change 135 (1977); Note, The Demise of Ozzie and Harriet: Effective Punishment of Domestic Abusers, 17 N. Eng. J. Crim. & Civ. Confinement 337 (1991).

108. See, e.g., Cahn, Civil Images of Battered Women: The Impact of Domestic Violence on Child Custody Decisions, 44 Vand. L. Rev. 1041 (1991); Note, Domestic Violence and Custody Litigation: The Need for Statutory Reform, 13 Hofstra L. Rev. 407 (1985). See also Developments in the Law, *supra* note 29, at 1597–1620.

109. See generally Ellis, Marital Conflict Mediation and Post-Separation Wife Abuse, 8 Law & Ineq. J. 317 (1990); Geffner & Pagelow, Mediation and Child Custody Issues in Abusive Relationships, 8 Behav. Sci. & L. 151 (1990); Germane, Johnson & Lemon, Mandatory Custody Mediation and Joint Custody Orders in California: The Danger for Victims of Domestic Violence, 1 Berkeley Women's L.J. 175 (1985); Lerman, Mediation of Wife Abuse Cases: The Adverse Impact of Informal Dispute Resolution on Women, 7 Harv. Women's L.J. 57 (1984); Stallone, Decriminalization of Violence in the Home: Mediation in Wife Battering Cases, 2 Law & Ineq. J. 493 (1984).

110. Robson, Lavender Bruises: Intra-Lesbian Violence, Law and Lesbian Legal Theory, herein; Robson & Valentine, Lov[h]ers: Lesbians as Intimate Partners and Lesbian Legal Theory, 63 Temple L. Rev. 511 (1990); Note, Battered Lesbians: Are They Entitled to a Battered Woman's Defense?, 29 J. Fam. L. 879 (1991).

111. See, e.g., K. Crenshaw, Mapping the Margins: Intersectionality, Identity Politics, and Violence Against Women of Color, in The Public Nature of Private Violence, *supra* note 91, at 93; Tong, *supra* note 104, at 169–172; Blackman, Emerging Images of Severely Battered Women and the Criminal Justice System, 8 Behav. Sci. & L. 121 (1990); Ruttenberg, *supra* note 42; Stallone, *supra* note 109, at 514–516 (dual problems of racism and sexism faced by victims who are women of color).

112. Tong, *supra* note 104, at 170 (Black women are more prone to excuse their husbands' behavior and to wonder whether arrest is best since the law deals more harshly with Black defendants).

113. Currie, Battered Women and the State: From the Failure of Theory to a Theory of Failure, 1 J. Human Just. 77, 88–89 (1990).

114. *Id.* at 93.

115. For an interesting critique of Schechter's book that analyzes contradictions within feminism, see Fine, Unearthing Contradictions: An Essay Inspired by *Women and Male Violence*, 11 Feminist Stud. 391 (1985). On divisions in the battered women's movement, see G. Arnold, Dilemmas of Feminist Coalitions: Collective Identity and Strategic Effectiveness in the Battered Women's Movement, in M. Ferree & P. Martin eds., Feminist Organizations: Harvest of the New Women's Movement 276 (Temple Univ. Press, 1995); Currie, *supra* note 113. On divisiveness within feminism generally, see M. Hirsch & E. Keller eds., Conflicts in Feminism (Routledge, 1990).

116. Schneider was co-counsel for the defendant in State v. Wanrow, 559 P.2d 548 (Wash. 1977), and co-counsel for *amicus curiae* in State v. Kelly, 478 A.2d 364 (N.J. 1984). See also Clare Dalton & Elizabeth M. Schneider, Cases and Materials on Battered Women and the Law (forthcoming, Foundation Press); Elizabeth M. Schneider, Feminist Lawmaking, Social Change and Woman-Abuse (forthcoming, Harvard Univ. Press).

117. The syndrome, based on theories of psychologist Lenore Walker, developed from the recognition that the legal treatment of self-defense discriminates against

women, primarily because of stereotypes regarding the passivity and masochism of battered women. By elucidating the psychological and social characteristics of battered women, the syndrome helps clarify that the accused herself was a victim. Specifically, the evidence sheds light on the reasonableness of the woman's acts: to explain her belief that the danger posed by the man's conduct was immediate and life threatening.

118. For an article making a similar point, see Jenkins & Davidson, Battered Women in the Criminal Justice System: An Analysis of Gender Stereotypes, 8 Behav. Sci. & L. 161 (1990). Feminist theorists criticize other aspects of the victimization paradigm. See, e.g., Kelly, The Continuum of Sexual Violence, in Women, Violence and Social Control, *supra* note 10, at 59 (cited in Liddle, Feminist Contributions, *supra* note 43, at 762) ("clear distinction cannot be made between 'victims' and other women" given that all women are subject to sexual violence). For Schneider's thoughts on victimization and agency in the context of pornography, see Schneider, Women, Censorship, and Pornography: Feminism and the False Dichotomy of Victimization and Agency, 38 N.Y.L. Sch. L. Rev. 387 (1993).

119. See generally Kelly, How Women Define Their Experiences of Violence, in Feminist Perspectives, *supra* note 1, at 117.

120. See generally Kelly, The Continuum of Sexual Violence, in Women, Violence and Social Control, *supra* note 10, at 46.

121. C. Renzetti, Violent Betrayal: Partner Abuse in Lesbian Relationships 115 (Sage, 1992). (Cf. Tong, *supra* note 104, at 189: "Such occurrences [referring to male rape of lesbians to cure them] are rare. So, too, are lesbian-on-lesbian rapes and lesbian-on-lesbian batteries.")

122. See, e.g., Renzetti, *supra* note 121, at 1 (author conducted research for ten years on violence against women which eventually highlighted lesbian battering). See also M. Eaton, Abuse by Any Other Name: Feminism, Difference, and Intralesbian Violence, in The Public Nature of Private Violence, *supra* note 91, at 198; B. Hart, Lesbian Battering: An Examination, in K. Lobel ed., Naming the Violence: Speaking Out About Lesbian Battering 173 (Seal Press, 1986).

123. On the role of lesbian experience in the stages of feminist legal scholarship, see Cain, Feminist Jurisprudence: Grounding the Theories, in D. Weisberg ed., Feminist Legal Theory: Foundations 359 (Temple Univ. Press, 1993). For recent works on lesbian legal theory, see Arriola, Gendered Inequality: Lesbians, Gays, and Feminist Legal Theory, 9 Berkeley Women's L.J. 103 (1994); Cain, Lesbian Perspective, Lesbian Experience, and the Risk of Essentialism, 2 Va. J. Soc. Pol'y & L. 43 (1994); Robson, Incendiary Categories: Lesbians/Violence/Law, 2 Tex. J. Women & L. 1 (1992); Robson, Embodiment(s): The Possibilities of Lesbian Legal Theory in Bodies Problematized by Postmodernisms and Feminisms, 2 Law & Sexuality: Rev. Lesbian & Gay Legal Issues 37 (1992); Robson, Lesbian Jurisprudence?, 8 Law & Ineq. J. 443 (1990); Robson, The Specter of a Lesbian Supreme Court Justice: Problems of Identity in Lesbian Legal Theorizing, 5 St. Thomas L. Rev. 433 (1993).

Although lesbian perspectives surfaced only recently in legal theory, they emerged early in the women's movement. See, e.g., G. Damon, The Least of These: The Minority Whose Screams Haven't Yet Been Heard, in Sisterhood Is Powerful, *supra* note 57; A. Koedt, Lesbianism and Feminism, in A. Koedt, E. Levine & A. Rapone eds., Radical Feminism 246 (Quadrangle Books, 1973).

124. For a review of this literature, see Tong, *supra* note 104, at 179–190.

125. See also Robson & Valentine, *supra* note 110.

126. Other commentators confirm that Schneider's fears are justified. See Developments in the Law, *supra* note 29, at 1560. ("The *DeShaney* decision has made it much more difficult for battered women to bring suits against unresponsive state actors.") The authors of this student note point to theories that overcome the obstacles posed by *DeShaney,* including substantive due process, procedural due process, equal protection, and tort. *Id.* at 1560–1573.

The Roots of the Battered Women's Movement: Personal and Political

SUSAN SCHECHTER

... THE FEMINISM which engendered the battered women's movement was itself the product of prior influences. In the 1950s and 1960s, the civil rights, anti-war, and black liberation movements challenged the nation. Although not all women who would become feminist activists were involved directly in these struggles, the movements of the 1960s deeply affected the development of feminism. Efforts to win equality for blacks set precedents for women's struggle for equality. As in the nineteenth century, women working against racial oppression came to question their own position—and gained political experience that would help them in building a feminist movement. . . .

There were, however, many other influences operating upon those who would start or join the feminist movement. Published in 1963, Betty Friedan's *The Feminine Mystique* captured the discontent of a whole generation of middle class women, caught between aspirations for fulfillment and an ideology that consigned them to the home. Feminism was influenced, too, by women's participation in the paid work force. . . . Low salaries, limited opportunities, and dead end jobs—juxtaposed to a rhetoric of equality and social justice and their families' economic problems—compelled many to scrutinize their own situation as women. From another direction, thousands of women, committing themselves to fight against poverty through welfare rights organizations and government agencies like the Office of Economic Opportunity or the Peace Corps, began to apply newly acquired political insights personally. As women saw others define the solutions to their life problems as political, they were inspired to act.[1]

By the late 1960s and early 1970s, feminism itself had developed into two major branches, a women's rights feminism, exemplified by organizations like NOW, and a women's liberation movement, embodied in socialist feminist and radical feminist groups, and small, autonomous organizing projects working on issues like abortion, women's schools, day care and prisoners' rights. Women's rights activism focused mainly on gaining access to the rights and opportunities held by men. Women's liber-

Reprinted by permission from Women & Male Violence: The Visions and Strategies of the Battered Women's Movement (South End Press, 1982), pp. 29–52.

ation encompassed this goal, but went far beyond it, exploring the unequal gender division of labor and women's lack of control over their bodies, sexuality, and lives. . . .

In addition to fighting discrimination, the women's liberation branch of the feminist movement declared that the private and the social were no longer separable categories. By claiming that what happened between men and women in the privacy of their home was deeply political, the women's liberation movement set the stage for the battered women's movement. Through small consciousness raising groups, women, often in fear or shame and then exhilaration, found that what they felt was "petty" or "private" was widely shared. Some of the most energizing topics for consciousness raising focused on previously undiscussed "personal" problems—feelings of isolation in maintaining a home or caring for small children, a sense of physical weakness, intense concern about appearance, the guilty feelings of never doing enough for men and children. In the early women's liberation anthologies and newsletters, articles proliferated on the unequal division of labor within the household, women's responsibilities for child care, the maintenance of rigid sex roles, the internalization of oppression expressed as women's self-hatred, low self-esteem and need for male affirmation, the socialization of women for passivity and caretaking, the continual and degrading sexual objectification by men, and the repression of female sexuality.

Although many political, strategic, and ideological differences were evident in the developing women's liberation movement, women agreed that men held power and privilege over women in personal life. Domination was uncovered operating, not only in the public political world, but also in the private political sphere of the family. This analysis moved women closer to a collective realization about violence. If women were dominated by men both outside and inside the family, women and men no longer had identical interests even within the family unit. Claiming conflicting interests, husband and wife were no longer "one." The importance of this message was twofold. First, women had rights as autonomous human beings which meant that their psychological and physical dignity could be asserted. Secondly, no longer could women be blamed for their own vague sense of dissatisfaction or for their husbands' unhappiness. Women's right to verbalize their pain without self-blame created an environment in which discussing violence was less shameful. In some consciousness raising groups women talked about violence,[2] while in others violence was too deeply buried or too painful to surface as a common element of many women's experiences.

As early as 1970, reference is made to male violence in the family in several of the women's liberation anthologies. An article in *Sisterhood Is Powerful* states that "the other crude and often open weapon that a man uses to control his wife is the threat of force or force itself. . . . In this circumstance it is difficult for a woman to pursue the argument which is bringing about the reaction, usually an argument for more freedom, respect, or equality in the marital situation."[3] And *Voices From Women's Liberation* suggests that "few radical women really know the worst of women's condition. . . . Few have experienced constant violence and drunkenness of a brutalizing husband or father."[4]

Although violence is acknowledged in these anthologies, its extent and impact, especially in middle class families, is understated. There are articles about self-defense and references to violence, but *Sisterhood Is Powerful* and *Voices From Women's Liberation* contain no articles about rape. It would take another year or two for the anti-rape movement to emerge; the battered women's movement would not begin for four or five more years.

The women's liberation movement not only helped create an atmosphere where women could understand and speak about battering; it also influenced the organization of work in the battered women's movement. Because male domination often inhibited women from talking and taught them to doubt their abilities, the women's liberation movement emphasized egalitarian and participatory organizational models. [T]he women's liberation movement developed a strong suspicion of hierarchy and leadership. Hierarchy only seemed to create differentials in power which could be misused either through acquiring personal privileges and status or through misrepresenting the group. Leadership was also suspect, so women's liberation organizations developed the idea of rotating leadership. The ideal insisted that many women were to be exposed to leadership positions and encouraged to develop skills in new areas. Having expertise was a dubious distinction, often negatively associated with a professionalism that deeply hurt women by labeling and excluding some at the same time that it elevated others. Egalitarian forms of working gave strength to the battered women's movement. . . .

The influence of the women's liberation movement on the battered women's movement is illustrated concretely in hundreds of shelters and women's crisis centers in the United States. In St. Paul, Minnesota, Women's Advocates, one of the oldest shelters solely for battered women, began as a consciousness raising group in 1971. Later wanting to move beyond their own small group experience, these women dreamed of opening a house for themselves and for any woman who needed a place to go. This house was to be a liberating, utopian community. Their early vision of a home never encompassed a battered women's shelter, although this is what it would become.

The first Boston shelter, Transition House, was also influenced by women's liberation ideas. Although the two women who started the shelter were former battered women, they were soon joined by two former members of Cell 16, one of Boston's earliest radical feminist groups. Women using the house were encouraged to explore their personal lives, learning the political parameters of "private" problems. For the activists at Transition House, physical abuse was not an isolated fact of daily existence. Battering was an integral part of women's oppression; women's liberation its solution.

The Influence of the Anti-Rape Movement

In the 1970s, applying feminist principles, women created hundreds of autonomous service and organizing projects throughout the United States. One of these projects, the rape crisis center, developed into an important movement that merits special attention here, both as an illustration of the large-scale feminist organizing that preceded the battered women's movement and as a path-breaking model for that movement.

In some cities, like Chicago, women active in anti-rape work formed part of the group that would later demand help for battered women. In Boston, close personal contact without organizational affiliations existed between feminists in the anti-rape and battered women's movements.[5] In still other places, women's crisis centers that originally provided rape counseling and anti-rape education added battered women's concerns to their tasks.

Although many activists in the battered women's movement never did rape crisis work, the battered women's movement maintains a striking and obvious resemblance to the anti-rape movement and owes it several debts. The anti-rape movement articulated that violence is a particular form of domination based on social relationships of unequal power. Through the efforts of the anti-rape movement, it became clear that violence is one mechanism for female social control. Today this sounds obvious; ten years ago it was a revelation. The anti-rape movement changed women's consciousness and redefined the parameters of what women would individually and collectively tolerate.

Susan Brownmiller, the first author to document the history of rape, described how unaware people were of the magnitude and significance of rape, noting that "few outside its victims thought it might be an important subject to explore. No one considered that it might have a history, and only a handful believed it was going to become an issue of international feminist concern."[6] Yet in 1971–72, Bay Area Women Against Rape formed; in June 1972, the first emergency rape crisis line opened in Washington, D.C.[7] Soon after, rape crisis centers appeared all across the country, started by former rape victims and active feminists.

The anti-rape movement first exposed the mythology that helps maintain rape: women like to be raped; women mean "yes" when they say "no"; women seduce their attackers through "provocative" clothes or gestures; rapists act impulsively; rapists are sex-starved; most rapists jump out of the bushes on dark streets to attack their victim; most rapists are poor and black. The Chicago Women Against Rape (CWAR) statement of purpose read in part:

> Rape violently reflects the sexism in a society where power is unequally distributed between women and men, black and white, poor and rich. . . . In rape, the woman is not a sexual being but a vulnerable piece of public property; the man does not violate society's norms so much as take them to a logical conclusion.[8]

The anti-rape movement not only exposed the mythology but also showed how it served to blame women for rape, let rapists go free, and provide ideological justification for legal and medical institutions to treat victims and people of color with hostility or indifference. It declared that rape reflected socialization patterns in which women learn to be passive and men learn to be dominating; rapists, the movement explained, were psychologically no different from most men.

Throughout the country, anti-rape groups conducted extensive educational campaigns. They distributed myth and fact sheets, with facts often based upon the one large-scale study of rape available, Menachem Amir's *Patterns in Forcible Rape*. A typical sheet explained:

the myth: Rape is predominantly an impulsive act.

the fact: In three quarters of the cases the rapist(s) planned it. Group-rape—90% planned; pair rape—83% planned; single rape—58% planned.[9]

In addition to establishing the facts, anti-rape literature interpreted them in a new way. One of the first and most profound explanations, Susan Griffin's 1971 "Rape: The All-American Crime,"[10] broke the choking hold of terror and shame and articulated a theory of rape [that rape is an act of male violence against women—a form of "mass terrorism." *Ed.*].

The anti-rape movement unearthed the multitude of ways in which victims historically had been blamed for the crime and silenced. Hundreds of articles about rape, many of them in mainstream journals and magazines, detailed this discovery, describing how, "the vast majority of victims fail to report the crime out of fear—fear of vengeance, of police, of publicity, of courtroom hassles—and out of shame. The fear is sensible. The shame is not, but it has been bred into our bones. . . . Women who go to the police often bitterly regret that they didn't keep their mouths shut. For at every level of our legal system they may find themselves treated like criminals, and worse: a murderer is innocent until proven guilty; a rape victim is guilty until proven innocent."[11] Exposing victim-blaming not only produced new theoretical understandings of rape but also laid the groundwork for pushing institutions to change the treatment of victims. Perhaps most profoundly, it gave women a way to relieve shame and guilt. . . .

Recognizing victims' needs for emotional and legal support and the movement's need to document and change sexist abuses in police stations and courts, rape crisis centers trained women to become legal advocates. Lay advocacy, as it was called, first meant that the rape crisis center staff or volunteers, often with the help of a few feminist lawyers, mastered the intricate details of local police and court procedures as well as local and state ordinances or laws.

Based on its understanding of how institutions revictimize women, the anti-rape movement demanded legal and institutional reforms. Activists insisted that women on witness stands not be grilled about their sexual behavior. Throughout the United States, women worked to overthrow laws that required corroboration of evidence by someone other than the victim. They focused on improving police arrest and evidence gathering procedures and some worked legislatively to change criminal sentencing procedures. Hospital policies that included administering dangerous drugs like DES to prevent pregnancy or that failed to provide privacy or concern for the victim were also targets of reform. . . .

In addition to replacing a sexist ideology with a feminist one and pushing for institutional reform, the anti-rape movement brought together thousands of women who continually developed new skills. Activists educated themselves and others politically. The Feminist Alliance Against Rape (FAAR) newsletter, started in 1974, was the movement's political sounding board and brought inspiration to hundreds of women, often working in isolated groups. Later it played a role in encouraging the battered women's movement to engage in the same kind of political and skill exchanges. . . .

By 1977, searching for more militant and public forums, thousands of women around the country marched annually to "Take Back The Night." During this single evening, they walked unafraid because of the collective presence of women. Turning individual fear into mass anger, women felt strength and temporary psychological liberation even as the number of reported rapes increased.

Borrowing ideas from the women's liberation movement, the counseling developed in rape crisis centers focused on the victim's need to retain control over decisions affecting her life and often used self-help methods. The victim was to decide whether to report the rape and who she would tell about the experience. Insisting that feminists and women who had experienced rape were the experts, rape crisis workers were often suspicious of professionally trained therapists who traditionally had blamed women for male violence. Although disagreement existed over the role of professionals in the work of rape crisis centers and tensions heightened as mainstream social service agencies or hospitals became involved, the idea of self-help and victim control remained primary to many feminists. . . .

The feminist anti-rape movement has not only laid the foundation to change public consciousness, but also has built organizations and networks of politically sophisticated and active women. The anti-rape movement has unmasked the domination that violence maintains, has torn away a veil of shame, and shown that women can aid one another, transforming individual silence and pain into a social movement. Such work handed ideological tools, collective work structures, and political resources to the battered women's movement. Without this precedent, the new movement might have faced far greater resistance and hostility from bureaucracies, legislatures, and the general public. By 1975, it was clear that since rape and battering had the same effects upon their victims and depended upon similar sexist mythology, battering had to be declared socially, not privately, caused.

Ideological and Personal Diversity Within the Movement

Women who started battered women's programs were motivated by diverse ideological and personal experiences. The meaning of this diversity, often invisible at first, became evident only later and partially accounts for tensions within the battered women's movement today. . . .

Feminists in the battered women's movement did not always agree on the meaning or implications of feminism. In its broadest sense, feminism means women's individual or collective rights to autonomy, to define their lives as they see fit. It thus suggests equality between the sexes. For some, the women's liberationists, feminism is both an analysis of how women are oppressed as a gender category and a commitment to organizing to end that oppression, gaining power and autonomy on many levels. Non-hierarchical organizational structures and interpersonal relationships are the embodiments of feminist theory. For others—those who are part of the women's rights branch of the movement—feminism primarily implies making the society better through winning concrete changes in the law and within institutions. In both of these large categories, analyses varied; and women did not necessarily label themselves as being in one or the other branch of the movement.

Those who entered the battered women's movement from a women's rights perspective often came with a social work or legal background. They assumed that equality with men would be gained through reforming the existing social system. While some women's rights activists defined their goals more broadly, most were primarily committed to ending discrimination. Questions of organizational structure and process were secondary; most often hierarchy was the preferred model in order to perform tasks quickly.

Unlike women's rights activists, radical feminists articulated a theory in which specific non-hierarchical organizational forms and self-help methods were a logical outcome of an analysis of violence against women. In many programs, locally and nationally, radical feminists organized first, setting the style and practice that continues to dominate in much of the battered women's movement. Radical feminists believe that historically and structurally the division of labor and power between men and women became the basis for other forms of exploitation, including class, ethnic, racial, and religious ones. Patriarchy is seen not only as a system that oppresses women, but also as one that structurally and conceptually creates, sustains, and justifies hierarchies, competition, and the unequal distribution of power and resources on an endless variety of levels. While some radical feminists embrace this analysis, others label the source of women's problems more broadly as male power, especially the advantages men gain through their control of women's labor and childrearing in the patriarchal family.

Theoretically, radical feminism claims women to be a class, challenging Marxist categories.

> No matter what social and economic class a woman's husband belongs to, when she leaves her husband she is leaving the money behind. In this sense all women are of one class: they receive no money for their work, put in unlimited hours of service, and can be beaten mercilessly on the whim of their masters.[12]

For some radical feminists, feminism implies socialism; social revolution, including a complete redistribution of wealth, is necessary to end women's oppression[13] and its first target must be the elimination of male supremacy.

A radical feminist analysis of battering suggests that "the present organization of home and family, whereby the husband wears the proverbial pants, and the wife and the children are commonly viewed as his dependents and his property, is a primary cause of the high incidence of wife abuse. It [battering] happens whenever a man perceives that a woman is either stepping out of her role, that she might be contemplating stepping out of her role, or even to insure that she would never dare so much as reflect on the possibility of contemplating stepping out of her role."[14]

From radical feminist theory emerged a specific practice. Collectivity was the assumed work structure; decisions belonged to the group through its use of consensus rather than voting. Radical feminists emphasized the need to organize autonomous women's programs, separate from male control or influence, where women would be encouraged to express their anger at men. Radical feminists combined caring for women with self-help methods, egalitarian work forms, and a staunch commitment to politicize women's understanding of personal problems. . . .

Socialist feminists who worked within the battered women's movement joined an analysis of male domination to one of class and race oppression. They grounded women's oppression within material reality: the unequal division of labor between the sexes inside and outside the home, female responsibility for childrearing, and women's work maintaining home and family. For socialist feminists, although male domination predated capitalism, class and race oppression could not be reduced to or explained by patriarchy. Each form of oppression had its unique historical foundations. Class and gender domination were intertwined through the benefits that both the capitalist class and individual men received from women's unpaid labor. But there were also ways in which men and women had interests in common, fighting against their exploitation as workers and as members of communities and families. Socialist feminists urged an examination of the changing nature of the family and the state under capitalism, refusing to label all women as one class and asserting that differences among women by class and race were as important as similarities. Like radical feminists, socialist feminists saw more than economic and political discrimination against women and believed that only profound transformations would end violence against women. At moments, socialist feminist analytic and strategic formulations sounded similar to those of radical feminists.

For socialist feminists, women's vulnerability to violence was a result not only of male domination in the family but also of a social system that sanctioned male violence and privatized the family, exploited women at home and at work, and left them few viable alternatives to escape from violence. Ending such conditions required that a movement against violence unite with other progressive movements for radical social change. This analysis meant that although socialist feminists argued that women needed to organize autonomous, women-only shelters, their anger at men often was more muted than that of radical feminists.

No analysis of battering has ever been explicitly labeled a lesbian feminist one. Because many lesbians also define themselves as radical feminists or socialist feminists, the distinctions blur. In the battered women's movement, lesbian feminist ideology speaks less to the analysis which relies heavily on radical feminism—and more to the form of working with women. . . .

In many locations, lesbian feminists were among those initiating battered women's services. Committing themselves to help women and children live free from terror and pain was their goal. As one woman said, "Lesbians were able to look at violence and its political ramifications and not freak out about its meaning for their relationships with men. If you live with men and work with battered women, you have to find a way to deal with anger and rage."[15] . . .

Third world feminists brought their own diverse experiences and political ideologies to the battered women's movement. Although their ideologies overlapped with the categories described above, their unique histories of cultural and racial oppression shaped their politics. The Combahee River Collective—a black feminist group whose members have worked on diverse projects and issues including sterilization abuse, abortion rights, rape, health care, and battered women—defines its goal as developing "a politics that was anti-racist, unlike those of white women, and anti-sexist, unlike those of black and white men." They go on to say:

> We also often find it difficult to separate race from class from sex oppression because in our lives they are most often experienced simultaneously. We know there is such a thing as racial-sexual oppression which is neither solely racial nor solely sexual, e.g., the history of rape of black women by white men as a weapon of political repression.
>
> Although we are feminists and lesbians, we feel solidarity with progressive black men and do not advocate the fractionalization that white women who are separatists demand. . . .
>
> We realize that the liberation of all oppressed peoples necessitates the destruction of the political-economic systems of capitalism and imperialism as well as patriarchy.[16]

Other black feminists had different analyses and different politics. However, almost all third world women within the battered women's movement asserted that their experiences as women were different from those of white women. . . .

If feminism is broadly defined, then the battered women's movement is a feminist movement. The goals of the movement are feminist as is the leadership in most, though not all, locales. However, women who do not consider themselves feminists have played a very significant role in the battered women's movement. Women who reject the label feminist have started shelters and worked in shelters; they have served on Boards of Directors of explicitly feminist shelters. Most important, battered women themselves are, obviously, not always feminists. Their political views cover a broad spectrum from feminist to anti-feminist—and like those of other women in the movement—are not static. . . .

For women of all races and classes, for feminists and non-feminists, for professionals and activists, reasons for joining the battered women's movement were and are complex and varied. Particular individual experiences, as well as feminist ideology, brought women into the movement. For many, a decisive factor was contact with a battered woman, as evidenced in the responses of a group of Pennsylvania women from diverse battered women's programs to the question, "Why did you first become involved in the issue of battered women?" One woman's motivation to take battered women into her home came from "radical church teachings that her family was not only her immediate family; from counter-cultural ideas that things don't have to be the way they are; that people must do what they believe in; and from women who came to the women's center with nowhere to go." Another woman, who had been adopted at six weeks and had felt the importance of a family taking her in, was also deeply influenced by the women's center and the homeless battered women she met there. One activist had been a battered woman herself and as a VISTA[17] worker in a low-income housing project she had also seen the lack of resources available to poor women. Another woman volunteered at a women's center out of a desire to reenter her former professional field, social work. A mother with two children, she sought paid part-time work at the center. Unable to find this, she volunteered and became deeply committed, first to the women's center and then to the shelter that emerged from it. Still others "fell" into the work by answering a few crisis calls at a women's center. Drawing the connection between one's own life and that of the woman calling was often a relatively easy step. Since women of all classes, races, and ethnic groups are battered, everyone heard a story that was hauntingly close to her own circumstances.

Once a part of the battered women's movement, women's analyses and understanding grew and changed over time, as they found themselves transformed through shelter and movement life.

Notes

1. Jo Freeman, The Politics of Women's Liberation: A Case Study of an Emerging Social Movement 28 (David McKay Co., 1975).

2. See Nanette Rainone ed., Men and Violence, transcript of a taped consciousness-raising session, WBAI Radio, New York, 1970.

3. Beverly Jones, The Dynamics of Marriage and Motherhood, in Robin Morgan ed., Sisterhood Is Powerful: An Anthology of Writings from the Women's Liberation Movement 47 (Vintage Books, Random House, 1970).

4. Kathy McAfee and Myrna Wood, Bread and Roses, in Leslie B. Tanner ed., Voices From Women's Liberation 421 (Signet, New American Library, 1970).

5. Author's interview with Freada Klein.

6. Susan Brownmiller, Introduction, in Florence Rush, The Best Kept Secret: Sexual Abuse of Children viii (McGraw-Hill, 1980).

7. Michelle Wasserman, Rape: Breaking the Silence, The Progressive 19 (November 1973).

8. Chicago Women Against Rape, undated brochure.

9. Material distributed by Chicago Women Against Rape, undated.

10. Susan Griffin, Rape: The All-American Crime, herein, at 422.

11. Martha Weinman Lear, The American Way of Rape, Viva 43 (November 1974).

12. Lisa Leghorn, Social Responses to Battered Women, Feminist Alliance Against Rape Newsletter 22 (March–April 1977).

13. Lisa Leghorn, personal communication.

14. Lisa Leghorn, Social Responses to Battered Women, *supra* note 12, at 19.

15. Anonymous interview.

16. The Combahee River Collective, A Black Feminist Statement, in Zillah R. Eisenstein ed., Capitalist Patriarchy and the Case for Socialist Feminism 365–366 (Monthly Review, 1979).

17. Volunteers in Service to America, a domestic peace corps which is now part of the federal agency ACTION.

STATE v. WANROW

559 P.2d 548 (Wash. 1977)

UTTER, Associate Justice.

Yvonne Wanrow was convicted by a jury of second-degree murder and first-degree assault. She appealed her conviction to the Court of Appeals. The Court of Appeals reversed. . . . We granted review and affirm the Court of Appeals.

   We order a reversal of the conviction [on the ground of] error committed by the trial court in improperly instructing the jury on the law of self-defense as it related to the defendant. On the afternoon of August 11, 1972, defendant's (respondent's) two children were staying at the home of Ms. Hooper, a friend of defendant. Defendant's son was playing in the neighborhood and came back to Ms. Hooper's house and told her that a man tried to pull him off his bicycle and drag him into a house. Some months earlier, Ms. Hooper's 7-year-old daughter had developed a rash on her body which was diagnosed as venereal disease. Ms. Hooper had been unable to persuade her daughter to tell her who had molested her. It was not until the night of the shooting that Ms. Hooper discovered it was William Wesler (decedent) who allegedly had violated her daughter. A few minutes after the defendant's son related his story to Ms. Hooper about the man who tried to detain him, Mr. Wesler appeared on the porch of the Hooper house and stated through the door, "I didn't touch the kid, I didn't touch the kid." At that moment, the Hooper girl, seeing Wesler at the door, indicated to her mother that Wesler was the man who had molested her. Joseph Fah, Ms. Hooper's landlord, saw Wesler as he was leaving and informed Shirley Hooper that Wesler had tried to molest a young boy who had earlier lived in the same house, and that Wesler had previously been committed to the Eastern State Hospital for the mentally ill. Immediately after this revelation from Mr. Fah, Ms. Hooper called the police who, upon their arrival at the Hooper residence, were informed of all the events which had transpired that day. Ms. Hooper requested that Wesler be arrested then and there, but the police stated, "We can't, until Monday morning." Ms. Hooper was urged by the police officer to go to the police station Monday morning and "swear out a warrant." Ms.

Hooper's landlord, who was present during the conversation, suggested that Ms. Hooper get a baseball bat located at the corner of the house and "conk him over the head" should Wesler try to enter the house uninvited during the weekend. To this suggestion, the policeman replied, "Yes, but wait until he gets in the house." (A week before this incident Shirley Hooper had noticed someone prowling around her house at night. Two days before the shooting someone had attempted to get into Ms. Hooper's bedroom and had slashed the window screen. She suspected that such person was Wesler.)

That evening, Ms. Hooper called the defendant and asked her to spend the night with her in the Hooper house. At that time she related to Ms. Wanrow the facts we have previously set forth. The defendant arrived sometime after 6 P.M. with a pistol in her handbag. The two women ultimately determined that they were too afraid to stay alone and decided to ask some friends to come over for added protection. The two women then called the defendant's sister and brother-in-law, Angie and Chuck Michel. The four adults did not go to bed that evening, but remained awake talking and watching for any possible prowlers. There were eight young children in the house with them. At around 5 A.M., Chuck Michel, without the knowledge of the women in the house, went to Wesler's house, carrying a baseball bat. Upon arriving at the Wesler residence, Mr. Michel accused Wesler of molesting little children. Mr. Wesler then suggested that they go over to the Hooper residence and get the whole thing straightened out. Another man, one David Kelly, was also present, and together the three men went over to the Hooper house. Mr. Michel and Mr. Kelly remained outside while Wesler entered the residence.

The testimony as to what next took place is considerably less precise. It appears that Wesler, a large man who was visibly intoxicated, entered the home and when told to leave declined to do so. A good deal of shouting and confusion then arose, and a young child, asleep on the couch, awoke crying. The testimony indicates that Wesler than approached this child, stating, "My what a cute little boy," or words to that effect, and that the child's mother, Ms. Michel, stepped between Wesler and the child. By this time Hooper was screaming for Wesler to get out. Ms. Wanrow, a 5'4" woman who at the time had a broken leg and was using a crutch, testified that she then went to the front door to enlist the aid of Chuck Michel. She stated that she shouted for him and, upon turning around to reenter the living room, found Wesler standing directly behind her. She testified to being gravely startled by this situation and to having then shot Wesler in what amounted to a reflex action. . . .

Reversal of respondent's conviction is . . . required by a . . . serious error committed by the trial court. Instruction No. 10, setting forth the law of self-defense, incorrectly limited the jury's consideration of acts and circumstances pertinent to respondent's perception of the alleged threat to her person. An examination of the record of the testimony and of the colloquies which took place with regard to the instructions on self-defense indicate the critical importance of these instructions to the respondent's theory of the case. Based upon the evidence we have already set out, it is obviously crucial that the jury be precisely instructed as to the defense of justification.

In the opening paragraph of instruction No. 10, the jury, in evaluating the gravity of the danger to the respondent, was directed to consider only those acts and circumstances occurring "at or immediately before the killing. . . ." This is not now, and never has been, the law of self-defense in Washington. On the contrary, the justification of self-defense is to be evaluated in light of all the facts and circumstances known to the defendant, including those known substantially before the killing.

In State v. Ellis, 30 Wash. 369, 70 P. 963 (1902), this court reversed a first-degree murder conviction obtained under self-defense instructions quite similar to that in the present case. The defendant sought to show that the deceased had a reputation and habit of carrying and using deadly weapons when engaged in quarrels. The trial court instructed that threats were insufficient justification unless "at the time of the alleged killing the deceased was making or immediately preceding the killing had committed some overt act . . ." State v. Ellis, *supra* at 371, 70 P. at 964. This court found the instruction "defective and misleading," stating "the apparent facts should all be taken together to illustrate the motives and good faith of the defendant . . ." *Ellis, supra* at 374, 70 P. at 965.

> [I]t is apparent that a man who habitually carries and uses such weapons in quarrels must cause greater apprehension of danger than one who does not bear such reputation. . . . The vital question is the reasonableness of the defendant's apprehension of danger. . . . The jury are (sic) entitled to stand as nearly as practicable in the shoes of defendant, and from this point of view determine the character of the act.

Ellis, at 373, 70 P. at 964. Thus, circumstances predating the killing by weeks and months were deemed entirely proper, and in fact essential, to a proper disposition of the claim of self-defense.

Similarly, in State v. Churchill, 52 Wash. 210, 100 P. 309 (1909), the court upheld self-defense instructions directing the jury to consider all relevant facts and circumstances, including those preceding the homicide. The trial court's instructions referred to an overt act of the person killed "'at or immediately before the killing . . . which, either by itself, or coupled with words, facts, or circumstances, *then or theretofore occurring,*'"which may establish a reasonable belief of imminent danger. (Italics ours.) State v. Churchill, *supra* at 219, 100 P. at 313. The instruction further requested the jury to "'take into consideration *all* the facts and circumstances bearing on the question and surrounding defendant, and existing at *or prior to the time of the alleged shooting* . . .'" (Italics ours.) *Churchill, supra* at 220, 100 P. at 313. This court found these instructions "clear, apt, and comprehensive" and free from error. *Churchill, supra* at 225, 100 P. 309.

State v. Tribett, 74 Wash. 125, 132 P. 875 (1913), is in accord. There this court approved an instruction which twice directed the jury to evaluate the reasonableness of the defendant's actions in defense of himself "'in the light of all the circumstances.'" *Tribett, supra* at 130, 132 P. at 877. Such circumstances included those existing and known long before the killing, such as the reputation of the place of the killing for lawlessness. . . . The rule firmly established by these cases has never been disapproved and is still followed today. "It is clear the jury is entitled to consider *all* of the circumstances surrounding the incident in determining whether [the] defendant had reasonable grounds to believe grievous bodily harm was about to be inflicted." State v. Lewis, 6 Wash.App. 38, 41, 491 P.2d 1062, 1064 (1971). By limiting the jury's consideration of the surrounding acts and circumstances to those occurring "at or immediately before the killing," instruction No. 10 in the present case was an erroneous statement of the applicable law on the critical focal point of the defendant's case. . . .

. . . Under the well-established rule, this error is presumed to have been prejudicial. Moreover, far from affirmatively showing that the error was harmless, the record demonstrates the limitation to circumstances "at or immediately before the killing" was of crucial importance in the present case. Respondent's knowledge of the victim's reputation for aggressive acts was gained many hours before the killing and was based upon events which occurred over a period of years. Under the law of this state, the jury should have been allowed to consider this information. . . .

The second paragraph of instruction No. 10 contains an equally erroneous and prejudicial statement of the law. That portion of the instruction reads:

> However, when there is no reasonable ground for the person attacked to believe that *his* person is in imminent danger of death or great bodily harm, and it appears to *him* that only an ordinary battery is all that is intended, and all that *he* has reasonable grounds to fear from *his* assailant, *he* has a right to stand *his* ground and repel such threatened assault, yet *he* has no right to repel a threatened assault with naked hands, by the use of a deadly weapon in a deadly manner, unless *he* believes, *and has reasonable grounds* to believe, that *he* is in imminent danger of death or great bodily harm. (Italics ours.)

In our society women suffer from a conspicuous lack of access to training in and the means of developing those skills necessary to effectively repel a male assailant without resorting to the use of deadly weapons.* Instruction No. 12 does indicate that the "relative size and strength of the persons involved" may be considered; however, it does not make clear that the defendant's actions are to be judged against her own subjective impressions and not those which a detached jury might determine to be objectively reasonable. The applicable rule of law is clearly stated in [State v. Miller 141 Wash. 104, 105, 250 P. 645, 645(1926)]:

> If the appellants, at the time of the alleged assault upon them, as reasonably and ordinarily cautious and prudent men, honestly believed that they were in danger of great bodily harm, they would have the right to resort to self-defense, and their conduct is to be judged by the condition appearing to them at the time, not by the condition as it might appear to the jury in the light of testimony before it.

---

*See B. Babcock, A. Freedman, E. Norton & S. Ross, Sex Discrimination and the Law: Causes and Remedies 943–1070 (1975); S. Brownmiller, Against Our Will: Men, Women and Rape (1975).

The second paragraph of instruction No. 10 not only establishes an objective standard, but through the persistent use of the masculine gender leaves the jury with the impression the objective standard to be applied is that applicable to an altercation between two men. The impression created—that a 5'4" woman with a cast on her leg and using a crutch must, under the law, somehow repel an assault by a 6'2" intoxicated man without employing weapons in her defense, unless the jury finds her determination of the degree of danger to be objectively reasonable—constitutes a separate and distinct misstatement of the law and, in the context of this case, violates the respondent's right to equal protection of the law. The respondent was entitled to have the jury consider her actions in the light of her own perceptions of the situation, including those perceptions which were the product of our nation's "long and unfortunate history of sex discrimination." Frontiero v. Richardson, 411 U.S. 677, 684 (1973). Until such time as the effects of that history are eradicated, care must be taken to assure that our self-defense instructions afford women the right to have their conduct judged in light of the individual physical handicaps which are the product of sex discrimination. To fail to do so is to deny the right of the individual woman involved to trial by the same rules which are applicable to male defendants. The portion of the instruction above quoted misstates our law in creating an objective standard of "reasonableness." It then compounds that error by utilizing language suggesting that the respondent's conduct must be measured against that of a reasonable male individual finding himself in the same circumstances.

We conclude that the instruction here in question contains an improper statement of the law on a vital issue in the case, is inconsistent, misleading and prejudicial when read in conjunction with other instructions pertaining to the same issue, and therefore is a proper basis for a finding of reversible error. . . .

❖ Describing and Changing: Women's Self-Defense Work and the Problem of Expert Testimony on Battering

Elizabeth M. Schneider

In [RECENT] YEARS . . . , many courts and commentators have been sensitized to issues of sex-bias in the law of self-defense. The overwhelming number of cases in which courts have addressed issues of women's self-defense have involved battered women charged with killing men who battered them. The primary legal issue relating to sex-bias in the law of self-defense which courts have addressed[1] and on which public attention has focused has been the issue of admissibility of expert testimony on "battered woman syndrome." A significant number of important legal victories have been won in the general area of what has become known as women's self-defense work and on the particular issue of the admissibility of expert testimony on battered woman syndrome.

Several cases which have admitted this testimony, such as the important 1984 decision of the New Jersey Supreme Court in State v. Kelly,[2] have done so on the basis of extraordinary acceptance of and insight into the feminist theoretical premises of women's self-defense work. Nevertheless, the main approach litigators developed and courts adopted on the issue of expert testimony on battering, the battered woman syndrome perspective, reflects ongoing tensions and paradoxes within women's self-defense work. . . .

. . . This article explores these problems. . . . [and considers] the implications of the work on expert testimony for feminist legal theory. . . .

The Problem of Expert Testimony

The question of the admissibility of expert testimony on battered woman syndrome has been the primary legal issue which appellate courts have addressed in the area of women's self-defense work. . . . Most appellate courts have ruled that this testimony is admissible, and commentators have almost unanimously supported admissibility.[3]

It is now well-established that homicide or assault cases involving battered women who killed their assailants pose serious problems to traditional self-defense. Women's self-defense work, beginning with State v. Wanrow [559 P.2d 548 (Wash. 1977)], has

---

9 Women's Rts. L. Rep. 195 (1986).

developed the perspective that self-defense requirements of reasonableness, imminent danger and equal force are sex-biased. A woman who kills her husband is viewed as inherently unreasonable because she is violating the norm of appropriate behavior for women. A battered woman who kills her batterer has to overcome special myths and misconceptions about battered women. . . .

The purpose of expert testimony has been to . . . give the judge and jury information concerning the common experiences and characteristics of battered women in order to refute widely held myths and misconceptions concerning battered women that would interfere with judge or juror ability to evaluate the woman's action fairly. Judges and jurors may accept the appropriateness of woman abuse as part of the marital relationship, assume the woman deserved or was responsible for the brutality, and blame her for not ending the relationship. Expert testimony can present a different picture by demonstrating that the battered woman was a victim. Introduction of expert testimony is important because a battered woman who explains a homicide as a reasonable and necessary response to abuse in the home, threatens deeply held stereotypes of appropriately submissive female conduct and of patriarchal authority. Expert testimony on the experiences of battered women can also answer specific questions that are in judges' and jurors' minds of why the battered woman didn't leave her home, why she may not have reported the battery to the police, and, most importantly, why she believed that the danger she faced on the particular occasion was life-threatening. In short, it can show that her conduct was reasonable.

In most of the cases in which expert testimony on battering has been presented, the expert has testified concerning battered woman syndrome, a pattern of severe physical and psychological abuse inflicted upon a woman by her mate. Dr. Lenore Walker, the leading researcher in this field, breaks down the pattern of abuse into a three-stage cycle of violence: a tension-building stage characterized by discrete abusive events; an acute battering stage characterized by uncontrollable explosions of brutal violence by the batterer; and a loving respite stage characterized by calm and loving behavior and pleas for forgiveness.[4] In the classical description, the battered woman lives in a constant state of fear that anything she does may precipitate another beating. She may be paralyzed by "learned helplessness," a sense of loss of predictability and control over her life, although she often has survival strategies. She may also have such a sense of low self-esteem and so few real and/or perceived options that she cannot leave the abusive relationship.

Battered woman syndrome can also include a description of the psychological impact of the common social and economic problems which battered women face. These problems have also been widely documented:[5] the police and the courts fail to protect women from abuse; battered women may not be able to leave their mates because they may have no job, child care, adequate housing or community social services; battered women suffer severe isolation and shame which strengthens their belief that they have no safe alternative; and that lack of alternatives and the cycle of battering in which the men promise to reform leads battered women to cling to the illusion that the men will change. When the violence recurs and escalates, battered women realize that they lack control over the situation and they deteriorate into depression and "learned helplessness," expecting unpredictable, more severe and increasingly frequent beatings.

Lawyers representing battered women have sought to introduce expert testimony to explain women's claims of self-defense and to show that the woman acted reasonably because she was in imminent danger of death or great bodily harm. The expert witness usually begins by explaining what is known about battering relationships and then describing battered woman syndrome and its effects on a woman's state of mind. The expert then points out the similarities between the battered woman syndrome model and the facts in the defendant's case. Finally, she will render an opinion as to whether the defendant was a victim of battered woman syndrome in order to explain why the defendant was in fear for her life. . . .

Admissibility of expert testimony at trial depends on a judicial finding that the testimony is both relevant to the issue at hand—either self-defense or some other issue—and that it meets the general standards governing the admissibility of expert testimony. In order for the testimony to be relevant to self-defense the court must determine that the testimony renders the desired inference—that the defendant reasonably believed she was in imminent danger and that the deadly force was necessary to avoid this danger—more probable than it would be without this evidence.[6] In order for the expert's testimony to be deemed admissible it must meet the jurisdiction's particular standard for admissibility of expert testimony generally.

Expert testimony on battered woman syndrome has had a substantial impact on the criminal process. . . . In general the expert testimony cases have demonstrated significant judicial recognition of the depth and severity of the problems of sex-stereotyping in the trial process for battered women claiming self-defense. . . .

From the beginning, literature on women's self-defense work has emphasized that expert testimony should not be used in isolation; expert testimony should be integrated with overall defense strategy, tied to the particular facts of the case and focused on the particular defense problems in the case. Commentators cautioned that an emphasis on expert testimony on battered woman syndrome, as the sole or even primary vehicle for remedying sex-bias in the trial process, was problematic because lawyers might not use the testimony carefully and tie it to the particular facts of the woman's case, because defense strategy might focus on evidence of battering rather than the reasonableness of the woman's act, and because there were risks that the substance of the expert testimony on battered woman syndrome would be presented or heard in a way that would unwittingly reinforce sex-stereotypes.

Virtually all of the cases that have considered the issue of expert testimony have done so in the context of testimony on battered woman syndrome and they have focused on Dr. Lenore Walker's work in her book *The Battered Woman*. The fact that the substance of the proffered or admitted testimony has been on battered woman syndrome has shaped judicial treatment of the issue in problematic ways. The phrase "battered woman syndrome" was intended to simply describe common psychological and social characteristics of battered women. Research on battered woman syndrome emerged from an effort to counteract the myths and misconceptions that women initiated, provoked and enjoyed the violence; it suggested that battered women were truly victims. Thus the initial focus of battered woman syndrome was a psychological analysis of battered women's victimization, their sense of paralysis or "learned helplessness." Although the term is purely descriptive, its psychological content and the language and import of the term carry a different message. Regardless of its more complex meaning, the term "battered woman syndrome" has been heard to communicate an implicit but powerful view that battered women are all the same, that they are suffering from a psychological disability and that this disability prevents them from acting "normally."

Recent experience with cases of expert testimony on battered woman syndrome confirms these early concerns. Precisely because expert testimony on battered woman syndrome has been commonly understood by lawyers and judges as the primary, perhaps even short hand, way to solve the problem of sex-bias in the trial process for battered women and to include battered women's voices in the courtroom, it is critical to examine both its importance and its risks. The New Jersey Supreme Court's opinion in State v. Kelly highlights both.

State v. Kelly

In State v. Kelly [478 A.2d 364 (N.J. 1984)], the New Jersey Supreme Court held that expert testimony concerning battered woman syndrome was admissible. The court ruled that the testimony was relevant under New Jersey's standard of self-defense, and that the testimony met the standards of New Jersey's rules for admissibility of expert testimony.

In *Kelly,* the defendant was charged with second degree murder of her husband. Gladys Kelly had been battered by her husband throughout their seven-year marriage. The beatings had begun on the day after her marriage, when she was beaten in public. On the day of the homicide, Mr. Kelly had been drinking and started beating her in public. During the physical struggle that ensued, she wounded him with a pair of scissors. She claimed that he was biting and clubbing her, and that she responded in self-defense.

At trial, defense counsel attempted to introduce the expert testimony of a clinical psychologist to explain why Gladys Kelly, as a battered woman, had a reasonable belief that she was in imminent danger of death or serious bodily harm and needed to act in self-defense. The trial judge . . . held that the testimony was not relevant under New Jersey's standard of self-defense and did not reach the issue of scientific reliability. On appeal, the Appellate Division affirmed the trial court's ruling. . . .

The [*amicus*] briefs submitted to the [New Jersey] Supreme Court emphasized the broad need for admissibility of this evidence on the issues of why Gladys Kelly did not leave her husband and the reasonableness of her perception of danger.

The Supreme Court's analysis of relevance reveals much about the dilemmas of using battered woman syndrome in women's self-defense work and the gains and limits of judicial understanding of the inherent issues. First, the court exhaustively and sensitively documented the severity of the problem of woman-abuse and the pervasiveness of stereotypes and myths concerning battered women. The vehicle for this discussion was the battered woman syndrome. The court described the experiences of battered women based upon the battered woman syndrome as "a series of common character- istics that appear in women who are abused physically and psychologically over an ex- tended period of time by the dominant male figure in their lives,"[7] and analyzed Dr. Walker's three stages of the battering cycle. The court discussed both these "psycho- logical impacts of battery" and the external social and economic factors which make it difficult for women to extricate themselves from the battering relationship: lack of money and support systems, primary responsibility for child care, and the fear and well- grounded belief that if the woman leaves the man will follow her and subject her to an even more brutal attack. Nonetheless, the court also recited the "symptoms" of the syn- drome and the common personality traits of the battered woman: "low self-esteem, tra- ditional beliefs about the home, the family, and the female sex role, tremendous feel- ings of guilt that their marriages are failing and the tendency to accept responsibility for the batterer's actions."[8]

Second, the court's understanding of the relevance and importance of this testi- mony was expansive. The court suggested that admission of the testimony was impor- tant because it would bolster Gladys Kelly's credibility in the eyes of the jury by demon- strating that her experiences, which the jury would find difficult to comprehend, were in fact common to women in abusive situations. The court ruled that in light of its in- terpretation of New Jersey's standard of self-defense, the expert testimony would be central to the *honesty* of Gladys Kelly's belief that she was in imminent danger of deadly harm, and it would aid the jury in determining whether a reasonable person could have believed that there was imminent danger to her life. The court characterized this as relevant under the "objective" standard of self-defense.

Third, the court held that the testimony was relevant because the expert could have responded to myths and misconceptions about battered women, particularly that the battered woman was free to leave, with information concerning battered women's in- ability to leave, "learned helplessness," and the lack of alternatives. . . .

[S]ignificantly, the court's analysis of relevance appears to focus on the woman's inability to leave. Indeed, the court contrasts the crucial nature of the expert testimony to rebut myths concerning why the battered woman does not leave with the relevance of the expert's testimony to the jury's determination of the reasonableness of the woman's act.

> The difficulty with the expert's testimony is that it sounds as if an expert is giv- ing knowledge to a jury about something the jury knows as well as anyone else namely, the reasonableness of a person's fear of imminent serious danger. That is not at all, however, what this testimony is directly aimed at. It is aimed at an area where the purported common knowledge of the jury may be very much mis- taken, an area where jurors' logic, drawn from their own experience, may lead to a wholly incorrect conclusion, an area where expert knowledge would enable the jurors to disregard their prior conclusions as being common myths rather than common knowledge. After hearing the expert, instead of saying Gladys

Kelly could not have been beaten up so badly for if she had, she certainly would have left, the jury could conclude that her failure to leave was very much part and parcel of her life as a battered wife. The jury could conclude that instead of casting doubt on the accuracy of her testimony about the severity and frequency of prior beatings, her failure to leave actually reinforced her credibility.[9]

This is underscored in the portion of the opinion in which the court defines the scope of the expert's testimony for retrial. The court again emphasizes that "the area of *expert* knowledge relates . . . to the reasons for defendant's failure to leave her husband."[10] *Kelly* exemplifies contradictory themes in the development of the issue of expert testimony. The Supreme Court's opinion reveals both the severity and tenacity of the problem of sex-bias in the law of self-defense. [T]he Supreme Court seems to perceive the testimony as primarily relevant to the issue of why Gladys Kelly did not leave, rather than the reasonableness of why she acted.

. . . On the one hand the court seems to say that admissibility of expert testimony on battering is important precisely because jurors' common sense experience with domestic relationships will give them the illusion of knowledge; jurors will not be aware of how their views have been shaped by common myths and stereotypes and tainted by bias. But the court's primary example is focused on why the battered woman didn't leave. Indeed, the opinion seems to suggest that if the testimony were focused on the issue of "reasonableness" of the woman's fear (and therefore the reasonableness of her *act* of self-defense as opposed to her failure to leave), the jury's perception that the expert was "giving knowledge to a jury about something the jury knows as well as anyone else, namely the reasonableness of a person's fear of imminent serious danger,"[11] would be right.

Certainly the court is correct that the question of why the battered woman did not leave (so as to avoid the possibility of death) is a threshold issue in the jury's mind. Her failure to leave raises the question of whether the woman was really battered (for if she was, why did she stay?), as well as the question of whether, by staying, she had in a sense "assumed the risk" of death. However, these questions only present the first issue for the jury. The second issue (and the more pressing one in many cases) is the reasonableness of the battered woman's belief that she was in particular jeopardy at the time that she responded in self-defense. A battered woman who has been the victim of abuse for many years and has survived it before must credibly explain why it was necessary to act on that occasion. Expert testimony, admitted for the purpose of explaining why the battered woman did not leave, does not help the jury answer the question whether she was reasonable in acting violently in order to save her life. It thus does not address the basic defense problem that the battered woman faces. Indeed, if the testimony is limited, or perceived as limited to the issue of why the woman does not leave, it highlights a contradiction implicit in the message of battered woman syndrome—if the battered woman was so helpless and passive, why did she kill the batterer?

. . . This highlights the dilemma of battered woman syndrome: explanation of the battered woman's actions from a solely victimized perspective cannot fully explain why she believed it was necessary to act. . . .

Expert Testimony: Dilemmas for Feminist Legal Theory

. . . The arguments first raised in *Wanrow* [reprinted herein, at 306] accepted by the plurality opinion of the Washington Supreme Court were based on several assumptions which have become basic: first, that women act in self-defense under different circumstances and in different ways than men; second, that the law of self-defense incorporates sex-bias;[12] and third, that sex-stereotypes of women as a group generally, and battered or raped women specifically, interfere with juror determinations of women's claims of self-defense. *Wanrow* and the substantial work on women's self-defense which flowed from it resulted from efforts to have the reasonableness standard of self-defense expand to include women's different experience and adjust to include sex-bias in the law. . . .

On the level of theory, as other commentators have noted,[13] *Wanrow* posed a radical challenge to a number of dichotomies in legal thought. . . .

A. Differences/Sameness

Wanrow squarely raised the issue of the different circumstances in which women killed in self-defense, the different means by which they killed, and the different factual contexts, as well as the history and experience of sex-discrimination. Women's self-defense work since *Wanrow* has emphasized those differences in the particular context of battered women.

Wanrow attempted to use acknowledgement of these different circumstances and experiences as the basis for accommodation to the same standard of self-defense. The court's opinion emphasized that failure to accommodate the law to these differences had consequences under the equal protection clause of the Fourteenth Amendment. Women could be denied equal rights to trial.

At the time *Wanrow* was litigated, only a few feminist litigators and legal scholars questioned the appropriateness of a formal equality model of analysis—an analysis which emphasized the sameness or similarity of men and women, as opposed to women's differences.[14] There was fear of acknowledging difference in any sphere either "real" or "socially constructed," or of arguing a need for different legal treatment, because women would then be subject to the "patriarchal protectionism" which constituted lesser and unequal treatment. Today many feminist thinkers and litigators are challenging formal models of equality. Much criticism has been raised about the extent to which formal equality models rest on a male standard and do not allow for accommodation of women's experiences and perspectives. This debate has recently centered on legal treatment of pregnancy, particularly state laws which single out pregnancy and maternity for special and more favorable treatment. Proponents of these laws have asserted the need to accommodate the law to women's physical differences and socially constructed discrimination. Yet the fear persists for many that acknowledgement of "difference" in the law necessarily implies unequal treatment.

In *Wanrow,* this concern over whether acknowledgement of difference necessarily implies inferiority is heightened by the Washington Supreme Court's use of the word "handicaps" to describe the effect of sex discrimination.[15] Sex discrimination is disabling to women as a class and to individual women. Nonetheless the court's use of the word "handicaps" to describe this effect was troubling. It played on the stereotype of victimized and mistreated women that has historically limited women's claims for equal treatment and suggested that the court's responsiveness to Yvonne Wanrow's claim was shaped by patriarchal solicitude.

The expert testimony cases are the net result of the "differences" approach—the goal of the expert testimony is to explain the content of battered women's *different* experiences and perceptions so that juries can fairly apply the *same* legal standards to them. But the question which the expert testimony cases squarely pose is this: if battered women's experiences are explained as different, can they ever be genuinely incorporated into the traditional standard and understood as equally reasonable? Are these different experiences inevitably perceived as inferior, as "handicaps"? If so, is it necessary to alter the traditional standard?

These tensions are heightened by the fact that the substance of the testimony is on battered woman syndrome. . . . Theoretically, it is a vehicle to set apart and describe battered women's "different" but common experiences. However, like the word "handicaps" in *Wanrow,* "battered woman syndrome" carries with it stereotypes of individual incapacity and inferiority. . . . Battered woman syndrome does not mean, but can be heard as reinforcing stereotypes of women as passive, sick, powerless and victimized. Although it was developed to merely *describe* the common psychological experiences and characteristics which battered women share, and it is undoubtedly an accurate description of these characteristics, battered woman syndrome can be misused and misheard to enshrine the old stereotypes in a new form. This repeats an historic theme of treatment of women by the criminal law—women who are criminals are viewed as crazy or helpless or both.[16] Thus the description of battered women's "different" experiences, although purely categorical in intent, carries with it the language and baggage of familiar stereotypes of female incapacity.

B. Excuse/Justification

Wanrow and subsequent women's self-defense work have been premised on the view that the traditional boundaries and definitions of self-defense, as a form of justification, were sex-biased and shaped by male experience. Assertion of self-defense was therefore not viewed as an available legal option, and women were more often shunted into some defense of incapacity; either insanity, heat of passion or extreme emotional disturbance. Although the line between justification and excuse is often not entirely clear, justification and excuse have different emphases. Self-defense as justification focuses on the act of defending oneself; it rests on a determination that the act was right because of its circumstances. In contrast, a finding of excuse, like insanity or heat of passion, focuses on the actor; it is a finding that the act, although wrong, should be tolerated because of the actor's characteristics or state of mind. . . .

[T]he danger of the battered woman syndrome approach is that it revives concepts of excuse. Even the New Jersey Supreme Court's thoughtful and comprehensive analysis of battered woman syndrome in *Kelly* has elements of a classic excuse description; it focuses on the woman's defects, the woman subject to the "syndrome." It implies that she is limited because of *her* weakness and *her* problems. . . . The opinion seems to suggest that admission of expert testimony is primarily important because the battered woman "suffers" from the syndrome and could not be expected to leave her home, not because it is relevant to the reasonableness of her act. The court is willing to extend its "protection" and admit the testimony because the battered woman is perceived as weak. Although the purpose of expert testimony on battered woman syndrome is to explain the reasonableness of the woman's action, the psychological aspect of the description sounds like incapacity and excuse.

By emphasizing a strain of excuse, battered woman syndrome tends to rigidify other dichotomies which, as others have suggested, are roughly correlated with excuse and justification. Excuse suggests that the act is personal to the defendant, a private act, in contrast with a more public and common sense of rightness which justification reflects. Excuse suggests a sense of the subject, while justification implies a more objective statement. Redrawing the boundaries of justification and excuse means recasting the boundaries of the private/public and subjective/objective oppositions, making women's experiences generally, and battered women's experiences and perceptions specifically, more public and legitimate, and also more objective.

The notion of battered woman syndrome contains the seeds of old stereotypes of women in new form—the victimized and the passive battered woman, too paralyzed to act because of her own incapacity.[17] From a defense standpoint, this perspective is potentially counterproductive in that it explains why the woman did not leave but not why she acted. It is in tension with the notion of reasonableness necessary to self-defense since it emphasizes the woman's defects and incapacity. It also does not adequately describe the complex experiences of battered women. The effect is that women who depart from this stereotype, because of their own life situations or because the facts of their cases do not fit this perspective, are not likely to be able to take advantage of judicial solicitude. This has already presented serious defense problems in several cases.[18] The stereotype of the reasonable battered woman who suffers from battered woman syndrome creates a new and equally rigid classification, which has the potential to exclude battered women whose circumstances depart from the model and force them once again into pleas of insanity or manslaughter rather than expanding our understandings of reasonableness. It thus reinforces and rigidifies the traditional boundaries of justification and excuse, rather than redrawing them. . . .

C. Individual/Group

Wanrow emphasized the importance of the individual's perspective as shaped by her experience as a woman. In *Wanrow* the court recognized the importance of the individual woman's own perspective as the standard of self-defense, but at the same time the court recognized that this perspective had a distinct and collective component to it. The court in *Wanrow* emphasized that a central aspect of the individual woman's perception was "those perceptions which were the product of our nation's long and unfortunate history of sex-discrimination."[19] The individual woman's experience thus was shaped by the history of sex discrimination. The court sees it as a *particular* experience (i.e. separate from that of men) and a *common* experience, an experience which women share together. Thus women share a common experience that is "different."

Wanrow challenged the dichotomy between individual and group perspective. Indeed, it stressed the necessary interrelationship between the individual and social perspective. *Wanrow*'s suggestion that an individual woman's distinct experience is a crucial aspect of her perspective set the foundation for the admission of testimony concerning the content of that woman's experience.

In the expert testimony area, courts have recognized that the experiences of battered women are distinct and shared, that these experiences are outside the common experience of jurors, and that it is necessary for the jury to learn about these experiences in order to overcome myths and misconceptions concerning battered women in order to evaluate whether the woman was acting in self-defense. This view is based on a recognition that the common ways that battered women have acted in self-defense (i.e., in not being able to leave, and in attacking assailants while asleep) will not be otherwise understandable to jurors.

Many courts have accepted the need for expert testimony. But consider what judicial acceptance of this testimony implies. It emphasizes the profound gap between the experiences of battered women and those of the rest of society; it reaffirms the notion of a woman's viewpoint *and* separate experience. It suggests that psychological and social factors are interrelated and that individual experience is necessarily shaped by group identity. It also suggests that women's own description of their experiences lacks credibility, because these experiences differ from the male norm, and because women generally are not viewed as believable.

Courts are effectively recognizing that an expert, a professional, someone not a battered woman, is needed to translate the experiences of large numbers of women in this society to the rest of society's representatives. It is arguable that expert testimony may be necessary only for a transitional period, until women's voices are strong enough to be heard on their own. But experience with the use of experts in the women's movement suggests that there may be risks. Courts may find experts particularly useful in cases involving women not as a complement to, but as a substitute for, women's voices.[20]

On a theoretical level, judicial acceptance of expert testimony has a profound impact because it affirmatively recognizes the substantive experience and content of sex discrimination and validates a "woman-centered" perspective. This collapses the dichotomy between individual experience and group experience by describing the experience as not just the individual's, but that of all battered women generally. At the same time, it is disturbing, for it suggests that only experts can bridge the gap between the individual and collective experience of women and counsel jurors and society that an individual woman's experience has a social validity and commonality and might be reasonable.

D. Subjective/Objective

The development of women's self-defense work from *Wanrow* to *Kelly* reveals change in our perspectives on the content of the standard of self defense.

Traditionally courts and commentators have distinguished "subjective" from "objective" standards of self-defense. The objective standard—the traditional "reasonable man standard"—looked at reasonableness from the perspective of the hypothetical reasonable man while the subjective standard looked at reasonableness from the individual's own perspective. It has been recognized that these characterizations of subjective and objective are poles on a continuum, since the jury must find that the actor acted reasonably under either approach.

The objective reasonable man standard of self-defense has been criticized from many perspectives, for failing to take account of complex social reality,[21] for embodying a rigid view of individual responsibility and for resulting in sex bias.[22] Recently objective standards in general have been criticized by feminist legal theorists who have argued that these standards inherently embody male values.[23] . . .

Wanrow arose in the context of a subjective individualized standard of self-defense and the arguments developed there about the need for an individualized perspective responded to the traditional "reasonable man" formulation. However, *Wanrow*, and the women's self-defense work which has developed from it, did not rest on the traditional subjective formulation. The content of the individualized perspective which *Wanrow* emphasized was clearly social and not simply psychological. It was the woman's individual perspective shaped by her experience as a woman within the collective and historical experience of sex discrimination. At the time, it seemed difficult enough to convince a jury that the woman might be reasonable even when applying a standard emphasizing the woman's own perspective. It was even more difficult to imagine arguing woman's experiences as objectively reasonable.

However, the expert testimony cases suggest that perhaps the *Wanrow* approach was too cautious. Expert testimony on battered woman syndrome necessarily challenges the dichotomy of subjective versus objective, as did *Wanrow*. The individual woman seeks expert testimony about the characteristics of the larger group of which she is a member to show that she acted reasonably both as an individual and as a member of that group. The very notion of expert testimony about the common character of battered women contains a subjective (individualized) component and an objective (group) component. The substance of the testimony describes experience which in some sense can be considered as objective. Courts have held that this testimony is relevant in jurisdictions with both objective and subjective standards.

Kelly demonstrates this development. The very issue in *Kelly* was whether the expert testimony was relevant under New Jersey's standard of self-defense. The trial court interpreted it as a traditional objective standard; counsel argued that under either standard the testimony was relevant. The court held that the testimony was relevant to the objective reasonableness of the defendant's belief as to whether she reasonably believe(d) deadly force to be necessary to prevent death or serious bodily harm. This recognition of a woman's and battered woman's experiences and perceptions as objectively reasonable is vitally important. The court thereby accords a woman's experience a group-based "public" dimension rather than merely an individual, "private" subjective one. At the same time, perhaps it is not surprising that the content of what is deemed "objective" is an image of a victimized, passive battered woman. Perhaps this is the reason the court sees it as objective and acceptable.

Describing and Changing: The Underlying Theme of Victimization and Agency

The underlying theme throughout this discussion of the expert testimony cases is the dilemma that the notion of victimization poses for feminist legal theory. Examination of the expert testimony cases on battering has suggested that a perspective like battered woman syndrome, which either emphasizes victimization or which is susceptible to being characterized as victimization, raises serious problems for women in theory and practice.

Over the last several years, victimization has increasingly become a powerful, pervasive and seductive theme in the women's movement and the women's legal rights movement. [T]his perspective on women's experience is important and useful, particularly on issues concerning violence against women, [however] the virtually exclusive focus on victimization by the women's movement in recent years has been problematic. Portrayal of women as solely victims or agents is neither accurate nor adequate to explain the complex realities of women's lives. It is crucial for feminists and feminist legal theorists to understand and explore the role of both victimization and agency in women's lives, and to translate these understandings into the theory and practice that we develop. . . .[24]

Other feminist theorists and legal thinkers have questioned the women's movement's reliance on victimization in a range of contexts,[25] including divorce and pornography. In the specific context of battered women, Susan Schechter has emphasized the dangers of an analysis premised on victimization. She suggests that the characterization of victim has been viewed as posing a complicated political problem for the battered women's movement

> because the focus on victimization helps to blur the insight that the struggle for battered women's rights is linked to the more general fight for women's liberation. When activists view battering as victimization rather than as an aspect of oppression, they have a tendency to see individual problems rather than collective ones.[26]

In addition, she observes that "victim" may be a label that battered women reject because "it fails to capture their complexity and strength."[27]

At the same time, a notion of the importance of women's agency without a social context of victimization is equally unsatisfactory. The notion of agency carries with it assumptions of liberal visions of autonomy, individual action, individual control and mobility that are also inadequate and incomplete. But women do act, . . . we act to make choices and shape our lives, we act even when there are few and terrible options. Sometimes, like battered women who kill, we act if only in order to survive.

In the battered woman context, recognition of the need to transcend the dichotomy and exclusivity of characterizations of victim versus agent and develop a theory and practice which encompasses both has consequences for the way we approach and handle the use of expert testimony in battered women's cases. Defense efforts should focus on the battering experience as well as the reasonableness of the woman's actions. Expert testimony on battering should be proffered and admitted, but lawyers should be sensitive to the way in which they understand, characterize and explain the testimony and its relevance, and they should not rely on it to the exclusion of other defense strategies. Battered women who kill need not be portrayed solely as victims with the focus on the battering, but as actors and survivors whose acts are reasonable. The psychological mechanisms that battered women develop, as in battered woman syndrome, can be explained as ways for battered women to cope and survive. If killing in self-defense can be understood as a reasonable act in terms of the context of victimization and other options, both the victimization and agency aspects of battered women's experiences are included. If battered women who kill are described as women who are victims but have fought back in order to survive, their actions in killing their batterers may be more effectively understood as reasonable.

Defense lawyers and experts must emphasize the common experiences of battered women, but must describe both the particular experience of the individual woman and be sensitive to the sex-stereotypical implications of the testimony. Defense lawyers and experts should emphasize the common aspects of the battered woman's experience, both her helplessness and her behavioral adjustments that allow her to survive, her desperate coping, her unique insight and ability to know and anticipate the degree of violence she faces, and her painful understanding of the paucity of alternatives available to women in this culture. This fuller description of battered women's experiences is both more accurate and better explains to judges and juries why a battered woman doesn't leave the house *and* why she kills to save her own life.

Explanation of aspects of both victimization and agency makes it possible for expert testimony to more accurately describe the complexity of battered women's experiences, respond to the hard defense problems presented in these cases, and allow for change by transcending static stereotypes. Feminist legal work must *both* describe *and* allow for change. As lawyers for battered women we must take account of battered women's experiences in being acted upon *and* acting. Our work must simultaneously capture the reality of battered women's lives, translate this reality more fully and effectively to courts, and push toward transforming this reality.

Notes

1. Appellate cases that have addressed the admissibility of expert testimony on battered woman syndrome and declined to admit this testimony include: State v. Edwards, 420 So. 2d 663 (La. 1982); State v. Burton, 464 So. 2d 421 (La. Ct. App. 1985); State v. Necaise, 466 So. 2d 660 (La. Ct. App. 1985); State v. Thomas, 66 Ohio St. 2d 518, 423 N.E.2d 137 (1981), *habeas petition denied sub nom.* Thomas v. Arn, 728 F.2d 813 (6th Cir. 1984), *aff'd,* 106 S. Ct. 466 (1985); Fielder v. State, 683 S.W.2d 565 (Tex. Ct. App. 1985); State v. Buhrle, 627 P.2d 1374 (Wyo. 1981). Appellate cases which have admitted testimony on battered woman syndrome include: Terry v. State, 467 So. 2d 761 (Fla. Dist. Ct. App. 1985); Borders v. State, 433 So. 2d 1325 (Fla. Dist Ct. App. 1983); Smith v. State, 247 Ga. 612, 277 S.E.2d 678 (1981); People v. Minnis, 118 Ill. App. 3d 345, 455 N.E.2d 209 (1983); State v. Anaya, 438 A.2d 892 (Me. 1981); State v. Kelly, 97 N.J. 178, 478 A.2d 364 (1984); State v. Branchall, 101 N.M. 498, 684 P.2d 1163 (Ct. App. 1984); State v. Allery, 101 Wash.2d 591, 682 P.2d 312 (1984).

2. 97 N.J. 178, 478 A.2d 364 (1984).

3. Crocker, The Meaning of Equality for Battered Women Who Kill Men in Self-Defense, 8 Harv. Women's L.J. 121 (1985); Donovan & Wildman, Is the Reasonable Man Obsolete? A Critical Perspective on Self-Defense and Provocation, 14 Loy. L. A. L. Rev. 435 (1981); Eber, The Battered Woman's Dilemma: To Kill or be Killed, 32 Hastings L. J. 895 (1981); Eisenberg & Seymour, The Self-Defense Plea and Battered Women, 14 Trial 34 (1978); Robinson, Defense Strategies for Battered Women Who Assault Their Mates: State v. Curry, 4 Harv. Women's L. J. 161 (1981); Schneider, Equal Rights to Trial for Women: Sex Bias in the Law of Self-Defense, 15 Harv. C.R.-C.L. L. Rev. 623 (1980); Schneider & Jordan, Representation of Women Who Defend Themselves in Response to Physical or Sexual Assault, 4 Women's Rts. L. Rep. 149 (1978); Walker, Thyfault, & Browne, Beyond the Juror's Ken: Battered Women, 7 Vt. L. Rev. 1 (1982). . . .

4. L. Walker, The Battered Woman 55–70 (1979).

5. . . . See generally R. Dobash & R. Dobash, Violence Against Wives (1979); R. Gelles, The Violent Home (1982); R. Langley & U. R. Levy, Wife Beating (1977); D. Martin, Battered Wives (1976); E. Pizzey, Scream Quietly or the Neighbors Will Hear (1974); S. Steinmetz, The Cycle of Violence (1977); U.S. Comm'n on Civil Rights, Battered Women: Issues of Public Policy (1978); S. Steinmetz & M. Straus eds., Violence in the Family (1974); L. Walker, *supra* note 4. . . .

6. C. McCormick, Evidence, 185 (E. Cleary ed. 3d ed., 1984).

7. *Kelly,* 97 N.J. at 191, 478 A.2d at 370.

8. 97 N.J. at 195, 478 A.2d at 372.

9. *Id.* at 206, 478 A.2d at 378.

10. *Id.*

11. *Id.*

12. Schneider and Jordan, *supra* note 3, at 159; the *Wanrow* opinion explains this insight in the following way: "The second paragraph of instruction No. 10 not only establishes an objective standard, but through the persistent use of the masculine gender leaves the jury with the impression the objective standard to be applied is that applicable to an altercation between two men. The impression created—that a 5'4" woman with a cast on her leg and using a crutch must, under the law, somehow repel an assault by a 6'2" intoxicated man without employing weapons in her defense, unless the jury finds her determination of the degree of danger to be objectively reasonable—constitutes a separate and

right to equal protection of the law. The respondent was entitled to have the jury consider her actions in the light of her own perceptions of the situation, including those perceptions which were the product of our nation's 'long and unfortunate history of sex discrimination.' Frontiero v. Richardson, 411 U.S. 677, 684 . . . (1973). Until such time as the effects of that history are eradicated, care must be taken to assure that our self-defense instructions afford women the right to have their conduct judged in light of the individual physical handicaps which are the product of sex discrimination. To fail to do so is to deny the right of the individual woman involved to trial by the same rules which are applicable to male defendants (citations omitted)." State v. Wanrow, 559 P.2d at 558–559.

13. See generally MacKinnon, Toward Feminist Jurisprudence (Book Review), 34 Stan. L. Rev. 703 (1982) (reviewing Ann Jones, Women Who Kill (1980); Crocker, *supra* note 3.

14. See generally Brown, Emerson, Falk & Freedman, The Equal Rights Amendment: A Constitutional Basis for Equal Rights for Women, 80 Yale L.J. 871 (1971); Williams, The Equality Crisis: Some Reflections on Culture, Courts and Feminism, 7 Women's Rts. L. Rep. 175 (1982).

15. "Until such time as the effects of that history are eradicated, care must be taken to assure that our self-defense instructions afford women the right to have their conduct judged in light of the *individual physical handicaps which are the product of sex discrimination.*" State v. Wanrow, 559 P.2d at 559 (emphasis added).

16. See A. Jones, Women Who Kill 158–166 (1980); E. Showalter, The Female Malady: Women, Madness and English Culture (1985). . . .

17. Phyllis Crocker calls this "the battered woman syndrome stereotype." She describes it in the following way: "A stereotype about battered women's behavior is emerging that threatens to create a separate standard of reasonableness for battered women. Some courts seem to treat battered woman syndrome as a standard to which all battered women must conform rather than as evidence that illuminates the defendant's behavior and perception. As a result, a defendant may be considered a battered woman only if she never left her husband, never sought assistance, and never fought back. Unless she fits this rigidly-defined and narrowly-applied definition, she is prevented from benefiting from battered woman syndrome testimony. Simultaneously, the prosecution characterizes her actions as unreasonable under the rubric of the reasonable man. Under that standard, the defendant must explain why her act of self-defense does not resemble a man's. The result is that the claims of the individual woman get caught between two conflicting stereotypes: the judicial construct of the battered woman based on the syndrome testimony, and the prosecutorial model that uses myths about battered women to prove their unreasonableness. Neither of these stereotypes allows a battered woman to portray the reasonableness of her actions accurately to the jury. The double bind of the two stereotypes is most apparent in the reactions to a defendant's physical response to prior abuse. If the defendant has tried to resist in the past, the court accepts this as evidence that rebuts her status as a battered woman. On the other hand, if the defendant has never attempted to fight back, the prosecution argues that the defendant did not act as a 'reasonable man.'" Crocker, *supra* note 3, at 144–145.

18. See generally *id.* Crocker suggests that in "non-traditional confrontation cases, in which the battered woman kills either in anticipation of or following a physical attack," expert testimony is often excluded "because the court views the battered woman's act as unreasonable." Even in "traditional confrontation cases, where the battered woman's act of self-defense seems to fit the traditional self-defense model, courts will admit battered woman syndrome expert testimony apparently because they doubt

the reasonableness of the battered woman's perception of danger." *Id.* at 138–139. Barbara Hart, an attorney in Pennsylvania, raised a similar issue in a letter describing the problems in a battered woman self-defense case involving a black woman who did not conform to the battered woman syndrome stereotype. She raises the question whether the battered woman syndrome was developed through interviews with women from middle- or upper-income families for whom the concept of self-defense was relatively unknown." Letter from Barbara Hart to author dated November 30, 1984. . . .

19. State v. Wanrow, 88 Wash. at 240, 559 P.2d at 559.

20. For a discussion of the historical and social role of experts in the women's movement, see B. Ehrenreich & D. English, For Her Own Good: One Hundred Fifty Years of Experts' Advice to Women (1978). Although experts can assist women so that courts can hear women's voices, experts may also be a more acceptable source of information than "ordinary" women. The dangers of professionalization of decision-making are serious, particularly where the realm of expertise is scientific or based on a medical model. For example, in Roe v. Wade, 410 U.S. 113 (1973), the Supreme Court discusses the decision to terminate a pregnancy as one to be made between a woman and her doctors. As subsequent cases unfold, courts seem to place the reproductive decision more in the hands of doctors. See Asaro, The Judicial Portrayal of the Physician in Abortion and Sterilization Decisions: The Use and Abuse of Medical Discretion, 6 Harv. Women's L.J. 51 (1983). For an interesting analysis of the changing social contexts in which the use and type of expert testimony relied upon by courts should be viewed, see Weisberg, The Discovery of Sexual Abuse: Experts' Role in Legal Policy Formulation, 18 U.C.D. L. Rev. 1 (1984). . . .

21. Donovan & Wildman, *supra* note 3.

22. Schneider & Jordan, *supra* note 3, at 30–31.

23. See generally MacKinnon, Feminism, Marxism, Method and the State: Toward Feminist Jurisprudence, in D. Weisberg ed., Feminist Legal Theory: Foundations 427 (Temple Univ. Press, 1993).

24. Perhaps using the words *action* and *agency* as parallels here is problematic. The woman has acted, but she has also been, as Catharine MacKinnon acutely observes, "acted upon." MacKinnon, *supra* note 13, at 734. It is not fair to say that she has been "self-acting" or really an agent, in the sense of free agent. Yet there is a sense in which the notion of victimization in its extreme form seems to deny any agency, the possibility of individual action, or the fact of action altogether.

25. See generally S. Schecter, Women and Violence, The Visions and Struggles of the Battered Women's Movement (1982); A. Jaggar, Feminist Politics and Human Nature (1983); K. Ferguson, The Feminist Case Against Bureaucracy (1984); Duggan, Hunter & Vance, False Promises: Feminist Antipornography Legislation in the United States in V. Burstyn ed., Women Against Censorship (1985); Fineman, Implementing Equality: Ideology, Contradiction and Social Change, A Study of Rhetoric in the Regulation of the Consequences of Divorce, 1983 Wis. L. Rev. 789; Feminist Discourse, Moral Values and the Law—A Conversation, 31 Buffalo L. Rev. 1 (1985).

26. Schecter, *supra* note 25, at 252.

27. *Id.* For an insightful analysis of the complex reasons that individuals who have been discriminated against do not want to experience themselves as victims, see also Bumiller, Anti-Discrimination Law and the Enslavement of the Victim: The Denial of Self-Respect by Victims Without a Cause (Working Paper, Disputes Processing Research Program, University of Wisconsin—Madison Law School).

Women's Experience and the Problem of Transition: Perspectives on Male Battering of Women

CHRISTINE A. LITTLETON

Try thinking without apology with what you know from being victimized.[1]

FEMINISM IS (or at least aspires to be) a theory and practice forged directly from women's experience as women. It thus directly implicates our biological status (as female), our sociological status (as those who are identified as, and treated as, women) and our political status (as those who identify with women). As Catharine MacKinnon notes, the "methodological secret" of feminism is that it is built on "believing women's accounts,"[2] on recognizing women's experience as central. When applied to (or in) law, feminism becomes feminist jurisprudence. Feminist jurisprudence refuses to take legal categories or doctrines as given, and thus refuses to limit itself to shaping women's experience to fit the current outlines of established law. Reversing the traditional process of introducing new ideas into law by trying to show that a new idea is very much like an old one, feminist jurisprudence takes women's experience as the starting point, whether or not our experience is "very much like" the experience of those who have previously made the rules and set the standards. . . .

Because women's experience is the central building block of feminist jurisprudence, it is necessary to deal explicitly . . . with the question of how to evaluate women's experience. . . . Feminist theorists have long struggled with potential approaches to . . . the paradox of diversity in commonality. . . .

One approach is to define accounts that do not fit a theorist's particular experience as "false consciousness.". . . A second approach to the diversity of women's accounts views feminism as made up of a variety of "feminisms"—all of which are inherently partial. . . .

Between the Scylla of false consciousness and the Charybdis of uncritical pluralism lies the possibility of a third option. . . . This option requires a dialectic between our own descriptions of our varying experience and the conditions under which such descriptions are made. Rather than viewing any woman's description as, on the one hand, potentially inaccurate, socially conditioned or merely the product of internalized oppression; or, on the other, individualized, attributable solely to determinants other

1989 U. Chi. Legal F. 23.

than gender, or exceptional, I suggest that we should use as a working hypothesis the assumption that women's descriptions of our experience are accurate, reasonable and potentially understandable *given the conditions under which we live.* Tensions and contradictions in women's descriptions give us a way to examine and criticize the conditions under which we live, rather than a reason to deny status to some descriptions or to consider other descriptions as relevant to some women but not others. The task for . . . this essay is to use this "third option" to examine the experience of women in one context—battering—where distortion of that experience seems ubiquitous.[3]

B. The Context of Battering

By some estimates, almost half of all marriages are marked by battering episodes,[4] and many more women are battered by their boyfriends, fiancés or lovers. Yet battering *per se* occupies very little of the legal landscape, at least as measured by law review pages and published opinions. "Law" seems to come in only at the extremes, as, for instance, when long-term victims of battering escape through the unusual route of killing their tormenters. For most battered women, "the police always come late if they come at all."[5]

It is often said that rape victims are raped twice—once by the rapist and once by the legal system. If that is so, then battered women are battered three times—once by the batterer, a second time by society and finally by the legal system. Traditional society blames the victim of battering for "deserving" the punishment. If only she had been a better wife, a more submissive helpmate, a more compliant sexual partner, then her nose would not have been broken, her eye would still be uncut, the bruises would never have marked her thighs. The legal system is somewhat more generous. It does not blame *all* battered women for their plight, only those who do not immediately sever their relationships and leave their batterers.

Women who have been battered tell stories that include fear (the one story law might listen to), love (a story usually heard as masochism), desire for connection (a story hardly heard at all) and absence of options (often dismissed as "objectively" inaccurate). Must we be forced, by either the lack of a unitary account or the pressure of existing conditions, to choose among them only one story? Will recognizing their multiplicity undermine efforts on behalf of women who are battered? Can the multifaceted nature of these descriptions be taken seriously and still provide the foundation of feminist critique?

The tension criminal law theorists identify in battered women's self-defense claims is between a commonly held image of battered women as passive and the actual action of those relatively few battered women who kill their batterers. The tension certainly seems real, especially when we consider *all* battered women. If these women are so passive, dependent and helpless, where do they get the strength and courage to live, day after day, with the abuse, humiliation and violence? Where do they get the intestinal fortitude to protect their children, pay their bills, maintain their facade of wedded bliss? And in those rare instances, where do they get the desperation to kill?

This lack of convergence between image and a full vision of action highlights two fundamental issues of feminist jurisprudence: the problem of evaluating women's experience and the problem of transition. . . .

I. Women's Experience

[T]he law's image of battered women . . . has its own set of adverse consequences. . . .

A. The Law's Picture of Battered Women

It was late evening when 23-year-old Josephine Smith returned to her apartment in Atlanta.[6] She was met outside by her live-in boyfriend David Jones. David lived at Jo's place "most of the time," leaving for days or weeks at a time to take care of business, hang out with his buddies or just get a little distance. Jo and David have had two children together, both of whom are spoken of as "her children," and only one of whom carries David's last name.

Jo finished the laundry while David hung around, then went upstairs to go to bed. Feeling amorous, David began to rub himself against Jo, who asked him to stop because she was tired. (By this time it was 1 or 2 A.M.) David grabbed Jo and shook her, saying, "You don't tell me when to touch you." Afraid, upset or just disgusted, Jo got out of bed, pulled on some street clothes and started to leave the bedroom. David held up a balled fist and told her she "wasn't going anywhere." Sighing, Jo sat down on the foot of the bed and started rolling her hair. David kicked her in the back. Jo placed her hair pick between her back and David's foot, and, as a result, his second kick gave him a flash of pain. He responded by hitting Jo in the head with his fist, grabbing her by the throat and choking her. Then he threw her against the door.

Jo ran to the bureau, grabbed her gun and ran downstairs. She tried to call her mother, but David had already taken the upstairs phone off the hook, and now took the receiver out of Jo's hand. Jo tried to run back to the bedroom, but David caught her. She tried to run out the door, but David slammed the door on her foot. Remembering the gun in her hand, Jo fired three times with her eyes closed, turned and ran. She begged a neighbor to let her in and used the telephone to call the police. When the police arrived, David was dead. Jo was arrested and charged with voluntary manslaughter.

Jo is not a typical battered woman. Most obviously, she had a gun and she used it. Over a million and a half women are beaten each year by the men they love,[7] but only a few hundred kill.[8] By contrast, several thousand women are killed each year by the men who supposedly love them.[9] She may also be unusual in another respect—she was not married to the man who beat her. . . . Nevertheless, Jo's case offers an opportunity to examine how the law distorts women's accounts, as well as to question why it does so.

At trial, Jo asserted that because she had acted in fear of her life, and thus in self-defense, she should be acquitted. In furtherance of this defense, she testified that:

[David] hit her in the eye with his fist about a month after they met, that he had beaten her periodically, particularly when she dated so she quit seeing other men, that she was scared to quit seeing the victim because he threatened her, that the beatings increased in frequency when she moved from her mother's house to the apartment, that after he beat her he would apologize and say he loved her, that she didn't call the police or tell her friends because she believed him when he said he wouldn't do it anymore, and that earlier on the day of the shooting the victim threatened her and she gave him ten dollars after asking him not to do that in the presence of her sister. She testified that on the night of the shooting the victim said he was going to do something to her and call her mother to come to get her, that she was scared he was going to hurt her more than before, and that she shot the victim in fear of her life.[10]

The jury found Jo guilty of voluntary manslaughter, and she was sentenced to 15 years. Jo appealed her conviction on the ground that the trial court had excluded expert psychological testimony during both the trial and the sentencing hearing. The court of appeals affirmed on the basis that such expert testimony would have invaded the province of the jury (that is, deciding whether Jo had acted out of fear for her life). The Georgia Supreme Court reversed, however, holding that "[e]xpert opinion testimony on issues to be decided by the jury, even the ultimate issue, is admissible where the conclusion of the expert is one which jurors would not ordinarily be able to draw for themselves; i.e., the conclusion is beyond the ken of the average layman."[11] The "average layman," the court reasoned, might think that the "logical reaction" of a battered woman would be to call the police or leave her husband (boyfriend).[12] Only through use of expert testimony on the "battered woman syndrome" could a jury learn that "typically victims of battered woman syndrome believe that their husbands are capable of killing them, that there is no escape, and that if they leave they will be found and hurt even more."[13] Without such expert testimony, a jury probably would not suspect that battered women believe "that they themselves are somehow responsible for their husbands' violent behavior, and that they are low in self-esteem and feel powerless."[14] Nor would they know that the primary emotion of a battered woman is fear.

Jo's conviction was reversed. . . . Yet the sub-text of the opinion is deeply troubling.

First, battered women were viewed by the *Smith* court as alien, their reasoning and actions "beyond the ken of the average layman." This view is indeed plausible: Not only battered women, but all women, may appear alien from a male perspective. In this sense, the court's characterization may be even truer than the court itself imagined. Second, whether accurate or not, the truth of an expert's assertion that the battered woman's "primary emotion is fear" is largely irrelevant. Unless she can convince the jury that she was afraid in a way they understand, she will go to jail. *That* is a powerful truth. Third, battered women are said to *believe* that there is no escape. This statement seems consistent with women's accounts, but it is also incomplete in a particularly insidious way. That is, not only is the objective accuracy of the belief deemed irrelevant, but so is its very reasonableness. It is precisely because the belief appears so incredible that expert testimony is introduced.

Whether or not Jo's belief that she could not safely escape the relationship with David was accurate is, or course, not the point. Whether her belief was *reasonable*, however, was precisely the point of feminist theorists and litigators who worked so hard to gain acceptance of expert testimony on behalf of battered women claiming self-defense.[15] There are, in fact, very strong empirical grounds for believing that escape is sometimes impossible, or at least as dangerous as staying. Every battered women's shelter has stories to tell of the men who follow "their" women, hammer at the door, and try to force their way through. Restraining orders do not prevent men from returning to threaten us again; moving only delays the day that they find us; even jail sentences do not assure safety.[16] . . . The statistical incidence of "recapture"—men finding women and beating again—makes a mockery of the standard self-defense analysis regarding "duty to retreat." It also makes battered women's belief that there is no safe escape rational. That rationality, however, is truly "beyond the ken of the average layman."

What difference does it make whether the belief that escape is impossible is rational, or an aspect of women's abnormal psychology? . . .

The characterization of the belief makes a difference in four interrelated ways. The first is that, paradoxically, the focus on the personal, interior, subjective nature of the belief without considering its class-wide, external, statistical rationality, denies the defense to those individual women who have not yet been beaten "enough." For example, in giving Jo Smith the benefit of expert testimony, the Georgia Supreme Court distinguished an Idaho case upholding the exclusion of psychiatric opinion "as to whether or not the defendant was in a state of fear at the time of shooting her husband."[17] That case was seen as different because there "the defendant testified as to *only one* prior occasion of physical abuse."[18]

A second consequence of focusing on subjective belief rather than social reality is that it allows society, and encourages women, to deny the extent of male violence and the threat of such violence to our lives. Thus, women who are battered are viewed by many other women as deviant, unusual, perhaps even rare. Such denial and lack of identification undermine the unity of women necessary to bring about political and legal change, as well as cutting off battered women from potential sources of support and nurturance.

The third consequence is even more subtle. In bypassing the question of *statistical frequency*, the law's imagery and categorization allows, perhaps even encourages, a notion of the *natural inevitability* of violence against women. In Dothard v. Rawlinson,[19] for example, the United States Supreme Court decided that a female prison guard's "very womanhood" and the resultant likelihood of sexual assault would undermine her ability to maintain control over male prisoners. By failing to identify the problem as one of male violence or as one of conditions that make male violence a real possibility, the Court made it impossible to see that changing the prison conditions was a viable alternative to excluding women from the job. In similar fashion, identifying the problem in battering by focusing on a woman's psychological reaction rather than on the battering itself makes it harder for the legal system to craft solutions that will stop the violence, and easier to blame the woman for not fleeing.

Finally, this notion of natural inevitability causes the jury immediately to accept the dead husband or boyfriend as "the victim." To gain acquittal, the battered woman's only option is to make herself even more of a victim. If she is successful, she will gain the sympathy of a jury, but not necessarily its respect. Rather, a successful showing of victimization will lead the jury to characterize her as incompetent rather than as reasonable. Labeling those women who finally and desperately resist the imposition of male power as unreasonable, incompetent, suffering from psychological impairment or just plain crazy supports, rather than undermines, the assumption that male power over women is natural and unalterable.

Beyond characterizing the battered woman as unreasonable, however, the law in its present cast is also able to maintain an absolute focus on whether the battered woman "chose" correctly between the risk of leaving and the risk of staying, and away from whether men should be able to impose *either* set of risks on us. This fact, above all others, leads me to think that the problem is much more than various judges' and juries' tendency to hold onto sex stereotypes. Translating women's victimization into a problem *with women* masks the pervasiveness and extent of men's ability to oppress, harm and threaten us. It protects the legal system from having to confront the central problems of battering—male violence, male power and gender hierarchy. . . .

C. Beyond Learned Helplessness

The phenomenon of some battered women choosing to remain in the relationship despite "objective" judgments that they would be safer if they left can be explained in several different ways—all of which have been, or could be, described as "feminist." One explanation accepts the accuracy of the outsider's judgment and ascribes the battered woman's behavior to some dysfunction in character, broadly described as "learned helplessness." [In an omitted section, Littleton describes Lenore Walker's psychological theory of learned helplessness. The theory, derived from animal behavior, explains battered women's passivity and submissiveness as a learned response to persistent abuse. *Ed.*] A second view has stressed the *un*safety of leaving, pointing out the lack of equal pay in female jobs, the practical problems of finding alternative housing and the difficulty of raising children alone.[20] Few, if any, commentators have suggested that women are doing anything other than misperceiving the danger to themselves, or settling for the lesser of two evils. A third explanation, however, is that those women who stay in battering relationships accurately perceive the risks of remaining, accurately perceive the risks of leaving, and choose to stay either because the risks of leaving outweigh the risks of staying *or* because they are trying to rescue something beyond themselves.

Broad-based acceptance by the legal system of the first explanation has already been explored. Focusing on women's reactions to what men do to them is an all too common strategy of male jurisprudence. The failure of the second explanation to gain similar acceptance in law could concomitantly be related to the law's reluctance to acknowledge the extent of male violence against, and oppression of, women outside the home. It is also plausible that, despite the dangers of leaving, women are indeed marginally safer in leaving a demonstrably violent relationship. But if women value connection enough to keep trying despite marginally greater risks of harm, both problems of evaluating women's accounts and problems of transition arise.

For most men to whom I have spoken about this issue, it seems literally incomprehensible that a battered woman is not lying—at least to herself if not to others—when she says that one reason she has not left yet is that she loves this man and believes that he will stop beating her. Love and pain are mutually exclusive, they say, at least outside of masochism.[21] It does not seem that men fail to value relationships per se, but rather that they value them for the *pleasure* they can give. That's what relationships are *for*, they seem to say.

I often wish it were that easy; I wish I could explain [Jo Smith's in Smith v. State] statements ("She continued the relationship for three basic reasons—she loved him, she believed him each time he said that he loved her and that he was never going to repeat the abuse, and she was afraid that if she tried to leave she would be endangering her life"[22]) as only one reason (fear), mixed with a large dose of false consciousness. Jo's love and hope made her intensely vulnerable to David's violence, and to the fear such violence engenders. Jo's love and hope led to tragedy. To ask society—and especially to ask the law—to take that love and hope seriously is to run headlong into the problem of transition. How could we possibly take seriously women's accounts of love and hope without undermining the little protection from male violence women have been able to wrest from the legal system, without indeed increasing our already overwhelming vulnerability?

II. The Problem of Transition

[In an earlier section, omitted here, Littleton points out that the distortion and silencing of women's experience raises "the problem of transition." Littleton identifies the problem as the discovery of strategies to improve women's situation without minimizing the dangers of partial reform. *Ed.*]

In its most general sense, the problem of transition is created by an existing system of power that makes any non-conforming patterns of behavior appear deviant, which in turn makes it relatively easy to maintain and increase the differential in the social rewards between conformist patterns of behavior and non-conformist ones. Phallocentrism is just such a hegemonic system. It systematically rewards those who conform to culturally male styles of behavior and systematically disadvantages those who resist, regardless of the biological sex of the actor. The existence of such a power structure has two related consequences. . . .

The first consequence of the asymmetry of power between women and men and between "deviance" and "normalcy" . . . makes it difficult to talk about battered women valuing the homes they have made without "home" being understood as the patriarchal and nuclear family. . . .

The second consequence of existing asymmetry is, however, even more troubling. When women's current access (albeit unequal access) to necessary resources is based on a system of allocation that assumes current economic structures, movement toward new structures threatens to deprive us of access entirely. The best recent description of this problem of transition is found in the work of Margaret Radin, who wrestles with (among other issues) the question of whether specifically female forms of labor should be commodified, in order to fit within male norms of deserving payment, or non-commodified, in order to fit within feminist or humanist ideals of sharing and community.[23] Even if everyone were to agree that human flourishing is best accomplished through non-commodification, abolition of markets and the acceptance of a model of human relationships based on caring and sharing, the social realities of a hegemonic exchange model of human nature would tend to subvert or destroy any *partial* attempts to prefigure the new social order.[24] Partial non-commodification, especially if it is maintained along sex lines, would keep women's labor out of the market while continuing to reward men's labor through the market. So long as money is readily translatable into political power, then non-commodification of women's labor will not alter the hegemony of the market, but only keep women poor and powerless in our separate sphere.

Similarly, the desire for connection expressed by women in battering relationships, even if understood and shared as an ideal, cannot simply be validated without taking account of the hegemony of male power. Leaving individual women to attempt to negotiate with their partners, even with a societal pat on the head for their good values and brave efforts, would be *worse* than the current situation. . . . If law is to help, rather than hinder, this project, it must not only overcome its presumption in favor of separation, but also *and simultaneously* stop men from battering us and foster alternative means of achieving connection. To fuse the desire for connection with the ability to resist or remove its abuses is the challenge of feminism *in* the law.

A. Separation and Connection

Robin West's exploration of the "separation thesis" of male jurisprudence and the "connection thesis" of feminism[25] is instructive at both the level of theory and the level of practice. In simplified terms, the separation thesis describes men as separate individuals whose awareness of separation "defines consciousness." Thus men, being separate, fear frustration of their individual ends by other separate individuals. The counter-story told by critical legal studies is that men also desire community, so that their lives are tragic, caught between unlimited desire for and unlimited fear of others. In contrast, the connection thesis describes women as connected to others (materially in the phenomenon of pregnancy), and as fearing abandonment and isolation. The counter-story told by radical feminism is of the violence of forced community, or invasion.

The practice of the legal system is consistent with these jurisprudential underpinnings of separation. Law's most common response to conflict is to separate, to keep individuals from interfering with each other's ends by removing them from one another. Contractual relationships begin outside the legal system (although sometimes with the help of lawyer-midwives) and litigation marks their rupture, either as symptom or as cause. While the marriage ceremony is accomplished with very little judicial oversight, divorce occupies enormous judicial resources. Those convicted of anti-social acts are removed from the community. . . .

Feminists facing the separationist impulse of the legal system have differed on how to react. . . . A great part of this difference is a result of the complexity of sexual inequality, consisting as it does of three interrelated phenomena—sex discrimination (different treatment because of sex); gender oppression (pressure to conform to expected sex roles) and sexual subordination (devaluing of what is associated with women).

At the level of simple sex discrimination, women have usually been *denied* the benefits of the legal system's impulse toward separation, even while feminists question the *value* of such an impulse. For the battered woman, even to get the police to respond, let alone arrest the batterer and separate him from the victim, takes incredible effort. . . .

Challenging the impulse toward separation on the civil side seems similarly fraught with danger. While feminist theorists such as Carrie Menkel-Meadow posit a "feminization of law practice" leading to, or at least encouraging, increased use of mediation and negotiation instead of litigation as a dispute resolution technique,[26] other feminists see in this trend the loss of what little power women derive from formal legal adjudication.[27] Caught between the emptiness of formal equality and rights discourses and the private coercion and violence that informal justice ignores and thereby permits, some feminists by contrast even appear to call for the abandonment of law altogether. The debate is completely understandable as a debate about instrumentalities—that is, how do we get there from here? It may also be a debate about ideals; that is, whether sexual equality *means* assimilation, androgyny, empowerment or acceptance. But it seems to me this issue will not be clear until all potential ends have been made equally safe (or equally dangerous) for women.

B. Toward Safe Connection

If battered women seek to maintain connection in the face of enormous danger, perhaps the key to accessing the legal system on their behalf lies in taking seriously *both* the connection they seek *and* the danger they face in that quest. What would legal doctrine and practice look like if it took seriously a mandate to make women safer *in* relationships, instead of offering separation as the *only* remedy for violence against women? This is a complex question, and I offer only a tentative agenda for research and programmatic development. Nevertheless, one thing already seems clear: We cannot afford to accept the terms of debate set by male jurisprudence. Moral theories of self-defense and excuse distract us from political theories of change. We cannot afford to treat our goal as the limited, albeit important one of gaining acquittal for battered women who kill; our goal must be the far more difficult one of stopping the violence. . . . The agenda, at least initially, seems to lead in several directions. . . .

1. CHANGE THE BATTERER.

If women choose, or are compelled, to remain in heterosexual marriages or marriage-like relationships, why should they have to take the batterer as they find him? Evidence indicates that therapy can overcome even long-ingrained patterns of violent behavior—but *only* if the therapy is completed. Many of the programs that require therapy for the batterer make his agreement to *enter* therapy a reason for diversion from the criminal system,[28] rather than making *completion* a condition of probation or parole. "Few would disagree that the concept of diversion, when it works, works well."[29] When it works is when the batterer remains in therapy; when it does not work is when he walks into court agreeing to enter therapy and, on that basis, has the case against him dropped. He then never shows up to another therapy session, and a cycle of battering begins again.

Effective behavioral change on the part of those who make connection dangerous to women might be accomplished through other means as well. Social disapproval—especially from other men—could be effective in some cases. Such disapproval might be mobilized through educational programs designed to rebut the mythology that wives are "appropriate" *targets of violence.*

2. DECREASE THE COST OF RUPTURE TO WOMEN.

As noted earlier, Lenore Walker suggests that the battered woman's threat to leave is the most effective means to stop any particular incident of battering. If the law really cares about stopping the violence against women, then it should use every means possible to make that threat credible. Instead, over and over, it has constructed means to make the threat seem empty.

First of all, the law assumes that the woman must leave the battering relationship. Why should the woman leave? It's her home, too. . . .[30] Evicting a batterer from the home, even if it is his home, is not unthinkable, and would reduce the costs of the rupture both to the battered woman and to the children who are usually additional victims of the violence.

Indeed, the need to care for the couple's children often acts to keep women in violent relationships, at least until they too are threatened with violence. Women have good reason to fear that when they leave they may lose their children, as custody is awarded to fathers in approximately 60% of cases in which custody is contested.[31]

Not only do men typically have access to greater economic resources to provide for the children, but they often know how to manipulate women's fear of losing them. . . .

Battered women usually do work outside the home, but—like all women—they work for significantly less pay than men. Continued legal indifference to comparable worth claims has the indirect effect of keeping women in relationships they would like to leave, but can't afford to. If women cannot afford to leave, they can't make credible threats to stop male violence. Paradoxically, if women are going to be able to maintain community, it may only be through the ability to make that community optional and not mandatory for the women. So long as discontinuing the relationship is costly to women but not to men, women lack the power to make credible threats to leave, and thus lack the power to use the single most effective (and non-violent) weapon in their arsenal.

3. INCREASE THE COSTS OF BATTERING—TO THE BATTERER.

Feminists have made some gains in getting the criminal law to take battering seriously. Police intervene more often; batterers are more likely to be arrested; meaningful sentences, although still characterized as "unusual," are at least not unheard of. But these gains are still too little, and, besides, have been made by increasing separation at the expense of connection. Even recognizing a complete defense for those women who finally turn and kill, while no doubt increasing the perceived costs of battering, does so only via the most extreme form of separation.

Perhaps this trade-off is unavoidable. It does seem that the general failure to date of restraining orders in keeping battering men away from the women who obtain such orders bodes ill for any attempt to use restraining orders to keep men from battering women while sharing the same space. Yet greater legal and social sanctions may discourage some men from engaging in the rupturing activity of battering in the first place, thus eventually leading to increased safe connections.

4. EXPAND THE OPTIONS FOR COMMUNITY.

Currently no state sanctions lesbian marriage. Given the statistics on battering, the legal definition of marriage as a relationship between a man and a woman subjects most women to a 50–50 chance of violence within the *only* type of relationship sanctioned by law. . . . While lesbian partnering does not guarantee the absence of battering, it does significantly reduce the odds. . . .

Similarly, committedly heterosexual women are not equally free to choose between singlehood and marriage. Jennifer Jaff has recently explored the myriad ways in which the legal system disadvantages unmarried people[32] and the concomitant legal pressure to marry. In addition to the social pressure to "couple," the law piles on disadvantages in health care, social security benefits, parenting rights and inheritance. Single women in partnership with each other (whether in dyads or larger communities), or in relation to their children, provide alternative models of community that need not be so expensive compared to legal partnership with a man.

Women who work in shelters for homeless or battered women often report that such women are reluctant to leave the shelter for the single apartments currently presumed to be their ultimate goal. Perhaps we should consider ways to expand the shelter movement from the perspective of providing potential long-term community rather than only short-term emergency housing.

The possibilities of alternative forms of connection are numerous. Why should the law be permitted to pressure women into the most dangerous form of social union? Making alternatives less costly and more available will help at least some women achieve connection without risking their lives and health.

The above suggestions are only the beginning of a search for ways to allow women safe space in order to explore connection. A full research agenda must include evaluation of what is actually available now, as well as what might come to be available if we were committed to a social, political and legal agenda that takes seriously both women's values as women express them *and* women's survival. . . .

Notes

1. Catharine A. MacKinnon, Feminism Unmodified:Discourses on Life and Law 9 (Harvard Univ. Press, 1987).

2. *Id.* at 5.

3. Even the terminology of battering is problematic. Resisting what has been viewed as sexism in the terms "wife battering" or "battered women," some have turned to neutral terminology such as "spousal abuse" or "domestic violence." Both the traditional and the quasi-equalitarian labels seem to me to miss the point. First, wives are battered as members of the class of women; wife battering is therefore gender related in a way that is different from occasional violence against men. Second, as developed later in this essay, treating battering as "the problem" of the person who is battered (whether she is called woman, wife or spouse) obscures the responsibility of the batterer. Why isn't battering considered "the problem" of violent husbands?

4. See, for example, Robin Morgan ed., Sisterhood Is Global 703 (Anchor Press/Doubleday, 1984) (50–70% of women experience battering during marriage). Exact figures are difficult to generate, both because battered women are often reluctant to acknowledge their situation and because serious study of the problem is a very recent phenomenon. "The problem of battered women has only come into the limelight in the past few years, its progression toward public awareness paralleling the growth of the women's movement. Historically, there has never been any public outcry against this brutality." Lenore E. Walker, The Battered Woman ix (Harper & Row, 1979). . . .

5. Tracy Chapman, Behind the Wall, from the album Tracy Chapman (Elektra/Asylum Records, 1988). . . .

6. This account paraphrases the Georgia Supreme Court report of Smith v. State, 247 Ga. 612, 277 S.E.2d 678 (1981). [H]er story is used to try to uncover the multiple meanings women may give to their relationships with violent men.

7. See Jeanne P. Deschner, The Hitting Habit: Anger Control for Battering Couples 6 (The Free Press, 1984) (3 million "battering couples"). Some estimates are much higher. . . .

8. In 1984, for example, approximately 477 husbands of boyfriends were killed by women. Comment, Provoked Reason in Men and Women: Heat-of-Passion Manslaughter and Imperfect Self-Defense, 33 UCLA L. Rev. 1679, 1681 n.10 (1986).

9. See Morgan, Sisterhood Is Global, *supra* note 4, at 704 ("2000–4000 women are beaten to death by husbands each year.").

10. Smith v. State, 277 S.E.2d at 679.

11. *Id.* at 683.

12. *Id.* (citing Ibn-Tamas v. U.S., 407 A.2d 626 (D.C. App. Ct. 1979).

13. *Id.*

14. *Id.*

15. See Susan B. Jordan and Elizabeth M. Schneider, Representations of Women Who Defend Themselves Against Physical or Sexual Assault, 4 Women's Rts. L. Rep.

149 (1978); Elizabeth M. Schneider, Describing and Changing: Women's Self-Defense Work and the Problem of Expert Testimony on Battering, herein, at 311.

16. "Lisa Bianco, an advocate for battered women who had been beaten for years by her former husband, took little comfort in his imprisonment for brutally attacking her two years ago, Instead, she lived in daily fear that he would make good his threats to kill her. Her nightmare came true March 4, officials say, when Alan Matheney got an 8-hour pass from a state prison near Indianapolis. They say his mother drove him to this small town near the Michigan border, where he broke into his former wife's house" and killed her. Isabel Wilkerson, Indianan Uses Prison Furlough to Kill Ex-Wife, N.Y. Times, Mar. 12, 1989, at 14.

17. Smith v. State, 277 S.E.2d at 683 n.3, distinguishing State v. Griffiths, 101 Idaho 163, 610 P.2d 522 (1980).

18. *Id.* (emphasis added).

19. 433 U.S. 321 (1977).

20. Deschner, The Hitting Habit, *supra* note 7, at 23; C. Guberman & M. Wolfe eds., No Safe Place: Violence Against Women and Children 53–54 (Women's Press, 1985).

21. The recent trial of New York attorney Joel Steinberg for the murder of the 6-year-old child he and Hedda Nussbaum had raised offered an unusually public view of a relationship marked by almost constant violence directed against a woman and child. Consider the following exchange between Nussbaum and Steinberg's attorney:

"Are you familiar with the term masochist?" Mr. London asked.

"Someone who likes pain," she replied.

"Isn't it someone who accepts pain?" he tried to correct her.

"No," she said. "It's someone who likes pain."

"Did you like pain?" he asked.

"No, I didn't," she replied.

"Then you must have been accepting of it," he said.

And later in the cross-examination:

"What was Joel's reaction when you told him you didn't like being beaten?" he asked.

"He said he hated himself for doing it," she said. "He said it wasn't him who was doing it. He felt it wasn't within his character."

"You had no anger or rage toward Joel?"

"No."

"Did he ever apologize for the beatings?"

"No," she replied.

"Did you ever ask him to?"

"No, I didn't."

"Why not?"

"Because I was very connected to him, not like someone who hurt me."

Ronald Sullivan, Defense Tries to Portray Nussbaum as a Masochist Who Liked Beatings, N.Y. Times, Dec. 9, 1988, at A18 (emphasis added).

22. Smith v. State, 277 S.E.2d at 680.

23. Margaret Jane Radin, Market-Inalienability, 100 Harv. L. Rev. 1849 (1987).

24. *Id.* at 1921–1925. Richard Wasserstrom explored the problems of transition in his very influential work on affirmative action. Wasserstrom, Racism, Sexism and Preferential Treatment: An Approach to Topics, 24 UCLA L. Rev. 581 (1977). He suggested that "much of the confusion in thinking and arguing about racism, sexism and

affirmative action results from a failure to see that there are three different perspectives within which the topics . . . can most usefully be examined." *Id.* at 583. From the first perspective, that of "social realities," the fundamental questions are about what is; the second ("ideals") concerns how things ought to be in the good society; and the third ("instrumentalities") asks how to move what "is" closer to what "ought" to be. . . . [H]is separation of the three perspectives is extremely useful.

25. Robin West, Jurisprudence and Gender, in D. Weisberg ed., Feminist Legal Theory: Foundations 75, 78–86 (Temple Univ. Press, 1993).

26. Carrie Menkel-Meadow, Portia in a Different Voice: Speculations on a Women's Lawyering Process, 1 Berkeley Women's L.J. 39, 55 (1985).

27. See, for example, Janet Rifkin, Mediation from a Feminist Perspective: Promise and Problems, 2 Law & Ineq. J. 21 (1984).

28. See, for example, Hallye Jordan, Diversion Program for Wife-Beaters Called Ineffective, L.A. Daily Journal, Sept 19, 1988, at 1.

29. *Id.*

30. See, for example, Smith v. State, 277 S.E.2d 678 (Ga. 1981). Even the popular film *Tootsie* (Columbia Picture Industries, Inc., 1982) got this part right in the scene in which Dustin Hoffman (Tootsie) finally decides to write his (her?) own lines:

> Battered woman: "I can't move out, Miss Kimberly, I have no place to go. I don't know what to do." Miss Kimberly (played by Tootsie, played by Dustin Hoffman): " . . . Why should you move out? It's your home too!"

Ultimately, however, Miss Kimberly can only conceive of ending the violence by escalating it in a culturally male way: "You know what I'd do if somebody did this to me? Why, if they came around again, I'd pick up the biggest thing around and I'd just take it like this and [crash of flower pot hitting wall] smash their brains right through the top of their skull before I'd let them beat me up again."

31. Lenore J. Weitzman, The Divorce Revolution 233 (The Free Press, 1985) (based on random samples of court records in Los Angeles County, California).

32. Jennifer Jaff, Wedding Bell Blues: The Position of Unmarried People in American Law, 30 Ariz. L. Rev. 207 (1988).

Legal Images of Battered Women:
Redefining the Issue of Separation

MARTHA R. MAHONEY

. . . [T]HIS ARTICLE proposes that we seek to redefine in both law and popular culture the issue of women's separation from violent relationships.[1] The question "why didn't she leave?" shapes both social and legal inquiry on battering; much of the legal reliance on academic expertise on battered women has developed in order to address this question. At the moment of separation or attempted separation—for many women, the first encounter with the authority of law[2]—the batterer's quest for control often becomes most acutely violent and potentially lethal.[3] Ironically, although the proliferation of shelters and the elaboration of statutory structures facilitating the grant of protective orders vividly demonstrate both socially and legally the dangers attendant on separation, a woman's "failure" to permanently separate from a violent relationship is still widely held to be mysterious and in need of explanation, an indicator of her pathology rather than her batterer's. We have had neither cultural names nor legal doctrines specifically tailored to the particular assault on a woman's body and volition that seeks to block her from leaving, retaliate for her departure, or forcibly end the separation. I propose that we name this attack "separation assault."

. . . As with other assaults on women that were not cognizable until the feminist movement named and explained them,[4] separation assault must be identified before women can recognize our own experience and before we can develop legal rules to deal with this particular sort of violence. . . .

To illustrate the contrast between women's lives and legal and cultural stereotypes, . . . this article offers narratives . . . from the lives of survivors of domestic violence. . . . Seven women's stories have come to me through their own accounts. Five of these have at some time identified themselves as battered women. Three of these women were Stanford Law School students or graduates; another was an undergraduate student at Stanford. One was an acquaintance in a support group. One is black, the rest are white. All but two were mothers when the violence occurred. Though our class backgrounds vary, only one was a highly educated professional before the battering

90 Mich. L. Rev. 1 (1991).

incidents described, but several have acquired academic degrees since the marriages ended. The other women's voices in this paper are drawn from identified published sources.

One of these stories is my own. I do not feel like a "battered woman."[5] Really, I want to say that I am not, since the phrase conjures up an image that fails to describe either my marriage or my sense of myself. It is a difficult claim to make for several reasons: the gap between my self-perceived competence and strength and my own image of battered women, the inevitable attendant loss of my own denial of painful experience, and the certainty that the listener cannot hear such a claim without filtering it through a variety of derogatory stereotypes. . . .

In fact, women often emphasize that they do not fit their own stereotypes of the battered woman. . . .

IV. Power, Control, Autonomy, and Separation

A. Identifying Domination in Violence Against Women

Battering is about domination: "Violence is a way of 'doing power' in a relationship,"[6] an effort by the batterer to control the woman who is the recipient of the violence.[7] . . . A decade ago, Dobash and Dobash placed battering in the context of patriarchy and described it as domination: "The fact that violence against wives is a form of a husband's domination is irrefutable in the light of historical evidence."[8] However, [l]egal literature, in particular, has often ignored the interplay of power and control, domination and subordination in the battering relationship. . . .

To bring women's experience into law and make it more comprehensible to women ourselves, we need litigation strategies aimed at exposing the power and control at the heart of battering. . . . Below, I develop an example of such a strategy, emphasizing the attacks on women's attempts to separate from violent relationships to help expose issues of power and control in both law and culture.

B. "Who Says She Didn't Leave?" Challenging Perceptions of Separation and Autonomy

The "shopworn question"[9] persists in the cases, legal scholarship, and social science literature. It reveals several assumptions about separation: that the right solution is separation, that it is the woman's responsibility to achieve separation, and that she could have separated. The question "why didn't she leave" is actually an objectifying statement that asserts that the woman did not leave. Asking this question often makes actual separations disappear.

If we ask the woman, "What did you do?" the answer very often turns out to be, "I sought help." Edward Gondolf, who studied women's helpseeking behavior, found that women responded to abuse by seeking help from both formal and informal sources.[10] The more apparent it became that the batterer would not change, or the worse the abuse became, the greater diversity the women showed in their efforts to find help. Gondolf concluded that it was the helping professions, rather than battered women, that were afflicted with "helplessness." He described battered women as "survivors" who developed self-transcendence to allow them to go on.

When we ask the woman, "Exactly what did you do in your search for help?" the answer often turns out to be that she left—at least temporarily. In Gondolf's study, more than seventy percent of the women had left home at some time in response to violence, though only fourteen percent had gone to shelters.[11] Of the women Walker studied, about one quarter left temporarily after each battering incident.[12] Walker does not indicate whether the intention of these women as they left was temporary or permanent separation or whether they were in fact uncertain when they left.

Some social scientists have criticized the assumption that the woman has a responsibility to—on her own—successfully accomplish a separation in her family on her first attempt to do so.[13] This assumption ignores the woman's substantial ties to her current family structures. Her initial goal in separating may have been to improve her family structure rather than end it. Participation by the batterer in a counseling program is a very significant factor in predicting a woman will end a separation, since his participation tends to increase her hope for safe return. Therefore, some experts recommend the credible threat to leave or attempt to separate as a measure for women who seek to end the violence against them but wish to preserve their relationships.[14] Finally, the assumption that the woman's first separation should be permanent ignores the real dangers that the man will seek actively—and sometimes violently—to end the separation. . . .

Finally, we ask the woman herself about the key behavior of the violent partner whose behavior actually defines her state as a "battered woman." We say, "What did he do when you left?" At that moment, we will hear the story of the attacks on her autonomy; all we need to do is listen. Often, a woman has left several times before she finally ends a marriage. Or, she may have been restrained from leaving by violent or coercive means: by being held prisoner in her home, by being threatened with custody suits, by having her savings taken away before she could depart. One feminist writer in the field recently wrote without apparent irony,

> [He] always found ways to get her to come back. He would come and tell her how sorry he was and how much he loved her; he would promise never to do it again. And she wanted to believe him. . . . When she wavered and it appeared his pleas and promises might not work, he would threaten to kill her if she refused to come home, threats which his past behavior gave her every reason to take seriously.[15]

There are many aspects to redefining separation: we need to comprehend the related power and control issues common to continuing relationships and to separation, rethink the implicit burden on the woman to leave her home and risk losing her family, and change our perceptions of what it means for her to separate. Finally, we need to reckon with the dangers she faces. The rest of this article discusses the assault on women's attempts to separate. The story of the violent pursuit of the separating woman must become part of the way we understand domestic violence to help eliminate the question "Why didn't she leave?" from our common vocabulary.

C. Strategies for Change and the Redefinition of Separation

How can we bring the issues of power and control into the courtroom? Can we explain how differently men and women may perceive control?

> I once told a man in a bar that if I was attacked by a man and could somehow fight him off enough to run away, I would consider that I had won the encounter—that I had beaten him. The man said, "No, no, you had to run away, therefore you lost." I said, "No, I was safe, I was unviolated, and therefore I won, I preserved myself." That's what we have to deal with. . . .

This reflection on the ways men and women perceive control has important implications for the concept of separation assault. The woman defines successful flight from attack as a victory. The man insists that this is not victory but defeat. The persistent accounts of the difficulty women encounter on separation, especially condemnation from their families and employers, suggest society's perceptions track men's interpretations: leaving a violent relationship is widely perceived as an admission of defeat rather than victory. The ways in which separation is similar to the escape from impliedly sexual assault discussed in the quotation above are generally not cognizable at all in law or social discourse. The dangers women face in the effort to separate make separation a victory. These dangers need a name.

Law assumes—pretends—the autonomy of women. Every legal case that discusses the question "why didn't she leave?" implies that the woman could have left. We need to challenge the coercion of women's choices, reveal the complexity of women's experience and struggle, and recast the entire discussion of separation in terms of the batterer's violent attempts at control.

Although it is still focused on successful and final separation as the key event, the recently developed term "postseparation woman abuse" begins to grapple with the problem of revealing the issue of power and control in women's experience of violence.[16] At least half of women who leave their abusers are followed and harassed or further attacked by them.[17] In one study of interspousal homicide, more than half of the men who killed their spouses did so when the partners were separated; in contrast, less than ten percent of women who killed were separated at the time.[18] Power and control are crucial here in several ways. Men who kill their wives describe their feeling of loss of control over the woman as a primary factor; most frequently, the man expresses the fear that the woman was about to abandon him, though in fact this fear may have been unfounded.[19] The fact that marital separation increases the instigation to violence shows that these attacks are aimed at preventing or punishing the woman's autonomy. They are major—often deadly—power moves.

However, the term "postseparation woman abuse" fails to capture the many cases where violence occurs in response to the decision itself: the essential attack is on the woman's autonomy. Barbara Hart notes that "[t]he *decision* by a battered woman to leave is often met with escalated violence by the batterer."[20] When the decision, rather than actual separation, triggers the attack, the circumstances of the violence may not reveal the assault on separation: the couple may still have been living together, and the attack may have taken place inside their mutual home—yet the attack may have been a direct response to her assertion of the will to separate or her first physical moves toward separation.

Defining Separation Assault

To expose the struggle for control, we should recognize the assault on the woman's separation as a specific type of attack that occurs at or after the moment she decides on a separation or begins to prepare for one. I propose that we call it "separation assault." The varied violent and coercive moves in the process of separation assault can be termed "separation attacks."

Separation assault is the attack on the woman's body and volition in which her partner seeks to prevent her from leaving, retaliate for the separation, or force her to return. It aims at overbearing her will as to where and with whom she will live, and coercing her in order to enforce connection in a relationship. It is an attempt to gain, retain, or regain power in a relationship, or to punish the woman for ending the relationship. It often takes place over time.

Attacks on separation pervaded the stories of the women who spoke with me. The announcement of intent to separate may be fraught with grave danger:

> He was on strike for the second time in a year. I was pregnant with the second baby in a row. There was absolutely no money. Every day, he yelled at me for a long time—an hour, two hours—about how awful I was. . . . I remember how desperate I felt and how much I needed it to stop.
>
> [One day, when he seemed receptive, she told him it had to stop.] He wouldn't listen. *I said I couldn't live like that anymore and would leave if he didn't stop. He kept saying I couldn't leave because we didn't have enough money to support two households. I said that only his failure to listen could make me leave—I couldn't live like that anymore. . . .*
>
> Suddenly he lost his temper. . . . He stormed upstairs, and I heard him pushing around in the closet. I thought, "That's funny. It sounds like he's getting the gun." And I didn't sit down or move—I stood in the middle of the living room floor and waited. He came down the stairs shouting and I saw that he really did have the shotgun. I knew it was fully loaded. I remember making the conscious decision that this was different than waiting through other outbursts, and that any argument would be deadly.
>
> I turned around and ran out the front door screaming that I was pregnant and ran up the landlady's front steps. I was going to call the police. But I realized that I had heard the baby crying upstairs. All the noise had wakened her from her nap.

I couldn't believe he would shoot his child, but I didn't know why he'd gotten the gun, how well he actually knew what he was doing . . . how irritating her crying might be. I turned around and went back into the house. I could hear him putting the gun away in the closet. We got to the baby at the same moment.

I dressed her, put on my own clothes, and left. I had $1.60 and no more money coming for several days. I took the better car. I drove away without knowing where I was going to go. (Emphasis added.)

Although women's stories recount many attacks triggered by separation, the nature of the attack *on separation itself* generally goes unrecognized. Similarly, women describe coercive violence escalating after separation—violence clearly aimed at denying their autonomy—in terms that show they may internalize self-blame rather than clearly identifying the man's attempt at control. . . .

Women describe protracted and inventive attacks on their moves to separate:

Well, leaving took months. When I first left, I really didn't even know I was leaving the marriage. I was just going to California to get the car that he had left there. But being on my own again, and away from him, I began to regain some of my self-confidence, and I liked it. And people liked me.

But then he came out to California to reclaim me. And totally humiliated me in front of my friends. ["Humiliation" including forcing her to have sex—essentially committing marital rape—in the back of a Volkswagen van while two other men were in the vehicle.] I was scared of him, I was still scared of his violence. As strong as I had been when he wasn't around, as soon as he came around, I would fall back into the baby talk, I would fall back into the patterns.

Then we got back to Michigan, and I left again and went to stay with my friends. I was in Ann Arbor, and I had a fever. And he came to check on me. . . . He got my heirloom ring off my finger that night. The ring that all my life I felt separated me from poor white trash. The ring that my great-great-grandmother brought over from Germany when she fled the failed revolution of 1848. I never saw that ring again. He threatened to burn down the house I was staying in, but he was satisfied when I gave him the ring because he knew I would come back for it.

I went back again [because he promised to return the ring]. I never got it. And then when it was time for my friends to leave town, they came to our house in Detroit, en masse, and said it was time to go. And I picked up, and I walked out. "Well, it's time to go, we're leaving." And I went.

Some of these attacks on separation will go unnoticed until we begin identifying them specifically:

I felt guilty, so I went back. That lasted a month, until Valentine's Day. . . . Finally, on Valentine's Day, he was throwing things. He was throwing glass—I was barefoot—it was totally absurd. I was being held prisoner in my bed by glass!

I picked the kids up, scrunched my feet so they were under the glass, dragged my feet over the floor so they weren't getting cut too much, and made it out of the house.

One of the best-known battered women in America is Francine Hughes, whose story was told in [the film] *The Burning Bed.* The trial and movie brought the atrocities against her to public attention, but there was little cultural attention to the lessons of her search for autonomy:

> Hughes' entire marriage—and her life after divorce—was a search for the exit. [Family], in-laws, friends, social services, police, sheriff's office, county prosecutor—she tried them all. And even when Mickey Hughes came within moments of choking her to death or cutting her throat, no one helped.[21]

We already recognize the danger of the attack on separation pragmatically and intuitively. This is a major reason for the existence of shelters, which protect women against attacks while giving them a place to live. It is the main reason that shelter numbers and addresses are not listed in telephone directories. It is the main reason women seek protective orders. It fills the pages of our newspapers with accounts of attacks on women by their separated husbands. Although we see this attack everywhere, we cannot analyze it until it has a name.

NAMING SEPARATION ASSAULT AND UNDERSTANDING BATTERING

Naming women's experience is an important component of feminist struggle for social and legal change. Naming separation assault has the potential to change consciousness in a manner comparable to the concept of "date rape." "Date rape" and "separation assault" name phenomena women know from our own experience, but which remain invisible without names. These terms do more, however, than merely identify hitherto unnamed experience. Each term identifies one aspect of a common attack on women in a way that illuminates the whole picture. Date rape is not all rape; separation assault is not the whole story of battering. Yet in each case, the act of identifying and describing the formerly invisible part transforms our understanding of the formerly misunderstood whole. . . .

Naming and recognizing separation assault will make women's experience more comprehensible to ourselves as well as to the legal system: We know it when we hear it. Attacks on our autonomy are one point at which women can—without stereotyping or invoking the likelihood of denial—locate our own experiences and those of our sisters and friends on a continuum of control attempts that includes those extremes of violence that become known through the sensational cases covered by the press. Women may find the current terminology of battering stigmatizing or alienating, yet be willing to admit that they have experienced inappropriate control attempts by their partners, including assaults on their capacity to separate from "bad" marriages. Exposing control attempts reveals the woman's struggle, rather than defining her according to the behavior of her assailant.

The name "separation assault" also helps women understand our own long-term reactions to violence or to the threats accompanying the end of relationships. Shelters and counseling provide short-term separation assistance, but the impact of separation assault goes on: Fear of an ex-husband becomes part of a woman's life.

> The first year I was at Stanford, I saw *The Burning Bed*. I couldn't *not* watch it, and I couldn't stop watching. I was so scared when it finished. I started calling my ex-husband. It was the middle of the night there. I kept calling him frantically for over an hour. He wasn't home. I became convinced he was on his way there with a gun on a plane. I was sure he would kill me.
>
> I locked the door and got in bed with the kids and shook all night, waiting for him. It was two and a half years later. I was two thousand miles away.

This woman had withstood physical attacks before and after separation, as well as poverty, the indignities inflicted by welfare workers, and the threat of a custody suit. . . . Naming the assault on separation may begin to pull loose the threads of intimidation from the fabric of feminine wisdom, and to legitimate women's perception of danger while directing our attention toward the resources and support we will need, rather than to our own deficiencies or inadequacies.

Popularizing the concept of separation assault is not without hidden dangers, however. Separation assault is effective in part because, rather than *directly* confronting existing stereotypes of battered women, it provides a partial explanation of women's actions that redirects attention toward the batterer. It works in part through its very resonance with existing stereotypes that ask why the woman didn't leave. Therefore, this concept alone cannot remake our understanding of domestic violence; by itself, separation assault becomes merely another explanation of the woman's apparent "failure" to separate—at worst, subtle reinforcement of existing stereotypes. Without further cultural redefinition of battering as a process of power and control, naming separation assault may not deeply challenge oppressive ideology regarding women and domestic violence. However, on a broader scale, separation assault should help the larger goal of shifting cultural perception because it helps change "objective" judgment—that is, shared cultural perceptions and wisdom—about what is normal in relationships. [Below] I explain how the redefinition of separation described above can help change legal doctrine . . . by shifting both cultural expectation and judicial inquiry.

V. The Uses of a Name: Separation Assault and Legal Doctrine

Naming separation assault is an attempt to use a social definition, a cultural concept, to resolve doctrinal problems in law. It should not articulate a new test for women's behavior ("did this woman in fact leave and how shall we judge the energy with which she attempted separation?") but rather promote a new understanding of violence against women. As it intervenes in cultural consciousness, separation assault allows legal actors (including attorneys, prosecutors, judges, jurors, social workers, and legal scholars) to reconceive many legal questions that depend on an understanding of women's lives and experiences. Our understanding of "objective" reasonableness depends on our cultural intuitions about normal experience and normal response. By reflecting a consciousness of power and control, and by emphasizing the dangers attendant on separation, separation assault helps make women's experience comprehensible in law.

In the following sections, I show how separation assault can be identified in cases in many areas of legal doctrine, and then explain how understanding separation assault can help resolve troubled areas in law. . . .

A. Recognizing Separation Assault in the Cases: The Problem of the Dead Woman's Voice

. . . There is a two-layered problem in seeing through the criminal cases involving abuse of women. First, these cases appear in various doctrinal guises, and few explicitly acknowledge that they concern domestic violence at all. Second, on closer examination, many of the "wife-murder" cases turn out to be "ex-wife murder," the most extreme violence turned against women at separation. Many of the women killed by their husbands are killed after they have separated.[22] Ironically, since those women are not alive to tell their stories, their voices disappear into the narrative voices of the courts, where the women are not usually identified as battered:

> On a day in early September in 1977, the petitioner and his wife of 28 years had a heated argument in their home. During the course of this altercation, the petitioner, who had consumed several cans of beer, threatened his wife with a knife and damaged some of her clothing. At this point, the petitioner's wife declared that she was going to leave him, and departed to stay with relatives. [This was not the first time that he and his wife had been separated as a result of his violent behavior.] That afternoon she went to a Justice of the Peace and secured a warrant charging the petitioner with aggravated assault. A few days later, while still living away from home, she filed suit for divorce. [A court hearing date was set and several efforts to persuade the wife to return home were rebuffed.] At some point during this period, his wife moved in with her mother. [Several angry phone calls were exchanged, while she refused to reconcile.]
>
> At this juncture, the petitioner got out his shotgun and walked with it down the hill from his home to the trailer where his mother-in-law lived. Peering through a window, he observed his wife, his mother-in-law, and his 11-year-old daughter playing a card game. He pointed the shotgun at his wife through the window and pulled the trigger. The charge from the gun struck his wife in the forehead and killed her instantly. He proceeded into the trailer, striking and injuring his fleeing daughter with the barrel of the gun. He then fired the gun at his mother-in-law, striking her in the head and killing her instantly.[23]

Godfrey v. Georgia [above] presents an almost perfect picture of the dangers for women at separation: Mrs. Godfrey had resolutely separated from her husband and energetically sought the protection of the law. However, her story does not enter the criminal law casebook as a domestic violence case. Rather, *Godfrey* is a death penalty case presenting the issue of whether this murder was unambiguously "outrageously or wantonly vile, horrible or inhuman," or whether the case revealed ambiguity and vagueness in the death penalty statute. The Supreme Court essentially found Mrs. Godfrey's death to be quite an ordinary murder. I believe the majority was correct—this was an ordinary murder—but the facts were even more ordinary than the majority realized.

Mary McNeill has shown that several torts cases on duty are actually domestic violence cases in disguise.[24] However, once the domestic violence is perceived, separation assault appears to be a further hidden issue in at least one of the cases. In Jablonski by Pahls v. United States,[25] Melinda Kimball had repeatedly approached the psychologists who examined the man she lived with, telling his doctors that she was afraid of him. They failed to commit him or to seek his medical records, which would have revealed that he had ten years earlier been diagnosed as schizophrenic and had then had homicidal ideas about his wife. One doctor told Kimball that she should avoid Jablonski if she heard him. Kimball left after a priest also urged her to separate from Jablonski. She was murdered when she returned to the apartment to pick up some baby diapers. Since there is no record of any attempt to kill her before she left, separation appears to be at least a precipitating factor in Kimball's death.

In Garcia v. Superior Court,[26] Grace Morales was killed by Napoleon Johnson, Jr., the man from whom she had recently separated. According to the complaint, Johnson's parole officer was aware that Johnson had killed his first wife after she left him. Although he was notified Johnson had threatened to kill Morales and that Morales was filing a temporary restraining order, the parole officer advised Morales that Johnson would not come looking for her. Johnson kidnapped Morales and killed her; her children sued. The court distinguished the parole officer's "negligent representations" from a failure to warn for which the officer might have been liable under Tarasoff v. Regents of the University of California,[27] and held that the plaintiffs must allege that Morales reasonably relied on the parole officer's advice.

The California case of People v. Berry,[28] doctrinally significant for its holding on cooling off periods when killers claim provocation by their victims, also concerns a hidden separation assault. The only account of the marriage is the one Berry gave the police and at trial. According to Berry's story, his wife, Rachel Pessah, had gone to Israel within days of their marriage; on her return, she taunted him about her love for another man and her plans to leave Berry. After repeated arguments and threats or attempts to separate, he tried to strangle her. He called a cab to take her to a hospital, and she later filed a police report that resulted in a warrant for his arrest. He told her he was leaving their home and going to stay with a friend. Two days later, he returned to the apartment and waited overnight. She returned the next day and said she supposed he had come to kill her. He was indecisive, but said he had. She screamed. He strangled her. . . .

B. Recognizing the Danger to Women at Separation

Recognizing the assault on separation can help disentangle a number of complex legal issues in cases in which women have been killed or harmed. In some areas of substantive law, identifying separation assault will change the questions posed by the court in its decisionmaking process. In other doctrinal areas, the shift in time frame made possible by highlighting the assault on separation can change judicial comprehension of the assault on the woman or of the probability that more assaults may occur. Separation assault may also, as in contested custody actions, help reveal underlying motivations in the legal action itself.

RESTRAINING ORDERS

In some jurisdictions, when women seek orders of protection against violent men, courts routinely grant mutual orders of protection rather than orders specifically protecting the women. Mutual orders of protection direct each party not to assault, endanger, or threaten the other. If mutual orders are violated, police officers believe they must either arrest both parties or do nothing. The New York Task Force on Women in the Courts concluded that a woman with a mutual order of protection is in a worse position than a woman with no order at all, since the mutual order makes her look equally violent in the eyes of the courts, and the husband may not be held responsible if there is another violent incident. Also, it may be harder for her to obtain a more restrictive order if the violence recurs.[29] The Task Force concluded that this was particularly dangerous if the mutual order was granted when the woman had requested protection for herself at the same time she filed an action to end the marriage—an especially dangerous period.[30] Even in jurisdictions that do not routinely grant mutual orders, battering men may make cross-accusations of violence against battered women. While many battered women do fight back against their husbands, their violence is largely defensive and less severe than the men's violence—yet since it is also described as "violence," these allegations can prove troubling and confusing to judges.

If we understood better the particular attacks women face at separation, courts could sort both cross-accusations of violence and requests for mutual orders of protection by examining the nature of current threats and the history of violence in relation to the issue of separation. The question then becomes: "Which of these people needs her [or his] capacity to separate protected?" Answering this question will help sort the dangers and should result in the grant of appropriate protective orders.

DUTY TO WARN

Recognizing the common occurrence of separation assault may also clarify professionals' duty to warn potential victims. For example, the *Jablonski* court upheld the district court's finding that the psychiatrists committed malpractice in failing to get Jablonski's records and failing to warn Kimball of his potential for violence.[31] Applying the concept of separation assault does not disturb this holding. Her foreseeability as a victim would be even clearer. However, the clergyman and doctors who advised Kimball to leave Jablonski might also have had a duty to warn her about extra care to be exercised in separating from a homicidal man, as well as a duty to warn her of his dangerousness.

In Garcia v. Superior Court,[32] Johnson's murder of his first wife was a separation assault of exactly the type that Johnson had threatened against Morales. The parole officer misrepresented Johnson's danger to Morales with respect to the very issue of measures regarding separation. Although the parole officer was legally barred from telling anyone the exact crime for which Johnson had previously been imprisoned, the court fails to reckon with the implications of the outright falsehood embodied in the parole officer's statement that Johnson's prior conviction was not for anything that endangered Morales' children.

A telling quote in the *Garcia* dissent shows that judges may inappropriately assume that separation assaults will inevitably culminate in murder: the court below had concluded "it [was] highly speculative to assume that [Morales] could have accomplished any improvement in her security. The frightening reality is that for one in Morales's position there is frequently nothing she can do to protect herself."[33] When courts rely on their own intuitions to state "truths" regarding violence against women, the dangers of cultural stereotyping are severe. A sense of the dangers of separation should have led the court to emphasize the need not to mislead Morales as to her safety and to recognize the implications of consciously identifying the assault on separation.

CUSTODY DETERMINATIONS: UNDERSTANDING DOMINANCE AND TIME-FRAMING ASSAULT

The concept of separation assault provides insight into the difficult bargains women strike during custody determinations. Women may accept mutual orders of protection, rather than orders that specifically protect them against their batterers, in exchange for the husband's agreement not to contest custody. Courts often award joint custody to batterers, and some courts that do not perceive violence against the mother as an aspect of the custody determination may even award them sole custody.[34] The problem is exacerbated for battered women by the professional analyses of the social workers in whom the court vests the power to evaluate women, and by the possibility that the judge will share a stereotypical, stigmatizing image of battered women.

Separation assault provides a link between past violence and current legal disputes by illuminating the custody action as part of an ongoing attempt, through physical violence and legal manipulation, to force the woman to make concessions or return to the violent partner. It reveals the potential for continuing danger from a batterer who may not have struck out physically in the recent past. Threats against the woman's separation attempts may reveal that the "domestic" violence has outlasted the marriage. Recognizing separation assault can therefore help judges understand the relevance of past violence and threats, and the relevance of the nature of present attacks, to custody cases. Also, when there is evidence of violent separation assault, a judge could give more intense scrutiny to the motives behind custody disputes and reconsider the appropriateness of joint custody awards or liberal visitation decrees. This would help diminish "legal separation assault" in custody cases. Finally, by remaking the cultural concept of separation, we may hope to affect positively the evaluation of women by the social workers in whom the legal system places so much power.

JUDGING THE WIFE-KILLER: TIME-FRAMING, PROVOCATION, AND
THE NATURE OF THE ASSAULT

In People v. Berry,[35] the defendant's arguments for a jury instruction on provocation depended entirely upon his statements that his wife had taunted him sexually and provoked her own murder. In fact, he did not kill her when she taunted him, but when she left him. Recognizing separation assault expands the relevant time frame to show his behavior was consistent with numerous prior assaults that seem at least as responsive to her departure as to sexual provocation. He had violently assaulted his first wife as well. *Berry* is cited for its holding that twenty hours of waiting in the apartment—some days after his wife's last "provocative" conduct—was not as a matter of law too long a period to permit an instruction on provocation. The court might have viewed the case differently had the assault on separation been as cognizable as his response to her alleged sexual taunts: it is difficult to find "heat-of-passion" in a repeatedly attempted assault carried out over a period of time.

A short time frame favors men in these cases, as it does in many types of cases, by removing violence from a context of power and struggle. Prior attacks on the woman's attempts to separate may essentially be rehearsals for the final killing.[36] Alternatively, the long-term assault on her separation may be perceived as one ongoing attack. If only the final, deadly assault is cognizable, the nature of the assault as an attack on separation, rather than on the woman's sexual provocation, may remain disguised. Separation assault can therefore change the time frame within which the man's mental state is to be evaluated by changing the perception of the ways in which the woman's autonomy is under attack.

C. Live Women and Dead Men: The Self-Defense Cases

The self-defense cases, which often have an extraordinarily high level of violence against women, have exercised a powerful influence on the literature on battering. Expert testimony on battered woman syndrome and learned helplessness was first introduced to explain the woman's actions and mental state in these cases. The idea that the woman should have left the relationship, and especially the idea that she failed to leave, shapes the courts' analyses of many aspects of self-defense cases, including the reasonableness of the woman's perceptions and reactions, the imminence of the threat of death or great bodily harm, and her duty to retreat from the confrontation. In this section I . . . illustrate the relevance of the concept of separation assault to the issues of imminent danger and the reasonableness of the woman's perception that self-defense is necessary. . . .

QUESTIONS OF TIMING, CAPTIVITY, AND "OBJECTIVE" PERCEPTION

The concept of "separation assault" brings the ghosts of dead women—women slain by their abusers—into court to stand beside the woman accused of killing an abusive spouse. The facts behind many. . . . self-defense cases reveal that the woman's separation has been repeatedly and successfully attacked before she finally kills her abuser.[37] With its implicit reminder of women killed during separation attacks, the concept of separation assault makes sense of the woman's fear of death and her compliance in the face of the violence that ended her previous separations. Further, by describing an assault that by its nature takes place over time, the concept of separation assault extends the time frame weighed by the court and expands the relevance of past attacks on the woman. Finally, of crucial importance in women's self-defense claims, this reconceptualization of the assault on the woman helps clarify the existence of imminent danger of death or great bodily harm.

Imminence has proved crucial in cases involving the death of sleeping husbands. Two states have recently held that women who shot sleeping husbands were not entitled to jury instructions on self-defense because the woman faced no imminent danger of death or grave bodily harm.[38] This meaning of imminent harm is not universal. "Imminent" is often distinguished from "immediate," and courts and scholars have criticized decisions that confuse the two.[39] The Model Penal Code does not require that the danger actually be immediate: rather, the actor must believe that the defensive action is immediately necessary and that the force against which she defends will be used on the present occasion, "but he [sic] need not apprehend that it will be immediately used."[40] Some states have overturned jury instructions that required that the attack on the woman pose an "immediate" danger of death or great bodily harm, and have upheld statutory standards that require only that the harm be "imminent," a term that broadens the context to include more of the facts and circumstances of the woman's experience in the relationship.[41] Even when a statute required "immediate danger," one court has required an overall consideration of the woman's circumstances and described as "imminent," rather than immediate, the threat necessary to justify the use of deadly force.[42] Therefore, the recent decisions construing imminence as virtually equivalent to immediacy place significant limits on the ability of women to raise claims that they acted in self-defense.

State v. Stewart[43] is the latest in a line of Kansas cases to grapple with the meaning of "imminent" and the relevant context for evaluating the woman's action. *Stewart* marks a return to a requirement of immediacy despite a factual background that strongly suggested an expanded contextual approach was relevant. Peggy Stewart married Mike Stewart in 1974. She had two young daughters, Carla and Laura, from previous marriages. Mike was abusive from the beginning. Peggy soon developed severe psychological problems and was treated for schizophrenia. Mike tampered with her medication, forcing her to take too much at times and to do without her medication at other times. Mike severely abused Peggy's daughter Carla. When he ordered Peggy to kill and bury Carla, Peggy filed for divorce, but the case does not indicate that she followed through with the divorce action. When Carla was twelve years old, Mike threw her out of the house with "no coat, no money, and no place to go." He forbade Peggy to have any contact with Carla. Laura left home as soon as she could.

Both the majority and dissenting opinions in *Stewart* chronicle an extraordinarily violent and abusive marriage in which Peggy's life was repeatedly threatened. Mike shot Peggy's cats and then held the gun to Peggy's head, threatening to shoot; another time, he threatened her with a loaded shotgun. She told her friends she believed he would kill her one day. Finally, Peggy ran away to Laura's house in another state. Peggy was suicidal, and Laura had her admitted to a mental hospital, where she was diagnosed as having reacted to an overdose of her medication. Though Peggy told a nurse that she felt like she wanted to shoot Mike, the nurse noted that Peggy's main emotion seemed to be hopelessness. Mike telephoned the hospital to say he was coming to get her, and she agreed to leave with him. At trial, she testified that she decided to go with him because the hospital did not provide the medical help she needed.

Mike drove Peggy back to Kansas. He told her that "if she ever ran away again, he would kill her." He "forced Peggy into the house and forced her to have oral sex several times" with such force that the inside of her mouth was bruised—that is, he raped her repeatedly—while telling her how much he preferred other women. She discovered bullets and a loaded gun, which frightened her because he had promised to keep his guns unloaded. She hid the gun. Mike made repeated remarks indicating that "she would not be there long, and could not take her things where she was going," which led her to think that he meant she would soon be dead. He ceased the abuse for a brief period while his parents came over to visit, then forced her to perform oral sex again and demanded that she come to bed with him. As he slept, she heard voices telling her "kill or be killed." Peggy got the gun she had found and hidden earlier, and she shot Mike as he slept.

The Kansas Supreme Court held Peggy was not entitled to a jury instruction on self-defense, since she was in no imminent danger when she shot Mike. "Under such circumstances, a battered woman cannot reasonably fear imminent life-threatening danger from her sleeping spouse."[44] The court distinguished three of its prior cases in which abused women had killed violent husbands. In State v. Hundley,[45] State v. Osbey,[46] and State v. Hodges,[47] the Kansas Supreme Court had held that the statutory requirement of imminence permitted consideration of the history and gradual build-up of violence within a relationship as well as the immediate acts of the batterer. Although none of these had directly confronted the question of the propriety of giving a self-defense instruction, they had rejected the use of the term "immediate" in explaining the imminence standard. The *Stewart* court did not directly overrule its prior holdings but distinguished the previous imminence cases as "involv[ing] a threat of death to the wife and a violent confrontation between husband and wife, contemporaneous with the shooting."[48] As the *Stewart* dissent pointed out, however, this holding effectively replaced the state's prior definition of "imminent" with an immediacy standard.

In holding that there was no "imminent" threat to Peggy, the majority ignored the imprisoning effect of Mike's bringing her back from another state after her effort to separate and his threat to kill her if she left again. In contrast, the dissent emphasized Mike's threat to kill Peggy if she separated from him again. The concept of an assault on separation continued over time may help courts appreciate the crucial distinction between imminence and immediacy in self-defense cases such as *Stewart*.

Separation assault can help reveal captivity. In *Hundley*, the Kansas Supreme Court drew an analogy between battered women and hostages or prisoners of war.[49] The *Stew-*

art dissent repeated this analogy and argued the *Stewart* holding would preclude finding imminence in "a hostage situation where the armed guard inadvertently drops off to sleep and the hostage grabs his gun and shoots him."[50] This could be a persuasive analogy: If a hostage were told, "you will be killed in three days," the danger would still appear imminent even if not immediate.[51] The question of imminence therefore appears to be affected by an assessment of the nature and degree of the hostage's captivity; the persuasive power of the hostage analogy depends on the recognition that the woman in an abusive relationship is not free to leave. At issue is our understanding of the woman's functional autonomy. The key difference between the analysis of the majority and dissent in *Stewart* is how seriously each takes the constraints Mike imposed on Peggy's capacity to separate.

Had the *Stewart* majority been able to perceive Mike's successful assault on Peggy's separation, they could have found a common thread of separation assault linking *Stewart* with *Hundley, Osbey,* and *Hodges.* In *Hundley,* the wife shot her husband as he attacked her in the motel room to which she had moved after leaving him. In *Osbey,* the wife had insisted on a separation after a history of substantial abuse. The husband was in the process of moving out when he changed his mind, telling a friend he had put too much time into his wife's house and that "it would be either [him] or her." He had [previously] threatened her with a gun. She shot him when she thought he reached for a weapon as he attempted to return some of his belongings to the apartment. In *Hodges,* the wife had continually left her husband early in their marriage only to have him pursue her and brutally fetch her back. On one such occasion

> [H]e took her to a wooded location where he beat her, broke her jaw, and said she was either going to live with him or she wasn't going to live. He left her there unconscious, but eventually returned, took her to the hospital, and told her to tell the hospital staff she fell down. She returned home with him because he had her children.[52]

She finally succeeded in divorcing him but reunited thirteen years later because he promised he had changed. When the beatings did not stop, she left again; however, when he again brought her back, she gave up trying to leave him. He had also threatened her family if they ever helped her leave him. She shot him as he engaged in yet another bout of violence.

The concept of separation assault thus bridges the difference between cases like *Stewart* that involve sleeping husbands and those like *Hundley, Osbey,* and *Hodges* that involve waking husbands. In *Hodges,* expert testimony on battered women was allowed in part to "help dispel the ordinary layperson's perception that a woman in a battering relationship is free to leave at any time."[53] This same "perception" clearly underlies the majority opinion in *Stewart,* which, in deciding that Peggy was not in imminent danger, specifically noted that Peggy had access to the car keys—without reviewing the threat to her life if she used them to escape.

Finally, the *Stewart* opinion emphasized a requirement of objective reasonableness in the battered woman's self-defense claims. In *Hodges,* Kansas had held that "the jury must determine, from the viewpoint of the defendant's mental state, whether defendant's belief in the need to defend herself was reasonable."[54] *Stewart* overruled *Hodges* on this point, holding that after determining whether the defendant subjectively sincerely and honestly believed it necessary to kill in self-defense, "We then use an objective standard to determine whether defendant's belief was reasonable—specifically, whether a reasonable person in defendant's circumstances would have perceived self-defense as necessary."[55] The objective standard to be applied is how a "reasonably prudent battered wife" would have perceived the aggressor's demeanor.[56] Separation assault is important here as well. The cultural redefinition of the dangers of separation goes beyond the individual woman's "subjective" perception of danger; it does not merely bolster her argument that under her particular, individual circumstances, her subjective perceptions (though unreasonable for a "normal person") persuaded her of danger. Rather, separation assault helps shift what judges and jurors "objectively" know as truth: To the extent that objective standards embody in law the shared cultural norms of society, separation assault helps restructure those norms to allow "objective" perception itself to track more closely the painfully accrued understanding of women who have lived with violent partners.

A recent North Carolina self-defense case involving a sleeping husband exemplifies perhaps even more dramatically than *Stewart* the urgent need for a better judicial understanding of separation assault. In State v. Norman,[57] a North Carolina court of appeals held that a woman who had shot her sleeping husband was entitled to a jury instruction on perfect self-defense. The North Carolina Supreme Court reversed,[58] holding that there was no imminent danger to the wife. Judy Norman had been subjected to vicious torture and degradation over a period of twenty years. Her husband, John Thomas (J. T.) Norman, had beaten her, thrown objects at her, put out cigarettes on her skin, and broken glass on her face. He forced her to prostitute herself daily to support him and then ridiculed her to family and friends. He called her a "dog," forced her to bark like a dog, eat pet food out of pet dishes, and sleep on the floor. He deprived her of food for days at a time and had "often stated both to defendant and others that he would kill [her] . . . [and] threatened to cut her heart out." She left him several times, but each time he found her, took her home, and beat her.

The thirty-six hours before Judy Norman shot her husband were marked by incredible violence, which escalated after her husband was arrested for drunken driving. He beat her almost continuously, refused to eat food that her hands had touched, refused to let her eat for a period of days, threatened to cut off her breast and "shove it up her rear end," and put out a cigarette on her chest.

On the first evening after the drunken driving arrest, Judy called the police for help. An officer told her they could only help if she filed a complaint ("[took] out a warrant on her husband"). She replied that "if she did so [her husband] would kill her." An hour later, she swallowed a bottle of "nerve" pills, and her family called for help. Her husband told the paramedics to let her die and repeatedly obstructed their attempts to save her. The police did not arrest him for attempting to block her rescue: "When he refused to respond to the officer's warning that if he continued to hinder the attendants, he would be arrested, the officer was compelled to chase him back into the house." At the hospital, Judy Norman spoke to a therapist and discussed filing charges against her husband and having him committed for treatment. She seemed depressed and said she should kill him for what he had done to her. She stayed at her grandmother's that night.

The next day, she went to the mental health center to discuss charges and the possibility of her husband's commitment and "confronted [him] with that possibility." Her husband told her that if he saw them coming to take him away, he would cut her throat before he could be committed. She went to apply for welfare benefits, but her husband followed her there, interrupted her interview, and forced her to return home with him. He continued to beat her and abuse her physically and would not permit her to eat or feed her children. He later lay down to take a nap, but made her lie on the concrete floor next to the bed, because "dogs" couldn't lie on beds. While he slept, her infant grandchild began to cry. She took the baby to her mother's house for fear it would awaken him. Judy's mother had placed a gun in her purse from fear of Judy's husband. At her mother's house, Judy asked for an aspirin, found the gun, returned home, and shot him.

The North Carolina Supreme Court held that all of the evidence tended to show that the defendant had ample time and opportunity to resort to other means of preventing further abuse by her husband. There was no action underway by the decedent from which the jury could have found that the defendant had reasonable grounds to believe either that a felonious assault was imminent or that it might result in her death or great bodily injury. Additionally, no such action by the decedent had been underway immediately prior to his falling asleep.

It is hard to know where to begin to discuss *Norman*. In the face of all the grave danger and murderous violence the opinion overlooks, it seems presumptuous to claim that the concept of separation assault could have remade the *Norman* holding. Yet the idea that Judy Norman was not captive is crucial to the majority's finding that she faced no imminent threat. The dissent is clearly groping for just such a concept in its attempt to describe what had happened to her. The dissent first quotes a psychologist, an expert witness, who compared Judy Norman to a brainwashed prisoner of war and described her as "a woman incarcerated by abuse, by fear, and by her conviction that her husband was invincible and inescapable . . .":[59]

> Mrs. Norman didn't leave because she believed, fully believed that escape was totally impossible. There was no place to go. . . . [S]he had left before; he had come and gotten her. She had gone to the Department of Social Services. He had come and gotten her. The law, she believed the law could not protect her, no one could protect her, and I must admit, looking over the records, that there was nothing done that would contradict that belief.[60]

The concept of separation assault addresses a major problem with sleeping husband cases like *Norman* and *Stewart*. These cases look to courts like executions; judges express concern over the specter of homicidal self-help for battered wives.[61] Separation assault replaces this image—as the dissenting judges in *Stewart* urged—with the paradigm of hostages resisting their captors. We believe the danger to a hostage is imminent both because the force used to hold them there is apparent and because our cultural knowledge includes the memory of the many hostages who have been harmed in the past. . . . By emphasizing the similarities between past and current uses of force, by emphasizing that force which holds the woman captive, and by persuasively invoking the shadow of many past assaults that have resulted in the death of women, separation assault helps shift the paradigm from the image of vigilantism to the image of a hostage resisting her own death. Here, at the intersection of legal standards and cultural perception, separation assault helps to reveal that by its very nature battering implicates questions of both violence and power, and to make possible a greater cultural understanding of the lives and experience of women. . . .

Notes

1. Redefining separation must include rethinking many assumptions—that it is the woman's job to separate from a battering relationship, that separation is the appropriate choice for all women when violence first occurs within a relationship, that appropriate separation is an immediate and final break rather than the process of repeated temporary separations made by many women—as well as identifying the violent assault on women's attempts to separate.

2. These encounters may take many forms, including the attempt to have a violent partner arrested, the filing of a temporary restraining order or legal separation, or the rush to find legal counsel because the partner has threatened to take custody of the children. . . .

3. See Desmond Ellis, Post-Separation Woman Abuse: The Contribution of Lawyers as "Barracudas," "Advocates," and "Counsellors," 10 Intl. J.L. & Psychiatry 403, 408 (1987). Many authors note the dangers of this period. See, e.g., Cynthia Gillespie, Justifiable Homicide 150–152 (1989); Ann Jones, Women Who Kill 298–299 (1980).

4. [One example] is "date rape." . . . Sexual harassment is another such example. . . .

5. . . . I would prefer some term that lets us discuss stereotyping without hopelessly dooming the discourse from the start. However, I think it is important to overcome our fear of the stigma and stereotype that come with the term "battered woman," so I accept it for this paper.

6. Jan E. Stets, Domestic Violence and Control 110 (1988) ("The men want to direct and determine how their partner behaves, and the way they do this is through violence. . . . [T]he men use violence to dominate, control, and force the women to conform to what they want."). *Id.* at 109.

7. Lee H. Bowker, Beating Wife-Beating 7–9 (1983) (discussing the balance of power in families); Susan Schechter, Women and Male Violence 219–224 (1982) (describing battering as a way to maintain control).

8. E. Emerson Dobash & Russell Dobash, Violence Against Wives ix (1979).

9. Ann Jones, The Burning Bed and Man Slaughter, 9 Women's Rts. L. Rep. 295, 296 (1986) (book review).

10. Edward Gondolf & Ellen Fisher, Battered Women as Survivors: An Alternative

to Treating Learned Helplessness 18, 27–28 (1988) (describing several studies show-ing helpseeking); see also Lenore Walker, The Battered Woman Syndrome 26 (1984) ("As the violence escalated, so did the probability that the battered woman would seek help.").

11. Gondolf & Fisher, *supra* note 10, at 77–78.

12. Walker, Syndrome, *supra* note 10, at 26.

13. Lewis Okun, Woman Abuse: Facts Replacing Myths 56 (1986); Gondolf & Fisher, *supra* note 10, at 82–83.

14. Bowker, *supra* note 7, at 65–67, 123 (husband's fear of divorce ended vio-lence); see also Christine A. Littleton, Women's Experience and the Problem of Tran-sition: Perspectives on Male Battering of Women, herein, at 327.

15. Gillespie, *supra* note 3, at 2.

16. See, e.g., Ellis, *supra* note 3, at 410.

17. Angela Browne, When Battered Women Kill 110 (1987).

18. George Barnard et al., Till Death Do Us Part: A Study of Spouse Murder, 10 Am. Acad. Psychiatry & L. 271, 224 (1982); see also Franklin Zimring et al., Intimate Violence: A Study of Intersexual Homicide, 50 U. Chi. L. Rev. 910 (1983).

19. Barnard et al., *supra* note 18, at 224.

20. Barbara Hart, Beyond the "Duty to Warn": A Therapist's "Duty to Protect" Bat-tered Women and Children, in Kersti Yllo & Michale Bograd eds., Feminist Perspec-tives on Wife Abuse 240 (1988) (emphasis added).

21. Jones, *supra* note 3, at 296.

22. No one has counted how many women are killed at the moment they an-nounce that they are leaving. However, the fact that more than half of women who leave their husbands are violently harassed was noted by Browne, *supra* note 17, at 110. The tendency for separation to actually increase the incidence of violence has also been noted. See Ellis, *supra* note 3, at 408 (citing several studies).

23. Godfrey v. Georgia, 446 U.S. 420, 424–425 (1980).

24. Mary McNeill, Domestic Violence: The Skeleton in Tarasoff's Closet, in Daniel J. Sonkin ed., Domestic Violence on Trial: Psychological and Legal Dimensions of Fam-ily Violence 197 (1978).

25. 712 F.2d 391 (9th Cir. 1983).

26. 789 P.2d 960, 961–962 (Cal. 1990).

27. 551 P.2d 334 (Cal. 1976), distinguished in *Garcia,* 789 P.2d at 963.

28. 556 P.2d 777 (Cal. 1976).

29. New York Task Force on Women in the Courts, Report of the New York Task Force Report on Women in the Courts, 15 Fordham Urb. L.J. 11, 38–39 (1986–1987).

30. *Id.* at 40.

31. Jablonski by Pahls v. United States, 712 F.2d 391, 398 (9th Cir. 1983).

32. 789 P.2d 960 (Cal. 1990).

33. Garcia v. Superior Court, 249 Cal. Rptr. 449, 454 (Cal. Ct. App. 1988), *quoted in* 789 P.2d 960 (Cal. 1990) (Mosk, J., dissenting). The dissent criticized the majority opinion for essentially adopting the same view the intermediate appellate court had held. 789 P.2d at 970 (Mosk, J., dissenting).

34. New York Task Force Report, *supra* note 29, at 41–42; Achieving Equal Justice for Victims of Domestic Violence, in Advisory Commission on Gender Bias in the Courts, California Judicial Council, Achieving Equal Justice for Men and Women in the Courts 37 (draft March 23, 1990) (less than half of judges surveyed viewed spousal abuse as a reason not to award joint custody).

35. 556 P.2d 777, 778–780 (Cal. 1976).

36. I am indebted to Donna Coker for suggesting this possibility.

37. Ann Jones vividly describes the assaults on the efforts to separate of many women who ultimately killed battering men, either during or after the separation attack, often after being held prisoner or prevented from leaving at all in a variety of ways: "Homicide is a last resort, and it most often occurs when men simply will not quit. As one woman testified at her murder trial, 'It seemed like the more I tried to get away, the harder he beat me.' Gloria Timmons left her husband, but he kept tracking her down, raping and beating her; finally when he attacked her with a screwdriver, she shot him. Patricia Evans filed for divorce, but her husband kept coming back to beat her with a dog chain, pistol-whip her, and shoot at her. At last, after she had been hospitalized seven times, she shot him. . . . Janice Strand was forced to return to her husband when he threatened her parents' lives. Patricia Gross' husband tracked her from Michigan to Mississippi and threatened to kill her relatives there to force her to return to him. . . . Mary McGuire's husband, teaching submission, made her watch him dig her grave, kill the family cat, and decapitate a pet horse. When she fled he brought her back with a gun held to her child's head. . . . Agnes Scott's husband found her and cut her up seven years after she left him. There are cases on record of men still harassing and beating their wives twenty-five years after the wives left them and tried to go into hiding. If researchers were not quite so intent upon assigning the pathological behavior to the women, they might see that the more telling question is not 'Why do the women stay?' but 'Why don't the men let them go?'" Jones, *supra* note 9, at 298–299.

38. *Stewart*, 763 P.2d at 573; *Norman*, 378 S.E.2d at 8–9; see also People v. Aris, 264 Cal. Rptr. 167 (Cal. Ct. App. 1989).

39. See, e.g., *Norman*, 378 S.E.2d at 13 (noting that interpreting "imminent" to mean "immediate" effectively denies a woman the right to self-defense); *Gillespie, supra* note 3, at 64–77, 185–187; see also State v. Hodges, 716 P.2d 563, 570–571 (Kan. 1986). But see Cathryn Jo Rosen, The Excuse of Self-Defense: Correcting a Historical Accident on Behalf of Battered Women Who Kill, 36 Am. U. L. Rev. 11, 29 n.107 (common law usually equated imminence with immediacy, though Model Penal Code does not).

40. Model Penal Code @ 3.04 cmt. 2(c) (1985), *quoted in Norman*, 378 S.E.2d at 19 n.1 (Martin, J., dissenting).

41. See Gillespie, *supra* note 3, at 185–187; see also *Hodges,* 716 P.2d 563; State v. Osbey, 710 P.2d 676 (Kan. 1985), State v. Hundley, 693 P.2d 475 (Kan. 1985).

42. State v. Gallegos, 719 P.2d 1268 (N.M. Ct. App. 1986); see also State v. Wanrow, 559 P.2d 548 (Wash. 1977). The jury instruction using an immediacy standard was held to overly restrict the inquiry into the defendant's circumstances. 559 P.2d at 555–556.

43. 763 P.2d 572 (Kan. 1988).

44. 763 P.2d at 578. The court also overruled an earlier holding that measured the reasonableness of perception of harm from the subjective viewpoint of the battered woman. 763 P.2d at 579 (overruling in part State v. Hodges, 716 P.2d 563 (Kan. 1986)). . . .

45. 693 P.2d 475 (Kan. 1985).

46. 710 P.2d 676 (Kan. 1985).

47. 716 P.2d 563 (Kan. 1985).

48. 763 P.2d at 578.

49. 693 P.2d 475, 479 (Kan. 1985).

50. 763 P.2d at 584 (Herd, J., dissenting).

51. I am indebted to Mary Coombs for this discussion. [S]ee also M. J. Willoughby, Comment, Rendering Each Woman Her Due: Can a Battered Woman Claim Self-

Defense When She Kills Her Sleeping Batterer?, 38 U. Kan. L. Rev. 169, 184–185 (1990) (comparing battered women to hostages).

52. 716 P.2d at 566–567.

53. *Id.* at 567.

54. *Id.* at 563.

55. 763 P.2d at 579.

56. *Id.*

57. 366 S.E.2d 586 (N.C. Ct. App. 1988), *rev'd.*, 378 S.E.2d 8 (N.C. 1989).

58. State v. Norman, 378 S.E.2d 8, 12 (N.C. 1989).

59. *Id.* at 17 (Martin, J., dissenting).

60. *Id.* The dissent concludes that a juror could have found "that defendant believed that her husband's threats to her life were viable, that serious bodily harm was imminent, and that it was necessary to kill her husband to escape that harm . . . [a] juror could find defendant's belief in the necessity to kill her husband not merely reasonable but compelling." *Id.* at 20 (Martin, J., dissenting).

61. See, e.g., *id.* at 15 ("Homicidal self-help would then become a lawful solution, and perhaps the easiest and most effective solution, to this problem."); see also State v. Stewart, 763 P.2d 572, 579 (Kan. 1988) ("To hold otherwise in this case would in effect allow the execution of the abuser for past or future acts and conduct.").

Mapping the Margins:
Intersectionality, Identity Politics,
and Violence Against Women of Color

KIMBERLÉ CRENSHAW

. . . MY OBJECTIVE [is to explore] the race and gender dimensions of violence against women of color. . . . I consider how the experiences of women of color are frequently the product of intersecting patterns of racism and sexism. . . .

[Based on] a brief field study of battered women's shelters located in minority communities in Los Angeles,[1] [I found that in most cases], the physical assault that leads women to these shelters is merely the most immediate manifestation of the subordination they experience. Many women who seek protection are unemployed or underemployed, and a good number of them are poor. Shelters serving these women cannot afford to address only the violence inflicted by the batterer; they must also confront the other multilayered and routinized forms of domination that often converge in these women's lives, hindering their ability to create alternatives to the abusive relationships that brought them to shelters in the first place. Many women of color, for example, are burdened by poverty, child care responsibilities, and the lack of job skills.[2] These burdens, largely the consequence of gender and class oppression, are then compounded by the racially discriminatory employment and housing practices women of color often face, as well as by the disproportionately high unemployment among people of color that makes battered women of color less able to depend on the support of friends and relatives for temporary shelter.[3]

Where systems of race, gender, and class domination converge, as they do in the experiences of battered women of color, intervention strategies based solely on the experiences of women who do not share the same class or race backgrounds will be of limited help to women who because of race and class face different obstacles.[4] Such was the case in 1990 when Congress amended the marriage fraud provisions of the Immigration and Nationality Act to protect immigrant women who were battered or exposed to extreme cruelty by the United States citizens or permanent residents these women immigrated to the United States to marry. Under the marriage fraud provisions of the Act, a person who immigrated to the United States to marry a United States cit-

---

43 Stan. L. Rev. 1241 (1991).

izen or permanent resident had to remain "properly" married for two years before even applying for permanent resident status,[5] at which time applications for the immigrant's permanent status were required of both spouses. Predictably, under these circumstances, many immigrant women were reluctant to leave even the most abusive of partners for fear of being deported.[6] When faced with the choice between protection from their batterers and protection against deportation, many immigrant women chose the latter. Reports of the tragic consequences of this double subordination put pressure on Congress to include in the Immigration Act of 1990 a provision amending the marriage fraud rules to allow for an explicit waiver for hardship caused by domestic violence.[7] Yet many immigrant women, particularly immigrant women of color, have remained vulnerable to battering because they are unable to meet the conditions established for a waiver. The evidence required to support a waiver "can include, but is not limited to, reports and affidavits from police, medical personnel, psychologists, school officials, and social service agencies."[8] For many immigrant women, limited access to these resources can make it difficult for them to obtain the evidence needed for a waiver. And cultural barriers often further discourage immigrant women from reporting or escaping battering situations. Tina Shum, a family counselor at a social service agency, points out that "[t]his law sounds so easy to apply, but there are cultural complications in the Asian community that make even these requirements difficult. . . . Just to find the opportunity and courage to call us is an accomplishment for many."[9] The typical immigrant spouse, she suggests, may live "[i]n an extended family where several generations live together, there may be no privacy on the telephone, no opportunity to leave the house and no understanding of public phones."[10] As a consequence, many immigrant women are wholly dependent on their husbands as their link to the world outside their homes.

Immigrant women are also vulnerable to spousal violence because so many of them depend on their husbands for information regarding their legal status.[11] Many women who are now permanent residents continue to suffer abuse under threats of deportation by their husbands. Even if the threats are unfounded, women who have no independent access to information will still be intimidated by such threats. And even though the domestic violence waiver focuses on immigrant women whose husbands are United States citizens or permanent residents, there are countless women married to undocumented workers (or who are themselves undocumented) who suffer in silence for fear that the security of their entire families will be jeopardized should they seek help or otherwise call attention to themselves.

Language barriers present another structural problem that often limits opportunities of non-English-speaking women to take advantage of existing support services. Such barriers not only limit access to information about shelters, but also limit access to the security shelters provide. Some shelters turn non–English-speaking women away for lack of bilingual personnel and resources.[12]

These examples illustrate how patterns of subordination intersect in women's experience of domestic violence. . . .

A. The Politicization of Domestic Violence

[T]he political interests of women of color are obscured and sometimes jeopardized by political strategies that ignore or suppress intersectional issues. [This] is illustrated by my [research]. I attempted to review Los Angeles Police Department statistics reflecting the rate of domestic violence interventions by precinct because such statistics can provide a rough picture of arrests by racial group, given the degree of racial segregation in Los Angeles.[13] L.A.P.D., however, would not release the statistics. A representative explained that one reason the statistics were not released was that domestic violence activists both within and outside the Department feared that statistics reflecting the extent of domestic violence in minority communities might be selectively interpreted and publicized so as to undermine long-term efforts to force the Department to address domestic violence as a serious problem. I was told that activists were worried that the statistics might permit opponents to dismiss domestic violence as a minority problem and, therefore, not deserving of aggressive action.

The informant also claimed that representatives from various minority communities opposed the release of the statistics. They were concerned, apparently, that the data would unfairly represent Black and Brown communities as unusually violent, potentially reinforcing stereotypes that might be used in attempts to justify oppressive police tactics and other discriminatory practices. These misgivings are based on the familiar and not unfounded premise that certain minority groups—especially Black men—have already been stereotyped as uncontrollably violent. Some worry that attempts to make domestic violence an object of political action may only serve to confirm such stereotypes and undermine efforts to combat negative beliefs about the Black community.

This account sharply illustrates how women of color can be erased by the strategic silences of antiracism and feminism. The political priorities of both were defined in ways that suppressed information that could have facilitated attempts to confront the problem of domestic violence in communities of color.

1. Domestic Violence and Antiracist Politics

Within communities of color, efforts to stem the politicization of domestic violence are often grounded in attempts to maintain the integrity of the community. The articulation of this perspective takes different forms. Some critics allege that feminism has no place within communities of color, that the issues are internally divisive, and that they represent the migration of white women's concerns into a context in which they are not only irrelevant but also harmful. At its most extreme, this rhetoric denies that gender violence is a problem in the community and characterizes any effort to politicize gender subordination as itself a community problem. This is the position taken by Shahrazad Ali in her controversial book, *The Blackman's Guide to Understanding the Blackwoman*.[14] In this stridently antifeminist tract, Ali draws a positive correlation between domestic violence and the liberation of African Americans. Ali blames the deteriorating conditions within the Black community on the insubordination of Black women and on the failure of Black men to control them.[15] Ali goes so far as to advise Black men to physically chastise Black women when they are "disrespectful."[16] While she cautions that Black men must use moderation in disciplining "their" women, she argues that Black men must sometimes resort to physical force to reestablish the authority over Black women that racism has disrupted.[17]

Ali's premise is that patriarchy is beneficial for the Black community, and that it must be strengthened through coercive means if necessary. Yet the violence that accompanies this will to control is devastating, not only for the Black women who are victimized, but also for the entire Black community. The recourse to violence to resolve conflicts establishes a dangerous pattern for children raised in such environments and contributes to many other pressing problems. It has been estimated that nearly forty percent of all homeless women and children have fled violence in the home,[18] and an estimated sixty-three percent of young men between the ages of eleven and twenty who are imprisoned for homicide have killed their mothers' batterers.[19] And yet, while gang violence, homicide, and other forms of Black-on-Black crime have increasingly been discussed within African-American politics, patriarchal ideas about gender and power preclude the recognition of domestic violence as yet another compelling incidence of Black-on-Black crime.

Efforts such as Ali's to justify violence against women in the name of Black liberation are indeed extreme. The more common problem is that the political or cultural interests of the community are interpreted in a way that precludes full public recognition of the problem of domestic violence. While it would be misleading to suggest that white Americans have come to terms with the degree of violence in their own homes, it is nonetheless the case that race adds yet another dimension to why the problem of domestic violence is suppressed within nonwhite communities. People of color often must weigh their interests in avoiding issues that might reinforce distorted public perceptions against the need to acknowledge and address intracommunity problems. Yet the cost of suppression is seldom recognized in part because the failure to discuss the issue shapes perceptions of how serious the problem is in the first place.

The controversy over Alice Walker's novel *The Color Purple* can be understood as an intracommunity debate about the political costs of exposing gender violence within the Black community.[20] Some critics chastised Walker for portraying Black men as violent brutes.[21] One critic lambasted Walker's portrayal of Celie, the emotionally and physically abused protagonist who finally triumphs in the end. Walker, the critic contended, had created in Celie a Black woman whom she couldn't imagine existing in any Black community she knew or could conceive of.[22]

The claim that Celie was somehow an unauthentic character might be read as a consequence of silencing discussion of intracommunity violence. Celie may be unlike any Black woman we know because the real terror experienced daily by minority women is routinely concealed in a misguided (though perhaps understandable) attempt to forestall racial stereotyping. Of course, it is true that representations of Black violence—

whether statistical or fictional—are often written into a larger script that consistently portrays Black and other minority communities as pathologically violent. The problem, however, is not so much the portrayal of violence itself as it is the absence of other narratives and images portraying a fuller range of Black experience. Suppression of some of these issues in the name of antiracism imposes real costs. Where information about violence in minority communities is not available, domestic violence is unlikely to be addressed as a serious issue.

The political imperatives of a narrowly focused antiracist strategy support other practices that isolate women of color. For example, activists who have attempted to provide support services to Asian- and African-American women report intense resistance from those communities.[23] At other times, cultural and social factors contribute to suppression. Nilda Rimonte, director of Everywoman's Shelter in Los Angeles, points out that in the Asian community, saving the honor of the family from shame is a priority.[24] Unfortunately, this priority tends to be interpreted as obliging women not to scream rather than obliging men not to hit.

Race and culture contribute to the suppression of domestic violence in other ways as well. Women of color are often reluctant to call the police, a hesitancy likely due to a general unwillingness among people of color to subject their private lives to the scrutiny and control of a police force that is frequently hostile. There is also a more generalized community ethic against public intervention, the product of a desire to create a private world free from the diverse assaults on the public lives of racially subordinated people. The home is not simply a man's castle in the patriarchal sense, but may also function as a safe haven from the indignities of life in a racist society. However, but for this "safe haven" in many cases, women of color victimized by violence might otherwise seek help.

There is also a general tendency within antiracist discourse to regard the problem of violence against women of color as just another manifestation of racism. In this sense, the relevance of gender domination within the community is reconfigured as a consequence of discrimination against men. Of course, it is probably true that racism contributes to the cycle of violence, given the stress that men of color experience in dominant society. It is therefore more than reasonable to explore the links between racism and domestic violence. But the chain of violence is more complex and extends beyond this single link. Racism is linked to patriarchy to the extent that racism denies men of color the power and privilege that dominant men enjoy. When violence is understood as an acting-out of being denied male power in other spheres, it seems counterproductive to embrace constructs that implicitly link the solution to domestic violence to the acquisition of greater male power. The more promising political imperative is to challenge the legitimacy of such power expectations by exposing their dysfunctional and debilitating effect on families and communities of color. Moreover, while understanding links between racism and domestic violence is an important component of any effective intervention strategy, it is also clear that women of color need not await the ultimate triumph over racism before they can expect to live violence-free lives.

2. Race and the Domestic Violence Lobby

Not only do race-based priorities function to obscure the problem of violence suffered by women of color; feminist concerns often suppress minority experiences as well. Strategies for increasing awareness of domestic violence within the white community tend to begin by citing the commonly shared assumption that battering is a minority problem. The strategy then focuses on demolishing this strawman, stressing that spousal abuse also occurs in the white community. Countless first-person stories begin with a statement like, "I was not supposed to be a battered wife." That battering occurs in families of all races and all classes seems to be an ever-present theme of anti-abuse campaigns. First-person anecdotes and studies, for example, consistently assert that battering cuts across racial, ethnic, economic, educational, and religious lines.[25] Such disclaimers seem relevant only in the presence of an initial, widely held belief that domestic violence occurs primarily in minority or poor families. Indeed some authorities explicitly renounce the "stereotypical myths" about battered women.[26] A few commentators have even transformed the message that battering is not exclusively a problem of the poor or minority communities into a claim that it equally affects all races and classes.[27] Yet these comments seem less concerned with exploring domestic abuse within "stereotyped" communities than with removing the stereotype as an obstacle to exposing battering within white middle- and upper-class communities.

Efforts to politicize the issue of violence against women challenge beliefs that violence occurs only in homes of "others." While it is unlikely that advocates and others who adopt this rhetorical strategy intend to exclude or ignore the needs of poor and colored women, the underlying premise of this seemingly universalistic appeal is to keep the sensibilities of dominant social groups focused on the experiences of those groups. Indeed, as subtly suggested by the opening comments of Senator David Boren (D-Okla.) in support of the Violence Against Women Act of 1991, the displacement of the "other" as the presumed victim of domestic violence works primarily as a political appeal to rally white elites. Boren said,

> Violent crimes against women are not limited to the streets of the inner cities, but also occur in homes in the urban and rural areas across the country.
>
> Violence against women affects not only those who are actually beaten and brutalized, but indirectly affects all women. Today, our wives, mothers, daughters, sisters, and colleagues are held captive by fear generated from these violent crimes—held captive not for what they do or who they are, but solely because of gender.[28]

Rather than focusing on and illuminating how violence is disregarded when the home is "othered," the strategy implicit in Senator Boren's remarks functions instead to politicize the problem only in the dominant community. This strategy permits white women victims to come into focus, but does little to disrupt the patterns of neglect that permitted the problem to continue as long as it was imagined to be a minority problem. The experience of violence by minority women is ignored, except to the extent it gains white support for domestic violence programs in the white community.

Senator Boren and his colleagues no doubt believe that they have provided legislation and resources that will address the problems of all women victimized by domestic violence. Yet despite their universalizing rhetoric of "all" women, they were able to empathize with female victims of domestic violence only by looking past the plight of "other" women and by recognizing the familiar faces of their own. The strength of the appeal to "protect our women" must be its race and class specificity. After all, it has always been someone's wife, mother, sister, or daughter that has been abused, even when the violence was stereotypically Black or Brown, and poor. The point here is not that the Violence Against Women Act is particularistic on its own terms, but that unless the Senators and other policymakers ask why violence remained insignificant as long as it was understood as a minority problem, it is unlikely that women of color will share equally in the distribution of resources and concern. It is even more unlikely, however, that those in power will be forced to confront this issue. As long as attempts to politicize domestic violence focus on convincing whites that this is not a "minority" problem but their problem, any authentic and sensitive attention to the experiences of Black and other minority women probably will continue to be regarded as jeopardizing the movement.

While Senator Boren's statement reflects a self-consciously political presentation of domestic violence, an episode of the CBS news program *48 Hours*[29] shows how similar patterns of "othering" nonwhite women are apparent in journalistic accounts of domestic violence as well. The program presented seven women who were victims of abuse. Six were interviewed at some length along with their family members, friends, supporters, and even detractors. The viewer got to know something about each of these women. These victims were humanized. Yet the seventh woman, the only nonwhite one, never came into focus. She was literally unrecognizable throughout the segment, first introduced by photographs showing her face badly beaten and later shown with her face electronically altered in the videotape of a hearing at which she was forced to testify. Other images associated with this woman included shots of a bloodstained room and blood-soaked pillows. Her boyfriend was pictured handcuffed while the camera zoomed in for a close-up of his bloodied sneakers. Of all the presentations in the episode, hers was the most graphic and impersonal. The overall point of the segment "featuring" this woman was that battering might not escalate into homicide if battered women would only cooperate with prosecutors. In focusing on its own agenda and failing to explore why this woman refused to cooperate, the program diminished this woman, communicating, however subtly, that she was responsible for her own victimization.

Unlike the other women, all of whom, again, were white, this Black woman had no name, no family, no context. The viewer sees her only as victimized and uncooperative. She cries when shown pictures. She pleads not to be forced to view the bloodstained room and her disfigured face. The program does not help the viewer to understand her predicament. The possible reasons she did not want to testify—fear, love, or possibly both—are never suggested. Most unfortunately, she, unlike the other six, is given no epilogue. While the fates of the other women are revealed at the end of the episode, we discover nothing about the Black woman. She, like the "others" she represents, is simply left to herself and soon forgotten.

I offer this description to suggest that "other" women are silenced as much by being relegated to the margin of experience as by total exclusion. Tokenistic, objectifying, voyeuristic inclusion is at least as disempowering as complete exclusion. The effort to politicize violence against women will do little to address Black and other minority women if their images are retained simply to magnify the problem rather than to humanize their experiences. Similarly, the antiracist agenda will not be advanced significantly by forcibly suppressing the reality of battering in minority communities. As the *48 Hours* episode makes clear, the images and stereotypes we fear are readily available and are frequently deployed in ways that do not generate sensitive understanding of the nature of domestic violence in minority communities.

3. Race and Domestic Violence Support Services

Women working in the field of domestic violence have sometimes reproduced the subordination and marginalization of women of color by adopting policies, priorities, or strategies of empowerment that either elide or wholly disregard the particular intersectional needs of women of color. While gender, race, and class intersect to create the particular context in which women of color experience violence, certain choices made by "allies" can reproduce intersectional subordination within the very resistance strategies designed to respond to the problem.

This problem is starkly illustrated by the inaccessibility of domestic violence support services to many non–English-speaking women. In a letter written to the deputy commissioner of the New York State Department of Social Services, Diana Campos, Director of Human Services for Programas de Ocupaciones y Desarrollo Economico Real, Inc. (PODER), detailed the case of a Latina in crisis who was repeatedly denied accommodation at a shelter because she could not prove that she was English-proficient. The woman had fled her home with her teenaged son, believing her husband's threats to kill them both. She called the domestic violence hotline administered by PODER seeking shelter for herself and her son. Because most shelters would not accommodate the woman with her son, they were forced to live on the streets for two days. The hotline counselor was finally able to find an agency that would take both the mother and the son, but when the counselor told the intake coordinator at the shelter that the woman spoke limited English, the coordinator told her that they could not take anyone who was not English-proficient. When the women in crisis called back and was told of the shelter's "rule," she replied that she could understand English if spoken to her slowly. As Campos explains, Mildred, the hotline counselor, told Wendy, the intake coordinator

> that the woman said that she could communicate a little in English. Wendy told Mildred that they could not provide services to this woman because they have house rules that the woman must agree to follow. Mildred asked her, "What if

the woman agrees to follow your rules? Will you still not take her?" Wendy responded that all of the women at the shelter are required to attend [a] support group and they would not be able to have her in the group if she could not communicate. Mildred mentioned the severity of this woman's case. She told Wendy that the woman had been wandering the streets at night while her husband is home, and she had been mugged twice. She also reiterated the fact that this woman was in danger of being killed by either her husband or a mugger. Mildred expressed that the woman's safety was a priority at this point, and that once in a safe place, receiving counseling in a support group could be dealt with.[30]

The intake coordinator restated the shelter's policy of taking only English-speaking women, and stated further that the woman would have to call the shelter herself for screening. If the woman could communicate with them in English, she might be accepted. When the woman called the PODER hotline later that day, she was in such a state of fear that the hotline counselor who had been working with her had difficulty understanding her in Spanish.[31] Campos directly intervened at this point, calling the executive director of the shelter. A counselor called back from the shelter. As Campos reports,

> Marie [the counselor] told me that they did not want to take the woman in the shelter because they felt that the woman would feel isolated. I explained that the son agreed to translate for his mother during the intake process. Furthermore, that we would assist them in locating a Spanish-speaking battered women's advocate to assist in counseling her. Marie stated that utilizing the son was not an acceptable means in communication for them, since it further victimized the victim. In addition, she stated that they had similar experiences with women who were non-English-speaking, and that the women eventually just left because they were not able to communicate with anyone. I expressed my extreme concern for her safety and reiterated that we would assist them in providing her with the necessary services until we could get her placed someplace where they had bilingual staff.[32]

After several more calls, the shelter finally agreed to take the woman. The woman called once more during the negotiation; however, after a plan was in place, the woman never called back. Said Campos, "After so many calls, we are now left to wonder if she is alive and well, and if she will ever have enough faith in our ability to help her to call us again the next time she is in crisis."[33]

Despite this woman's desperate need, she was unable to receive the protection afforded English-speaking women, due to the shelter's rigid commitment to exclusionary policies. Perhaps even more troubling than the shelter's lack of bilingual resources was its refusal to allow a friend or relative to translate for the woman. This story illustrates the absurdity of a feminist approach that would make the ability to attend a support group without a translator a more significant consideration in the distribution of resources than the risk of physical harm on the street. The point is not that the shelter's image of empowerment is empty, but rather that it was imposed without regard to the disempowering consequences for women who didn't match the kind of client the shelter's administrators imagined. And thus they failed to accomplish the basic priority of the shelter movement—to get the woman out of danger.

Here the woman in crisis was made to bear the burden of the shelter's refusal to anticipate and provide for the needs of non–English-speaking women. Said Campos, "It is unfair to impose more stress on victims by placing them in the position of having to demonstrate their proficiency in English in order to receive services that are readily available to other battered women."[34] The problem is not easily dismissed as one of well-intentioned ignorance. The specific issue of monolingualism and the monistic view of women's experience that set the stage for this tragedy were not new issues in New York. Indeed, several women of color reported that they had repeatedly struggled with the New York State Coalition Against Domestic Violence over language exclusion and other practices that marginalized the interests of women of color.[35] Yet despite repeated lobbying, the Coalition did not act to incorporate the specific needs of nonwhite women into its central organizing vision.

Some critics have linked the Coalition's failure to address these issues to the narrow vision of coalition that animated its interaction with women of color in the first place. The very location of the Coalition's headquarters in Woodstock, New York—an area where few people of color live—seemed to guarantee that women of color would play a limited role in formulating policy. Moreover, efforts to include women of color came, it seems, as something of an afterthought. Many were invited to participate only after the Coalition was awarded a grant by the state to recruit women of color. However, as one "recruit" said, "they were not really prepared to deal with us or our issues. They thought that they could simply incorporate us into their organization without rethinking any of their beliefs or priorities and that we would be happy."[36] Even the most formal gestures of inclusion were not to be taken for granted. On one occasion when several women of color attended a meeting to discuss a special task force on women of color, the group debated all day over including the issue on the agenda.[37]

The relationship between the white women and the women of color on the Board was a rocky one from beginning to end. Other conflicts developed over differing definitions of feminism. For example, the Board decided to hire a Latina staffperson to manage outreach programs to the Latino community, but the white members of the hiring committee rejected candidates favored by Latina committee members who did not have recognized feminist credentials. As Campos pointed out, by measuring Latinas against their own biographies, the white members of the Board failed to recognize the different circumstances under which feminist consciousness develops and manifests itself within minority communities. Many of the women who interviewed for the position were established activists and leaders within their own community, a fact in itself suggesting that these women were probably familiar with the specific gender dynamics in their communities and were accordingly better qualified to handle outreach than other candidates with more conventional feminist credentials.[38]

The Coalition ended a few months later when the women of color walked out.[39] Many of these women returned to community-based organizations, preferring to struggle over women's issues within their communities rather than struggle over race and class issues with white middle-class women. Yet as illustrated by the case of the Latina who could find no shelter, the dominance of a particular perspective and set of priorities within the shelter community continues to marginalize the needs of women of color.

The struggle over which differences matter and which do not is neither an abstract nor an insignificant debate among women. Indeed, these conflicts are about more than difference as such; they raise critical issues of power. The problem is not simply that women who dominate the antiviolence movement are different from women of color but that they frequently have power to determine, either through material or rhetorical resources, whether the intersectional differences of women of color will be incorporated at all into the basic formulation of policy. Thus, the struggle over incorporating these differences is not a petty or superficial conflict about who gets to sit at the head of the table. In the context of violence, it is sometimes a deadly serious matter of who will survive—and who will not. . . .

Notes

1. During my research in Los Angeles, California, I visited Jenessee Battered Women's Shelter, the only shelter in the Western states primarily serving Black women, and Everywoman's Shelter, which primarily serves Asian women. I also visited Estelle Chueng at the Asian Pacific Law Foundation, and I spoke with a representative of La Casa, a shelter in the predominantly Latino community of East L.A.

2. One researcher has noted, in reference to a survey taken of battered women's shelters, that "many Caucasian women were probably excluded form the sample, since they are more likely to have available resources that enable them to avoid going to a shelter. Many shelters admit only women with few or no resources or alternatives." Mildred Daley Pagelow, Woman-Battering: Victims and Their Experiences 97 (1981). On the other hand, many middle- and upper-class women are financially dependent upon their husbands and thus experience a diminution in their standard of living when they leave their husbands.

3. More specifically, African Americans suffer from high unemployment rates, low incomes, and high poverty rates. According to Dr. David Swinton, Dean of the School of Business at Jackson State University in Mississippi, African Americans "receive three-fifths as much income per person as whites and are three times as likely to have annual incomes below the federally defined poverty level of $12, 675 for a family of four." Urban League Urges Action, N.Y. Times, Jan 9, 1991, at A14. In fact, recent statistics indicate that racial economic inequality is "higher as we begin the 1990s than at any other time in the last 20 years." David Swinton, The Economic Status of African Americans: "Permanent" Poverty and Inequality, in The State of Black America 1991, 25 (1991).

The economic situation of minority women is, expectedly, worse than that of their male counterparts. Black women, who earn a median of $7,875 a year, make considerably less than Black men, who earn a median income of $12,609 a year, and white women, who earn a median income of $9,812 a year. *Id.* at 32 (Table 3). Additionally, the percentage of Black female-headed families living in poverty (46.5%) is almost twice that of white female-headed families (25.4%). *Id.* at 43 (Table 8). Latino households also earn considerably less than white households. In 1988, the median income of Latino households was $20,359 and for white households, $28,340—a difference of almost $8,000. Hispanic Americans: A Statistical Sourcebook 149 (1991). Analyzing by origin, in 1988, Puerto Rican households were the worst off, with 34.1% earning below $10,000 a year and a median income for all Puerto Rican households of $15, 447 per year. *Id.* at 155. 1989 statistics for Latino men and women show that women earned an average of $7,000 less than men. *Id.* at 169.

4. . . . Racial differences marked an interesting contrast between Jenessee's policies and those of other shelters situated outside the Black community. Unlike some other shelters in Los Angeles, Jenessee welcomed the assistance of men. According to the Director, the shelter's policy was premised on a belief that given African American's need to maintain healthy relations to pursue a common struggle against racism, anti-violence programs within the African American community cannot afford to be antagonistic to men. For a discussion of the different needs of Black women who are battered, see Beth Richie, Battered Black Women: A Challenge for the Black Community, Black Scholar 40 (Mar./Apr. 1985).

5. §U.S.C. §1186a (1988). . . .

6. Immigration activists have pointed out that "[t]he 1986 Immigration Reform Act and the Immigration Marriage Fraud Amendment have combined to give the spouse applying for permanent residence a powerful tool to control his partner." Jorge Banales, Abuse Among Immigrants; As Their Numbers Grow So Does the Need for Services, Wash. Post, Oct. 16, 1990, at E5. . . . In one egregious instance described by Beckie Masaki, executive director of the Asian Women's Shelter in San Francisco, the closer the Chinese bride came to getting her permanent residency in the United States, the more harshly her Asian-American husband beat her. Her husband, kicking her in the neck and face, warned her that she needed him, and if she did not do as he told her, he would call immigration officials. Deanna Hodgin, "Mail-Order" Brides Marry Pain to Get Green Cards, Wash. Times, Apr. 16, 1991, at E1.

7. Immigration Act of 1990, Pub. L. No. 101-649, 104 Stat. 4978. . . .

8. H.R.Rep. No. 723(1), 101st Cong., 2d. Sess. 79 (1990), *reprinted in* 1990 U.S.C.C.A.N. 6710, 6759.

9. Hodgin, *supra* note 6.

10. *Id.*

11. A citizen or permanent resident spouse can exercise power over an alien spouse by threatening not to file a petition for permanent residency. If he fails to file a petition for permanent residency, the alien spouse continues to be undocumented and is considered to be in the country illegally. These constraints often restrict an alien spouse from leaving. Dean Ito Taylor tells the story of "one client who has been hospitalized—she's had him arrested for beating her—but she keeps coming back to him because he promises he will file for her. . . . He holds that green card over her head." Hodgin, *supra* note 6. . . .

12. . . . To combat this lack of appropriate services for women of color at many shelters, special programs have been created specifically for women from particular communities. A few examples of such programs include the Victim Intervention Project in East Harlem for Latina women, Jenessee Shelter for African American women in Los Angeles, Apna Gar in Chicago for South Asian women, and, for Asian women generally, the Asian Women's Shelter in San Francisco, the New York Asian Women's Center, and the Center for the Pacific Asian Family in Los Angeles. Programs with hotlines include Sakhi for South Asian Women in New York, and Manavi in Jersey City,

also for South Asian women, as well as programs for Korean women in Philadelphia and Chicago.

13. Most crime statistics are classified by sex or race but none are classified by sex and race. Because we know that most rape victims are women, the racial breakdown reveals, at best, rape rates for Black women. Yet, even given this head start, rates for other non-white women are difficult to collect. While there are some statistics for Latinas, statistics for Asian and Native American women are virtually non-existent. Cf. G. Chezia Carraway, Violence Against Women of Color, 43 Stan. L. Rev. 1301 (1993).

14. Shahrazad Ali, The Blackman's Guide to Understanding the Blackwoman (1989). Ali's book sold quite well for an independently published title, an accomplishment no doubt due in part to her appearances on the Phil Donahue, Oprah Winfrey, and Sally Jesse Raphael television talk shows. For public and press reaction, see Dorothy Gilliam, Sick, Distorted Thinking, Wash. Post, Oct. 11, 1990, at D3; Lena Williams, Black Woman's Book Starts a Predictable Storm, N.Y. Times, Oct 2, 1990, at C11; see also Pearl Cleague, Mad at Miles: A Black Woman's Guide to Truth (1990). The title clearly styled after Ali's Mad at Miles responds not only to issues raised by Ali's book, but also to Miles Davis's admission in his autobiography, Miles: The Autobiography (1989), that he had physically abused, among other women, his former wife, actress Cicely Tyson.

15. Shahrazad Ali suggests that the "[Blackwoman] certainly does not believe that her disrespect for the Blackman is destructive, nor that her opposition to him has deteriorated the Black nation." S. Ali, *supra* note 14, at viii. Blaming the problems of the community on the failure of the Black woman to accept her "real definition," Ali explains that "[n]o nation can rise when the natural order of the behavior of the male and the female have been altered against their wishes by force. No species can survive if the female of the genus disturbs the balance of her nature by acting other than herself." *Id.* at 76.

16. Ali advises the Blackman to hit the Blackwoman in the mouth, "[b]ecause it is from that hole, in the lower part of her face, that all her rebellion culminates into words. Her unbridled tongue is a main reason she cannot get along with the Blackman. She often needs a reminder." *Id.* at 169. Ali warns that "if [the Blackwoman] ignores the authority and superiority of the Blackman, there is a penalty. When she crosses this line and becomes viciously insulting, it is time for the Blackman to soundly slap her in the mouth." *Id.*

17. Ali explains that, "[r]egretfully some Blackwomen want to be physically controlled by the Blackman." *Id.* at 174. "The Blackwoman, deep inside her heart" Ali reveals, "wants to surrender but she wants to be coerced." *Id.* at 72. "[The Blackwoman] wants [the Blackman] to stand up and defend himself even if it means he has to knock her out of the way to do so. This is necessary whenever the Blackwoman steps out of the protection of womanly behavior and enters the dangerous domain of masculine challenge." *Id.* at 174.

18. [Women and Violence: Hearings Before the Senate Comm. on the Judiciary on Legislation to Reduce the Growing Problem of Violent Crime Against Women, 101st Cong., 2d Sess., pt. 2, at 142] (statement of Susan Kelly-Dreiss) (discussing several studies in Pennsylvania linking homelessness to domestic violence).

19. *Id.* at 143 (statement of Susan Kelly-Dreiss).

20. Alice Walker, The Color Purple (1982). The most severe criticism of Walker developed after the book was filmed as a movie. Donald Bogle, a film historian, argued that part of the criticism of the movie stemmed from the one-dimensional portrayal of

Mister, the abusive man. See Jacqueline Trescott, Passions Over Purple; Anger and Unease Over Film's Depiction of Black Men, Wash. Post, Feb. 5, 1986, at C1. Bogle argues that in the novel, Walker linked Mister's abusive conduct to his oppression in the white world—since Mister "can't be himself, he has to assert himself with the black woman." The movie failed to make any connection between Mister's abusive treatment of Black women and racism, and thereby presented Mister only as an "insensitive, callous man." *Id.*

21. See, e.g., Gerald Early, Her Picture in the Papers: Remembering Some Black Women, Antaeus, Spring 1988, at 9; Daryl Pickney, Black Victims, Black Villains, N.Y. Review of Books, Jan. 29, 1987, at 17; Trescott, *supra* note 20.

22. Trudler Harris, On the Color Purple, Stereotypes, and Silence, 18 Black Am. Lit. F. 155, 155 (1984).

23. The source of the resistance reveals an interesting difference between the Asian-American and African-American communities. In the African-American community, the resistance is usually grounded in efforts to avoid confirming negative stereotypes of African-Americans as violent; the concern of members in some Asian-American communities as to avoid tarnishing the model minority myth. Interview with Nilda Rimonte, Director of the Everywoman Shelter, in Los Angeles, California (April 19, 1991).

24. Nilda Rimonte, A Question of Culture: Cultural Approval of Violence Against Women in the Pacific-Asian Community and the Cultural Defense, 43 Stan. L. Rev. 1311 (1991); see also Nilda Rimonte, Domestic Violence Against Pacific Asians, in Asian Women United of California ed., Making Waves: An Anthology of Writings By and About Asian American Women 327, 328 (1989). . . .

When—or, more importantly, how—to take culture into account when addressing the needs of women of color is a complicated issue. Testimony as to the particularities of Asian "culture" has increasingly been used in trials to determine the culpability of both Asian immigrant women and men who are charged with crimes of interpersonal violence. A position on the use of the "cultural defense" in these instances depends on how "culture" is being defined as well as on whether and to what extent the "cultural defense" has been used differently for Asian men and Asian women. See Leti Volpp, (Mis) Identifying Culture: Asian Women and the "Cultural Defense," (unpublished manuscript).

25. See, e.g., Lenore F. Walker, Terrifying Love: Why Battered Women Kill and How Society Responds 101–102 (1989) ("Battered women come from all types of economic, cultural, religious, and racial backgrounds. . . . They are women like you. Like me. Like those whom you know and love."); Murray A. Straus, Richard J. Gelles & Suzanne K. Steinmetz, Behind Closed Doors: Violence in the American Family 31 (1980) ("Wife-beating is found in every class, at every income level."). . . .

26. For example, Susan Kelly-Dreiss states: "The public holds many myths about battered women—they are poor, they are women of color, they are uneducated, they are on welfare, they deserve to be beaten and they even like it. However, contrary to common misperceptions, domestic violence is not confined to any one socioeconomic, ethnic, religious, racial or age group." Hearings on Violent Crime Against Women, *supra* note 18, pt. 2, at 139 (testimony of Susan Kelly-Dreiss, Executive Director, Pa. Coalition Against Domestic Violence). Kathleen Waits offers a possible explanation for this misperception: "It is true that battered women who are also poor are more likely to come to the attention of governmental officials than are their middle- and upper-class counterparts. However, this phenomenon is caused more by the lack of alterna-

tive resources and the intrusiveness of the welfare state than by any significantly higher incidence of violence among lower-class families." Kathleen Waits, The Criminal Justice System's Response to Battering: Understanding the Problem, Forging the Solutions, 60 Wash. U. L. Rev. 267, 276–277 (1985).

27. However, no reliable statistics support such a claim. In fact, some statistics suggest that there is a greater frequency of violence among the working classes and the poor. See M. Straus, R. Gelles & S. Steinmetz, *supra* note 25, at 31. Yet these statistics are also unreliable because, to follow Waits's observation, violence in middle- and upper-class homes remains hidden from the view of statisticians and governmental officials alike. I would suggest that assertions that the problem is the same across race and class are driven less by actual knowledge about the prevalence of domestic violence in different communities than by advocates' recognition that the image of domestic violence as an issue involving primarily the poor and minorities complicates efforts to mobilize against it.

28. 137 Cong. Rec. S611 (daily ed. Jan. 14, 1991) (statement of Sen. Boren). Senator William Cohen (D-Me.) followed with a similar statement. . . . *Id.* (statement of Sen. Cohen).

29. *48 Hours: Till Death Do Us Part* (CBS television broadcast, Feb. 6, 1991).

30. Letter of Diana M. Campos, Director of Human Services, PODER, to Joseph Semidei, Deputy Commissioner, New York State Department of Social Services (Mar. 26, 1992).

31. The woman had been slipping back into her home during the day when her husband was at work. She remained in a heightened state of anxiety because he was returning shortly and she would be forced to go back out into the streets for yet another night.

32. PODER Letter, *supra* note 30 (emphasis added).

33. *Id.*

34. *Id.*

35. Roundtable Discussion on Racism and the Domestic Violence Movement (April 2, 1992). The participants in the discussion—Diana Campos, Director, Bilingual Outreach Project of the New York State Coalition Against Domestic Violence; Elsa A. Rios, Project Director, Victim Intervention Project (a community-based project in East Harlem, New York, serving battered women); and Haydee Rosario, a social worker with the East Harlem Council for Human Services and a Victim Intervention Project volunteer—recounted conflicts relating to race and culture during their association with the New York State Coalition Against Domestic Violence, a state oversight group that distributed resources to battered women's shelters throughout the state and generally set policy priorities for the shelters that were part of the Coalition.

36. *Id.*

37. *Id.*

38. *Id.*

39. Ironically, the specific dispute that led to the walk-out concerned the housing of the Spanish-language domestic violence hotline. The hotline was initially housed at the Coalition's headquarters, but languished after a succession of coordinators left the organization. Latinas on the Coalition board argued that the hotline should be housed at one of the community service agencies, while the board insisted on maintaining control of it. The hotline is now housed at PODER. *Id.*

Lavender Bruises: Intra-Lesbian Violence, Law and Lesbian Legal Theory

RUTHANN ROBSON

. . . INTRA-LESBIAN violence is not a new phenomenon, although the legal reaction it has provoked has at times penalized lesbian sexuality rather than violence. A 1721 German trial transcript, for example, documents intra-lesbian violence: the "two women did not get along. Because the codefendant complained that she did not earn anything, the defendant beat her frequently."[1] However, it was not the violent expressions that prompted judicial intervention, but the sexual ones. The women were on trial for the crime of lesbianism. Found guilty, the defendant Catharina Linck was sentenced to death. The codefendant Catharina Mühlhahn received the lesser sentence of three years in the penitentiary and then banishment, not because she was the victim of physical abuse, but because she was "simple-minded."[2] The violence between the women was superfluous from the legal perspective: what was criminalized was sexuality.

This essay seeks to elucidate the confusion between sexuality and violence that confounds legal treatments of intra-lesbian violence. This confusion is both explicitly and implicitly revealed in judicial decisions and legislative enactments. A distinct but intertwined task of this essay is to situate intra-lesbian violence within the development of a lesbian legal theory. . . .

. . . Intra-lesbian violence may consist of three types of possible relationships between the lesbians. The first type of relationship, a "non-relationship" of strangers, is apparently a very rare form of violence between lesbians. The second type of possible relationship is that of acquaintances or friends within the lesbian community. The third type of relationship is that of lovers, and in this form of intra-lesbian violence the dynamics often parallel the patterns of domestic violence that have been so well documented in heterosexual relationships. The latter two types of relationships, of course, are not mutually exclusive, for the boundaries between "friend" and "lover" may be fluid among lesbians. Another example of intra-lesbian violence that straddles the latter two categories is violence revolving around a love triangle. In a recent situation, a woman murdered her former lover who ended the relationship and had found a new lover.[3] In a famous historical trial in the Netherlands, two lesbian lovers were convicted

20 Golden Gate U. L. Rev. 567 (1990).

of conspiring and committing the murder of a former lover.[4] Whatever the type of intra-lesbian violence, however, such violence . . . proves problematic for the present legal system as it attempts to address the violence.

Intra-Lesbian Violence and the Law

The legal sanctions in cases of intra-lesbian violence have often been directed more at the "lesbian" sexual component than at the act(s) of violence. The punishment of sexuality may be explicit, [or] implicit. . . . The legal response to such sensationalism was not increased prosecutions for murder, but increased prosecutions for lesbianism.

In addition to sensationalizing, another legal response to intra-lesbian violence which implicitly privileges sexuality over violence is the insistence on the erasure of lesbianism. While this appears paradoxical, this strategy operates to insulate lesbianism from candid consideration as it relates or does not relate to the violence. Thus, the lesbianism may be denied[5] or it may be "hetero-relationized."[6] In modern American cases in which judges refer to lesbianism, lesbianism is often an issue of the defendant's "character." For example, in a recent Florida appellate opinion, the court rejects the defendant's claim that her lesbianism was improperly before the jury:

> Wiley further contends on appeal that her character was impermissibly placed in issue when the State elicited the fact that she was a "bull dagger"—a lesbian that assumes the male role during intercourse. This contention is without merit. The record undeniably shows that the question of Wiley's sexual preferences came into the trial as a part of her own confession. According to Wiley, the victim hurled this invective at her during the quarrel that occurred between them on that fateful evening. This accusation perhaps constitutes an explanation for the flailing received by the victim some moments later. The State's only crime here was to try to explain to the jury exactly what a "bull dagger" is.[7]

Thus, the court conceptualizes the defendant's lesbianism in a hetero-patriarchal manner ("male role") and disparages it ("invective") even while trivializing it ("the State's only crime"). . . . In an earlier Texas case in which the victim is the defendant's putative lover although the defendant denies she is a lesbian, the appellate court is more straightforward about rejecting the defendant's claim that evidence of her lesbian relation with the murder victim was prejudicial.[8] What is troublesome, however, is that during the Texas trial the "evidence" of the relationship consisted in part of photographs and testimony that the defendant "dressed like a man; kept her hair cut like a man; wore men's clothing, including men's shoes."[9] The appellate court is comfortable in relying on heterosexual stereotypes to confirm the defendant's lesbianism, despite the defendant's denials.

The judicial discourse relating to lesbian violence thus finds it relevant to denominate the male-identified lesbian, even absent a partner-relationship as in *Wiley*. Perhaps this denomination is a cipher for categorizing the defendant as the aggressor. . . .

Determining the aggressor in a violent lesbian relationship becomes especially crucial when the defense to murder is self-defense. In Crawford v. State,[10] the appellate court provides excerpts of the defendant's interrogation in which the law enforcement officers unceasingly reiterate disbelief that the defendant was beaten by her lover and that defendant was not the "aggressor." The appellate court reversed, on the basis of the prejudicial nature of the trial admission of the law enforcement officer's statements during the interrogation, after categorizing the victim as the one who had assumed "the dominant role" in the lesbian relationship.[11] While the court's conclusion that the admission of the officer's statements during interrogation was prejudicial error seems a fair one, one wonders to what extent this conclusion is buoyed by the finding that the victim was the "dominant" one. The court does not relate any prior incidents of violence for its conclusion of "dominance." What I am suggesting is that "dominance" is a hetero-relational concept that may not be applicable to lesbian relationships; the operative consideration in murder trials in which self-defense is raised should be related to abuse rather than heterosexist notions of dominance that are based on stereotypical gender roles.

Not only does hetero-relationality impact upon legal responses to intra-lesbian violence, but homophobia does as well. In an . . . unreported trial apparently involving the first use of the "battered woman syndrome" defense in a lesbian relationship,[12] Annette Green was convicted of the first degree murder of her lover Ivonne Julio by a Palm Beach County, Florida, jury. The trial judge allowed the "battered woman syndrome defense," construing it as a "battered person defense."[13] The prosecutor had argued that the defense was inappropriate, despite his admission that defendant Green had been "battered. She was shot at before by the victim. She had a broken nose, broken ribs."[14] Nevertheless, even with the complicated issues presented by the "battered person" defense before the jury, it took only two and one-half hours to return a guilty verdict. Green's defense attorney attributed this to homophobia, noting that it usually takes a jury much longer to deliberate, even in routine cases.[15] One jury member related an incident to the judge in which two venire members spoke in the women's restroom about their desire to be selected as jurors in order to "hang that lesbian bitch."[16] The court personnel also exhibited what the defense attorney termed homophobic conduct. Further, the defense attorney attributes homophobia to the first degree murder charge, although the situation of battering and self-defense was a "classic murder-two case."[17]

After her conviction, Annette Green has appeared on television shows . . . in order to tell battered lesbians to "get help":

> I want to tell them that to not be afraid to get help. To please go and get help. There's someone out there that could help because, if they don't do that, one of them is going to be dead. Sooner or later, it's going to happen.[18]

Yet the legal help available to battered lesbians may be chimerical. In Florida, where Annette Green was surviving abuse before she killed her lover, Green was not within the statutory definitions of a victim of domestic abuse. Annette Green was not entitled to shelter or services from "domestic violence centers," partially funded by the state, because domestic violence is defined as violence "by a person against the person's spouse."[19] Further, Annette Green was not entitled to avail herself of the judicial system to obtain an injunction for protection against domestic violence. Such injunctions, often called protective orders or temporary restraining orders are available to victims of domestic abuse in order to prevent further abuse. These civil orders have just recently become available in every state; however, not every state extends protection to lesbians in battering relationships. [In some states,] often because of recent amendments—lesbians who cohabit, or who have cohabited, may apply for protective orders in cases of domestic violence.[20] For lesbians who have never lived together, judicial protection from an abusive relationship is much more rare.

Even where legal assistance is statutorily available, applications for restraining orders may be denied by courts because of the parties' lesbianism. The courts may reason that the situation is one of "mutual combat." The term "mutual combat" indicates a situation where the parties are "really just fighting" rather than one in which abuse is occurring. Within the battering relationship, the concept of mutual combat may have some currency. In the domestic violence movement itself, there is some controversy about the validity of the notion of "mutual combat" between lesbians. The majority view is that "mutual combat" is a myth, and a dangerous one.[21] Another view, proposed by battered women advocate Ginny NiCarthy, is that there are lesbians who are violent toward each other but do not ultimately succeed in controlling each other: two-way violence.[22] In the legal arena, the mutual combat concept may be more attractive in situations where hetero-relational factors are less evident. Many judges and legal officials have been educated in domestic violence issues in ways which emphasize the dominant/submissive patriarchal arrangement based on objective criteria such as gender. When such factors are absent, judges may be more likely to feel inadequate to determine against whom the restraining order should issue. In the face of such inadequacy, such judges may either deny the restraining order or issue a mutual restraining order.

The denying of a restraining order has obvious import: the violence is legally sanctioned. The issuing of a mutual restraining order may have a less obvious significance. To be "restrained" from doing some act one has never done and apparently has no desire to do, appears insignificant. Yet this very irrelevance conveys the message of its relevance. A mutual restraining order apportions responsibility for the violence between the parties. Despite the civil nature of the order, it serves as an adjudication that "fighting" rather than abuse is occurring.

In addition to its rhetoric, the mutual restraining order has practical legal effects. [P]enalties are applied to persons against whom restraining orders have been issued. In some states, a finding of "domestic violence," including findings based upon the issuance of temporary retraining orders, may disqualify one from state employment, or from employment with mental health facilities, alcohol treatment facilities, drug treatment facilities, nursing homes, or child care facilities, or from working with the developmentally disabled, working with youth services or providing foster care. Thus, a mutual restraining order might impact upon one's livelihood. . . .

In addition to the problems for a battered lesbian seeking help from the legal community, battered lesbians may have difficulty obtaining assistance from the lesbian community. Annette Green's defense attorney complained of lack of support from the lesbian and gay community, describing the communities' "parochial attitude" that there is enough homophobia without publicizing lesbian violence. Yet the silence about intra-lesbian violence, both intimate and nonintimate, is founded on an acute—and very real—awareness of societal homophobia. Internalized homophobia also impacts upon the reactions of individuals within the lesbian community, often in complex and contradictory ways. For example, internalized homophobia may lead one to become rigidly defensive about one's lesbianism and thus susceptible to denying intra-lesbian violence even when witnessed or experienced. . . . .

Developing a Lesbian Legal Theory of Intra-Lesbian Violence

Intra-lesbian violence in all forms presents a complex and vital issue for resolution by any attempts to articulate a lesbian legal theory. Lesbian legal theory could, of course, embrace either of two extremes: eschewing the "patriarchal" legal system altogether; or embracing the legal system as if lesbianism was irrelevant. The first alternative is based upon the politics of lesbian separatism[23] and upon the realistic suspicion of a disenfranchised group. The second alternative is based upon the politics of the domestic violence movement which has stressed that the "legal response to family violence must be guided primarily by the nature of the abusive act, not the relationship between the victim and the abuser."[24]

Both of these extremes are unsatisfactory, yet the tension between these extremes appears again and again in lesbian discourse about intra-lesbian violence. In a fictional example, the lesbian characters discuss the relative merits of using the legal system as opposed to a lesbian arbitration to redress the trashing of the victim's apartment by two lesbians whose acts were motivated by politics.[25] In another example, a battered lesbian relates:

> The response of the local lesbian community to the arrest of my former lover was demoralizing. Lesbians were upset—even angry—that I had called the police. "I can see turning in a batterer and calling the cops," said one woman. "But a lover? What does that say about your ability to be intimate with anyone?". . . Several women put a lot of pressure on me to drop the charges. They said things like: "Oh, come on. Haven't you ever hit a lover? It wasn't all that bad." "You're dragging your lover's name through the mud. It was in the newspapers." "Do you realize that the state could take away her children because of what you have done?" They suggested setting up a meeting between my former lover and me. They volunteered to mediate so we could reach an "agreement."
>
> I can think of few crueler demands on a woman who has been attacked than to insist she sit down with her attacker and talk things out. I would guess that

none of the lesbians who wanted me to do that would consider demanding such a thing from a straight woman who had just been attacked by her boyfriend. . . . The lowest blow came when a friend called me the day before a pretrial hearing. "You should drop the charges," she said. "We in the lesbian community can take care of our own." "But what about me? Who's going to guarantee my safety and see that my house doesn't get trashed?" She had no response.[26]

In this instance, the battered lesbian went to court and related her story, but the "story" was partial. The defendant's lawyer "covered up the relationship" stating that the lesbian lovers were "just two good friends" and the battered lesbian "did not say we had been lovers."[27] In addition to erasure of lesbian existence, another cost of resort to legal adjudication could be hetero-relationizing (and thus also erasing) lesbian existence. In yet another instance, the battering lesbian availed herself of the judicial procedure to contest the restraining order, resulting in the order being made mutual. . . .

Because we are only beginning our attempts to formulate a lesbian legal theory, the problem of intra-lesbian violence has not been addressed. Domestic violence in feminist legal theory is not necessarily applicable to lesbian legal theory because feminist legal theory is often based upon heterosexist assumptions. If lesbianism is mentioned at all, it is distorted. For example, feminist theorist Catharine MacKinnon explicitly connects domestic violence to heterosexual activity and heterosexualized (and sado-masochistic) lesbianism:

Marital rape and battery of wives have been separated by law. A feminist analysis suggests that assault by a man's fist is not so different from assault by his penis, not because both are violent, but because both are sexual. Battery is often precipitated by women's noncompliance with gender requirements. Nearly all incidents occur in the home, most in the kitchen or bedroom. Most murdered women are killed by their husbands or boyfriends, usually in the bedroom. The battery cycle accords with the rhythms of heterosexual sex. The rhythm of lesbian sadomasochism is the same. Perhaps violent interchanges, especially between genders, make sense in sexual terms.[28]

[T]he simplistic equation of lesbian sadomasochism with heterosexual domestic violence does not elucidate the issues involved in intra-lesbian violence. Many lesbians in the battered women's movement whose work included daily confrontations with heterosexual battering theorized that domestic abuse could be attributed to disparities in gender.[29] Yet, it soon became obvious that inextricably linking intimate violence with sexuality is problematic for lesbian legal theory. For, if lesbian legal theory were to adopt such a view, it would hetero-relationize itself in the same manner in which the legal system often hetero-relationizes lesbian relationships. To sanction MacKinnon's view would be to make relevant an inquiry into "who is the man" in order to determine the identity of the batterer. Obviously, lesbian legal theory cannot countenance such a result. . . .

[A]lso useful is the work that is beginning in lesbian moral philosophy on intra-lesbian violence. In the recent work *Lesbian Ethics,* Sarah Hoagland addresses intra-lesbian violence. . . .

Ultimately, any words I have here are inadequate. This is a crisis, and lesbians in crisis have to use all our wits, ingenuity, skill, and resources to get through it. But there is a difference between making choices in crisis and reaching for community social justice.

The problem with crises is that they interrupt all else that we're doing and rivet us on someone else's agenda which we didn't agree to, often one we wanted to ignore. However, a system of punishment . . . structures our agendas too. . . .

If, instead, we attend the crisis, asking for help from friends, doing whatever is necessary to take care of ourselves, and go through the time it takes to dissolve it (sometimes years, if one can't let go), as has been happening, we may begin gaining understanding of ways to keep similar situations from reaching crises in the future.[30]

The rejection of concepts such as "social justice" and legalism is consonant with Hoagland's lesbian separatist politics, yet "doing whatever is necessary to take care of ourselves" does seem to allow legal intervention as a potential. . . .

. . . Although ethicist Hoagland specifically rejects the concept of ostracism [of the batterer], as attorney Barbara Hart conceptualizes it, the issue is one of "safe space."[31] Hart contends that the community and the battered women's movement take responsibility for providing a safe space for battered women by excluding all "lesbians who have battered and who have not been accountable to the person battered and to their community of friends."[32] While it is unclear whether Hart is defining community with reference to the "battered women's community" or the "lesbian community," what is intensely interesting is the insistence on accountability not only to the woman battered but also to "their community of friends." . . .

While the concept of community responsibility is a vital one, the existence or not of a lesbian community and the degree of intimacy experienced within that community by lesbians involved with violence, seem to me to be crucial variables in the expression of any lesbian legal theory that addresses intra-lesbian violence. Even if one were to adopt the extreme that resort to patriarchal legal mechanisms is unacceptable in situations of intra-lesbian disputes because lesbians "can take care of our own," such a position is nonsensical if there are no available lesbians to accomplish the taking care. Many lesbians do not live within lesbian communities. Even battered lesbians who live within lesbian communities, even small lesbian communities, may be isolated. Any reference to lesbian community within lesbian legal theory to solve battering situations must be cognizant of the tendency of the batterer to isolate her lover, and must also acknowledge the segregation that the violence itself causes. Thus, lesbian legal theory cannot assume the existence of a lesbian community.

Lesbian legal theory cannot assume the character of lesbian community, even presupposing that one exists. For although much lesbian discourse posits politically sensitive groups of lesbians, for many other lesbian communities, this is simply not the case. Further, there is no guarantee that individuals within such communities will act according to their pronounced politics. Even given the variability in available lesbian communities, I think it is nevertheless possible to attempt some principles that might guide the development of lesbian legal theory in the area of intra-lesbian violence. . . .

A necessary foundation for lesbian legal theory in the area of intra-lesbian violence, especially as it confronts the extant legal system, is an insistence on recognition. Recognition for lesbians and lesbianism in the law is paradoxical: it demands both relevance and irrelevance. Recognition is that which does not privilege sexuality over violence by punishing sexuality, by erasing sexuality, or by distorting sexuality.

Thus, lesbianism must be recognized by including intimate lesbian violence in legal discourse and enactments relating to domestic violence. Statutes that deny lesbians the ability to obtain judicial protective orders on the same basis as married persons, related persons, or heterosexuals are discriminatory and limiting. Further, the judicial enforcement of such statutes should preclude mutual restraining orders except in those instances in which "fighting" truly occurs. The evidentiary standard should not be different in cases involving two persons of a shared gender from cases involving persons of different genders. To do otherwise is not only to erase lesbian sexuality, but also to punish the expression of that sexuality by deeming it sufficient to deserve violence.

Lesbianism must also be recognized as lesbianism. Hetero-relationism disguises intra-lesbian violence in ill-fitting heterosexist apparel. Lesbian relationships are not synonymous with heterosexual relationships. This is not to say that lesbian relationships, whether violent or not, are completely dissimilar from all other relationships. Violence occurs in heterosexual, gay and lesbian relationships, and in many ways this violence may be remarkably similar. Nevertheless, attempting to adapt lesbian relationships to heterosexual ones brutalizes and erases lesbian existence. It also distorts, provokes, maintains and justifies intra-lesbian violence.

Intra-lesbian violence presents one of the most important issues for a lesbian legal theory to confront. Intra-lesbian violence makes impossible a separatist lesbian jurisprudence that eschews all involvement with the extant legal system. Intra-lesbian violence also makes impossible an assimilationist position that lesbians should participate in the legal system as if they were not lesbians. Intimate intra-lesbian violence exhibits the incompleteness of both the extant legal system and feminist attempts to reform that system. As we begin to confront these issues, we come closer to not only acknowledging the problem but attempting to use the law and legal theory for the benefit of all. . . .

Notes

1. A Lesbian Execution in Germany, 1721: The Trial Records, 6 J. Homosexuality 27, 32 (1980/1981) (trans. Brigitte Eriksson).

2. *Id.* at 40.

3. Relying on newspaper reports, one commentator describes the events thusly: "On Friday the 13th of this January [1989], Catharine Rouse, former manager of Madison's former feminist restaurant Lysistrata, took a gun purchased a few days before, drove to the house of her ex-lover, Joan, who had recently ended their relationship,

and shot her three times, dead. She did not find Joan's new lover. She then drove home and shot herself, dead." Card, Defusing the Bomb: Lesbian Ethics and Horizontal Violence, 3 Lesbian Ethics 91 (1989).

4. In this murder trial, two women were arrested and tried for murdering a third in 1792. R. Dekker & L. vandePol, The Tradition of Female Transvestism in Early Modern Europe 70 (1989).

5. As scholar Rhonda Rivera notes, judges in opinions may never refer to homosexuality and cases involving homosexual issues may be unpublished more often than other cases. Rivera, Our Straight-Laced Judges: The Legal Position of Homosexual Persons in the United States, 30 Hastings L.J. 799, 805 (1979).

6. This phrase is from Janice Raymond's concept of the re-definition of women in "hetero-relational terms" to fit prevailing models of heterosexuality and patriarchy. See J. Raymond, A Passion for Friends 64–66 (1986).

7. Wiley v. State, 427 So. 2d 283, 285 (Fla. Dist. Ct. App. 1983).

8. Perez v. State, 491 S.W. 672, 675 (Tex. Crim. App. 1973) ("the relationship between the appellant and the deceased was clearly admissible" under the Texas Evidence Code, citing cases).

9. Id. at 673.

10. 285 Md. 431, 404 A.2d 244 (1979).

11. Id. at 451, 404 A.2d at 254.

12. For a discussion of the applicability of the battered woman syndrome defense to lesbians, see Comment, The Defending of Accused Homosexuals: Will Society Accept Their Use of the Battered Wife Defense?, 4 Glendale L. Rev. 208 (1982).

13. Telephone conversation with William Lasley, attorney for Annette Green (Nov. 13, 1989) [hereinafter Lasley conversation].

14. Assistant State Attorney Bob Johnson, quoted in Gay Community News, Sept. 17–23, 1989, at 1.

15. Lasley conversation, *supra* note 13.

16. Id.

17. Id.

18. Geraldo: Battered Lesbians—Battered Lovers? (television broadcast, Nov. 21, 1989) at 12. . . .

19. Fla. Stat. 415.602(3) (1989). . . .

20. See, e.g., Colo. Rev. Stat. §14–4–101(2) (Supp. 1987) (domestic abuse defined as violence committed or threatened by an adult or emancipated minor against another adult or emancipated minor living "in the same domicile"); . . . Wis. Stat. Ann. §813.12 (West. Supp. 1989)(expanding the definition of "domestic abuse" in 1985 to include acts by a "family member or household member"). But see Mo. Rev. Stat. §455.010(5) (Supp. 1990) . . . (protected household members as "spouses, persons related by blood or marriage, and other persons of the *opposite sex* jointly residing in the same dwelling unit" [emphasis added]). . . .

21. See, e.g., Hart, Lesbian Battering: An Examination, in K. Lobel ed., Naming the Violence: Speaking Out About Lesbian Battering 173 (1986). For a critique of the concept of mutual combat between gay men, see Kingston, The Truth Behind Mutual Combat, Coming Up!, Dec. 1987, at 12.

22. NiCarthy, Lesbian Battering, Political Principles and Therapeutic Methods: Feminist Therapy Conference (May 1987) (unpublished manuscript). . . .

23. See generally, S. Hoagland & J. Penelope eds., For Lesbians Only: A Separatist Anthology (1988).

24. U.S. Attorney General's Task Force on Family Violence, Final Report 4 (Sept. 1984). . . .

25. D. Allison, Violence Against Women Begins at Home, in Trash 141 (1988).

26. Dietrich, Nothing Is The Same Anymore, in Naming the Violence, *supra* note 21, at 155, 159–160.

27. *Id.* at 161–162.

28. C. MacKinnon, Toward a Feminist Theory of the State 178 (1989).

29. For example, Del Martin, author of Battered Wives (1976) and co-author of Lesbian/Woman (1974), testified before the United States Commission on Civil Rights that "wife beating" could be attributed to the historical emergence of "monogamous pairing relationships," resulting in a "father right" which brought about "the complete subjugation of one sex by the other." U.S. Comm'n on Civil Rights, Battered Women: Issues of Public Policy 5 (1978). . . .

30. S. Hoagland, Lesbian Ethics 266 (1988).

31. Hart, *supra* note 21, at 95.

32. *Id.* at 95–96.

The Violence of Privacy

ELIZABETH M. SCHNEIDER

... THIS ESSAY explores the ways in which concepts of privacy permit, encourage, and reinforce violence against women, focusing on the complex interrelationship between notions of "public" and "private" in our social understandings of woman-abuse.[1] Historically, male battering of women was untouched by law, protected as part of the private sphere of family life. Over the last twenty years, however, as the battered women's movement in this country has made issues of battering visible, battering is no longer perceived as a purely "private" problem and has taken on dimensions of a "public" issue. There has been an explosion of legal reform and social service efforts: the development of battered women's shelters and hotlines, many state and federal governmental reports and much state legislation. New legal remedies for battered women have been developed which have been premised on the idea of battering as a "public" harm. However, at the same time, there is widespread resistance to acknowledgment of battering as a "public" issue. . . .

The concept of privacy poses a dilemma and challenge to theoretical and practical work on woman-abuse. The notion of marital privacy has been a source of oppression to battered women and has helped to maintain women's subordination within the family. However, a more affirmative concept of privacy [may be developed].

Historically, the dichotomy of "public" and "private" has been viewed as an important construct for understanding gender. The traditional notion of "separate spheres" is premised on a dichotomy between the "private" world of family and domestic life (the "women's" sphere), and the "public" world of marketplace (the "men's" sphere).[2] Nadine Taub and I have discussed elsewhere the difference between the role of law in the public and private spheres.[3] In the public sphere, sex-based exclusionary laws join with other institutional and ideological constraints to directly limit women's participation. In the private sphere, the legal system operates more subtly. The law claims to be absent in the private sphere and has historically refused to intervene in ongoing family relations.

23 Conn. L. Rev. 973 (1991).

Tort law, which is generally concerned with injuries inflicted on individuals, has traditionally been held inapplicable to injuries inflicted by one family member on another. Under the doctrines of interspousal and parent-child immunity, courts have consistently refused to allow recoveries for injuries that would be compensable but for the fact that they occurred in the private realm. In the same way, criminal law fails to punish intentional injuries to family members. Common law and statutory definitions of rape in most states continue to carve out a special exception for a husband's forced intercourse with his wife. Wife beating was initially omitted from the definition of criminal assault on the ground that a husband had the right to chastise his wife. Even today, after courts have explicitly rejected the definitional exception and its rationale, judges, prosecutors, and police officers decline to enforce assault laws in the family context.[4]

Although a dichotomous view of the public sphere and the private sphere has some heuristic value, and considerable rhetorical power, the dichotomy is overdrawn.[5] The notion of a sharp demarcation between public and private has been widely rejected by feminist and Critical Legal Studies scholars.[6] There is no realm of personal and family life that exists totally separate from the reach of the state. The state defines both the family, the so-called private sphere, and the market, the so-called public sphere. "Private" and "public" exist on a continuum.

Thus, in the so-called private sphere of domestic and family life, which is purportedly immune from law, there is always the selective application of law. Significantly, this selective application of law invokes "privacy" as a rationale for immunity in order to protect male domination. For example, when the police do not respond to a battered woman's call for assistance, or when a civil court refuses to evict her assailant, the woman is relegated to self-help, while the man who beats her receives the law's tacit encouragement and support.[7] . . .

The rhetoric of privacy that has insulated the female world from the legal order sends an important ideological message to the rest of society. It devalues women and their functions and says that women are not important enough to merit legal regulation. . . .

Definitions of "private" and "public" in any particular legal context can and do constantly shift. Meanings of "private" and "public" are based on social and cultural assumptions of what is valued and important, and these assumptions are deeply gender-based. Thus, the interrelationship between what is understood and experienced as "private" and "public" is particularly complex in the area of gender, where the rhetoric of privacy has masked inequality and subordination. The decision about what we protect as "private" is a political decision that always has important "public" ramifications.[8]

In general, privacy has been viewed as problematic by feminist theorists.[9] Privacy has seemed to rest on a division of public and private that has been oppressive to women and has supported male dominance in the family. Privacy reinforces the idea that the personal is separate from the political; privacy also implies something that should be kept secret. Privacy inures to the benefit of the individual, not the community. The right of privacy has been viewed as a passive right, one which says that the state cannot intervene.[10]

However, some feminist theorists have also explored the affirmative role that privacy can play for women.[11] Privacy is important to women in many ways. It provides an opportunity for individual self-development, for individual decisionmaking and for protection against endless caretaking.[12] In addition, there are other related aspects of privacy, such as the notion of autonomy, equality, liberty, and freedom of bodily integrity, that are central to women's independence and well-being. For women who have been battered, these aspects of privacy are particularly important. . . .

Dimensions of Privacy

A. *The Denial of Power and the Power of Denial*

The battered women's movement grew out of the rebirth of the women's movement in the 1960s, and it is one of the areas in which the women's movement has made an enduring contribution to law. Like sexual harassment, the "problem" of battering and the social and legal construct of a "battered woman" did not exist in this country until the women's movement named it.[13] The battered women's movement revealed to the public hidden and private violence. Over the last 20 years, the battered women's movement has been involved in efforts to provide services for battered women, to create legal remedies to end abuse, and to develop public education efforts to change consciousness about battering. The battered women's movement saw battering as an aspect of fundamental gender relations, as a reflection of male power and female subordination.[14] . . .

. . . When the battered women's movement began, battered women, had, effectively no legal remedies.

Over the last twenty years, there has been considerable change. . . . Federal and state task forces have recommended reforms of legal, social welfare and health care systems.[15] Lawsuits have resulted in improved police and court practices. Lawsuits against the police have compelled police departments to arrest batterers vigorously.[16] Almost all states now have domestic violence legislation providing for orders of protection for women, and legal sanctions for their violation and/or criminal remedies for battering.[17] In short, there has been an explosion of law reform efforts to assist battered women.

Work on issues of battered women is now at a turning point. Some reforms have been institutionalized, and problems of battered women have achieved credibility and visibility. To some degree, a public dimension to the problem is now recognized. However, federal, state and private funding resources put into these efforts have been small. There has been little change in the culture of female subordination that supports and maintains abuse. At the same time, there is a serious backlash to these reform efforts and many of the reforms that have been accomplished are in serious jeopardy. For the last several years, while writing a report on national legal reform efforts for battered women for The Ford Foundation,[18] I have been amazed at the enormous accomplishments of the battered women's movement over the last 20 years. Indeed, I can think of few recent social movements that have accomplished so much in such a short time.

However, I have also been stunned by the depth of social resistance to change. Although battering has evolved from a "private" to a more "public" issue, it has not become a serious political issue, precisely because it has profound implications for all of our lives.[19] Battering is deeply threatening. It goes to our most fundamental assumptions about the nature of intimate relations and the safeness of family life. The concept of male battering of women as a "private" issue exerts a powerful ideological pull on our consciousness because, in some sense, it is something that we would like to believe.[20] By seeing woman-abuse as "private," we affirm it as a problem that is individual, that only involves a particular male-female relationship, and for which there is no social responsibility to remedy. Each of us needs to deny the seriousness and pervasiveness of battering, but more significantly, the interconnectedness of battering with so many other aspects of family life and gender relations. Instead of focusing on the batterer, we focus on the battered woman, scrutinize her conduct, examine her pathology and blame her for not leaving the relationship, in order to maintain that denial and refuse to confront the issues of power. Focusing on the woman, not the man, perpetuates the power of patriarchy. Denial supports and legitimates this power; the concept of privacy is a key aspect of this denial.

Denial takes many forms and operates on many levels.[21] Men deny battering in order to protect their own privilege. Women need to deny the pervasiveness of the problem so as not to link it to their own life situations. Individual women who are battered tend to minimize the violence in order to distance themselves from some internalized negative concept of "battered woman." I see denial in the attitudes of jurors, who try to remove themselves and say that it could never happen to me; if it did, I would handle it differently.[22] I see denial in the public engagement in the Hedda Nussbaum/Joel Steinberg case which focused on Hedda Nussbaum's complicity, and involved feminists in active controversy over the boundaries of victimization.[23] The findings of the many state task force reports on gender bias in the courts have painstakingly recorded judicial attitudes of denial.[24] Clearly, there is serious denial on the part of state legislators, members of Congress and the Executive Branch who never mention battering as an important public issue. In battering, we see both the power of denial and the denial of power. The concept of privacy is an ideological rationale for this denial and serves to maintain it.

The concept of privacy encourages, reinforces and supports violence against women. Privacy says that violence against women is immune from sanction, that it is permitted, acceptable and part of the basic fabric of American family life. Privacy says that what goes on in the violent relationship should not be the subject of state or community intervention. Privacy says that it is an individual, and not a systemic problem. Privacy operates as a mask for inequality, protecting male violence against women.

B. The Shifting Parameters of Private and Public

As work on battered women has evolved, social meanings of what is private and public, and the relationship between them, have become more complex. Traditionally, battering has been viewed as within the private sphere of the family, and therefore unprotected by law. Yet, as Martha Minow has suggested, this social failure to intervene in male battering of women on grounds of privacy should not be seen as separate from the violence, but as part of the violence.

> When clerks in a local court harass a woman who applies for a restraining order against the violence in her home, they are part of the violence. Society is organized to permit violence in the home; it is organized through images in mass media and through broadly based social attitudes that condone violence. Society permits such violence to go unchallenged through the isolation of families and the failures of police to respond. Public, rather than private, patterns of conduct and morals are implicated. Some police officers refuse to respond to domestic violence; some officers themselves abuse their spouses. Some clerks and judges think domestic violence matters do not belong in court. These failures to respond to domestic violence are public, not private, actions.[25]

Although social failure to respond to problems of battered women has been justified on grounds of privacy, this failure to respond is an affirmative political decision that has serious public consequences. The rationale of privacy masks the political nature of the decision. Privacy thus plays a particularly subtle and pernicious ideological role in supporting, encouraging, and legitimating violence against women. The state plays an affirmative role in permitting violence against battered women by protecting the privileges and prerogatives of battering men and failing to protect battered women, and by prosecuting battered women for homicide when they protect themselves. These failures to respond, or selective responses, are part of "public patterns of conduct and morals."[26]

Over the last several years, the meaning of what has been traditionally viewed as public and private, concerning issues of battered women, has shifted. In some sense, a public dimension of the problem has increased. There are now legal decisions that have held police forces liable for money damages for failure to intervene to protect battered women, an explosion of state legal remedies to protect battered women, and federal legislation to assist battered women in implementing remedies. All of these approaches suggest a more public dimension to the problem, or at least a recognition by governmental bodies, speaking with a public voice, that they must acknowledge and deal with the problem. Some of the rhetoric surrounding issues of violence against women has shifted from the language of private to the language of public.

However, at the same time, the notion of family violence as within the private sphere has been given additional support by the Supreme Court's decision in De-Shaney v. Winnebago County Department of Social Services.[27] In *DeShaney*, the Supreme Court held that the state had no affirmative responsibility to protect a child who had been permanently injured as a result of abuse committed by his custodial father, even when the state had been investigating the child abuse for several years. The majority opinion reflects a crabbed view of the world that reasserts a bright-line distinction between public and private. Family violence is private and therefore immune from state scrutiny because, implicitly, the state has no business to be there in the first place and no responsibility to intervene at all. *DeShaney* revives the notion that family violence is private and the distinction between public and private action places this violence beyond public control.[28] *DeShaney* is already being interpreted by courts around the country to limit police liability in suits brought by battered women.[29]

The tension between public and private also is seen in the issue of what legal processes are available to battered women, and the social meaning of those processes to battered women, in particular, and to society at large.[30] Over the last several years, the range of legal remedies has expanded and there has been an explosion of statutory reforms. For example, there are civil remedies, known as restraining orders or orders of protection. These are court orders with flexible provisions that a battered woman can obtain to stop a man from beating her, prevent him from coming to the house, or evict him from the house.[31] There are also criminal statutes that provide for the arrest of batterers, either for beating or for violation of protective orders.[32] Although there remain serious problems in the enforcement and implementation of these orders, the fact that such formal legal processes exist is evidence of a developing understanding of the public dimension of the problem. By giving battered women remedies in court there is, at least theoretically, public scrutiny, public control and the possibility of public sanction. In addition, some states impose marriage license fees to generate funds to be used for battered women's services, thus making an important statement about the public impact of purportedly private conduct as well as implying an important ideological link between marriage and violence.[33] On the other hand, some of these extensive state statutory provisions have been challenged by battering men on constitutional grounds, including invasion of rights to marital privacy.[34]

At the same time that these remedies have been developing, there has been a move towards more private and informal processes, notably mediation. Most battered women's advocates are critical of mediation, because they believe that informal modes of dispute resolution substantially hurt battered women who are disadvantaged with respect to power, money and resources.[35] Mediation is viewed as signaling that battering is the women's individual and private "problem" that should be "worked out," and that the state has no role. A general mood in legal circles, in favor of alternative dispute resolution and less adversarial forms of problem solving, has helped to legitimate mediation and obscure its problematic implications in this circumstance.[36] However, it is more accurate to see the move to mediation and more informal processes as a reflection of the low priority accorded family law issues, generally, and battered women's problems, in particular, by the law.[37]

Recently, the importance of criminal remedies for battering, particularly mandatory arrest provisions, has been increasingly recognized.[38] Activists have argued that criminal remedies, generally, and mandatory arrest, in particular, are important remedies that send a clear social message that battering is impermissible, and, because criminal remedies are prosecuted by the state, give more public force to the sanction. However, even civil remedies, such as orders of protection and tort suits against batterers, initiated by individual women against individual men, can send a social message. These lawsuits use formal court process, are subject to public scrutiny, and the legal decisions arrived at in those cases also make a public statement. In particular, the tort action may carry a greater social meaning in light of the demise of the historic bar of interspousal immunity, the social dimension of the claimed harm, and the affirmative nature of the claim for damages.[39] Other examples of alternative procedural frameworks that carry more public meaning include the articulation of battering as a civil rights violation,[40] an international human rights violation,[41] and as involuntary servitude.[42]

Indeed, the development of these more formal processes has several important ramifications in promoting public education and helping to redefine violence as a public issue. . . . The development of more formal processes also has been important to battered women [in other ways]. A recent empirical study of battered women's experiences in obtaining restraining orders in New Haven, Connecticut, concluded that temporary restraining orders can help battered women in ways other than increasing police responsiveness or deterring violent men; "the process is (or can be) the empowerment."[43] The authors emphasize that "[t]his occurs when attorneys listen to battered women, giving them time and attention, and when judges understand their situation, giving them support and courage."[44] . . .

This study underscores the importance of legal representation, another issue that reveals the tension between public and private. Although battered women now have remedies that are available to them "on the books," they have no assured access to lawyers to represent them. Many battered women have limited resources and cannot afford to hire a lawyer. Moreover, there are few lawyers who are sensitive to their issues and problems. State statutory schemes do not provide for counsel; indeed many of the protective order statutes specifically provide the option for battered women to represent themselves.[45] Battered women's advocates, formerly battered women or shelter workers, usually without formal legal training, are now the crucial link between battered women and the legal system, and also frequently the child welfare and social service systems. Battered women's advocates help battered women to navigate the legal system, and assist them in every facet of the process. Although battered women's advocacy has played a critical role for battered women and has contributed a woman-centered form of representation, it is necessarily limited. Even the simplest litigation concerning restraining orders may involve complex issues of divorce, support and custody, and the lack of skilled legal representation effectively discriminates against battered women.

These examples illustrate the contradictions posed by more informal processes. The problem of lack of legal representation highlights the dilemma that a more formal process would pose. Because counsel is not provided, and has not been required by any of these statutes, battered women's advocates have been able to assist many battered women who would not otherwise have been represented. If counsel were required, but not provided by the state, those battered women who cannot pay for representation would be severely disadvantaged. Only the provision of free counsel, knowledgeable about these issues, would make a substantial difference. Thus, although in theory we might prefer a more formal legal process for battered women, in practice, under present conditions of scarce legal resources, it may not be realistic.

Finally, the complex interrelationship between private and public can be seen within the battered women's movement itself. Until about fifteen years ago, the terms "woman-abuse" and "battered woman" did not exist. "Linguistically, it was classed with the disciplining of children and servants as a 'domestic,' as opposed to a 'political' matter."[46] Feminist activists in the battered women's movement named the problem in a different way; they claimed that battery was not a personal, domestic problem but a systemic, political problem. Battering was not the result of a particular man or woman's difficulties, but part of a larger problem of male domination and female subordination. Nancy Fraser describes the meaning of this redefinition in the following way:

> Feminist activists contested established discursive boundaries and politicized a previously depoliticized phenomenon. In addition, they reinterpreted the experience of battery and posited a set of associated needs. Here they situated battered women's needs in a long chain of in-order-to relations that spilled across conventional separations of "spheres"; they claimed that in order to be free from dependence on batterers, battered women needed not just temporary shelter but also jobs paying a "family wage," day care and affordable permanent housing.[47]

The battered women's movement began with a clearly political and public agenda. Battered women are not viewed primarily as individual victims but as potential feminist activists. Activists organized battered women's shelters, which were woman-centered refuges and sites of consciousness-raising. The organization of shelters was nonhierarchical and egalitarian; many formerly battered women went on to become counselors or advocates. Many battered women who had blamed themselves developed a more political perspective, and began to identify more with other women, rather than with the men who battered them.[48]

However, as the issue of woman-abuse became a more legitimate political issue, and battered women's organizations and shelters began to receive government funding, "a variety of new, administrative constraints ranging from accounting procedures to regulation, accreditation and professionalization requirements were imposed."[49] Many organizations began to develop a service, rather than activist, perspective.

> As a consequence, publicly funded shelters underwent a transformation. Increasingly, they were staffed by professional social workers, many of whom had not themselves experienced battering. Thus, a division between professional and client supplanted the more fluid continuum of relations that characterized the early shelters. Moreover, many social work staff have been trained to frame problems in a quasi-psychiatric perspective. This perspective structures the practices of many publicly funded shelters even despite the intentions of individual staff, many of whom are politically committed feminists. Consequently, the practices of such shelters have become more individualizing and less politicized. Battered women tend now to be positioned as clients. They are increasingly psychiatrized, addressed as victims with deep, complicated selves. They are only rarely addressed as potential feminist activists. Increasingly, the language game of therapy has supplanted that of consciousness raising. And the neutral

scientific language of "spouse abuse" has supplanted more political talk of "male violence against women." Finally, the needs of battered women have been substantially reinterpreted. The very far-reaching earlier claims for the social and economic prerequisites of independence have tended to give way to a narrower focus on the individual woman's problems of "low self-esteem."[50]

Thus, the battered women's movement has experienced the tension between a more systemic "public" definition of the problem and an individualistic "privatized" vision. Even within the movement, we see internal tensions and pressures to move to a more privatized definition and experience of battering. Privacy encourages a focus on the individual, and avoidance of collective definition, systemic analysis and social responsibility. . . .

Conclusion

The challenge is to develop a right to privacy which is not synonymous with the right to state noninterference with actions within the family,[51] but which recognizes the affirmative role that privacy can play for battered women. Feminist reconstruction of privacy should seek to break down the dichotomy of public and private that has disabled legal discourse and public policy in this area. Male battering of women is a serious public problem for which we need to accept collective responsibility; it requires a dramatic program of mass public re-education similar to the drunk driving campaigns over the last several years. At the same time, while claiming woman-abuse as a public problem, we do not want to suggest that state intervention is always the answer. Frank Michelman has observed that even if we understand that the personal is political, this insight does not answer the question of the appropriate boundaries of state intervention.[52] Others have detailed the ways in which state intervention will always be problematic for women,[53] . . .

However, we also do not want to reject the genuine values and benefits of privacy for battered women. Thinking about privacy as something that women who have been battered might want makes us think about it differently. Battered women seek the material and social conditions of equality and self-determination that makes privacy possible.[54] Privacy that is grounded on equality, and is viewed as an aspect of autonomy, that protects bodily integrity and makes abuse impermissible, is based on a genuine recognition of the importance of personhood. . . . Such a notion of privacy could challenge the vision of individual solution, rather than social responsibility, for abuse. Conceived differently, privacy could help keep women safe, not battered.

Notes

1. I use the words "private" and "public" in quotes in order to emphasize there is no single natural meaning to the terms, but several socially constructed meanings.

2. Olsen, The Family and the Market: A Study of Ideology and Legal Reform, 96 Harv. L. Rev. 1497, 1499–1501 (1983).

3. Taub & Schneider, Women's Subordination and the Role of Law, in D. Weisberg ed., Feminist Legal Theory: Foundations 9 (Temple Univ. Press, 1993).

4. *Id.* at 12.

5. Kerber, Separate Spheres, Female Worlds, Women's Place: The Rhetoric of Women's History, 75 J. Am. Hist. 9, 17 (1988)

6. See Freeman and Mensch, The Public-Private Distinction in American Law and Life, 36 Buff. L. Rev. 237; Minow, Adjudicating Differences, Conflicts Among Feminist Lawyers, in M. Hirsh & E. Fox Keller eds., Conflicts in Feminism 156–160 (1990); Symposium, The Public/Private Distinction, 130 U. Pa. L. Rev. 1289 (1982).

7. Olsen, *supra* note 2, at 1507 n.39, 1537.

8. Michelman, Private, Personal But Not Split: Radin v. Rorty, 63 S. Cal. L. Rev. 1783, 1794 (1990).

9. C. MacKinnon, Toward a Feminist Theory of the State (1989); Copelon, Unpacking Patriarchy: Reproduction, Sexuality, Originalism and Constitutional Change, in J. Lobel ed., A Less Than Perfect Union: Alternative Perspectives on the U.S. Constitution 303 (1988); Minow, *supra* note 6.

10. Copelon, *supra* note 9.

11. A. Allen, Uneasy Access: Privacy for Women in a Free Society (1988).

12. *Id.* at 70–72.

13. For a discussion of the history and development of the battered women's movement, see S. Schechter, Women and Male Violence: The Vision and Struggles of the Battered Women's Movement (1982).

14. *Id.* at 43–52. According to feminist analysis of women battering, violence has traditionally been a means of maintaining control over women as a class by men as a class: "When a husband uses violence against his wife, people often view this as a random, irrational act. In contrast, feminists define wife abuse as a pattern that becomes understandable only through examination of the social context. Our society is structured along the dimensions of gender: Men as a class wield power over women." Bograd, Feminist Perspectives on Wife Abuse: An Introduction, in K. Yllo & M. Bograd eds., Feminist Perspectives on Wife Abuse 14 (1988).

15. See Schneider, Legal Reform Efforts to Assist Battered Women: Past, Present and Future 20–24 (1990) (unpublished manuscript).

16. See, e.g., Thurman v. Torrington, 595 F. Supp. 1521, 1527–1528 (D. Conn. 1984); Bruno v. Codd, 90 Misc. 2d 1047, 1049, 396 N.Y.S.2d 974 (N.Y. Sup. Ct. 1977), *rev'd on other grounds,* 64 A.D.2d 582, 407 N.Y.S.2d 165 (N.Y. App. Div. 1978), *aff'd,* 47 N.Y.2d 582, 393 N.E.2d 976, 419 N.Y.S.2d 901 (1979); Nearing v. Weaver, 295 Or. 702, 704, 670 P.2d 137, 139 (1983); *but see* DeShaney v. Winnebago County Dep't of Social Servs., 409 U.S. 189 (1989).

17. See Finn, Statutory Authority in the Use and Enforcement of Civil Protection Orders Against Domestic Abuse, 23 Fam. L.Q. 43, 60–73 (1989), for an overview of civil restraining legislation enacted across the country.

18. Schneider, *supra* note 15.

19. Bunch, Global Feminism, Human Rights and Sexual Violence, in First Annual Women's Policy Research Conference Proceedings 74 (Institute for Women's Policy Research, May 1989).

20. For an exploration of the phenomenon of denial and the importance of naming violence generally, see Kelly, How Women Define Their Experiences of Violence, in Feminist Perspectives, *supra* note 14, at 114–131.

21. Martha Mahoney's discussion of the problem of denial in Mahoney, Legal Im-

ages of Battered Women: Redefining the Issue of Separation, [herein at 341, 342, 347], was very helpful to me.

22. For a discussion of jury attitudes toward battered women, see Bochnak, Krauss, McPherson, Sternberg & Wiley, Case Preparation and Development, in E. Bochnak ed., Women's Self-Defense Cases: Theory and Practice (1981); Koonan & Waller, Jury Selection in a Woman's Self-Defense Case, CACJ/Forum May–June 1989 at 18; Note, Juror Misconduct and Juror Composition, 18 Golden Gate U.L. Rev. 589, 598 (1988).

23. The Joel Steinberg/Hedda Nussbaum case involved the murder of their adopted daughter, Lisa Steinberg, who was beaten to death by Joel Steinberg. This case focused on examination of Hedda Nussbaum as both a victim of abuse and a neglect-ful mother. See Sullivan, Defense Tries to Show Nussbaum Liked Pain, N.Y. Times, Dec. 9, 1988, at B2. Some feminist response to the case centered on Hedda Nuss-baum's "complicity," and not upon Joel Steinberg's terrorization of the family: "Sys-tematic battering combined with misguided, though culturally inculcated, notions of love is not a sufficient excuse to exonerate Hedda Nussbaum from her share of culpa-bility in Lisa Steinberg's death. . . . When decent, honorable women insist that a piece of Hedda Nussbaum resides in us all, they give the Joel Steinbergs of this world far too much credit and far too much power. More insidiously, they perpetuate the specious notion that women are doomed to be victims of the abnormal psychology of love at all cost." Brownmiller, Hedda Nussbaum, Hardly a Heroine, N.Y. Times, Feb. 2, 1989, at A25.

24. See e.g., Report of the New York Task Force on Women in the Courts, 15 Ford-ham Urb. L.J. 11 (1986); First Year Report of the New Jersey Supreme Court Task Force on Women in the Courts, 9 Women's Rts. L. Rep. 129 (1986); Report of the Gender Bias Study of the Court System in Massachusetts, 24 New Eng. L. Rev. 745 (1990).

25. Minow, Words and the Door to the Land of Change: Law, Language, and Fam-ily Violence, 43 Vand. L. Rev. 1665, 1671–1672 (1990).

26. *Id.*

27. 489 U.S. 189 (1989).

28. For a thoughtful analysis of *DeShaney*, see Minow, *supra* note 25, at 1666–1676.

29. *DeShaney* has made it difficult for victims of woman-abuse to bring section 1983 claims against the state for failure to protect them from battering. Courts are rejecting substantive due process claims, which are typically based on the alleged existence of a "special relationship" between the victims and the state (whether as a result of previ-ous knowledge of the harm they faced at the hands of their abusers or because the state had issued a protective order), as incompatible with *DeShaney*. See, e.g., Balistreri v. Pacifica Police Dep't, 901 F.2d 696, 700 (9th Cir. 1990); Luster v. Price, No. 90–0115-CV-W-8, at 10 (W.D. Mo. July 5, 1990) (LEXIS, Genfed library, Dist. file); Hynson v. City of Chester, 731 F. Supp. 1236, 1239 (E.D. Pa. 1990); Dudosh v. City of Allentown, 722 F. Supp. 1233, 1235 (E.D. Pa. 1989). Only in two cases involving battering men who were arguably more "public" actors, where batterers were either close friends of the po-lice chief, Freeman v. Ferguson, 911 F.2d 52, 53 (8th Cir. 1990) (plaintiff alleged that the husband was a close friend of the police chief and the chief in fact directed other police officers not to intervene on behalf of the wife), or a member of the police force himself, Muhammed v. City of Chicago, No. 89-C-6903 (N.D. Ill. Jan. 15, 1991) (LEXIS, Genfed library, Dist. file) have district courts held that plaintiffs should be given the opportunity to prove a duty-to-protect claim. But see Borgmann, Battered Women's Substantive Due Process Claims: Can Orders of Protection Deflect *DeShaney*, 65 N.Y.U. L. Rev. 1280, 1314–1317 (1990) (arguing that issuance of protective orders should

overcome *DeShaney*). One court has held, post-*DeShaney,* that a court's protective order issued pursuant to Pennsylvania's Protection from Abuse Act might create a property interest in police protection. Coffman v. Wilson Police Dep't, 739 F. Supp. 257, 264 (E.D. Pa. 1990).

As a result of the diminishing availability, after *DeShaney,* of section 1983 due process claims based on the notion of a special relationship, battered women may have to turn to alternative theories to sue the state for its failure to protect them. Such theories include equal protection violations, claims that the state has failed adequately to train its agents in domestic violence situations, or claims based on state tort law. Some courts dismissing section 1983 special relationship claims at least have been willing to permit plaintiffs the opportunity to bring such claims. See, e.g., *Balistreri,* 901 F.2d at 701–702; *Freeman,* 911 F.2d at 55 (permitting plaintiff to pursue an equal protection claim based on city's failure to train adequately its police force). See generally Note, Battered Women Suing Police for Failure to Intervene: Viable Legal Avenues After DeShaney v. Winnebago County Department of Social Services, 75 Cornell L. Rev. 1393 (1990) (arguing that, post-*DeShaney,* battered women's best chances of suing state actors for failure to intervene lie with due process suits not dependent on a special relationship theory, such as a state failure to train, equal protection challenges, and state tort theories).

30. For a discussion of the social meaning of rights claims, see Schneider, The Dialectic of Rights and Politics: Perspectives from the Women's Movement, in D. Weisberg ed., Feminist Legal Theory: Foundations 507 (Temple Univ. Press, 1993).

31. See Finn, *supra* note 17, at 43–44.

32. Buel, Mandatory Arrest for Domestic Violence, 11 Harv. Women's L.J. 213, 214–215 (1988).

33. Mo. Rev. Stat. §455.205 (Supp. 1989) authorizes a surcharge of $10.00 in each marriage dissolution case for domestic violence shelters. Ariz. Rev. Stat. Ann. §12–284 (1989) provides that 80 percent of monies gathered for marriage licenses shall be deposited in a domestic violence shelter fund. Minn. Stat. §357.021 (1990) provides that a portion of the marriage dissolution fee shall be used for emergency shelter and support services to battered women.

34. For constitutional challenges to some of the marriage license fee provisions, see Browning v. Corbett, 153 Ariz. 74, 734 P.2d 1030 (1987); Boynton v. Kusper, 112 Ill.2d 356, 494 N.E.2d 135 (1986); Crocker v. Finley, 99 Ill.2d 444, 459 N.E.2d 1346 (1984); Villars v. Provo, 440 N.W.2d 160 (Minn. Ct. App. 1989).

Griswold [v. Connecticut, 381 U.S. 479 (1965)] has been raised as a defense by men to marital rape on the ground that it protects marital privacy. These challenges have been rejected by courts. In Commonwealth v. Shoemaker, 359 Pa. Super. 111, 518 A.2d 591 (1986), the court rejected the defendant's privacy challenge on the ground that the right to privacy should be overridden by the compelling state interest protecting the "fundamental right of all individuals to control the integrity of his or her body." *Id.* at 116, 518 A.2d at 594. Other cases involving privacy challenges to marital rape have taken a stronger position, suggesting that marital privacy was never intended to cover nonconsensual acts. Williams v. State, 494 So. 2d 819, 828–829 (Ala. Crim. App. 1986); People v. Liberta, 64 N.Y.2d 152, 165, 474 N.E.2d 567, 574, 485 N.Y.S.2d 207, 214 (1984), *cert. denied,* 471 U.S. 1020 (1985). Significantly, in rejecting this argument, some courts drew analogies to woman-abuse with one court suggesting that "[j]ust as a husband cannot invoke a right to marital privacy to escape liability for beating his wife, he cannot justifiably rape his wife under the guise of a right to privacy." *Liberta,* 64

N.Y.2d at 165, 474, 485 N.Y.S.2d at 214. See also Merton v. State, 500 So. 2d 1301, 1304 (Ala. Crim. App. 1986); State v. Rider, 449 So. 2d 903, 906 n.6 (Fla. Dist. Ct. App. 1984). But see People v. Forman, 145 Misc. 2d 115, 121, 546 N.Y.S.2d 755, 760 (N.Y. Crim. Ct. 1989), where the defendant argued that his associational liberty interests protected by *Griswold* were violated by the issuance of a temporary order of protection.

35. See M. Sun & L. Woods, A Mediator's Guide to Domestic Abuse (1989); Hart, Gentle Jeopardy: The Further Endangerment of Battered Women and Children in Custody Mediation, 7 Mediation Q. 317 (1990); Lerman, Mediation of Wife Abuse Cases: The Adverse Impact of Informal Dispute Resolution on Women, 7 Harv. Women's L.J. 57 (1984). For a more general analysis of the problems with mediation for women, see Grillo, The Mediation Alternative: Process Dangers for Women, 100 Yale L.J. 1545 (1991).

36. Lerman, *supra* note 35, at 88–89.

37. *Id.*

38. Buel, *supra* note 32, at 215–216.

39. For analysis of the developing area of domestic violence and torts, see L. Karp & C. Karp, Spousal Abuse, in Domestic Torts: Family Violence, Conflict and Sexual Abuse (1989). . . .

40. Lawyers in some states are exploring whether their civil rights statutes can be interpreted to cover domestic violence. See Mass. Gen. L. Ann. ch. §265, 37 (West 1990); N.J. Stat. Ann. §10:5–1–10:5–42 (West 1976 & Supp. 1991) (the New Jersey Law Against Discrimination). The proposed Violence Against Women Act of 1991, also defines gender bias as a civil rights violation in Title III of the Act. See S. 15, 101st Cong., 1st Cong., 1st Sess. (1991).

41. For a discussion of domestic violence as an international human rights violation, see Baer, Human Rights at the United Nations: Women's Rights Are Human Rights, 24 In Brief, Nov. 1989, at 1; Heise, Crimes of Gender, World Watch, Mar.–Apr. 1989, at 12; Sullivan, Human Rights at the United Nations: The Implementation of Women's Rights: The Effectiveness of Existing Procedures, 29 In Brief, Oct. 1990, at 1 (International League for Human Rights).

42. McConnell, Beyond Metaphor: Battered Women, Involuntary Servitude, and the Thirteenth Amendment, 4 Yale J.L. & Feminism (1992).

43. Chaudhuri & Daly, Do Restraining Orders Help? Battered Women's Experience with Male Violence and Legal Process, in E. Buzawa ed., Domestic Violence: The Changing Criminal Justice Response (1992).

44. *Id.*

45. Most civil restraining order statutes have no provisions for counsel and are designed for pro se applicants. Though legal advocates are bridging the representational gap in new and creative ways, battered women are still in desperate need of adequate legal representation because civil restraining order litigation inevitably involves issues of custody, support, and visitation. Schneider, *supra* note 15, at 51–52, 56–59. For a discussion of the problem of legal representation in restraining order litigation, see P. Finn & S. Colson, Civil Protection Orders: Legislation, Current Court Practice, and Enforcement 19 (U.S. Dep't of Justice, Nat'l Trust of Justice, March 1990).

46. Fraser, Struggle Over Needs: Outcome of a Socialist-Feminist Critical Theory of Late-Capitalist Political Culture, in L. Gordon ed., Women, The State, and Welfare 199, 213 (1990).

47. *Id.* at 213–214.

48. *Id.* at 214.

49. *Id.*

50. *Id.* at 214–215.

51. Eisler, Human Rights: Toward an Integrated Theory for Action, 9 Hum. Rts. Q. 287, 282–293 (1987).

52. Michelman, *supra* note 8, at 1794.

53. See Olsen, The Myth of State Intervention in the Family, 18 U. Mich. J.L. Ref. 835, 858–861 (1985).

54. See Copelon, Losing the Negative Right of Privacy: Building Sexual and Reproductive Freedom, 18 N.Y.U. Rev. L. & Soc. Change 15, 44–50 (1990–1991), for a discussion of privacy and equality.

Section 4

Rape

Introduction

FEMINIST CONCERN with rape emerged early in the women's movement.[1] Although the feminist agenda was first dominated by other issues (employment discrimination, passage of the Equal Rights Amendment, abortion),[2] attention soon focused on male sexual violence toward women.[3] Early feminists' views on rape reflected a singular consensus:

> Within the women's movement . . . rape in the early 1970s was *the* feminist issue. It symbolized women's unique vulnerability to attack from men at any time and an attack involving a fundamental violation of their physical and sexual being. Unlike other issues at the time, such as prostitution or abortion, rape had the advantage of uniting all women, whatever their status, values or beliefs. Indeed, it has been wryly observed that on rape, and on rape alone, women on the radical right and on the radical left find themselves in agreement.[4]

Scholars credit 1971 as the year marking the beginning of scholarly attention to rape.[5] In that year appeared Susan Griffin's "Rape: The All-American Crime" (included herein)[6] and Barbara Mehrhof and Pamela Kearon's "Rape: An Act of Terror."[7] Griffin's discovery of the fear of rape spawned other studies exploring the consequences of this fear.[8] Mearhof and Kearon introduced the radical feminist view of rape as a political act that keeps women subordinate.

With the publication of Susan Brownmiller's classic in 1975,[9] the topic of rape took center stage. Brownmiller made several important contributions. First, she placed rape in historical perspective, from Biblical times to the present, thereby revealing rape as a pervasive although largely unexplored practice.[10] Her book sparked further historical feminist studies of sexual violence.[11]

Brownmiller's work is noteworthy, too, for its reliance on sociological research. Behavioral scientists had long been interested in the subject of sex offenders.[12] In 1971 Menachem Amir, an Israeli sociologist and student of famed criminologist Marvin Wolfgang, had conducted the first in-depth study of rape.[13] Amir explored patterns and characteristics of the crime, including such factors as age, race, relationship, and previous arrest record of both victim and offender; modus operandi; and temporal and spatial patterns of the offense.

Brownmiller's book disseminated Amir's research to a broader audience and thereby refuted rape myths. Among the most common myths are: (1) African-American men are more likely to attack white, rather than African-American, women; (2) rape usually occurs between persons unknown to each other; (3) rape is predominantly an explosive, unpremeditated act; (4) rape is always a violent crime in which physical force is inflicted; and (5) rape is always characterized by a showing of resistance by the victim. Although Amir's work had its feminist critics,[14] his findings played a role in the law reform movement.

Brownmiller made another contribution with her feminist analysis of the legal response to rape.[15] In particular, she criticized the requirement of corroboration; the admissibility of the victim's past sexual history; the requirement of resistance by the victim; evidentiary rules (inapplicable to other crimes) stemming from the male fear of a false rape charge; the chastity requirement; and the prejudicial effect of a previous sexual relationship between offender and victim.

Prior to 1971, legal scholars had directed little attention to the topic of rape. However, in that year, references to rape escalate.[16] Early commentary emphasized the defendant's rights, statutory rape, prior sexual history as evidence of character, consent as a defense, and corroboration. Subsequent studies call for law reform and criticize reforms as they are enacted. In addition, the focus shifts to the victim rather than the defendant, largely due to the concerns of feminist scholars.[17]

Also, at that time, women formed consciousness-raising groups. They organized more structured discussions of rape soon thereafter. In 1971 a woman's group, the New York Radical Feminists (NYRF), held two conferences on rape. At the New York Radical Feminists Speak-out on Rape, participants revealed personal experiences. Conference participants criticized the criminal justice system for its insensitive handling of victims. The subsequent New York Radical Feminist Rape Conference concentrated on statutory criticisms, especially in regard to New York's legislation.[18]

The issue of rape also captured attention on the federal level. A major achievement of the anti-rape movement was the establishment of rape crisis centers.[19] In 1972 the National Institute of Justice's Law Enforcement Assistance Administration funded the first rape crisis centers in Los Angeles; Washington, D.C.; and Ann Arbor, Michigan.[20] By 1978, 550 rape crisis centers existed,[21] many receiving federal funding.

The centers had a dual purpose: to provide emotional support and to promote institutional change.[22] Rape crisis centers offered such services as telephone hotlines, counseling services, support personnel to accompany victims to hospitals and police stations, and self-help therapy groups.[23] Centers were founded on the belief that victims needed alternatives to traditional legal, medical, and mental health services. Some centers, such as the prototype Bay Area Women Against Rape, served as springboards for legal reform.[24]

As a result of intensive lobbying by feminist groups,[25] Congress established the National Center for the Prevention and Control of Rape in the National Institute of Mental Health.[26] The national center became a major source of funding for research and treatment.[27]

Rape Law Reform

Early rape reform laws were the result of campaigns by feminist organizations.[28] In some jurisdictions, feminists formed coalitions with law-and-order advocates.[29] These efforts resulted in considerable success. Law enforcement handling of rape victims improved.[30] Also, from 1976 through 1979, thirty-two states amended their rape statutes.[31] Lobbying efforts in 1973 by the Michigan Women's Task Force on Rape resulted in the first comprehensive rape reform legislation—legislation that became a prototype for other states'.[32]

Feminist reformers benefited from groundwork laid earlier by efforts to revise the Model Penal Code (MPC).[33] In the 1950s legal reformers had proposed statutory revisions to overcome shortcomings in rape law. In particular, the MPC drafters proposed three major changes: removal of the requirement that the woman resist her attacker; alteration of the law's focus on the victim's nonconsent; and creation of differentiated categories of offenses.[34] A number of states enacted reforms based on MPC proposals.[35] As state legislatures debated the MPC proposals, a feminist critique emerged. Although feminists supported the MPC's purpose of improving the rape conviction rate, they argued that the proposals manifested serious shortcomings.[36]

Principal among feminist concerns were the MPC's attempts to protect men from false accusations by imposing a corroboration requirement,[37] as well as the prompt complaint rule[38] and marital rape exemptions.[39] Feminists attacked, in particular, the belief that women frequently make false reports of rape.[40] They ultimately expanded their struggle to include additional reforms: redefining the offense as a crime of assault (violence) rather than as a sexual crime;[41] phrasing statutes in gender-neutral terms;[42] repealing statutory spousal exceptions;[43] eliminating the use of implied consent[44] and the resistance requirement;[45] attempting to punish defendants for their culpable actions, rather than victims for their failure to communicate nonconsent effectively; and changing evidentiary rules both to remove the requirement of corroboration[46] and to prevent the victim's past sexual history from being introduced at trial as evidence of present consent ("rape shield laws").[47]

The rape law reform movement resulted in repeal or modification of many rape laws. "As of 1980, every state has considered, and most states have passed, some form of rape reform legislation."[48] Reform was effected along several dimensions: (1) redefinition of the offense and replacement of rape as a single offense with a series of graded offenses varying according to the presence of aggravating factors; (2) change in the consent standard by eliminating the victim resistance requirement; (3) elimination of the corroboration requirement; (4) restrictions on the admissibility of the victim's prior sexual conduct via rape shield laws; and (5) changes in the law of marital rape to eliminate the husband's exemption.[49]

Reform recently has reached the national level. Congress enacted the Violence Against Women Act (VAWA) in 1994 as part of the Violent Crime Control and Law Enforcement Act. The VAWA enables victims of "gender-motivated violence" (presumably, victims of rape and battering) to recover damages from perpetrators[50]—a novel remedy for rape victims who may be unable to secure convictions against offenders. The VAWA also indirectly targets rape by providing increased funding for security measures on public transportation.[51]

Despite statutory reform, commentators criticize the reform movement for its failure to achieve feminist goals. Some scholars charge that state evidentiary reforms, for example, have only limited effectiveness.[52] And VAWA has been criticized for mirroring the deficiencies of state laws.[53] Researchers of a multijurisdiction empirical study conclude that

> legal changes did not produce the dramatic results anticipated by those who lobbied for reform. In spite of the elimination of legal requirements, criminal justice officials in every jurisdiction still believe that resistance by the victim and corroboration of her testimony are important determinants of whether a rape case will result in conviction. Officials also assume that evidence of a prior sexual relationship between the victim and the defendant will be admitted at trial. . . .
>
> Most disappointing, in terms of reformers' expectations, is our finding that the legal changes had limited effects on reports of rape and the processing of rape cases. The reforms did not produce an increase in the likelihood of conviction.[54]

Scholars voice additional criticisms. Ellis, for example, argues that the shift to gender neutral laws, by ignoring the gender-specific nature of the crime, removes women's voices, thereby lodging control in the hands of bureaucrats and politicians.[55] Berger, Searles, and Neuman point out that, despite some legislative successes, feminist goals have been hampered by the ideologies of both the criminal justice system and nonfeminist political groups.[56]

Many theorists argue that women's experience of rape is still absent from the legal model of rape.[57] Rape continues to be defined in male terms. The essays herein illustrate these and other feminist criticisms of rape reform. The various schools of feminist thought provide helpful background for an understanding of these essays.

Liberal Feminist Perspectives of Rape

Liberal feminist perspectives are reflected in both practice and theory on rape. The National Organization for Women (NOW) played a prominent role in rape reform, advocating the liberal feminist agenda.[58] NOW chapters focusing on rape-related activities increased from thirteen in 1973 to two hundred in 1975.[59] NOW organized more than three hundred state and local rape task forces to study rape and to implement reform.[60] With the establishment of a National Task Force on Rape in 1973 at NOW's sixth annual conference,[61] NOW began advocating reform at the national level. In 1974, NOW members submitted to the National Board Meeting a resolution with the following objective:

> To revise the present laws which overwhelmingly favor the defendant, impede convictions, allow victims, as witnesses, to be treated in a manner which is both humiliating and damaging to their emotional health, and which further discourage victims from reporting the crime to the officials.[62]

Additional support for reform came from the American Bar Association in 1975. Largely through the efforts of the Law Student Division, a resolution was drafted and adopted by the ABA House of Delegates which urged a revision of the rules of evidence, reevaluation of penalties for rape, development of new police and prosecutorial procedures, and establishment of rape treatment centers.[63]

Scholarly treatment of rape, as well as rape law reform, reflect the liberal feminist perspective:

> Given liberalism's stress on the autonomous individual and choice, sexual coercion came to be viewed as individual and gender neutral rather than institutional and sex specific. Moreover, its violent rather than its sexual aspects were emphasized. According to liberals, coercion consists of force or threats of force that violate natural human rights. Because liberalism established that women should be treated as individuals, not as women classified by their sex, legal standards of objectivity determining whether coercion existed in any circumstance regardless of sex were preferred to the gender-biased standards adhered to in traditional legal practices.[64]

Other commentators, as well, have noted the intertwining of classic liberal theory and feminist views of rape. Judith Vega, for example, argues that the views of radical feminists Susan Brownmiller and Catherine MacKinnon contain strains of liberal beliefs in their conceptualizations of the victim and the state.[65] These radical feminist views are explored below.

Marxist Feminist Views

Marxist feminist writers have also propounded views of rape. The Marxist perspective of Schwendinger and Schwendinger[66] emphasizes the interrelationship of rape, sexual inequality, and capitalist systems. Schwendinger and Schwendinger disagree with the radical feminist view of the universality of rape. By examining anthropological studies, they conclude that male violence is neither inborn nor universal.[67] Rather, rape is related to levels of violence that vary from society to society. They hypothesize that the social mechanisms that give rise to rape operate in societies dominated by capitalist modes of production.

They substantiate their hypothesis by secondary analysis of anthropological data from four African tribes in precapitalist societies which reflect varying degrees of modes of production. The tribes include the highly egalitarian Mbuti of Zaire, the Lovedu and Mpondo of South Africa, reflecting an intermediate level of egalitarianism, and the inegalitarian class society of the Baganda in Uganda. ("Egalitarian" here signifies equality in terms of both sexual and class relations.[68])

Schwendinger and Schwendinger find that the societies manifesting greater sexual and class inequality reveal more violence generally, as well as increased sexual violence against women.[69] Their solution to the problem of rape is to direct social policies at changing the socioeconomic factors that contribute to violence: improving the opportunities and working conditions of unemployed men and reducing female dependency at home and in the labor force, to provide women with greater power.[70]

Other Marxists, too, have addressed the topic of rape. Rafter and Natalizia highlight rape and marital rape as examples of women's oppression under capitalism:

> Rape is an act that symbolizes the political and economic oppression of women in capitalist society. Traditionally, rape has been regarded as a property crime, an offense whose victim is the man whose property (i.e. wife or daughter) has been defiled. This interpretation is reinforced by the fact that in most jurisdictions, it is legally impossible for a man to rape his wife, for she is his possession and he may demand sexual gratification from her at will. Patriarchal capitalism thus reduces the body and spirit of woman to their property value and then takes from her the control over that property.[71]

One Marxist scholar has applied Marxist theory specifically to marital rape.[72] Collins analyzes a British case, Rex v. Miller,[73] in which a court held that the absence of a separation order precluded a husband's conviction for marital rape. Collins uses the case to illustrate judicial reconciliation of conflicting authorities which supports the "autonomy thesis" (that legal decisions are independent of the interests of the dominant class). He thereby debunks the instrumentalist view of law that is often attributed to Marxists (that the formalism of legal reasoning disguises law that is formulated in the interests of the ruling class).[74]

Marxists' analysis of rape has been criticized by radical feminists and others. Susan Griffin, for example, believes that the view of rape as the product of capitalism is "nonsense" and, further, that such a theory is disproved by rape in Soviet society and by Cuban troops in Angola.[75] MacKinnon's criticism is included in an essay herein.

Schwartz and Slatin also criticize the application of Marxist theory to the example of marital rape. They cite a number of problems in attempts to generalize Marxist theory to marital rape. One such problem is the Marxist assumption that law serves the interests of the ruling class, an assumption that glosses over the need to identify those bourgeois interests.[76] In addition, they criticize the "dead end" approach of Marxist analysis "where all roads eventually lead back to the maintenance of the existing social order."[77] Instead, their explanation of the endurance of the marital rape exemption results from a synthesis of Marxism and feminist perspectives, notions of male hegemony,[78] and historical inertia theory.[79]

Radical Feminist Views

Radical feminists believe that rape functions as a mechanism of social control. "Feminists scholars who take this position believe that rape and the fear of rape enable men to assert their power over women and maintain the existing system of gender stratification."[80] Radical feminists also believe that pornography causes rape by reflecting and encouraging male dominance, objectifying women, and serving as a behavioral model for the perpetration of misogynistic acts.[81]

Radical feminists view the root of women's oppression as male control of women's bodies—specifically, control of their fertility and sexuality.[82] Set against this emphasis on sexuality, radical feminists regard rape as a political act. According to one of the earliest radical feminist works:

> Rape, then, is an effective political device. It is not an arbitrary act of violence by one individual on another; it is a political act of oppression (never rebellion) exercised by members of a powerful class on members of the powerless class. Rape is supported by a consensus in the male class. It is preached by male-controlled and all-pervasive media with only a minimum of disguise and restraint. It is communicated to the male population as an act of freedom and strength and a male right never to be denied.[83]

Brownmiller's early classic *Against Our Will* elaborates on radical feminist views. She claims that men rape women to affirm their domination. Rape is political in the sense of making women's bodies into pawns of men—whether it be medieval husbands with proprietary rights over wives, fathers whose daughters are marketable commodities, or aggressors in war who violate and humiliate their adversaries. Brownmiller also shares the view of other radical feminists, such as Robin Morgan, Andrea Dworkin, and Catharine MacKinnon, that pornography causes rape.[84]

Brownmiller's work amplifies on the views of radical feminist Kate Millett, author of *Sexual Politics*.[85] Millett argues that the state maintains its rule through force as well as ideological hegemony. That is, patriarchal ideology permeates women's lives and conditions women to accept certain social roles which benefit men. According to Millett, rape is one of the ways in which force is exerted to keep women in their place.[86]

Radical feminists believe that, as a political act, rape constitutes oppression against women along individual as well as societal dimensions. As Griffin explains:

> Rape is an act of aggression in which the victim is denied her self-determination. It is an act of violence, which, if not actually followed by beatings or murder, nevertheless always carries with it the threat of death. And finally, rape is a form of mass terrorism, for the victims of rape are chosen indiscriminately, but the propagandists for male supremacy broadcast that it is women who cause

rape by being unchaste or in the wrong place at the wrong time—in essence by behaving as though they were free.[87]

Radical feminists emphasize the similarity of rape to "normal" heterosexual relations.[88] In a society characterized by male hegemony, all sexual relations may be regarded as violent, they argue, because such relations are coerced by male power. Rape then becomes merely an end on the same continuum as normal heterosexual relations. Early second-wave radical feminists (such as Shulamith Firestone and Kate Millett) explained that the myth of romantic love dupes women in heterosexual relationships by concealing this element of sexual coercion.[89]

Some feminists are critical of this radical feminist perception. For example, Henderson argues that such a view denies women's pleasurable sexual experiences. She also suggests that this conception promotes a simplistic, Victorian idea of sex that makes woman the victim and blames the man.[90]

Criticism of victimization ideology is present as well in the literature on the pornography debate and on battered women.[91] Some critics take the criticism further as part of an antifeminist backlash. Author Katie Roiphe has suggested that rape activists exaggerate the dangers of rape and that their overemphasis on victimization serves only to oppress women.[92]

Another subject of debate between radical feminists and others concerns the sources of rape. For Brownmiller and other radical feminists, rape is a crime of power and violence.[93] This is refuted by those who regard rape as motivated by a desire for sexual gratification. For example, historian Edward Shorter argues that "the sexual frustration theory"[94] provides a better historical explanation. Many feminists,[95] including many radical feminists, reject this theory, by pointing to the persistence of rape in today's sexually liberated society. Indeed, it might be stated that a major contribution of radical feminism is the debunking of this theory. Currently, as Hartmann and Ross observe: "A consensus is emerging among both feminists and criminologists that rape is quintessentially a crime of aggression and hostility, not a form of sexual release."[96]

The essays in this chapter examine rape from different feminist perspectives. Radical feminist Susan Griffin's classic identifies the gender-specific nature of the fear of rape. Especially insightful is Griffin's identification of the behavioral consequences for women of this fear.

Susan Estrich's essay provides one of the earliest examples of feminist narratives in legal scholarship.[97] Estrich's personal experience enables her to view the many ways in which rape law is shaped by stereotypically male notions. Challenging the role of neutrality in scholarship,[98] she pleads for law reform to take women's perspective into account by adopting a communicative model of sexual relations in which consent or nonconsent is not presumed.[99] In addition to highlighting rape law as an illustration of sexism in the criminal law,[100] Estrich illuminates the tensions between legal doctrine, practice, and experience.

Fran Olsen explores the advantages and disadvantages of rights analysis as applied to statutory rape and, specifically, to the Supreme Court case of Michael M. v. Superior

Court, 450 U.S. 464 (1981). Olsen's point of departure is that laws prohibiting statutory rape serve to protect, as well as to undermine, women's rights.[101] Olsen uses the context of statutory rape to illustrate the limits of law reform.

Catharine A. MacKinnon's essay provides the most cogent illustration of her views on rape.[102] MacKinnon's point of departure, reflecting her radical feminist perspective, regards sexuality as a sphere of male power. MacKinnon argues that rape is defined in male terms; namely, its emphasis on penetration and the level of force that is unacceptable. MacKinnon also questions the meaningfulness of consent.[103]

Lois Pineau focuses on a special type of rape[104]—sexual assault by a casual acquaintance on a date. The critical dilemma in rape reform, Pineau explains, is the consent requirement. To be convicted of rape (to be held to have the requisite mental state, or *mens rea*), an offender must believe that the victim did not consent. Consent is implied unless the victim evidences resistance. However, if the offender is known to the victim (common in date rape), the victim must demonstrate more resistance to establish lack of consent. Similar to Estrich, Pineau proposes a reformulation of the consent requirement through adoption of a model of communicative sexuality. This model, advocated by these and other legal scholars, has garnered considerable feminist support.[105]

Jennifer Wriggens shifts the focus to the relationship between race, gender, and sexual violence. Her essay reflects the recent broadening of feminist theory on rape to include the concerns of African-American women.[106] Wriggens highlights the law's longstanding neglect of African-American female victims and its emphasis on the African-American rapist of white women.

Robin West focuses on the context of marital rape to explore equality theory. Although most analyses examine the constitutionality of the marital rape exemption (in which a husband is exempt from rape of his wife) under the equal protection model, West assesses its constitutionality against other formulations, including MacKinnon's antisubordination approach. Given the shortcomings of traditional constitutional doctrine, West concludes that law reformers should seek equality through legislative, rather than judicial, means.

Notes

1. Clark and Lewis note that the first articles dealing with rape were "a direct result of the women's movement developing in the late 1960s [which] first appeared in feminist publications [and] were written by avowed feminists." L. Clark & D. Lewis, Rape: The Price of Coercive Sexuality 24 (Women's Press, 1977). See also Rose, Rape as a Social Problem: A Byproduct of the Feminist Movement, 24 Soc. Probs. 75–76 (1977) (feminists were the most active group in the 1970s addressing rape).

2. F. Davis, Moving the Mountain: The Women's Movement in America Since 1960 49 (Simon & Schuster, 1991).

3. The first women's liberation anthologies contained several general references to male violence. S. Schechter, Women and Male Violence: The Visions and Struggles

of the Battered Women's Movement 32–33 (South End Press, 1982) (citing R. Morgan ed., Sisterhood Is Powerful: An Anthology of Writings from the Women's Liberation Movement (Vintage Books, Random House, 1970) and L. Tanner ed., Voices from Women's Liberation (Signet, New American Library, 1970)). Feminist attention on male sexual violence focused initially on prostitution and only subsequently on rape. D. Chappell, R. Geis & G. Geis eds., Forcible Rape: The Crime, the Victim, and the Offender 4 (Columbia Univ. Press, 1977). Author Susan Brownmiller, for example, was first interested in prostitution. As a member of the New York Radical Feminists, Brownmiller organized a meeting on prostitution and, later, a conference on rape. *Id.* at 4–5.

4. A. Edwards, Male Violence in Feminist Theory: An Analysis of the Changing Conceptions of Sex/Gender Violence and Male Dominance, in J. Hanmer & M. Maynard eds., Women, Violence and Social Control 18 (London, MacMillan, 1987).

5. L. Bourque, Defining Rape 13 (Duke Univ. Press, 1989); F. Davis, *supra* note 2, at 310.

6. The essay was originally published in Ramparts, Sept. 1971, at 26, 31–32.

7. B. Mehrhof & P. Kearon, Rape: An Act of Terror, in Notes from the Third Year (1971), reprinted in A. Koedt, E. Levine & A. Rapone eds., Radical Feminism 228–233 (Quadrangle, 1973). For another early popular article, see Greer, Seduction Is a Four-Letter Word, Playboy, Jan. 1973, at 80 (attacking the myth that women desire to be raped and elaborating on the fear of rape).

8. See, e.g., Riger & Gordon, The Fear of Rape: A Study of Social Control, 37 J. Soc. Issues 71 (1981).

9. S. Brownmiller, Against Our Will: Men, Women and Rape (Simon & Schuster, 1975). Brownmiller's book, although not the first scholarly work on rape, is the most famous. For other early works, see A. Burgess & L. Holmstrom, Rape: Victims of Crisis (Bowie, Md., Brady, 1974); N. Gager & C. Schurr, Sexual Assault: Confronting Rape in America (Grosset & Dunlap, 1976); A. Medea & K. Thompson, Against Rape (Farrar, Straus, & Giroux, 1974); D. Russell, The Politics of Rape: The Victim's Perspective (Stein & Day, 1975).

10. Brownmiller also explores the origins of rape law, pointing out that before the Norman Conquest the penalty for rape was death and dismemberment, but only for the rape of a virgin of the nobility. William the Conqueror reduced the punishment to castration and blinding. King Henry III modernized criminal procedure generally, including procedures regarding rape, providing for trial by jury rather than combat or duel.

By the thirteenth century, legal protection was extended to women of other social classes. Also, the Statutes of Westminster, enacted at the end of the thirteenth century during the reign of Edward I, broadened the offense to include statutory rape and rape of a married woman by someone other than her husband. Brownmiller, *supra* note 9, at 15–22.

11. See, e.g., A. Clark, Women's Silence, Men's Violence: Sexual Assault in England 1770–1845 (Pandora Press, 1987); Pleck, Feminist Responses to Crimes Against Women, 1868–1896, 8 Signs 450 (Spring 1983); Walkowitz, Jack the Ripper and the Myth of Male Violence, 8 Feminist Stud. 543 (1982).

12. See, e.g., M. Forst, Civil Commitment and Social Control (Lexington Books, 1978) (tracing the interest in the mentally disordered sex offender to the 1930s).

13. M. Amir, Patterns in Forcible Rape (Univ. of Chicago Press, 1971). Amir collected data in 1961 on six hundred rape cases in Philadelphia over two one-year periods (1958 and 1960).

14. Amir's concept of "victim-precipitated rape," in particular, came in for its share of criticism. Amir theorized that in some cases the victim initially agreed to sexual intercourse but later retracted her consent, thereby precipitating the rape. Amir, *supra* note 13, at 266. See also Amir, Victim-Precipitated Forcible Rape, 58 J. Crim. L. & Criminology 493 (1967). Amir adopted the term from Marvin Wolfgang's classic work on homicide. See M. Wolfgang, Patterns of Criminal Homicide (Univ. Pennsylvania Press, 1958). Feminists and others chastised Amir for holding the victim responsible. Although victim precipitation may play a role in homicide, critics argued that the concept feeds into rape myths by blaming the victim. See, e.g., Chappell, Geis & Geis, *supra* note 3, at 20–21; Clark & Lewis, *supra* note 1, at 152–155; Rose, *supra* note 1, at 78; Weis & Borges, Victimology and Rape: The Case of the Legitimate Victim, 8 Issues Criminology 71 (1973); J. Schwendinger & H. Schwendinger, Rape and Inequality 26, 66–68 (Sage, 1983).

15. Brownmiller, *supra* note 9, at 183–235. For other early criticisms, see generally LeGrand, Rape and Rape Laws: Sexism in Society and Law, 63 Cal. L. Rev. 919 (1973); Sasko & Sesek, Rape Reform Legislation: Is It the Solution?, 24 Clev. St. L. Rev. 463 (1975); Note, The Rape Corroboration Requirement: Repeal Not Reform, 81 Yale L.J. 1365 (1972); Note, The Victim in a Forcible Rape Case: A Feminist View, 11 Am. Crim. L. Rev. 335 (1972).

16. Bourque, *supra* note 5, at 108–109. Bourque's study focused on citations in the Index of Legal Periodicals and the Current Law Index. Bourque notes that, beginning in 1916 through 1970, the average number of citations to rape was two annually; however starting in 1971, references increase to 135 for the years 1971 to 1979. *Id.* at 108.

17. Bourque notes: "Between 1980 and mid-1986, 382 comments, notes, and research articles on the subject were listed in Current Law Index, and female authors were increasingly prevalent." *Id.* at 108.

18. Davis, *supra* note 2, at 311. In her description of the second 1971 NYRF conference, Davis notes feminist criticisms of the corroboration requirement. See also the discussion of the first "Rape Speak-Out" in M. Manhart & F. Rush, New York Radical Feminists Manifesto, in N. Connell & C. Wilson eds., Rape: The First Sourcebook for Women (New American Library, 1974), unpaginated.

19. Rose, *supra* note 1, at 76. See generally N. Matthews, Feminist Clashes with the State: Tactical Choices by State-Funded Rape Crisis Centers, in M. Ferree & P. Martin eds., Feminist Organizations: Harvest of the New Women's Movement 291 (Temple Univ. Press, 1995); Gornick, Burt & Pittman, Structure and Activities of Rape Crisis Centers in the Early 1980's, 31 Crime & Delinq. 247 (1985).

20. Bourque, *supra* note 5, at 13. See also Largen, History of the Women's Movement in Changing Attitudes, Laws, & Treatment Toward Rape Victims, in M. Walker & S. Brodsky eds., Sexual Assault 69 (D.C. Heath, 1976); Schechter, *supra* note 3, at 35; Schwendinger & Schwendinger, *supra* note 14, at 9.

21. King & Webb, Rape Crisis Centers: Progress and Problems, 37 J. Soc. Issues 93, 99 (1981) (citing the National Coalition Against Sexual Assault, a newsletter edited by Ann Pride, Pittsburgh Action Against Rape, Pittsburgh PA, 1978).

22. Clark & Lewis, *supra* note 1, at 25.

23. Davis, *supra* note 2, at 319; King & Webb, *supra* note 21, at 97; Rose, *supra* note 1, at 76.

24. Schechter, *supra* note 3, at 36–37; Schwendinger and Schwendinger, *supra* note 14, at 9–10.

25. Largen, *supra* note 20, at 72.

26. 42 U.S.C. §2689(q)(1976)(repealed 1981). See also Bourque, *supra* note 5, at 13.

27. Bourque, *supra* note 5, at 13. Practice also nourished theory. Two leading scholars, for example, initially were rape counselors in emergency rooms. See Burgess & Holmstrom, *supra* note 9. See also Schwendinger & Schwendinger, *supra* note 14, at 9 (founder of Bay Area Women Against Rape and later researcher).

28. Brownmiller, *supra* note 9, at 421–454; Bienen, Rape III—National Developments in Rape Reform Legislation, 6 Women's Rts. L. Rep. 170, 171 (1980).

29. Bienen, *supra* note 28, at 171. See also J. Marsh, A. Geist, & N. Caplan, Rape and the Limits of Law Reform 11 (Auburn House, 1982).

30. Rose, *supra* note 1, at 76.

31. Bienen, *supra* note 28, at 171.

32. Bourque, *supra* note 5, at 13. See Mich. Comp. Laws Ann. §750.520 (West 1977)("Criminal sexual conduct"). On the passage of the Michigan legislation, see Bourque, *supra* note 5, at 107; Marsh, Geist & Caplan, *supra* note 29, at viii, 3; Sasko & Sesek, *supra* note 15, at 496; Note, Michigan's Criminal Sexual Assault Law, 8 U. Mich. J.L. Ref. 217 (1974).

33. Bienen, *supra* note 28, at 176.

34. The three offenses were as follows: "rape" was defined as two offenses, and reserved for defendants who engaged in life-threatening conduct involving "imminent death, serious bodily injury, extreme pain, or kidnapping." Rape was to be punished as a first-degree offense if the parties were strangers, but second-degree if the parties were acquaintances. A third category called "gross sexual imposition" was created to punish men who compelled women (not their wives) to submit to sexual intercourse "by any threat that would prevent resistance by a woman of ordinary resolution." Model Penal Code §213.1(2)(a) (Tentative Draft No. 4, 1955).

35. See Schulhofer, Taking Sexual Autonomy Seriously: Rape Law and Beyond, 11 Law & Phil. 35, 37–39 (1992)(discussing state reforms). See also Model Penal Code and Commentaries, Part II, §213.1 Cmt. at 276 (1980).

36. Bienen, *supra* note 28, at 175.

37. The MPC stated that "no person shall be convicted of any felony . . . upon the uncorroborated testimony of the alleged victim." Model Penal Code §213.6 (5)(Tentative Draft No. 4, 1955). Feminists since the 1960s have argued that this requirement institutionalizes the belief that women falsely accuse men of rape. See Estrich, Rape, herein, at 431, 434 & 453 n.24.

38. The MPC requirement that a sexual assault complaint be filed within three months is indicative of its concern that women falsely accuse men. "The requirement of prompt complaint springs in part from a fear that an unwanted pregnancy . . . or a relationship gone bad might convert a willing participant in sexual relations into a vindictive complainant." Model Penal Code and Commentaries §213.6 Cmt. at 421 (1980). The MPC concern with the problem of vindictive women is important, especially when compared to the absence of concern with the victim's worries about the receptiveness of the criminal justice system. See also Estrich, Rape, herein, at 431, 436; Greenfield, The Prompt Complaint: A Developing Rule of Evidence, 9 Crim. L.Q. 286 (1967).

39. Usage of the term *marital rape* has engendered feminist criticism. See D. Russell, Rape in Marriage 9, 108 (Indiana Univ. Press, 1990).

40. It is generally thought that women fabricate rape because they are ashamed; desire a socially acceptable justification for pregnancy; or desire revenge, blackmail, or notoriety. Tchen, Rape Reform and a Statutory Consent Defense, 74 J. Crim. L. & Crimi-

nology 1518, 1519–1524 (1983); Note, The Rape Corroboration Requirement: Repeal Not Reform, 81 Yale L.J. 1365, 1373 (1972). For other explanations for the belief, see United States v. Wiley, 492 F.2d 547, 554–555 (D.C. Cir. 1973) (Bazelon, concurring).

The belief has longstanding roots in English legal history. Lord Chief Justice Mathew Hale wrote in 1680 that rape "is an accusation easily to be made and hard to be proved, and harder to be defended by the party accused, tho never so innocent." Quoted in Wiley, *supra,* at 554 (Bazelon, concurring). In a famous treatise on evidence, Wigmore reiterates the belief in women's proclivity to make false accusations and argues that the dangers of miscarriage of justice militate in favor of psychiatric examinations of rape victims. 3A Wigmore, Evidence §924a (Chadbourn rev. 1970) [cited in Estrich, herein, at 453 n. 24]. For a criticism of the sources on which this belief is based, see B. Babcock, A. Freedman, E. Norton & S. Ross, Sex Discrimination and the Law: Causes and Remedies 855–860 (Little, Brown, 1975). See also S. Katz & M. Mazur, Understanding the Rape Victim 209 (Wiley, 1979) (research disputing the myth); Nemeth, Character Evidence in Rape Trials in Nineteenth Century New York: Chastity and the Admissibility of Specific Acts, 6 Women's Rts. L. Rep. 214, 224 (1980) (historical perspective on the myth).

41. Theoretically, defining the act in assault terms would limit or remove the requirement of proof of a woman's nonconsent from these crimes, because the law generally holds that one cannot consent to an assault. However, even in the face of statutes specifically omitting a nonconsent element, courts have judicially imposed their own requirement of proof of nonconsent. Bienen, *supra* note 28, passim; Gager & Schurr, *supra* note 9, at 246.

42. Bienen, *supra* note 28, at 177–178. Feminists, especially those in the equality tradition, supported this reform, arguing that it removes the stigma of woman as victim and supports the contention that rape is a crime of violence, not of sex. Brownmiller, *supra* note 9. But see MacKinnon, Sex Equality, 100 Yale L.J. 1281, 1286 (1991) ("The reform of rape law to gender neutrality denies reality; women are . . . raped on the basis of their sex, defined by gender within a social reality of male supremacy.").

43. Historically, the common law and a majority of state statutes contained a marital rape exemption which prevented a wife from charging her husband with rape. In these states, a woman is deemed to have consented to sex upon marriage, having no right to refuse her husband's advances. See generally D. Finkelhor & K. Yllo, License to Rape: Sexual Abuse of Wives, (1985); Schwartz & Slatin, The Law on Marital Rape: How Do Marxism and Feminism Explain Its Persistence, 8 ALSA Forum 244 (1984); West, Equality Theory, Marital Rape, and the Promise of the Fourteenth Amendment, herein, at 511; Marital Rape Exception: Time for Legal Reform, 21 Tulsa L.J. 355 (1985); Adamo, The Injustice of the Marital Rape Exception: A Survey of Common Law Countries, 4 Am. U.J. Int. Law & Pol'y 555 (1989).

44. Courts have held that drinking, hitchhiking, sexually promiscuous behavior and provocative clothing are a signal of a woman's sexual availability. Although these behaviors fall short of actual consent, and have no relationship to communicating in affirmative terms a desire to engage in sexual activity, courts have implied consent to "incriminate the testimony of the female complainant and pardon the actions of the male defendant." Tchen, *supra* note 40, at 1524.

45. Traditionally, women had to manifest resistance, in many jurisdictions, to the maximum extent possible. Bienen, *supra* note 28, at 182.

46. Many states prevented an accused from being convicted solely on the basis of the victim's uncorroborated testimony. This can be viewed only as a confirmation of

the underlying legal presumption that women lie about their consent in sexual matters. See Estrich, Rape, herein, at 444–448.

47. The shield laws, designed to protect women against invasive exposure of prior sexual history, created obstacles to introduction of such evidence. See Althouse, Thelma and Louise and the Law: Do Rape Shield Rules Matter?, 25 Loy. L.A. L. Rev. 757 (1992); Bienen, *supra* note 28, at 179, 200–209; Galvin, Shielding Rape Victims in the State and Federal Courts: A Proposal for a Second Decade, 70 Minn. L. Rev. 763 (1986); Murphy, Rejecting Unreasonable Sexual Expectations: Limits on Using a Rape Victim's Sexual History to Show the Defendant's Mistaken Belief in Consent, 79 Cal. L. Rev. 541 (1991); Tuerkheimer, A Reassessment and Redefinition of Rape Shield Laws, 50 Ohio St. L.J. 1245 (1989).

48. Bienen, *supra* note 28, at 171. See also J. Temkin, Women, Rape and Law Reform, in S. Tomaselli & R. Porter eds., Rape 16 (Basil Blackwell, 1986).

49. Several of these dimensions are discussed in detail in C. Spohn & J. Horney, Rape Law Reform: A Grassroots Revolution and Its Impact (Plenum Press, 1992).

50. Pub. L. No. 103–322, §40001, 108 Stat. 1796 (codified as amended at 42 U.S.C. §13981 (1994)).

51. Safe Streets for Women Act, Pub. L. No. 103–366, §40131, 108 Stat. 1796 (codified as amended at 42 U.S.C. §13931 (1994)).

52. For example, although some states enacted rape shield laws excluding the victim's prior sexual history as evidence of her present consent, these same jurisdictions nonetheless admitted this evidence to impeach the victim's credibility. Bienen, *supra* note 28, at 198–201.

53. Willis, The Gun Is Always Pointed: Sexual Violence and Title III of the Violence Against Women Act, 80 Geo. L.J. 2197, 2201 (1992) (because of its adoption of traditional definitions of rape, the act "threatens to repeat the errors and omissions of state criminal laws").

54. Spohn & Horney, *supra* note 49, at 159–160.

55. Ellis, Redefining Rape: Re-Victimization of Women, 17 Resources for Feminist Research: Documentation sur la Recherche Feministe 96–99 (1988); Chappell, The Impact of Rape Legislation Reform: Some Contemporary Trends, 7 Int. J. Women's Stud. 70–80 (1984) (concludes progress was more symbolic than actual).

56. Berger, Searles & Neuman, The Dimensions of Rape Reform Legislation, 22 Law & Soc'y Rev. 329–357 (1988). See also Balos & Fellows, Guilty of the Crime of Trust: Nonstranger Rape, 75 Minn. L. Rev. 599, 600 (1991) ("Most feminists . . . continue to believe that the criminal justice system's treatment of rape remains inadequate.")

57. See Estrich, Rape, herein, at 431, 433; Henderson, Rape and Responsibility, 11 Law & Phil. 127, 132 (1992); Henderson, Review Essay: What Makes Rape a Crime? 3 Berkeley Women's L.J. 193 (1987–1988); MacKinnon, Sex Equality, *supra* note 42, at 1300.

58. See Z. Eisenstein, The Radical Future of Liberal Feminism 193 (Longman, 1981): "I think it is important to recognize that NOW as a national organization adopts a *liberal feminist* analysis." (emphasis in the original)

59. Bourque, *supra* note 5, at 13.

60. Schechter, *supra* note 3, at 36–37. See also Rose, *supra* note 1, at 76.

61. Bourque, *supra* note 5, at 13; Largen, *supra* note 20, at 70; Rose, *supra* note 1, at 76.

62. Resolution No. 20 on Rape, National Organization for Women National Board Meeting, August 3–4, 1974, (cited in Sasko & Sesek, *supra* note 15, at 499).

63. ABA Law Student Division Report No. 112, February 1975, in House of Delegates Redefines Death, Urges Redefinition of Rape and Undoes the Houston Amendments, 61 A.B.A.J. 463, 465 (1975) (cited in Sasko & Sesek, *supra* note 15, at 500–501)).

64. J. Dixon, Feminist Reforms of Sexual Coercion Laws, in E. Grauerholz & M. Koralewski eds., Sexual Coercion: A Sourcebook on Its Nature, Causes, & Prevention 166 (Lexington Books, 1991).

65. Vega, Coercion and Consent: Classic Liberal Concepts in Texts on Sexual Violence, 16 Int.'l J. Soc. L. 77 (1988).

66. Schwendinger & Schwendinger, *supra* note 14. See also Schwendinger & Schwendinger, Rape Myths in Legal, Theoretical and Everyday Practice, 1 Crime & Soc. Just. 18 (1974).

67. Schwendinger & Schwendinger, *supra* note 14, at 13.

68. K. Sacks, Sisters and Wives: The Past and Future of Sexual Equality (Greenwood Press, 1979).

69. Schwendinger and Schwendinger, *supra* note 14, at 179.

70. *Id.* at 215–217. For a sociological study exploring the relationship today between gender inequality and rape, see L. Baron & M. Straus, Four Theories of Rape in American Society: A State-Level Analysis 61–94 (Yale Univ. Press, 1989).

71. Rafter & Natalizia, Marxist Feminism: Implications for Criminal Justice, 27 Crime & Delinq. 88 (Jan. 1981).

72. H. Collins, Marxism and the Law 63–66 (Oxford Univ. Press, 1982). See also Schwartz & Slatin, *supra* note 43, at 248–249 (discussing Collins's Marxist application).

73. Rex v. Miller, (1954) 2 Q.B. 282.

74. Collins, *supra* note 72, at 63–66.

75. Susan Griffin, personal communication, 1976 (cited in Chappell, Geis & Geis, *supra* note 3, at 41).

76. Schwartz & Slatin, *supra* note 43, at 250.

77. *Id.* at 251.

78. The authors rely on the views of Antonio Gramsci. *Id.* at 255–256 (citing E. Greer, Antonio Gramsci and Legal Hegemony, in David Kairys ed., The Politics of Law: A Progressive Critique 304 (Pantheon, 1982)).

79. *Id.* at 257–258 (citing J. Reiman, The Rich Get Richer and the Poor Get Prison: Ideology, Class and Criminal Justice (Wiley, 1984)).

80. Baron & Straus, *supra* note 70, at 61. They term this theory of rape "gender inequality." *Id.*

81. *Id.* at 95–96. Baron and Straus term their four theories of rape "gender inequality," "pornography," "social disorganization," and "legitimate violence" (cultural spillover theory). For additional discussion of the link between pornography and rape, see Introduction to Chapter 1 on pornography, *supra*.

82. A. Jaggar, Feminist Politics and Human Nature 267 (Rowman & Littlefield, 1988). Jaggar suggests that the patriarchal definition of women as mothers and sex objects may accurately reflect the reality of women under patriarchy in the advanced western capitalist nations in which radical feminism flourishes. She remarks that the radical feminist emphasis on fertility and sexuality may be a necessary counterbalance to patriarchal political theories that exclude these aspects from systematic critical scrutiny. *Id.*

83. Mehrhof & Kearon, *supra* note 7 (cited in Jaggar, *supra* note 82, at 263).

84. Brownmiller, *supra* note 9, at 394. Also, see Introduction to Section 1 herein, at 5.

85. K. Millett, Sexual Politics (Ballantine, 1970).

86. Other similar instances of "sexual politics" include footbinding, the veil, and clitoridectomies. *Id.* at 64. "Politics" occurs in the personal realm of sexual intimacy, hence the title of Millett's work.

87. S. Griffin, Rape: The Power of Consciousness 21 (Harper & Row, 1979) (cited in Jaggar, *supra* note 82, at 262).

88. Jaggar, *supra* note 82, at 265.

89. S. Firestone, The Dialectic of Sex 126 (Bantam Books, 1971); Millett, *supra* note 85, at 51.

90. Henderson, Rape and Responsibility, *supra* note 57, at 131–132.

91. See, e.g., Hunter & Law, Brief Amici Curiae of Feminist Anti-Censorship Taskforce, herein, at 127; Strossen, A Feminist Critique of "The Feminist Critique of Pornography," herein, at 135–136; Schneider, Describing and Changing, herein, at 319.

92. See Katie Roiphe, The Morning After: Sex, Fear, and Feminism on Campus (Little, Brown, 1993).

93. Brownmiller, *supra* note 9, at 283. See also Clark & Lewis, *supra* note 1, at 27.

94. Shorter, On Writing the History of Rape, 3 Signs 471, 473 (1977). See also E. Shorter, The Making of the Modern Family (Basic Books, 1975), especially Chapter 3.

95. Hartmann & Ross, Comment on "On Writing the History of Rape," 3 Signs 931, 931–932 (1978).

96. *Id.* at 933.

97. Abrams, Hearing the Call of Stories, 79 Cal. L. Rev. 971, 983 (1991). Estrich illustrates the "subtle epistemological point that we learn from experience, as well as from the kind of professional training" (*id.* at 983–984) and also provides an analysis of the law and law reform that is influenced by experience. See also Scheppele, The Re-Vision of Rape Law, 54 U. Chi. L. Rev. 1095 (1987) (reviewing S. Estrich, Real Rape: How the Legal System Victimizes Women Who Say No (1987)).

98. For a more detailed discussion of the feminist critique of the neutral subject, see the essays on "Feminist Legal Methods" in Volume I of this collection.

99. Other scholars also refer to the communicative model. See Henderson, Rape and Responsibility, *supra* note 57; Pickard, Culpable Mistakes and Rape: Relating Mens Rea to the Crime, 30 U. Toronto L.J. 217, 276–277 (1980); Pineau, Date Rape: A Feminist Analysis, [reprinted herein, at 484, 490–491]; West, Legitimizing the Illegitimate: A Comment on *Beyond Rape*, 93 Colum. L. Rev. 1442, 1445 n.19 (1993). Estrich stops short of adopting the term *communicative approach*. However, her proposal that a man be subject to criminal liability for failure to ensure consent before proceeding with a sexual act, though less comprehensive, is very similar to this model.

100. See generally Erickson & Taub, Final Report: Sex Bias in the Teaching of Criminal Law, 42 Rutgers L. Rev. 309 (1990).

101. See also Oberman, Turning Girls Into Women: Re-Evaluating Modern Statutory Rape Law, 85 J. Crim. L. & Criminology 15 (1994).

102. MacKinnon's essay is presented here in its complete and unabridged form, as the author wishes.

103. For other theoretical discussions of consent in the context of rape, see Dripps, Beyond Rape: An Essay on the Difference Between the Presence of Force and the Absence of Consent, 92 Colum. L. Rev. 1780 (1992); West, *supra* note 99.

104. See also Balos & Fellows, *supra* note 56 (arguing that doctrine of confidential relationship should be made applicable to criminal prosecution of nonstranger rape).

For an intriguing discussion of date rape in the law-and-literature context, see Cairney, Recognizing Acquaintance Rape in Potentially Consensual Situations: A Re-Examination of Thomas Hardy's Tess of the D'Urbervilles, 3 Am. U. J. Gender & L. 301 (1995).

105. Although much of the feminist support has been theoretical, feminists at Antioch College in Yellow Springs, Ohio, in Fall 1992, secured adoption of a sexual code whereby the initiator of sexual touching must request a partner's verbal consent for each stage of the encounter. Approximately 150 other colleges and universities contacted the school to inquire about the policy. See Jason Vest, The School That's Put Sex to the Test, at Antioch, a Passionate Reaction to Consent Code, Wash. Post, Dec. 3, 1993, (Style Section), at 1.

106. See also Bumiller, Rape as a Legal Symbol: An Essay on Sexual Violence and Racism, 42 U. Miami L. Rev. 75 (1987); Burrell, Myth, Stereotype, and the Rape of Black Women, 4 UCLA Women's L.J. 87 (1993); M. Hall, The Mind That Burns in Each Body: Women, Rape, and Racial Violence 328, in A. Snitow, C. Stansell & S. Thompson eds., Powers of Desire (Monthly Review Press, 1983); Merchan, Rape, Ethnicity and Culture: Spirit Injury from Bosnia to Black America, 25 Colum. Hum. Rts. L. Rev. 1 (1993).

Rape: The All-American Crime

SUSAN GRIFFIN

I HAVE NEVER been free of the fear of rape. From a very early age I, like most women, have thought of rape as part of my natural environment—something to be feared and prayed against like fire or lightning. I never asked why men raped; I simply thought it one of the many mysteries of human nature.

. . . I was never certain why the victims were always women . . . but I did guess that the world was not a safe place for women. I observed that my grandmother was meticulous about locks, and quick to draw the shades before anyone removed so much as a shoe. I sensed that danger lurked outside.

At the age of eight, my suspicions were confirmed. My grandmother took me to the back of the house where the men wouldn't hear, and told me that strange men wanted to do harm to little girls. I learned not to walk on dark streets, not to talk to strangers, or get into strange cars, to lock doors, and to be modest. She never explained why a man would want to harm a little girl, and I never asked.

If I thought for a while that my grandmother's fears were imaginary, the illusion was brief. That year, on the way home from school, a schoolmate a few years older than I tried to rape me. Later, in an obscure aisle of the local library (while I was reading *Freddy the Pig*) I turned to discover a man exposing himself. Then, the friendly man around the corner was arrested for child molesting. . . .

But though rape and the fear of rape are a daily part of every woman's consciousness, the subject is so rarely discussed by that unofficial staff of male intellectuals (who write the books which study seemingly every other form of male activity) that one begins to suspect a conspiracy of silence. And indeed, the obscurity of rape in print exists in marked contrast to the frequency of rape in reality, for forcible rape is the most frequently committed violent crime in America today. . . .

When I asked Berkeley, California's Police Inspector in charge of rape investigation if he knew why men rape women, he replied that he had not spoken with "these people and delved into what really makes them tick, because that really isn't my job. . . ." However, when I asked him how a woman might prevent being raped, he was not so reticent, "I wouldn't advise any female to go walking around alone at night . . . and she should lock her car at all times." The Inspector illustrated his warning with a grisly story about a man who lay in wait for women in the back seats of their cars, while they were shopping in a local supermarket. This man eventually murdered one of his rape victims. "Always lock your car," the Inspector repeated, and then added, without a hint of irony, "Of course, you don't have to be paranoid about this type of thing."

The Inspector wondered why I wanted to write about rape. Like most men he didn't understand the urgency of the topic, for, after all, men are not raped. But like most women I had spent considerable time speculating on the true nature of the rapist. When I was very young, my image of the sexual offender was a nightmarish amalgamation of the boogie-man and Captain Hook: he wore a black cape, and he cackled. As I matured, so did my image of the rapist. Born into the psychoanalytic age, I tried to understand the rapist. Rape, I came to believe, was only one of many unfortunate evils produced by sexual repression. Reasoning by tautology, I concluded that any man who would rape a woman must be out of his mind.

Yet, though the theory that rapists are insane is a popular one, this belief has no basis in fact. According to Professor Menachem Amir's study of 646 rape cases in Philadelphia, *Patterns in Forcible Rape*, men who rape are not abnormal. . . . Alan Taylor, a parole officer who has worked with rapists in the prison facilities at San Luis Obispo, California, stated the question in plainer language, "Those men were the most normal men there. They had a lot of hang-ups, but they were the same hang-ups as men walking out on the street."

Another canon in the apologetics of rape is that, if it were not for learned social controls, all men would rape. Rape is held to be natural behavior, and not to rape must be learned. But in truth rape is not universal to the human species. Moreover, studies of rape in our culture reveal that, far from being impulsive behavior, most rape is planned. Professor Amir's study reveals that in cases of group rape (the gangbang of masculine slang) 90 percent of the rapes were planned, in pair rapes, 83 percent of the rapes were planned, and in single rapes, 58 percent were planned. These figures should significantly discredit the image of the rapist as a man who is suddenly overcome by sexual needs society does not allow him to fulfill. . . .

This culture's concept of rape as an illegal, but still understandable, form of behavior is not a universal one. In her study *Sex and Temperament*, Margaret Mead describes a society that does not share our views. The Arapesh do not ". . . have any conception of the male nature that might make rape understandable to them." Indeed our interpretation of rape is a product of our conception of the nature of male sexuality. A common retort to the question, why don't women rape men, is the myth that men have greater sexual needs, that their sexuality is more urgent than women's. And it is the nature of human beings to want to live up to what is expected of them.

And this same culture which expects aggression from the male expects passivity from the female. Conveniently, the companion myth about the nature of female sexuality is that all women secretly want to be raped. Lurking beneath her modest female exterior is a subconscious desire to be ravished. The following description of a stag movie, written by Brenda Starr in Los Angeles' underground paper, *Every woman,* typifies this male fantasy. The movie "showed a woman in her underclothes reading on her bed. She is interrupted by a rapist with a knife. He immediately wins her over with his charm and they get busy. . . ."

[T]he male psyche persists in believing that, protestations and struggles to the contrary, deep inside her mysterious feminine soul, the female victim has wished for her own fate. A young woman who was raped by the husband of a friend said that days after the incident the man returned to her home, pounded on the door and screamed to her, "Jane, Jane. You loved it. You know you loved it."

The theory that women like being raped extends itself by deduction into the proposition that most or much of rape is provoked by the victim. But this too is only myth. Though provocation, considered a mitigating factor in a court of law, may consist of only a gesture, according to the Federal Commission on Crimes of Violence, only 4 percent of reported rapes involved any precipitative behavior by the woman.

The notion that rape is enjoyed by the victim is also convenient for the man who, though he would not commit forcible rape, enjoys the idea of its existence, as if rape confirms that enormous sexual potency which he secretly knows to be his own. It is for the pleasure of the armchair rapist that detailed accounts of violent rapes exist in the media. Indeed, many men appear to take sexual pleasure from nearly all forms of violence. Whatever the motivation, male sexuality and violence in our culture seem to be inseparable. James Bond alternately whips out his revolver and his cock, and though there is no known connection between the skills of gun-fighting and love-making, pacifism seems suspiciously effeminate. . . .

And in the spectrum of male behavior, rape, the perfect combination of sex and violence, is the penultimate act. Erotic pleasure cannot be separated from culture, and in our culture male eroticism is wedded to power. Not only should a man be taller and stronger than a female in the perfect love-match, but he must also demonstrate his superior strength in gestures of dominance which are perceived as amorous. Though the law attempts to make a clear division between rape and sexual intercourse, in fact the courts find it difficult to distinguish between a case where the decision to copulate was mutual and one where a man forced himself upon his partner.

The scenario is even further complicated by the expectation that, not only does a woman mean "yes" when she says "no," but that a really decent woman ought to begin by saying "no," and then be led down the primrose path to acquiescence. Ovid, the author of Western Civilization's most celebrated sex manual, makes this expectation perfectly clear:

> . . . and when I beg you to say "yes," say "no." Then let me lie outside your bolted door. . . . So Love grows strong. . . .

That the basic elements of rape are involved in all heterosexual relationships may explain why men often identify with the offender in this crime. But to regard the rapist as the victim, a man driven by his inherent sexual needs to take what will not be given him, reveals a basic ignorance of sexual politics. For in our culture heterosexual love finds an erotic expression through male dominance and female submission. A man who derives pleasure from raping a woman clearly must enjoy force and dominance as much or more than the simple pleasures of the flesh. . . . According to Amir's study of forcible rape, on a statistical average the man who has been convicted of rape [tended] to be different from the normal, well-adjusted male only in having a greater tendency to express violence and rage.

And if the professional rapist is to be separated from the average dominant heterosexual, it may be mainly a quantitative difference. For the existence of rape as an index of masculinity is not entirely metaphorical. *[G]ood boys* engage in the same rites [as bad boys] to prove their manhood. In Stockton, a small town in California which epitomizes silent-majority America, a bachelor party was given . . . for a young man about to be married. A woman was hired to dance *topless* for the amusement of the guests. At the high point of the evening the bridegroom-to-be dragged the woman into a bedroom. No move was made by any of his companions to stop what was clearly going to be an attempted rape. Far from it. As the woman described, "I tried to keep him away—I told him of my Herpes Genitalis, et cetera, but he couldn't face the guys if he didn't screw me." After the bridegroom had finished raping the woman and returned with her to the party, far from chastising him, his friends heckled the woman and covered her with wine.

It was fortunate for the dancer that the bridegroom's friends did not follow him into the bedroom for, though one might suppose that in group rape, since the victim is outnumbered, less force would be inflicted on her, in fact, Amir's studies indicate, "the most excessive degrees of violence occurred in group rape." Far from discouraging violence, the presence of other men may in fact encourage sadism, and even cause the behavior. In an unpublished study of group rape by Gilbert Geis and Duncan Chappell, the authors refer to a study by W. H. Blanchard which relates, "The leader of the male group . . . apparently precipitated and maintained the activity, despite misgivings, because of a need to fulfill the role that the other two men had assigned to him. 'I was scared when it began to happen,' he says. 'I wanted to leave but I didn't want to say it to the other guys—you know—that I was scared.' "

Thus it becomes clear that not only does our culture teach men the rudiments of rape, but society, or more specifically other men, encourage the practice of it.

If a male society rewards aggressive, domineering sexual behavior, it contains within itself a sexual schizophrenia. For the masculine man is also expected to prove his mettle as a protector of women. To the naive eye, this dichotomy implies that men fall into one of two categories: those who rape and those who protect. In fact, life does not prove so simple. In a study euphemistically entitled *Sex Aggression by College Men*, it was discovered that men who believe in a double standard of morality for men and women, who in fact believe most fervently in the ultimate value of virginity, are more liable to commit "this aggressive variety of sexual exploitation."

(At this point in our narrative it should come as no surprise that Sir Thomas Malory, creator of that classic tale of chivalry, *The Knights of the Round Table*, was himself arrested and found guilty for repeated incidents of rape.)

In the system of chivalry, men protect women against men. This is not unlike the protection relationship which the mafia established with small businesses in the early part of this century. Indeed, chivalry is an age-old protection racket which depends on rape for its existence.

According to the male mythology which defines and perpetuates rape, it is an animal instinct inherent in the male. The story goes that sometimes in our pre-historical past, the male, more hirsute and burly than today's counterparts, roamed about an uncivilized landscape until he found a desirable female. . . . Her mate does not bother with courtship. He simply grabs her by the hair and drags her to the closest cave. Presumably, one of the major advantages of modern civilization for the female has been the civilizing of the male. We call it chivalry.

But women do not get chivalry for free. . . . For the female, civilized behavior means chastity before marriage and faithfulness within it. Chivalrous behavior in the male is supposed to protect that chastity from involuntary defilement. The fly in the ointment of this otherwise peaceful system is the fallen woman. She does not behave, and therefore she does not deserve protection. . . .

The assumption that a woman who does not respect the double standard deserves whatever she gets (or at the very least *asks for it*) operates in the court today. While in some states a man's previous rape convictions are not considered admissible evidence, the sexual reputation of the rape victim is considered a crucial element of the facts upon which the court must decide innocence or guilt.

The court's respect for double standard manifested itself particularly clearly in the case of the People v. Jerry Plotkin. Mr. Plotkin, a 36-year-old jeweler, was tried for rape . . . in a San Francisco Superior Court. According to the woman who brought the charges, Plotkin, along with three other men, forced her at gunpoint to enter a car one night in October 1970. She was taken to Mr. Plotkin's fashionable apartment where he and the three other men first raped her and then, in the delicate language of the *S.F. Chronicle,* "subjected her to perverted sex acts." She was, she said, set free in the morning with the warning that she would be killed if she spoke to anyone about the event. She did report the incident to the police who then searched Plotkin's apartment and discovered a long list of names of women. Her name was on the list and had been crossed out.

In addition to the woman's account of her abduction and rape, the prosecution submitted four of Plotkin's address books containing the names of hundreds of women. Plotkin claimed he did not know all of the women since some of the names had been given to him by friends and he had not yet called on them. Several women, however, did testify in court that Plotkin had, to cite the *Chronicle,* "lured them up to his apartment under one pretext or another, and forced his sexual attentions on them."

Plotkin's defense rested on two premises. First, through his own testimony, Plotkin established a reputation for himself as a sexual libertine who frequently picked up girls in bars and took them to his house where sexual relations often took place. He was the Playboy. He claimed that the accusation of rape, therefore, was false—this incident had simply been one of many casual sexual relationships, the victim one of many playmates. The second premise of the defense was that his accuser was also a sexual libertine. . . .

Through skillful questioning fraught with innuendo, Plotkin's defense attorney James Martin MacInnis portrayed the young woman as a licentious opportunist and unfit mother. MacInnis began by asking the young woman (then employed as a secretary) whether or not it was true that she was *familiar with liquor* and had worked as a *cocktail waitress.* The young woman replied (the *Chronicle* wrote *admitted*) that she had worked once or twice as a cocktail waitress. The attorney then asked if she had worked as a secretary in the financial district but had "left that employment after it was discovered that you had sexual intercourse on a couch in the office." The woman replied, "That is a lie. I left because I didn't like working in a one-girl office. It was too lonely." Then the defense asked if, while working as an attendant at a health club, "you were accused of having a sexual affair with a man?" Again the women denied the story, "I was never accused of that."

Plotkin's attorney then sought to establish that his client's accuser was living with a married man. She responded that the man was separated from his wife. Finally he told the court that she had spent the night with another man who lived in the same building.

At this point in the testimony the woman asked Plotkin's defense attorney, "Am I on trial? . . . It is embarrassing and personal to admit these things to all these people. . . . I did not commit a crime. I am a human being." The lawyer, true to the chivalry of his class, apologized and immediately resumed questioning her, turning his attention to her children. (She is divorced, and the children at the time of the trial were in a foster home.) . . .

The jury, divided in favor of acquittal ten to two, asked the court stenographer to read the woman's testimony back to them. After this reading, the Superior Court acquitted the defendant of both the charges of rape and kidnapping.

According to the double standard, a woman who has had sexual intercourse out of wedlock cannot be raped. Rape is not only a crime of aggression against the body, it is a transgression against chastity as defined by men. When a woman is forced into a sexual relationship, she has, according to the male ethos, been violated. But she is also defiled if she does not behave according to the double standard, by maintaining her chastity, or confining her sexual activities to a monogamous relationship.

One should not assume, however, that a woman can avoid the possibility of rape simply by behaving. Though myth would have it that mainly *bad girls* are raped, this theory has no basis in fact. . . . In a study of rape committed in the District of Columbia, it was found that 82 percent of the rape victims had a *good reputation.* Even the Police Inspector's advice to stay off the streets is rather useless, for almost half of reported rapes occur in the home of the victim and are committed by a man she has never before seen. Like indiscriminate terrorism, rape can happen to any woman, and few women are ever without this knowledge.

But the courts and the police, both dominated by white males, continue to suspect the rape victim, *sui generis,* of provoking or asking for her own assault. According to Amir's study, the police tend to believe that a woman without a good reputation cannot be raped. The rape victim is usually submitted to countless questions about her own sexual mores and behavior by the police investigator. This preoccupation is partially justified by the legal requirements for prosecution in a rape case. The rape victim must have been penetrated, and she must have made it clear to her assailant that she did not want penetration (unless of course she is unconscious). A refusal to accompany a man to some isolated place to allow him to touch her does not in the eyes of the court, constitute rape. She must have said "no" at the crucial genital moment. And the rape victim, to qualify as such, must have put up a physical struggle—unless she can prove that to do so would have been to endanger her life.

But the zealous interest the police frequently exhibit in the physical details of a rape case is only partially explained by the requirements of the court. A woman who was raped in Berkeley was asked to tell the story of her rape four different times "right out in the street," while her assailant was escaping. She was then required to submit to a pelvic examination to prove that penetration had taken place. Later, she was taken to the police station where she was asked the same questions again: "Were you forced?" "Did he penetrate?" "Are you sure your life was in danger and you had no other choice?" This woman had been pulled off the street by a man who held a ten-inch knife at her throat and forcibly raped her. She was raped at midnight and was not able to return to her home until five in the morning. Police contacted her twice again in the next week, once by telephone at two in the morning and once at four in the morning. In her words, "The rape was probably the least traumatic incident of the whole evening. If I'm ever raped again, . . . I wouldn't report it to the police because of all the degradation. . . ."

If white women are subjected to unnecessary and often hostile questioning after having been raped, third world women are often not believed at all. According to the white male ethos (which is not only sexist but racist), third world women are defined from birth as *impure*. Thus the white male is provided with a pool of women who are fair game for sexual imperialism. Third world women frequently do not report rape and for good reason. . . .

As a final irony, that same system of sexual values from which chivalry is derived has also provided womankind with an unwritten code of behavior, called femininity, which makes a feminine woman the perfect victim of sexual aggression. If being chaste does not ward off the possibility of assault, being feminine certainly increases the chances that it will succeed. To be submissive is to defer to masculine strength; to lack muscular development or any interest in defending oneself; to let doors be opened, to have one's arm held when crossing the street. To be feminine is to wear shoes which make it difficult to run; skirts which inhibit one's stride; underclothes which inhibit the circulation. Is it not an intriguing observation that those very clothes which are thought to be flattering to the female and attractive to the male are those which make it impossible for a woman to defend herself against aggression?

Each girl as she grows into womanhood is taught fear. Fear is the form in which the female internalizes both chivalry and the double standard. Since, biologically speaking, women in fact have the same if not greater potential for sexual expression as do men, the woman who is taught that she must behave differently from a man must also learn to distrust her own carnality. She must deny her own feelings and learn not to act from them. She fears herself. This is the essence of passivity, and of course, a woman's passivity is not simply sexual but functions to cripple her from self-expression in every area of her life.

Passivity itself prevents a woman from ever considering her own potential for self-defense and forces her to look to men for protection. The woman is taught fear, but this time fear of the other, and yet her only relief from this fear is to seek out the other. Moreover, the passive woman is taught to regard herself as impotent, unable to act, unable even to perceive, in no way self-sufficient, and, finally, as the object and not the subject of human behavior. It is in this sense that a woman is deprived of the status of a human being. She is not free to be. . . .

The laws against rape exist to protect rights of the male as possessor of the female body, and not the right of the female over her own body. . . . It is in the sense of rape as theft of another man's property that Kate Millett writes, "Traditionally rape has been viewed as an offense one male commits against another—a matter of abusing his woman." In raping another man's woman, a man may aggrandize his own manhood and concurrently reduce that of another man. Thus a man's honor is not subject directly to rape, but only indirectly, through *his* woman.

If the basic social unit is the family, in which the woman is a possession of her husband, the superstructure of society is a male hierarchy, in which men dominate other men (or patriarchal families dominate other patriarchal families). And it is no small irony that, while the very social fabric of our male-dominated culture denies women equal access to political, economic and legal power, the literature, myth and humor of our culture depicts women not only as the power behind the throne, but the real source of the oppression of men. . . . Through a media which is owned by men, censored by a State dominated by men, all the evils of this social system which make a man's life unpleasant are blamed upon the wife. The theory is: were it not for the female who waits and plots to *trap* the male into marriage, modern man would be able to achieve Olympian freedom. She is made the scapegoat for a system which is in fact run by men. . . .

Indeed, the existence of rape in any form is beneficial to the ruling class of white males. For rape is a kind of terrorism which severely limits the freedom of women and makes women dependent on men. Moreover, in the act of rape, the rage that one man may harbor toward another higher in the male hierarchy can be deflected toward a female scapegoat. For every man there is always someone lower on the social scale on whom he can take out his aggressions. And that is any woman alive. . . .

Rape is an act of aggression in which the victim is denied her self-determination. It is an act of violence which, if not actually followed by beatings or murder, nevertheless always carries with it the threat of death. And finally, rape is a form of mass terrorism, for the victims of rape are chosen indiscriminately, but the propagandists for male supremacy broadcast that it is women who cause rape by being unchaste or in the wrong place at the wrong time—in essence, by behaving as though they were free.

The threat of rape is used to deny women employment. (In California, the Berkeley Public Library, until pushed by the Federal Employment Practices Commission, refused to hire female shelvers because of perverted men in the stacks.) The fear of rape keeps women off the streets at night. Keeps women at home. Keeps women passive and modest for fear that they be thought provocative.

It is part of human dignity to be able to defend oneself, and women are learning. Some women have learned karate; some to shoot guns. And yet we will not be free until the threat of rape and the atmosphere of violence is ended, and to end that the nature of male behavior must change. . . .

 *Rape*

SUSAN ESTRICH

I. Introduction

ELEVEN YEARS AGO, a man held an ice pick to my throat and said: "Push over, shut up, or I'll kill you." I did what he said, but I couldn't stop crying. A hundred years later, I jumped out of my car as he drove away.

I ended up in the back seat of a police car. I told the two officers I had been raped by a man who came up to the car door as I was getting out in my own parking lot (and trying to balance two bags of groceries and kick the car door open). He took the car, too.

They asked me if he was a crow. That was their first question. A crow, I learned that day, meant to them someone who is black.

They asked me if I knew him. That was their second question. They believed me when I said I didn't. Because, as one of them put it, how would a nice (white) girl like me know a crow?

Now they were on my side. They asked me if he took any money. He did; but while I remember virtually every detail of that day and night, I can't remember how much. But I remember their answer. He did take money; that made it an armed robbery. Much better than a rape. They got right on the radio with that.

We went to the police station first, not the hospital, so I could repeat my story (and then what did he do?) to four more policemen. When we got there, I borrowed a dime to call my father. They all liked that.

By the time we went to the hospital, they were really on my team. I could've been one of their kids. Now there was something they'd better tell me. Did I realize what prosecuting a rape complaint was all about? They tried to tell me that "the law" was against me. But they didn't explain exactly how. And I didn't understand why. I believed in "the law," not knowing what it was.

Late that night, I sat in the Police Headquarters looking at mug shots. I was the one who insisted on going back that night. My memory was fresh. I was ready. They had

---

Reprinted by permission of the Yale Law Journal Company and Fred B. Rothman & Company from The Yale Law Journal, Vol. 95, pp. 1087–1184.

four or five to "really show" me; being "really shown" a mug shot means exactly what defense attorneys are afraid it means. But it wasn't any one of them. After that, they couldn't help me very much. One shot looked close until my father realized that the man had been the right age ten years before. It was late. I didn't have a great description of identifying marks, or the like: No one had ever told me that if you're raped, you should not shut your eyes and cry for fear that this really is happening. You should keep your eyes open focusing on this man who is raping you so you can identify him when you survive. After an hour of looking, I left the police station. They told me they'd be back in touch. They weren't.

A clerk called me one day to tell me that my car had been found minus tires and I should come sign a release and have it towed—no small matter if you don't have a car to get there and are slightly afraid of your shadow. The women from the rape crisis center called me every day, then every other day, then every week. The police detectives never called at all.

I learned, much later, that I had "really" been raped. Unlike, say, the woman who claimed she'd been raped by a man she actually knew, and was with voluntarily. Unlike, say, women who are "asking for it," and get what they deserve. I would listen as seemingly intelligent people explained these distinctions to me, and marvel; later I read about them in books, court opinions, and empirical studies. It is bad enough to be a "real" rape victim. How terrible to be—what to call it—a "not real" rape victim.

Even the real rape victim must bear the heavy weight of the silence that surrounds this crime. At first, it is something you simply don't talk about. Then it occurs to you that people whose houses are broken into or who are mugged in Central Park talk about it all the time. Rape is a much more serious crime. If it isn't my fault, why am I supposed to be ashamed? If I shouldn't be ashamed, if it wasn't "personal," why look askance when I mention it?

As this introduction makes clear, I talk about it. I do so very consciously. Sometimes, I have been harassed as a result. More often, it leads women I know to tell me that they too are victims, and I try to help them. I cannot imagine anyone writing an article on prosecutorial discretion without disclosing that he or she had been a prosecutor. I cannot imagine myself writing on rape without disclosing how I learned my first lessons or why I care so much.

The rapes that I examine in this essay are, like my own, the rapes of adult, competent women by men. . . . I have put . . . to one side the issue of race as a dominant theme. The history of rape, as the law has been enforced in this country, is a history of both racism and sexism. [B]ut I cannot do justice to both. My focus is sexism.

In recent years, rape has emerged as a topic of increasing research and attention among feminists, in both popular and scholarly journals.[1] But much of the feminist writing is not focused on an analysis of the *law* of rape. . . .

This essay examines rape within the criminal law tradition in order to expose and understand that tradition's attitude toward women. It is, first and foremost, a study of rape law as an illustration of sexism in the criminal law. A second purpose is to examine the connections between the law as written by legislators, as understood by courts, as acted upon by victims, and as enforced by prosecutors. Finally, this essay is an argument for an expanded understanding of rape in the law.

To examine rape within the criminal law tradition is to expose fully the sexism of the law. Much that is striking about the crime of rape—and revealing of the sexism of the system—emerges only when rape is examined relative to other crimes, which the feminist literature by and large does not do. . . .

The study of rape as an illustration of sexism in the criminal law also raises broader questions about the way conceptions of gender and the different backgrounds and perspectives of men and women should be encompassed within the criminal law.[2] . . . In rape, the male standard defines a crime committed against women, and male standards are used not only to judge men, but also to judge the conduct of women victims. Moreover, because the crime involves sex itself, the law of rape inevitably treads on the explosive ground of sex roles, of male aggression and female passivity, of our understandings of sexuality—areas where differences between a male and a female perspective may be most pronounced. . . .

. . . At one end of the spectrum is the "real" rape, what I will call the traditional rape: A stranger puts a gun to the head of his victim, threatens to kill her or beats her, and then engages in intercourse. In that case, the law—judges, statutes, prosecutors and all—generally acknowledge that a serious crime has been committed. But most cases deviate in one or many respects from this clear picture, making interpretation far more complex. Where less force is used or no other physical injury is inflicted, where threats are inarticulate, where the two know each other, where the setting is not an alley but a bedroom, where the initial contact was not a kidnapping but a date, where the woman says no but does not fight, the understanding is different. In such cases, the law, as reflected in the opinions of the courts, the interpretation, if not the words, of the statutes, and the decisions of those within the criminal justice system, often tell us that no crime has taken place and that fault, if any is to be recognized, belongs with the woman. In concluding that such acts—what I call, for lack of a better title, "non-traditional" rapes—are not criminal, and worse, that the woman must bear any guilt, the law has reflected, legitimized, and enforced a view of sex and women which celebrates male aggressiveness and punishes female passivity. And that vision, while under attack in recent years, continues to be a dominant force in our society and in the law of rape. . . .

Some of those who have written about rape from a feminist perspective intimate that nothing short of political revolution can redress the failings of the traditional approach to rape, that most of what passes for "sex" in our capitalist society is coerced, and that no lines can or should be drawn between rape and what happens in tens of millions of bedrooms across America.[3]

So understood, this particular feminist vision of rape shares one thing with the most traditional sexist vision: the view that non-traditional rape is not fundamentally different from what happens in tens of millions of bedrooms across America. According to the radical feminist, all of it is rape; according to the traditionalist, it is all permissible sex and seduction. In policy terms, neither is willing to draw lines between rape and permissible sex. As a result, the two visions, contradictory in every other respect, point to the same practical policy implications.

My own view is different from both of these. I recognize that both men and women in our society have long accepted norms of male aggressiveness and female passivity which lead to a restricted understanding of rape. And I do not propose, nor do I think it feasible, to punish all of the acts of sexual intercourse that could be termed coerced. But lines can be drawn between these two alternatives. . . .

II. The Definition of Rape: The Common Law Tradition

The traditional way of defining a crime is by describing the prohibited act (*actus reus*) committed by the defendant and the prohibited mental state (*mens rea*) with which he must have done it. We ask: What did the defendant do? What did he know or intend when he did it?

The definition of rape stands in striking contrast to this tradition, because courts, in defining the crime, have focused almost incidentally on the defendant—and almost entirely on the victim. . . .

But while the focus is on the female victim, the judgment of her actions is entirely male. If the issue were what the defendant knew, thought, or intended as to key elements of the offense, this perspective might be understandable; yet the issue has instead been the appropriateness of the woman's behavior, according to male standards of appropriate female behavior.

To some extent, this evaluation is but a modern response to the longstanding suspicion of rape victims. As Matthew Hale put it three centuries ago: "Rape is . . . an accusation easily to be made and hard to be proved, and harder to be defended by the party accused, tho never so innocent."[4]

But the problem is more fundamental than that. . . .

At its simplest, the dilemma lies in this: If nonconsent is essential to rape (and no amount of force or physical struggle is inherently inconsistent with lawful sex), and if no sometimes means yes, and if men are supposed to be aggressive in any event, how is a man to know when he has crossed the line? And how are we to avoid unjust convictions?

This dilemma is hardly inevitable. Partly, it is a product of the way society (or at least a powerful part of it) views sex. Partly, it is a product of the lengths to which the law has gone to enforce and legitimize those views. We could prohibit the use of force and threats and coercion in sex, regardless of "consent." We could define consent in a way that respected the autonomy of women. Having chosen neither course, however, we have created a problem of fair warning, and force and consent have been defined in an effort to resolve this problem.

Usually, any discussion of rape begins (and ends) with consent. I begin instead with *mens rea*, because if unjust punishment of the blameless man is our fear (as it was Hale's), then *mens rea* would seem an appropriate place to start addressing it. At least a requirement of *mens rea* would avoid unjust convictions without adjudicating the "guilt" of the victim. It could also be the first step in expanding liability beyond the most traditional rape. . . .

A. Mens Rea

It is difficult to imagine any man engaging in intercourse accidentally or mistakenly. It is just as difficult to imagine an accidental or mistaken use of force, at least as force is conventionally defined. But it is not at all difficult to imagine cases in which a man might claim that he did not realize that the woman was not consenting to sex. He may have been mistaken in assuming that no meant yes. He may not have bothered to inquire. He may have ignored signs that would have told him that the woman did not welcome his forceful penetration.

In doctrinal terms, such a man could argue that his mistake of fact should exculpate him because he lacked the requisite intent or *mens rea* as to the woman's required nonconsent. American courts have altogether eschewed the *mens rea* or mistake inquiry as to consent, opting instead for a definition of the crime of rape that is so limited that it leaves little room for men to be mistaken, reasonably or unreasonably, as to consent. The House of Lords, by contrast, has confronted the question explicitly and, in its leading case [*Morgan*, discussed *infra. Ed.*], has formally restricted the crime of rape to men who act recklessly, a state of mind defined to allow even the unreasonably mistaken man to avoid conviction. . . .

. . . In *mens rea* terms, the question is whether negligence suffices, that is, whether the defendant should be convicted who claims that he thought the woman was consenting, or didn't think about it, in situations where a "reasonable man" would have known that there was not consent. In mistake of fact terms, the question is whether a mistake as to consent must be reasonable in order to exculpate the defendant.

In defining the crime of rape, most American courts have omitted *mens rea* altogether. [For example,] [i]n Pennsylvania, the Superior Court held in 1982 that even a reasonable belief as to the victim's consent would not exculpate a defendant charged with rape.[5] . . .

To treat what the defendant intended or knew or even should have known about the victim's consent as irrelevant to his liability sounds like a result favorable to both prosecution and women as victims. But experience makes all too clear that it is not. To refuse to inquire into *mens rea* leaves two possibilities: turning rape into a strict liability offense where, in the absence of consent, the man is guilty of rape regardless of whether he (or anyone) would have recognized nonconsent in the circumstances; or defining the crime of rape in a fashion that is so limited that it would be virtually impossible for any man to be convicted where he was truly unaware or mistaken as to nonconsent. In fact, it is the latter approach which has characterized all of the older, and many of the newer, American cases. In practice, abandoning *mens rea* produces the worst of all possible worlds: The trial emerges not as an inquiry into the guilt of the defendant (is he a rapist?) but of the victim (was she really raped? did she consent?). The perspective that governs is therefore not that of the woman, nor even of the particular man, but of a judicial system intent upon protecting against unjust conviction, regardless of the dangers of injustice to the woman in the particular case.

The requirement that sexual intercourse be accompanied by force or threat of force to constitute rape provides a man with some protection against mistakes as to consent. A man who uses a gun or knife against his victim is not likely to be in serious doubt as to her lack of consent, and the more narrowly force is defined, the more implausible the claim that he was unaware of nonconsent.

But the law's protection of men is not limited to a requirement of force. [C]ourts have demanded that the victim demonstrate her nonconsent by engaging in resistance that will leave no doubt as to nonconsent. The definition of nonconsent as resistance . . . functions as a substitute for *mens rea* to ensure that the man has notice of the woman's nonconsent.

The choice between focusing on the man's intent or focusing on the woman's is not simply a doctrinal flip of the coin. First, the inquiry into the victim's nonconsent puts the woman, not the man, on trial. Her intent, not his, is disputed; and because her state of mind is key, her sexual history may be considered relevant (even though utterly unknown to the man). . . . Second, the issue for determination shifts from whether the man is a rapist to whether the woman was raped. A verdict of acquittal thus does more than signal that the prosecution has failed to prove the defendant guilty beyond a reasonable doubt; it signals that the prosecution has failed to prove the woman's sexual violation—"her innocence"—beyond a reasonable doubt. . . . Third, the resistance requirement is not only ill-conceived as a definition of nonconsent, but is an overbroad substitute for *mens rea* in any event. [T]he resistance standard requires women to risk injury to themselves in cases where there may be no doubt as to the man's intent or blameworthiness. . . .

Finally, by ignoring *mens rea,* American courts and legislators have imposed limits on the fair expansion of our understanding of rape. As long as the law holds that *mens rea* is not required, and that no instructions on intent need be given, pressure will exist to retain some form of resistance requirement and to insist on force as conventionally defined in order to protect men against conviction for "sex." Using resistance as a substitute for *mens rea* unnecessarily and unfairly immunizes those men whose victims are afraid enough, or intimidated enough, or, frankly, smart enough, not to take the risk of resisting physically. In doing so, the resistance test may declare the blameworthy man innocent and the raped woman guilty.

While American courts have unwisely ignored the entire issue of *mens rea* or mistake of fact, the British courts may have gone too far in the other direction. To their credit, they have squarely confronted the issue, but their resolution suggests a highly restrictive understanding of criminal intent in cases of sexual assault. The focal point of the debate in Great Britain and the Commonwealth countries was the House of Lords' decision in Director of Public Prosecutions v. Morgan,[6] in which the certified question was: "Whether in rape the defendant can properly be convicted, notwithstanding that he in fact believed that the woman consented, if such belief was not based on reasonable grounds." The majority of the House of Lords answered the question in the negative. . . .

My view is that such a "negligent rapist" should be punished, albeit—as in murder— less severely than the man who acts with purpose or knowledge, or even knowledge of the risk. First, he is sufficiently blameworthy for it to be just to punish him. Second, the injury he inflicts is sufficiently grave to deserve the law's prohibition.

The traditional argument against negligence liability is that punishment should be limited to cases of choice, because to punish a man for his stupidity is unjust and, in deterrence terms, ineffective. Under this view, a man should only be held responsible for what he does knowingly or purposely, or at least while aware of the risks involved. As one of Morgan's most respected defenders put it:

> To convict the stupid man would be to convict him for what lawyers call inadvertent negligence—honest conduct which may be the best that this man can do but that does not come up to the standard of the so-called reasonable man. People ought not to be punished for negligence except in some minor offences established by statute. Rape carries a possible sentence of imprisonment for life, and it would be wrong to have a law of negligent rape.[7]

If inaccuracy or indifference to consent is "the best that this man can do" because he lacks the capacity to act reasonably, then it might well be unjust and ineffective to punish him for it.[8] But such men will be rare. . . . More common is the case of the man who could have done better but didn't; could have paid attention, but didn't; heard her say no, or saw her tears, but decided to ignore them. Neither justice nor deterrence argues against punishing this man.

Certainly, if the "reasonable" attitude to which a male defendant is held is defined according to a "no means yes" philosophy that celebrates male aggressiveness and female passivity, there is little potential for unfairness in holding men who fall below *that* standard criminally liable. Under such a low standard of reasonableness, only a very drunk man could honestly be mistaken as to a woman's consent, and a man who voluntarily sheds his capacity to act and perceive reasonably should not be heard to complain here—any more than with respect to other crimes—that he is being punished in the absence of choice.

But even if reasonableness is defined—as I argue it should be—according to a rule that "no means no," it is not unfair to hold those men who violate the rule criminally responsible, provided that there is fair warning of the rule. I understand that some men in our society have honestly believed in a different reality of sexual relations, and that many may honestly view such situations differently than women. But, it is precisely because men and women may perceive these situations differently, and because the injury to women stemming from the different male perception may be grave, that it is necessary and appropriate for the law to impose a duty upon men to act with reason, and to punish them when they violate that duty.

In holding a man to such standard of reasonableness, the law signifies that it considers a woman's consent to sex to be significant enough to merit a man's reasoned attention. In effect, the law imposes a duty on men to open their eyes and use their heads before engaging in sex—not to read a woman's mind, but to give her credit for knowing her own mind when she speaks it. The man who has the inherent capacity to act reasonably, but fails to do so, has made the blameworthy choice to violate this duty. While the injury caused by purposeful conduct may be greater than that caused by negligent acts, being negligently sexually penetrated without one's consent remains a grave harm, and being treated like an object whose words or actions are not even worthy of consideration adds insult to injury. This dehumanization exacerbates the denial of dignity and autonomy which is so much a part of the injury of rape, and it is equally present in both the purposeful and negligent rape.

By holding out the prospect of punishment for negligence, the law provides an additional motive for men to "take care before acting, to use their faculties and draw on their experience in gauging the potentialities of contemplated conduct."[9] We may not yet have reached the point where men are required to ask verbally. But if silence does not negate consent, at least the word "no" should, and those who ignore such an explicit sign of nonconsent should be subject to criminal liability. . . .

B. Force and Threats

. . . Virtually every jurisdiction has traditionally made "force" or "threat of force" an element of the crime of rape. Where a defendant threatens his victim with a deadly weapon, beats her, or threatens to hurt her, and then proceeds immediately to have sex, few courts have difficulty finding that force is present. These facts fit the schoolboy definition of force. But when some time elapses between the force and intercourse, when the force is more of the variety considered "incidental" to sex, or when the situation is threatening but no explicit threat of harm is communicated, "force" as defined and required by the criminal law may not be present at all. In such cases, the law fails to recognize, let alone protect, a woman's interest in bodily integrity.

In Mills v. United States,[10] in 1897, the defendant seized his victim at gunpoint, told her he was a notorious train robber named "Henry Starr," threatened to kill her, and proceeded to have intercourse with her twice. The trial court instructed the jury:

> The fact is that all the force that need be exercised, if there is no consent, is the force incident to the commission of the act. If there is non-consent of the woman, the force, I say, incident to the commission of the crime is all the force that is required to make out this element of the crime.[11]

The jury convicted, and the defendant appealed on the ground that this instruction was in error as to the amount of force necessary to constitute rape. The Supreme Court agreed, and reversed the conviction:

> In this charge we think the court did not explain fully enough so as to be understood by the jury what constitutes in law non-consent on the part of the woman, and what is the force, necessary in all cases of non-consent, to consti-

tute the crime. . . . But the charge in question. . . covered the case where no threats were made; where no active resistance was overcome; where the woman was not unconscious, but where there was simply non-consent on her part and no real resistance whatever. . . . More force is necessary when that is the character of non-consent than was stated by the court to be necessary to make out that element of the crime. That kind of non-consent is not enough, nor is the force spoken of then sufficient, which is only incidental to the act itself.[12]

. . . The distinction between the "force" incidental to the act of intercourse and the "force" required to convict a man of rape is one commonly drawn by courts. Once drawn, however, the distinction would seem to require the courts to define what additional acts are needed to constitute prohibited rather than incidental force. This is where the problems arise. For many courts and jurisdictions, "force" triggers an inquiry identical to that which informs the understanding of consent. Both serve as substitutes for a *mens rea* requirement. Force is required to constitute rape, but force—even force that goes far beyond the physical contact necessary to accomplish penetration—is not itself prohibited. Rather, what is required, and prohibited, is force used to overcome female nonconsent. The prohibition is defined in terms of a woman's resistance. Thus, "forcible compulsion" becomes the force necessary to overcome reasonable resistance. When the woman does not physically resist, the question becomes then whether the force was sufficient to overcome a reasonable woman's will to resist. Prohibited force turns on the judge's evaluation of a reasonable woman's response.

In State v. Alston,[13] Mr. Alston and the victim had been involved in a "consensual" relationship for six months. That relationship admittedly involved "some violence" by the defendant and some passivity by the victim. The defendant would strike the victim when she refused to give him money or refused to do what he wanted. As for sex, the court noted that "she often had sex with the defendant just to accommodate him. On those occasions, she would stand still and remain entirely passive while the defendant undressed her and had intercourse with her." This was their "consensual" relationship. It ended when, after being struck by the defendant, the victim left him and moved in with her mother.

A month later, the defendant came to the school which the victim attended, blocked her path, demanded to know where she was living and, when she refused to tell him, grabbed her arm and stated that she was coming with him. The victim told the defendant she would walk with him if he released her arm. They then walked around the school and talked about their relationship. At one point, the defendant told the victim he was going to "fix" her face; when told that their relationship was over, the defendant stated that he had a "right" to have sex with her again. The two went to the house of a friend. The defendant asked her if she was "ready," and the victim told him she did not want to have sexual relations. The defendant pulled her up from the chair, undressed her, pushed her legs apart, and penetrated her. She cried.

The defendant was convicted of rape, and his conviction was affirmed by the intermediate court of appeals. On appeal, the North Carolina Supreme Court agreed that the victim was not required to resist physically to establish nonconsent: The victim's testimony that she did not consent was "unequivocal" and her testimony provided substantial evidence that the act of sexual intercourse was against her will.

But the North Carolina Supreme Court nonetheless reversed on the ground that, even viewing the evidence in the light most favorable to the state, the element of force had not been established by substantial evidence. The victim did not "resist"—physically, at least. And her failure to resist, in the court's evaluation, was not a result of what the defendant did before penetration. Therefore, there was no "force."

The force used outside the school, and the threats made on the walk, "although they may have induced fear," were considered to be "unrelated to the act of sexual intercourse." Indeed, the court emphasized that the victim testified that it was not what the defendant said that day, but her experience with him in the past, that made her afraid. Such past experience was deemed irrelevant. . . .

State v. Alston is not a unique case, but it is an unusual one. Rape cases between individuals who have had what passes in the law for a "consensual" sexual relationship are rare in the system. . . .

Later in 1984, the North Carolina Court of Appeals applied *Alston* to another case where the defendant and the victim knew each other and had previous sexual relations. In this case, however, the parties were not "boyfriend" and "girlfriend." They were a father and his 15-year-old daughter.

The defendant in State v. Lester[14] was the father of three daughters and a son. Prior to the parents' divorce, the defendant frequently beat the children's mother in their presence. He also beat his girlfriend and his son. He had a gun and on one occasion pointed it at his children. He engaged in sexual activity with all three of his daughters. He first had sexual relations with the daughter whose rape was at issue when she was 11 years old. Her mother found out and confronted the defendant. He swore never to touch her again, and then threatened to kill both mother and daughter if they told anyone of his actions. On both of the occasions in question, the victim initially refused her father's demand to take her clothes off and "do it." In both cases, she complied when the demand was repeated and she sensed that her father was becoming angry. The court held that the defendant could be convicted of incest, but not of rape:

> In the instant case there is evidence that the acts of sexual intercourse between defendant and his fifteen-year-old daughter . . . were against her will. There is no evidence, however, that defendant used either actual or constructive force to accomplish the acts with which he is charged. As *Alston* makes clear, the victim's fear of defendant, however justified by his previous conduct, is insufficient to show that defendant *forcibly* raped his daughter on 25 November and 18 December.[15]

. . . Decisions such as *Lester* and *Alston* are vulnerable to attack on traditional doctrinal grounds. The courts' unwillingness to credit the victim's past experience of violence at the hands of the defendant stands in sharp contrast to the black letter law that a defendant's knowledge of his attacker's reputation for violence or ownership of a gun is relevant to the reasonableness of his use of deadly force in self-defense.

That these decisions depart so straightforwardly from established criminal law doctrine is noteworthy but not unusual in the law of rape. More interesting is the apparent paradox that they create. In each case, the court says—and this is explicit, not implicit—that sex was without the woman's consent. It also says that there was no force. In other words, the woman was not forced to engage in sex, but the sex she engaged in was against her will.

Such a paradox is almost inevitable if one adopts, and then enforces, the most traditional male notion of a fight as the working definition of "force." In a fight, you hit your assailant with your fists or your elbows or your knees. In a fight, the one attacked fights back. In these terms, there was no fight in *Alston*. Therefore, there was no force.

I am not at all sure how the judges who decided *Alston* would explain the victim's simultaneous refusal to consent and failure to resist. For myself, it is not at all difficult to understand that a woman who had been repeatedly beaten, who had been a passive victim of both violence and sex during the "consensual" relationship, who had sought to escape from the man, who is confronted and threatened by him, who summons the courage to tell him their relationship is over only to be answered by his assertion of a "right" to sex—a woman in such a position would not fight. She wouldn't fight; she might cry. Hers is the reaction of "sissies" in playground fights. Hers is the reaction of people who have already been beaten, or who never had the power to fight in the first instance. Hers is, from my reading, the most common reaction of women to rape. It certainly was mine.

To say that there is no "force" in such a situation is to create a gulf between power and force, and to define the latter solely in schoolboy terms. Mr. Alston did not beat his victim —at least not with his fists. He didn't have to. She had been beaten—physically and emotionally—long before. But that beating was one that the court was willing to go to great lengths to avoid recognizing.

That the law prohibiting forced sex understands force in such narrow terms is frustrating enough for its women victims. Worse, however, is the fact that the conclusion that no force is present may emerge as a judgment not that the man did not act unreasonably, but as a judgment that the woman victim did. . . .

[T]he "reasonable" woman under the view of [many judges] is not a woman at all. Their version of a reasonable person is one who does not scare easily, one who does not feel vulnerability, one who is not passive, one who fights back, not cries. The reasonable woman, it seems, is not a schoolboy "sissy." She is a real man. . . .

. . . Technically, . . . threats of force may be implicit as well as explicit. But implicit to whom? That a woman feels genuinely afraid, that a man has created the situation that she finds frightening, even that he has done it intentionally in order to secure sexual satisfaction, may not be enough to constitute the necessary force or even implicit threat of force which earns bodily integrity any protection under the law of rape.

In Goldberg v. State,[16] a high-school senior working as a sales clerk was "sold a story" by the defendant that he was a free-lance agent and thought she was an excellent prospect to become a successful model. She accompanied him to his "temporary studio" where she testified that she engaged in intercourse because she was afraid. Her reasons for being afraid, according to the appellate court which reversed the conviction, were: "1) she was alone with the appellant in a house with no buildings close by and no one to help her if she resisted, and 2) the appellant was much larger than she was." According to the appellate court, "[i]n the complete absence of any threatening words or actions by the appellant, these two factors, as a matter of law, are simply not enough to have created a reasonable fear of harm so as to preclude resistance and be 'the equivalent of force.'"

The New York Supreme Court, sitting as the trier of fact in a rape case, reached a similar conclusion with respect to the threatening situation facing an "incredibly gullible, trusting, and naive" college sophomore. In People v. Evans,[17] the defendant posed as a psychologist conducting a sociological experiment, took the woman to a dating bar to "observe" her, and then induced her to come to an apartment he used as an "office." When she rejected his advances, he said to her: "'Look where you are. You are in the apartment of a strange man. How do you know that I am really who I say I am? How do you know that I am really a psychologist? . . . I could kill you. I could rape you. I could hurt you physically.'" The trial court found his conduct "reprehensible," describing it as "conquest by con job." But it was not criminal; the words were ambiguous, capable of communicating either a threat to use ultimate force or the chiding of a "foolish girl." While acknowledging that the victim might be terrified, the court was not persuaded beyond a reasonable doubt that the guilt of the defendant had been established.

In both *Goldberg* and *Evans,* a woman finds herself alone and potentially stranded in a strange place with a man who is bigger than she. One need not be "incredibly gullible" to find oneself in this situation; one need only . . . agree to give an average man (who is bigger than an average woman) a ride home. There are at least four possible doctrinal approaches to these threatening situations, even accepting the courts' understanding that "force" can only be understood in relation to a woman's resistance. It is noteworthy that all the decisions discussed above adopt the approach that not only makes conviction most difficult, but also operates to place guilt most squarely on the victim.

The simplest approach would be to ask whether this woman's will to resist was in fact overcome by this defendant's actions. Is she lying, or did she submit because she was truly frightened? If she is not lying— and none of the courts suggested that any of the women in these cases were actually lying—then affirm the conviction. But what about the poor man who didn't realize that the woman was overcome by fear of him, rather than desire for him? Properly regarded, such a man lacks *mens rea* as to force or consent.

A second approach resolves that problem without relying explicitly on *mens rea*. It asks instead: Were the defendant's acts and behavior intended to overcome this woman's will to resist? Under such a standard, at least Mr. Lester, Mr. Alston, Mr. Goldberg, and Mr. Evans . . . will have a hard time claiming that they didn't mean to succeed, and that success was not defined as creating a situation that would frighten the woman into submission.

A third approach probes whether the defendant's acts and statements were calculated to overcome the will of a reasonable woman. This standard, very close to the "reasonable calculation" standard actually used in earlier decisions in [some jurisdictions], obviously allows men greater freedom than the second approach. It tolerates their exploitation of naive and gullible women by claiming that, in their "reasonableness calculation," the tactics should not have been threatening enough. Even at its best, the "reasonably calculated" standard creates something of a paradox: If most women have a different understanding of force than most men, then the reasonable calculation standard is one that asks how a reasonable man understands the mind of a reasonable woman. But at least it focuses primarily on the defendant's actions and thoughts and makes his guilt or innocence the center of the trial.

The final approach doesn't even do that. It judges the woman, not the man. It asks—as did the court in each of these cases—whether the will of the reasonable woman would have been overcome given the circumstances. The focus is on women generally, and on the victim as she compares (poorly) to the court's assessment of the reasonable woman. The court then proceeds to conclude that a reasonable woman's will would not have been overcome in those circumstances, because there is no "force" as men understand it.

Such an approach accomplishes two things. First, it ensures broad male freedom to "seduce" women who feel powerless, vulnerable, and afraid; the force standard guarantees men freedom to intimidate women and exploit their weaknesses, as long as they don't "fight" with them. Second, it makes clear that the responsibility and blame for such seductions belong with the woman. Because the will of a reasonable woman by definition would not have been overcome, a particular woman's submission can only mean that she is sub-par as women go or that she was complicitous in the intercourse.

It is one thing to argue that none of the men in these cases should be considered in the same category (in terms of their blameworthiness, their dangerousness, or the harm caused by their actions), as the man who puts a gun to his victim's head and threatens to kill her if she refuses to have sex. It is quite another to argue that these men have committed no crime.

Most striking about these cases is the fact that had these men been seeking money instead of sex, their actions would plainly violate traditional state criminal prohibitions. Had Mr. Goldberg used his modeling agent story to secure money rather than sex, his would be a case of theft by deception or false pretenses. As for Mr. Evans, had he sought money rather than sex as part of his "sociological test," he too could have been found guilty of theft. Neither Goldberg nor Evans could have escaped liability on the ground that a "reasonable person" would not have been deceived, any more than a victim's leaving his front door unlocked or his keys in the automobile ignition serves as a defense to burglary or larceny. . . . And had Mr. Lester threatened to expose the nude pictures were he not paid, he might well have been guilty of state law extortion.

Lying to secure money is unlawful theft by deception or false pretenses, a lesser crime than robbery, but a crime nonetheless. Yet lying to secure sex is old-fashioned seduction—not first-degree rape, not even third-degree rape. . . .

. . . I am suggesting that we . . . prohibit fraud to secure sex to the same extent we prohibit fraud to secure money, and prohibit extortion to secure sex to the same extent we prohibit extortion to secure money. [L]oss of bodily integrity is a different and greater injury than loss of money and thus merits greater punishment. . . .

C. Consent

. . . Rape is unique . . . in the definition which has been accorded to consent. That definition makes all too plain that the purpose of the consent rule is not to protect female autonomy and freedom of choice, but to assure men the broadest sexual access to women. In matters of sex, the common law tradition views women ambivalently at best: Even when not intentionally dishonest, they simply cannot be trusted to know what they want or to mean what they say. While the cases that engendered this tradition date from the 1870's and 1880's, [recent cases] have perpetuated it.

The justification for the central role of consent in the law of rape is that it protects women's choice and women's autonomy in sexual relations. Or, as one leading commentator put it: "In all cases the law of rape protects the woman's discretion by proscribing coitus contrary to her wishes."[18] Not exactly. As discussed in the preceding section, the law does not protect the woman from "coitus contrary to her wishes" when there is no "force." Secondly, the definition of nonconsent requires victims of rape, unlike victims of any other crime, to demonstrate their "wishes" through physical resistance.

A 1906 Wisconsin case, Brown v. State,[19] provides an example of the classic definition of nonconsent in rape as it was applied for most of this century. In a modified form, it continues to apply in some courts and jurisdictions. The victim in *Brown,* a sixteen-year-old (and a virgin), was a neighbor of the accused. She testified at trial that on a walk across the fields to her grandmother's home, she greeted the accused. He at once seized her, tripped her to the ground, and forced himself upon her. "I tried as hard as I could to get away. I was trying all the time to get away just as hard as I could. I was trying to get up; I pulled at the grass; I screamed as hard as I could, and he told me to shut up, and I didn't, and then he held his hand on my mouth until I was almost strangled." Whenever he removed his hand from her mouth she repeated her screams. The jury found the defendant guilty of rape.

On appeal, the Supreme Court of Wisconsin did not reverse Brown's conviction on the ground that the force used was insufficient to constitute rape. Nor did the court conclude that the defendant lacked the necessary *mens rea* for rape. Rather, the court reversed the conviction on the ground that the victim had not adequately demonstrated her nonconsent:

> Not only must there be entire absence of mental consent or assent, but there must be the most vehement exercise of every physical means or faculty within the woman's power to resist the penetration of her person, and this must be shown to persist until the offense is consummated.[20]

Here, the victim failed to meet that standard: She only once said "let me go;" her screams were considered "inarticulate;" and her failure to actually "resist," to use her "hands and limbs and pelvic muscles"—obstacles which the court noted that "medical writers insist . . . are practically insuperable"—justified reversal of the conviction.[21] Indeed, the court noted that "when one pauses to reflect upon the terrific resistance which the determined woman should make," the victim's absence of bruises and torn clothing was "well-nigh incredible."

Brown is almost eighty years old. But the problem it illustrates is not merely of historical interest. Virtually every jurisdiction has eliminated the requirement of "utmost resistance" to establish nonconsent. But by statute and in practice, many courts continue to inquire into the victim's "earnest resistance" to establish that she did not consent to intercourse. . . .

. . . In Goldberg v. State,[22] where the defendant brought a would-be modeling prospect to his fictitious and deserted "temporary studio," his conviction of rape was reversed both on the ground that the force used was insufficient and on the ground that the victim had failed to offer "real resistance." On the latter point, the court drew a bright line between verbal and physical resistance: "It is true that she *told* the appellant she 'didn't want to do that [stuff].' But the resistance that must be shown involves not merely verbal but *physical* resistance 'to the extent of her ability at the time.' "[23]

No similar effort is required of victims of other crimes for which consent is a defense. . . .

In robbery, claims that the victim cooperated with the taking of the money or eased the way, and thus consented, have generally been unsuccessful. . . .

In the 1950's and 1960's, the leading law journals in this country provided detailed explanations of why women could not be relied upon to know what they wanted or mean what they said; how it was that many women enjoyed physical struggle as a sexual stimulant; and how unfair it would be to punish men who realized that "no" means "yes," only to have their ambivalent partners lie after the fact.[24] According to a student author published in the *Stanford Law Review*:

> Although a woman may desire sexual intercourse, it is customary for her to say, "no, no, no" (although meaning "yes, yes, yes") and to expect the male to be the aggressor. . . . It is always difficult in rape cases to determine whether the female really meant "no." . . . The problem of determining what the female "really meant" is compounded when, in fact, the female had no clearly determined attitude—that is, her attitude was one of ambivalence. Slovenko explains that often a woman faces a "trilemma"; she is faced with a choice among being a prude, a tease, or an "easy lay." Furthermore a woman may note a man's brutal nature and be attracted to him rather than repulsed.[25]

In order to remedy these problems, the author concluded that the resistance standard must be "high enough to assure that the resistance is unfeigned and to indicate with some degree of certainty that the woman's attitude was not one of ambivalence or unconscious compliance and that her complaints do not result from moralistic after-thoughts," but must be "low enough to make death or serious bodily injury an *unlikely outcome* of the event."[26] That death or serious bodily injury remains a possible result of ignoring a woman's words is apparently not too great a cost to pay.

Perhaps the most influential of all such commentary was the often and still-cited *Yale Law Journal* Note on what women want.[27] Relying on Freud, the author pointed out that it is not simply that women lie, although there is an "unusual inducement to malicious or psychopathic accusation inherent in the sexual nature of the crime." Even the "normal girl" is a confused and ambivalent character when it comes to sex. Her behavior is not always an accurate guide to her true desires; it may suggest resistance when in fact the woman is enjoying the physical struggle:

> When her behavior looks like resistance although her attitude is one of consent, injustice may be done the man by the woman's subsequent accusation. Many women, for example, require as part of preliminary "love play" aggressive over-tures by the man. Often their erotic pleasure may be enhanced by, or even de-pend upon, an accompanying physical struggle. The "love bite" is a common, if mild, sign of the aggressive component in the sex act. And the tangible signs of struggle may survive to support a subsequent accusation by the woman.[28]

And if women are ambivalent toward sex, it follows that it would be unfair to pun-ish the man who was not acting entirely against her wishes:

> [A] woman's need for sexual satisfaction may lead to the unconscious desire for forceful penetration, the coercion serving neatly to avoid the guilt feelings which might arise after willing participation. . . .
>
> Where such an attitude of ambivalence exists, the woman may, nonetheless, exhibit behavior which would lead the factfinder to conclude that she opposed the act. To illustrate. [T]he anxiety resulting from this conflict of needs may cause her to flee from the situation of discomfort, either physically by running away, or symbolically by retreating to such infantile behavior as crying. The scratches, flight, and crying constitute admissible and compelling evidence of non-consent. But the conclusion of rape in this situation may be inconsistent with the meaning of the consent standard and unjust to the man. [F]airness to the male suggests a conclusion of not guilty, despite signs of aggression, if his act was not contrary to the woman's formulated wishes.[29]

In short, the problem is not only that some women lie, but that many women do not in fact know what they want, or mean what they say—at least when they say no. And the presence of force does not even prove rape, because many women enjoy and de-pend on force. According to this view, insisting that women do more than simply say no to sex is an essential means of protecting the man who exercises his judgment to ig-nore a woman's words of protestation.

Nonconsent, defined as physical resistance, serves this notice function in two ways. First, resistance defines the limits of force. The law avoids the task of inquiring into how much force in sex is too much by defining proscribed force according to victim resistance. Second, physical resistance means that this woman in fact means what she says; men are free to ignore words, but resistance signifies that no, in this case, means no. Resistance thus serves to give notice that sex is indeed unwelcome, that force is just that, and that the man has crossed the line.

Under this view, the "utmost resistance" standard could be understood by judges to reflect their view that a truly unwilling woman would fight nearly to the death to protect her virtue. If the judges believed this, then certainly a male defendant did not deserve the serious punishment of a rape conviction for acting on the same belief. Unless the woman offered utmost resistance, or had good reason (fear of death, unconsciousness, incompetence) for not doing so, the man presumably could not be held to be on notice that his advances were truly unwelcome.

In practice, the nonconsent standard has served a second important function as well. It has provided a convenient means for distinguishing between those victims deserving of the law's protection, characteristically the chaste, white victim, and those who were not. Thus the Court of Appeals of Virginia reasoned, in reversing the conviction of a black man for attempted rape of a black woman (who, the court thought it important to note, had never been married and had two children, and attended a performance with the prisoner paying all the expenses):

> The evidence indicates that he had wooed her pretty roughly in a way that would have been horrible and a shocking outrage toward a woman of virtuous sensibilities, and should have subjected him to the severest punishment which the law would warrant. But how far it affected the sensibilities of the prosecutrix does not appear. It by no means appears, from the facts certified, that it was an attempt to ravish her, against her will, or that it was not only an attempt to work upon her passions, and overcome her virtue, which had yielded to others before—how often it does not appear. . . . Without any interference, or any outcry on her part, together with his after conduct, shows, we think, that his conduct, though extremely reprehensible, and deserving of punishment, does not involve him in the crime which this statute was designed to punish.[30]

Eventually, the "utmost resistance" standard came to be replaced by a "reasonable resistance" standard: Chastity may be valuable, but judges came to realize that it may not be more valuable than life itself. The reasonable resistance standard spares the woman the choice of risking her life or serious injury to prevent unwanted sex, instead asking whether she had offered reasonable resistance. But for many courts, saying "no" —passive resistance—does not count as resistance. In those courts, the understanding of the law review authors of the 1950's and 1960's, that "no means yes," continues to have the force of law.

The consent standard, like the force standard, thus emerges as another means to protect men against unfair convictions by giving them full and fair warning that their (forceful) advances constitute an unwelcome rape rather than a welcome, or at least accepted, seduction. An alternative approach to this fair warning problem would be to spell out the crime or crimes of "rape" in detail, without regard to the response of the woman. In fact, most courts recognize the use of deadly weapons or a threat of imminent death as criminal without the need for too much reliance on the woman's response, at least most of the time. But to go further and prohibit all forms of physical force would inject the criminal law into what many conceive as private and appropriate choices: It is one thing to ban guns and deadly weapons, or even fraud and extortion, but quite another to say that "love bites" or vigorous thrashing or pushing is criminal regardless of consent.

Our inability or unwillingness to detail the sexual practices that we as a society will not tolerate, regardless of consent, creates the law's heavy reliance on the behavior of the woman. Because the law has provided that if the woman "consents"—regardless of the amount of force used—intercourse is not rape, men have a right to fair warning as to consent. But the consent standard does not necessarily lead to the denial of autonomy to women, or to the "no means yes" philosophy. Quite the contrary, the consent standard could be viewed as a means to afford women their deserved freedom to engage in sex however they choose—whether that is sex with women or sex with forcible penetration. The harm of rape, or part of it, is the denial of that freedom. Indeed, a consent standard that allowed the individual woman to say "yes" as well as "no," to define all of the limits of permissible sex for herself and then to have that definition incorporated and respected in law, would be a means of empowering women. It could also expand liability for criminal sex to any man who refuses to respect those limits.

Many feminists would argue that as long as women are powerless relative to men, viewing a "yes" as a sign of true consent is misguided. Yet if a "yes" might really mean "no," we might at least agree to respect the courage of a woman who dared to say "no." The insistence that men are entitled not only to presume consent from silence but actually to ignore a woman's explicit words makes all too clear the law's absolute determination not to empower women at all. The fear that women, acting from shame or spite or vengeance, will abuse any power they are afforded in sexual relations at the expense of "innocent" men is the most pervasive theme in the legal commentary on rape. A consent standard that further empowered women and potentially eased the burden of proving rape—limited sexual access—has been plainly unacceptable.

The refusal of the law (and the society it reflects) either to limit the scope of seduction regardless of consent or to empower women through the consent standard creates the fair warning problem that demands a resistance standard as its answer. We could seek to prohibit certain forms of seduction. We could seek to empower women, at least when they say no. Both alternatives would mean less freedom for men to coerce submission and secure sexual access. Both would eliminate the need for women to resist physically. Having chosen neither, we have created a fair warning problem whose only solution, at least to many courts and commentators, is to interpret force and consent in ways that punish women for "complicity" in sex, making their conduct the determinant of liability and the subject of our verdicts. There is nothing inevitable about either the problem or the solution. . . .

Toward a Broader Understanding

The conduct that one might think of as "rape" ranges from the armed stranger who breaks into a woman's home to the date she invites in who takes silence for assent. In between are literally hundreds of variations: the man may be a stranger, but he may not be armed; he may be armed, but he may not be a stranger; he may be an almost, rather than a perfect, stranger—a man who gave her a ride or introduced himself through a ruse; she may say yes, but only because he threatens to expose her to the police or the welfare authorities; she may say no, but he may ignore her words.

[Today] the woman raped at gunpoint by the intruding stranger should find most of the legal obstacles to her complaint removed. That was not always so ... she might well have faced a corroboration requirement, a cautionary instruction, a fresh complaint rule, and a searing cross-examination about her sexual past to determine whether she had nonetheless consented to sex. In practice, she may still encounter some of these obstacles; but to the extent that the law communicates any clear message, it is likely to be that she was raped.

But most rapes do not as purely fit the traditional model, and most victims do not fare as well. Cases involving men met in bars ... or at work ... or at airports ... let alone cases involving ex-boyfriends ..., still lead some appellate courts to enforce the most traditional views of women in the context of the less traditional rape. And in the system, considerations of prior relationship and the circumstances of the initial encounter, as well as force and resistance and corroboration, seem to reflect a similarly grounded if not so clearly stated view of the limits of rape law.

In thinking about rape, it is not as difficult to decide which rapes are more serious or which rapists deserving of more punishment: Weapons, injury, and intent—the traditional grading criteria of the criminal law—are all justifiable answers to these questions. Most jurisdictions that have reformed their rape laws [recently] have focused on creating degrees of rape—aggravated and unaggravated—based on some combination of the presence of weapons and injury.[31] While *mens rea* or mistake needs to be addressed more clearly in some rape laws, and bodily injury more carefully defined in others, these are essentially problems of draftsmanship which are hardly insurmountable.

The more difficult problem comes in understanding and defining the threshold for liability—where we draw the line between criminal sex and seduction. Every statute still uses some combination of "force," "threats" and "consent" to define the crime. But in giving meaning to those terms at the threshold of liability, the law of rape must confront the powerful norms of male aggressiveness and female passivity which continue to be adhered to by many men and women in our society.

The law did not invent the "no means yes" philosophy. Women as well as men have viewed male aggressiveness as desirable and forced sex as an expression of love; women as well as men have been taught and have come to believe that when a woman "encourages" a man, he is entitled to sexual satisfaction. From the sociological surveys to prime time television, one can find ample support in society and culture for even the most oppressive views of women, and the most expansive notions of seduction enforced by the most traditional judges.

But the evidence is not entirely one-sided. For every prime time series celebrating forced sex, there seems to be another true confession story in a popular magazine detailing the facts of a date rape and calling it "rape." . . .

We live, in short, in a time of changing sexual mores—and we are likely to for some time to come. In such times, the law can cling to the past or help move us into the future. We can continue to enforce the most traditional views of male aggressiveness and female passivity, continue to adhere to the "no means yes" philosophy and to the broadest understanding of seduction, until and unless change overwhelms us. That is not a neutral course, however; in taking it, the law (judges, legislators, or prosecutors) not only reflects (a part of) society, but legitimates and reenforces those views.

Or we can use the law to move forward. It may be impossible—and even unwise—to try to use the criminal law to change the way people think, to push progress to the ideal. But recognition of the limits of the criminal sanction need not be taken as a justification for the *status quo*. Faced with a choice between reenforcing the old and fueling the new in a world of changing norms, it is not necessarily more legitimate or neutral to choose the old. There are lines to be drawn short of the ideal: The challenge we face in thinking about rape is to use the power and legitimacy of law to reenforce what is best, not what is worst, in our changing sexual mores. . . .

In a better world, I believe that men and women would not presume either consent or nonconsent. They would ask, and be certain. There is nothing unromantic about showing the kind of respect for another person that demands that you know for sure before engaging in intimate contact. In a better world, women who said yes would be saying so from a position of equality, or at least sufficient power to say no. In a better world, fewer women would bargain with sex because they had nothing else to bargain with; they would be in at least as good a position to reject demands for sexual access as men are to reject demands for money.

If we are not at the point where it is appropriate for the law to presume nonconsent from silence, . . . then at least we should be at the point where it is legitimate to punish the man who ignores a woman's explicit words of protestations. I am quite certain that many women who say yes—whether on dates or on the job—would say no if they could; I have no doubt that women's silence is sometimes the product not of passion and desire but of pressure and pain. But at the very least the criminal law ought to say clearly that women who actually say no must be respected as meaning it; that nonconsent means saying no; that men who proceed nonetheless, claiming that they thought no meant yes, have acted unreasonably and unlawfully.

So, too, for threats of harm short of physical injury, and for deception and false pretenses as methods of seduction. The powerlessness of women and the value of bodily integrity are great enough to argue that women deserve more comprehensive protection for their bodies than the laws of extortion or fraud provide for money. But if going so far seems too complicated and fraught with difficulty, as it does to many, then we need not. For the present, it would be a significant improvement if the law of rape in any state prohibited exactly the same threats as that state's law of extortion and exactly the same deceptions as that state's law of false pretenses or fraud.

In short, I am arguing that "consent" should be defined so that "no means no." And the "force" or "coercion" that negates consent ought be defined to include extortionate threats and deceptions of material fact. As for *mens rea,* unreasonableness as to consent, understood to mean ignoring a woman's words, should be sufficient for liability: Reasonable men should be held to know that no means no, and unreasonable mistakes, no matter how honestly claimed, should not exculpate. Thus, the threshold of liability—whether phrased in terms of "consent," "force" or "coercion," or some combination of the three, should be understood to include at least those non-traditional rapes where the woman says no or submits only in response to lies or threats which would be prohibited were money sought instead. The crime I have described would be a lesser offense than the aggravated rape in which life is threatened or bodily injury inflicted, but it is, in my judgment, "rape." One could, I suppose, claim that as we move from such violent rapes to "just" coerced or nonconsensual sex, we are moving away from a crime of violence toward something else. But what makes the violent rape different—and more serious—than an aggravated assault is the injury to personal integrity involved in forced sex. That same injury is the reason that forced sex should be a crime even when there is no weapon or no beating. In a very real sense, what does make rape different from other crimes, at every level of the offense, is that rape is about sex and sexual violation. Were the essence of the crime the use of the gun or the knife or the threat, we wouldn't need—and wouldn't have—a separate crime.

Conduct is labeled as criminal "to announce to society that these actions are not to be done and to secure that fewer of them are done."[32] As a matter of principle, we should be ready to announce to society our condemnation of coerced and nonconsensual sex and to secure that we have less of it. The message of the substantive law to men, and to women, should be made clear.

That does not mean that this crime will, or should, be easy to prove. The constitutional requirement of proof beyond a reasonable doubt may well be difficult to meet in cases where guilt turns on whose account is credited as to what was said. . . .

The message of the substantive law must be distinguished from the constitutional standards of proof. In this as in every criminal case, a jury must be told to acquit if it is in doubt. The requirement of proof beyond a reasonable doubt rests on the premise that it is better that ten guilty should go free than that one innocent man should be punished. But if we should acquit ten, let us be clear that we are acquitting them not because they have an entitlement to ignore a woman's words, not because what they allegedly did was right or macho or manly, but because we live in a system that errs on the side of freeing the guilty.

Notes

1. See, e.g., S. Brownmiller, Against Our Will: Men, Women and Rape (1975); N. Gager & C. Schurr, Sexual Assault: Confronting Rape in America (1976); A. Medea & K. Thompson, Against Rape (1974); D. Russell, The Politics of Rape: The Victim's Per-

spective (1975); Griffin, Rape: The All American Crime, herein, at 422; MacKinnon, Feminism, Marxism, Method, and the State: Toward Feminist Jurisprudence, 8 Signs 635 (1983).

2. Similar questions may be raised, for example, when a woman is prosecuted for killing the husband who battered her, see, e.g., Ibn-Tamas v. United States, 407 A.2d 626 (D.C. 1979), or a man suspected of sexually molesting her children, see, e.g., State v. Wanrow, 88 Wash. 2d 221, 559 P.2d 548 (1977). The law must define the standard of "reasonableness" against which the woman's conduct must be judged for purposes of self-defense or provocation. Is the question what a "reasonable person" would have done in such a situation, or what a "reasonable woman" would have done? Is there such a thing, in life or in law, as reasonable people, or only men and women, with all their differences?

3. See, e.g., MacKinnon, *supra* note 1; see also Russell, *supra* note 1.

4. 1 M. Hale, The History of the Pleas of the Crown 635 (1778). This statement is the usual basis for the "cautionary" instructions traditionally given in rape cases.

5. . . . Commonwealth v. Williams, 294 Pa. Super. 93, 99–100, 439 A.2d 765, 769 (1982).

6. Director of Pub. Prosecutions v. Morgan, 1976 A.C. 182, 2 All. E.R. 347, [1975] 2 W.L.R. 913 (H.L.). [Mr. Morgan and his three drinking companions failed to find some female company. Mr. Morgan invited the three men home to have intercourse with his spouse, telling them not to be surprised if she resisted, because this was the way she got sexually excited. The four men were convicted of rape and their convictions affirmed by the Court of Appeals. Although holding that negligence was not a sufficient basis for liability for rape, the House of Lords upheld the convictions, reasoning that no jury could have concluded that defendants' belief was reasonable. *Ed.*]

7. Prof. Glanville Williams in a letter to The Times (London), May 8, 1975, at 15.

8. See H. L. A. Hart, Punishment and Responsibility 152–154 (1968). Professor Hart argues that what is critical to just punishment is not the defendant's awareness of the risks of his conduct, but "that those whom we punish should have had, when they acted, the normal capacities, physical and mental, for doing what the law requires and abstaining from what it forbids, and a fair opportunity to exercise these capacities." *Id.* at 152.

9. Model Penal Code §2.02 comment at 126–127 (Tent. Draft No. 4 1955). The Model Penal Code commentators thus recognized the deterrence rationale of negligence liability in justifying its inclusion as a potential basis for criminal liability (albeit for a limited number of crimes, not including rape).

10. 164 U.S. 644 (1897).

11. *Id.* at 647.

12. *Id.* at 647–648. The reader may be puzzled as to why I am devoting any attention to a decision, even a decision of the United States Supreme Court, which dates from the 1890's. Were *Mills* simply a historical curiosity, the reader would surely be right to question my priorities; it is far too easy to attack 100-year-old cases. But when cases from the 1890's reflect an understanding of force which survives into cases from the 1980's—and *Mills* does—it is no longer a matter of slaying straw men. *Mills* is a living dragon.

13. 310 N.C. 399, 312 S.E.2d 470 (1984).

14. State v. Lester, 70 N.C. App. 757, 321 S.E.2d 166 (1984), *aff'd*, 313 N.C. 595, 330 S.E.2d 205 (1985).

15. *Id.* at 761, 321 S.E.2d at 168 (emphasis in original).

16. 41 Md. App. 58, 395 A.2d 1213 (Ct. Spec. App. 1979).

17. 85 Misc. 2d 1088, 379 N.Y.S.2d 912 (Sup. Ct. 1975), *aff'd*, 55 A.D. 2d 858, 390 N.Y.S.2d 768 (1976).

18. Note, Forcible and Statutory Rape: An Exploration of the Operation and Objectives of the Consent Standard, 92 Yale L.J. 55, 71 (1952); see also Model Penal Code §213.1 comment 4, at 301 (1980) ("The law of rape protects the female's freedom of choice and punishes unwanted and coerced intimacy.").

19. 127 Wis. 193; 106 N.W. 536 (1906).

20. *Id.* at 199; 106 N.W. at 538.

21. *Id.* at 199–200; 106 N.W. at 538. According to the court, a woman "is equipped to interpose most effective obstacles by means of hands and limbs and pelvic muscles. Indeed, medical writers insist that these obstacles are practically insuperable in absence of more than the usual relative disproportion of age and strength between man and woman, though no such impossibility is recognized as a rule of law." *Id.* The latter qualification is, by the court's own opinion and holding, open to question. The view that an unwilling woman physically could not be raped was not limited to Wisconsin or to the nineteenth century. It provided support for insisting that the least women should do was resist to the utmost. . . .

22. 41 Md. App. 58, 395 A.2d 1212 (1979). . . .

23. *Id.* at 68, 395 A.2d at 1219 (citation omitted). See also Hazel v. State, 221 Md. 464, 469–70, 157 A.2d 922, 925 (1960): "The authorities are by no means in accord as to what degree of resistance is necessary to establish the absence of consent. However, the generally accepted doctrine seems to be that a female—who was conscious and possessed of her natural, mental and physical powers when the attack took place—must have resisted to the extent of her ability at the time, unless it appears that she was overcome by numbers or was so terrified by threats as to overpower her will to resist."

24. Similar concerns led leading commentators to advocate special rules of proof in rape cases. Professor Wigmore, for example, thought all women rape victims to be sufficiently suspect to argue that the complainant be examined by a psychiatrist, and that no case go to the jury unless such an examination had been performed and the physician had testified as to her personal history and mental health. According to Professor Wigmore: "[Rape complainants'] psychic complexes are multifarious, distorted partly by inherent defects, partly by diseased derangements or abnormal instincts, partly by bad social environment, partly by temporary physiological or emotional conditions. . . . The unchaste . . . mentality finds incidental but direct expression in the narration of imaginary sex incidents of which the narrator is the heroine or the victim. On the surface the narration is straight-forward and convincing." 3A J. Wigmore, Evidence §924a, at 736 (Chadbourn rev. ed. 1970). . . .

25. Note, The Resistance Standard in Rape Legislation, 18 Stan. L. Rev. 680 (1966), at 682 (footnotes omitted) (quoting Slovenko, A Panoramic Overview: Sexual Behavior and the Law, in Sexual Behavior and the Law 5, 51 (1965)).

26. Note, Resistance Standard, *supra* note 25, at 685 (emphasis added).

27. Note, Forcible and Statutory Rape, *supra* note 18. This Note is cited, and its influence apparent, not only in the Model Penal Code provisions adopted in the 1950's, but in the comments to them edited in the 1970's and published in 1980. . . .

28. *Id.* at 66 (footnotes omitted).

29. *Id.* at 67–68 (footnotes omitted).

30. Christian v. Commonwealth, 64 Va. (23 Gratt.) 954, 955, 959 (1873). The Virginia Court subsequently upheld the death penalty for the attempted rape of a white "simple, good, unsophisticated country girl" by a black man. Hart v. Commonwealth,

131 Va. 726, 729, 109 S.E. 582 (1921). But even virginity could have its costs, at least in cases involving simple white country boys as defendants; the story of Brown v. State, 127 Wis. 193, 106 N.W. 536 (1906), discussed earlier, is, after all, the story of Little Red Ridinghood on her way to her grandmother's house when attacked in the fields by the accused. In her case, it appears, virginity was seen not as a factor earning her the court's protection but one which would motivate her to lie about her sexual indiscretion. According to the court, when she found that she was bleeding, she realized that she would have to lie: "[The] prosecutrix turned from her way to friends and succor to arrange her underclothing and there discovered a condition making silence impossible. . . . She could not conceal from her family what had taken place." *Id.* at 201, 106 N.W. at 539.

31. See H. Field & L. Bienen, Jurors and Rape (1980), at 207-458 (state-by-state listing of rape provisions); Bienen, Rape III—National Developments in Rape Reform Legislation, 6 Women's Rts. L. Rep. 170, 171 (1980).

32. H. L. A. Hart, *supra* note 8, at 6.

MICHAEL M. v. SUPERIOR COURT

450 U.S. 464 (1981)

Justice REHNQUIST announced the judgment of the Court and delivered an opinion, in which THE CHIEF JUSTICE, Justice STEWART, and Justice POWELL joined.

The question presented in this case is whether California's "statutory rape" law, §261.5 of the Cal. Penal Code Ann. (West Supp. 1981), violates the Equal Protection Clause of the Fourteenth Amendment. Section 261.5 defines unlawful sexual intercourse as "an act of sexual intercourse accomplished with a female not the wife of the perpetrator, where the female is under the age of 18 years." The statute thus makes men alone criminally liable for the act of sexual intercourse.

In July 1978, a complaint was filed in the Municipal Court of Sonoma County, Cal., alleging that petitioner, then a 17½-year-old male, had had unlawful sexual intercourse with a female under the age of 18, in violation of §261.5. The evidence, adduced at a preliminary hearing showed that at approximately midnight on June 3, 1978, petitioner and two friends approached Sharon, a 16½-year-old female, and her sister as they waited at a bus stop. Petitioner and Sharon, who had already been drinking, moved away from the others and began to kiss. After being struck in the face for rebuffing petitioner's initial advances, Sharon submitted to sexual intercourse with petitioner. Prior to trial, petitioner sought to set aside the information on both state and federal constitutional grounds, asserting that §261.5 unlawfully discriminated on the basis of gender. The trial court and the California Court of Appeal denied petitioner's request for relief and petitioner sought review in the Supreme Court of California.

The Supreme Court held that "section 261.5 discriminates on the basis of sex because only females may be victims, and only males may violate the section." 25 Cal.3d 608, 611, 159 Cal.Rptr. 340, 342, 601 P.2d 572, 574. The court then subjected the classification to "strict scrutiny," stating that it must be justified by a compelling state interest. It found that the classification was "supported not by mere social convention but by the immutable physiological fact that it is the female exclusively who can become pregnant." Ibid. Canvassing "the tragic human costs of illegitimate teenage pregnancies," including the large number of teenage abortions, the increased medical risk associated with teenage pregnancies, and the social consequences of teenage childbearing, the court concluded that the State has a compelling interest in preventing such pregnancies. Because males alone can "physiologically cause the result which the law properly seeks to avoid," the court further held that the gender classification was readily justified as a means of identifying offender and victim. . . .

. . . Unlike the California Supreme Court, we have not held that gender-based classifications are "inherently suspect" and thus we do not apply so-called "strict scrutiny" to those classifications. Our cases have held, however, that the traditional minimum rationality test takes on a somewhat "sharper focus" when gender-based classifications are challenged. In Reed v. Reed, 404 U.S. 71 (1971), for example, the Court stated that a gender-based classification will be upheld if it bears a "fair and substantial relationship" to legitimate state ends, while in Craig v. Boren, 429 U.S. 190, 197 (1976), the Court restated the test to require the classification to bear a "substantial relationship" to "important governmental objectives."

Underlying these decisions is the principle that a legislature may not "make overbroad generalizations based on sex which are entirely unrelated to any differences between men and women or which demean the ability or social status of the affected class." Parham v. Hughes, 441 U.S. 347, 354 (1979). But because the Equal Protection Clause does not "demand that a statute necessarily apply equally to all persons" or require "'things which are different in fact . . . to be treated in law as though they were the same,'" Rinaldi v. Yeager, 384 U.S. 305, 309 (1966), quoting Tigner v. Texas, 310 U.S. 1497, 1499 (1966), this Court has consistently upheld statutes where the gender classification is not invidious, but rather realistically reflects the fact that the sexes are not similarly situated in certain circumstances. As the Court has stated, a legislature may "provide for the special problems of women." Weinberger v. Wiesenfeld, 420 U.S. 636, 653 (1975).

Applying those principles to this case, the fact that the California Legislature criminalized the act of illicit sexual intercourse with a minor female is a sure indication of its intent or purpose to discourage that conduct. Precisely why the legislature desired that result is of course somewhat less clear. . . .

The justification for the statute offered by the State, and accepted by the Supreme Court of California, is that the legislature sought to prevent illegitimate teenage pregnancies. That finding, of course, is entitled to great deference. . . .

We are satisfied not only that the prevention of illegitimate pregnancy is at least one of the "purposes" of the statute, but also that the State has a strong interest in preventing such pregnancy. At the risk of stating the obvious, teenage pregnancies, which have increased dramatically over the last two decades, have significant social, medical, and economic consequences for both the mother and her child, and the State. Of particular concern to the State is that approximately half of all teenage pregnancies end in abortion. And of those children who are born, their illegitimacy makes them likely candidates to become wards of the State.

We need not be medical doctors to discern that young men and young women are not similarly situated with respect to the problems and the risks of sexual intercourse.

Only women may become pregnant, and they suffer disproportionately the profound physical, emotional and psychological consequences of sexual activity. The statute at issue here protects women from sexual intercourse at an age when those consequences are particularly severe.

The question thus boils down to whether a State may attack the problem of sexual intercourse and teenage pregnancy directly by prohibiting a male from having sexual intercourse with a minor female. We hold that such a statute is sufficiently related to the State's objectives to pass constitutional muster.

Because virtually all of the significant harmful and inescapably identifiable consequences of teenage pregnancy fall on the young female, a legislature acts well within its authority when it elects to punish only the participant who, by nature, suffers few of the consequences of his conduct. It is hardly unreasonable for a legislature acting to protect minor females to exclude them from punishment. Moreover, the risk of pregnancy itself constitutes a substantial deterrence to young females. No similar natural sanctions deter males. A criminal sanction imposed solely on males thus serves to roughly "equalize" the deterrents on the sexes.

We are unable to accept petitioner's contention that the statute is impermissibly underinclusive and must, in order to pass judicial scrutiny, be broadened so as to hold the female as criminally liable as the male. It is argued that this statute is not necessary to deter teenage pregnancy because a gender-neutral statute, where both male and female would be subject to prosecution, would serve that goal equally well. The relevant inquiry, however, is not whether the statute is drawn as precisely as it might have been, but whether the line chosen by the California Legislature is within constitutional limitations.

In any event, we cannot say that a gender-neutral statute would be as effective as the statute California has chosen to enact. The State persuasively contends that a gender-neutral statute would frustrate its interest in effective enforcement. Its view is that a female is surely less likely to report violations of the statute if she herself would be subject to criminal prosecution. In an area already fraught with prosecutorial difficulties, we decline to hold that the Equal Protection Clause requires a legislature to enact a statute so broad that it may well be incapable of enforcement. . . .

There remains only petitioner's contention that the statute is unconstitutional as it is applied to him because he, like Sharon, was under 18 at the time of sexual intercourse. Petitioner argues that the statute is flawed because it presumes that as between two persons under 18, the male is the culpable aggressor. We find petitioner's contentions unpersuasive. Contrary to his assertions, the statute does not rest on the assumption that males are generally the aggressors. It is instead an attempt by a legislature to prevent illegitimate teenage pregnancy by providing an additional deterrent for men. The age of the man is irrelevant since young men are as capable as older men of inflicting the harm sought to be prevented. . . .

Accordingly, the judgment of the California Supreme Court is affirmed.

Justice BRENNAN, with whom Justices WHITE and MARSHALL join, dissenting.

It is disturbing to find the Court so splintered on a case that presents such a straightforward issue: Whether the admittedly gender-based classification in Cal. Penal Code Ann. §261.5 bears a sufficient relationship to the State's asserted goal of preventing teenage pregnancies to survive the "mid-level" constitutional scrutiny mandated by Craig v. Boren. . . . I am convinced that there is only one proper resolution of this issue: the classification must be declared unconstitutional. I fear that the plurality opinion and Justices Stewart and Blackmun reach the opposite result by placing too much emphasis on the desirability of achieving the State's asserted statutory goal—prevention of teenage pregnancy—and not enough emphasis on the fundamental question of whether the sex-based discrimination in the California statute is *substantially* related to the achievement of that goal. . . .

The plurality assumes that a gender-neutral statute would be less effective than §261.5 in deterring sexual activity because a gender-neutral statute would create significant enforcement problems. The plurality thus accepts the State's assertion that

> a female is surely less likely to report violations of the statute if she herself would be subject to criminal prosecution. In an area already fraught with prosecutorial difficulties, we decline to hold that the Equal Protection Clause requires a legislature to enact a statute so broad that it may well be incapable of enforcement.

However, a State's bare assertion that its gender-based statutory classification substantially furthers an important governmental interest is not enough to meet its burden of proof under Craig v. Boren. Rather, the State must produce evidence that will persuade the court that its assertion is true.

The State has not produced such evidence in this case. Moreover, there are at least two serious flaws in the State's assertion that law enforcement problems created by a gender-neutral statutory rape law would make such a statute less effective than a gender-based statute in deterring sexual activity.

First, the experience of other jurisdictions, and California itself, belies the plurality's conclusion that a gender-neutral statutory rape law "may well be incapable of enforcement." There are now at least 37 States that have enacted gender-neutral statutory rape laws. Although most of these laws protect young persons (of either sex) from the sexual exploitation of older individuals, the laws of Arizona, Florida, and Illinois permit prosecution of both minor females and minor males for engaging in mutual sexual conduct. California has introduced no evidence that those States have been handicapped by the enforcement problems the plurality finds so persuasive. . . .

In addition, the California Legislature in recent years has revised other sections of the Penal Code to make them gender-neutral. . . . Again, the State has introduced no evidence to explain why a gender-neutral statutory rape law would be any more difficult to enforce than those statutes.

The second flaw in the State's assertion is that even assuming that a gender-neutral statute would be more difficult to enforce, the State has still not shown that those enforcement problems would make such a statute less effective than a gender-based statute in deterring minor females from engaging in sexual intercourse. Common sense, however, suggests that a gender-neutral statutory rape law is potentially a *greater* deterrent of sexual activity than a gender-based law, for the simple reason that a gender-neutral law subjects both men and women to criminal sanctions and thus arguably has a deterrent effect on twice as many potential violators. Even if fewer persons were prosecuted under the gender-neutral law, as the State suggests, it would still be true that twice as many persons would be *subject* to arrest. The State's failure to prove that a gender-neutral law would be a less effective deterrent than a gender-based law, like the State's failure to prove that a gender-neutral law would be difficult to enforce, should have led this Court to invalidate §261.5.

Until very recently, no California court or commentator had suggested that the purpose of California's statutory rape law was to protect young women from the risk of pregnancy. Indeed, the historical development of §261.5 demonstrates that the law was initially enacted on the premise that young women, in contrast to young men, were to be deemed legally incapable of consenting to an act of sexual intercourse. Because their chastity was considered particularly precious, those young women were felt to be uniquely in need of the State's protection. In contrast, young men were assumed to be capable of making such decisions for themselves; the law therefore did not offer them any special protection.

It is perhaps because the gender classification in California's statutory rape law was initially designed to further these outmoded sexual stereotypes, rather than to reduce the incidence of teenage pregnancies, that the State has been unable to demonstrate a substantial relationship between the classification and its newly asserted goal. But whatever the reason, the State has not shown that Cal.Penal Code §261.5 is any more effective than a gender-neutral law would be in deterring minor females from engaging in sexual intercourse. It has therefore not met its burden of proving that the statutory classification is substantially related to the achievement of its asserted goal.

I would hold that §261.5 violates the Equal Protection Clause of the Fourteenth Amendment. . . .

Statutory Rape: A Feminist Critique of Rights Analysis

FRANCES OLSEN

. . . STATUTORY RAPE laws provide a concrete example of the advantages and disadvantages of rights analysis. These laws pose a classic political dilemma for feminists. On one hand, they protect females; like laws against rape, incest, child molestation, and child marriage, statutory rape laws are a statement of social disapproval of certain forms of exploitation. To some extent they reduce abuse and victimization. On the other hand, statutory rape laws restrict the sexual activity of young women and reinforce the double standard of sexual morality.[1] The laws both protect and undermine women's rights, and rights arguments can be used to support, attack, or urge changes in the laws.

Although feminists initially supported such laws, in recent years they have been among the most trenchant critics of gender-based statutory rape laws. I examine their two major objections to the laws: that they restrict women and that they reinforce sexist stereotypes.[2] To illustrate the indeterminacy of rights analysis, I suggest a variety of rights-oriented arguments that could be made in favor of very different revisions of gender-based statutory rape laws. Although some of the revisions are more appealing than others, rights analysis does not explain why this is so. The problem is not that one is unable to choose among equally persuasive arguments, but that the basis for the choices one makes and urges upon others has little or nothing to do with the abstract categories employed in rights analysis.

A. Historical Background

The complexity of the feminist position is illustrated by a bill introduced into the English Parliament in 1885 to raise the age of consent from thirteen to sixteen. Radical separatist feminists spearheaded the bill and intended it to be an attack on male sexual aggression and on the double standard of sexual morality.[3] Their opponents in the House of Lords openly supported the double standard; they warned one another that the proposed legislation posed a threat to themselves and their sons.[4] These upper

Published originally in 63 *Texas Law Review* 387 (1984). Copyright 1984 by the Texas Law Review Association. Reprinted by permission.

class men wanted young women of the lower classes to remain sexually available to them. Two additional factors complicated these struggles. First, some of the feminists' support came from repressive moralists with whom the feminists were in general disagreement.[5] Second, some of the people who opposed the bill did so to protect the right of young females to make their own sexual choices.[6] The feminists understood, however, that this sexual freedom in practice would be freedom primarily for men.

Feminists in the United States launched similar attacks against aggressive male sexuality in the nineteenth century. Judith Walkowitz has argued that in America, even more than in Britain, conservative antivice elements dominated the reform movement and coopted the feminists' efforts.[7] Although American feminists sometimes were able to "structure public discourse on sex and arouse popular female anger at male sexual license,"[8] they were not able to muster the cultural and political power necessary to reshape the standards of acceptable sexual conduct.[9]

Statutory rape laws came to America with the common law of England.[10] The age of consent, originally ten, was gradually raised by individual states, sometimes to eighteen or even twenty-one. Several states tailored their laws to provide greater penalties for adult men who had intercourse with prepubescent females and lesser penalties when the females were older or the males younger.[11]

The nineteenth century concern with oppressive male initiative was replaced in the mid-twentieth century by concern with state repression of sexuality. Twentieth century feminists understood that when the dominant ideology advocated social control of sexuality, in practice it meant social control of women, not of men. Women's rights advocates criticized gender-based statutory rape laws for reinforcing sexist stereotypes and restricting the sexual autonomy of young women. Partly in response to these criticisms and partly to avoid constitutional challenge, most states revised their statutory rape laws to make them gender-neutral, and many states decriminalized sex among teenagers. These gender-neutral age-of-consent laws protect both boys and girls from sexual exploitation by any person who is significantly older than the victim or who exercises various kinds of official authority over the youngster. Although these developments may reduce the practical importance of gender-based laws, they do not solve the theoretical and constitutional problems that such laws present.

B. A Feminist Critique of Gender-Based Statutory Rape Laws

California's law against "unlawful sexual intercourse" is typical of the gender-based statutory rape laws that remain on the books in a minority of states. The California statute prohibits any "act of sexual intercourse accomplished with a female not the wife of the perpetrator, where the female is under the age of 18 years."[12]

Feminists charge that statutes such as this one are harmful to women on both a practical and an ideological level. First, as an effort to control the sexual activities of young women, statutory rape laws are an unwarranted governmental intrusion into their lives and an oppressive restriction upon their freedom of action. An unmarried woman under eighteen cannot legally have intercourse in California. Whether the prohibition is enforced by prosecuting her partner or by prosecuting her as an aider and abettor, the statute interferes with the sexual freedom of the underage female. In the language of rights analysis, statutory rape laws violate the female's right to privacy and her right to be as free sexually as her male counterpart.

Feminists' second common objection to statutory rape laws is ideological.[13] Gender-based statutory rape laws reinforce the sexual stereotype of men as aggressors and women as passive victims. The laws perpetuate the double standard of sexual morality. For males, sex is an accomplishment; they gain something through intercourse. For women, sex entails giving something up. Further, for the myth of male sexual accomplishment to exist, some females must give in. The double standard divides females into two classes—virgins and whores, "good girls" whose chastity should be protected and "bad girls" who may be exploited with impunity. Even if young women need more protection from sexual coercion and exploitation than the laws against forcible rape and incest provide, many feminists nevertheless oppose gender-based laws. They argue that males and females should be protected equally and that gender-based laws stigmatize women as weaker than men. In terms of rights theory, gender-based statutory rape laws violate the right of all women to be treated equally to men.

Although these two objections to statutory rape laws are analytically distinct, they nonetheless are related. Ideology affects people's lives, and daily life can limit and reshape ideology. The restrictive aspects of statutory rape laws are practically objectionable because they exalt female chastity and treat women as lacking in sexual autonomy. This view of women both provides a reason (although a false and pernicious one) for state restrictions upon young women's sexual freedom and reinforces damaging stereotypes. At the same time, the laws imply that young men do not need the protection that they afford. This implication reinforces the ideology that sex is okay for young men; it also means that some women will have to be available to have sex with them.

The state restricts the young woman's sexual behavior for reasons related to sexist notions of what makes female valuable. The state does not merely restrict the young woman's freedom: it also treats her sexuality as a thing that has a value of its own and must be guarded. By refusing to grant women autonomy and by protecting them in ways that men are not protected, the state treats women's bodies—and therefore women themselves—as objects. Men are treated differently. Their bodies are regarded as a part of them, subject to their free control.

C. Changing Statutory Rape Laws to Protect Women's Rights

There are several ways statutory rape laws could be altered to overcome these grounds for objection. There are at least two ways the law could be altered to free young women from state-enforced sexual constraint and four ways the laws could be changed to help overcome debilitating stereotypes.

1. Freeing Women from Sexual Constraints

(A) DISEMPOWERING THE STATE

The simplest way to prevent statutory rape laws from restricting women's sexual freedom and treating women as objects would be to repeal the laws or declare them unconstitutional.[14] This approach would support the rights of young women by freeing them from one form of state domination and giving them the same status as adult women.

Unfortunately, invalidating statutory rape laws altogether and putting young women in the same position as adult women might undermine the right of young women to be free of unwanted sexual contact. Adult women occupy a position of pervasive and economic social subordination to men. Adult women are seduced, pressured, coerced, and even forced into unwanted sexual relations, for which they have no legal recourse.[15] Underage females might discover that although the abolition of statutory rape laws would protect their rights against the state, it would remove some of their already-minimal protection against individual men. Young women and their sexuality would still be treated as objects, but instead of being controlled by state legislation, sex would be "taken" from them by individual men, one at a time.[16] Nice as it is to be freed from state oppression, domination by private individuals can be equally oppressive.[17] Despite their negative aspects, statutory rape laws may provide some protection for females. Recognizing this, even opponents of such laws support some form of age-of-consent statute—at least to protect six-year-olds, if not twelve-year-olds.

Statutory rape laws can also protect females against forms of oppression that other laws do not reach. For example, statutory rape laws may prohibit certain instances of sexual assault that should be considered illegal, but cannot be prosecuted as forcible rape.[18] Similarly, abuses of authority that do not fit the statutory definition of incest may be punishable under statutory rape laws.

(B) EMPOWERING WOMEN

Instead of restricting women's freedom, it might be possible to protect women by empowering them against male coercion.[19] This alternative would free women from state domination without removing all protection against private domination. For example, statutory rape laws could be amended or interpreted to give the underage woman control over the prosecution decision. Such a law could either permit charges to be brought only upon the woman's complaint[20] or require that they be dropped upon her request.[21] Either version would increase the protective aspects of statutory rape laws and reduce the negative, repressive aspects.[22] A young woman would be free to engage in sex or accept the protection of statutory rape laws.[23] Her characterization of a sexual encounter as voluntary intercourse or as rape would be determinative.[24] Although giving the woman control over prosecution would not guarantee that her decision would be her choice and not coerced, it might at least enable her to play the various pressures against one another.[25]

Despite its merits, many feminists would oppose this revision of statutory rape laws because it would treat women differently from men and therefore could stigmatize all women by implying that underage women are vulnerable and in need of protection. But the ideological significance attached to the label "vulnerable" depends in good measure upon the concrete context in which the label is attached and the practical effect of the labeling. Women rightly object when their alleged vulnerability is used as an excuse to deny them certain opportunities or to foreclose choices that should be available to them.[26] Statutory rape laws that gave a young woman power over the prosecution decision, however, would treat her vulnerability as a reason to empower her against coercion rather than to take power away from her.

Nevertheless, it is certainly possible that women would be stigmatized as well as empowered. Indeed, it may be impossible to predict whether the ideological damage to women from being treated as vulnerable would in the long run outweigh the practical and ideological advantages of empowerment.[27]

2. *Overcoming Debilitating Stereotypes*

The second feminist objection to statutory rape laws is that they stigmatize women and reinforce sexist stereotypes. There are at least four possible solutions to this problem.

(A) ABOLITION

One could meet the objection that statutory rape laws perpetuate debilitating sexual stereotypes by abolishing the laws. Although this approach might increase the practical basis for the woman-as-powerless-victim stereotype by allowing more young women to be victimized by male aggression, it would at least avoid ideological reinforcement of the stereotype.

(B) EFFECTIVE ENFORCEMENT

If it were possible to enforce or revise statutory rape laws so that they actually prevented men from victimizing women, the stereotypes might become so false that they would lose their power. This approach imposes significant risks, however. Legal reform may be insufficient to prevent victimization; laws alone seldom change behavior. Moreover, in our present society, it may be impossible to empower women without stigmatizing them.[28]

In a sense, this second approach is the converse of the first. The first proposal would undermine the stereotype of men as aggressors and women as victims but allow the reality; the second would support the stereotype but undermine the reality.

(C) SIMPLE EXTENSION

A third approach—criminalizing sexual intercourse when either party is underage—would seem neither to stigmatize women nor to reinforce sexist stereotypes. This approach benefits underage males by protecting them from being pressured into premature sex[29] and harms them by curtailing their freedom.[30]

Although this change seems to address the issue of stereotyping, it obscures the issue of social power. Extending the age-of-consent laws to males may effect merely a cosmetic change, without altering images or practices under the law. Moreover, it leaves untouched the repressive aspects of statutory rape laws. In our present society, these repressive aspects hurt females more than males. Extension of the legal rule to males might not bring extension of these repressive aspects. This solution therefore is actually less neutral than it initially appears.

(D) EXTENSION WITH AGE GAP

As a variation of the third approach, one could decriminalize most sex between teenagers but extend protection to minors of both sexes against exploitation by an older person. For example, statutory rape laws might provide criminal penalties for anyone who engaged in sexual intercourse with a minor four or more years younger than the person charged.[31] Such a law would restrict freedom less than the previous proposal because it would allow teenagers to engage in sexual intercourse with partners near their own age.[32] In addition, the law would provide for criminal prosecution in many of the worst kinds of exploitative situations, but would avoid overt sexual stereotyping. Unfortunately, such a law would not address the problem of male sexual aggression that characterizes society at large. Underage males are likely to relate to underage females in illegitimate ways, just as their older counterparts relate to adult women in illegitimate ways.

D. Conclusion

A commitment to establish and protect rights for women provides us with little guidance in deciding whether to support any particular statutory rape law or to oppose all statutory rape laws. Even if we artificially simplify our task by focusing only upon the rights of women, we cannot determine how to protect these rights. Rights analysis does not help us as an analytic tool because it is indeterminate. Every effort to protect young women against private oppression by individual men risks subjecting women to state oppression, and every effort to protect them against state oppression undermines their power to resist individual oppression.

Further, any acknowledgment of the actual difference between the present situation of males and females stigmatizes females and perpetuates discrimination. But if we ignore power differences and pretend that women and men are similarly situated, we perpetuate discrimination by disempowering ourselves from instituting effective change. The strategy of protecting rights runs afoul of the conflict between rights as freedom of action and rights as security; the strategy of promoting equality runs afoul of the conflict between formal equality of opportunity and substantive equality of outcome.

Despite the circularity of arguments about rights and equality, however, effective reforms do take place and do change people's lives. Some of the proposed changes in statutory rape laws are better than others. It is even possible that most feminists would agree on the best change. But this agreement would not be reached by discovering the "real" meaning of women's rights or by logically deducing the "true implications" of gender equality. Rather, it would rest upon sociological calculations and political and moral commitments. An abstract commitment to women's rights does not help us decide concrete cases. . . .

[For a more detailed discussion of rights analysis in terms of legal theory, see Olsen, Statutory Rape: A Feminist Critique of Rights Analysis, in D. Weisberg ed., Feminist Legal Theory: Foundations 485 (Temple Univ. Press, 1993).]

Notes

1. The double standard of sexual morality has two important aspects. First, nonmarital sex or sexual activity separated from emotional commitment, is considered desirable for men but devaluing for women. The second aspect is a corollary of the first: some women have to be "immoral" in order to serve as sexual partners for males outside of marriage. Thus, women are categorized as moral or immoral, good girls or bad girls, virgins or whores, wife material or playmate material.

2. It is important to consider a third ground upon which the statutes might be attacked. It can be argued that the statutes legitimate the pervasive reality of male sexual aggression by attempting to police a border between "good" shared sex and "bad" coercive sex. In fact, there is no clear distinction; the exploitative content of so much of sexuality in our society pervades all of its forms. Outlawing certain forms of male coercion to protect particularly vulnerable females can be seen cynically as necessary to prevent us all from becoming aware of the relationship of domination and submission that is built into our basic definitions of heterosexuality. As Catharine MacKinnon puts it: "[I]s ordinary sexuality, under conditions of gender inequality, to be presumed healthy? What if inequality is built into the social conceptions of male and female sexuality, of masculinity and femininity, of sexiness and heterosexual attractiveness? [M]ale sexual desire itself may be aroused by female vulnerability. [S]exual intercourse normally occurs between economic (as well as physical) unequals." C. MacKinnon, Sexual Harassment of Working Women 219 (1979). Sexual intercourse also normally occurs between older men with some social power and younger, less powerful women. MacKinnon concludes: "In this context, the apparent legal requirement that violations of women's sexuality appear out of the ordinary before they will be punished helps prevent women from defining the ordinary conditions of their own consent." *Id.* By isolating those cases in which it is obvious that a young woman had no meaningful choice and that her sexuality was expropriated, statutory rape laws may pacify women by encouraging them to believe that their own choices are voluntary and that they are not exploited in their sexual encounters.

3. See J. Weeks, Sex, Politics and Society 88–89 (1981); Gorham, The "Maiden Tribute of Modern Babylon" Re-examined: Child Prostitution and the Idea of Childhood in Late-Victorian England, 21 Victorian Stud. 353, 357 (1978); Walkowitz, The Politics of Prostitution, in C. Stimson & E. Person eds., Women: Sex and Sexuality 145, 146–148 (1980).

4. Feminists accused these men of wanting to set aside "a large section of female society . . . to administer to the irregularities" of the men. J. Weeks, *supra* note 3, at 88–89; see Gorham *supra* note 3, at 366.

5. See Walkowitz, *supra* note 3, at 148. The bill that raised the age of consent also extended the summary jurisdiction of the police over poor women and children and outlawed male homosexuality. See *id.* at 150. Homosexuality was thought to be related to men's exploitation of women in that both resulted from an "undifferentiated male lust." *Id.* at 151 (quoting J. Weeks, Coming Out: Homosexual Politics in Britain From the 19th Century to the Present 18 (1977)).

6. See J. Weeks, *supra* note 3, at 89. It should be emphasized that the feminists who supported strengthening the statutory rape law were not repressive moralists. Indeed, their campaign began as a defense of prostitutes against repressive state registration laws. See *id.* at 85–86. . . .

7. See Walkowitz, *supra* note 3, at 153.

8. *Id.* at 157.

9. See *id.* Under these circumstances, the women's anger was "easily diverted into repressive campaigns against male vice and sexual variation, controlled by men and corporate interests whose goals were antithetical to the values and ideals of feminism." *Id.*

10. See Comment, The Constitutionality of Statutory Rape Laws, 27 UCLA L. Rev. 757, 762 (1980). . . .

11. *Id.* at 765–766.

12. Cal. Penal Code §261.5 (West Supp. 1981).

13. By "ideological" I simply mean "having an effect on people's ideas." For an elaborate description of this and other uses of "ideology," see R. Geuss, The Idea of a Critical Theory 4–25 (1981).

14. It could be argued that the statutory rape laws are so seldom enforced, see G. Fletcher, Rethinking Criminal Law §9.3 at 729 (1978), that they are practically irrelevant. Men, who control our legal system, are often not interested in enforcing statutory rape laws. I believe that their existence does have a practical effect, however, even if they are seldom enforced, because the threat of enforcement may deter some men from particularly exploitative behavior. . . . Moreover, statutory rape laws affect ideology, and ideology affects behavior.

15. On the ineffectiveness of current rape laws, see Note, Shifting the Communication Burden: A Meaningful Consent Standard in Rape, 6 Harv. Women's L.J. 143, 146–149 (1983). Civil remedies, such as tort actions for assault and battery, have not yet proved effective, in part because many rapists are judgment proof and their insurance does not cover claims of this sort.

16. Laws and judicial decisions that establish the home and sexuality as spheres of privacy can be seen as protecting the right of individual men to oppress individual women. See MacKinnon, Feminism, Marxism, Method, and the State: Toward Feminist Jurisprudence, in D. Weisberg ed., Feminist Legal Theory: Foundations 427, 434–435 (Temple Univ. Press, 1993). Catharine MacKinnon has noted the similarities between the Marxist assertion that workers' labor is expropriated from them and the feminist assertion that women's sexuality is expropriated from them. See *id.* at 437. For an excellent development of the notion that a woman does not own or control her sexuality, but merely acts as its trustee, see L. Clark & D. Lewis, Rape: The Price of Coercive Sexuality (1977).

17. This is not to say that the two forms of oppression are identical. Some argue that state oppression is worse than "private" oppression, some argue that "private" oppression is worse, and others that it depends upon the particular circumstances of the oppression. House arrest probably feels about the same to someone whether "the state" tells its sheriffs to keep her in her house or whether it allows her husband to do the same.

18. See Comment, *supra* note 10, at 811. The testimony at the preliminary hearing in Michael M. v. Superior Court, 450 U.S. 464 (1981), provides one example. The male hit the female in the face two or three times as she resisted his efforts at sexual intercourse. Presumably this could be prosecuted as forcible rape because before intercourse took place the female gave what is considered legal consent. According to Sharon, "I just said to myself, 'Forget it' and I let him do what he wanted to do. . . ." *Id.* at 485n* (Blackmun, J., concurring). To the State's argument that prosecutors would "commonly invoke [the statutory rape] statute only in cases that actually involve a forcible rape," *id.* at 501 (Stevens, J., dissenting), Justice Stevens responded that this would result in "convicting a [rape] defendant on evidence that is constitutionally insufficient." *Id.* . . .

19. The question whether the coercive apparatus of the state can be used effectively on behalf of women or whether attempts to do so will always divert, coopt, or patronize women has been treated in literature on rape, wife beating, and sexual harassment. See MacKinnon, Introduction, 10 Cap. U. L. Rev. i, viii (Spring 1981); M. Freeman, Violence Against Women: Does the Legal System Provide Solutions or Itself Constitute the Problem? 3 Can. J. Fam. L. 377 (1980); see also S. Schechter, Women and Male Violence 125, 185–202, 241–255 (1982) (arguing that grass-roots movements may be coopted and subverted by government enforcement efforts).

20. For this scheme to be effective, the law would have to be amended so that underage women could not be charged with aiding and abetting statutory rape by consenting to or initiating sexual intercourse. Between 1975 and 1979 approximately 14% of the juveniles arrested for violating California's statutory rape laws were females. See Michael M. v. Superior Court, 450 U.S. 464, 477 n.5 (1981) (Stewart, J., concurring). Justice Stewart does not indicate how frequently charges against the female may have been brought to coerce her cooperation in a prosecution initiated against her wishes by her parents or another third party.

21. Another, slightly different approach would allow the state to press charges despite the wishes of the female, but would allow as a defense her testimony that the defendant did not exploit her. Alternatively, the law could allow a female to institute criminal charges only if she asserted that the defendant coerced or exploited her. Under any of these formulations a female still might be coerced (by the defendant or his friends) to drop charges or (by her parents) to initiate charges, but the provisions would tend to empower her, increasing her control over her own sexuality.

A girl too young to understand sex presumably would be too young to ask to have charges dropped against her molester, while a girl old enough to seek sexual contact would be old enough to protect her voluntary partner. The only probable exceptions to this approach would involve cases of serious parental abuse or neglect and should be dealt with under those rubrics.

Any such laws could, however, be abused. For example, forcible rape law has been used to repress black men, and such racist abuse could also occur with statutory rape laws. See Wriggens, Rape, Racism, and the Law, herein, at 495.

22. To a male wishing to have sexual intercourse with an underage woman, however, this law may seem quite oppressive. He might argue that it delegates the power of prosecutorial discretion to the underage woman in violation of the due process clause of the fourteenth amendment and that it violates his right to equal protection. The first argument should fail, because allowing victims to drop prosecution is common and is not considered a delegation of state authority, but treatment of the second is not clear.

23. Indeed, if such a law could actually empower women, perhaps we should remove the age limit and give all women this power. I recognize that this is a startling proposal: it would give a woman considerable power over any man with whom she has had intercourse, and women could misuse this power. But whatever the proposal lacks in practical value, I believe it makes up for as a heuristic device. It is often assumed that a man increases his power over a woman when he has intercourse with her. This proposal would certainly reverse this conventional power-shift, and it would generally increase the power of women in their sexual relations with men. Intercourse would empower the woman and render the man vulnerable. . . .

24. Under present laws of forcible rape, the man's characterization of the encounter as consensual or forced is too often determinative. A man's actual belief that the woman consented to intercourse may be a defense, as long as his belief was not grossly unreasonable. See Note, *supra* note 15, at 144–145.

25. Although it might be unpleasant for a teenager to be pressured by her family to prosecute a man with whom she had had sex and pressured by the male's friends not to do so, she would at least have some room to decide whether she felt she was coerced or was a voluntary participant. Females lack even this power under current statutory rape laws. As "victims" they can choose only whether to cooperate in prosecution and the degree of cooperation to extend. Even this choice can be coerced by threats of prosecution for aiding and abetting. Ironically, victims of forcible rape probably have more power to prevent prosecution than do victims of statutory rape.

26. Statutory rape laws traditionally have been interpreted to deny women the legal right to consent to sexual intercourse on the ground that their vulnerability warrants special protection. Similarly, in Muller v. Oregon, 208 U.S. 412 (1908), the Supreme Court upheld gender-based protective labor legislation on the basis of women's presumed vulnerability. It is important to distinguish between the reactionary claim that protective labor legislation demeans all workers by treating them as inferior and the progressive feminist criticism of *Muller*. Limiting protective legislation to women undermined the effectiveness of the protection, because employers could replace women with men instead of improving conditions for women. See Olsen, The Family and The Market: A Study of Ideology and Legal Reform, 7 Harv. L. Rev. 1497, 1555–1557 (1983). The overall effect of the legislation was to make it more difficult for women to compete against men. The legislation thus denied women the opportunity to compete effectively in the marketplace and to relate to work in the same way men did. Protective labor legislation itself is not offensive, however, and, when applied equally to women and men, can serve progressive goals.

27. The ideological damage would also include reinforcement of the damaging sexist stereotype of the woman who tempts a man into sexual contact and then cries rape.

28. It may be that the difference between stigma and power is one of perspective. What women see as empowerment, men may see as stigmatizing to women.

29. There is some debate whether there is such a thing as "premature sex" or whether the term simply reflects a moralistic bias. The term seems to me to have meaning.

30. This purports to be a more "neutral" approach than it really is. First, the focus on sexual intercourse, or penetration, is a gender-specific, masculine focus. See MacKinnon, Feminism, Marxism, and the State: Toward Feminist Jurisprudence, 8 Signs 635, 647 (1983); Moulton, Sex and Reference, in R. Baker & F. Elliston eds., Philosophy and Sex 34, 34–44 (1975). Further, state control of female sexuality has a different history and a different social meaning than state control of male sexuality. Some peo-

ple assert that male sexuality has never been effectively controlled, much less expropriated, while others claim that the sexuality of working class black men has been expropriated. See generally Note, *supra* note 15.

An interesting variation of this proposal would give the underage person of either sex power over the decision to prosecute. Depending on the exact nature of that power, this approach could give the state either significant control over minors' sexual behavior (e.g., if the minor had to prove that her or his decision not to prosecute was not coerced), or very little control (e.g., if the minor was not required to show that her or his decision was not coerced).

31. Such a law would rest on the assumption that the evil to be addressed is the coercion of a younger person by an older person. Thus, the age differential approach may be seen as an effort to criminalize intercourse that is presumed to be exploitative, using the age differential as a proxy for exploitation. . . .

32. But see North American Man/Boy Love Association, The Case for Abolishing the Age of Consent Laws, in D. Tsang ed., The Age Taboo 93, 99–100 (1981) (arguing that laws forbidding men from having sexual relations with young boys violate important rights of the boys).

Rape: On Coercion and Consent

Catharine A. MacKinnon

Negotiations for sex are not carried on like those for the rent of a house. There is often no definite state on which it can be said that the two have agreed to sexual intercourse. They proceed by touching, feeling, fumbling, by signs and words which are not generally in the form of a Roman stipulation.

—Honoré, twentieth-century British legal scholar and philosopher

Rape is an extension of sexism in some ways, and that's an extension of dealing with a woman as an object. . . . Stinky [her rapist] seemed to me as though he were only a step further away, a step away from the guys who sought me on the streets, who insist, my mother could have died, I could be walking down the street and if I don't answer their rap, they got to go get angry and get all hostile and stuff as though I walk down the street as a . . . that my whole being is there to please men in the streets. But Stinky only seemed like someone who had taken it a step further . . . he felt like an extension, he felt so common, he felt so ordinary, he felt so familiar, and it was maybe that what frightened me the most was that how similar to other men he seemed. They don't come from Mars, folks.

—Carolyn Craven, reporter

If you're living with a man, what are you doing running around the streets getting raped?

—Edward Harrington, defense attorney in New Bedford gang rape case

IF SEXUALITY IS CENTRAL to women's definition and forced sex is central to sexuality, rape is indigenous, not exceptional, to women's social condition. In feminist analysis, a rape is not an isolated event or moral transgression or individual interchange gone wrong but an act of terrorism and torture within a systemic context of group subjection, like lynching. The fact that the state calls rape a crime opens an inquiry into the state's treatment of rape as an index to its stance on the status of the sexes.

Under law, rape is a sex crime that is not regarded as a crime when it looks like sex. The law, speaking generally, defines rape as intercourse with force or coercion and without consent.[1] Like sexuality under male supremacy, this definition assumes the sadomasochistic definition of sex: intercourse with force or coercion can be or become consensual. It assumes pornography's positive-outcome-rape scenario: dominance plus submission is force plus consent. This equals sex, not rape. Under male supremacy, this is too often the reality. In a critique of male supremacy, the elements "with force and without consent" appear redundant. Force is present because consent is absent.

Like heterosexuality, male supremacy's paradigm of sex, the crime of rape centers on penetration.[2] The law to protect women's sexuality from forcible violation and expropriation defines that protection in male genital terms. Women do resent forced penetration. But penile invasion of the vagina may be less pivotal to women's sexuality, pleasure or violation, than it is to male sexuality. This definitive element of rape centers upon a male-defined loss. It also centers upon one way men define loss of exclusive access. In this light, rape, as legally defined, appears more a crime against female monogamy (exclusive access by one man) than against women's sexual dignity or intimate integrity. Analysis of rape in terms of concepts of property, often invoked in marxian analysis to criticize this disparity, fail to encompass the realities of rape.[3] Women's sexuality is, socially, a thing to be stolen, sold, bought, bartered, or exchanged by others. But women never own or possess it, and men never treat it, in law or in life, with the solicitude with which they treat property. To be property would be an improvement. The moment women "have" it—"have sex" in the dual gender/sexuality sense—it is lost as theirs. To have it is to have it taken away. This may explain the male incomprehension that, once a woman has had sex, she loses anything when subsequently raped. To them women have nothing to lose. It is true that dignitary harms, because nonmaterial, are ephemeral to the legal mind. But women's loss through rape is not only less tangible; it is seen as unreal. It is difficult to avoid the conclusion that penetration itself is considered a violation from the male point of view, which is both why it is the centerpiece of sex and why it is the centerpiece of sex and why women's sexuality, women's gender definition, is stigmatic. The question for social explanation becomes not why some women tolerate rape but how any women manage to resent it.

Rape cases finding insufficient evidence of force reveal that acceptable sex, in the legal perspective, can entail a lot of force. This is both a result of the way specific facts are perceived and interpreted within the legal system and the way the injury is defined by law. The level of acceptable force is adjudicated starting just above the level set by what is seen as normal male sexual behavior, including the normal level of force, rather than at the victim's, or women's, point of violation.[4] In this context, to seek to define rape as violent not sexual is as understandable as it is futile. Some feminists have reinterpreted rape as an act of violence, not sexuality, the threat of which intimidates all women.[5] Others see rape, including its violence, as an expression of male sexuality, the social imperatives of which define as well as threaten all women.[6] The first, epistemologically in the liberal tradition, comprehends rape as a displacement of power based on physical force onto sexuality, a preexisting natural sphere to which domination is alien. Susan Brownmiller, for example, examines rape in riots, wars, pogroms, and revolutions; rape by police, parents, prison guards; and rape motivated by racism. Rape in normal circumstances, in everyday life, in ordinary relationships, by men as men, is barely mentioned.[7] Women are raped by guns, age, white supremacy, the state—only derivatively by the penis. The view that derives most directly from victims' experiences, rather than from their denial, construes sexuality as a social sphere of male power to which forced sex is paradigmatic. Rape is not less sexual for being violent. To the extent that coercion has become integral to male sexuality, rape may even be sexual to the degree that, and because, it is violent.

The point of defining rape as "violence not sex" has been to claim an ungendered and nonsexual ground for affirming sex (heterosexuality) while rejecting violence (rape). The problem remains what it has always been: telling the difference. The convergence of sexuality with violence, long used at law to deny the reality of women's violation, is recognized by rape survivors with a difference: where the legal system has seen the intercourse in rape, victims see the rape in intercourse. The uncoerced context for sexual expression becomes as elusive as the physical acts come to feel indistinguishable. Instead of asking what is the violation of rape, their experience suggests that the more relevant question is, what is the nonviolation of intercourse? To know what is wrong with rape, know what is right about sex. If this, in turn, proves difficult, the difficulty is as instructive as the difficulty men have in telling the difference when women see one. Perhaps the wrong of rape has proved so difficult to define because the unquestionable starting point has been that rape is defined as distinct from intercourse,[8] while for women it is difficult to distinguish the two under conditions of male dominance.

In the name of the distinction between sex and violence, reform of rape statutes has sought to redefine rape as sexual assault.[9] Usually, assault is not consented to in law; either it cannot be consented to, or consensual assault remains assault.[10] Yet sexual assault consented to is intercourse, no matter how much force was used. The substantive reference point implicit in existing legal standards is the sexually normative level of force. Until this norm is confronted as such, no distinction between violence and sexuality will prohibit more instances of women's experienced violation than does the existing definition. Conviction rates have not increased under the reform statutes.[11] The question remains what is seen as force, hence as violence, in the sexual arena.[12] Most rapes, as women live them, will not be seen to violate women until sex and violence are confronted as mutually definitive rather than as mutually exclusive. It is not only men convicted of rape who believe that the the only thing they did that was different from what men do all the time is get caught.

Consent is supposed to be women's form of control over intercourse, different from but equal to the custom of male initiative. Man proposes, woman disposes. Even the ideal is not mutual. Apart from the disparate consequences of refusal, this model does not envision a situation the woman controls being placed in, or choices she frames. Yet the consequences are attributed to her as if the sexes began at arm's length, on equal terrain, as in the contract fiction. Ambiguous cases of consent in law are archetypically referred to as "half won arguments in parked cars."[13] Why not half lost?

Why isn't half enough? Why is it an argument? Why do men still want "it," feel entitled to "it," when women do not want them? The law of rape presents consent as free exercise of sexual choice under conditions of equality of power without exposing the underlying structure of constraint and disparity. Fundamentally, desirability to men is supposed a woman's form of power because she can both arouse it and deny its fulfillment. To woman is attributed both the cause of man's initiative and the denial of his satisfaction. This rationalizes force. Consent in this model becomes more a metaphysical quality of a woman's being than a choice she makes and communicates. Exercise of women's so-called power presupposes more fundamental social powerlessness.[14]

The law of rape divides women into spheres of consent according to indices of relationship to men. Which category of presumed consent a woman is in depends upon who she is relative to a man who wants her, not what she says or does. These categories tell men whom they can legally fuck, who is open season and who is off limits, not how to listen to women. The paradigm categories are the virginal daughter and other young girls, with whom all sex is proscribed, and the whorelike wives and prostitutes, with whom no sex is proscribed. Daughters may not consent; wives and prostitutes are assumed to, and cannot but.[15] Actual consent or nonconsent, far less actual desire, is comparatively irrelevant. If rape laws existed to enforce women's control over access to their sexuality, as the consent defense implies, no would mean no, marital rape would not be a widespread exception,[16] and it would not be effectively legal to rape a prostitute.

All women are divided into parallel provinces, their actual consent counting to the degree that they diverge from the paradigm case in their category. Virtuous women, like young girls, are unconsenting, virginal, rapable. Unvirtuous women, like wives and prostitutes, are consenting, whores, unrapable. The age line under which girls are presumed disabled from consenting to sex, whatever they say, rationalizes a condition of sexual coercion which women never outgrow. One day they cannot say yes, and the next day they cannot say no. The law takes the most aggravated case for female powerlessness based on gender and age combined and, by formally prohibiting all sex as rape, makes consent irrelevant on the basis of an assumption of powerlessness. This defines those above the age line as powerful, whether they actually have power to consent or not. The vulnerability girls share with boys—age—dissipates with time. The vulnerability girls share with women—gender—does not. As with protective labor laws for women only, dividing and protecting the most vulnerable becomes a device for not protecting everyone who needs it, and also may function to target those singled out for special protection for special abuse. Such protection has not prevented high rates of sexual abuse of children and may contribute to eroticizing young girls as forbidden.

As to adult women, to the extent an accused knows a woman and they have sex, her consent is inferred. The exemption for rape in marriage is consistent with the assumption underlying most adjudications of forcible rape: to the extent the parties relate, it was not really rape, it was personal.[17] As marital exemptions erode, preclusions for cohabitants and voluntary social companions may expand. As a matter of fact, for this purpose one can be acquainted with an accused by friendship or by meeting him for the first time at a bar or a party or by hitchhiking. In this light, the partial erosion of the marital rape exemption looks less like a change in the equation between women's experience of sexual violation and men's experience of intimacy, and more like a legal adjustment to the social fact that acceptable heterosexual sex is increasingly not limited to the legal family. So although the rape law may not now always assume that the woman consented simply because the parties are legally one, indices of closeness, of relationship ranging from nodding acquaintance to living together, still contraindicate rape. In marital rape cases, courts look for even greater atrocities than usual to undermine their assumption that if sex happened, she wanted it.[18]

This approach reflects men's experience that women they know do meaningfully consent to sex with them. *That* cannot be rape; rape must be by someone else, someone unknown. They do not rape women they know. Men and women are unequally socially situated with regard to the experience of rape. Men are a good deal more likely to rape than to be raped. This forms their experience, the material conditions of their epistemological position. Almost half of all women, by contrast, are raped or victims of attempted rape at least once in their lives. Almost 40 percent are victims of sexual abuse in childhood.[19] Women are more likely to be raped than to rape and are most often raped by men whom they know.[20]

Men often say that it is less awful for a woman to be raped by someone she is close to:

> The emotional trauma suffered by a person victimized by an individual with whom sexual intimacy is shared as a normal part of an ongoing marital relationship is not nearly as severe as that suffered by a person who is victimized by one with whom that intimacy is not shared.[21]

Women often feel as or more traumatized from being raped by someone known or trusted, someone with whom at least an illusion of mutuality has been shared, than by some stranger. In whose interest is it to believe that it is not so bad to be raped by someone who has fucked you before as by someone who has not? Disallowing charges of rape in marriage may, depending upon one's view of normalcy, "remove a substantial obstacle to the resumption of normal marital relationships."[22] Note that the obstacle is not the rape but the law against it. Apparently someone besides feminists finds sexual victimization and sexual intimacy not all that contradictory under current conditions. Sometimes it seems as though women and men live in different cultures.

Having defined rape in male sexual terms, the law's problem, which becomes the victim's problem, is distinguishing rape from sex in specific cases. The adjudicated line between rape and intercourse commonly centers on some assessment of the woman's "will." But how should the law or the accused know a woman's will? The answer combines aspects of force with aspects of nonconsent with elements of resistance, still effective in some states.[23] Even when nonconsent is not a legal element of the offense, juries tend to infer rape from evidence of force or resistance. In Michigan, under its reform rape law, consent was judicially held to be a defense even though it was not included in the statute.[24]

The deeper problem is that women are socialized to passive receptivity; may have or perceive no alternative to acquiescence; may prefer it to the escalated risk of injury and the humiliation of a lost fight; submit to survive. Also, force and desire are not mutually exclusive under male supremacy. So long as dominance is eroticized, they never will be. Some women eroticize dominance and submission; it beats feeling forced. Sexual intercourse may be deeply unwanted, the woman would never have initiated it, yet no force may be present. So much force may have been used that the woman never risked saying no. Force may be used, yet the woman may prefer the sex—to avoid more force or because she, too, eroticizes dominance. Women and men know this. Considering rape as violence not sex evades, at the moment it most seems to confront, the issue of who controls women's sexuality and the dominance/submission dynamic that has defined it. When sex is violent, women may have lost control over what is done to them, but absence of force does not ensure the presence of that control. Nor, under conditions of male dominance, does the presence of force make an interaction nonsexual. If sex is normally something men do to women, the issue is less whether there was force than whether consent is a meaningful concept.[25]

To explain women's gender status on a rape theory, Susan Brownmiller argues that the threat of rape benefits all men.[26] How is unspecified. Perhaps it benefits them sexually, hence as a gender: male initiatives toward women carry the fear of rape as support for persuading compliance, the resulting appearance of which has been considered seduction and termed consent. Here the victims' perspective grasps what liberalism applied to women denies: that forced sex as sexuality is not exceptional in relations between the sexes but constitutes the social meaning of gender.

> Rape is a man's act, whether it is a male or a female man and whether it is a man relatively permanently or relatively temporarily; and being raped is a women's experience, whether it is a female or a male woman and whether it is a woman relatively permanently or relatively temporarily.[27]

To be rapable, a position that is social not biological, defines what a woman is.

Marital rape and battery of wives have been separated by law. A feminist analysis suggests that assault by a man's fist is not so different from assault by a penis, not because both are violent but because both are sexual. Battery is often precipitated by women's noncompliance with gender requirements.[28] Nearly all incidents occur in the home, most in the kitchen or bedroom. Most murdered women are killed by their husbands or boyfriends, usually in the bedroom. The battery cycle accords with the rhythms of heterosexual sex.[29] The rhythm of lesbian sadomasochism is the same.[30] Perhaps violent interchanges, especially between genders, make sense in sexual terms.

The larger issue raised by sexual aggression for the interpretation of the relation between sexuality and gender is: what is heterosexuality? If it is the erotization of dominance and submission, altering the participants' gender does not eliminate the sexual, or even gendered, content of aggression. If heterosexuality is males over females, gender matters independently. Arguably, heterosexuality is a fusion of the two, with gender a social outcome, such that the acted upon is feminized, is the "girl" regardless of sex, the actor correspondingly masculinized. Whenever women are victimized, regardless of the biology of the perpetrator, this system is at work. But it is equally true that whenever powerlessness and ascribed inferiority are sexually exploited or en-joyed—based on age, race, physical stature or appearance or ability, or socially reviled or stigmatized status—the system is at work.

Battery thus appears sexual on a deeper level. Stated in boldest terms, sexuality is vi-olent, so perhaps violence is sexual. Violence against women is sexual on both counts, doubly sexy. If this is so, wives are beaten, as well as raped, as women—as the acted upon, as gender, meaning sexual, objects. It further follows that acts by anyone which treat a woman according to her object label, women, are in a sense sexual acts. The extent to which sexual acts are acts of objectification remains a question of one's account of women's freedom to live their own meanings as other than illusions, of individuals' abil-ity to resist or escape, even momentarily, prescribed social meanings short of political change. Clearly, centering sexuality upon genitality distinguishes battery from rape at exactly the juncture that both existing law, and seeing rape as violence not sex, do.

Most women get the message that the law against rape is virtually unenforceable as applied to them. Women's experience is more often delegitimated by this than the law is. Women, as realists, distinguish between rape and experiences of sexual violation by concluding that they have not "really" been raped if they have ever seen or dated or slept with or been married to the man, if they were fashionably dressed or not provably virgin, if they are prostitutes, if they put up with it or tried to get it over with, if they were force-fucked for years. The implicit social standard becomes: if a woman proba-bly could not prove it in court, it was not rape.

The distance between most intimate violations of women and the legally perfect rape measures the imposition of an alien definition. From women's point of view, rape is not prohibited; it is regulated. Even women who know they have been raped do not believe that the legal system will see it the way they do. Often they are not wrong. Rather than deterring or avenging rape, the state, in many victims' experiences, perpetuates it. Women who charge rape say they were raped twice, the second time in court. Un-der a male state, the boundary violation, humiliation, and indignity of being a public sexual spectacle makes this more than a figure of speech.[31]

Rape, like many other crimes, requires that the accused possess a criminal mind (*mens rea*) for his acts to be criminal. The man's mental state refers to what he actually understood at the time or to what a reasonable man should have understood under the circumstances. The problem is that the injury of rape lies in the meaning of the act to its victim, but the standard for its criminality lies in the meaning of the act to the as-sailant. Rape is only an injury from women's point of view. It is only a crime from the male point of view, explicitly including that of the accused.

The crime of rape is defined and adjudicated from the male standpoint, presum-ing that forced sex is sex and that consent to a man is freely given by a woman. Under male supremacist standards, of course, they are. Doctrinally, this means that the man's perceptions of the woman's desires determine whether she is deemed violated. This might be like other crimes of subjective intent if rape were like other crimes. With rape, because sexuality defines gender norms, the only difference between assault and what is socially defined as a noninjury is the meaning of the encounter to the woman. Interpreted this way, the legal problem has been to determine whose view of that meaning constitutes what really happened, as if what happened objectively exists to be objectively determined. This task has been assumed to be separable from the gender of the participants and the gendered nature of their exchange, when the objective norms and the assailant's perspective are identical.

As a result, although the rape law oscillates between subjective tests and objective standards invoking social reasonableness, it uniformly presumes a single underlying reality, rather than a reality split by the divergent meanings inequality produces. Many women are raped by men who know the meaning of their acts to their victims perfectly well and proceed anyway.[32] But women are also violated every day by men who have no idea of the meaning of their acts to the women. To them it is sex. Therefore, to the law it is sex. That becomes the single reality of what happened. When a rape prosecution is lost because a woman fails to prove that she did not consent, she is not considered to have been injured at all. It is as if a robbery victim, finding himself unable to prove he was not engaged in philanthropy, is told he still has his money. Hermeneutically unpacked, the law assumes that, because the rapist did not perceive that the woman did not want him, she was not violated. She had sex. Sex itself cannot be an injury. Women have sex every day. Sex makes a woman a woman. Sex is what women are for.

Men set sexual mores ideologically and behaviorally, define rape as they imagine women to be sexually violated through distinguishing that from their image of what they normally do, and sit in judgment in most accusations of sex crimes. So rape comes to mean a strange (read Black) man who does not know his victim but does know she does not want sex with him, going ahead anyway. But men are systematically conditioned not even to notice what women want. Especially if they consume pornography, they may have not a glimmer of women's indifference or revulsion, including when women say no explicitly. Rapists typically believe the woman loved it. "Probably the single most used cry of rapist to victim is 'You bitch . . . slut . . . you know you want it. You all want it' and afterward, 'there now, you really enjoyed it, didn't you?'"[33] Women, as a survival strategy, must ignore or devalue or mute desires, particularly lack of them, to convey the impression that the man will get what he wants regardless of what they want. In this context, to measure the genuineness of consent from the individual assailant's point of view is to adopt as law the point of view which creates the problem. Measuring consent from the socially reasonable, meaning objective man's, point of view reproduces the same problem under a more elevated label.[34]

Men's pervasive belief that women fabricate rape charges after consenting to sex makes sense in this light. To them, the accusations are false because, to them, the facts describe sex. To interpret such events as rapes distorts their experience. Since they seldom consider that their experience of the real is anything other than reality, they can only explain the woman's version as maliciously invented. Similarly, the male anxiety that rape is easy to charge and difficult to disprove, also widely believed in the face of overwhelming evidence to the contrary, arises because rape accusations express one thing men cannot seem to control: the meaning to women of sexual encounters.

Thus do legal doctrines, incoherent or puzzling as syllogistic logic, become coherent as ideology. For example, when an accused wrongly but sincerely believes that a woman he sexually forced consented, he may have a defense of mistaken belief in consent or fail to satisfy the mental requirement of knowingly proceeding against her will.[35] Sometimes his knowing disregard is measured by what a reasonable man would disregard. This is considered an objective test. Sometimes the disregard need not be reasonable so long as it is sincere. This is considered a subjective test. A feminist inquiry into the distinction between rape and intercourse, by contrast, would inquire into the meaning of the act from women's point of view, which is neither. What is wrong with rape in this view is that it is an act of subordination of women to men. It expresses and reinforces women's inequality to men. Rape with legal impunity makes women second-class citizens.

This analysis reveals the way the social conception of rape is shaped to interpret particular encounters and the way the legal conception of rape authoritatively shapes that social conception. When perspective is bound up with situation, and situation is unequal, whether or not a contested interaction is authoritatively considered rape comes down to whose meaning wins. If sexuality is relational, specifically if it is a power relation of gender, consent is a communication under conditions of inequality. It transpires somewhere between what the woman actually wanted, what she was able to express about what she wanted, and what the man comprehended she wanted.

Discussing the conceptually similar issue of revocation of prior consent, on the issue of the conditions under which women are allowed to control access to their sexuality from one penetration to the next, one commentator notes: "Even where a woman revokes prior consent, such is the male ego that, seized of an exaggerated assessment of his sexual prowess, a main might genuinely believe her still to be consenting; resistance may be misinterpreted as enthusiastic cooperation; protestations of pain or disinclination, a spur to more sophisticated or more ardent love-making; a clear statement to stop, taken as referring to a particular intimacy rather than the entire performance."[36] This vividly captures common male readings of women's indications of disinclination under many circumstances[37] and the perceptions that determine whether a rape occurred. The specific defense of mistaken belief in consent merely carries this to its logical apex. From whose standpoint, and in whose interest, is a law that allows one person's conditioned unconsciousness to contraindicate another's violation? In conceiving a cognizable injury from the viewpoint of the reasonable rapist, the rape law affirmatively rewards men with acquittals for not comprehending women's point of view on sexual encounters.

Whether the law calls this coerced consent or defense of mistaken belief in consent, the more the sexual violation of women is routine, the more pornography exists in the world the more legitimately, the more beliefs equating sexuality with violation become reasonable, and the more honestly women can be defined in terms of their fuckability. It would be comparatively simple if the legal problem were limited to avoiding retroactive falsification of the accused's state of mind. Surely there are incentives to lie. The deeper problem is the rape law's assumption that a single, objective state of affairs existed, one that merely needs to be determined by evidence, when so many rapes involve honest men and violated women. When the reality is split, is the woman raped but not by a rapist? Under these conditions, the law is designed to conclude that a rape did not occur. To attempt to solve this problem by adopting reasonable belief as a standard without asking, on a substantive social basis, to whom the belief is reasonable and why—meaning, what conditions make it reasonable—is one-sided: male-sided.[38] What is it reasonable for a man to believe concerning a woman's desire for sex when heterosexuality is compulsory? What is it reasonable for a man (accused or juror) to believe concerning a woman's consent when he has been viewing positive-outcome-rape pornography?[39] The one whose subjectivity becomes the objectivity of "what happened" is a matter of social meaning, that is, a matter of sexual politics. One-sidedly erasing women's violation or dissolving presumptions into the subjectivity of either side are the alternatives dictated by the terms of the object/subject split, respectively. These alternatives will only retrace that split to women's detriment until its terms are confronted as gendered to the ground.

Notes

1. W. LaFave & A. Scott, Substantive Criminal Law 688–689 (West, 1986), sec. 5. 11; R. M. Perkins & R. N. Boyce, Criminal Law 210 (Foundation Press, 1980).

2. One component of Sec. 213.0 of the Model Penal Code (American Law Institute, 1980) defines rape as sexual intercourse with a female not the wife of the perpetrator, "with some penetration however slight." Most states follows. New York requires penetration (sec. 130.00 [1]). Michigan's gender-neutral sexual assault statute includes penetration by objects (sec. 750.520a[h]; 720.520[b]). The 1980 Annotation to Model Penal Code (Official Draft and Revised Comments, sec. 213.1[d]) questions and discusses the penetration requirement at 346–348. For illustrative case law, see Liptroth v. State, 335 So. 2d 683 (Ala. Crim. App. 1976), *cert. denied,* 429 U.S. 963 (1976); State v. Kidwell, 556 P.2d 20, 27 Ariz. App. 466 (Ariz. Ct. App. 1976); People v. O'Neal, 50 Ill. App. 3d 900, 365 N.E. 2d 1333 (Ill. App. Ct. 1977); Commonwealth v. Usher, 371 A.2d 995 (Pa. Super. Ct. 1977); Commonwealth v. Grassmyer, 237 Pa. Super. 394, 352 A.2d 178 (Pa. Super. Ct. 1975) (statutory rape conviction reversed because defendant's claim that five-year-old child's vaginal wound was inflicted with a broomstick could not be disproved and commonwealth could therefore not prove requisite penetration; indecent assault conviction sustained). Impotence is sometimes a defense and can support laws that prevent charging underage boys with rape or attempted rape; Foster v. Commonwealth, 31 S.E. 503, 96 Va. 306 (1896) (boy under fourteen cannot be guilty of attempt to commit offense that he is legally assumed physically impotent to perpetrate).

3. In the manner of many socialist-feminist adaptations of marxian categories to women's situation, to analyze sexuality as property short-circuits analysis of rape as male sexuality and presumes rather than develops links between sex and class. Concepts of property need to be rethought in light of sexuality as a form of objectification. In some ways, for women legally to be considered property would be an improvement, although it is not recommended.

4. For contrast between the perspectives of the victims and the courts, see Rusk v.

State, 43 Md. App. 476, 406 A.2d 624 (Md. Ct. Spec. App. 1979) (*en banc*), rev'd, 289 Md. 230, 424 A.2d 720 (1981); Gonzales v. State, 516 P.2d 592 (1973).

5. Susan Brownmiller, Against Our Will: Men, Women, and Rape 15 (Simon & Schuster, 1975).

6. Diana E. H. Russell, The Politics of Rape: The Victim's Perspective (Stein & Day, 1977); Andrea Medea & Kathleen Thompson, Against Rape (Farrar, Straus and Giroux, 1974); Lorenne M. G. Clark & Debra Lewis; Rape: The Price of Coercive Sexuality (Women's Press, 1977); Susan Griffin, Rape: The All-American Crime, Ramparts, September 1971, pp. 26–35, reprinted herein, at 422. Ti-Grace Atkinson connects rape with "the institution of sexual intercourse," Amazon Odyssey: The First Collection of Writings by the Political Pioneer of the Women's Movement 13–23 (Links Books, 1974). Kalamu ya Salaam, Rape: A Radical Analysis from the African-American Perspective, in Our Women Keep Our Skies from Falling 25–40. (Nkombo, 1980).

7. Racism is clearly everyday life. Racism in the United States, by singling out Black men for allegations of rape of white women, has helped obscure the fact that it is men who rape women, disproportionately women of color.

8. Pamela Foa, What's Wrong with Rape? in Vetterling-Braggin, Frederick A. Elliston, & Jane English eds., Feminism and Philosophy 347–359 (Littlefield, Adams, 1977); Michael Davis, What's So Bad about Rape? Paper presented at the annual meeting of the Academy of Criminal Justice Sciences, Louisville, Ky., March 1982. "Since we would not want to say that there is anything morally wrong with sexual intercourse per se, we conclude that the wrongness of rape rests with the matter of the woman's consent"; Carolyn M. Shafer & Marilyn Frye, Rape and Respect, in Vetterling-Braggin et al., *supra* this note at 334. "Sexual contact is not inherently harmful, insulting or provoking. Indeed, ordinarily it is something of which we are quite fond. The difference is [that] ordinary sexual intercourse is more or less consented to while rape is not"; Davis, What's So Bad?, *supra* this note at 12.

9. Leigh Bienen, Rape III—National Developments in Rape Reform Legislation, 6 Women's Rts. L. Rep. 170 (1980). See also Camille LeGrande, Rape and Rape Laws; Sexism in Society and Law, 61 Cal. L. Rev. 919 (1973).

10. People v. Samuels, 58 Cal. Rptr. 439, 447 (1967).

11. Julia R. Schwendinger & Herman Schewendinger, Rape and Inequality 44 (Sage, 1983); K. Polk, Rape Reform and Criminal Justice Processing, 31 Crime & Delinq. 191–205 (April 1985). "What can be concluded about the achievement of the underlying goals of the rape reform movement? . . . If a major goal is to increase the probability of convictions, then the results are slight at best . . . or even negligible" (*id.* at 199) (California data). See also P. Bart and P. O'Brien, Stopping Rape: Successful Survival Strategies 129–131 (Pergamon, 1985).

12. See State v. Alston, 310 N.C. 399, 312 S.E. 2d 470 (1984) and discussion in Susan Estrich, Real Rape 60–62 (Harvard Univ. Press, 1987).

13. Note, Forcible and Statutory Rape: An Exploration of the Operation and Objectives of the Consent Standard, 62 Yale L. J. 55 (1952).

14. A similar analysis of sexual harassment suggests that women have such "power" only so long as they behave according to male definitions of female desirability, that is, only so long as they accede to the definition of their sexuality (hence, themselves, as gender female) on male terms. Women have this power, in other words, only so long as they remain powerless.

15. See Comment, Rape and Battery between Husband and Wife, 6 Stan. L. Rev. 719 (1954). On rape of prostitutes, see, e.g., People v. McClure, 42 Ill. App. 952, 356

N.E. 2d 899 (1st Dist. 3d Div. 1976) (on indictment for rape and armed robbery of prostitute where sex was admitted to have occurred, defendant acquitted of rape but "guilty of robbing her while armed with a knife"); Magnum v. State, 1 Tenn. Crim. App. 155, 432 S.W. 2d 497 (Tenn. Crim. App. 1968) (no conviction for rape; conviction for sexual violation of age of consent overturned on ground that failure to instruct jury to determine if complainant was "a bawd, lewd or kept female" was reversible error; "A bawd female is a female who keeps a house of prostitution, and conducts illicit intercourse. A lewd female is one given to unlawful indulgence of lust, either for sexual indulgence or profit. . . . A kept female is one who is supported and kept by a man for his own illicit intercourse"; complainant "frequented the Blue Moon Tavern; she had been there the night before . . . she kept company with . . . a married man separated from his wife. . . . There is some proof of her bad reputation for truth and veracity"). Johnson v. State, 598 S.W. 2d 803 (Tenn. Crim. App. 1979) (unsuccessful defense to charge of rape that "even [if] technically a prostitute can be raped . . . the act of the rape itself was no trauma whatever to this type of unchaste woman"); People v. Gonzales, 96 Misc. 2d 639, 409 N.Y.S. 2d 497 (Crm. Crt. N.Y. City 1978) (prostitute can be raped if "it can be prove beyond a reasonable doubt that she revoked her consent prior to sexual intercourse because the defendant . . . used the coercive force of a pistol).

16. People v. Liberta, 64 N.Y. 2d 152, 474 N.E. 2d 567, 485 N.Y.S. 2d 207 (1984) (marital rape recognized, contrary precedents discussed). For a summary of the current state of the marital exemption, see Joanne Schulman, State-by-State Information on Marital Rape Exemption Laws, in Diana E. H. Russell ed., Rape in Marriage 375–381 (Macmillan, 1982); Patricia Searles & Ronald Berger, The Current Status of Rape Reform Legislation: An Examination of State Statutes, 10 Women's Rts. L. Rep. 25 (1987).

17. On "social interaction as an element of consent" in a voluntary social companion context, see Model Penal Code, sec. 213.1. "The prior social interaction is an indicator of consent in addition to actor's and victim's behavioral interaction during the commission of the offense"; Wallace Loh, Q: What Has Reform of Rape Legislation Wrought? A: Truth in Criminal Labeling, 37 J. Soc. Issues 47 (1981).

18. E.g., People v. Burnham, 176 Cal. App. 3d 1134, 222 Cal. Rptr. 630 (Cal. App. 1986).

19. Diana E. H. Russell & Nancy Howell, The Prevalence of Rape in the United States Revisited, 8 Signs: Journal of Women in Culture and Society 668–695 (Summer 1983); and D. Russell, The Secret Trauma: Incestuous Abuse of Women and Girls (Basic Books, 1986).

20. Pauline Bart found that women were more likely to be raped—that is, less able to stop a rape in progress—when they knew their assailant, particularly when they had a prior or current sexual relationship; A Study of Women Who Both Were Raped and Avoided Rape, 37 J. Soc. Issues 132 (1981). See also Linda Belden, Why Women Do Not Report Sexual Assault (Portland, Ore.: City of Portland Public Service Employment Program, Portland Women's Crisis Line, March 1979); Menachem Amir, Patterns in Forcible Rape 229–252 (Univ. Chicago Press, 1971).

21. Answer Brief for Plaintiff-Appellee, People v. Brown, Sup. Ct. Colo., Case No. 81SA102 (1981): 10.

22. Note, Forcible and Statutory Rape, *supra* note 13, at 55.

23. La. Rev. Stat. 14.42. Delaware law requires that the victim resist, but "only to the extent that it is reasonably necessary to make the victim's refusal to consent known to the defendant"; 11 Del. Code 761(g). See also Sue Bessmer, The Laws of Rape (Praeger, 1984).

24. See People v. Thompson, 117 Mich. App. 522, 524, 324 N.W. 2d 22, 24 (Mich. App. 1982); People v. Hearn, 100 Mich. App. 749, 300 N.W. 2d 396 (Mich. App. 1980).

25. See Carol Pateman, Women and Consent, 8 Pol. Theory 149–168 (May 1980): "Consent as ideology cannot be distinguished from habitual acquiescence, assent, silent dissent, submission, or even enforced submission. Unless refusal of consent or withdrawal of consent are real possibilities, we can no longer speak of 'consent' in any genuine sense. . . . Women exemplify the individuals whom consent theorists declared are incapable of consenting. Yet, simultaneously, women have been presented as always consenting, and their explicit non-consent has been treated as irrelevant or has been reinterpreted as 'consent'" (*id.* at 150).

26. Brownmiller, *supra* note 5, at 5.

27. Shafer and Frye, *supra* note 8, at 334.

28. See R. Emerson Dobash & Russell Dobash, Violence against Wives: A Case against the Patriarchy 14–21 (Free Press, 1979).

29. On the cycle of battering, see Lenore Walker, The Battered Woman (Harper & Row, 1979).

30. Samois, Coming to Power (Alyson Publications, 1983).

31. If accounts of sexual violation are a form of sex, victim testimony in rape cases is a form of live oral pornography.

32. This is apparently true of undetected as well as convicted rapists. Samuel David Smithyman's sample, composed largely of the former, contained self-selected respondents to his ad, which read: "Are you a rapist? Researchers Interviewing Anonymously by Phone to Protect Your Identity. Call . . ." Presumably those who chose to call defined their acts as rapes, at least at the time of responding; The Undetected Rapist (Ph.D. diss., Claremont Graduate School, 1978), 54–60, 63–76, 80–90, 97–107.

33. Nancy Gager & Cathleen Schurr, Sexual Assault: Confronting Rape in America 244 (Grosset & Dunlap, 1976).

34. Susan Estrich proposes this; see Estrich, *supra* note 12, at 102–103. Her lack of inquiry into social determinants of perspective (such as pornography) may explain her faith in reasonableness as a legally workable standard for raped women.

35. See Director of Public Prosecutions v. Morgan, 2 All E.R.H.L. 347 (1975) [England]; Pappajohn v. The Queen, 111 D.L.R. 3d 1 (1980) [Canada]; People v. Mayberry, 542 P. 2d 1337 (Cal. 1975).

36. Richard H. S. Tur, Rape: Reasonableness and Time, 3 Oxford J. Legal Stud. 432, 441 (Winter 1981). Tur, in the context of the *Morgan* and *Pappajohn* cases, says the "law ought not to be astute to equate wickedness and wishful, albeit mistaken, thinking" (*id.* at 437). Rape victims are typically less concerned with wickedness than with injury.

37. See Silke Vogelmann-Sine, Ellen D. Ervin, Reenie Christensen, Carolyn H. Warmsun, & Leonard P. Ullmann, Sex Differences in Feelings Attributed to a Woman in Situations Involving Coercion and Sexual Advances, 47 J. Personality 429 (September 1979).

38. Estrich has this problem in Real Rape, *supra* note 12.

39. E. Donnerstein, Pornography: Its Effect on Violence against Women in N. Malamuth & E. Donnerstein eds., Pornography and Sexual Aggression 65–70 (Academic Press, 1984). Readers who worry that this could become an argument for defending accused rapists should understand that the reality to which it points already provides a basis for defending accused rapists. The solution is to attack the pornography directly, not to be silent about its exonerating effects, legal or social, potential or actual.

Date Rape: A Feminist Analysis

LOIS PINEAU

... DATE RAPE is nonaggravated sexual assault, nonconsensual sex that does not involve physical injury, or the explicit threat of physical injury. But because it does not involve physical injury, and because physical injury is often the only criterion that is accepted as evidence that the *actus reas* is nonconsensual, what is really sexual assault is often mistaken for seduction. The replacement of the old rape laws with the new laws on sexual assault have done nothing to resolve this problem. . . .

. . . A woman on a casual date with a virtual stranger has almost no chance of bringing a complaint of sexual assault before the courts. One reason for this is the prevailing criterion for consent. According to this criterion, consent is implied unless some emphatic episodic sign of resistance occurred, and its occurrence can be established. But if no episodic act occurred, or if it did occur, and the defendant claims that it didn't, or if the defendant threatened the plaintiff but won't admit it in court, it is almost impossible to find any evidence that would support the plaintiff's word against the defendant. This difficulty is exacerbated by suspicion on the part of the courts, police, and legal educators that even where an act of resistance occurs, this act should not be interpreted as a withholding of consent, and this suspicion is especially upheld where the accused is a man who is known to the female plaintiff.

In Glanville Williams's classic textbook on criminal law we are warned that where a man is unknown to a woman, she does not consent if she expresses her rejection in the form of an episodic and vigorous act at the "vital moment." But if the man is known to the woman she must, according to Williams, "make use of all means available to her to repel the man."[1] Williams warns that women often welcome a "mastery advance" and present a token resistance. He quotes Byron's couplet,

A little still she strove, and much repented
And whispering "I will ne'er consent"—consented[2]

by way of alerting law students to the difficulty of distinguishing real protest from pretense. Thus, while in principle, a firm unambiguous stand, or a healthy show of temper

8 Law & Phil. 217 (1989). © 1989 Kluwer Academic Publishers. Reprinted by permission of Kluwer Academic Publishers.

ought to be sufficient, if established, to show nonconsent, in practice the forceful over-riding of such a stance is apt to be taken as an indication that the resistance was not se-riously intended, and that the seduction had succeeded. The consequence of this is that it is almost impossible to establish the defendant's guilt beyond a reasonable doubt.

Thus, on the one hand, we have a situation in which women are vulnerable to the most exploitive tactics at the hands of men who are known to them. On the other hand, almost nothing will count as evidence of their being assaulted, including their having taken an emphatic stance in withholding their consent. The new laws have done almost nothing to change this situation. Yet clearly, some solution must be sought. Moreover, the road to that solution presents itself clearly enough as a need for a reformulation of the criterion of consent. . . .

The purpose of this paper is to develop such a criterion. . . .

The Problem of the Criterion

The reasoning that underlies the present criterion of consent is entangled in a number of mutually supportive mythologies which see sexual assault as masterful seduction, and silent submission as sexual enjoyment. Because the prevailing ideology has so much in-formed our conceptualization of sexual interaction, it is extraordinarily difficult for us to distinguish between assault and seduction, submission and enjoyment, or so we imagine. At the same time, this failure to distinguish has given rise to a network of rationalizations that support the conflation of assault with seduction, submission with enjoyment. . . .

The position of the courts is supported by the widespread belief that male aggres-sion and female reluctance are normal parts of seduction. Given their acceptance of this model, the logic of their response must be respected. For if sexual aggression is a part of ordinary seduction, then it cannot be inconsistent with the legitimate consent of the person allegedly seduced by this means. And if it is normal for a woman to be reluctant, then this reluctance must be consistent with her consent as well. The posi-tion of the courts is not inconsistent just so long as they allow that some sort of protest on the part of a woman counts as a refusal. [H]owever, it frequently happens that no sort of a protest would count as a refusal. Moreover, if no sort of protest, or at least if precious few count, then the failure to register these protests will amount to "asking for it," it will amount, in other words, to agreeing.

The court's belief in "natural" male aggression and "natural" female reluctance has increasingly come under attack by feminist critics [as discussed below]. . . .

Rape Myths

The belief that the natural aggression of men and the natural reluctance of women somehow makes date rape understandable underlies a number of prevalent myths about rape and human sexuality. These beliefs maintain their force partly on account of a logical compulsion exercised by them at an unconscious level . . . . These myths are not just popular, however, but often emerge in the arguments of judges who acquit date rapists, and policemen who refuse to lay charges.

The claim that the victim provoked a sexual incident, that "she asked for it," is by far the most common defense given by men who are accused of sexual assault.[3] Feminists, rightly incensed by this response, often treat it as beneath contempt, singling out the defense as an argument against it. On other fronts, sociologists have identified the response as part of an overall tendency of people to see the world as just, a tendency which disposes them to conclude that people for the most part deserve what they get.[4]

. . .

The least sophisticated of the "she asked for it" rationales, and in a sense, the easiest to deal with, appeals to an injunction against sexually provocative behavior on the part of women. If women should not be sexually provocative, then, from this standpoint, a woman who is sexually provocative deserves to suffer the consequences. Now it will not do to respond that women get raped even when they are not sexually provocative—or that it is men who get to interpret (unfairly) what counts as sexually provocative. The question should be: Why shouldn't a woman be sexually provocative? Why should this behavior warrant any kind of aggressive response whatsoever?

Attempts to explain that women have a right to behave in sexually provocative ways without suffering dire consequences still meet with surprisingly tough resistance. Even people who find nothing wrong or sinful with sex itself, in any of its forms, tend to suppose that women must not behave sexually unless they are prepared to carry through on some fuller course of sexual interaction. The logic of this response seems to be that at some point a woman's behavior commits her to following through on the full course of a sexual encounter as it is defined by her assailant. At some point she has made an agreement, or formed a contract, and once that is done, [the promisee] is entitled to demand that she satisfy the terms of that contract. Thus, this view about sexual responsibility and desert is supported by other assumptions about contracts and agreement. But we do not normally suppose that casual nonverbal behavior generates agreements. What rationale would support our conclusion in this case?

The rationale, I believe, comes in the form of a belief in the especially insistent nature of male sexuality, an insistence which lies at the root of natural male aggression, and which is extremely difficult, perhaps impossible to contain. At a certain point in the arousal process, it is thought, a man's rational will gives way to the prerogatives of nature. His sexual need can and does reach a point where it is uncontrollable, and his natural masculine aggression kicks in to assure that this need is met. Women, however, are naturally more contained, and so it is their responsibility not to provoke the irrational in the male. If they do go so far as that, they have both failed in their responsibilities, and subjected themselves to the inevitable. One does not go into the lion's cage and expect not to be eaten. . . .

This belief about the normal aggressiveness of male sexuality is complemented by common knowledge about female gender development. Once, women were taught to deny their sexuality and to aspire to ideals of chastity. Things have not changed so much. Women still tend to eschew conquest mentalities in favor of a combination of sex and affection. Insofar as this is thought to be merely a cultural requirement, however, there is an expectation that women will be coy about their sexual desire. The assumption that women both want to indulge sexually, and are inclined to sacrifice this desire for higher ends, gives rise to the myth that they want to be raped. After all, doesn't rape give them the sexual enjoyment they *really* want, at the same time that it relieves them of the responsibility for admitting to and acting upon what they want? And how then can we blame men, who have been socialized to be aggressively seductive precisely for the purpose of overriding female reserve? If we find fault at all, we are inclined to cast our suspicions on the motives of the woman. For it is on her that the contradictory roles of sexual desirer and sexual denier has been placed. Our awareness of the contradiction expected of her makes us suspect her honesty. In the past, she was expected to deny her complicity because of the shame and guilt she felt at having submitted.[5] This expectation persists in many quarters today, and is carried over into a general suspicion about her character, and the fear that she might make a false accusation out of revenge, or some other low motive.

But if women really want sexual pleasure, what inclines us to think that they will get it through rape? This conclusion logically requires a theory about the dynamics of sexual pleasure that sees that pleasure as an emergent property of overwhelming male insistence. For the assumption that a raped female experiences sexual pleasure implies that the person who rapes her knows how to cause that pleasure independently of any information she might convey on that point. Since her ongoing protest is inconsistent with requests to be touched in particular ways in particular places, to have more of this and less of that, then we must believe that the person who touches her knows these particular ways and places instinctively, without any directives from her.

Thus we find, underlying and reinforcing this belief in incommunicative male prowess, a conception of sexual pleasure that springs from wordless interchanges, and of sexual success that occurs in a place of meaningful silence. The language of seduction is accepted as a tacit language: eye contact, smiles, blushes, and faintly discernible gestures. It is, accordingly, imprecise and ambiguous. It would be easy for a man to make mistakes about the message conveyed, understandable that he should mistakenly think that a sexual invitation has been made, and a bargain struck. But honest mistakes, we think, must be excused.

In sum, the belief that women should not be sexually provocative is logically linked to several other beliefs, some normative, some empirical. The normative beliefs are that (1) people should keep the agreements they make, (2) that sexually provocative behavior, taken beyond a certain point, generates agreements, (3) that the peculiar nature of male and female sexuality places such agreements in a special category, one in which the possibility of retracting an agreement is ruled out, or at least made highly unlikely, (4) that women are not to be trusted, in sexual matters at least. The empirical belief, which turns out to be false, is that male sexuality is not subject to rational and moral control.

Dispelling the Myths

The "she asked for it" justification of sexual assault incorporates a conception of a contract that would be difficult to defend in any other context. . . .

The belief that a woman generates some sort of contractual obligation whenever her behavior is interpreted as seductive is the most indefensible part of the mythology of rape. In law, contracts are not legitimate just because a promise has been made. In particular, the use of pressure tactics to extract agreement is frowned upon. Normally, an agreement is upheld only if the contractors were clear on what they were getting into, and had sufficient time to reflect on the wisdom of their doing so. . . . But whatever the terms of a contract, there is no private right to enforce it. So that if I make a contract with you on which I renege, the only permissible recourse for you is through due legal process.

Now it is not clear whether sexual contracts can be made to begin with, or if so, what sort of sexual contracts would be legitimate. But assuming that they could be made, the terms of those contracts would not be enforceable. To allow public enforcement would be to grant the state the overt right to force people to have sex, and this would clearly be unacceptable. Granting that sexual contracts are legitimate, state enforcement of such contracts would have to be limited to ordering nonsexual compensation for breaches of contract. So it makes no difference whether a sexual contract is tacit or explicit. There are no grounds whatsoever that would justify enforcement of its terms.

Thus, even if we assume that a woman has initially agreed to an encounter, her agreement does not automatically make all subsequent sexual activity to which she submits legitimate. If during coitus a woman should experience pain, be suddenly overcome with guilt or fear of pregnancy, or simply lose her initial desire, those are good reasons for her to change her mind. Having changed her mind, neither her partner nor the state has any right to force her to continue. But then if she is forced to continue she is assaulted. Thus, establishing that consent occurred at a particular point during a sexual encounter should not conclusively establish the legitimacy of the encounter. What is needed is a reading of whether she agreed throughout the encounter.

If the "she asked for it" contractual view of sexual interchange has any validity, it is because there is a point at which there is no stopping a sexual encounter, a point at which that encounter becomes the inexorable outcome of the unfolding of natural events. If a sexual encounter is like a slide on which I cannot stop halfway down, it will be relevant whether I enter the slide of my own free will, or am pushed.

But there is no evidence that the entire sexual act is like a slide. While there may be a few seconds in the "plateau" period just prior to orgasm in which people are "swept" away by sexual feelings to the point where we could justifiably understand their lack of heed for the comfort of their partner, the greater part of a sexual encounter comes well within the bounds of morally responsible control of our own actions. . . . Modern sexual therapy assumes that such control is universally accessible, and so far there has been no reason to question that assumption. Sexologists are unanimous, moreover, in holding that mutual sexual enjoyment requires an atmosphere of comfort and communication, a minimum of pressure, and an ongoing check-up on one's partner's state. . . . These findings show that the way to achieve sexual pleasure, at any time at all, let alone with a casual acquaintance, decidedly does not involve overriding the other person's express reservations and providing them with just any kind of sexual stimulus.[6] And while we do not want to allow science and technology a voice in which the voices of particular women are drowned, in this case science seems to concur with women's perception that aggressive incommunicative sex is not what they want. But if science and the voice of women concur, if aggressive seduction does not lead to good sex, if women do not like it or want it, then it is not rational to think that they would agree to it. Where such sex takes place, it is therefore rational to presume that the sex was not consensual.

The myth that women like to be raped, is closely connected, as we have seen, to doubt about their honesty in sexual matters, and this suspicion is exploited by defense lawyers when sexual assault cases make it to the courtroom. It is an unfortunate consequence of the presumption of innocence that rape victims who end up in court frequently find that it is they who are on trial. For if the defendant is innocent, then either he did not intend to do what he was accused of or the plaintiff is mistaken about his identity, or she is lying. Often the last alternative is the only plausible defense, and as a result, the plaintiff's word seldom goes unquestioned. Women are frequently accused of having made a false accusation, either as a defensive mechanism for dealing with guilt and shame, or out of a desire for revenge.

Now there is no point in denying the possibility of false accusation, though there are probably better ways of seeking revenge on a man than accusing him of rape. However, we can now establish a logical connection between the evidence that a woman was subjected to high-pressure aggressive "seduction" tactics, and her claim that she did not consent to that encounter. Where the kind of encounter is not the sort to which it would be reasonable to consent, there is a logical presumption that a woman who claims that she did not consent is telling the truth. Where the kind of sex involved is not the sort of sex we would expect a woman to like, the burden of proof should not be on the woman to show that she did not consent, but on the defendant to show that contrary to every reasonable expectation she did consent. The defendant should be required to convince the court that the plaintiff persuaded him to have sex with her even though there are no visible reasons why she should.

In conclusion, there are no grounds for the "she asked for it" defense. Sexually provocative behavior does not generate sexual contracts. Even where there are sexual agreements, they cannot be legitimately enforced either by the state, or by private right, or by natural prerogative. Secondly, all the evidence suggests that neither women nor men find sexual enjoyment in rape or in any form of non-communicative sexuality. Thirdly, male sexual desire is containable, and can be subjected to moral and rational control. Fourthly, since there is no reason why women should not be sexually provocative, they do not "deserve" any sex they do not want. . . .

Communicative Sexuality: Reinterpreting the Kantian Imperative

The present criterion of consent sets up sexual encounters as contractual events in which sexual aggression is presumed to be consented to unless there is some vigorous act of refusal. As long as we view sexual interaction on a contractual model, the only possibility for finding fault is to point to the presence of such an act. But it is clear that whether or not we can determine such a presence, there is something strongly disagreeable about the sexual aggression described above.

In thinking about sex we must keep in mind its sensual ends, and the facts show that aggressive high-pressure sex contradicts those ends. Consensual sex in dating situations is presumed to aim at mutual enjoyment. It may not always do this, and when it does, it might not always succeed. There is no logical incompatibility between wanting to continue a sexual encounter, and failing to derive sexual pleasure from it.

But it seems to me that there is a presumption in favor of the connection between sex and sexual enjoyment, and that if a man wants to be sure that he is not forcing himself on a woman, he has an obligation either to ensure that the encounter really is mutually enjoyable, or to know the reasons why she would want to continue the encounter in spite of her lack of enjoyment. A closer investigation of the nature of this obligation will enable us to construct a more rational and a more plausible norm of sexual conduct.

Onara O'Neill has argued that in intimate situations we have an obligation to take the ends of others as our own, and to promote those ends in a non-manipulative and non-paternalistic manner.[7] Now it seems that in honest sexual encounters just this is required. Assuming that each person enters the encounter in order to seek sexual satisfaction, each person engaging in the encounter has an obligation to help the other seek his or her ends. To do otherwise is to risk acting in opposition to what the other desires, and hence to risk acting without the other's consent.

But the obligation to promote the sexual ends of one's partner implies the obligation to know what those ends are, and also the obligation to know how those ends are attained. Thus, the problem comes down to a problem of epistemic responsibility, the responsibility to know. The solution, in my view, lies in the practice of a communicative sexuality, one which combines the appropriate knowledge of the other with respect for the dialectics of desire.

So let us, for a moment, conceive of sexual interaction on a communicative rather than a contractual model. Let us look at it the way I think it should be looked at, as if it were a proper conversation rather than an offer from the Mafia. . . .

Just as communicative conversationalists are concerned with more than didactic content, persons engaged in communicative sexuality will be concerned with more than achieving coitus. They will be sensitive to the responses of their partners. They will, like good conversationalists, be intuitive, sympathetic, and charitable. Intuition will help them to interpret their partner's responses; sympathy will enable them, to share what their partner is feeling; charity will enable them to care. Communicative sexual partners will not overwhelm each other with the barrage of their own desires.

They will treat negative, bored, or angry responses as a sign that the erotic ground needs to be either cleared or abandoned. Their concern with fostering the desire of the other must involve an ongoing state of alertness in interpreting her responses.

Just as a conversationalist's prime concern is for the mutuality of the discussion, a person engaged in communicative sexuality will be most concerned with the mutuality of desire. As such, both will put into practice a regard for their respondent that is guaranteed no place in the contractual language of rights, duties, and consent. The dialectics of both activities reflect the dialectics of desire insofar as each person's interest in continuing is contingent upon the other person wishing to do so too, and each person's interest is as much fueled by the other's interest as it is by her own. Each respects the subjectivity of the other not just by avoiding treading on it, but by fostering and protecting the quality of that subjectivity. Indeed, the requirement to avoid treading on the subjectivity of the other entails the obligation to respect the dialectics of desire. . . . And only by respecting the dialectics of desire can we have any confidence that we have not misused our position of trust and knowledge.

Cultural Presumptions

. . . Friendship . . . is a relation that is greatly underdetermined by what we usually include in our sets of rights and obligations. For the most part, rights and obligations disappear as terms by which friendship is guided. They are still there, to be called upon, in case the relationship breaks down, but insofar as the friendship is a friendship, it is concerned with fostering the quality of the interaction and not with standing on rights. Thus, because we are friends, we share our property, and property rights between us are not invoked. Because we are friends, privacy is not an issue. Because we are friends we may see to each other's needs as often as we see to our own. The same can be said for relations between lovers, parents and dependent children, and even between spouses, at least when interaction is functioning at an optimal level. . . .

But is there a similar conceptual relation between the kind of activity that a date is, and the sort of moral practice that it requires? My claim is that there is, and that this connection is easily established once we recognize the cultural presumption that dating is a gesture of friendship and regard. Traditionally, the decision to date indicates that two people have an initial attraction to each other, that they are disposed to like each other, and look forward to enjoying each other's company. Dating derives its implicit meaning from this tradition. It retains this meaning unless other aims are explicitly stated, and even then it may not be possible to alienate this meaning. It is a rare woman who will not spurn a man who states explicitly, right at the onset, that he wants to go out with her solely on the condition that he have sexual intercourse with her at the end of the evening, and that he has no interest in her company apart from gaining that end, and no concern for mutual satisfaction. Explicit protest to the contrary aside, the conventions of dating confer on it its social meaning, and this social meaning implies a relationship which is more like friendship than the cutthroat competition of opposing teams. As such, it requires that we do more than stand on our rights with regard to each other. As long as we are operating under the auspices of a dating relationship, it requires that we behave in the mode of friendship and trust. But if a date is more like a friendship than a business contract, then clearly respect for the dialectics of desire is incompatible with the sort of sexual pressure that is inclined to end in date rape. And clearly, also, a conquest mentality which exploits a situation of trust and respect for purely selfish ends is morally pernicious. Failure to respect the dialectics of desire when operating under the auspices of friendship and trust is to act in flagrant disregard of the moral requirement to avoid manipulative, coercive, and exploitive behavior. Respect for the dialectics of desire is *prima facie* inconsistent with the satisfaction of one person at the expense of the other. The proper end of friendship relations is mutual satisfaction. But the requirement of mutuality means that we must take a communicative approach to discovering the ends of the other, and this entails that we respect the dialectics of desire.

But now that we know what communicative sexuality is, and that it is morally required, and that it is the only feasible means to mutual sexual enjoyment, why not take this model as the norm of what is reasonable in sexual interaction? The evidence of sexologists strongly indicates that women whose partners are aggressively uncommunicative have little chance of experiencing sexual pleasure. But it is not reasonable for women to consent to what they have little chance of enjoying. Hence it is not reasonable for women to consent to aggressive noncommunicative sex. Nor can we reasonably suppose that women have consented to sexual encounters which we know and they know they do not find enjoyable. With the communicative model as the norm, the aggressive contractual model should strike us as a model of deviant sexuality, and sexual encounters patterned on that model should strike us as encounters to which *prima facie* no one would reasonably agree. But if acquiescence to an encounter counts as consent only if the acquiescence is reasonable, something to which a reasonable person, in full possession of knowledge relevant to the encounter, would agree, then acquiescence to aggressive noncommunicative sex is not reasonable. Hence, acquiescence under such conditions should not count as consent.

Thus, where communicative sexuality does not occur, we lack the main ground for believing that the sex involved was consensual. Moreover, where a man does not engage in communicative sexuality, he acts either out of reckless disregard, or out of willful ignorance. For he cannot know, except through the practice of communicative sexuality, whether his partner has any sexual reason for continuing the encounter. And where she does not, he runs the risk of imposing on her what she is not willing to have. All that is needed then, in order to provide women with legal protection from "date rape" is to make both reckless indifference and willful ignorance a sufficient condition of *mens rea* and to make communicative sexuality the accepted norm of sex to which a reasonable woman would agree. Thus, the appeal to communicative sexuality as a norm for sexual encounters accomplishes two things. It brings the aggressive sex involved in "date rape" well within the realm of sexual assault, and it locates the guilt of date rapists in the failure to approach sexual relations on a communicative basis.

The Epistemological Implications

Finding a proper criterion for consent is one problem, discovering what really happened, after the event, when the only eye witnesses give conflicting accounts is another. But while there is no foolproof way of getting the unadulterated truth, it can make a significant difference to the outcome of a prosecution, what sort of facts we are seeking. On the old model of aggressive seduction we sought evidence of resistance. But on the new model of communicative sexuality what we want is evidence of an ongoing positive and encouraging response on the part of the plaintiff. This new goal will require quite different tactics on the part of the cross-examiners, and quite different expectations on the part of juries and judges. Where communicative sexuality is taken as the norm, and aggressive sexual tactics as a presumption against consent, the outcome . . . would be quite different. It would be regarded as sexual assault rather than seduction.

Let us then consider a date rape trial in which a man is cross-examined. He is asked whether he was presuming mutual sexual enjoyment. Suppose he answers in the negative. Then he would have to account for why he persisted in the face of her voiced reluctance. He cannot give as an excuse that he thought she liked it, because he believes that she did not. If he thought that she had consented even though she didn't like it, then it seems to me that the burden of proof would lie with him to say why it was reasonable to think this. Clearly, her initial resistance, her presumed lack of enjoyment, and the pressure tactics involved in getting her to 'go along' would not support a reasonable belief in consent, and his persisting in the face of her dissatisfaction would surely cast doubt on the sincerity of his belief in her consent.

But suppose he answers in the affirmative. Then the cross-examiner would not have to rely on the old criteria for non-consent. He would not have to show either that she had resisted him, or that she was in a fearful or intimidated state of mind. Instead he could use a communicative model of sexuality to discover how much respect there had been for the dialectics of desire. Did he ask her what she liked? If she was using contraceptives? If he should? What tone of voice did he use? How did she answer? Did she make any demands? Did she ask for penetration? How was that desire conveyed? Did he ever let up the pressure long enough to see if she was really that interested? Did he ask her which position she preferred? Assuming that the defendant does not perjure himself, he would lack satisfactory answers to these questions. But even where the defendant did lie, a skilled cross-examiner who was willing to go into detail could probably establish easily enough when the interaction had not been communicative. It is extraordinarily difficult to keep up a consistent story when you are not telling the truth.

On the new criterion, the cross-examination focuses on the communicative nature of the ongoing encounter, and the communicative nature of an encounter is much easier to establish than the occurrence of an episodic act of resistance. For one thing, it requires that a fairly long, yet consistent story be told, and this enables us to assess the plausibility of the competing claims in light of a wider collection of relevant data. Secondly, in making noncommunicative sex the primary indicator of coercive sex it provides us with a criterion for distinguishing consensual sadomasochism from brutality.

For even if a couple agree to sadomasochistic sex, bondage and whippings and the rest of it, the court has a right to require that there be a system of signals whereby each partner can convey to the other whether she has had enough. Thirdly, the use of a new criterion of communicative sexuality would enable us to introduce a new category of nonaggravated sexual assault which would not necessarily carry a heavy sentence but which would nonetheless provide an effective recourse against "date rape." . . .

. . . If we are serious about date rape, then the next step is to take this criterion as objective grounds for establishing that a date rape has occurred. The proper legislation is the shortest route to establishing this criterion. . . .

Notes

1. Glanville Williams, Textbook of Criminal Law 238 (Stevens, 2d ed., 1983).

2. *Id.*

3. See Jeanne C. Marsh, Allison Geist & Nathan Caplan, Rape and the Limits of Law Reform 61 (Auburn House, 1982), for a particularly good example of this response. Also see John M. MacDonald, Victim-Precipitated Rape, in Rape: Offenders and Their Victims 78–89 (Charles C. Thomas, 1971), for a good example of this response in academic thinking. Also see Menachem Amir, Patterns in Forcible Rape 259 (Univ. Chicago Press, 1972).

4. See Eugene Borgida & Nancy Brekke, Psycholegal Research on Rape Trials, in Ann Wolbert Burgess ed., Rape and Sexual Assault: A Research Handbook 314 (Garland Press, 1985). Also see M. J. Lerner, The Desire for Justice and Reactions to Victims, in Jacqueline Macaulay & Leonard Berkowitz eds., Altruism and Helping Behavior (Academic Press, 1970).

5. See Sue Bessner, The Laws of Rape 111–121 (Praeger, 1984), for a discussion of the legal forms in which this suspicion is expressed.

6. It is not just women who fail to find satisfaction in the "swept away" approach to sexual interaction. Studies of convicted rapists, and of conquest-oriented men, indicate that men are frequently disappointed when they use this approach as well. In over half of aggravated sexual assaults penetration fails because the man loses his erection. Those who do succeed invariably report that the sex experienced was not enjoyable. This supports the prevailing view of sexologists that men depend on the positive response of their partners in order to fuel their own responsive mechanisms. See A. Nicholas Groth, Men Who Rape (Plenum, 1979). Also see Sylvia Levine & Joseph Koenig eds., Why Men Rape (Toronto: Macmillan, 1982). . . .

7. Onora O'Neill, Between Consenting Adults, 14 Phil. & Pub. Aff. 252 (1985).

Rape, Racism, and the Law

JENNIFER WRIGGINS

... THERE ARE MANY different kinds of rape.[1] Its victims are of all races, and its perpetrators are of all races. Yet the kind of rape that has been treated most seriously throughout this nation's history has been the illegal forcible rape of a white woman by a Black man. The selective acknowledgement of Black accused/white victim rape was especially pronounced during slavery and through the first half of the twentieth century. Today a powerful legacy remains that permeates thought about rape and race.

During the slavery period, statutes in many jurisdictions provided the death penalty or castration for rape when the convicted man was Black or mulatto and the victim white.[2] These extremely harsh penalties were frequently imposed.[3] In addition, mobs occasionally broke into jails and courtrooms and lynched slaves alleged to have raped white women, prefiguring Reconstruction mob behavior.

In contrast to the harsh penalties imposed on Black offenders, courts occasionally released a defendant accused of raping a white woman when the evidence was inconclusive as to whether he was Black or mulatto.[4] The rape of Black women by white or Black men, on the other hand, was legal;[5] indictments were sometimes dismissed for failing to allege that the victim was white. In those states where it was illegal for white men to rape white women, statutes provided less severe penalties for the convicted white rapist than for the convicted Black one.

During slavery, then, the legal system treated seriously only one racial combination of rape—rape involving a Black offender and a white victim. This selective recognition continued long after slavery ended.

After the Civil War, state legislatures made their rape statutes race neutral, but the legal system treated rape in much the same way as it had before the war. Black women raped by white or Black men had no hope of recourse through the legal system. White women raped by white men faced traditional common-law barriers that protected most rapists from prosecution.

Allegations of rape involving Black offenders and white victims were treated with heightened virulence. This was manifested in two ways. The first response was lynch-

6 Harv. Women's L. J. 103 (1983). Permission granted by the Harvard Women's Law Journal © 1983 and the President and Fellows of Harvard College.

ing, which peaked near the end of the nineteenth century.[6] The second, from the early twentieth century on, was the use of the legal system as a functional equivalent of lynching, as illustrated by mob coercion of judicial proceedings special doctrinal rules, the language of opinions, and the markedly disparate numbers of executions for rape between white and Black defendants.

Between 1882 and 1946 at least 4715 persons were lynched, about three-quarters of whom were Black.[7] Although lynching tapered off after the early 1950s, occasional lynch-like killings persist to this day.

The most common justification for lynching was the claim that a Black man had raped a white woman.[8] The thought of this particular crime aroused in many white people an extremely high level of mania and panic. One white woman, the wife of an ex-Congressman, stated in 1898, "If it needs lynching to protect woman's dearest possession from human beasts, then I say lynch a thousand times a week if necessary."[9] The quote resonates with common stereotypes that Black male sexuality is wanton and bestial, and that Black men are wild, criminal[10] rapists of white women.

Many whites accepted lynching as an appropriate punishment for a Black man accused of raping a white woman. The following argument made to the jury by defense counsel in a 1907 Louisiana case illustrates this acceptance:

> Gentlemen of the jury, this man, a nigger, is charged with breaking into the house of a white man in the nighttime and assaulting his wife, with the intent to rape her. Now, don't you know that, if this nigger had committed such a crime, he never would have been brought here and tried; that he would have been lynched, and if I were there I would help pull on the rope.[11]

It is doubtful whether the legal system better protected the rights of a Black man accused of raping a white woman than did the mob. Contemporary legal literature used the term "legal lynching" to describe the legal system's treatment of Black men.[12] Well past the first third of the twentieth century, courts were often coerced by violent mobs, which threatened to execute the defendant themselves unless the court convicted him.[13] Such mobs often did lynch the defendant if the judicial proceedings were not acceptable to them. A contemporary authority on lynching commented in 1934 that "the local sentiment which would make a lynching possible would insure a conviction in the courts."[14] Even if the mob was not overtly pressuring for execution, a Black defendant accused of raping a white woman faced a hostile, racist legal system. State court submission to mob pressure is well illustrated by the most famous series of cases about interracial rape, the Scottsboro cases of the 1930s.[15] Eight young Black men were convicted of what the Alabama Supreme Court called "a most foul and revolting crime," which was the rape of "two defenseless white girls." The defendants were summarily sentenced to death based on minimal and dubious evidence, having been denied effective assistance of counsel. The Alabama Supreme Court upheld the convictions in opinions demonstrating relentless determination to hold the defendants guilty regardless of strong evidence that mob pressure had influenced the verdicts and the weak evidence presented against the defendants. In one decision, the appellate court affirmed the trial court's denial of a change of venue on the grounds that the mobs' threats of harm were not imminent enough although the National Guard had been called out to protect the defendants from mob executions. The U.S. Supreme Court later recognized that the proceedings had in fact taken place in an atmosphere of "tense, hostile, and excited public sentiment."[16] After a lengthy appellate process, including three favorable Supreme Court rulings, all of the Scottsboro defendants were released, having spent a total of 104 years in prison.

In addition, courts applied special doctrinal rules to Black defendants accused of the rape or attempted rape of white women.[17] One such rule allowed juries to consider the race of the defendant and victim in drawing factual conclusions as to the defendant's intent in attempted rape cases. If the accused was Black and the victim white, the jury was entitled to draw the inference, based on race alone, that he intended to rape her. One court wrote, "In determining the question of intention, the jury may consider social conditions and customs founded upon racial differences, such as that the prosecutrix was a white woman and defendant was a Negro man."[18] The "social conditions and customs founded upon racial differences" which the jury was to consider included the assumption that Black men always and only want to rape white women, and that a white woman would never consent to sex with a Black man.

The Georgia Supreme Court of 1899 was even more explicit about the significance of race in the context of attempted rape, and particularly about the motivations of Black men. It held that race may properly be considered "to rebut any presumption that might otherwise arise in favor of the accused that his intention was to obtain the consent of the female, upon failure of which he would abandon his purpose to have sexual intercourse with her."[19] Such a rebuttal denied to Black defendants procedural protection that was accorded white defendants. . . .

The outcome of this disparate treatment of Black men by the legal system was often the same as lynching—death.[20] Between 1930 and 1967, thirty-six percent of the Black men who were convicted of raping a white woman were executed.[21] In stark contrast, only two percent of all defendants convicted of rape involving other racial combinations were executed.[22] As a result of such disparate treatment, eighty-nine percent of the men executed for rape in this country were Black.[23] While execution rates for all crimes were much higher for Black men than for white men, the differential was most dramatic when the crime was the rape of a white *woman*.[24]

The Legacy Today

The patterns that began in slavery and continued long afterwards have left a powerful legacy that manifests itself today in several ways. Although the death penalty for rape has been declared unconstitutional,[25] the severe statutory penalties for rape continue to be applied in a discriminatory manner. A recent study concluded that Black men convicted of raping white women receive more serious sanctions than all other sexual assault defendants.[26] A recent attitudinal study found that white potential jurors treated Black and white defendants similarly when the victim was Black. However, Black defendants received more severe punishment than white defendants when the victim was white.[27]

The rape of white women by Black men is also used to justify harsh rape penalties. One of the few law review articles written before 1970 that takes a firm position in favor of strong rape laws to secure convictions begins with a long quote from a newspaper article describing rapes by three Black men, who at 3 A.M. on Palm Sunday "broke into a West Philadelphia home occupied by an eighty-year-old widow, her forty-four-year-old daughter and fourteen-year-old granddaughter," brutally beat and raped the white women, and left the grandmother unconscious "lying in a pool of blood."[28] This introduction presents rape as a crime committed by violent Black men against helpless white women. It is an image of a highly atypical rape—the defendants are Black and the victims white, the defendants and victims are strangers to each other, extreme violence is used, and it is a group rape. Contemporaneous statistical data on forcible rapes reported to the Philadelphia police department reveals that this rape case was virtually unique. Use of this highly unrepresentative image of rape to justify strict rape laws is consistent with recent research showing that it is a prevalent, although false, belief about rape that the most common racial combination is Black offender and white victim.[29]

Charges of rapes committed by Black men against white women are still surrounded by sensationalism and public pressure for prosecution. Black men seem to face a special threat of being unjustly prosecuted or convicted. One example is Willie Sanders.[30] Sanders is a Black Boston man who was arrested and charged with the rapes of four young white women after a sensational media campaign and intense pressure on the police to apprehend the rapist. Although the rapes continued after Sanders was incarcerated, and the evidence against him was extremely weak, the state subjected him to a vigorous twenty-month prosecution. After a lengthy and expensive trial, and an active public defense, he was eventually acquitted. Although Sanders was clearly innocent, he could have been convicted; he and his family suffered incalculable damage despite his acquittal.

Another recent example is the Alabama case of Thomas Lee Hines.[31] Hines is a young mentally retarded Black man who was accused of raping several white women. The trial judge granted a change of venue, noting, "the facts of the race of the defendant and victims have so overpowered the case as to make it appear to the community as a racial incident."[32] Hines' trial was transferred to a nearby county, where he was convicted by an all-white jury in proceedings marked by frequent outbursts from spectators, sensationalist press coverage, and extensive security to protect the courtroom participants. The appellate court granted a new trial because police behavior coupled with the degree of Hines' retardation called into question the voluntariness of his statements to the police, and stated that the court found that the racially charged trial conditions justified a second change of venue. Hines was eventually declared incompetent for trial and committed to a state institution. . . .

From slavery to the present day, the legal system has consistently treated the rape of white women by Black men with more harshness than any other kind of rape. The punishment for Black offender/white victim rape has ranged historically from castration, to death by torture and lynching, to executions. Today Black men convicted of raping white women receive longer prison sentences than other rape defendants. Innocent Black men also face the threat of racially motivated prosecutions.

This selective focus is significant in several ways. First, since tolerance of coerced sex has been the rule rather than the exception, it is clear that the rape of white women by Black men has been treated seriously not because it is coerced sex and thus damaging to women, but because it is threatening to white men's power over both "their" women and Black men.[33] Second, in treating Black offender/white victim illegal rape much more harshly than all coerced sex experienced by Black women and most coerced sex experienced by white women, the legal system has implicitly condoned the latter forms of rape. Third, this treatment has contributed to a paradigmatic but false concept of rape as being primarily a violent crime between strangers where the perpetrator is Black and the victim white. Finally, this pattern is perverse and discriminatory because rape is painful and degrading to both Black and white victims regardless of the attacker's race.

The Denial of the Rape of Black Women

> Who knows what the black woman thinks of rape? Who has asked her? Who cares?
>
> —*Alice Walker*[34]

The selective acknowledgement of the existence and seriousness of the rape of white women by Black men has been accompanied by a denial of the rape of Black women that began in slavery and continues today. Because of racism and sexism, very little has been written about this denial. Mainstream American history has ignored the role of Black people to a large extent; systematic research into Black history has been published only recently. The experiences of Black women have yet to be fully recognized in those histories. . . .

The rape of Black women by white men during slavery was commonplace and was used as a crucial weapon of white supremacy.[35] White men had what one commentator called "institutionalized access" to Black women.[36] The rape of Black women by white men cannot be attributed to unique Southern pathology, however, for numerous accounts exist of northern armies raping Black women while they were "liberating" the South.

The legal system rendered the rape of Black women by any man, white or Black, invisible. The rape of a Black woman was not a crime. In 1859 the Mississippi Supreme Court dismissed the indictment of a male slave for the rape of a female slave less than 10 years old, saying:

> [T]his indictment can not be sustained, either at common law or under our statutes. It charges no offense known to either system. [Slavery] was unknown to the common law . . . and hence its provisions are inapplicable. . . . There is

no act (of our legislature on this subject) which embraces either the attempted or actual commission of a rape by a slave on a female slave. Masters and slaves can not be governed by the same system or laws; so different are their positions, rights and duties.[37]

This decision is illuminating in several respects. First, Black men are held to lesser standards of sexual restraint with Black women than are white men with white women. Second, white men are held to lesser standards of restraint with Black women than are Black men with white women. Neither white nor Black men were expected to show sexual restraint with Black women.

After the Civil War, the widespread rape of Black women by white men persisted. Black women were vulnerable to rape in several ways that white women were not. First, the rape of Black women was used as a weapon of group terror by white mobs and by the Ku Klux Klan during Reconstruction.[38] Second, because Black women worked outside the home, they were exposed to employers' sexual aggression as white women who worked inside the home were not.[39]

The legal system's denial that Black women experienced sexual abuse by both white and Black men also persisted, although statutes had been made race-neutral. Even if a Black victim's case went to trial—in itself highly unlikely—procedural barriers and prejudice against Black women protected any man accused of rape or attempted rape.[40] The racist rule which facilitated prosecutions of Black offender/white victim attempted rapes by allowing the jury to consider the defendant's race as evidence of his intent, for instance, was not applied where both persons were "of color and there was no evidence of their social standing."[41] That is, the fact that a defendant was Black was considered relevant only to prove intent to rape a white woman; it was not relevant to prove intent to rape a Black woman. By using disparate procedures, the court implicitly makes two assertions. First, Black men do not want to rape Black women with the same intensity or regularity that Black men want to rape white women. Second, Black women do not experience coerced sex in the sense that white women experience it.

These attitudes reflect a set of myths about Black women's supposed promiscuity which were used to excuse white men's sexual abuse of Black women. An example of early twentieth century assumptions about Black women's purported promiscuity was provided by the Florida Supreme Court in 1918. In discussing whether the prior chastity of the victim in a statutory rape case should be presumed subject to defendant's rebuttal or should be an element of the crime which the state must prove, the court explained that:

What has been said by some of our courts about an unchaste female being a comparatively rare exception is no doubt true where the population is composed largely of the Caucasian race, but we would blind ourselves to actual conditions if we adopted this rule where another race that is largely immoral constitutes an appreciable part of the population.[42]

Cloaking itself in the mantle of legal reasoning, the court states that most young white women are virgins, that most young Black women are not, and that unchaste women are immoral. The traditional law of statutory rape at issue in the above-quoted case provides that women who are not "chaste" cannot be raped. Because of the way the legal system considered chastity, the association of Black women with unchastity meant not only that Black women could not be victims of statutory rape, but also that they would not be recognized as victims of forcible rape.

The Legacy Today

The criminal justice system continues to take the rape of Black women less seriously than the rape of white women. Studies show that judges generally impose harsher sentences for rape when the victim is white than when the victim is Black.[43] The behavior of white jurors shows a similar bias. . . .

Evidence concerning police behavior also documents the fact that the claims of Black rape victims are taken less seriously than those of whites.[44] A 1968 study of Philadelphia police processing decisions concluded that the differential in police decisions to charge for rape "resulted primarily from a lack of confidence in the veracity of Black complainants and a belief in the myth of Black promiscuity."[45]

The thorough denial of Black women's experiences of rape by the legal system is especially shocking in light of the fact that Black women are much more likely to be victims of rape than are white women. Based on data from national surveys of rape victims, "the profile of the most frequent rape victim is a young woman, divorced or separated, Black and poverty stricken."[46]

. . . The statistics concerning Black women's rape by white men, however, may be too low. Black women apparently underreport illegal rape to the police—especially rape by white men[47]—and may do the same with victim survey interviewers.

. . . Today women continue to suffer rape in disproportionate numbers, while the criminal justice system still takes the claims of Black rape victims less seriously than the claims of white victims.

The Denial of the Significance of Sexual Coercion

The legal system and American society have acknowledged the existence and seriousness of one racial combination of rape—that of white women by Black men. Courts and commentators justified this focus by exaggerating the trauma white women face when raped by Black men. This characterization allowed the crime of rape to be narrowly defined and treated in a way that denied to all women an effective legal shield against rape. Moreover, the myth that rape is only a crime committed by Black men against white women has obscured and deflected attention from the varied nature, pervasiveness, and influence of the sexual subordination to which all women are subjected. . . .

The attitudes manifested in the rape laws and expressed in the legal literature extend to other areas of the criminal justice system. Police have often been extremely insensitive to rape victims. Rape complainants have been disbelieved by police more frequently than complainants of other crimes. . . . While denial of any experience is a significant indication of powerlessness, the widespread denial of women's experiences of coerced sex is the denial of a phenomenon which deeply affects every woman's life.

The crime of illegal rape is a terrifying, traumatic experience which often has long-term damaging effects on its victims. Illegal rape is much more widespread than is reported to police. . . . Additionally, the fear and threat of rape influences many women who are never actually raped. It restricts movement and forces women to maintain a special wariness about the situations in which they place themselves.

Illegal rape is neither the only nor necessarily the most harmful kind of coerced sex for women. . . . Spousal rape is legal in most states, and its incidence is widespread. Other forms of sexual coercion are also pervasive. The incidence of incest is difficult to calculate, but it is certainly widespread. . . . A large proportion of working women are sexually harassed on the job. . . .

Very little is done about these forms of sexual abuse, and what has been done has largely been done by women themselves, in the last decade. Widespread societal ignorance and general denial of sexual coercion by the legal system persist.[48] . . .

The legal system's treatment of rape is not designed to protect women from sexual coercion. Through discriminatory punishment, the language of opinions, scholarly writing, and the manipulation of doctrine, the legal system has implicitly defined rape so as to limit it to the rape of white women by Black men. The social meaning of rape is thus limited to a Black offender and white victim. In addition, because of the legal system's traditionally narrow definition of rape, coupled with the widespread acceptance of other forms of sexual coercion, the legal system has also implied that illegal rape is the only form of sexual abuse. In fact, both of these implications are false. . . .

Because of the specific social meaning of rape, sole responsibility for the coerced sex of white women has been placed on the shoulders of Black men, and Black women have been ignored as rape victims. Those who work against rape and other forms of sexual coercion must be vigilant not to support this racist social meaning. . . .

Recasting the Form of the Debate—Beyond Legal Reform

. . . The pervasiveness of racism and its historical connection to rape raise complex issues for those who oppose sexual coercion. As leaders of the movement against rape,[49] feminists are responsible for examining closely the implications of their actions and proposals.[50] The foregoing analysis raises considerations often neglected in feminist writing and thus leads to some conclusions about strategies to fight sexual coercion that differ in emphasis from other feminist work.

The legal system has historically ignored or denied the claims of women who have been victims of rape. At the same time, women have been traumatized by the criminal justice system, few men have been convicted of rape, and women continue to be victimized by rape in appalling numbers.

Feminist strategies to combat rape have included encouraging self defense and protection, improving the treatment rape victims receive after their attack, and reforming rape laws so as to increase the conviction rate.

One of the most degrading aspects of rape for victims has been the treatment they receive from the criminal justice system. One of the critical contributions of feminist anti-rape work has been to increase public awareness of this unsympathetic treatment. One proposal to improve the treatment rape victims receive has been to increase the representation of women who deal with rape victims within the criminal justice system.[51] A second proposal has been to exclude evidence of a complainant's prior sexual experiences at trial.[52]

The first proposal is a positive one as far as it goes, but placing more women in law enforcement is not in itself adequate to improve the treatment victims receive. If the women participants are all white, or have little understanding of racism, many of the problems pointed out . . . will remain. Black women's rape claims will continue to lack credibility because white women share with white men notions of Black people's promiscuity and untrustworthiness. The special harshness reserved for Black men who are accused of raping white women will also continue.

If increasing the number of women involved in the legal and criminal justice systems is to create a system more sympathetic to all women, it is imperative that substantial numbers of these women be Black and that all individuals working with rape victims are keenly aware of, and strongly opposed to, racism.

Another proposal for improving the legal system's treatment of rape victims has been the reform of rape statutes to exclude evidence of rape victims' sexual history from trial. Cross-examination on the details of one's sexual history, a common defense technique, is one of the victim's most traumatic contacts with the legal system.[53] Another rationale for this proposal is that the introduction of the rape victim's sexual history as evidence reflects and reinforces misogynistic attitudes about women and sexuality.

In Michigan, where the law has forbidden the introduction of evidence of past sexual behavior since 1975,[54] the overall experiences of victims, as reported by rape crisis center workers and criminal justice participants, seem to have improved markedly.[55] . . .

Another major goal of feminists has been to increase rape convictions. Law reform proposals offered to accomplish this have included limiting the admissibility of evidence of a victim's sexual history, reducing the penalties allowed for rape,[56] and introducing degrees of rape. . . .

It is understandable that many white feminists initially perceive an increased rape conviction rate as a victory. Rape has been denied so consistently by the criminal justice system until so recently that any type of recognition of it by the legal system seems positive. Also, upperclass white women until recently have been fairly isolated in a private sphere in which their subordination to men has been furthered by the law's absence,[57] so that the prospect of the law's presence in an area, seemingly acting on behalf of women, is attractive.

However, the subordination of other groups has been furthered by the law's presence, and rape laws in particular have functioned to further white supremacy. In light of the racist history surrounding the legal system's treatment of rape, the goal of increasing the rape conviction rate must be examined in more detail.

Working to increase the conviction rate for rape is not necessarily a constructive tactic in the struggle against sexual coercion for several reasons. First, most pragmatically, raising the conviction rate has not been shown to have any impact on the incidence of rape, although long-term data are not yet available. Second, given the existing disparities in punishments between whites and Blacks, an across-the-board increase would simply reproduce these disparities. Third, the increasingly racist political climate, and the Supreme Court's destruction of various constitutional procedures to protect defendants, suggest that the punishment disparities are likely to increase. Fourth, to the extent these disparities implicitly indicate that men are being punished on racial grounds and not because they committed rape, the credibility of the underlying claim of sexual abuse is undermined. Fifth, to press for convictions under rape laws suggests that women accept the narrow definitions and limited conceptions of sexual abuse that underlie those laws. Finally, to say that rape should be treated like other crimes is problematic in that it implicitly validates the way other crimes have been and are treated. The criminal justice system has radical shortcomings—the treatment, definition, and punishment of many other crimes should be deplored rather than endorsed. It has refused to protect and indeed has consistently worked against the interests of Black men, Black women, and white women. . . .

Attempting to reform rape laws to increase convictions thus has numerous shortcomings as a feminist strategy. Improving the criminal justice system's treatment of the victim is a positive goal but does not change the fact of women's victimization. A problem with both approaches is that they only address the problems of women who are known victims of illegal rape. This focus is insufficient. First, even if the activity forbidden by rape laws stopped, other powerful forms of women's sexual subordination would persist. Second, given the racist content of the social meaning of rape, struggles limited to illegal rape are likely to have the racist repercussion of targeting Black men.

A response must be devised which goes beyond the formulation of rape as an extraordinary crime to which only some unlucky women fall victim, to a conception that the sexual coercion of women is pervasive, multivariate, and wholly unacceptable in every form. If women go beyond the formulation given by the legal system they may be able to escape some of the traps of racism, and claim their own lives and sexuality.

This means linking rape issues with other issues of sexual coercion such as incest, spousal abuse, and sexual harassment. It also means recognizing that rape will be treated by the criminal justice system in a racist way as long as this society is racist.

Conclusion

> . . . Eyes that only see the bruises inflicted by men miss seeing other bruises and deep scars.
>
> —*Janet Howard* [58]

The legal system's treatment of rape both has furthered racism and has denied the reality of women's sexual subordination. It has disproportionately targeted Black men for punishment and made Black women both particularly vulnerable and particularly without redress. It has denied the reality of women's sexual subordination by creating a social meaning of rape which implies that the only type of sexual abuse is illegal rape and the only form of illegal rape is Black offender/white victim. Because of the interconnectedness of rape and racism, successful work against rape and other sexual coercion must deal with racism. Struggles against rape must acknowledge the differences among women and the different ways that groups other than women are disempowered. In addition, work against rape must go beyond the focus on illegal rape to include all forms of coerced sex, in order to avoid the racist historical legacy surrounding rape and to combat effectively the subordination of women.

Notes

1. By "rape" this article refers not to the legal definition of rape or sexual assault, but rather to "any attempted or completed sexual act that is forced on an individual against his or her will." L. Bowker ed., Rape and Other Sexual Assaults, Women and Crime in America 180, 180 (1981). The term thus includes a wide range of situations, from a stranger assaulting a woman in a dark alley to a husband forcing sex on his wife, regardless of whether penetration is involved or the act is illegal. The term "illegal rape" refers to situations where the imposition of sex is prohibited by law.

This Article addresses only the rape of women by men. Besides being the most prevalent and widely studied kind of rape, it is also an important manifestation of, and means of perpetuating, male dominance. This article argues that the treatment of this kind of rape by the legal system also serves as a weapon of white dominance.

2. See, e.g., Alabama Code of 1852 (death penalty for rape of a white woman by a slave or free Black); Mississippi 1857 Statute (death penalty for attempted carnal connection with or rape of a white female under fourteen by a slave); Tennessee 1858 Law (death by hanging for rape of a free white woman by a slave or free Black); Missouri 1825 Statute (castration for rape or attempted rape by a Black or mulatto); Arkansas Code of 1838 (death penalty for assault with intent to commit rape by a Black or mulatto). Bienen, Rape III—National Developments in Rape Reform Legislation, 6 Women's Rights L. Rep. 170, 173 n.14 (1980). . . . . Although concentrated in the South, statutes distinguishing between the races for sexual crimes were enacted in other states as well. [S]ee also Burns, Race Discrimination—Law and Race in America, in D. Kairys ed., The Politics of Law 89 (1982).

3. . . .H. Catterall ed., 1–3 Judicial Cases Concerning American Slavery and the Negro (1926–1932); see M. Hindus, Prison and Plantation: Crime, Justice and Authority in Massachusetts and South Carolina 1767–1878, 150–161 (1980); K. Stampp, The Peculiar Institution 210–211 (1956).

4. Thurman v. State, 18 Ala. 276 (1850); Dick, a slave, v. State, 30 Miss. 631 (1856).

5. S. Brownmiller, Against Our Will 176 (1975); Evans, Rape, Race, and Research, in C. Owens & J. Bell eds., Blacks and Criminal Justice 75, 79 (1977); see W. Bowers, Executions in America 173 (1974); A. L. Higginbotham, In the Matter of Color 282

(1978); Blackwell, Social and Legal Dimensions of Interracial Liaisons, in D. Wilkinson & R. Taylor eds., The Black Male in America 219, 225 (1977)....

6. A. Raper, The Tragedy of Lynching 1–2 (1933); C. Woodward, The Strange Career of Jim Crow 43 (1974); Note, Constitutionality of Proposed Federal Anti-Lynching Legislation, 34 Va. L. Rev. 944 (1948).

7. A. Rose, The Negro in America 185 (1948) (citing a Tuskegee Institute study). A study by the NAACP found the number of lynchings acknowledged by white officials between 1882 and 1927 to be 4951, with approximately 70% of the victims being Black. White, A Statement of Fact [on Lynching], in H. Aptheker ed., A Documentary History of the Negro People in the United States 1910–1932, 610 (1973).

8. Rose, *supra* note 7, at 185; Woodward, *supra* note 6, at 43; Hall, "The Mind that Burns in Each Body": Women, Rape, and Racial Violence, in A. Snitow, C. Stansell & S. Thompson eds., Powers of Desire: The Politics of Sexuality (1983); Reynolds, The Remedy for Lynch Law, 7 Yale L.J. 20, 20 (1897–1898) (quoting an article that refers to the lynching of a Black man for the alleged rape of a white woman as "the usual crime").

9. Reynolds, *supra* note 8, at 20.

10. The association of Black men with criminality extends back at least to the nineteenth century. Rose, *supra* note 7, at 303. White criminals often capitalized on and perpetuated this stereotype by dyeing their faces black before committing crimes. *Id.* at 304; Johnson, The Negro and Crime, in M. Wolfgang, L. Santz & N. Johnston eds., The Sociology of Crime and Delinquency 419, 422 (2d ed. 1970). The alleged propensity of Black men to rape white women can be seen partly as a manifestation of the criminality stereotype. In 1933, Arthur Raper made this link in trying to explain lynching: "[A]ccording to the popular estimate, all Negroes are essentially alike and are inclined to commit certain crimes, chief of which is the rape of white women." Raper, *supra* note 6, at 50; see Rose, *supra* note 7, at 305. Note that "all Negroes" refers only to Black men; Black women are left out of this formulation.

11. State v. Petit, 119 La. 1013, 1016, 44 So. 848, 849 (1907) (quoting defense counsel)....

12. Chadbourn, Plan for Survey of Lynching and the Judicial Process, 9 N.C. L. Rev. 330, 332 (1931).

13. Raper, *supra* note 6, at 143; Chadbourn, *supra* note 12, at 332–333; see Thompson v. State, 117 Ala. 67, 23 So. 676 (1898) (change of venue granted for Black defendant accused of rape because threats of mob violence threatened defendant's imminent death or would pressure jury into convicting); see also R. Wilkins, Rape: A Case History of Murder, Terror and Injustice Visited Upon a Negro Community (1949).

14. Chadbourn, Lynching and the Law, 20 A.B.A.J. 71 (1934).

15. Patterson v. State, 224 Ala. 531, 141 So. 195 (1932); Powell v. State, 224 Ala. 540, 141 So. 201 (1932); Weems v. State, 224 Ala. 524, 141 So. 215 (1932).

16. Powell v. Alabama, 287 U.S. 45, 51 (1932)....

17. Chastity evidence, for example, was treated differently for Black and white defendants....

18. McQuirter v. State, 36 Ala. App. 707, 709, 63 So. 2d 388, 390 1953) (citations omitted)....

19. Dorsey v. State, 108 Ga. 477, 480, 34 S.E. 135, 136–137 (1899)....

20. In 1965, 18 American jurisdictions allowed the death penalty for rape. Wolfgang & Reidel, Race, Judicial Discretion and the Death Penalty, 407 Annals 120 (1973). Hugo Bedau has written that most criminologists think capital punishment for rape

was "introduced in order to *Keep the Nigras in line*" and "had nothing to do with its deterrent effect." Bailey, Rape and the Death Penalty: A Neglected Area of Deterrence Research, in H. Bedau & C. Pierce eds., Capital Punishment in the United States 336 (1975) (citing unpublished letter) (emphasis in the original).

21. Wolfgang, Racial Discrimination in the Death Sentence for Rape, in Executions in America, *supra* note 5, at 116. A systematic analysis of 1238 convictions for rape between 1945 and 1965 examined many variables in addition to race, such as presence of a weapon and prior record of the defendant, to attempt to account for the disparate numbers of executions. The study concluded that race was the only factor that accounted for the disparities.

22. *Id.* at 110–113. . . .

23. Wolfgang & Reidel, *supra* note 20.

24. Wolfgang, *supra* note 21, at 110–113. The NAACP-LDEF challenged the constitutionality of the death penalty partly on the grounds that the execution rate disparities for rape constituted racial discrimination. M. Meltsner, Cruel and Unusual 73–105 (1973). This argument was not accepted by the Supreme Court in its decision limiting the circumstances in which the death penalty could constitutionally be imposed. See Furman v. Georgia, 408 U.S. 238 (1972). . . .

25. Coker v. Georgia, 433 U.S. 584 (1977).

26. LaFree, The Effect of Sexual Stratification by Rape on Official Reactions to Rape, 45 Am. Soc. Rev. 842, 852 (1980).

27. H. Field & L. Bienen, Jurors and Rape 117–118 (1980). This difference is not solely attributable to the type of crime at issue, since many studies show that Black defendants usually receive stricter sentences than white defendants for crimes committed against whites other than rape, *id.* at 117, and that white jurors are generally lenient on Black defendants who commit crimes against Blacks. Note, The Case for Black Jurors, 79 Yale L.J. 531, 534 (1970). But the degree of misinformation and sensationalism associated with the accusation of rape is unique. . . .

28. Schwartz, The Effect in Philadelphia of Pennsylvania's Increased Penalties for Rape and Attempted Rape, 59 J. Crim. L., Criminology & Police Behavior 509 (1968).

29. . . . Recent victim survey data contradicts this prevalent belief; more than four-fifths of illegal rapes reported to researchers were between members of the same race, and white/Black rapes roughly equaled Black/white rapes. Bowker, Women as Victims: An Examination of the Results of L.E.A.A.'s National Crime Survey Program, in L. Bowker ed., Women and Crime in America 158–164 (1981). . . .

30. Suffolk Superior Court Indictment No. 025027–36, 025077 (1980).

31. Hines v. State, 384 So. 1171 (Ala. Crim. App. 1980). . . .

32. *Id.* at 1183.

33. Part of the reason for this social meaning of rape is that laws against rape originate in the conception of women as property. See Brownmiller, *supra* note 5, at 7–10, 201; L. Clark and D. Lewis, Rape: The Price of Coercive Sexuality 115–132 (977). . . .

34. A. Walker, Advancing Luna—and Ida B. Wells, in You Can't Keep a Good Woman Down 85, 93 (1981).

35. Brownmiller, *supra* note 5, at 165; A. Davis, Women, Rape and Class 24–27 (1981); B. Hooks, Ain't I a Woman: Black Women and Feminism 24–27 (1981); G. Lerner, Black Women in White America 149–150 (1972); J. Noble, Beautiful also Are the Souls of My Black Sisters 35 (1978); see DuBois, Divine Right, in A Documentary History, *supra* note 7, at 53.

36. L. Curtis, Criminal Violence 22 (1974).

37. George, a slave, v. State, 37 Miss. 306 (1859). The following year the state legislature, evidently shocked by the decision, outlawed attempted or actual rape of a Black or mulatto female under 12 by a Black or mulatto male, and made it punishable by death or whipping. 1860 Miss. Laws 62. The legislature refused to recognize the rape of adult Black females and the rape of any Black females by white men.

38. See Lerner, *supra* note 35, at 172–181.

39. See Hooks, *supra* note 35, at 56–59. . . .

40. . . . Black women's claims were not taken seriously regardless of the offender's race. In a 1971 study on judges' attitudes toward rape victims, a judge was quoted as saying: "with the Negro community, you really have to redefine rape. You never know about them." Bohmer, Judicial Attitudes Towards Rape Victims, 57 Judicature 303 (1974). A vivid example of the judicial system's response to Black women's claims of sexual harassment is the account by a nurse published in 1912: "I remember well the first and last work place from which I was dismissed. I lost my place because I refused to let the madam's husband kiss me. . . . I didn't know then what has been a burden to my mind and heart ever since; that a colored woman's virtue in this part of the country has no protection. When my husband went to the man who had insulted me, the man . . . had him arrested! I . . . testified on oath to the insult offered me. The white man, of course, denied the charge. The old judge looked up and said: "'This court will never take the word of a nigger against the word of a white man.'" More Slavery at the South, 72 The Independent, Jan. 25, 1912, at 197–200, *reprinted in* G. Lerner, Black Women in White America 155–156 (1972).

41. Washington v. State, 38 Ga. 370, 75 S.E. 253 (1912).

42. Dallas v. State, 76 Fla. 358, 79 So. 690 (1918), quoted in Note, Statutory Rape: Previous Chaste Character in Florida, 13 U. Fla. L. Rev. 201, 203–204 (1960).

43. LaFree, *supra* note 26, at 847–848. A 1968 study of rape sentencing in Maryland revealed that in *all* 55 cases where the death penalty was imposed the victim had been white, and that between 1960 and 1967, 47% of all Black men convicted of criminal assaults on Black women were immediately released on probation. The average sentence received by Black men, exclusive of cases involving life imprisonment or death, was 4.2 years if the victim was Black, 16.4 years if the victim was white. Howard, Racial Discrimination in Sentencing, 59 Judicature 121, 123 (1975).

44. See M. Amir, Patterns in Forcible Rape 11 (1971); Peters, The Philadelphia Rape Survey, in I. Drapkin & E. Viano eds., Victimology: A New Focus, vol. III, Crimes, Victims and Justice 186 (1975); Note, The Victim in a Forcible Rape Case: A Feminist View, 11 Am. Crim. L. Rev. 335, 343 (1973). The relatively high credibility accorded white women's accusations of rape against Black men was mitigated if the woman was known to socialize with Blacks.

45. Comment, Police Discretion and the Judgment that a Crime Has Been Committed—Rape in Philadelphia, 117 U. Pa. L. Rev. 277, 304 (1968).

46. Karmen, Women Victims of Crime: Introduction 185, 188, in B. Price & N. Sokoloff eds., The Criminal Justice System and Women: Offenders, Victims, Workers (1982).

47. There is conflicting commentary as to whether Black women are more or less likely than white women to report rape to the police. Lee Bowker explains that the National L.E.A.A. Survey published in 1976 found that, "white rape victims were much more likely to report the crime to the police (59%) than were Black rape victims (36%)." Bowker, *supra* note 29, at 173. Allen Johnson, however, claims, "the available

evidence suggests that nonwhites are more likely than whites to report their assaults." Johnson, On the Prevalence of Rape in the United States, 6 Signs 136, 145 (1980). . . . Police behavior may be an especial deterrent to Black women's reporting. When the race of the assailant is taken into account, there is agreement that Black women tend not to report rapes by white men. In a 1971 study of rape in Oakland, California, few Black women would report being raped by white men. One respondent told the questioners: "No black woman would report being raped by a white man to the police in Oakland. They might report it to the Panthers, but never the police." Agopian, Chappell & Geis, Black Offender and White Victim: A Study of Forcible Rape in Oakland, California, in Victimology III, *supra* note 44, at 101. See Curtis, *supra* note 36; see also Socialist Women's Caucus of Louisville, The Racist Use of Rape and the Rape Charge 5–6 (July 1975) (discussion of the rape of Black women by Alabama police during the Civil Rights movement); Davis, *supra* note 35, at 173 (the rape of Black women by Chicago police in 1974).

48. The problems of sexual harassment, incest, and spousal abuse have received very little attention and action until very recently. For examples of recent discussions of these problems, see C. MacKinnon, Sexual Harassment of Working Women 158–174 (1979) (sexual harassment); F. Rush, The Best Kept Secret: The Sexual Abuse of Children 137–138 (1980) (incest); L. Walker, The Battered Woman 212–213 (1979) (spousal abuse).

49. See Rose, Rape as a Social Problem: A By-Product of the Feminist Movement, 25 Soc. Probs. 75, 75–77 (1977).

50. Various commentators have noted that white feminists often demonstrate ignorance of the racist uses of the rape charge, and have pointed out the limitations of anti-rape theories and strategies that fail to deal with issues of racism. See, e.g., Davis, *supra* note 35, at 178–182, 196–199; A. Edwards, Rape, Racism and the White Women's Movement: An Answer to Susan Brownmiller (2d printing 1979); The Racist Use of Rape and the Rape Charge, *supra* note 47; Braden, A Second Open Letter to Southern White Women, 4 Southern Exposure 50 (Winter 1977); Does the Women's Movement Compromise the Struggle of Minorities? 4 Women's Rts. L. Rep. 27, 31 (1977); Friedman, Rape, Racism and Reality, Aegis, Summer 1981, at 14; Hare, Revolution Without A Revolution: The Psychology of Sex and Race 13, The Black Scholar, Summer 1982, at 14; 1981, at 14; Sagarin, Forcible Rape and the Problem of the Rights of the Accused, in D. Chappell, R. Geis & G. Geis eds., Forcible Rape 146 (1977); Sands, Rape and Racism in Boston: An Open Letter to White Feminists, Off Our Backs, Jan. 1980, at 16–17.

51. See Brownmiller, *supra* note 5, at 434–437; Note, *supra* note 44, at 352.

52. See J. Marsh, A. Geist & N. Caplan, Rape and the Limits of Law Reform 22–23 (1982); L. Holmstrom & A. Burgess, The Victim of Rape: Institutional Reactions 279 (1978); Rose, *supra* note 49, at 80; Note, *supra* note 44, at 353.

53. Holmstrom & Burgess, *supra* note 52, at 179–183; Note, *supra* note 51, at 350–351; Comment, The Rape Victim: A Victim of Society and the Law, 11 Willamette L.J. 36, 45–56 (1974).

54. Michigan's sexual assault statute, which took effect in 1975, is widely considered one of the nation's most innovative and comprehensive rape laws and has served as the model for many states. Bienen, *supra* note 2, at 172. The most detailed published research on the impact of rape laws deals with Michigan. See Marsh, Geist & Caplan, *supra* note 52. For these reasons, the discussion on reforming rape laws is limited to Michigan.

55. J. Marsh, A. Geist & N. Caplan, *supra* note 52, at 68–71.

56. Many reformers favor reducing penalties for rape because they think the severity of traditional penalties deters juries from convicting. Bienen, *supra* note 2, at 173.

57. See Taub & Schneider, Perspectives on Women's Subordination and the Role of Law, in D. Weisberg ed., Feminist Legal Theory: Foundations 9 (Temple Univ. Press, 1993).

58. Howard, Battered and Raped: The Physical/Sexual Abuse of Women, in F. Delacoste & F. Newman eds., Fight Back! 80 (1981).

Equality Theory, Marital Rape, and the Promise of the Fourteenth Amendment

ROBIN WEST

DURING THE 1980s a handful of state judges either held or opined in dicta what must be uncontrovertible to the feminist community, as well as to most progressive legal advocates and academics: the so-called marital rape exemption, whether statutory or common law in origin, constitutes a denial of a married woman's constitutional right to equal protection under the law.[1] Indeed, a more obvious denial of equal protection is difficult to imagine: the marital rape exemption denies married women protection against violent crime solely on the basis of gender and marital status. . . .

[T]hat a number of feminist commentators[2] and a few state court appellate judges[3] felt it necessary to argue to a still skeptical and often hostile listening audience that marital rape exemptions constitute a denial of the Fourteenth Amendment's guarantee . . . evidences the degree to which women's injuries still are trivialized and rendered invisible by a pervasively misogynist legal, political, and social culture. That the arguments of these advocates met with such limited success in abolishing the exemption reveals how short a distance women have come, and how far we have yet to travel, toward full equality and the necessary result of equality: an assurance that the state will provide a modicum of safety in our private lives against sexual assault.

States [made] limited progress in reforming marital rape law during the 1980s. A few abolished the exemption entirely[4]—but only a few. The majority continue to permit rape or sexual assault within marriage by according it a lower level of criminality than extramarital rape of sexual assault, by criminalizing only certain kinds of marital rape, or by criminalizing only first-degree rapes. Some states, ironically in the name of reform, may have worsened the problem of marital rape by extending the exemption to include women who rape their husbands in order to make the exemptions appear "gender neutral."[5] This extension provides a false neutrality to an institution that almost invariably endangers only women's lives. . . . Furthermore, movements in other states to extend the marital rape exemption offset [gains]. For example, some states have extended the marital rape exemption to include cohabitants and formerly married persons.

42 Fla. L. Rev. 45 (1990). Reprinted with the permission of the Florida Law Review. Copyright 1990.

This pattern of one-step-forward, two-steps-back progress on the criminalization of marital rape illustrates the general pattern of thinking in the 1980s regarding marital rape. While virtually every progressive commentator, judge, or legislator (feminist and otherwise) who seriously has considered the issue readily has concluded that these laws violate equal protection, and while explicit vocal support from conservatives for the exemption almost entirely has disappeared from scholarly literature, no major upheaval of the law reflects or foreshadows such progressive unanimity. . . . Those who understand the exemption view it as an antiquated holdover from an earlier and discarded view of women. But the educated public, and even the legal community, lacks general awareness that these laws not only inflict extensive damage on innumerable women's lives, but also constitute a constitutional outrage.

[In this essay], I want to use the marital rape laws and the movements directed toward their reform to raise two related issues about equal protection ideology and equality theory. The first issue is theoretical; the second is strategic.

The theoretical issue is the following: Why is it that this overwhelmingly obvious constitutional flaw in our criminal law has not, in the last ten years, attracted more attention, generated more outrage, and simply collapsed of its own unconstitutional weight? Why, after several decades of case law and academic commentary on the meaning, original intent, and political vision embodied in the equal protection guarantee of the Fourteenth Amendment, do we still have marital rape exemptions, the express purpose of which is to deprive married women of the state's protection against rape? My argument will be that the endurance of marital rape exemptions, despite their apparent unconstitutionality, partly results from the dominant understanding of the meaning of equality and constitutionally guaranteed equal protection. [It] illustrates the inadequacies and ambiguities in the equality theory within which equal protection arguments must be framed. In other words, the endurance of marital rape exemptions partly is a function of the inadequacy of the dominant or mainstream political theory of equality, which informs dominant legal understandings of the constitutional mandate of equal protection.

This much of the argument should not be surprising or unfamiliar to a feminist audience; feminist and progressive discontent with traditional equality theory and equal protection law reached an all-time high in the 1980s.[6] The endurance of marital rape exemptions simply illustrates the inadequacies in modern equal protection law alleged by feminists and progressives over the last decade. More specifically, however, and perhaps more controversially, I will argue that the inadequate theories of equality and equal protection that we have inherited and that have muted the force of constitutional challenges to the marital rape exemption are not solely the product of the bad faith, sexist, racist, classist, or conservative politics of the Supreme Court Justices who authored those doctrines. They also are a product of the adjudicative institutional context in which those theories have evolved. Mainstream views of the meaning of equality and equal protection respond not only to political biases, but also to the institutional constraints of their judicial origins. The Supreme Court, and therefore the rest of us, including the feminist community, generally have examined, developed, and debated the meaning of the Fourteenth Amendment equal protection guarantee in the particular context of judicial challenges to state classifications. This adjudicative context, I believe, has skewed and limited our understanding of equal protection and our understanding of how we should make the promise of equal protection a reality. More specifically, our confinement to the judicial forum has truncated a wide range of potential constitutional claims, including the particular claim that marital rape exemptions violate the Fourteenth Amendment.

This paper proposes not so much a novel approach to marital rape exemption or to the Fourteenth Amendment, but rather a new direction of progressive and feminist-informed constitutional arguments. I will urge that we should direct our arguments away from a hypothetical judicial audience and toward a congressional audience. If the dominant understandings of equal protection truly are inadequate, and if judicially developed law has determined the content of those inadequate understandings, then "equal protection" might take on a very different and more helpful meaning if developed in a congressional, rather than a judicial, context. . . .

[T]his essay discusses three contrasting understandings of the meaning of equal protection: the Supreme Court's dominant rationality approach; Professor MacKinnon's proposed dissident "antisubordination" approach; and what I label the "pure protection" understanding, which may be closest to the original meaning of the clause. [Finally,] this essay will then re-examine the constitutionality of marital rape exemptions in light of these competing views of the meaning of equal protection. . . .

II. Three Theories of Equality

A. The Rationality Model

The dominant judicial interpretation of the equal protection clause is that the clause generally seeks to ensure that legislators govern in a fair-handed and well-motivated way, rather than out of a malicious desire to hurt some groups or a biased desire to help others.[7] Of course, all legislation unavoidably burdens some groups while helping others, but the Constitution requires the legislative allocation of those burdens and benefits to be directed toward legitimate governmental ends. Accordingly, legislation must be rational, or evenhanded: legislation must not be the product of bias, malice, or differing levels of concern for some citizens over others. Rather, legislation and the classifications of legislation must be rationally related to legitimate state ends. In accord with general usage, I call this dominant view the rationality model of equal protection.[8]

The rationality model, as it has developed doctrinally, imposes three easily summarized constraints upon legislative classifications. First, as the name of the model implies, legislative classifications must be rational: "like groups must be treated alike." Thus, a legislative classification that defines groups A and B, divides them, and then treats them differently must "map on to" or "mirror" a distinction in the world between groups A and B that is relevant to some legitimate state objective. If no relevant difference between groups A and B exists, then legislation that treats them differently is irrational and unconstitutional because it denies the citizens in the burdened group equal protection of the laws. . . .

The rationality model imposes a second constraint on classification. The legislative classification must be relevant to a legitimate end. If the classification furthers a legitimate state objective only marginally or not at all and imposes a significant cost on the burdened class, then the legislation might be unconstitutional. . . .

Finally, the rationality model requires that the articulated legislative end be a legitimate one. Legislators may classify and differentially assist or burden certain groups, but only if they are doing so in the public interest or toward the vindication of some public value. Moreover, the end toward which the classification is directed must be an end that legislators are permitted to pursue. . . .

These three basic principles of rationality, relevance, and legitimacy provide the foundation for modern equal protection jurisprudence. These three constraints motivated the Court to adopt various levels of "scrutiny" for different types of legislation. . . . Under the rationality, relevance, and legitimacy principles summarized above, the Court has conceded that most economic or social legislation is presumptively rational, relevant to legitimate governmental ends, and, hence, constitutional. . . . Classifications that involve race, however, are entirely another matter. The Court generally has held that most racially explicit classifications are presumptively suspect, and, therefore, their rationality, their relevance, and their legitimacy must be strictly scrutinized. Such strict scrutiny typically has resulted in the invalidation of these statutes. . . .

The Court seems to believe that gender classifications fall somewhere between economic classifications (presumptively legitimate) and racial classifications (presumptively illegitimate). According to the Court, some biological and social "real differences" between men and women do exist; consequently, some legislative classifications that distinguish men and women may be rational. Further, women have not been targeted as a class in the same way as blacks have, and, therefore, the Court does not as readily presume that gendered classifications are badly motivated.[9] Unlike racial classifications, gender classifications are not necessarily irrational, and the ends toward which they aim are not necessarily illegitimate. Thus, the judicial scrutiny that the Court applies to gender classifications is higher than that which the Court applies to economic legislation, but not as strict as that which the Court applies to racial classifications. While the Court has struck down some gender-based statutes,[10] it has upheld more than a few.[11]

Finally, as the Court held in Washington v. Davis,[12] legislation that does not facially discriminate between men and women or whites and blacks, but nevertheless adversely affects the interests of persons in those classes, is not, for that reason alone, unconstitutional. Rather, facially neutral legislation is unconstitutional only if the law-making body intended its adverse impact. . . . Therefore, for such legislation to violate Fourteenth Amendment norms, the challenger must show a specific legislative intent to harm. Absent a showing of specific intent, the Court will uphold a facially neutral statute as constitutional.

B. The Attack on Formal Equality and the Rationality Model

The central judicial presumption of the rationality model, that racial classifications always are irrational and that gender classifications usually are irrational, rests on a theory of equality grounded in a universalist vision of our shared human nature. That vision is unquestionably noble and appealing in its aspiration. Its guiding assumption is that all persons—women, men, blacks, and whites—are more or less the same with respect to the traits and issues that affect or should affect political decisionmaking.[13] Women as well as men, and blacks as well as whites, wish to lead and can lead meaningful lives ennobled by participation in the shared, political life of the public sphere, enriched by fairly compensated and intrinsically rewarding work in the private sphere, and enlivened by stimulating, nurturant relationships in the intimate sphere. Blacks no less than whites, and women no less than men, benefit from the liberal arts and educational opportunities deepening intellectual adult life. Blacks and women, like whites and men, need and value opportunities to develop athletic potential. Many women, like many men, treasure and pursue the opportunity to enlist in the country's armed services and willingly devote their lives to strengthen the country's defense capabilities against outside aggression. Women, like men, and blacks, like whites, can be competent and fair jurors, estate executors, lawyers, and doctors. The list could be extended endlessly. Legislation that classifies on the basis of gender or race and that burdens women's or blacks' political, economic, athletic, or educational opportunities in any sphere in which women and men and blacks and whites are similarly situated is irrational, and hence, unconstitutional. The universalist vision promotes this formal or legal ideal of equality and provides the basis for the rationality interpretation of the equal protection clause. In all areas of life in which blacks and whites and women and men are the same, the legislator must treat them as the same.

During the 1980s feminist legal theorists registered increasing dissatisfaction with the rationalist model of equal protection, the formal or legal vision of equality toward which it aspires, and the universalist conception of human nature in which it is rooted. Such feminist dissatisfaction with formal equality stems not so much from a suspicion that the Court's practice cannot live up to the promise of equal treatment, but from the nature of the promise itself. Formal equality—across-the-board equal treatment of women and men—would have only a limited effect on women's lives for two basic reasons. First, women and men are not similar, the universalist premises of the rationality model notwithstanding. To summarize a great deal of recent feminist writings: women have different perceptions and experiences of the social world, different understandings of moral obligations, different perspectives of the biological role in reproduction, different ways of assimilating knowledge, different feelings toward housework and childraising, different vulnerabilities toward different potential harms, different life patterns, and a radically different history. Insistence upon the "same-

ness" of men and women in the fact of undeniable differences between them and social subordination of women by men enshrines male attributes as the "norm" and denies the existence and value of female attributes, pursuits, and ways of life. Any constitutional standard based on the theory that men and women are the same will
benefit only those women *least* in need of the law's protection—women, such as the
"professional women" of the 1980s, who already are most like men. Formal equality
will ignore or even hurt those women "least" like men: traditional homemakers and
women trapped in low-paying and gender-segregated jobs. Finally, formal equality is
irrelevant to *all* women in those spheres of our lives in which we are most clearly unlike men: our more marked vulnerability to sexual assault, our greater involvement in
childraising and housework, and our different role in the reproductive process. The
rationality model fails because it rests on a false assumption of sameness and aspires
toward a goal of similar treatment that will help only marginally a few already-privi-
leged women. Its consequence will be not true equality but further harm to most
women.

The "sameness-difference" problem with the dominant rationality model has
prompted several feminists, notably Christine Littleton, to advocate a modification or
reform of the rationality doctrine itself.[14] Littleton has argued that equality should
mean not just treating groups the same when they are the same, but also treating them
differently when they are different, and doing so in such a way as to ensure a rough
equality of outcomes. Under this modified view of the rationality model of equality,
which Littleton calls the equal acceptance model, the equal protection clause requires
legislators to be "equally accepting" of men and women. If women are the same as men
in certain aspects, they should be treated similarly. But in aspects in which women and
men differ, the law should be as equally responsive to men's and women's differing
characteristics, attributes, needs, values, vulnerabilities, and aspirations. The impulse
behind the "acceptance" picture of equality is strikingly feminist: the acceptance
model requires legislators not only to treat like groups alike, but also to refrain from
inscribing the imprimatur of "normalcy" upon male attributes, characteristics, preferences, and modes of life.

Other feminists, notably Catharine MacKinnon, Ruth Colker, and Mary Becker, argue that the rationality model had a second and deeper problem that Littleton's reform, although well-meaning and even welcome, failed to address. The larger problem
with the rationality model is not just that women are different from men in ways which
formal equality ignores, but that formal equality itself, whether or not modified by Littleton's "acceptance" amendment, targets the wrong evil. Irrationality, or treating like
groups differently, should not be the target of the equal protection clause, nor should
rationality, treating like groups alike, be regarded as its goal. Rather, antisubordina-
tionists argue that the social subordination of some groups by others (women by men
and blacks by whites) is the target of the equal protection clause. Hence, only substantive equality between these groups, or the end of social subordination, is its goal.
The rationality model fails to target the social, economic, and political differences that
account for women's subordinate status. . . .

C. Alternative Understandings of Equal Protection: Antisubordination and Pure Protection

The critiques of the rationality model summarized above have given rise to a second, and dissident, understanding of the mandate of equal protection. Catharine MacKinnon has delineated this second understanding with great force and eloquence in her writings. Often called the antisubordination model of equal protection, this view perceives the equality that equal protection guarantees as substantive, not formal. Hence, the test of legislation under the equal protection clause is not whether the legislative classification "fits" a pre-existing reality, but rather whether the classification furthers the subordination of women vis-à-vis men or attempts to end that subordination. MacKinnon explained the antisubordination model:

> [T]he only question for litigation is whether the policy or practice in question integrally contributes to the maintenance of an underclass or a deprived position because of gender status. This disadvantage which constitutes the injury of discrimination is not the failure to be treated "without regard to" one's sex that is the injury of arbitrary differentiation. The unfairness lies in being deprived because of being a woman or a man, a deprivation given meaning in the social context of the dominance or preference of one sex over the other.[15]

The antisubordination model, then, aspires not to formal equality, but to substantive equality. The goal is not a world in which state legislators treat men and women "the same," but rather a world in which men and women, whether the same or different, are social equals. The antisubordination model envisions a world in which women are no more vulnerable to assault than men are, no less valued than men are, no more underpaid than men are, no less cared for than men are, no less represented than men are, and no less participatory in the public sphere than men are. In sharp contrast to the rationality model, the antisubordination model rests not on a universalist vision of our "shared" human nature, but on a political vision of our present unequal social reality. For constitutional purposes, the relevant issue is decidedly not that women are "the same" as men but are treated differently or that women are different from men and are treated the same. The relevant issue is that women are subordinate to men in the public, social, economic, private, and intimate spheres. Thus, the aim of the equal protection clause should be to highlight and rectify that political reality and not to highlight and mirror similarities or differences between men and women. Legislation that promotes or encourages social equality is constitutional, but that which promotes or encourages social subordination is unconstitutional.[16]

A third possible understanding of equal protection that has received relatively little attention in either feminist commentary or cases, but which may be closer to the plain meaning, intent, and history of the clause than either the rationality or the antisubordination models, is what I call the pure protection model. To deny equal protection might mean that a state refuses to grant to some citizens the protection against private wrongdoing that it grants to others. For example, a state's refusal to protect black citizens from homicidal attacks by whites or a state's passivity in the fact of widespread lynching and private violence would constitute a paradigmatic violation of the constitutional guarantee of equal protection of the law. . . . The pure protection model views the target of the equal protection clause as the denial of the state's protection to some of its citizens from private violence, aggression, and wrongdoing. The goal is a community in which all are equally protected by the state against private encroachment of rights.

One way to describe the vision behind this pure protection model of equal protection, and to a lesser extent behind the antisubordination model, is in terms of state sovereignty. The pure protection model envisions a world in which the state is the sole, legitimate repository of organized force exercised by some individuals against others. The equal protection clause would not tolerate the existence of separate "regimes" of sovereignty, backed by unchecked and private systems of organized violence. The pure protection model requires that we live under only one sovereign—the state. The white race cannot constitute a separate sphere of sovereignty over the black race, nor can men constitute a separate sovereignty over women. Only the state has the power to exercise dominion, through the use of organized violence, over its citizens. Any other exercise of violence and power by one group of citizens over another is criminal, and the state is constitutionally obligated to guard its citizens against such domination.

III. The Constitutionality of the Marital Rape Exemption

Predictably, most of the scholarly commentary and virtually all of the judicial opinions that have addressed the constitutionality of marital rape exemptions have analyzed the constitutionality of marital rape exemptions under the rationality model of equality and equal protection. The commentary and opinions illustrate not only the strength and sensibility of the rationality model, but also the problems and limits of its formal vision of equality, its universalist vision of human nature, and its doctrinal tests of "rationality." These arguments take several different forms, depending on whether the law under scrutiny is gender-specific (exempts wives from rape laws) or gender neutral (exempts "spouses"). A summary of these arguments follows:

First, some states employ marital rape exemptions that are explicitly gendered: rape is defined as nonconsensual intercourse with a woman other than one's wife. The two-step argument that these gender-specific statutes are unconstitutional is straightforward. First, such gender-specific statutes explicitly legislate on the basis of either gender alone or gender plus marital status. Either classification constitutes a suspect class giving rise to at least the mid-level scrutiny. As the Court has noted on multiple occasions, women have been the objects of stereotypical and stultifying thinking that has seriously compromised their enjoyment of and participation in the public world. For that reason alone, legislation that treats women differently from men deserves heightened scrutiny. Furthermore, although the Court never has held as much, historically oppressive treatment renders married women a suspect class. In America and English common law heritage, the law did not acknowledge a married woman's existence.[17] Thus, a law that burdens either women or married women, and marital rape exemptions can do both, should be subject to heightened scrutiny.

Second, under a heightened scrutiny, if the gender-specific legislation is to be sustained, the state must articulate an "important governmental interest" which is "substantially related" to the statutory classification. This articulation, the argument proceeds, a state cannot possibly do. Proponents of the marital rape exemption typically assert that the state's important interest in promoting marital harmony and intimacy, or, alternatively, its interest in encouraging reconciliation of warring spouses, justifies the statute. Yet, the state undeniably has little or no legitimate interest in protecting the harmony or intimacy of a marriage deteriorated to the point of violent sexual abuse, and it has equally as little interest in encouraging the reconciliation of spouses whose relations no longer are consensual, much less harmonious. Thus, because these statutory classifications are not "substantially related" to an important governmental interest, gender-specific marital exemption laws are unconstitutional.

On the other hand, marital exemptions that define rape as nonconsensual sex with anyone except one's spouse, rather than nonconsensual sex with anyone except one's wife, are gender neutral. While these statutes avoid the heightened scrutiny triggered by gender explicit classifications, they nevertheless also are unconstitutional under traditional rationality standards. A gender-neutral classification that adversely impacts upon women and appears to be motivated by an intention to hurt women is as unconstitutional as is a sex-specific classification. Marital rape exemptions are strikingly easy to trace to misogynist roots, from Hale's infamous argument that a married woman is presumed to consent to all marital sex and, therefore, cannot be raped,[18] to the common law's assumption that marriage results in the unification of husband and wife and that marital rape thus constitutes rape of oneself, a legal impossibility.[19] Whether cleansed through the filter of sex-neutral language or not, the marital rape exemption clearly is rooted in an intention to deprive the married woman of the protection of the state and to subject her to the will, sovereignty, and unchecked violence of her spouse. Because this intention serves no "important governmental interest," gender-neutral marital rape exemptions are unconstitutional as well.

Furthermore, whether gender-specific or gender-neutral, marital rape exemptions create a host of irrational distinctions that underscore their unconstitutionality: between married couples and unmarried couples who cohabitate; between married, but estranged partners still living together and married partners living apart (who often are not included in the scope of the exemption); between partners who have filed for divorce and those who have not; and between partners who have indicated their intentions to end the marital union and those who have not. Apart from the effects of the marital rape exemption on women, and even granting the importance of the state's interest in protecting marital harmony, these distinctions are irrational. What rational, legitimate state goal could possibly justify the lines drawn between these groups?

Paradoxically, perhaps the strongest traditional, rationality-based argument against marital rape exemptions has not appeared in case law. This argument asserts that these statutes create an irrational distinction between married women and all other persons and that this distinction is not justified by real differences between those two groups. The classification and differential treatment of married women rests on the assumption that married women, unlike all other persons, have no interest in receiving protection from the state against violent and sexual assault. But, married women, exactly like men and unmarried women, clearly need physical security in their private spheres. Just as all human beings without the security and dignity of knowing that the state ensures their protection, women cannot lead autonomous, meaningful, and pleasurable lives. Married women need to know that sexual assault against them is criminal and punishable when committed by their husbands. For that matter, they need to know that sexual assault is as criminal when committed against them as would be any intrafamilial crime of violence. The irrational distinction of the marital rape exemption is between the protected needs and rights of the average citizen to be safe from criminal assault and the unprotected same needs and rights of married women. The creation of a class of citizens subject to legalized violence is the core effect, if not the purpose, of the marital rape exemption. Surely, the constitutional guarantee of equal protection must guard against that effect.

Marital rape exemptions, then, are arguably unconstitutional, even under the traditional rationality model of equal protection, for reasons that are at the heart of that model's utopian vision. We do indeed share a common humanity, part of which is to need protection against private violence. Women are as much in need of that protection as are men. Like men, without that protection women are rendered vulnerable to the whim, will, sovereignty, instincts, fiat, and command of those who are stronger. And, like men, when women are rendered weak. they become incapable of living the kinds of lives the ideal liberal state is surely meant to foster: autonomous, pleasurable, productive, civic, and educated. When state passivity renders women vulnerable to private violence, women, like men, become stunted, fearful, self-alienated, childlike, and servile. Women are no more naturally suited to such servility and dominance than are their brothers, fathers, sons, and husbands.

All of these arguments, however, pose serious doctrinal problems. These problems reflect the inadequacies of the rationality model of equal protection and formal equality that have troubled feminists throughout the 1980s. Simply stated, for each argument catalogued above, a fairly obvious legal rejoinder is available, which is equally, if not better, grounded in modern equal protection doctrine. I am not using a linguistic quirk or playing a lawyer's game. My point is not the familiar indeterminacy claim that any legal argument gives rise to an equally credible rejoinder. Rather, the doctrinal and legal basis for the legal rejoinders rest on the fundamental, political reality of women's lives—the irreducible fact of women's subordination to men through unchecked sexual violence. The universalist vision and formal equality aspirations of the rationality model of equal protection simply fail to address this reality. Thus, the very existence and viability of these rejoinders evidence the limits and dangers of current under-standings of the equal protection clause.

First, the argument for the unconstitutionality of gender-specific rape exemptions summarized above is anything but airtight. As noted earlier, in contrast to the impossi-ble requirement of a compelling state interest required to sustain racially explicit legis-lation, gender-specific legislation is constitutional if the state can articulate an "impor-tant governmental objective" substantially furthered by the gendered classification. Nothing prohibits a court from determining that protection of marital privacy, insular-ity, and harmony is such an important state interest that protection of the husband against criminal charges of rape substantially furthers that interest.[20] The political real-ity that the availability of this legal rejoinder reflects is that, to the mainstream, the very sphere of private subordination that harms women and concerns feminists appears to be not only a legitimate, but also an important or even compelling state interest. This political reality also reflects a deeper social reality. The obstacles to women's equal par-ticipation in public life and enjoyment of private life are so thoroughly ingrained in our societal habits, institutions, and thought patterns that they appear not as obstacles to equality, but as the essence of private life. Surely, protecting the allure of romance, the domain of sentiment, and the pleasures of intimacy is a compelling state interest. The bottom line is that the same reality experienced by the raped wife as a daily ritual of vi-olence, abuse, and horror strikes the feminist as unconscionable state passivity in the face of private subordination and strikes the feminist lawyer as the denial of equal pro-tection. But it conceivably appears to the Court as an "important" or "compelling" state interest in marital privacy, marital harmony, and spousal reconciliation.

The argument for the unconstitutionality of gender-neutral marital rape exemp-tions also rests on shaky ground. The legal uncertainty reflects not the uncertainty or indeterminacy of legal arguments generally, but rather societal ambivalence towards women's equality. Gender-neutral marital rape exemptions undoubtedly are the prod-uct of a history of discriminatory attitudes toward women. Nevertheless, a court con-ceivably could decide that, ancient history notwithstanding, a statute recently cleansed of gender-specific language is freed of its misogynist heritage and that its recent leg-islative history provides the sole source of its constitutionality. Surely one could argue that gender-neutral marital rape exemptions, similar to the one in the Model Penal Code[21] endorsed in this decade, rest not on a desire to harm women, but on a desire to protect the institution of marriage.

As is evidenced by this theory, the presumption that the gender-neutral marital rape exemptions are constitutional because they respect the sameness of men and women ignores the very real differences between husbands and wives. Women and men are very differently situated within marriage. Overwhelmingly, husbands are larger, stronger, and wealthier than wives. A gender-neutral statute that treats spouses similarly by ac-cording them the same immunities from rape prosecution and hence the same vulner-ability to marital rape ignores these crucial differences and perpetuates the marital sub-ordination of women. As many feminists suggest, in the light of the societal differences between women and men, the presumption of fairness and constitutionality on universalist grounds typically accorded gender-neutral statutes may be generally unwarranted. In the case of marital rape exemptions, however, the presumption of sameness in the face of life-threatening differences looks not only unwarranted but also grotesque.

Most importantly, the arguable constitutionality of all marital rape exemptions, both gender-specific and gender-neutral, vividly exemplifies the antisubordinationist reservations about the rationality model of equal protection. The rationality arguments that underlie traditional equal protection analysis not only are doctrinally unstable, they also overlook the terrifying injustice of these statutes—for precisely the reasons MacKinnon's, Becker's, and Colker's critiques of formal equality suggest. Indeed, the virtue of rationality and the vice of irrationality is worse than irrelevant to the real injustice of these exemptions. After all, rationality problems with these statutes can and sometimes have been cured by extending rather than eliminating the scope of the exemption. If married couples and cohabitants cannot rationally be treated differently, the marital rape exemption should be extended to include cohabitants. By the same perverse logic, if married women and unmarried women cannot rationally be treated differently, rape law should be eliminated altogether. At the extreme, if married women and all other persons cannot rationally be treated differently, the criminal sanction should be eliminated. Presumably, these arguments would and should fail, but a model of equal protection that implies their coherence is profoundly wrong.

The irrationality of marital rape exemptions is not their fundamental flaw. The evil flaw of these exemptions is not that they irrationally treat married couples differently from cohabitants, or married women differently from unmarried women, or husbands differently from rapists unacquainted with their victims, or women differently from men. The evil is that they legalize, and hence legitimate, a form of violence that does inestimable damage to all women, not only those who are raped. In addition to the obvious violence, brutality, and terror marital rape exemptions facilitate, marital rape exemptions, like the rapes they legalize, also sever the central connection to selfhood that links a woman's pleasure with her desires, will, and actions.[22] The will of the married woman who learns to accept routinized rape is no longer ruled by or even connected to her desires. Eventually, her desires are no longer a product of what she enjoys or what she has learned to enjoy. What the victim of routinized rape within marriage does, sexually, is a product not of what the victim wills but of what her attacker demands. As an immediate consequence, her will becomes a function not of her desires but of his desires. Eventually her desires become a function not of her pleasures, but of his pleasures; she wants literally to please him rather than herself because to please herself is too dangerous. The victim of marital rape gains survival, but she sacrifices self-sovereignty. In other words, she sacrifices the ability to control her own will and to determine her own actions, pleasures, and desires free from external influence. In short, she sacrifices selfhood.[23]

To call the damage occasioned by statutes protecting this direct subordination of self to the necessity of survival an irrationality simply is wrong. The damage occasioned by these statutes is the subordination, and in many cases the annihilation, of the psychic, physical, emotional, and erotic female self. Under a rationality model th⸲ clear fact entirely escapes constitutional notice. The exemption is constitutional if rational and unconstitutional if irrational. Surely, the state acts irrationally when it complies with this profoundly personal, violent subordination. The determination of rationality depends on the Court's assessment of the importance of the state's goals. If the state wants to pursue the goal of marital privacy, harmony, and spousal reconciliation at the cost of female self-sovereignty, and if the Court decides that the goal of marital privacy is important (which surely it could), then the marital rape exemption is an imminently rational, hence constitutional, way to achieve this goal. But, whether the law is rational or irrational, the state's complicity in this pervasive regime of private domestic violence is clearly unequal. It denies married women, in the most literal sense, the protection of its laws. The rationality model of equal protection quite dramatically fails to target the state's complicity in this subordinating annihilation of married women's selfhood.

In contrast, both the evil and the inequality perpetuated by marital rape exemptions become strikingly apparent under either the dissident antisubordination or historical pure protection model of equal protection. Under the antisubordination model a state action violates the Fourteenth Amendment guarantee if the state complies with the subordination of women by men. Without question, marital rape exemptions do precisely that. The antisubordination model locates the target of the Fourteenth Amendment equal protection guarantee, not in the irrationality of a state's legislative scheme, but in a state's complicity in private or social subordination. When the state encourages or permits a significant increase in the illegitimate power of one social group over another, the state defies the safeguards of the equal protection clause. The marital rape exemption is an instance of state complicity in men's subordination of women through routinized violent sexual assault and the threat of violent assault. Each assault spurs self-denial, self-abnegation, and self-diminution for women and furthers political ratification of women's psychological and psychic subservience. Each assault constitutes a political act of subordination. Under the antisubordination model even state complicity, not to mention explicit state endorsement, in this private subordination clearly is unconstitutional.

Similarly, the pure protection model highlights the unconstitutionality of these statutes rather than obscures it. This model recognizes that the Fourteenth Amendment ensures that all citizens equally enjoy the basic terms of the social contract, that the state protects all from private assault, that the state protects all from their own vulnerability, that the state recognizes the equality of all citizens under law, and that the state assures that they live under no separate sovereign authority. Only with such protection may persons construct the public, productive, responsible, autonomous lives that the liberal state and its rule of law ideal envisions. A marital rape exemption, regardless of its intent, its history, or its purported state purpose, creates precisely the insulated, separate sphere of sovereignty that the pure protection view of the equal protection clause forbids. With the exemption in place, a marriage becomes not a nurturant, safe haven offering shelter from the storm, but a separate political world in which the husband is sovereign and the wife subject. Moreover, her vulnerability to this organized, dehumanizing, and alienating violence is fully legitimated by the state under which she lives. Sexual force and violence within marriage is unleashed and legalized, and legalized force and violence, of course, is the precondition of political power. A marriage thus becomes a separate state of sovereignty. The marital rape exemption creates, fosters, and encourages not marital intimacy, harmony, or reconciliation, but a separate state of sovereignty ungoverned by law and insulated from state interference. Whatever other "legitimate" goals the state may thereby further, such a separate political order, under a pure protection model, precisely is what the Fourteenth Amendment forbids the state to tolerate. . . .

Whether or not the United States Supreme Court or state supreme courts ever rule on the unconstitutionality of marital rape exemptions, Congress has the power, the authority, and arguably the duty, to do so, under section five of the Fourteenth Amendment.[24] Congress could enact a federal law guaranteeing protection to all women against violent sexual assault. Consistent with rationality requirements, this law would prohibit irrational discrimination against married women in the making and enforcement of rape laws. This federal law also would guarantee, consistent with the antisubordination mandate of the Fourteenth Amendment, that states would not perpetuate or insulate the sexualized social, private, or intimate subordination of women by men. Lastly, consistent with the "protection" mandate of the Fourteenth Amendment, it would guarantee that no state would deny to women protection of the state against private criminality. The political will may or may not be sufficient to sustain such a bill, but the constitutional authority for it surely exists.

A law of this sort at least would remove the anomaly that, while the marital rape exemptions strike most concerned lawyers and legal academicians as spectacularly unconstitutional, under present doctrine, no clear-cut argument presents itself. Perhaps the main reason for this lag between consensus, argument, and action is logistic. Given a court-based system of constitutional adjudication in which courts have near exclusive responsibility for interpreting and enforcing constitutional law, cases that properly raise issues of this sort will be extremely rare. Thus, when a rape defendant raises the issue of the unconstitutionality of the marital rape exemption—indeed, to the best of my knowledge, the only scenario to date in which the issue has been raised—he is likely to be arguing that the state's refusal to extend the exemption to him, is an unconstitutional denial of his equal protection rights. A court could respond to this sort of argument by striking the exemption in its entirety. However, a court faced with this argument could avoid ruling on the constitutionality of the exemption by simply rejecting the contention that the failure of the state to extend the exemption constitutes a denial of equal protection. A suit for damages under the Civil Rights Act or directly under the Fourteenth Amendment, the other major vehicles for bringing a constitutional infirmity to a court's attention, also lacks logistical viability. A court hardly could find any branch or agent of state government liable for failing to arrest or prosecute when no state statute criminalizing the conduct exists. State immunity doctrines, of course, would bar an action against the legislature for failing to criminalize conduct. For logistic reasons alone, the issue seems ripe for legislative, rather than judicial, constitutional decisionmaking.

The second reason for urging a congressional rather than judicial response to the unconstitutionality of marital rape exemption lies in the fact that Congress may be more willing than the judiciary to interpret seriously the Fourteenth Amendment as forbidding marital rape exemptions. Congress is more likely to view marital rape exemptions as subordinating women and insulating a separate sovereignty of legitimized force, thereby denying women's rights to equal protection under law. Congress may be more open to these arguments not only because of its present political composition, but for institutional and theoretical reasons as well. Under the Court, Congress is not obligated to ensure that legislation rationally map on the pre-existing real distinctions. Furthermore, at least on occasion, Congress aggressively has sought to dismantle and restructure the social, private, and even intimate structures that collectively create and mask the hierarchies of daily life. Unlike the Court, Congress does not recoil inevitably at the prospect of undertaking significant reconstructions of social life. . . .

If we think of the Fourteenth Amendment as a moral and political guide for reconstructive legislation aimed at eradicating illegitimate social subordination and private spheres of insulated, violent sovereignty, marital rape exemptions surely are a sensible place for Congress to start to fulfill its constitutional obligations. A dismantling of the private regime of sexual violence against women could affect socially women's public and private lives as greatly as the dismantling of private regimes of segregation and institutionalized racism has affected blacks. As was the case with the desegregation campaign, the legal recognition of a constitutional right to protection against private sexual violence in the domestic sphere, without more, could change and expand not only women's rights, privacy, security, and safety, but also women's senses of self and others' senses of women as fully participatory, represented, acknowledged, and respected members of society. . . .

Finally, the foundational and permanent recognition of women's rights to be free from forced marital sex that can come about only through constitutional decisionmaking may be a prerequisite to further progress on a range of related issues regarding women's physical and sexual security. Date rape and acquaintance rape, for example, unlike marital rape, clearly are criminal, but they may be insulated from legal prosecution and public condemnation at least in part because of their shadow resemblance to marital rape, which is still fully protected in many states and underprosecuted in virtually all. The marital exemption, in brief, is simply the most brutal of all possible expressions of the social inclination to trivialize women's interest in physical sexual security. Until women have physical and sexual security, both their public contributions and their private lives will be stunted, not only by personal fears, but by social and legal inferiority fueled by a public perception of female personhood perverted by the deep knowledge of women's legal vulnerability. Women will not have that security until they have established their constitutional right to be equally protected against laws that encourage their physical and sexual subordination and render them subject to private states of separate sovereignty. Conversely, when the law guarantees women that security, the gains will be immense. All women, married and single, and all men might learn what it means to live in a truly democratic home, in a truly nurturant social world, transformed and inspired by a newly empowered, equally respected feminist community.

Notes

1. See, e.g., Merton v. State, 500 So. 2d 1301, 1305 (Ala. Crim. App. 1986); Williams v. State, 494 So. 2d 819, 830 (Ala. Crim. App. 1986); People v. Liberta, 64 N.Y. 2d 152, 474 N.E. 2d 567, 573–576, 485 N.Y.S. 2d 207, 213–216 (1984); People v. DeStefano, 121 Misc. 2d 113, 163–164, 170, 467 N.Y.S. 2d 506, 515–516 (County Ct. 1983); Shunn v. State, 742 P. 2d 775, 778 (Wyo. 1987).

2. See Freeman, But If You Can't Rape Your Wife, Who(m) Can You Rape?: The Marital Rape Exemption Re-Examined, 15 Fam. L.Q. 1, 29 (1981); Note, To Have and To Hold: The Marital Rape Exemption and the Fourteenth Amendment, 99 Harv. L. Rev. 1255 (1986); Note, 24 J. Fam. L. 87, 87–93 (1985); Comment, For Better or for Worse: Marital Rape, 15 N. Ky. L. Rev. 611, 631–634 (1988).

3. See, e.g., People v. Liberta, 64 N.Y. 2d 152, 163–164, 170, 474 N.E.2d 567, 573–576, 485 N.Y.S. 2d 207, 213–216 (1984) (opinion by Judge Wachtler advancing the most complete argument).

4. For examples of judicial abolishment of the marital rape exemption, see *supra* note 1. For examples of legislative abolishment of the exemption, see Alaska Stat. §11.41.443 (repealed 1989); Colo. Rev. Stat. §18-3-409 (Supp. 1989); Fla. Stat. §794.011 (1989); Me. Rev. Stat. Ann. tit. 17A, §251 (1983 & Supp. 1989); *id.* §252 (repealed 1989); Neb. Rev. Stat. §§28-319 to -320 (1985); N.J. Stat. Ann. §2C:14-4(b) (West 1982); N.D. Cent. Code §12.1-20-01 to -03 (1985 & Supp. 1989); Or. Rev. Stat. §§163.355–.375 (1987); Vt. Stat. Ann. tit. 13, §3252 (Supp. 1989); Wis. Stat. Ann. §940.225(6) (West Supp. 1989).

5. Cf. S.D. Codified Laws Ann. §22-22-1.1 (1988) (recognizing spousal rape).

6. See, e.g., C. MacKinnon, Toward a Feminist Theory of the State 215–237 (1989); Becker, Prince Charming: Abstract Equality, in D. Weisberg ed., Feminist Legal Theory: Foundations 221 (Temple Univ. Press, 1993).

7. For a general discussion, see L. Tribe, American Constitutional Law §16-13 to -17, at 1465–1488 (1988).

8. For general discussions of the rationality approach to equal protection, see J. Ely, Democracy and Distrust 145–148 (1980); Gunther, Foreword: In Search of Evolving Doctrine on a Changing Court: A Model for a Newer Equal Protection, 86 Harv. L. Rev. 1, 20–24 (1972); Michelman, Politics and Values or What's Really Wrong with Rationality Review?, 13 Creighton L. Rev. 487 (1979); Sunstein, Naked Preferences and the Constitution, 84 Colum. L. Rev. 1689, 1697–1698, 1713–1714 (1984); Westen, The Empty Idea of Equality, 95 Harv. L. Rev. 537, 569–577 (1982).

9. This insight explains the Court's uncertainty over whether gender-based discriminations hurt or help women, or discriminate against men rather than women. See, e.g., Califano v. Webster, 430 U.S. 313 (1977) (per curiam) (more lenient formula to calculate social security benefits for women than men); Califano v. Goldfarb, 430 U.S. 199, 207–208 (1977) (plurality opinion); *id.* at 217–218 (Stevens, J., concurring in the judgment) (gender-based difference between widow and widowers for social security benefits).

10. See, e.g., Craig v. Boren, 429 U.S. 190 (1976); Stanton v. Stanton, 421 U.S. 7 (1975); Weinberger v. Wiesenfeld, 420 U.S. 636 (1975); Frontiero v. Richardson, 411 U.S. 677 (1973); Reed v. Reed, 404 U.S. 71 (1971).

11. See, e.g., Califano v. Webster, 430 U.S. 313 (1977); Schesinger v. Ballard, 419 U.S. 498 (1975); Kahn v. Shevin, 416 U.S. 351 (1974).

12. 426 U.S. 229 (1976).

13. The vision is also, in some of its forms, unquestionably feminist. For a strong defense and explication of the virtues of the model from a feminist point of view, see Williams, Notes from a First Generation, 1989 U. Chi. Legal F. 99.

14. See Littleton, Reconstructing Sexual Equality, in D. Weisberg ed., Feminist Legal Theory: Foundations 248 (Temple Univ. Press, 1993).

15. C. MacKinnon, Sexual Harassment of Working Women 117 (1979).

16. The antisubordination model has much to commend it, not only to women's progress, but also as a constitutional rule. It is the essence of simplicity. Doctrine developed under this model would not bear the burdens of two-tiered review, suspect class analysis, the real difference doctrine, and the intent requirement. As Professor MacKinnon noted, "the *only* question for litigation" is whether the statute subordinates women, or challenges that subordination. MacKinnon, *supra* note 15, at 117 (emphasis added); see also *supra* text accompanying note 15. The antisubordination model of equal protection, however, also is riddled with problems, many of them pragmatic. Most importantly, because of its simplicity, the antisubordination model could be extremely difficult to apply to particular cases: it is much easier to state the standard than to ascertain whether a particular piece of legislation has met the standard. Feminist scholar and lawyer Sylvia Law explains: "Professor MacKinnon's approach is ambitious, but it adds unnecessary complexity to the application of sex equality doctrine in a large number of cases. The determination of what reinforces or undermines a sex-based underclass is exceedingly difficult. Professor MacKinnon may overestimate judges' capacities to identify and avoid socially imposed constraints on equality. She disregards our history in which laws justified as protecting women have been a central means of oppressing them. Most fundamentally, her proposed standard may incorporate and perpetuate a false belief that a judicially enforced constitutional standard can, by itself, dismantle the deep structures that 'integrally contribute' to sex-based deprivation." Law, Rethinking Sex and the Constitution, 132 U. Pa. L. Rev. 955, 1005 (1984). Even accepting Professor Law's criticism, the major problem with the model is somewhat simpler: for whatever reasons, antisubordination approaches to equal protection, regarding sex or race, have not met with judicial acceptance.

17. See Note, To Have and To Hold, *supra* note 2, at 1256–1258.

18. M. Hale, Historia Plactorum Coronae: The History of the Pleas of the Crown 636 (1936).

19. For a good discussion of the history of the exemption, see Note, To Have and To Hold, *supra* note 2, at 1255–1258.

20. Indeed, the "privacy" cases under the substantive due process doctrine, including Roe v. Wade, 410 U.S. 113 (1973), itself, seems to bolster such an argument. See generally Griswold v. Connecticut, 381 U.S. 479 (1965); Pierce v. Society of Sisters, 268 U.S. 510 (1925); Meyer v. Nebraska, 262 U.S. 390 (1923).

21. Model Penal Code §213.0, .6 (1989).

22. See generally D. Russell, Rape in Marriage (1983) (describing effects of marital rape exemptions). . . .

23. See generally West, The Difference in Women's Hedonic Lives, herein at 162.

24. See U.S. Const. Amend. XIV, §5; see also Katzenbach v. Morgan, 384 U.S. 641, 650 (1966) (section 5 of the Fourteenth Amendment is a positive grant of legislative power authorizing Congress to exercise its discretion in determining the need for and nature of legislation to secure Fourteenth Amendment guarantees).

◈ PART III

EMPLOYMENT

Section 5

Employment

A. The Work-Family Conflict, Occupational Segregation, and Comparable Worth

Introduction

FEMINISTS IN BOTH the first and the second waves of feminism have been concerned with ameliorating women's work life. In the nineteenth century feminists worked to improve conditions for women factory workers, to secure equal pay, and to permit married women to retain their earnings.

From 1868 to 1870, Elizabeth Cady Stanton and Susan B. Anthony advocated reform of women's working conditions in their journal *The Revolution*.[1] Sarah Grimke deplored the fact that women failed to receive equal pay.[2] Among the "grievances" listed in the Declaration of Sentiments, authored by Elizabeth Cady Stanton and others, were married women's common law disability to retain their wages; women's difficulties securing "profitable employment"; their inability to receive "equitable pay"; and their exclusion from many professions.[3]

Early liberal feminists argued that, because women were men's equals, they were entitled to equal rights in the economic as well as the political sphere.[4] Legal reform was a primary means of securing those rights. Nineteenth-century feminists were staunch advocates of a wave of state legislation (referred to as Married Women's Property Acts) that improved the economic status of married women.[5]

Twentieth-century feminists, similarly, have utilized legal channels to secure rights. Feminists championed protective labor laws that restricted women's hours of employment and prohibited employers from employing women in occupations that were thought to be injurious to their physical and moral well-being.[6] The Supreme Court examined the constitutionality of such legislation in Muller v. Oregon,[7] upholding restrictions on working conditions based on women's differences from men. As one commentator describes the rationale on which *Muller* was based:

First, women are inherently more in need of protection from overwork because of their physical structure, especially when performing their 'maternal functions,' and are inherently incapable of asserting fully their own rights as well as men. Secondly, women are the bearers of the race; therefore, the well-being of society depends on their well-being, and their freedom can be restricted for the sake of the unborn child and society.[8]

Muller signaled a major triumph in the struggle to improve working conditions.

Today, however, feminists view *Muller* in a different light,[9] debating whether protective legislation represents a victory or a defeat for women. *Muller*'s rationales are increasingly regarded as suspect. Feminists see the justification of women's weaker physical condition as paternalistic, in protecting women who are capable of decision making and in reinforcing gender stereotypes. The justification of women's role as childbearers is objectionable in that it treats women as objects and subordinates their rights to those of children.[10]

Feminists have continued the battle, through legislative and judicial channels, to improve working conditions for women. Their work builds on the New Deal legislation, the Fair Labor Standards Act,[11] which first recognized the legitimacy of government regulation of working conditions. The Equal Pay Act of 1963[12] requires employees to receive equal wages for equal work; Title VII of the Civil Rights Act of 1964[13] prohibits employment discrimination on the grounds of race, color, religion, sex, or national origin.[14]

Feminists urged legal reforms, campaigning to ensure maternity leave, to end occupational segregation by sex, to secure pay equity by means of "comparable worth" (job reclassification to raise wages in female-dominated occupations to the level paid in male occupations of comparable worth), and to end sexual harassment in the workplace.[15] Underlying these efforts is a central concern with women's differences from men and whether these differences necessitate special protection.

The essays in this chapter explore several issues concerning women and employment, including the work-family conflict, occupational segregation, and comparable worth.

The Work-Family Conflict

The work-family conflict (the difficulties women encounter juggling work and family responsibilities) stems from women's increasing participation in the labor force, especially among mothers of young children. Concern with the work-family conflict surfaced early in the women's movement, as research explored women's primary responsibility for housework and their attitudes toward it.[16]

Although contemporary feminist theory continues to focus on the conflicting demands of family and work, especially in the sociological literature,[17] the legal literature has been slow to address this issue. For a long time, legal attention emphasized only the need for maternity/family leaves in the context of the special treatment/equal treatment debate.[18] This lacuna in the legal literature has now been remedied. Mary

Joe Frug was one of the first legal scholars to suggest that the labor market is "hostile" to working mothers.[19] She argued that the traditional work schedule is inflexible for primary caretakers of young children. Women often must compromise their employment opportunities to accommodate childrearing. In order to achieve equality for working mothers, Frug concluded that legislation was necessary.[20]

Still another legal scholar, Kathryn Abrams, has explored workplace norms that contribute to the work-family conflict.[21] She concurs with sociologists (discussed subsequently) who suggest that the workplace is a gendered institution. Abrams advocates transformation of workplace norms to obtain equality in the workplace. The work-family conflict is explored further in an essay herein by Nancy Dowd.

Occupational Segregation

This chapter turns next to the problem of occupational segregation, or the classification and stereotyping of certain jobs by gender. Since the beginning of this century, women have made dramatic gains in labor force participation. In 1890 women constituted 18 percent of the labor force; by 1992, this number had risen to 58 percent.[22] Nonetheless, segregation remains a major obstacle.

Specifically, in 1990, of the 56 million women in the labor force, one-third worked in 10 of 503 occupations listed by the Census Bureau, predominating in retail sales, food preparation, elementary school teaching, nursing, and cashiering.[23] The disparity is especially pronounced for women of color.[24] Reskin and Padavic conclude pessimistically, "Despite World War II, the women's liberation movement, and affirmative action, the most common occupations for women in 1990 were almost identical to those that employed the most women in 1940."[25]

Scholars have noted some encouraging trends, however. England finds that sex segregation declined slowly until about 1970, when the decline accelerated, reflecting women's increased entry into male jobs. The decline continued in the 1980s, although at a slower pace.[26] However, she adds that, rather than culminating in occupational integration, new patterns of resegregation may be emerging *within* occupations.[27]

What are the consequences of sex segregation in employment? Reskin and Padavic respond:

> Separating groups into different places and different roles makes it easier to treat them unequally, and it implies that treating them differently is acceptable. In contemporary societies, which use people's jobs to place them in the status system and distribute income and prestige, segregating the sexes into different jobs contributes to women's lower pay and lesser social power—at work, in their families, and in the larger society.[28]

A primary consequence, then, is the gap between men's and women's salaries. The disparity is substantial: salaries of white females are 67 percent of those of white males; salaries of African-American females are 82 percent of those of African-American males.[29] Richmond-Abbott amplifies: "Wage differentials occur with job segregation because, by concentrating in only certain fields, women increase the supply of workers for these jobs and decrease their own wages."[30] Still another consequence is the lowered prestige of predominantly female occupations.[31] In addition, occupational segregation wastes talent and "plays a fundamental role in maintaining sex inequality."[32]

Several sociological and economic explanations have been offered to explain occupational segregation.[33] England characterizes these explanations as employees' *choices* versus structural *constraints*.[34] Explanations stemming from choice include human capital theory and gender role socialization. Constraints include male power or resistance, institutional inertia, statistical discrimination, taste discrimination, and gendered organizations.

"Choice" Explanations of Occupational Segregation

HUMAN CAPITAL THEORY [35]

Human capital theory is based on a belief that women's primary commitment is to their family. This preoccupation, the theory holds, contributes to women's being less attached or committed to the labor force. It prevents them from obtaining the necessary education, job training, and experience. In short, women become less productive than men in the workplace.[36]

This theory also provides an explanation for occupational segregation. That is, women's family orientation, the theory argues, leads them to choose traditionally female occupations—for example, those that require less effort and permit intermittent employment. This theory assumes that women choose occupations based on rational choice, that is, occupations compatible with family responsibilities.[37]

GENDER ROLE SOCIALIZATION [38]

Another theory for occupational segregation suggests that socialization predisposes women and men to choose certain jobs. Because of childhood socialization, boys and girls learn appropriate gender roles. This process inculcates different values and preferences that influence occupational selection. For example, studies reveal that men place higher value on salary, status, autonomy or freedom from supervision, and the potential for promotion and leadership. On the other hand, women value altruism, creativity, and working with people.[39] These values, learned through the socialization process, predispose women to choose employment that is easy to combine with family responsibilities.

"Constraints" Explanations of Occupational Segregation

MALE POWER OR RESISTANCE [40]

Explanations of occupational segregation also include external factors. One sociological theory posits that men, as a dominant group, seek to preserve their advantage in the workplace. They perceive women as a threat to their position. They fear that women will fail to contribute their share or that women will change the workplace. Men then resist women's entry into the labor market. "Sometimes the resistance is simply exclusion; at other times it is subtle barriers that block women's advancement or open harassment."[41] Male resistance is so pervasive that it leads Reskin to conclude pessimistically that neither occupational segregation nor comparable worth will improve women's employment status because men will subvert these remedies.[42]

INSTITUTIONAL INERTIA

The theory of institutional inertia posits that industries manifest an inertia to change.[43] That is, if an industry or firm hires only men, this pattern continues due to custom or tradition. Institutional inertia contributes to occupational segregation because, once sex discrimination occurs in the initial hiring process, it persists as more employees of only one sex are promoted.

STATISTICAL DISCRIMINATION

Another theory posits models of employers' discrimination based on beliefs about statistical data. England describes various such models.[44] In the first, employers base hiring decisions on sex group average productivity (using a group's average to gauge individual qualifications). Alternatively, employers base hiring decisions on sex group differences in *variances* rather than averages. That is, employers may prefer a group that reflects a smaller variance from the average in terms of productivity. Finally, employers base employment decisions on the assumption that race or sex differences affect the predictive validity of selection instruments, such as tests. Discrimination in employment, then, constitutes the employer's rational response based on these beliefs.

TASTE DISCRIMINATION

Economists have proposed other models of discrimination. Gary Becker has theorized a "taste model"—that employers may have a "taste for" discrimination.[45] Although Becker applied his theory to race discrimination, sociologist Paula England suggests that the model applies equally to sex discrimination.[46] Taste discrimination encompasses employers' personal tastes as well as their consideration of the tastes of customers or coworkers.[47] Employers may be willing to offset their distaste for employing women or minorities, but only if women or minorities are willing to work at lower wages.[48]

GENDERED ORGANIZATIONS

One sociological theory maintains that the work environment is gendered.[49] That is, the workplace has a culture that is socially constructed. In this way organizations, in formal and informal ways, institutionalize the sexual hierarchy that advantages men. Employers construct gendered workplaces both intentionally and unintentionally.[50]

Employers, of course, are not alone in constructing gendered workplaces. Employees also contribute, as men and women create a workplace culture with masculine or feminine values and ideologies. Engendering the workplace, Reskin and Padavic argue, has four functions: (1) to socialize new employees to informal workplace rules; (2) to dignify the job; (3) to exclude unwelcome outsiders; and (4) to minimize oppressive aspects of the job.[51] The gendered workplace thus impedes opportunities for integrating the labor market.

Sociological studies have revealed that organizations reflect a resistance to integrating women, despite a legal mandate to do so.[52] Studies suggest that, even in occupations with significant increases in the proportion of women, organizational resistance contributes to a process known as "resegregation,"[53] as subfields adapt to the influx of women by creating new divisions of labor. Newly integrated entry-level positions may become female ghettos. Alternatively, devaluation or marginalization may occur as newly female-dominated fields decrease in status.[54] In addition to the preceding sociological and economic explanations, feminist philosophical perspectives also enhance our understanding of occupational segregation.

Feminist Theoretical Perspectives

LIBERAL FEMINISM

Liberal feminists believe that women's underrepresentation in the public arena, rather than "a result of choices made freely by women," is a result of discrimination.[55] NOW, usually thought of as a liberal feminist organization, reflects the objective of eliminating discrimination.[56] Resolutions adopted at NOW's national conventions have focused on discrimination in employment, in addition to abortion, childcare, marriage, and lesbians' custody rights.[57] NOW's liberal philosophy encompasses the belief that legal reform can create equality of opportunity and protect freedom of choice.

Liberal feminists subscribe to a view that physical differences between women and men are irrelevant. Thus, they support sex-blindness, generally, in the application and formulation of the law.[58] Although some liberal feminists believe that physical differences should play no role in the workplace, others have abandoned their original requirement of sex-blindness to support maternity leaves and affirmative action programs.[59]

Most liberal feminists also support comparable worth as an important weapon to combat employment discrimination.[60] As Paula England points out, liberal feminist organizations (such as NOW and the National Women's Political Caucus) support this strategy to achieve equal pay, perceiving it as an issue of equal treatment.[61]

England rebuts the position of those liberals who argue that comparable worth is too radical.[62] She counters the claim that equal treatment should be limited only to ensuring equal access to hiring and promotions, by arguing that "without equality between men and women in distributions across occupations and earnings, young women cannot have equal opportunity for mentors with similar experiences, role models, and so forth."[63]

MARXIST FEMINISM

Marxist analysis of women's oppression rests on the assumption that women wage laborers suffer the same oppression as the working class. Wives suffer a double burden, oppressed by both their husbands and their exclusion from public life.[64] To many Marxist feminists, the family contributes to women's subordination by relegating women to the private sphere.[65] Many modern thinkers criticize the Marxist belief that women will achieve liberation by entering the labor force. For example, Tong cites such theorists as Eli Zaretsky, Ann Foreman, Michele Barrett, Johanna Brenner, Nancy Holmstrom and Maria Ramos for concurring that both family and work must be transformed.[66]

Marxist feminists joined some union leaders in challenging the market basis of wages via the comparable worth movement.[67] For Marxist feminists, the comparable worth movement has revolutionary potential to equalize wages and alleviate women's poverty.[68] Tong cites, in particular, the work of Marxist feminists Theresa Amott and Julie Matthaei for the proposition that the comparable worth movement could undermine capitalist assumptions about the value of work.[69] Amott and Matthaei urge pursuing comparable worth in conjunction with demands for job security, retraining programs, and plant-closing legislation.

SOCIALIST FEMINISM

Socialist feminists resist the attempt to label class as the primary agent of women's oppression. In contrast to Marxist feminists, socialist feminists address both capitalism and patriarchy, believing that economic conditions and socially imposed differences must be remedied.[70] Unlike liberal feminists or Marxist feminists, socialist feminists emphasize women's differences.[71] In their preoccupation with sexuality and reproduction, they believe that change must target childbearing and childrearing. Socialist feminists concur that the sexual division of labor must be eliminated.

Socialist feminists recognize that women's productive work differs from men's: women's work is less prestigious, lower paid, and defined as less skilled.[72] Heidi Hartmann, author of a classic work on occupational segregation, argues that the root of women's disadvantaged status lies in an interaction between patriarchy and capitalism.[73] By keeping women's wages low outside the home, men keep women dependent so that women will continue to perform labor at home.[74] Women's domestic roles further weaken their position in the labor market. Thus, men benefit from their own higher wages as well as from the domestic division of labor.[75]

The solution to women's subordination, according to Hartmann, is for men to yield their favored positions (both at home and in the market) in the division of labor.[76] It is essential, she argues, to address subconscious behavior patterns and socially imposed gender differences before we can eradicate the sex-ordered division of labor.[77]

Several socialist feminists view comparable worth as a reform with significant potential. Feldberg, for example, advocates comparable worth as a partial solution to the feminization of poverty.[78] Hartman also advocates comparable worth, urging that the increase in women's wages will result in women's increased independence. She argues further that reform efforts to implement comparable worth are beneficial to the fight for socialism.[79]

Acker urges that comparable worth can be especially beneficial to socialists by revealing how work is valued, evaluated, and organized into "structures of dominance and subordination."[80] Some socialist feminists urge the adoption of comparable worth, not as an end in itself, but rather for its potential to "expose the social values and priorities underlying the wage hierarchy."[81]

Not all socialist feminists offer unqualified support for comparable worth. Some argue that it does not go far enough to achieve equality. Feldberg, for example, argues that comparable worth, although contributing to equal treatment and the amelioration of wages within the existing wage hierarchy, fails to challenge the hierarchy itself.[82] Brenner argues that comparable worth fails to challenge the distribution of wealth, the hierachical division of labor, or inequality in the distribution of wages.[83] She is also concerned that comparable worth may exacerbate race and class divisions among workers.[84]

Steinberg, although conceding that comparable worth may exacerbate workplace tensions in the short run, counters that the comparable worth movement has effected far-reaching reforms.[85] It has raised fundamental issues about the meaning of work, she suggests, by questioning such social values as, for example, why people who work with money earn more than those who work with people, and why supervision of work is valued more highly than performing that work. Not only has comparable worth improved wages, it also "has broadened public thinking on what discrimination is and redefined standards of fairness."[86]

RADICAL FEMINISM

Radical feminists, traditionally, have not been particularly interested in the topic of women and work.[87] Radical feminists believe that the source of women's oppression is not economic, but biological.[88] Radical feminists are not united in their conceptualizations of equality or the best methods of achieving it. Some advocate a gender-free society; others a matriarchy.[89] Radical feminists also differ in terms of the optimum method by which to challenge patriarchy. Many radical feminists eschew political or legal reform.[90]

Although radical feminists themselves have not devoted much attention to comparable worth, England points out that radical feminist values are compatible with this reform. Radical feminists would view the problem as "a cultural devaluation of some jobs because of their association with traditionally female spheres."[91] However, she notes that methods of implementation of comparable worth fall short of radical feminist goals.

The essays in this chapter raise fundamental issues for equality theory. They focus on whether women have different employment interests than men; if so, whether these differences account for women's underrepresentation in certain jobs; and, on a broader policy level, what reforms are necessary to achieve equality in the labor market.[92]

The chapter first focuses on the work-family conflict. Nancy Dowd, in "Work and Family: The Gender Paradox and the Limitations of Discrimination Analysis in Restructuring the Workplace," explores the limitations of existing legislation to remedy the work-family conflict.[93] Exploring the shortcomings of Title VII, she concludes that discrimination analysis provides an ineffective vehicle for reform. She suggests alternative strategies to restructure the work-family relationship.

The famous case of Equal Employment Opportunity Commission (EEOC) v. Sears, Roebuck & Company[94] highlights opposing positions in the sameness-versus-difference debate. This debate has proven extremely divisive for feminists. Two arenas in which this conflict has occupied center stage are employment (in the context of the *Sears* case) and pregnancy (in the context of maternity leave policies).[95]

The *Sears* case captured public[96] and scholarly[97] attention. *Sears* highlights issues of individual choice versus labor market constraints. That is, does women's underrepresentation in certain jobs result from women's differences or from discrimination? For purposes of legal analysis, if women's different natures and aspirations contribute to their choice of specific jobs and that choice is formed outside the labor market (because of socialization, for example), then the cause of occupational segregation is not legally remediable. On the other hand, if the source of the problem resides in the employer (for example, statistical discrimination or taste discrimination), then this constitutes illegal discrimination, and the employer must correct hiring, promotion, or other employment practices.

The origins of the lawsuit may be found in the period following enactment of Title VII of the 1964 Civil Rights Act[98] when many large corporations established programs to hire and train female and nonwhite male employees. In the 1970s the Equal Employment Opportunity Commission (the agency charged with enforcement of Title VII), initiated investigations of several corporations, including Sears, for failure to implement affirmative action plans adequately.

After negotiation failed, the EEOC filed a class action suit charging the company with violations of Title VII.[99] The case, based on statistical evidence, pitted two self-proclaimed feminist historians against each other.[100] At trial, Alice Kessler-Harris[101] refuted Rosalind Rosenberg's[102] "lack of interest" argument in an attempt to attribute job segregation to employer discrimination.[103] However, Judge John Nordberg ruled that the EEOC failed to prove sex discrimination, and the Seventh Circuit Court of Appeals affirmed.[104]

Several essays herein explore the implications of the case. Alice Kessler-Harris's first-person account explores the consequences of emphasizing women's differences for the purpose of effecting legal reform. She also provides a powerful critique of essentialism.[105]

Joan Scott, moving the debate to a more theoretical level, turns to the body of knowledge known as poststructuralism[106] to identify alternative ways of thinking about gender. For Scott, *Sears* illustrates the perils of dichotomous thinking. She urges a recognition that difference and equality are highly contextualized.

Joan Williams, in "Deconstructing Gender," adds the perspective of relational feminism (a school of difference theorists) to reveal the power of gender stereotypes. Williams urges contemporary feminists not to rely on negative stereotypes which perpetuate oppression, but rather to challenge the "gendered structure of wage labor." Vicki Schultz, based on empirical research, isolates two competing judicial approaches to occupational segregation. She explores the shortcomings of both the "conservative story of choice" and the "liberal story of coercion."

Turning to remedies for occupational segregation, Marion Crain's feminist agenda proposes an increase in women's union membership to ensure access to positions of power,[107] as well as a "deconstruction" of labor law to transform the legal concept of the worker as male. The final three essays explore comparable worth, sometimes referred to as "pay equity"—a remedy to eliminate the undervaluation of women's labor by requiring equal pay for jobs demanding the same level of training and skill.

Litigation has been a primary vehicle to accomplish this objective. In County of Washington v. Gunther,[108] women prison guards argued that they were being paid unequal wages. Although technically their claim was not based on comparable worth, the women scored a victory by means of the Supreme Court's interpretation of Title VII's Bennett Amendment.[109] By limiting the reasons for unequal pay to seniority, merit, quality and quantity of work, and factors other than sex, the Court opened the door to possible comparable worth claims under Title VII.

In American Federation of State, County, and Municipal Employees (AFSCME), AFL-CIO v. State of Washington,[110] state employees alleged that the state discriminated by paying women in female-dominated jobs lower wages. The district court held that the state had violated Title VII based on statistical proof that facially neutral employee policies had a disparate impact on women. Although the appellate court reversed on the grounds that disparate impact analysis was inapplicable,[111] the impact of *AFSCME* as well as *Gunther* was pronounced. As Evans and Nelson remark:

> *Gunther* and AFSCME v. State of Washington encouraged proponents of comparable worth to broaden their efforts. Legislation joined litigation and labor negotiations as a strategy to win comparable worth. In rapid succession many states outside of the South established comparable worth study commissions, passed comparable worth legislation, and even began to distribute comparable worth raises [focusing on the public sector].[112]

In the essays herein, Julianne Malveaux, with her focus on the problems affecting women of color,[113] adds an important perspective to the debate about women's differences, the dangers of essentialism, and strategies of law reform. Mary Becker rebuts arguments by economists[114] who assert that comparable worth fails to respond to various explanations of occupational segregation (human capital theory, statistical discrimination, and taste discrimination). And Ronnie Steinberg, from a sociological perspective, reveals how deeply gendered are the influences on our compensation system.

Notes

1. J. Donovan, Feminist Theory: The Intellectual Traditions of American Feminism 36 (Frederick Ungar, 1985).

2. *Id.* at 15.

3. *Id.* at 7. For an interesting study of nineteenth century reformers' efforts regarding women's work, see generally Siegel, Home as Work: The First Woman's Rights Claims Concerning Wives' Household Labor, 1850–1880, 103 Yale L.J. 1073 (1994) (suggesting that early feminists advocated recognition of household labor, which legislators transformed into protection for market labor); Siegel, The Modernization of Marital Status Law: Adjudicating Wives' Rights to Earnings, 1860–1930, 82 Georgetown L.J. 2127 (1994) (analysis of early "earnings statutes").

4. See also A. Kraditor, The Ideas of the Woman Suffrage Movement 1890–1920, 105–137 (Anchor, 1971) (subsequent concern by suffragists with plight of working women).

5. On the history of married women's property laws, see generally N. Basch, In the Eyes of the Law: Marriage and Property in Nineteenth-Century New York (Cornell Univ. Press, 1982); M. Salmon, Women and the Law of Property in Early America (Univ. North Carolina Press, 1986); Linda Speth, The Married Women's Property Acts, 1839–1865: Reform, Reaction, or Revolution? in D. Weisberg ed., 2 Women and the Law: The Social Historical Perspective (Schenkman, 1982).

6. On the background of Muller v. Oregon, see J. Baer, The Chains of Protection: The Judicial Response to Women's Labor Legislation 56–67 (Greenwood Press, 1978). See also Taub & Schneider, Women's Subordination and the Role of Law, in D. Weisberg ed., Feminist Legal Theory: Foundations 9, 15–16 (Temple Univ. Press, 1993).

7. 208 U.S. 412 (1908).

8. N. Erickson, Historical Background of "Protective" Labor Legislation: Muller v. Oregon, in Women and the Law, *supra* note 5, at 156.

9. For some of the extensive feminist criticism of *Muller,* see Erickson, *supra* note 8; Olsen, The Family and the Market: A Study of Ideology and Legal Reform, 96 Harv. L. Rev. 1497, 1546 (1983); Taub & Schneider, *supra* note 6, at 15–16; Becker, From Muller v. Oregon to Fetal Vulnerability Policies, 53 U. Chi. L. Rev. 1219, 1222–1223 (1986). On the background of protective labor legislation, see Baer, *supra* note 6; S. Lehrer, Origins of Protective Labor Legislation for Women (State Univ. New York Press, 1987).

10. Erickson, *supra* note 8, at 156–157.

11. 29 U.S.C. §201 (1988 & Supp. V 1993). See generally R. Steinberg, Wages and Hours: Labor and Reform in Twentieth Century America (Rutgers Univ. Press, 1982).

12. 29 U.S.C. §206(d) (1988 & Supp. V 1993). The Equal Pay Act of 1963 was added as an amendment to the Fair Labor Standards Act of 1938, 29 U.S.C. §§201–219 (1988 & Supp. V 1993).

13. 42 U.S.C. §2000e-2 (1988 & Supp. V 1993).

14. The prohibition against discrimination on the grounds of gender was originally proposed as a joke. See F. Davis, Moving the Mountain: The Women's Movement in America Since 1960 39–42 (Simon & Schuster, 1991).

15. On the battle to secure pregnancy benefits, see the essays on The Equality Debate: Equal Treatment versus Special Treatment, in D. Weisberg ed., Feminist Legal Theory: Foundations 121–207 (Temple Univ. Press, 1993). For the legislation that re-

sulted from feminist efforts, see the Family and Medical Leave Act of 1993, Pub. L. No. 103–3, 107 Stat. 6 (codified at 5 U.S.C. §§6381–6387 and 29 U.S.C. §§2601–2654 (Supp. V 1993)).

16. See generally M. Ferree, She Works Hard for a Living: Gender and Class on the Job, in B. Hess & M. Ferree eds., Analyzing Gender: A Handbook of Social Science Research 337–339 (Sage, 1987) (review of research). For early classics that focused on the malaise resulting from domestic responsibilities, see B. Friedan, The Feminine Mystique (Dell, 1963); J. Bernard, The Future of Marriage (World, 1972); P. Mainardi, The Politics of Housework, in R. Morgan ed., Sisterhood Is Powerful: An Anthology of Writings from The Women's Liberation Movement 501 (Vintage, 1970); J. Syfers, Why I Want a Wife, in A. Koedt, E. Levine & A. Rapone eds., Radical Feminism 60–62 (1973).

17. See, e.g., A. Hochschild, The Second Shift (Viking, 1989).

18. See the essays in Weisberg, *supra* note 6, at 335–395. Feminist Legal Theory: Foundations, Part II, ch. 4.

19. See, e.g., Frug, Securing Job Equality for Women: Labor Market Hostility to Working Mothers, 59 B.U. L. Rev. 55 (1979).

20. *Id.* at 94–103.

21. Abrams, Gender Discrimination and the Transformation of Workplace Norms, 42 Vand. L. Rev. 1183 (1989).

22. B. Reskin & I. Padavic, Women and Men at Work 23–24 (Sage, 1994). See also M. Richmond-Abbott, The World of Work, in J. Kourany, J. Sterba & R. Tong eds., Feminist Philosophies 135 (Prentice-Hall, 1992).

23. Reskin & Padavic, *supra* note 22, at 52–54.

24. *Id.* at 58. African-American women and Hispanic women, like white women, work in predominantly female occupations. Women of color are disproportionately found in such jobs as secretary, office clerk, cashier, elementary school teacher, janitor/cleaner, cook, and domestic service.

25. *Id.* at 54.

26. P. England, Comparable Worth: Theories and Evidence 15 (Aldine, 1992).

27. *Id.* at 16–18.

28. Reskin & Padavic, *supra* note 22, at 46.

29. Richmond-Abbott, *supra* note 22, at 137.

30. *Id.* at 139. Richmond-Abbott attributes the wage gap to three factors: human capital inequalities (characteristics of workers that enable them to produce more for the firm); overt discrimination; and institutional barriers. *Id.* at 138.

31. Reskin & Padavic, *supra* note 22, at 46.

32. *Id.*

33. For an excellent review and criticism of these theories, see generally England, *supra* note 26.

34. *Id.* at 37.

35. See *id.* at 28–34, 51–54; Reskin & Padavic, *supra* note 22, at 39–41, 76.

36. Reskin & Pavlic, *supra* note 22, at 39–40.

37. England, *supra* note 26, at 17.

38. See England, *supra* note 26, at 18–19, 34–35; Reskin & Padavic, *supra* note 22, at 41–42, 76–77.

39. See England, *supra* note 26, at 18–19 (citing studies).

40. See Reskin, Bringing the Men Back In: Sex Differentiation and the Devaluation of Women's Work, 2 Gender & Soc'y 58, 68 (1988) (citing additional studies documenting men's resistance to women entering male jobs).

41. *Id.* at 68.

42. *Id.* at 61, 69.

43. England, *supra* note 26, at 21–22, 108. See also M. Hannan & J. Freeman, Structural Inertia and Organization Change, 49 Am. Soc. Rev. 149 (1984).

44. England, *supra* note 26, at 55–60.

45. G. Becker, The Economics of Discrimination 5–9 (Univ. Chicago Press, 1957).

46. England, *supra* note 26, at 54.

47. *Id.* at 56.

48. *Id.* at 54.

49. On the gendered workplace, see generally R. Kanter, Men and Women of the Corporation (Basic Books, 1977); Reskin & Padavic, *supra* note 22, at 127–141; Acker, Hierarchies, Jobs, Bodies: A Theory of Gendered Organizations, 4 Gender & Soc'y 139 (1990). For a fascinating study of the ways in which feminist organizations differ, see M. Ferree & P. Martin eds., Feminist Organizations: Harvest of the New Women's Movement (Temple Univ. Press, 1995).

50. Reskin & Padavic, *supra* note 22, at 127.

51. *Id.* at 134–141.

52. For studies of organizational resistance, see C. Burton, The Promise and the Price: The Struggle for Equal Opportunity in Women's Employment (Allen & Unwin, 1991) (reasons for lack of success of legislation in New South Wales); C. Cockburn, In the Way of Women: Men's Resistance to Sex Equality in Organizations (ILR Press, 1991) (study of strategies that limit opportunities in different organizations). See also Steinberg, Gender on the Agenda: Male Advantage in Organizations, 21 Contemp. Soc. 576 (1992) (book review of the preceding books).

53. See Reskin, Bringing the Men Back In, *supra* note 40, at 70. See also B. Reskin & P. Roos, Job Queues, Gender Queues: Explaining Women's Inroads in Male Occupations 70–71 (Temple Univ. Press, 1990); B. Reskin & P. Roos, Status Hierarchies and Sex Segregation, in C. Bose & G. Spitze eds., Ingredients for Women's Employment Policy 3, 16 (SUNY Press, 1987) (exploring trends of resegregation).

54. See L. Blum, Constrained Choices: Women's Interest in Women's Work, in Beyond Feminism and Labor: The Significance of the Comparable Worth Movement 137 (Univ. California Press, 1991); Reskin & Roos, Status Hierarchies, *supra* note 53, at 15 (furnishing examples of this "feminization/degradation process"). The sequence occasionally may be unclear—Reskin points out that sometimes women gain access to male-dominated occupations after a change in work content or professional status makes the job less attractive to men. Reskin, *supra* note 40, at 70.

55. A. Jaggar, Feminist Politics and Human Nature 181 (Rowman & Allanheld, 1983).

56. See Z. Eisenstein, The Radical Future of Liberal Feminism 177–200 (Longman, 1981) (criticizing liberal feminist author Betty Friedan and NOW).

57. *Id.* at 195–196.

58. Many feminists have criticized this liberal feminist goal of androgyny. See, e.g., Raymond, The Illusion of Androgyny, in Building Feminist Theory: Essays from Quest 59, 61 (Longman, 1981). Compare J. Sterba, Feminist Justice and the Family, in Feminist Philosophies, *supra* note 22, at 271 (discussion of defenses of androgyny).

59. Jaggar, *supra* note 55, at 183.

60. See, e.g., England, *supra* note 26, at 263–264. See also Pinzler & Ellis, Wage Discrimination and Comparable Worth: A Legal Perspective, 45 J. Soc. Issues 51 (1989) (arguing that Title VII can be used to implement comparable worth).

61. England, *supra* note 26, at 263.

62. England, A Dissenting View in Favor of Pay Equity, 9 Harv. J.L. & Pub. Pol'y 99 (1986).

63. England, *supra* note 26, at 263–264.

64. Jaggar, *supra* note 55, at 217, 220.

65. See R. Tong, Feminist Thought: A Comprehensive Introduction 67 (Westview Press, 1989). Other feminists, however, criticize this negative view of the family under capitalism. See especially J. Elshtain, Public Man, Private Woman 254–286 (Princeton Univ. Press, 1981); Tong, Feminist Thought, *supra* this note, at 61–63.

66. Tong, *supra* note 65, at 68. See also Brenner & Holmstrom, Women's Self-Organization: Theory and Strategy, 34 Monthly Rev., Apr. 1983, at 40; Brenner & Ramos, Rethinking Women's Oppression, New Left Rev., Mar.–Apr. 1984, at 49.

67. On the collaboration, see generally S. Evans & B. Nelson, Wage Justice: Comparable Worth and The Paradox of Technocratic Reform 69–91 (Univ. Chicago Press, 1989).

68. Tong, *supra* note 65, at 59.

69. *Id.* (citing Amott and Matthaei, Comparable Worth, Incomparable Pay, Radical America, Sept.–Oct. 1984, at 21, 26).

70. Jaggar, *supra* note 55, at 331.

71. For psychoanalytic explanations by socialist feminists about the manner in which masculinity and femininity evolve, see N. Chodorow, The Reproduction of Mothering: Psychoanalysis and the Sociology of Gender (Univ. Calif. Press, 1978); D. Dinnerstein, The Mermaid and the Minotaur: Sexual Arrangements and Human Malaise (Harper & Row, 1977); J. Mitchell, Psychoanalysis and Feminism (Pantheon, 1974). But cf. Jaggar, *supra* note 55, at 126 (labeling Chodorow and Dinnerstein as socialist feminists) with Tong, *supra* note 65, at 149–161 (labeling Chodorow and Dinnerstein as representatives of psychoanalytic feminism). Socialist feminists also recognize that class differences and historical influences affect conceptions of masculinity and femininity. Jaggar, *supra* note 55, at 129–130.

72. Jaggar, *supra* note 55, at 129.

73. Hartmann, Capitalism, Patriarchy, and Job Segregation by Sex, 1 Signs 193, 223 (1976).

74. *Id.* at 211.

75. *Id.* at 195.

76. *Id.* at 223.

77. *Id.* at 225.

78. Feldberg, Comparable Worth: Toward Theory and Practice in the United States, 10 Signs 312, 313 (1984).

79. H. Hartmann, Comparable Worth and Women's Economic Independence, in Ingredients for Women's Employment Policy, *supra* note 53, at 251, 257.

80. J. Acker, Doing Comparable Worth: Gender, Class and Pay Equity 227 (Temple Univ. Press, 1989).

81. *Id.* at 226.

82. Feldberg, *supra* note 78, at 323.

83. Brenner, Feminist Political Discourses: Radical Versus Liberal Approaches to the Feminization of Poverty and Comparable Worth, 1 Gender & Soc'y 457, 457–458 (1987).

84. *Id.* at 459–460.

85. Steinberg, Radical Challenges in a Liberal World: The Mixed Success of Comparable Worth, 1 Gender & Soc'y 466, 468 (1987).

86. *Id.* at 468.

87. The exception, of course, is Catharine MacKinnon, who was influential in the legal recognition of sexual harassment. Her views are explored in the next chapter.

88. Donovan, *supra* note 1, at 147; Tong, *supra* note 65, at 73.

89. Jaggar, *supra* note 55, at 103.

90. *Id.* at 104.

91. England, *supra* note 26, at 272.

92. See Milkman, Women's History and the *Sears* Case, 12 Feminist Stud. 375 (1986) (characterizing thus the equal treatment/special treatment focus raised by *Sears*).

93. See also Dowd, Work and Family: Restructuring the Workplace, 32 Ariz. L. Rev. 431 (1990).

94. 628 F. Supp. 1264 (N.D. Ill. 1986), *aff'd*, 839 F.2d 302 (7th Cir. 1988).

95. See Herma Hill Kay, Sex-Based Discrimination: Text, Cases and Materials 574 n.53 (West, 3d ed., 1988) (claiming that *Sears* triggered a debate among feminist scholars "every bit as intense as that generated among feminist legal practitioners and scholars by the *Miller-Wohl* and *Cal. Fed.* cases").

96. See, e.g., Freedman, Of History and Politics: Bitter Feminist Debate, N.Y. Times, June 6, 1986, at B1; Sternhell, Life in the Mainstream: What Happens When Feminists Turn Up on Both Sides of the Courtroom? Ms., July 1986, at 15, 48–51, 86–91; Wiener, The *Sears* Case: Women's History on Trial, The Nation, Sept. 7, 1985, at 161, 176–180; Winkler, 2 Scholars' Conflict in Sears Sex-Bias Case Sets Off War in Women's History, Chron. Higher Educ., Feb. 5, 1986, at 1; Yardley, When Scholarship and the Cause Collide, Wash. Post, June 16, 1986, at C2; Misusing History, Wash. Post, June 9, 1986, at A20.

97. See generally Davis, *supra* note 1, at 339–340; S. Faludi, Backlash: The Undeclared War Against Women 378–388 (Crown, 1991); J. Scott, Gender and the Politics of History 166–177 (Columbia Univ. Press, 1988); Boris, Looking at Women's Historians Looking at "Difference," 3 Wis. Women's L.J. 213 (1987); Hall, Women's History Goes to Trial: EEOC v. Sears, Roebuck and Company, 11 Signs 751 (1986); Haskell & Levinson, Academic Freedom and Expert Witnessing: Historians and the *Sears* Case, 66 Tex. L. Rev. 1629 (1988); Kessler-Harris, Academic Freedom and Expert Witnessing: A Response to Haskell and Levinson, 67 Tex. L. Rev. 429 (1988); Milkman, *supra* note 92; Rhode, The "No-Problem" Problem: Feminist Challenges and Cultural Change, 100 Yale L.J. 1731, 1768 (1991).

Sears has special relevance, too, for historians and sociologists for its focus on the role of history in legal proceedings; the use of social science data, especially statistical evidence, in legal proceedings; the problems of expert witnesses, especially historians, attempting to convey "truth" in the context of an adversarial proceeding; and the role of scholarship in the formulation of legal policy.

98. 42 U.S.C. 2000e-2 (1988 & Supp. V 1993). Title VII prohibits, as an unlawful employment practice, the refusal to hire or otherwise discriminate against an individual in employment because of the individual's race, color, religion, sex, or national origin.

99. The EEOC subsequently dropped charges of alleged violations of the Equal Pay Act. 839 F.2d at 340.

100. Historian Rosalind Rosenberg's role, in particular, attracted virulent criticism. See, e.g., Milkman, *supra* note 92, at 376; *id.* at 391 (noting criticisms by historian Ellen DuBois regarding the implications of Rosenberg's testimony for affirmative action). In December 1985, feminist scholars at a conference at Columbia University sharply criticized Rosenberg. *Id.* See also Sternhell, *supra* note 96, at 48; Wiener, *supra* note 96, at 1;

Winkler, *supra* note 96, at 1. For Rosenberg's response to the criticisms, see Rosenberg, What Harms Women in the Workplace, N.Y. Times, Feb. 27, 1986, at A23.

101. See A. Kessler-Harris, Out to Work: A History of Wage-earning Women in the United States (Oxford Univ. Press, 1982); A. Kessler-Harris, Women Have Always Worked (Feminist Press, 1981). See also A. Kessler-Harris, A Woman's Wage: Historical Meanings and Social Consequences (Univ. Press Kentucky, 1990). For background on the two historians' involvement, see Faludi, *supra* note 97, at 381–382.

102. See R. Rosenberg, Beyond Separate Spheres: The Intellectual Roots of Modern Feminism (Yale Univ. Press, 1982).

103. Recent qualitative research also supports this position. R. Needleman & A. Nelson, Policy Implications: The Worth of Women's Work, in A. Stratham, E. Miller & H. Mauksch eds., The Worth of Women's Work: A Qualitative Synthesis 296 (State Univ. New York Press, 1988) (commenting on the research findings of a study of working women).

104. 839 F.2d 302 (7th Cir. 1988). The appeal also decided other issues raised on Sears' cross-appeal, such as an alleged conflict of interest by an EEOC attorney—affirming the district court's denial of the motion to dismiss the EEOC's suit on this basis.

105. Research now reveals that women of color have played an important role historically in the labor force, although their role differed from that of white middle-class women. For an excellent study of the factors of race, class, and gender in women's labor history, see T. Amott & J. Matthaei, Race Gender, and Work: A Multicultural Economic History of Women in the United States (South End Press, 1991). See also E. DuBois & V. Ruiz eds., Unequal Sisters: A Multicultural Reader in U.S. Women's History (Routledge, 1990).

106. Feminist legal theorists have increasingly been interested in the potential of this school of thought. See generally Ashe, Mind's Opportunity: Birthing a Poststructuralist Feminist Jurisprudence, 38 Syracuse L. Rev. 1129 (1987); Frug, A Postmodern Feminist Legal Manifesto (An Unfinished Draft), 105 Harv. L. Rev. 1045 (1992); Williams, Feminism and Post-Structuralism, 88 Mich. L. Rev. 1776 (1990) (reviewing Z. Eisenstein, The Female Body and the Law (1988)). See also L. Nicholson ed., Feminism/Post-Modernism (Routledge, 1990); C. Weedan, Feminist Practice and Poststructuralist Theory (Basil Blackwell, 1987). The terms *poststructuralism* and *postmodernism* are often used interchangeably.

107. On the role of the labor movement in representing working women, see also Blum, *supra* note 54, at 6–11; D. Cobble, Women and Unions: Forging a Partnership (ILR Press, 1993); Milkman, Women Workers, Feminism and the Labor Movement Since the 1960s, in R. Milkman ed., Women, Work and Protest 300 (Routledge & Kegan Paul, 1985).

108. 623 F.2d 1303 (9th Cir. 1979), *aff'd*, 452 U.S. 161 (1981).

109. 42 U.S.C. 2000e-2(h)(1988).

110. 578 F. Supp. 846 (W.D. Wash. 1983), *rev'd*, 770 F.2d 1401 (9th Cir. 1985).

111. 770 F.2d 1401, at 1405.

112. Evans & Nelson, Wage Justice, *supra* note 67, at 40.

113. For other discussions of this issue, compare Brenner, *supra* note 83, at 449 (criticism of comparable worth as remedy for women of color) with Scales-Trent, Comparable Worth: Is This a Theory for Black Workers?, 8 Women's Rts. L. Rep. 50 (1984) (defense of comparable worth).

114. See Fischel & Lazear, Comparable Worth and Discrimination in Labor Markets, 53 U. Chi. L. Rev. 891 (1986).

Work and Family: The Gender Paradox and the Limitations of Discrimination Analysis in Restructuring the Workplace

NANCY E. DOWD

TALK ABOUT WORK and family is assumed to be women's talk. It is talk about women's lives, our feelings. Talk about work and family is tied to women's entry into the workforce and the concomitant redefinition of ourselves and our roles. It is also talk about responsibility and conflict, the conflict between work and family. . . .

But talk about work and family ought not to be assumed to be only women's talk. Men are harmed and affected by the existing work-family structure. . . .

Moreover, if we accept the circumscription of "women's talk," we not only limit our perspective, but also obscure the powerful impact of factors other than gender on the structure of work and family. . . .

I argue that it is essential that we recognize this fundamental paradox about work and family: that the structure of work and family, and the nature of the conflict between work and family, is not just a women's issue and a gender issue. We must constantly take women and gender into account because they are inseparable from the existing structure and assumptions of family and work. . . . At the same time, however, we must get beyond gender, to redefining the relationship between work and family. . . .

The Context: The Nature of Work-Family Conflict

The conflict between work and family responsibilities is pervasive and serious.[1] Between one-third and one-half of working parents report nearly daily conflict between their work and family roles; this translates into one-quarter or more of the workforce.[2] The manifestations of that conflict are complex and multi-layered. . . .

A. Levels of Conflicts

At the simplest level, the conflict between work and family is expressed as conflicts of time. While they are the easiest to identify and potentially resolve, time conflicts include some of the most intractable work-family problems.[3] Due to the number of hours com-

24 Harv. C.R.-C.L. L. Rev. 79 (1989). Permission granted by the Harvard Civil Rights Civil Liberties Review. © 1989 by the President and Fellows of Harvard College.

mitted to work and the scheduling of work, many men and women do not have enough time for both family and wage work. Contrary to the assumptions of social and economic theorists, increasing industrialization and the continued entry of more individuals into the paid workforce has not led to a more collective or commodified approach to household or caregiving work.[4] There is a particularly strong need for care-giving work, which is socially essential, highly individualized, and very time-consuming. Thus, a fundamental conflict exists between the time needed to perform family and wage work.

For women, the time conflict is exacerbated by an overload of family and childcare work. Women's entry into the paid workforce has not led to equitable redistribution of work. Rather, the predominant pattern has been the addition of wage work to women's existing unpaid household and childcare work.[5] While men are doing more, they are not doing much more.[6] As one researcher observed, "Under optimal conditions, we note the wife doing five times as much domestic work as her spouse and usually more."[7] Even if the inequity in the distribution of family work responsibilities were resolved, however, it would not alleviate the conflict in the time demands of work and family roles; it would only more equally distribute the stress. The workplace structure presumes a worker with minimal or no family work responsibilities.

In addition to problems caused by insufficient time, there are problems related to the use and control of time. On a regular basis, the time schedules of the school day and the school calendar clash with the workplace day and workplace calendar. The lack of flexibility in the workplace creates particularly difficult problems when family emergencies, such as a sick child or an unexpected snow-day, occur during working hours. Non-emergency situations are no less a problem, since the scheduling of routine appointments, or attendance at significant events, is never guaranteed.

Even more fundamentally, family time and work time conflict due to the clash between the occupational cycle of the workplace and the life cycle of the family and individual family members. Our occupational patterns are in many respects geared to the family life of a single individual or a worker who is supported by a non-working wife. The demands are greatest and the stakes are highest at the earlier stages of one's worklife, both in professional and blue-collar occupations. However, during this same period, the psychological and economic demands on the family are also the greatest. The family life cycle revolves around marital or partner patterns, and childrearing patterns, and is particularly vulnerable at the commencement of the partnership and the beginning of childrearing. Thus, during the early stages of career and family, the demands of each are on a predictable collision course.

This clash between occupational and family life cycles has produced starkly different patterns of labor force attachment for men and women. Women continue to fit work to families, and men vice versa. While there has been a marked decline in the stereotypical pattern of women leaving the workforce for childbearing, the presence of children nevertheless has a very strong impact on women's career patterns, even more so than marriage.[8] In contrast to a linear, uninterrupted, upward progression which characterizes the work pattern of most men (tapering off more quickly for blue-collar men) women's career patterns have varied from the typical male pattern to patterns of interrupted and second careers. Women most often make their strongest work contribution in mid-life, whereas men hit the high point in their careers or occupations much earlier in their lives.[9]

This clash between occupational and family life cycles is also reflected in highly gendered occupational patterns. Roughly sixty to seventy percent of either male or female workers would have to change occupations in order to equalize the sexual division of labor.[10] Even more disturbingly, job segregation is extremely pronounced within individual establishments, even where the occupation is one that aggregate figures would indicate is gender neutral. Those who argue that these patterns are not the result of discrimination, but rather of "choice," nevertheless concede that the choice is required due to the conflict of occupational time or career demands with family responsibilities and priorities.[11]

Work-family conflict arises not only from time and life cycle clashes, but also from deep psychological stress intimately tied to views of appropriate roles. The perception of conflict between work and family arises from fundamental conceptions of self and a shift in our ideals and visions of those selves. The conflict is highly gendered, both in the perception of the conflict and in the difficulty of its resolution. The source and perpetuation of this conflict lies in the social stereotypes of appropriate roles which are embedded in institutional structures.

Role conflict operates on at least two levels. First, there is the conflict arising from the ideal roles or stereotypes for men and women, which construct very different gendered paradigms of the work-family relationship. Those roles conflict with changing concepts of marriage and parenting, and with the workplace. Second, there is the conflict arising out of the role of parent and the role of worker. The workplace culture denies that both roles can exist simultaneously, requiring any conflict between them to be buried or resolved in favor of the worker role. The workplace and the family also demand and reward different sets of values and priorities.

For each sex, the ideal relation between work and family is constructed differently, and the sense of conflict between the ideal and changing social mores is experienced differently. For women, the primary role is one of family and childrearing. It is a role that presumes dependence on a male provider. Women perceive work as presenting a conflict with parenting and family. This is so not only because it conflicts with their family role, but also because women perceive that they are judged at work not simply on their achievement, but also on their gender.[12] Women's perception of conflict is strongly affected by social context and role models. Thus, women often report greater satisfaction from family than from work,[13] but that is only logical, since women have largely been confined to the family sphere, and have felt more conflict with the workplace.

For men, concepts of masculinity support an entirely different work-family relationship. Men are socialized to define themselves by work and to measure their life success occupationally, as epitomized by the breadwinner or good provider role. Men feel entitled to receive emotional support for their career efforts, while they commonly fail to provide that support for their partner; some men even feel hostile or competitive with their career-oriented spouses. Despite professions of equality, men still view their career as primary.[14]

This highly gendered construction of marital work-family roles is mirrored in the gendered construction of parenting roles. Many authors have examined our complex images of motherhood and its disfunction from reality.[15] The role of mother encourages nurturing and caregiving, but at the price of economic dependence and domination. "Central to our experience of our mothers and our mothering is a poignant conjunction of power and powerlessness."[16] Traditionally, the idealized role of mother did not conflict with work roles because mothers did not work—or at least they did not perform paid work. While as wives their work role was to be supportive, or a secondary earner, as mothers, women's work role was not to work at all.

Conversely, the image of fatherhood lacks social support for nurturing, involved parenting. The role of father is viewed almost entirely as economic. Both legal and social policies make it difficult for men to parent.[17] Employers are less tolerant of work-family conflicts in men than women, and continue to see men as primarily breadwinners in relation to their families, an image that continues to be reinforced by women's lower earnings.

These stereotypes of marital and parenting roles presume the existence of work-family conflict and resolve it in a gendered assignment of roles. Any step outside of a role is made mechanically difficult by a structure which presumes these divisions, and psychologically difficult by the felt conflict between the ideal role and one's measure of oneself. At the same time, these strongly gendered marital and parenting work-family roles sharply conflict with emerging, more egalitarian visions of gender roles which reject the sexual division of work and family as "natural" or biologically determined.

This disfunction between the rhetoric of equality and the persistence of inequality is the source of role overload and role frustration. This is experienced very differently by men and women. Women most frequently experience role overload.[18] Women see the assumption of a paid work role as a positive role expansion, but feel compelled to *add* this role to their primary family role. The attempt to be "superwoman" reflects an attempt to preserve a concept of femininity tied to dependency, not strength, that is associated with the primary family role. It also reflects women's struggle to maintain the value of nurturance within a workplace structure which does not recognize its worth and which continues to evaluate women's work role from a strongly gendered perspective. At the same time, the rhetoric of equality pushes women to adopt the male work role as a neutral role, silencing women from criticizing that role.

Men feel that they have little to gain by changing gender roles and adopting more egalitarian marital roles. While the benefits for women to enter the workforce seem clear (after all, they are simply adopting the valued male breadwinner role), the benefits of sharing family responsibilities are less clear both individually and societally.[19] Furthermore, in order for men to truly achieve the egalitarian model, they must undergo nothing less than a reconstruction of self: "Because male power over women is central to extant views of masculinity and because wives traditionally sustained husbands' personal and work life, men in dual-career families also need to revise their sense of self. This is not a one-time task, and it is not easily accomplished."[20]

The struggle to attain less gendered, more egalitarian roles is closely related to the development of alternative role models and social supports. The choice of role models is strongly affected by so-called "environmental" factors, which include the workplace structure. "A still basic question is how men (and women) surrounded by patriarchal institutions and attitudes can survive, grow, and develop in an egalitarian . . . lifestyle."[21] This is the second level of role conflict: the infusion of gendered workfamily roles in the construction of gendered employee stereotypes, and the conflict between the values and priorities of work and family.

Work-family role models are not only personal guideposts, but are also the basis for the perceptions of appropriate roles in the workplace culture. The view of what is appropriate powerfully affects the management of the workplace, the content of employee conduct and the nature of the communication about work-family issues. . . .

A source of much work-family conflict for many employees is the attitude of their supervisors, as well as of management in general. Supervisors develop their perception of appropriate work-family roles from their own socialization, experience and the content of the workplace culture. One of the ironies of the workplace is that management reflects a work-family pattern at odds with the bulk of the workforce. The management pattern is disproportionately one of a male single-earner married to a nonworking spouse, while the predominant workforce pattern is one of dual-earners or single head of household earners.[22] The majority of corporate decision-makers today are men whose mothers stayed home to care for them, and whose wives do the same for their children.

The infusion of this gendered perspective is also reflected in the pervasive stereotyping of male and female employees. This stereotyping contributes to occupational segregation, as well as to the limitation of available flexibility for parenting to female employees (and then only, and always, at a significant workplace price).

Finally, there is a similar, if more general, conflict between the values associated with the roles of parent and worker. The nurturing, caregiving, relational role of parent, presumably motivated by love and connection, sharply conflicts with the competitive, hierarchical workplace role of employee where the assumed motivators are fear and greed. This is also reflected in the devaluation of caregiving work in the market. Even to the extent that a different basis of employee motivation is accepted, or that caregiving work within the market or the family is valued, it is nevertheless assumed that no conflict exists between the employee role and family responsibilities because they are kept separate. In part, this is viewed as an implicit term of the employer-employee contract. It also reflects a social/cultural assumption that the work-family issues are private, not public, issues.

This ideology of work and family separation and individual responsibility means that work-family conflict is strongly felt as individual conflict.[23] Inability to handle work and family responsibilities is viewed as an individual failure, not as a societal problem. This discourages connecting individual work-family issues to broader structural issues or to values that create or magnify the conflict. Public policy toward families has emphasized limited intervention. Such a policy stance promotes values of autonomy and self-sufficiency. Additionally, social policy has reinforced the idea that home and workplace should be treated as functionally separate and has supported a sexual division of labor.

The struggle to think of work and family *together* requires overcoming the tendency to separate the two and conceive of them as opposites, in contradiction and conflict with each other. The family and market are assumed to embody a fundamental and radical separation: "[T]he market structures our productive lives and the family structures our affective lives."[24] It is an unnatural separation, contrary to our felt connection of the two.

B. Structural Features

The various levels of work-family conflict are not surprising in view of several structural features of the workplace. . . .

First, the workplace is premised upon a singular male stereotype of the employee as an economic parent and the work-family relation as one of separation.[25] This stereotype is a standard that denies the existence of work-family conflict or presumes the accommodation of family to work. Thus, not surprisingly, the workplace is remarkably rigid and inflexible. With respect to time and schedules, most jobs require an eight hour day, a five day week, with a uniform starting and quitting time. Barely fifteen percent of all workers have the option of working a flexible schedule.[26] The problems created by the standard work pattern are magnified for shift workers and overtime workers, who by virtue of economics or mandatory work requirements work a schedule even more in conflict with family schedules.

The same rigidity is characteristic of occupational patterns in the workplace structure. The content and demands of individual occupations, as well as the interrelation between occupations, have been impervious to two of the implicit causes of the stark pattern of occupational segregation: the "choices" forced by work-family conflict, and employers' construction and assignment of jobs based upon a presumed allocation of work family roles. Little questioning or change has occurred regarding occupational life cycles or occupational demands.[27]

The rigidity of time and occupational patterns might be offset by the benefit structure. That structure, too, however, is almost totally unresponsive to work-family concerns. Legally mandated benefits (social security, workers' compensation and unemployment) are oriented toward events which separate the worker from the workplace due to age, injury, or lack of employment, and are designed to support a male breadwinner. The model is based on temporary, short-term job disruption, and provides no protection for job security or for managing the disruptions of work-family conflict.

The same primary wage earner, male breadwinner presumption underlies the fringe benefit structure. The primary benefits offered, apart from those legally mandated, include health and life insurance, a private retirement plan, and paid holidays and vacations. Time benefits are rarely available to alleviate time conflicts or to resolve family emergencies. Sick leave, for instance, is confined to the illness of the employee, and personal leave is an uncommon benefit. Only about ten percent of employers provide any childcare-related benefits or services to their employees.[28] Even the most essential of necessary work family policies, maternity leave for pregnancy-related disability, is by no means a universal benefit, and where it is provided, it is commonly without the guarantee of job security. [This article was written before the federal Family and Medical Leave Act, mandating that employers of *over 50 employees* provide 12 weeks of *unpaid* leave for care of a newborn, adopted child or seriously ill family member, while simultaneously guaranteeing job security, and health benefits. *Ed.*]

In addition to the incorporation of this male standard, the workplace structure incorporates a rigid conception of family. That conception is one of a patriarchal family: a male wage earner in the paid workforce married to a stay-at-home female spouse who performs the unpaid housework and childcare. However, only a small minority of families, fewer than ten percent, conform to this pattern and are served by the existing benefit structure.[29]

The great majority of families are characterized by enormous diversity and fluidity. The diversity includes single parent, blended, unmarried and homosexual families.[30] The dominant earner patterns in the workforce are now dual-earner and single-parent/single-earner families.[31] An estimated half of all children under the age of thirteen live in one- or two-parent families in which all parents are in the labor force.[32] The fluidity (some might say instability) of families is tied to the decline in marriage and fertility rates, the increase in divorce rates, the increase in unwed mothers and the increase in single-parent households.

Yet, the workplace structure makes no allowance for this diversity, and unduly burdens the majority of families. The families most hurt by the maintenance of the patriarchal family model in the workplace are those families headed by women and minorities, and all families that are poor, which disproportionately are the families of women and minorities.

At the same time that the workplace structure creates problems for the vast majority of families by its support of a minority family form, economic and demographic dynamics both push and pull family members into the workplace. The push is the decline in real family income which has been responsible, in part, for the rise in dual-earner families and the economic losses of single-parent families unable to compensate for the increased financial burden. The pull is the demographic reality that new workers will primarily be women and minorities, who constitute the largest untapped pools of workers. The ironic twist to the pull of the market is that many of the jobs in the existing labor market and a significant proportion of those likely to be created in the foreseeable future barely provide a minimal income sufficient for a primary or sole wage earner to support a family. . . .

Beyond the Paradox: A Preliminary Agenda

Gender is one of the primary determinants of the existing work-family structure. The content and assignment of work-family roles are divided on gender lines, and limited, gendered roles of mothering, fathering and parenting are widely accepted. Gender is also present in the perpetuation of a myth of care that belies the reality of the undervaluation of care. Recognition of this mandates an agenda of reform that will take work-family restructuring beyond the paradox. The agenda must include both women's issues and gender issues: improving the status of women and exposing, analyzing and reconstructing concepts of gender.

Getting beyond the paradox requires real equality for women in the workplace structure. We must eliminate the disadvantages based on biological difference without sacrificing the health, safety or potential for procreation of either sex. Where biological difference has been ignored by the workplace structure, resulting in disadvantage to women, the structure must change to accommodate difference. Where difference has been used as a basis to exclude women, such exclusion must not be permitted. Both insensitivity to biological difference and discriminatory attention to biological difference must be eliminated. . . .

At the very least, [e]limination of biological disadvantage would require job-protected, paid maternity leave for pregnancy-related disability and accommodating pregnancy-related modifications in work tasks. It would also require the guarantee of a safe, healthful workplace that would not present the risk of harm to either sex's reproductive potential. . . .

Economic equality also is essential to transcending the paradox, both for women's and children's basic survival and maintenance, and for the elimination of the economic basis for dominance and patriarchy. Achieving economic equality for women will require sexual desegregation of the workplace and revaluation of women's work in conformity with its true worth. It may also require the guarantee of a minimal level of sustenance to ensure survival and choice, and a reevaluation of home and family work in market/economic terms.

Sexual desegregation of the occupational structure and within occupational structures is a particularly complex task. It requires elimination of the gender stereotypes in hiring and promotion that steer women into particular occupations and infect the evaluation process. It also requires consideration of the underlying assumptions in particular occupational progressions, which may betray male bias or other assumptions about work and family roles.

Job segregation must be viewed not only from the employer's perspective, scrutinizing the decision-making process to eliminate gender stereotyping, but also from the perspective of potential employees, to determine what constraints the employment structure imposes on individual choice by its assumption and incorporation of the traditional, gendered division of work and family roles. We must eliminate occupational constructs that arise from presumed gender roles or that value a particular gender role.

The elimination of gender stereotypes and the preference for the traditional male work-family role also requires that we rethink the traditional female work-family role. At least a part of this task is to recognize and provide room for alternative work-family roles without tying them to economic devaluation or patriarchal domination. For example, the workplace structure may need to be reformed to permit women or men to follow the traditional female work-family role without the consequence of occupational limitation and economic impoverishment. An individual would be free to choose that role, with the choice not framed by learned gender constructs, but rather by factors not tied to sex or gender.

Getting beyond the paradox may also involve an entire reconstruction of the relation between work and family, a redefinition of the relationship and the creation of some new role-models or models. . . .

A further aspect of the project, then, is to focus on the stereotypes and gendered work-family roles of both sexes and to eliminate aspects of the workplace structure that dictate or encourage a division of responsibilities and construction of roles based on gender. This is not aimed at eliminating gender. Gender as a social construct will not disappear; that is not only unimaginable, but undesirable. Instead, we should eliminate gender as the primary determinant of the assignment of work-family roles.

This process of examination and restructuring requires exposing gender stereotypes and the assignment and division of work and family responsibilities in the structure, and the resonance of those divisions in the constructs of gender roles. For example, how can men be encouraged to share family responsibilities, and how can employers become reoriented to viewing both sexes this way? Imagine that every time something occurred which required at least one parent to leave the workplace (pregnancy, childbirth, recovering from childbirth, initial parenting, sick child, child's activities) that *both* parents left the workplace as a means to ensure necessary caregiving and to equalize the consequences that flow from absence (loss of contacts and experience, perception by others of lack of commitment or different priorities) that at present fall disproportionately on women. How can such restructuring be accomplished short of coercion?

Achievement of this goal requires identifying gender roles and their reflection in the structure, and analyzing the validity or invalidity of gender stereotypes assumed in the roles, as well as determining the value or worth of the roles apart from untrue stereotypes. The analysis of gender stereotypes involves examining untrue assumptions. The analysis of gender roles includes questioning the roles themselves.

Essential to that exposure and analysis is revealing the pattern of dominance and hierarchy in the division of roles. The gendered structure of work and family as it currently exists is not simply a division of work and family tasks into gender complements; rather, it is a division infused with patriarchy, by the domination of the male role over the female role, by the valuing of the work role over the family role, thereby preserving male power and dominance even in the female sphere of the home. The pattern of patriarchy is accomplished by simultaneous devaluation and elevation of the female work-family role, while also requiring the separation and limitation of the male work-family role. It is essential to eliminate patriarchy if we are to have any meaningful sense of equality and liberty, freedom and choice.

Exposing and eliminating patriarchal power points to one of the greatest difficulties in getting beyond the paradox. Dealing with gender in work and family roles as they are manifested in the workplace structure is a difficult task, but it is further complicated if it is separated from the family structure. If we limit ourselves to the workplace, then arguably, it can at best be reflective of the needs of the existing family structure. There would be only partial, limited and ineffective change. To reach the family structure, however, requires breaching public/private lines, intruding into the individual and private in the name of the state. We must confront the concept of public and private, and consider individual privacy and choice.

Part of the challenge is to conceive of public policy as supportive rather than coercive or intrusive. Such a supportive public policy might encourage diversity in the rethinking and reconstruction of work-family roles, as long as those roles do not reconstitute patriarchy. Furthermore, the public/private distinction might be transcended by supporting work-family roles beyond the workplace. For example, if part of our analysis is the recognition of the devaluation of nurturing, caregiving work by separating it from the valued public sphere of work (making it difficult for those who perform such work to participate in the paid workplace while simultaneously relegating them to a position of economic and social powerlessness), then perhaps we should not merely value and permit nurturing work in the workplace, or provide flexibility to perform paid work and nurturing work at home, but rather develop a support structure for nurturing and caregiving functions that is not limited to the workplace.

While a focus on the gender paradox is essential, it is also necessary to reemphasize the limits of that focus for resolving work-family conflict. [A]n analysis limited to the gender perspective does not adequately provide a means to resolve the myriad additional policy and philosophical issues presented by the conflict between work and family. . . .

[C]an the project of resolving the gender paradox be accomplished through the use of discrimination law? I argue in the next section that discrimination analysis is an extremely limited tool for the project. . . .

The Gender Paradox and the Discrimination Framework

Existing discrimination analysis is divided between intentional or disparate treatment discrimination, and unintended or disparate impact discrimination. Very few of the conflicts between work and family responsibilities can be ascribed to conduct which would fall within intentional discrimination analysis. With the exception of certain pregnancy or pregnancy-related classifications or policies, those aspects of the workplace which cause work-family conflict are largely structural features that have resulted from the adoption of facially neutral policies, or from the inaction and inadequacies of the structure which generate conflict between work-family roles. Identifying and eliminating work-family conflict, particularly degenderization of work-family conflict, is not, then, a process of determining blame or guilt, but rather is a process of uncovering the impact of structural factors on work and family roles.

If such structural discrimination, or "unconscious" discrimination, can be reached, therefore, it is only under Title VII disparate impact analysis. Stated in its classic *Griggs*[33] formulation, disparate impact analysis provides that policies fair in form but sexually discriminatory in operation, which cannot be justified as a business necessity, are illegally discriminatory. To what extent can disparate impact analysis contribute to the resolution of the gender paradox?

One way to try to answer that question is to try to fit particular sex/gender aspects of work-family conflict within the disparate impact framework. The attempt to do so reveals the limited reach of this analysis. . . . It refracts complex work-family issues into a single image of women and biological sex, and away from the social construction of gender and the political and power issues of patriarchy.

Consider, for example, trying to deal with the assertion that the existing workplace structure incorporates a male standard by its assumption of a masculine ideal and therefore discriminates against those who do not conform to that ideal, who are disproportionately female. At the same time, try to argue that the singular male standard, based on a particular male stereotype, disadvantages both men and women who do not conform to the ideal or stereotype. Or consider the assertion that any aspect of the employment structure which imposes a hardship on parents (lack of parenting leave, lack of sick leave to care for a sick child, required overtime, required travel, long hours, etc.) disproportionately impacts on women because women disproportionately bear total or primary care responsibility for children. At the same time, try to argue that the structure reinforces gender roles for both men and women (by restraining men from being parents and women from being workers), and perhaps falls even more harshly on men (by disallowing nonconformity with gender role stereotypes). Or try to argue that the structure is discriminatory if it fails to provide an individual who is a primary caretaker with the means to meet job performance standards without detriment to the individual's parenting role or employment opportunities.

Where claims of discrimination identify disproportionate impact based on sex, they appear to fit within the disparate impact framework. This demonstrates the push of the disparate impact framework towards biological sex. Yet the basis of each claim is inextricably intertwined with gender roles, not with biological determinism. At the same time, if the claim expressly raises gender issues by attempting to demonstrate the concurrent harm to both sexes from a structure premised on a single gender standard, the claim will be frustrated by the very duality of the sex/gender system. That duality is the harm to both men and women by the constrictions of gender roles reinforced by the workplace structure. Disparate impact analysis, however, rests upon demonstrating the comparative disadvantage of one sex to the other. It does not comprehend mutual disadvantage.

As a defense to a discrimination claim, an employer might argue that the disproportionate pattern results from the plaintiff's individual choice, not the employer's policy. The employer might further argue that there is no discrimination because of sex, but at best a differential employment pattern based on a different pattern of choices by the sexes. The "maleness" in the structure is tied to gender, not sex, so it is social/cultural discrimination, not sex discrimination, a value choice which is sex-linked but not sex-determined. Women are not precluded from participating in the structure except because of their socialization in and acceptance of "female" social/cultural roles. Finally, the employer would argue that the male standard disadvantages all parents, whether the parent is male or female, and therefore is not discriminatory on the basis of sex. The difficulty in trying to fit work-family issues and the project of degenderization within disparate impact analysis springs from several aspects of that analysis.

A. Inability to Reach Structural Change

. . . Discrimination analysis is designed to ensure that no one is denied an equal opportunity within the existing structure; it is not designed to change the structure to the least discriminatory, most opportunity-maximizing pattern. Discrimination analysis is geared to providing the same opportunity for all, not the best opportunity for all. Equality as a principle has no substance or content. It merely requires that likes be treated alike but does not judge the content of the like treatment nor the nature of the structure within which treatment is given or received. It basically accepts the existing structure as a given, and accomplishes the goal of equal opportunity by minor tinkering and adjustment, removing unnecessary pieces of the structure if they have a disproportionate discriminatory effect. It can, at best, eliminate unjustified barriers; it cannot mandate a fundamental change in the structure. . . .

Since the concept of equality in discrimination analysis accepts the basic workplace structure, it also implicitly accepts the moral choices underlying that structure. It accepts the existing structure as legitimate, rather than asserting a new structure of rights or a new structure not based on rights. Also, by focusing on individual rights and the opportunity to exercise those rights, discrimination analysis obscures the potential for discrimination based upon one's group identification.

The limited structural reach of discrimination analysis is exemplified by the permit/require distinction. Under that distinction, affirmative efforts to restructure the workplace, most commonly compensatory affirmative action (which is really a bridging mechanism, not a type of permanent restructuring), are permitted as long as equality goals are justified and the extraordinary means chosen are narrowly confined. On the other hand, affirmative restructuring is not required by the absence of structures essential or useful to equality goals. The U.S. Supreme Court drew this distinction in two cases involving pregnancy. In California Federal Savings & Loan v. Guerra (*Cal. Fed.*),[34] the Court upheld the validity of the California maternity leave statute against the claim that the statute's sex-specific benefit discriminated against men. The Court reasoned that it was *permissible* for the state to enact legislation which furthered equal opportunity by ensuring that the consequences of procreation were equal between women and men by taking into account and providing for pregnancy-related disability. One week later, the Court decided in Wimberly v. Labor and Industrial Relations Commission of Missouri (*Wimberly*)[35] that a prohibition against pregnancy discrimination in the award of unemployment benefits did not *require* taking pregnancy into account in the design of benefit denials for voluntary termination of employment. The Court upheld the denial of benefits where all employees disabled by a non–work-related disability were denied benefits. The sex-specific impact of a structure based on this "gender-neutral" standard was ignored. Moreover, the recognition in *Cal. Fed.* of the inequality in employment opportunity that results if the workplace structure fails to recognize both female and male reproductive roles is totally absent in *Wimberly.*

The limited potential of discrimination analysis is also related to its inability to reach cases in which an employer has failed to adopt *any* policy, or has merely incorporated market or industry standards or structures. . . .

As many feminist critics have noted, the effect of these analytical limitations is to preserve structures built on a "male" image or standard. The male standard is objectified as neutral and universal. All that is required is that women have the same opportunity under that standard. Similarly, if the presence of women in the workplace generates the creation of new benefits based on a female standard, it requires extending the same benefits to men. The only justification for sex-specific benefits is biological uniqueness and the necessity of minimal benefits to ensure equal opportunity. This permits the continuation of the existing structure as long as its impact is equally felt, positively or negatively, on both sexes as their biological selves.

Yet simply treating women "the same" as men means stifling any change in the concept of parenting; it also suggests that non-support is acceptable. . . . Another way of looking at this is to examine the problem of difference. . . . Discrimination analysis does not celebrate or support difference except by requiring that it be ignored—tending to leave the existing structure in place, supporting the status quo.

B. Sex vs. Gender

Discrimination analysis focuses on biological sex, not socially constructed gender. The heart of work-family conflict, however, arises from the way in which the workplace is structured around powerful gender constructs. The assumption and adoption of a male standard is at the core of that structure. While discrimination analysis attacks some issues of gender, it seems profoundly ill-suited for a frontal assault on the gendered structure of the workplace.

Discrimination analysis identifies as most offensive the denial of access or opportunity on the basis of immutable attributes of biology. Accordingly, discrimination analysis is preoccupied with generalizations related to biological sex (i.e., assumptions about consequences of biology: that women are weaker, slower, etc.). Such generalizations are either untrue for all or most women;[36] or are untrue for individual members of the class of women.[37] Even when the generalizations about women upon which employment benefits are premised seem to be statistically true, courts may nevertheless hold that the connection is arbitrary and irrational. . . .

Discrimination analysis is more difficult to apply to social and cultural gender constructs. First, while one sex may be more disadvantaged than the other, both sexes are harmed by gender constructs because they assign roles, characteristics and choices on the basis of sex. Second, the gender constructs are paired, interrelated and interlocked, which makes the isolation of a single construct or role seem arbitrary and artificial and precludes the comparison essential to equality analysis. Fundamentally, the difficulty of dealing with gender revolves around its social/cultural origin.[38]

While most persons agree that biological difference should not be the basis for work-family distinctions, we are not sure whether to condemn or support roles that have become associated with gender. Analytically, we have difficulty identifying the evil: is it that since there is no biological basis for the division of work and family responsibilities, any characteristic of the structure which reinforces a sexual division of those responsibilities is discriminatory? Or is it that any structure which only incorporates the male standard is discriminatory because it fails to permit the female role to exist on an equal basis, with equal consequences? It is not clear whether we can, or should, attack socially constructed concepts of male and female roles, masculinity and femininity.

This debate is related to the question of whether employers should be held responsible for societal discrimination. Specifically, to what extent should an employer be held responsible for individuals' perception of their range of employment opportunities, or for the extent to which that perception is constrained by a structure that incorporates a gendered view of who belongs in the workplace.

When discrimination analysis *has* focused on gender, it has done so primarily through an analysis of sex stereotypes. Discrimination analysis has focused on the extent to which stereotypes are "anti-individual," i.e., the fact that some individuals don't fit the stereotype (they aren't like other women or they have managed to be like men). But it is unclear how employers should treat specific men or women who fit the stereotype or gender construct. Should employers be allowed to discriminate on that basis when the effect is to adopt a sex-specific model (male) for the workplace? Should such decisions be condemned because they adopt a "male" structure, because they exclude certain individuals on the basis of socially constructed gender?

Alternatively, what is the consequence of "choosing" a gendered role, or "voluntarily" adopting such a role? For example, what is the consequence of choosing the traditional female work-family role, or of choosing traditionally female work, or the consequence of a reluctance to apply for traditionally male positions? The *Sears* case exemplifies a number of these difficulties.[39] In that case, "choice" became a defense to a statistical pattern of discrimination, while the underlying stereotype, the gendered construction of the job and the gendered constraint on choice, was not addressed. The focus of the case shifted from the employment structure and the definition of particular jobs according to a male standard to the reasons why particular employees made their choices, independent of any consideration of the structural or cultural discouragement of making those choices.

C. Issues of Power and Patriarchy

Existing discrimination analysis also fails to deal effectively with problems of power. With the possible exception of sexual harassment, discrimination analysis has not been a means to attack patriarchy. It may be a means to prevent the recreation of patriarchy if any affirmative restructuring occurs, but it seems inadequate to mandate redistribution of existing power or to change the pattern of power relations. This is tied to the structural and gender limitations of the analysis. . . .

Another limitation of discrimination analysis in reaching power issues is its individualistic emphasis. As Fran Olsen points out:

> Antidiscrimination law promotes market individualism and promises each individual woman that she can win success in the market if only she chooses to apply herself. It obscures for women the actual causes of their oppression and treats discrimination against women as an irrational and capricious departure from the normal objective operation of the market, instead of recognizing such discrimination as a pervasive aspect of our dichotomized system. The reforms reinforce free market ideology and encourage women to seek individualistic, inward-looking solutions to social problems.[40]

Rather than empowering, the discrimination framework can disempower. It puts the victim off by requiring that the individual identify as a victim, who must pinpoint the aberration from an otherwise presumably non-discriminatory structure.[41] It ignores the relational constraints that pull against the assertion of rights. The value of the equality framework then becomes largely symbolic, or, through publicized litigation, it occasionally acts as a constraint upon employers. It does not, however, affirmatively expand the choices of potential victims.

Furthermore, commentators have argued that discrimination analysis disempowers when it is used to strike down protectionist legislation under the banner of the equality principle.[42] The practical result of this equality approach (dropping barriers to the workplace without attacking the male bias of the structure) has been, at best, a minor improvement in the lot of most women, and at worst a sanction of the decline of women's status. Employers have gained by being able to treat women like men, rather than "as people with different needs."[43] The result has been:

> a relative increase in the amount of female poverty, little reduction of unemployment in poorly paid work force sectors, a rather small narrowing in the wage-gap . . . and only selective relief from occupational segregation. In short, for all its euphoric and insistent tone, the notion of dropping barriers to equality for women at work has not prevented women from becoming poorer and has only marginally increased opportunities for genuine mobility.[44]

A final problem of discrimination analysis is the limited reach of the statutory structure across family/work and public/private divisions. The discrimination framework reinforces the work/family split by leaving family out of the analysis. There is no parallel "family discrimination" alongside employment discrimination; such a concept would breach the sphere of "private" activity. In addition, use of existing discrimination analysis ties the solutions of work-family issues to employment-related benefits, leaving other nurturers unprotected and unsupported. Finally, it reinforces the definition of work as including only paid work; discrimination analysis does not value, empower, or provide economic independence for caregivers.

The Role of Discrimination Analysis

Given the limitations and inadequacies of existing discrimination analysis, we are faced with two different strategies for unraveling work-family conflict: (1) To continue to try to pull, stretch, or force equality analysis to encompass expanded notions of equality that would achieve some measure of structural change; or (2) to acknowledge the limited reach of discrimination analysis, articulate that limit, and move on in search of a broader framework. Although we should do both, our primary focus should be upon the construction of another framework. This conclusion rests on the theory that work-family conflict is not solely an issue of gender. . . .

We should not, however, discard or reject discrimination analysis wholesale. The discrimination framework remains useful because it takes advantage of an existing set of ideas and legal categories that retain great power and persuasive capacity. Although limited and partial, it nevertheless may be a part of a broader framework. It potentially can contribute to the project of resolving work-family conflict in three ways: (1) by continuing to force confrontation of the gendered reality of the existing occupational and wage structure; (2) by further reconstructing fundamental concepts of equality and liberty; and (3) by acting as a "preventer" with respect to new, affirmative legislation, to prohibit the perpetuation or reinstitutionalization of patriarchal structures. . . .

The issues raised by work and family go beyond discrimination analysis, requiring not only equalizing treatment, opportunity, and access to the workplace, but also changing the structure of the workplace to include room for parenting. Even in its most expansive form, discrimination analysis is an inadequate, limited tool for restructuring the workplace, a task that requires a deconstruction of gender roles and an attack on patriarchy within family and work and within the relationship between work and family. The restructuring also reaches beyond gender issues: it is not simply a matter of adding women to work and men to family, or integrating the values of each sphere to reflect the other, but requires rethinking and changing work and family and their relationship to each other by imagining that relationship without the framework of gender.

The difficulty in envisioning a non-gendered ideal of work and family attests to the depth of gendered thinking and conceptualization of self, work, family and society. It also demonstrates the need to take gender into account in order to eliminate its predominance in work and family and prevent its reinstitutionalization. Resolving issues of work and family are essential to women's equality, in a real and meaningful sense (as opposed to the sense of formal rights and privileges), and to liberating both women and men from the limited universe of gender-prescribed roles. Work and family is also more than that—it challenges us to reexamine workers and the relation between work and family, the nature and necessity for workplace hierarchy, and the economic consequences of post-industrial capitalism.

Discrimination analysis is at best a partial means to address women's issues and gender issues, and is inadequate to define the restructuring of the workplace that work-family conflict exposes as necessary. Feminist thought contributes to both the project of resolving the gender paradox and the project of transformation: to improving women's position and exposing the anti-female, anti-family bias of the existing work-family structure. It also encourages us to promote values devalued as merely "female" in transforming the workplace and providing support for the functions of families. It begins and is grounded in the inter-woven paradoxes of work and family that are the premises which we must get beyond in order to transform the structure of work and family.

Notes

1. Various disciplines have documented the work-family conflict, and each discipline reflects its own set of values, assumptions and changing biases about the nature of work and family and their relationship. . . . The primary focus of much of the sociological and psychological data has been on dual career, i.e., dual profession, married couples. The data is thus limited to that perspective, although several scholars have begun to research blue collar and dual earner families. Brinkerhoff, Introduction, in M. B. Brinkerhoff ed., Family and Work 3–30 (1984); Rapoport & Rapoport, The Next Generation in Dual-Earner Family Research, in J. Aldous ed., Two Paychecks: Life in Dual-Earner Families 229–243 (1982); Walshok, Occupational Values and Family Roles: Women in Blue-Collar and Service Occupations, in K. W. Feinstein ed., Working Women and Families 63, 64 (1979). Much of the literature examines the impact of work on the family, but some researchers are beginning to argue that the impact is reciprocal. Brinkerhoff, supra. Finally, most of the studies focus on white couples. . . .

2. Economic Policy Council of UNA-USA, Work and Family in the United States: A Policy Initiative 51 (1985) [hereinafter Work and Family]; D. Burden & B. Googins, Boston University Balancing Job and Homelife Study 23–25 (1987). . . .

3. The precise issue of schedule conflict has been closely studied. Pleck & Staines, Work Schedules and Work-Family Conflict in Two-Earner Couples, in Aldous, *supra* note 1, at 63–87; G. L. Staines & J. H. Pleck, The Impact of Work Schedules on the Family (1983). These studies indicate the need for flexibility and, to the extent possible, control by the worker of his or her schedule. Staines & Pleck, *supra* this note, at 3.

4. See, e.g., C. P. Gilman, Women and Economics 145–146 (1898, reprinted 1966); E. Malos, The Politics of Housework 16–17 (1980). . . .

5. The basic pattern is that men do slightly more paid work than women, while women shoulder the vast amount of both household and childcare work. There is some movement toward a more egalitarian ideal, but that trend has not been matched by equal changes in reality. Most of the reduction in the female household role has come from simply doing less; very little reduction has come from redistribution of work. To the extent there has been redistribution, it more frequently occurs with respect to childcare than with respect to housework. [See] B.U. Study, *supra* note 2, at 13. . . ; Levitan & Belous, Working Wives and Mothers: What Happens to Family Life? 104 Monthly Lab. Rev. 26, 27 (Sept. 1981). . . .

6. . . . Some researchers had theorized that the effect of greater workforce participation by women would be the equalization of work and family responsibilities, based on the exchange model of division of marital responsibilities, whereby the division of tasks was explained by the wife's greater resource of time. Feminist critics argued that such an expectation ignored the power element in marital roles and the use of that power to avoid undesirable work. The feminist critique, combined with insights

from Marxist theorists, led to the articulation of role overload theory. Pleck, Working Wives/Working Husbands 15–23 (1985); Simpson & England, Conjugal Work Roles and Marital Solidarity, in Aldous, *supra* note 1, at 147–171.

There has been, however, some shift in the male family role. Despite the meager evidence of any major redistribution of family work, there is at least some evidence of a shifting paradigm toward more equity in family roles. It seems clear that the failure of redistribution stems at least partly from the identification of this work as "women's work," or devalued work. It also appears that for those men who are committed to actual equalization of tasks and a redefined role of fathering, there is virtually no external support. Beyond the structural problems in the workplace that disadvantage all parents, fathers are discouraged from being caregivers in addition to breadwinners. See generally Gilbert & Rachlin, Mental Health and Psychological Functioning of Dual-Career Families, 15 Counseling Psychologist 7, 15–18 (1987); Pleck, *supra* this note.

7. Model, Housework by Husbands, in Aldous, *supra* note 1, at 193–205. Pleck argues that the only solution is to reduce men's paid work time and to increase women's sharing of the breadwinner role; the structural issue is whether that alternative is even possible under existing work structures. Pleck, *supra* note 6, at 157–158. Pleck also points out, however, that a reduction in men's work role will have little impact absent ideological change in the view of men's role. Current variations in the amount of housework and child care a man does is not related as much to work factors as to the man's perspective of his work-family role. Pleck, The Work-Family Role System, in Kahn-Hut, Daniels & Colvard eds., Women and Work: Problems and Perspective 101, 104 (1982). According to researchers, the factors contributing to the unequal distribution of family work are not simply attitudinal problems (such as lack of motivation, role models, or the support of others), but also are tied to structural barriers of the workplace. Pleck, *supra* note 6, at 157; Model, *supra,* at 194–195.

8. Poloma, Pendleton & Garland, Reconsidering the Dual-Career Marriage, in Aldous, *supra* note 1, at 173, 181.

9. *Id.* at 180–189.

10. Bielby & Baron, Men and Women at Work: Sex Segregation and Statistical Discrimination, 91 Am. J. Soc. 759, 760 (Jan. 1986). . . .

11. Indeed, human capital theorists point to this very choice as the non-discriminatory basis for occupational patterns, neither questioning the gender roles nor the occupational structure. See, e.g., Women's Work, Men's Work: Sex Segregation on the Job 70–75 (1986); M. Gold, A Dialogue on Comparable Worth (1983).

12. Gilbert & Rachlin, *supra* note 6, at 14.

13. Sekaran, The Paths to Mental Health: An Exploratory Study of Husbands and Wives in Dual-Career Families, 58 J. Occupational Psychol. 129, 135–136 (1985). In this study of the relationship between job and life satisfaction in dual-career couples, Sekaran concluded that the paths to mental health differ by sex: husbands' well-being depended roughly equally on job and life satisfaction, while wives' well-being rested on life satisfaction, not job satisfaction. *Id.*

14. Gilbert & Rachlin, *supra* note 6, at 15–16.

15. A. Rich, Of Woman Born (1986); see also A. Daly, Inventing Motherhood (1983); Ruddick, Maternal Thinking, 6 Feminist Stud. 342 (1980).

16. Ruddick, *supra* note 15, at 343. . . .

17. Lamb, Russell & Sagi, Summary and Recommendations for Public Policy, in M. Lamb & A. Sagi eds., Fatherhood and Family Policy 248–250 (1983). This is gen-

erally true for Western countries, not just the United States. *Id.* See also Note, Fathers and Families: Expanding the Familial Rights of Men, 36 Syracuse L. Rev. 1265, 1266, 1283–1284 (1986). While the social, cultural, economic consequences of mothering are well documented, only fairly recently have researchers begun to study the poverty of the image of fatherhood. The results of these preliminary studies underscore once again the different experience of work for men and women, and the strong institutional barriers to more involved parenthood for fathers. Eisikovits, Paternal Child Care as a Policy Relevant Social Phenomenon and Research Topic: The Question of Values, in Lamb & Sagi, *supra* this note, at 15; Rodman & Safilios-Rothschild, Weak Links in Men's Worker-Earner Roles: A Descriptive Model, in Brinkerhoff, *supra* note 1, at 55.

18. Pleck, *supra* note 6, at 23. Role overload is not the result of the multiplicity of roles—indeed, such multiplicity is often viewed as healthy. See studies surveyed in R. K. Malmaud, Work and Marriage: The Two Profession Couple (1984), at Introduction. Role overload means the inability to meet the demands of the defined role, with that definition tied to socio-cultural definitions of roles.

19. Gilbert & Rachlin, *supra* note 6, at 16. "Thus, men who support equality for women often do so from an ideological commitment to equality in general, but this commitment is not part of their personal identity or consciousness. For such men *feminism is an abstract issue of rights and obligations, a set of rules to be followed.* This perception can cause difficulties because the tendency is for the man to decide what is fair (or convenient) from his perspective, to do this, and then to expect everything to be fine and perhaps even to be applauded. . . . He feels a sense of entitlement and recognition that she finds irritating to have to respond to." *Id.* (emphasis added).

20. *Id.* at 19. . . .

21. *Id.* at 16.

22. D. Friedman, Encouraging Employer Supports to Working Parents: Community Strategies for Change 101 (1983). In the B.U. Study, 11% of the workforce was composed of married males with wives at home. An even smaller number, 8.7%, were married parents with wives at home. The predominant pattern was dual-earner couples or single employees. B.U. Study, *supra* note 2, at 12. However, those who had wives full time at home tended to be males in upper level management positions. *Id.* "In other words, the men making the management decisions and setting human resource policy for the workforce may have little first hand knowledge of the lifestyles and multiple job/homelife responsibilities of the great majority of their employees." *Id.* . . .

23. Walker, Rozee-Koker & Wallston, Social Policy and the Dual-Career Family: Bringing the Social Context into Counseling, 15 Counseling Psychologist 97, 102 (1987).

24. Olsen, The Family and The Market: A Study of Ideology and Legal Reform, 96 Harv. L. Rev. 1497, 1498 (1983); see also Voydanoff, The Implications of Work-Family Relationships for Productivity 1–2 (1980) (discussing the myth of the separate worlds, and associating it with the Protestant work ethic).

25. The strong connection between the family and the workforce traditionally has meant that the family is a primary source of socialization and support for work. Nevertheless, the workplace has required separation between work and family. That is, attention to family responsibilities has usually meant temporary or long-term absence from the workforce. This is most clearly seen in the pattern of job interruptions and the reasons for job interruptions experienced by employed persons 21 to 64 years of

age. Women have more frequent job interruptions, which are almost entirely for family reasons; men have far fewer interruptions, with the most frequent cause being involuntary unemployment. . . . Bureau of the Census, Lifetime Work Experience and Its Effect on Earnings at 10, 20 (1984) (retrospective data from the 1979 Income Survey Development Program, Special Studies Series P-23, No. 136); Bureau of the Census, Male-Female Differences in Work Experience, Occupation, and Earnings: 1984, at 2, 3 (1987) (Data from the Survey of Income and Program Participation, Household Economic Studies, Series P-70, No. 10). . . .

26. Daily Lab. Rep. (BNA) No. 153, at B-1 (Aug. 8, 1986). . . . This type of convenient scheduling is most available in the finance, insurance, and real estate industries. *Id.* Even fewer workers have flexibility in the place where they work; only 8% of civilian workers work at home for eight or more hours in their sole or principal job. *Id.* Among alternate schedules, the most common is the compressed work schedule, that is, working forty hours in fewer than five days, usually four days. Smith, The Growing Diversity of Work Schedules, 109 Monthly Lab. Rev. 7, 9 (Nov. 1986). There is a general movement toward more diverse schedules, but it is not yet very strong. *Id.* at 13.

27. Women's Work, Men's Work, *supra* note 11, at 69–70. Two examples of this are academic tenure and law firm partnership decisions. Each decision is supposed to determine one's fitness and promise for the future, and is critical to one's career. To the extent that this decision has changed in recognition of family responsibilities, it has been to allow women with family responsibilities to "get off the track" for a limited period of time for childbearing. The track itself, however, has not been questioned; the structure of this key professional decision is simply viewed as a neutral custom.

28. Child-related benefits are more likely to be found in the public sector than the private sector, in large establishments rather than small ones, and in the service sector rather than the goods-producing industries. Of the small proportion of employers who provide child-related benefits or services, more provide information, counselling or referral than on-site day care or assistance with childcare expenses. A much larger proportion of employers claim to have some work schedule policies aiding childcare (just over 60%), but on closer scrutiny those policies provide very little beyond the ability to vary one's starting time or quitting time, to voluntarily work part-time at reduced earnings and benefits for a temporary period, or to utilize vacation or sick leave for childcare related reasons. Bureau of Labor Statistics, Childcare-Related Benefits Survey, reprinted in Daily Lab. Rep. (BNA) No. 10, at B-1 (Jan. 15, 1988).

29. Work and Family, *supra* note 2, at 1. . . .

30. . . . Despite the predominance of dual-parent families, this family form has dramatically declined in the past 20 years: as a proportion of all households, married couples with children under age 18 constituted 40% of all households in 1970; by 1984, these households only constituted 29% of all households, a drop of 11%. Bureau of the Census, Household and Family Characteristics: March 1984, at 1 (1985). The concurrent rise in single-parent families has been dramatic. For nearly a century, single-parent families represented approximately 10% of all households; since 1980, however, they have constituted at least 20% of all households, and . . . , now represent one-quarter of all families with children under the age of 18. Bureau of National Affairs (BNA), Work and Family: A Changing Dynamic 17 (1986). The number of single-parent families has nearly doubled since 1970. Household and Family Characteristics, *supra* this note, at 3. . . .

31. Work and Family, *supra* note 2, at 45. . . .

32. Hayghe, Married Couples: Work and Income Patterns, 106 Monthly Lab. Rev. 28 (Dec. 1983) (most children have at least one employed parent).

33. Griggs v. Duke Power Co., 401 U.S. 424 (1971).

34. 479 U.S. 272 (1987).

35. *Id.* at 511.

36. For example, mandatory maternity leave policies, which were widespread prior to 1974, were based on the assumption that pregnancy disables women long before childbirth actually occurs. Dowd, Maternity Leave: Taking Sex Differences Into Account, 54 Fordham L. Rev. 699, 706 n.36 (1986). See also Finley, Transcending Equality Theory: A Way Out of the Maternity and the Workplace Debate, 86 Colum. L. Rev. 118, 126–144 (1986) (traditional treatment of pregnancy in the workplace).

37. These include policies excluding women on the basis of presumed inability to meet height, weight or strength requirements. See, e.g., Dothard v. Rawlinson, 433 U.S. 321 (1977); United States v. North Carolina, 512 F. Supp. 968 (E.D.N.C. 1981), *aff'd,* 679 F.2d 890 (4th Cir. 1982), *cert. denied,* 459 U.S. 1103 (1983); Berkman v. City of New York, 536 F. Supp. 177 (E.D.N.Y. 1982); EEOC v. Spokane Concrete Prods. Inc., 534 F. Supp. 518 (E.D. Wash. 1982). These cases represent stereotypical judgments: often the job "requirements" favor male attributes simply because the job is typically performed by males. Indeed, many of these requirements have been struck down on the basis that they are not demonstrably job-related, but rather are tied to gendered assumptions.

38. I have argued in the past that the distinction between biological and socially constructed difference is an important one. Dowd, Maternity Leave, *supra* note 36, at 762–763. I still believe that it is. Biological difference must be recognized and incorporated into the workplace framework. Socially constructed difference is quite distinct: to merely ameliorate its consequences, but accept its existence, would simply perpetuate the dominance that lies at the heart of that difference.

Scholars debate, however, where the line between biological and cultural differences should be drawn. See, e.g., Rossi, A Biosocial Perspective on Parenting, 106 Daedalus 1 (1977). . . .

39. EEOC v. Sears, Roebuck & Co., 839 F.2d 302 (7th Cir. 1988).

40. Olsen, Family and Market, *supra* note 24, at 1547.

41. Bumiller argues that: "[t]he acceptance of a situation of sexual or racial discrimination as a legal problem (a bipolar, rights-oriented, isolated dispute) structures the interpretation for both the participants and outsiders. In such a system, interaction with the law is alienating for social victims just as the language of legality is alienated from everyday discourse." Bumiller, Victims in the Shadow of the Law: A Critique of the Model of Legal Protection, 12 Signs 421, 423 (1987). Bumiller's analysis alludes to the rights critique, raising the question whether creating new rights to achieve a resolution of work-family issues is a viable, meaningful means to achieve that end. As Bumiller points out, the method may significantly affect whether the end is achieved. See generally Sparer, Fundamental Human Rights, Legal Entitlements, and the Social Struggle: A Friendly Critique of the Critical Legal Studies Movement, 36 Stan. L. Rev. 509 (1984); Schneider, The Dialectic of Rights and Politics: Perspectives from the Women's Movement, in D. Weisberg ed., Feminist Legal Theory: Foundations 507 (Temple Univ. Press, 1993). Awareness of the uses and limitations of rights (awareness of paradox) may permit a reasoned use of the concept as a conscious political choice. Singer, The Legal Rights Debate in Analytical Jurisprudence from Bentham to Holifield,

1982 Wis. L. Rev. 975 (the exposure of political agenda in the law simply makes the choice conscious instead of unconscious)....

42. See, e.g., McCloud, Feminism's Idealist Error, 5 N.Y.U. Rev. L. & Soc. Change 277, 284–285 (1986); see also Kessler-Harris, The Debate over Equality for Women in the Work Place, in Women and Work: An Annual Review 141, 154 (1985).

43. Kessler-Harris, *supra* note 42, at 154.

44. *Id.*

EEOC v. SEARS, ROEBUCK & CO.

628 F. Supp. 1264 (N.D. Ill. 1986)

NORDBERG, District Judge.

This opinion [of the U.S. District Court for the Northern District of Illinois] marks the culmination of a lengthy dispute between the Equal Employment Opportunity Commission ("EEOC") and Sears, Roebuck & Co. ("Sears"), the world's largest retail seller of general merchandise. . . . After an extensive investigation and extensive conciliation discussions, EEOC filed this suit in 1979, alleging nationwide discrimination by Sears against women in virtually all aspects of its business, in violation of Title VII of the Civil Rights Act of 1964, as amended, 42 U.S.C. §2000e et seq.

The . . . allegations EEOC sought to prove at trial were that Sears engaged in a nationwide pattern or practice of sex discrimination: by failing to hire female applicants for commission selling on the same basis as male applicants, and by failing to promote female noncommission salespersons into commission sales on the same basis as it promoted male noncommission salespersons into commission sales (commission sales claim). . . . The allegations are limited to the time period beginning March 3, 1973, and ending December 31, 1980.

A trial before the court was held lasting 10 months. . . .

Based on all of the testimony presented, the credibility of the witnesses and the weight to be given their testimony, the exhibits received in evidence, and the law governing this case, the court concludes that the EEOC has failed to prove its case on either claim of discrimination and finds that Sears has not discriminated against women in hiring, promotion, or pay, as claimed. . . .

The court must first determine the legal standards to apply to this case. Two separate legal analyses are applied to Title VII cases, disparate treatment and disparate impact. Each has its distinct elements and burdens of proof. . . .

In this case, the EEOC relies principally on the disparate treatment theory. . . .

The disparate treatment theory evolved under §703(a)(1) of Title VII, 42 U.S.C. §2000e-2(a)(1). Under this theory, employers are prohibited from treating an employee less favorably than the employee's peers because of the employee's sex, race, color, religion, or national origin. In a disparate treatment case, a plaintiff must prove discriminatory intent. This is the most common type of discrimination claim. It may be

571

brought by an individual, or as a "pattern and practice" claim alleging systemic disparate treatment of a protected group. . . .

To establish a prima facie case of intentional discrimination, the plaintiff must prove that he is a member of the protected class, has substantially the same qualifications as those not in protected classes, but was not treated on an equal basis by the employer. A plaintiff's prima facie case creates a rebuttable presumption that the defendant unlawfully discriminated against the plaintiff. . . .

The plaintiff then must persuade the court that the defendant's explanation is unworthy of credence, or that a discriminatory reason more likely motivated the defendant. Importantly, the plaintiff always retains the ultimate burden of persuasion. . . .

Since the EEOC admits that it has not identified any specific, facially neutral policy of Sears which disproportionately excludes women from the jobs at issue in this case, the court will apply only the disparate treatment theory to this case.

Virtually all the proof offered by the EEOC in this case is statistical in nature, or related to the statistical evidence. Statistics are an accepted form of circumstantial evidence of discrimination. In some cases, where "gross disparities" are shown, statistics alone may constitute a prima facie case. . . .

Statistical evidence, like other evidence, must not be accepted uncritically. . . . Without a sound theoretical basis, which is carefully reasoned and closely tailored to the factual circumstances of the case, the statistical results can be meaningless. Close attention will therefore be paid in this case to the assumptions made by the experts and their relation to reality. . . .

[Discussion of the concepts of statistical significance and multiple regression is omitted. *Ed.*]

Hiring and Promotion into Commission Sales

EEOC attempted to prove at trial that Sears intentionally discriminated against women in hiring and promotion into commission sales on a nationwide basis from 1973 until 1980. . . .

A. *General Background*

Sears is the nation's largest retailer of general merchandise, employing approximately 380,000 persons in over 4,000 facilities across the country. During the relevant time period, Sears had approximately 920 retail stores. Its corporate headquarters is located in Chicago, Illinois. . . .

General corporate policies at Sears are formulated at the corporate headquarters, communicated to the territorial organizations, and eventually disseminated to individual stores. Although Sears has some very strongly enforced corporate policies, its entire management system overall is highly decentralized. This includes its hiring and compensation practices. Maximum flexibility, within bounds, is given to individual store managers to respond to the surrounding markets. Each store manager's compensation is significantly tied to the profitability of his or her store. Commission sales is a major source of store profits, and having a qualified and successful commission salesforce is of great importance to individual store managers. All of this has been very important to Sears' success over the years.

1. COMMISSION SALES AT SEARS

During 1973–1980, Sears retail stores were divided into approximately 55 retail divisions. Salespersons in these divisions were paid either on a commission or noncommission basis. Merchandise sold on commission was usually much more expensive and complex than merchandise not sold on commission. Commission selling usually involved "big ticket" items, meaning high cost merchandise, such as major appliances, furnaces, air conditioners, roofing, tires, sewing machines, etc. Noncommission selling normally involved lower priced "small ticket" items, such as apparel, linens, toys, paint and cosmetics.

Until 1977, commission salespeople were paid on a "draw versus commission" basis. Commissions ranged between six and nine percent. Under this system, salespersons were guaranteed a "draw" each week, usually not exceeding 70% of average or estimated earnings. However, if the salesperson's commissions did not equal the amount of his weekly "draw", he incurred a deficit. This deficit was carried over to the next week. If the salesperson exceeded his draw for the next week, the excess would be applied against the preceding week's deficit. If the deficit was not eliminated in the following week, the deficit would be cleared. Thus, the deficit would be carried over for only one week. However, if the salesperson failed to meet his draw over a period of time, his employment could be terminated. Thus, there was substantial risk attached to commission selling.

After 1977, this risk was ameliorated to some extent when Sears changed its method of compensating commission salespersons to a "salary plus commission" basis. This change was implemented primarily to reduce the financial risk of selling on commission in an effort to attract more women to commission sales. Under this system, the salesperson earned a nominal salary plus a three percent commission. However, the salesperson's income was still substantially dependent on the amount of sales made, and failure to make sufficient sales could result in termination.

Noncommission salespeople were compensated on a straight hourly rate, except that a nominal 1% commission was earned by full time salespersons on all sales until January 1979. Throughout the period from 1973 through 1980, full time and part time commission salespersons on average earned substantially more than full time and part time noncommission sales persons.

Commission selling techniques varied from division to division, depending on the nature and price of the merchandise. Technical skills required to sell also varied widely between divisions. Some divisions required a high level of technical knowledge and expertise, while others required less technical knowledge. For example, selling in the Installed Home Improvements divisions required substantial technical knowledge and a high degree of motivation. The selling of some products was done on an "outside basis," at the customer's home or place of business. Products requiring "outside" selling included central air conditioning, heating, and plumbing systems. Merchandise sold "inside" included water heaters, attic fans, and other big ticket items which did not require complicated estimates or installations. . . . All commission sales positions required a high degree of motivation. The salesperson's income and continued employment was dependent upon his ability to sell. In addition, as noted above, a substantial part of the store's revenues, and the store manager's income, was dependent upon commission sales. Managers therefore endeavored to hire the most highly qualified commission salespeople.

2. QUALIFICATIONS FOR COMMISSION SALES POSITIONS

No written document at Sears specifically identifies the qualifications for commission sales positions. Sears' Retail Testing Manual (entitled "Psychological Tests for Use in Sears Retail Stores," Pl. Ex. 108, Def. Ex. 34), contains the only written description of a desirable commission sales candidate. The commission salesperson is described as a "special breed of cat," with a sharper intellect and more powerful personality than most other retail personnel. According to the manual, a good commission salesperson possesses a lot of drive and physical vigor, is socially dominant, and has an outgoing personality and the ability to approach easily persons they do not know. A good commission salesperson needs the ability to react quickly to a customer's verbal suggestions and modify the approach accordingly. Thus, according to the Retail Testing Manual, a higher level of "salesmanship" is required of the commission salesperson than is required of the general salesperson.

However, the Retail Testing Manual generally was not relied on to any significant extent in selecting commission salespersons. . . .

First, in reviewing applications to identify potential commission sales candidates, Sears managers and interviewers look for: prior commission selling experience, prior experience selling a product line sold on commission at Sears, any specific indication of interest in commission sales, knowledge or experience of any kind in a product line, availability during the hours required for a particular job, a work or personal background reflecting a history of achievement, prior experience involving significant public contact, and any special training, education or experience indicating an active, outgoing personality. Previous product line experience was particularly important when there was a commission sales vacancy in an installed home improvements division, the automotive divisions, or custom draperies.

However, most of the essential qualities for commission selling could be determined only from an interview, not from a written application. . . . During the interview, managers looked for a number of important qualities, including aggressiveness or assertiveness, competitiveness, the ability to communicate effectively, persuasiveness, an outgoing, social or extraverted personality, self-confidence, personal dominance, a strong desire to earn a substantial income, resilience and the ability to deal with rejection, a high level of motivation and enthusiasm for the job, maturity, and a good personal appearance. The extent that each of these characteristics was required depended on the particular job opening. . . . However, as with all hiring decisions at Sears, the qualifications sought in commission sales applicants were often modified or relaxed to comply with Sears' Affirmative Action Plan, described below. . . .

4. AFFIRMATIVE ACTION AT SEARS

Sears has for many years had a far ranging and effectively enforced affirmative action program. Sears was the first major retail employer in the nation to institute an affirmative action program. Sears' program became a model plan followed by other corporations in the retail industry and in other industries as well.

Sears' commitment to affirmative action began in 1968, when it appointed its first Equal Opportunity Director. . . .

In 1968, Sears began to develop its affirmative action program by distributing a questionnaire to obtain information about minorities and women at Sears. One of the pages of the questionnaire was specifically devoted to the movement of women into commission sales. (Sears Ex. 247, Tab. 1268, at 7). Sears then began to formulate its affirmative action program, which required Sears managers to consider the race, sex, and national origin of applicants and employees in making every employment decision. Because Sears was decentralized and each Sears unit hired independently, each unit had its own specially tailored plan.

In 1969, Sears set a long-term goal of 38 percent women in all jobs at Sears. This figure was derived from the government's estimates of women in the labor force. Because the female percentage of Sears employees substantially exceeded 38 percent, Sears concentrated on promoting women into non-traditional areas. . . .

In April, 1970, Sears instituted a centralized, company-wide affirmative action program for women and minorities. In 1971, full time executives were hired to administer the program from the corporate headquarters and territorial offices. . . . Sears' plan was revised in 1972. The stated long term goal of the plan was to obtain parity with the proportion of women and minorities in the total work force. Hiring goals were set for each unit to reflect the local populations. Managers were required to report efforts to contact minority and women's groups and other recruiting efforts. They were also required to identify and develop promotable women and minority employees, and to encourage minorities and women to participate in training programs. . . .

In February, 1973, A. Dean Swift became president of Sears. One of his first actions as president was to call a conference of Sears' top 250 executives, for the first time in 23 years, to discuss affirmative action. The topic of the conference was the personal accountability of managers for affirmative action. Out of this conference grew the Mandatory Achievement of Goals ("MAG") Plan. The MAG Plan set long term goals for both timecard and checklist women. To meet these goals for timecard employees (including commission sales), the Plan required that managers fill one out of every two positions with women or minorities. . . .

Each store's compliance was monitored at the group and territorial level. Regularly scheduled personnel meetings always included discussions of affirmative action. . . .

In addition to imposing these hiring and promotion goals, in 1972, Sears implemented an Equal Pay Affirmative Action Plan. Under the plan, a nationwide formula was established for setting timecard salary to ensure that male and female timecard employees received equal pay. . . .

The sincere dedication and commitment of Sears management at all levels to affirmative action was evident from the testimony of the Sears' officials and employees, whom the court found to be highly credible witnesses. Sears' program exceeded the requirements of Title VII or any other governmental regulation. . . .

NONSTATISTICAL EVIDENCE

Despite the comprehensive, nationwide scope of its lawsuit, EEOC did not produce any victims of discrimination by Sears, or any persons who claimed they witnessed discrimination against women by Sears. EEOC points, instead, to two aspects of Sears' selection process to support its statistical analyses: the subjective nature of Sears' selection process, and its testing practices. First, EEOC asserts that the absence of objective criteria for selection provides a ready mechanism for discrimination. It presented evidence showing a lack of written guidelines for selection of commission salespersons, and the lack of formal training of interviewers, both of which permitted subjective hiring decisions. . . . Interviewers were expected to learn the desirable characteristics for commission salespersons from observation of those persons presently selling on commission, and from managers' guidance as to the types of individuals who had been successful in the past.

EEOC also relies on Sears' Retail Testing Manual, discussed above, which apparently contains the only written descriptions of the desirable characteristics of a commission salesperson. EEOC focuses on the original version of the manual, issued in 1953, which describes a commission salesperson as a man who is "active," "has a lot of drive," possesses "considerable physical vigor," "likes work which requires physical energy," etc. References to males were eliminated in the 1960's. . . .

EEOC also presented evidence of Sears' testing practices, EEOC focused its presentation on the Vigorous Dimension of the Thurstone Temperament Schedule. Some of the questions from which the vigor score is determined would more likely be answered affirmatively by males.[29] . . .

D. Analysis of EEOC's Evidence: Hiring

EEOC has relied almost exclusively on its statistical analyses to meet its burden of persuasion on its commission sales claim. There is so much imprecision in all of the underlying data being used that the mathematical presentation connoting precision is highly misleading. EEOC's statistical evidence is so flawed that it is not sufficient to meet its burden of persuasion.

---

[29]Questions asked include: "Do you have a low pitched voice?" "Do you swear often?" "Have you ever done any hunting?" "Have you played on a football team?" However, as will be discussed below, men and women were evaluated using different scales.

First, one of the most serious flaws pervading all of EEOC's statistical analyses is in its selection of the applicant pool for commission sales jobs at Sears. Dr. [Bernard] Siskin arbitrarily included in his "sales" applicant pool, on which he based all of his statistical analyses, any individual in the sampled stores who applied for any job at Sears, except those who specifically applied for nonsales jobs only. Thus, he considered that any person who checked the "sales" box on the application, or "sales" and any other box, or even those who checked the "any of the above" box, were applying specifically for a commission sales position at Sears. He also arbitrarily assumed that all of these members of his "sales" pool were applying for all commission sales positions at Sears in all divisions. EEOC presented no material evidence to support either assumption, and Sears' evidence proved that both assumptions were false. . . .

A second major flaw in EEOC's analysis is its failure to include in its analysis many important factors that significantly affect the hiring process. . . .

First, with respect to excluded factors, the one single most important factor intentionally excluded by EEOC is the applicant's interest in commission sales and in the product to be sold. Dr. Siskin simply assumed that all applicants in his "sales" pool were equally interested in and qualified for all commission sales jobs at Sears. There was no basis in the evidence for this assumption; the evidence is overwhelmingly to the contrary. As will be discussed below, many applicants for sales jobs at Sears were not in fact interested in selling on commission, and women were considerably less interested in commission sales than men. Moreover, many women were not interested in selling those product lines which have been called "non-traditional." . . .

FAULTY BASIC ASSUMPTIONS

Even more important than EEOC's errors in constructing its data base and adjusting for factors important to commission sales hires, EEOC's statistical analyses are based on two essential assumptions for which there is no credible support in the record. In designing all of his statistical analyses relating to commission sales, Dr. Siskin made the important assumptions that (1) all male and female sales applicants are equally likely to accept a job offer for all commission sales positions at Sears, and (2) all male and female sales applicants are equally qualified for all commission sales positions at Sears. . . .

EEOC has offered no credible evidence to support its assumption of equal interest by male and female applicants in all commission sales positions at Sears. Sears, on the other hand, has offered much credible evidence that employees' and applicants' interests, preferences and aspirations are extremely important in determining who applies for and accepts commission sales jobs at Sears. Sears has proven, with many forms of evidence, that men and women tend to have different interests and aspirations regarding work, and that these differences explain in large part the lower percentage of women in commission sales jobs in general at Sears, especially in the particular divisions with the lowest proportion of women selling on commission.

(1) Store Witnesses. The most credible and convincing evidence offered at trial regarding women's interest in commission sales at Sears was the detailed, uncontradicted

testimony of numerous men and women who were Sears store managers, personnel managers and other officials, regarding their efforts to recruit women into commission sales. As discussed above, attracting women to commission sales has been an important priority in Sears' affirmative action programs since the first affirmative action questionnaire was circulated in 1968. Sears managers and other witnesses with extensive store experience over the entire relevant time period testified that far more men than women were interested in commission selling at Sears. Numerous managers described the difficulties they encountered in convincing women to sell on commission. Sears managers continually attempted to persuade women to accept commission selling or other non-traditional jobs. Women who expressed an interest in commission selling were given priority over men when an opening occurred. Managers attempted to persuade even marginally qualified women to accept commission selling positions. They would sometimes guarantee a woman her former position if she would try commission selling for a certain period. Store managers reported that they had interviewed every woman in the store and none were willing to sell on commission. Managers often had to "sell" the job to reluctant women, even though enthusiasm and interest in the positions were qualities management valued highly in commission salespeople. Despite these unusual efforts, managers had only limited success in attracting women to commission sales.

Female applicants who indicated an interest in sales most often were interested in selling soft lines of merchandise, such as clothing, jewelry, and cosmetics, items generally not sold on commission at Sears. Male applicants were more likely to be interested in hard lines, such as hardware, automotive, sporting goods and the more technical goods, which are more likely to be sold on commission at Sears. These interests generally paralleled the interest of customers in these product lines. Men, for example, were usually not interested in fashions, cosmetics, linens, women's or children's clothing, and other household small ticket items. Women usually lacked interest in selling automotives and building supplies, men's clothing, furnaces, fencing and roofing. Women also were not as interested as men in outside sales in general,[30] and did not wish to invest the time and effort necessary to learn to sell in the home improvements divisions. Women often disliked Division 45 (men's clothing) because it sometimes involved taking personal measurements of men. . . . As is evident from the above discussion, interests of men and women often diverged along patterns of traditional male and female interest.

This lack of interest of women in commission sales was confirmed by the number of women who rejected commission sales positions. . . . Women at Sears who were not interested in commission sales expressed a variety of reasons for their lack of interest. Some feared or disliked the perceived "dog-eat-dog" competition. Others were uncomfortable or unfamiliar with the products sold on commission. There was fear of be-

---

[30]Outside sales were required in Division 32 (fencing), Division 37 (floor coverings), Division 42 (plumbing and heating), Division 64 (building materials), and Division 65 (kitchens, dishwashers). Outside sales often required night calls on customers.

ing unable to compete, being unsuccessful, and of losing their jobs. Many expressed a preference for noncommission selling because it was more enjoyable and friendly. They believed that the increased earnings potential of commission sales was not worth the increased pressure, tension, and risk.

These reasons for women not taking commission sales jobs were confirmed in a study performed by Juliet Brudney[40] on behalf of Sears. Ms. Brudney conducted structured interviews of women in nontraditional jobs at Sears, including women in automotive and service technician jobs, and their supervisors. She also interviewed women who were seeking jobs or changing jobs, and found that they perceived commission sales as requiring cut-throat competitiveness that prevents friendships at work. They were also reluctant to sell products with which they were unfamiliar and preferred the security of a steady salary to the risks of making less in commission sales.

The results of Ms. Brudney's study were supported by the testimony of Sears' expert, Dr. Rosalind Rosenberg,[42] who testified that women generally prefer to sell soft-line products, such as apparel, housewares or accessories sold on a noncommission basis, and are less interested in selling products such as fencing, refrigeration equipment and tires. Women tend to be more interested than men in the social and cooperative aspects of the workplace. Women tend to see themselves as less competitive. They often view noncommission sales as more attractive than commission sales, because they can enter and leave the job more easily, and because there is more social contact and friendship, and less stress in noncommission selling. This testimony is consistent with the uncontradicted testimony of Sears' witnesses regarding the relative lack of interest of women in commission selling at Sears, and with the testimony of Ms. Brudney,[43] and is further evidence that men and women were not equally interested in commission sales at Sears.

(2) Survey Evidence. Sears also introduced a number of surveys taken of Sears employees and applicants which also demonstrate that women were much less interested than men in commission selling at Sears. This evidence also showed that women were

---

[40]Juliet Brudney is a consultant and writer on employment issues, particularly issues concerning women.

[42]Dr. Rosenberg is an associate professor of history at Barnard College, Columbia University, where she specializes in American women's history. The court found her to be a well-informed witness who offered reasonable, well-supported opinions. She was a highly credible witness.

[43]Neither Ms. Brudney nor Dr. Rosenberg contend that all women have these tendencies or preferences, and the court has not drawn any such inference from their testimony. They have merely attempted to describe the overall tendencies of many women. EEOC presented witnesses with contrary views, whose testimony is discussed below. Suffice it to say at this point that few sweeping generalities can be accurately made about women (or men) overall in the workplace or in society. The court continually throughout trial exhorted witnesses to quantify their generalizations by estimating some percentage of women with the interests or views being discussed. Few witnesses were able to do so. The court therefore gave little weight to much of the testimony generalizing about women in the workforce from the actions of a few. However, the testimony of Ms. Brudney, although not based on a scientific study, reflected actual views of women at Sears, and was corroborated by the testimony of credible Sears' witnesses discussed above. The testimony of Dr. Rosenberg was also consistent with the experience of Sears' managers and other personnel, and with other evidence discussed below, and has also accordingly been given some weight by the court.

particularly less interested than men in selling products in divisions where EEOC found the greatest disparities between the expected and actual proportions of women.

First, Sears presented extensive evidence of differences in the general interests and attitudes of men and women in American society over the past 50 years. This evidence was developed by Dr. Irving Crespi from an exhaustive study of national surveys and polls taken from the mid-1930's through 1983 which related to the changing status of women in American society. Although the evidence presented by Dr. Crespi demonstrated many changes in attitudes over the past 50 years, he made a number of conclusions directly relevant to women's interest in commission sales. Dr. Crespi found that: (1) men were more likely than women to be interested in working at night or on weekends, (2) women were more likely than men to be interested in regular daytime work; (3) men were more likely than women to be interested in sales jobs involving a high degree of competition among salespersons; (4) men were more likely to be interested in jobs where there was a chance of making more money, even though it involved a risk of losing the job if they did not sell enough; and (5) men were more likely than women to be motivated by the pay of a job than by the nature of the job and whether they like it. All of these conclusions support Sears' contention that women were less likely than men to be interested in commission selling in general. . . .

In addition, specific surveys of the interests of Sears employees reveal that far more men than women are interested in commission sales. Sears has taken regular morale surveys of its employees in every retail store approximately once every three years since 1939. Sears has also conducted a number of special surveys to ascertain employee opinions on particular subjects.

The morale surveys demonstrated that most noncommission salespeople were happy with their work, and that more noncommission saleswomen preferred to stay in their present jobs than noncommission salesmen. . . .

This survey evidence, which has not been challenged by EEOC, demonstrates that noncommission saleswomen were generally happier with their present jobs at Sears, and were much less likely than their male counterparts to be interested in other positions, such as commission sales. These results confirm the reports of Sears' witnesses that women were less interested in commission sales than men. . . .

(4) Other Evidence of Interest. The only evidence introduced by EEOC regarding the interest of women in commission sales is the testimony of several witnesses regarding women's interests and aspirations in the workforce in general.[60] These witnesses described the general history of women in the workforce, and contend essentially that there are no significant differences between the interests and career aspirations of men and women. They assert that women are influenced only by the opportunities presented to them, not by their preferences. They often focused on small segments of women, rather than the majority of women, in giving isolated examples of women who

---

[60]These witnesses were Dr. Alice Kessler-Harris, Dr. Janice Fanning Madden, and Eileen Appelbaum. . . .

have seized opportunities for greater income in nontraditional jobs when they have arisen.[62]

However, these experts provided little persuasive authority to support their theories. The particular examples of unknown numbers and proportions of women in history to which they refer generally focus on small groups of unusual women and their demonstrated abilities in various historical contexts, not on the majority of women or their interests at the time of this case. The sweeping generalizations these witnesses sought to make are not supported by credible evidence.[63] None of these witnesses had any specific knowledge of Sears, or provided any specific evidence to contradict the strong evidence presented by Sears of the actual differences between the interests of men and women in commission sales positions at Sears.

More convincing testimony in this area was offered by Sears expert Dr. Rosalind Rosenberg. Dr. Rosenberg testified that, although differences between men and women have diminished in the past two decades, these differences still exist and may account for different proportions of men and women in various jobs. She offered the more reasonable conclusion that differences in the number of men and women in a job could exist without discrimination by an employer.

In conclusion, EEOC's statistical analyses are dependent upon the crucial arbitrary assumption that men and women are equally interested in commission sales jobs at Sears. As is evident from the above discussion, EEOC has provided nothing more than unsupported generalizations by expert witnesses with no knowledge of Sears to support that assumption. Sears has offered a wide variety of credible evidence that, during 1973 to 1980, women in fact were far less interested in commission selling at Sears than men. All the evidence presented by Sears indicates that men are at least two times more interested in commission selling than women. Thus, EEOC's assumption of equal interest is unfounded and fatally undermines its entire statistical analysis. . . .

In addition to assuming equal interest, EEOC also assumed that male and female applicants in its "sales" pool are equally qualified for all commission sales positions at Sears. However, as EEOC's Commission Sales Report itself demonstrated, this assumption is also false. The report indicates that, on average, female applicants in the "sales" pool were younger, less educated, less likely to have commission sales experience, and less likely than male applicants to have prior work experience with the products sold on commission at Sears. Therefore, its erroneous assumption of equal quali-

---

[62]For example, Dr. Kessler-Harris testified about the experience of women during both World Wars, who took jobs such as welders, shipfitters, and crane operators, as well as similar experiences of other women in unusual circumstances throughout history. It is not an issue in this case that some women are both capable and interested in holding commission sales jobs in traditional male product areas, such as automotive, plumbing, furnaces and fencing. This is obviously true. The real question is what percentage of women versus men, who applied for those jobs at Sears stores during 1973 to 1980, were capable and interested.

[63]For example, Dr. Kessler-Harris insisted that numerical differences between men and women within jobs in the workforce can only be explained by sex discrimination by employers. Written Testimony of Alice Kessler-Harris; Tr. 16, 545–546. She offered no evidence to support this bald assertion. Also, Dr. Madden insisted that women's preferences play no part in their decisions regarding jobs. Written Direct Testimony of Dr. Janice Fanning Madden, at 1–2. She later admitted that interest may have some effect on female job decision-making.

fications of male-female applicants also undermines the validity of its statistical analyses, particularly its unadjusted analysis. . . .

EEOC'S NONSTATISTICAL EVIDENCE

Some of EEOC's nonstatistical evidence also merits discussion. First, EEOC has focused considerable attention on Sears' testing practices. Although EEOC has stated throughout this litigation that it does not claim that Sears' testing practices violate Title VII, it has attempted to show that Sears' psychological tests "disadvantaged" women.

However, many Sears applicants were not tested, and often those who were tested were not tested until after they were hired. . . . The credible evidence shows that test scores for women were often completely ignored in hiring women into commission sales.

[T]he actual scores of women on the "vigor" scale of the test shows that the vigor scores of women hired were substantially lower than those of the men hired. Sears Exhibit 6-III, 6-JJJ. [However] [t]here is no credible evidence that a woman's "vigor" score ever prevented her from being hired into commission sales at Sears. The court therefore finds that Sears' testing program did not discriminate against women, and provides no support for EEOC's claim.

EEOC also relies on what it characterizes as Sears' "masculine" description of a commission salesperson in Sears' Retail Testing Manual. However, there is no evidence that this historical description had any influence on hiring decisions, particularly during the years in question. To the contrary, Sears managers often paid no attention to information in the manual. . . .

Finally, EEOC presented two witnesses in its rebuttal case, two women who had applied for commission sales positions at Sears and were not hired. These witnesses were not called specifically to testify that Sears' had discriminated against them. They were called to rebut testimony of a Sears witness regarding coding of applications. Their testimony illustrated the difficulty of determining interest and qualifications of applicants solely from an application form. Neither witness provided any evidence that Sears discriminated against women.

One witness, Alice Howland, applied to a store which had hired only one commission salesperson from outside of Sears for nine years, from 1976 to the present. Consequently, at the time Ms. Howland applied, applications for full time commission sales generally were not even processed. Thus, her testimony provides no proof of discrimination by Sears.

The second witness, Lura Nader, applied for a commission sales position in draperies in response to an advertisement. She was not hired, and testified at trial that, while she didn't think so at the time, she now thought Sears had discriminated against her. However, Sears proved that it hired in that position at that time two other women who had applied on the same date as Ms. Nader and who had better qualifications for the job than she did. Faced with this evidence, Ms. Nader refused to alter her claim of discrimination. Obviously, however, her testimony provides no credible evidence that Sears discriminated against women.

Therefore, none of the nonstatistical evidence offered by EEOC supports its statistical analyses or provides any credible proof of discrimination by Sears. All of the deficiencies in EEOC's evidence discussed above leave its statistical analyses with virtually no persuasive value. . . .

Viewing all of this evidence together, considering the credibility of the witnesses and the reasonableness of their testimony, the court finds that EEOC has failed to carry its burden of persuasion. . . .

The most egregious flaw is EEOC's failure to take into account the interests of applicants in commission sales and products sold on commission at Sears. EEOC turned a blind eye to reality in constructing its artificial, overinclusive "sales" pool, and assuming away important differences in interests and in qualifications. . . .

Moreover, evidence presented by Sears provided a more reasonable basis for evaluating Sears, and showed that Sears met all reasonable estimates of the proportion of qualified and interested women. Its evidence demonstrated that, when interest and qualifications are taken into account, EEOC's alleged disparities are virtually eliminated.

Equally important, EEOC has failed to counter Sears' highly convincing evidence of its affirmative action programs. Sears has proven that it has had a long and serious commitment to affirmative action, which applied to the recruitment of women for its commission sales force. . . . EEOC has not presented any credible evidence to cast doubt on the commitment of Sears to affirmative action. The court therefore finds that Sears' evidence of its strictly enforced affirmative action programs is strong evidence that it did not in fact intentionally discriminate against women.

Finally, notably absent from EEOC's presentation was the testimony of any witness who could credibly claim that Sears discriminated against women by refusing to hire or promote women into commission sales. It is almost inconceivable that, in a nationwide suit alleging a pattern and practice of intentional discrimination for at least 8 years involving more than 900 stores, EEOC would be unable to produce even one witness who could credibly testify that Sears discriminated against her.[82] EEOC's total failure to produce any alleged victim of discrimination serves only to confirm the court's conclusion that no reasonable inference of sex discrimination can be drawn from EEOC's statistical evidence regarding hiring into commission sales.

Therefore, based on all of the evidence presented, the court concludes that EEOC has failed to prove that Sears had a pattern or practice of intentionally discriminating against women in hiring into commission sales. . . . Sears has proven legitimate, non-

---

[82]EEOC has argued that victims of discrimination often do not know that they have been discriminated against, and that therefore the court should not view its failure to produce persons who were discriminated against in a negative light. The number of Title VII suits filed by individuals alone seems to fairly refute EEOC's contention. More specifically, however, this dispute between EEOC and Sears has lasted for over ten years. With EEOC's vast investigation, and the enormous amount of information provided by Sears to it, EEOC had ample time and information available to identify at least some members of the alleged huge class of victims it purports to represent. . . . Moreover, particularly in the area of promotions, the EEOC should have presented evidence of actual applications for commission sales positions that were discriminatorily denied, or evidence that, had a woman employee who claims discrimination known of an opening in commission sales, she actually would have applied for that position.

discriminatory reasons for the alleged statistical disparities between the hiring of men and women into commission sales from 1973 until 1980, and EEOC has not proven them pretextual.

Much of the evidence discussed above with respect to hiring is relevant to EEOC's promotion claim against Sears, particularly the evidence regarding interest in commission sales, the qualities sought in commission salespeople, the characteristics of commission salespeople, and affirmative action. All of the court's findings above relating to these and all other relevant matters are incorporated here. . . .

EEOC v. SEARS, ROEBUCK & CO.

839 F.2d 302 (7th Cir., 1988)

HARLINGTON WOOD, Jr., Circuit Judge.

These appeals [to the United States Court of Appeals, Seventh Circuit] are the outgrowth of protracted litigation stemming from an EEOC commissioner's charge filed against Sears, Roebuck & Company. [T]he EEOC sought to prove that Sears engaged in a nationwide pattern or practice of discrimination against women from March 3, 1973, to December 31, 1980, by failing to hire and promote females into commission sales positions on the same basis as males and by paying female checklist management employees less than similarly situated male employees. The district court on January 31, 1986, held for Sears on all claims. [The EEOC here appeals the district court judgment.]

The district court in this case made a multitude of factual findings. Some of those findings rested on determinations of the credibility of various witnesses, and some were based on the district court's evaluation of statistical evidence. We accord [considerable] deference to the district court's findings based on evaluations of those types of evidence. . . .

We must also defer to the district court to a certain extent regarding the court's factual findings based on statistical evidence. [T]he primary statistical experts for each side—Dr. Bernard R. Siskin for the EEOC and Dr. Joan G. Haworth for Sears . . . together produced 5,275 pages of trial testimony. The judge specifically stated regarding this testimony that "[t]he credibility of statistical experts and the weight to be given their testimony were . . . of great importance." *Sears II,* 628 F.Supp. at 1279 & n.2. [The court also heard testimony of other expert witnesses, including historians Rosalind Rosenberg and Alice Kessler-Harris. *Ed.*]

B. Absence of Individual Victim Testimony

Regarding all major claims at issue—hiring, promotion and compensation—the district court found that EEOC's failure to present testimony of any witnesses who claimed that they had been victims of discrimination by Sears confirmed the weaknesses of the EEOC's statistical evidence. The EEOC, conceding it did not present any witnesses who testified to individual acts of discrimination,[8] argues that the district court gave undue weight to the absence of individual victim testimony. . . . We believe the district court accorded this lack of evidence the proper weight. . . .

The district court properly recognized the value of anecdotal evidence when it determined that lack of individual victim testimony reinforced its conclusions regarding the deficiencies in the EEOC's statistical evidence. . . . In this case the district court considered the lack of anecdotal evidence only after finding there were major problems with the EEOC's labor pool and determining that the EEOC's statistical evidence was severely flawed. . . . When experts disagree, as they did here, the court may need the help of live witnesses to relate their actual experiences.

The EEOC's reasons for not presenting such individual testimony are not satisfying. The EEOC argues that such evidence would be "inappropriate" because "where 47,000 hires and promotions were at issue . . . it would have been impossible to present enough individual demonstrations [sic] of discrimination to meaningfully reflect on the statistics." We do not agree that examples of individual instances of discrimination must be numerous to be meaningful. Even a few examples would have helped bring "cold numbers convincingly to life." International Brotherhood of Teamsters v. United States, 431 U.S. 324, 339 (1977). Furthermore, we agree with the district judge that considering the ten-year length of the lawsuit and the amount of investigation by the EEOC and information passed by Sears to the EEOC, it is difficult to see how the EEOC could fail to "identify at least some members of the alleged huge class of victims it purports to represent." Sears II, 628 F.Supp. at 1325 & n.82. The EEOC also argues that an individual applicant would not know if she had been discriminated against. While this speculative argument may be more apt for the hiring situation, in which an applicant may not know whether there was a vacancy or the qualifications of other persons who were hired, we agree with the district judge that in the area of promotions and compensation at least, the number of Title VII suits filed by individuals against employers in general "seems to fairly refute EEOC's contention." Id. . . .

C. Hiring

The district judge found a plethora of problems in the statistical analyses that the EEOC had offered to support the claim that Sears discriminated against women in hiring into commission sales positions from 1973 to 1980. Before addressing the EEOC's specific challenges to the district court's criticisms of its statistical evidence, it is help-

---

[8]Although the EEOC claims that two of its witnesses "testified in rebuttal that [they were] definitely interested in a commission sales position at the time [they] applied," the district court found, we believe correctly, that neither witness provided any evidence that Sears discriminated against women. [O]ne applied at a store in which applications for full-time commission sales were not usually processed because the store had done so little hiring outside of Sears for commission sales, while Sears showed that the store to which the other witness applied had hired two other women who had better qualifications than the witness.

ful to discuss . . . key findings made by the district court, which we believe are not clearly erroneous. Those findings are that during the period at issue in this case (1973–1980): . . . women were not as interested in commission selling as were men; and . . . women were not as qualified for commission selling as were men.

The court's . . . major findings, that there were different interests and qualifications among men and women for commission selling, were grounded in part on the court's recognition of differences between noncommission and commission selling at Sears. The court based these findings on the large amount of evidence presented by Sears on these issues. The court extensively discusses this evidence. Again, we cannot say that these findings are clearly erroneous.

Regarding the question of differing interests in general among men and women in commission selling, we have already briefly reviewed the types of evidence presented by Sears to the district court on this issue. We need only highlight some significant findings of the court in support of our determination that the court's finding was not clearly erroneous. The court found that "[t]he most credible and convincing evidence offered at trial regarding women's interest in commission sales at Sears was the detailed, uncontradicted testimony of numerous men and women who were Sears' store managers, personnel managers and other officials, regarding their efforts to recruit women into commission sales." *Id.* at 1306. These witnesses testified to their only limited success in affirmative action efforts to persuade women to sell on commission, and testified that women were generally more interested in product lines like clothing, jewelry, and cosmetics that were usually sold on a noncommission basis, than they were in product lines involving commission selling like automotives, roofing, and furnaces. The contrary applied to men. Women were also less interested in outside sales which often required night calls on customers than were men, with the exception of selling custom draperies. Various reasons for women's lack of interest in commission selling included a fear or dislike of what they perceived as cut-throat competition, and increased pressure and risk associated with commission sales. Noncommission selling, on the other hand, was associated with more social contact and friendship, less pressure and less risk. This evidence was confirmed by a study of national surveys and polls from the mid-1930's through 1983 regarding the changing status of women in American society, from which a Sears expert made conclusions regarding women's interest in commission selling; morale surveys of Sears employees, which the court found "demonstrate[ ] that noncommission saleswomen were generally happier with their present jobs at Sears, and were much less likely than their male counterparts to be interested in other positions, such as commission sales," *id.* at 1310; a job interest survey taken at Sears in 1976; a survey taken in 1982 of commission and noncommission salespeople at Sears regarding their attitudes, interests, and the personal beliefs and lifestyles of the employees, which the court concluded showed that noncommission salesmen were "far more interested" in commission sales than were noncommission saleswomen, *id.* at 1312; and national labor force data.

The court recognized the EEOC's expert witness testimony [by Alice Kessler-Harris] regarding women's general interests in employment, which essentially was that there were no significant differences between women and men regarding interests and career aspirations. We cannot determine the district court clearly erred in finding the evidence not credible, persuasive or probative. These expert witnesses used small samples of women who had taken traditional jobs when opportunities arose. Larger samples would have been more persuasive. In addition as the court found, "[n]one of these witnesses had any specific knowledge of Sears." *Id.* at 1314. The court found Sears' evidence [by Rosalind Rosenberg] clearly more persuasive on the issue of different interest in commission selling between men and women. The court also found significant Sears' evidence that women became increasingly willing to accept commission sales positions between 1970 and 1980 due to, among other things, changes in commission sales positions from mostly full-time and largely part-time (more women preferred part-time), change in compensation to salary plus commission (which eliminated a lot of risk), increased availability of day care, and a group of successful saleswomen who served as role models. . . .

Furthermore, we find the district court did not clearly err in crediting the testimony of Sears' store management witnesses regarding efforts to encourage women to take commission sales positions and women's lack of interest in those positions. . . .

If it is argued that there was no interest in commission selling only because there were no opportunities, which disputes Sears' argument that there was instead an actual lack of interest in the existing opportunities, we are faced with the problem of which comes first, interest or opportunity, a chicken-egg problem. This is again an area where EEOC might have called a representative group of disappointed witnesses who preferred commission selling, but were rebuffed. It did not.

In short, we hold that the district court did not clearly err in finding that women were not as interested in commission sales positions as were men.

We similarly find that the district court did not clearly err in concluding that women applicants had different qualifications than did men applicants. The court noted that the EEOC's Commission Sales Report indicated that "on average, female applicants in the 'sales' pool were younger, less educated, less likely to have commission sales experience, and less likely than male applicants to have prior work experience with the products sold on commission at Sears." *Sears II*, 628 F.Supp. at 1315. The EEOC does not challenge this finding.

All . . . of the court's findings discussed above—that commission selling is significantly different from noncommission selling, that women were not equally interested with men in commission selling at Sears, and that women applicants were not equally qualified with men for commission selling at Sears—form the bases for the court's criticisms of the EEOC's statistics regarding hiring at Sears.

HIRING PRACTICES

The EEOC maintains that the district court erred in determining that none of its evidence regarding the subjective nature of Sears' hiring process or regarding Sears' testing practices supported the EEOC's statistical analyses or provided any credible proof of discrimination by Sears. With respect to the subjectivity of Sears' hiring process, the

EEOC argued that there was no formal training and a lack of written instructions for Sears' interviewers regarding the qualities to look for in commission sales applicants. In addition, the EEOC pointed to what it referred to as a "highly masculine" description of a commission salesperson found in the Retail Testing Manual, which included phrases such as "active," "has a lot of drive," possesses "considerable vigor," and "likes work which requires physical energy." The EEOC also notes that a Sears official admitted that this reflected characteristics that "on average more men possess than women." The EEOC cites numerous cases for the proposition that a lack of objective standards regarding employment decisions can be a discriminatory practice because such a system with its lack of safeguards may easily be subject to abuse. . . .

Sears concedes that its hiring process was subjective, but argues that subjectivity is a necessary part of the hiring process and it does not follow that because a hiring process is subjective, it is necessarily discriminatory. . . .

The question, then, is how much subjectivity is permissible. . . . While it may have been better policy for Sears to have had written instructions and formal training for interviewers regarding qualities to look for in commission sales applicants, we cannot say on this record that Sears exercised so much subjectivity as to engage in a discriminatory practice. In addition, the court's finding regarding Sears' affirmative action efforts appears to obviate impermissible subjectivity on the part of Sears' interviewers. . . .

The EEOC also argues that the district court erred in finding that one aspect of Sears' testing practices was not discriminatory. The EEOC contends that a "vigor" scale, one of seven scales on the Thurstone Temperament Schedule, contained questions that would more likely be answered affirmatively by men, such as "Have you played on a football team?" The district court agreed that these questions would more likely be answered affirmatively by men, but chose to believe Sears' witnesses, who testified that many Sears applicants were not tested, or if they were tested, it was not until after they were hired. The court also believed Sears' managers, who testified that the test had little impact on any decision to hire and that test scores were adjusted for women. The EEOC argues that it is implicit in the district court's phrasing of the impact of the test that it had at least some impact. In light of the court's conclusion that there was no credible evidence that a woman's vigor score ever prevented her from being hired for commission sales at Sears, however, we find the court did not clearly err in determining this aspect of Sears' testing did not have enough impact, on its own, to prove a case of discrimination. . . .

D. Promotions

. . . Sears' general evidence regarding differences in men's and women's interest in commission selling that we discussed in the context of the hiring claim applies to the promotion claim as well. . . .

The district court's conclusions regarding the promotion claim also incorporated its decisions regarding the absence of individual victim testimony and Sears' affirmative action efforts. We have previously determined that these considerations were justified in the context of the claim of hiring discrimination, and see no reason not to apply them to the promotion context as well. Indeed, we think that the absence of individual victim testimony is even more difficult to understand in the promotion context.

Although there may have been some reliability problems in Sears' interest adjustments, the question is not whether the interest adjustments alone totally eliminate the promotion disparities. The question is rather whether the court clearly erred in determining that interest adjustments along with other considerations such as differences in qualifications, the lack of individual victim testimony, and Sears' affirmative action efforts negate any inferences of intentional discrimination against women in promotions to commission selling. We conclude that the district court did not clearly err. . . .

IV. Affirmative Action

The district court concluded that Sears' affirmative action evidence demonstrated that Sears had no intent to discriminate against women in either hiring, promotions, or pay. The EEOC argues that the district court erred in this determination, and clearly erred in finding that Sears had an affirmative action program since 1968 that made the movement of women into commission sales a priority. . . .

We cannot say that the district court's finding that Sears had no intent to discriminate against women in hiring or promotions into commission sales is clearly erroneous. The EEOC contends that the existence of an affirmative action program is not enough to support a finding of no intent to discriminate. The Second Circuit has noted, however, that "[t]he existence of a comprehensive affirmative action program is the antithesis of a pattern and practice of discrimination based on sex. Such a program is evidence of an intent to eliminate gender as an employment criteria [sic] and to root out subtle forms of discrimination. It thus directly controverts a claim that discrimination is the 'standard operating procedure.' " Coser v. Moore, 739 F.2d 746, 751 (2d Cir. 1984) (quoting International Brotherhood of Teamsters v. United States, 431 U.S. 324, 336 (1977)).

The EEOC essentially argues that the evidence of affirmative action is weak and cannot support a finding of no intent to discriminate. . . . The EEOC then argues that although according to Sears it had set a long range goal of 38% as early as 1969, "at no time prior to the full implementation of the MAG program (nor for some time thereafter) did the full time hiring rate for women even approach 38%, much less exceed it."

We nonetheless find the district court's finding that Sears actually had "a long and serious commitment to affirmative action" was not clearly erroneous. *Sears II,* 628 F.Supp. at 1324. . . . The district court in this case found that "attracting women to commission sales at Sears has been an important priority in Sears' affirmative action programs since . . . 1968." *Id.* at 1306. The EEOC argues that this finding is clear error, but the record evidences support for the court's finding. . . .

Regarding Sears' affirmative action program during the period of the charges at issue (roughly 1972 to 1980), the court relied on the description of the Mandatory

Achievement of Goals (MAG) affirmative action program, fully implemented in 1974, and "the testimony of the Sears' officials and employees, whom the court found to be highly credible witnesses," *Sears II,* 628 F.Supp. at 1294, who testified based on their own personal experiences how Sears tried to recruit women into commission sales positions. We do not find the court's findings that the requirements of Sears' affirmative action programs "highly influenced" all aspects of the hiring process or that the testimony of Sears' witnesses reflected the "sincere dedication and commitment of Sears management at all levels to affirmative action," *id.* at 1294, to be clearly erroneous. . . .

[The EEOC also appealed the district court's findings regarding a day's-leave-with-pay issue. The Sears Personnel Manual allowed a male employee a day of paid leave when his wife gave birth, although female employees were not given this benefit when they gave birth. The district court held that the EEOC failed to establish a prima facie case of discrimination under Title VII; the Court of Appeals affirmed. Another issue determined by the Court of Appeals concerned the district court's failure to dismiss the EEOC's suit based on a conflict of interest by the EEOC attorney investigating Sears, who was also a member of the board of directors of the NOW Legal Defense Fund. Although rebuking the EEOC for its actions, the Court of Appeals affirmed the district court's denial of the motion to dismiss. *Ed.*]

Conclusion

It appears from the record that this has been a war between two parties that both profess commitment to equality for employees regardless of sex. If Sears in fact did not have such a commitment during 1973–1980, then the EEOC has simply failed to prove that lack of commitment, which was the burden it had assumed. We defer, as we must, to the trial court's factual findings unless they are clearly erroneous. We also defer to the trial court's judgment of the credibility of the witnesses heard and observed by it, and not by us. We view this as a difficult case which was as well-handled by the trial court as was reasonably possible. . . . We hope this determination will not be considered all loss and will instead assist the EEOC in various ways in the future pursuit of its worthy objectives.

CUDAHY, Circuit Judge, concurring in part and dissenting in part:

It is extremely difficult to distinguish superficial blemishes from structural defects in this oversized and confusing case. Although its efforts are impressive and, in many respects, commendable, the majority has been only partially successful. Its opinion properly identifies some important shortcomings in the EEOC's case; but it overstates the significance of others and seems to overlook entirely certain equally serious flaws in Sears' argument. Thus, it is true that the EEOC's internal machinations in initiating this case deserve condemnation. It is equally true that the EEOC as much as gave the case away by failing to produce any flesh and blood victims of discrimination. [T]he

EEOC's failure to present first-hand evidence makes Sears' lopsided victory far easier to understand. I would reiterate, however, that key elements in Sears' case have escaped critical examination.

Perhaps the most questionable aspect of the majority opinion is its acceptance of women's alleged low interest and qualifications for commission selling as a complete explanation for the huge statistical disparities favoring men. The adoption by the district court and by the majority of Sears' analysis of these arguments strikes me as extremely uncritical. Sears has indeed presented varied evidence that these gender-based differences exist, both in our society as a whole and in its particular labor pool. But it remains a virtually insuperable task to overcome the weight of the statistical evidence marshalled by the EEOC or the skepticism that courts ought to show toward defenses to Title VII actions that rely on unquantifiable traits ascribed to protected groups.

I start with the expectation that commission salespeople generally see themselves as the elite of the sales force. They make more money than noncommission sales people and obtain their positions through a more selective hiring process. As a consequence, they enjoy greater prestige. They are people with confidence in their ability to captivate customers and move merchandise. I would expect them to look with condescension, if not contempt, upon retail clerks working as order-takers for a straight wage. I do not therefore quarrel with the majority's proposition that retail order-taking is a "different" task from commission selling. But I would expect that the jobs are most often seen in a vertical alignment with commission selling on top. Whether or not the perspective that gives rise to this hierarchical ranking is commendable, it is certainly pervasive. I think my view differs from that of the majority, who seem to believe that the tasks are perceived as coequal not as occupying distinct tiers in a vertical pecking order.

These perspectives are important because the majority's more benign view tends to minimize the significance of Sears' contentions that women lack the interest and qualifications to sell on commission. Women, as described by Sears, the district court and the majority, exhibit the very same stereotypical qualities for which they have been assigned low-status positions throughout history. The majority states that [the] reasons for women's lack of interest in commission selling included a fear or dislike of what they perceived as cut-throat competition, increased pressure and risk associated with commission sales. Noncommission selling, on the other hand, was associated with more social contact and friendship, less pressure and less risk.

The district court found that noncommission saleswomen were generally happier with their present jobs at Sears, and were much less likely than their male counterparts to be interested in other positions, such as commission sales. . . . 628 F.Supp. at 1313.

These conclusions, it seems to me, are of a piece with the proposition that women are by nature happier cooking, doing the laundry and chauffeuring the children to softball games than arguing appeals or selling stocks. The stereotype of women as less greedy and daring than men is one that the sex discrimination laws were intended to address. It is disturbing that this sort of thinking is accepted so uncritically by the district court and by the majority. Perhaps they have forgotten that women have been hugely successful in such fields as residential real estate, door-to-door sales and other direct outside merchandising. There are abundant indications that women lack neither the desire to compete strenuously for financial gain nor the capacity to take risks.

Sears, the district court and the majority hang much of their refutation of the EEOC's hiring and promotion claims on the putative difference between men's and women's interest in undertaking commission sales. Huge statistical disparities in participation in various commission selling jobs are ascribed to differences in "interest." Yet there is scarcely any recognition of the employer's role in shaping the "interests" of applicants. Even the majority is willing to concede that lack of opportunity may drive lack of interest, but dismisses the matter as a "chicken-egg" problem. I concede that the government's case would be stronger if it had produced even a handful of women willing to testify that Sears had frustrated their childhood dreams of becoming commission sellers of roofing, sewing machines or air conditioners. However, even absent flesh and blood victims, I find the willingness of the district court and the majority to accept the interest defense uncritically, and without recognition of its close parallel to the stereotypes that Title VII seeks to eradicate, perplexing and unacceptable. . . .

Equal Employment Opportunity Commission v. Sears, Roebuck & Company: A Personal Account

ALICE KESSLER-HARRIS

THE CASE EXPLODED into my life in early September of 1984. Had I heard of the suit against Sears, Roebuck, said the lawyer for the Equal Employment Opportunity Commission on the telephone? Did I know that it was the last of the class action cases and that Sears was the largest employer of women outside the federal government? Discrimination, retail sales, a female work force—would I be willing to testify for the EEOC? But why, I asked, confusedly processing bits of information, do you need a historian to testify? "Well, they've got one," came the answer, "and we want you to rebut her testimony. She argues that women were not interested in commission sales, and she cites your work as evidence that Sears was not guilty of discrimination. Do you agree?"

No, I thought, I did not agree that women's lack of "interest" could absolve a company of charges of discrimination. Nor could I accept that the complex reality embodied in the notion of "interest" could be so readily simplified. I did think that there was some as yet undefined difference between men and women. I had argued as much myself. But I had not yet figured out what that meant in terms of historical analysis. And to equate different "interests" with an acceptance of the current distribution of rewards from wage work was, in my judgment, to misunderstand the process by which women struggled for change, as well as to simplify the way difference and inequality have played themselves out historically.

Layers peeled back in the months that followed and the clarity that now seems possible only slowly became visible. A female historian, identified as a feminist, had taken a position in a political trial. She was prepared to testify that other women—working class women, poor women, non-white women—had not wanted well-paying jobs, and would not willingly make the kinds of compromises she herself had made in order to succeed at them. What was to be gained by such testimony? A successful argument would damage women who worked at Sears as well as past and future applicants. Worse, it would set a legal precedent that would inhibit affirmative action cases in the future. For if defendants could justify the absence of women in certain kinds of jobs on the

35 Radical Hist. Rev. 57 (1986). Copyright 1986 The Radical Historians Organization. Reprinted with the permission of Cambridge University Press.

grounds that insufficient numbers of women possessed any interest in them, one could foresee the resulting cycle. Expectations and aspirations conditioned by generations of socialization and labor market experience would now be used to justify continuing discrimination against women. The potential consequences were terrifying. The absence of women from the ranks of plumbers, automobile mechanics or airline pilots could become evidence of their lack of interest in preparing for these jobs. Neither employers nor unions could be held responsible for their absence. Women were themselves to blame. . . .

The elements of the case fell into place slowly. Accused of discriminating against women by failing to hire either new applicants or present employees into commission sales jobs, and by paying managerial women less than men in the same jobs, the company did not dispute the essential facts of the case. Before 1973 (when the EEOC, acting on the complaints of scores of women, and in the wake of the A.T.& T. decision, first brought charges), few women worked in Sears' well paying commission sales categories.[1] Between 1974 and 1979, under pressure from the EEOC's threatened action, Sears had made some progress in some commission sales categories nationwide. Women had begun to sell such items as sewing machines and draperies, furniture and shoes. In one of the five regional territories into which Sears stores were divided, progress had been substantial.[2] But everywhere, the most lucrative jobs in automotive accessories, large appliances, home entertainment, sporting goods and installed home improvements remained stubbornly resistant to female workers. Overall, the EEOC argues, the proportion of women hired or promoted into such jobs was fifty per cent lower than they estimated it should have been. Efforts to reach an agreement with the company on an enforceable affirmative action plan failed, and in 1980 the EEOC determined on court action.

In court, the EEOC relied on statistical methods to prove its case. Producing a few complainants among the more than one million people who had applied for jobs over the seven-year period in contention would, lawyers feared, create vulnerability if the company could undermine the character of one or two witnesses. Aware that statistical data had been successfully used in the past to demonstrate discrimination in cases involving both women and minorities, EEOC lawyers chose what they thought would be a sure path. They attempted to demonstrate that the absence of women in certain kinds of jobs revealed a pattern of discrimination. Using elaborate statistical techniques that took account of the general and specific work-force experience and educational background of men and women who applied for sales jobs at Sears, the EEOC contended that Sears had fallen far short of good faith efforts at placing women in commission sales jobs. Particularly in contention were the most lucrative jobs selling "big ticket" items such as installed home improvements, carpets, home appliances and auto parts.

Sears' lawyers countered by challenging the notion that a pool of women was available for the jobs it had to offer. The company, they argued, should not be held responsible for the relatively low numbers of women hired in certain categories. Sears had tried, and failed, to find women willing to take those jobs. They were simply not interested in them. A team of lawyers from the Washington-based firm of Charles Morgan and Associates presented a series of Sears personnel officials to the court, all of whom testified that even after 1973, when Sears presumably had a goal-oriented affirmative action program, they had had great difficulty in persuading women to take commission sales jobs. As one affirmative action officer testified, "Sears tried very hard to get women into commission selling, despite women's general reluctance to accept these positions."[3] Women, personnel officers agreed, would not willingly undertake the greater competition and financial risk involved in such jobs. And besides, women preferred not to sell items such as men's clothing, fencing equipment, appliances and autoparts because they had no "interest" in them. "Women had to be persuaded to accept commission sales positions . . . " claimed one personnel officer. "Women were very reluctant to accept positions in the larger appliances, installed home improvements, and automotive divisions because they were uncomfortable with selling those product lines or felt they lacked the capacity for the technical aspects of the job."[4]

To prove there was no pool of women available for commission sales jobs, Sears' lawyers drew on the experts of survey researchers and economists who cited national opinion polls taken in the '50s and '60s that unanimously indicated the prevalence of "traditional" attitudes among women and men regarding the family and women's role within it. And, finally, Sears called on historian Rosalind Rosenberg to provide the broader picture. Women, born and reared before the onset of the contemporary women's movement, she testified, were likely to have internalized traditional values and would thus be less likely than men to accept certain kinds of jobs, even when they carried substantial increases in income.[5]

The EEOC, in rebuttal, contended that Sears had never really tried to find women. The company's affirmative action program was a sham; its personnel people, who kept meticulous records about everything else, could not recall the name of any female job applicant who had actually turned down a job; its interviewing tests for commission sales people were biased. In short, Sears was blind to its own discrimination. "The reasonable inference," argued the EEOC, "to be drawn from the consistent pattern of disparities between the expected and actual female proportion of promotions from full and part time noncommission sales positions to full and part time commission sales position is that such disparities resulted from discrimination in Sears' practices, policies and positions."[6] When only women who had in fact applied for jobs at Sears were counted, EEOC counsel argued, Sears had hired less than fifty percent of the expected number of women overall. In some departments and regions the figures were much worse, even after the Company was under EEOC investigation.

Sears, drawing once again on Rosalind Rosenberg and others, replied that the EEOC's figures were flawed: the commission incorrectly assumed that men and women were alike and would seek the same kinds of jobs. Sears had tried. Its failure was a result of social circumstances beyond its control. It was, as Rosenberg argued, "naive to believe that the natural effects of these differences was evidence of discrimination by Sears."[7]

How important was the historical evidence in the context of a case that used the expertise of economists, sociologists and survey research experts? To exonerate itself from the charge of discrimination, Sears had to demonstrate that the disproportionately low numbers of women in its most lucrative commission sales jobs could be explained by some factor other than discrimination. A statistical pattern alone would not prove discrimination if Sears could come up with some logical explanation for the absence of women. Sears chose to try to convince the court of three things: that commission sales jobs in fact required competitive, aggressive and risk-oriented personalities; that Sears had made enormous attempts to induce women to take these jobs; and finally, that women's family values and domestic roles had undermined Sears' efforts. It was in this third category that the historical testimony played a role, for an important part of the company's defense rested on whether lawyers could demonstrate that an exceedingly limited pool of women willing to take commission sales jobs had been available in the years before 1973 when charges were first brought, and between 1973 and 1979 when the suit was filed.

Sears apparently counted on finding historical support from the beginning. The case went to trial in Chicago (company headquarters) in early September 1984. It concluded at the end of the following June, the longest case to be tried to date in the seventh circuit. Rosenberg prepared an "offer of proof," a summary of the evidence she was to present in court, sometime before July 1984. On the basis of this, she was deposed (examined by the opposing side as to the content of her testimony) in early July 1984, before the trial began. I did not know when the EEOC decided it needed a historian to rebut her testimony. I was first contacted in the fall of 1984, and deposed in April 1985, after Rosenberg had testified, and it was clear that my rebuttal would be needed. Because the case was lengthy and drawn out, Judge John Nordberg, a Reagan appointee who was relatively new on the bench, decided about halfway through the trial to ask all witnesses to prepare their direct testimony in writing. This was intended to save time at the trial itself and to facilitate cross-examination. Rosenberg's slightly modified and annotated offer of proof served as her written testimony. Because my offer of proof was prepared under extreme pressure of time, it presented only a two-page outline of my position, on which the written testimony I prepared in May elaborated. After my court appearance in early June, Rosenberg prepared a "sur-rebuttal" on the basis of which she was cross-examined in late June. Neither the EEOC nor I had a chance to respond to this sur-rebuttal, except under the restricted conditions of cross-examination. The unusual circumstance of having two written testimonies (about twenty pages from each of us), as well as Rosenberg's rebuttal, provides a set of documents that lay out the two historical positions in a relatively coherent way, as court proceedings go.[8]

These documents pose a series of challenges to historians of women, the most important of which is why the documents came into existence at all. Historians and other social scientists frequently serve as expert witnesses, and even the unusual circumstance of testifying as to general ideology rather than to particular cases has precedent. According to anthropologist Lawrence Rosen the 1949–1954 school desegregation cases relied heavily on the expertise of anthropologists who testified that there was no rational basis for keeping schoolchildren of different races apart.[9] But the testimony in the *Sears* case raises two hotly debated issues. First is the nature of truth and the possibility of claiming it in a case of this kind, and under the conditions that a court of law offers. Given the nature of adversarial proceedings, the historian who does not acknowledge (as C. Vann Woodward did in 1954) that he is "constrained by the limits of his craft" must wonder whether expertise is not merely a cover for more complicated rationalizations of our own values.[10] This raises a second issue: the politics of history. Lawrence Rosen argues that experts must set their own standards for the form of the argument used in a court of law as opposed to those "employed when writing for a scholarly or popular audience," implying what nearly everyone suggests: that witnesses who engage themselves in an adversarial situation necessarily take on the mission of their side. . . .

Rosenberg studied the data that Sears' lawyers provided and concluded on the basis of it, as well as, presumably, on the basis of her general knowledge of the history of women, that the company was not guilty of discrimination.[11] I looked at the same material (or at any rate the material that the EEOC provided) and concluded in the light of my work on wage-earning women that an absence of women was more likely to be a consequence of discrimination than of any other cause. There is no point in obscuring these essentially political perceptions or the political decisions that followed from them. Neither of us would have been selected as expert witnesses had we come to the opposite conclusions. Rosenberg later defended her participation in the case on the grounds that discrimination *alone* could not account for the absence of women. Of course not. But this was never the issue. The point is that, in a case that is about discrimination, to argue that discrimination was not the likely explanation is to lend one's expertise to the argument that other explanations are more plausible. What followed was to be expected. Rosenberg marshalled evidence to demonstrate that the absence of women was consistent with a lack of discrimination. I marshalled evidence to demonstrate that the absence of women was probably a result of it.

The capacity to take opposing positions on such a crucial issue deserves scrutiny. How does it happen that two feminist historians faced with the same question could come to such different conclusions? The answer may lie in different understandings of why and how we study the past. For many of us, history is about exploring the nature of social change. We engage in it as professional historians not to explore the past for its own sake but to explain how change happened. Some of us go one step further. In this respect I identify with a comment of Natalie Zemon Davis: "I want to show that even when times were hard, people found ways to cope with what was happening and maybe to resist it. . . . Especially I want to show that it could be different, that it was different, that there are alternatives."[12] As feminist historians, we are particularly concerned to discover what women's lives were like because we know that they simultaneously lived within oppressive systems and found ways to search for the elusive goal of equality. So we are drawn to write the biographies of all kinds of women not because they mirrored the social realities of their worlds, but because they transcended them. We use our knowledge to try to figure out how, despite the overwhelming weight of tradition, change occurs.

The attempt to understand mechanisms of change, then, requires questions about how women have pushed at the boundaries of opportunity. Under what historical circumstances did culture operate to inhibit change and under what circumstances to enhance opportunity? Recent historiography of wage-earning women has involved a search for answers to such questions. We began with the knowledge that most women worked at relatively poor jobs that they sought for a variety of reasons and in a variety of ways. We quickly rejected the biases of an early twentieth-century literature that accepted the values of domesticity, moving beyond its descriptions and illustrations of women's repeated victimization. Instead, we turned to sorting out how particular groups of women were constrained by force (economic and physical) as well as by self-justifying belief systems, and how they took advantage of unique moments to make incremental gains in their positions.

These concerns for the mechanisms of change are negated in the testimony offered by Rosenberg. Sears, seeking to justify the status quo, had set the terms of the discourse. Were there plausible alternative explanations other than discrimination, lawyers asked, for the absence of women in some jobs? Rosenberg had responded with what she later described as a "multicausal" view of history: one in which socialization, family responsibilities, educational practices, government policies, cultural attitudes and employer discrimination all played a part in shaping the contemporary labor force.[13] But, far from explaining the absence of women in certain sectors of the labor market, throwing out a variety of causes merely begs the question of how to order and assess them. As we shall see, Rosenberg had done precisely that. Having accepted the issues as Sears, Roebuck and Co. had chosen to define them, she had responded by presenting a plausible array of alternatives that together added up to a defense of the status quo.

The structure of the argument made to the court followed logically from this essential political perspective. Rosenberg's position was deceptively simple. "Men and women had different interests, goals and aspirations regarding work," she wrote.[14] The EEOC ignored the fact that "many workers, especially women, have goals and values other than realizing maximum economic gain . . . , values shaped in earlier eras."[15] These different goals and values, reinforced by government policies, had led women to emphasize traditional, family-oriented roles, and to make choices about wage work from that perspective. Rosenberg wrote:

> Even the semi-subsistence, farming families in seventeenth-century America divided work according to sex. Women cared for the children, prepared the food, nursed the sick, made the clothes, and tended the garden. Men worked the fields, cared for the livestock, and represented the family in the outside world. Many of the jobs that men and women perform in the labor force today are the modern equivalents of traditional male and female tasks. For women these modern equivalents are simply added on to the traditional male and female tasks, especially if the woman is a wife and mother. Even as they have entered the labor force in increasing numbers, women have retained their historical commitment to the home. Women's role in American society and in the American family unit has fostered the development of "feminine" values that have been internalized by women themselves and reinforced by society, through its customs, its culture, and its laws.[16]

For a "multicausal" view of women's condition, these observations reflect a singularly monocausal view of history. They take into account only the suppliers of labor—women—and offer up their domestic roles as the central explanation for the continuation of occupational segregation in the work force. Women had chosen not to look for jobs in non-traditional areas such as commission sales, Rosenberg concluded. Their absence from these jobs was consistent with a finding that there had been no discrimination at Sears.

Given the difficulty of presenting a nuanced historical argument before a court of law (a difficulty I was to experience later), I don't want to debate here the details of the evidence offered. Still, the absence of nuance exposes clearly the structure of the argument on both sides, and it is the outlines of the two positions and their implications that deserve scrutiny. Rosenberg's position lent itself to the uses that Sears' lawyers, Morgan and Associates, made of it.

The case turned on whether Sears' employment practices reflected female preferences and values as opposed to those of employers. Lawyers for Sears emphasized women's goals and values, focused on the desire of individuals to fulfill their interests at work, and asserted employers' willingness to hire anyone qualified. Similarly, Rosenberg's testimony assumed the existence of genuine choice for women within an unrestricted labor market. "Because housework and child care continue to affect women's labor force participation even today," she wrote, "many women choose jobs that complement their family obligations over jobs that might increase and enhance their earning potential."[17] This vision of a labor market operating in response to the needs of women and the family pervades a testimony that lacks any sense that employers, too, make choices in terms of their preconceptions about workers. While no one would want to argue that employers alone discriminate, the decisions made by employers take into account the real costs of equity, and are often buttressed by an ideology that obscures discrimination in which employers and workers alike participate. Rosenberg's position implicitly holds women responsible for the sexual division of labor, offering the reality of a segmented labor market as though it were the product of women's will, but failing to acknowledge that women must confront it whether or not their own inclinations are family oriented.[18]

Such a vision of the labor market suggests that higher wages are incompatible with family responsibilities, an idea affirmed by Rosenberg's statement that "Many workers, especially women, have goals and values other than realizing maximum economic gain."[19] On one level, this statement is of course accurate. Recent research indicates that neither men nor women are interested *solely* in maximizing income. Men tend to choose between work and leisure; women between work, housework and leisure. In the neoclassical paradigm, a rise in wages tips the balance in favor of wage work, so it is hardly radical to view higher wages or available opportunity as responsible for women's willingness to trade housework for a job.

In this context, the notion that some workers have goals and values other than realizing maximum economic gain reveals the essential issue at Sears. According to the EEOC's undisputed calculations, the median salary of full-time commission salespeople in their first year at Sears averaged between three and four dollars an hour more than the average salary of full-time non-commission salespeople. Gaining this wage involved little or no risk. Between 1973 and 1977, Sears paid commission sales people a "draw" against commissions, but the company made up the difference if after one week the employee had not earned the rate of draw. After 1977, Sears guaranteed a minimum salary (estimated on the basis of sales performance) to all commission sales people and salespeople retained their commissions. Personnel officers testified in court that they could recall few people ever fired for failing to make their base salaries. To believe Sears, in short, we would have to believe not only that women were not interested in maximizing income, but that the competition involved in such jobs and their lack of interest in the products sold would deter them from nearly doubling their wages. Since the hours in both non-commission and commission jobs were substantially the same and since earning income is seen by most wage-earning women as a way of meeting family needs, women's objections to commission sales jobs are reduced to the ideological sphere.

Who, then, were the women who preferred to avoid competition and were uninterested in nontraditional jobs? In Rosenberg's testimony, they were the women for whom the nineteenth century prescription of domesticity had become reality. "Throughout American history," wrote Rosenberg, "there has been a consensus, shared by women, that, for women, working outside the home is subordinate to family." Rosenberg wrote as if all women were middle class. Black, immigrant, and poor women existed only at the periphery of the labor market, instead of at the center of most past and present decisions about wage work. Conceptions such as "traditional" and "nontraditional" work were never defined, and "family life" was reified, wiping out the diverse forms women had adopted to sustain themselves and their dependents.

The result was a conception in which "nontraditional" work and family life appeared as opposites, while "traditional" work was located not in labor market terms but in jobs that sustained notions of the "ideal" family—nursing, part-time, etc.[20] The evident tautology here (if women are doing the job, it must be consistent with family life; if it was consistent with family life, women would do it), was resolved in this schema by the assumption that women, after all, wanted these, and only these jobs. Women's interest in family life led them, with the encouragement of government and educational institutions, to seek out jobs that sustained their family roles and so on in a circular pattern that neatly fit the needs of employers and reaffirmed family life. One can admit the half truth here, namely that many women have accepted prevailing stereotypes about their roles, without negating the ways in which change in women's roles as a whole has resulted from the efforts of a minority of women to break down restrictive barriers. All women have not needed to be construction workers, telephone linemen or tool and die makers to demonstrate that those options are available to other women.

What is at issue, then, is a conception that is so unalterably middle class and white that the notion of "family needs" is separable from the productive labor of women, inside or outside the home. Historically, women have met the needs of their families where, and as, necessity has required and opportunity has existed. To offer a view of history that suggests that working outside the home is somehow an evasion of family responsibility is to invoke turn-of-the-century middle class condemnation of poor working women.

The unstated assumption of this testimony is that the social root of ideological change lay within the family, as opposed to the sphere of production. Alterations in family demography and inflationary pressures on the family accounted for the surge of interest in jobs in the 1970s. Denying the impact of greater accessibility of jobs through affirmative action plans and legislative intervention, Rosenberg argued that women themselves have been forced, in consequence of demographic and family changes, to seek jobs. Still, they chose to work in areas consistent with her conception of family roles, and thus she could account for the flood of women into the workforce while holding that Sears could not be held responsible for failing to hire women in jobs they and she deemed inconsistent with an unchanging conception of women's roles. In this interpretation, the family was, and remained, the source of women's perceptions of the world around them. Avoiding this pattern was possible, according to the testimony, largely for educated women, who constituted the vanguard of change in the past as in the present.[21] Gone was the tradition of radical womanhood embodied in the anarchist experience, or in the lives of black women. Gone too the legion of female trade union activists whose struggles to create opportunity for women highlight the pages of nineteenth- and twentieth-century history. Those were women who often identified with women's "sphere" and nevertheless attempted to fight their disadvantaged status at work. Gone too any conception of consciousness in which the production of household and factory formed a unity in women's minds.

The testimony lacked any conception that the job market and the world of work could and did influence how young girls thought about themselves and how women assessed their possibilities. Failure to understand that aspirations are themselves conditioned by perceptions of available opportunity (that Sears was an important part of this world and complicit in the socialization process) or to put it in another way, that ideology and consciousness are both rooted in an everyday experience of which the family is a form as well as a creator, provided the curious gap in perception that allowed Rosenberg to acknowledge on the stand that black women might have had goals and aspirations that varied from those of white women without altering the direction of her testimony a notch.

There was another particularly disturbing problem from the perspective of women's history, however. Rosenberg's testimony offered an interpretation to which many of us had come. Namely, that women's social and cultural differences from men could and should be the subject of historical analysis. And yet, no student of history of working women that I knew of inferred from that interpretation what was suggested by Rosenberg. What, then, was the level of truth in the argument? That women of all classes and racial groups had had a special relationship to home and family, no one could deny. But the circumstances surrounding that relationship were not merely minor details in an otherwise homogeneous past. An enormous variety of specific experiences divided women and encouraged them to make dramatically different assessments of their work and home options. Granted the differences between men and women, women themselves had understood and used them in varied ways.

Indeed, one of the tensions in women's history that arguably described much of the dynamic of change in women's lives over time was the tension between women's own conception of "difference" and the objective condition of inequality. We had all observed that women, to live, had participated in, even colluded in, their own oppression. But that was not the sum total of their perceptions and understandings of the world around them. Nor did that truth wipe out the ways in which women had continually exerted themselves (in ways consonant with their access to money, resources and education) in a centuries-long struggle for emancipation. If women had sometimes accepted the difference as a justification for inequality, they had frequently used it to reach for opportunity when it appeared, and to struggle for political and social change. Changing understandings of cultural difference over time had provided the entering wedges in what could only be interpreted as an effort to achieve greater equality: the domestic feminism of the mid-nineteenth century, the battles for suffrage, and the struggle for protective legislation are cases in point. To use the notion that women had "different" interests to justify their absence from the workplace was to assume that "difference" inevitably affirmed the traditional family.

Historians of working class women have generally not used the idea that way. The notion that women brought with them to the workforce a sense of self and an orientation that was not identical to that of men offered a way of distinguishing their behavior, their values, their commitments and their aspirations from those of men.[22] It helped us to think about workers in gendered terms, as we had earlier learned to think of them in ethnic and racial terms. But gender was one among many patterns that influenced how women worked. To think about women as workers who make choices, conditioned by and responsive to their life experiences, is to say one thing. To think about the generic constraints of a universal female experience defining work orientation is to say something entirely other.

Rosenberg had turned on its head the position to which most students of the subject had come—namely, that women's behavior could be interpreted in light of their own constraints. Instead, she had chosen to universalize her assumptions about what those constraints were likely to be—to saddle all women with a particular interpretation of the domestic code. The result was a series of conclusions that trapped women within a domestic ideology isolated from class, race, ethnicity or region. She had then taken the next step which was to assert that the mechanism of entrapment lay within their own power to remove. Sears was not responsible for women's choices; women were. By implication, corporations that did not hire women were merely responding to women's own needs and interests. This linear and deterministic view of history had inexorably placed responsibility on women's own shoulders—a classic example of blaming the victim.

Reconciling the notion that women could simultaneously operate within and against their society posed little problem for me. Women were part of the society in which they lived, and continually pushed at the boundaries of opportunity within the contexts of their class and race positions. It was not difficult to explain the existence of simultaneous, seemingly opposite directions in individuals. People could and did have a range of needs and experiences, as well as a range of social understanding within which to place them. Women's behavior was, as much as anything else, a function of their social experience. Change the context, and people would respond in different ways. . . .

Rosenberg's testimony lent itself to precisely the purposes for which it was used. That this was no accident is confirmed by the language of the first paragraph of Rosenberg's sur-rebuttal. "It is my professional opinion," she wrote,

> that the overwhelming weight of modern scholarship in women's history and related fields supports the view that other Sears experts and I have put forward—namely, that disparities in the sexual composition of an employer's workforce, as well as disparities in pay between men and women in many circumstances, are consistent with an absence of discrimination on the part of the employer.[23]

Well, yes, but they are also consistent with the presence of discrimination. And if so, why would one want to place one's services at the disposal of, at best, a potentially discriminatory employer?

Rosenberg provided, as her own explanations, two puzzling answers to this question. She had studied Sears' affirmative action program and found it satisfactory; she believed that a successful defense by Sears would encourage other employers to develop good programs. And, she thought, not telling what she had become persuaded was the truth about women would do them "more harm than good."[24] Neither of these is convincing. Whatever we think of the Sears' affirmative action program, by its own admission, in a period when goals and targets were widely met by other employers, it failed to meet even its own goals. If her position was based on a study of Sears, why generalize, and why not give women, rather than employers, the benefit of the doubt? Were we to revert to the position that only the slow passage of time would reap change? Rosenberg had never made it clear how women would be harmed by the discussion of a more complex truth.

I prefer to argue that we would never know what women wanted until the doors of opportunity were fully opened. The historical evidence viewed from the perspective of what women had been able to achieve, suggested that given available opportunity, sufficient numbers of women had never been lacking for jobs offered at good pay, even when those jobs were defined as male. An occupationally segregated labor force provided only a description of the labor market constraints, not an explanation of labor market behavior. Labor force needs and the socialization process together explained the structure of the labor force. Neither was independent of the other, I testified, and therefore notions of women's socialization and culture had to be seen in the context of the whole picture. I suggested that women had not "internalized" values and goals. Rather, they had continually modified and altered them as circumstances made it possible to do so.

I acknowledged what all of my work had indicated—namely, that women had operated within social constraints that varied for different groups of women as they varied between men and women.[25] But, I argued, those constraints were not unrelated to available opportunities. The existence of something called female culture was not in dispute; this function was. Rosenberg had presented its role as preserving the status quo. I saw it as malleable, as part of the process of change. The key in court would be to demonstrate that sex roles were not rigid as Rosenberg had portrayed them; that women differed widely among themselves; and crucially, that employers, who used all kinds of differences to discriminate among workers, certainly used gender as well.

These goals were more easily developed than executed. One intuits the difference between working in a library and participating in a court room drama, but until one has experienced it, the disjunction between the two remains abstract. Accustomed to developing the subtle distinctions of an argument, to negotiating about fine points of interpretation, the historian quickly discovers that these skills must be abandoned in testifying. Maintaining a position is as important as the position taken. Consistency is not merely a virtue but evidence of one's expertise. Yet the temptation to overgeneralize or to state a case in its sharpest form must also be resisted. I discovered to my sorrow that either one can be quickly penetrated in a cross examination.

My written testimony emerged out of an attempt to avoid these two danger points, the product of a two-day ordeal in deposition, and of negotiation with the EEOC lawyer over how much to say and how to say it. Of the two, the deposition was clearly the stronger influence. There, I got my first taste of the clear distinction made by the legal profession between learning the truth and constructing a case; between understanding and persuading. And there, I also learned for the first time, that precisely what I as a historian cared most about would most surely destroy my testimony if I pursued it. My job, I was told, was to answer all questions, but to provide no more information than was demanded. The job of the examining lawyer, Denise Leary, an employee of the firm defending Sears, was to find out as much as she could about what I would testify in writing, and at the trial. Any attempt I made to introduce controversy, disagreement and analysis merely revealed that history was an uncertain tool and invalidated both its findings and my conclusions. She was interested in authority, clarity and weaknesses in my level of knowledge. The basis of both questions and answers was the "offer of proof": in my case a two-page statement defining the boundaries within which I was prepared to testify.

I had begun my "offer of proof" with two statements: the first negating the value of prescriptive literature in understanding the behavior of wage-earning women; and the second attacking Rosenberg's testimony for its "numerous omissions and misunderstandings." What, the lawyer wanted to know, were these omissions and misunderstandings? What were the areas where I disagreed? Over a two-day period, we moved item by item through Rosenberg's testimony as the lawyer asked about, and I responded to every item. Sometimes the exchanges were funny. More often, they were brutal. Did I not agree that Nancy Cott was a well-respected historian? Well, yes, of course. Then it followed that this point of Rosenberg's for which she had cited Cott as a source must be correct. No, as I understood Cott's position, it did not sustain Rosenberg's argument. Had not Mary Beth Norton argued that women in the revolution knew little about family finances? Yes, but . . . Did not this support the notion that women's roles were restricted? Not necessarily—after all, Kerber had said X and Berkin said Y, and even Norton in other places modified the argument. Besides, I wanted to scream, this was all irrelevant.

I wanted to explain that history was about change; that to drag the American revolution into today's labor market practices had no meaning at all. That the women those historians had studied, pre-industrial, pre-urban, and white had little in common with contemporary women workers. But my job was to answer questions. When I tried to introduce diversity, my answers were demeaned. What percentage of married women in 1890 were black or immigrants? What percentage of those worked? Was not the total a relatively small proportion of women as a whole? It depended on how you defined work, I countered: agricultural work, home work, boarders, those added up to significant numbers. And besides, wasn't this case about women *in* the workforce, not about women who could afford to stay out of it? She could ask the questions, thank you. This case was about statistics, she kept reminding me. And when I retreated behind the scattered information that historians possess, she sneered; you just don't know. Oh, for the opportunity to explain what it was that historians did, and how they generalized from limited data!

Rosenberg cited more than a dozen historians and sociologists in support of points with which I disagreed. Over a weekend break between questions, I looked up as many as I could to see whether and how the citation supported her generalizations. Again and again, I pinpointed misinterpretations, discovered quotes out of context and arguments made from evidence that pointed in contrary directions. By the second day, I had the hang of it. My answers were more precise, my evidence more targeted, my rebuttals more positive. To refute Rosenberg's argument, I found myself constructing a rebuttal in which subtlety and nuance were omitted, and in which evidence was marshaled to make a point while complexities and exceptions vanished from sight.

In the end, it did not matter. It was not history but its use that went on trial. Just as so much of what we do is not about what is true and what false, what happened and what did not, so the issue here was not about who had correctly interpreted the past, but about how that interpretation was presented in different contexts. Testimony had a double-edged quality. In this case, once given and written, it had a life of its own, at the mercy of cross-examining lawyers, and not subject to qualification. Because it constituted the boundaries within which examination could happen, it had to encompass the totality of my expertise: broad enough to meet the needs of the plaintiff, and yet sufficiently restrained as to offer few loopholes that the defendants could use to undermine it. What sorts of claims to truth could be justified by such expertise? The speculation and tentativeness of an article or a lecture had no place in the courtroom. In a statement of one's own making, one had both leisure and time to play out an argument, to present the negative in order to come to the positive. In a judicial proceeding, not only was there no such time, but doing so jeopardized the case, because it could be and, in my limited experience was, so often cited out of context.

It was no surprise, for example, when the cross examining lawyer challenged not the substance of my testimony, but the language in which it was phrased in a sometimes successful attempt to reduce it to its absurd extremes. So, for example, "women had never failed to take jobs when opportunities presented themselves" (which I had written to mean that sufficient numbers of women were available to fill any job opportunity) got turned into a query about whether it could possibly be true that *all* women availed themselves of opportunity. An argument that the need for income rather than the pursuit of interest drove women into certain kinds of jobs led to a dispute about whether "interest" played any role at all in the kinds of jobs women would take. Though I gathered that such attempts to attack the credibility of witnesses and reduce statements to absurdity were routine parts of every cross-examination, I was nevertheless astonished at how easy it was, within the yes or no format demanded by the court, to agree with statements simply because I could not deny them, not because they represented my understanding of the issues involved.

Deposition, written testimony, cross-examination: if I had not fully understood before, they taught me now that with whatever virtue and justice I entered the lists, skill in the fight would tell the tale. What then was a feminist doing in the courtroom at all? I had reacted viscerally to seeing my own work, badly distorted, put to the service of a politically destructive cause. I believed that the success of Sears' lawyers would undermine two decades of affirmative action efforts and exercise a chilling effect on women's history as a whole. To allow the tale told by Sears to pass unchallenged as women's view of their history would encourage others to use it to rationalize an unequal past.

It did not surprise me that history was brought to trial. We have long appealed to the past to justify and rationalize present beliefs and behavior. But I continue to be disturbed that a feminist historian should fail to see the implications of her testimony for working women and for women's history. Rosenberg argued after the trial that she was serving the cause of "careful scholarship." "If we insist on pretending that no factors other than employer discrimination play a significant role in shaping women's role in the workforce, we will do women more harm than good," she wrote. But in fact, she had offered as "careful scholarship" a single-minded interpretation that played down the role of discrimination. She had done this, not in the cause of ordinary women, but in the name of an employer accused of denying women jobs. The past had once again become the creature of conserving ideology—ideology all the more dangerous for remaining unspoken.

The case has been instructive for me. Excited by the possibility of exploring working women's conceptions of gender in order to find a way of probing the pressures to retain and alter tradition, I began, several years ago, to explore the language and symbols with which wage-earning women described their own experiences. I believed—I still believe—that the self-experience of work, as it changes over time, could provide clues about women's relationship to work in the past and in the future. Such symbols were not themselves explanatory, nor could they be interpreted outside the context of material pressures and other social needs. Yet in the search for the dynamism of change, they demanded attention. This would be my way of challenging the particular universalism of labor history. We would, for the first time, have to write books in which "workers" meant women as well as men. One could argue (as I have) that such distinctions, such a breakdown of the universal male would enable women to fight for working conditions that met the legitimate needs of workers who were not male. It could therefore become a political rallying point. But if understanding the way difference can move us toward change offers one way to think about the past, understanding how difference reinforces tradition and legitimizes inequality suggests another.

This case reminds us that whether we will or not, writing history is a political act. For my part, then, I am troubled less by the question of how easily careful scholarship is abandoned than by how readily it is distorted and misinterpreted when placed in the service of a political cause.

This case, then, should not serve to stifle our thoughts but to heighten awareness of their political context. Feminist historians have struggled for more than a decade and a half now, not merely to include the experiences of women in history books, but to explore how history itself would be altered by their inclusion. To do that required new frameworks for thought, new ways of thinking. What historical theory, in its vaunted universalism, could not provide, we hungrily absorbed from psychology, philosophy, sociology and anthropology. But this case demonstrates that historians have something to return to these disciplines: the empirical evidence that demonstrates that culture is not a static framework, but a moving force. Among the lessons we should learn from this experience is what happens when one historian forgets that history is about change and makes claims to value-free evidence in order to demonstrate that past behavior justifies present injustice. Not the politics but the ethics of history is then called into question.

I don't think that means we should abandon the effort to explore "women's culture" nor should we fail to use the concept to help define the parameters within which a sex-gender system works. Surely there is something useful to the notion that women are somehow "different" from men: such a conception has led us to begin to think of non-universal methodologies in anthropology and psychology; to identify research questions and issues in which distinctions become ways of pursuing knowledge about how and where and when they are created and overcome. The notion has led us to the highest reaches of critical and philosophical speculation. But I think it does mean that we have to remember and articulate, explicitly and consciously, the historical context of the culture about which we speak, for as Ellen Dubois warned us several years ago, what is offered as explanation, can also be used as justification.[26]

The use of historical argument in the *Sears* case affirms the degree to which historical interpretation is subject to the whims of time. In a period when the politics of the family and efforts to reassert traditional sex roles are in the forefront of a new morality, it illustrates yet again the ease with which political positions are rationalized in the name of scholarship.

Notes

1. Percentages of women varied by commission sales category. In 1973, 73.5 per cent of Sears 14,794 full time noncommission sales employees were women, but only 15.4 per cent of its 23,867 full time commission sales people were women. Plaintiff's Proposed Finding of Fact and Conclusions of Law—Commission Sales, p. 9 (all documents were filed with the district court).

2. Figures for the Midwest were substantially higher than for the four other regions in all commission sales categories. One can speculate that this means that midwestern women were more willing to take such jobs, or that management in this region was more amenable to hiring them.

3. Testimony of Carolyn Rogers, May 7, 1985, p. 6; cf. also, pp. 22, 38, 55, 64, 65.

4. Testimony of J. Richard Howie, May 7, 1985; pp. 4–5.

5. Offer of Proof concerning the Testimony of Dr. Rosalind Rosenberg, items 18, 19, 20. The annotated version, which became Rosalind Rosenberg's written testimony, and which I cite herein, was filed in court on March 11, 1985. The document is not paginated.

6. Plaintiff's Pre-trial Brief, p. 15.

7. Rosenberg, Offer of Proof, item 24.

8. All of these documents as well as the transcripts of both depositions and the trial testimonies are available from the Clerk of the Court, United States District Court for the Northern District of Illinois, Eastern Division, and on deposit in the Schlesinger Library in Cambridge, Mass. Rosenberg has claimed that Sears' lawyers wrote the Offer of Proof that was the basis for her deposition and was submitted to the court on March 11, 1985, as her written testimony. Whether or not she actually penned the words, Rosenberg certainly testified to the specific and general contents of the document, as the court transcript makes clear. See pp. 10345–10347.

9. Lawrence Rosen, The American Anthropologist as Expert Witness, 79 Am. Anthropologist 560 (1978).

10. Woodward is cited in Paul Soifer, The Litigation Historian: Objectivity, Responsibility, 5 Pub. Historian 51 (1983).

11. On March 11, 1985, toward the end of her first cross examination, Rosenberg admitted that discrimination was a possible explanation for the data. Asked in re-direct questioning if she thought this was likely, she answered that it was not. Cf. trial transcript pp. 10453, 10459, 10463.

12. Natalie Zemon Davis, Politics, Progeny, and French History: An Interview with Natalie Zemon Davis, 24 Radical Hist. Rev. 133 (1980).

13. A Feminist for Sears, The Nation, Oct. 26, 1985, at 394.

14. Rosenberg, Offer of Proof, item 1.

15. *Id.* at item 2.

16. *Id.* at items, 5, 10, 16.

17. *Id.* at item 11.

18. In the event, this turned out to be one of the most interesting historical issues. Rosenberg characterized my attempt to assert the other side of the dialectical process as "monocausal." I claimed, she held, that employers were solely responsible for discrimination. In charging that my depiction of limited choice for women, within the framework of available opportunity, assumed them to be passive and dependent, she concluded (Written Rebuttal Testimony of Dr. Rosalind Rosenberg, June 25, 1985, p.

11), that I was guilty of portraying them as victims. I take this attack as demonstration of the validity of my assertion here, and as evidence of the value of a dialectical view of history.

19. Rosenberg, Offer of Proof, item 2.

20. *Id.*, item 4; Deposition of Rosalind Rosenberg, July 2, 1984, p. 44; and July 3, 1984, p. 54.

21. Offer of Proof, item 23, Rosenberg Deposition, July 3, 1984, p. 6.

22. See Carole Turbin, Reconceptualizing Family, Work and Labor Organizing: Working Women in Troy, 1860–1890, 16 Rev. Radical Pol. Econ. 1 (1984); Ardis Cameron, Bread and Roses Revisited: Women's Culture and Working-class Activism in the Lawrence Strike of 1912, in Ruth Milkman ed., Women, Work and Protest: A Century of Women's Labor History 42–61 (Routledge & Kegan Paul, 1985); and Alice Kessler-Harris, The Debate over Equality for Women in the Workplace: Recognizing Differences, in Laurie Larwood et al. eds., 1 Women and Work: An Annual Review 141–161 (Sage, 1985).

23. Rosenberg, Written Rebuttal Testimony, p. 1.

24. A Feminist for Sears, *supra* note 13, at 394.

25. Rosenberg's use of my work to make her case deserves attention. Accusing me of contradicting my own written work in court, she cited twelve pages of examples from my writing that purportedly supported the idea that women operated in obedience to certain kinds of social constraints, never acknowledging that in virtually every instance I had played out both sides of a dialectical process, and repeatedly misquoting, and quoting out of context to make her case.

26. Ellen DuBois, Politics and Culture in Women's History: A Symposium, 6 Feminist Stud. 28 (1980).

Deconstructing Equality-Versus-Difference: Or, the Uses of Poststructuralist Theory for Feminism

JOAN W. SCOTT

THAT FEMINISM needs theory goes without saying. . . . We need theory that can analyze the workings of patriarchy in all its manifestations—ideological, institutional, organizational, subjective—accounting not only for continuities but also for change over time. We need theory that will let us think in terms of pluralities and diversities rather than of unities and universals. We need theory that will break the conceptual hold, at least, of those long traditions of (Western) philosophy that have systematically and repeatedly construed the world hierarchically in terms of masculine universals and feminine specificities. We need theory that will enable us to articulate alternative ways of thinking about (and thus acting upon) gender without either simply reversing the old hierarchies or confirming them. And we need theory that will be useful and relevant for political practice.

It seems to me that the body of theory referred to as poststructuralism best meets all these requirements. . . . Poststructuralism and contemporary feminism are late-twentieth-century movements that share a certain self-conscious critical relationship to established philosophical and political traditions. It thus seemed worthwhile for feminist scholars to exploit that relationship for their own ends.[1] . . . The first part of this article is a brief discussion of concepts used by poststructuralists that are also useful for feminists. The second part applies some of these concepts to one of the hotly contested issues among contemporary (U.S.) feminists—the "equality-versus-difference" debate.

Among the useful terms feminists have appropriated from poststructuralism are language, discourse, difference, and deconstruction.

LANGUAGE

Following the work of structuralist linguistics and anthropology, the term is used to mean not simply words or even a vocabulary and set of grammatical rules but, rather, a meaning-constituting system: that is, any system—strictly verbal or other—through which meaning is constructed and cultural practices organized and by which, accordingly, people represent and understand their world, including who they are and how

This article is reprinted from *Feminist Studies*, Volume 15, number 2 (Summer 1989) 237–254, by permission of the publisher, Feminist Studies, Inc., c/o Women's Studies Program, University of Maryland, College Park, MD 20742.

they relate to others. [T]he analysis of language provides a crucial point of entry, a starting point for understanding how social relations are conceived, and therefore—how institutions are organized, how relations of production are experienced, and how collective identity is established. . . .

. . . Poststructuralists insist that words and texts have no fixed or intrinsic meanings, that there is no transparent or self-evident relationship between them and either ideas or things, no basic or ultimate correspondence between language and the world. The questions that must be answered in such an analysis, then, are how, in what specific contexts, among which specific communities of people, and by what textual and social processes has meaning been acquired? More generally, the questions are: How do meanings change? How have some meanings emerged as normative and others have been eclipsed or disappeared? What do these processes reveal about how power is constituted and operates?

DISCOURSE

Some of the answers to these questions are offered in the concept of discourse, especially as it has been developed in the work of Michel Foucault. A discourse is not a language or a text but a historically, socially, and institutionally specific structure of statements, terms, categories, and beliefs. Foucault suggests that the elaboration of meaning involves conflict and power, that meanings are locally contested within discursive "fields of force," that (at least since the Enlightenment) the power to control a particular field resides in claims to (scientific) knowledge embodied not only in writing but also in disciplinary and professional organizations, in institutions (hospitals, prisons, schools, factories), and in social relationships (doctor/patient, teacher/student, employer/ worker, parent/child, husband/wife). Discourse is thus contained or expressed in organizations and institutions as well as in words; all of these constitute texts or documents to be read.[2]

Discursive fields overlap, influence, and compete with one another; they appeal to one another's "truths" for authority and legitimation. These truths are assumed to be outside human invention, either already known and self-evident or discoverable through scientific inquiry. Precisely because they are assigned the status of objective knowledge, they seem to be beyond dispute and thus serve a powerful legitimating function. Darwinian theories of natural selection are one example of such legitimating function. Darwinian theories of natural selection are one example of such legitimating truths; biological theories about sexual differences are another. The power of these "truths" comes from the way they function as givens or first premises for both sides in an argument, so that conflicts within discursive fields are framed to follow from rather than question them. The brilliance of so much of Foucault's work has been to illuminate the shared assumptions of what seemed to be sharply different arguments, thus exposing the limits of radical criticism and the extent of the power of dominant ideologies or epistemologies.

In addition, Foucault has shown how badly even challenges to fundamental assumptions often fared. They have been marginalized or silenced, forced to underplay their most radical claims in order to win a short-term goal, or completely absorbed into an existing framework. . . . Although some have read Foucault as an argument about the futility of human agency in the struggle for social change, I think that he is more appropriately taken as a warning against simple solutions to difficult problems, as advising human actors to think strategically and more self-consciously about the philosophical and political implications and meanings of the programs they endorse. From this perspective, Foucault's work provides an important way of thinking differently (and perhaps more creatively) about the politics of the contextual construction of social meanings about such organizing principles for political action as "equality" and "difference."

DIFFERENCE

An important dimension of poststructuralist analyses of language has to do with the concept of difference, the notion (following Ferdinand de Saussure's structuralist linguistics) that meaning is made through implicit or explicit contrast, that a positive definition rests on the negation or repression of something represented as antithetical to it. Thus, any unitary concept in fact contains repressed or negated material; it is established in explicit opposition to another term. Any analysis of meaning involves teasing out these negations and oppositions, figuring out how (and whether) they are operating in specific contexts. Oppositions rest on metaphors and cross-references, and often in patriarchal discourse, sexual difference (the contrast masculine/feminine) serves to encode or establish meanings that are literally unrelated to gender or the body. In that way, the meanings of gender become tied to many kinds of cultural representations, and these in turn establish terms by which relations between women and men are organized and understood. The possibilities of this kind of analysis have, for obvious reasons, drawn the interest and attention of feminist scholars.

Fixed oppositions conceal the extent to which things presented as oppositional are, in fact, interdependent—that is, they derive their meaning from a particularly established contrast rather than from some inherent or pure antithesis. Furthermore, according to Jacques Derrida, the interdependence is hierarchical with one term dominant or prior, the opposite term subordinate and secondary. The Western philosophical tradition, he argues, rests on binary oppositions: unity/diversity, identity/difference, presence/absence, and universality/specificity. The leading terms are accorded primacy; their partners are represented as weaker or derivative. Yet the first terms depend on and derive their meaning from the second to such an extent that the secondary term can be seen as generative of the definition of the first terms.[3] If binary oppositions provide insight into the way meaning is constructed, and if they operate as Derrida suggests, then analyses of meaning cannot take binary oppositions at face value but rather must "deconstruct" them for the processes they embody.

DECONSTRUCTION

Although this term is used loosely among scholars—often to refer to a dismantling of destructive enterprise—it also has a precise definition in the work of Derrida and his followers. Deconstruction involves analyzing the operations of difference in texts, the ways in which meanings are made to work. The method consists of two related steps:

the reversal and displacement of binary oppositions. This double process reveals the interdependence of seemingly dichotomous terms and their meaning relative to a particular history. It shows them to be not natural but constructed oppositions, constructed for particular purposes in particular contexts.[4] The literary critic Barbara Johnson describes deconstruction as crucially dependent of difference.

> The starting point is often a binary difference that is subsequently shown to be an illusion created by the working of differences much harder to pin down. The differences *between* entities . . . are shown to be based on a repression of differences *within* entities, ways in which an entity differs from itself. . . . The "deconstruction" of a binary opposition is not thus an annihilation of all values or differences; it is an attempt to follow the subtle, powerful effects of differences already at work within the illusion of a binary opposition.[5]

Deconstruction is, then, an important exercise, for it allows us to be critical of the way in which ideas we want to use are ordinarily expressed, exhibited in patterns of meaning that may undercut the ends we seek to attain. A case in point—of meaning expressed in a politically self-defeating way—is the "equality-versus-difference" debate among feminists. Here a binary opposition has been created to offer a choice to feminists, of either endorsing "equality" or its presumed antithesis "difference." In fact, the antithesis itself hides the interdependence of the two terms, for equality is not the elimination of difference, and difference does not preclude equality.

In the past few years, "equality-versus-difference" has been used as a shorthand to characterize conflicting feminist positions and political strategies.[6] Those who argue that sexual difference ought to be an irrelevant consideration in schools, employment, the courts, and the legislature are put in the equality category. Those who insist that appeals on behalf of women ought to be made in terms of the needs, interests, and characteristics common to women as a group are placed in the difference category. In the clashes over the superiority of one or another of these strategies, feminists have invoked history, philosophy, and morality and have devised new classificatory labels: cultural feminism, liberal feminism, feminist separatism, and so on.[7] Most recently, the debate about equality and difference has been used to analyze the *Sears* case . . .

[In an article on the *Sears* case], Milkman insists that we attend to the political context of seemingly timeless principles: "We ignore the political dimensions of the equality-versus-difference debate at our peril, especially in a period of conservative resurgence like the present." She concludes:

> As long as this is the political context in which we find ourselves, feminist scholars must be aware of the real danger that arguments about "difference" or "women's culture" will be put to uses other than those for which they were originally developed. That does not mean we must abandon these arguments or the intellectual terrain they have opened up; it does mean that we must be self-conscious in our formulations, keeping firmly in view the ways in which our work can be exploited politically.[8]

Milkman's carefully nuanced formulation implies that equality is our safest course, but she is also reluctant to reject difference entirely. She feels a need to choose a side, but which side is the problem. Milkman's ambivalence is an example of what the legal theorist Martha Minow has labeled in another context "the difference dilemma." Ignoring difference in the case of subordinated groups, Minow points out, "leaves in place a faulty neutrality," but focusing on difference can underscore the stigma of deviance. "Both focusing on and ignoring difference risk recreating it. This is the dilemma of difference."[9] What is required, Minow suggests, is a new way of thinking about difference, and this involves rejecting the idea that equality-versus-difference constitutes an opposition. . . . Instead of remaining within the terms of existing political discourse, we need to subject those terms to critical examination. Until we understand how the concepts work to constrain and construct specific meanings, we cannot make them work for us.

A close look at the evidence in the *Sears* case suggests that equality-versus-difference may not accurately depict the opposing sides in the *Sears* case. During testimony, most of the arguments against equality and for difference were, in fact, made by the Sears lawyers or by Rosalind Rosenberg. They constructed an opponent against whom they asserted that women and men differed, that "fundamental differences"—the result of culture or long-standing patterns of socialization—led to women's presumed lack of interest in commission sales jobs. In order to make their own claim that sexual difference and not discrimination could explain the hiring patterns of Sears, the Sears defense attributed to EEOC an assumption that no one had made in those terms—that women and men had identical interests.[10] Alice Kessler-Harris did not argue that women were the same as men; instead, she used a variety of strategies to challenge Rosenberg's assertions. First, she argued that historical evidence suggested far more variety in the jobs women actually took than Rosenberg assumed. Second, she maintained that economic considerations usually offset the effects of socialization in women's choices. The question of women's choices could not be resolved, Kessler-Harris maintained, when the hiring process itself predetermined the outcome, imposing generalized gendered criteria that were not necessarily relevant to the work at hand. The debate joined then not around equality-versus-difference but around the relevance of general ideas of sexual difference in a specific context.

To make the case for employer discrimination, EEOC lawyers cited obviously biased job applicant questionnaires and statements by personnel officers, but they had no individuals to testify that they had experienced discrimination. Kessler-Harris referred to past patterns of sexual segregation in the job market as the product of employer choices, but mostly she invoked history to break down Rosenberg's contention that women as a group differed consistently in the details of their behavior from men, instead insisting that variety characterized female job choices (as it did male job choices), that it made no sense in this case to talk about women as a uniform group. She defined equality to mean a presumption that women and men might have an equal interest. Rather, Kessler-Harris and the EEOC called into question the relevance for hiring decisions of generalizations about the necessarily antithetical behaviors of women and men. EEOC argued that Sears's hiring practices reflected inaccurate and inapplicable notions of sexual difference; Sears argued that "fundamental" differences between the sexes (and not its own actions) explained the gender imbalances in its labor force.

The *Sears* case was complicated by the fact that almost all the evidence offered was statistical. The testimony of the historians, therefore, could only be inferential at best. Each of them sought to explain small statistical disparities by reference to gross generalizations about the entire history of working women; furthermore, neither historian had much information about what had actually happened at Sears. They were forced, instead, to swear to the truth or falsehood of interpretive generalizations developed for purposes other than legal contestation, and they were forced to treat their interpretive premises as matters of fact. Reading the cross-examination of Kessler-Harris is revealing in this respect. Each of her carefully nuanced expressions of women's work history was forced into a reductive assertion by the Sears lawyers' insistence that she answer questions only by saying yes or no. Similarly, Rosalind Rosenberg's rebuttal to Alice Kessler-Harris eschewed the historian's subtle contextual reading of evidence and sought instead to impose a test of absolute consistency. She juxtaposed Kessler-Harris's testimony in the trial to her earlier published work (in which Kessler-Harris stressed differences between female and male workers in their approaches to work, arguing that women were more domestically oriented and less individualistic than men) in an effort to show that Kessler-Harris had misled the court.[11] Outside the courtroom, however, the disparities of the Kessler-Harris argument could also be explained in other ways. In relationship to a labor history that had typically excluded women, it might make sense to overgeneralize about women's experience, emphasizing difference in order to demonstrate that the universal term "worker" was really a male reference that could not account for all aspects of women's job experiences. In relationship to an employer who sought to justify discrimination by reference to sexual difference, it made more sense to deny the totalizing effects of difference by stressing instead the diversity and complexity of women's behavior and motivation. In the first case, difference served a positive function, unveiling the inequity hidden in a presumably neutral term; in the second case, difference served a negative purpose, justifying what Kessler-Harris believed to be unequal treatment. Although the inconsistency might have been avoided with a more self-conscious analysis of the "difference dilemma," Kessler-Harris's different positions were quite legitimately different emphases for different contexts; only in a courtroom could they be taken as proof of bad faith.[12]

The exacting demands of the courtroom for consistency and "truth" also point out the profound difficulties of arguing about difference. Although the testimony of the historians had to explain only a relatively small statistical disparity in the numbers of women and men hired for full-time commission sales jobs, the explanations that were preferred were totalizing and categorical.[13] In cross-examination, Kessler-Harris's multiple interpretations were found to be contradictory and confusing, although the judge praised Rosenberg for her coherence and lucidity.[14] In part, that was because Rosenberg held to a tight model that unproblematically linked socialization to individual choice; in part it was because her descriptions of gender differences accorded with prevailing normative views. In contrast, Kessler-Harris had trouble finding a simple model that would at once acknowledge difference and refuse it as an acceptable explanation for the employment pattern of Sears. So she fell into great difficulty maintaining her case in the face of hostile questioning. On the one hand, she was accused of assuming that economic opportunism equally affected women and men (and thus of believing that women and men were the same). How, then, could she explain the differences her own work had identified? On the other hand, she was tarred (by Rosenberg) with the brush of subversion, for implying that all employers might have some interest in sex typing the labor force, for deducing from her own (presumably Marxist) theory, a "conspiratorial" conclusion about the behavior of Sears.[15] If the patterns of discrimination that Kessler-Harris alluded to were real, after all, one of their effects might well be the kind of difference Rosenberg pointed out. Caught within the framework of Rosenberg's use of historical evidence, Kessler-Harris and her lawyers relied on an essentially negative strategy, offering details designed to complicate and undercut Rosenberg's assertions. Kessler-Harris did not directly challenge the theoretical shortcomings of Rosenberg's socialization model, nor did she offer an alternative model of her own. That would have required, I think, either fully developing the case for employer discrimination or insisting more completely on the "differences" line of argument by exposing the "equality-versus-difference" formulation as an illusion.

In the end, the most nuanced arguments of Kessler-Harris were rejected as contradictory or inapplicable, and the judge decided in Sears's favor, repeating the defense argument that an assumption of equal interest was "unfounded" because of the differences between women and men. Not only was EEOC's position rejected, but the hiring policies of Sears were implicitly endorsed. According to the judge, because difference was real and fundamental, it could explain statistical variations in Sears's hiring. Discrimination was redefined as simply the recognition of "natural" difference (however culturally or historically produced), fitting in nicely with the logic of Reagan conservatism. Difference was substituted for inequality, the appropriate antithesis of equality, becoming inequality's explanation and legitimation. The judge's decision illustrates a process literary scholar Naomi Schor has described in another context: it "essentializes difference and naturalizes social inequality."[16]

The *Sears* case offers a sobering lesson in the operation of a discursive, that is, a political field. Analysis of language here provides insight not only into the manipulation of concepts and definitions but also into the implementation and justification of institutional and political power. References to categorical differences between women and men set the terms within which Sears defended its policies and EEOC challenged them. Equality-versus-difference was the intellectual trap within which historians argued not about tiny disparities in Sears's employment practices, but about the normative behaviors of women and men. Although we might conclude that the balance of power was against EEOC by the time the case was heard and that, therefore, its outcome was inevitable (part of the Reagan plan to reverse affirmative action programs of the 1970s), we still need to articulate a critique of what happened that can inform the next round of political encounter. How should that position be conceptualized?

When equality and difference are paired dichotomously, they structure an impossible choice. If one opts for equality, one is forced to accept the notion that difference is antithetical to it. If one opts for difference, one admits that equality is unattainable. That, in a sense, is the dilemma apparent in Milkman's conclusion cited above. Feminists cannot give up "difference"; it has been our most creative analytic tool. We cannot give up equality, at least as long as we want to speak to the principles and values of our political system. But it makes no sense for the feminist movement to let its arguments be forced into preexisting categories and its political disputes to be characterized by a dichotomy we did not invent. How then do we recognize and use notions of sexual difference and yet make arguments for equality? The only response is a double one: the unmasking of the power relationship constructed by posing equality as the antithesis of difference and the refusal of its consequent dichotomous construction of political choices.

Equality-versus-difference cannot structure choices for feminist politics; the oppositional pairing misrepresents the relationship of both terms. Equality, in the political theory of rights that lies behind the claims of excluded groups for justice, means the ignoring of differences between individuals for a particular purpose or in a particular context. Michael Walzer puts it this way: "The root meaning of equality is negative; egalitarianism in its origins is an abolitionist politics. It aims at eliminating not all differences, but a particular set of differences, and a different set in different times and places."[17] This presumes a social agreement to consider obviously different people as equivalent (not identical) for a stated purpose. In this usage, the opposite of equality is inequality or inequivalence, the noncommensurability of individuals or groups in certain circumstances, for certain purposes. Thus, for purposes of democratic citizenship, the measure of equivalence has been, at different times, independence or ownership of property or race or sex. The political notion of equality thus includes, indeed depends on, an acknowledgement of the existence of difference. Demands for equality have rested on implicit and usually unrecognized arguments from difference; if individuals or groups were identical or the same there would be no need to ask for equality. Equality might well be defined as deliberate indifference to specified differences.

The antithesis of difference in most usages is sameness or identity. But even here the contrast and the context must be specified. There is nothing self-evident or transcendent about difference, even if the fact of difference—sexual difference, for example—seems apparent to the naked eye. The questions always ought to be, What qualities or aspects are being compared? What is the nature of the comparison? How is the meaning of difference being constructed? Yet in the Sears testimony and in some debates among feminists (sexual) difference is assumed to be an immutable fact, its meaning inherent in the categories female and male. The lawyers for Sears put it this way: "The reasonableness of the EEOC's a priori assumptions of male/female sameness with respect to preferences, interests, and qualifications is . . . the crux of the issue."[18] The point of the EEOC challenge, however, was never sameness but the irrelevance of categorical differences.

The opposition men/women, as Rosenberg employed it, asserted the incomparability of the sexes, and although history and socialization were the explanatory factors, these resonated with categorical distinctions inferred from the facts of bodily difference. When the opposition men/women is invoked, as it was in the *Sears* case, it refers a specific issue (the small statistical discrepancy between women and men hired for commission sales jobs) back to a general principle (the "fundamental" differences between women and men). The differences within each group that might apply to this particular situation—the fact, for example, that some women might choose "aggressive" or "risk-taking" jobs or that some women might prefer high- to low-paying positions— were excluded by definition in the antithesis between the groups. The irony is, of course, that the statistical case required only a small percentage of women's behaviors to be explained. Yet the historical testimony argued categorically about "women." It thus became impossible to argue (as EEOC and Kessler-Harris tried to) that within the female category, women typically exhibit and participate in all sorts of "male" behaviors, that socialization is a complex process that does not yield uniform choices. To make the argument would have required a direct attack on categorical thinking about gender. For the generalized opposition male/female serves to obscure the differences among women in behavior, character, desire, subjectivity, sexuality, gender identification, and historical experience. In the light of Rosenberg's insistence on the primacy of sexual difference, Kessler-Harris's insistence on the specificity (and historically variable aspect) of women's actions could be dismissed as an unreasonable and trivial claim.

The alternative to the binary construction of sexual difference is not sameness, identity, or androgyny. By subsuming women into a general "human" identity, we lose the specificity of female diversity and women's experiences; we are back, in other words, to the days when "Man's" story was supposed to be everyone's story, when women were "hidden from history," when the feminine served as the negative counterpoint, the "Other," for the construction of positive masculine identity. It is not sameness or identity between women and men that we want to claim but a more complicated history of variable diversity than is permitted by the opposition male/female, a diversity that is also differently expressed for different purposes in different contexts. In effect, the duality this opposition creates draws one line of difference, invests it with biological explanations, and then treats each side of the opposition as a unitary phenomenon. Everything in each category (male/female) is assumed to be the same; hence, differences within each category are suppressed. In contrast, our goal is to see not only differences between the sexes but also the way these work to repress differences within gender groups. The sameness constructed on each side of the binary opposition hides the multiple play of differences and maintains their irrelevance and invisibility.

Placing equality and difference in antithetical relationship has, then, a double effect. It denies the way in which difference has long figured in political notions of equality and it suggests that sameness is the only ground on which equality can be claimed. It thus puts feminists in an impossible position, for as long as we argue within the terms of a discourse set up by this opposition, we grant the current conservative premise that because women cannot be identical to men in all respects, we cannot expect to be equal to difference and insist continually on differences—differences as the condition of individual and collective identities, differences as the constant challenge to the fixing of those identities, history as the repeated illustration of the play of differences, differences as the very meaning of equality itself.

Alice Kessler-Harris's experience in the *Sears* case shows, however, that the assertion of differences in the face of gender categories is not a sufficient strategy. What is required in addition is an analysis of fixed gender categories as normative statements that organize cultural understandings of sexual difference. This means that we must open to scrutiny the terms women and men as they are used to define one another in particular contexts—workplaces, for example. The history of women's work needs to be retold from this perspective as part of the story of the creation of a gendered workforce. [T]he meaning of "worker" was established through a contrast between the presumably natural qualities of women and men. If we write the history of women's work by gathering data that describes the activities, needs, interests, and culture of "women workers," we leave in place the naturalized contrasts and reify a fixed categorical difference between women and men. We start the story, in other words, too late, by uncritically accepting a gendered category (the "woman worker") that itself needs investigation because its meaning is relative to its history.

If in our histories we relativize the categories women and man, it means, of course, that we must also recognize the contingent and specific nature of our political claims. Political strategies then will rest on analyses of the utility of certain arguments in certain discursive contexts, without, however, invoking absolute qualities for women and men. There are moments when it makes sense for mothers to demand consideration for their social role, and contexts within which motherhood is irrelevant to women's behavior; but to maintain that womanhood is motherhood is to obscure the differences that make choice possible. There are moments when it makes sense to demand a reevaluation of the status of what has been socially constructed as women's work ("comparable worth" strategies are the current example) and contexts within which it makes much more sense to prepare women for entry into "non-traditional" jobs. But to maintain that femininity predisposes women to certain (nurturing) jobs or (collaborative) styles of work is to naturalize complex economic and social processes and, once again, to obscure the differences that have characterized women's occupational histories. An insistence on differences undercuts the tendency to absolutist, and in the case of sexual difference, essentialist categories. It does not deny the existence of gender difference, but it does suggest that its meanings are always relative to particular constructions in specified contexts. In contrast, absolutist categorizations of difference ends up always enforcing normative rules.

It is surely not easy to formulate a "deconstructive" political strategy in the face of powerful tendencies that construct the world in binary terms. Yet there seems to me no other choice. Perhaps as we learn to think this way solutions will become more readily apparent. Perhaps the theoretical and historical work we do can prepare the ground. Certainly we can take heart from the history of feminism, which is full of illustrations of refusals of simple dichotomies and attempts instead to demonstrate that equality requires the recognition and inclusion of differences. Indeed, one way historians could contribute to a genuine rethinking of these concepts, is to stop writing the history of feminisms as a story of oscillations between demands for equality and affirmations of difference. This approach inadvertently strengthens the hold of the binary construction, establishing it as inevitable by giving it a long history. When looked at closely, in fact, the historical arguments of feminists do not usually fall into these neat compartments; they are instead attempts to reconcile theories of equal rights with cultural concepts of sexual difference, to question the validity of normative constructions of gender in the light of the existence of behaviors and qualities that contradict the rules, to point up rather than resolve conditions of contradiction, to articulate a political identity for women without conforming to existing stereotypes about them.

In histories of feminism and in feminist political strategies there needs to be at once attention to the operations of difference and an insistence on differences, but not a simple substitution of multiple for binary difference for it is not a happy pluralism we ought to invoke. The resolution of the "difference dilemma" comes neither from ignoring nor embracing difference as it is normatively constituted. Instead, it seems to me that the critical feminist position must always involve two moves. The first is the systematic criticism of the operations of categorical difference, the exposure of the kinds of exclusions and inclusions—the hierarchies—it constructs, and a refusal of their ultimate "truth." A refusal, however, not in the name of an equality that implies sameness or identity, but rather (and this is the second move) in the name of an equality that rests on differences—differences that confound, disrupt, and render ambiguous the meaning of any fixed binary opposition. To do anything else is to buy into the political argument that sameness is a requirement for equality, an untenable position for feminists (and historians) who know that power is constructed on and so must be challenged from the ground of difference.

Notes

1. On the problem of appropriating poststructuralism for feminism, see Biddy Martin, Feminism, Criticism, Foucault, 27 New German Critique 3 (1982).

2. Examples of Michel Foucault's work include The Archaeology of Knowledge (Harper & Row, 1976); The History of Sexuality, vol. 1, An Introduction (Vintage, 1980); and Power/Knowledge: Selected Interviews and Other Writings, 1972–1977 (Pantheon, 1980). See also Hubert L. Dreyfus & Paul Rabinow, Michel Foucault: Beyond Structuralism and Hermeneutics (Univ. Chicago Press, 1983).

3. The Australian philosopher Elizabeth Gross puts it this way: "What Derrida attempts to show is that within these binary couples, the primary or dominant term derives its privilege from a curtailment or suppression of its opposite. Sameness or identity, presence, speech, the origin, mind, etc. are all privileged in relation to their opposites, which are regarded as debased, impure variants of the primary term. Difference, for example, is the lack of identity or sameness; absence is the lack of presence; writing is the supplement of speech, and so on." See her Derrida, Irigaray, and Deconstruction, 20 Leftwright, Intervention (Sydney, Australia) 73 (1986). See also Jacques Derrida, Of Grammatology (Johns Hopkins Univ. Press, 1976); and Jonathan Culler, On Deconstruction: Theory and Criticism After Structuralism (Cornell Univ. Press, 1982).

4. Again, to cite Elizabeth Gross's formulation: "Taken together, reversal and its useful displacement show the necessary but unfounded function of these terms in Western thought. One must both reverse the dichotomy and the values attached to the two terms, as well as displace the excluded term, placing it beyond its oppositional role, as the internal condition of the dominant term. This move makes clear the violence of the hierarchy and the debt the dominant term owes to the subordinate one. It also demonstrates that there are other ways of conceiving these terms than dichotomously. If these terms were only or necessarily dichotomies, the process of displacement would not be possible. Although historically necessary, the terms are not logically necessary." See Gross, *supra* note 3, at 74.

5. Barbara Johnson, The Critical Difference: Essays in the Contemporary Rhetoric of Reading x–xi (Johns Hopkins Univ. Press, 1980).

6. Most recently, attention has been focused on the issue of pregnancy benefits. . . . [See the essays in Part II of D. Weisberg ed. Feminist Legal Theory: Foundations (Temple Univ. Press, 1993). *Ed.*]

7. Recently, historians have begun to cast feminist history in terms of the equality-versus-difference debate. Rather than accept it as an accurate characterization of antithetical positions, however, I think we need to look more closely at how feminists used these arguments. . . . I think it is a mistake for feminist historians to write this debate uncritically into history for it reifies an "antithesis" that may not actually have existed. We need instead to "deconstruct" feminist arguments and read them in their discursive contexts, all as explorations of "the difference dilemma."

8. Ruth Milkman, Women's History and the *Sears* Case, 12 Feminist Stud. 394 (1986). In my discussion of the *Sears* case, I have drawn heavily on this careful and intelligent article, the best so far of the many that have been written on the subject.

9. Martha Minow, Learning to Live with the Dilemma of Difference: Bilingual and Special Education, 48 Law & Contemp. Probs. 157 (1984). Quotation is from p. 160; see also pp. 202–206.

10. There is a difference, it seems to me, between arguing that women and men have identical interests and arguing that one should presume such identity in all aspects of the hiring process. The second position is the only strategic way of not building into the hiring process prejudice or the wrong presumptions about difference of interest.

11. Appendix to the Written Rebuttal Testimony of Dr. Rosalind Rosenberg, 1–12.

12. On the limits imposed by courtrooms and the pitfalls expert witnesses may encounter, see Nadine Taub, Thinking about Testifying, Perspectives (American Historical Association Newsletter) 24 (November 1986): 10–11.

13. On this point, Taub asks a useful question: "Is there a danger in discrimination cases that historical or other expert testimony not grounded in the particular facts of the case will reinforce the idea that it is acceptable to make generalizations about particular groups?" *Id.* at 11.

14. See the cross-examination of Kessler-Harris, EEOC vs. Sears, 16376–619.

15. The Rosenberg "Rebuttal" is particularly vehement on this question: "The assumption that all employers discriminate is prominent in her [Kessler-Harris's] work. . . . In a 1979 article, she wrote hopefully that women harbor values, attitudes, and behavior patterns potentially subversive to capitalism" (p. 11). "There are, of course, documented instances of employers limiting the opportunities of women. But the fact that some employers have discriminated does not prove that all do" (p. 19). The rebuttal

raises another issue about the political and ideological limits of a courtroom or, perhaps it is better to say, about the way the courtroom reproduces dominant ideologies. The general notion that employers discriminate was unacceptable (but the general notion that women prefer certain jobs was not). This unacceptability was underscored by linking it to subversion and Marxism, positions intolerable in U.S. political discourse. Rosenberg's innuendos attempted to discredit Kessler-Harris on two counts—first, by suggesting she was making a ridiculous generalization and, second, by suggesting that only people outside acceptable politics could even entertain that generalization. Joan Scott, 14 Feminist Stud. 33 (1988).

16. Naomi Schor, Reading Double: Sand's Difference, in Nancy K. Miller ed., The Poetics of Gender 256 (Columbia Univ. Press, 1986).

17. Michael Walzer, Spheres of Justice: A Defense of Pluralism and Equality xii (Basic Books, 1983). See also Minow, *supra* note 9, at 202–203.

18. Milkman, *supra* note 8, at 384.

❖ Deconstructing Gender

JOAN C. WILLIAMS

EEOC v. Sears: The Perils of Modern Domesticity

IN EEOC V. SEARS, Roebuck & Co.,[1] Sears argued successfully that women were underrepresented in its relatively high-paying commission sales positions not because Sears had discriminated against them, but because women lacked "interest" in commission sales. Sears used the language of relational feminism to support its core argument that women's focus on relationships at home and at work makes them choose to sacrifice worldly advancement in favor of a supportive work environment and limited hours that accommodate their devotion to family.[2] [Williams uses the term *relational feminism* to describe the view put forth by Carol Gilligan, Suzanne Lebsock, and others: that women are more focused on relationships than are men. *Ed.*] An unmistakable undertone is Sears' subtle intimation that women's sacrifice is limited, since their "different voice" makes the fast track unappealing. Women's "ethic of care" enables them to rise above the fray, so they are not truly hurt when they are excluded from high-powered, competitive jobs in commission sales.[3]

The brilliance of Sears' lawyers lies in their success in enshrining gender stereotypes at the core of Title VII. *Sears* provides a dramatic illustration of the power of relational feminism to provide a respectable academic language in which to dignify traditional stereotypes. The case holds the potential to transform Title VII law in a way that pits gender discrimination plaintiffs against stereotypes in a battle the stereotypes are designed to win, for in effect *Sears* establishes a legal assumption that all women fit gender stereotypes and imposes on plaintiffs a burden to disprove that assumption as part of their prima facie case. Understanding the potential impact of *Sears* requires some background in Title VII law.

The usual focus of a Title VII class action lawsuit is on statistics comparing the proportion of women in a given job category with the proportion of women in the relevant labor market. Statistics are direct proof that a facially neutral hiring policy has a disparate impact on a group protected under Title VII. Statistics also are evidence of

---

87 Mich. L. Rev. 797 (1989).

intent, as is illustrated by the "billiard ball" example. Say one begins with a barrel containing 50 black and 50 white billiard balls. If balls were removed in a random fashion, one would expect half black and half white balls to be chosen. The further the results are from a 50/50 split, the greater the likelihood some other factor is at work. Because defendants who discriminate are rarely open about it, the law helps plaintiffs through a presumption that the "other factor" involved is discrimination. Thus, courts have required only evidence of a statistically significant disparity by a plaintiff to establish a prima facie case of discrimination.[4] Thereafter, the burden shifts to the defendant to articulate some nondiscriminatory reason for the disparity documented.

In contrast to courts prior to *Sears*, both the trial and appellate *Sears* courts required the EEOC to prove not only statistical disparities but also men's and women's "equal interest." Under *Sears*, therefore, a class of gender discrimination plaintiffs cannot prove their prima facie case simply by proving a disparity between the proportion of women in the relevant labor market and the proportion of women in the jobs at issue. Instead they have the additional burden of establishing what percentage of women in the otherwise relevant labor market was truly "interested" in the jobs at issue.

Sears based its argument, first, upon testimony of managers, one of whom made the now famous claim that women did not want commission sales jobs because such salesmen were required to work outside the store and women do not like to go out when "it's snowing or raining or whatever."[5] The managers' testimony was bolstered by a sociologist who testified about a survey of Sears employees, by a writer on women's issues, and by historian Rosalind Rosenberg, who cited Gilligan and other relational feminists to support her assertion that the EEOC's "assumption that women and men have identical interests and aspirations regarding work is incorrect. Historically, men and women have had different interests, goals and aspirations regarding work."[6]

To support this statement, Rosenberg offered portraits of men and women that closely echoed Gilligan's. Women she depicted as "humane and nurturing," focused on relationships, and averse to capitalist virtues such as competition. Again echoing Gilligan, she painted men as competitive and motivated by self-interest: possessive individualists *par excellence*.

Sears proceeded to use against women the gender stereotypes rehabilitated by relational feminism.[7] The implication of Sears' successful use of domesticity's insults is that relational feminists delude themselves if they think they can rehabilitate domesticity's compliments without its insults. To relational feminists, the key point of domesticity may be women's higher morality; to Sears managers it was that women are weak and dependent, delicate and passive.

A closer look at the trial transcript dramatizes the power of these stereotypes once unleashed, for it shows how Sears systematically used stereotypes to override information about the desires and the aspirations of actual women. The most obvious example of this occurs in the testimony of Joan Haworth, Sears' major statistical witness, who argued that even female applicants who appeared to be interested in commission sales, in fact, were not interested. When the EEOC challenged this statement, Haworth chose three applications that indicated background and experience in commission sales and explained how she knew none was truly interested.[8] The EEOC located two of the three women Haworth discussed, both of whom testified they had in fact been seeking jobs in commission sales.[9] The trial judge glossed over this rebuttal in his opinion.[10]

Sears also systematically discounted interests expressed by female applicants in "male" jobs such as auto sales. Haworth, who argued that those applicants were puffing up their interest, guarded against this by "normalizing" the scores of female applicants. Her methodology functioned to ensure that sales applicants who indicated interest in working both in "male" areas such as auto sales and in "female" areas such as the baby department had their "male" interests systematically discounted.[11]

Sears' attorneys had help from the trial judge in policing gender stereotypes.[12] Judge John A. Nordberg, a Reagan appointee, played an active role in shaping the evidence to support his eventual holdings that women lack interest in "male" jobs. Whenever EEOC witnesses made statements about women's commitment to the home and their lack of commitment to wage labor that contradicted gender stereotypes, Nordberg insisted they specify the precise percentage of women whose interests diverged from those of women in general (i.e., from gender stereotypes). Here's one example from the testimony of historian Alice Kessler-Harris, who countered Rosenberg's testimony by arguing that women generally have taken higher paying jobs when they became available despite the mandates of domesticity.

> Could I just interrupt for one second, Dr. Harris, or Kessler-Harris. This is what I have said to others, and if you had sat through all the testimony, you would understand the reason for my saying this. One of the difficulties in analyzing and dealing with the evidence in the case is a tendency of witnesses to use the phrase "men and women" as though it is 100 percent of men or 100 percent of women. I think that the testimony makes it clear that there are a range of personalities, interests, experiences, achievements, and everything in both sexes. . . . And what this case in a sense is getting down to, because of the statistical nature of the case, is percentages. It would be very helpful to me during the course of your testimony to try to quantify the percentage or the proportion or possible number that you are dealing with in any particular thing that you say. I [know] it is hard, because you are, in a sense, seeking to generalize. But it makes it very difficult when it is asserted that either women so and so or men so and so, when we all know that it isn't 100 percent correct.[13]

Judge Nordberg repeated the same point as a constant refrain to the testimony of EEOC witnesses. Women behave like this, they testified. What percentage, Nordberg asked again and again.[14] When Sears witnesses made generalized statements about women that *confirmed* stereotypes derived from domesticity, Nordberg's concern for quantification evaporated. I found no instance in which Nordberg felt the need for this type of quantification from Sears witnesses.[15] Nordberg's opinion shows why: he adopted the argument advanced by Sears (through Rosalind Rosenberg) that women who did not fit conventional stereotypes were a marginal group of (uppity?) college women. No statistical evidence supported this assertion.

Nordberg's insistence on quantification in effect required plaintiffs to specify the precise percentage of women interested in nontraditional jobs such as commission sales. By not requiring Sears to provide equivalent proof of the specific percentage of women who *fit* gender stereotypes, the *Sears* district court opinion in effect establishes a legal presumption that all women fit traditional gender stereotypes. The Seventh Circuit opinion [on appeal] wholeheartedly adopted this approach.

Sears' doctrinal innovation clashes at a fundamental level with the thrust of Title VII. *Sears* allows information about *gender*, about women *as a group*, to be used to establish a legal presumption about individual plaintiffs consolidated into a class. This is inappropriate because Title VII is designed to protect women who do not fit gender stereotypes, who want to work as physicists, or in auto sales. Title VII's underlying goal is to protect women who want nontraditional work. Establishing a legal presumption that every class of female plaintiffs conforms to gender stereotypes frustrates this goal.

Sears is thus a dramatic reversal of existing Title VII law and should be overruled. From a theoretical standpoint, *Sears* shows the power of gender stereotypes to overshadow evidence about actual women. *Sears* also shows how relational feminism's critique of possessive individualism serves to marginalize both women and the critique itself.

Unlike the critique of capitalism from traditional radical discourse,[16] domesticity's critique does not compel its followers to confront capitalist practice and to change it. Instead, an abiding tenet of domesticity is that women's aversion to capitalist virtues makes them "choose" home and family. This is an argument that encourages women to "choose" economic marginalization and celebrate that choice as a badge of virtue. This analysis of domesticity as an ideology designed to enlist women in their own oppression will be more fully developed [elsewhere]. For now the important thing is how Sears mobilized domesticity's critique of possessive individualism against women.

One can see how domesticity's compliments add up to its critique: women reject crass competition; they favor a friendly, cooperative, working environment over mere material advancement; they value their commitments to family over career success.[17] Sears' argument demonstrates how domesticity's critique of possessive individualism rests on a claim that women are psychologically unsuited to the economic mainstream. All Sears did was pick this up and use it to argue that women are psychologically unsuited to work in commission sales.

Sears thus illustrates how domesticity's gendered critique of possessive individualism functions to marginalize the women who espouse it. It also shows that domesticity's power derives from its ability to make arguments about women's "choice" vaguely complimentary instead of clearly insulting. When defendants prior to *Sears* tried to mobilize the interest argument, they met with little success because their "interest" arguments so clearly mobilized racist or sexist insults. For example, the assertion in a 1976 race discrimination case that blacks lacked interest in law enforcement evidently smacked too much of a claim that blacks are lazy and shiftless, or inherently not law-abiding.[18] In another case, the defendant's argument that women did not need the vocational training available to men since women choose unskilled jobs anyway also struck a jarring note.[19] In both cases, the interest argument evidently struck the courts as a blatant attempt to use against minorities the insulting stereotypes to which they traditionally have been subjected. Sears' lawyers succeeded because they used against women not the insults but the compliments of domesticity. Once the interest argument was linked with women's *virtues,* the trial judge and the conservative Seventh Circuit found it easier to frame complimentary holdings asserting that women choose their relative poverty, while framing their argument as a paean to female virtue.

If *Sears* contains some disturbing messages for relational feminists, it also contains a comforting one: that by giving up domesticity's critique of possessive individualism, they are abandoning a singularly ineffective critique. A key source of the attraction of "women's voice" for feminists and other progressive thinkers is that, in a society where radicals have had trouble being taken seriously, relational feminism offers a critique of capitalism that avoids the perceived stridency of traditional radical discourse. It is Marxism you can take home to mother.[20] But, as *Sears* shows, this strength is also a weakness, for what domesticity offers is a singularly "domesticated" critique that accepts the notion that anyone who rejects the values of contemporary capitalism freely chooses to eschew the spoils of capitalist endeavor. As traditional radical discourse makes clear, the whole point of critiquing capitalism is to challenge the way in which wealth is created and distributed. Domesticity's critique is designed to evade the central issue of whether society should be transformed.

Suzanne Lebsock offered a balanced assessment of relational feminism when she noted that the "emphasis on gender differences has great promise and great strategic risks. The risks derive from the difficulty we have in thinking in genuinely egalitarian terms. . . . The promise lies farther off."[21] With *Sears,* the risks associated with relational feminism have been played out. Moreover, I have argued that the promise of relational feminism, its critique of possessive individualism, is fundamentally flawed. Plenty of less dangerous, nongendered critiques exist to help progressives in their search for words against the resurgence of classical economic liberalism: The ongoing fascination with republicanism offers a possible alternative.[22] Neither this approach, nor traditional radical discourse—nor, for that matter, standard New Deal rhetoric—holds the pitfalls of relational feminism.[23] Instead of rehabilitating inherently loaded stereotypes, contemporary feminists should follow through domesticity's insights into the gendered structure of American capitalism to their logical conclusion [by challenging the gendered structure of the division of labor]. . . .

II. Challenging the Gendered Structure of Wage Labor

The challenge to "male norms" offered by the feminism of difference is comprised of two quite different elements. The first is the critique of "male" behavior and values, which in essence is the critique of possessive individualism. A second element is the critique of men's traditional life patterns. . . .

A rejection of men's traditional life patterns entails a fundamental challenge to the structure of wage labor. In articulating such a challenge, I begin from Catharine Mac-

Kinnon's analysis of gender as a system of power relations . . . that inequalities of power are the core feature of the gender system as we know it.[24] MacKinnon and her followers have explored the implications of this insight primarily in the context of sexuality. [T]he Western wage labor system [is] a system of power relations that leaves women economically and socially vulnerable.

Western wage labor is premised on an ideal worker with no child care responsibilities.[25] In this system men and women workers are allocated very different roles. Men are raised to believe they have the right and the responsibility to perform as ideal workers. Husbands as a group therefore do far less child care, and earn far more, than their wives. Women are raised with complementary assumptions. They generally feel that they are entitled to the pleasure of spending time with their children while they are small. Moreover, even upon their return to work, the near-universal tendency is to assume that women's work commitment must be defined to accommodate continuing child-care responsibilities. . . .

Before the mid-1970s, many women's historians concentrated on documenting how domesticity cramped women's lives.[26] This early focus on how domesticity oppressed women was replaced after 1975 by a revisionist movement initiated by Carroll Smith-Rosenberg's influential article entitled "The Female World of Love and Ritual: Relations Between Women in Nineteenth-Century America."[27] Smith-Rosenberg's article began a celebration of nineteenth-century women's culture, as historians explored the close emotional ties as well as the empowering aspects of women's separate sphere. This literature, which developed simultaneously with Gilligan's feminism and echoed its celebration of women's different voice, takes on new meaning when it is combined with the earlier literature documenting the oppressive aspects of nineteenth-century women's culture. To put it bluntly, women's rich emotional relationships in their disempowered sphere and the seductive compliments of domesticity—in particular, the notion that women were more moral than men—encouraged women to "choose" their own repression. This analysis need not deny the positive elements of women's culture. But it does demonstrate the need to assess how those positive elements sought to enlist women in their own oppression, and the extent to which that effort has been successful. *Sears* showed how traditionalist judges can use women's culture against women. The more troubling question is the extent to which women use it against themselves, as they do every time a woman "chooses" to subordinate her career "for the good of the family" and congratulates herself on that choice as a mature assessment of her own "priorities."

Feminists need to arm women to resist the argument that women's economic marginalization is the product of their own choice. . . . When we speak of women's "choices" to subordinate their careers, we are so blinded by gender prescriptions that we can forget that the husband's decision to be an ideal-worker rests upon the assumption that his wife will choose not to be in order to allow him that privilege. This is true whether the wife eschews a career altogether or whether (in the modern pattern) she merely subordinates her career to child-care responsibilities.[28] The point is that the husband is doing neither. Women know that if they do not sacrifice no one will, whereas men assume that if they do not, women will.

Thus women do not enjoy the same choices as men. But the underlying point is a deeper one: that society is structured so that everyone, regardless of sex, is limited to two unacceptable choices—men's traditional life patterns or economic marginality. Under the current structure of wage labor, people are limited to being ideal workers, which leaves them with inadequate time to devote to parenting, and being primary parents condemned to relative poverty (if they are single parents) or economic vulnerability (if they are currently married to an ideal worker). Wage labor does not have to be structured in this way.

The increasing onerousness of the gender system makes a challenge to the structure of wage labor a priority of the highest order. Moreover, a historic opportunity exists for a challenge: the current revolution in wage labor itself.

This revolution is not that women work; women have always worked.[29] The change is that the majority of *mothers* now engage in wage labor. In 1890, only 2.5 percent of married white women did so,[30] but 59 percent of married women do today, including 51 percent of those with children under three, and 54 percent of those with children with six.[31] Not only have married women gone out to work, but the social taboos against such work, a crucial policing mechanism of domestic ideology, also are disappearing. . . .

The massive shift in the gendered distribution of wage labor has produced intense pressures to challenge the assumption that the ideal worker has no child care responsibilities. But this pressure is being evaded by a cultural decision to resolve the conflicts between home and work where they have always been resolved: on the backs of women. In the nineteenth century, married women "chose" total economic dependence in order to fulfill family responsibilities. Today, many women with children continue to make choices that marginalize them economically in order to fulfill those same responsibilities, through part-time work, "sequencing," the "mommy track" or "women's work."[32] In each case, the career patterns that accommodate women's child care responsibilities often are ones that hurt women's earning potential.

Day care, widely assumed to be the key to incorporating mothers into the labor force, is part of the emerging gender system that reinforces women's traditional condemnation to the margins of economic life, for even mothers with day care cannot truly perform as ideal workers. The ideal worker is one who can work a minimum of 40 hours a week and has no career interruptions (such as time out for childbirth, infant care, or care of the sick) and who can do the things required for "normal" career advancement—which frequently include the ability to work overtime and the willingness to travel and (for white-collar jobs) to be transferred to a different city. Employers are taught they can expect this, but mothers cannot fulfill this career profile even with most types of day care—the single exception may be the mother with a full-time housekeeper, a solution available only to the relatively rich.

The child-care options available to the great bulk of workers often require someone to take time from work when the child or the caretaker is sick or for other appointments that must take place during business hours. Moreover, many day care centers and many family-care situations offer sharply limited hours that do not accommodate many employers' requirements for overtime work. So long as mothers systematically take up the slack, the traditional gender system will not change: mothers will remain at the margins of economic life. . . .

Women can work without insisting on a redefinition of the ideal worker, but most can do so only at the cost of failing to fulfill the ideal. This is not happening. Consequently, what we are seeing today is the adjustment of the gender system to these new conditions in a way that ensures women's continued relegation to the margins of economic life. We are living through a reinvention of the gender system, when we as feminists should be proposing a paradigm shift that entails a redesign of wage labor to take parenting activities into account. There are three basic options for changing the status quo. One is for each individual woman to rebel against the traditional demand that she sacrifice in order for her husband to be an ideal worker. But what will that mean: that *she* will become the ideal worker and he will play the supportive role? This is an alternative most men would find unthinkable because they are socially conditioned to believe that the option to be an ideal worker is their birthright. Most women, moreover, would find this option unattractive because society has nourished in them the belief that it is their birthright to be able to take time off the grind and enjoy their children while they are small.

A second alternative is for both men and women to give a little, so that they share the family responsibilities that preclude ideal worker status. But then neither husband nor wife functions as an ideal worker—a risky strategy in an age of economic uncertainty.[33]

The only remaining alternative is to challenge the structure of wage labor. Since the current structure, and the gender system of which it is a part, increasingly condemns women to poverty, this should be at the core of a feminist program.

Such a program would build upon many reforms that currently exist. These include programs such as day care, flex-time, and four day work weeks, organized labor contracts that provide for unconditional personal days that can be used for care of sick children, as well as paid maternity leave (for the physical disability associated with childbirth) and parental leave. More sweeping proposals are those offered by noted child care specialists Benjamin Spock and Penelope Leach[34] and by noted economist Heidi Hartmann, who advocates a six-hour work day for all workers.[35]

Feminists' goal must be to redesign wage labor to take account of reproduction. Such a goal today seems utopian—but then the eight hour work day seemed utopian in the mid-nineteenth century. The notion that the wage-labor system should take account of the human life cycle has always faced the argument that such "private costs" as aging or raising children are of no concern to employers. Even in the United States, this view has been successfully challenged: old age is now acknowledged as a reality, and wage-labor expectations have been modified accordingly. That, too, once seemed a utopian goal. But expectations change: hegemony is never complete. Feminists should begin to work both towards cultural change and towards the kind of small, incremental steps that will gradually modify the wage-labor system to acknowledge the reality of society's reproductive needs. . . .

Notes

[The author explains that she is not using "deconstruction" in the technical sense used by critical legal scholars influenced by Jacques Derrida, see, e.g., Dalton, An Essay in the Deconstruction of Contract Doctrine, 94 Yale L.J. 997 (1985), but in the emerging popular sense of deconstructing a social phenomenon into its component parts.]

1. 628 F. Supp. 1264 (N.D. Ill. 1986), *aff'd*, 839 F.2d 302 (7th Cir. 1988).

2. This argument was made most clearly through the testimony of Rosalind Rosenberg. See Offer of Proof Concerning the Testimony of Dr. Rosalind Rosenberg at paras. 11, 16–22, EEOC v. Sears (No. 79-C-4373). Sears' testimony at times made it seem that all women prefer part-time work.

3. [The terms *ethic of care* and women's *different voice* refer to ideas in the work of psychologist Carol Gilligan. See Carol Gilligan, In a Different Voice (1982). *Ed.*]

4. For a good general discussion, see Boardman & Vining, The Role of Probative Statistics in Employment Discrimination Cases, 46 Law & Contemp. Probs. 189 (1983); for an advanced discussion, see D. Baldus & J. Cole, Statistical Proof of Discrimination 26–31, 290–293 (1980).

5. Trial Transcript at 8439, Testimony of Ray Graham, EEOC v. Sears, Roebuck & Co., 628 F. Supp. 1264 (N.D. Ill. 1986) (No. 79-C-4373), *aff'd*, 839 F.2d 302 (7th Cir. 1988). Graham, Sears' corporate director of equal opportunity, repeatedly expressed the opinion that some jobs (hardware, for example) have "natural appeal" for men, *id.* at 8435, while others (draperies) are "a natural" for women, *id.* at 8432. His assessments were based on assertions that women are averse to competition, *id.* at 8433, and pressure, *id.* at 8434–8435.

6. Offer of Proof Concerning the Testimony of Dr. Rosalind Rosenberg, at para. 1, EEOC v. Sears (No. 79-C-4373).

7. Some thoughtful comments on drafts of this paper have suggested that all *Sears* proves is that relational feminism can be misused. I disagree. The fact that stereotypes drawn from relational feminism can so successfully be used against women suggests, to me, their inherent limitations (namely, that they were designed to be used against women), not that Rosenberg and Nordberg distorted Gilligan's imagery. I want to stress that my charge that Gilligan's description of gender is inaccurate and potentially harmful does not mean that I think feminists should stop exploring gender differences . . . ; it means only that our explorations should break free from the grip of verities derived from domestic ideology.

In addition to using domesticity's compliments against women, Sears also subtly mobilized the insults that are an integral part of the traditional stereotypes. Rosenberg notes women's traditional association with dependence, *id.* at para 17; Ray Graham's testimony is pervaded by notions of women as weak, Trial Transcript at 8425–8426, 8436, delicate, *id.* at 8425, 8439, and vulnerable, *id.* at 9435, 8438, EEOC v. Sears (No.79-C-4373). Other managers also stressed women's sexual vulnerability, see Offer of Proof Concerning the Testimony of Thomas Biczak at para. 26, EEOC v. Sears (No. 79-C-4373); Offer of Proof Concerning the Testimony of Daniel Mihalovich at para. 12, EEOC v. Sears (No. 79-C-4373).

8. Trial Transcript at 14625–29, Testimony of Joan Haworth, EEOC v. Sears (No. 79-C-4373). Haworth was analyzing applications that provided a single box marked "sales" for applicants to check, without a breakdown into commission and noncommission sales. The EEOC's analysis incorporated the assumption that female applicants who checked sales and had background and experience in commission sales were in-

terested in commission sales positions. Sears challenged this assumption by putting Haworth on the stand to testify that such women were not in fact interested in commission sales.

9. One stated, "[C]ommission sales is exactly what I was looking for and was the reason I came to Sears and put in an application." Written Testimony of Lura L. Nader at 1, EEOC v. Sears (No. 79-C-4373). See also Written Testimony of Alice Howland at 4.

10. Judge Nordberg's opinion discounted these witnesses' testimony on the ground that the EEOC had not proven that they were discriminated against. EEOC v. Sears, 628 F. Supp. 1264, 1318 (N.D. Ill. 1986), *aff'd*, 839 F.2d 302 (7th Cir. 1988). This of course was not the purpose for which these witnesses' testimony was submitted.

11. This arose in Sears' lawyers' analysis of Sears' Applicant Interview Guides (AIG's), in which applicants were asked to rate their interest in selling various categories of items from one to five in terms of interest, and skill. In Judge Nordberg's words, "The scores were normalized to take into account that some applicants might inflate their scores to increase their chances of being hired." 628 F. Supp. at 1322. Normalization is a commonly used statistical technique, but two of EEOC's experts testified they had never seen it used as Dr. Haworth used it. . . .

12. Sears also had help from the EEOC. The Agency's decision not to provide testimony from victims of discrimination made it much easier for Sears to make general arguments on the basis of stereotypes. The EEOC's position is that if it had provided witnesses, the trial judge would have discounted their testimony on the grounds that the witnesses were too few in number or were otherwise unrepresentative of the nationwide class. Brief of the Equal Employment Opportunity Commission as Appellant at 151–153, EEOC v. Sears, 839 F.2d 302 (7th Cir. 1988). However, the testimony of live women interested in nontraditional jobs might have made it more awkward for the courts to accept Sears' assertions about women's interests. . . . But the existence of victim testimony so labelled would at the least have required the Seventh Circuit to write its opinion differently. It relied heavily on the lack of testimony from "real" victims. See 839 F.2d at 310–312.

13. Trial Transcript at 16501–16502, EEOC v. Sears (No. 79-C-4373).

14. For example, Nordberg repeated this point to Alice Kessler-Harris six times. Trial Transcript, *passim*, EEOC v. Sears (No. 79-C-4373).

15. I have not read the entire 19,000-page transcript. However, I note that Nordberg never pressed Sears' complementary witness Rosalind Rosenberg to attach a percentage to her claims about women, although those claims often were as unqualified as Kessler-Harris', or more so. To Rosenberg, Nordberg stressed the need to qualify her statements by designating the time period to which they applied. Trial Transcript at 10374–76, EEOC v. Sears (No. 79-C-4373). That objection was much easier to meet: it is easier for a historian to limit generalized statements to a given century than to specify what precise percentage of women during a given period wanted nontraditional jobs (or otherwise diverged from women's traditional roles).

16. I use the term "radical discourse" to refer to a radical rhetoric in the Marxist tradition. This includes both classical Marxism and the neo-Marxist critical theorists.

17. Compare Offer of Proof Concerning the Testimony of Dr. Rosalind Rosenberg, EEOC v. Sears (No. 79-C-4373), at paras. 19(c), 20(a) (women reject competitiveness) *and* para. 19(a) ("Women tend to be more interested than men in the cooperative, social aspects of the work situation.") *with* para. 10 ("Even as they have entered the labor force in increasing numbers, women have retained their historic commitment to the home.").

18. Castro v. Beecher, 334 F. Supp. 930, 936 (D. Mass. 1971).

19. Glover v. Johnson, 478 F. Supp. 1075, 1086–1088 (E. D. Mich. 1979), *aff'd. sub nom.* Cornish v. Johnson, 774 F.2d 1161 (6th Cir. 1985), *cert. denied,* 478 U.S. 1020 (1986).

20. This phrase was first applied to Antonio Gramsci. See Romano, But Was He a Marxist? (Book Review), Village Voice, Mar. 29, 1983, at 41, quoted in Lears, The Concept of Cultural Hegemony: Problems and Possibilities, 90 Am. Hist. Rev. 567 (1985).

21. Suzanne Lebsock, The Free Women of Petersburg: Status and Culture in a Southern Town, 1784–1860, 144 (1984).

22. See, e.g., Sunstein, Interest Groups in American Public Law, 38 Stan. L. Rev. 29 (1985); Michelman, The Supreme Court, 1985 Term—Foreword: Traces of Self-Government, 100 Harv. L. Rev. 3 (1986); Sherry, Civic Virtue and the Feminine Voice in Constitutional Adjudication, 72 Va. L. Rev. 543 (1983); Horwitz, Republicanism and Liberalism in American Constitutional Thought, 29 Wm. & Mary L. Rev. 57 (1987); Forbath, The Ambiguities of Free Labor: Labor and the Law in the Gilded Age, 1985 Wis. L. Rev. 767. For critiques of possessive individualism not framed in gendered terms, see R. Bellah, R. Madsen, W. Sullivan, A. Swidler & S. Tipton, Habits of the Heart: Individualism and Commitment in American Life 275–296 (1985); Cornell, Toward a Modern/Postmodern Reconstruction of Ethics, 133 U. Pa. L. Rev. 291 (1985); Gottlieb, Relationism: Legal Theory for Relational Society, 50 U. Chi. L. Rev. 567 (1983); Lynd, Communal Rights, 62 Texas L. Rev. 1417 (1984); Simon, The Invention and Reinvention of Welfare Rights, 44 Md. L. Rev. 1 (1985); Sparer, Fundamental Human Rights, Legal Entitlements, and the Social Struggle; A Friendly Critique of the Critical Legal Studies Movement, 36 Stan. L. Rev. 509 (1984). I find it particularly disturbing when feminists cite ungendered critiques and characterize them as "feminine." See, e.g., Sherry, *supra,* at 543–544. Indeed, Hendrik Hartog has argued that, to the extent republicanism is gendered, it is patriarchal. See Hartog, remarks in a round table discussion on The Constitution, Republicanism, and Women in the New Nation, at the Seventeenth Annual Meeting of the American Society for Legal History, Oct. 23–24, 1987. The only overlap I can see between Sherry's description of republicanism and that of the "feminine voice" is that both constitute critiques of liberal individualism. This overlap does not make republicanism "feminine." See also Schneider, The Dialectic of Rights and Politics: Perspectives From the Women's Movement, 61 N.Y.U. L. Rev. 589, 612–613 (discussing parallels between feminist theory and Sparer's non-gendered critiques of capitalism).

23. See Tronto, Beyond Gender Difference to a Theory of Care, 12 Signs: J. Women Culture & Soc'y 644 (1987).

24. See, e.g., C. MacKinnon, Sexual Harassment of Working Women—A Case of Sex Discrimination 92, 101–129, 215–221 (1979) [hereinafter Sexual Harassment]; C. MacKinnon, Feminism Unmodified 32–42 (1987) [hereinafter Feminism Unmodified].

25. I would like to thank Ann Freeman for insights and encouragement in developing this argument, of which she has a somewhat different version. Mary Joe Frug has articulated the core insight that Western wage labor assumes a worker with no child care responsibilities in her seminal study, Frug, Securing Job Equality for Women: Labor Market Hostility to Working Mothers, 59 B.U. L. Rev. 55 (1979). . . .

26. See, e.g., Welter, The Cult of True Womanhood: 1820–1860, 18 Am. Q. 151, 152 (1966). A sampling of other representative works: Faragher & Stansell, Women and Their Families on the Overland Trail to California and Oregon, 1842–1867, 2 Feminist Stud. 150 (1975); Smith-Rosenberg, The Hysterical Woman: Sex Roles and Role Conflict in 19th-Century America, 39 Soc. Res. 652 (1972); Wood, The "Scribbling

Women" and Fanny Fern: Why Women Wrote, 23 Am. Q. 3 (1971). Welter and other contemporary writers of women's history were directly influenced by Betty Friedan's *The Feminist Mystique*. See Kerber, Separate Spheres, Female Worlds, Women's Place: The Rhetoric of Women's History, 75 J. Am. Hist. 9, 11 (1988). Kerber offers an astute reassessment of women's history designed to move beyond the stages I discuss here.

27. Smith-Rosenberg, The Female World of Love and Ritual: Relations Between Women in Nineteenth-Century America, reprinted in N. Cott & E. Pleck, A Heritage of Her Own 311 (1979).

28. In a recent Gallup poll, 28% of working and 57% of nonworking mothers said they had quit work since having children; 43% of working and 37% of nonworking mothers said they had changed jobs or hours to spend more time with family; 35% of working and 45% of nonworking mothers said they had cut back on career goals. Kantrowitz, Witherspoon, Burgower, Weathers & Huck, A Mother's Choice, Newsweek, Mar. 31, 1986, at 46, 51.

29. See A. Kessler-Harris, Women Have Always Worked (1981); A. Kessler-Harris, Out to Work (1982). Kessler-Harris' title illustrates the difficulty of trying to be consistent about not referring to wage labor as "work," a usage that implies that women's traditional activities, from bearing children to housework, are leisure.

30. Smith, Family Limitation, Sexual Control, and Domestic Feminism in Victorian America, in Cott & Pleck, *supra* note 27, at 225. Married black women have always worked outside the home in greater numbers. See J. Jones, Labor of Love, Labor of Sorrow 6–8 (1985). . . .

31. U.S. Dept. of Commerce, Bureau of the Census, Statistical Abstract of the United States 383 (1987). . . .

32. . . . The ten leading occupations of women are ones in which it is relatively easy for workers to leave and reenter. See Marshall & Paulin, Employment and Earnings of Women: Historical Perspective, in Working Women: Past, Present, Future 10, 24 (1987).

33. Both these options are doomed politically, as is any political strategy that attempts to gain equality for women by insisting men share women's traditional disabilities. This strategy has been tried before, with notably unsuccessful results. An example is the Victorian attempt to eliminate the sexual double standard by insisting that men join them in adhering to the sexual purity expected of women. Modern reformers have been careful to disassociate advancements for women from sacrifices for men. . . .

In addition, it is likely that men face even greater career difficulties than women when they demand accommodation of child care responsibilities. . . .

34. "Go after our industries!" advises Doctor Spock. He recommends more flexibility in hours, six-hour work days and subsidized day care. Both Penelope Leach, a psychology Ph.D., and Dr. T. Barry Brazelton believe that current trends have potentially adverse psychological consequences for today's families. Brazelton has stressed the need for improved pay for day care workers; Leach advocates extensive paid maternity leave (6 months) and part-time work by both parents (next 18 months). See Work and Families, Washington Parent 1, 3, 5 (Nov. 1988) (report of a panel discussion in Boston, Apr. 1988). See also Brazelton, Stress for Families Today, Infant Mental Health J., Spring 1988, at 65.

35. See Hartmann, Achieving Economic Equity for Women, in M. Raskin & C. Hartman eds., Winning America: Ideas and Leadership for the 1990s, 99 (1988).

Telling Stories about Women and Work: Judicial Interpretations of Sex Segregation in the Workplace in Title VII Cases Raising the Lack of Interest Argument

Vicki Schultz

HOW DO WE MAKE sense of that most basic feature of the world of work, sex segregation on the job? . . . Social science research has documented, and casual observation confirmed, that men work mostly with men, doing "men's work," and women work mostly with women, doing "women's work."[1] We know also the serious negative consequences segregation has for women workers. Work traditionally done by women has lower wages, less status, and fewer opportunities for advancement than work done by men. Despite this shared knowledge, however, we remain deeply divided in our attitudes toward sex segregation on the job. What divides us is how we interpret this reality, the stories we tell about its origins and meaning. Why does sex segregation on the job exist? Who is responsible for it? Is it an injustice, or an inevitability?

In EEOC v. Sears, Roebuck & Co.,[2] the district court interpreted sex segregation as the expression of women's own choice. . . . In the court's eyes, Sears had done nothing to segregate its salesforce; it had merely honored the preexisting employment preferences of working women themselves.

Few recent cases have received more attention—or provoked more controversy—than Sears. The extraordinary attention given the case suggests that it was somehow unusual and therefore noteworthy. . . .

In fact, neither the issues nor the outcome in *Sears* are new. For almost two decades, employers have argued successfully that they had no role in creating sex segregation in their workforces. "It's not our fault," they say. "We don't exclude women from men's jobs. In fact, we've been trying to move women into those jobs. The trouble is, women won't apply for them—they just aren't interested. They grow up wanting to do women's work, and we can't force them to do work they don't want to do." Almost half the courts to consider the issue have accepted this explanation and attributed women's disadvantaged place in the workplace to their own lack of interest in more highly valued nontraditional jobs.

This essay places the *Sears* case in historical and theoretical context. It studies all published Title VII decisions since 1965 in which employers have sought to justify sex

---

103 Harv. L. Rev. 1749 (1990). Copyright © 1990 by the Harvard Law Review Association.

segregation as the expression of women's own lack of interest in nontraditional jobs. An analysis of the results, evidentiary approaches, and reasoning in these cases shows that there has been a continuing (if not always conscious) sexism in the way working women have been envisioned within the law. The women who predominate in these cases are working-class women. Many are women of color,[3] seeking jobs traditionally held by men rather than jobs held by white women.[4] Working-class women have shared the experience of being marginalized at work, but being unable to opt out.[5] [Society] has long viewed these women as inauthentic workers, uncommitted to wage work as an important life interest and source of identity. This view has justified relegating them to dead-end, female-dominated jobs at the lowest rung of the economic ladder.

Title VII promised working women change. But, consciously or unconsciously, courts have interpreted the statute with some of the same assumptions that have historically legitimated women's economic disadvantage. Most centrally, courts have assumed that women's aspirations and identities as workers are shaped exclusively in private realms that are independent of and prior to the workworld. By assuming that women form stable job aspirations before they begin working, courts have missed the ways in which employers contribute to creating women workers in their images of who "women" are supposed to be. Judges have placed beyond the law's reach the structural features of the workplace that gender jobs and people, and disempower women from aspiring to higher-paying nontraditional employment. . . .

I write, then, from a conviction that what judges say and do matters. Courts have authority to help or hinder working women in their struggle against marginalization and segregation into low-paying, low-status jobs. Judges' interpretations of sex segregation enter a broader stock of cultural knowledge that organizes people's experience and gives meaning to what we see when we observe men and women doing separate tasks in everyday life.[6] An interpretation that portrays women as having formed their job preferences before they ever enter the workworld renders invisible all the ways in which employers disempower women from claiming nontraditional jobs. As such, it rationalizes the sex-segregated status quo. But if law organizes meaning, it also orchestrates power. . . . When judges impose liability, they can dramatically alter the sexual composition of employers' workforces or job classifications. Conversely, when courts refuse to intervene, segregation will likely continue. Thus, judges have the power to create the conditions that make their stories about sex segregation come true.

The story of how courts have dealt with sex segregation in the workplace is necessarily a story about how they have treated statistical evidence in Title VII cases. The purpose of statistical evidence is to demonstrate that women or minorities are significantly underrepresented in the employer's workforce or in certain jobs, thereby proving the existence of the patterns of segregation that the plaintiffs seek to dismantle. [A]s quickly as plaintiffs began to use statistical evidence, employers began to devise strategies to undermine its probative value.

One central strategy has been the lack of interest argument. Since 1967,[7] employers have sought to justify patterns of sex and race segregation in their workforces by arguing that these patterns resulted not from any actions they had taken, but rather from women's and minorities' own lack of interest in higher-paying nontraditional jobs. The lack of interest argument attacks the meaningfulness even of statistical evidence showing egregious, long-standing patterns of segregation. For if these patterns are the expression of women's or minorities' independent work preferences, then employers cannot be blamed. Whether such preferences are attributable to biological influences or to pre-work socialization, the point is that employers are not responsible. . . .

. . . Before the first sex discrimination case raising the lack of interest argument was decided, the courts had already decided a landmark series of race discrimination cases. . . . In these early race discrimination cases, the courts applied evidentiary standards that presumed that continuing patterns of racial segregation were attributable to historical labor market discrimination, rather than to minorities' independent preferences for lower-paying, less-challenging jobs. This approach recognized that human choices are never formed in a vacuum and that people's work aspirations are inevitably shaped by the job opportunities that have historically been available to them, as well as by their experiences in the work structures and relations of which they have been a part. . . . That the courts have never taken such an approach in sex discrimination cases is a testimonial to the degree to which judges have accepted the dominant societal view of women as marginal workers. This view is linked to the cultural image of women as beings formed in and for the private domestic sphere, rather than actors shaped like their male counterparts by and for the public world of wage work. . . .

Stories About Women and Work: A Rhetorical Study of the Two Competing Judicial Interpretations of Sex Segregation

[J]udges have used the "choice" and "coercion" explanations to legitimate accepting or rejecting the lack of interest argument. Even though both explanations rest in a common evidentiary framework, each of them also stands as a separate narrative that justifies a different legal outcome. I refer to the rhetorical justification used by courts who have accepted the lack of interest argument as the conservative story of choice, and to the one used by courts who have rejected that argument as the liberal story of coercion. Each of these justifications may be envisioned as a "story" with a beginning, middle, and end. There is dramatic tension and resolution, as each story draws on a particular set of images of women and work to explain why women are underrepresented in nontraditional work. Each story ends with a "moral" that legitimates a certain way of understanding sex segregation in the workplace.[8]

The critical assumption that binds the two stories within a single interpretive universe is the assumption that women form stable job preferences, independently of employer action, in early social realms. In the conservative story, this assumption is accompanied by a naturalized, totalizing account of gender. Sex segregation exists because women are "feminine," and the feminine role is so all-encompassing that it implies by definition a preference for "feminine" work. In the liberal story of coercion, by contrast, the assumption that women's job preferences are fixed before they begin working means that gender difference must be suppressed. Liberal courts can justify holding employers liable only to the extent that judges can represent women as "ungendered" subjects who emerge from a gender-free social order with the same aspirations and values as men.

That these two stories constitute the entire interpretive universe creates problems for plaintiffs challenging sex segregation. By accepting the premise that only women who escape early sex-role socialization can aspire to nontraditional jobs, the liberal story reinforces the conservative one. By failing to develop an account of how employers create jobs and job aspirations along gendered lines, both stories ultimately assume away the major problem Title VII should be addressing: the organization of work structures and workplace cultures to disempower large numbers of women from aspiring to and succeeding in more highly rewarded nontraditional work.

A. The Conservative Story of Choice

The conservative story of choice is the familiar one told by the *Sears* court: women are "feminine," nontraditional work is "masculine," and therefore women do not want to do it. The story rests on an appeal to masculinity and femininity as oppositional categories. . . . Work itself is endowed with the imagined human characteristics of masculinity or femininity based on the sex of the workers who do it. . . .

In the blue-collar context, the story begins by describing the work in heavily gendered terms. Courts invoke oppositional images of work as heavy versus light, dirty versus clean, and explicitly align the left side of the equation with masculinity (while implicitly aligning the right side with femininity). Thus, nontraditional jobs in bakeries are described as "hot, heavy, and hard work."[9] Males, of course, do this "heavy work," while females do the "lighter," "less demanding" work.[10] Work in a cardboard box factory is "dirty and somewhat heavy"; the factory is located in a "very poor section of the city," where women fear to tread.[11] Road maintenance work is "outside laboring work" that is "physically demanding and generally unappealing" to women.[12] Working as a food inspector for a railroad association is characterized as "nocturnal prowling in railroad yards inspecting rotten food" that is not "attractive" to "young women."[13]

In such cases, conservative courts did not bother to question whether the work fit the gendered characteristics ascribed to it. Indeed, employers did not assert that being male was a bona fide occupational qualification for these jobs. Although some of the jobs may have required considerable physical strength, the courts made no inquiry into whether this was true and if so, whether only men had sufficient strength to perform them. Similarly, although some of the settings may have been dirty, a tolerance for dirt is surely not a "job qualification" possessed only by men. Within the story of coercion, nontraditional work is simply reified, endowed with characteristics typically thought of as masculine, as though there were a natural connection between heavy, dirty work and manhood itself. Ironically, courts associated such work with masculinity even in some cases where the employer's traditionally female jobs involved equally dirty and physically demanding work.

Once the court described the work in reified, masculine terms, women's lack of interest followed merely as a matter of "common sense." "The defendant manufactures upholstered metal chairs,"[14] said one court. "Common sense tells us that few women have the skill or the desire to be a welder or a metal fabricator, and that most men cannot operate a sewing machine and have no desire to learn."[15] Or, as another court put it: "Common practical knowledge tells us that certain work in a bakery operation is not attractive to females. . . . The work is simply not compatible with their personal interests and capabilities."[16] In these blue-collar cases, courts almost never state their specific assumptions about women workers' traits or attitudes. Just what is it about women's "personal interests" that causes them not to want to be welders or bakers? Interestingly, employers and courts almost never invoke women's family roles as the reason for their lack of interest in male-dominated blue-collar jobs. They appeal instead to a much broader, naturalized conception of femininity that draws on physical images of weakness and cleanliness and applies even to women without family responsibilities.

While in blue-collar cases, the story begins by describing the work as "masculine," in white-collar cases, it begins instead by describing women as "feminine." In the white-collar context, courts invoke social and psychological characteristics rather than physical images. In particular, employers invoke women's domestic roles to explain their lack of interest in traditionally male white-collar work,[17] and conservative courts accept these explanations. In Gillespie v. Board of Education,[18] the court explained why women teachers did not want to be promoted to administrative positions as follows:

> [M]ales who are pursuing careers in education are often the principal family breadwinners. Women . . . , on the other hand, have frequently taken teaching jobs to supplement family income and leave when this is no longer necessary or they are faced with the exigencies of raising a family. We regard this as a logical explanation and find as a matter of fact that there has been no discrimination in the North Little Rock School District.[19]

In some cases the appeal to women's domestic roles is less direct, but even broader in its implications. In Sears, for example, the court invoked women's experience in the family as the underlying cause of a whole host of "feminine" traits and values that lead them to prefer lower-paying noncommission sales jobs. According to the court:

> Women tend to be more interested than men in the social and cooperative aspects of the workplace. Women tend to see themselves as less competitive. They often view noncommission sales as more attractive than commission sales, because they can enter and leave the job more easily, and because there is more social contact and friendship, and less stress in noncommission selling.[20]

To support these generalizations, the court cited the testimony of the historian Sears hired as an expert witness, who attributed the "nurturing" aspects of women's personalities directly to their historic domestic roles. This reasoning transforms the observation that women have been family caretakers into the far more general proposition that they do not aspire to nontraditional work.

Even though the white-collar story begins by portraying women as "feminine," the story nonetheless depends on a contrasting image of nontraditional white-collar work as "masculine." In the *Sears* case, women were romanticized as friendly and noncompetitive, but this mattered only because such traits were the opposite of the ones allegedly needed for successful commission selling. Sears' retail testing manual described a commission salesperson as . . . someone who is "active" and "'has a lot of drive,'" has "'considerable physical vigor,'" and "'likes work which requires physical energy.'" Sears also administered to sales applicants a test that included such questions as, "'Do you have a low-pitched voice?,'" "'Do you swear often?,'" "'Have you ever done any hunting?,'" and "'Have you played on a football team?'" Yet, it did not occur to the court to ask whether Sears had used the sales manual and test to construct the job in masculine terms. Like the courts in blue-collar cases, the judge simply took for granted that the gendered characteristics Sears ascribed to the commission sales position were an inherent, necessary part of the job. Once the court endowed the job with these stereotypically masculine characteristics, it became a foregone conclusion that women would find it unappealing.

In the end, the logic of the story of choice converges in both blue-collar and white-collar cases. . . . In both contexts, the story portrays gender as so complete and natural as to render invisible the processes through which gender is socially constructed by employers. The story is powerful because it appeals to the widely held perception that the sexes are different. It extends this perception into an account of gendered job aspirations: if women have different physical characteristics or have had different life experiences from men, then they must have different work interests, too. There is no room for the possibility that women are different from men in certain respects, yet still aspire to the same types of work. If gender is all-encompassing, it is also so natural as to be unalterable. . . . Because there is no room for change, employers do not and cannot contribute to shaping women's job preferences.

The flip side of the coin is that work itself is somehow inherently "masculine" or "feminine," apart from anything employers do to make it that way. With the world neatly compartmentalized into gendered people and jobs, sex segregation becomes easy to explain. Women bring to the workplace their preexisting preferences for traditionally female work, and employers merely honor those preferences. In the story of choice, workplace segregation implies no oppression or even disadvantage for women. Courts telling this story often describe women's jobs as "more desirable" than men's jobs, even where women's jobs pay lower wages, afford less prestige, and offer fewer opportunities for advancement than men's. The implicit point of reference for evaluating the desirability of the work, is, of course, the courts' own construction of women's point of view: no court would describe women's work as more desirable to men. The moral of the conservative story is that working women choose their own economic disempowerment.

B. The Liberal Story of Coercion

Like their conservative counterparts, liberal courts assume that women form their job preferences before they begin working. This shared assumption, however, drives liberal courts to a rhetoric that is the opposite of conservative rhetoric. Whereas the conservative story has a strong account of gender that implies a preference for "feminine" work, the liberal story has no coherent account of gender. To the contrary, liberal courts suppress gender difference, because the assumption of stable, preexisting preferences means that they can hold employers responsible for sex segregation only by portraying women as ungendered subjects who emerge from early life realms with the same experiences and values, and therefore the same work aspirations, as men.

The liberal story centers around the prohibition against stereotyping. Courts reject the lack of interest argument by reasoning that "Title VII was intended to override stereotypical views" of women.[21] "[T]o justify failure to advance women because they did not want to be advanced is the type of stereotyped characterization which will not stand."[22] This anti-stereotyping reasoning is the classic rhetoric of gender neutrality: it invokes the familiar principle that likes are to be treated alike. The problem lies in determining the extent to which women are "like" men. On its face, the anti-stereotyping reasoning seems to deny the existence of group-based gender differences and assert that, contrary to the employer's contention, the women in the proposed labor pool are no less interested than the men in nontraditional work. Below the surface, however, this reasoning reflects a basic ambiguity (and ambivalence) about the extent of gender differences. For the anti-stereotyping rule may be interpreted to admit that women are as a group less interested than men in nontraditional work, and to assert only that some individual women may nonetheless be exceptions who do not share the preferences of most women. Under such an individualized approach, the employer is forbidden merely from presuming that all women are so "different" from men that they do not aspire to nontraditional work.

This individualized approach finds support in a number of cases, which emphasize the exceptional woman who does not "share the characteristics generally attributed to [her] group."[23] Some courts condemn employers who raise the lack of interest argument for "stereotyping" all women as being uninterested in nontraditional work.[24] Other courts reject the interest argument by observing that although some women do not desire nontraditional jobs, others do.[25] These courts reason that "Title VII rights are peculiar to the individual, and are not lost or forfeited because some members of the protected classes are unable or unwilling to undertake certain jobs."[26] Logically, however, this reasoning does not suffice to refute the lack of interest argument. The employer is not asserting that no individual woman is interested in nontraditional work, but rather that, within the pool of eligible workers, the women are as a group sufficiently less interested than men to explain their underrepresentation.

The focus on individual women thus serves a largely symbolic function. The liberal story invokes the image of the victim, the modern woman who comes to the labor market with a preexisting interest in nontraditional work, to signify the presence of a new social order in which the sexes are equal and ungendered. In this brave new world free of gender, women emerge from pre-work realms with the same life experiences and values, and therefore the same work aspirations, as men. The liberal story suppresses gender difference outside the workplace to attribute sex segregation within the workplace to employer coercion. Insofar as women approach the labor market with the same experiences and values as men, they must have the same job preferences as men, and to the extent that women end up severely underrepresented in nontraditional jobs, the employer must have discriminated.

The symbolic use of the victim, however, does not resolve the underlying issue of how representative of other women the victim is. This poses no practical difficulty when the only women who testify are the plaintiff's witnesses, who say that the employer prevented them from realizing their preferences for nontraditional jobs. But when employers present testimony from other women, who say that they are happier doing traditionally female jobs and that they would not take more highly rewarded nontraditional jobs even if offered, the liberal story confronts a dilemma. Often, liberal courts have simply characterized these women as unrepresentative of the larger group of women in the labor pool.[27] But they have no way of explaining why these women should be considered less representative of most women than the victims, or how they came to have more gendered job aspirations than other women. Because liberal courts have no coherent explanation for gender difference, more conservative courts can easily portray the victims, rather than those satisfied with traditionally female work, as the anomalous, unrepresentative group.[28]

Indeed, at a conceptual level, the liberal suppression of gender difference actually reinforces the conservative story. Because the liberal story assumes that women form their job preferences through pre-workworld socialization, it accepts the notion that only women who are socialized the same as men desire such work. To secure legal victory under the liberal approach, women must present themselves as ungendered subjects without a distinctive history, experience, culture, or identity. But this approach only validates the conservative notion that women who are "different" ("feminine") in non-work aspects automatically have "different" ("feminine") work preferences, as well.

The EEOC's position in *Sears* illustrates this dynamic. The EEOC emphasized that contrary to the district court's findings, it had not assumed that female sales applicants were as interested as males in commission sales jobs. Instead, the EEOC had recognized that the women were less interested than the men, and it had controlled for sex differences in interest by isolating the subgroup of female applicants who were similar to the males on a number of different background characteristics and who therefore could be presumed to be equally interested in commission sales. The EEOC argued that "men and women who are alike with respect to [these] . . . characteristics . . . would be similar with respect to their interest in commission sales."[29] Judge Cudahy, in a dissent from the Seventh Circuit's opinion, agreed. Although he condemned the majority and the district court for "stereotyping" women, his acceptance of the EEOC's argument suggests that the only women whose job interests were being inaccurately stereotyped were those whose earlier life experiences resembled men's. Judge Cudahy's and the EEOC's position assumed that the women had formed specific preferences for commission or noncommission saleswork before they applied at Sears. Indeed, Judge Cudahy expressed this assumption explicitly, emphasizing that the EEOC's case would have been much stronger if it had produced "even a handful of witnesses to testify that Sears had frustrated their childhood dreams of becoming commission sellers."[30] Once this assumption was accepted, it was impossible to analyze seriously the extent to which Sears had shaped its workers' preferences. The only alternative was to identify the illusive group of women whose personal histories were so similar to men's that one might safely presume that they had been socialized to prefer the same jobs.

This liberal approach faces two strategic difficulties that leave working women vulnerable to the conservative explanation for segregation. The first may be termed a credibility problem. Insofar as the liberal story relies on an image of women as "ungendered," it is less believable than the conservative story. Like most people, judges tend to find implausible the suggestion that women have the same characteristics, experiences, and values as men. Employers are able to turn this perception to their advantage by arguing that even feminists have acknowledged that our sexist society socializes girls and women into "feminine" roles. In *Sears*, for example, the historian retained by Sears was able to cite the feminist consciousness-raising movement to the company's advantage, asserting that the very need for consciousness-raising was premised on the "recognition that men and women have internalized different personality traits and different attitudes."[31] In the end, it made no difference that the EEOC had controlled for sex differences in background, for the judge believed that even women whose life experiences resembled men's remained sufficiently "different" that they lacked interest in commission sales jobs. The conservative story thus capitalizes on the widely held perception of sexual difference to imply that, because girls are conditioned to conform to "feminine" sex roles, adult women will automatically aspire to "feminine" work.

This same dynamic emerges more subtly in connection with the "different family roles" explanation for women's underrepresentation in nontraditional jobs. The liberal approach refuses to credit this explanation, but fails to make clear whether this refusal is based on a denial that women have heavier family responsibilities than men or rather a rejection of the notion that women's concededly heavier family responsibilities lead them to choose female-dominated jobs. This ambiguity weakens the liberal story, for women do assume a greater burden than men for sustaining family life.[32] Again, the result is greater credibility for the conservative story, which clearly acknowledges that domestic labor is gendered. The flaw in the conservative story is not that it unfairly "stereotypes" women as family caretakers, but rather that it portrays women's domestic roles as the fulfillment of a broader set of unalterable "feminine" attributes that dictates a preference for low-paying, traditionally female jobs.

This leads to the second, related problem with the liberal story. Because it denies gender difference, the liberal approach misses the ways in which employers draw upon societal gender relations to produce sex segregation at work. The liberal prohibition against stereotyping assumes that the problem is that the employer has inaccurately identified the job interests of (at least some exceptional) women who have already formed preferences for nontraditional work. By stopping at this level of analysis, however, liberal courts fail to inquire into or discover the deeper processes through which employers actively shape women's work aspirations along gendered lines. . . .

The story one tells about women and work has profound implications for the power of law to dismantle sex segregation in the workplace. . . . The conservative story implies that law does not and cannot influence women's work aspirations. There is a natural order of gender and work that even "an Act of Congress cannot overcome."[33] . . .

[T]he liberal story . . . shares the conservative assumption that women form their work preferences exclusively in early pre-work realms. This assumption, in turn, leads the liberal approach to adopt an overly restrictive view of the role Title VII can play in dismantling sex segregation in the workplace. If women have already formed their job preferences before seeking work, the most the law can do is to ensure that employers do not erect formal barriers to prevent women from realizing their preexisting preferences.

There is a need for a new story to make sense of sex segregation in the workplace. Gender conditioning in pre-work realms is too slender a reed to sustain the weight of sex segregation. To explain sex segregation, the law needs an account of how employers actively construct gendered job aspirations—and jobs—in the workplace itself.

An Alternative Account of Gender and Work

[A] rich body of recent sociological research exists which construct[s] an alternative account of sex segregation in the workplace. Unlike the liberal story, this account recognizes the reality of gender in social life. It acknowledges that women and men are subjected to different expectations and experiences growing up, and that, as a result, they tend to express preferences for different types of work early in their lives. But unlike the conservative story, the new account does not find sex-role conditioning so monolithic or so powerful that it dictates irrevocably gendered job aspirations. Girls may be taught to be "feminine," but this does not imply that adult women will aspire only to traditionally female work throughout their adult lives. Rather, women's work preferences are formed, created, and recreated in response to changing work conditions.

This new account traces gendered work attitudes and behaviors to organizational structures and cultures in the workplace. Like all workers, women adapt their work aspirations and orientations rationally and purposefully, but always within and in response to the constraints of organizational arrangements not of their own making. Providing women the formal opportunity to enter nontraditional jobs is a necessary but insufficient condition to empower them to claim those jobs, because deeper aspects of work systems pose powerful disincentives for women to enter and remain in nontraditional employment. The new account of work and gender thus reverses the causation implicit in the current judicial framework. Sex segregation persists not because most women bring to the workworld fixed preferences for traditionally female jobs, but rather because employers structure opportunities and incentives and maintain work cultures and relations so as to disempower most women from aspiring to and succeeding in traditionally male jobs.

The new account suggests a more transformative role for the law in dismantling sex segregation at work. Once we realize that women's work aspirations are shaped not solely by amorphous "social" forces operating in early pre-work realms, but primarily by the structures of incentives and social relations within work organizations, it becomes clear that Title VII can play a major role in producing the needed changes. Title VII cases challenging segregation seek to alter (at least indirectly) the very structural conditions that prevent women from developing and realizing aspirations for higher-paid, more challenging nontraditional jobs. By attributing women's aspirations to forces external and prior to the workworld, courts deny their own ability to (re)construct workplace arrangements and the work aspirations that arise out of those arrangements. In a very real sense, the legal system has perpetuated the status quo of sex segregation by refusing to acknowledge its own power to dismantle it.

A. The Inadequacy of the Pre-Labor Market Explanation for Sex Segregation in the Workplace

The current judicial framework proceeds from the view that women bring to the labor market stable, fixed preferences for certain types of work. Whether women's preferences for traditionally female work are traced to biological influences or early socialization to "feminine" sex roles, this view attributes workplace segregation to social forces operating prior to the labor market rather than to forces operating within the workplace itself. I will refer to this view as the pre-labor market explanation for workplace segregation by sex.

The pre-labor market explanation depends on two different sets of assumptions. The first is the assumption that young women emerge from early life experiences articulating preferences for different types of work than young men. This assumption is correct. There is, however, nothing "natural" about the process through which young people come to express gendered job aspirations. Girls and boys are regularly subjected to sex-role conditioning in the family, the schools, and other early realms of life; they are constantly bombarded with messages that link "femininity" or "masculinity" to sex-appropriate work. It is therefore unsurprising that numerous studies have documented sex differences in the vocational aspirations of children, adolescents, teenagers, and young adults.

This evidence alone, however, is insufficient to support the claim that workplace segregation exists because women have been socialized to prefer traditionally female jobs. Women may change their initial preferences for jobs sex-typed as "female" to jobs sex-typed as "male" as a result of their experiences at work. If young women change the sex-type of their early job preferences after they begin working and if women's initial preferences do not predict the sex-type of the jobs they perform as their careers unfold, then it is difficult to explain segregation as a function of women's pre-labor market socialization. Thus, the pre-labor market explanation depends also on a second set of assumptions that link the sex-type of women's early work aspirations to the sex-type of the work they do over the course of their careers.

Recent sociological research has demonstrated the weakness of this link. In his book *Revolving Doors,* sociologist Jerry Jacobs presents the most comprehensive quantitative analyses of these issues to date.[34] Jacobs' research presents three propositions that refute the claim that workplace segregation is attributable to women's pre-labor market preferences. First, the sex-type of the work to which young women initially aspire does not remain stable over time, but changes substantially after they start working. For the more than eighty percent of young women who changed their aspirations between 1970 and 1980, the sexual composition of the occupation to which they aspired in 1970 was only very weakly associated with the sexual composition of the occupation to which they aspired ten years later. Second, the sex-type of the work to which young women initially aspire does not predict the sex-type of the work they do as their careers unfold. For the eighty percent of young women who changed occupations, the sexual composition of the occupations they said they desired in 1970 was not correlated with the sexual composition of the occupations they actually held in 1980. Third, the sex-type of women's early work does not predict the type of work they do later in life. For those who changed occupations, there was no correlation between the sexual composition of the occupations in which they began and the sexual composition of the occupations in which they were employed a decade later. Furthermore, not only young women change the sex-type of their occupations over time; older women do also.[35] Mature women who move into nontraditional occupations mid-career are almost equally likely to move into them from male-dominated, female-dominated, and more sexually integrated occupations.

Taken together, Jacobs' analyses provide strong evidence that workplace segregation cannot be attributed solely to women's pre-labor market preferences. Even if young women's early preferences perfectly predicted the sex-type of their first jobs, the sex-type of the occupations to which they aspire changes substantially over time. Indeed, most young women aspire to both female-dominated and male-dominated occupations at some point or another during their early careers. In addition, women's early aspirations bear almost no relationship to the sex-type of the occupations they hold over time. If sex segregation were attributable to the fact that women emerged from early life experiences with stable preferences for work of a certain sex-type, we would not expect to see so many women moving between female-dominated and male-dominated occupations.

Furthermore, the fact that women in male-dominated and female-dominated employment have similar personal histories suggests that nothing in their backgrounds has led them to approach the labor market with permanent preferences for "masculine" or "feminine" work. That women employed in nontraditional occupations often began in traditionally female ones undercuts the view that nontraditional women workers are an anomalous group of women who somehow managed to escape socialization to feminine roles. To explain segregation as a function of women's early socialization, proponents of this explanation must be able to identify and account for the personal characteristics that distinguish women who work in nontraditional occupations from the majority who do not. However, researchers have been unable to identify any such demographic characteristics. Mobility studies have found that women's probability of moving across sex-typed occupational boundaries over time does not vary significantly by race, age, marital status, or parental status.[36] These mobility studies are consistent with other studies finding that various personal, family-related characteristics—such as marital status, continuity of labor force participation, or number of children—do not predict women's likelihood of being employed in a male-dominated or female-dominated occupation at any given time. These studies demonstrate that workplace segregation cannot be attributed to women's different family roles.[37] The studies do not imply that women do not assume a greater burden for caring for families than men. Women do. The studies show only that contrary to the conventional wisdom, sex segregation does not persist because women's commitment to the family leads them to "choose" to consign themselves to lower-paid, female-dominated occupations.[38]

If sociological evidence refutes the view that workplace segregation is a function of women's early socialization, it also challenges the theoretical account of gender implicit in that view. By positing that women have chosen traditionally female work, the pre-labor market explanation initially appears to portray women as agents actively involved in constructing their own work aspirations and identities. Instead, this explanation eliminates women's capacity for agency. To explain segregation as a function of women's own choice, one must presume that the content of early sex-role conditioning is so coherent and its hold on women so permanent that it predetermines what they do throughout their lives. In adopting this static view of women's work preferences, the pre-labor market explanation reduces women to little more than walking embodiments of other people's early role-expectations for them. Adult women are limited to acting out "feminine" scripts others wrote for them while they were children.

In fact, the content of early socialization is neither monolithic nor uniform. Girls receive ambiguous and inconsistent signals that encourage them in some stereotypically masculine behavior as well as stereotypically feminine behavior. In addition, children do not always conform to even the clearest parental expectations, but respond to parental and other messages with their own interpretations. In light of these factors, it is not surprising that women emerge from early socialization with work attitudes and preferences that are open and subject to revision. Neither life nor people are static. Even if the main thrust of women's early training is to reward them for appropriate sex-role behavior, socialization is not a straitjacket that predetermines that adult women will aspire only to work defined by the dominant culture as feminine. . . .

B. The Construction of Gender in the Workplace

An emerging perspective in the sociological literature provides an alternative to the pre-labor market explanation for sex segregation in the workplace. This alternative perspective begins from the premise that people's work aspirations are shaped by their experiences in the workworld.[39] It examines how structural features of work organizations reduce women's incentive to pursue nontraditional work and encourage them to display the very work attitudes and behavior that come to be viewed as preexisting gender attributes.

The central insight of this perspective is that adults' work attitudes and behavior are shaped by the positions they occupy within larger structures of opportunity, rewards, and social relations in the workplace. Perhaps for this reason, this perspective has been coined "the new structuralism."[40] But it should not be mistaken for deterministic theories that portray people as having no capacity for agency, for it emphasizes that people act reasonably and strategically within the constraints of their organizational positions in an effort to make the best of them.[41] Indeed, this perspective endows people with an ongoing capacity for agency that is missing from early socialization theories. People's work aspirations and behavior are "the result of a sense-making process involving present experiencing and future projecting, rather than of psychological conditioning in which the dim past is a controlling force."

This perspective sheds light on the workplace dynamics that limit women's ability to claim higher-paid nontraditional work as their own. Women's patterns of occupational movement suggest that there are powerful disincentives for women to move into and to remain in nontraditional occupations. The mobility studies show that women in higher-paying, male-dominated occupations are much less likely to remain in such occupations over time than are women in lower-paying female-dominated occupations, who are more likely to stay put.[42] Thus, just as employers appear to have begun opening the doors to nontraditional jobs to women, almost as many women have been leaving those jobs as have been entering them. To the extent that women have been given the formal opportunity to do nontraditional work, something is preventing them from realizing that opportunity.

The new structuralism perspective instructs us to look beyond formal labor market opportunity and to ask what it is about the workplace itself that disempowers women from permanently seizing that opportunity. Research in this tradition directs us toward the "culture-producing" aspects of work organizations,[43] examining whether there is "something in the relations of employment, in work culture, the way jobs are defined and distinguished from each other, that conspires to keep women from even aspiring to [nontraditional] work."[44] I analyze below two structural features of work organizations that discourage women from pursuing nontraditional work.[45] . . .

1. THE STRUCTURES OF MOBILITY AND REWARD FOR TRADITIONALLY FEMALE JOBS

It is an old insight that people who are placed in jobs that offer little opportunity for growth or upward mobility will adapt to their situations by lowering their work aspirations and turning their energies elsewhere. Decades ago, researchers documented this phenomenon among male workers.[46] Indeed, men in low-mobility positions display orientations toward work that conventional stereotypes reserve for women. They do not define work as a central life interest, but focus instead on non-work activities. They dream of escape from their jobs and often interrupt their careers. They value extrinsic aspects of their jobs, including sociability with their co-workers, more than the intrinsic aspects of the work itself. They also insist that they are content not to be promoted.

It was not until recently, however, that this same insight began to be applied to female workers. Within firms, jobs are highly segregated by sex. Female-dominated jobs tend to be on distinct promotional ladders that offer far less opportunity for advancement than do those for male-dominated jobs. In light of these unequal mobility structures, "[w]omen in low-mobility . . . situations develop attitudes and orientations that are sometimes said to be characteristic of those people as individuals or 'women as a group,' but that can more profitably be viewed as universal *human* responses to blocked opportunities."[47]

Kanter's study of secretaries in a major industrial corporation vividly portrays this point. The corporation recruited its secretaries from parochial high schools, attended mostly by young women who were accustomed to taking orders and who had had little opportunity to develop habits of independence and initiative. Once hired, secretaries had no opportunity to move upward in the organization. . . . Bosses rewarded secretaries for their attitudes instead of their skills and their loyalty instead of their talent. [S]ecretaries were offered non-utilitarian, symbolic rewards—such as "praise" and "love"—rather than money or career advancement.

The corporation's secretaries tended to display work attitudes and behaviors that are commonly perceived to be attributes of "femininity." Many were narrowly devoted to their individual bosses, timid and self-effacing, dependent on praise, and given to emotionality and gossip. But it was their position within the organization and the structure of incentives attached to their jobs that led them to develop these orientations. To be good secretaries, they were required to display the "feminine" behaviors that are commonly viewed as an extension of women's intrinsic personalities.

Like the blue-collar men studied by an earlier generation of sociologists, Kanter's secretaries adjusted to their realistically nonexistent possibility of advancement by rating the desirability of promotion relatively low. Similarly, they began to value social relations at work over the intrinsic aspects of the job itself, developing close relationships with their peers in a counterculture that valued mutual aid and loyalty over individual mobility and "success." . . . Thus, women's work aspirations and orientations are, like men's, shaped by their opportunities for mobility and the social organization of their jobs.

The stories of blue-collar tradeswomen illustrate the converse effect on women's aspirations created by the opportunity to enter nontraditional jobs offering higher wages, challenge, and the chance for advancement. These women's interest and commitment to nontraditional work seemed almost fortuitous, the by-product of being lucky enough to encounter some opportunity to move into a job offering greater personal growth and rewards. However, the fact that they encountered such an opportunity was not mere happenstance, but a direct consequence of the fact that their employers felt legal pressures to hire women. Many of these women cited the significance of affirmative action in influencing them to pursue nontraditional work. . . . When they heard that some nontraditional job was opening up specifically for women[48] or saw other women performing nontraditional work,[49] or made contact with community-based programs designed specifically to attract and support women in nontraditional work, many of them perceived for the first time that they could aspire to nontraditional jobs.

Once they began doing nontraditional jobs, these women became highly motivated workers who defined work as a central life interest and who valued the intrinsic aspects of their work. Although many of the women had originally moved into nontraditional work because they needed the money, the job quickly became more than a paycheck. The women in Walshok's study valued four things most highly about their work: (1) productivity . . . ; (2) challenge . . . ; (3) autonomy, or the opportunity to work independently and to exercise discretion about how to control the timing and sequencing of one's work; and (4) relatedness, or "feeling as if one's 'in the swim of things', in the 'mainstream' of life."[50] Indeed, women may appreciate these features of nontraditional work even more than men do, because they contrast so favorably with the characteristics of female-dominated jobs available to working-class women.

If there is tragedy in this account of how work aspirations and behaviors come to be gendered, there is also potential for hope. If women's work orientations are attributable not to their individual "feminine" characteristics, but rather to the structures of mobility and rewards attached to jobs, then the solution is to change the work structures. Classwide Title VII suits challenging sex discrimination in promotion hold the promise to do just that. In alleging that women on the female job ladder are systematically being denied promotion into better jobs on the male job ladder, plaintiffs seek to restructure internal career ladders to create new paths up and out of entry-level female jobs for all women (and not just an exceptional few). Courts can order remedies that will prompt employers to restructure those ladders in ways that will infuse women workers with new hopes and aspirations. In doing so, they may also stimulate employers to redefine the content of entry-level jobs traditionally done by women in less stereotypically feminine terms.

Unfortunately, the courts all too often fail to respond, and in the process, they reproduce the very rationalizations for the two-tier system that keeps so many women in their place. When courts accept employers' arguments that women in female jobs lack interest in being promoted, they reinforce the sexist notion that there is something about womanhood itself that endows women with a penchant for low-paying, dead-end jobs. By refusing to intervene, they permit employers to continue to structure career ladders in ways that will encourage women to develop the depressed aspirations that can later be identified as "proof" that they preferred to be stuck at the bottom all along. Through their statements and their actions, these courts undercut women's ability to form and exercise the very choice they purport to defend.

2. THE WORK CULTURES OF TRADITIONALLY MALE JOBS

While separate-but-unequal job structures encourage women to lower their work aspirations, they also imply that segregation is natural in a way that encourages male workers to adopt proprietary attitudes toward "their" jobs. These attitudes encapsulate male-dominated jobs in a web of social relations that are hostile and alienating to women who dare to upset the "natural" order of segregation. I refer to the entire bundle of practices and processes through which these relations are created and sustained as harassment.[51] Overtly sexual behavior is only the tip of a tremendous iceberg that confronts women in nontraditional jobs. They face a wide-ranging set of behaviors and attitudes by their male supervisors and co-workers that make the culture of nontraditional work hostile and alienating. The following statement by a woman welder captures a sense of what is involved:

> It's a form of harassment every time I pick up a sledgehammer and that prick laughs at me, you know. It's a form of harassment when the journeyman is supposed to be training me and it's real clear to me that he does not want to give me any information whatsoever. . . . It's a form of harassment when the working foreman puts me in a dangerous situation and tells me to do something in an improper way and then tells me, Oh, you can't do that! It's a form of harassment when someone takes a tool out of my hand and said, Oh, I'm going to show you . . . and he grabs the sledgehammer from my hand and proceeded to . . . show me how to do this thing . . . you know, straighten up a post . . . it's nothing to it, you just bang it and it gets straight. . . . It's a form of harassment to me when they call me honey and I have to tell them every day, don't call me that, you know, I have a name printed right on my thing. . . . Ah, you know, it's all a form of harassment to me. It's not right. They don't treat each other that way. They shouldn't treat me that way.[52]

Harassment is a structural feature of the workplace that sex segregation engenders.[53] It creates a serious disincentive for women to enter and remain in nontraditional jobs. Even overtly sexual harassment is widespread. Furthermore, women in male-dominated occupations are more likely to be subjected to harassment than are women in other occupations.[54] Women in female jobs understand that they will be likely to experience harassment if they attempt to cross the gender divide;[55] they may conclude that the price of deviance is too high. Harassment is also driving the small number of women in nontraditional jobs away.[56] Blue-collar tradeswomen report that women are leaving the trades because they cannot tolerate the hostile work cultures, and there are signs that this is occurring in male-dominated professions as well.[57]

One of the most debilitating forms of harassment is conduct that interferes with a woman's ability to do her job. In nontraditional blue-collar occupations, virtually all training is acquired informally on the job. Thus, a woman's ability to succeed depends on the willingness of her supervisors and co-workers to teach her the relevant skills. Yet women's stories of being denied proper training are legion.[58] Indeed, it is sometimes difficult to distinguish inadequate training from deliberate sabotage of women's work performance, both of which can endanger a woman's physical safety.[59] To the extent that foremen and co-workers succeed in undermining women's job performance, they convert the notion that women are not cut out for nontraditional work into a self-fulfilling prophecy.

In nontraditional white-collar occupations, male workers—including elite professionals—also guard their territory against female incursion. Their conduct, too, runs the gamut from overtly sexual behavior,[60] to discriminatory work assignments and performance evaluations, to day-to-day personal interactions that send women the message that they are "different" and "out of place."[61] The white-collar equivalent of work sabotage may lie in evaluating women's work by differential and sexist standards, a practice which occurs even within the upper echelons of professional life.[62] . . .

By driving women out of nontraditional jobs, harassment reinforces the idea that women are inferior workers who cannot meet the demands of a "man's job." More subtly, for women who stay in nontraditional jobs, harassment exaggerates gender differences to remind them that they are women who are "out of place" in a man's workworld. By labeling the women as "freaks" or "deviants,"[63] and simultaneously pressuring them to conform to the dominant culture,[64] men mediate the contradiction posed by the presence of women doing "masculine" work. Thus, harassing behavior that marks nontraditionally employed women workers as exceptions for their gender—yet still women and therefore never quite as competent or as committed as the men—enables men to continue to define their work (and themselves) in masculine terms.

Cynthia Cockburn's study of engineers illustrates this process.[65] By defining women as inherently incapable of possessing technological competence, the men appropriated engineering as a masculine preserve. They viewed the relationship between manhood and technology in essentialist terms, as a natural affinity between "man" and "machine." "In contrast to the way the men [perceived] themselves—as striving, achieving, engaging in the public sphere of work—they [viewed] women as static, domestic, private people, as nonworkers."[66] They defined women as "aspect[s] of the decor" who "create a pleasant atmosphere," as interested in and good at "boring and repetitive tasks," and as soft, weak creatures who "'couldn't do' the *man*handling" required to master technology.[67] They exceptionalized the few women engineers as "performing seals," who must have been "train[ed] . . . up a bit" by some man behind the scene.[68] They also created an occupational culture that was built around "sexual stories, references and innuendo that are directly objectifying and exploitative of women."[69] By creating such a hostile work culture, the men ensured that few women would try to invade their jobs. They could then point to the absence of women as evidence that these jobs demand "masculine" skills and abilities not possessed by women.

This analysis of the relationship between harassment and the "masculinity" of nontraditional work makes clear why many women are reluctant to apply for such work. Women understand that behind the symbolism of masculinized job descriptions lies a very real force: the power of men to harass, belittle, ostracize, dismiss, marginalize, discard, and just plain hurt them as workers. The legal system does not adequately protect women from this harassment and abuse.[70] Courts have erected roadblocks to recovery, abandoning women to cope with hostile work environments on their own. The general attitude of the legal system seems to mirror that held by many male workers and managers: if women want to venture into a man's workworld, they must take it as they find it.[71]

The legal system thus places women workers in a Catch-22 situation. Women are disempowered from pursuing or staying in higher-paid nontraditional jobs because of the hostile work cultures. The only real hope for making those work cultures more hospitable to women lies in dramatically increasing the proportion of women in those jobs. Eliminating those imbalances is, of course, what Title VII lawsuits challenging segregation promise. But when women workers bring these suits, too often the courts tell them that they are underrepresented in nontraditional jobs not because the work culture is threatening or alienating, but rather because their own internalized sense of "femininity" has led them to avoid those jobs.

And so the cycle continues. A few women continue to move in and out the "revolving door," with little being done to stop them from being shoved back out almost as soon as they enter. The majority of working women stand by as silent witnesses, their failure to enter used to confirm that they "chose" all along to remain on the outside. There is no need for a sign on the door. Women understand that they enter at their own risk.

Conclusion: The Implications of the New Account for the Law

The new account of the dynamics of gender and work brings us back full circle to where we began: to the role of interpretation in creating meaning and power. Judicial interpretations of sex segregation at work simultaneously flow from and feed back into a larger stream of cultural understandings and practices. . . .

I have elaborated a new account of the dynamics of job segregation [as] a truer story about women and work—than the stock of cultural images judges have used to ground their interpretations in the past.

The central insight of the new account is that working women do not bring with them to the workworld fixed preferences for traditionally female or traditionally male work. Rather, the workplace is a central site of development for women's aspirations and identities as workers. In a very real sense, employers create women's job preferences. Once judges realize that women's preferences are unstable and always potentially in transition depending on work conditions, it will no longer do to imagine that women have a static set of "true" preferences independent of employer action that courts can discover as a factual matter and use to ground legal decisionmaking. Indeed, the notion that women have stable preferences for traditional or nontraditional work becomes a legal fiction that is plausible only by accepting as given the very structural features of the workplace that women seek to challenge through the lawsuit.

The new account of gender and work thus exposes the myths underlying the conservative "choice" explanation. What is more, it does so in a way that moves beyond, and holds more transformative potential than, the existing liberal alternative. The new account has three implications for legal analysis that, taken together, transform the current judicial framework for interpreting sex segregation.

First, the new account frees courts to reject the conservative "choice" explanation without resorting to the liberal suppression of gender difference. Once judges acknowledge that women's early work preferences remain tentative and temporary, they need not deny the force of gender in social life to hold employers responsible for sex segregation in their workforces. Courts may acknowledge that our society pressures girls to conform to appropriately "feminine" roles, that it is women who assume the lion's share of the load of caring for families, and even that it is important to most women to think of themselves as "feminine," for none of these observations imply that women will aspire only to the lower-paying, dead-end jobs considered appropriate for their sex. To put it more positively, courts may acknowledge that women have a distinctive history, culture and identity, without concluding as a corollary that they are marginal workers content to do only unremunerative, unchallenging jobs. The new account thus frees courts to portray "women" and "workers" as involving no contradiction in terms.

Second, the new account demands deeper judicial scrutiny of the way employers have structured their workplaces. Once the assumption that women approach the labor market with fixed job preferences is abandoned, it will no longer do to conceptualize discrimination in terms of whether the employer has erected specific "barriers" that prevent individual women from exercising their preexisting preferences. Employers do not simply erect "barriers" to already formed preferences: they create the workplace structures and relations out of which those preferences arise in the first place. Thus, in resolving the lack of interest argument, courts must look beyond whether the employer has provided women the formal opportunity to enter nontraditional jobs. Judges should be skeptical about employers' claims to have made efforts to attract women to nontraditional work. Such efforts are likely to be ineffective unless they . . . describe the work in terms that will appeal to women. Moreover, even extensive recruiting efforts will fail if the firm manages only to convey an all too accurate picture of organizational life that serves more as a warning than a welcome to women. Through its hiring criteria, training programs, performance evaluation standards, mobility and reward structures, response to harassment, and its managers' and male workers' day-to-day attitudes and actions, the firm may have created an organizational culture that debilitates most women from aspiring to nontraditional jobs. These sorts of work cultures can be changed, but only if courts recognize that the firm's practices create a disempowering culture for women. . . .

[T]he third and most fundamental implication of the new account is that the judicial system is itself inevitably implicated in creating women's work preferences. Once we understand that women form their job preferences in response to employers' practices, it becomes clear that courts participate in shaping women's work aspirations all the time. Preference shaping is an unavoidable part of the job judges do when they decide Title VII cases challenging workplace segregation. Every time a plaintiff brings such a case, the legal system is confronted with a decision whether to affirm or alter the status quo. When courts accept the lack of interest argument, they permit employers to organize their workplaces in ways that disable women from forming an interest in nontraditional work. When courts impose liability instead, they prompt employers to restructure their workplaces in ways that empower women to aspire to nontraditional jobs. Judicial decisions that reject the lack of interest argument also create a climate in which it is more likely that employers not involved in litigation will undertake genuine affirmative action through creative efforts to dismantle old patterns of sexual hierarchy. . . .

The new account of gender and work thus reminds judges that they, too, are the authors of women's work aspirations. This awareness should bring a new sensitivity to the way judges exercise their responsibility to resolve the factual determination of whether women lack interest in nontraditional jobs. If this is a daunting responsibility, it is one that courts have been assuming since the earliest days of Title VII enforcement. Courts can acknowledge their own constitutive power and use it to help create a workworld in which the majority of working women are empowered to choose the more highly rewarded work that Title VII has long been promising them. To create that world, they must refuse to proclaim that women already have that choice.

Notes

1. Although the degree of sex segregation declined modestly during the 1970's, work remains highly segregated by sex. Throughout the 1980's, for example, roughly 60% of all men and women workers would have been required to switch to occupations atypical for their sex to achieve sex integrated occupations. See, e.g., J. Jacobs, Revolving Doors: Sex Segregation and Women's Careers 20, 28–29 (1989); Beller, Trends in Occupational Segregation by Sex and Race 1960–1981, in B. Reskin ed., Sex Segregation in the Workplace: Trends, Explanations, Remedies II (1984). As recently as 1985, over two-thirds of working women were employed in occupations in which at least 70% of the workers were female. See Jacobs, Long-Term Trends in Occupational Segregation by Sex, 95 Am. J. Soc. 160, 160 (1989). These estimates of occupational segregation understate the degree of sex segregation, because even workers employed in apparently sex-neutral occupations often work in industries, firms, departments, and jobs that are highly segregated by sex. . . . For general discussions of sex segregation at work, see B. Bergmann, The Economic Emergence of Women (1986); P. England & G. Farkas, Households, Employment, and Gender: A Social, Economic, and Demographic View 121–196 (1986); Jacobs, *supra;* B. Reskin & H. Hartmann eds., Women's Work, Men's Work: Sex Segregation on the Job (1986).

2. 628 F. Supp. 1264 (N.D. Ill. 1986), *aff'd,* 839 F.2d 302 (7th Cir. 1988).

3. . . . Faced with the intersecting disadvantage of racial and sexual discrimination, women of color have often been excluded from work deemed appropriate for white women. For accounts of labor market discrimination against African-American, Hispanic, and Chinese-American women, see, for example, J. Jones, Labor of Love, Labor of Sorrow: Black Women, Work, and the Family from Slavery to the Present (1985); P. Zavella, Women's Work and Chicano Families: Cannery Workers of the Santa Clara Valley (1987); Glenn, Racial Ethnic Women's Labor: The Intersection of Race, Gender, and Class Oppression, in C. Bose, R. Feldberg & N. Sokoloff eds., Hidden Aspects of Women's Work 46 (1987); and Malveaux & Wallace, Minority Women in the Workplace, in K. Koziara, M. Moskow & L. Tanner eds., Working Women: Past, Present, Future 265 (1987).

4. . . . Since the enactment of Title VII, women of color have made more progress

entering occupations traditionally held by white women than they (or white women) have made in entering occupations traditionally held by men. . . . See Albelda, Occupational Segregation by Race and Gender, 1958–81, 39 Indus. & Lab. Rel. Rev. 404, 405–406 (1986). . . .

5. Historically, African-American women, immigrant women, and low-income native-born white women have engaged in wage work in large numbers, despite being relegated to undesirable jobs. See, e.g., Jones, *supra* note 3; S. Kennedy, If All We Did Was to Weep at Home: A History of White Working-Class Women in America (1979); A. Kessler-Harris, Out to Work: A History of Wage-Earning Women in the United States (1982); Milkman, A Statistical Portrait, in 2 N. Hewitt, Women, Families, and Communities: Readings in American History 249 (1990). . . .

6. As my use of the metaphor of interpretation suggests, I believe that what courts say about sex segregation influences more broadly how people not involved in the immediate legal contest understand that reality. For earlier work in the interpretive tradition, see, for example, Delgado, Storytelling for Oppositionists and Others: A Plea for Narrative, 87 Mich. L. Rev. 2411 (1989), which examines the use of storytelling in the struggle for racial justice; Fineman, Dominant Discourse, Professional Language, and Legal Change in Child Custody Decisionmaking, 101 Harv. L. Rev. 727 (1988), which explores how social workers helped shape legal discourse in child custody cases so as to disempower custodial mothers; and Minow, Interpreting Rights: An Essay for Robert Cover, 96 Yale L.J. 1860 (1987), which argues for an interpretive approach to law that defends rights as tools for expressing communal aspirations.

7. The earliest case I found that addresses the lack of interest argument is Cypress v. Newport News Gen. & Nonsectarian Hosp. Ass'n, 375 F.2d 648, 653 (4th Cir. 1967). . . .

8. I have borrowed heavily from Martha Fineman's insightful description of the role of narrative in legal decisionmaking about child custody. See Fineman, *supra* note 6, at 753–758.

9. EEOC v. Mead Foods, Inc., 466 F. Supp. 1, 3 (W.D. Okla. 1977).

10. See *id.* at 4.

11. EEOC v. Service Container Corp., 19 Fair Empl. Prac. Cas. (BNA) 1614, 1616 (W.D. Okla. 1976). . . .

12. Mazus v. Dept. of Transp., 489 F. Supp. 376, 388 (M.D. Pa. 1979), *aff'd*, 629 F.2d 870 (3d Cir. 1980), *cert. denied*, 449 U.S. 1126 (1981).

13. Ste. Marie v. Eastern R.R. Ass'n, 650 F.2d 395, 403 (2d Cir. 1981).

14. Logan v. General Fireproofing Co., 6 Fair Empl. Prac. Cas. (BNA) 140, 144 (W.D.N.C. 1972).

15. *Id.*

16. EEOC v. Mead Foods, Inc., 466 F. Supp. 1, 3 (W.D. Okla. 1977).

17. See, e.g., Kraszewski v. State Farm Ins. Co., 38 Fair Empl. Prac. Cas. (BNA) 197, 222 (N.D. Cal. 1985); EEOC v. Akron Nat'l Bank & Trust Co., 497 F. Supp. 733, 748 (N.D. Ohio 1980). It is not clear why employers use different explanations for sex segregation in the blue-collar and white-collar contexts. Perhaps employers have realized that it would be implausible to try to attribute sex segregation to women's domestic roles in blue-collar settings, in which women with family responsibilities have long labored in jobs that demand as much of their time as the higher-paying jobs done by men. See generally L. Weiner, From Working Girl to Working Mother 86–87 (1985) (describing the relegation of married women to lower-paid blue-collar work before 1940). . . . Conversely, employers may have realized that they could not plausibly de-

fend women's absence from white-collar work with images of physical difference, because white-collar work is light, clean work of the type associated with femininity in the blue-collar context. Thus, in white-collar cases, employers have had to resort to imputed social and psychological characteristics to ground their conceptions of femininity and masculinity.

18. 528 F. Supp. 433 (E.D. Ark. 1981), *aff'd on other grounds,* 692 F.2d 529 (8th Cir. 1982).

19. *Id.* at 437.

20. 628 F. Supp. at 1308.

21. EEOC v. Cook Paint & Varnish Co., 24 Fair Empl. Prac. Cas. (BNA) 51, 56 (W.D. Mo. 1980).

22. Ostapowicz v. Johnson Bronze Co., 369 F. Supp. 522, 537 (W.D. Pa. 1973), *aff'd in part and vacated in part on other grounds,* 541 F.2d 394 (3d Cir. 1976), *cert. denied,* 429 U.S. 1041 (1977).

23. *Ostapowicz,* 369 F. Supp. at 537.

24. See, e.g., Mitchell v. Mid-Continent Spring Co., 583 F.2d 275, 281–283 (6th Cir.), *modified,* 587 F.2d 841 (6th Cir. 1978), *cert. denied,* 441 U.S. 922 (1979); EEOC v. Cook Paint & Varnish Co., 24 Fair Empl. Prac. Cas. (BNA) 28, 51, 56 (W.D. Mo. 1980). . . .

25. See, e.g., Kohne v. Imco Container Co., 480 F. Supp. 1015, 1027–1028 (W.D. Va. 1979); *Ostapowicz,* 369 F. Supp. at 537–38.

26. *Rath,* 40 Fair Empl. Prac. Cas. (BNA) at 566; *accord Mitchell,* 583 F.2d at 281; *Chrapliwy,* 458 F. Supp. at 278.

27. See, e.g., Palmer v. Shultz, 815 F.2d 84, 110 (D.C. Cir. 1987); *Kohne,* 480 F. Supp. at 1027–1028 & n.6; *Rath,* 40 Fair Empl. Prac. Cas. (BNA) at 565–566; *Ostapowicz,* 369 F. Supp. at 537–538. Employers tend to present testimony from women who were hired for traditionally female jobs, rather than from women who were rejected from employment altogether, as examples of women who prefer traditionally female work. But as Judge Thornberry has observed, the fact that women already working in traditionally female jobs have grown accustomed to them says little about whether women who were denied employment altogether "might well have taken [nontraditional jobs], if not precluded from doing so by a discriminatory hiring policy." Durant v. Owens-Illinois Glass Co., 656 F.2d 89, 91 (5th Cir. 1981) (Thornberry, J., dissenting).

28. As one court who accepted the lack of interest argument stated: "To be sure there are some females who would be interested in this type of physical [road maintenance] work but a reliable percentage has not yet been developed." Mazus v. Department of Transp., 489 F. Supp. 376, 388 (M.D. Pa. 1979), *aff'd,* 629 F.2d 870 (3d Cir. 1980), *cert. denied,* 449 U.S. 1126 (1981); see also EEOC v. Sears, Roebuck & Co., 628 F. Supp. 1264, 1314 (N.D. Ill. 1986) (dismissing the EEOC's historical examples of women who have responded to nontraditional job opportunities as isolated instances involving only "small groups of unusual women" rather than "the majority of women"), *aff'd,* 839 F.2d 302 (7th Cir. 1988).

29. Brief for EEOC as Appellant at 38.

30. See EEOC v. Sears, Roebuck & Co., 839 F.2d 302, 360–366 (7th Cir. 1988) (Cudahy, J., concurring in part and dissenting in part).

31. Offer of Proof Concerning the Testimony of Dr. Rosalind Rosenberg, EEOC v. Sears, Roebuck & Co., 628 F. Supp. 1264 (N.D. Ill. 1986) (No. 79-C-4373) [hereinafter Testimony of Rosalind Rosenberg] at 766; see also Davis v. City of Dallas, 483 F. Supp. 54, 61 (N.D. Tex. 1979) (attributing women's failure to apply for police work to "job preferences . . . born of attitudes conditioned by societal sexist values").

32. Studies have universally found that women do far more child care and other domestic work than men and that married men increase their share of housework very little in response to increases in their wives' paid employment. See, e.g., Bergmann, *supra* note 1, at 261–269; S. Berk, The Gender Factory: The Apportionment of Work in American Households (1985); M. Geerken & W. Gove, At Home and at Work: The Family's Allocation of Labor (1983). See generally P. England & G. Farkas, *supra note* 1, at 94–99 (1986) (summarizing these studies and the prevailing explanation for men's low participation in housework).

33. EEOC v. Mead Foods, Inc., 466 F.Supp. 1, 3 (W.D. Okla. 1977).

34. See Jacobs, *supra* note 1. Jacobs examined data from the National Longitudinal Survey of Young Women (NLS Young Women), a survey of a representative sample of more than 5000 women between the ages of 14 to 24 in 1968. Each year between 1968 and 1980, the women were asked to name the occupation in which they were employed that year, as well as the occupation to which they aspired at age 35. . . .

35. Jacobs also examined data from the NLS Survey of Mature Women, a representative sample of over 5000 women between the ages of 30 and 44 in 1967. See *id.* at 11. . . .

36. See *id.* at 148–149. Jacobs also found that other independent variables—including number and ages of children, weeks employed, and hours worked per week—did not dramatically alter women's occupational mobility patterns. See *id.* at 149–150. Jacobs' findings are consistent with Rosenfeld's, who found that, for both black and white women, the likelihood of changing the sex-type of their occupations was independent of marital status and whether they had interrupted their careers to care for children. See Rosenfeld, Job Changing and Occupational Sex Segregation: Sex and Race Comparisons, in Sex Segregation in the Workplace, *supra* note 1, at 72–76. Ironically, Rosenfeld found that "[t]he only effect of family responsibility . . . [was] for white *men*," who were less likely to move from a male-dominated to a female-dominated occupation if they were married. *Id.* at 74 (emphasis in original).

37. See Jacobs, *supra* note 1, at 190–191 ("[M]arital and family responsibilities simply are not powerful factors in producing mobility from male-dominated into female-dominated occupations."); Rosenfeld, *supra* note 36, at 77 ("For neither white nor black women was there much support for the idea that extent of family responsibilities influences the chance to move from or to a sex-typical occupation.").

38. The fact that women with primary family responsibilities are about as likely as women without such responsibilities to be found in, or to move to, nontraditional occupations may reflect a number of underlying phenomena. First, many nontraditional jobs probably do not pose any greater barriers to family life than do traditionally female jobs. . . . Indeed, portraying the jobs men do as inherently more demanding than the jobs women do is part of the ideological framework that stigmatizes women as marginal workers and justifies keeping them out of the higher-paying "men's jobs." This is part of the insight of the comparable worth movement. See Clauss, Comparable Worth—The Theory, Its Legal Foundation, and the Feasibility of Implementation, 20 U. Mich. J.L. Ref. 7 (1986). Second, to the extent that certain nontraditional jobs may make demands that are difficult for primary family caretakers, many such women are willing to undertake those demands despite the back-breaking double burden. Particularly for working-class women, the higher wages for nontraditional jobs enable them to give their children greater opportunities, such as a college education. See, e.g., M. Walshok, Blue-Collar Women: Pioneers on the Male Frontier 252 (1981). . . .

39. As Rosabeth Moss Kanter has written: "[T]o a very large degree, organizations

make their workers into who they are. Adults change to fit the system. . . . [O]rganizations often act as though it is possible to predict people's job futures from the characteristics they bring with them [to] a recruiting interview. What really happens is that predictions get made on the basis of stereotypes and current notions of who fits where in the present system; people are then 'set up' in positions which make the predictions come true." R. Kanter, Men and Women of the Corporation 263 (1977).

40. See England & Farkas, *supra* note 1, at 140. "[R]esearch [in this tradition] implies that individuals develop the psychological styles required to survive in the structural position they hold. . . . [B]ehavioral differences between groups are a product of the jobs they have been allowed to enter, rather than being exogenous to actual work experience." *Id.* at 138.

41. See Kanter, *supra* note 39, at 252.

42. See Jacobs, *supra* note 1, at 141. . . .

43. C. Cockburn, Machinery of Dominance: Women, Men and Technical Know-How 167 (1985). . . .

44. *Id.* at 165.

45. By focusing on these two phenomena, I do not mean to suggest that they are the only features of the workplace that contribute to women's disempowerment. See, e.g., Roos & Reskin, Institutional Factors Contributing to Sex Segregation in the Workplace, in Sex Segregation and the Workplace, *supra* note 1, at 235–260 (describing numerous institutional mechanisms that limit women's ability to enter nontraditional jobs). . . .

46. See, e.g., R. Blauner, Alienation and Freedom (1964); E. Chinoy, Automobile Workers and the American Dream (1955); T. Purcell, Blue Collar Man: Patterns of Dual Allegiance in Industry (1960); Dubin, Industrial Workers' Worlds: A Study of the "Central Life Interests" of Industrial Workers, 3 Soc. Probs. 131 (1956); Guest, Work Careers and Aspirations of Automobile Workers, 19 Am. Soc. Rev. 155 (1954); see also Kanter, *supra* note 39, at 140, 143, 147–148 (summarizing these and other similar studies).

47. Kanter, *supra* note 39, at 159 (emphasis in original); see also Laws, Psychological Dimensions of Labor Force Participation of Women, in P. Wallace ed., Equal Employment Opportunity and the AT&T Case 125, 141 (1976). . . .

48. As one former secretary explained: "I didn't start thinking about non-traditional work until I heard the carpenters were looking for women. . . . But as soon as the possibility was mentioned, my imagination went with it." J. Schroedel, Alone in a Crowd: Women in the Trades Tell Their Stories 35 (1985).

49. One woman described the transformative power of seeing women doing nontraditional work as follows: "When I came out here I fell in with some women who worked in the trades and they had some potlucks for women in the building trades and I went there and I saw all these women and I was real excited—I thought, 'Oh, yeah, that's who I am, I'm like those women over there.'" Walshok, *supra* note 38, at 137–138; see also *id.* at 163–164 (describing a similar transformation).

50. *Id.* at 145. Other studies have reported that women in blue-collar trades value the challenge, freedom, and intrinsic rewards of the job, just as their male co-workers do. See, e.g., K. Deaux & J. Ullman, Women of Steel: Female Blue-Collar Workers in the Basic Steel Industry 131–133 (1983). The women speak movingly of the exhilaration that comes with challenge and freedom on the job. See, e.g., M. Martin, Hard-Hatted Women: Stories of Struggle and Success in the Trades 167–168 (1988). One female firefighter stated: "For nine days, I was part of the biggest [fire] incident I ever expect to see. . . . I've never worked as hard as I did on some of those hot afternoons, pulling those lines around in the mud and rocks. . . . Events that demand everything you can give leave

you with an unconquerable feeling of exuberance that lasts well beyond fatigue. Given the choice, there was no place in the world I would rather have been." *Id.* . . .

51. In contrast to my definition of harassment, the legal system focuses on conduct that is explicitly "sexual" in nature. . . .

52. Martin, *supra* note 50, at 221–222.

53. The literature documenting the effects of skewed sex ratios on work groups makes this clear. See, e.g., B. Gutek, Sex and the Workplace 129–152 (1985); Kanter, *supra* note 39, at 206–242.

54. See, e.g., Gutek & Morasch, Sex-Ratios, Sex-Role Spillover, and Sexual Harassment of Women at Work, J. Soc. Issues, Winter 1982, at 55, 67–68 (finding that women in male-dominated occupations and jobs were more likely to report harassment and to have experienced negative consequences from it than women in other work settings); Martin, Sexual Harassment: The Link Joining Gender Stratification, Sexuality, and Women's Economic Status, in Women: A Feminist Perspective 57, 61 (J. Freeman 4th ed. 1989) (citing studies showing that the greater the proportion of men in a work group, the more likely women were to be harassed).

55. See, e.g., O'Farrell & Harlan, 29 Soc. Probs. 252, 259 (1982) (finding that half the women in white-collar, female-dominated occupations who considered moving into blue-collar, male-dominated occupations expected that they would be subjected to harassment if they did so).

56. See Gutek, *supra* note 53, at 119 ("By making insulting comments and touching women sexually, some men may try to 'make life miserable' for women in the [nontraditional] jobs, encouraging them to leave. The relatively high turnover rate among women in [these jobs] suggests that this is a successful strategy to force women out."); Gutek & Morasch, *supra* note 54, at 68 (finding that 20% of women in nontraditional work quit a job at some point because of sexual harassment, while only 9% of the larger sample did so).

This research exposes a methodological problem in most surveys attempting to measure the extent of harassment, particularly among women in male-dominated occupations. Most of the surveys are not based on longitudinal data and thus do not include women who left because of harassment. For this reason, they probably underestimate the prevalence of harassment. See Jacobs, *supra* note 1, at 153.

57. A recent newspaper article noted, for example, that a growing number of women engineers have become so discouraged by their discriminatory treatment that they are leaving engineering to pursue alternative careers. See Arundel, Stagflation for Female Engineers, N.Y. Times, Oct. 1, 1989, at F32. Other studies have documented the disproportionate attrition of women attorneys from law firms, see, e.g., Menkel-Meadow, Exploring a Research Agenda on the Feminization of the Legal Profession: Theories of Gender and Social Change, 14 Law & Soc. Inquiry 289, 307 (1989); Weisenhaus, Still a Long Way to Go for Women, Minorities, Nat'l L.J., Feb. 8, 1988, at 48, and there is evidence that women leave in part because of discrimination, see, e.g., Liefland, Career Patterns of Male and Female Lawyers, 35 Buffalo L. Rev. 601, 609–611 (1986); Quade, Myth v. Ms.: Why Women Leave the Law, 13 Barrister 28 (1986).

58. In Walshok's study, when the women were asked about the negative aspects of their job during the first year, the most frequently voiced criticism (expressed by 68% of the women) was that they felt they were being trained poorly. See Walshok, *supra* note 38, at 188.

59. Stories like electrician Sue Eisenberg's are still far too common: "For some men, getting rid of the invaders was a personal mission. Ron, one of my first foremen,

constantly warned me of the ways I might get killed in this dangerous trade: be electrocuted, have my head severed from my body, be boiled alive by steam. Without giving any instruction on how to do it safely, he told me one day to open up a 200-foot-long snake. . . . A snake is a thin piece of steel, used by electricians to pull wires through pipes. It comes tightly coiled, bound with wire ties, and if not opened carefully, will spring apart with great force. 'I had a Chinese kid open one up,' Ron told the crew, laughing. 'He got it caught up his nose and wound up in the hospital. Quit right after that.' I haven't opened up a snake since without remembering how I sweated through it that first time, while my co-workers hid." Eisenberg, Women Hard Hats Speak Out, Nation, Sept. 18, 1989, at 272. For other stories of how women have been subjected to acts by foremen or co-workers that threatened them with, or caused them, physical harm, see, for example, Martin, *supra* note 50, at 33–34. . . .

60. For example, one of Atlanta's most prestigious corporate law firms, King & Spalding, planned to hold a "wet T-shirt" contest featuring its female summer associates, even while the firm faced a sex discrimination lawsuit in the Supreme Court. See Burleigh & Goldberg, Breaking the Silence: Sexual Harassment in Law Firms, A.B.A. J., Aug. 1989, at 46. (The lawsuit was Hishon v. King & Spalding, 467 U.S. 69 (1984).) After complaints, the firm decided to hold a swimsuit competition instead. One of the firm's partners later told the Wall Street Journal that the "winner" of the competition had been offered a job upon graduation, remarking: "She has the body we'd like to see more of." Burleigh & Goldberg, *supra*, at 46.

61. In one recent case, for example, the lone female resident in a general surgery program was forced to endure sexual advances and touching; sexually explicit drawings of her body and other pornography in public meeting rooms; her supervisors' refusal to talk to her, permit her to operate, or assign her work tasks; discriminatory standards for evaluating her performance; sabotage of her work, including falsification of medical records to make it appear as though she and another female resident had made an error, see Lipsett v. University of Puerto Rico, 864 F.2d 881, 886–94 (1st Cir. 1988), and "a constant verbal attack, one which challenged their capacity as women to be surgeons, and questioned the legitimacy of their being in the program at all." *Id.* at 905.

62. See, e.g., Price Waterhouse v. Hopkins, 490 U.S. 228 (1989). Ann Hopkins brought suit against Price Waterhouse, perhaps the nation's most prestigious public accounting firm, claiming that she was discriminatorily denied partnership. Among other outstanding achievements, she had helped secure a multimillion dollar contract with the Department of State, an accomplishment that none of the other candidates for partnership that year had matched. See *id.* at 1782. But, when it came time to consider her for partnership, her colleagues evaluated her by criteria by which no man would be judged: "One partner described her as 'macho' . . .; another suggested that she 'overcompensated for being a woman' . . . ; a third advised her to take 'a course at charm school'. . . . Several partners criticized her use of profanity. . . . [Another advised her to] 'walk more femininely, talk more femininely, dress more femininely, wear make-up, have her hair styled, and wear jewelry.'" *Id.* (citations omitted).

63. One of the tactics men use to make nontraditional women workers feel deviant is "lesbian-baiting." See Martin, *supra* note 50, at 14. . . .

64. Kanter discusses how male workers subject token women to "loyalty tests," in which the women are required to affirm their loyalty to the dominant culture by turning against other women. Pressuring women to tolerate sexist jokes and comments are examples. See Kanter, *supra* note 39, at 227–229. . . .

65. See Cockburn, *supra* note 43.

66. *Id.* at 185.

67. *Id.* at 101 (emphasis in original).

68. *Id.* at 188.

69. *Id.* at 176.

70. It remains unclear, for example, whether hostile but not sexually explicit behavior of the type so often encountered by nontraditional women workers even falls within the scope of sexual harassment prohibited by Title VII. Compare McKinney v. Dole, 765 F.2d 1129, 1138 (D.C. Cir. 1985) (holding that acts that are hostile but not sexually explicit may constitute sexual harassment prohibited by title VII) with Rabidue v. Osceola Refining Co., 805 F.2d 611, 619 (6th Cir. 1986), *cert. denied,* 481 U.S. 1041 (1987) (implicitly refusing to recognize hostile conduct as harassment when it is not explicitly sexual in nature). For discussions of this issue, see R. Austin, Employer Abuse, Worker Resistance, and the Tort of Intentional Infliction of Emotional Distress, herein, at 797; and Pollack, Sexual Harassment: Women's Experience vs. Legal Definitions, 13 Harv. Women's L.J. 35, 75 n.164.

71. The clearest expression of this attitude appears in the Sixth Circuit's opinion in Rabidue v. Osceola Refining Co., 805 F.2d 611 (6th Cir. 1986), *cert. denied,* 481 U.S. 1041 (1987). The plaintiff was the only woman with managerial responsibilities over male employees in a refining company. Despite the fact that the work environment was extremely hostile and degrading to women, the court held that it was not so offensive as to have interfered with the work performance, or to have affected seriously the "psychological well-being of a reasonable person." *Id.* at 620. To support this holding, the majority quoted favorably from the following passage from the district court's opinion: "[I]t cannot seriously be disputed that in some work environments, humor and language are rough hewn and vulgar. Sexual jokes, sexual conversations and girlie magazines may abound. Title VII was not meant to—or can—change this. . . . Title VII is the federal court mainstay in the struggle for equal employment opportunity for the female workers of America. But . . . Title VII was [not] designed to bring about a magical transformation in the social mores of American workers." *Id.* at 620–621 (quoting Osceola v. Rabidue, 584 F. Supp. 419, 430 (E.D. Mich. 1984)).

Feminizing Unions: Challenging the Gendered Structure of Wage Labor

Marion G. Crain

FEMINIST SCHOLARS in increasing numbers are calling for a feminist agenda that challenges directly the economic, social, and political power imbalance between women and men. . . .

. . . I argue that labor unions can be an effective, central tool in a feminist agenda targeting the gendered structure of wage labor. Collective action is the most powerful and expedient route to female empowerment; further, it is the only feasible means of transforming our deeply gendered market and family structure. Others have laid the groundwork by showing how existing individual-model challenges have been unable to accomplish such broad-based reform.[1] I begin where they leave off. . . .

A brief historical overview is necessary to appreciate the very rational ambivalence and distrust for labor unions expressed by many feminists. . . .

Before 1873, nearly all male-dominated trade societies and unions completely barred women.[2] When the Knights of Labor began to flourish in the 1880s, its open membership policy encouraged women to organize in relatively large numbers.[3] The Knights of Labor gave way, however, to the American Federation of Labor (AFL), a group of trade unions founded in 1886. The AFL developed a "'philosophy of pure wage consciousness,'" signifying "'a labor movement reduced to an opportunistic basis, accepting the existence of capitalism and having for its object the enlarging of the bargaining power of the wage earner in the sale of his labor.'"[4] The AFL's focus was thus on short-run objectives rather than political goals; it "refused to allow its energies to be diverted from the task of improving the immediate economic position of its members."[5] The AFL's narrow, shortsighted focus produced a willingness to sacrifice solidarity for wage gains, and ultimately led to the creation of a partnership of organized labor and organized capital which supported exclusionary policies against marginalized workers such as women and immigrants.[6]

The AFL's short-term focus on increasing the wages of its members resulted in considerable ambivalence by the AFL toward organizing female workers. Despite rapid expansion in the numbers of working women in the industrial labor force between 1897

89 Mich. L. Rev. 1155 (1991).

664

and 1920, the AFL was able to organize no more than 1.5% of the women engaged in industrial occupations by the year 1910; only new organizing among garment workers was responsible for raising the figure to 6.6% by 1920.[7] The AFL's ambivalence derived from competing and conflicting concerns between a fear of being undercut by cheap female labor, and a commitment to the patriarchal view of women's role as home-makers. The former concern generated a shaky commitment to unionize women and to demand equal pay for them, while the latter suggested that women "ought not to be in the labor force at all."[8]

The AFL resolved the conflict by pledging to organize women. Despite its rhetorical commitment to organizing women, however, the AFL's efforts were half-hearted at best: although it did not take affirmative steps to exclude women from its member unions, it took no action against gender restrictions on membership imposed by member unions. Moreover, the AFL did little to assist unionized women in obtaining entry into the ap-propriate parent unions, which frequently ignored them or denied them access.[9] Even unions that did admit women sometimes directed exclusionary tactics at female mem-bers; these unions held meetings at late hours, in meeting places such as saloons.

The lone exception was the Women's Trade Union League. . . . The League was founded in 1903 at an AFL meeting. . . . The League's purpose was to provide money, publicity, tactical advice, and political support for nonunionized women seeking to build their own unions, while simultaneously maintaining connections with male-dom-inated labor unions. The League's eventual alliance with the Industrial Workers of the World (the Wobblies), a leftist group that advocated the abolition of capitalism and the modern political state through direct action by workers, prompted a split between the AFL and the League. Ultimately, the League, dependent on the AFL for support, ac-quiesced in the AFL's policy regarding organizing women workers, and turned away from activist organizing efforts. The League sought instead to solve the problems of fe-male wage-earners through political action, an activity that proved largely unsuccessful.

The AFL's ideological resistance to organizing women was based on gendered stereotypes. These stereotypes were predicated upon three assumptions about women: (1) women's primary interests and talents lay in homemaking and caretaking; (2) it was inappropriate for women to work or to be members of unions, because both tended to denigrate women's respectable, morally pure status; and (3) women were not competent to understand or appreciate the traditional work issues utilized by or-ganizers during union campaigns to rally support from the workers.

The AFL female stereotype was packaged and marketed as the "family-wage ideol-ogy." This ideology proclaimed the social right of the working class to the ideal family and gender roles—female domesticity and male responsibility. It expressed serious concern over the effects of industrial development on family life. Specifically, unions argued that if women were forced to work because their husbands were poorly paid or had little job security, women would be unable to fulfill their obligations to their hus-bands and children.[10] The ideology connected class issues of subsistence and justice with gender, thereby establishing the parameters of the relationship between men, women, and work. The National Trades' Union's proclamation of the ideology was typical: "The physical organization, the natural responsibilities, and the moral sensibilities of woman, prove conclusively that her labor should only be of a domestic nature."[11]

The AFL continued the ideology in the early 1900s. [I]t was man's role and right to serve as the breadwinner, and it was woman's responsibility to remain in the home. Trade unionists worried that the shop atmosphere would be "morally corrupting" for women. Similarly, they expressed concern that men would lose respect for women if they worked together:

> Respect for women is apt to decrease when they are compelled to work in the factory or store. . . . More respect for women brings less degeneration and more marriages . . . if women labor in factories and similar institutions they bring forth weak children who are not educated to become strong and good citizens.[12]

Finally, the cultural expectation that wage-earning women would eventually marry and leave the workforce spawned the argument that women were transient and temporary members of the workforce; therefore, allowing them to occupy positions that could be filled by men was pointless and unfair to the ousted male workers. Women themselves internalized these cultural stereotypes and behaved accordingly. Wage-earning women were sometimes reluctant to join unions due to their desire to marry and the consequent belief that work was merely a temporary interval between childhood and marriage. Some women believed that "no nice girl would belong to [a union],"[13] apparently either because they felt that such an allegiance would undermine the primary loyalty or obedience which they owed to their fathers, or because it was considered socially inappropriate for women "to act militantly or to wield power directly," which they would be required to do if they organized or joined a union.[14] Women's life situations—their exclusions from many of the best jobs because of the perception that women were only temporarily in the workforce, and the low pay available in the jobs they did hold—served to increase the economic pressure on young women to marry. The message was clear: "[F]ind some nice young man and form a union of two, for life; that's the best form of union."[15]

Widespread acceptance of the assumptions underlying the family-wage ideology in large part generated the gendered stereotypes that crept into the workplace and affected women who did work. The family-wage ideology portrayed women as the weaker sex, in need of protection. Women were regarded either as mothers or potential mothers, who needed protection from threats on their chastity or excessive strains upon their health. Consequently, women were channeled into jobs thought to be less demanding physically and safer. Women were also assumed to be especially good at certain tasks suited for women; thus, working women's problems differed from those of male workers. . . .

In sum, women were not thought of, nor were they supposed to be, "real" workers. Joining a union meant publicly proclaiming one's status as a worker. Instead, women became

> members of a secondary labor force, performing marginal tasks, receiving lower wages, occupying a narrower range of jobs, even serving as a reserve army of la-

bor. Indeed, they constituted so different, so other, a category of labor that, like slaves in colonial economies, they were scarcely regarded as part of the labor force. They became—and remained for more than a century—invisible.[16]

. . .

As a result of the sudden need for female workers during World War II, large numbers of married as well as unmarried women joined the workforce. The family-wage ideology was abandoned and the major unions were forced to ease restrictions on the employment of married women. After the war, pressure by female trade unionists caused the major unions to abandon openly discriminatory policies and contract provisions blocking the hiring of married women.[17] The influence of the women's movement on the outlook of female trade unionists was evident: women argued for the first time that they possessed the right to equal protection under union contracts despite their marital status, asserting that union discrimination against married women was counter to the democratic principles of industrial unionism. . . .

. . . After World War II, the market reverted to prewar patterns of job segregation. Ruth Milkman has argued that the reversion to prewar patterns was fundamentally capital's conscious choice, rather than simply the result of either a postwar resurgence of the ideology of domesticity, or the operation of union-instituted seniority systems and their manipulation by male unionists.[18] Milkman attributes postwar capitalist policy to two factors: (1) the traditional sexual division of labor was embodied in the structure of each industry and so remained compelling when demobilization occurred; and (2) capital had assessed labor's position on the subject of retaining women in "men's jobs" as ambivalent, at best, and with sex differentials in wages having been narrowed considerably during the war, female substitution was no longer as profitable. Job segregation patterns, wage structures that discriminated against women, and separate seniority systems continued to exist.

The 1960s, 1970s, and 1980s brought an increased consciousness of women's rights, and along with it changes in social mores. The rise of feminism, particularly during the 1970s, encouraged a more independent and assertive role for women. Militancy and unionism also increased. The media portrayed women's position in the labor market as radically altered. The influx of women into the workforce increased the percentage of women who were union members.

Nevertheless, women remain underrepresented on union rolls. Unions blame employers for past discrimination against women in hiring, arguing that if women are not workers, they will never become union members. Yet women are grossly underrepresented in union leadership proportionate to female union membership, particularly at the national level.[19] As power and control over union affairs becomes increasingly centralized at the national level, the lack of female union leadership and, consequently, attention to women's concerns at the national level makes it increasingly difficult for prospective female members to identify with unions. In addition, only a small percentage of union organizers are female. . . .

Researchers attribute unions' failure to admit women into the ranks of officers and organizers to gendered stereotypes held by male union members. One study shows that, applying stereotypical notions about attributes of the sexes, men rank higher than do women in perceived competence to perform the tasks of a union organizer and officer.[20] Women are perceived as lacking competence in negotiation and interpersonal skills (using effective power tactics, being assertive and strong, and empathizing with and responding to members); industrial relations knowledge and political savvy; and availability of time for union duties and accessibility. Men are perceived as more aggressive, uncompromising, competitive, assertive, intelligent and as having better judgment than women. Men also are assumed to use more expert, direct tactics; therefore they are perceived as better negotiators. Men are perceived as more emotionally stable than women, and hence may be perceived as more approachable; men possess more self-confidence than women when evaluating personal industrial relations skills, and are more likely to be accepted as equals by management: therefore, they are viewed as better negotiators. Men generally have more seniority than women, and with experience comes industrial relations knowledge. Finally, union members still believe that women should bear primary responsibility for childcare and homemaking; because men do not have these family responsibilities, they have more time for their roles as union officers, and thus are more accessible.

Moreover, unions continue to represent their female membership with ambivalence. Title VII litigation over the effect of union seniority and security clauses on women hired under affirmative action programs reflects unions' continued willingness to serve the needs of the white male majority and to sacrifice those of women and other marginalized groups.[21] Similarly, litigation over unions' failure to fairly represent female members is evidence of unions' continuing tendency to ignore women's interests.[22] . . .

Current gender discrimination is supported by a new ideology, labeled the "public-private spheres ideology" of work and home, male and female. Under the public-private spheres view of the world, "the [male-dominated] market structures our productive lives and the [female-dominated] family structures our affective lives."[23] The market is particularly suited to men; the family is particularly the domain of women. This dichotomy is firmly embedded in our traditions, culture, workplace structure, and law. And it is nothing more than the family-wage ideology in another, more sinister, guise. . . .

Until very recently, the conventional wisdom has been that women are "hard to organize," which is shorthand for the notion that women are harder to organize than men.[24] Indeed, the influx of women into the workforce has been cited as a major barrier to union growth.[25]

Early conclusions about women's organizability were based in part on study by researchers whose gendered assumptions about women tainted their methodologies and conclusions.[26] Observations of union leaders indicated that women workers had accepted and internalized the gendered assumptions underlying the studies, and that male union leaders had done nothing to address women's particular needs. Karen Nussbaum, President of District 925, Service Employees International Union (and the founder of the Working Women's Organization, 9 to 5), believes that the consciousness-raising done by the women's movement laid the foundation for increased organizability of women.[27] Nussbaum lists three principal reasons why women did not join unions in large numbers prior to the 1960s: (1) women saw themselves as secondary wage earners; (2) consequently, women were more afraid than men of antagonizing their employers by engaging in organizing activity; (3) women perceived male-dominated unions as insensitive to issues such as equal pay, child care, and maternity leave.

Recent studies, however, indicate that women are now and may have always been *more* organizable than men. One study, by sociologist Thomas Moore, examines the conclusions of postindustrialist sociologists and concludes that the gender differential in union membership is not simply a consequence of the differing labor force location of male and female workers, as many had theorized. After controlling for variables previously identified in studies of attitudes about unions, Moore finds that "unorganized women workers are *more* likely to desire union representation than [are] their male counterparts," and that women view unions and their leadership more favorably than men.[28] . . . Other recent studies also have found that many of the assumed barriers to union organization of women presupposed worker attitudes that had never been demonstrated.[29]. . .

Although it has become unfashionable to speak of women's unorganizability in light of these studies, the gendered assumptions that spawned the term remain. . . . Union adoption of these gendered assumptions . . . can be demonstrated by reference to two explanations frequently advanced by union leaders and organizers to explain their failure to organize women. . . .

A. Women Are Secondary Wage Earners

The justification for women's lack of interest in their work lives—and hence, in unionism—has two aspects: first, jobs are of secondary importance to women from an economic standpoint because women typically can rely upon a husband as a primary breadwinner, and second, women value family over jobs. The idea that most women are secondary wage earners whose earnings are "pin money" in the family economic situation is patently false. Statistics show that women are increasingly either heads of households or remaining single.[30] This phenomenon is attributable to the divorce rate, longevity of women relative to men, and the cultural practice of men of a particular age marrying into younger and younger age groups, creating an artificial "man shortage" for those in higher age groups. Thus, many women simply do not have the so-called luxury of being a secondary breadwinner. Fifty percent of the nine million working poor in this country are women, and one and a half million of these women head families. Further, more than half of all poor families are headed by women, with forty percent working outside the home.[31]

Second, statistics demonstrate that most two-earner couples today find *both* incomes necessary to sustain their standard of living. The so-called typical American family—a husband supporting a nonworking wife and two children—represents less than five percent of married-couple families.[32] Nearly two thirds of families with a husband and wife present have two wage earners. Half of all working wives work year round, full time, and contribute forty percent of their families' income.[33] Thus, even women in two-earner marriages may have economic needs pushing them into the labor force.[34] Over twenty percent of all poor families contain two or more workers.[35]

Finally, the notion that people work solely to meet economic needs, and that they would not be in the workforce if they were not required to be by economic necessity, is itself an anachronism.[36] For many, work may be the only source of a sense of community and connection. Further, paid work often nurtures self-esteem and feelings of worth and purpose in society. Roberta Goldberg, who surveyed women office workers in the Baltimore area, writes that women's motivations for working are complex. Her research indicates that most of the women did not consider their earnings to be as supplemental as the literature suggests. For unmarried respondents, working for a living was an unquestioned assumption. Among married and unmarried, divorced, separated, or widowed women, "over half reported that they alone provided 100% of their family income. An additional 13% provided 75 to 90 percent of their family income. Only 22% reported that they provided 50% or less."[37]

The second aspect of the justification for unions' failure to organize women—primary commitment to the family—is equally flawed. According to this argument, women choose low-paying, dead-end jobs because they are uninterested in their careers, preferring to devote their energies to their families. It is true that women themselves describe sex role expectations as guiding decisions they make about careers:

> We've been geared by society, by the male population especially, that we're suited for clerical work. We're suited for teaching and keeping house. And the worst thing in the world would be for us to be piloting a plane, or be on the board of directors for some corporation . . . . My first thought out of high school was, "I got to make some money and the best way to do that is get some clerical skills and get a job as a secretary." I didn't think about getting technical training in plumbing.[38]

Nevertheless, the "pre-labor market explanation" for women's "lack of interest" in market work[39] is not sufficient to explain why women change career aspirations after they have entered the workplace, nor does it explain how women in nontraditional occupations escape early conditioning to feminine sex roles while still remaining "feminine." Instead, women's work aspirations evolve and are shaped by their experiences in the work world.

At best, women who occupy roles as both workers and mothers are seen as having a "conflict of allegiance" between home and work. Because complete loyalty to the employer and the job is the male norm in the public sphere, attempts by women to accommodate the two spheres are perceived as evidencing a lack of commitment to the work world. Thus, women workers are caught in a Catch-22: they are perceived as aggressive and unfeminine if they do not assume primary responsibility for child care and family obligations, and as uninterested in market work if they attempt to juggle both roles.

Unions have played a significant part in maintaining this situation. . . . Because unions still view women as primarily responsible for child care, the issues are personal issues *for women*. Despite liberal legal rhetoric's success in gaining important private

rights for women in other contexts (such as the right to private, autonomous reproductive choice for women who can afford it), in this arena it operates as a "double-edged
sword" for women: private choice means having the individual responsibility for it.

The consequences of the privatization of women's issues like child care, maternity
leave, and parental leave have been dramatic for working women. The unavailability
and expense of child care leaves many working women no choice but to stay home and
care for their children until they reach school age, leading inevitably to a break in
women's market careers that sentences them to dead-end jobs when they return to the
workforce. Many women, however, simply cannot afford to stay at home. Women sometimes rely on friends and relatives to care for their children. This arrangement is unstable because the caregivers themselves move in and out of the workforce, forcing
working mothers to alternate periods of work with periods of caring for their children,
or to take part-time jobs. The ultimate result, again, is a sporadic work history, which
traps working mothers in low-income jobs. Similarly, the absence of flexible job scheduling and adequate parental or maternity leave have contributed to the restriction of
labor force participation for working mothers.

Several unions have noticed that unions' historical neglect of so-called women's issues has been a barrier to organizing women, and have asserted a new commitment to
advancing women's interests through collective bargaining and national legislation.
The approach has proved most effective where the union leadership itself is female.
Unions with primarily male leadership have been hardpressed to demonstrate their
commitment to these issues, however. . . .

B. Women Are Concentrated in Nonunionizable Occupations

Unions and scholars also contend that women are underrepresented because women
tend to work in occupations that do not lend themselves to unionization.[40] Labor market segmentation theorists argue that the low wages, high turnover, and vulnerable
working conditions that characterize many female-dominated occupations pose barriers to unionization.[41] Another study suggests female-dominated occupations are less
unionizable because (1) "managerial opposition to unionism is more intense in disproportionately female firms," and (2) "union leaders perceive the costs of organizing
and servicing predominantly female bargaining units [as] relatively high."[42] The researchers view the second reason as more compelling; they argue that a higher expected
turnover rate for women, a lack of understanding by male union leaders of the needs
of women working in predominantly female occupations, and the concentration of
female-dominated jobs in smaller, less capital-intensive firms located in more competitive industries, increase perceived organizing costs. Thus, the presence of women in bot-
tom-tier, undesirable, high-turnover jobs is self-determining as far as collective organization opportunities are concerned: unions do not seek to organize them to begin with.

Further, the nonunionizable jobs held by women are typically associated with "female" character traits, such as passivity, docility, and a preference for working in a hierarchy beneath a male superior. So, for example, conventional wisdom suggests that

women are less militant than men, and therefore more difficult to organize. Women are also perceived to be more loyal to the company than men, and thus more reluctant to challenge its authority. Because most women work for men, this observation is generally expressed in terms of the patriarchal dimensions of the work: sexual hierarchy in the office restrains efforts to organize women, preventing the development of a critical consciousness in women. In many female-dominated jobs, the very behavior that reinforces traditional sex roles in the home is also desirable behavior at the office. Essentially, women are socialized to be submissive both at home and at work.

A striking example of unions' incorporation of the public-private spheres ideology in this context is unions' lack of commitment to issues of pay equity. Unions historically have demonstrated little ability to close the wage gap between men and women through collective bargaining. Some commentators attribute unions' failure in this area to discriminatory attitudes towards women, unions' inability to protect part-time workers, and their tendency to divert pay equity issues to their lobbying agendas for national legislation.[43] These scholars conclude that despite courts' initial inhospitable reception of pay equity litigation, union attitudes render litigation a more promising strategy for reducing the male-female wage gap than collective bargaining.

In short, unions continue the public-private spheres ideology by privatizing issues that affect women disproportionately, such as child care, maternity leave, parental leave, and pay equity. . . .

[U]nions have traditionally blamed women's unorganizability on women themselves or on employers. . . . The "lack of interest"/"women are secondary earners" argument seeks to place the blame on women themselves for their economic subordination, while the argument that most women are employed in "nonunionizable" workforces is directed primarily at employers. . . .

The key feature of the lack of interest argument is "individual-model thinking," sometimes referred to as a "blame the victim" approach.[44] Individual-model thinking about women is characterized by the conception of women as "different," which provides organizations with a set of excuses for the slow pace of change. Worse, because individual-model thinking compares women to a male norm of the worker, it attributes responsibility or fault for the difference to women.

The argument that women are secondary wage earners who often choose low-paying part-time or temporary jobs to accommodate their primary obligation—child care—provides an illustration of this type of thinking. Women can hardly be condemned for participating in their own victimization by making choices that are not really choices at all. . . .

Labor unions could alter the gendered structure of labor and thus change the constraints on women's choice whether to work for pay or not. Unions hold promise because they offer an opportunity to open communication channels between women workers, and they may serve as a vehicle for collective female access to the power structure. To the extent cultural feminists' observations about women's natures are accurate, women should be easier to organize because of their predisposition to value relationships, their awareness of the connection between people, and their recognition of responsibility for one another. . . .

Further, nothing in mainstream cultural feminist theory limits women's ability to care for others, and the value which they place on relationships, to the family sphere. Those relationships are not achievable only outside the workplace. Indeed, many women, both single and married, form enduring friendships with their colleagues at work. The assumption that women's ability and interest in caring for others is limited to the sphere of home is simply another manifestation of the public-private spheres ideology.

Radical feminists have also acknowledged women's willingness to sacrifice for the larger good, an essential element of the union philosophy. Dworkin has written that "[w]omen are especially given to giving up what we know and feel to be right and true for the sake of others or for the sake of something more important than ourselves."[45] Although radical feminists criticize this trait in women, they make their criticism in the context of women's willingness to sacrifice for men rather than for the good of other women.[46]

Finally, critical race feminists suggest that the very notion that priorities in one's life must be ordered in some hierarchical fashion—for example, work first, family second—reflects an essentialist view of the world.[47] Poor women and women of color have historically worked both inside and outside the home. For these women, organizing work and family values hierarchically is a foreign practice, more consistent with male, competitive either/or thinking. Women of color in particular have long dealt with multiple, overlapping identities (race, class, sex, mother, daughter, worker), and the practice of prioritizing and compartmentalizing relationships or identities is inconsistent with their life experience.

Another aspect of the "lack of interest" argument is the assumption that unions are political institutions, and women lack interest in political issues. If this is true, it can be explained [as follows]. First, within unions as in the larger political world, a white, male majority sets the prevailing societal definition of what is publicly relevant or political; in other words, whatever interests men is called political, while anything that specifically affects women is called "private." . . .

The second possible explanation for women's perceived failure to show interest in the politics of unionism derives from a male vision of the *process* of politics that conflicts with a feminist understanding of the process of politics. In the male liberal democratic world of politics, the political community exists for instrumental purposes: its goal is "to provide the least restrictive environment possible in which each may pursue his or her own ends."[48] . . . By contrast, for cultural feminists the opportunity for connection and relationship presented by the political process is *itself* the goal. . . .

By adopting the public-private ideology, unions miss an opportunity to embrace workers for whom connection and relationship—that is, the process of politics—comes easily. Unions also limit the agenda for change in the workplace that could advantage both male and female workers. As Lucinda Finley has pointed out, even though it is women who get pregnant and who still bear most of the responsibility for raising children, men are affected as well: those men affiliated with these women feel the effects when the women cannot get paid leave, cannot maintain sufficient health insurance, must return to work before they are physically ready, and suffer sleepless nights during the first few months of a baby's life.[49] Finally, unions have by-passed an opportunity to revolutionize parenting by distributing equally the obligation to care for children. Many feminists argue that a dramatic change in parenting roles must precede elimination of the stereotypical notion that women are inherently better suited to parent.[50] . . .

The second argument advanced by unionists for their failure to organize women in significant numbers purports to be gender-neutral. Women themselves are not un-organizable, rather the occupations in which they tend to work—like clerical work or nursing—are difficult to organize. Despite its initial appeal, this justification is actually deeply gendered: these "difficult to organize" occupations reflect sexual stereotyping (women are good at tasks requiring manual dexterity and nurturing) and so are female-dominated; in other words, they are sex-segregated jobs. Radical feminists posit that the feminization of particular jobs results from a conscious effort by men to maintain women's inferior economic position. Dworkin asserts that sex-typing of an occupation can occur in any field where jobs are low-paying relative to other areas where men can find employment.[51] She describes the ways in which the market operates to create and maintain women's low economic status as follows:

(1) Women are paid lower wages than men for doing the same work. . . .
(2) Women are systematically excluded from work of high status, concrete power, and financial reward. . . .
(3) Women are consigned the lowest ranks within the field, no matter what the field. . . .
(4) When women enter any industry, job, or profession in great numbers, the field itself becomes feminized, that is, acquires the low status of the female.[52]

Others add that sex-typing of an occupation is especially likely to occur where the job "combine[s] a need for a fairly high level of training and education with very low pay (stenography, nursing, teaching)."[53] Such jobs provide valuable labor for less-than-market wages while simultaneously keeping skilled and trained workers from taking the existing higher-paying (male) jobs.

Critical race feminists argue that the low wage resulting from the sex segregation of work disproportionately affects women of color and working-class women.[54] . . . Unions must shoulder some of the blame for these statistics. Unionized women undoubtedly are economically better off than nonunionized women. Because unions have been successful in raising the wages of the poor and of other disadvantaged groups, unions' failure to organize women, particularly women of color, implicitly helps to institutionalize the economic subordination of women. . . .

Unions will only be capable of increasing the numbers of women and their locus of power within labor unions if they can overcome the admittedly poor image of unions in the eyes of many women workers. Moreover, many women have internalized the sexist ideology they have encountered from unions and employers, and in some cases have accepted the apparent naturalness of their own inferior economic, social, and political status. Thus, unions will need to reeducate themselves and women about the role women can play in unions. . . .

In addition, unions must rethink traditional, male-oriented models of union organizing. The traditional model is as follows: (1) the union targets "hot shops," shops where the workers already have indicated a desire for organization; (2) the organizers attempt to entice workers, promising better wages and fringe benefits; (3) the organizing strategy is based entirely upon appealing to workers' identities as workers, rather than appealing to their other identities—racial, gender, religious, ethnic, and so on; (4) the union views organizing ability as a technical skill rather than an ability that grows out of a shared experience of community-building; (5) classic organizing tactics are those developed to reach a workforce employed by a large, centralized plant, including, for example, leafletting and mass meetings; (6) the union places nearly all its efforts on winning the representation election—shops where a quick victory seems unlikely, or where an election has already been lost, are largely ignored by unions; further, once an election has been won, the organizing task is considered to be over.[55]

By contrast, a feminized union might focus first on building a nurturing community that can withstand and flourish in the face of inevitable employer antiunion pressure. Because this style of organization relies upon establishing an emotional connection between employees as well as on intellectual commitment to the goals of the union, it requires nontraditional organizing strategies that are more personal in nature, and which take into account differences of age, race, and class. . . .

We must simultaneously begin the process of deconstructing and ungendering the labor laws to facilitate organization of women and bargaining on behalf of women. . . . The primary goal of a feminist perspective on labor law must be to recast the law's conception of the worker as a male, full-time breadwinner with a wife and children at home. . . .

Labor law focuses upon "work," which it defines implicitly as that which is done for wages outside the home. The paradigm of the male worker, with a wife at home tending to the necessities of life, is woven into the National Labor Relations Act [NLRA]. This gendered paradigm is perhaps best illustrated by the definition of an "employee" covered by the NLRA. The Act explicitly excludes from the definition of "employee" spouses who "work" for their spouses.[56] Further, the Act maintains the public-private spheres ideology by excluding from coverage those who perform housework and child care.[57]

Labor law jurisprudence also impedes unions' organization of employees in sex-segregated occupations. Some of these categories of workers are specifically excluded from the Act's coverage. [For example, "confidential employees," who may be secretaries or administrative assistants, are excluded. In addition,] domestic employees are also excluded from coverage under the Act; they are almost exclusively female.

Finally, independent contractors are expressly excluded from the Act's coverage. Contract work is particularly common in the sex-typed occupations of clerical and service worker. The flexibility of independent contractor arrangements, and their consequent suitability for working mothers who have assumed primary responsibility for child care, ensure that women will continue to be drawn to these positions. Technological innovations, such as telecommuting, make it possible to perform many sex-typed clerical jobs from home. These jobs, too, are attractive to working mothers. As employers seek to restructure relationships with employees to reduce labor costs and deter unionization, they are increasingly utilizing these innovations. Because of the difficulties in organizing isolated workers, the AFL/CIO is pressing for a total ban on telecommuting.[58]

Other sex-typed categories of employees, while not explicitly excluded from the Act's coverage, are a difficult target for union organization efforts because of employer job-structuring. Part-time and temporary workers often are the subject of bargaining unit composition litigation because their interests are potentially dissimilar to those of full-time employees in the unit. Part-time and temporary workers now comprise almost one third of the workforce, and 64% of all temporary workers and 65% of all part-time workers are women.[59] . . .

If union efforts to organize women are to be facilitated—or at least, not blocked—by the labor laws, an expanded definition of the term "employee" is required. . . .

The gendered definition of the typical employee as a male with no household obligations is also reflected in the National Labor Relations Board's rulings concerning allowable restrictions on union solicitations. The Board has upheld employer no-solicitation rules that limit employee solicitation to nonwork time, such as breaks or lunchtime, in nonwork areas.[60] Further, outside organizers may be denied access to an employer's property when "reasonable access" to employees may be gained through other means.[61] These limitations on access to employees disproportionately affect working women because of their double burden of housework and child care; most women have little time to listen to the appeals of union organizers. A less restrictive approach to union solicitation is necessary if unions are to gain access to working mothers.

As the feminist studies of worker militancy styles described above make clear, women often choose nontraditional means of protesting working conditions imposed by their employers. Current law fails to protect many of these methods of employee protest. For example, sit-downs and slow-downs are generally unprotected.[62] Employees who engage in these forms of protest may be discharged with impunity. Expanded protection for female-style collective action should be another feature of a gender-neutral labor law.

The gendered definition of work and the conditions under which it is performed are reinforced by the public-private spheres ideology, encapsulated in the NLRA's mandatory/permissive subject dichotomy. The obligation to bargain collectively under the NLRA is statutorily limited to issues involving "wages, hours, and other terms and conditions of employment."[63] All subjects falling within the scope of the statutory obligation are mandatory, and must be bargained over; all others are permissive, and may be discussed but not insisted upon to impasse. Because issues such as child care, maternity benefits, and parental leave have not been pressed by unions at the bargaining table, the Board has never faced the question whether they are mandatory subjects of bargaining. As feminized unions cement their commitment to advancing the interests of working women at the bargaining table, the NLRA's definition of mandatory subjects must evolve. For example, the term "hours" should be contrued to include flexible shift schedules for child care. "Wages" and "terms and conditions of employment" should be construed to encompass child care benefits, maternity leave benefits, parental leave provisions, and other subjects of interest to women. . . . Much additional deconstructive work remains for feminists and labor lawyers. . . .

Notes

1. See Dowd, Work and Family: The Gender Paradox and the Limitations of Discrimination Analysis in Restructuring the Workplace, herein, at 549; (discussing existing discrimination analysis); Schultz, Telling Stories About Women and Work: Judicial Interpretations of Sex Segregation in the Workplace in Title VII Cases Raising the Lack of Interest Argument, herein, at 636; (examining judicial interpretations of sex segregation under Title VII, and proposing deeper judicial scrutiny of employer responsibility for sex segregation); Browne & Giampetro-Meyer, The Overriding Importance of Market Characteristics for the Selection of Pay Equity Strategies: The Relative Efficacy of Collective Bargaining and Litigation in the Nursing Industry, 11 Indus. Rel. L.J. 414, 428–432 (1989) (discussing courts' lack of receptivity to comparable worth claims under Title VII).

2. May, Bread Before Roses: American Workingmen, Labor Unions and the Family Wage, in R. Milkman ed., Women, Work and Protest 6 (1985).

3. A. Kessler-Harris, Out to Work 152 (1982). The Knights of Labor brand of unionism has been described as "romantic," and "reformist" as contrasted with the American Federation of Labor's approach. See H. Millis & R. Montgomery, Organized Labor 59 (1945). The Knights emphasized equality of opportunity and sought "panaceas" which would "lift the wage earners out of their class." A. Cox, D. Bok & R. Gorman, Cases and Materials on Labor Law 7 (10th ed. 1986).

4. Cox, Bok & Gorman, *supra* note 3, at 8 (quoting S. Perlman, History of Trade Unionism in the U.S. (1922)).

5. *Id.* at 8.

6. See Kessler-Harris, *supra* note 3, at 152; Perlman, *supra* note 4, at 66. The AFL's short-term perspective was not solely a product of shortsightedness and self-interest; political expedience was an important element as well. The capitalist system restrained the labor movement. The demise of the American Socialist Party and the Red Scare were instrumental in destroying labor's larger political and social goals. See M. Harrington, Socialism: Past & Future 28–59 (1989). . . .

7. By 1920, more than 20% of the labor force was female. Kessler-Harris, *supra* note 3, at 152.

8. *Id.* at 153.

9. *Id.* at 157. Kessler-Harris describes the methods by which the AFL effectively denied women's unions access. The methods included stalling until the employer had dissipated union support through discharge of union leaders, outright refusals to issue charters, disputes over jurisdiction of the parent body, and assessing unreasonably high dues and fees. *Id.* at 157–158.

10. Indeed, unionists urged that woman's full-time presence in the home was critical to the very survival of the family: "'The demand for female labor' . . . is 'an insidious assault upon the home . . . it is the knife of the assassin aimed at the family circle.'" *Id.* at 154 (quoting statement of an official of the Boston Central Labor Union, made in 1897).

11. National Laborer, Nov. 12, 1836, at 133, reprinted in J. Commons & H. Sumner, A Documentary History of American Industrial Society 281 (1958). William Sylvis of the National Labor Union carried the analysis one step further during an 1867 speech: "It will be fatal to the cause of labor, when we place the sexes in competition, and jeopardize those social relations which render woman queen of the household. Keep her in the sphere which God designed her to fill, by manly assistance. . . ." J. Sylvis, The Life, Speeches, Labors, and Essays of William H. Sylvis 220 (1872).

Although most feminists are critical of the family-wage ideology, Martha May points out that the family-wage ideal had its origins in a politics of class *unity* rather than class division. See May, *supra* note 2, at 2. Historically, May argues, the family-wage ideal constituted a class aspiration, supported by both men and women of the working class—and the ideology was strenuously resisted by capital. *Id.* at 7. May quotes an AFL spokesperson who described the ideology in more positive terms: "The workers are tired of having themselves, their wives and children, used as chips for our commercial, financial, and industrial gamblers . . . What is the price we pay for children free from factory life, for mothers burdened by no duties outside the home, for fathers who have leisure for homes and families? . . . The living wage is the right to be a man and to exercise freely and fully the rights of a free man. [T]o realize that is the sure and true destiny of organized labor." *Id.* at 8–9. Note that even in this explication, however, the family-wage ideology—and, indeed, the goals of organized labor itself—were defined in terms of gender roles. It was only when the presence of women wage earners in the labor market threatened to upset the balance between home and shop, that the family-wage ideology took on the aspect of female exclusion. *Id.* at 7. Ultimately, May agrees, the family-wage ideology operated to divide the working class along gender lines. *Id.*

12. Kessler-Harris, *supra* note 3, at 153–154.

13. *Id.* at 159.

14. Feldberg, "Union Fever": Organizing Among Clerical Workers, 1900–1930, Radical Am., May–June 1980, at 53, 60–61. Even those who sympathized with the condition of working women believed that improvements in working conditions should only be achieved through "appropriate methods" and in "ladylike fashion, through the exercise of quiet influence and moral suasion among men who would champion their cause." *Id.* at 61. In short, "[women] were to be protected, not to become their own guardians." *Id.*

15. *Id.* at 53 (quoting Typewriter Tappings, 24 The Typewriter and Phonographic World 90 (1904), to the "typewriter girls" of Montreal, Canada, who had "the fever" and were talking about forming a union).

16. Cook, Introduction to A. Cook, V. Lorwin & A. Daniels, Women and Trade Unions in Eleven Industrialized Countries 14 (1984).

17. Examples of these policies included contracts forbidding the hiring of married women and requiring the resignation of single female employees who married; contracts that required a married woman to show "cause" for her employment (e.g., her husband was either incapacitated or in the service); contracts restricting the accumulation of seniority for women; and contracts requiring women to pay a special fee to the local union for "permission to work." *Id.*

18. See Milkman, *supra* note 2, at 100–101.

19. See Koziara & Pierson, The Lack of Female Union Leaders: A Look at Some Reasons, 104 Monthly Lab. Rev. 30, 31 (1981); see also K. Amundsen, A New Look at the Silenced Majority 89–91 (1977) (describing phenomenon of predominantly white male oligarchy controlling organized labor).

20. See, e.g., Koziara & Pierson, *supra* note 19, at 31.

21. See Goldberg, The Economic Exploitation of Women, in Capitalist System 343 (1972); W.R. Grace & Co. v. Rubber Workers, 461 U.S. 757 (1983) (company's departmental and plantwide seniority systems, mandated by its collective bargaining agreement, violated Title VII; company was required to comply with EEOC conciliation agreement, and to bear costs of breach of collective bargaining agreement); Wallace, Increased Labor Force Participation of Women and Affirmative Action, in P. Wallace ed., Women in the Workplace 1, 16–20 (1982) (describing legal battle between AT&T and telephone unions over EEOC consent decree requiring implementation of an affirmative action plan in conflict with seniority provisions in collective bargaining agreement; unions fought implementation of affirmative action plan). . . .

22. See, e.g., Jones v. Truck Drivers Local Union No. 299, 748 F.2d 1083, 1086 (6th Cir. 1984) (breach of duty of fair representation action by five female office clericals against union for blocking them from bidding on nonoffice jobs despite accrued seniority after merger which left them jobless, held barred by statute of limitations).

23. Olsen, The Family and the Market: A Study of Ideology and Legal Reform, 96 Harv. L. Rev. 1497, 1498 (1983).

24. Strom, Challenging "Woman's Place": Feminism, the Left, and Industrial Unionism in the 1930s, 9 Feminist Stud. 359, 359–360 (1983) (citing as an example L. Tentler, Wage-Earning Women: Industrial Work and Family Life in the United States, 1900–1930 (1979)); see Okafor, White-Collar Unionization: Why and What To Do, 62 Personnel 17, 18 (1985) (militancy of women office workers "has been especially surprising to traditional labor leaders who have long regarded women office workers as largely unorganizable"); Green & Tilly, Service Unionism: Directions for Organizing, 38 Lab. L.J. 486, 488 (1987) ("it is a time-honored complaint among male organizers that women are difficult to organize"); Browne & Giampetro-Meyer, *supra* note 1, at 439 (citing studies by economists that "indicate that women are less likely than men to join unions because they see themselves as temporary, secondary workers [and] because women perceive that unions discriminate against them and fail to emphasize wage and benefit issues that are important to women."). . . .

25. Moore, Are Women Workers "Hard to Organize"?, 13 Work & Occupations 97, 97–98 (1986).

26. See *id.* at 99. . . .

27. See Narod, Labor Woos Women, Dunn's Bus. Month, Sept. 1984, at 83.

28. Moore, *supra* note 25, at 107 (emphasis added). . . .

29. See *id.* at 98; R. Freeman & J. Medoff, What Do Unions Do? 28–29, Table 2–2 (1984) (female nonunion workers were more likely to favor unions than were male nonunion employees, a fact which is consistent with analyses of actual voting behavior in union representation elections); Green & Tilly, *supra* note 24, at 488 (nonunionized women actually desire unionization at a higher rate than men) (citing paper presented by Freeman and Leonard); Leigh & Hills, Male-Female Differences in the Potential for Union Growth Outside Traditionally Unionized Industries, 8 J. Lab. Res. 131, 141–142 (1987) ("the lower extent of unionization found for females employed in private sector industries outside the unionized sectors is due almost entirely to a greater degree of frustration among women who desire a union job but are unable to get one").

30. See Too Late for Prince Charming, Newsweek, June 2, 1986, at 54, 55 (reporting unpublished study by Yale sociologists and Harvard economist predicting that marriage rates for college-educated single women 30 and over are only 20%, decrease to 5% by age 35, and to 2.6% by age 40).

31. National Commn. of Working Women of Wider Opportunities for Women, No Way Out: Working Poor Women in the United States 2,4 (1988).

32. Norwood Sees Encouraging Signs in Narrowing of Earnings Gap, 3 Lab. Rel. Wk. (BNA) 1095 (Nov. 22, 1989) (summarizing Bureau of Labor Statistics data).

33. *Id.*

34. Increased household dependence on women's incomes, even in middle- and upper-class households, is evidenced by the fact that, for example, life insurance companies are now selling more policies to women than to men. Cetron, Rocha & Luckins, Into the Twenty-First Century: Long-Term Trends Affecting the United States, Futurist, July–Aug. 1988, at 29, 38.

35. No Way Out, *supra* note 31, at 4.

36. See R. Goldberg, Organizing Women Office Workers 21, 99 (1983) (One study found that women who had to work out of economic necessity often continued to work after the necessity had passed, "finding it a relief from household drudgery" and enjoying "the personal qualities of competence, importance, and independence gained through their jobs.").

37. *Id.* at 60.

38. *Id.* at 95 (quoting a survey respondent).

39. The phrase "prelabor market explanation" was coined by Vicki Schultz to describe the attribution of "workplace segregation to social forces operating prior to the labor market," whether traceable to biological influences or to "early socialization to 'feminine' sex roles." Schultz, *supra* note 1, at 646.

Some have employed the "lack of interest" argument to justify the gender-wage gap, couching it in more "neutral" economic terms. See R. Posner, Economic Analysis of Law 313–334 (3d ed. 1986). Posner suggests that higher wages for males may reflect a compensatory premium for the "dirty, disagreeable, and strenuous jobs that men dominate presumably because their aversion to such work is less than women's"; and/or that lower wages for women represent "differences in investments in market-related human capital (earning capacity). [T]his will show up in the choice of occupations: women will be attracted to occupations that don't require much human capital." *Id.* Posner allows that "irrational or exploitive discrimination," *id.*, is another possible explanation, but he emphasizes the economic justifications, which boil down to lack of interest arguments with a decidedly negative twist: in blunt terms, women earn less either because they do not want to get dirty, or because they are lazy.

40. See also Fiorito & Greer, Gender Differences in Union Membership, Preferences, and Beliefs, 7 J. Lab. Res. 145, 161–162 (1986) (gender variations in unionism measures are due, in part, to industrial and occupational distributions, and thus may "diminish as occupational and industrial distributions become more gender-neutral"); Freeman & Medoff, *supra* note 29, at 28 (limiting the comparison between men and women union membership rates to individuals working in the same industry and occupation, the difference in unionization rates is reduced by over 60%); Hirsch, The Determinants of Unionization: An Analysis of Interarea Differences, 33 Indus. & Lab. Rel. 147, 149 (1980) (women are more likely to work in less-unionized industries and in white-collar occupations, which are difficult to organize).

41. See R. Edwards, M. Reich & D. Gordon, Labor Market Segmentation (1975);

Barron & Norris, Sexual Divisions and the Dual Labor Market, in D. Barker & S. Allen eds., Dependence and Exploitation in Work and Marriage 47 (1976). For a feminist critique of labor market segmentation theory, see Beechey, Women and Production: A Critical Analysis of Some Sociological Theories of Women's Work, in A. Kuhn & A. Wolpe eds., Feminism and Materialism 155 (1978).

Some female-dominated occupations, such as clerical work, have always been considered difficult to organize, regardless of whether men or women filled the jobs. The reasons for this belief include the fact that clericals identify with the boss for whom they work; clericals identify with white collar workers and with the middle class, which have traditionally been opposed to unionism because of its identification with the working class; and isolation by work roles, office organization, and status hierarchies within the office. See Goldberg, *supra* note 36, at 19. Alternatively, the argument has explicitly assumed a sex-stereotyped form: women are by nature passive and adaptable, rendering them ideally suited to performing repetitive, routine tasks without complaint; their docility makes it unlikely that they will aspire to rise above their station. See Davies, Woman's Place Is at the Typewriter: The Feminization of the Clerical Labor Force, Radical Am., July–Aug. 1974, at 1, 18.

42. Leigh & Hills, Male-Female Differences in the Potential for Union Growth Outside Traditionally Unionized Industries, 8 J. Lab. Res. 131, 139 (1987). Actually, the two reasons can be collapsed into a single reason: cost-effectiveness for the union. The more intense management opposition to a union campaign is, the lengthier and costlier it will be for the union to win.

43. Browne & Giampetro-Meyer, *supra* note 1, at 434.

44. See R. Kanter, Men and Women of the Corporation 261 (1977) (individual-model thinking); W. Ryan, Blaming the Victim (1971) (victim-blaming approach).

45. A. Dworkin, Letters from a War Zone 128 (1988).

46. See *id.* (women have developed this trait because they are colonized by men).

47. See B. Hooks, Feminist Theory: From Margin to Center 29 (1984). Hooks was referring to the fact that black feminists are often asked to rank-order their gender or racial identities and to assert that either the "feminist struggle to end sexist oppression is more important than the struggle to end racism," or vice versa. Her comments apply equally, however, to the assumptions underlying requests that women prioritize their commitment to feminism and to unionism, or to the roles of worker and mother.

48. Ackelsberg, Communities, Resistance, and Women's Activism: Some Implications for a Democratic Polity, in A. Bookman & S. Morgen eds., Women and the Politics of Empowerment 301 (1988).

49. Finley, Transcending Equality Theory: A Way Out of the Maternity and the Workplace Debate, 86 Colum. L. Rev. 1118, 1138 (1986). . . .

50. See, e.g., Hooks, *supra* note 47, at 133–146.

51. Dworkin, *supra* note 45, at 123. . . .

52. *Id.* at 122–123.

53. Goldberg, *supra* note 36, at 345.

54. See generally Hooks, *supra* note 47.

55. Green & Tilly, *supra* note 24, at 487.

56. See National Labor Relations Act §2(3), 29 U.S.C. §152(3) (1988) ("'employee' . . . shall not include any individual employed by his [sic] parent or spouse"). The original basis for this exclusion was apparently a conflict of interest rationale: Congress wanted to avoid the divided loyalties that might exist if an employer's spouse or

children were included in a bargaining unit along with nonfamily employees. See NLRB v. Action Automotive, 469 U.S. 490, 499 (1985).

57. See National Labor Relations Act §2(3), 29 U.S.C. §152(3) (1988) (excluding domestic workers). The reason for the exclusion of domestic workers has been described as reflective of "political and economic realities." See T. Khell, 4 Labor Law §14.02[1] (1989).

58. D. Nye, Alternative Staffing Strategies 156 (1988).

59. J. Sweeney & K. Nussbaum, Solutions for the New Workforce 55 (1989). Part-time workers are distributed as follows: 27.7% service; 19.3% technical and sales; 18.8% clerical and administrative; 15.5% managerial and professional; 12.7% unskilled laborers; 5.7% skilled craft; and 0.4% agricultural. Id. Temporary workers (only those hired through agencies are included in this definition) are distributed as follows: 43.4% clerical and administrative; 16.9% unskilled laborers; 11% managerial and professional; 10.8% service; 8.8% technical and sales; 4.6% skilled craft; and 4.4% agricultural. Id.

60. See Peyton Packing Co., 49 N.L.R.B. 828, 843 (1943), enforced, 142 F.2d 1009 (5th Cir.), cert. denied, 323 U.S. 730 (1944).

61. See NLRB v. Babcock & Wilcox Co., 351 U.S. 105, 112 (1956).

62. See NLRB v. Fansteel Metallurgical Corp., 306 U.S. 240 (1939) (sit-downs unprotected); Audubon Health Care Center, 268 N.L.R.B. 135 (1983) (partial or intermittent strike not protected activity).

63. National Labor Relations Act §8(d), 29 U.S.C. §158(d) (1988).

Comparable Worth and Its Impact on Black Women

JULIANNE MALVEAUX

. . . COMPARABLE WORTH is an issue that has maintained a high place on the "women's agenda" for social and economic equity since 1980, when then EEOC Director Eleanor Holmes Norton described it as "the civil rights issue of the 1980's."[1] Given its visibility, it is amazing that little research has focused on the ramifications of comparable worth in the black community, or on the implications of comparable worth for black women. In fact, there seems to be an assumption that because comparable worth is on the "women's agenda" it will have uniform impacts on black and white women. Or, alternatively, the assumption has been that there is no reason to focus on the special needs of black women because comparable worth will "help us all."

The failure to analyze differences among women, and to note different ways policy can impact women makes the use of the term "a women's agenda" more exclusive than inclusive. This exclusion (of women who are "other") is not restricted to analysis of comparable worth. In fact, when one views the use of the word "woman" in the social science literature, one is most frequently struck with disappointment at the intellectual myopia that allows researchers to use the word "woman" globally, but at the same time to indirectly assert that "women" have similar labor force characteristics, regardless of race.

Marianne Ferber, for example, criticizes male researchers for the global use of terms, while at the same time writing about women and failing to note that all of them are not white. Cynthia Epstein similarly writes about black women in some of her work, but blatantly ignores them in her book, *Women and Law*.[2]

Maybe these women ignore the status of minority women because they think it is identical to the status of white women. After all, a growing literature on "convergence" asserts that racial biases among women have been eliminated while gender biases remain. This growing literature ignores or rejects the Darity and Myers argument that wage "convergence" is (1) not dramatic, given the historical differences between black and white women's labor force participation, and (2) the result of two very different phenomena— of white women entering the labor market, and of black women doing different jobs.[3]

The convergence argument might retire to the obscure cobwebs of theory were it not for the policy implications of the assertion that black and white women are similar. An assertion of similarity suggests that policies designed to improve the status of white women will also improve the status of black women, in the same amounts and for the same reason. But much of my own work shows that this assertion is not true.[4]

This article explores ways comparable worth affects black women. While detailed data on comparable worth cases is not presented, this article explores my assertion that there are a different set of benefits that black and white women will derive from comparable worth.

Comparable Worth: Definitions

Comparable worth is defined as "equal pay for jobs of equal value." The concept emerged from a frustration that despite the Equal Pay Act of 1963 and the Civil Rights Act of 1964, women's relative wages remained at about their 1960 level throughout the succeeding twenty year period. The most frequent male-female wage ratio quoted is that women earn 59% of what men earn. Depending on how wages are measured, the number may range from 50% to 75%. No matter how wage gaps are measured, though, researchers agree that a portion of the wage gaps can only be explained by gender (and not by differences in education, occupation, or other factors).

Comparable worth activists assert that women earn much less than men do because they work in "typically female" jobs, or jobs "crowded" by women. A number of researchers have addressed this question, noting that the majority of women work in jobs that are typically female.[5] Even though the proportion of women working in typically female jobs is dropping, the pace is slow, and the prospects of pay equity are dim if occupation switching is the only way this goal can be achieved.

This is true for several reasons. Firstly, substantial employment growth is scheduled to take place in jobs that are currently defined as "typically female."[6] Secondly, it will be difficult for some women to immediately shift their occupational affiliations, especially since their occupational choice some years ago was determined by the segregation women faced in the workplace. Finally, individual strategies to improve women's wages ignore global tendencies to devalue women's work, especially in "typically female" jobs.

Still many researchers have taken the approach that women need merely get more education, change fields, or pick new occupations to earn more money. These "supply-side" theories suggest that something is wrong with the workers who earn low wages, not with the markets that systematically generate low wages for women. Some economic theorists have, in fact, hypothesized that women "supply" their labor to segregated occupations, choosing to work for lower pay because they "protect" themselves from problems they may face by leaving the labor force for childbearing and attempting to reenter later.[7]

Others assert that pay differentials are a function of institutional distortions in the way wages are paid. In hierarchical workplaces, for example, job evaluation systems, rather than "free markets" determine the ways jobs are evaluated in a workplace. A set of compensable factors is identified and point values are assigned for each of these factors. A first set of gender biases may become part of the system when compensable factors are identified, and when points are assigned. Bergmann notes, for example, that the Hay System job evaluators equated the skill necessary to operate a mimeograph machine with the skill necessary to "operate a typewriter." A second set of gender biases may become incorporated into a job evaluation system when compensable factors are weighed.[8]

While one focus of comparable worth is to correct biases that exist in job evaluation systems, another focus is to make sure that those similarly evaluated receive similar pay. Thus, those whose jobs are assigned 200 points will earn more money than those whose jobs are assigned 100 points. But most job evaluations do not measure *every* job, especially in a large workplace. Instead "job clusters" are determined and one "benchmark" job is evaluated in a cluster. The choice of clusters and benchmark jobs is another potential source of bias in job evaluation systems.

Sometimes "typically female" jobs and "typically male" jobs are similarly clustered, and then "typically female" jobs are compensated at a different level than "typically male" jobs. In this case, a woman with 200 points may earn more than a woman with 100 points. It is not clear, though, that a woman whose job is assigned 200 points will earn as much as a man with the same point allocation. Comparable worth seeks to remedy the gaps in pay between men and women whose jobs are assigned the same number of points in an evaluation process.

Examples of the pay inequities found in existing job evaluation studies are illustrative. In the State of Washington the job "Food Service Worker I" was evaluated at 93 points. Average salary for that job was $472 per month. A "Delivery Truck Driver I" was evaluated comparably, with 94 points, but average salary for that job was $792. A "Nurse Practitioner II" had 385 points and average pay of $832 per month. A "Boiler Operator" with just 144 points earned the same level of pay.[9]

Applying the results of job evaluations will not necessarily solve problems of gender bias in wage rates, although they may move toward elimination of such biases. Remick details the set of biases that are possible in job evaluation processes. Beatty and Beatty list a set of problems with job evaluations. McArthur details the basis of potential biases in the job evaluation process, not the least of which is the fact that biases about the person holding a job at present (and his or her gender) may influence an "impersonal" evaluation. But in an attempt to develop a definition of an ideal comparable worth system, Remick calls for "the application of a single, bias-free point factor evaluation system within a given establishment, across job families, to both rank order jobs and to set salaries." Fully cognizant of problems in the job evaluation process, then, Remick insists that gender biases be removed from them. Her discussion represents the essence of the comparable worth argument—that jobs with similar point ratings receive similar wages. In the AFSCME v. State of Washington case (578 F.Supp. 848), as well as in other cases, the issue has been that male and female jobs have been evaluated differently, so that men and women with the same number of points earn very different wages.[10]

Some policymakers have argued against comparable worth by noting that a comparable worth system compares different things, like "apples and oranges." The suggestion has been that if women want to earn "men's" wages they should work in "men's" jobs. This suggestion ignores the subjectivity inherent in job evaluation systems that currently allow faulty evaluation of "apples and oranges" and the fact that comparable worth merely asks that evaluation be more systematic and less biased.[11] The suggestion that women switch jobs ignores the labor market realities that suggest more job growth in "women's" than "men's" jobs, and further ignores the fact that "women's jobs" may be undervalued precisely because women work in them.

The "market" wage is frequently cited as the reason that "typically female" jobs have lower renumeration than "typically male" jobs. But a quarter of all workers are covered by nonmarket collective bargaining agreements. Another third or so work in hierarchical firms where job evaluation studies are used. The "market" sets wages for secondary labor market workers, and indirectly for those who use the results of the other firm's job evaluation to set their pay levels. And the market recursively justifies discriminatory wages. In other words, if one firm pays tellers less than it pays comparably evaluated couriers, another will do the same, citing the "market" as the reason these pay differentials exist. But if, in fact, two or three firms paid equitable wages, other firms would, based on "the market," follow suit.

Discussions of "market" wages also fail to differentiate between internal and external labor markets. Pay for jobs at the port of entry may well be based on certain "market" factors. But job evaluations are internal labor market evaluative tools that assess the value of workers in a given organization. Comparable worth strategies question the way value has been assigned, especially when women's jobs are consistently undervalued.

Comparable worth does not advocate a massive government wage-setting process, as some opponents have asserted. Instead, as Killingsworth notes, comparable worth would not establish uniform national wages, but would implement comparability for those workers who worked for a single employer. The implementation of comparable worth, then, would not preclude pay from varying from location to location, or even, in the same location, from employer to employer.[12]

Actually, the adherence to "market" wages is amusing when one notes that markets only work for some of the people some of the time. Research on the economics of discrimination, and on different racial returns to education and training suggests, in Bergmann's words, markets that are neither free nor competitive. As Remick and Steinberg note, markets are tampered with in a number of ways. Subsidies to Chrysler and Amtrak are examples. Choices to regulate import and export activities are others.[13] One might argue that our policy toward developing countries has been a way of tampering with the labor market. Border controls (or lack of controls), combined with restrictive immigration policies might also be considered labor market "tampering" because they keep wages for undocumented workers down. It is my assertion that the sanctity of "markets" is only raised infrequently: when the consumer or nonwhite nonmale stands to gain from "tampering," even though tampering may be remedial.

Some have argued that comparable worth hurts blue-collar workers, or blacks, or some combination thereof. But comparable worth activists have never proposed cutting the wages of some workers to provide higher wages for others. Instead, to bring women's pay up "to par" the rates of change in wages would differ by job category. In other words, once a comparable worth settlement takes place, all workers may be granted a 5% pay increase, while those workers whose jobs are undervalued may get 15% pay increases to help close the wage gap.

A final argument against comparable worth has been the cost argument. Opponents say the national costs of comparable worth range from $2 billion to $150 billion.[14] However, comparable worth is not likely to be implemented immediately, but in steps, as we have seen in those cities and states where comparable worth has been implemented. San Jose allocated $1.5 million for "pay equity adjustments" over a two year period to begin correcting for wage discrimination. In Minnesota, just 1.25% of the personnel budget was allocated for pay equity adjustments.[15] And in the AFSCME v. State of Washington case, the award amount is projected to be high because both pay adjustments and back pay are included.

San Francisco's mayor implicitly blamed comparable worth for changing the city's budget picture from rosy to ravaged in just one year.[16] Other legislators that oppose comparable worth paint gloomy pictures of high costs, reduced services, job layoffs, and other dire consequences if comparable worth is implemented. Some have sympathized with pay gaps but argued against comparable worth because they say municipalities cannot afford to address pay inequities (that are not their fault). But what is the price of fairness? If cost is the only consideration, the black community should certainly support comparable worth—after all, cost considerations have been used to oppose affirmative action, full employment, educational access and other issues.

Comparable Worth and Black Women

Can comparable worth improve the economic status of black women? To answer this question it is useful to review the occupational status of black women. Like white women, the majority of black women (more than 60%) work in typically female clerical and service occupations. Proportionately fewer black than white women work in management, sales, and professional jobs, while proportionately more black women work in service, operative (manufacturing), and private household jobs.[17]

Within occupational categories, though, there are differences in the status of black and white women. Among clerical workers, black women are more likely to be found as file clerks, typists, calculating machine operators, and social welfare clerical assistants. Except for social welfare clerical assistants, all of these occupations have wages below the median clerical wage.[18] Among service workers, black women are heavily represented as chambermaids, nurses aides, and practical nurses. Again, pay was lower in those occupations where black women were heavily represented.

Another key difference between black and white women's employment is the heavy concentration of black women in public sector employment. In 1981, 16% of all workers were employed by federal, state or local governments. In contrast, 26% of black women held government employment. Proportionately more black women than any other race-sex group were employed by governments—18% of black men, 17.5% of white women, and 12.9% of white men were so employed. Twenty percent of all clerical workers are employed by governments; but nearly a third of black female clerical workers (compared to less than 18% of white clerical workers) are so employed.[19]

Because of differences in the occupational status and employers of black and white women, one can conclude that implementation of comparable worth pay strategies will have a positive impact on the wage status of black women. Comparable worth's positive impact will come both because black women work in typically female clerical jobs that are underpaid, and because a disproportionate number of black women work for governments, where comparable worth strategies are most likely to be implemented.

There is an additional reason why black women will gain from comparable worth. Although black women work in clerical jobs similar to the clerical jobs in which white women work, they work in a set of clerical jobs that earn lower pay than the clerical jobs in which white women work. Malveaux explores the concept of "black women's crowding," which is defined as distinct from the "women's crowding" that white women experience.[20] It is noted that although black women are just 5.4% of the labor force, their representation in some jobs is as high as 35%. In this article, I suggest that this form of crowding results in lower wages for black women, and note that, in clerical occupations, black women are overrepresented in some of the lowest-paying clerical jobs. This means that black women in clerical occupations tend to be underpaid relative to their white counterparts.

This overrepresentation among the lowest paying jobs suggests differential effects from the implementation of comparable worth. Table 1 (below) shows the results of an exercise that illustrates this point. Pay gaps revealed by Remick in State of Washington data were supplemented by data on the percentage of black women in certain jobs.[21] Where all women were overrepresented, but black women were underrepresented, workers were paid an average of 94% of what they should have been paid based on job evaluation estimates. But in jobs where black women were overrepresented (with their representation in a job category at 15% or more), workers were paid 76% of what they should have been paid. Implementation of comparable worth, in this case, would improve the relative position of black women in "typically black female" jobs.

Table 1
Black Women's Pay When They Are Overrepresented
and Underrepresented in Occupations

Job Title	Actual Salary	Predicted Salary	Ratio	% Female, Washington State	% Black Female, National
Black women are overrepresented as:					
Intermediate clerk	921	1208	76.2	81.0	17.9
Intermediate clerk/typist	968	1269	76.3	96.7	16.3
Telegraph operator	887	1239	71.6	95.7	15.5
Data entry operator	1017	1239	82.1	96.5	18.1
Licensed practical nurse	1030	1367	75.3	89.5	18.5
Average			76.3	91.9	17.3
Black women are underrepresented as:					
Legal secretary	1269	1401	90.6	98.7	5.0
Word processor	1082	1301	83.2	98.3	5.0
Bookkeeper	1122	1269	88.4	87.0	5.2
Administrative assistant	1334	1472	90.6	95.1	2.6
Intermediate accountant	1585	1585	100.0	60.2	4.4
Lab technician	1208	1401	86.2	84.1	5.2
Retail sales clerk	921	1239	74.3	100.0	4.9
Pharmacist	1980	1666	118.8	60.0	2.7
Librarian	1625	1794	90.6	84.6	5.1
Community program developer	1932	1750	110.4	60.0	4.7
Administrative services manager	1839	1794	102.5	73.4	2.6
Average			94.1	81.9	4.3

Data source: Remick (1981); unpublished BLS data; Malveaux (1984).

Comparable Worth and Black Community Gains

The black community, as well as black women, will accrue gains when comparable worth is implemented. The first gain is an obvious one—the gain from higher black family wages when black women earn equitable pay. Given the large number of black women heading households, the need for black women to earn equitable pay cannot be overstated. But even where there is another household earner, black women's contribution to black family income frequently makes the difference between black family poverty and black family survival.[22]

Black men will also gain from comparable worth because they are more likely than white men to hold those "typically female" jobs in which pay would be adjusted. Malveaux notes differences in the distribution of black and white men and speculates this may be because black men have, in the past, been excluded from the professional, managerial, and craft jobs in which white men have been concentrated. In the same vein, Giddings writes of the Moynihan suggestion that black women's jobs be "re-designed" for black men as one way to combat high levels of black male unemployment.[23]

There is another potential gain to the black community from adopting a comparable worth strategy. Comparable worth relies on the implementation of a "single, neutral" job evaluation process and uncovers systematic gender bias that results in very different rates of pay for workers whose jobs have a comparable number of evaluation points. Once flaws in the job evaluation process are uncovered, and examination of job evaluations begin, it is likely that pay inequities will be revealed in job categories where minority males are heavily concentrated. In San Francisco, job evaluation revealed that janitors, mostly minority males, received 97 evaluation points and $18,000 in pay. Truck drivers, mostly white males, had 98 evaluation points, but $27,000 in pay.[24] In Alameda County, California, a contrast of the job classifications dominated by minorities and those dominated by nonminorities revealed a 76% pay gap, a smaller gap than revealed when job classifications dominated by women, and those dominated by men are compared. (This gap was 37%).[25] Thus, because systematic racial bias is as likely to occur as systematic gender bias, the adoption of comparable strategies may have a benefit to the black community that is greater than the gain to black women.

Although there is potential for blacks to gain from comparable worth in municipalities, it is critical to note that comparable worth gains will not accrue to the black community merely because comparable worth is being considered in a community. The process of examining job evaluations merely opens the door for black activists and trade unionists to evaluate racial biases that may exist in job evaluations. Clearly, the subjectivity inherent in job evaluation processes has affected blacks (and other minorities) as much as it has affected women. But because comparable worth has been seen as a "women's issue," the inclusion of jobs that are "typically" minority in settlement processes may be one that requires political coalition building tactics.

Some researchers and activists detail ways to include the crowding of minorities into comparable worth consideration; others see the inclusion of minorities in comparable worth strategies as "muddying the waters."[26] Still others, for reasons of political pragmatism, choose not to see the connection between race and sex discrimination. But whenever one acknowledges that job evaluations have allowed the introduction of subjective biases in the way wages are paid, then it is a small step to move from correction of gender biases to correction of racial biases.

Limitations to Comparable Worth Strategy

While comparable worth strategies promise clear gains for black women (and men) who are employed in the public sector, the implementation of comparable worth will not solve all of the employment problems of the black community. In fact, some have argued that comparable worth is a strategy limited to solving the problems of workers in low-paying, typically female jobs.[27] In any case, no assessment of comparable worth's impact on the black community is complete without a discussion of strategy limitations.

Comparable Worth's Benefits Are Limited to Public-Sector Employees

Unless far-reaching national legislation is passed, . . . comparable worth is likely to be implemented in cities and states, and to apply solely to those workers employed in the public sector. Private-sector employers are not likely, in the absence of legislation, to implement comparable worth.

Even as comparable worth is discussed as a strategy, however, workers who were formerly employed in the public sector have found their jobs subcontracted to private employers. These workers are employed primarily in food and cleaning service occupations, and are mostly minorities.[28]

When jobs leave the civil service structure, the question of "comparable pay" for those jobs is irrelevant. Instead, because subcontractors compete for contracts on the basis of a low bid, it is likely that the wages and working conditions of workers will decline when their jobs move from the public sector to the private sector. Strategies to ensure fair wages, hours and working conditions for these workers are not likely to include comparable worth strategies.

While this discussion is not meant to minimize the importance of comparable worth strategies, it makes it clear that a substantial segment of employed black women (more than 22% of whom hold service jobs) are likely to find comparable worth an inapplicable strategy to their situation. Strategies to limit contracting out are more appropriate strategies for improving the status of these women.

Comparable Worth Strategies Are Limited to Employed Workers

Black female unemployment rates are more than twice white female rates (15.4% and 6.5%, respectively, in 1984). Strategies to improve the status of employed women will, of necessity, exclude the unemployed. For these women, affirmative action strategies are likely to facilitate entry into paid employment, while comparable worth will facilitate the equitable pay process.

Comparable Worth Strategies May not Include Women Who Participate in "Workfare" Programs

Although the mechanics of employment and pay in workfare programs are in draft stage (at least in California where legislation was passed in 1985), it is clear that a disproportionate number of black women will work in these jobs because a disproportionate number of black women receive public assistance. If jobs are not available in the private sector, then workfare women will be provided with public sector, below "market" wages, and possibly "make-work" jobs. These women may be substitutes for unionized civil service workers who perform the same tasks. Given the low pay rates built into workfare legislation, the issue of comparable pay will also not be an issue for these women.

Comparable Worth Strategies Will not Affect Women Forced to Participate in the Underground Economy

Women on welfare are likely to participate in underground economy employment because welfare payments are not large enough to provide for the needs of their families. Though there is little solid information on employment sources for these women, anecdotal information suggests that these women work in the service sector, in laundries and as hotel maids, and in related "typically female" service jobs.

It is important to note that discussion of welfare women's participation in the underground economy is not an attempt to "blame the victim" or put further restrictions on welfare women (many of whom are penalized for school attendance by reduction in welfare checks), but rather an attempt to point out the implicit subsidy offered those employers who hire these women and pay them minimum or below minimum wages. Reform in this area should begin with investigation of employers, not employees.

In any case, while the number of welfare women participating in the underground economy cannot be estimated, it is likely that a disproportionate number of them are black (because a disproportionate number of the women on welfare are black). Comparable worth strategies, no matter what their importance to women employed in the public sector, will not help these women.

Comparable Worth Will not Help Women Who Hold Semiskilled and Unskilled Jobs

Comparable worth may improve the status of women working in jobs where their skills are undervalued, but those women who work in semiskilled and unskilled jobs will not benefit from implementation of comparable worth. Unionization is possibly the most direct way to ensure fair wages, hours, and working conditions for these women.

While comparable worth offers the opportunity for improvement of the wages of some black workers, it is a strategy that will not address the employment situation of many others. It is important to view comparable worth, then, as one of a set of strategies to improve the employment status of black workers. Other strategies include affirmation action, full employment legislation, job creation, encouragement of unionization, and legislation to limit contracting out.

Distributional Aspects of Comparable Worth

Comparable worth is an activist strategy; it is one that requires activists to agitate and lobby legislators to support revising the way state or local civil service jobs are evaluated. While the thrust of this article his been to highlight the benefits accruing to black women as a result of implementation of comparable worth, this section raises questions about activist priorities and ways they may change depending on the demographics and fiscal realities in a state or municipality. Again, this discussion is not meant to detract from the real value of comparable worth strategies, but to suggest ways to evaluate the benefits from comparable worth.

How Are Black Women Distributed in a Given Community?

If more are service workers than clerical workers, greater impact may be gained by encouraging unionization and limiting contracting out of service activities. While comparable worth will help clerical workers gain equitable pay, institutional arrangements will determine how service workers are paid.

Where Will Money to Pay Comparable Worth Pay Adjustments Come From?

If it will come from education budgets, from community service budgets, or from other budgets beneficial to the black community, then legislators opposed to comparable worth are likely to make that point. (In San Francisco, the mayor has asked all city departments to take a 5% budget cut, supposedly to pay for a $28 million comparable worth settlement.) If money will come from budget items particularly helpful to the black community, then careful evaluation of the budget process is in order. While comparable worth wage adjustments should not take the blame for budget shifts (what cost fairness?), activists should be cognizant of budget battles likely to emerge from comparable worth settlements, and be prepared to fight these battles with broad-based coalitions of black community activists, trade unionists, and feminist activists.

Will Workers in Subcontracted Jobs Be Affected?

This question (and its answer) is related to the previous one, but is raised separately because so many minority women are found in subcontracted service jobs. Are there ways the impact of such tradeoffs can be reduced? It may be appropriate to consider supporting the rights of workers whose jobs may be subcontracted with a coalition similar to the one described above.

Will There Be a Tax Increase to Pay for Comparable Worth?

If so, what is the tax incidence? Tax increases may provide black taxpayers with a springboard for demanding that issues of racial crowding and bias in job evaluation processes be considered.

What Is the Relationship Between Comparable Worth and Affirmative Action?

Since affirmative action deals with all of the terms and conditions of employment, including hiring, recruitment, promotion, transfer, and wages, comparable worth should be considered a subset of an overall affirmative action strategy. However, comparable worth has too frequently been considered a self-standing strategy, and in some cases a sole strategy instead of one in a series of strategies. Black workers who support comparable worth should not lose sight of broader affirmative action tactics, and should consider brokering their support of comparable worth for stronger support of affirmative action efforts.

In general, comparable worth will have a positive impact on black women's wages. But the size of the impact will differ by community, and will depend on the proportion and distribution of black women in the public sector. Additionally, the positive impact of comparable worth on black women will depend on how legislators propose to pay for comparable worth and whether black community services or tax payments are adversely affected by comparable worth costs.

A key point for the black community to consider is the fact that questions about gender bias in job evaluation lead to related questions about racial bias. Comparable worth strategies are most likely to raise these questions when black workers are involved in defining those strategies. To the extent that comparable worth strategies raise these questions, and ultimately change these pay scales, black women and the black community are both beneficiaries.

Conclusion

Clearly, many aspects of this article are conjectural. But it lays out a framework for an empirical investigation of the impact of comparable worth on the black community. Preliminary investigation suggests that comparable worth is likely to have clear positive effects. A discussion of distributional issues highlights ways comparable worth concepts may be used to strengthen the entire employment position of black workers in municipalities.

When employment policies are considered for the black community, an important factor is the diversity of the black population and their employment status. From this standpoint comparable worth should be viewed as one of a series of strategies to improve the status of black women. While comparable worth will not help black women who are unemployed, who work in the private sector, who participate in underground economies or in workfare programs, it will have a positive effect on black women (and some black men) in public-sector jobs. As long as comparable strategies are developed in tandem with other strategies to improve the employment status of black women, the black community has nothing to lose and much to gain by supporting comparable worth.

Notes

1. Eleanor Holmes Norton, Speech to Conference on Pay Equity, Daily Labor Reporter 211 (Bureau of National Affairs), October 30, 1980.

2. Marianne Ferber, Women and Work: Issues of the 1980s, 8 Signs 273 (Winter 1982); Cynthia Fuchs Epstein, Women in Law (Basic Books, 1981).

3. James P. Smith The Convergence to Racial Equality in Women's Wages, in Cynthia Lloyd et al. eds., Women in the Labor Market 173 (Columbia Univ. Press, 1979); William Darity & Sam Myers, Changes in Black-White Income Inequality, 1968–78: A Decade of Progress? 10 Review of Black Political Economy 354 (Summer 1980).

4. Julianne Malveaux, The Economic Interests of Black and White Women: Are They Similar? 14 Review of Black Political Economy (Summer 1985).

5. Andrea Beller, Trends in Occupational Segregation by Sex and Race, 1960–1981, in Barbara F. Reskin ed., Sex Segregation in the Workplace: Trends, Explanations, and Remedies 11 (National Academy Press, 1984).

6. Pamela Stone Cain, Prospects for Pay Equity in a Changing Economy, in Heidi Hartmann ed., Comparable Worth: New Directions for Research (National Academy Press, 1985).

7. Solomon Polachek, Occupational Segregation Among Women: Theory, Evidence, and a Prognosis, in Cynthia Lloyd et al. eds., Women in the Labor Market 137 (Columbia Univ. Press, 1979).

8. Barbara Bergmann, The Economic Case for Comparable Worth, in Heidi Hartmann ed., Comparable Worth: New Directions for Research (National Academy Press, 1985); Helen Remick, Major Issues in a Prior Applications, in Helen Remick ed., Comparable Worth and Wage Discrimination (Temple Univ. Press, 1984).

9. Remick, *supra* note 8, at 103.

10. Richard Beatty and James R. Beatty, Some Problems with Contemporary Job Evaluation Systems, in Helen Remick ed., Comparable Worth and Wage Discrimination (Temple Univ. Press, 1984); Leslie Zebrowitz McArthur, Social Judgment Biases in Comparable Worth Analysis, in Heidi Hartmann ed., Comparable Worth: New Directions for Research (National Academy Press, 1985); see also Helen Remick, The Comparable Worth Controversy, 10 IMPA Public Personnel Management Journal (December 1981), for a definition of comparable worth.

11. Mark Killingsworth, The Economics of Comparable Worth: Analytical, Empirical, and Policy Questions, in Heidi Hartmann ed., Comparable Worth: New Directions for Research (National Academy Press, 1985).

12. *Id.*

13. Barbara Bergmann, The Economic Case for Comparable Worth, in Heidi Hartmann ed., Comparable Worth: New Directions for Research (National Academy Press, 1985); Helen Remick & Ronnie J. Steinberg, Technical Possibilities and Political Realities: Concluding Remarks, in Helen Remick ed., Comparable Worth and Wage Discrimination (Temple Univ. Press, 1984).

14. Remick & Steinberg, *supra* note 13.

15. *Id.*

16. Phillip Matier, Feinstein Orders Hiring Freeze, Trims in Budget, San Francisco Examiner, October 8, 1985.

17. See Malveaux, *supra* note 4, for more details.

18. Julianne Malveaux, Low Wage Black Women: Occupational Descriptions, Strategies for Change, unpublished paper, NAACP Legal Defense and Education Fund, 1984.

19. *Id.*

20. *Id.*

21. *Id.*; see also Remick, *supra* note 10.

22. Phyllis A. Wallace, Black Women in the Labor Force (MIT Press, 1980).

23. Julianne Malveaux, Recent Trends in Occupational Segregation by Race and Sex, paper presented May 1982 to the Committee on Women's Employment and Related Social Issues, National Academy of Science; Paula Giddings, When and Where I Enter: The Impact of Black Women on Race and Sex in America (William Morrow Co., 1984).

24. Tim Shreiner, How Comparable Worth Plan Works, San Francisco Chronicle, February 13, 1985.

25. SEIU 250, 535, 616, Wage Gap and Job Classification Data, Exhibits B and G (Alameda County: SEIU), 1985.

26. Comparable Worth Project, First Steps to Identifying Sex and Race-Based Pay Inequities in a Workplace (Oakland: Comparable Worth Project, 1982); Julianne Malveaux, An Activist's Guide to Comparable Worth, 1 North Star (May 1985 [a]), at 22–31.

27. Killingsworth, *supra* note 11.

28. Malveaux, *supra* note 18.

Barriers Facing Women in the Wage-Labor Market and the Need for Additional Remedies: A Reply to Fischel and Lazear

MARY E. BECKER

FISCHEL AND LAZEAR [in their critique of comparable worth][1] perceive a world in which women's jobs pay less than men's jobs either because women face barriers to entry into male occupations or because women choose jobs that pay less. They believe that barriers to entry can effectively be eliminated by direct remedies, especially Title VII and the Equal Pay Act. Were these perceptions shared by all, comparable worth would not be the hot issue it is today.

Fischel and Lazear suggest that women may "choose" lower paying, more flexible, less skilled, jobs because of their specialization in non-wage labor.[2] Although this theory seems intuitively plausible, it is not likely to explain, for example, why tree trimmers are paid more than nurses.[3]

Other more precise empirical studies[4] suggest that this choice, or human capital theory, does not explain sexual segregation of the wage-labor market and the associated wage gap.[5] Women with less continuous employment experience are about as likely to be in male fields as women with more continuous employment experience, and the depreciation rates associated with temporary withdrawal from the wage-labor market are not significantly higher for male jobs than for female jobs.[6] Skill differences explain little of the gap in pay because the manual skills of many predominantly male jobs are negatively correlated to earnings, and male and female jobs are "nearly equal" in demands for the skills positively correlated to earnings.[7] Single women are only slightly (1%) more likely to be in nontraditional fields than are married women, and the probability of a woman being in a nontraditional field actually increases with the number of children (0.4% per child).[8]

There is a more basic flaw in Fischel and Lazear's narrow description of discrimination: the neoclassical models they use are inherently incapable of describing many of the barriers women face in the wage-labor market. Fischel and Lazear present the two models developed by neoclassical economics—discrimination caused by a taste for discrimination and discrimination based on statistical differences—augmented by an occasional reference to discriminatory socialization. But, sexual segregation of labor

53 U. Chi. L. Rev. 934 (1986).

and the subordinate status of women did not begin with capitalism. Capitalism developed in societies in which women were regarded as less important than men, were subordinate to men, and performed different tasks than men. Any economic system which develops in a society in which power and opportunities are differentially allocated on the basis of sex is likely to operate in a manner that will perpetuate those differentials, regardless of the particulars of economic theory. For example, opportunities and wages may be allocated on the basis of productivity and potential in a capitalist economy, but productivity and potential are assessed by those with the ability to pay. As a result, the preferences, values, biases, and blind spots of the powerful determine the allocation of wages and opportunities, and the meaning of "productivity" and "potential." Thus, neoclassical models of discrimination cannot describe many of the barriers women face in the wage-labor market.

Equally troubling is Fischel and Lazear's characterization of discrimination based on accurate statistical differences between men and women as "non-invidious."[9]. . .

I. Efficient Discrimination: "Non-invidious?"

According to Fischel and Lazear, women are treated differently from men in a "non-invidious" way when male sex is an accurate statistical proxy for such factors as productivity, attachment, and commitment to wage labor.[10] Anti-discrimination legislation should not unnecessarily prohibit efficient discrimination;[11] comparable worth should, therefore, be rejected. Thus, if the pay gap between men and women is the result of employers paying less for women's jobs because the incumbents are predominantly women (and women as a group have been less attached to the wage-labor market in the past,[12] discrimination is "non-invidious" and should be legal.

This view—that, ideally, anti-discrimination legislation should not prohibit efficient discrimination—deprives equality of opportunity of all meaningful content by equating it with the norm of efficiency. But equality of opportunity (whatever it means)[13] is a quite different norm from efficiency.

Using gender as a proxy for desirable attributes denies equal opportunity in every sense to women who would prefer nontraditional roles. "Efficient" statistical discrimination is a vicious circle, perpetuating the subordinate status of women in the wage-labor market. Women can be paid less than men because women have been the primary caretakers of children and primarily responsible for housework. Women will therefore continue to have these responsibilities (and to be economically dependent on men) because their alternative opportunities are less attractive than their husbands'. Individual women will thus have no opportunity to break out of the circle. All women can be relegated to subordinate status on the basis of gender without any discrimination visible to neoclassical economists.

More fundamentally, the acceptance of efficient discrimination as non-invidious ignores the fact that efficiency (which is based on willingness to pay) is a product of existing distributions of wealth, entitlements, and preferences, all of which have been affected by discrimination based on gender. Given the context in which efficient, statistical discrimination occurs, three additional objections may be made on moral grounds.

First, statistical discrimination, even if accurate on average, may not be efficient: it may impose a greater cost on women than the costs saved (or losses avoided) by employers. Women should be able to overcome this obstacle by making it worthwhile for employers to search for better information.[14] But because of the existing distribution of wealth (and transaction costs), women may be unable to offer employers enough to cover the additional costs even though the benefits to women may outweigh these costs.[15]

Second, even if statistical discrimination is consistent with the preferences of women, their preferences may be "adaptive," because of the human tendency to adjust one's desires to what is attainable. Women might have quite different preferences if their opportunities were not limited because of their gender.[16]

Third, statistical discrimination, even when accurate, can have systemic distributional effects when the costs of individual errors and inefficiencies are borne disproportionately by an economic minority.[17] Even accurate and efficient statistical discrimination against women will tend, systematically, to make men ever wealthier relative to women.

One can view efficient discrimination as non-invidious only by focusing almost exclusively on the person in power. But the primary reason for ending discrimination should not be to make those in power better persons, or more rational. Instead, the primary purpose should be to eliminate real-world problems faced by the victims of discrimination. Women paid less because of their gender face the same real-world consequences regardless of the motives and possible good faith of the discriminator.

II. Socialization

Fischel and Lazear concede that the crowding of women into female-dominated occupations may be the result of discriminatory socialization. They argue that direct remedies are superior to comparable worth but they never suggest any concrete remedy. Even ignoring its lack of a concrete remedy, their proposal is impractical. The effects of discriminatory socialization cannot be eliminated easily and quickly by direct remedies because, among other things, many direct remedies would be considered unconstitutional.[18] It is also too late for direct remedies for many women and men who are already socialized. Comparable worth should therefore be considered, along with other partial and indirect remedies.

If wages for women's jobs under comparable worth are closer to the wages that would prevail in a nondiscriminatory world, comparable worth would be an appropriate way to compensate some women, in part, for the effects of discriminatory socialization. Comparable worth has the further potential to change socialization practices. If, as Fischel and Lazear suggest, more men would be interested in becoming nurses if nurses were paid more than janitors, girls and boys would be less likely to be socialized to consider nursing women's work. Comparable worth will not—any more than any other possible remedy—immediately eliminate discriminatory socialization. But it should, over time, help to weaken current socialization patterns, and should be pursued together with other partial or indirect remedies.

III. Current Remedies for "Neoclassical" Discrimination

Fischel and Lazear identify two forms of invidious discrimination: an employer's conscious preference for men over women because of the employer's own taste for discrimination or the tastes of employees or customers, and an employer's mistaken use of male sex as a proxy for desired traits actually shared equally by women.[19] Title VII and the Equal Pay Act were probably designed with such discrimination in mind; at the time, discrimination was often overt as well as conscious.

To some extent, Title VII and the Equal Pay Act have been effective. Perhaps their greatest effect has been to change cultural norms; no longer is explicit discrimination on the basis of sex widely regarded as natural and unobjectionable. Explicitly different wage scales for men and women no longer exist and most jobs are no longer formally closed to women.

These statutes are not, however, effective remedies for covert discrimination. Unless the plaintiff can produce a smoking gun, individual cases alleging differential treatment are notoriously hard to win. The plaintiff must, for example, convince a judge that an employer refused to hire her because she is a woman. The employer typically responds that the decision was based on some neutral factor and some difference between applicants can always be found to support the claim. Judges are very reluctant to second- guess employers' judgments in such cases.[20]

In addition, Title VII and the Equal Pay Act often give the victim little incentive to sue. Monetary relief, under both statutes, is often limited to back pay for a relatively short period. If the victim is able to find other employment (which she is obligated to try to do), the monetary award is usually relatively small. She is also unlikely to be interested in a court order forcing the discriminator to hire her. If she is still an employee, there are obvious reasons not to sue if she is interested in continued employment. For any victim, a suit against an employer or potential employer may damage her chances for successful employment elsewhere.

Although Fischel and Lazear consider the novelty of comparable worth a reason to avoid it, the fact that it is, to some extent,[21] a break with traditional approaches to discrimination is one of its advantages. Comparable worth—because it does not require proof of any decision to treat men and women differently—is a more viable remedy for a period like the present in which discrimination is seldom documented and is less likely even to be conscious.

Comparable worth also insulates most recipients from the consequences of suing employers. If even one nurse, for example, is willing to sue for a comparable-worth adjustment to wages, all the nurses employed by that employer will benefit. And individual women will have more incentive to seek a comparable worth remedy because, if successful, the remedy is more likely to increase earnings for life.

IV. Other Barriers Facing Women

Women face many barriers to access and advancement in the wage market for labor, many of which have nothing to do with any conscious decision to prefer men over women.

1. The Ideology of Gender and Sexual Identity

At a very young age, girls and boys are taught an ideology of gender under which girls and boys (women and men) are essentially different with different roles and abilities. Both girls and boys are pressured to make the ideology of gender part of their personal sexual identity. A girl can become a true woman, a boy a true man, only if each acts in a manner which accords with the reigning ideology of what is appropriate for her or his sex. An important part of the unconscious personal identity of each is, therefore, the internalization of sex-specific behavioral norms and roles.

If an individual chooses work traditionally performed by the other sex, she faces considerable tension between her work and her sexual identity, and threatens the sexual identity of those around her. Employers are often reluctant to hire a woman for a man's job because it requires behavior inconsistent with their view of femininity.[22] There are, therefore, powerful barriers to women performing men's jobs and vice versa. The internal barriers appear to be especially strong for men who might otherwise enter certain nurturative female fields, such as nursing.[23]

Since gender ideology has become part of sexual identity, it is not surprising that the workplace has been resistant to integration. Moreover, both the ideology of gender and the sexual segregation of work preceded capitalism; we have no reason to think that capitalism can eliminate either. Traditional remedies, requiring only that women be treated like men if they want a job traditionally held by men, and vice versa, do little to change this aspect of socialization.

Comparable worth, however, would weaken male reluctance to enter female fields by lowering the economic disincentive for men who have other options, and easing some of the social and personal stigma attached to male entry into a female field. If, for example, nursing were higher paying, nursing might be regarded as more appropriate work for men. If more men perform jobs traditionally held by women, women would have greater opportunity to pursue jobs traditionally held by men, and employers might be more willing to hire women for male jobs if fewer men were available.

2. Unconscious Bias in Valuing the Work of Women

Sexual segregation is troubling because women are valued less than men in most cultures,[24] and in our own. The work of women is devalued, just as women are devalued. Hence, jobs held predominantly by women pay less because of unconscious, and even inadvertent, discrimination in valuing women. In addition, in our society, only a few positions are regarded as women's jobs, whereas men have a wide range of occupations open to them. As a result, employers are likely to have an abundance of those employees whose work they regard as least valuable. Market forces will, therefore, only further depress the wages of undervalued women.

This is the core of the moral case for comparable worth. Study after study reveals that a woman is likely to be rated less competent and less valuable than an identical man.[25] For example, in one study female and male students regarded an article as less important when it was presented as having a female author than when presented as having a male author.[26] It is not surprising that women's jobs pay less than men's jobs.

Moreover, subordination and undervaluation of women preceded current job evaluation studies and contemporary notions of the relative productivity and difficulty of specific tasks. We tend to rate as undemanding and unskilled tasks requiring "feminine" skills, and to rate as more demanding and skilled tasks requiring objectively similar "masculine" skills.[27] Job evaluation studies are "highly illuminating," not because they reveal actual differences in skills between female and male jobs, but because they reveal a sexual hierarchy so pervasive that it is often invisible.[28]

The choice theory cannot answer the moral claim for comparable worth. Even if it were true that most women freely choose women's jobs (rather than being socialized to serve such functions), it would still be immoral to pay workers less *because* they are women, members of the low-valued second sex.

Fischel and Lazear characterize the moral claim for comparable worth as either a rhetorical flourish or as a penalty arbitrarily imposed on innocent employers to compensate roughly for discrimination elsewhere in society. But the moral claim for comparable worth is that this employer is paying these people doing women's work less than it would pay in a world without discrimination, in a world in which the work of women is not undervalued and in which as many (and as valuable) opportunities are open to women as to men.

Neither Title VII nor the Equal Pay Act provides direct remedies for the undervaluing of tasks performed predominantly by women. Comparable worth, however, would be an appropriate and fairly direct remedy for such discrimination. By forcing employers to pay more for women's work, comparable worth should result in the work of women (and women themselves)[29] actually being valued more, both when women work in women's jobs and when women work in integrated jobs or in men's jobs.

3. Unconscious Use of Stereotypes to Fill in Information Gaps

Most employment decisions are made on the basis of incomplete evidence. Empirical data indicates that when decisions must be made in such circumstances, sexual stereotypes (perhaps accurate, perhaps inaccurate, but in any event discriminatory) are used to fill in the gaps.[30] This tendency to rely on stereotypes in the absence of other evidence is likely to disadvantage women, relative to men, when they apply for higher-paying traditionally male jobs. Men are likely to be preferred because of common stereotypes holding that men have more attachment to the wage market, are better supervisors, or are more assertive.[31] Women are likely to be given more routine tasks and fewer opportunities for training or advancement. Comparable worth may be more effective (though less direct) as a remedy for these forms of discrimination than existing antidiscrimination legislation. If work done by women is seen as more valuable, women will be seen as more valuable, and stereotypes which assume that men are better, more effective, or more reliable workers should begin to break down.

4. Sex-linked External and Internal Barriers to Women's Advancement in Jobs Traditionally Held by Men

In both blue-collar and white-collar settings, the fact that women must advance into male territory to succeed creates a number of external and internal barriers to success. I mention only a few. A woman entering a traditionally male, blue-collar field often faces hostility from co-workers who resent the intrusion.[32] Often, such women face sexual harassment. Much training in skilled crafts is informal on-the-job training given by older workers to newcomers; it may be difficult for a woman to get such training from hostile fellow workers. And women may be required to prove that they can really do a man's job by, for example, performing unusually arduous tasks. A female apprentice does not "fit in" the way a male apprentice does.

Similar obstacles face women trying to advance into traditionally male levels of upper management. Again, I mention only a few. Women are often protected by those around them, and thus denied the opportunity to be effective in difficult tasks.[33] At this level, having a powerful mentor is an important prerequisite for success, and women are less likely to have a mentor since mentors usually sponsor younger employees with whom they can identify.[34] As one employee put it, "Who can look at a woman and see themselves?"[35] For these reasons and others, employees tend to perceive a woman as less likely (than a similar man) to have substantial upward mobility or real power.[36] These perceptions are often self-fulfilling.

Those at the top tend to promote people of the same sex with similar social backgrounds for another reason. Such people are seen as more trustworthy and more likely to behave in a manner consistent with the behavioral code of those at the top. To promote a person of another sex to a high policy-making position is to introduce an unnecessary element of uncertainty.[37]

In addition, male bonding (learned in clubs, sports, and other activities from which women are excluded) is a barrier to the advancement of women into high levels of management.[38] A woman simply does not fit in with the guys the way a guy does.

The first women who enter into previously all-male groups feel these barriers particularly acutely.[39] In addition, they feel considerable pressure to perform well so as not to hurt the chances of the women who will follow them, yet they lack any intragroup support system analogous to that enjoyed by men. Internalization of sex-specific behavioral norms, by the women breaking in and those around them, makes finding an effective and comfortable style in a male environment difficult. If the work place is to be desegregated, woman after woman in department after department in company after company must survive—indeed, succeed—amid such pressures and isolation.

Theoretically, Title VII is available as a remedy for much discrimination of this type, though not all. For example, Title VII provides no remedy for differential treatment by customers or students. Even when Title VII affords a remedy, it is not an effective one. Filing a sex discrimination suit is more likely to end a woman's career than to lessen the pressures she faces and provide a more supportive environment.

The only effective way to eliminate these barriers is to integrate the workforce at all levels. Strong affirmative action quotas or goals would be an effective direct remedy, but such legislation has not been enacted. Comparable worth should help (though indirectly) since it gives both men and women more incentive to pursue jobs held predominantly by the other sex. If fewer men are available for traditionally male jobs, women may be seen as more valuable for such positions, and may receive more acceptance and support from male colleagues.

5. Institutionalized Rules Unnecessarily Restrict the Entry or Advancement of Women in Male Jobs

Many traditionally male jobs are unnecessarily geared to male employment patterns. There is, for example, no reason why continuity of employment should be critical for employment in a unionized skilled craft, though not in nursing. But seniority systems, established to secure jobs for certain workers when discrimination against women was both legal and overt, are now formidable barriers to women's entry and advancement in many male fields.[40]

Similarly, age limits on apprenticeship programs and other common conditions of apprenticeships are compatible with male employment patterns. Women, however, are likely to be interested in skilled trades only after learning something about the realities of life and their need for financial independence; at that point, it is often impossible for women to enter apprenticeship programs.

These "neutral" requirements and conditions are likely to crowd women into women's jobs because of the differences between the life patterns of young men and young women, though often these differences could easily be accommodated. Direct remedies to overcome these institutionalized barriers have not been enacted. Comparable worth should help to overcome these barriers, although indirectly, since employers may be more willing to make traditionally male jobs flexible enough to accommodate (valuable) women, especially if there are fewer men interested in such jobs.

6. Information Problems

Information about opportunities in skilled, traditionally male, blue-collar jobs is often unavailable to women. Such information is typically passed through male networks, or presented in a form suggesting that the jobs are for men.[41] Traditional remedies do not reach such practices. Under a comparable worth regime, women may be seen as more valuable. Employers may therefore be more interested in making information available to women in a form indicating that the job is open to them. If more men work in traditionally female jobs, the shortage of men for traditionally male jobs may result in employers making real efforts to give information to valuable women.

7. Steering of Women into Women's Jobs

Women continue to be steered into women's jobs by guidance counselors, employment agencies (including governmental agencies), and personnel departments.[42] Remedies, even when theoretically available, will not be pursued if women do not know about their missed opportunities. Under comparable worth, employers would no longer have an incentive to maintain a dual labor market—one for men and one for women. If women have to be paid comparably to men no matter what they do, employers and their agents will have less incentive to steer women into women's jobs, and shortages of males for male jobs would give employers an incentive to change their practices.

V. Conclusion

The case for comparable worth is even stronger than suggested thus far. We are all socialized to undervalue women and the work of women, and women are channeled into only a few occupations. Women, as a result, tend to earn less than men, to consider themselves (and their careers) less important than their husbands (and their careers), and to have less power in marriage. Further, women tend to be channeled into a few low-paying jobs regardless of individual potential and interest.

But there is more. Girls are socialized to serve others, to be interested in women's jobs, to be primarily responsible for child care, and to regard their roles as wage earners as secondary to their other material responsibilities. Boys, but not girls, are raised with the expectation that they will be primarily responsible, financially, for their children. These assumptions are mirrored in employers' attitudes: "Women get penalized for having children, and men get promoted for having children to support."[43]

But marriage is no longer a reliable institution. Most divorced fathers do not pay child support. Most divorced mothers (90% of whom have custody) are the only source of support for their children, and virtually all non-welfare custodial mothers are the primary source of support for their children. Most support their children, often in poverty, by performing low-paying women's jobs.[44]

Comparable worth will not eliminate all of the barriers women face in the wage-labor market, any more than existing anti-discrimination legislation has. But comparable worth would be a fairly direct remedy for much discrimination—i.e., unconscious and inadvertent undervaluing of women's work—and would be valuable as an indirect remedy for many other forms of discrimination. In light of the diversity of barriers facing women, and their need adequately to support their children, we should pursue as many means as possible.[45]

Notes

1. Fischel & Lazear, Comparable Worth and Discrimination in Labor Markets, 53 U. Chi. L. Rev. 891 (1986).

2. *Id.* at 897 (1986) (citing Polacheck, Women in the Economy: Perspectives on Gender Inequality, in 1 U.S. Comm'n on Civil Rights, Comparable Worth: Issue for the 80's 34 (1984)). Polacheck maintains that "close to 100% of the wage gap can be explained" by the choice, or human capital, theory. *Id.* at 45.

3. See Killingsworth, The Economics of Comparable Worth: Analytic, Empirical, and Policy Questions, in H. Hartmann ed., Comparable Worth: New Directions for Research 86, 100 (1985) [hereinafter New Directions] (this disparity was at issue in Lemons v. City and County of Denver, 620 F.2d 228, (10th Cir.) *cert. denied*, 449 U.S. 888 (1980))....

4. Such studies, for example, rely on time-specific data, unlike the Polachek study, which uses census data and combines male and female jobs. See, e.g., Blau, Occupation Segregation and Labor Market Discrimination, in B. Reskin ed., Sex Segregation in the Workplace: Trends, Explanations, Remedies 117, 139 (1984) [hereinafter Trends].

5. For reviews concluding that Polachek's thesis—that women's lower wages are due to their lower lifetime participation in the labor force and to the division of labor within the family—is not supported by the empirical evidence, see, e.g., B. Reskin & H. Hartmann eds., Committee on Women's Employment and Related Social Issues, Women's Work, Men's Work: Sex Segregation on the Job 70–73 (1986); Blau, Occupational Segregation and Labor Market Discrimination, in Trends, *supra* note 4, at 117; see also Osterman, Sex Discrimination in Professional Employment: A Case Study, 32 Indus. & Lab. Rel. Rev. 451 (1979) (rejecting human capital explanation on basis of firm-specific data).

6. Corcoran, Duncan & Ponza, Work Experience, Job Segregation, and Wages, in Trends, *supra* note 4, at 171, 189; England, Wage Appreciation and Depreciation: A Test of Neoclassical Economic Explanations of Occupational Sex Segregation, 62 Soc. Forces 726, 741–742 (1984); England, The Failure of Human Capital Theory to Explain Occupational Sex Segregation, 17 J. Hum. Resources 358, 369 (1982).

7. England, Chassie & McCormack, Skill Demands and Earnings in Female and Male Occupations, 66 Soc. & Soc. Research 147, 163–164 (1982). The study on skill differences is important since, as its authors note, "the greater productivity of males seems

unlikely unless male occupations require more skill. Otherwise, it is unclear how men's greater human capital manifests itself in greater productivity." *Id.* at 148.

8. Beller, Occupational Segregation by Sex: Determinants and Changes, 17 J. Hum. Resources 371, 384 (1982).

9. Fischel & Lazear, *supra* note 1, at 913–915.

10. Fischel and Lazear present an economic definition of discrimination—i.e., that discrimination occurs only when groups with the same average productivity receive different average compensation—as if it were widely accepted in other contexts. It is not. See, e.g., Lundberg & Startz, Private Discrimination and Social Intervention in Competitive Labor Markets, 73 Am. Econ. Rev. 340, 341–342 (1983) (noting that economists and the legal system address different concerns with the term "discrimination").

Recent research suggests that even when groups appear to differ, statistical discrimination may be inefficient and discriminatory (in the economic sense described above). See *id.* (arguing that statistical discrimination leads to underinvestment in human capital); Schwab, Is Statistical Discrimination Efficient?, 76 Am. Econ. Rev. 228 (1986).

11. Some non-invidious discrimination is illegal under existing anti-discrimination legislation, but Fischel and Lazear maintain that the only possible reason for the prohibition is the difficulty of distinguishing between "non-invidious" and invidious discrimination. See Fischel & Lazear, *supra* note 1, at 913–915.

12. Such assumptions are often inaccurate. See Lloyd, The Division of Labor between the Sexes: A Review, in C. Lloyd ed., Sex Discrimination and the Division of Labor 1, 17 (1975).

13. See, e.g., Alison Jagger, Feminist Politics and Human Nature 17, 193–197 (1983) (discussing the meaning of "equality," "opportunity," and "equal opportunity" from a feminist perspective).

14. See Coase, The Problem of Social Cost, 3 J.L. & Econ. 1 (1960).

15. See, e.g., Dworkin, Is Wealth a Value?, 9 J. Legal Stud. 191, 191–194, 204 (1980); Kennedy, Cost-Benefit Analysis of Entitlement Problems: A Critique, 33 Stan. L. Rev. 387, 392–393, 401–403 (1981).

16. See Mary Walshok, Blue-Collar Women 155–170 (1981) (describing how women's job preferences are created by their job opportunities and on-the-job experience).

17. See Richard Posner, The Economics of Justice 355 (1981).

18. A comprehensive direct remedy would require wide-ranging governmental regulation of speech to prevent discriminatory socialization, including, for example, regulation of books, movies, television, parental speech and practices, and the teachings of historically male-dominated religions.

19. See Fischel & Lazear, *supra* note 1, at 914. Fischel and Lazear do not use the word "conscious," but in each of their detailed examples, an employer decides to treat men one way, and women another. Such discrimination is "conscious" in the sense that the employer knows it is treating men one way and women another.

20. See, e.g., Texas Dep't of Community Affairs v. Burdine, 450 U.S. 248, 254–257 (1981).

21. Comparable worth is entirely consistent with the disparate impact strand of Title VII; it would allow women to challenge employers' use of facially-neutral market wages which have a disparate impact on women. See Stone, Comparable Worth in the Wake of AFSCME v. State of Washington, 1 Berkeley Women's L.J. 78, 81, 101–112 (1985).

22. See, e.g., United States Comm'n on Civil Rights, Women Still in Poverty 16 (1979) (e.g., an employer refused to hire a female auto mechanic with two years of experience because "she'll get too dirty.").

23. As the nursing example suggests, the risk of a man being labeled homosexual often seems higher than the analogous risk for women. In addition, the homosexual label may be more threatening to men. For evidence that "the occupational aspirations of males are . . . more highly sex typed than those of females," see Marini & Brinton, Sex Typing in Occupational Socialization, in Trends, *supra* note 4, at 192, 200.

24. See, e.g., Leviticus 27:3–4 (men to be valued at 50 shekels, and women at 30, the same ratio as the current pay gap).

25. See, e.g., Dipboye, Arvey & Terpstra, Sex and Physical Attractiveness of Raters and Applicants as Determinants of Resume Evaluations, 62 J. Applied Psychol. 288 (1977); Etaugh & Kasley, Evaluating Competence: Effects of Sex, Marital Status, and Parental Status, 6 Psychol. Women Q. 196 (1981); McArthur, Social Judgment Biases in Comparable Worth Analysis, in New Directions, *supra* note 3, at 53, 55–64; Mischel, Sex Bias in the Evaluation of Professional Achievements, 66 J. Educ. Psychol. 157 (1974); Placente, Penner, Hawkins & Cohen, Evaluation of the Performance of Experimenters as a Function of Their Sex and Competence, 4 J. Applied Psychol. 321 (1974).

26. Goldberg, Are Women Prejudiced Against Women, Transaction, Apr. 1968, at 28.

27. For example, the Department of Labor's Dictionary of Occupational Titles for 1974 rated the positions of nursery school teacher and foster mother as less skilled than the position of horse pusher (someone who feeds, waters, and tends horses en route to train). See M. Witt & P. Naherny, Women's Work—Up from 878, Report on the DOT Research Project 24–25, 29–33 (1975).

28. Phillips & Taylor, Sex and Skill: Notes Towards a Feminist Economics, 6 Feminist Rev. 79, 84 (1980).

29. Because of space constraints, I do not discuss an important and pervasive problem with traditional remedies. Women are unlikely to perceive discrimination because they, almost inevitably, share their culture's view: men are superior, more powerful, and so on. Here, too, comparable worth may help; if women are paid more, we may regard ourselves as more valuable.

30. Fischel and Lazear do discuss the use of male sex as a proxy for productivity, etc., but always in the context of a conscious decision to treat men one way and women another. See Fischel & Lazear, *supra* note 1, at 914.

31. See Rosabeth Kanter, Men and Women of the Corporation 197–205 (1977) (also explaining that the stereotype image of a female supervisor describes the behavior of male and female supervisors without real power); Rosen & Jerdee, Influence of Sex Role Stereotypes on Personnel Decisions, 59 J. Applied Psychol. 9 (1974); Terborg & Ilgen, A Theoretical Approach to Sex Discrimination in Traditionally Masculine Occupations, 13 Organizational Behav. & Hum. Performance 352 (1975).

32. See M. Walshok, *supra* note 16, at 13, 188, 192–193, 211–212, 221–232.

33. See Kanter, *supra* note 31, at 187–188.

34. See *id.* at 181–184.

35. *Id.* at 184. Also, men often have difficulty relating to women on a professional, nonsexual basis. This difficulty may directly deter powerful men from sponsoring younger women. Powerful men may also avoid sponsoring younger women because of the possibility of rumors that the relationship is sexual.

36. See *id.* at 181–184, 197–205; Terborg & Ilgen, *supra* note 31, at 374 (also, success of a woman is more likely to be attributed to luck, whereas a man's success is more likely to be attributed to competence; therefore, a so-far-successful woman is less likely to be seen as having as much upward mobility as a similar man).

37. See Kanter, *supra* note 31, at 48–63, 222; Wiley & Eskilson, Scaling the Corporate Ladder: Sex Differences in Expectations for Performance, Power and Mobility, 46 Soc. Psychol. Q. 351, 357–358 (1983).

38. See Kanter, *supra* note 31, at 58–59; Nazario, Gentlemen of the Club, Wall St. J., Mar. 24, 1986, §4, at 19D (part of A Special Report—The Corporate Woman); Freedman, How To Do Everything Better, Wall St. J., Mar. 24, 1986, §4, at 25D.

39. See Macke, Token Men and Women, 8 Soc. Women & Occupations 25 (1981).

40. See Roos & Reskin, Institutional Factors Contributing to Sex Segregation in the Workplace, in Trends, *supra* note 4, at 235, 242, 248–250.

41. See *id.* at 237–238, 241, 245. When given information about blue collar jobs in a form indicating that the jobs are also for women, women are interested. *Id.*; see also Walshok, *supra* note 16, at 155–170.

42. See Still in Poverty, *supra* note 22, at 19–23.

43. Sylvia Hewlett, A Lesser Life 360 (1986) (quoting school teacher in England). For empirical support, see Hill, The Wage Effects of Marital Status and Children, 14 J. Hum. Resources 4 (1978); Osterman, *supra* note 5.

44. See generally Lenore Weitzman, The Divorce Revolution: The Unexpected Social and Economic Consequences for Women and Children in America (1985).

45. In their reply, Fischel and Lazear criticize me for failing to explain how a comparable worth remedy would work. As they note, I have not identified when comparable worth should be used "to intervene in markets, against whom, and how much." Fischel & Lazear, Comparable Worth: A Rejoinder, 53 U. Chi. L. Rev. 950, 951 (1986).

In the limited space allocated to me, I have purported only to note problems with the objections to comparable worth which Fischel and Lazear consider compelling. They conclude that the "standard market critique of comparable worth is not entirely convincing," since "[m]any situations exist where market prices are not accepted as final." Fischel & Lazear, *supra* note 1, at 894. Fischel and Lazear attempt to build a case against comparable worth independent of the difficulty of measuring worth with a nonmarket standard. Their objections to comparable worth hold even if comparable worth would eliminate discrimination reflected in market wages. I therefore assume, throughout my discussion, that wages under comparable worth would more closely approximate wages in a world without discrimination than do market wages. . . . The purpose of my discussion has been to show that the objections Fischel and Lazear regard as compelling are not. In this, it seems that I have been successful. The debate must therefore shift to whether comparable worth would be a workable and effective remedy.

Social Construction of Skill: Gender, Power, and Comparable Worth

RONNIE J. STEINBERG

... PRIOR TO COMPARABLE WORTH, the wage gap was viewed largely as the result of some combination of inadequate human capital on the part of women and of labor market discrimination. Most economists viewed discrimination as a problem of access —of barriers that either blocked appropriately trained women from entering more complex male jobs or blocked women from obtaining the skills needed to qualify for these jobs.[1] Wage determination was not viewed as distorted but as subject to economic forces. A few economists did stress the role of "market power" as a catchall for empirical outcomes that couldn't be accounted for by economic factors. But even then, discussion of discrimination emphasized flawed analysis.

Comparable worth proponents agreed that allocation processes were flawed. . . . They also suggested that the wage determination process was itself discriminatory. . . .

As pay equity proponents examined job evaluation systems, they uncovered pervasive sex bias in design and application. Since the labor market has never been gender-neutral, assumptions about gender have saturated the structure of compensation. In the nineteenth century, few married women worked outside the home. Single women were only expected to work until marriage.[2] Bound strictly by the "cult of domesticity," these women served as status symbols for their husbands. A successful man was one who could support his family. Women may have taken in boarders, washed clothes, taught school, nursed the sick, worked in factories, or even, by the late nineteenth century, replaced men as clerical workers. But wages paid had built into them the assumption that the woman received primary support from fathers, brothers, and husbands.

Paying women less than men has been built on the ideology that men are the main breadwinners, while women are secondary earners who rely on a man's wage and benefit package. The struggle in the United States over the family wage in the late nineteenth and twentieth centuries was premised entirely on the assumption that men supported families. Both labor and management agreed with these assumptions. The substantial wage increases for men were justified on this basis, allowing for the institutionalization of a two-tiered wage structure.[3]

Such assumptions and ideologies became further institutionalized in the job evaluation systems that rationalize and legitimate the wage structure. The systems of job evaluation currently in widespread use were developed at a time when hiring advertisements said, "Help Wanted—Male" or "Help Wanted—Female." When used today, they impose assumptions about work complexity and work context drawn from the 1940s and 1950s onto an employment situation and a set of jobs that have profoundly changed since that time. . . . Since women's work was especially low-paying at the time of the development of these systems, this method of constructing job evaluation systems assured that the characteristics associated with female jobs would remain uncompensated.

Job evaluation systems were developed largely in manufacturing, craft, and administrative contexts[4] sometimes explicitly designed for male-dominated managerial jobs. For example, Hay offered his Guide Chart-Profiled Method as especially suited to managerial jobs:

> In recent years, a method of evaluating high level jobs has been developed which uses management thinking. Called the Guide Chart-Profile Method, . . . it was developed seven years ago in response to the demand of the Owens-Illinois Company for some explanation, or "rationalization," of a high level salary structure established for one of the company's divisions. . . . The "guide chart" was devised to explain the reasons for suggested job and salary standards—to show management how to evaluate high level jobs by thinking of them in management terms. . . . We have seen that the Guide Chart-Profile Method was designed for a specific purpose—evaluating managerial and technical jobs in order to set equitable salary standards.[5]

The Hay system has undergone minor modifications and is now widely used to evaluate *all* jobs in a firm. Evaluating nonmanagerial jobs in managerial terms has, I suggest in the following, a decided gender effect.

There are several ways in which conventional job evaluation systems embed in their design outdated cultural assumptions about work that have the effect of devaluing activities performed by women. The major sources of sex bias found in evaluation frameworks and job descriptions are summarized here.[6] Few specific systems of job evaluation include all of these problems, but most systems contain many biases.

The Prerequisites, Tasks, and Work Content Associated with Women's Work Are Invisible

The central defining characteristics of jobs are often perceived in terms that are consistent with sex-role stereotypes. Authority is part of the male sex role, and everyone sees the authority associated with male work, while the authority associated with female work is invisible. Male managers are perceived as running offices and departments. Yet the daily work of the secretary in passing on messages, responding to emergencies, training new employees, and coordinating schedules for meetings and other activities remains invisible, especially if she performs these responsibilities competently. So too is the authority and coordination involved in the provision of services, where teamwork requires that the work get performed without resorting to formal authority. Thus the invisibility of women's work may extend beyond job tasks to alternative forms of work organization.

Hospital settings provide a good example of how sex stereotypes inform perceptions of jobs. Ward clerks are thought to perform routine clerical functions. Yet one of the things they do routinely is handle the family of a patient in a crisis situation, allowing medical staff to treat the patient. When these workers execute their tasks smoothly, no one notices what they are doing.

For another example, compare firefighters and flight attendants in relation to perceived responsibilities for handling crisis that involve decisions about life and death. The skills of firefighters in handling emergencies are central to conventional understandings about their job. Even though the time spent by a firefighter in handling these emergencies is relatively small, he is fully compensated for this aspect of his work. Few realize that the position of flight attendant emerged as a result of Federal Aviation Administration regulations requiring trained staff to work with passengers in case of an emergency. The emotional, communication, and food distribution skills of flight attendants evolved as a way to make use of the extra personnel under normal circumstances. Nonetheless, the emergency skills of the flight attendant—while not as complex as those of a firefighter—remain invisible and uncompensated.[7]

Frequently overlooked characteristics in job evaluation systems include the following:

Skill in the area of communication, coordination, emotional work in crisis situations, fine motor movement, operating and calibrating technical equipment, establishing and maintaining recordkeeping systems, and writing and editing others' correspondence and reports;

Effort, such as concentration, stress from inflexible deadlines, lifting people, listening for long periods, sitting for long periods, getting work accomplished without resort to formal sources of control and authority, and performing multiple tasks simultaneously;

Responsibility, such as protecting confidentiality, caring for patients, clients and inmates, representing the organization through communications with the public, preventing damage to technical equipment and instruments, and actual or proximate (as opposed to formal or ultimate) responsibility;

Working condition, such as exposure to disease and human waste, emotional overload, stress from communication with difficult and angry clients, working in open office spaces, and stress from multiple role demands.

In job evaluation systems, working with mentally ill or retarded persons may be overlooked as a stressful working condition, while working with noisy machinery is not. The range of undesirable working conditions out-of-doors is elaborated in a job evaluation framework, while the range of office arrangements is treated as if all clerical, administrative, professional, and managerial workers are given the same type of office space and privacy. The concentration involved in reading heating system gauges may be recognized and evaluated, while the eyestrain associated with reading technical instruments or working on VDTs is ignored. Often this form of bias arises when job evaluation systems developed for one set of (primarily male administrative) job classes are applied to other (primarily clerical, service, and health) job classes.

The invisibility of tasks and prerequisites found in women's work extends into the composite descriptions that are used to evaluate jobs. In general, pay equity proponents found that male jobs were described in considerably greater detail than female jobs. . . . These descriptions are problematic because they serve as the information source for the evaluation process. [Also,] the more vague the job description, the greater the likelihood that preconceived stereotypes about jobs will enter into determinations of job complexity. . . .

One reason why skills and responsibilities in female jobs remained invisible until recently may be that, for women's work, we not only selectively perceive job content on the basis of sex stereotypes but we confuse the content of the *job* with stereotypic notions about the characteristics of the *jobholder*. Why else would a dog catcher's work be viewed as more complex than that of a nursery school teacher? While the commonly held assumption that women have better fine-finger coordination has been used to hire them as typists and in electronic assembling work, it has also been used to dismiss the complexity of these jobs.[8] Yet no job evaluation system of which I am aware acknowledges the skills necessary to perform this work at the pace required in most industrial and clerical settings.

A second reason why women's skills remained invisible may be that until the emergence of comparable worth, women did not contest the values embedded in job evaluation systems. Job evaluation systems emerged to legitimate and gain further control of existing wage hierarchies. They proved useful to employers in union contexts, enabling them to point to an external seemingly nonarbitrary technical rationale for paying some workers more than others.[9] . . .

The Prerequisites, Tasks, and Work Context Associated with Women's Work Are Included in the Evaluation Framework but Are Not Valued at Equivalent Levels of Complexity as Those That Favor Male Classes

Another way in which job evaluation frameworks embed gender bias is by defining factors and the levels of complexity within factors, such that characteristics differentially found in male work are emphasized and rated as more complex. For example, conventional job evaluation frameworks usually include a measure of contact with people. [C]omplexity of contact is defined as a function of the level in the organizational hierarchy of the person being contact: The contact with higher-status persons is defined as inherently more complex. Yet because higher positions tend to be male-dominated while female jobs are much more likely to involve contact with clients and patients, the definition of this factor is biased in the direction of more highly valuing the content of male jobs.

Similarly, responsibility factors are typically oriented toward scope of financial assets: The greater one's fiscal responsibility, the higher the job evaluation points. Few conventional systems give any points for the responsibility of caring for troubled, sick, or dying patients. Even those organizations that have recently modified such systems to achieve pay equity give responsibility for human life considerably lower complexity levels than fiscal responsibility. . . .

Women's work is treated as invisible in the definition of job factors, just as in the description of jobs. Since nurses aides' work requires few education or experience prerequisites in most jurisdictions, it is likely to be rated as involving a lower level of knowledge than that of a parking lot attendant, simply because the definition of knowledge in most systems allows for more points when jobs involve working with "simple equipment and machines." Most clerical positions are rated below entry-level craft work, because such features as knowledge of grammar, the ability to compose original letters, and being able to perform several skills simultaneously are not included in definitions of technical skill. While credentials for engineers translate into a high rating on technical know-how, the credentials and technical knowledge of librarians are not regarded as "specialized knowledge."[10]

Gender bias on job evaluation measures sometimes occurs because job evaluation systems designed for one type of work organization are uncritically applied to another type organized on a different basis. The Ontario (Canada) Hospital Association endorsed a nine-factor job evaluation system for all the province's hospitals, which was strongly oriented to job classes found in administrative settings where decision making is organized bureaucratically with clear, formal lines of command. Six of the nine factors define managerial decision making and responsibilities as involving the most complex work.[11] This creates problems for evaluating professional and service-provision hospital jobs, where decision making and work are organized less hierarchically, involving more teamwork. In this job evaluation system, by definition, any job class involved in the provision of medical care is less complex than any job class involved in administrative or managerial work. This lack of organizational fit has a strong gender effect: Hospital administration positions have historically been male-dominated. Professional and service-provision occupations in hospitals are overwhelmingly female-dominated. While seemingly neutral, such systems are biased in favor of job content found in historically male job classes and against historically female job classes. . . .

The Weights Assigned to Factors Differentially Associated with Men's Job Classes Are Substantially Higher Than the Weights Assigned to Factors Differentially Associated with Women's Classes

Gender bias also results because job characteristics associated with men's work are differentially and positively valued in the construction of factors and factor weights while the job characteristics found in women's work are either not valued or negatively valued when other job characteristics are taken into account. In the Hay Guide-Chart system, one of the major a priori job evaluation systems available to firms, the skill factor, labeled Know-How, is constructed as a matrix of three subfactors: technical know-how, managerial know-how, and human relations know-how. Each job class receives one score for Know-How, which is a function of the level of complexity of the class on each subfactor. The managerial know-how scale, defined largely in terms of the characteristics of male managerial work,[12] is allocated five times the weight assigned to human relations know-how. Technical know-how receives seven times the point value of human relations know-how. Although human relations skills are differentially associated with women's work, the Hay system defines it to include both working with people and supervising other employees.

This has two consequences. First, all managers receive points for supervision on both the managerial and the human relations subfactors. By contrast, nurse supervisors receive points only for their client responsibilities. This double-counts managerial human relations and penalizes those whose jobs require both managerial human relations and skills and responsibilities associated with service provision and caretaking.

Consider two jobs—RN and carpenter. The fact that the RN works with patients is likely to increase her know-how points from 175 to 230. However, a carpenter promoted to a supervisory position might increase one's total know-how points from 230 to 400 because of the combined effect of technical know-how and human relations know-how.[13]

The weighting of factors also favors male job classes by evaluating the same job content in several different factors, a so-called double-counting. Since the act of supervision is already part of the definition of different levels of organizational know-how, giving additional points for supervision under human relations know-how means counting the same characteristic twice. . . .

Evaluation Committees Used Inconsistent Standards for Assessing the Complexity of Male Jobs and Female Jobs

Bias in the treatment of women's work often enters into the process of evaluation. A frequently used approach involves establishing evaluation committees comprising personnel staff or a diverse group of employees who are trained in the application of the evaluation system by compensation consultants. [J]ob evaluation points have been unevenly applied across female and male jobs by such committees.

[One] example is drawn from the job evaluation phase of a pay equity study of Oregon. . . . Job evaluation committees of nonmanagerial employees were created to evaluate all nonmanagerial jobs. The committees contained both male and female employees from a diverse range of occupations. As part of the evaluation process, committee members routinely supplemented specifications with their personal knowledge of the tasks and responsibilities associated with a job. [Male committee members] questioned the women's authority when they suggested that the jobs being evaluated were more complex than the specification suggested. This made it difficult to achieve a consensus on job worth. As a result, the points assigned to the female jobs in question were always lower than what they would have been had the information been taken into account. By contrast, the women on the committee never questioned the authority of the men or the information they added to the job specifications. This information was taken into account in determining job complexity, resulting in higher point scores than would be the case based on the specifications alone. Even when women are represented on evaluation committees, their ability to effectively win their claims about the complexity of women's work is limited by male images of women's jobs.[14]

Redesigning Job Evaluation: The Politics of Skill Reconstruction

How have advocates of comparable worth fared in their efforts to redefine the concepts and techniques used to evaluate women's work? Not well, as the following case material illustrates. As recently as the mid-1970s, federal court judges found it possible to rule against comparable worth suits even as they acknowledged the validity of their claims. For example, in a case comparing registered nurses to more highly paid tree trimmers, the judges remarked:

> [The] skills [of nurses] are such that in a truly egalitarian society, [they] would receive more money [than tree trimmers] . . . [the nurses] have established that, by and large, male-dominated occupations probably pay more for comparable work than is paid in occupations dominated by females.

These same judges also viewed this case as "pregnant with the possibility of disrupting the entire economic system of the United States."[15]

The roots of comparable worth can be found in the 19th-century demand for equal pay for equal work, although the first national test case was brought before the War Labor Board in 1945 by the electrical workers union against General Electric and Westinghouse. The Board sustained the union's claims of sex discrimination in sex-segregated compensation practices. Unfortunately, the Board's powers provided only for voluntary compliance. The companies failed to comply.[16]

In 1962, comparable worth (then called equal pay for work of equal value) resurfaced momentarily in early drafts of federal equal pay legislation. Even with the strong endorsement of the Kennedy administration and intense lobbying by unions and women's groups, direct business opposition prevailed and the bill's standards were watered down to allow only for equal pay for equal work.[17]

Comparable worth did not surface again as a political demand until the early 1970s, when a number of states and municipalities undertook comparable worth studies using job evaluation methodologies. From its inception in World War II, comparable worth has been closely associated with job evaluation, to the extent that the most widely used definition sees it as "the application of a single, bias-free point factor job evaluation system within a given establishment, across job families, both to rank-order jobs and to set salaries."[18] Ironically, in their efforts to achieve pay equity, proponents have invoked the very job evaluation systems they identified as the source of the problem. To a certain extent they viewed these systems as tools that would facilitate their claims to undervaluation. As we shall see, existing job evaluation systems have proved to be a two-edged sword.

Comparable worth has been a decentralized reform focused mainly on public sector employment.[19] The National Committee on Pay Equity[20] estimated that, by 1989, all but four states have taken some action on pay equity and that over 2,000 political subdivisions have implemented pay equity adjustments. For the purpose of understanding the essential features of the struggle over the redefinition of women's work, these initiatives can be divided into three broad phases.

Phase 1

Early pay equity initiatives . . . relied primarily on unmodified job evaluation systems, largely for reasons of political expediency. In Washington State, a pay equity study was funded on the heels of a job evaluation study of management jobs. State managerial jobs had been found to be undervalued relative to comparable private sector jobs. Proponents were able to get the same procedures applied to a comparison of male and female jobs within the state.[21] Sixteen years, one major court case, and four studies later, the state agreed to a modest implementation plan that would adjust female wages over 5-year period.

In San Jose, proponents also piggybacked their study off of a study of management salaries. The management study was implemented without controversy. The pay equity study was not. After lengthy attempts to negotiate, the union went out on strike, which facilitated a settlement with the female-headed city council.[22]

In Minnesota, a study of state jobs had already been conducted using a conventional job evaluation system, but it had not been implemented. The state's Commission on the Status of Women reanalyzed the data to determine the pay gap for male and female jobs of equivalent complexity. The gap in pay averaged between 5% and 20%. The Commission drafted legislation proposing that inequities be eliminated. The legislation passed. The relative success of this initiative rests on a unique conjunction of factors: (a) a completed job evaluation study that had not been proposed by feminists, (b) the Commission on the Status of Women with close ties to the governor and legislative leadership, (c) little interest group organization for or against, and (d) reasonable wage adjustments. The legislature was operating with a budget surplus, and the unions were supportive. To implement this among state employees, the governor promoted the executive director of the Commission to be the head of the personnel department that would implement the wage adjustments.[23]

Yet, in each of these cases, existing systems of job evaluation remained intact, perpetuating gender bias and the invisibility of skills and responsibilities found in women's jobs.[24] Indeed, in two of the three early studies, the job evaluation system used to estimate wage discrimination was the one that had been most visibly criticized by technical proponents. Despite their knowledge of these more general critiques of this system, the Minnesota Commission leadership believed that to modify the job evaluation system would have been costly in terms of money, time, and political success. They didn't risk it. Incumbents of female jobs received salary increases of 5% to 20%.

Only Connecticut set out to conduct a job evaluation from scratch. The first study resulted in a second, general classification study of all state jobs, partially as a result of the final report of the compensation consultant who conducted the first study. This recommendation, of course, is in the interest of the consultant, as it could generate more business. In this case, the study is still underway over a decade later, impeded by labor-management battles that created long delays. Each modification to the job evaluation system has involved months of conflict, with little change in the end.

These early precedents resulted in modest pay equity adjustments. Not surprising, the implementation plans that grew out of further political negotiations watered down even more the already limited technical results. In Washington State, pay equity adjustments for incumbents of female jobs are being brought up to 5% below the average pay line—which includes female wages that had been found to be discriminatory. In San Jose, California, wages for undervalued female jobs are being brought up to 10% below the male pay line, meaning that female classes will now make, on average, 10% less than male classes of equivalent job complexity. In Connecticut, interim adjustments varied by union.

The impact of these early outcomes on later initiatives was contradictory. On one hand, they translated a political demand into a policy outcome, making it easier for later proponents to argue that it was a feasible political objective. Yet, on the other hand, they set tight boundaries on how others could use job evaluation. Any attempt to modify existing systems of job evaluation was now made even more difficult because policymakers and administrators faced with demands for comparable pay could point to Washington, Minnesota, San Jose, and a few other early efforts as evidence that using an unmodified system was good enough to achieve pay equity.

Phase 2

A second phase of pay equity initiatives emerged in the early 1980s. Spurred by the first round of successes, the impact of the gender gap of the 1982 elections, positive court cases, and a favorable report on the feasibility of pay equity released by the National Research Council, proponents in many states and municipalities fought for pay equity studies that would be based on the use of modified systems of job evaluation.

By this point, many proponents were aware of the technical difficulties involved in the design and use of conventional job evaluation systems. Yet political and organizational factors often kept them from translating this knowledge into policy initiatives. Often, proponents lost control over efforts to redesign the job evaluation process, with serious consequences for the resulting pay equity adjustments. In addition, proponents underestimated the strength and strategies of administrators and policymakers in containing comparable worth initiatives.[25]

Most strategies of containment involved manipulation of the process and results of job evaluation. Tactics generally involved taking control of job evaluation away from proponents, while maintaining the appearance of their full participation. The result is that existing job evaluation systems emerge largely intact, are relegitimated, and adjustments for wage discrimination turn out to be less costly than annual cost-of-living adjustments.[26]

In some cases, administrators and policymakers have succeeded in turning political decisions into technical decisions that can then be removed from the realm of negotiation. In such cases, unilateral control over the study of wage discrimination has often been placed in the hands of personnel administrators, who can then select which consultants will be used. This seems to be the price for achieving a study in the first place. Personnel administrators have defended their expertise, neutrality, and jurisdiction over this matter with great success. Often a condition for allocating labor-management monies for a study has been this unilateral control, on the grounds that the wage structures—opposed to the wage levels not bargainable under the law.

Even when a compensation consultant agrees to modify a system, it is easy to do so in appearance only. An Oregon task force debated with the consultant hired to conduct their study about gender bias in several factor definitions. With great resistance, the consultant agreed to several modifications, one of which was to a "Human Relations" factor. It stretched a three-level factor into five levels. After the State jobs had been evaluated, the consultant admitted that "a job with [the highest] level of skill probably did not exist in the state of Oregon."[27] By the time the task force understood this, most of the evaluations had been completed. To undo this consultant manipulation would cost additional money, delay the announcement of the findings, and require the task force members to explain to their constituencies how they had allowed this to happen.

In other cases, administrators have sought to contain comparable worth initiatives by withholding information, making it impossible for advocates to develop a counter-proposal in a timely fashion. In New York State, for example, a proponent-directed study was followed by a second, state-controlled "interim study," employing a technical staff of 17 full-time state employees. Funded by joint labor-management monies, the technical unit was unilaterally controlled by management, arguing that the union was entitled to "meet and confer" on issues of classification. The unions were updated regularly on the progress of the unit and had no reason to believe that the state was acting in bad faith.

Some two years later, the pay equity adjustments recommended by the state were a shock to the leadership of the two unions, especially to the union representing entry-level professional employees. With no warning, the state recommended significant wage downgrades for almost one half of all the classes in the professional bargaining unit. The leadership of this union, caught off guard and without its own information base, and with its membership having waited over 5 years for the study results, ended up trading off any pay equity adjustments in order to avoid pay downgrades. The state recommendations were timed to dovetail with union elections, forcing the leadership to accommodate state offers of tradeoffs rather than jeopardize their elected positions. For the other union, representing clerical and hospital workers as well as operational jobs, the recommendations, while low, were good enough for their leadership to save face.

In still other cases, administrators have placed proponents in a minority position on a task force or advisory committee, seeking to divide them, or to push them out entirely after they have succeeded in gaining monies to undertake a study. In Hawaii, New Hampshire, North Carolina, and Vermont, advocates were excluded from all decisions surrounding the job evaluation study. Not one of these studies was completed.

One group is often offered special privileges or fuller information as a way to divide a potential coalition. Unions are frequently privileged and women's groups marginalized, on the argument that unions formally represent the incumbents of historically male jobs. Unfortunately, not all unions have supported pay equity. Others must balance the claims of their women workers with those of the more powerful male membership. This has been used to great advantage by administrators. Acker showed that in Oregon, unions representing male employees actively opposed the reform in the legislature, facilitating managerial objectives.[28]

Even during this second phase of the evolution of pay equity policy, the reconstruction of evaluation systems for women's jobs took second place to other routes for obtaining wage adjustments. Specifically, with little consensus over this reform and an intractable compensation consultant, it proved easier to achieve consistency in the application of existing systems (i.e., to receive the same number of job complexity points and the same point-to-pay relationship for a given educational requirement, for example) than to achieve the redesign of systems.

Thus pay equity has resulted in wage adjustments to millions of employees working in historically female jobs. But it has not yet resulted in the social redefinition of women's work. In taking the very systems of job evaluation that they have criticized and utilizing them to estimate the extent of wage discrimination, they failed to appreciate the extent to which these systems, in the hands of others, could be used to legitimate the existing wage hierarchy. . . .

Phase 3

Fortunately, the efforts to achieve comparable worth have moved into a third phase that builds on these lessons. Utilizing technical knowledge of gender bias, proponents are conducting unilateral pay equity studies. The Pay Equity Program of the National Education Association has designed a job evaluation system customized to positively value the distinctive characteristics of nonteacher school staff, including food service workers, librarians, secretaries, and teaching assistants. The Collective Bargaining Committee of Local 34, Federation of University Employees, at Yale University realigned the jobs in its bargaining unit without recourse to a job evaluation study. It placed the new wage structure on the bargaining table. Yale accepted the union's proposed reorganization. Wage adjustments amounted to an average of 28%. The union and the university are jointly supervising a job evaluation study to create a new evaluation system that will legitimate the new ordering of jobs.

Proponents are also maintaining greater control of every phase of the job evaluation process. In Philadelphia, a proponent consulting firm was hired to feminize the standard job evaluation system operating in the jurisdiction. In Ann Arbor, Michigan, the same consulting firm designed a customized system based on achieving gender neutrality given state-of-the-art technical knowledge. Among other actions to protect their interests, proponents in both cities hired a technical monitor to review the work of the consultant at every juncture of the study. In Boston, a coalition of union and women's organizations has turned an advisory committee into an advocate-controlled decision-making body that reviews all the details of the job evaluation process. This group stopped the initiative when the city excluded it from choosing the job evaluation consultant and went public with their complaints. The consulting firm chosen was one of the two proponent firms that had submitted proposals. While none of these initiatives has been implemented, they already have gone farther than any undertaken in Phases 1 or 2.

Finally, legislation in Ontario, Canada, explicitly prohibits gender bias in systems of job evaluation and extends pay equity to the private sector.[29] Unfortunately, the government has thus far only issued guidelines about gender neutrality, preferring instead to allow its scope to be determined through labor-management negotiations. The law established the Pay Equity Tribunal to consider unresolved issues.[30]

The comparable worth movement offers a unique opportunity . . . to examine basic questions about the character of work, the dynamics of complex organizations, the contours of new social movements, and determinants of social reform. [W]e must develop a more sophisticated understanding of the political and cultural factors that surround economic processes, especially an understanding of the gendered character of the labor market. We need to understand how our ideas about gender shape what we see and don't see and influence what is considered appropriate, productive, and valuable work.

Notes

1. P. England & D. Dunn, Evaluating Work and Comparable Worth, 14 Ann. Rev. Soc. 227 (1988).

2. A. Kessler-Harris, Out to Work: A History of Wage-Earning Women in the United States (Oxford Univ. Press, 1982); J. Matthaei, An Economic History of American Women (Schocken, 1982).

3. E. Boris & P. Bardaglio, The Impact of the State on the Family and the Economy, 1790–1945, in N. Gerstel and H. Gross eds., Families and Work, 132 (Temple Univ. Press, 1987); M. May, The Historical Problem of the Family Wage: The Ford Motor Company and the Five-Dollar Pay, in Gerstel and Gross, *supra*, at 111–131.

4. D. Treiman, Job Evaluation: An Analytic Review (Washington, D.C.: National Research Council, 1979).

5. E. Hay, Setting Salary Standards for Executive Jobs, 34 Personnel 63–65, 72 (1958).

6. This review of types of sex bias is not comprehensive. It emphasizes those fea-

tures of job evaluation systems that treat characteristics found in historically female work differently than characteristics more prevalent in male jobs. A second, major category of bias in job evaluation systems involves inconsistencies in valuing the same job characteristics in historically female and male jobs.

7. A. Hochschild, The Managed Heart: Commercialization of Human Feeling (Univ. California Press, 1983).

8. J. Brecher, The Roots of Power: Employers and Workers in the Electrical Products Industry, in A. Zimbalist ed., Case Studies in the Labor Process 229 (Monthly Review Press, 1979); M. Davies, Women's Place Is at the Typewriter (Temple Univ. Press, 1982).

9. Treiman, *supra* note 4, at 4–5.

10. Blake and Schneider, personal communication, 1989.

11. L. Haignere, Pay Equity Implementation: Experimentation Negotiation, Mediation, Litigation Aggravation and Compensation (paper presented at the Conference on Pay Equity: Theory and Practice, York Univ., May 1990).

12. J. Acker, Doing Comparable Worth (Temple Univ. Press, 1989).

13. R. Steinberg & L. Haignere, Review of Massachusetts Statewide Classification and Compensation System for Achieving Comparable Worth 170 (Albany, NY: Center for Women in Government, 1987).

14. Acker, *supra* note 12, at 91–98.

15. Lemons v. City and County of Denver, 17 FEP Case 906, as quoted in R. Feldberg, Comparable Worth and Nurses in the United States (unpublished manuscript, 1990).

16. R. Milkman, Gender at Work: The Dynamics of Job Segregation by Sex During World War II (Univ. Illinois Press, 1987).

17. G. Milkovich & A. Broderick, Pay Discrimination: Legal Issues and Implications for Research, 21 Indus. Rel. 309 (1982).

18. H. Remick, Major Issues in A Priori Applications in H. Remick ed., Comparable Worth and Wage Discrimination (Temple Univ. Press, 1984).

19. There are several reasons why pay equity emerged first in the public sector. Proponents wanted to avoid direct confrontation with business opposition in getting the reform off the ground. The emergence of comparable worth also intersected with a vigorous organizing drive of public sector employees. Since a disproportionate percentage of women workers are found in public sector employment, comparable worth becomes an obvious way for unions to establish their commitment to the needs of women workers. Finally, comparable worth was pushed forward by state and local groups, such as the Commission on the Status of Women.

20. Pay Equity Activity in the Public Sector, 1979–1989 (Washington, D.C., National Committee on Pay Equity, 1989).

21. F. Hutner, Equal Pay for Comparable Worth: The Working Women's Issue of the Eighties (New York: Praeger, 1986); H. Remick, Beyond Equal Pay for Equal Work: Comparable Worth in the State of Washington, in R. Steinberg Ratner ed., Equal Employment Policy for Women 405 (Temple Univ. Press, 1980).

22. J. Flammang, Effective Implementation: The Case of Comparable Worth in San Jose, 5 Pol'y Stud. Rev. 815 (1986); J. Flammang, Women Make a Difference: Comparable Worth in San Jose, in M. Katzenstein & C. Mueller eds., The Women's Movements in the United States and Western Europe (Temple Univ. Press, 1987).

23. S. Evans & B. Nelson, Wage Justice: Comparable Worth and the Paradox of Technocratic Reform (Univ. Chicago Press, 1989).

24. Although the methods for describing and evaluating jobs were not modified, the studies corrected for part of the wage gap. This occurred because the study carried out consistent procedures between historically female and male jobs. In addition, all jobs were evaluated by the same job evaluation framework. While these represent modifications, they do not positively value job characteristics differentially found in women's work.

25. R. Steinberg, Job Evaluation and Managerial Control: The Politics of Technique and the Techniques of Politics (paper presented at the Conference on Pay Equity: Theory and Practice, York University, May 1990).

26. Haignere, *supra* note 11; Steinberg, *supra* note 25.

27. Acker, *supra* note 12, at 189.

28. *Id.* The role of unions and comparable worth has been mixed. Unions have been responsible for moving the reform forward and for limiting its impact. In some instances, unions representing different and sex-segregated bargaining units have fought each other. In other instances the same union has acted differently in different places, depending on whether the specific bargaining unit represented female classes or male classes. Most common, bargaining units with a mix of segregated classes will negotiate a settlement with management without much stand against low wage adjustments.

29. Pay Equity Act, R.S.O., ch. 34 (1988) (Can.). The Pay Equity Act, enacted in the province of Ontario in 1987, required that employers with 100 or more employees review their job classifications in selected female-dominated occupations to determine the extent of gender discrimination in pay practices. Where unions represent employees, it requires that corrections for wage discrimination be undertaken through joint labor-management negotiation and through the use of job comparison systems that are gender neutral. The "value" of the work carried out in the normal performance of the job is the basis upon which wage adjustments between equivalent male and female jobs are made. For a discussion of the Act and especially of its shortcomings, see, N. Kubasek, J. Johnson, and N.M. Browne, Comparable Worth in Ontario: Lessons the United States Can Learn, 17 Harv. Women's L.J. 103.

30. For a discussion of Tribunal decisions on gender neutrality in job evaluation see R. Steinberg, & L. Walters, Making Women's Work Visible: The Case of Nursing; First Steps in the Design of a Gender-Neutral Comparison System, Proceedings, Third Institute for Women's Policy Research Conference. Washington, D.C., June 1992; R. Steinberg, & J. Jacobs, Pay Equity in Nonprofit Organizations: Making Women's Work Visible, in M. O'Neill & T. Odendahl, eds., Women and Power in the Nonprofit Sector 79 (John Wiley, 1994).

B. Sexual Harassment

Introduction

Despite the increase in the proportion of women in the labor force, women workers continue to face significant problems in the workplace. One gender-specific problem is sexual harassment.[1] Studies suggest that between 40 percent to 80 percent of working women have experienced some form of sexual harassment.[2] Many feminists currently regard sexual harassment as a form of violence similar to rape and battering.[3]

Sexual harassment in employment poses a serious barrier to women's equality. As writer Lin Farley notes:

> [J]ob segregation by sex is to a large degree sustained by male sexual harassment. This abuse is already rolling back the momentum of affirmative action and it will continue to coerce women by means of severe economic and emotional abuse into over-crowded, sexually-segregated job categories. . . . At the same time, the abuse also impacts destructively [by] disrupting female job attachment, promoting female unemployment and inhibiting female solidarity.[4]

Law professor Nadine Taub concurs that sexual harassment is a barrier to equal opportunity, although she describes the problem somewhat differently:

> Unreciprocated sexual advances do not represent harmless expressions of interpersonal attraction. Rather, like rape, they are exercises in male power and reminders of women's inferior status and traditional role as sexual object. As such, they are an important cause of absenteeism and job turnover; they also make it harder for women to perform their jobs well.[5]

Catharine MacKinnon, probably the most famous scholar on the subject, believes that sexual harassment impedes equality in two ways: "by using [woman's] employment position to coerce her sexually, while using her sexual position to coerce her economically."[6] Every incident of sexual harassment reproduces, MacKinnon writes, "the inequitable social structure of male supremacy and female subordination which [anti-discrimination legislation] seeks to eliminate."[7]

Sexual harassment is related to women's position in the workplace, although the nature of that link is subject to speculation. While some writers concur with Farley (above) that sexual harassment is a causal factor of sex segregation in employment,[8] other writers suggest that, perhaps, sexual harassment is the result of occupational segregation. For example, Goodman writes that sexual harassment is a consequence of women's subordinate place in the labor market.[9] She explains that, because of the sexual stratification of the workplace, many women workers are subordinate to male superiors. Women's low status, she suggests, makes them especially vulnerable to harassment.[10]

Catharine MacKinnon takes a more interactive view. MacKinnon argues that sexual harassment is both cause and consequence of women's segregation in the labor force.

> [T]he sexual harassment of women can occur largely because women occupy inferior job positions and job roles; at the same time, sexual harassment works to keep women in such positions. Sexual harassment then, uses and helps create women's structurally inferior status.[11]

Another subject of speculation concerns the extent to which sexual harassment in sex-segregated jobs differs from that in nontraditional jobs. Sexual harassment may be more prevalent in the latter.[12] Moreover, the function of sexual harassment may differ. One commentator suggests: "The function of sexual harassment in nontraditional jobs is to keep women out; its function in the traditional female job section is to keep women down."[13]

Although evidence reveals that sexual harassment of women workers is longstanding,[14] the practice first garnered public attention in 1975.[15] Prior to that time, no term existed to describe the phenomenon.[16] In that year, two feminist activists at Cornell University's Human Affairs Program received a request for assistance from administrative assistant Carmita Wood, who was employed in a university laboratory.[17] Unable to endure sexual harassment by her supervisor, Wood resigned. After the denial of her application for unemployment insurance, she requested assistance from the Human Affairs Program. The feminist investigators sent requests for case studies to three hundred women's organizations and organized a conference in Ithaca. Later, the activists, with Wood and a university professor, formed Working Women United. Although the organization originally focused on unionizing women, it subsequently altered its focus to sexual harassment.[18]

The women's movement was slow to recognize sexual harassment as a feminist issue. Scholars suggests several reasons: (1) women (especially the successful and highly skilled) deny sexual harassment, in part because of being threatened by being judged as sexual objects; (2) some victims (especially middle class women) resolve the harassment by quitting; and (3) women perceive harassment as personal, feeling guilty that they may have provoked it.[19] Backhouse and Cohen pose additional explanations, suggesting that the recent increase in the numbers of women employed outside the home has augmented the incidence of sexual harassment and also that more middle-class women recognize the centrality of work, making them take harassment more seriously.[20]

Backhouse and Cohen point, too, to the influence of the rape crisis movement in focusing attention on sexual harassment.

> Another theory ties the discussion of sexual harassment to that of rape—pointing out that rape, too was a closet issue about which few people spoke out until recently. Women rape victims feared reprisals and personal attack from a society which viewed rape victims with some suspicion and dislike. . . . Sexual harassment can be seen as a sub-issue of rape, and in the more enlightened climate of the present, women are less afraid to challenge sexual harassment in the workplace.[21]

Literature continues to emphasize the relationship between sexual harassment and rape. Some researchers suggest that victims of rape and harassment experience similar effects.[22] Legal theorists also explore theoretical links in the essays herein. Early literature on sexual harassment, prompted by the 1975 Ithaca conference, consists of anecdotal accounts.[23] Studies were conducted, such as the 1976 *Redbook* survey, that revealed that 88% of women had experienced sexual harassment and 92% considered it serious.[24] Researchers conducted additional studies as well.[25]

Sociological and psychological studies focus on myths concerning sexual harassment, paradigms, and causal factors. Myths include the following: men view harassment as "fun" or as "compliments"; sexual harassment is regarded as trivial; sexual harassment affects only women in low-status jobs; women have responsibility to control the expression of sexuality in the workplace; and women can handle harassment with ease.[26] Another myth, present in the rape context too, is that women make false accusations.[27]

Theory also consists of relevant paradigms. Early contributions to feminist theory analogize sexual harassment to prostitution.[28] Silverman applies this analogy to understand the causes of sexual harassment, leading her to speculate that women's inferior economic condition requires them to trade sexual services for economic benefits.[29]

Other early writing analogizes sexual harassment to rape.[30] One article terms sexual harassment "the executive's alternative to rape."[31] A sociological study likens sexual harassment to "economic rape"[32]—coercion exerted on women so needy of employment that they believe they must suffer sexual advances. Gutek explains the rape analogy as illustrative of "the power perspective" of sexual harassment.[33]

Literature also proposes additional conceptual frameworks. Tangri, Burt, and Johnson develop the following models to explain harassment: (1) the natural/biological model (sexual harassment is a manifestation of natural attractions between people); (2) the organizational model (sexual harassment is the result of certain opportunity structures within organizations, such as hierarchies); and (3) the sociocultural model (sexual harassment reflects male dominance over women in society in general and work in particular).[34] Gutek contributes the "sex role spillover" model, consisting of the carryover of gender-based expectations into the workplace (that women are expected to be sex objects).[35] Still other authors identify the variables contributing to harassment as follows:

> 1) at the macro level: socioeconomic inequalities, societal sex roles attitudes, societal sex ratios, economic conditions, the nature of the labor market, and legal sanctions;
> 2) at the organizational level: status or power differentials in the workplace, organizational climate, type of technology, task design, employee composition, and sex ratios;
> 3) at the individual level: intent, motivation, attitudinal and demographic variables, attitudes about harassment, and information processing styles and strategies of the victim and offender.[36]

Also exploring the causal factors, sociologist Diana Russell suggests the role of sex role socialization, social control, and the pursuit of men's economic self-interest.[37] Russell adds that cultural values (the view that woman's place is in the home) encourage men to sexually harass women.[38]

Feminist Philosophical Perspectives on Sexual Harassment

Feminist writing on sexual harassment stems from several philosophical perspectives. Early theory associated sexual harassment with the emergence of capitalism.[39] From a socialist feminist perspective, Lin Farley draws on the work of political economist Heidi Hartmann[40] to argue that, before capitalism, men controlled the work of women and children in the family. Capitalism threatened male power by instituting a market for women's labor. Sexual harassment, according to Farley, is a manifestation of this continuing patriarchal control.[41]

Early writing, as mentioned above, propounded the view that sexual harassment, similar to rape, is characterized by power rather than by sex.[42] Subsequent writers continue this theme.[43] Radical feminists, especially, assert that both employment discrimination and sexual harassment are the results of male dominance.[44] Men's dominant role in the labor force results in the "sexualization of the woman worker as a part of the job."[45]

For liberal feminist theorists, women's equality in employment is only one of many issues. Although they have sought laws requiring equal pay for equal work, and prohibitions against employment discrimination (hiring, promotion, and so forth), they have not targeted sexual harassment as a special concern.

Socialist feminists, however, have addressed the practice, based on their concern with problems facing women workers. On a practical level, socialist feminists have organized women workers in an effort to improve working conditions in general,[46] and to eliminate sexual harassment in particular.[47]

By far the most important contribution to the field has come from radical feminist Catharine MacKinnon, who played a major role in legal recognition of sexual harassment as a form of sex discrimination in employment. Professor Cass Sunstein characterizes MacKinnon's impact as "one of the more dramatic and rapid changes in legal and social understanding in recent years."[48] Specifically, MacKinnon crafted Title VII into a tool to combat sexual harassment[49] and also facilitated judicial recognition of the "hostile environment theory." Her role is explained further below.

Development of Legal Theory

Legal literature on sexual harassment dates to 1976, the same time as psychological and sociological research on the subject. Early law review articles discussed particular cases[50] and possible legal remedies,[51] and furnished advice for practitioners confronted with these new causes of action.[52] Gradually, commentators turned their focus to Title VII[53] and, after promulgation of the EEOC Guidelines in 1980, criticized these guidelines.[54] Some commentators explored sexual harassment in other contexts (such as educational and medical settings).[55] Despite the steady growth of the body of legal articles, legal theory has been slow to develop. With the exception of Catharine MacKinnon's work,[56] early legal theory was virtually nonexistent.

In 1974, when MacKinnon began writing her landmark work, *Sexual Harassment of Working Women,* no court had held that sexual harassment was sex discrimination. In fact, as MacKinnon points out, several courts had held that it was not.[57] A number of federal courts dismissed initial cases that questioned whether employers' conduct constituted sexual discrimination that violated Title VII.[58]

In 1975 MacKinnon began circulating her manuscript.[59] Although its influence on early cases is not well documented, it is known that drafts came to the attention of early litigators.[60] The central thesis of MacKinnon's book is that sexual harassment constitutes a form of sex discrimination and that, as such, it should be actionable under federal law.[61] MacKinnon identifies two forms of workplace harassment: quid pro quo and condition-of-work.[62] She defines quid pro quo harassment as an exchange, in which the woman must comply sexually or forfeit an employment benefit.[63] In other situations, the woman is not promised or denied anything, but harassment is a condition of her work that simply makes her work unbearable.[64]

The first federal court recognized sexual harassment as a Title VII violation in 1976. In Williams v. Saxbe,[65] a male supervisor's retaliatory actions following an employee's resisting his sexual advances were actionable as sexual discrimination under Title VII. Several other federal courts subsequently adopted this line of reasoning.[66]

MacKinnon's next victory occurred in 1980, when the Equal Employment Opportunity Commission adopted her legal framework as part of their regulations of discrimination in the workplace.[67] The EEOC promulgated guidelines adopting MacKinnon's proposition that sexual harassment constitutes a violation of Title VII.[68] Specifically, under current Title VII doctrine, sexual harassment affects the "compensation, terms, conditions, or privileges of employment."[69]

The EEOC guidelines also adopted MacKinnon's delineation of the different forms of harassment. The guidelines prohibit sexual harassment either when it is linked to an economic benefit (MacKinnon's quid pro quo form of harassment) or when it "has the purpose or effect of unreasonably interfering with an individual's work performance or creating an intimidating, hostile, or offensive working environment"[70] (MacKinnon's condition-of-work form of harassment, subsequently characterized as "hostile environment").

With sexual harassment suits becoming increasingly common,[71] MacKinnon scored another victory in a case for which she wrote the plaintiff's brief. In Meritor Savings Bank v. Vinson,[72] bank employee Mechelle Vinson's employer forced her to have intercourse, even raping her on several occasions. For the first time, the Supreme Court held that such conduct was a form of sexual discrimination violating Title VII. Specifically, the Court unanimously held that Title VII prohibits sexual harassment of the hostile environment form (as well as the quid pro quo form).[73]

Recognition of the hostile environment claim was especially important because it is "[l]ess clear, and undoubtedly more pervasive"[74] than the quid pro quo type. Pollock explains that hostile environment cases are more difficult for several reasons: offenders are often coworkers, triggering the assumption that the coworker has no power to harm the victim; the victim's loss may be defined in economic or psychological, rather than monetary, terms, which courts fail to recognize; and behavior that women find offensive is regarded as normal by men.[75]

The feminist response to *Meritor Savings* was not entirely favorable. Scholars criticized the decision for its failure to adopt a strict standard of employer liability (the standard in quid pro quo cases)[76] and for its holding that evidence of the woman's speech, clothing, and conduct is relevant and admissible.[77]

Following *Meritor Savings,* courts wrestled with the requisite degree of seriousness of the conduct. Some courts adopted an objective approach, requiring that the conduct offend a reasonable person in order to be actionable.[78] This standard, however, often results in defeat for victims because men's definitions of harassment differ from women's.[79] Commentators began to urge recognition of a subjective standard.[80] Some courts followed commentators' recommendations and adopted a subjective standard.[81] In Ellison v. Brady[82] the Ninth Circuit Court of Appeals employed the "reasonable woman" standard in a hostile environment case. Since *Ellison,* other circuit courts have followed suit.[83]

Although some feminists have hailed the adoption of this standard, support has not been unanimous. Nancy Ehrenreich, for example, argues that the reasonable woman standard creates a false sense of security, reinforcing the idea of the law as neutral and objective.[84] Ehrenreich also criticizes the standard for ignoring racial and class differences, thereby perpetuating the same wrongs inherent in the reasonable person standard.[85]

Paradoxically, recognition of the subjective standard raises the equal treatment/special treatment debate.

> At worst the reasonable woman standard [adopted in *Ellison*] could be used in other contexts as a rationale to support the idea that women require special

treatment. Women need only look at the debate affirmative action laws have engendered, particularly toward racial minorities, to understand the destructive potential of the reasonable woman standard.[86]

One commentator fears that the new standard may send women the message that they are "inherently unreasonable" and that sexual harassment may only be recognized "when seen through the eyes of a woman," rather than by anyone.[87] The choice of legal standard also raises issues of the importance of perspective,[88] an issue explored further in an essay herein by Martha Chamallas.

The equal treatment/special treatment debate is part and parcel of the broader debate regarding whether objective standards represent an advance or a defeat for women. Some feminist legal theorists have argued that objective standards in other legal contexts, such as rape[89] and battering,[90] merely reflect dominant male ideology.

Sexual harassment law continues to evolve. A significant development is the revision of remedial damages in the Civil Rights Act of 1991.[91] Section 102 of the Civil Rights Act now makes compensatory and punitive damages available for claims alleging intentional discrimination under Title VII including sexual harassment.[92] Prior to the act, victims of sexual harassment were afforded only equitable relief, such as back pay and reinstatement. Now, plaintiffs can recover even when they have suffered no economic loss.[93]

Commentators predict that the availability of these damages will facilitate litigation in the federal courts.[94] Another positive note is the United States Supreme Court's decision in Harris v. Forklift,[95] holding that a victim of sexual harassment need not prove *severe* psychological injury in order to recover under a hostile work environment claim.

Legal theory now contains many insightful theoretical explorations of sexual harassment, as the essays herein reveal. The essays share an emphasis on the importance of the victim's perspective and the necessity for legal reform, although the nature of the proposed reforms varies. The section begins with two important cases: Meritor Savings Bank v. Vinson and Ellison v. Brady. Next, Susan Estrich makes an important contribution to reform efforts by her illumination of the similarities between rape and sexual harassment law.

Elvia Arriola suggests the insightful theory that issues of color, class, and sexual orientation contribute to blue-collar women's unique experience of sexual harassment. Regina Austin's essay, emphasizing the victim's perspective, is valuable for its exploration of the different forms harassment takes and its identification of a new weapon in the arsenal of legal strategies to combat harassment.

Comparing sexual and racial harassment, Martha Chamallas explores competing standards of litigation: the reasonable person standard and the victim-oriented reasonable victim standard. Her study also contributes to the equal treatment/special treatment debate with its focus on the appropriateness of a special gendered standard.

Kimberlé Crenshaw explores the significance of sexual harassment from the perspective of women of color who appear to be especially vulnerable to such harassment.[96] She expands our understanding by her application of intersectionality theory[97] to the Senate confirmation hearings of Clarence Thomas.[98]

Continuing the focus on the Clarence Thomas hearings, Martha Mahoney takes the analysis in a different direction. Unlike those feminists who analogize sexual harassment to rape, Mahoney compares harassment to battering. By her study of the departure from abusive relationships, Mahoney's powerful essay contributes an analytical tool with which to analyze power and agency in the context of social relationships.[99]

Notes

1. Although there have been instances of sexual harassment of men by women, there are few studies of this phenomenon. One study (sample unspecified) notes that such harassment consists of irritants or embarrassments, rather than sexual coercion. C. Backhouse & L. Cohen, The Secret Oppression: Sexual Harassment of Working Women 160 (MacMillan of Canada, 1978). Based on informal interviews, author Lin Farley explains the reasons for the low incidence: women tend to be neither in positions of authority nor inclined to harass men. L. Farley, Sexual Shakedown: The Sexual Harassment of Women on the Job 181 (McGraw-Hill, 1978).

By the same token, few studies exist of same-sex harassment. For a rare study, see U.S. Merit Systems Protection Board, Office of Merit Review and Studies, Final Report, Sexual Harassment in the Federal Workplace: Is It a Problem? 58–60 (Government Printing Office, 1981) (22% of men are harassed by men, 3% of women harassed by women).

2. D. Russell, Sexual Exploitation: Rape, Child Sexual Abuse, and Workplace Harassment 270 (Sage, 1981) (citing Merit Systems Protection Board, Final Report, *supra* note 1, at 3) (42% of women victims in study of 20,000 federal employees); U.S. Merit Systems Protection Board, Sexual Harassment in the Federal Government; An Update 2 (Government Printing Office, 1988) (similar results in followup study); Hill & Behrens, Love in the Office: A Guide for Dealing with Sexual Harassment Under Title VII of the Civil Rights Act of 1964, 30 DePaul L. Rev. 581, 581 (1981) (citing D. Neugarten & J. Shafritz eds., Sexuality in Organizations: Romantic and Coercive Behaviors at Work 4–6 (Moore Pub. Co., 1980)) (50% to 80%); L. Evans, Sexual Harassment: Women's Hidden Occupational Hazard, in J. Chapman & M. Gates eds., The Victimization of Women 203, 204 (Sage, 1978) (citing Working Women United Institute, Sexual Harassment on the Job: Results of a Preliminary Survey (Working Women United Institute, 1975)) (70%). See also B. Gutek, Sex and the Workplace: The Impact of Sexual Behavior and Harassment on Women, Men and Organizations 46 (Jossey Bass, 1985); Gutek, Understanding Sexual Harassment at Work, 6 Notre Dame J.L. Ethics & Pub. Pol'y 335, 343–346 (1992); Gutek, Nakamura, Gahart & Handschumacher, Sexuality in the Workplace, 1 Basic & Applied Soc. Psychol. 255, 260 (1980); Gutek, Morasch & Cohen, Interpreting Social-Sexual Behavior in a Work Setting, 22 J. Vocational Behav. 30, 42 (1983) (discussing incidence studies).

3. See, e.g., C. MacKinnon, Feminism Unmodified 5 (Harvard Univ. Press, 1987); New York Radical Feminists, Rape: The First Sourcebook for Women 1–2 (New American Library, 1974). See also Backhouse & Cohen, *supra* note 1, at 49.

4. Farley, *supra* note 1, at xvii.

5. Taub, (Lin Farley's) Sexual Shakedown: The Sexual Harassment of Women on the Job, 5 Women's Rts. L. Rep. 311, 316 (1979) (book review).

6. C. MacKinnon, Sexual Harassment of Working Women: A Case of Sex Discrimination 7 (Yale Univ. Press, 1979).

7. *Id.* at 235.

8. See, e.g., Gutek, Understanding Sexual Harassment, *supra* note 2, at 349 ("sexual harassment helps to maintain the sex segregation of work when it is used to coerce women out of nontraditional jobs").

9. Goodman, Sexual Demands on the Job, Civ. Liberties Rev., Mar.-Apr. 1979, at 55, 56.

10. *Id.* at 56; Taub, *supra* note 5, at 312.

11. MacKinnon, Sexual Harassment, *supra* note 6, at 235. She elaborates that sexual harassment has a negative impact on women's employment opportunities if they quit or lose their jobs as a result.

12. See, e.g., Gutek, Understanding Sexual Harassment, *supra* note 2, at 345. See also C. Carothers & P. Cruell, Contrasting Sexual Harassment in Female and Male Dominated Occupations, in K. Brodkin-Sachs & D. Remy eds., My Troubles are Going to Have Trouble with Me 219, 222 (Rutgers Univ. Press, 1984); Merit Systems Protection Board, Final Report, *supra* note 1, at 51–52; Merit Systems Protection Board, Update, *supra* note 2, at 20.

13. Farley, *supra* note 1, at 90. See also Taub, *supra* note 5, at 312 (concurring with Farley).

14. See, e.g., Backhouse & Cohen, *supra* note 1, at 53–72 ("The History of Sexual Harassment"); Farley, *supra* note 1, at 28–44 ("The Historical Imperative"); and A. Jaggar, Feminist Politics and Human Nature 327 (Rowman & Allanheld, 1983) (citing Bularzik, Sexual Harassment at the Workplace: Historical Notes, Radical America, July–Aug. 1978, at 2).

15. For accounts pointing to 1975, see Silverman, Sexual Harassment: Working Women's Dilemma in Building Feminist Theory: Essays from Quest 84 (Longman, 1981); R. Tong, Women, Sex, and the Law 66 (Rowman & Littlefield, 1984). Occasionally, sexual harassment was mentioned by other names prior to that date. See e.g., Greer, Seduction Is a Four-Letter Word, Playboy, Jan. 1973, at 80, 228 ("petty rapes" by men who have the power to hire or fire).

16. It is unclear who coined the term *sexual harassment*. MacKinnon suggests that Working Women United Institute was the first, although the term was used also by the Alliance Against Sexual Coercion and appears, as well, in an early book by Carroll Brodsky, The Harassed Worker (D.C. Heath, Lexington Books, 1976). See MacKinnon, Sexual Harassment, *supra* note 6, at 250 n.13.

On the other hand, Bowman attributes the term to author Lin Farley. Bowman, Street Harassment and the Informal Ghettoization of Women, 106 Harv. L. Rev. 517, 518 n.2 (1993). However, Farley makes no such claim at the page cited by Bowman.

17. In re Carmita Wood, Case No. 75–92437, New York State Department of Labor Unemployment Insurance Appeals Board, Decision and Notice of Decision, Mar. 7, 1975 (unreported case discussed in Backhouse & Cohen, *supra* note 1, at 157, and MacKinnon, *supra* note 6, at 78–80).

18. They also changed the name to Working Women United Institute. According to Evans, the organization is now defunct. Evans, *supra* note 2, at 203.

19. Silverman, *supra* note 15, at 90–91.

20. Backhouse & Cohen, *supra* note 1, at 71.

21. *Id.* at 72. The link between sexual harassment and rape reform is also apparent in the formation of the organization Alliance Against Sexual Coercion. Three counselors at the Rape Crisis Center in Washington D.C. received so many requests for assistance by victims of sexual harassment that they decided to establish the organization in 1976 to provide education and counseling for victims. *Id.* at 157–159.

22. See, e.g., Gutek, Understanding Sexual Harassment, *supra* note 2, at 352; Jensen & Gutek, Attribution and Assignment of Responsibility in Sexual Harassment, 38 J. Soc. Issues 121, 130–132 (1982); M. Koss, Changed Lives: The Psychological Impact of Sexual Harassment, in M. Paludi ed., Ivory Power: Sexual Harassment on Campus 73 (SUNY Press, 1990); K. Quina, The Victimization of Women, in *id.* at 93.

23. Silverman, *supra* note 15, at 84. See also Evans, *supra* note 2, at 222–223 (citing Bralove, A Cold Shoulder: Career Women Decry Sexual Harassment by Bosses and Clients, Wall St. J., Jan. 29, 1976, at 1; Nemy, Women Begin to Speak out Against Sexual Harassment at Work, N.Y. Times, Aug. 19, 1975, at 38; Christensen, Sexual Harassment—the Quiet Job Threat, Chicago Daily News, Aug. 20, 1975, at 33; Peterman, Sex and the Working Girl, St. Petersburg Times, Sept. 12, 1975; Rosenberg, A Woman Must Persevere in Battle Against Sexism, Santa Clara Sun, Aug. 20, 1975, at 6). See also Farley, *supra* note 1, at 214 (citing Nolan, Sex and the Working Woman—Harassment on the Job, Louisville Courier Journal & Times, Nov. 16, 1975).

24. See Safran, What Men Do to Women on the Job: A Shocking Look at Sexual Harassment, Redbook, Nov. 1976, at 148, 216–217.

25. See, e.g., Backhouse & Cohen, *supra* note 1, at 41 (citing S. Carey, Sexual Politics in Business, paper delivered at Southwestern Sociological Association, 1977, in which a University of Texas sociologist discussed interviews of 481 working women, all of whom reported suffering sexual harassment); Comment, Employment Discrimination—Sexual Harassment and Title VII, 51 N.Y.U. L. Rev. 148, 149 n.6 (1976) (reporting on study by United Nations Ad Hoc Group on Equal Rights for Women that surveyed female U.N. employees, of whom 49% reported the existence of sexual pressure on the job). On the UN study, see also Farley, *supra* note 1, at 20–21.

The largest study, initiated by the Subcommittee on Investigations of the House Committee on Post Office and Civil Service, was conducted by the Merit Systems Protection Board. See Merit Systems Protection Board, Final Report, *supra* note 1. See also Russell, *supra* note 2, at 269–273 (discussing Merit Systems Board findings); U.S. Merit Systems Protection Board, Update, *supra* note 2.

26. Evans, *supra* note 2, at 205–208.

27. Backhouse & Cohen, *supra* note 1, at 48–50.

28. Silverman, *supra* note 15, at 85.

29. *Id.* at 89.

30. See, e.g., Estrich, Sex at Work, herein, at 755; MacKinnon, Sexual Harassment of Working Women, *supra* note 6, at 220; Russell, *supra* note 2, at 274.

31. Rivers, Sexual Harassment: The Executive's Alternative to Rape, Mother Jones, June 1978, at 21.

32. Evans, *supra* note 2, at 210.

33. Gutek, Understanding Sexual Harassment, *supra* note 2, at 351.

34. Tangri, Burt & Johnson, Sexual Harassment at Work: Three Explanatory Models, 38 J. Soc. Issues 33, 47 (1982).

35. Gutek, Understanding Sexual Harassment, *supra* note 2, at 352–357. See also V. Nieva & B. Gutek, Women and Work: A Psychological Perspective 60–61 (Praeger, 1981); Gutek, Sex and the Workplace, *supra* note 2, at 15–16.

36. Terpstra & Baker, A Framework for the Study of Sexual Harassment, 7 Basic & Applied Soc. Psychol. 17, 21–22 (1986).

37. Russell, *supra* note 2, at 273–274. Margaret Mead also supports the view of sex role socialization as a causal factor. See Mead, A Proposal: We Need Taboos on Sex at Work, Redbook, Apr. 1978, at 31.

38. Russell, *supra* note 2, at 276. See also Goodman, *supra* note 9, at 57.

39. Farley, *supra* note 1, at 28.

40. Hartmann, Capitalism, Patriarchy, and Job Segregation By Sex, 1 Signs 193 (1976).

41. Farley, *supra* note 1, at 34.

42. See, e.g., Russell, *supra* note 2, at 274; Rivers, *supra* note 31, at 29.

43. See, e.g., Backhouse & Cohen, *supra* note 1, at 42; Terpstra & Baker, *supra* note 36, at 19 (citing both the economic power differential and individual factors). But compare Russell, *supra* note 2, at 272 (citing Merit Systems Protection Board, Final Report, casting doubt on the power differential because victims report being harassed by coemployees more often than by supervisors).

44. See generally Jaggar, *supra* note 14, at 86.

45. MacKinnon, Sexual Harassment of Working Women, *supra* note 6, at 18.

46. Jaggar, *supra* note 14, at 327.

47. *Id.* Jaggar points to several socialist feminist organizations focusing on sexual harassment.

48. Sunstein, Feminism and Legal Theory, 101 Harv. L. Rev. 826, 829 (1988)(reviewing C. MacKinnon, Feminism Unmodified (Harv. Univ. Press, 1987)).

49. Although other remedies for sexual harassment exist, Title VII has been heralded as the most promising. Other remedies include Title IX for sexual harassment in education; unemployment insurance for women forced to leave their jobs because of harassment; criminal law (e.g., rape, sexual assault, solicitation for prostitution); tort (e.g., battery, assault or intentional infliction of emotional distress); and contract doctrine. See generally MacKinnon, Sexual Harassment of Working Women, *supra* note 6, at 158–174; Dworkin, Ginger & Mallor, Theories of Recovery for Sexual Harassment: Going Beyond Title VII, 25 San Diego L. Rev. 125, 127–156 (1988).

50. See, e.g., Comment, Employment Discrimination—Sexual Harassment and Title VII—Female Employees' Claim Alleging Verbal and Physical Advances By a Male Supervisor Dismissed as Nonactionable (Corne v. Bausch and Lomb, Inc.), 51 N.Y.U. L. Rev. 148 (1976); Discrimination: Sex—Title VII—Cause of Action under Title VII Arises When Supervisor, with Employer's Knowledge and Acquiescence, Makes Sexual Advances toward Subordinate Employee and Conditions Employee's Job Status on Favorable Response—Tomkins v. Public Service Electric & Gas Co., 9 Seton Hall L. Rev. 108 (1978).

51. See, e.g., Note, Legal Remedies for Employment-Related Sexual Harassment, 64 Minn. L. Rev. 151 (1979).

52. See, e.g., Babiskin, Sexual Harassment: How Can the Arbitrator Help?, 54 N.Y. St. B.J. 278 (1982); Marmo, Arbitrating Sex Harassment Cases, Arb. J., Mar. 1980, at 35; Sexual Harassment in the Workplace: A Practitioner's Guide to Tort Actions, 10 Golden Gate U. L. Rev. 879 (1980).

53. See, e.g., Bryan, Sexual Harassment as an Unlawful Discrimination under Title VII of the Civil Rights Act of 1964, 14 Loy. L.A. L. Rev. 25 (1980); Schupp, Windham & Draughn, Sexual Harassment Under Title VII: The Legal Status, 32 Labor L.J. 238 (1981); Comment, Sexual Harassment Claims of Abusive Work Environment Un-

der Title VII, 97 Harv. L. Rev. 1449 (1984); Comment, Sexual Harassment in the Employment Context: An Analysis of the New Title VII Cause of Action, 32 Baylor L. Rev. 605 (1980); Note, Sexual Harassment in the Workplace: Title VII's Imperfect Relief, 6 J. Corp. L. 625 (1981).

54. See, e.g., Leventer, Sexual Harassment and Title VII: EEOC Guidelines, Conditions Litigation, and the United States Supreme Court, 10 Cap. U. L. Rev. 481 (1981); Oneglia & Cornelius, Sexual Harassment in the Workplace: The Equal Employment Opportunity Commission's New Guidelines, 26 St. Louis U. L.J. 39 (1981); Comment, New EEOC Guidelines on Discrimination Because of Sex: Employer Liability for Sexual Harassment under Title VII, 61 B.U. L. Rev. 535 (1981); Comment, Sexual Harassment in the Workplace: New Guidelines from the EEOC, 27 Loyola L. Rev. 512 (1981).

55. See, e.g., Crocker & Simon, Sexual Harassment in Education, 10 Cap. U. L. Rev. 541 (1981); Yollick & Hirsh, Sexual Harassment in the Hospital Workplace, 31 Med. Trial Tech. Q. 484 (1984).

56. MacKinnon, Sexual Harassment of Working Women, *supra* note 6. See also C. MacKinnon, Introduction, Sexual Harassment: A Symposium, 10 Cap. U. L. Rev. i (1981).

57. MacKinnon, Sexual Harassment of Working Women, *supra* note 6, at xi.

58. See, e.g., Corne v. Bausch & Lomb, Inc., 390 F. Supp. 161 (D. Ariz. 1975) (supervisor's conduct merely personal proclivity and thus not within reach of Title VII) (*vacated by* 562 F.2d 55 (1977)); Miller v. Bank of America, 418 F. Supp. 233 (N.D. Cal. 1976) (isolated and unauthorized sexual misconduct by co-worker is not an injury cognizable under Title VII), *rev'd,* 600 F.2d 211 (1979).

59. MacKinnon, Sexual Harassment of Working Women, *supra* note 6, at xi.

60. See Kay & Brodsky, Protecting Women from Sexual Harassment in the Workplace, 58 Tex. L. Rev. 671, 673 (book review) (MacKinnon's book was "widely circulated in manuscript as early as 1975 among many of the lawyers working on cases of sexual harassment prior to its publication").

61. MacKinnon suggests that sexual harassment constitutes unlawful discrimination within the meaning of the Equal Protection Clause (when it occurs in conjunction with operations of government) and also within the scope of Title VII. The development of sexual harassment law has followed MacKinnon's second view.

62. MacKinnon, Sexual Harassment of Working Women, *supra* note 6, at 32.

63. *Id.*

64. *Id.* at 40.

65. 413 F.Supp. 654 (D.D.C. 1976), *rev'd on other grounds sub nom.* Williams v. Bell, 587 F.2d 1240 (D.C. Cir. 1978).

66. See, e.g., Munford v. James T. Barnes & Co., 441 F. Supp. 459 (D.C. Mich. 1977); Heelan v. Johns-Manville Corp., 451 F. Supp. 1382 (D. Colo. 1978); Elliott v. Energy Air Freight (D.N.C. 1977).

67. See generally Equal Employment Opportunity Commission, Guidelines on Discrimination Because of Sex, 29 C.F.R. §1604.11 (1992).

68. *Id.* at 1604.11(a).

69. Title VII states (in relevant part): "It shall be an unlawful employment practice for an employer—(1) to fail or refuse to hire or to discharge any individual, or otherwise to discriminate against any individual with respect to his compensation, terms, conditions or privileges of employment, because of . . . sex. . . ." 42 U.S.C. §2000e-2(a)(1)(Supp V 1993). For purposes of Title VII, the Guidelines define sexual harassment as: "[u]nwelcome sexual advances, requests for sexual favors, and other verbal or physical conduct of a sexual nature." 29 C.F.R. §1604.11(a)(1995).

70. 29 C.F.R. §1604.11(a)(3)(1995).

71. McKinney & Maroules, Sexual Harassment, in E. Grauerholz & M. Koralewski eds., Sexual Coercion: A Sourcebook on Its Nature, Causes, and Prevention 29 (D.C. Heath, Lexington Books, 1991).

72. 477 U.S. 57 (1986).

73. *Id.* at 65–68. In so doing, the Court adopted a distinction which the lower federal courts first recognized in Bundy v. Jackson, 641 F.2d 934 (D.C. Cir. 1981).

74. MacKinnon, Sexual Harassment of Working Women, *supra* note 6, at 40.

75. Pollack, Sexual Harassment: Women's Experience vs. Legal Definitions, 13 Harv. Women's L.J. 35, 52–53 (1990).

76. See, e.g., Dodier, Meritor Savings Bank v. Vinson: Sexual Harassment at Work, 10 Harv. Women's L.J. 203, 218–219 (1987); Note, Meritor Savings Bank v. Vinson: Title VII Liability for Sexual Harassment, 17 Golden Gate U.L. Rev. 379, 396–398 (1987).

77. See, e.g., Dodier, *supra* note 76, at 218–219; Estrich, herein, at 755; Krieger & Fox, Evidentiary Issues in Sexual Harassment Litigation, 1 Berkeley's Women's L.J. 115, 116–128 (1985); Note, Did She Ask for It?: The "Unwelcome" Requirement in Sexual Harassment Cases, 77 Cornell L. Rev. 1558, 1573 (1992); Note, Meritor Savings Bank v. Vinson: Title VII Liability for Sexual Harassment, 17 Golden Gate U. L. Rev. 379, 396–398 (1987).

78. See, e.g., Scott v. Sears, Roebuck and Co., 605 F. Supp. 1047 (N.D. Ill. 1985); Jennings v. D.H.L. Airlines, 34 FEP Cases 1432 (N.D. Ill. 1984).

79. See, e.g., Gutek, Morasch & Cohen, *supra* note 2, at 34 (finding that men were more likely to view potentially sexual behaviors positively). See also Collins & Blodgett, Sexual Harassment . . . Some See it . . . Some Won't, Harv. Bus. Rev., Mar.–Apr. 1981, at 76; Powell, Effects of Sex Role Identity and Sex on Definitions of Sexual Harassment, 14 Sex Roles 9 (1986).

80. See, e.g., Estrich, Sex at Work, herein at 767–768; Pollack, *supra* note 75, at 53, 82–83.

81. See, e.g., Rabidue v. Osceola Refining Co., 584 F. Supp. 419, 439 (E.D. Mich. 1984), *aff'd*, 805 F.2d 611 (1986); Yates v. Avco Corp. 819 F.2d 630 (6th Cir. 1987); Andrews v. City of Philadelphia, 895 F.2d 1469 (3d Cir. 1989).

82. 924 F.2d 872 (9th Cir. 1991).

83. Dey v. Colt Constr. & Dev. Co., 28 F.3d 1446 (7th Cir. 1994); Steiner v. Showboat Operating Co., 25 F.3d 1459 (9th Cir. 1994); Munday v. Waste Management, 858 F. Supp. 1364 (D. Md. 1994); Burns v. McGregor, 989 F.2d 959 (8th Cir. 1993); T.L. v. Toys 'R' Us, Inc., 605 A.2d 1125 (N.J. Super. Ct. App. Div. 1992); Trotta v. Mobil Oil Corp., 788 F. Supp. 1336 (S.D.N.Y. 1992); Harris v. Int'l Paper Co., 765 F. Supp. 1509 (2d Cir. 1991); Jenson v. Eveleth Taconite Co., 139 F.R.D. 657 (D. Minn. 1991); Smolsky v. Consolidated Rail Corp., 780 F. Supp. 283 (E.D. Penn. 1991).

84. Ehrenreich, Pluralist Myths and Powerless Men: The Ideology of Reasonableness in Sexual Harassment Law, 99 Yale L.J. 1177, 1218 (1990).

85. *Id.* at 1220. For additional discussion of the reasonable person and reasonable woman standards, see Eileen Blackwood, The Reasonable Woman in Sexual Harassment Law and the Case for Subjectivity, 16 Vt. L. Rev. 1005 (1992); Jane Dolkart, Hostile Environment Harassment: Equality, Objectivity, and the Shaping of Legal Standards, 43 Emory L.J. 151 (1994); Caroline Forell, Essentialism, Empathy, and The Reasonable Woman, 1994 U. Ill. L. Rev. 769 (1994).

86. Kenealy, Sexual Harassment and the Reasonable Woman Standard, 8 Lab. L.J. 203, 204 (1992).

87. *Id.* at 204, 210.

88. See, e.g., Minow, Justice Engendered in D. Weisberg ed., Feminist Legal Theory: Foundations 306–308 (Temple Univ. Press, 1993) (discussing unstated assumptions in thinking about difference that the observer can see without a perspective. See also Dalton, Where We Stand: Observations on the Situation of Feminist Legal Thought, *id.* at 34; Scales, The Emergence of Feminist Jurisprudence, An Essay, *id.* at 41–42, 45: Littleton, Reconstructing Sexual Equality, *id.* at 254; MacKinnon, Feminism, Marxism, Method, and the State: Toward Feminist Jurisprudence, *id.* at 432–433; Minow, Feminist Reason: Getting It and Losing It, *id.* at 339; Bartlett, Feminist Legal Methods, *id.* at 558–559; and Finley, Breaking Women's Silence in Law: The Dilemma of the Gendered Nature of Legal Reasoning, *id.* at 574.

89. See, e.g., S. Estrich, Real Rape 20–23, 31, 36–40 (Harvard Univ. Press, 1987) (criticism of "neutral" factors and of resistance requirement); Estrich, Rape, herein (reasonable resistance standard often defined as requiring force more characteristic of man).

90. See, e.g., Donovan & Wildman, Is the Reasonable Man Obsolete? A Critical Perspective on Self-Defense and Provocation, 14 Loyola L.A. L. Rev. 435 (1981); Schneider, Equal Rights to Trial for Women: Sex Bias in the Law of Self-Defense, 15 Harv. C.R.-C.L. L. Rev. 623 (1980). See also G. Calabresi, Ideals, Beliefs, Attitudes, and the Law 21–44 (Syracuse Univ. Press, 1985) (reasonable standard excludes perspective of the powerless).

91. Civil Rights Act of 1991, §102–166, 42 U.S.C. §1981 (1991 & Supp. 1995).

92. *Id.* §102.

93. See generally Cathcart & Snyderman, The Civil Rights Act of 1991, 8 Lab. L.J. 849, 857 (1992).

94. *Id.*

95. 114 S.Ct. 367 (1993). For other recent positive developments, see Karibian v. Columbia University, 14 F.3d 773 (2d Cir. 1994), *cert. denied,* 114 S. Ct. 2963 (1994) (plaintiff may prove threatened, rather than actual, economic loss for quid pro quo sexual harassment claims); Steiner v. Showboat Operating Co., 25 F.3d 1459 (9th Cir. 1994), *cert. denied,* 115 S. Ct. 733 (1995) (rejecting the defense that plaintiff welcomed the harassment because of her behavior, i.e., vulgar language).

96. Pollack, *supra* note 75, at 76 n.167 (observation based on personal experiences as tradeswoman); MacKinnon, Sexual Harassment of Working Women, *supra* note 6, at 53 (suggesting black women are most vulnerable "both because of the image of black women as the most sexually accessible and because they are the most economically at risk"). But compare Merit Systems Board, *supra* note 2, at 44–45 (race and ethnicity not overrepresented in harassment cases).

97. See Crenshaw, Demarginalizing the Intersection of Race and Sex: A Black Feminist Critique of Antidiscrimination Doctrine, Feminist Theory and Antiracist Politics, in D. Weisberg ed., Feminist Legal Theory: Foundations 383 (Temple Univ. Press, 1993). For an application of "intersectionality" to battering, see Crenshaw, Mapping the Margins: Intersectionality, Identity Politics, and Violence Against Women of Color, herein, at 363.

98. For other accounts of the significance of the Clarence Thomas hearings, see T. Phelps & H. Winternitz, Capitol Games: Clarence Thomas, Anita Hill, and the Story of a Supreme Court Nomination (Hypenon, 1992); R. Crisman & R.L. Allen eds., Court of Appeal: The Black Community Speaks Out on the Racial and Sexual Politics of Clarence Thomas vs. Anita Hill (Ballantine, 1992); Jordan, Race, Gender and Social

Class in the Thomas Sexual Harassment Hearings: The Hidden Fault Lines in Political Discourse, 15 Harv. Women's L.J. 1 (1992); Nagel, The Thomas Hearings: Watching Ourselves, 63 U. Colo. L. Rev. 945 (1992); Taylor, Invisible Woman: Reflections on the Clarence Thomas Confirmation Hearing, 45 Stan. L. Rev. 443 (1993); Symposium, Gender, Race, and the Politics of Supreme Court Appointments: The Import of the Anita Hill/Clarence Thomas Hearings, 65 S. Cal. L. Rev. 1283 (1992).

99. See also M. Mahoney, Victimization or Oppression? Women's Lives, Violence, and Agency, in M. Fineman ed., The Public Nature of Private Violence: The Discovery of Domestic Abuse 59 (Routledge, 1994).

MERITOR SAVINGS BANK v. VINSON

477 U.S. 57 (1986)

Justice REHNQUIST delivered the opinion of the Court.

This case presents important questions concerning claims of workplace "sexual harassment" brought under Title VII of the Civil Rights Act of 1964. . . .

I

In 1974, respondent Mechelle Vinson met Sidney Taylor, a vice president of what is now petitioner Meritor Savings Bank (bank) and manager of one of its branch offices. When respondent asked whether she might obtain employment at the bank, Taylor gave her an application, which she completed and returned the next day; later that same day Taylor called her to say that she had been hired. With Taylor as her supervisor, respondent started as a teller-trainee, and thereafter was promoted to teller, head teller, and assistant branch manager. She worked at the same branch for four years, and it is undisputed that her advancement there was based on merit alone. In September 1978, respondent notified Taylor that she was taking sick leave for an indefinite period. On November 1, 1978, the bank discharged her for excessive use of that leave.

Respondent brought this action against Taylor and the bank, claiming that during her four years at the bank she had "constantly been subjected to sexual harassment" by Taylor in violation of Title VII. She sought injunctive relief, compensatory and punitive damages against Taylor and the bank, and attorney's fees.

At the 11-day bench trial, the parties presented conflicting testimony about Taylor's behavior during respondent's employment. Respondent testified that during her probationary period as a teller-trainee, Taylor treated her in a fatherly way and made no sexual advances. Shortly thereafter, however, he invited her out to dinner and, during the course of the meal, suggested that they go to a motel to have sexual relations. At first she refused, but out of what she described as fear of losing her job she eventually agreed. According to respondent, Taylor thereafter made repeated demands upon her for sexual favors, usually at the branch, both during and after business hours; she estimated that over the next several years she had intercourse with him some 40 or 50 times. In addition, respondent testified that Taylor fondled her in front of other employees, followed her into the women's restroom when she went there alone, exposed himself to her, and even forcibly raped her on several occasions. These activities ceased after 1977, respondent stated, when she started going with a steady boyfriend.

Respondent also testified that Taylor touched and fondled other women employees of the bank, and she attempted to call witnesses to support this charge. But while some supporting testimony apparently was admitted without objection, the District Court did not allow her "to present wholesale evidence of a pattern and practice relating to sexual advances to other female employees in her case in chief, but advised her that she might well be able to present such evidence in rebuttal to the defendants' cases." Respondent did not offer such evidence in rebuttal. Finally, respondent testified that because she was afraid of Taylor she never reported his harassment to any of his supervisors and never attempted to use the bank's complaint procedure.

Taylor denied respondent's allegations of sexual activity, testifying that he never fondled her, never made suggestive remarks to her, never engaged in sexual intercourse with her, and never asked her to do so. He contended instead that respondent made her accusations in response to a business-related dispute. The bank also denied respondent's allegations and asserted that any sexual harassment by Taylor was unknown to the bank and engaged in without its consent or approval.

The District Court denied relief [finding that]

> [i]f [respondent] and Taylor did engage in an intimate or sexual relationship during the time of [respondent's] employment with [the bank], that relationship was a voluntary one having nothing to do with her continued employment at [the bank] or her advancement or promotions at that institution.

Although it concluded that respondent had not proved a violation of Title VII, the District Court nevertheless went on to address the bank's liability. After noting the bank's express policy against discrimination, and finding that neither respondent nor any other employee had ever lodged a complaint about sexual harassment by Taylor, the court ultimately concluded that "the bank was without notice and cannot be held liable for the alleged actions of Taylor."

The Court of Appeals for the District of Columbia Circuit reversed. 753 F.2d 141 (1985). Relying on its earlier holding in Bundy v. Jackson, 641 F.2d 934 (1981), decided after the trial in this case, the court stated that a violation of Title VII may be predicated on either of two types of sexual harassment: harassment that involves the conditioning of concrete employment benefits on sexual favors, and harassment that, while not affecting economic benefits, creates a hostile or offensive working environment. The court drew additional support for this position from the Equal Employment

Opportunity Commission's Guidelines on Discrimination Because of Sex, 29 CFR §1604.11(a) (1985), which set out these two types of sexual harassment claims. Believing that "Vinson's grievance was clearly of the [hostile environment] type," and that the District Court had not considered whether a violation of this type had occurred, the court concluded that a remand was necessary.

The court further concluded that the District Court's finding that any sexual relationship between respondent and Taylor "was a voluntary one" did not obviate the need for a remand. "[U]ncertain as to precisely what the [district] court meant"by this finding, the Court of Appeals held that if the evidence otherwise showed that "Taylor made Vinson's toleration of sexual harassment a condition of her employment," her voluntariness "had no materiality whatsoever." The court then surmised that the District Court's finding of voluntariness might have been based on "the voluminous testimony regarding respondent's dress and personal fantasies," testimony that the Court of Appeals believed "had no place in this litigation."

As to the bank's liability, the Court of Appeals held that an employer is absolutely liable for sexual harassment practiced by supervisory personnel, whether or not the employer knew or should have known about the misconduct. . . .

In accordance with the foregoing, the Court of Appeals reversed the judgment of the District Court and remanded the case for further proceedings. A subsequent suggestion for rehearing en banc was denied, with three judges dissenting. We granted certiorari, and now affirm but for different reasons.

II

Title VII of the Civil Rights Act of 1964 makes it "an unlawful employment practice for an employer . . . to discriminate against any individual with respect to his compensation, terms, conditions, or privileges of employment, because of such individual's race, color, religion, sex, or national origin." 42 U.S.C. §2000e-2(a) (1). . . .

Respondent argues, and the Court of Appeals held, that unwelcome sexual advances that create an offensive or hostile working environment violate Title VII. Without question, when a supervisor sexually harasses a subordinate because of the subordinate's sex, that supervisor "discriminate[s]" on the basis of sex. Petitioner apparently does not challenge this proposition. It contends instead that in prohibiting discrimination with respect to "compensation, terms, conditions, or privileges" of employment, Congress was concerned with what petitioner describes as "tangible loss" of "an economic character," not "purely psychological aspects of the workplace environment." In support of this claim petitioner observes that in both the legislative history of Title VII and this Court's Title VII decisions, the focus has been on tangible, economic barriers erected by discrimination.

We reject petitioner's view. First, the language of Title VII is not limited to "economic" or "tangible" discrimination. . . . Petitioner has pointed to nothing in the Act to suggest that Congress contemplated the limitation urged here.

Second, in 1980 the EEOC issued Guidelines specifying that "sexual harassment," as there defined, is a form of sex discrimination prohibited by Title VII. . . . The EEOC Guidelines fully support the view that harassment leading to noneconomic injury can violate Title VII.

In defining "sexual harassment," the Guidelines first describe the kinds of workplace conduct that may be actionable under Title VII. These include "[u]nwelcome sexual advances, requests for sexual favors, and other verbal or physical conduct of a sexual nature." Relevant to the charges at issue in this case, the Guidelines provide that such sexual misconduct constitutes prohibited "sexual harassment," whether or not it is directly linked to the grant or denial of an economic quid pro quo, where "such conduct has the purpose or effect of unreasonably interfering with an individual's work performance or creating an intimidating, hostile, or offensive working environment."

In concluding that so-called "hostile environment" (i.e., non quid pro quo) harassment violates Title VII, the EEOC drew upon a substantial body of judicial decisions and EEOC precedent holding that Title VII affords employees the right to work in an environment free from discriminatory intimidation, ridicule, and insult. Rogers v. EEOC, 454 F.2d 234 (CA5 1971), *cert. denied,* 406 U.S. 957 (1972), was apparently the first case to recognize a cause of action based upon a discriminatory work environment. In *Rogers,* the Court of Appeals for the Fifth Circuit held that a Hispanic complainant could establish a Title VII violation by demonstrating that her employer created an offensive work environment for employees by giving discriminatory service to its Hispanic clientele. The court explained that an employee's protections under Title VII extend beyond the economic aspects of employment:

> [T]he phrase "terms, conditions or privileges of employment" in [Title VII] is an expansive concept which sweeps within its protective ambit the practice of creating a working environment heavily charged with ethnic or racial discrimination. . . . One can readily envision working environments so heavily polluted with discrimination as to destroy completely the emotional and psychological stability of minority group workers. . . . 454 F.2d at 238.

Courts applied this principle to harassment based on race, religion, and national origin. Nothing in Title VII suggests that a hostile environment based on discriminatory *sexual* harassment should not be likewise prohibited. The Guidelines thus appropriately drew from, and were fully consistent with, the existing case law.

Since the Guidelines were issued, courts have uniformly held, and we agree, that a plaintiff may establish a violation of Title VII by proving that discrimination based on sex has created a hostile or abusive work environment. As the Court of Appeals for the Eleventh Circuit wrote in Henson v. Dundee, 682 F.2d 897, 902 (1982):

> Sexual harassment which creates a hostile or offensive environment for members of one sex is every bit the arbitrary barrier to sexual equality at the workplace that racial harassment is to racial equality. Surely, a requirement that a

man or woman run a gauntlet of sexual abuse in return for the privilege of being allowed to work and make a living can be as demeaning and disconcerting as the harshest of racial epithets.

Of course, as the courts in both *Rogers* and *Henson* recognized, not all workplace conduct that may be described as "harassment" affects a "term, condition, or privilege" of employment within the meaning of Title VII. . . . For sexual harassment to be actionable, it must be sufficiently severe or pervasive "to alter the conditions of [the victim's] employment and create an abusive working environment." Respondent's allegations in this case—which include not only pervasive harassment but also criminal conduct of the most serious nature—are plainly sufficient to state a claim for "hostile environment" sexual harassment.

The question remains, however, whether the District Court's ultimate finding that respondent "was not the victim of sexual harassment," effectively disposed of respondent's claim. The Court of Appeals recognized, we think correctly, that this ultimate finding was likely based on one or both of two erroneous views of the law. First, the District Court apparently believed that a claim for sexual harassment will not lie absent an *economic* effect on the complainant's employment. . . . Since it appears that the District Court made its findings without ever considering the "hostile environment" theory of sexual harassment, the Court of Appeals' decision to remand was correct.

Second, the District Court's conclusion that no actionable harassment occurred might have rested on its earlier "finding" that "[i]f [respondent] and Taylor did engage in an intimate or sexual relationship . . . , that relationship was a voluntary one." But the fact that sex-related conduct was "voluntary," in the sense that the complainant was not forced to participate against her will, is not a defense to a sexual harassment suit brought under Title VII. The gravamen of any sexual harassment claim is that the alleged sexual advances were "unwelcome." While the question whether particular conduct was indeed unwelcome presents difficult problems of proof and turns largely on credibility determinations committed to the trier of fact, the District Court in this case erroneously focused on the "voluntariness" of respondent's participation in the claimed sexual episodes. The correct inquiry is whether respondent by her conduct indicated that the alleged sexual advances were unwelcome, not whether her actual participation in sexual intercourse was voluntary.

Petitioner contends that even if this case must be remanded to the District Court, the Court of Appeals erred in one of the terms of its remand. Specifically, the Court of Appeals stated that testimony about respondent's "dress and personal fantasies," which the District Court apparently admitted into evidence, "had no place in this litigation." The apparent ground for this conclusion was that respondent's voluntariness *vel non* in submitting to Taylor's advances was immaterial to her sexual harassment claim. While "voluntariness" in the sense of consent is not a defense to such a claim, it does not follow that a complainant's sexually provocative speech or dress is irrelevant as a matter of law in determining whether he or she found particular sexual advances unwelcome. To the contrary, such evidence is obviously relevant. The EEOC Guidelines emphasize that the trier of fact must determine the existence of sexual harassment in light of "the record as a whole" and "the totality of circumstances, such as the nature of the sexual advances and the context in which the alleged incidents occurred."

Respondent's claim that any marginal relevance of the evidence in question was outweighed by the potential for unfair prejudice is the sort of argument properly addressed to the District Court. In this case the District Court concluded that the evidence should be admitted, and the Court of Appeals' contrary conclusion was based upon the erroneous, categorical view that testimony about provocative dress and publicly expressed sexual fantasies "had no place in this litigation." While the District Court must carefully weigh the applicable considerations in deciding whether to admit evidence of this kind, there is no *per se* rule against its admissibility.

III

Although the District Court concluded that respondent had not proved a violation of Title VII, it nevertheless went on to consider the question of the bank's liability. Finding that "the bank was without notice" of Taylor's alleged conduct, and that notice to Taylor was not the equivalent of notice to the bank, the court concluded that the bank therefore could not be held liable for Taylor's alleged actions. The Court of Appeals took the opposite view, holding that an employer is strictly liable for a hostile environment created by a supervisor's sexual advances, even though the employer neither knew nor reasonably could have known of the alleged misconduct. The court held that a supervisor, whether or not he possesses the authority to hire, fire, or promote, is necessarily an "agent" of his employer for all Title VII purposes, since "even the appearance" of such authority may enable him to impose himself on his subordinates.

The parties and amici suggest several different standards for employer liability. Respondent, not surprisingly, defends the position of the Court of Appeals. Noting that Title VII's definition of "employer" includes any "agent" of the employer, she also argues that "so long as the circumstance is work-related, the supervisor is the employer and the employer is the supervisor." Notice to Taylor that the advances were unwelcome, therefore, was notice to the bank.

Petitioner argues that respondent's failure to use its established grievance procedure, or to otherwise put it on notice of the alleged misconduct, insulates petitioner from liability for Taylor's wrongdoing. A contrary rule would be unfair, petitioner argues, since in a hostile environment harassment case the employer often will have no reason to know about, or opportunity to cure, the alleged wrongdoing.

The EEOC, in its brief as amicus curiae, contends that courts formulating employer liability rules should draw from traditional agency principles. Examination of those principles has led the EEOC to the view that where a supervisor exercises the authority actually delegated to him by his employer, by making or threatening to make decisions affecting the employment status of his subordinates, such actions are properly imputed to the employer whose delegation of authority empowered the supervisor to undertake them. Thus, the courts have consistently held employers liable for the discriminatory discharges of employees by supervisory personnel, whether or not the employer knew, should have known, or approved of the supervisor's actions.

The EEOC suggests that when a sexual harassment claim rests exclusively on a "hostile environment" theory, however, the usual basis for a finding of agency will often disappear. In that case, the EEOC believes, agency principles lead to

> a rule that asks whether a victim of sexual harassment had reasonably available an avenue of complaint regarding such harassment, and, if available and utilized, whether that procedure was reasonably responsive to the employee's complaint. If the employer has an expressed policy against sexual harassment and has implemented a procedure specifically designed to resolve sexual harassment claims, and if the victim does not take advantage of that procedure, the employer should be shielded from liability absent actual knowledge of the sexually hostile environment (obtained, e.g., by the filing of a charge with the EEOC or a comparable state agency). In all other cases, the employer will be liable if it has actual knowledge of the harassment or if, considering all the facts of the case, the victim in question had no reasonably available avenue for making his or her complaint known to appropriate management officials.

Brief for United States and EEOC as Amica Curiae 26. As respondent points out, this suggested rule is in some tension with the EEOC Guidelines, which hold an employer liable for the acts of its agents without regard to notice. The Guidelines do require, however, an "examin[ation of] the circumstances of the particular employment relationship and the job [f]unctions performed by the individual in determining whether an individual acts in either a supervisory or agency capacity."

This debate over the appropriate standard for employer liability has a rather abstract quality about it given the state of the record in this case. We do not know at this stage whether Taylor made any sexual advances toward respondent at all, let alone whether those advances were unwelcome, whether they were sufficiently pervasive to constitute a condition of employment, or whether they were "so pervasive and so long continuing . . . that the employer must have become conscious of [them]," Taylor v. Jones, 653 F.2d 1193, 1197–1199 (CA8 1981) (holding employer liable for racially hostile working environment based on constructive knowledge).

We therefore decline the parties' invitation to issue a definitive rule on employer liability, but we do agree with the EEOC that Congress wanted courts to look to agency principles for guidance in this area. While such common-law principles may not be transferable in all their particulars to Title VII, Congress' decision to define "employer" to include any "agent" of an employer, 42 U.S.C. §2000e(b), surely evinces an intent to place some limits on the acts of employees for which employers under Title VII are to be held responsible. For this reason, we hold that the Court of Appeals erred in concluding that employers are always automatically liable for sexual harassment by their supervisors. For the same reason, absence of notice to an employer does not necessarily insulate that employer from liability.

Finally, we reject petitioner's view that the mere existence of a grievance procedure and a policy against discrimination, coupled with respondent's failure to invoke that procedure, must insulate petitioner from liability. While those facts are plainly relevant, the situation before us demonstrates why they are not necessarily dispositive. Petitioner's general nondiscrimination policy did not address sexual harassment in particular, and thus did not alert employees to their employer's interest in correcting that form of discrimination. Moreover, the bank's grievance procedure apparently required an employee to complain first to her supervisor, in this case Taylor. Since Taylor was the alleged perpetrator, it is not altogether surprising that respondent failed to invoke the procedure and report her grievance to him. Petitioner's contention that respondent's failure should insulate it from liability might be substantially stronger if its procedures were better calculated to encourage victims of harassment to come forward.

Justice MARSHALL, with whom Justice BRENNAN, Justice BLACKMUN, and Justice STEVENS join, concurring in the judgment.

I fully agree with the Court's conclusion that workplace sexual harassment is illegal, and violates Title VII. Part III of the Court's opinion, however, leaves open the circumstances in which an employer is responsible under Title VII for such conduct. Because I believe that question to be properly before us, I write separately.

The issue the Court declines to resolve is addressed in the EEOC Guidelines on Discrimination Because of Sex. . . . The Guidelines explain: "Applying general Title VII principles, an employer . . . is responsible for its acts and those of its agents and supervisory employees with respect to sexual harassment regardless of whether the specific acts complained of were authorized or even forbidden by the employer and regardless of whether the employer knew or should have known of their occurrence. . . ."

. . . The question thus arises as to the circumstances under which an employer will be held liable under Title VII for the acts of its employees.

The answer supplied by general Title VII law, like that supplied by federal labor law, is that the act of a supervisory employee or agent is imputed to the employer. Thus, for example, when a supervisor discriminatorily fires or refuses to promote a black employee, that act is, without more, considered the act of the employer. The courts do not stop to consider whether the employer otherwise had "notice" of the action, or even whether the supervisor had actual authority to act as he did. E.g., *Flowers v. Crouch-Walker Corp.*, 552 F.2d 1277, 1282 (CA7 1977). Following that approach, every Court of Appeals that has considered the issue has held that sexual harassment by supervisory personnel is automatically imputed to the employer when the harassment results in tangible job detriment to the subordinate employee.

The brief filed by the Solicitor General on behalf of the United States and the EEOC in this case suggests that a different rule should apply when a supervisor's harassment "merely" results in a discriminatory work environment. The Solicitor General concedes that sexual harassment that affects tangible job benefits is an exercise of authority delegated to the supervisor by the employer, and thus gives rise to employer liability. But, departing from the EEOC Guidelines, he argues that the case of a supervisor merely creating a discriminatory work environment is different because the supervisor "is not exercising, or threatening to exercise, actual or apparent authority to make personnel decisions affecting the victim." In the latter situation, he concludes, some further notice requirement should therefore be necessary.

The Solicitor General's position is untenable. A supervisor's responsibilities do not begin and end with the power to hire, fire, and discipline employees, or with the power to recommend such actions. Rather, a supervisor is charged with the day-to-day supervision of the work environment and with ensuring a safe, productive workplace. There is no reason why abuse of the latter authority should have different consequences than abuse of the former. In both cases it is the authority vested in the supervisor by the employer that enables him to commit the wrong: it is precisely because the supervisor is understood to be clothed with the employer's authority that he is able to impose unwelcome sexual conduct on subordinates. There is therefore no justification for a special rule, to be applied only in "hostile environment" cases, that sexual harassment does not create employer liability until the employee suffering the discrimination notifies other supervisors. . . .

. . . I would apply in this case the same rules we apply in all other Title VII cases, and hold that sexual harassment by a supervisor of an employee under his supervision, leading to a discriminatory work environment, should be imputed to the employer for Title VII purposes regardless of whether the employee gave "notice" of the offense.

ELLISON v. BRADY

924 F.2d 872 (9th Cir. 1991)

BEEZER, Circuit Judge.

. . . Kerry Ellison worked as a revenue agent for the Internal Revenue Service in San Mateo, California. During her initial training in 1984 she met Sterling Gray, another trainee, who was also assigned to the San Mateo office. The two co-workers never became friends, and they did not work closely together.

Gray's desk was twenty feet from Ellison's desk, two rows behind and one row over. Revenue agents in the San Mateo office often went to lunch in groups. In June of 1986 when no one else was in the office, Gray asked Ellison to lunch. She accepted. Gray had to pick up his son's forgotten lunch, so they stopped by Gray's house. He gave Ellison a tour of his house.

Ellison alleges that after the June lunch Gray started to pester her with unnecessary questions and hang around her desk. On October 9, 1986, Gray asked Ellison out for a drink after work. She declined, but she suggested that they have lunch the following week. She did not want to have lunch alone with him, and she tried to stay away from the office during lunch time. One day during the following week, Gray uncharacteristically dressed in a three-piece suit and asked Ellison out for lunch. Again, she did not accept.

On October 22, 1986 Gray handed Ellison a note he wrote on a telephone message slip which read: "I cried over you last night and I'm totally drained today. I have never been in such constant term oil (sic). Thank you for talking with me. I could not stand to feel your hatred for another day." When Ellison realized that Gray wrote the note, she became shocked and frightened and left the room. Gray followed her into the hallway and demanded that she talk to him, but she left the building.

Ellison later showed the note to Bonnie Miller, who supervised both Ellison and Gray. Miller said "this is sexual harassment." Ellison asked Miller not to do anything about it. She wanted to try to handle it herself. Ellison asked a male co-worker to talk to Gray, to tell him that she was not interested in him and to leave her alone. The next day, Thursday, Gray called in sick.

Ellison did not work on Friday, and on the following Monday, she started four weeks of training in St. Louis, Missouri. Gray mailed her a card and a typed, single-spaced, three-page letter. She describes this letter as "twenty times, a hundred times weirder" than the prior note. Gray wrote, in part: "I know that you are worth knowing with or without sex. . . . Leaving aside the hassles and disasters of recent weeks. I have enjoyed you so much over these past few months. Watching you. Experiencing you from O so far away. Admiring your style and elan. . . . Don't you think it odd that two people who have never even talked together, alone, are striking off such intense sparks . . . I will [write] another letter in the near future."

Explaining her reaction, Ellison stated: "I just thought he was crazy. I thought he was nuts. I didn't know what he would do next. I was frightened."

She immediately telephoned Miller. Ellison told her supervisor that she was frightened and really upset. She requested that Miller transfer either her or Gray because she would not be comfortable working in the same office with him. Miller asked Ellison to send a copy of the card and letter to San Mateo.

Miller then telephoned her supervisor, Joe Benton, and discussed the problem. That same day she had a counseling session with Gray. She informed him that he was entitled to union representation. During this meeting, she told Gray to leave Ellison alone.

At Benton's request, Miller apprised the labor relations department of the situation. She also reminded Gray many times over the next few weeks that he must not contact Ellison in any way. Gray subsequently transferred to the San Francisco office on November 24, 1986. Ellison returned from St. Louis in late November and did not discuss the matter further with Miller.

After three weeks in San Francisco, Gray filed union grievances requesting a return to the San Mateo office. The IRS and the union settled the grievances in Gray's favor, agreeing to allow him to transfer back to the San Mateo office provided that he spend four more months in San Francisco and promise not to bother Ellison. On January 28, 1987, Ellison first learned of Gray's request in a letter from Miller explaining that Gray would return to the San Mateo office. The letter indicated that management decided to resolve Ellison's problem with a six-month separation, and that it would take additional action if the problem recurred.

After receiving the letter, Ellison was "frantic." She filed a formal complaint alleging sexual harassment on January 30, 1987, with the IRS. She also obtained permission to transfer to San Francisco temporarily when Gray returned.

Gray sought joint counseling. He wrote Ellison another letter which still sought to maintain the idea that he and Ellison had some type of relationship.

The IRS employee investigating the allegation agreed with Ellison's supervisor that Gray's conduct constituted sexual harassment. In its final decision, however, the Treasury Department rejected Ellison's complaint because it believed that the complaint did not describe a pattern or practice of sexual harassment covered by the EEOC regulations. After an appeal, the EEOC affirmed the Treasury Department's decision on a different ground. It concluded that the agency took adequate action to prevent the repetition of Gray's conduct.

Ellison filed a complaint in September of 1987 in federal district court. The court granted the government's motion for summary judgment on the ground that Ellison had failed to state a prima facie case of sexual harassment due to a hostile working environment. Ellison appeals. . . .

. . . Courts have recognized different forms of sexual harassment. In "quid pro quo" cases, employers condition employment benefits on sexual favors. In "hostile environment" cases, employees work in offensive or abusive environments. This case, like Meritor Savings Bank v. Vinson, 477 U.S. 57 (1986), involves a hostile environment claim. . . .

The parties ask us to determine if Gray's conduct, as alleged by Ellison, was sufficiently severe or pervasive to alter the conditions of Ellison's employment and create an abusive working environment. The district court, with little Ninth Circuit case law to look to for guidance, held that Ellison did not state a prima facie case of sexual harassment due to a hostile working environment. It believed that Gray's conduct was "isolated and genuinely trivial." We disagree.

. . . We have closely examined *Meritor* and our previous cases, and we believe that Gray's conduct was sufficiently severe and pervasive to alter the conditions of Ellison's employment and create an abusive working environment. We first note that the required showing of severity or seriousness of the harassing conduct varies inversely with the pervasiveness or frequency of the conduct. . . .

Next, we believe that in evaluating the severity and pervasiveness of sexual harassment, we should focus on the perspective of the victim. If we only examined whether a reasonable person would engage in allegedly harassing conduct, we would run the risk of reinforcing the prevailing level of discrimination. Harassers could continue to harass merely because a particular discriminatory practice was common, and victims of harassment would have no remedy.

We therefore prefer to analyze harassment from the victim's perspective. A complete understanding of the victim's view requires, among other things, an analysis of the different perspectives of men and women. Conduct that many men consider unobjectionable may offend many women. See, e.g., Lipsett v. University of Puerto Rico, 864 F.2d 881, 898 (1st Cir. 1988) ("A male supervisor might believe, for example, that it is legitimate for him to tell a female subordinate that she has a 'great figure' or 'nice legs.' The female subordinate, however, may find such comments offensive"); Yates v. Avco Corp., 819 F.2d 630, 637 n.2 (6th Cir. 1987) ("men and women are vulnerable in different ways and offended by different behavior"). See also Ehrenreich, Pluralist Myths and Powerless Men: The Ideology of Reasonableness in Sexual Harassment Law, 99 Yale L.J. 1177, 1207–1208 (1990) (men tend to view some forms of sexual harassment as "harmless social interactions to which only overly-sensitive women would object"); Abrams, Gender Discrimination and t he Transformation of Workplace Norms, 42 Vand. L. Rev. 1183, 1203 (1989) (the characteristically male view depicts sexual harassment as comparatively harmless amusement).

We realize that there is a broad range of viewpoints among women as a group, but we believe that many women share common concerns which men do not necessarily share.[1] For example, because women are disproportionately victims of rape and sexual assault, women have a stronger incentive to be concerned with sexual behavior. Women who are victims of mild forms of sexual harassment may understandably worry whether a harasser's conduct is merely a prelude to violent sexual assault. Men, who are rarely victims of sexual assault, may view sexual conduct in a vacuum without a full appreciation of the social setting or the underlying threat of violence that a woman may perceive.

In order to shield employers from having to accommodate the idiosyncratic concerns of the rare hyper-sensitive employee, we hold that a female plaintiff states a prima facie case of hostile environment sexual harassment when she alleges conduct which a reasonable woman[2] would consider sufficiently severe or pervasive to alter the conditions of employment and create an abusive working environment.[3]

We adopt the perspective of a reasonable woman primarily because we believe that a sex-blind reasonable person standard tends to be male-biased and tends to systematically ignore the experiences of women. The reasonable woman standard does not establish a higher level of protection for women than men. Instead, a gender-conscious examination of sexual harassment enables women to participate in the workplace on an equal footing with men. By acknowledging and not trivializing the effects of sexual harassment on reasonable women, courts can work towards ensuring that neither men nor women will have to "run a gauntlet of sexual abuse in return for the privilege of being allowed to work and make a living." Henson v. Dundee, 682 F.2d 897, 902 (11th Cir. 1982).

We note that the reasonable victim standard we adopt today classifies conduct as unlawful sexual harassment even when harassers do not realize that their conduct creates a hostile working environment. Well-intentioned compliments by co-workers or supervisors can form the basis of a sexual harassment cause of action if a reasonable victim of the same sex as the plaintiff would consider the comments sufficiently severe or pervasive to alter a condition of employment and create an abusive working environment.[4] . . . To avoid liability under Title VII, employers may have to educate and sensitize their workforce to eliminate conduct which a reasonable victim would consider unlawful sexual harassment.

---

[1]One writer explains: "While many women hold positive attitudes about uncoerced sex, their greater physical and social vulnerability to sexual coercion can make women wary of sexual encounters. Moreover, American women have been raised in a society where rape and sex-related violence have reached unprecedented levels, and a vast pornography industry creates continuous images of sexual coercion, objectification and violence. Finally, women as a group tend to hold more restrictive views of both the situation and type of relationship in which sexual conduct is appropriate. Because of the inequality and coercion with which it is so frequently associated in the minds of women, the appearance of sexuality in an unexpected context or a setting of ostensible equality can be an anguishing experience." Abrams, Gender Discrimination and the Transformation of Workplace Norms, 42 Vand. L. Rev. 1183, 1205 (1989).

[2]Of course, where male employees allege that co-workers engage in conduct which creates a hostile environment, the appropriate victim's perspective would be that of a reasonable man.

[3]We realize that the reasonable woman standard will not address conduct which some women find offensive. Conduct considered harmless by many today may be considered discriminatory in the future. Fortunately, the reasonableness inquiry which we adopt today is not static. As the views of reasonable women change, so too does the Title VII standard of acceptable behavior.

[4]If sexual comments or sexual advances are in fact welcomed by the recipient, they, of course, do not constitute sexual harassment. Title VII's prohibition of sex discrimination in employment does not require a totally desexualized work place.

The facts of this case illustrate the importance of considering the victim's perspective. Analyzing the facts from the alleged harasser's viewpoint, Gray could be portrayed as a modern-day Cyrano de Bergerac wishing no more than to woo Ellison with his words. There is no evidence that Gray harbored ill will toward Ellison. He even offered in his "love letter" to leave her alone if she wished. Examined in this light, it is not difficult to see why the district court characterized Gray's conduct as isolated and trivial.

Ellison, however, did not consider the acts to be trivial. Gray's first note shocked and frightened her. After receiving the three-page letter, she became really upset and frightened again. She immediately requested that she or Gray be transferred. Her supervisor's prompt response suggests that she too did not consider the conduct trivial. When Ellison learned that Gray arranged to return to San Mateo, she immediately asked to transfer, and she immediately filed an official complaint.

We cannot say as a matter of law that Ellison's reaction was idiosyncratic or hypersensitive. We believe that a reasonable woman could have had a similar reaction. After receiving the first bizarre note from Gray, a person she barely knew, Ellison asked a coworker to tell Gray to leave her alone. Despite her request, Gray sent her a long, passionate, disturbing letter. He told her he had been "watching" and "experiencing" her; he made repeated references to sex; he said he would write again. Ellison had no way of knowing what Gray would do next. A reasonable woman could consider Gray's conduct, as alleged by Ellison, sufficiently severe and pervasive to alter a condition of employment and create an abusive working environment.

Sexual harassment is a major problem in the workplace. Adopting the victim's perspective ensures that courts will not "sustain ingrained notions of reasonable behavior fashioned by the offenders." *Lipsett*, 864 F.2d at 898, *quoting*, Rabidue v. Osceola Refining Co., 805 F.2d 611, 626 (6th Cir. 1986) (Keith, J., dissenting), *cert. denied*, 481 U.S. 1041 (1987). Congress did not enact Title VII to codify prevailing sexist prejudices. To the contrary, "Congress designed Title VII to prevent the perpetuation of stereotypes and a sense of degradation which serve to close or discourage employment opportunities for women." Andrews v. City of Phila., 895 F.2d at 1483. We hope that over time both men and women will learn what conduct offends reasonable members of the other sex. When employers and employees internalize the standard of workplace conduct we establish today, the current gap in perception between the sexes will be bridged. . . .

Reversed and remanded.

STEPHENS, District Judge, dissenting:

. . . I believe that [this case] is an inappropriate case with which to establish a new legal precedent which will be binding in all subsequent cases of like nature in the Ninth Circuit. I refer to the majority's use of the term "reasonable woman," a term I find ambiguous and therefore inadequate.

Nowhere in section 2000e of Title VII, the section under which the plaintiff in this case brought suit, is there any indication that Congress intended to provide for any other than equal treatment in the area of civil rights. The legislation is designed to achieve a balanced and generally gender neutral and harmonious workplace which would improve production and the quality of the employees' lives. . . . I believe that it is incumbent upon the court in this case to use terminology that will meet the needs of all who seek recourse under this section of Title VII. Possible alternatives that are more in line with a gender neutral approach include "victim," "target," or "person."

The term "reasonable man" as it is used in the law of torts, traditionally refers to the average adult person, regardless of gender, and the conduct that can reasonably be expected of him or her. For the purposes of the legal issues that are being addressed, such a term assumes that it is applicable to all persons. Section 2000e of Title VII presupposes the use of a legal term that can apply to all persons and the impossibility of a more individually tailored standard. It is clear that the authors of the majority opinion intend a difference between the "reasonable woman" and the "reasonable man" in Title VII cases on the assumption that men do not have the same sensibilities as women. This is not necessarily true. A man's response to circumstances faced by women and their effect upon women can be and in given circumstances may be expected to be understood by men.

It takes no stretch of the imagination to envision two complaints emanating from the same workplace regarding the same conditions, one brought by a woman and the other by a man. Application of the "new standard" presents a puzzlement which is born of the assumption that men's eyes do not see what a woman sees through her eyes. I find it surprising that the majority finds no need for evidence on any of these subjects. . . .

The creation of the proposed "new standard" which applies only to women will not necessarily come to the aid of all potential victims of the type of misconduct that is at issue in this case. I believe that a gender neutral standard would greatly contribute to the clarity of this and future cases. . . .

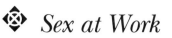 *Sex at Work*

Susan Estrich

I. Introduction: The Modern Law of Rape

During the 1970s and 1980s, rape law reform occupied a prominent place on the agendas of feminist organizations across the country. It was said by many, and with good reason, that the history of rape law was a history of both sexism and racism; that too often the victim was victimized a second time by a legal system which focused more on determining her fault than the man's. . . . All of these criticisms were voiced loudly; all were largely true. And, unfortunately, they still are.

This is not to say that feminist law reformers lacked the ability or skill to change the laws. In fact, the laws *were* changed, in virtually every state. So why wasn't the problem solved?

Part of the answer is that in practice the law had long drawn distinctions between different kinds of rape. These distinctions survived, and in some cases obscured, attempts at law reform. When a woman was raped by a stranger, or better yet, by two strangers jumping from the bushes and brandishing weapons, courts waved aside the substantive requirement of resistance. . . . These are the cases that the system has long considered to be "real rapes," and "real rape" has always been considered a serious crime. . . .

That has not been the case when the man is a friend, neighbor, or co-worker; or when the force consists of words and hands instead of guns and knives. . . . Reform or no reform, most such cases are never reported by their victims, most that are reported do not lead to prosecution and conviction. . . .

Even so, the new statutes *could* easily have served as vehicles for meaningful reform. . . . In practice, [however] the revised statutes have not always protected women from being judged blameworthy. The inquiry has too often remained focused on the appropriateness of the male-female relationship and the woman's role in provoking, accepting, endorsing, and affirming the rightness of her rape.[1]

In the last analysis, reform failed not because feminists are not good at writing statutes, but because if there is one area of social behavior where sexism is entrenched

43 Stan. L. Rev. 813 (1991). © 1991 by the Board of Trustees of the Leland Stanford Junior University.

in law . . . it is in the area of sex itself, even forced sex. Guns and gangs may be recognized as criminal, but to go beyond that is to enter a man's protected preserve, in life and in law. In life, this male domain is protected by the wielding of real power—economic, physical, psychological, and emotional. In law, it is protected by doctrines of consent, corroboration, fresh complaint, and provocation. It is protected by manipulating these doctrines to embrace female stereotypes which real women cannot meet. . . . It is protected, in short, by the operation of sexism in law. . . .

These very same doctrines, unique in the criminal law, are becoming familiar tools in sexual harassment cases. The rules and prejudices have been borrowed almost wholesale from traditional rape law. The focus on the conduct of the woman—her reactions or lack of them, her resistance or lack of it—reappears with only the most minor changes. The evaluative stance is distressingly familiar: One judges the woman's injury from a perspective which ignores women's views; or one compares her view to that of some ideal reasonable woman, or that of women afraid to speak out against harassment for fear of losing their jobs; and thus one applies a standard that the victim cannot and does not meet. The old demons, such as corroboration and fresh complaint, are invoked as if decades of criticism of the criminal law had never taken place. All this is attached to a cause of action which carries no prison sentence, nor even the possibility of compensatory damages, let alone punitive ones, and where relief is limited to an often toothless remedy in equity. . . .

Given their recent vintage, sexual harassment suits presented unique opportunities to shape the cause of action with a heightened awareness of the traditional sexist doctrines which the feminist efforts to reform rape laws highlighted. The fact that many federal courts jettison such opportunities daily, that the worst of rape litigation stands more as an example followed than one rejected, is the most persuasive and painful evidence of the durability of sexism in the law's judgement of the sexual relations of men and women. This essay seeks to present and evaluate just that evidence, in the hope that in the harshness of light such evidence will appear, as it should, untenable.

II. Finding a Cause of Action: The Application of Title VII to Sexual Harassment

A. *The Title VII Cause of Action*

Title VII of the Civil Rights Act of 1964 prohibits discrimination in employment on the basis of race, religion, national origin, or sex. The inclusion of the category of sex was something of an accident, at best. It was added as an amendment one day before House passage of the Civil Rights Act; its proponents included a number of Congressmen opposed to the Act, who hoped that the inclusion of "sex" would highlight the absurdity of the effort as a whole, and contribute to its defeat.[2] The strategy obviously failed, but it explains why there was no legislative history to guide the courts and the Equal Employment Opportunity Commission (EEOC), the statutorily created enforcement agency, in deciding what discrimination based on sex means.

Early decisions struggled with issues which to most people now seem easy. . . . Even so, Title VII emerged as a powerful tool in many respects. First, it afforded a federal cause of action, to be tried before a federal judge, thus avoiding the strictures of state tort law and the possible prejudices of state court juries. Second, its procedural rules were . . . structured to ease the plaintiff's burden of establishing a prima facie case, by having the plaintiff show . . . the discriminatory effects of policies, rather than by having the plaintiff meet the far more elusive constitutional requirement of proving invidious intent.[3] Therefore, it was not very surprising that as feminist scholars and popular magazines focused attention on the problems of sexual coercion and harassment in the workplace,[4] Title VII's prohibitions on sex discrimination would be viewed as a possible and desirable avenue for litigation.

In a landmark theoretical work published in 1979, Professor Catharine MacKinnon argued that sexual harassment, which she defined as "the unwanted imposition of sexual requirements in the context of a relationship of unequal power," should be considered sex discrimination, actionable under Title VII.[5] The following year the EEOC agreed, and issued guidelines finding harassment on the basis of sex to be a violation of Title VII, and labelling as sexual harassment sexual advances, requests for sexual favors, and other verbal or physical conduct of a sexual nature," when such behavior occurred in any of three circumstances:

> (1) [where] submission to such conduct is made either explicitly or implicitly a term or condition of an individual's employment, (2) [where] submission to or rejection of such conduct by an individual is used as the basis for employment decisions affecting such individual, or (3) [where] such conduct has the purpose or effect of unreasonably interfering with an individual's work performance or creating an intimidating, hostile, or offensive working environment.[6]

The various definitions are obviously fraught with uncertainties. . . . At least in the EEOC's eyes, these were . . . for the courts to resolve on a case-by-case basis. First, however, the courts had to accept the existence of the cause of action.

B. The Early Decisions—and the Usual Arguments

The early cases focused on a rather standard set of arguments.[7] . . . Not all of the arguments, however, were . . . predictable. . . . At least two of the major arguments put forth by employers in the 1970s, and accepted by a number of courts, presaged some of the basic theoretical tensions inherent in the Title VII sexual harassment action. Both arguments were ultimately resolved to allow suits to go forward, but in a larger sense, the failure to address these issues at their core continues to plague the cause of action that the suits ostensibly support.

The first argument was, in its narrow form, based on the slippery slope to bisexuality. Even if one takes the view that homosexual advances (e.g., by a man to man) would also be sex discrimination (because if he weren't a man . . .), the possibility of a bisexual supervisor making advances to both sexes illustrates the folly of considering homosexual or heterosexual overtures to be sex discrimination. . . .

The narrow answer to this argument is that if a woman is being sexually harassed, or denied higher wages, because she is a woman, then she is suffering from gender discrimination. When conditions are imposed on a person that would not be imposed but for her being a woman, that is sex discrimination regardless of the nature of the offensive conditions. . . . This is the conventional response. Eventually, this view came to be accepted, sometimes reluctantly to be sure, by all district courts. Today, it seems so obvious that commentators barely pause to consider it.

Unfortunately, this conventional answer ignores the "sexual" aspect of sexual harassment and the unique meaning of such harassment in a male-female context. We fit such cases into the Title VII rubric by pretending that they are no different than wage cases or other working condition cases. We treat the issue of sexuality, and the special nature of sexual coercion, as entirely beside the point: The sole issue becomes whether the coercion, whatever form it takes, would have been imposed on a man. But this issue is not analogous to issues in other Title VII cases. . . . What makes sexual harassment more offensive, more debilitating, and more dehumanizing to its victims than other forms of discrimination is precisely the fact that it is sexual. Not only are men exercising power over women, but they are operating in a realm which is still judged according to a gender double standard, itself a reflection of the extent to which sexuality is used to penalize women. In my view, these cases are such a disaster in doctrinal terms precisely because, as with rape, they involve sex and sexuality. And yet however clear all that might be, the argument for treating these cases as violations of Title VII begins from the premise that the sexuality which lies at their core is legally invisible: They are simply cases of differential treatment based on gender. . . .

The second argument, heard even more often in the early cases, rests on the alleged pervasiveness of what attorneys for one employer termed "sexual consideration" in the workplace.[8] To find Title VII liability in such cases, another court reasoned, would mean "a potential federal lawsuit every time any employee made amorous or sexually oriented advances toward another. The only sure way an employer could avoid such charges would be to have employees who were asexual."[9] . . .

There is no question that sexual consideration, flirtation, and advances *are* as pervasive in the workplace as these opinions suggest, although their victims surely find them more offensive and threatening than did . . . particular courts. In 1976, *Redbook* magazine (hardly a mouthpiece of the feminist left) asked its readers whether they had been subject to unwanted sexual "attention" at work from male bosses or colleagues; 9 out of 10 women who responded said yes, and 75 percent called the advances embarassing, demeaning, or intimidating.[10] In a more scientific study by the federal government four years later, 42 percent of the women respondents reported being subjected to some form of "sexual harassment," . . .[11] The harassment figures were roughly the same when the government resurveyed in 1987. . . .[12] Smaller surveys during this period, sometimes phrased in terms of harassment or unwelcome advances, consistently found that anywhere from 36 to 53 percent of the women questioned identified themselves as victims.[13]

But the facts of many of the early cases provided an all too easy route to evade the reality of pervasive sexual harassment. None of these early cases involved what anyone would consider minor episodes of harassment. All of them involved, as early test cases often do, rather egregious incidents in which, at least for motion purposes, courts accepted as true complaints that women were being coerced into sexual intercourse with their bosses as a condition of keeping their jobs or receiving a promotion.[14] It is often said that hard cases make bad law. Sometimes easy cases are worse still. The obvious answer in easy cases like these—the one which appellate courts and commentators seized upon most when reversing or criticizing denials of liability by lower courts—was to use the egregious facts of the particular case to paint a picture of sexual harassment as an extreme and rare event. In real life, sexual harassment is a pervasive and common problem, but the cause of action was premised on its being unusual and rare. Perhaps there was no other way to win the early battles. But the choice ensured that the war would be a long one.

In hindsight, it seems that the early district courts were, as the law reviews often like to put it, wrong—but for the right reasons. They were right in recognizing that the fact that such cases involved sex made them inherently different from, and not simply another form of, the usual Title VII wage-and-hours or hiring-and-firing cases. And they were right to recognize that sexual harassment (although they certainly would not have called it that) was pervasive in the workplace. To prohibit it in all cases, rather than in only the most egregious, presented a fundamental challenge to the way business is conducted in America. These early district courts were, in my view, very wrong in citing these facts as reasons *not* to act, rather than as imperatives demanding strong action. But by treating sex as irrelevant and harassment as a rare event, the courts that reversed the district courts sowed the seeds of what so drastically limits the efficacy of the current cause of action for sexual harassment.

C. Meritor Savings Bank v. Vinson

In 1986, the Supreme Court finally resolved the question of the *existence* of a Title VII cause of action for sexual harassment, even though by that point most courts seemed willing to accept such an action in some form. However, the Supreme Court's decision in Meritor Savings Bank v. Vinson[15] can hardly be construed as an unqualified victory.

Mechelle Vinson began work at the Meritor Savings Bank as a teller-trainee. Her boss, who had also hired her, was Sidney Taylor, a vice president of the bank and manager of one of its branch offices. With Taylor as her supervisor for the next four years, Vinson was promoted to teller, head teller, and finally assistant branch manager; according to the Court, it was "undisputed that her advancement there was based on merit alone."[16] In September 1978, she notified Taylor that she intended to take sick leave for an indefinite time; on November 1 of that year, the bank fired her for overusing her leave. Vinson sued, alleging that during her employment she had "constantly been subjected to sexual harassment" by Taylor.[17] According to Vinson's trial testimony, shortly after her probationary period as a teller-trainee, Taylor invited her out to dinner—and to have sex with at a motel. At first she refused, but, afraid of losing her job, she eventually agreed. Over the next three years, Taylor repeatedly demanded sexual relations with Vinson. She testified that she had intercourse with him forty or fifty times. He fondled her in front of other employees, followed her into the women's restroom, exposed himself to her, and forcibly raped her on several occasions.[18]

Taylor denied everything, claiming that Vinson fabricated the allegations due to a business-related dispute. The bank also denied everything, and denied knowledge or approval of any sexual harassment.

The district court found it unnecessary to resolve the conflicting testimony, concluding that no sex discrimination existed in any event. "If [Vinson] and Taylor did engage in an intimate or sexual relationship during the time of [her] employment with [the bank], that relationship was a voluntary one . . . having nothing to do with her continued employment [at the bank] or her advancement or promotions at that institution."[19] Furthermore, the trial judge concluded that given the bank's policy against sexual harassment and Vinson's failure to lodge an internal complaint, the bank would not be liable even if sexual harassment did take place.

The trial court's insistence on proof of a "nexus" between alleged sexual harassment and job-related decisions imposed strict limits on the sexual harassment cause of action. Under this view, which a number of courts shared at the time, unless the woman could prove that her sexual relationship affected job-related decisions by her employer, no claim for employment discrimination would stand. . . . As modern cases demonstrate, the theory leads to a great deal of testimony about the woman's tardiness, or other minor infractions, which is paraded with great energy as the reason for her firing.[20] But the most curious cases of all are those like *Vinson,* where a woman's competence is used against her: The circuit court found it "undisputed" that Mechelle Vinson was promoted not because she was sleeping with her boss (and being fondled by him in public, and even occasionally raped by him in private), but because of her merit. . . . The reality, of course, as even some of the worst early district courts almost recognized, is that sex may enter into a decision that could and should have been made strictly on the merits. Competent people are not always promoted, and tardy ones not always fired.

Not all courts at the time of *Vinson* viewed establishing a nexus between sex and job-related decisions as the only means to prove sex discrimination. The Court of Appeals for the District of Columbia reversed the trial judge and held that a Title VII violation might rest on either of two types of sexual harassment claims: harassment that conditions concrete employment benefits on granting sexual favors (often called the quid pro quo type, the functional expression of the nexus theory), and harassment that creates a hostile or offensive work environment without affecting economic benefits.[21] The court concluded that Vinson's grievance was of the hostile environment type, that the district court had not considered this claim, and that a remand was necessary as a result. . . .

The bank appealed, making Meritor Savings v. Vinson the first . . . sexual harassment case to reach the Supreme Court. The Court's holding marks the conclusion of the first part of our story, the birth of a federal cause of action, and the introduction to the second, the dominance of sexism in defining that cause of action.

Then Justice and now Chief Justice Rehnquist delivered the opinion of the Court. The Court rejected the bank's claim that only sexual harassment which related to a "tangible loss" of "an economic character," as opposed to "purely psychological aspects of the workplace environment," could give rise to Title VII liability. Pointing to the EEOC guidelines, precedent in racial harassment cases, and recent appellate court decisions, the Court held that "hostile environment" harassment, like quid pro quo harassment, may violate Title VII.[22]

To this holding, however, the Court attached three very significant reservations. First, "not all workplace conduct that may be described as 'harassment' affects a 'term, condition, or privilege' of employment within the meaning of Title VII."[23] . . . To be actionable, sexual harassment "must be sufficiently severe or pervasive 'to alter the conditions of [the victim's] employment and create an abusive working environment.' "[24]

Second, while "voluntariness" in the sense of consent is not a defense to a claim of sexual harassment, "[t]he gravamen of any sexual harassment claim is that the alleged sexual advances were 'unwelcome.' . . . The correct inquiry is whether respondent by her conduct indicated that the alleged sexual advances were unwelcome, not whether her actual participation in sexual intercourse was voluntary."[25] And contrary to the Court of Appeals, the Court held that "it does not follow that a complainant's sexually provocative speech or dress is irrelevant as a matter of law in determining whether he or she found particular sexual advances unwelcome. *To the contrary, such evidence is obviously relevant.*"[26]

Third, while finding that the question of the employer's liability had "a rather abstract quality about it given the state of the record," the Court nonetheless held that the appellate court "erred in concluding that employers are always automatically liable for sexual harassment by their supervisors."[27] The usual rule in Title VII cases is strict liability, and four Justices, concurring in the judgment, argued that the same rule should apply to sexual harassment claims, too. The majority disagreed. . . .

Thus, having established a Title VII cause of action, the Court immediately imposed restrictions on it. Whether by design or not, these restrictions not only make litigation more difficult for particular claimants like Mechelle Vinson, but also reinforce some of the most demeaning sexual stereotypes of women. Such restrictions operate to preserve male access to "traditional" workplace sex. . . .

III. The Gravamen of the Action: Unwelcomeness

"Unwelcomeness" has served as a vehicle to import some of the most pernicious doctrines of rape law into Title VII cases. Given the additional prerequisites for establishing sexual harassment in any event, the unwelcomeness requirement is unnecessary even as a means to protect what some would consider legitimate, consensual sex in the workplace.

The district court's holding that Mechelle Vinson engaged in voluntary sexual intercourse with Sidney Taylor ignores the coercive nature of their employer-employee relationship, including . . . any implicit threat of retaliation should she reject his advances. There were, apparently, no guns or knives involved; under the strictest definitions of the criminal law, this coercion was not rape. But that does not make it simply sex.

. . . The Court held that the district court had erred in focusing on the "voluntariness" of Ms. Vinson's participation in the claimed sexual episodes. Rather than completely abandon the inquiry into consent, however, the Court held that "[t]he correct inquiry is whether respondent by her conduct indicated that the alleged sexual advances were unwelcome," terming unwelcomeness the "gravamen of any sexual harassment claim."[28]

The shift in inquiry from the voluntariness of the sexual act to the welcomeness of the sexual advances can be counted as a victory for women, at least in legal terms, for it provided a basis for concluding that the district court had erred. But the victory is limited at best: Unwelcomeness has emerged as the doctrinal stepchild of the rape standards of consent and resistance. . . . On its face, the standard presents at least three serious problems. First, as in rape cases, the focus is on the victim, not on the man: She may be less powerful, and economically dependent, but she still is expected to express unwelcomeness. Unless she does, no burden is placed on him to refrain from abusing his position of power. . . .

The second problem with the unwelcomeness standard, as defined by the Supreme Court, is that "conduct" is the yardstick by which we measure assent. The plain implication is that a polite "no" may not suffice. Though it is bad enough to presume consent in the absence of words, it is worse still to presume it notwithstanding a woman's words.

Third, and most pernicious of all, since the focus of inquiry is on the plaintiff, and since the unwelcomeness test must be met by her conduct, should we be surprised if the trial focuses on what the plaintiff wears, how she talks, even who else she sleeps with? Whatever unwelcomeness means, the Court in *Vinson* squarely held that a "complainant's sexually provocative speech or dress" is "obviously relevant" in determining whether she found the particular sexual advances unwelcome.[29]

What is "sexually provocative" dress? Does the Court mean that women who wear short skirts intend to invite sexual advances? That tight sweaters may justly be pled as provocation for otherwise offensive conduct? That men are legally entitled to treat women whose clothes fit snugly with less respect than women whose clothes fit loosely? By accepting the notion of "sexually provocative" clothing, the Court effectively denies women the right to dress as they wish. . . .

The consequences of this approach are devastating for women. Women are invisible as anything other than potential sexual objects of men—invisible to the Court and, ultimately by its rules, invisible to themselves. And in making the determination of the harassment *of* women dependent upon the extent of "sexually provocative" behavior *by* women, the Court adopts a rule which holds women responsible for their own torment. Thus, the victim of harassment, like the rape victim, suffers not only the direct injury of sexual abuse, but also the indignity of the Court's presumption that she is to blame. . . .

In practice, both traditional and nontraditional women may find that their own actions are used against them in the unwelcomeness analysis. A woman who behaves in the most stereotypical ways—complimenting men, straightening their ties, "moving her body in a provocative manner,"[30] . . . may find that the sexual advances she rejects are, as a matter of law, not unwelcome. Similarly, women who act too much like men—who use "crude and vulgar language," or choose to eat with the men in the employee lunchroom—cannot be heard to complain of a worksite which is "permeated by an extensive amount of lewd and vulgar conversation and conduct."[31] Their "unfeminine" behavior apparently deprived them of protection, whatever the statutory mandate. Like women in rape cases who have sexual pasts, their conduct makes them fair game.

In short, the unwelcomeness requirement performs the doctrinal dirty work of the consent standard in rape law. At a minimum, it shifts the focus from the man to the woman. In too many cases, her conduct is evaluated in terms which see women only as the sexual objects of men. The standard of judgment is painfully male. . . . The apparent difficulty that many judges have finding the deserving victim raises the question whether, at least in some courts, the very point of the inquiry might be in effect to protect a broad category of sexual relations in the workplace, so long as these relations appear, at least to the men judging them, typical and acceptable.

Certainly, that is the rule in rape cases. The consent standard—and the corresponding inquiries into what a woman did or said . . . have, at least until recently, made successful prosecution of acquaintance rape all but impossible. Where the relationship is "appropriate," at least to the court's eyes, judges tend to see sex, not rape. Similarly, in Title VII cases they see sex, not sexual harassment. In both types of cases, they are often wrong. That a certain relationship might be appropriate does not necessarily mean that the man's behavior has been.

The strongest justification for the welcomeness doctrine is that the rule ensures that consensual workplace sex does not provide the basis for a civil action. The more radical response to this argument is that there is no such thing as truly "welcome" sex between a male boss and a female employee who needs her job. And if there is, then the women who welcome it will not be bringing lawsuits in any event. Certainly from my experience teaching this subject, it seems much easier for men putting themselves in the shoes of the powerful to assume that their advances are welcome than it is for women putting themselves in the shoes of the powerless to think that even a "yes" is a real or free choice.

One need not adopt the more radical approach, however, to reject the welcomeness inquiry as unnecessary. The fact is that in both the quid pro quo and the hostile environment cases, additional requirements exist for proving that sex is harassment, making the unwelcomeness inquiry superfluous, and leaving no justification for the burden it imposes.

Consider, first, the case of quid pro quo harassment. In such a case, the woman is required to establish a direct connection between her acceptance or rejection of sexual advances and a job benefit or loss. The prototype fact pattern is simple: If you sleep with me, you'll be promoted; if you don't, you'll be fired. The question of whether such a bargain is "welcomed" by the woman should startle even those who reject the more radical approach to workplace sex. Even if you believe that I might freely consent to sex with my supervisor in some other circumstances, can free will exist in the face of coercion? With a gun to my head, would you even ask about philanthropy?

. . . Title VII leaves the employer free to hire or fire for any reason he chooses other than sex; here, it is plainly sex—both the gender of the offeree, which renders her subject to such a bargain, and the very terms of the bargain—that functions as the basis for the employment decision. And this is so regardless of welcomeness. . . .

Thus, eliminating unwelcomeness as an element in quid pro quo cases would not, for better or worse, bar sex that many men and some women might consider welcome or consensual. Rather, doing so would prohibit only conditioning job benefits upon sex. The man who chooses to make the workplace his sexplace would in theory remain free to do so. He would simply be barred from using extortion—threats of harm and promises of benefit—to win his welcome.

Unwelcomeness is no more necessary in hostile environment cases, although for different reasons. The irony of the hostile environment case is that the subjective welcomeness inquiry, gravamen or not, is fundamentally at odds with all the other elements of the cause of action. A hostile environment, the courts have consistently held, must be based on objective criteria, evaluated from an "objective" viewpoint. The fact that a particular woman found the environment totally debilitating is beside the point; the question is what other persons, often mythic, would think. Thus the welcomeness inquiry is either utterly gratuitous or gratuitously punitive. . . . In either case, welcomeness serves as a means to keep the focus on the woman rather than the supervisor; on what she, rather than he, has done wrong; and on whether *she* deserves to be treated with human decency, rather than whether *he* violated the standards of decency and humanity.

Under the old rule in rape cases, a woman's sexual history might be relevant regardless of the circumstances of the assault. In most cases, the effect was not to improve the truth-seeking process of the courts, but to discourage women from filing complaints in the first instance. "Welcomeness"—defined in sexual harassment doctrine to include the woman's dress, language, habits, and even sex life—may play a similar role.

It should be obvious that the system already contains serious disincentives to women filing sexual harassment complaints. Start with embarrassment, loss of privacy, and sometimes shame. . . . Anything which adds another disincentive, as the Supreme Court's unwelcomeness requirement surely does, ought to be supported by a strong justification. In my view, the unwelcomeness inquiry certainly is not.

IV. Proving the Quid Pro Quo

The division between quid pro quo harassment and hostile environment harassment rests on the assumption that only in the former, and not the latter, does harassment directly determine economic benefits and losses. In practice, this is rarely so; the distinction between these two forms of harassment takes the form of a continuum rather than a divide. . . .

The distinction is, however, significant in legal terms. The plaintiff in a quid pro quo case is not required, as a hostile environment claimant is, to prove that the harassment is pervasive and objectively intolerable. In practice, less harassment is necessary to satisfy the threshold requirement of a quid pro quo case.

There is, not surprisingly, a catch: While the quid pro quo plaintiff need not establish that harassment was pervasive, she faces two obstacles so substantial as to spell failure for many claimants. First, she must establish the existence of an actual threat. Second, she must prove that her reaction to the threat, rather than some other factor, resulted in her firing or demotion. In practice, these obstacles produce a working definition of quid pro quo harassment that may be so narrow as to make all but the most perfect plaintiff unable to establish the requisite nexus, and all but the most perfectly stupid defendants able to rebut successfully a prima facie case.

Establishing the requisite threat is no easy matter. Only on rare occasions will a boss admit that he threatened a female employee with termination if she refused to sleep with him. Indeed, in all the cases I have reviewed, I cannot recall one instance where an employer admitted to threatening a female employee. As in many rape cases, there are rarely witnesses, leaving the factfinder to weigh one person's word against another's. Moreover, no word need ever be spoken to make such a threat effective. . . .

[M]ost quid pro quo cases focus not so much on whether a threat was made, but on the related question of whether the woman's response to her boss's proposition or threat motivated the decision to deprive her of an economic benefit. If the nexus between proposition and economic deprivation is established, her claim that there was at least an implicit threat will usually be accepted.[32] Not surprisingly, establishing that nexus is even more difficult than establishing the threat.

Obviously, the easiest way to establish the basis for a personnel decision is from personnel files or statements. [E]ven at their most naive, most employers would not write letters to women, or place notes in personnel files, explaining that Mrs. S. did not receive a promotion because she refused sexual intercourse with her boss. These are things one seldom writes down, or even tells to close friends.

The absence of perfectly stupid employers necessitates the perfect employee. An employer can always find good reasons to fire people, as labor organizers have long understood. In case after case, one reads of women who were tardy for work, women (like Mechelle Vinson) who were out sick too often, women whose typing or phone skills are found, after some time on the job, to be less than par.[33] In theory, if one could show that other equally sick, tardy, or incompetent workers are not fired, one might convince a court that the stated reason is a pretext. In practice, finding other identically situated women may prove difficult if not impossible. Generally, only in cases where harassment was truly endemic to the workplace—and other women came forward to attest to it—have plaintiffs succeeded in establishing that the stated reason for their firing was only a pretext.[34]

At a more fundamental level, the quest for perfection begs the real question. For a fired employee, the real question is not whether she is perfect, but whether her sexual rejection of her boss played a role in his concluding that she is not. Or, to frame the inquiry in a more telling way, *would she still have been fired if she had said yes?* One sees many cases of women who said no and were fired, and very few of women who said yes and lost their jobs. . . . If a woman understands that she can keep her job by saying yes, she should be protected from firing if she says no. If an employer allows sex to have currency in his workplace, then Title VII at a bare minimum should require that those who say no be treated no worse than those who say yes. But that is not the way the courts ask the question, or answer it. . . .

. . . If the goal is to protect all women from sexual blackmail, and there is no basis to argue that it should be anything less, then the governing doctrines should be structured to serve that goal, and not to protect sexual access to everyone who might later be termed "unqualified." This means that we should find a prima facie case of sexual harassment whenever a woman can establish that she was subjected to an adverse employment action—whether she was fired, demoted, or not promoted—and that she rejected sexual advances of her superior. The law should impose on the employer the burden of showing not simply that she was "unqualified," but that the adverse action would have been taken even if she had said yes to sex.

Such a rule would be a significant advance for women in two respects. First, it would relieve them of the obligation of proving the elusive nexus between their responses to their bosses' propositions and the deprivation of an economic benefit. Instead it would place the burden of proving the absence of a nexus on the employer. Second, it would require the blackmailer or his employer to bear the responsibility for his blackmail: If an employer chooses to make sex a positive consideration in employment decisions, then all women should be entitled to the benefit, *regardless of whether they say yes or no.*

To be sure, an employer under this rule would be less free to fire than if he had never resorted to sexual extortion in the first place. So be it. No one forced him to engage in blackmail. Surely the law does not need to *encourage* sex in the workplace, let alone do so by affirmatively protecting sexual blackmail. It hardly seems too much to expect that as between the powerful blackmailer and his less powerful victim, he, rather than she, should bear the burden of the blackmail. Perhaps most important, once sexual blackmail has been introduced, it is foolish and even punitive for courts to close their eyes and pretend that employment decisions can somehow be made and judged without regard to it.

Of course, no legal rule will stop all blackmail in the workplace. There will always be women who cannot afford the risk of unemployment, cannot bear the expense of litigation, and cannot stomach the pains of disclosure and discovery. But the legal rule should say to all women, even if it cannot make good its assurance in every case, that they are protected from sexual blackmail. Women are entitled to know that saying no will leave them no worse off than if they had said yes. Hopefully, such a rule will make at least a few more women feel a little more free to choose for themselves.

V. Establishing a Hostile Environement

The great victory of *Vinson,* if it can be called that, was the Supreme Court's willingness to recognize the second and less widely accepted form of sexual harassment: the hostile environment. But the acceptance was hardly unconditional. Hostile environment claimants, before and since *Vinson,* have faced substantial difficulties establishing that their worksites violate Title VII.[35]

At least two obstacles regularly complicate hostile environment lawsuits, in addition to the unwelcomeness gravamen. First, the woman must prove that the offensive conduct was "based upon sex." Second, she must show that the harassment was "sufficiently pervasive so as to alter the conditions of employment and create an abusive working environment."

A. The "Based on Sex" Requirement

. . .

In theory, one could argue that the "based on sex" requirement is an absolute mandate of Title VII. After all, the Act bars only discrimination in the conditions of employment based on sex. But Title VII in no way mandates the practical obstacle which the "based on sex" requirement has come to represent in many courts.

While the test is often stated, in legal terms, as whether the harassment is "equally offensive" to both sexes, it is often applied in practice as a question of whether the action is itself sexual. Presumably, nonsexual acts are directed at both men and women, and are equally offensive to both. Sexual acts, by contrast, are directed at women and are offensive only to them. Such a test might work for women if "sexual" acts were broadly defined, and viewed from a woman's perspective. The problem is that courts tend to define "sexual" very narrowly, based on a man's view of a man's acts.

In Wendorf v. Metropolitan Life Insurance Co.,[36] for example, the court found that the boss "was a 'physical person' and felt a need to touch people in order to communicate."[37] The court had no doubt that his behavior was "impolite and possibly annoying"; nor did the court question that he might have been "unpleasant to the plaintiff" on a number of occasions. But the court concluded that his acts did not constitute sexual harassment, since "this behavior . . . was directed at both male and female workers and was clearly not sexual in nature."[38]

What is striking about *Wendorf* is the court's rather facile assumption that a physical touch is the same behavior when done by a man to a man as when done by a man to a woman. Perhaps that is true among some groups of family and friends, but it is hardly typical of the American workplace, let alone the workplace where the man is a boss and the woman his employee. There was no showing, nor did the court require one, that Metropolitan Life was a uniquely familial work environment. The fact that men were touched as well may not be irrelevant to a sexual harassment claim, but it surely should not be dispositive.

One problem, plainly, is perspective: Even if the man who touched (the boss) and the man who reviewed his behavior (the judge) view such touching as nonsexual, it does not follow that it would be viewed that way either by the woman touched (Ms. Wendorf) or by most women. So the dispositive question here may be simply this: *Whose perspective should govern?* And if that is the right question, the male perspective is not necessarily the right answer. . . .

If there are strong reasons for adopting a reasonableness standard in the criminal law, and I believe there are, these grounds are even more persuasive in the civil context, where the very purpose of the law is to protect women, and where the deprivation of liberty and the stigma inherent in criminal punishment are absent. Why, after all, should the courts protect a man's right to maul women? This is the only "right" to be lost if courts presume what most women would indeed assume: that being touched by a man is different than being touched by a woman, and that as a rule, men should keep their hands off. . . .

B. The Pervasiveness Requirement

The second obstacle women complainants face is the requirement that they prove that the harassment is sufficiently severe or pervasive. As the Supreme Court held in *Vinson,* it is not enough that the employee herself is offended. It is not enough, for example, that the source of offense is an intentionally insulting, gender-based comment. For sexual harassment to be actionable, the woman must establish that it was sufficient "'to alter the conditions of [the victim's] employment and create an abusive working environment.'"[39] Or, as one leading appellate court decision put it, the harassment must be "sufficiently severe and persistent to affect seriously the psychological well being of employees, is a question to be determined with regard to the totality of the circumstances."[40]

Certainly the pervasiveness of the harassment should be relevant to the question of what relief is appropriate: For example, was the harassment sufficiently severe as to result in a constructive discharge of the plaintiff? But it does not inevitably follow that there is no harm in harassing, so long as it is sporadic.

One justification for the pervasiveness requirement seems, plainly, that every workplace insult should not be treated, quite literally, as a federal case. But in defining what counts as trivial or "de minimis," many courts have wrongly looked to social interaction outside the workplace as the standard, ignoring not only the "captive audience" nature of the employment context but also the fact that "society" hardly reflects a normative standard which women have had an equal role in shaping. . . .

A second and related justification for the pervasiveness requirement may be the recognition by federal courts that what even *they* would consider nontrivial harassment is itself pervasive in the workplace. . . . The early federal courts recognized the highly sexualized atmosphere of many workplaces, and cited it as a reason not to afford protection under Title VII. More recent decisions that have reached the opposite result, including *Vinson,* have done so by stressing the limited application of the Title VII action to only the most extreme cases of sexual harassment.[41]

But the fact that a hazard is widespread should be a reason to ban it, not to tolerate it. The greater the number of women who are exposed to sexual harassment, the more of a reason strict standards are needed. If harassment is viewed as a wrong, then its very commonness is an argument to "get tough." Consider the analogy to drug use. Few would accept the argument that its prevalence means that employers should be more tolerant of it. There is no analogous view in the narcotics situation of "There's no harm in trying—as long as it's sporadic or casual." On the contrary, spot checks of everyone, suspected or not, have become the rule of the day. . . . Yet harassment can destroy a woman's health and well-being more quickly than marijuana use. Our insistence on thinking about sexual harassment differently reveals the depth of our acceptance of sexual harassment as appropriate workplace behavior.

Even in this context, however, the standards applied by some courts in enforcing the "pervasiveness" requirement remain extreme. Formally, the pervasiveness test is wholly objective: The harassment must be "so significant a factor that the average female employee finds that her overall work experience is substantially and adversely affected by the conduct."[42] Who is this average female? Sometimes, she is constructed out of whole cloth by the court. For example, the average female, according to a Michigan judge, would not consider herself harassed if a flashlight were shined up her skirt, but would merely dismiss it as "childish."[43] In other cases, she is not even a woman, but a "reasonable person" of no explicit gender. This construct is at best meaningless, given that men and women do not view harassment in the same way; at worst, it implies that the reasonable person is male. More often, she is fashioned out of the court's view of the *other* women in the workplace: other women who, according to one court, "simply ignored" pictures of naked women on doors and sexual objects in the work area;[44] or other women who find their bosses sitting on their laps, talking about his tongue and penis, to be merely "horseplay" that is "funny and inoffensive."[45]

Women who fail to meet this objective standard—women who find flirtation by their boss debilitating, or who are adversely affected by the "romantic ambience" of the boss's conduct—are vulnerable to being judged "hypersensitive to conduct by men."[46] But while women who complain too much are "hypersensitive," women who do not complain at all may fare no better. Those who suffer in silence often find that their silence is used against them, either because of the courts' assumption that had they complained the harassment would have stopped, or, more often, because of the presumption that the harassment couldn't have been so bad—and therefore not so pervasive or debilitating—if the woman didn't even complain.

Superwomen—women who not only do not complain, but also continue to get their jobs done, at least for a time, and even excel at them—often fare least well of all. Where a woman was able to work regular shifts for ten days after an alleged instance of forced intercourse, [for example] the court found the harassment did not impact significantly upon the conditions of employment.[47] . . .

These cases illustrate at least two problems that go beyond their particular facts. First, for at least some of the courts, the objective standard of pervasiveness is defined by an idealized woman who simply may not exist. Such a woman is tough, not "hypersensitive"; she is aggressive, not passive. Such a woman complains in a way that effectively stops the harassment. Such a woman does not suffer in silence or confide only in other women. In short, the "reasonable woman" is very much a man.

By requiring women to behave like men, Title VII courts are following a pattern well established in rape cases. . . . Moreover, even those courts that base their standard on the reactions of real women—of the particular plaintiff, or of others in the workplace—end up with a definition of pervasiveness that is often no broader than that of courts which cling to the idealized model. Few of these courts recognize that the extent to which women react to insults, propositions, and physical abuse may have far less to do with the severity of the harassment than with the need of women to keep their jobs. . . .

Because courts fail to recognize this, or perhaps choose not to, many courts in hostile environment cases end up . . . translating the tolerance of powerless women for offensive conditions into a normative standard of acceptable workplace conduct. Thus, what the powerless must tolerate because of their need becomes what the law defines as acceptable conduct.

And yet, the very point of Title VII—indeed, the only point—should be to ensure that precisely this kind of "tolerance" by the powerless *not* define the prerogatives of the powerful. That women would be "willing" to work with hazardous chemicals, or for subminimum pay, or for fifty hours without overtime, is hardly a justification for those unlawful working conditions. Because the market does not protect women against these conditions, the law does. So, too, for discrimination—at least in theory. But the pervasiveness requirement, particularly as it has been most strictly interpreted, signals our (or at least judges') unwillingness to clearly state that sexual insults have no place on the worksite. Sexual harassment, unlike sweatshop conditions, remains an acceptable aspect of the American workplace. . . .

VI. Questions of Credibility

While doctrinal elements like unwelcomeness, nexus, and pervasiveness decide many sexual harassment cases, my reading of the case law suggests that credibility questions probably decide nearly as many. By credibility, I mean, quite simply, whether the judge believes the woman's account of victimization or the man's exhortations of innocence.

One problem with addressing questions of credibility is that their resolution ultimately depends on being there. If you weren't at the trial, if you didn't hear the evidence and see the witnesses yourself, or even read the transcript in its entirety, you are certainly in no position to second-guess the court's judgment. At least that is the approach of most appellate courts, and it works quite effectively to protect credibility judgments from reversal.

But my point is not so much whether case X or case Y was rightly decided, as whether there emerges, from the courts' discussions of fact-finding, patterns of judgment which raise legitimate questions as to the enterprise as a whole. Based on my review, serious questions are raised in at least three respects. First, some courts, though perhaps only a minority, have structured the relevancy rules in sexual harassment cases to frame the credibility question as a one-way ratchet against women. Second, and even more troubling, virtually every decision on credibility seems to assume the relevance of factors such as the presence of corroboration and the freshness of the woman's complaint, treating these factors as neutral indicia of credibility rather than as cards categorically stacked against women. Finally, in making judgments about women's motivations, a number of courts have embraced stereotypes of women which punish real women for both their strengths and their weaknesses, and leave unchallenged the most traditional "scorned woman" explanations for why women complain of harassment.

The 1988 decision in Kresko v. Rulli[48] serves as the worst example of the one-way ratchet. In *Kresko,* a Minnesota court upheld the trial court's simultaneous *exclusion* of evidence of the boss's sexual relations with other workers and *inclusion* of evidence of the plaintiff's subsequent relations with other men. As to the former, the court emphasized that "most of the other women did not consider the incidents sexual harassment," and that since he admitted that most of the incidents occurred, but claimed they were consensual, they were not necessary to show motive or opportunity.[49] As for the woman's sex life, the court held the evidence relevant and probative because she "affirmatively placed this aspect of her life at issue."[50]

Kresko is easy to attack. In criminal cases, there may be a justification for applying different rules of proof to victim and defendant, for such cases are contests not between plaintiff and defendant, but between the state and the individual, and the deck is supposed to be stacked on the individual's side. But that justification disappears in a civil suit. . . .

Ultimately, though, what makes *Kresko* and other cases like it so vulnerable to attack is the unjustifiable lack of symmetry which lies at their core: the application of harsher evidentiary rules to her than to him. But the most important question is whether the system *should* be symmetrical.

Plainly, whether a man has had sexual relations with other female employees seems relevant, regardless of whether they "consented" at the time. Such a pattern might well define the "understandings" at work on the job site. Indeed, in a number of cases, it is the third or fourth woman who brings the suit, and often she succeeds only because of the testimony of her heretofore uncomplaining predecessors.[51] And it is not always obvious, at least in his case, that the line should be drawn at work: If he has harassed women outside of work, that seems relevant; if he is a "Don Juan" on the outside claiming to be a choirboy at the office, even that may seem relevant. But are these same patterns equally relevant to the woman complainant: Does it matter if she has had relationships with other men at work, or with other men outside of work, or if she has complained before or since, as Ms. Kresko apparently did, of date rape outside the office?

Symmetry is neat, applying the same rules of relevancy to both men and women, to both aggressor and victim; with symmetry, the ratchet runs both ways. Unfortunately, we do not live in a neat world. A rule treating evidence of a woman's other sexual relationships the same as such evidence about the man may seem egalitarian; the impact of such evidence may not be. Men with active sex lives are normal, desirable, successful. Women are loose, easy, unworthy. . . . The fear of having one's sex life paraded before a court, and the fear that what is average for women will, when exposed, look exceptional (because for women, the gap between the male-defined ideal and the usually male-imposed average is so great) lead not only to shame in the courtroom but acquiescence in the workplace. If this form of evidentiary symmetry is enforced, it may substantially enhance the asymmetry of power and powerlessness inside the workplace.

So if there is to be symmetry—and I have yet to read an opinion embracing a one-way ratchet *favoring* women—it must be of a more limited kind. Lines must be drawn to limit the admissibility of evidence in order to protect women, even if those legal parameters also protect men. We must draw evidentiary lines at the workplace which render purely personal life irrelevant. We must draw lines between sex and aggression which make evidence of the latter admissible, even if the line between the two is an artificial one. I want to know if the man has been prosecuted or sued for rape elsewhere, or arrested for domestic assault, and I want to know even if the cost of knowing is also asking whether the woman has ever complained of rape.

At least most judges, most of the time, recognize the need to be at least somewhat careful when dealing with evidence of other sexual activity. They may still fail to admit or exclude the proper amount of evidence, but generally they are paying attention. This is not so when dealing with factors such as corroboration and the freshness of the complaint. For most judges, it seems, these look like neutral criteria, beyond reproach as a basis for judging. Few even hesitate before embracing them in making credibility decisions. They should.

In rape law, similar rules were established, both formally and informally, to guide the fact-finding process, rules which emphasized such things as the presence of corroboration, the availability of eyewitness accounts, and the freshness of the woman's complaint.[52] . . . With law reform in the 1960s and 1970s, American jurisdictions formally abandoned these special proof rules. . . .

It is therefore somewhat surprising, and even more disquieting, to read again and again in sexual harassment suits not only that the woman loses, but that her credibility suffers because no witnesses were present, or because she did not complain swiftly or publicly enough. Ironically, the forms of harassment most likely to occur in public, and thus be corroborated, are also those which courts are most likely to dismiss as trivial jokes and gestures rather than treat as harassment. But one should rarely expect nontrivial harassment, at least as judicially defined, to take place in public in front of witnesses, or to be memorialized in personnel files. More serious forms of harassment—explicit sexual overtures, threats of firing or promises of promotion, and actual acts of sexual intercourse—are less likely to be accompanied by corroboration, and consequently, the woman is less likely to be believed.

Similarly, to read the judges' opinions, one would expect that the first response of a harassed woman is to complain, both officially *and* privately. But in fact, one sees few cases of women who do this. Indeed, the opinions which most emphatically announce this standard of conduct almost always involve women who did *not* complain.[53] The surveys . . . bear out the pattern: One survey found that while over half of the women questioned reported having experienced sexual harassment, only 22.5 percent reported having ever even talked about the general subject matter—let alone the particular instance—with a co-worker.[54]

Yet the corroboration rule lives on in sexual harassment cases as if it were a neutral criterion, as if absence of corroboration were as probative as its presence. In reality, corroboration *should* be treated as a one-way ratchet. It should be persuasive when present—for no one would argue that witnesses should be ignored, bruises discounted, or cries for help dismissed—and irrelevant when not. The fact that the corroboration rule continues to be embraced unembarrassedly in sexual harassment cases, long after it has at least been formally rejected in rape cases, raises the question of whether it serves, here as there, its more traditional and deservingly vilified purpose: not as a neutral guide to truth, but as a mechanism reflecting the disfavored status of sexual complaints and complainants.[55] . . .

VIII. Conclusion

The pitfalls for women in current Title VII doctrine suggest a number of doctrinal changes that the federal courts and Congress should adopt to protect women against sexual harassment at the workplace. . . . At least some courts may be ready to meet the challenge. . . . The Court of Appeals for the Ninth Circuit held in Ellison v. Brady that the appropriate perspective for judging a hostile environment claim is that of the "reasonable woman" and recognized that a woman's perspective may differ substantially from a man's.[56]

But the broader prospects for making any of these changes are uncertain at best. At its inception, Title VII's grounding in the federal equity jurisdiction seemed an ideal alternative to conservative and unsympathetic state judges and juries. Today, while some exceptions remain, the increasing conservatism of the federal judiciary raises the question of whether state courts and state juries might not be at least equally sympathetic, particularly in states like California, where laws provide for both compensatory and punitive damages in harassment cases.[57]

Whether in state or federal court, however, the challenge of making the law work for women, and not against them, is more than a matter of doctrinal manipulation. Underlying the system as it is currently structured and enforced rests a set of assumptions and attitudes about women and work that support both the rules and results of which I am most critical.

One of the leading theorists of sexual harassment in the workplace has argued that such behavior represents an inappropriate spillover into the workplace of the norms of conduct which exist in society generally. Under this view, socially accepted forms of male aggressiveness become unacceptable in the workplace because of the additional elements of economic power and dependence.[58]

Aggressive fondling, drunken lurches, exclusive attention to anatomy, abusive language, and the treatment of women solely as sexual objects may, empirically speaking, be considered acceptable behavior outside of the workplace, but that is in large part a reflection of the very sorts of power imbalances which we at least recognize, reluctantly, at work. What makes such conduct generally acceptable outside of work is that men say it is, and that women have no say.

It is precisely this attitude of easy acceptance, at least outside of work, which makes it so difficult to limit sexual harassment at work. The problem with the court decisions, and the attitudes they reflect, is that offensive sexuality is so routinely considered normal, abuse of power acceptable, and the dehumanizing of women in sexual relations unremarkable, that when we (or the courts, at least) see such things at work, it hardly seems a "federal case." On the contrary, both courts and commentators have expressed the view that such activity is not only common but desirable. As Judge MacKinnon of the U.S. Court of Appeals pointed out, "Sexual advances may not be intrinsically offensive . . . . [they involve] social patterns that to some extent are normal and expectable."[59] Indeed, according to one commentator writing in the *Harvard Law Review,* "relations between the sexes may be chilled if men fear that behavior offensive to a sensitive woman may be actionable in court."[60]

The courts' answer to this concern has been the creation of the limited and inadequate legal doctrine addressed in this essay. Only where they find the explicit quid pro quo, only where the employee is otherwise perfect in terms of both job performance and personal worthiness, only where the hostile environment seems hostile even to the men judging it are the courts willing to say that something aberrant is happening, and that it needs to be stopped. The Title VII action, by and large, limits its redress to the most unusual; the problem, by and large, is what is considered usual.

But this is not the only answer. As things stand now, we protect the right of a few to have "consensual" sex in the workplace (a right most women, according to the studies, do not even want), at the cost of exposing the overwhelming majority to oppression and indignity at work. Is the benefit to the few so great as to outweigh the costs to so many more? I think not. For my part, I would have no objection to rules which prohibited men and women from sexual relations in the workplace, at least with those who worked directly for them. Men and women could, of course, violate the rule; but the power to complain, once in the hands of the less powerful, might well "chill" sexual relations by evening the balance of power between the two.

I do not see this as going too far. After all, in cases of true love, one could wait a semester, or transfer to another department, or even trust the woman not to file a lawsuit. But for those who shy away from such a clear rule, the courts' sexism is not the only alternative. The doctrinal changes recommended in this essay, for example, would not mean an end to all sexual relations at work. They would, however, enhance the scrutiny of employment decisions which men make about women with whom they have been sexually involved, and about women who have rejected them sexually. These changes would also require employers to take responsibility for their workplaces, to ensure that they are no more dangerous to a woman's psyche than to her body. Though not a major revolution perhaps, and not as clearcut as I would ideally like, these changes would nonetheless be steps in the right direction.

As with rape, the reality is that many men will not change unless and until forced to change. After all, few give up power, or its perquisites, without a fight. But there are some signs that the fight has begun. Women who for years routinely accepted harassment as part of the environment—indeed, by men's definition, as a prize of it—are beginning to say "no," to speak out, to force employers and institutions to recognize and address the question of what counts as harassment.

Take, for instance, the case of Congressman Jim Bates (D-CA), whose idea of "just joking around" apparently included requests for daily hugs from female staffers, during which he patted their buttocks; discussions of whether an aide would sleep with him if she were stranded on a desert island; and wrapping his legs around the leg of another staffer, in full view of his office staff, and swaying back and forth, grinning.[61] Representative Bates is surely not the first member of Congress to engage in such "joking around." But his staffers complained to the House Ethics Committee, which found the allegations sufficiently serious to investigate and to require an apology. This is at least a beginning.

It is a beginning because the women had the courage to speak up, and because the men of the Ethics Committee knew that however acceptable such behavior was in the past, today it could not be officially approved. This case was not a "federal" one perhaps, but it was not acceptable either. For all the grousing, my guess is that Congressional offices are a little more pleasant to work in today because of the complaint against Congressman Bates. And that is certainly a step in the right direction.

Notes

1. A major study of the Michigan reform statute, for example, concluded that "the law has very little impact on the system's approach to sexual assault cases." Jeanne Marsh, Alison Geist & Nathan Caplan, Rape and the Limits of Law Reform 65 (1982)....

2. See 110 Cong. Rec. 2577–2584 (1964) (remarks of Reps. Smith, Tuten, Andrews, and Rivers). See generally Francis J. Vaas, Title VII: Legislative History, 7 B.C. Indus. & Com. L. Res. 431, 441–442 (1966).

3. See McDonnell Douglas Corp. v. Green, 411 U.S. 792, 802–806 (1972) (discussing allocation of burdens of proof in racial discrimination cases); Griggs v. Duke Power Co., 401 U.S. 424 (1971) (use of pre-employment test having discriminatory impact violates Title VII despite absence of discriminatory intent)....

4. See, e.g., Paula Bernstein, Sexual Harassment on the Job, Harper's Bazaar, Aug. 1976, at 12; Judith Coburn & Mary Cunningham, So Successful, She Had to Fail, Mademoiselle, Jan. 1981, at 24; Claire Safran, What Men Do to Women on the Job: A Shocking Look at Sexual Harassment, Redbook, Nov. 1976, at 149; Nancy J. White, Sex in the Office: It's Mostly Bad Business, Ladies Home Journal, Oct. 1982, at 104.

5. Catharine A. MacKinnon, Sexual Harassment of Working Women 1 (1979).

6. 29 C.F.R. §1604.11(a) (1990).

7. See, e.g, Corne v. Bausch & Lomb, Inc., 390 F. Supp. 161, 163 (D. Ariz. 1975), *vacated without opinion,* 562 F.2d 55 (9th Cir. 1977); Barnes v. Train, 13 Fair Empl. Prac.

Cas. (BNA) 123, 124 (D.D.C. 1974), *rev'd sub. nom.* Barnes v. Costle, 561 F.2d 983 (D.C. Cir. 1977).

8. Williams v. Saxbe, 413 F. Supp. 654, 657 (D.D.C. 1976), *rev'd sub nom.* Williams v. Bell, 587 F.2d 1240 (D.C. Cir. 1978) (on procedural grounds), *on remand,* Williams v. Civiletti, 487 F. Supp. 1387 (D.D.C. 1980). . . . [The contract term *consideration* implies a quid pro quo. *Ed.*]

9. Corne v. Bausch & Lomb. Inc., 390 F. Supp. 161, 163–164 (D. Ariz. 1975), *vacated without opinion,* 562 F.2d 55 (9th Cir. 1977).

10. Safran, *supra* note 4, at 217. The Redbook survey found: "[N]early 9 out of 10 women report that they have experienced one or more forms of unwanted attentions on the job. This can be visual (leering and ogling) or verbal (sexual remarks and teasing). It can escalate to pinching, grabbing and touching to subtle hints and pressures, to overt requests for dates and sexual favors—with the implied threat that it will go against the woman if she refuses."

11. United States Merit Systems Protection Board, Sexual Harassment in the Federal Workplace: Is It a Problem? 2–3 (1981).

12. United States Merit Systems Protection Board, Sexual Harassment in the Federal Government: An Update 39 (1988).

13. See Barbara A. Gutek, Sex and the Workplace 46 (1985) (53.1% of women surveyed identified themselves as victims of sexual harassment); . . . Donald E. Maypole, Sexual Harassment at Work: A Review of Research and Theory, 2 Affilia 24, 30 (1987) (36% of women surveyed identified themselves as victims of sexual harrassment). . . .

14. See, e.g., Williams v. Civiletti, 487 F. Supp. 1387 (D.D.C. 1980) (supervisor kept changing his story; plaintiff consistently alleged that she was fired because she failed to accede to his demands); Miller v. Bank of America, 418 F. Supp. 233, 234 (N.D. Cal. 1976) (allegation by black female employee that her male supervisor promised her a better job if she would be sexually cooperative and caused her dismissal when she refused).

15. 477 U.S. 57 (1986). Mechelle Vinson, the plaintiff, is an African-American woman. Whether and to what extent racism plays a role in sexual harassment, and in the legal system's treatment of such cases, is an important question which is beyond the scope of this essay.

16. *Id.* at 60.

17. *Id.*

18. *Id.* Vinson also testified that Taylor "touched and fondled" other female employees, *id.* at 60, but the district court did not permit her "to present wholesale evidence of a pattern and practice relating to sexual advances to other female employees in her case in chief, but advised her that she might well be able to present such evidence in rebuttal to the defendants' case." *Id.* at 61 (quoting Vinson v. Taylor, 23 Fair Empl. Prac. Cas. (BNA) 37, 38 n.1 (D.D.C. 1980)).

19. *Vinson,* 23 Fair Empl. Prac. Cas. (BNA) at 42.

20. See, e.g., Dockter v. Rudolf Wolff Futures, Inc., 684 F. Supp. 532, 534–535 (N.D. Ill. 1988), *aff'd,* 913 F.2d 456 (7th Cir. 1990); Christoforou v. Ryder Truck Rental, Inc., 668 F. Supp. 294, 296–297 (S.D.N.Y. 1987). . . .

21. *Vinson,* 753 F.2d at 145 n.30.

22. *Vinson,* 477 U.S. at 65–66.

23. *Id.* at 67.

24. *Id.* (quoting Henson v. Dundee, 682 F.2d 897, 904 (11th Cir. 1982)).

25. *Id.* at 68 (citing 29 C.F.R. §1604.11(a) (1985)).

26. *Id.* at 69 (emphasis added).

27. *Id.* at 72.

28. *Id.* at 68.

29. *Id.* at 69.

30. Reichman v. Bureau of Affirmative Action, 536 F. Supp. 1149, 1164 (M.D. Pa. 1982).

31. Gan v. Kepro Circuit Sys., 28 Fair Empl. Prac. Cas. (BNA) 639, 640–641 (E.D. Mo. 1982). . . .

32. See Joan Vermeulen, Preparing Sexual Harassment Litigation Under Title VII, 7 Women's Rts. L. Rep. 331, 340–342 & n.81 (1982).

33. See, e.g., Valdez v. Church's Fried Chicken, Inc., 683 F. Supp. 596 (W.D. Tex. 1988) (absenteeism); Ramsey v. Olin Corp., 39 Fair Empl. Prac. Cas. (BNA) 959 (S.D.N.Y. 1984) (high error rate); Sand v. Johnson Co., 33 Fair Emp. Prac. Cas. (BNA) 716 (E.D. Mich. 1982) (tardiness). . . .

34. See, e.g., Horn v. Duke Homes, 755 F.2d 599, 602 (7th Cir. 1985) (three other women employees came forward to testify that the same supervisor had repeatedly harassed them). . . .

35. See, e.g., Drinkwater v. Union Carbide Corp., 904 F.2d 853 (3d Cir. 1990). . . .

36. 47 Empl. Prac. Dec. (CCH) ¶38,316, at 53,788 (E.D.N.Y. 1988).

37. *Id.* at 53,795.

38. *Id.* . . .

39. Meritor Sav. Bank v. Vinson, 477 U.S. 57, 67 (1986) (quoting Henson v. City of Dundee, 682 F.2d 897, 904 (11th Cir. 1982)).

40. Henson v. City of Dundee, 682 F.2d 897, 904 (11th Cir. 1982). Applying this standard, courts have been reluctant to recognize sexual harassment in the absence of at least the old "quid" of the quid pro quo cases—repeated sexual demands. Mere "sexual derision," as Professor Kathryn Abrams terms it, has generally been held insufficient to create a hostile environment, and even sporadic sexual demands have often proven insufficient. Kathryn Abrams, Gender Discrimination and the Transformation of Workplace Norms, 42 Vand. L. Rev. 1183, 1199–1200 (1989). . . .

41. See Meritor Sav. Bank v. Vinson, 477 U.S. 57, 67; Henson v. City of Dundee, 682 F.2d 897, 904 (11th Cir. 1982).

42. Rabidue v. Osceola Ref. Co., 584 F. Supp. 419, 433 (E.D. Mich. 1984), *aff'd,* 805 F.2d 611 (6th Cir. 1986).

43. Vermett v. Hough, 627 F. Supp. 587, 607 (W.D. Mich. 1986).

44. Kelsey-Andrews v. City of Philadelphia, No. 88–4101, 1988 WL 137284, at *2 (E.D. Pa. Dec. 19, 1988).

45. Spencer v. General Elec. Co., 697 F. Supp. 204, 214 (E.D. Va. 1988).

46. Sand v. Johnson Co., 33 Fair Empl. Prac. Cas. (BNA) 716, 720, 727 (E.D. Mich. 1982).

47. Staton v. Maries County, 868 F.2d 996, 998 (8th Cir. 1989).

48. 432 N.W.2d 764 (Minn. Ct. App. 1988). . . .

49. *Id.* at 768–769.

50. *Id.* at 770.

51. See, e.g., Horn v. Duke Homes, 755 F.2d 599 (7th Cir. 1985) (two former female employees testified that they had been harassed, and another that she had had a "voluntary" affair with the same man).

52. While most jurisdictions have formally abandoned such rules, the Model Penal Code retains a corroboration provision and a fresh complaint rule in its proposals. See Model Penal Code §213.6(4)–(5); Susan Estrich, Real Rape, 95 Yale L.J. 1087 (1986).

53. See, e.g., *Spencer,* 697 F. Supp. at 210–211 (failure to complain, except to one friend, considered particularly telling given that victim, according to several co-workers, often inappropriately discussed her personal life at work). . . .

54. Gutek, *supra* note 13, at 46, 54.

55. This disfavored status seems to be reflected not only in the tone that many opinions take toward the complaining witnesses, but also in the reluctance of courts to reach a conclusion of "sexual harassment" in the absence of more proof than is generally required in civil cases. Formally, the standard of proof may be a preponderance of the evidence; in practice, the standard applied seems much heavier.

56. 924 F.2d 872 (9th Cir. 1991).

57. See Commodore Home Systems, Inc. v. Superior Court, 32 Cal.3d 211, 649 P.2d 912, 185 Cal. Rptr. 270 (1983). [The Civil Rights Act of 1991 permits a plaintiff to recover both compensatory and punitive damages if she establishes that the defendant acted with discriminatory intent. *Ed.*]

58. See Gutek, *supra* note 13. . . .

59. Barnes v. Costle, 561 F.2d 983, 1001 (D.C. Cir. 1977) (MacKinnon, J., concurring).

60. Sexual Harassment Claims of Abusive Work Environment Under Title VII, 97 Harv. L. Rev. 1449 (1984) (student author).

61. See Sex Probes to Target 3 Lawmakers, L.A. Times, Aug. 5, 1989, at 2, col. 1.

"What's the Big Deal?" Women in the New York City Construction Industry and Sexual Harassment Law, 1970–1985

Elvia R. Arriola

. . .

THE RECENT HISTORY of women's participation in the New York City construction industry provides historians and lawyers with an opportunity to broaden their perspectives on gender as a tool for social and legal historical analysis.[1] At the same time, it offers the opportunity to assess the effectiveness of the legal system as a tool for social change. . . .[2]

[T]he emergence of a "sexual harassment" law in the 1970s was a significant accomplishment. Any assessment of this law's place in history must ask, however, not only if the law enhanced the body of women's legal rights, but also if it actually improved working women's lives. Furthermore, this assessment must be sensitive to issues of class, color, ethnicity and sexual orientation. . . .

I. The Socio-Historical Groundwork for a Sexual Harassment Legal Theory: National Developments

A. Early 1970s Feminist Body Politics and the Emergence of the "New Working Woman"

In 1970, the idea of a woman choosing non-traditional work as an electrician or a plumber in New York City was a "big deal"—an improbability. [I]n 1970 the feminist fever was reaching women of all social and economic backgrounds.

By 1971, the women's liberation movement made its greatest impact on employment. The size of the female labor force had more than doubled since World War II, and it continued to grow throughout the decade.[3] White married women accounted for the most dramatic increases, mostly in white collar jobs. However, other groups of working women also made changes. Large numbers of black women left domestic service and entered clerical and other service industries.[4] Data are unreliable on the em-

22 Colum. Hum. Rts. L. Rev. 21 (1990).

ployment of Puerto Rican, Mexican, Chinese, Japanese and other Hispanic and Asian women during this period because existing reports tend to group all Hispanics and Asians together. By 1971, however, the civil rights movement and the inclusion of prohibitions against sex discrimination in Title VII helped lift the pre-war social barriers that discouraged women of color from taking office and industrial jobs.[5]

Although participation of women in the labor force had consistently risen since World War II, the overall earning capacity of women in comparison to that of men had not. For good reason, therefore, feminists made better wages a primary focus of the national women's movement. . . . The time seemed ripe for women to seek better paying "men's work.". . .

The rising participation of women in the white-collar sector throughout the 1970s was consistent with the movement's white middle-class character. In comparison, women's participation in the blue-collar trades started low and never returned to the high levels of participation once seen in the 1940s.[6] Post-war declines in female employment hit hardest in the blue-collar sector. The war effort marketed the image of "Rosie the Riveter" to encourage women to take blue-collar jobs. After the war, however, an expulsion campaign to get "Mom" back into the home resulted in a severe drop in the number of tradeswomen. By the end of the 1960s, women of all racial backgrounds accounted for approximately 2% of the work force employed in craft jobs.[7]

B. Origins of a Feminist Jurisprudence: Legitimating the Social and Legal Claim for "Sexual Harassment"

. . . Sexual harassment had historically been a part of the experience of working-class women. The "new working woman," formerly the white middle-class housewife or daughter, was not exempt from the same range of harassment—from flirtations, verbal or physical expressions of sexual interest, to coercive sexual demands. Larger numbers of women in white-collar employment increased the opportunities for incidents of sexual harassment. In some cases, harassment may have been a reaction to the perceived threat of female encroachment on "male territory." In other cases, harassment might have functioned as a means to preserve a heterosexual, male-dominated social order from gradual erosion by an expanding feminist consciousness. Yet, in contrast to the economically vulnerable working-class woman of the past, the "new working woman," backed by a growing feminist political strength, felt empowered to challenge unwarranted male sexual advances in the workplace.

Among the first to challenge the legality of sexually harassing behavior were women who had taken traditionally male-occupied positions in the business world. In the New York–New Jersey area, for example, public attention to the treatment of women at work coincided with the beginning of the women's movement. In 1971, preeminent labor attorney Judith Vladeck filed a Title VII action against a division of the Western Electric Corporation in New Jersey on behalf of Kyriaki Cleo Kyriazi. Kyriazi, an engineer, claimed that her firing in November 1970 was discriminatory and that prior to her firing she was sexually ridiculed and harassed by her male co-workers. The case evolved into a more than ten-year battle on behalf of a class of women at Western Electric. Eventually, it brought an $8.5 million judgment as well as separate fines against five bosses who had harassed Kyriazi.[8] Kyriazi's case prompted local feminists to create the Working Women's Institute, which opened in 1971 in Manhattan to promote awareness of the discrimination and harassment of working women. By 1972, feminist activists were gearing up to turn a growing social and political conflict between the sexes into a consistent legal battle to establish the claim of "sexual harassment." The Working Women's Institute had been in service for one year providing working women, activists and lawyers with forums, workshops and an information clearinghouse on discrimination and harassment.[9] The Institute's resources empowered feminist lawyers to begin the process of codifying the political argument that unwanted sexual advances towards working women constituted abuse, harassment and employment discrimination. . . .

C. Public Reception of the New Woman's Right to a Sexual-Harassment-Free Working Environment: A White-Collar Picture

By the late 1970s, popular culture began to reflect the social and legal developments initiated by white-collar working women and the feminist bar. Women's magazines that grew out of the feminist movement, such as *Ms.* and *Working Woman,* began to publish articles about sexual harassment lawsuits beginning in the fall of 1977. . . .

Feminist politics, legal theory and practice had produced a powerful principle that could, theoretically, be used by any working woman in the United States. In reality, however, the success of the new legal remedy depended on whether all women could obtain sufficient support for their right to work in sexual-harassment-free environments. Popular culture depicted sexual harassment as if it were an exclusively white-collar problem; it excluded the experience of blue-collar working women. As a result, only middle- and upper-class women—who were predominantly white—benefitted from society's attention. Blue-collar working women, many of whom were women of color and ethnic women, remained unaffected by changes in the law and popular culture.

Also, by 1979 sharp differences appeared in the impact of the women's movement on the labor force. At the movement's start, activists defined non-traditional work broadly—as any field in which the representation of women was not commensurate with their 38% availability in 1970. Activists, in their efforts to improve the socioeconomic standing of women as a whole, made no distinction between the divergent needs and interests of working-class and middle-class women. Efforts to place working-class women in blue-collar "men's jobs" were marginalized by the overall effort, which was not immune to class bias; the mostly white, middle-class movement concentrated much of its efforts on placing mostly white, middle-class women in the privileged jobs once reserved for their husbands, fathers and brothers. As a result, while the number of women in white-collar jobs greatly increased, women's participation in highly paid "non-traditional" blue-collar fields like construction remained negligible at the decade's close.[10] A working-class woman like Jane Doe,[11] for example, who had neither a college education nor a significant interest in white-collar work, could not get the plumber's apprenticeship that she sought as early as 1968 and still wanted in 1979.

The numerical presence of women in the white-collar sector, when compared to their virtual absence in the blue-collar trades, suggests that the greatest prospects for the feminist strategy to reform male sexual behavior existed in the former workplace only.[12] As the next Part of this Article demonstrates, work culture, color and class issues in the blue-collar sector accounted for significant levels of difference and similarity in the experience of sexual harassment. . . .

II. Blue-Collar Feminist Organizing: The Negligible Impact of Sexual Harassment Remedies on the New York City Construction Industry

A. The Essential Backdrop: Entrenched Patterns of Racism in the Construction Trades, 1970–1978

In New York City, significant efforts to place women in jobs in the blue-collar trades did not occur until the late 1970s. This simple historical fact affected the overall impact that the feminist strategy to reform problems of sexual harassment would have on all American working women after the second national women's movement. At the beginning of the 1970s, women were completely absent from the city's high-paying construction trades. In fact, in 1971, the New York City Building Trades Council did not even bother to mention the "sex" of industry apprentices in its apprenticeship enrollment records;[13] all apprentices, of course, were male. Any woman seeking non-traditional blue-collar work would have needed strong institutional backing by women's groups, the government or unions to get into the trades. Yet women who wanted to work as plumbers, carpenters or electricians and who were motivated by personal and/or political interests to break into this traditionally male industry clearly existed.

Individual women like Jane Doe, a Jewish lesbian who is now a plumber, typify a kind of woman who may have embraced the spirit of the national feminist movement of the early 1970s despite her differences from its mostly white, middle-class and educated constituency. Doe was in her late twenties in 1970, and she was fully caught up in feminist politics as the movement progressed. Growing up as an only child in a working-class neighborhood in the Bronx, Doe remembers "always" wanting to perform the kind of hard physical labor that she enjoys on construction sites today. From an early age, both of her parents served as role models for learning to work with tools. Doe's father was a car mechanic, and her mother worked in factories. Doe recalls trying "to build things" with her father's tools "behind his back." Despite her socioeconomic differences from most women in the movement, Doe's expectations that feminist activism could fulfill her wish to become a tradeswoman were not unusual at a time when so much public attention was focused on a "women's liberation movement." Motivated by feminist ideals and a lifelong interest in working with her hands, Doe applied to plumbers' apprenticeship school around 1968, only to be rejected. By 1970, her desire to work as a plumber seemed like an elusive dream, and, like most other working-class women at the time, she performed "some kind of clerical work."[14]

The closed character of the construction industry, which effectively shut out not only women but also most minorities, was clear at the decade's start. Small neighborhood organizations that reached out to the black or Hispanic community had been fighting racism in the New York City construction trades at least since 1964.[15] In the early 1970s, for example, the federal government joined a local battle, a law suit initiated by state and city agencies along with members of Harlem Fight Back, a neighborhood organization which was headed by Jim Haughton, against Local 28 of the International Brotherhood of Sheet Metal Workers. The lawsuit charged that union officers had discriminated against blacks and Hispanics. Plaintiffs alleged that union officers had employed nepotism and closed hiring halls to prevent blacks and Hispanics from enjoying equal opportunities, and that blacks and Hispanics were unlawfully denied membership in the union and enrollment in the apprenticeship school.[16]

Systematic racist exclusionary practices were not limited to the Sheet Metal Workers. During the same period, Puerto Rican electricians like Samuel Lopez fought against the discriminatory practices of Local 3 of the International Brotherhood of Electrical Workers (IBEW). By the mid-1970s, Lopez and other mostly black and Hispanic tradesmen formed the United Third Bridge (UTB) in an effort to dismantle a power structure that kept the IBEW and other construction unions in the city wholly dominated by white men. . . .[17]

The uphill battle against racism in the construction industry was marked by numerous court orders, contempt sanctions against obstructionist union leaders and affirmative action programs. By the mid-1970s, however, legal developments were just starting to make breaks in a wall of white-male trade unionist hostility. By 1974, political and legal pressure increased minority representation in construction and mechanical apprenticeships to 22%.[18] Against this background of entrenched racism, the prospects for women's participation in a tightly closed industry remained grim.

In the early 1970s, even though public attention to the issue of "women's liberation" increased, it appears that only one woman, Liz Young, broke into the New York City construction trades. In 1972, Young, a feminist Chinese-American, used her personal contacts with members of Fight Back to become a plumber trainee.[19] By 1974, only 4 of the total 4,500 construction and mechanical apprentices under the jurisdiction of the Building Trades Council were women.[20] Without organizational support or encouragement, working-class women like Jane Doe, who also wanted to be a plumber at this time, did not have a chance. In 1978, Fight Back urged city officials to encourage significant social change; the organization appealed to Mayor Ed Koch to create a city-administered hiring hall that would serve as an alternative to the racist and sexist hiring halls of the unions.[21] Even as recently as the late 1970s, the New York City construction industry was plainly closed to anyone not white or male.

B. Early Efforts to Sexually Integrate the Construction Trades: Women's Organizations, 1978–1980

Around 1978, a few local advocacy groups took steps to increase the presence of women in the New York City construction industry. These groups worked to place women from a wide range of social, economic, racial and ethnic backgrounds in jobs in the industry. Some of the women had college degrees; others never completed high school. Women born inside and outside of the United States; middle-class women and working-class women; former welfare recipients; some just out of high school, others in their forties and fifties; former nurses and teachers; lesbian, black, Chinese-American, Puerto Rican, Jewish, and white women—all began to seek careers as electricians, laborers, latherers, carpenters, plumbers, ironworkers and sheetmetal workers.

One such woman was electrician Cynthia Long. Long immigrated to Tarrytown, New York, from La Tuque, Quebec, with her Chinese-Canadian parents and two brothers when she was in the sixth grade. As a child, Cynthia was drawn to "non-traditional" activities. She enjoyed making house repairs with her father. Later she took a mechanical drawing course in Tarrytown's high school; she had even thought of becoming a doctor or a lawyer. Her mother's work in the male-dominated field of computer systems design analysis probably encouraged her to become an electrician. After high school, Long found career prospects very depressing; as she put it, she could either "work at McDonald's" or become a low-paid clerk or secretary with no opportunities for advancement. Corporate employers to which she applied for work noted her intelligence and verbal skills, but declined to hire her because she lacked a college degree. In 1976, when Long was twenty-one years old and living on her own, her low earnings record qualified her for a training program that would make her employable in the construction trades.

Funding for women's groups or community outreach organizers during this period often came through government programs like the Comprehensive Employment Training Act (CETA).[22] The U.S. Department of Labor, which administered CETA, funded "prime sponsors," public agencies at the state and local level that assessed local needs for training the "economically disadvantaged, unemployed, and underemployed."[23] CETA's drafters were concerned with the economic survival of many of the nation's inner cities; in particular they were concerned with finding employment for youths in low-income black and Hispanic neighborhoods that were scarred by the race riots of the late 1960s. . . .

One of the first programs created that had as its specific purpose the introduction of women into the construction trades was the Manhattan-based Women in Apprenticeships Project (WAP). WAP was formed in 1977 or 1978; it was later renamed Non-Traditional Employment for Women (NEW). [Another organization] was the Allcraft

Center, which . . . was headed by a woman named Joyce Hartwell. . . . Because Allcraft reached out to women and men of many minority groups, the organization successfully attracted a broad social spectrum of women.

Despite the initiatives of organizations like Allcraft and WAP, however, several factors combined to frustrate and undermine the overall success of efforts to integrate the construction industry. Racism, the inopportune timing of the first organizing efforts, the limited institutional support provided by women's job placement organizations, and a deeply entrenched and resistant masculine work culture gave shape to an environment which, when it did not completely bar women, left them with little or no protection from abusive treatment on the job.

1. THE FIRST FACTOR: RACISM

Organizations like Allcraft or WAP, the primary purposes of which were to make women "employable" in the trades, designed short-term training programs to prepare an individual to perform a variety of basic trade skills and pass the trade apprenticeship entry exams. At Allcraft, Cynthia Long joined about thirty women in a one-month program that taught them how to use the basic tools for plumbing, carpentry, cabinetmaking or electrical wiring. Long remembers that her classmates were black, Hispanic, Asian and white, and that they ranged in age from the teens to the late fifties. A few were from white middle-class college backgrounds and drawn to the trades because of their feminist politics or the prospects of leaving low-paying "female professions" like nursing, teaching and social work.[24]

Although the training programs looked promising, graduates were often left on their own to find steady work as trainees or union apprentices in an industry that historically had shown signs of hostility toward social minorities. Most trades offered a limited number of spaces in their union apprenticeship schools, and spaces were available only about once per year. Nevertheless, the nepotistic network that gave preference to the friends and relatives of union officials enabled hundreds of white men to obtain employment while avoiding the apprenticeship examination system. In theory, the New York State Department of Labor and a Joint Apprenticeship Committee comprised of employers and union officials for each trade regulated the trade apprenticeships system for all of New York City's five boroughs. In practice, however, the city's white male trade union leadership tightly controlled all aspects of hiring, layoffs, promotion and benefits.[25]

Therefore, the women who first entered the New York City construction trades—many of whom were women of color—faced formidable obstacles to acceptance by a white male-dominated industry. Joyce Hartwell, the director of Allcraft Center, reputedly quickly gave up trying to get the unions to accept her mostly black, Hispanic or Asian graduates.[26] Long's difficulties in getting work after leaving Allcraft and the experiences of women like Sadie Baxter and Michelle Jackson, both black single mothers and former welfare recipients, typified the problem. The difficulty of getting into the trade apprenticeships or any union job meant that many Allcraft graduates endured long periods of unemployment, or they performed non-union odd jobs. Some women graduates arranged for small jobs through Mothers and Daughters Construction Company, a construction company formed by Joyce Hartwell that advertised in the Village Voice, a progressive New York weekly. Sadie Baxter, for example, did not find work as a plumber for almost one year except through Mothers and Daughters; it took Michelle Jackson an entire year to find steady work as a carpenter.[27]

2. THE SECOND FACTOR: THE INOPPORTUNE TIMING OF FEMINIST ORGANIZING

By the late 1970s, programs like WAP were offering more direct support to women who were trying to get into trade apprenticeship schools. By 1978, however, the ideal moment for raising the issue of "non-traditional employment" of women in the blue-collar sector had passed. Entrenched racism in the construction industry was a continuing reality. Also, public support for the women's movement had started to wane. . . . Shifting political attitudes to the right detracted from the efficacy of efforts to organize to sexually integrate the construction industry.

Insensitivity on the part of movement organizers to the social and political heterogeneity of women in the movement created internal divisions. For example, in 1978, Jane Doe was thrilled—at least initially—to be referred to WAP for assistance in obtaining membership in the plumbers' union. As a radical feminist, however, Doe found the recruitment process to be unpleasant and offensive. Mary Garvin, WAP's founder and the recruiter with whom Doe consulted, anticipated that Doe would encounter resistance from male union officers and she offered Doe some advice in the form of a "survival technique" that was wholly at odds with Doe's personal and political values. "Cover up your arms," she told Doe. She also said, "I don't mind showing a little leg or tit to get a job."[28] Despite the social, legal and political developments that had occurred, many women involved in the effort to integrate the trades did not operate from a comprehensive feminist perspective, nor did they employ a developed feminist strategy to achieve gender equality in the workplace. Women like New York State Division of Labor Industrial Commissioner Louise Finney, who monitored WAP, were identifiably feminist, but other activists, like Garvin, were not. Therefore, the one and only issue that united women organizers and activists was not ideology, but the pragmatic belief that more women should be hired.

3. THE THIRD FACTOR: THE LACK OF POST-HIRING INSTITUTIONAL SUPPORT

The feminist activism of the 1970s, which emphasized more and better jobs for women, had its most profound effect in the business world, where a significant number of middle-class women were hired. It is not unusual, therefore, that the increased hiring of women became the central goal of blue-collar organizations like WAP also. This emphasis on hiring blinded organizers to many obstacles that were in the way of opening up the construction industry to women. Issues of discrimination based not only on sex, but also on class, race and sexual orientation, as well as reactionary politics and misogynistic characteristics of the blue-collar male work culture, frustrated efforts to sexually integrate the construction industry. The situation was exacerbated by the fiscal and political reality that groups like WAP relied on public funds to keep their recruitment programs going. Funding, moreover, was conditioned on proof that funds were used to gain access into apprenticeship programs; no funds were available to finance the counseling and support of women who had been hired. Without such funds for post-hiring support, concerns about job security and discrimination were relegated to the back burner.

Once a woman obtained employment, the typical government-supported organization ceased to function as a source of support, and no assistance was available to help her cope with post-hiring problems like sexual or racial harassment. Michelle Jackson experienced continuous sexual harassment, such as threats that she would be fired if she did not have sex with her supervisor; she also found that pornography and a poster entitled "The Making of a Cunt" had been placed in her locker. Allcraft, the organization that placed Jackson, could offer no help. In fact, Jackson even felt Allcraft's Joyce Hartwell had tried to dissuade her from lodging a complaint with the union.[29] Elaine Major, a black carpenter who also graduated from Allcraft, was another target of persistent racial and sexual slurs and harassment. Aside from finding pornography in her locker, she once found that someone had placed a dead mouse in her tool box.[30]

4. THE FOURTH FACTOR: BLUE-COLLAR MEN AND THE USE OF HARASSMENT AS A SHIELD AGAINST THE EROSION OF A WHITE MASCULINE BLUE-COLLAR WORK CULTURE

The feminist move to integrate an industry with a history of exclusionary practices against minorities also brought to the surface dominant white masculine attitudes about women. Organizations like Allcraft, which heavily recruited people of color, believed that it would be a waste of time to take a black woman's complaint of sexual harassment to the white-dominated unions. The most likely beneficiaries of the recruitment surge of the late 1970s were white women. For example, Elly Spicer, a carpenter and former recruiter for WAP's successor entity, Non-traditional Employment for Women (NEW), recalls that sexist racism often came to bear on the hiring process. Spicer is from a white, middle-class family in New Jersey; she is also college-educated. Her involvement with radical feminist organizing got her the job as a NEW recruiter in the early 1980s. To get work, graduates of a trade skills program like NEW were taken on a "shape," a process that involved appearing at a construction site at the start of the workday, usually at about 7:00 A.M. While the women who sought work waited in a van, a recruiter talked to the site supervisor to try to get him to hire one or more of the women. Attending the shape did not guarantee getting work, especially for women of color. Spicer recalls that white male site supervisors would barely glance at the mostly black and Hispanic women on the shape. In contrast they would often offer Spicer a job "on the spot."[31]

Although all women experienced pervasive sexism, tradeswomen of color appeared most vulnerable. Plumber Carolyn Nowodzinski is white and from a working-class background. She never had a problem getting work, and she believes that her being white has been an employment asset. Nowodzinski recalls that black tradeswomen and tradesmen were frequently assigned to the worst locations and the most difficult or dangerous jobs.[32] Gladys Lopez, a Puerto Rican apprentice, says that in her nine years as an electrician she experienced both sexual and racial discrimination—"most of the time" because of her skin color. For example, her apprenticeship director once told her to "get a job as a cook like your father; you're not cut out for this business."[33]

Union officials frequently transferred a woman from one construction site to another, rather than deal with her complaints of harassment, intimidation and racial or sexual discrimination. The most vulnerable tradeswoman was the apprentice. Gladys Lopez remembers frequently being assigned to "coffee duty"; she also describes being laid-off during her six-month probation period on grounds that she was "not suited for this type of work." In fact, frequent layoffs kept many women, especially women of color, from fulfilling the requirements of their apprenticeships, which in turn prevented them from qualifying for higher paying, steadier jobs with "journeyman" or "mechanic" status. Zaiah Martinez' case is illustrative. Martinez, a small black ironworker, who was the only woman in her local for years, was repeatedly assigned to a job site where the foreman refused to put her to work. On another site, the foreman stated that he was "anti-women and anti-black" and that the only reason that Martinez was tolerated there was "the law." On one occasion, Martinez was forced to singlehandedly use the "hell dog," a sixty-pound piece of equipment that usually required operation by two people. On many other jobs, Martinez was denied proper safety equipment.[34]

Understanding racism, which, like sexism, is an historical manifestation of patriarchal structures,[35] is essential to understanding the swift merging of racial and sexual harassment as a functional aspect in the defense of the traditional working conditions of the construction industry. Cultural theorist Susan Jeffords argues that from the late 1960s to about 1987 American culture was in the process of renegotiating and regenerating images and constructions of "the masculine." Examining cultural images of the Vietnam War, Jeffords suggests that when challenges to a certain prejudice appear "taboo" to the dominant white male structure, exclusionary practices emerge within the culture to bolster or uplift "masculinity."[36] Jeffords argues that the civil rights movements of blacks and of women shook the stability of the foundation on which patriarchal power in America rested. Consequently, tradeswomen encountered a barrage of "remasculinization" from their male co-workers, supervisors and trade union officials. What posed a greater threat to "the masculine" than the fact that a woman dared to take a job culturally believed to require "brute male force"? . . .

The hostility that women confronted on the job took on numerous forms, which ran the gamut from expressions of sexist or racist resentment to frequent layoffs and harassment. Sometimes hostility was expressed in behavior that bordered on criminal assault and battery. Such extreme behavior suggests that men on the job perceived a need to preserve the construction industry as one of the last "pure" bastions of masculine values in the blue-collar work culture. . . .

While in certain respects the experience of sexual harassment in the construction industry was no different from the experience of sexual harassment in white-collar settings, a study of sexual harassment in the construction industry reveals how deeply embedded masculine values were in blue-collar work culture. The mere presence of a woman in a hardhat threatened the masculine assumptions of male physical superiority on which the culture was based because masculine attitudes subordinated women to men—sexually, physically and socially. Tradeswomen, who could do a "man's job" competently, were perceived as threats to the heterosexual social order. As a result, male workers viewed most of the early tradeswomen as "unfeminine"; they verbally attacked the women as "dykes." Those women who actually were lesbian had to hide their identities or endure expressions of intense male hostility. Carpenter Alyssa Melnick, for example, is certain that her open lesbian identity led to her being the only member of a work crew not to be invited to a male co-worker's wedding.[37]

By ignoring or penalizing women who complained of or reacted to extreme male sexual taunts, the construction industry became a "hostile work environment" for pioneer tradeswomen. By the early 1980s, while lawsuits brought by women in the white-collar sector were strengthening the jurisprudential trend that was started in the late 1970s,[38] the frequently isolated tradeswomen had no public or private recourse for help. Consequently, out of fear or a sense of futility, many tradeswomen tolerated aggressive behavior aimed at displaying or preserving masculine superiority. One of Cynthia Long's transfers resulted from an incident involving a male co-worker who asked her for a date every day for two months. One day, as she stood on a ladder and he described a "wet dream" he had about her, Long finally "blew up" and threw a hammer at him. Long was off the job the next day. Plumber Jane Doe remembers one job where a male co-worker twice exposed his genitals to her and another relieved himself against the wall of the women's changing room. Gladys Lopez does not remember ever being sexually touched or teased, but recalls that men were "constantly dropping their pants in front of [her]."

The case of Pam Berdebes, a lesbian who was formerly an ironworker and plumber, illustrates the full range of intimidating and hostile behavior aimed at preserving masculine values and keeping women out of the industry. Berdebes was drawn to the trades; as a child, she worked with her father on plumbing and sewer cleaning jobs for the Roto-Rooter Company. Berdebes remembers being hired while on a NEW shape because she was the only white woman in the group. On her first job as a laborer, she experienced "constant" sexual flirtations and touchings from the site foreman. The union officer she complained to urged her to leave the trades. On another job, she experienced intense ostracism; the men "truly believed a woman should stay at home." Ten days into a new job, her partner intentionally dropped a heavy fence that they were carrying and Berdebes fell, breaking a leg. Determined not to quit, Berdebes went back to work—"cast and all"—one week later. With that, she became "one of the guys." Thereafter her male co-workers resorted to "kinder things" like sexual teasing and jokes, grabbing her breasts, and "peeing in front of [her]." In particular, one experience illustrates the misogyny that Berdebes often faced on the job. As Berdebes worked down in a sewer, a partner "with real problems" tried to "jerk off" on her.[39]

C. The Search for Empowerment Against Sexual Hostility

Encouraged by a lack of effective institutional support, and in the historical tradition of gender solidarity, pioneer tradeswomen of New York City looked to each other for understanding and solace. Long, for example, feels that she became a feminist because of her work experiences and her labor studies at the Cornell School of Industrial Relations. She survived her apprenticeship years by forming Women Electricians with three colleagues: Beth Goldman, a feminist; Melinda Hernandez, an Hispanic "street-wise feminist"; and Jackie Simmons, a black woman who was not an activist but supported the group's formation. Women Electricians defined its membership as any woman in Local 3 of the IBEW. An indication of the industry's success in keeping women out is that even in the 1980s only 50 women were members of Women Electricians. Eliminating pornography at job sites, which many women viewed as overtly hostile, was on the group's immediate agenda. In some places pornography was "wall to wall," something "you [had] to be in . . . to experience." Long felt that pornography nurtured male insensitivity to the desire of women to work and earn a living without being treated "like tits and asses." However, despite repeated attempts to get the IBEW to order the removal of the pornography, by the mid-1980s Women Electricians' complaints were still being ignored.[40] United Tradeswomen (UT) originated in December 1979 as a female support network committed to addressing the issues of discrimination, sexual harassment, racism, pornography and exclusionary practices such as the lack of women's toilets, changing rooms or adequate safety equipment. By 1984, however, UT was struggling to stay alive for lack of funds. Although it was able to conduct a survey of 200 diverse tradeswomen on these issues, lack of resources prevented the results from ever being published.[41] The need for effective alternatives to compensate for the glaring lack of institutional support cut across all the trades.

III. Sexual Harassment Law and All Working Women: Concluding Thoughts on the Relationship Between Feminist Theory and Practice

By the mid-1980s, the likelihood that a developed theory of sexual harassment would improve the working conditions of construction tradeswomen seemed remote. As long as the focus of women's organizations and government funding remained on hiring, as was the case, problems of sexual and racial harassment and abuse were relegated to silence and obscurity. In both the white-collar and blue-collar sectors, a complaint of harassment often promised retaliation. In the especially male-dominated culture of construction workers, retaliation took on a more threatening character. Complaints invited long-term layoffs, the loss of apprenticeships and a forced return to the "pink-collar ghetto," unemployment and welfare—consequences not typically faced by women in white-collar jobs. Even the potential for violence could not be taken lightly. Like Pamela Berdebes, who suffered a broken leg, a woman might even get hurt. As Long put it, "'accidents' can happen, and who would ever know or care?"

When, in the late 1970s, feminists decided to sexually integrate the construction industry, they might have taken on more than they realized. Placement in a construction job was equivalent to an invitation to become "invisible" in a "sea of men." Given the risks of complaining about harassment without effective institutional support, it hardly mattered that sophisticated social and legal theories to take on the issue of sexual harassment in the workplace had developed. The law and feminist politics had no meaningful impact on the entrenched masculine attitudes of the construction workplace. The marginal increase in the number of New York City tradeswomen suggests that sexual harassment and abuse were effective in keeping women out. Some tradeswomen thought the men just "didn't get it"; others felt that on issues of women and sexuality these men were "not educable." And yet, despite the harshness of some women's experiences, many expressed love for their work as plumbers, carpenters or electricians. It was a "big deal" for these women to go after a "man's job" in the construction industry. It was an even more significant triumph for them to stay in the industry when those with the power to assess and support women's experiences inside the industry, also seemed not to "get it."

The story of how the body of sexual harassment law developed demonstrates that law, politics and changing social values are intricately related. By examining and assessing the impact of the social and legal developments through the personal experiences of working women who were, theoretically, intended to benefit from the social and legal changes, we are also given an opportunity to see how issues of class, race, ethnicity and sexuality have affected and can continue to affect the ultimate path of a feminist legal strategy for reform.

This recent historical survey suggests that feminist jurisprudence can never be socially responsible or true to the goals of feminism if discourse about "patriarchal relations" is allowed to rest in the ivory towers of legal theory. Feminist scholars need to critically examine instances of the individual and societal experience of power and lack of power in relation to the law and particularly to those laws designed to affect the direction of women's history and women's rights.

In order to tighten the relationship between feminist theory and feminist practice, issues of class, race, ethnicity and sexuality must inform the perspectives from which we evaluate the impact of feminist politics on the society we seek to change. After all, it is the experiential basis that has historically given feminism its theoretical and political strength. Such empirical perspectives enhance the social responsibility of the feminist legal theorist and strategist. As demonstrated by the experiences of New York City tradeswomen, what good is a new "woman's right" without enforcement or without evidence that what has been fought for in the courts and legislatures has actually improved women's lives?

Appendix
Selected Interviews*

Name	Age Group**	Occupation	Race/Ethnicity	Recruited
Baxter	40–50	Plumber	Black	Allcraft
Berdebes	40–50	Plumber	White	NEW
Doe	40–50	Plumber	White (Jewish)	WAP
Jackson	40–50	Electrician	Black	Allcraft
Long	30–40	Electrician	Chinese	WAP
Lopez	20–30	Electrician	Puerto Rican	City-RTP***
Lurie	30–40	Carpenter	White (Jewish)	Independent
Major	40–50	Plumber	Black	Allcraft
Martinez	30–40	Ironworker	Black	NEW
Melnick	20–30	Carpenter	White (Jewish)	Independent
Nowodzinski	40–50	Plumber	White	Independent
Reyes	30–40	Carpenter	Puerto Rican	Independent
Spicer	30–40	Carpenter	White (Jewish)	Independent

* Some interviews were conducted as part of an investigation on racism and sexism in the New York City construction industry that the author initiated in January 1987 in her capacity as an Assistant Attorney General for the New York State Department of Law, Civil Rights Bureau (June 1986 to Sept. 1989). Many of the women interviewed were unwilling to identify themselves publicly for fear of reprisal or even physical abuse. On April 3, 1987, the author met approximately 25–35 members of Women Electricians at a meeting in New York City. Throughout that year, the author spoke to approximately 30 other women in person or by telephone. Although many of the interviewees readily identified themselves as lesbians, others who depend on union hiring halls to obtain work did not reveal their sexual orientation for fear of reprisal.

** At time of interview.

*** City Recruitment & Training Program.

Notes

1. The working-class women whose statements appear in this chapter do not, of course, represent all women who work or have worked in the New York City construction industry. Over the past three years, I spoke to approximately four times as many women as are identified in the Appendix about experiences of sexism and racism on the job or at the hands of employers and trade unions. . . .

Over a period of time, I noticed a consistent pattern emerge as the women whom I interviewed, regardless of their trades, described how they experienced or witnessed sexually and/or racially offensive, violent and harassing behavior. The systemic patterns of sexism and racism observed and described herein match the largely anonymous testimony recently compiled by the National Organization for Women Legal Defense and Education Fund (NOW-LDEF) for hearings on the extent of discrimination in the construction industry that were conducted by the New York City Commission on Human Rights on March 12–13 and April 24–26, 1990. Letter from Sarah Burns, Legal Director of NOW-LDEF, to Elvia Arriola (Mar. 22, 1990).

One characteristic that unites all of the interviews . . . is that all of the interviewees had worked on a major public construction site. Large contractors generally employ from 240 to 400 workers on any particular project and may receive millions of dollars in public funding for the construction of highways, housing complexes and public buildings. Interview with Kendall Argrette, of Argrette Enterprises Corp., in New York City (Sept. 21, 1989). . . .

2. . . . The legal system's inability to integrate sexually the construction industry [also] has been noted and discussed by Sylvia Law. Law, "Girls Can't Be Plumbers"— Affirmative Action for Women in Construction: Beyond Goals and Quotas, 24 Harv. C.R.-C.L. L. Rev. 45 (1989). . . .

3. L. Weiner, From Working Girl to Working Mother: The Female Labor Force in the United States, 1820–1980, 4 (1985). The 1940 U.S. census estimated that 12,951,000 women were working in 1940. These women accounted for approximately 25% of the American labor force. The 1970 U.S. census estimated that 30,547,000 women were working. In 1970, they accounted for 37% of the labor force. *Id.*

4. *Id.;* R. Milkman, Gender at Work: The Dynamics of Job Segregation by Sex During World War II 103 (1987); J. Jones, Labor of Love, Labor of Sorrow: Black Women, Work and the Family, From Slavery to the Present, 236–239, 301–302 (1986).

5. Before World War II, women of color were effectively barred from most industrial and office settings. As a result, many black, Hispanic and Asian women were forced to find work elsewhere. Nakano-Glenn, The Dialectics of Wage Work: Japanese-American Women and Domestic Service, 1905–1940, 6 Feminist Stud. 432 (1980). Most took domestic service jobs. . . . Domestic service continues to be the only viable employment option for many women of color. . . .

6. During the period between 1940 and 1945, the number of women in the U.S. labor force increased by nearly 32%, from 14.8 million in 1940 to 19.5 million in 1945. Jones, *supra* note 4, at 234. Most working women of this period were married and white; many took blue-collar "men's jobs" for the first time. *Id.* Women historians have increasingly called into question the "Rosie the Riveter" stereotype of the white housewife who supported the war effort by taking on a "man's job." See, e.g., Quick, Rosie the Riveter: Myths and Realities, 9 Radical America 115 (1975). . . .

7. By 1970, although the number of women working in the trades—as carpenters, construction workers, mechanics, electricians, plumbers, tool and die makers, machinists and typesetters—increased to about 500,000, women workers accounted for only 2–3% of employees for most trades. A. Kessler-Harris, Out to Work: A History of Wage-Earning Women in the United States 312 (1982). As late as 1976, figures for minority women were even lower. See, e.g., A. Mirande & E. Enriquez, La Chicana: The Mexican-American Woman 122–123 (1979).

8. Kyriazi v. Western Elec. Co., 461 F. Supp. 894 (D.N.J. 1978). . . .

9. C. MacKinnon, Sexual Harassment of Working Women xiv (1979).

10. Nationally, by 1979 women accounted for only 1.1% of all carpenters, 0.9% of electricians, and 1.9% of sheetmetal workers. Josephs, Latack, Roach & Levine, The Union as Help or Hindrance: Experiences of Women Apprentices in the Construction Trades, 13 Lab. Stud. J. 3, 3–4 (1988). Available information suggests that at the decade's close not much improvement had been made in the negligible representation of women in the New York City construction trades; women accounted for only .09% of the industry. The Committee for Women in Non-Traditional Jobs, Proposal to the U.S. Dep't of Labor, Women's Bureau (Apr. 18, 1980) [hereinafter Dept. of Labor Proposal].

Oral histories of the first women who entered the trades in the late 1970s strongly suggest that most trade unions admitted an insignificant number of women and that the representation of women was only marginally increased. Unions continued this hiring pattern throughout the 1980s. . . .

11. Jane Doe is a plumber in New York City who requested to be anonymous throughout this Article. She believed that her job security would be jeopardized if the comments that she made, which are referred to in this Article, were to be attributed to her by name. Interview with Jane Doe, in New York City (Dec. 29, 1989).

12. By no means do I claim that the problem of sexual harassment was erased in the business world or the "pink-collar ghetto" by the social and legal developments of the 1970s and the early 1980s. In the opinion of one woman who works as a legal secretary in a large New York City law firm: "It hasn't stopped in places like this; the men just go after the young and vulnerable ones, or those with such low self-esteem that they would never file a complaint." Interview with Roseann Bucca, in New York City (Mar. 28, 1990). Or as one tradeswoman and former office clerk put it, "white-collar men are more hypocritical; blue-collar men tell you more what they're thinking." Interview with Carolyn Nowodzinski, a plumber, in New York City (Dec. 26, 1989). Nevertheless, the social and legal developments of the period from 1970 to 1985 sufficiently affected middle-class consciousness so as to encourage many white-collar employers to adopt policies, post notices and provide female employees with some assurances that blatant acts of sexual harassment would no longer be tolerated. Such assurances or formal support measures (e.g., the appointment of equal employment opportunity officers or the implementation of functional grievance mechanisms) are non-existent in the construction industry.

13. New York City Mayor's Office of Construction Industry Relations, Chart: 1971–1981 Building Trades Survey (1982).

14. Interview with Jane Doe, in New York City (Dec. 29, 1989).

15. Fight Back, Blacks, Hispanics, Asian-Americans, Mexican-Americans, Women in Construction in the 80's (May 1980); Bivens, A Firm Foundation of Bias: Minorities' Uphill Fight for Construction Jobs, Newsday, Jan. 29, 1987, at 7, col. 3; Carpenter Who Spoke Up Finds Himself Walled Out, *id.* at 7, col. 1.

16. Local 28 of the Sheet Metal Workers Int'l Ass'n v. Equal Employment Opportunity Comm'n, 478 U.S. 421 (1985). . . .

17. Interview with Samuel Lopez, in New York City (Mar. 18, 1990).

18. Dept. of Labor Proposal, *supra* note 10.

19. Interview with Cynthia Long, in New York City (Nov. 3, 1989).

20. See Dept. of Labor Proposal, *supra* note 10, at 39.

21. Haughton, Two Steps Back at the Job Site, Newsday, Jan. 23, 1989, at 48, col. 1. Fight Back reissued its appeal to the New York City Commission on Human Rights at the Commission's hearings on the extent of discrimination in the construction industry on March 12, 1990. Bunis, Claims of Prejudice Leveled at Unions, Newsday, Mar. 12, 1990, at 7, col. 1.

22. Comprehensive Employment and Training Act of 1973, Pub. L. No. 93–203, 87 Stat. 839 (1973). In 1982, CETA was replaced by the Job Training Partnership Act, Pub. L. No. 97–300, 96 Stat. 1322 (1982) (codified as amended at 29 U.S.C. §§49–491, 801–999, 1501–1592, 1601–1781 (1988) & 42 U.S.C. §§602, 632–633 (1988)). . . .

23. CETA §2.

24. Interview with Cynthia Long, in New York City (Nov. 3, 1989). Some of the white women employed in the construction industry today are the relatives of men who have been involved with the trade for many years. As a result, on the job these women

benefit from a knowledge of the trade and job culture that they developed at home. They also benefit from the paternalistic "protection" of male relatives and friends. These advantages are unavailable—and in fact, unknown—to women of color who work in the industry. Law, *supra* note 2, at 51–52.

25. Interview with James MacNamara, of the New York State Organized Crime Task Force, in New York City (Jan. 25, 1987); Benson, Blacklisting in Construction, in Ass'n for Union Democracy, Democracy in the Construction Trades (1985); Construction Corruption Inquiry Hampered by Fears of Retaliation, N.Y. Times, Apr. 25, 1982, at A1, col. 5.

26. Interview with Elly Spicer, in New York City (Jan. 2, 1990).

27. Interview with Sadie Baxter and Michelle Jackson, in New York City (Apr. 11, 1987).

28. Interview with Jane Doe, in New York City (Dec. 29, 1989). The statement has been attributed to Mary Garvin by interview sources who felt that, as an experienced carpenter and not necessarily a feminist, Garvin could be controversial in her organizing tactics. Telephone interview with Cynthia Long (Feb. 4, 1990).

29. Interview with Michelle Jackson, in New York City (Mar. 4, 1987).

30. Complainant's Request for Reconsideration of Finding of No Probable Cause, Major v. Cosmopolitan Corp. (1987) (N.Y. State Div. Hum. Rts. Charge No. 021–85-2411).

31. Interview with Elly Spicer, in New York City (Jan. 2, 1990).

32. Interview with Carolyn Nowodzinski, in New York City (Dec. 26, 1989).

33. Interview with Gladys Lopez, an electrician, in New York City (Mar. 18, 1990).

34. Interview with Zaiah Martinez, in New York City (Feb. 5, 1987).

35. Shulamith Firestone has argued that "racism is sexism extended" because, at least for Western cultures, it can only be understood in terms of the power hierarchies of the nuclear family. S. Firestone, The Dialectic of Sex: The Case for Feminist Revolution 118–141 (1970). . . .

Similarly, according to historian Gerda Lerner, sexism and racism are both ideologies that enable the dominant class to believe that it is extending paternalistic benevolence to a class of people that is inferior and weaker. Lerner points out that sexism and racism can persist even where institutionalized patriarchal relations, such as slavery, have been abolished. In fact, the persistence of sexism and racism weakens legislative attempts to eliminate them; and unless they are eliminated completely, institutionalized sexism and racism can be reestablished. G. Lerner, The Creation of Patriarchy 239–241 (1986). Consider, as an illustration of this proposition, the ineffectiveness of civil rights legislation due to the persistent force of racist beliefs. Cf. Kaplan, Female Consciousness and Collective Action: The Case of Barcelona, 1910–1918, in E. Keohane, M. Rosaldo & B. Gelpi eds., Feminist Theory: A Critique of Ideology 55, 57 (1981).

36. S. Jeffords, The Remasculinization of America: Gender and the Vietnam War xiii–xiv (1983).

37. Interview with Alyssa Melnick, a carpenter, in New York City (Mar. 12, 1990). Cynthia Long estimates that between 75% and 80% of the first tradeswomen admitted to apprenticeships in the late 1970s were lesbians. My interview data strongly suggest that lesbian representation remains high. However, the nature of the hostility that might be directed by male construction workers, foremen and union officers towards those who do not conform to conventional notions of "femininity" or "masculinity" forces most lesbian and gay workers on large construction jobs to hide their sexual

identity despite improvements in the law of discrimination pertaining to sexual orientation. Interview with Cynthia Long, in New York City (Feb. 6, 1990).

There is no federal law prohibiting discrimination on the basis of sexual orientation. . . .

38. See, e.g., Henson v. City of Dundee, 682 F.2d 897 (11th Cir. 1982) (holding that women employees and applicants in federal employment have a right to be free from sexual harassment); Bundy v. Jackson, 641 F.2d 934 (D.C. Cir. 1981) (construing Title VII to prohibit pervasive on-the-job sexual harassment).

39. Interview with Pamela Berdebes, in New York City (Dec. 28, 1989).

40. Letter from Thomas Van Arsdale, Business Manager of Local No. 3 of the IBEW to Women Electricians (Apr. 10, 1987) (revealing that at that time pornography was still present at certain sites).

As this [article] went to print, feminists were celebrating Robinson v. Jacksonville Shipyards, 760 F. Supp. 1486 (M.D. Fla. 1991), the first Title VII case to hold that the presence in a workplace of pictures of women in sexually submissive or suggestive poses creates a sexually hostile and intimidating work environment. The extent to which *Robinson* signals meaningful change, however, remains unclear. . . .

41. Interview with Elly Spicer, in New York City (Jan. 2, 1990). Spicer reported that UT is technically "defunct." . . .

42. [Data reveal] [citations omitted] that by the early 1980s very few women were working or apprenticed in the major construction trades. Of the 65,190 people employed in the construction labor force, only 1,142, or 1.75%, were women; of the 10,417 apprentices, only 383, or 3.68%, were women. These figures might even be highly inflated because of the "revolving door" characteristic of the industry's exclusionary patterns. A woman or a member of a racial minority could be admitted to an apprenticeship program but in actuality work so few hours in a year as to never accumulate the requisite on-the-job training to achieve "journeyman" or mechanic status. For example, although theoretically Zaiah Martinez should have been able to achieve "journeyman" status after three years, after six years she had not yet accumulated the requisite years of experience as an apprentice. Interview with Zaiah Martinez, in New York City (Feb. 5, 1987).

Employer Abuse, Worker Resistance, and the Tort of Intentional Infliction of Emotional Distress

REGINA AUSTIN

THE CONVENTIONAL wisdom is that, in the workplace, abuse can be a legitimate instrument of worker control and an appropriate form of discipline.[1] By "abuse" I mean treatment that is intentionally emotionally painful, offensive, or insulting. . . .

It is generally assumed that employers and employees alike agree that some amount of such abuse is a perfectly natural, necessary, and defensible prerogative of superior rank. It assures obedience to command. Bosses do occasionally overstep the bounds of what is considered reasonable supervision, but, apart from contractually based understandings[2] and statutory entitlements to protection from harassment, there are few objective standards of "civility" by which to judge a superior's treatment of a subordinate. Workers for their part are expected to respond to psychologically painful supervision with passivity, not insubordination and resistance. They must and do develop stamina and resilience. If the supervision is intolerable, they should quit and move on to another job.

In sum, there is little reason for workers to take undue umbrage at the treatment they receive at work. The pain, insults, and indignities they suffer at the hands of employers and supervisors should be met with acquiescence and endurance. That's life.

WHO BELIEVES THIS?

My experiences as a "subordinate" and as an observer of life among the "subordinates" who work where I do[3] suggest that employees' attitudes toward, and actions against supervisors are frequently at odds with any concept of deference to authority. The conventional wisdom is reflected in the appellate court opinions applying the tort of intentional infliction of emotional distress in suits brought by employees against their employers and supervisors. It is not, however, reproduced in the everyday actions and attitudes of workers. . . .

The focus of concern throughout this essay will be the working conditions and experiences of black and Latino employees of both sexes, and female workers, black, brown and white, all of whom occupy the lower tiers of the labor force. To be sure, the sources of the material circumstances of these minority men, minority women, and majority women are not the same. There are dangers in ignoring the particularities of the ideological and economic conditions and cultural responses that separate each group from the others as well as from the group of white male low status workers. Yet many members of these groups historically subject to multiple oppressions share a common experience of abusive supervision. For them, it is not isolated and sporadic rudeness, but a pervasive phenomenon that causes and perpetuates economic and social harm as well as emotional injury. In the places where these workers labor, racism and sexism obscure and are obscured by the perniciousness of class oppression. Mistreatment that would never be tolerated if it were undertaken openly in the name of white supremacy or male patriarchy is readily justified by the privileges of status, class, or color of collar. Moreover, minority and female low status workers appear to have little economic clout with which to combat such supervisory abuse. They do, however, criticize their work situations and resist them to a limited extent. This essay explores how the law might be useful in maximizing the affirmative politically progressive potential of their informal, local, and largely defensive cultural opposition to mistreatment on the job. . . .

I. In Support of Authoritative Abuse

[C]ourts and commentators have [addressed] abuse in the workplace in the context of the tort of outrage. . . . In delineating the requirements of a cause of action for the intentional infliction of emotional distress, the courts generally rely on Section 46 of the Restatement (Second) of Torts.[4] Section 46 requires that the plaintiff prove that the defendant's conduct was

> so outrageous in character, and so extreme in degree, as to go beyond all possible bounds of decency, and to be regarded as atrocious, and utterly intolerable in a civilized community. . . .[5]

If the conduct does not rise to the requisite level, it is dismissed as being among those "mere insults, indignities, threats, annoyances, petty oppressions, or other trivialities" to which the victim "must necessarily be expected and required to be hardened."[6] As applied to the employment relationship, this means that every practice or pattern of emotional mistreatment except the outrageous, atrocious, and intolerable is treated as the ordinary stuff of everyday work life.

The approach mandated by Section 46 immediately focuses on whether the employer's or supervisor's coercion was excessive and skips the threshold issue of whether any amount of emotional mistreatment was justified. In this regard, it differs from the 1948 version of the section which required that the defendant show that abuse of the plaintiff was privileged.[7] . . .

A. Traditional Employer Prerogatives

The courts accord employers wide latitude in directing their employees' activities in ways that cause them emotional distress. The courts leave little doubt as to who is in charge of the workplace. The employer is free to ignore any interest workers may have in performing particular tasks, using particular skills, or doing a job at a particular level of proficiency or ease. Thus, work assignments are "managerial decisions . . . [that do] not qualify as intentional infliction of severe mental distress."[8] Similarly, while imposition of an inordinate work load may "creat[e] an environment which is oppressive to function within . . . it is not the type of action to arouse resentment, by the average member of the community. . . ."[9]

The courts recognize that emotional disturbance is an inherent aspect of being reprimanded, demoted, or discharged. But they allow the victim no cause of action if the emotional harm is an unintended or incidental result of an exercise of legitimate workplace authority, civilly undertaken. The courts are particularly wary of attempts to use Section 46 to evade the rules sanctioning the summary discharge of at-will employees.[10] Assertions to the effect that "if the firing of . . . [plaintiff] was done in an outrageous manner, then every firing that occurs would be considered outrageous," are quite common.[11]

Liability does not always follow, even when the supervisor is rude or insensitive in carrying out a personnel action. . . .

In lieu of the relatively straightforward, aboveboard forms of discipline, supervisors sometimes engage in indirect methods of disapproval that take their toll on the employee's psyche because they are insidious and underhanded. Instead of firing an employee, supervisors may undertake a campaign to make the job so unbearable that she or he will resign. The law of outrage poses little or no impediment to the indirect, "constructive discharge" approach. . . .

When investigating theft and dishonesty, employers frequently use emotionally distressful techniques. The courts have often condoned interrogation techniques and summary dismissals that the employees have felt to be arbitrary, insulting, humiliating, embarrassing, and painful. But they have also given victims a few victories. The successful claimants have been almost uniformly innocent, and most have been young female service workers. It may be that courts are somewhat more sympathetic to workers in this context, but a more likely explanation is that they consider the female plaintiffs especially deserving of compassion because of the emotional vulnerability that is associated with their sex and age.

B. Abuse and Status Group Distinctions

The nature of the employee's work setting, the color of her or his collar, and the employee's age, sex, race, or ethnicity can explicitly affect the kind and amount of abuse the employee is expected to bear. In general, the claims that are most likely to survive court review are those attacking harassment based on race, ethnicity, national origin, and sex. The cases involving minority group members generally involve overt racist or ethnocentric slurs. Similarly, the suits of the successful female plaintiffs have included conduct that falls squarely within the definition of sexual harassment developed by the Equal Employment Opportunity Commission[12] under Title VII.[13] The courts will act positively when there is blatant conduct, but do not extend protection against forms of discriminatory abuse that are less explicit or demonstrative.

The courts' formalistic perspective means that employees of the same race or sex who work together and see themselves as similarly abused may be accorded different degrees of legal protection. Hogan v. Forsyth Country Club Co.,[14] for example, involved three female plaintiffs who worked in the defendant's dining room. While all were verbally harassed by superiors, one was also subjected to suggestive remarks and physical sexual contact. The second was given assignments she could not perform because she was pregnant. The third had menus thrown in her face and her duties were interfered with, but there was no specific explanation given for this treatment. The intentional infliction of emotional distress claim of the first plaintiff withstood defendant's motion for summary judgment because it was easily identified as "sexual harassment." The claims of the remaining two plaintiffs did not. . . .

Status group characteristics can sometimes increase the amount of abusive behavior a worker must tolerate. More endurance is expected from males in general and from blue-collar employees in particular than from women, for example. . . . However, where the abuse is racial in form, the rough nature of the work and the workplace may not suffice to insulate an employer from liability. . . .

C. Severe Harm and the Implicit Requirement of Surrender

Whether they agree or not, workers are by and large expected to develop the fortitude and stamina to endure intentionally inflicted distress on the job. Their best protection is their own emotional mettle. In the courts' view, learning to accept abuse is necessary because personal liberty and good mental health require that employers, like all individuals, have the "freedom to get mad or be impolite."[15] Furthermore, a certain amount of rudeness simply has to be tolerated. . . .

In order to recover under Section 46, the plaintiff must show that the extent of her or his harm is exceptional. . . . In the words of the Restatement, "[t]he law intervenes only where the distress inflicted is so severe that no reasonable man could be expected to endure it."[16]

The severe harm requirement presents formidable obstacles to recovery. . . . The result of this reasoning is that the more pervasive the form of abuse, the more ordinary it is, and the more it must be tolerated. The humiliation and embarrassment endured by the many who are disciplined or dismissed simply will not be considered sufficiently egregious to warrant relief. Furthermore, the injury of the plaintiff who survives without seeking treatment by doctors or psychiatrists and gets on with her or his life may . . . not satisfy the standard. . . . Finally, the employee whose suffering exceeds that which the hypothetical reasonable person would incur will be adjudged maladjusted or supersensitive and denied a recovery.[17] The psychological frailty of

such a person may even be advanced as the explanation for the supervisor's behavior.
. . .

Contentious assertiveness and counteraggression are clearly not preferred reactions. Plaintiffs who immediately replied to their supervisor's abuse did not fare well in their subsequent tort actions. For example, a cashier who was accused by her employer's security supervisor of giving unauthorized discounts became angry and hysterical during the course of a polygraph session, and she responded with "strong language."[18] In denying her claim the court concluded that her "language and tone of voice were at least as bellicose and lacking in delicacy as [the supervisor's]."[19] It appears that the law encourages employees to adopt a stance of emotional detachment from their jobs and the supervisory mistreatment they may incur. . . .

While the legal community customarily thinks about the impact of the law on workers and of workers on the law in vague and global terms, such an analysis ignores the role that real, ordinary working people play in perpetuating and attacking abuse on the job. . . .

II. Authoritative Abuse from the Workers' Perspective

Workers' opinions about supervisory abuse . . . surface in ethnographic studies by sociologists and anthropologists, as well as in fiction, popular books employing interview techniques, and newspaper and magazine accounts. This literature portrays ordinary people responding to and coping with emotionally painful, degrading, and insulting working conditions and supervision as a matter of everyday life.

The people who are the particular focus of attention here . . . are black and Latino women and men and white women, all of whom hold low-paying, low-status, unskilled, or low-skilled jobs. These workers theoretically have the least to gain from adhering to the prevailing wisdom regarding authoritative abuse but, perhaps, the most to lose from defiance of its message. Their understanding of and response to abuse stand in opposition to the outlook of the law and suggest why anyone interested in justice should be less tolerant of supervisory abuse than the courts presently are. . . .

[M]inority and female workers in particular rely on their group cultural norms in accommodating and resisting the demands and adverse effects of their jobs. The sexual division of labor encourages both females and males to create a sense of group solidarity and superiority with which to absorb and challenge the strictures of workplace authority. The cultural devices that minorities employ to deal with the racism and ethnocentricity that permeate society allow them to endure low-paying, low status work. Constantly confronted with insults and abuse that are the product of white supremacist thinking, minority people have developed mechanisms for maintaining their dignity and fighting for their self-respect without endangering their jobs. The values and activities of these overlapping sexual, racial, and ethnic communities provide alternative "localized" standards for determining self-worth and the worth of one's work.[20] . . .

Workers would agree with the law's assessment that supervisory abuse is an ordinary, everyday occurrence in the workplace. They would, however, part company with the courts and commentators when the latter argue that it is so mundane and commonplace that it should escape severe censure. On the contrary, from the workers' perspective, the frequency with which they encounter supervisory mistreatment means that it cannot be warranted or justified in the way the law and the conventional wisdom assert.

Among workers, there is widespread condemnation of close, coercive supervision. It is not acceptable behavior. The hostility of this sort of abusive authority is manifested in the words and actions of workers performing disparate jobs, in disparate work-places.[21] A tuna factory worker interviewed in Barbara Garson's book *All the Livelong Day*[22] elaborated on the techniques used by the line ladies trying to meet the day's production quotas. She said that "they figure out who they can push—the ones who really need the job. And believe me they push them. They're on their backs. . . . " She continued, "Now some women can't work any faster no matter how much they're pushed. They get upset. You can see their eyes tearing. Others speed up and those are the ones the line ladies will go for."[23] As discipline for not working fast enough, workers were sent to other lines or made to count bones. Of such treatment, the worker said that "you feel like a kid in school being stepped out by the monitor" and "[e]veryone knows you're being punished."[24] Studs Terkel's *Working*[25] describes a . . . black domestic worker [who] expressed her sentiments regarding close supervision as follows:

> The younger women, they don't pay you too much attention. Most of 'em work. The older women, they behind you, wiping. I don't like nobody checkin' behind me. When you go to work, they want to show you how to clean. That really gets me, somebody showin' me how to clean. I been doin' it all my life. They come and get the rag and show you how to do it. (Laughs.) I stand there, look at 'em. Lotta times I ask her, "You finished?"[26]

As the comments of the domestic worker indicate, abuse can be objectionable to workers because it does not reflect objective assessments of their productivity. Whereas the law assumes that abuse is utilized because workers are not contributing to the enterprise as they should be, workers view abuse as a calculated devaluation of themselves and their work. . . .

Minority and female employees have reason to suspect that the disparagement and mistreatment they receive on the job is motivated by racial prejudice and sexist animosity, not merely by a concern for productivity and profits or by individualized assessments of merit. . . .

Consider as well the work experiences of the black hospital ward secretaries described by Karen Brodkin Sacks.[27] The ward secretaries were the victims of the compound interaction of racism, sexism, and occupational elitism. Jobs at the hospital were segregated by both race and sex. Secretarial positions, which were allocated to women, were further segregated by race; the higher paid administrative and medical secretaries were white, while the ward secretaries who were two pay grades beneath the other secretaries, were predominately black. . . .

Because of their race, low status, and unrecognized coordination role, the ward secretaries were particularly vulnerable to abuse from doctors, nurses, and supervisors. Sacks quotes the views of one of the secretaries as being representative of their feelings in general:

> Their attitudes are really, really nasty. You have to count to fifty. Sometimes I just walk away. I don't like being yelled at. I'm an adult; I'm grown. If you can't speak to me without yelling, don't speak to me at all. Often they yell about something the ward secretaries don't know about. . . . What they're saying is that they think you're ignorant; and they never apologize when they accuse you wrongly. They don't try to learn your name; they call us "hey you." Very few say "good morning." It takes everything to keep this job.[28]

Abuse was a way of pulling institutional and racial rank on the secretaries. . . . "For some doctors, tantrums and loud abuse were an automatic response to anything other than instant gratification; they acted as though they had a *right* to yell without regard for anyone's feelings and felt no obligation to apologize when they were wrong."[29] In other words, those occupying superior status in the hospital viewed abuse of subordinates as a prerogative. . . .

In sum, although the law and the conventional wisdom see something wrong with the workers that justifies their abuse, the workers know that it is the employers, supervisors, and bosses who are wrong, and on two counts. They are wrong in using slurs, close scrutiny, and onerous or insulting assignments to push workers to work harder, demand less, and know their place. And they are wrong again if they think that these tactics are wholly effective. The rude, insensitive behavior the courts condone is the very sort of behavior the workers criticize by their words and their actions. The melding of racism, sexism, class bias, and occupational elitism generates a critique that does not finely differentiate among the possible sources of worker oppression. . . .

In order to protect minority and female workers fully, abuse that is justified by a worker's status, class, or color of collar must be considered on a par with harassment that is overtly racist and sexist. Workers victimized by supervisory conduct that explicitly manifests a racial, ethnic, national origin, or sexual animus have successfully invoked the tort of outrage, but the courts have been reluctant to extend similar protection in cases of treatment of a more subtle sort, such as the close supervision and reprimands workers attribute to racism and sexism. If the ascriptive categories were discrete, or if job segregation did not make comparisons impossible, or if the same sort of abusive conduct were not considered an acceptable feature of the working conditions of secondary market workers whatever their skin color or sex, then insisting that objectionable supervisory conduct be categorized as either the product of white supremacy or male patriarchy might be a fruitful exercise. The reality of the subordination of minority and female workers is otherwise, and the workers' critique reflects this reality. Moreover, the absence of a multidimensional anti-harassment challenge furthers employers' ability to avoid judicial regulations.

While linking racial and sexual harassment to "class harassment" would render covertly racist or sexist abuse more vulnerable, it may also have pragmatic political benefits. The availability of causes of action against racial and sexual harassment, a legacy of the civil rights movement, has generated expectations that other kinds of arbitrary and capricious employer behavior can be curbed. Protection against worker harassment should appeal to those who feel that their oppression has been ignored because of the attention focused on the claims of minorities and women. At the same time, however, minority and female workers should be wary of losing sight of their distinct economic, political, and cultural existences. While the resort to class represents a recognition of the commonality of poor working conditions across color and gender lines, it is also a deliberate maneuver necessitated by the limitations that a strict racist/sexist categorization places on their ability to denounce the conduct of employers and supervisors (which, as far as the workers are concerned, remains racist and sexist at its core).

If the full implications of the workers' critique are considered, it appears that the idea of freedom from worker harassment contradicts the notion, touted by employers and accepted by courts, that the supervisory treatment accorded workers can vary with their sex, race, ethnicity, and class. For all of their masculine posturing, male employees no more deserve to be cursed than do female employees. Blue-collar factory workers should not be required to tolerate harassing practical jokes from supervisors any more than white-collar office workers. It is inappropriate to treat female employees as if they were "girls" even when they refer to themselves by such a term. Moreover, it is wrong for employers and supervisors to scrutinize the conduct of young black employees for signs of thievery or to hold their brash demeanors against them. . . .

The right to freedom from workplace harassment is concerned with preserving the peace of mind and emotional tranquility of workers by shoring up their economic security and reinforcing the power of their work and cultural alliances. The workers do not and cannot assess the propriety of supervision based on the amount of individual psychological harm it causes, as tort law does. The severe harm requirement of Section 46 insulates outrageous supervisory conduct from attack and penalizes those workers who, because of their own personal or social resources, have the strength to withstand abuse. Thus, the very collective cultural mechanism on which secondary market workers rely in protecting themselves from supervisory mistreatment become the justification for the perpetuation of authoritative abuse. . . . Finally, condemning an employer's or supervisor's abusive behavior because of the emotional distress it causes carries with it the implication that severe distress was a reasonable reaction to the supervisor's or employer's conduct. The attack upon workplace harassment must proclaim the propriety of the more aggressive responses work and group culture generate. The emphasis must be on the conduct of the employers, not on the suffering and misery of the aggrieved workers. If their mental states are pertinent at all, anger, antipathy, and sullen contempt should suffice. . . .

The idea of an entitlement to freedom from worker harassment as it is proposed here is only intended to be an organizing tool. It can do little more than lend coherence to the vision of antiauthoritarianism that is exemplified by the informal work and group culture of unorganized, low-skilled, low-paid minority and female workers. The acuity, originality, and dynamism of their workplace critiques cannot possibly be captured by a single static statement. Furthermore, any gains that overt political activity or tort litigation may produce must be maintained through continued resistance in the workplace. There must be constant local struggle that is an extension of the workers' everyday existences. The workers must take their critique as they live it and as it is (re)reflected in the counterideology that is disseminated from above, exploit the contradictions thereby created between the real and the ideal, and extend the vision of what it means to be free of abuse in the workplace through commonplace cultural activities and attitudes.

Epilogue

As a black person and a woman, I found it extremely difficult to accept the assumption advanced in the outrage cases that employer abuse and the emotional pain it causes workers are too subjective, ephemeral, trivial, and mundane to warrant judicial relief. Studies of the working conditions of minority and female workers who hold low-paying, low-status jobs and are subject to simple control confirmed my assessment of the inadequacy of the law's response to the supervisory mistreatment of subordinates. If the minority and female workers who experience abuse can, through informal cultural devices, make it sufficiently concrete and objective to denounce it, resist it, and cleverly subvert it, then the courts are without excuse. The analysis of simple control and secondary market working conditions adds weight to the workers' assessments. The courts' view of the inevitability of the status quo is not universally shared. The workers do not seem to be completely resigned to their fate as harassed subordinates, nor do they appear to be totally beaten down. . . .

There is no adequate justification for society's abandonment of these workers. Their critique of their working conditions should have the benefit of a formal articulation at the highest levels of visibility and legitimacy, and the overt and covert resistance they are brave enough to mount on their own behalf should receive the support and sanction of those interested in justice in the workplace. The workers themselves have done, and will continue to do, the hard work. They have already conceptualized the problem and made it discrete. They have also supplied alternatives to the traditional ways of evaluating the worth of jobs and encouraging maximum productivity. *Attention must be paid* to those whose endurance and struggle are so much the ordinary stuff of everyday life that they are too easily taken for granted.

Notes

1. See, e.g., C. Brodsky, The Harassed Worker 6, 149–150 (1976).
2. Some workers are protected by bureaucratic safeguards that are codified in union contracts and employee handbooks. . . .

3. As a teenager growing up in black Washington, D.C. . . . . I got jobs through summer youth employment programs. I mainly worked in offices and laboratories. Now that I am a law professor, I suppose that I am more of a superordinate. . . . I have spent most of my professional life as a token, one of two or three or four blacks and/or women occupying high-level positions. I have felt especially comfortable with and supported by the secretaries, office help, library personnel, security guards, and housekeeping staff. I share deep cultural ties with them, and their common sense and critical assessments of their working situations have been of immeasurable instruction and encouragement.

4. Restatement (Second) of Torts §46 (1965) reads as follows: "One who by extreme and outrageous conduct intentionally or recklessly causes severe emotional distress to another is subject to liability for such emotional distress, and if bodily harm to the other results from it, for such bodily harm."

5. *Id.* at comment d.

6. *Id.* In addition, First Amendment concerns may dictate that insulting language, slurs, and epithets be immune from liability. See generally First Amendment Limits on Tort Liability for Words Intended to Inflict Severe Emotional Distress, 85 Colum. L. Rev. 1749 (1985) (student author).

7. The 1948 version of section 46 provided that "[o]ne who, without a privilege to do so, intentionally causes severe emotional distress to another is liable (a) for such emotional distress, and (b) for bodily harm resulting from it." Restatement of the Law: 1948 Supplement, Torts §46 (1948). Daniel Givelber, in his extensive article on the tort, suggests that the privilege approach was subsequently rejected because it required that "issues such as the legitimacy of coercion" be directly addressed. Givelber, The Right to Minimum Social Decency and the Limits of Evenhandedness: Intentional Infliction of Emotional Distress by Outrageous Conduct, 82 Colum. L. Rev. 42, 62 (1982).

8. Hall v. May Dept. Stores, 292 Or. 131, 139, 637 P.2d 126, 132 (1981). . . .

9. Hooten v. Pennsylvania College of Optometry, 601 F. Supp. 1151, 1155 (E.D. Pa. 1984). . . .

10. See, e.g., Blades, Employment at Will vs. Individual Freedom: On Limiting the Abusive Exercise of Employer Power, 67 Colum. L. Rev. 1404 (1967).

11. Meierer v. E.I. Dupont De Nemours & Co., 607 F. Supp. 1170, 1182 (D.C.S.C. 1985). . . .

12. Guidelines of Sexual Harassment, 29 C.F.R. §1604.11 (1986).

13. 42 U.S.C. §§2000(e)(1)–2000(e)(17)(1982).

14. 79 N.C. App. 483, 340 S.E.2d 116 (1986).

15. Givelber, *supra* note 7, at 57.

16. Restatement (Second) of Torts §46 comment j.

17. *Id.;* see, e.g., Cafferty v. Garcia's of Scottsdale, 375 N.W.2d 850 (Minn. Ct. App. 1985).

18. [Bridges v. Winn-Dixie Atlanta, Inc., 335 S.E.2d 445, 446 (Ga. 1985).]

19. *Id.* at 448.

20. R. Horowitz, Honor and the American Dream: Culture and Identity in a Chicano Community 51 (1983).

21. See, e.g., L. Rubin, Worlds of Pain: Life in the Working-Class Family 168 (1976) (former file clerk complains someone was always looking over her shoulder); S. Terkel, Working 202–203 (1971) (bus driver complains of constant and surreptitious overseeing and of discipline at the "whims of the superintendent"); P. Zavella,

Women's Work and Chicano Families 104–105, 112–117 (1987) (Chicano cannery workers criticize close, unfair, discriminatory, and disrespectful supervision).

22. B. Gerson, All the Livelong Day (1975).

23. *Id.* at 38.

24. *Id.*

25. Terkel, *supra* note 21.

26. *Id.* at 117.

27. Sacks, Computers, Ward Secretaries, and a Walkout in a Southern Hospital, in K. Sacks & D. Remy eds., My Troubles Are Going to Have Trouble with Me 173 (1984).

28. *Id.* at 181.

29. *Id.*

Feminist Constructions of Objectivity: Multiple Perspectives on Sexual and Racial Harassment Litigation

MARTHA CHAMALLAS

IN A VARIETY of disciplines, feminist and postmodern scholars have changed the face of their fields by their persistence in investigating the relationship between knowledge and power.[1] There is now a rich body of scholarship demonstrating how particular views of the world come to dominate discourse, how our "knowledge" is far less diverse than our people. A central feature of these new critical inquiries is their skepticism about claims of "objectivity" and "neutrality" and about statements that purport to have "universal" applicability.[2] The take-home message of much of this work is that frequently what passes for the whole truth is instead a representation of events from the perspective of those who possess the power to have their version of reality accepted. The search is on for multiple meanings and multiple perspectives, whether attached to language, texts, or human events.

The challenge to claims of objectivity is becoming increasingly visible in the area of anti-discrimination law and discourse, particularly sexual and racial harassment cases. Harassment is a context in which it is easy to grasp the meaning of the critique of objectivity made by feminist and critical race legal scholars. As the Clarence Thomas hearings so graphically demonstrated, it is no longer sufficient to provide a single description of human relationships in a workplace and declare it to be the true, factual account. Most people would not resist the proposition that what constitutes an insult is open to multiple interpretations.

I. Choosing a Perspective: Variations on the Theme of a Reasonable Person

The question of perspective or point of view arises most often in cases alleging offensive work environments. The issue of perspective is important as a theoretical matter; it lies at the heart of much feminist and critical race scholarship aimed at creating new definitions of equality for marginalized groups of people. . . .

Originally published in full in *Texas Journal of Women and the Law*, Volume 1 (1992).

As framed by most courts, the issue of perspective translates into the narrow doctrinal issue of defining the standard that should be used in what are known as offensive or hostile working environment cases. In these cases, the plaintiff must prove that the harassing conduct had "the purpose or effect of unreasonably interfering with an individual's work performance or creating an intimidating, hostile, or offensive working environment."[3] On this issue, the courts have been reluctant to embrace as authoritative either the subjective perspective of the plaintiff, or that of the person charged with harassment. The stated fear is that using plaintiff's subjective viewpoint as the standard could lead unjustifiably to liability in cases involving hypersensitive or idiosyncratic responses to challenged conduct. Similarly, courts reject the harasser's subjective perspective because to do otherwise would limit Title VII protection to only the clearest cases of consciously retaliatory abuse.

The two standards currently vying for acceptance are both labeled "objective." The division is drawn between courts that employ a "reasonable person"[4] standard and those that adopt a more victim-specific standard modified to reflect the gender or racial group to which the plaintiff belongs,[5] for example, a "reasonable woman" or a "reasonable black person" standard. Choice of the standard in itself, of course, does not dictate who will win the lawsuit. However, as the cases have been litigated, plaintiffs typically argue for a modified victim-perspective standard, while defendants generally align themselves with the unitary standard.

The case that first highlighted the issue of perspective is the Sixth Circuit case Rabidue v. Osceola Refining Co.[6] The plaintiff was what social psychologists sometimes refer to as a "solo" or a "token," the only woman in a salaried management position at the workplace.[7] In polite terms, the refinery would be described as a highly sexualized worksite: male employees posted pornography in common areas, and one of the male supervisors consistently called women employees derogatory names such as "cunt," "pussy," "whores," and "tits." The major claim in the case centered around plaintiff's discharge: she alleged sex discrimination as the cause and used the evidence of the offensive environment to show that defendant's actions were biased. By defendant's account, it was plaintiff's bad personality that prompted her firing. Her employer said she was rude, too aggressive, and did not follow company policies.

The issue of perspective surfaced in the case as a rhetorical formula to aid the court in deciding whether the sexualized environment at the refinery amounted to a Title VII violation. Judge Robert B. Krupansky's majority opinion invoked the familiar reasonable person standard and concluded that a reasonable employee would not be damaged seriously by the environment. Krupansky based his judgment principally on the belief that society condoned graphic sexual depictions in the mass media, including prime time TV, and that plaintiff assumed the risk of harassment when she took the job at a plant where such sexual conduct was prevalent.

In a dissent that has become well known, Judge Damon J. Keith voiced his objection to the majority's willingness to accept the status quo as the normative measure by which to gauge the offensiveness of a work environment. The fact that male workers at refineries and other blue collar settings often used profanity and displayed sexually graphic pictures demeaning women should not control, in Keith's view, because Title VII was intended to prevent and change even ingrained behaviors.

Keith proposed that the courts adopt an objective victim-oriented standard which would allow them to take into account "salient sociological differences" among persons, including gender. For Keith, such a reasonable woman standard differed from the reasonable person standard in that the modified standard recognized that women have not played an important role in fashioning societal standards of appropriate behavior, and it acknowledged that prevailing standards can simply be a reflection of male prerogative. Keith's objection to the reasonable person standard was not only that it failed to recognize that men and women may have differing views of what is appropriate, although he relied in part on studies documenting such divergences. Keith also maintained that societal standards were premised on a system of sexual inequality that "stifled female potential" and could only prove debilitating and stigmatic for women as a class. The pervasiveness of commercial exploitation of female sexuality in American culture did not convince Keith that pornography in the workplace and anti-female language should be legally acceptable, noting that at one point in history society also condoned slavery. Instead, Keith argued, the law should fashion its definition of discrimination by resort to the perceptions of those less powerful groups whose equality Title VII was designed to bring about.

Keith was also convinced that no reasonable woman would condone such degradation. His confidence elided an important and recurring question in feminist scholarship: whether any one position or even range of positions can be claimed to be "the woman's view." Keith focused on differences between the sexes (or more properly, between dominant and subordinate groups), without considering diversities among women.

It is ironic that the gulf between the majority and the dissent in *Rabidue* found its legal expression in the choice of perspective. Many of the important features of the Krupansky opinion—reliance on societal standards as exemplified by the mass media, blaming the plaintiff for accepting a job at a crude workplace—were also present in Judge Stewart A. Newblatt's opinion at the trial court level.[8] In his ruling for the defendant, however, Newblatt described his role as that of determining what the "average female employee" would find offensive. The crucial difference was that Newblatt's conclusions about the perceptions of the average woman proved radically different from those of Keith.

After *Rabidue,* the cases splintered in many directions, touching upon the issue of perspective in a confusing and contradictory fashion. Some courts appeared to follow the majority in *Rabidue,* adopting the reasonable person standard.[9] Other courts, as well as the EEOC, seemed to agree partially with the dissent in *Rabidue* but drew different conclusions with respect to perspective. . . .[10]

Rabidue also provided an occasion for feminist scholars to deepen their critiques of traditional objective standards in the law. By the early 1980s, Catharine MacKinnon's work on sexual coercion had laid the groundwork for feminist criticism of hidden male-oriented viewpoints embedded in much of the law governing sexual conduct.[11] . . . Much of Martha Minow's work also dealt with perspective.[12] . . .

During the same period, feminist litigators also challenged the use of the reasonable person as the standard for determining the legitimacy of a claim of self defense in homicide cases.[13] Central to their critique was the claim that the responses of many women—most prominently women who had been the victims of domestic violence—did not fit the masculine mode of self defense and were unfairly labeled as unreasonable. They sought an alternative to the reasonable person standard which, without stereotyping all women as victims, would recognize the vulnerability of women to violence.

By the late 1980s, a growing group of feminist legal scholars had the benefit of MacKinnon's and Minow's critical methodologies as well as the critiques of objectivity emanating from a variety of schools of feminist thought and from postmodern scholarship. A well-developed body of theoretical work now existed to challenge the *Rabidue* majority's claim of objectivity and to suggest ways to change the law of sexual harassment to make it more responsive to victims and to the aspirations of feminist theory.

In one of the first important commentaries on *Rabidue*,[14] Lucinda Finley focused on the nonneutrality of the reasonable person standard as employed by the *Rabidue* majority. She emphasized that only by excluding women from the reasonable person standard could the court have concluded that a "work environment, repeatedly complained of by women workers as being harmful, degrading, disruptive to their ability to work and the source of extreme physical stress, was acceptable to the reasonable person." For Finley, the case graphically illustrated what feminist scholars meant when they asserted that purportedly objective universal standards were based on the partial perspective of those framing and enforcing the standards.

At the same time, however, Finley questioned Keith's reasonable woman standard. Her concern was that the standard suggested that women were a special breed of people, and that rather than expand the concept of reasonableness, the standard could actually backfire and reinforce stereotypes of women as unreasonable. She recognized the danger of constructing a new stereotype that might obscure diversities among women and ignore important dimensions of identity such as class, race, and sexual orientation. Rather than create a modified standard for women only, Finley argued, courts should engage in a constant testing of the reasonable person standard to "include the perspectives of many people—or more accurately, the majority of the population—who have been considered outside the mainstream in this society."[15]

In a similar vein, Nancy Ehrenreich voiced doubts [about the reasonable woman standard].[16] In Ehrenreich's view, any purportedly objective standard—whether modified or not—was too dependent on a liberal vision of the world in which mediation of interests among groups is possible and all groups are equally protected. Ehrenreich also found fault with the construct of reasonableness, arguing that use of the construct suggests that judicial decisions are apolitical and takes the focus away from the substantive content of particular judgments. The search for the viewpoint of the reasonable woman could readily translate into a futile search for a consensus viewpoint among women, with the danger that the values of the more dominant in the group—namely white, affluent, heterosexual women—are construed as representative of the whole.

The concerns expressed in these two commentaries represent familiar dilemmas in feminist legal theory. Once the bias underlying neutral legal constructs is exposed, there remains the problem of replacing the constructs within a legal system that has not undergone fundamental change. Finley's chief concerns echo those of liberal feminists who are wary of explicit gender lines in the law and who have grown up mistrusting separate treatment for women only. Feminists attentive to American legal history might worry that an explicitly gendered concept such as the reasonable woman standard resonates as easily with the old "separate spheres" mentality as it does with new feminist definitions of appropriate sexual conduct. Particularly when the federal courts are filled with conservative . . . judges, there is reason to fear that acknowledging women's difference will be construed as a license to renew old stereotypes of women as naturally unsuited for paid employment.

Beyond the separate/equal treatment aspect of the problem, both Finley and Ehrenreich struggle with . . . the issue of interlocking systems of subordination and the consequent difficulty of identifying inclusive strategies, policies, or even slogans that speak for all subordinated groups. . . . There is widespread agreement that the new standards—whatever they may be—should be more inclusive, but it is difficult to find forms to express this inclusiveness in the law. . . .

The post-*Rabidue* article that has received the most judicial attention is Kathryn Abrams' treatment of hostile environment cases.[17] . . . Abrams described with particularity the ways in which she believes that women's responses to sexual harassment differ from men's. . . .

Abrams' arguments, particularly her emphasis on the significant differences between the responses of men and women to sexual conduct in the workplace, can easily be used to support adoption of the reasonable woman standard. In her article, however, Abrams proposed a somewhat altered standard that she hoped would temper the danger of essentialism, the danger that the reasonable woman standard would prompt courts to create new stereotypes of appropriate behavior for all women. Under her proposal, liability would be imposed unless the defendant was able to prove that plaintiff's subjective reaction was idiosyncratic, in the sense that the sexual conduct in the workplace was unlikely to create in women either "a fear of sexual coercion or a sense of devaluative sexualization among women."[18] By discarding the term "reasonable" and specifying more precisely the harm that women often suffer as a result of harassment, Abrams offered the courts an explicitly gendered standard using terminology more familiar to feminist theory than to traditional legal analysis.

Not long after the publication of these critiques in the law reviews, some courts began to justify their rejections of the majority's approach in *Rabidue* by resorting to more elaborate, and more identifiably feminist, rationales. . . .

II. Modifying the Objective Standard: Ellison v. Brady[19]

The most prominent appellate decision to endorse the reasonable woman standard is Ellison v. Brady, decided by a divided panel in the Ninth Circuit. Depending on the choice of perspective, the case could be called the "love letters" case or the "delusional romance" case. The plaintiff, Kerry Ellison, received three letters from Sterling Gray, a man in her office who was also a trainee for the IRS. The letters described Gray's intense feelings for Ellison. . . . [See Ellison v. Brady, herein, at 749 . *Ed.*] This pursuit frightened Ellison because, as far as she was concerned, no such relationship existed. . . .

In ruling that the case should proceed to trial, the panel majority conceptualized the litigation as one in which perspective made a crucial difference. Viewed from the victim's perspective, this was a case of "delusional romance," involving a nontrivial threat of sexual coercion. Through no action of her own, Ellison had become the object of a man's fantasies, a man who had ignored her clear requests to stop his aggressive behavior toward her. . . .

Judge Robert R. Beezer's opinion for the panel majority started from the premise that men and women tend to have different evaluations of sexual conduct in the workplace. Citing a lengthy passage from the Abrams article, Beezer attempted to explain why a woman might fear that conduct such as Gray's could be a "prelude to [a] violent sexual assault," even though the conduct was verbal and Gray made no explicit threats. [Also, he recognized that as] newcomers in the workplace whose jobs are felt to be expendable, women are also likely to view sexual conduct at work as a threat to maintaining their precarious hold as serious employees.

Beezer justified the court's choice of the reasonable woman standard by accepting the core feminist criticism of objectivity: that a "sex-blind reasonable person standard tends to be male-biased and tends to systematically ignore the experiences of women." This acknowledgment of the partiality of the reasonable person standard also allowed the court to view equality and discrimination in a new light. Implicit in the opinion is a counter to the argument that the reasonable woman standard is an unjustified form of special treatment for women. Undeniably, the reasonable woman standard is asymmetric; it is premised on an explicit gender distinction and calls for nonidentical treatment of men and women. In the court's view, however, this asymmetry did not mean that the standard was discriminatory. Instead, the asymmetry was desirable and consistent with the aims of Title VII because it would promote substantive equality for women. Elimination of the gender-specific barrier of sexual harassment required a gender-conscious standard. Because this reasoning rejected formal equality as the sole measure of justice, it simultaneously abolished any meaningful distinction between special treatment and equal treatment in this context.

The *Beezer* opinion did not address at any length the other problems with the reasonable woman standard identified by feminist commentators. . . .

III. Contesting the Content of the Reasonable Woman Standard: Robinson v. Jacksonville Shipyards, Inc.[20]

The most significant case to give content to the reasonable woman standard is Judge Howell W. Melton's opinion in Robinson v. Jacksonville Shipyards, Inc., decided shortly before *Ellison*. In this litigation, the NOW Legal Defense and Education Fund represented Lois Robinson, one of a very few women who worked in a skilled crafts position at the shipyards. The debate in the case did not center on the choice of the standard; Melton simply announced that the reasonable woman standard would control. Instead, the contest focused on application of the standard, with each side presenting expert witnesses to debate the issue of how reasonable women would respond to the environment at the shipyards.

No one disputed that the shipyards presented a highly sexualized worksite. . . . Pictures of nude or partially nude women were visible all over the workplace. . . . Several of the pictures very explicitly demeaned women and women's bodies. . . .

The management at the shipyards clearly condoned the sexually graphic displays. . . . Company and union officials told Robinson that she had no cause to complain about the pornography, and defended the practice by arguing that the men had a First Amendment right to post sexually explicit materials. . . . They also offered the theory that such pictures were a "natural thing" in a shipyard because "nautical people always had displayed pinups and other images of nude or partially nude women, like figureheads on boats."[21]

In addition to the visual displays, Robinson and other women employees recounted that they had been personally targeted for harassment of both a sexual and a nonsexual, but sexist, variety. The harassment often contained an element of retaliation. For example, after Robinson complained about a calendar that she found offensive, male employees posted a "Men Only" sign in one area and began to bring in hard-core pornography and show it to women employees. Robinson's workstation became the site for abusive graffiti. . . .

Factually, the case resembled *Rabidue* in that the conflict centered on whether women entering male-dominated blue collar jobs had a right to be accepted, particularly when acceptance required a change in the way the men spoke about women and sex and in the way they expressed their views about women through jokes, pornography, and graffiti. The innovation in *Robinson,* however, was that the plaintiff offered the testimony of two expert witnesses—a social psychologist who specialized in stereotyping and a consultant who had previously worked for the Working Women's Institute. The plaintiff's strategy was to use this academic and practical knowledge to provide a theoretical framework for placing the sexual behavior of the men at the shipyards into the larger pattern of gender stereotyping that typically occurs when women enter nontraditional jobs. The experts gave the court a vocabulary to describe both how gender subordination is enacted in the workplace and how sexual behavior differentially affects women workers. By using the theory of stereotyping to tie the kind of sexual behavior prevalent at the shipyard to gender discrimination, the plaintiff was able to cast her claim as a serious and systemic form of discrimination, and to offer empirical support for her contention that a reasonable woman would regard the environment as hostile.

The primary thrust of Dr. Susan Fiske's testimony on stereotyping was that there is a pattern to the obstacles faced by women who are in the extreme minority in a predominantly male workplace. . . . Fiske explained how "rarity"—making up less than 15%–20% of the workforce—can make individuals highly visible and susceptible to stereotyped evaluations based on group affiliation rather than individual behavior.[22] . . .

Overall, Fiske characterized the situation at the shipyards as one of "sex role spillover," where women were evaluated "in terms of [their] sexuality . . . and their worth as sex objects rather than their merit as craft workers." Fiske theorized that the presence of pornography at the worksite set in motion a process called "priming," which encouraged men to think about women in categorical, sexually objectified terms. Fiske also thought it highly significant that men controlled all positions of power at the shipyards. This factor made it more likely that any complaints brought by members of the out-group would likely be dismissed as trivial and that the complainer would be perceived as the real problem. Finally, Fiske cited studies drawing a correlation between the nonprofessional ambience of a workplace, evidenced by toleration of profanity and sexual joking, and the existence of stereotyping. Her final conclusion was that a sexualized workplace like that present at the shipyards imposed burdens on women that are not borne by men.

K. C. Wagner, the plaintiff's other expert witness, based her testimony on her experience counseling sexual harassment victims and providing sexual harassment training in male-dominated jobs. Wagner focused on women's diverse responses to sexually harassing behavior, ranging from blocking out the event, to avoiding the workplace or the harasser, to trying to defuse the situation by joking, to telling the harasser to stop, to lodging a formal complaint. These coping strategies tend to vary with the personal style of the individual and with her assessment of the possibilities for remediation. The range of coping strategies, Wagner concluded, indicated that not all women could be expected to have the same response to a sexualized environment.

Together the Fiske and Wagner testimony provided an elaborate response to the majority's conclusion in *Rabidue* that there was little connection between a sexualized workplace and harmful sexual harassment. The defense attempted to counter this showing by offering two of its own academic experts, who gave their account of the responses of reasonable women to pornography in the workplace. Both experts had conducted studies in which female college students were asked to rate the offensiveness of sexually explicit materials, namely a *Playboy* playmate calendar and cartoons and pictures of *Hustler*. The studies found that female subjects' reactions to the material tended not to be seriously negative. From this research, the experts concluded that the average woman would not be seriously offended by the visual materials at the shipyards. Finally, the defense introduced evidence of an increase in sexual explicitness of certain women's magazines in an attempt to show that the reasonable woman would not be offended by sexually graphic materials.

The primary task for the court in *Robinson* was to choose between these conflicting versions of the reasonable woman standard. Melton preferred the account offered by plaintiff's experts because many of their studies were conducted in the workplace and were more obviously relevant to the specific situation at the shipyards where women were in the extreme minority. The court discounted defendant's experts because the important element of context was missing from their testimony. In one of the studies on which the defendant relied, for example, the ratings of the sexually explicit pictures were done by women in small groups. Melton saw this as qualitatively different from the workplace setting at the shipyard. . . .

By adopting Fiske's theoretical framework over that offered by the defendant's experts, the court tacitly accepted the assumptions underlying Fiske's theory of stereotyping. These assumptions fit well with many feminist accounts of the dynamics of sexual harassment in the workplace. . . .

Fiske's analysis is also feminist in orientation in its attention to the connection between sexualization of the work environment and female subordination. Fiske stressed that issues of sexuality form an important component of gender stereotyping. Female sexuality, as constructed by men, becomes women's salient attribute, to the exclusion of other characteristics. Women become judged in sexual terms, and anger directed toward women often takes on a sexual dimension. That sexuality is deployed as an expression of male power is an observation central to MacKinnon's work and other radical feminist theories. To this extent, the social science literature forming the basis for Fiske's views provides for legal change in a feminist direction. . . .

IV. Race and the Reasonable Person: Harris v. International Paper[23]

Discussions of perspective have been associated primarily with the issue of sexual harassment, and have only very recently had an impact in race discrimination cases. The distinction is not rooted in the statutory language of Title VII because the statute makes no explicit distinction between race and sex discrimination that would be relevant for hostile environment cases. The distinction may, however, be traced to a difference in the traditional understandings of the nature and effects of the two types of discrimination. The conventional wisdom has been that racial harassment is less subtle than sexual harassment and that perspective is less important in race cases because the law is called upon principally to deal with cases of blatantly racist behavior.[24] . . .

In legal circles, the conventional wisdom about the nature of race discrimination began to be challenged in the late 1980s by a group of scholars—sometimes referred to as critical race theorists[25]—who argued that there was an appreciable difference between the perspectives of whites and African Americans on what types of conduct should be considered racist and objectionable. In an important article about unconscious racism,[26] Charles Lawrence drew upon psychoanalysis, anthropology, and cognitive psychology to show the power of tacit stereotypes that perpetuate racism, despite an official ideology condemning race discrimination. In constitutional cases, Lawrence urged the courts to go beyond the statutory language or the conscious motivations of lawmakers and to judge the race-based nature of an action by its "cultural meaning."[27] By this time, black feminist scholarship had made its way into legal scholarship and was having a major impact on the development of feminist theory. A central premise of this body of work was that black women had been excluded both from traditional discourses, which were grounded on the perspective of white men, and from progressive discourses, which tended to focus only on the situation of either white women or black men.[28] . . . These intellectual developments laid a foundation for thinking about race and sex discrimination in ways that intersected or converged. . . .

In Harris v. International Paper, the first race harassment case to adopt a modified victim standard, Judge Gene Carter connected the developments on perspective in *Ellison* and *Robinson* to the approach of the critical race theorists. A common theme in the scholarship is that racism, like sexism, is practiced not only by self-aware bigots who intend to harm their targets, but by white liberals and others who act upon unconscious cultural stereotypes of blacks as inferior. [Carter] ruled that the appropriate standard to apply in a hostile environment racial harassment case is that of a reasonable black person.

Much as in *Rabidue* and *Robinson*, the plaintiffs in *Harris* cited to a number of racially charged incidents, and the question was whether the cumulative effect amounted to a racially hostile environment. Plaintiffs were part of a group of black workers who had transferred from Mobile to defendant's paper mill in Maine to become permanent replacement workers when the unionized workers there went on strike. At the same time, defendant also brought in white supervisors and white employees from its Southern plants. Supervisors and co-workers at the mill commonly used racial epithets such as "lazy nigger," "black ass," "watermelon man," and "Buckwheat" to refer to the plaintiffs and to blacks generally. Vicious racist jokes with punchlines suggesting that blacks were ignorant and worthless were told, and friends of the plaintiffs were called "nigger lovers." Images of the Ku Klux Klan figured prominently in the hazing of the black workers: KKK was written on the paper rolls where one plaintiff worked, and on more than one occasion white employees dressed up as Klan members and taunted or bullied the plaintiffs. Someone put up a postcard of the Little Rascals, including the Buckwheat character, with the caption "the new generation of papermakers."

The *Harris* court had no doubt that these incidents added up to a racially hostile work environment and the opinion suggests that the plaintiffs would have prevailed regardless of the standard of review chosen. Given that the law in the First Circuit was uncertain,[29] it is a bit surprising that Carter chose this case to announce the new reasonable black person standard. One plausible explanation for this choice is that the use of the victim's perspective helped to explain why the KKK imagery and the Buckwheat jokes should not be dismissed as tasteless humor. Just as the *Ellison* court viewed the harasser's love letters in the context of a rape-prone society that requires women to be wary of sexual conduct, the *Harris* court recognized that images of the KKK amounted to a code that threatened racial violence against blacks. And not unlike the pornography in *Robinson,* the Buckwheat stereotype depicting blacks as fools and as physically comical posed a threat to the black workers' status as credible employees. Without the aid of the victim's perspective, courts might be included to view such verbal taunts and epithets categorically as a lesser evil than physical threats and might fail to see the physical threat behind the epithet.

By applying a modified standard in a racial harassment context, *Harris* responds to the concern, shared by feminists and critical race theorists, that new standards be inclusive and recognize differences within various groups. Although *Harris* involved racial harassment of black men, the court drew an analogy to sexual harassment of the white female plaintiffs in *Ellison* and *Robinson,* presumably viewing the mechanisms of discrimination—stereotyping, ridicule, and exclusion of the out-group—as sufficiently similar to justify a parallel doctrine. The similar treatment of racial and sexual discrimination in this context also suggests that the court accepted the critical race theorists' insight about the subtlety and unconscious nature of some forms of racism. In my view, *Harris* does not equate race to sex discrimination simply for the sake of legal symmetry, but accepts an account of both types of discrimination that places importance on the social construction of difference and on the socially specific experience of each subordinated group.

The *Harris* opinion contains one statement explicitly relevant to the issue of diversity within subordinated groups. Observing that there is no unanimity of perspective among black Americans, the court cited an article by Professor Judith Scales-Trent[30] that makes the point that black women are subject to discrimination in ways that differ from either black men or white women. Apparently, the court was aware of the danger that the reasonable black person standard could be applied in ways that respond only the situation of black men, while the reasonable woman standard could reflect the perspective of white women only. To avoid replicating the false universality problem that prompted reconsideration of the reasonable person standard in the first place, the court recognized that the standard might need to be modified further to focus specifically on the perspective of black women. On this point, the court stated that "[t]he appropriate standard to be applied in hostile environment harassment is that of a reasonable person from the protected group of which the alleged victim is a member."[31] Although ambiguous, the standard suggests that if the target of harassment identifies with more than one subordinated group, the standard should be structured accordingly, for example, the reasonable black woman standard if the victim is a black woman.

V. Shaping the Modified Standards: New Constructions of Objectivity

Together, *Ellison, Robinson,* and *Harris* strike me as potentially very influential cases because their arguments for modifying the reasonable person standard have an unusually strong theoretical foundation. . . .

In selecting modified standards, the courts seem to have been convinced by the commentators' arguments that the reasonable person standard was infused with sexual and racial bias. The text of each opinion indicates a willingness to look behind gender- and race-neutral formulations to test whether the standards perpetuate an unequal status quo. The courts seemed less responsive, however, to the reservations expressed in the literature about the efficacy of simple modification of the traditional standards to include the suppressed perspective. The courts respected the critique of objectivity but were not ready to accept a more dramatic revision of the law that would eliminate familiar terms such as "reasonable" and replace them with standards drawn from feminist and critical race theory. Although the courts in both *Ellison* and *Robinson* cited Abrams extensively, they did not adopt her proposed test centering on sexual coercion and devaluative sexualization. Likewise, *Harris* was influenced by Lawrence's analysis of the victim's perspective in racial contexts, but did not adopt his proposed cultural meaning standard for use in Title VII litigation. . . .

The linguistic feature of the modified standards that might prove the most resistant to feminist interpretations is the retention of the concept of "reasonableness." As used by the courts, reasonableness determines which victim responses will be legitimated and which will be discredited. The focus is on the plaintiff. If she loses the suit because her response to the challenged behavior is deemed unreasonable, even from the perspective of persons in her situation, this sends a clear message that the blame lies within the individual making the complaint.[32] Perhaps even more so than a plaintiff who loses a claim because of a blanket rule—for example, a rule immunizing pornography in the workplace or sexual behavior not targeted at a specific individual—the plaintiff who fails the reasonable woman test runs a high risk of revictimization.

Reasonableness is such a familiar legal concept that pressing it into service to delimit worthy harassment claims poses problems. There is the danger of essentialism, the risk that if courts regard the viewpoint of the reasonable woman as having a determinate content, they will tend to reconstruct stereotypes of women that will do little to change the distribution of power in the workplace. Yet if reasonableness is not bounded to some degree, subjective judgments of individual women will become the measure of sex equity in the workplace. As the debate about false consciousness or ideological determinism demonstrates,[33] it is risky to rely exclusively on subjective judgments that have been formulated under conditions of gender inequality. . . .

One possible construction of reasonableness is easy to reject. This is the contention that there must be a unanimity of views among women before a position can authentically be called a women's viewpoint and be shared by reasonable women as a position reflective of their situation and experience. It is still the case that to discredit a claim of sexual harassment or sex discrimination, opponents will point to the one woman who takes the counterposition. The assumption apparently is that if one woman disagrees, the contrasting viewpoints are degendered. Such an argument may stem from a naturalistic notion that a woman's perspective has a biological basis which is constant for every individual female. The argument may also represent a dramatic version of gender stereotyping, one that cannot comprehend differences among women and therefore classifies any noticeable differences as having nothing to do with gender. Or the insistence of unanimity might be thought of in more strategic terms: in predominantly male environments, great pressure is often placed on token women to acquiesce to male structures and social patterns and to show their allegiance to the dominant group by distancing themselves from other women. With such built-in incentives to be loyal to the group in power, there will rarely come a time when the need for change is acknowledged, if a prerequisite is unanimous support from the affected class.

In litigation, the issue tends to surface when employers offer the testimony of female workers who state that they did not experience the environment as hostile and were not personally offended by the sexual comments and other behavior that form the basis for their co-worker's claim. The courts have generally not regarded such testimony, even if credible, as precluding the plaintiff's claim and thus have not required unanimity as a matter of formal legal doctrine. . . .

A construction of reasonableness that is harder to dismiss equates the reasonable woman to the average or typical or the majority of women. Such a standard is familiar in tort law, in which custom is regarded as highly probative to establish the standard of care of the reasonable person in negligence cases. In torts, reasonableness is most often measured by the status quo, and it is deviation from the normal that is most readily labeled unreasonable. . . .

As in *Robinson,* defendants can be expected to argue that if most women would not regard conduct as objectionable, it is not reasonable for the plaintiff to have such a response. This search for the average victim might also be attractive to a judge who wants to appear neutral or impartial because it casts the decision as an empirical inquiry. . . .

This majoritarian construction of reasonableness is problematic, however, if the goal is to use the victim's perspective as a legal incentive for sex and race equity in the workplace. As *Robinson* demonstrated, courts must often confront the difficult preliminary question of which women's views should count in determining the majority view. . . . In deciding which evidence was the most convincing to establish the reasonable woman's response, [Judge] Melton embraced a theoretical framework that placed sex equity at the center of its concern and assumed that the status quo was unfair and nonneutral. The social science literature upon which Fiske drew assumes that if there is only a small percentage of women in a given sector of the workplace this signals a problem. The studies were designed to detect those mechanisms that increase the chances that women will be less favorably evaluated than men and that keep the number of women low. One of the prescriptions for change that Fiske and others in her field advocate, for example, is the hiring of women in significant numbers in management positions to moderate the effects of a gender-stratified workplace. In contrast, the defendant's experts did not start from the premise that there was a need for change in male-dominated workplaces. . . .

The construction of the reasonable woman's perspective I find implicit in *Robinson* could be restated as the perspective that might reasonably be taken by women consciously interested in improving their status in the workplace. Under this construction, reasonableness is tied specifically to women's interests and is a standard that contemplates change. This version of reasonableness is compatible with feminist and critical race theories insofar as it questions traditions and common practices that develop in segregated settings. . . . This construction of reasonableness comports with an asymmetrical justification for adoption of modified standards that regards gender and race-specific standards as a useful strategy to focus on the inequities caused by gender or race hierarchies. Putting this feminist gloss on reasonableness may well mean that the hypothetical reasonable woman will not be the average woman who has found a way to cope with, but not to challenge, sexually harassing conduct. . . .

Putting such a woman-centered gloss on reasonableness could have an impact on the quantum and quality of conduct that the courts regard as sufficient to create a hostile environment. In deciding how much is too much, the courts have barely begun to develop standards that measure severity and pervasiveness from the victim's standpoint. . . .

Placing women's interests at the center of the inquiry might allow us to frame the inquiry in more positive and more expansive terms. For example, a persuasive argument could be made that it is reasonable for women to expect to work in an environment that is no more onerous than they would experience if they worked in a female-dominated workplace. This comparative claim seems modest from the perspective of the victim, because the claim is only that women are entitled to experience what men already have—a working environment that is receptive to their sex. Framing the issue in terms that use women's institutions or organizations as a model would be unusual for most courts because women's activities are so seldom used as reference points. If the reasonable woman is not expected to tolerate sexist behavior as inevitable, however, it is necessary to search for new ways to express the level of protection the law should provide, beyond the minimum of prohibiting intolerable conditions. . . .

An important value in recognizing differing perspectives in the law is the respect accorded to distinct groups whose experiences have traditionally been discounted or ignored. This recognition of distinctive group experiences immediately raises the problem, however, of deciding which groups qualify for separate legal treatment. In the context of modifications to the reasonable person standard, this entails consideration of which groups can meaningfully be said to share a perspective about their working environment. Stated another way, how many modifications of the reasonable person standard should the courts endorse?

. . . The *Harris* court indicated that in offensive work environment cases, the legal standard used should be shaped to fit the protected group of which plaintiff is a member. Most probably the court's reference to "protected group" means the list contained in the text of Title VII which, in addition to race, sex, and color, prohibits discrimination based on religion and national origin. . . . Additionally, because Title VII has been used as a model for adjudicating claims of age discrimination and discrimination based on disability grounded in other federal statutes, the courts may be asked to consider the perspectives of older workers and disabled employees.

This multiplicity of perspectives admittedly complicates the law, but theoretically does not pose any insuperable problems. Before further modifying the standard, the courts may want some assurance that the modification is truly needed to express substantially different viewpoints that arise from disparities in power or numbers in the workplace. . . .

[Another problem is that in] cases of compound discrimination, the ordinary legal practice of classifying incidents as *either* racial *or* sexual harassment minimizes the injury to persons who experience both types of discrimination. It also means that a fragmented identity is the only identity the law affords to minorities within a minority group.

Moreover, as Kimberle Crenshaw's analysis of Title VII cases so powerfully demonstrates,[34] African American women sometimes are subjected to forms of discrimination that have no counterpart in the discrimination faced by white woman or African American men. In these cases, use of a distinctive black women's perspective is perhaps the best way to assure that the offensive qualify of the harassment directed at black women as a group is made visible and is understood. A similar analysis may also be applied to other identifiable subgroups.

Allowing legal standards to reflect subgroup identities, however, only begins to address the problem of how law should respond to the existence of multiple oppression and interlocking discrimination. If identity is not a fixed attribute but rather is linked to specific human relationships and situations, it may make sense to allow for some flexibility in describing the appropriate perspective in any given Title VII case. Crenshaw's analysis also suggests that perspective should not automatically be assigned by the court to specific plaintiff groups, for example, if the plaintiff is an Asian woman, her case should not automatically be judged by the perspective of the reasonable Asian woman. Instead, perhaps plaintiffs should have the ability to claim that a particular perspective fits the circumstances of the case. If an Asian woman suffers discrimination she believes that Asian men also face at her workplace, she might choose to argue that the case should be viewed from the perspective of the reasonable Asian worker. The modifications of the reasonable person standard do not need to be fixed but could respond to plaintiff's descriptions of her community and the relationships among workers. This seems preferable to having the court decide for the plaintiff at the outset what form of discrimination she suffered.

As long as the modification fits within one or more of the statutory categories, there seems to be nothing to prevent judicial adoption of a perspective that helps plaintiff explain the full extent of her injury. However, for at least two important dimensions of identity—sexual orientation and class—there is no explicit protection in Title VII or other federal anti-discrimination laws. This makes it difficult to argue that these groups ought to be treated as protected groups and that their perspectives ought to be legally recognized. Particularly when the harassment of lesbians and gay men is so prevalent and so virulent, exclusion of their perspectives is an injustice that highlights the pressing need to amend the laws and to provide explicit protection against discrimination based on sexual orientation. The current limitation on protected groups in Title VII law also underscores the general lack of attention to class in law generally. Class hierarchies imbedded in the structures of jobs and occupations are often invisible and do not even become a topic for progressive legal change. . . .

This argument for inclusion of the perspectives of subgroups beyond the categories specifically mentioned in the legislation would be a practical application of Elizabeth Spelman's philosophical critique of legal and other analytical processes of categorization.[35] Spelman's reasoning presents a challenge to the meaning of the category "women" and to conventional legal meanings of "sex discrimination." . . . A Spelman-like deconstruction of legal categories would ultimately mean that any law directed at oppression would reach all forms of oppression simultaneously.

Such a thoroughgoing attack on legal categories is considerably more radical than the modifications of the reasonable person standard the courts have so far been willing to discuss. . . .

In her postmodern critique of legal feminist scholarship, Angela Harris has argued for categories that are tentative, relational, and unstable.[36] However, legal categories are generally treated as being fixed, intrinsic, and unchanging. Throughout this essay I have tried to keep in mind that it is not the words of the legal standards that give them this quality; it depends on how the words are interpreted. I think it is possible to modify the reasonable person standard in a progressive direction—in a way that does not naturalize difference, that challenges conventional understandings of reasonableness, and that recognizes diversity within subordinated groups.

Notes

1. See generally Martha Minow, Making All the Difference: Inclusion, Exclusion and American Law 184–214 (1990); Kathryn Abrams, Hearing the Call of Stories, 79 Cal. L. Rev. 971, 1013–1016 (1991); Dennis M. Patterson, Postmodernism/Feminism/Law, 77 Cornell L. Rev. 254 (1992).

2. Two often-cited articles addressing this topic in feminist studies are Katharine T. Bartlett, Feminist Legal Methods, in D. Weisberg ed., Feminist Legal Theory: Foundations 550 (Temple Univ. Press, 1993), and Mary E. Hawkesworth, Knowers, Knowing, Known: Feminist Theory and Claims of Truth, 14 Signs 533 (Spring 1989). Perhaps the earliest call for a victim's perspective in the law came from Alan Freeman. See Alan Freeman, Anti-Discrimination Law: A Critical Review, in David Kairys ed., The Politics of Law: A Progressive Critique 96 (1982).

3. EEOC Guidelines on Discrimination Because of Sex, 29 C.F.R. 1604.11(a)(3) (1982). This language was cited with approval in Meritor Sav. Bank v. Vinson, 477 U.S. 57, 65 (1986). . . .

4. See, e.g., Brooms v. Regal Tube Co., 881 F.2d 412, 419 (7th Cir. 1989); Highlander v. K.F.C. Nat'l Management Co., 805 F.2d 644, 650 (6th Cir. 1986).

5. See Ellison v. Brady, 924 F.2d 872, 878–879 (9th Cir. 1991); Andrews v. City of Philadelphia, 895 F.2d 1469, 1482, 1486 (3d. Cir. 1990); Yates v. Avco Corp., 819 F.2d 630, 637 (6th Cir. 1987); Harris v. Int'l Paper, 765 F. Supp. 1509, 1516 (D. Me. 1991); Austen v. Hawaii, 759 F. Supp. 612, 628 (D. Haw. 1991); Robinson v. Jacksonville Shipyards, Inc., 760 F. Supp. 1486 (M.D. Fla. 1991).

6. 805 F.2d 611 (6th Cir. 1986), *cert. denied,* 481 U.S. 1041 (1987).

7. See Rosabeth Moss Kanter, Men and Women of the Corporation 206–242 (1977).

8. 584 F. Supp. 419 (E.D. Mich. 1984), *aff'd*, 805 F.2d 611 (6th Cir. 1986), *cert. denied*, 481 U.S. 1041 (1987).

9. E.g., Brooms v. Regal Tube Co., 881 F.2d 412 (7th Cir. 1989); Highlander v. K.F.C. Nat'l Management Co., 805 F.2d 644, 650 (6th Cir. 1986).

10. E.g., Waltman v. Int'l Paper Co., 875 F.2d 468, 477 n.3 (5th Cir. 1989); Bennett v. Corroon & Black Corp., 845 F.2d 104, 106 (5th Cir. 1988), *cert. denied*, 489 U.S. 1010 (1989); EEOC Policy Guidance on Sexual Harassment, Daily Lab. Rep. (BNA) No. 201, at E-5 (Oct. 18, 1988).

11. The most significant of MacKinnon's early writings were: Catharine A. MacKinnon, Sexual Harassment of Working Women (1979); Catharine A. MacKinnon, Feminism, Marxism, Method and the State: Toward Feminist Jurisprudence, in Feminist Legal Theory: Foundations, *supra* note 2, at 427; Catharine A. MacKinnon, Feminism, Marxism, Method and the State: An Agenda for Theory, in *id.* at 437.

12. The fullest elaboration of Minow's social-relations approach to difference can be found in Minow, *supra* note 1. Two important earlier articles addressing the same theme are: Martha Minow, When Difference Has Its Home, in Feminist Legal Theory: Foundations, *supra* note 2, at 320, and Martha Minow, Foreward: Justice Engendered, in *id.* at 301.

13. Professor Elizabeth Schneider's articles document and analyze the history of women's self-defense litigation from her perspective as a litigator and feminist theorist. Elizabeth Schneider, Describing and Changing: Women's Self-Defense Work and the Problem of Expert Testimony on Battering, herein, at 311; Elizabeth Schneider, The Dialectic of Rights and Politics: Perspectives from the Women's Movement, in Feminist Legal Theory: Foundations, *supra* note 2, at 507; Elizabeth Schneider, Equal Rights to Trial for Women: Sex Bias in the Law of Self-Defense, 15 Harv. C.R.-C.L. L. Rev. 623 (1980).

14. Lucinda M. Finley, A Break in the Silence: Including Women's Issues in a Torts Course, 1 Yale J.L. & Feminism 41 (1989).

15. *Id.* at 64.

16. Nancy S. Ehrenreich, Pluralist Myths and Powerless Men: The Ideology of Reasonableness in Sexual Harassment Law, 99 Yale L. J. 1177, 1216–1232 (1990).

17. Kathryn Abrams, Gender Discrimination and the Transformation of Workplace Norms, 42 Vand. L. Rev. 1183 (1989).

18. *Id.* at 1211.

19. 924 F.2d 872 (9th Cir. 1991).

20. 760 F. Supp. 1486 (M.D. Fla. 1991).

21. *Id.* at 1516.

22. Trial Testimony of Dr. Susan Fiske, Record vol. 4, at 184–185, Robinson (No. 86–927-Civ-J-12). Fiske estimated that women made up only five percent of the workforce and less than one percent of the skilled workers at Jacksonville Shipyards. *Id.*

23. 765 F. Supp. 1509 (D. Me. 1991), *vacated in* part, 765 F. Supp. 1529 (1991).

24. This did not mean, however, that the law was more protective of one class of victims over another. Instead, the conventional wisdom about both forms of discrimination tended to limit what the law would address. In the traditional view, sexual harassment was naturalized, with the result that much abuse, exclusion, and segregation could be rationalized as inevitable based on biological differences between men and women. When sex discrimination was acknowledged, it was often categorized as subtle and said to be less harmful than blatant discrimination. Racially based disparate treatment was

not so easily dismissed because of the widely shared official view that race discrimination was wrong and that there were no natural differences between racial groups. . . .

25. For some notable examples from this body of scholarship, see e.g., Derrick Bell, And We Are Not Saved: The Elusive Quest for Racial Justice (1987); Patricia Williams, The Alchemy of Race and Rights (1991); Kimberle Crenshaw, Race, Reform, and Retrenchment: Transformation and Legitimation in Anti-Discrimination Law, 101 Harv. L. Rev. 1331 (1988); Jerome McCristal Culp, Toward A Black Legal Scholarship: Race and Original Understandings, 1991 Duke L.J. 39; Richard Delgado, When a Story Is Just a Story: Does Voice Really Matter? 76 Va. L. Rev. 95 (1990); Mari J. Matsuda, Looking to the Bottom: Critical Legal Studies and Reparations, 22 Harv. C.R.-C.L. L. Rev. 323 (1987). Randall Kennedy's skepticism that legal academic scholars of color could speak with a distinctive voice generated a well-publicized debate. See Randall Kennedy, Racial Critiques of Legal Academia, 102 Harv. L. Rev. 1745 (1989); Scott Brewer, Colloquy, Responses to Randall Kennedy's Racial Critiques of Legal Academia, 103 Harv. L. Rev. 1844, 1844–1886 (1990) (comprising responses to Scott Brewer, Milner S. Ball, Robin D. Barnes, Richard Delgado, and Leslie G. Espinosa to Randall Kennedy's Racial Critiques of Legal Academia, 102 Harv. L. Rev. 1745 (1990)).

26. Charles Lawrence, The Id, the Ego, and Equal Protection: Reckoning with Unconscious Racism, 39 Stan. L. Rev. 317 (1987).

27. *Id.* at 343.

28. Some influential texts are: Gloria T. Hull et al. eds., All the Women Are White, All the Blacks Are Men, But Some of Us Are Brave (1982); Angela J. Davis, Women, Race and Class (1981); Paula Giddens, When and Where I Enter: The Impact of Black Women on Race and Sex in America (1984); bell hooks, Ain't I a Woman: Black Women and Feminism (1981); Audre Lorde, Sister Outsider (1984).

29. Harris v. Int'l Paper, 765 F. Supp. at 1513–1514 (noting that in Lipsett v. University of P.R., 864 F.2d 881 (1st Cir. 1988), the court mentioned the victim's perspective, but in Morgan v. Massachusetts Gen. Hosp., 901 F.2d 186 (1st Cir. 1990), the court used the traditional reasonable person standard).

30. Id. at 1516 n.12 (citing Judith Scales-Trent, Black Women and the Constitution: Finding Our Place, Asserting Our Rights, 42 Harv. C.R.-C.L. L. Rev. 9 (1989)).

31. *Id.*

32. Because of the potential for law and litigation to "blame the victim" and intensify and renew the injury suffered, a recurring theme in some feminist scholarship is a skepticism or even hostility to legal reform strategies. See, e.g., Kristin Bumiller, The Civil Rights Society: The Social Construction of Victims (1988); Carol Smart, Feminism and the Power of Law (1989).

33. See, e.g., Kathryn Abrams, Ideology and Women's Choices, 24 Geo. L. Rev. 761 (1990).

34. Kimberle W. Crenshaw, Demarginalizing the Intersection of Race and Sex: A Black Feminist Critique of Antidiscrimination Doctrine, Feminist Theory, and Antiracist Policies, in Feminist Legal Theory: Foundations, *supra* note 2, at 383.

35. Elizabeth V. Spelman, Inessential Woman: Problems of Exclusion in Feminist Thought (1988).

36. Angela Harris, Race and Essentialism in Feminist Legal Theory, in Feminist Legal Theory: Foundations, *supra* note 2, at 348.

◈ *Whose Story Is It, Anyway? Feminist and Antiracist Appropriations of Anita Hill*

KIMBERLÉ CRENSHAW

As TELEVISION, the Clarence Thomas/Anita Hill hearings played beautifully as an episode right out of "The Twilight Zone." Stunned by the drama's mystifying images, its misplaced pairings, and its baffling contradictions, viewers found themselves in a parallel universe where political allegiances barely imaginable a moment earlier sprang to life: an administration that won an election through the shameless exploitation of the mythic black rapist took the offensive against stereotypes about black male sexuality; a political party that had been the refuge of white resentment won the support, however momentary, of the majority of African Americans; a black neoconservative individualist whose upward mobility was fueled by his unbounded willingness to stymie the advancement of other African Americans was embraced under the wings of racial solidarity; and a black woman, herself a victim of racism, was symbolically transformed into the role of a would-be white woman whose unwarranted finger-pointing whetted the appetites of a racist lynch mob.

But it was no "Twilight Zone" that America discovered when Anita Hill came forward. America simply stumbled into the place where African-American women live, a political vacuum of erasure and contradiction maintained by the almost routine polarization of "blacks and women" into separate and competing political camps. Existing within the overlapping margins of race and gender discourse and in the empty spaces between, it is a location whose very nature resists telling. This location contributes to black women's ideological disempowerment in a way that tipped the scales against Anita Hill from the very start. While there are surely many dimensions of the Thomas-Hill episode that contributed to the way it played out, my focus on the ideological plane is based on the idea that at least one important way social power is mediated in American society is through the contestation between the many narrative structures through which reality might be perceived and talked about. By this I mean to focus on the intense interpretive conflicts that ultimately bear on the particular ways that realities are socially constructed. Ideology, seen in the form of the narrative tropes available for representing our experience, was a factor of social power to the extent that Anita Hill's inability to be heard outside the rhetorical structures within which cultural power has been organized hampered her ability to achieve recognition and support. Thus, Anita Hill's status as a black female—at the crossroads of gender and race hierarchies—was a central feature in the manner in which she was (mis)perceived. . . .

The particular experience of black women in the dominant cultural ideology of American society can be conceptualized as intersectional. Intersectionality captures the way in which the particular location of black women in dominant American social relations is unique and in some senses unassimilable into the discursive paradigms of gender and race domination. One commonly noted aspect of this location is that black women are in a sense doubly burdened, subject in some ways to the dominating practices of both a sexual hierarchy and a racial one. In addition to this added dimension, intersectionality also refers to the ways that black women's marginalization within dominant discourses of resistance limits the means available to relate and conceptualize our experiences as black women.

In legal doctrine this idea has been explored in terms of doctrinal exclusion, that is, the ways in which the specific forms of domination to which black females are subject sometimes fall between the existing legal categories for recognizing injury.[1] Underlying the legal parameters of racial discrimination are numerous narratives reflecting discrimination as it is experienced by black men, while the underlying imagery of gender discrimination incorporates the experiences of white women. The particularities of black female subordination are suppressed as the terms of racial and gender discrimination law require that we mold our experience into that of either white women or black men in order to be legally recognized.

. . . When feminism does not explicitly oppose racism, and when antiracism does not incorporate opposition to patriarchy, race and gender politics often end up being antagonistic to each other and both interests lose. The Thomas/Hill controversy presents a stark illustration of the problem as evidenced by the opposition between narratives of rape and of lynching. These tropes have come to symbolize the mutually exclusive claims that have been generated within both antiracist and feminist discourses about the centrality of sexuality to both race and gender domination. In feminist contexts, sexuality represents a central site of the oppression of women; rape and the rape trial are its dominant narrative trope. In antiracist discourses, sexuality is also a central site upon which the repression of blacks has been premised; the lynching narrative is embodied as its trope. (Neither narrative tends to acknowledge the legitimacy of the other; the reality of rape tends to be disregarded within the lynching narrative; the impact of racism is frequently marginalized within rape narratives. Both these tropes figure prominently in this controversy, and it was in this sense that the debacle constituted a classic showdown between antiracism and feminism. The tropes, whether explicitly invoked, as lynching, or implicitly referred, as rape, served to communicate in shorthand competing narratives about the hearings and about what "really" happened between Clarence Thomas and Anita Hill. Anita Hill was of course cast in both narratives, but because one told a tale of sexism and the other told an opposing tale of racism, the simultaneity of Hill's race and gender identity was essentially denied. In this sense, both feminist and anti-racist told tales on Anita Hill, tales in which she was appropriated to tell everybody's story but her own.

These competing appropriations of Anita Hill within feminist and antiracist discourses represent a persistent dilemma that confronts black women within prevailing constructions of identity politics: dominant conceptions of racism and sexism render it virtually impossible to represent our situation in ways that fully articulate our subject position as black women. While Thomas was able to invoke narratives that linked his situation to the sexual oppression of black men and thus have his story understood as relevant to the entire black community, Hill remained unable to represent even herself, much less other similarly situated black women.

In this essay I want to elaborate how the cultural dynamics surrounding the Thomas-Hill conflict are better understood in terms of Hill's intersectional disempowerment. . . .

I. Anita Hill as a Victim of Sexual Domination— The Rape Trope

Anita Hill was primarily presented to the American public as simply a woman complaining about sexual harassment. Her plausibility in that role was dependent upon the degree to which she could be fit within the dominant images of sexual victimization. . . . While many elements of the dominant feminist discourse about gender power and sexuality clearly did apply to Anita Hill—for example, the tradition of impugning charges of sexual aggression with baseless allegations of psychic delusions or vengeful spite—the grounding of the critique on white women meant that, in a sense, Hill (and Thomas) had to be deraced, so that they could be represented as actors in a recognizable story of sexual harassment. While white feminists were in general the most consistent and vocal supporters of Hill, the fact remains that both her lack of fit into the dominant imagery of the violated madonna and, more specifically, the feminist movement's inability to develop alternative narratives comprehending the ways that women of color experience gender power, led to the particular dynamics that many of her supporters themselves were unable to understand, dynamics that included the rejection of Hill by the majority of black women as well as white women.

Feminist legal scholars have frequently used rape as a framework to capture both the way women experience sexual harassment and the way the law shapes the claims of the few courageous women who come forward. Feminist scholars and activists have long criticized the way the adjudication of sexual aggression is animated by myths about women, about assumptions regarding their veracity and their integrity, and by doubts about their grasp on reality. In both rape and sexual harassment cases the inquiry tends to focus more on the woman's conduct and character rather than on the conduct and character of the defendant. As a consequence, rape law does less to protect the sexual autonomy of women than it does to reinforce established codes of female sexual conduct.

Part of the regulation of sexuality through rape law occurs in the perception of the complaining witness at the rape trial. Building on the idea that reality is socially constructed in part through ideologically informed images of "men" and "women," feminist legal work has emphasized the ways that perceptions of the credibility of witnesses, for example, are mediated by dominant narratives about the ways that men and women "are." Within this framework, the vast disparity between male and female characterization reflects a gendered zero-sum equation of credibility and power. The routine focus on the victim's sexual history functions to cast the complainant in one of several roles, including the whore, the tease, and vengeful liar, the mentally or emotionally unstable, or, in a few instances, the madonna. Once these ideologically informed character assignments are made, "the story" tells itself, usually supplanting the woman's account of what transpired between the complainant and the accused with a fiction of villainous female intentionality that misleads and entraps the "innocent" or unsuspecting male in his performance of prescribed sexual behavior. Such displaying narratives are overwhelmingly directed toward interrogating and discrediting the woman's character on behalf of maintaining a considerable range of sexual prerogatives for men. Even the legal definitions of the crime of rape itself are inscribed with male visions of the sexual sphere—the focus on penetration, the definitions of consent (with the once-conventional requirement of "utmost resistance"),[2] the images of female provocation and spiteful false accusation, and the links between desirability, purity, chastity, and value.[3]

The feminist narrative of the rape trial did in many ways account for the dynamics that Anita Hill put into play. For example, a good deal of the hearings was allegedly devoted to determining the credibility of the parties. Anita Hill's subordination through the notion of credibility is revealed in the relatively wide range of narratives that Thomas's defenders could invoke by simply describing events and impressions that had little to do with what transpired between Hill and Thomas in private. For example, the conversation that Anita Hill allegedly had with John Doggett was deemed relevant within a narrative that presented Hill as an undesirable woman who constructed relationships with men who rejected her. Testimony that she was aloof, ambitious, and hard to get along with was relevant within a narrative that presented her as calculating and careerist. The continuous focus on failure to resign after the harassment began fit into a narrative that presented her as a woman who did not meet the utmost-resistance standard because she was apparently unwilling to exchange her career for her "honor"; she was thus unworthy to make the claim.

Yet there were many narratives that could have been told about Thomas that bore on his credibility. For example, his quite startling shift in philosophy during the eighties and his subsequent "confirmation conversion" could have been understood as bearing on his reputation for truthfulness;[4] his derogatory public references to his sister could be seen as further evidence of his willingness to bend the truth;[5] his participation in an administrative position paper recommending reduced enforcement of sexual harassment could have been interpreted as suggesting a dismissive attitude toward the problem of sexual harassment. Moreover, the testimony of Angela Wright and two other corroborating witnesses could have been used to suggest that there was in fact a pattern of harassment,[6] and most obviously, evidence relating to his consumption of pornography could have been used to suggest a source for the elusive Long Dong Silver. That none of these narratives were seriously pursued while countless narratives about Anita Hill were—though they were arguably less relevant—demonstrates how the interpretive structures we use to reconstruct events are thoroughly shaped by gender power.

II. Race and Chastity: The Limitations of the Feminist Paradigm

Feminist discourse speaks to the particular way in which Anita Hill was disempowered through the very structuring of the inquiry, yet it could account for only part of the context within which Anita Hill acted. The particular intersectional identity of Hill, as both a woman and an African American, lent dimensions to her ideological placement in the economy of American culture that could not be translated through the dominant feminist analysis.[7] Again using the parallel between rape and sexual harassment, these race-specific aspects of black women's experiences are accessible.

Rape and other sexual abuses in the work context, now termed sexual harassment, have been a condition of black women's work life for centuries. Forced sexual access to black women was of course institutionalized in slavery and was central to its reproduction. During the period when the domination of white women was justified and reinforced by the nineteenth-century separate-spheres ideology, the few privileges of separate spheres were not available to black women at all. Instead, the subordination of African-American women recognized few boundaries between public and private life. Rape and other sexual abuses were justified by myths that black women were sexually voracious, that they were sexually indiscriminate, and that they readily copulated with animals, most frequently imagined to be apes and monkeys. Indeed, their very anatomy was objectified. . . .[8]

The stereotypes and myths that justified the sexual abuse of black women in slavery continue to be played out in current society. They are apparent in the experiences of women who are abused on their jobs and in the experiences of black women elsewhere in society. For example, in many of the sexual harassment cases involving African-American women, the incidents they report often represent a merging of racist myths with the victims' vulnerability as women. Black female plaintiffs tell stories of insults and slurs that often go to the core of black women's sexual construction. While black women share with white women the experience of being objectified as "cunts," "beavers," or "pieces," for them those insults are many times prefaced with "black" or "nigger" or "jungle." Perhaps this racialization of sexual harassment explains why black women are disproportionately represented in sexual harassment cases. Racism may well provide the clarity to see that sexual harassment is neither a flattering gesture nor a misguided social overture but an act of intentional discrimination that is insulting, threatening, and debilitating.

Pervasive myths and stereotypes about black women not only shape the kinds of harassment that black women experience but also influence whether black women's stories are likely to be believed. Historically, a black woman's word was not taken as truth; our own legal system once drew a connection—as a matter of law—between lack of chastity and lack of veracity. In other words, a woman who was likely to have sex could not be trusted to tell the truth. Because black women were not expected to be chaste, they were likewise considered less likely to tell the truth. Thus, judges were known to instruct juries to take a black woman's word with a grain of salt. One judge admonished jurors not to apply the ordinary presumption of chastity to black women, for if they were to do so, they "would be blinding themselves to actual conditions."[9] . . . Lest it be believed that such doubts have been banished to the past, a very recent study of jurors in rape trials revealed that black women's integrity is still very deeply questioned by many people in society. One juror, explaining why a black rape victim was discredited by the jury, stated, "You can't believe everything they say. They're known to exaggerate the truth."[10]

Even where the facts of our stories are believed, myths and stereotypes about black women also influence whether the insult and injury we have experienced is relevant or important. One study concluded, for example, that men who assault black women are the least likely to receive jail time; when they do, the average sentence given to black women's assailants is two years; the average for white women's assailants is ten years. Again, attitudes of jurors seem to reflect a common belief that black women are different from white women and that sexual aggression directed toward them is less objectionable. In a case involving the rape of a black preteen, one juror argued for acquittal on the grounds that a girl her age from "that neighborhood . . . probably wasn't a virgin anyway."

These responses are not exceptional, as illustrated by the societal response to the victimization of Carol Stuart, the Boston woman whose husband murdered her and then fingered a black male. It would strain credibility to say that the Boston police would have undertaken a door-to-door search of any community had Carol Stuart and her fetus been black. . . . Surely the black woman who was gang-raped during that same week, whose pelvis and ankles were shattered when she was thrown down an elevator shaft and left to die, along with the twenty-eight other women who were raped that week and received no outpouring of public concern, would find it impossible to deny that society views the victimization of some women as being less important than that of others.

Black women experience much of the sexual aggression that the feminist movement has articulated but in a form that represents simultaneously their subordinate racial status. While the fallen-woman imagery that white feminists identify does represent much of black women's experience of gender domination, given their race, black women have in a sense always been within the fallen-women category. For black women the issue is not the precariousness of holding on to the protection that the madonna image provides or the manner in which the madonna image works to regulate and thereby constrain black women's sexuality. Instead, it is the denial of the presumption of "madonna-hood" that shapes responses to black women's sexual victimization.

White feminists have been reluctant to incorporate race into their narratives about gender, sex, and power. Their unwillingness to speak to the race-specific dimensions of black women's sexual disempowerment was compounded by their simultaneous failure to understand the ways that race may have contributed to Anita Hill's silence. Their attempts to explain why she remained silent spoke primarily to her career interests. Yet the other reasons why many black women have been reluctant to reveal experiences of sexual abuse—particularly by African-American men—remained unexamined. In fact, many black women fear that their stories might be used to reinforce stereotypes of black men as sexually threatening. Others who may not share this particular concern may nevertheless remain silent fearing ostracism from those who do. Black women face these kinds of dilemmas throughout their lives; efforts to tell these stories may have shaped perceptions of Anita Hill differently among black women, perhaps providing some impetus for breaking through the race-versus-gender dichotomy. Content to rest their case on a raceless tale of gender subordination, white feminists missed an opportunity to span the chasm between feminism and antiracism. Indeed feminists actually helped maintain the chasm by endorsing the framing of the event as a race versus a gender issue. In the absence of narratives linking race and gender, the prevailing narrative structures continued to organize the Hill and Thomas controversy as either a story about the harassment of a white woman or a story of the harassment of a black man. Identification by race or gender seemed to be an either/or proposition, and when it is experienced in that manner, black people, both men and women, have traditionally chosen race solidarity. Indeed, white feminist acquiescence to the either/or frame worked directly to Thomas's advantage: with Hill thus cast as simply a de-raced—that is, white—woman, Thomas was positioned to claim that he was the victim of racial discrimination with Hill as the perpetrator. However, that many black people associated Hill more than Thomas with the white world is not solely based on the manner in which feminist discourse is perceived as white. As discussed below, the widespread embrace of Thomas is also attributable to the patriarchal way that racial solidarity has been defined within the black community.

III. Anita Hill as Villain: The Lynching Trope

One of the most stunning movements in the history of American cultural drama occurred when Clarence Thomas angrily denounced the hearings as a "high-tech lynching." Thomas's move to drape himself in a history of black male repression was particularly effective in the all-white male Senate, whose members could not muster the moral authority to challenge Thomas's sensationalist characterization. Not only was Thomas suddenly transformed into a victim of racial discrimination, but Anita Hill was further erased as a black woman. Her racial identity became irrelevant in explaining or understanding her position, while Thomas's play on the lynching metaphor racially empowered him. Of course, the success of this particular reading was not inevitable; there are several competing narratives that could conceivably have countered Thomas's move. Chief among them was the possibility of pointing out that allegations relating to the sexual abuse of black women have had nothing to do with the history of lynching, a tradition based upon white hysteria regarding black male access to white women. Black women's relationship to the lynch mob was not as a perpetrator but as one of its victims, either through their own lynching or the lynching of loved ones. Moreover, one might have plausibly predicted that, given Thomas's persistent denunciation of any effort to link the history of racism to ongoing racial inequalities, the American public would have scornfully characterized this play as a last-ditch effort to pull his troubled nomination out of the fire. African Americans in particular might have easily rejected Thomas's bid for racial solidarity by concluding that a man who has adamantly insisted that blacks be judged on the content of their character rather than the color of their skin should not be supported when he deploys the color of his skin as a defense to judgments of his character. Yet the race play was amazingly successful; Thomas's approval ratings in the black community skyrocketed from 54 percent to nearly 80 percent immediately following his performance. Indeed, it was probably his solid support in the black community, particularly in the South, that clinched the seat on the Court. Implicit in this response was a rejection, at times frighteningly explicit, of Anita Hill.

The deification of Thomas and the vilification of Anita Hill were prefigured by practices within the black community that have long subordinated gender domination to the struggle against racism. In the process the particular experiences of black men have often come to represent the racial domination of the entire community, as is demonstrated by the symbolic currency of the lynching metaphor and the marginalization of representations of black female domination. Cases involving sexual accusations against black men have stood as hallmarks of racial injustice; Emmett Till, the Scottsboro boys, and others wrongly accused are powerful symbolic figures in our struggle for racial equality. Black women have also experienced sexualized racial violence; the frequent and unpunished rape and mutilation of black women by white men is a manifestation of racial domination. Yet the names and faces of black women whose bodies also bore the scars of racial oppression are lost to history. To the limited extent that sexual victimization of black women is symbolically represented within our collective memory, it is as tragic characters whose vulnerability illustrates the racist emasculation of black men. The marginalization of black female narratives of racism and sexuality thus worked directly to Thomas's advantage by providing him with the ready means to galvanize the black community on his behalf. Thomas's angry denunciations of Hill's allegations as a "high-tech lynching" invoked powerful images linking him to a concrete history that resonated deeply within most African Americans. Hill, had she been so inclined, could have invoked only vague and hazy recollections in the African-American memory, half-digested experiences of black female sexual abuse that could not withstand the totalizing power of the lynching metaphor.

The discourse of racial liberation, traditionally built around the claim of unequal treatment of black and white people, is of course relevant to the Thomas-Hill conflict, but only partially. In one sense the racial narrative of differential treatment based on race partly comprehends the situation that Hill was in. It seems relatively clear that had Hill been white she would have been read differently by most Americans; as a black female, she had to overcome not only the burdens that feminists have so well articulated in the rape-trial trope but the additional obstacles of race. But, like the dominant feminist narrative, it is again only partial; the abstract description of differential subordination based on skin color is crystallized into narrative tropes that translate racial inequality into the terms of inequality between men.

The relative potency of male-centered images of sexual racism over female-centered ones is manifested in the contemporary marginalization of black female sexual abuse within black political discourse. Dominant narratives representing the intersections of racism and sexual violence continue to focus on the way that black men accused of raping white women are disproportionately punished relative to black-on-black or white-on-white rape. Within traditional antiracism formulations, this disproportionality has been characterized as racial discrimination against black men. Yet the pattern of punishing black men accused of raping white women more harshly than those accused of raping black women is just as surely an illustration of discrimination against black women. Indeed, some studies suggest that the race of the victim rather than the race of the defendant is the most salient factor determining the disposition of men convicted of rape. Clearly, black women are victims of a racial hierarchy that subordinates their experiences of sexual abuse to those of white women. Yet this intersectional oppression is rarely addressed in antiracist discourses in part because traditional readings of racism continue to center on power differentials between men. Consequently, there is relatively little emphasis on how racism contributes to the victimization of black women both inside and outside the criminal-justice system. The rape of black women has sometimes found its way to the center of antiracism politics, particularly when the rapist is white. But the more common experience of interracial rape is often disregarded within antiracist political discourses, perhaps as a consequence of the view that politicizing such rapes conflicts on some level with efforts to eradicate the prevailing stereotype of the black male rapist. While racism may help explain why white victims are more likely to see their assailants punished than are black victims, one must look to gender power within the black community in order to understand why this persistent devaluation of black women is marginalized within the prevailing conceptions of racism.

Interracial rape and other abusive practices have not been fully addressed within the African-American community in part because African Americans have been reluctant to expose any internal conflict that might reflect negatively on the black community. Although abiding by this "code of silence" is experienced by African Americans as a self-imposed gesture of racial solidarity, the maintenance of silence also has coercive dimensions. Coercion becomes most visible when someone—male or female—breaks the code of silence. Elements of this coercive dimension of gender silence is illustrated in part by the coverage of the hearings of the black press. In many such accounts Hill was portrayed as a traitor for coming forward with her story. Many commentators were less interested in exploring whether the allegations were true than in speculating why Hill would compromise the upward mobility of a black man and em-barrass the African-American community. Anger and resentment toward Hill was reflected in opinions of commentators traversing the political spectrum within black political discourses. Liberal, centrist, and conservative opinion seemed to accept a view of Hill as disloyal and even treasonous.[11] One columnist, a teacher, reported—without criticism—that one of her third-grade students advocated that Hill be taken out and shot. The theme of treachery was also apparent in a column authored by psychologists Nathan and Julia Hare. In an article titled "The Many Faces of Anita Faye Hill,"[12] they linked Hill to other black women who had in some way violated the code by linking gender issues to black women. . . .

The rhetorical deployment of race-based themes to ostracize Anita Hill as an outlaw in the black community received an unexpected boost from noted Harvard sociologist Orlando Patterson in a widely circulated opinion piece that appeared in the New York Times.[13] While many critics who lambasted Hill for voicing her complaints shied away from offering a direct defense of the behavior of which she complained, Patterson deployed race to normatively embrace such behavior and to ostracize Anita Hill for having been offended by it at all. Themes of treachery and betrayal, so central in Hill's indictment for breaking the code of silence, reemerged as disingenuity and inauthenticity under Patterson's indictment of Hill for acting white. Setting forth what the preconversion Thomas might have pejoratively labeled an affirmative-action defense to sexual harassment, Patterson argued that Thomas's sexual taunting of Professor Hill was defensible as a "down-home style of courting," one that black women are accustomed to and apparently flattered by. According to Patterson, even if Thomas did say the things Anita Hill claimed he said, not only must Thomas's behavior be weighed against a different racial standard, but Thomas's identity as a black man must be taken into account in determining whether he was justified in perjuring himself. Patterson concludes that in this case perjury was a justifiable means toward winning a seat on the highest court of the land because white America could never understand that such sexual repartee was in fact common among black men and women.

Patterson's text warrants extensive analysis because it articulates and exemplifies the underlying ways in which certain notions of race and culture function to maintain patriarchy and deny or legitimize gender practices that subordinate the interests of black women. Patterson's argument basically functions as a cultural defense of the harassment Hill complained about. Similar defenses have been articulated in various forms to justify other misogynistic or patriarchal practices perpetuated by some black men. Indeed, were the thesis not so readily available in the rhetorical discourse within the black community, one might follow Senator Hatch's allegation that Hill found Long Dong Silver in a court case and wonder whether Patterson's defense of Thomas was found in the case of California v. Jacinto Rhines.[14] Mr. Rhines, a black man, appealed his conviction for raping two black women, arguing that his conviction should be overturned because the trial court failed to take into account cultural differences between blacks and whites. This failure, he claimed, transformed an ordinary consensual encounter into an actionable rape. According to Rhines, the victim implicitly consented to having intercourse with him when she agreed to accompany him to his apartment. Rhines also argued that the victim was unreasonable in feeling threatened and coerced by his behavior. Black people are often quite animated and talk loudly to each other all the time, he contended. Because the social meaning of the event in the black community differed dramatically from the way whites would read the event, Rhines concluded that he was wrongly convicted. This "cultural defense," trading on familiar stereotypes of black women as hardier than white women, and more accustomed to aggressive, gritty, even violent sex, essentially amounted to a claim that the complainant was not really a rape victim because she was black.

What caused the downfall of Rhines's argument was that he was unable to explain why the "victims" were apparently unaware of these cultural codes. Whether unreasonable or not, if the women were frightened, the sexual intercourse that occurred was coerced. The court was not only unconvinced that race had any bearing on a woman's reaction to coercion; it also deemed Rhines's argument an "inexcusable slur" designed to "excuse his own conduct by demeaning females of the Black race."

For Rhines's argument to have worked, he would have had to convince the court that the cultural practice he identified was so pervasive that the victim's claims of fear and nonconsent were implausible. In effect, Rhines had to convince the court that the black woman should be held to a different standard of victimhood because she was black. Patterson's argument picks up where Rhines's argument failed. Through labeling Hill's reaction to Thomas's "flirtations" disingenuous, Patterson implies that either Hill was not, in fact, emotionally injured by Thomas's barrage of sexual innuendo or that if she was, she was influenced to reinterpret her experience through the lens of middle-class white feminism. Indeed, he suggests that the harassment may have actually served to affirm their common origins. This pattern of "bonding" is apparently so readily acceptable that any black woman who is offended or injured by it must be acting on a white feminist impulse rather than a culturally grounded black female sensibility.

Patterson has subsequently defended his argument as an attempt to counter the failure of white feminists to comprehend the many ways that gender issues differ across race and class lines.[15] There should be, of course, little question that sexism often manifests itself in varying ways within racial contexts. The complexities of racism present black women with many issues that are unfamiliar to white feminists. Yet one of the thorniest issues that black women must confront is represented by Patterson's own descent into cultural relativism. Patterson subtly transformed the quite perceptive claim that black women often have different issues with black men than white women do with white men into a claim that sexual harassment as described in the testimony of Anita Hill is not one of them. He seemed to ground this assertion on a claim that black women have played along with and apparently enjoyed this "sexual repartee." Thus, like Rhines, he argued that attempts to sanction this behavior as abusive or offensive to black women are grounded in a white feminist misreading of black cultural practices.

There are a number of reasons why Patterson's analysis is off the mark in explaining the particularities of black women's sexual subordination, yet it succeeds wonderfully as a discursive illustration of it. Patterson's argument initially rests on a failure to draw any distinction between sexual practices that occur privately and those that occur within the work environment. More fundamentally, the argument reflects a failure to understand the power dynamics that shape those sexual practices in the first place. His argument thus amounts to an uncritical acceptance of sexual practices that he observes in some social settings, an assumption that these practices are characteristic of the whole, and a use of these practices as a normative base to discredit black women who claim to be offended and injured by them.

Patterson's misunderstanding of the nature of sexual harassment is exemplified by his failure to take into account the particular consequences of sexualizing relationships in a highly stratified work environment. In defending Thomas's alleged banter by claiming that such behavior is typical among black men and black women, Patterson constructs the relationship between black men and women as essentially personal and self-contained, no matter what the context. Thus, the rules that prevail in the private social world dictate the terms and conditions of interaction in the more public work world. Setting aside for the moment the power dynamics that shape sexual repartee elsewhere, Patterson overlooks the fact that the highly stratified workplace so thoroughly raises the stakes for black women that engaging in this sexual competition, however skilled at or familiar with the "game" they might be, is a dangerously risky proposition. In a work context, black women are not dealing with a man who, when rebuffed or bested by a woman, will simply move on. Often they are dealing with a supervisor who can wield his superior institutional power over them either to impose sanctions for their response or to pressure them to compromise their sexual autonomy. Patterson's failure to understand these workplace consequences of sexual harassment is actually consistent with the response of federal judges who initially refused to see sexual harassment as anything other than private sexual banter that routinely occurs between men and women. Because these practices are quite common throughout society, judges saw them as normative and indeed essential to relations between men and women. Women plaintiffs, however, eventually succeeded in forcing courts to recognize that regardless of the currency of sexual game-playing elsewhere, the perpetuation of these practices in the workplace significantly contributes to women's subordination in the work force.

Black and white women thus share the burden of overcoming assumptions that sexual harassment in the workplace is essentially a "private" issue. Yet race does shape the problem somewhat differently for black women. The racial specificity is grounded in the fact that there is a certain connection between black men and black women born from a common social history of racial exclusion. Often there is a sense of camaraderie between African Americans a "we're in this together" sensibility. I call this a zone of familiarity, one that creates expectations of support and mutuality that are essential to survival in a work world that is in some ways alien. In fact, this camaraderie is based on a belief that ultimately came to bear on Thomas's behalf—a belief that the interests of African Americans as a whole are advanced by efforts to increase the number of successful and well-placed blacks. However, this zone of familiarity can sometimes be seen as one of privileged sexual access as well. Consequently, one of the workplace dilemmas faced by black women is trying to negotiate between overlapping expectations in this zone, to maintain much-needed relationships but to avoid unwanted intimacy. This camaraderie and the notions of a shared fate make many black women reluctant to complain about or even decisively reject the harasser. No doubt this silence contributes to some degree of confusion as to exactly where the boundaries between desired camaraderie and unwanted intimacy exist. This confusion, however, does not render sexual harassment a nonissue. Quite the contrary: claims similar to those made by Patterson contribute to the problem by reinforcing attitudes that feminist critiques of sexuality and power are inapplicable to the sexual dynamic between black men and women. This failure to confront and debate the terms of sex and power allows men to continually dismiss the possibility that their actions or advances might be unwelcome.

Even if we acknowledge that confusion about boundaries might sometimes contribute to harassment, this possibility does little to account for occasions when black men intentionally use and abuse power over black women. Indeed, it was this misuse of power that was consistently misinterpreted or intentionally mischaracterized during the hearings. Ironically, Patterson's characterization of Thomas's alleged behavior as "down-home courting" recalls Hatch's disbelief that any man who wanted to date a woman would use such an offensive approach. Although Patterson, of course, seems to be saying "Yes, he would, if they were black" while Hatch maintains that such a man would be a pervert, they are actually in agreement that sexual harassment is really about a miscommunicated negotiation over dating. Yet the kind of sexual harassment that women find threatening and harmful is seldom about dating but is, instead, often an expression of hostility or an attempt to control. All women have probably experienced abusive, sexually degrading comments that are almost routinely hurled our way when we initially decline or ignore a solicitation from strangers. Sexual harassment is often no different, particularly in contexts where the harasser believes for whatever reason that the woman needs to be "loosened up," "brought down to size," or "taught a lesson."

Patterson's defense of the kind of behavior Hill described remains troubling even outside a formally stratified work context. Patterson's argument takes as a given the sexual repartee that he believes is simply endemic to the black community "down home." Since he has observed black women responding to such sexual verbal gestures by putting men in their place, he contends that it was somehow "out-of-character" and consequently disingenuous for a black woman to claim that she was repulsed and injured by it. Moreover, such verbal gestures are not only typical but somewhat desirable as down-home courting. Of course, Patterson's failure to specify where "down home" is (it later turns out to be working-class Jamaica) gives uninformed readers the impression that all African Americans are familiar with, participate in, and enjoy this "Rabelaisian humor." The fact that many black people—African-American and Afro-Caribbean alike—do not participate in this "down-home" style is actually beside the point. The more troubling issue is how his attempt to defend this mode of sexual repartee by focusing on black women's participation in it so completely overlooks the way in which this sexual discourse reflects a differential power relationship between men and women.

Patterson assumes that simply because black women have responded to such behavior by displacing aggressive sexual overtures onto a plane of humor and wit, they are neither offended nor threatened by it, and that somehow this "style" is defensible as cultural. Yet merely because black women have developed this particular style of self-defense does not mean that they are not defending themselves against unwanted sexual gestures. A description of the particular way in which women participate and respond to this sexual repartee does not suffice as an analysis of its power dimensions or as a reasonable defense of its subordinating characteristics. Patterson's claims do succeed in centering white women's patterns of interactions by implying that since black women respond differently to verbal aggression, then what they experience is not sexual harassment. Yet women of all races, classes, and cultures no doubt respond in different ways, ways that probably reflect to some degree their particular sociocultural position. White middle-class women have a repertoire of responses to deflect verbal aggression as do working-class black women and middle-class black women, and these responses are likely to differ. The humor or verbal competition that typifies the way some black women react to harassment probably results from the dearth of options available to nonelite black women within a society that has demonstrated manifest disregard for their sexual integrity. After all, to what authority can women who have been consistently represented as sexually available appeal? Since they have little access to any rhetorical or social power from which to create a sphere of sexual autonomy, it is not surprising that some women have learned to displace the aggression onto a humorous, discursive plane. The paradox of Patterson's position is that, given the greater exposure of black women to various forms of sexual aggression, many have developed defense mechanisms that Patterson then points to, in effect to confirm the racist stereotypes that black women are tougher than white women and thus not injured by the same practices that would injure white women. Black women's historical lack of protection becomes a basis for saying no protection is necessary.

Finally, it may be that Patterson's argument, while intellectually and politically indefensible, might in fact provide a clue into how someone like Clarence Thomas might differentiate between women. The plausibility of the People magazine image of Thomas and his wife together reading the Bible in their home as a counterimage to Hill's charges made sense for a public that would assume that he would in fact treat all women the same.[16] In other words, sexual harassment is read as only implicating a deraced notion of gender power. But like many men, black and white, Patterson perpetuates images that give a ready rationale for different treatment of black and white women. White women could be pure, madonna-like figures needing vigilant protection, but black women can take care of themselves—indeed, they even implicitly consent to aggression by participating in a cultural repartee.

The overall strategy of Patterson's defense seems to rest on an assumption that merely identifying the culturally specific dimensions of some practice or dynamic constitutes a normative shield against any criticism of it. But mere descriptions of the practices do little to engage the conditions of power that created them. This point is not unfamiliar to African-American scholars and activists. Indeed, there was a time when "cultural defense" arguments were made against those who opposed the racial caste system that prevailed in the South. Many white community leaders argued that patterns of interaction between blacks and whites were maintained by mutual consent and that local blacks were content in their subordinate role. Having portrayed blacks as willing participants in the racial regime, defenders of the southern way of life were able to claim that demands for equality were imposed from without by northern agitators who did not share the cultural mores of the South.

African Americans as a group refused to allow these arguments to deter their quest for equality. Focusing on the coercive conditions under which consent had been maintained and enforced, critics revealed the way that white supremacy was manifest in relationships not only between dominant whites and subordinate blacks but among blacks as well. Most important, critics exposed the role of coercion in creating these "voluntary" racial practices. This critique included a full accounting of the way that dissent and other counterhegemonic practices were suppressed.

Drawing on this history, the deployment of the cultural defense where gender subordination is alleged requires that we examine not only the way that cultural practices among African-American men and women are an expression of particular power arrangements but also the different means by which these practices are maintained and legitimated. A critical dimension of this examination involves acknowledging the ways that African-American women have contributed to the maintenance of sexist and debilitating gender practices. For example, the Anita Hill controversy and the commentary it has spawned have shed light on how women's own participation in this conspiracy of silence has legitimated sexism within our community. Our failure to break ranks on the issue of misogyny permits writers like Patterson to argue not only that these behaviors are harmless but that they function to affirm our cultural affinity. Our historical silence functions in much the same way that Hill's silence did: we have played along all this time; thus it is far too late in the game for black women to voice offense.

Of course, not all black women have silently acquiesced in sexism and misogyny within the African-American community. Indeed, many writers, activists, and other women have voiced their opposition and paid the price: they have been ostracized and branded as either man-haters or pawns of white feminists, two of the more predictable modes of disciplining and discrediting black feminists. Patterson's argument is of course a model illustration of the latter mode.

In the ongoing debates over black feminism, some critics argue that their objective is not to suppress discussions of gender power within the black community but to stem the tide of negative black stereotypes. Yet even this principle, when examined, reveals a pattern of criticism that seems to suggest that the concern over black male stereotypes functions in a specifically gendered way. For example, the black community has sometimes been embroiled in a debate over political and literary representations of black women's experience of sexism and misogyny.[17] Yet there is a remarkable willingness to accept, virtually without debate, similar images of black men when these images are valorized and sometimes politicized. Ranging from political tracts such as Eldridge Cleaver's Soul on Ice to movies such as Boyz 'N the Hood to rap lyrics such as those of NWA, the Geto Boys, and 2 Live Crew, black men have been depicted in sexist and often violently misogynistic terms. In these "scripts" black women serve simply as the objects of masculine rage or sexuality. Yet when the objects take on the voice and the same male images are re-presented through the eyes of the newly empowered subjects, accusations fly. This suggests that it is not the perpetuation of the images themselves that enrages these writers' harshest critics but rather the implicit critique and complaint that is being lodged against patriarchy in the black community. . . .

The framing of these conflicts, along with Patterson's defense of Clarence Thomas, reveals how politics and culture are frequently deployed to suppress or justify many of the troubling manifestations of patriarchal power within the black community. Of course, cultural integrity and political solidarity are important values in the black community. Yet the ways in which these values have functioned to reinscribe gender power must constantly be interrogated. That black people across a political and class spectrum were willing to condemn Anita Hill for breaking ranks is a telling testament to how deep gender conflicts are tightly contained by the expectations of racial solidarity. But more specifically it is a testament to the greater degree to which differences over gender are suppressed as compared with other political differences. The vilification of Anita Hill and the embracing of Clarence Thomas reveal that a black woman breaking ranks to complain of sexual harassment is seen by many African-Americans as a much greater threat to our group interests than a black man who breaks ranks over race policy. . . .

IV. Political Implications

Now, . . . after one of the most extraordinary public spectacles involving race and gender in this country's history, we are left asking what have we learned. Among the most painful of the lessons to be drawn from the Thomas-Hill affair is that feminism must be recast in order to reach women who do not see gender as relevant to an understanding of their own disempowerment. In an attempt to recast the face of feminism, women organizers have to begin to apply gender analysis to problems that might initially appear to be shaped primarily by exclusively racial or class factors. Nonwhite and working-class women, if they are ever to identify with the organized women's movement, must see their own diverse experiences reflected in the practice and policy statements of these predominantly white middle-class groups.

The confirmation of Clarence Thomas, one of the most conservative voices to be added to the Court in recent memory, carries a sobering message for the African-American community as well. As he begins to make his mark upon the lives of African Americans, we must acknowledge that his successful nomination is due in no small measure to the support he received from black Americans.[18] On this account, it is clear that we still operate under a reflexive vision of racial solidarity that is problematic on two fronts. First, our failure to readily criticize African Americans, based on a belief that our interests are served whenever a black rises through the ranks of power, will increasingly be used to undermine and dismantle policies that have been responsible for the moderate success that group politics have brought about. Already, African-American individuals have played key roles in attacking minority scholarships, cutting back on available remedies for civil rights injuries, and lifting sanctions against South Africa. While group-based notions of solidarity insulate these people from serious criticism and scrutiny, it is precisely their willingness to pursue a ruthlessly individualist agenda that renders this strategy effective and ultimately profitable. Yet the Thomas-Hill story is about more than the political ways that racial solidarity must be critically examined. It is also about the way that our failure to address gender power within our community created the conditions under which an ultimately self-destructive political reaction took place. If we are not to continue to be victimized by such understandable but still counterproductive responses, we must achieve a more mature and purposeful vision of the complex ways in which power is allocated and withheld in contemporary American politics. In particular, we must acknowledge the central role that black women's stories play in our coming to grips with how public power is manipulated. If black women continue to be silenced and their stories ignored, we are doomed to have but a limited grasp of the full range of problems we currently face. The empowerment of black women constitutes therefore the empowerment of our entire community.

Notes

1. See Crenshaw, Demarginalizing the Intersection of Race and Gender in Antidiscrimination Law, Feminist Theory, and Antiracist Politics, in D. Weisberg ed., Feminist Legal Theory: Foundations 383 (Temple Univ. Press, 1993).

2. As recently as 1978, Wigmore's Treatise on Evidence, Section 62, provided that where the nonconsent of a rape complainant is a material element in a rape case, "the character of a woman for chastity is of considerable probative value in judging of the likelihood of that consent." Wigmore went on to say that "the same doctrine should apply . . . in a charge of mere assault with intent to commit rape or of indecent assault, or the like, not because it is logically relevant where consent is not in issue, but because a certain type of feminine character predisposes to imaginary or false charges of this sort." Some states continue to admit such evidence in certain instances.

3. Historically, a woman was required to fight off her attacker until her resistance was overcome. If a woman failed to struggle, or if she gave in before she was subdued, the conclusion drawn was that she was not raped. See Susan Estrich, Rape, 95 Yale L.J. 1087, 1184 n.105 (1986): "in effect, the 'utmost resistance' rule required both that the woman resist to the 'utmost' and that such resistance must not have abated during the struggle."

4. See An Analysis of the Views of Judge Clarence Thomas, NAACP Legal Defense and Education Fund, Inc., August 13, 1991, pointing out the contradiction between Thomas's pre-1986 speeches and writings and the speeches and writings he produced starting in late 1986. His earlier statements explicitly condemned only three Supreme Court decisions—Dred Scott, Plessy v. Ferguson, and a conservative decision. In contrast, the later statements contained "an outburst of denunciations of both the Supreme Court and its civil rights decisions." The Legal Defense Fund position paper

also points out Thomas's shift from praising Justices Black, Douglas, Frankfurter, and Warren to praising Scalia and Bork.

5. Thomas's criticism of his sister as a welfare dependent created an image that contrasted starkly with her actual work history, which included both work-force participation and caring for family members. See Joel Handler, The Judge and His Sister: Growing Up Black, N.Y. Times, July 23, 1991.

6. Wright, a former employee of the Equal Employment Opportunity Commission during Thomas's tenure with the commission, is quoted as saying that Judge Thomas pressured her for dates, asked her breast size, and showed up at her apartment uninvited. Peter Applebom, Common Threads Between the Two Accusing Thomas of Sexual Improprieties, N.Y. Times, October 12, 1990.

7. I do not mean to suggest that race is only relevant in the sexual domination of black women. Race is clearly a factor—though a hidden one—in white women's experiences, just as gender also figures in the experiences of black men. However, because white is the default race in feminism and male is the default gender in antiracism, these identity characteristics usually remain unarticulated.

8. Patricia Hill Collins, The Sexual Politics of Black Womanhood, in Black Feminist Thought: Knowledge, Consciousness, and the Politics of Empowerment 168 (Unwin Hyman, 1990).

9. See Jennifer Wriggins, Race, Racism and the Law, herein, at 495.

10. See Gary LaFree, Rape and Criminal Justice: The Social Construction of Sexual Assault (Wadsworth, 1991).

11. Hamil R. Harris, Hill Is Lying, Says EEOC Staffer, Washington Afro-American, October 12, 1991, quoting Armstrong Williams, who called Hill "an outrageous liar"; Betrayal of Friendship, Bay State Banner, October 17, 1991, attacking Anita Hill's credibility and stating that the case "demonstrates the vulnerability of all men in important positions to bogus sexual harassment charges as a power play by ambitious women." And in the white press, many of the black women interviewed expressed little or no sympathy for Hill, ignoring the reality of their own experiences with gender-based abuses of power, and placing the responsibility for avoiding harassment squarely on the shoulders of the victim. See Felicity Barringer, The Drama as Viewed by Women, N.Y. Times, October 18, 1991, at A12, documenting women's adverse reactions to Hill: "It's unbelievable that a woman couldn't stop something like that at its inception," said one. Another asked, "Wouldn't you haul off and poke a guy in the mouth if he spoke in that manner?" And still another had this to say: "You have to make sure you get across that you're a professional. If someone isn't willing to accept that, you make sure you're not in a room alone with him."

12. See Nathan Hare and Julia Hare, The Many Faces of Anita Hill, in The Final Call, the newspaper published by The Nation of Islam under Minister Louis Farrakhan. The headline on the paper in which the Hare's article appeared read "Thomas Survives High-Tech Lynching."

13. Orlando Patterson's "Race, Gender, and Liberal Fallacies" appeared in the New York Times on October 20, 1991, the Sunday following Thomas's confirmation.

14. People v. Jacinto Aniello Rhines, 131 Cal. App. 3d. 498, (1982).

15. See Roundtable: Sexuality in America After Thomas/Hill, Tikkun, January/February 1992, at 25.

16. Virginia Lamp Thomas, Breaking Silence, People, November 11, 1991, at 111. Virginia Thomas tells how she and her husband invited two couples to their home to

pray for two to three hours each day. "They brought over prayer tapes, and we would read parts of the Bible," she stated.

17. Mel Watkins, Sexism, Racism, and Black Women Writers, N.Y. Times, June 15, 1986; Donna Britt, What About the Sisters? With All the Focus on Black Men, Somebody's Getting Left Out, Washington Post, February 2, 1992, citing black male objections to Alice Walker's and Ntozake Shange's work, and questioning where those black male voices are when black male violence is being condoned . . . glamorized, ignored; Susan Howard, Beware of "Blacklash," Newsday, February 12, 1992, arguing that there is a blacklash against black women, and citing the communities' unwillingness to forgive Alice Walker and Ntozake Shange for writing *The Color Purple* and *For Colored Girls Who Have Considered Suicide When the Rainbow Is Enuf* to support this proposition.

18. In Other Words, USA Today, March 7, 1992: "Rookie Justice Clarence Thomas already is leaving his mark on America's legal system. Based on the dissent he wrote in a recent case, it's not just a mark—it's more like a welt. Fortunately, all but one other justice on the high court viewed the actions of a Louisiana prison guard—who shackled and beat a prisoner—as the kind of cruel and unusual punishment that the Eighth Amendment forbids. . . . Those who harbored hopes that Justice Thomas might feel a shred of concern for society's victims got a firm sock in the kisser" [Hudson v. McMillian, 112 S. Ct. 995 (1992) (Thomas, J. dissenting)]. In another of his more notable contributions, in Presley v. Etowah County Commission [502 U.S. 491 (1992)] Thomas paid tribute to his southern roots by denying the voting-rights claims of a newly *elected* black official who was deprived of decision-making authority. Even the Bush administration agreed that the actions violated the Voting Rights Act.

Exit: Power and the Idea of Leaving in Love, Work, and the Confirmation Hearings

MARTHA R. MAHONEY

How could she have brought herself to follow Judge Thomas so faithfully and so long in her career, given the sordid remarks he allegedly made to her?[1]

On cross-examination, when discussing an occasion when Mr. Kelly temporarily moved out of the house, the State repeatedly asked Ms. Kelly: "You wanted him back, didn't you?" The implication was clear: domestic life could not have been too bad if she wanted him back.[2]

EXIT—THE DOOR with the glowing red sign—marks the road not taken that proves we chose our path. Prevailing ideology in both law and popular culture holds that people are independent and autonomous units, free to leave any situation at any time, and that what happens to us is therefore in some measure the product of our choice. When women are harmed in love or work, the idea of exit becomes central to the social and legal dialogue in which our experience is processed, reduced, reconstructed and dismissed. Exit is so powerful an image that it can be used both to dispute the truth of our statements and to keep people from hearing what we say at all. The image of exit hides oppression behind a mask of choice, forces upon us a discourse of victimization that emphasizes individualism and weakness rather than collectivity and strength, and conceals the possibility and necessity of alliance and resistance to oppression.

I began writing this essay [when] the Senate confirmed the appointment of Clarence Thomas to the Supreme Court. [I]mages of the hearings are still before me: of Anita Hill testifying—graceful and composed, tiring as the day wears on, maintaining dignity, clarity, directness, honesty.[3] Of Orrin Hatch's face, filling the screen—the Grand Inquisitor, reprocessing her testimony. Of Clarence Thomas, rigid in his chair, claiming he is being lynched for his independence.[4]

[T]his essay addresses the ways in which failure to exit was used against Anita Hill in the Senate and in public discourse. I compare the treatment of exit in the confirmation hearings with cases involving battered women.

65 S. Cal. L. Rev. 1283 (1992), reprinted with the permission of the Southern California Law Review.

Love and work are the most important areas of life, from which life gains meaning, satisfaction and pleasure. Battering and sexual harassment are abuses of power within the relational worlds of love and work. Battering is about power over the lover: the attempt to exercise power and control marked by a pattern of violent and coercive behaviors. Sexual harassment is an abuse of power associated particularly with the workplace. . . .

The Importance of Exit

[A]n "outraged person" would [not] stay with a mentor who psychologically abused her, until she was secure enough to make her own way. . . .[5]

[O]ne of the common myths, apparently believed by most people, is that battered wives are free to leave. To some, this [suggests masochism] . . . to others, however, the fact that [she] stays on unquestionably suggests that the "beatings" could not have been too bad for if they had been, she certainly would have left.[6]

During the week of the confirmation hearings, newspapers repeatedly cited studies of working women, including lawyers, who said that they neither filed complaints nor left their jobs when they encountered sexual harassment.[7] Many women said they would just tell the offender to stop ("just say knock it off"). Anita Hill's story generally tracked this course of action: She said she told her supervisor, Clarence Thomas, that she would not go out with him and that she didn't enjoy sexual conversations; she believed she had successfully handled the situation when the harassment stopped, found the recurrence of harassment distressing, and finally left for academic employment.

Nevertheless, those who supported the confirmation discussed Anita Hill's story as if it did *not* follow a plausible course. In particular, the fact that she continued to work for Clarence Thomas was used to discredit her account of harassment: first, she continued to work for him at the Department of Education, then she moved to the EEOC and continued to work for him there. The move to the EEOC lent a heightened sense of affirmative choice, since she continued working with him rather than trying to continue in an unknown job in the same department.

Failure to exit was raised to dispute the truth of her claims of fact, her account of words spoken by Clarence Thomas (if he really said that, why did she follow him to the EEOC?). Failure to exit was also raised to argue that, if he indeed said those things, his statements could not have been entirely unsought and unwelcome. . . . Failure to exit was seen as an indication of inconsistency between her actions and her report of her feelings, making suspect her overall credibility (she couldn't be telling the truth, because if she felt the disgust she claimed, she would have left). Finally, failure to exit was used in a sort of waiver argument to imply at least political opportunism, if not dishonesty (if it wasn't bad enough to leave or bring charges then, why bring this up now?).

These concepts of exit in the confirmation hearings bear striking similarity to the uses of exit in social and legal discussion of battered women. The woman's very presence in the battering relationship is used against her in several ways. Most important, as in the confirmation hearings, failure to exit is raised to dispute the truth of descriptions of physical violence (if it was so bad, why didn't she leave?). The issue of exit also shapes perception of the woman's functionality, as in custody cases (if she didn't leave, how can she be a strong or competent person—or a fit mother?). In self-defense cases when women kill or harm their abusers, other doctrinal points can also hinge on exit (could danger have been imminent if she could have left instead?).

Anita Hill's move to the EEOC was presented in the hearings as a choice of Clarence Thomas as supervisor rather than a choice of particular work or federal department within which to work. The move was then raised to cast doubt upon the truth of her account and, indirectly, to support challenges to her motives or rationality (she had "fantasies"; she was in love with him).[8] Battered women who separate temporarily and return to their partners encounter similar perceptions. Failure to exit comes to include a very high degree of intentionality. Exit is now clearly defined as possible. The woman is seen as choosing to return to a batterer, rather than to a husband; the act of choosing a batterer throws into question either the truth of her claims or her sanity.

The image of exit in battering cases is inconsistent with the realities of separation from violent relationships. Half of all marriages may include violence.[9] A significant number of divorced women report that their husbands were physically violent with them.[10] Violence is everywhere; *both* staying and leaving are normal activities when women encounter violence. . . . The question "why didn't she leave" hides the commonality of violence, the ways women actually behave in the face of violence, and the dangers of exit.

Similarly, the image presented in the confirmation hearings—exit as the normal prompt response to harassment—is inconsistent with the actions of the majority of women who neither report harassment nor leave their jobs. In Meritor Savings Bank v. Vinson,[11] . . . the plaintiff had been harassed continually during virtually the entire four years of her employment with the firm. She sued only after she was fired for taking too much sick leave. . . . Similarly, a government lawyer who successfully sued the Securities and Exchange Commission after enduring several years of sexual harassment on the job recently pointed out that she had not brought suit until she was "forced into it" when her job was threatened.[12]

Exit is also not the norm for many workers who encounter painful choices about work. Workers threatened by plant closings or job cuts make givebacks on wages and working conditions. When women face particularly agonizing choices in relation to work, they often internalize the pain and keep the job. This is why there were sterilized plaintiffs in the fetal protection cases. . . .

So the normal responses to abuse and harassment in love and work conflict with the image of exit. Yet exit retains great rhetorical power. Exit shaped at least the public rationales of several senators for their votes to confirm Clarence Thomas, and it continues to shape doctrine, juror perception, and litigation strategy in many cases involving battered women. Failure to exit promptly can affect the way a woman's account—or even uncontested facts—are heard, remembered, or weighed.

These images of exit are particularly dangerous because they are used against women when analyzing harms that are particular to women. Women's lives are constructed under conditions of inequality, and any gains we make are built on unequal ground. The ideology of exit implicitly denies inequality in relationships by emphasizing mutual freedom to leave. This rhetoric actually increases inequality by strengthening the position of the abuser, because it makes suspect the choice most women make—neither leaving nor suing.

Albert Hirschman noted some time ago that exit has a powerful ideological hold on our society: "With the country having been founded on exit and having thrived on it, the belief in exit as a fundamental and beneficial social mechanism has been unquestioning."[13] As Hirschman explained, however, exit effects change only indirectly; voice (any effort to change the situation rather than escape) is important as an option in its own right and particularly important when loyalty or structural barriers make exit difficult or undesirable.[14] In the context of sexual harassment, voice would include, among other actions, telling the perpetrator to "knock it off," filing complaints through company mechanisms, bringing lawsuits, or taking political action.

In sexual harassment, both exit—the possibilities of new jobs—can be shaped by the good will of the harasser. But the public exercise of "voice" carries a stigma and may also involve traumatic recounting of personal experience, including experience of the abuse itself.[15] The private exercise of voice—the one that women adopt when they tell the harasser to stop—is invisible at the time and is hidden in retrospect in the question "why didn't she leave?" In battering, both loyalty—identification with the family rather than simply as an individual—and the batterer's determination to block exit may create a similarly invisible attempt to effectuate change.

The concept of exit that pervaded the confirmation hearings denied the importance of work. Similarly, exit denies the importance of love in the context of violence that starts during an intimate, loving relationship. Relationships in both love and work are extended and multiple. Working women form ties to the people with whom they work and often ties to their work as well. They have pride in their work, or in their capacity for hard work, for holding on to work, for survival.[16] In the context of family, women often have ties to both the relationships with their husbands *and the* relationships between their husbands and their children. As a test of facts or authenticity of response, exit makes all these ties invisible and eliminates from our understanding of agency the time and effort required to shape one's life under adverse conditions. . . .

Explanation and Victimization

Fairness means . . . understanding . . . why victims often do not, or can not, leave their jobs. Perhaps fourteen men sitting here today cannot understand. I know there are many people watching today who suspect that we never will understand.[17]

The expert could clear up these myths, by explaining that one of the common characteristics of a battered wife is her inability to leave despite such constant beatings; her "learned helplessness"; her lack of anywhere to go; her feeling that if she tried to leave, she would be subjected to even more merciless treatment; her belief in the omnipotence of her battering husband; and sometimes her hope that her husband will change his ways.[18]

Exit centers inquiry on the individual who was harmed and the reasons she acted in a particular way, rather than on the person who sought power and control abusively. With the context of power and control invisible, failure to exit generates a demand for explanation: either these events did not happen, or they were not truly harmful, or *this individual has exceptional problems,* qualities that caused failure to exit, qualities that need to be explained. This process of explaining the individual, now defined by *failure* to exit, has brought with it a discourse of victimization in the areas of both battering and sexual harassment that is heard as denying agency in those who are harmed, with important cultural and political consequences.

Beginning in the early 1970s, feminists identified and fought against rape, sexual harassment, and battering, as well as other forms of abuse of women, as part of a project of articulating experience and undertaking transformation in the lives of women and in society. The feminist method of consciousness raising was based on articulating women's experience through discussions with other women.[19] This experience was then publicly asserted in speakouts in which women told their stories at public meetings organized by feminists, breaking down the walls of silence that had surrounded many aspects of the oppression of women. The first speakout on rape took place in 1971.[20] A speakout on sexual harassment was held in Ithaca, New York in 1975.[21] Women founded battered women's shelters and rape crisis centers. And knowledge was produced with pioneering books about several sorts of violence against women in print by the late 1970s.[22]

Shaping legal claims was part of this process of political action. But legal doctrine itself creates categories that affect the articulation of experience. When doctrine shifts sufficiently to bring aspects of women's experience into law, it is filtered through the consciousness of legal actors and (including judges, jurors, prosecutors, policemen called to the scene of assault, social workers evaluating custody claims) in ways that further reshape the articulation of experience. Therefore, defining legal terms that reflect the oppression of women creates new contests over meaning. Each block of progress shifts the style or locus of struggle over how to understand harm to women, reveal it, discuss it, and work against it, raising questions of the possibility and method of mobilization and transformation.

Law forces upon us a discourse of victimization. Either you are on the playing field of liberal competition, in which case you require no protection, or you prove into a category as a victim who is being kept off the field. The goal of remedy is to lift you back on to the playing field, to the starting line of the race, so you too can "play." Resistance may merely show your ability to function on the field.[23] Therefore, while a generation of social historians have painted a complex world of oppression and resistance—slaves both suffer and resist, battered women gradually shape the consciousness of social workers[24]—law has not managed to incorporate this duality and struggle, pain and strength, but filters it to a sense of victimization.

One important mechanism of constructing victimization, related to the vision of the person as wholly autonomous and mobile, is to make women explain failure to exit. When women are harmed, exit tests the existence of abuse by looking to conformity with *predicted* response that contradicts both resistance and the presence of social and legal constraint. Rather than challenge the prediction of exit, the woman must explain "inconsistency" through victimization. Once battering is dragged into the light, for example we explain why the woman didn't leave through a syndrome she develops in response to battering.[25] We explain why a woman "feels" she cannot tell or leave work,[26] defensively, *as if* the norms were "leaving," because of how the question has been set up.

This problem of explanation rapidly becomes acute because, in the course of shaping our lives under conditions of oppression, women both leave and stay. The fact that we sometimes do leave is used to challenge the legitimacy of staying to fight for what we need and to deny the difficulties we face in exit. The ideology of exit is extremely powerful, so we make concessions to it in legal explanation. Our concessions are shaped by the urgency of need when encountering law: The legal system broadly interacts with social expectation, shaping and shaped by our beliefs about women, but law intersects the lives of particular individuals at moments of crisis, when attempting to remake social expectations is too large a task. However, concessions may reinforce cultural stereotypes about exit, and even when we carefully articulate duality, stereotypes may result in the irony of having this heard as victimization.

Self-defense killings by battered women are the most dramatic example. Juries often see failure to leave as discrediting the defendant's account of violence and her perceptions of danger. Feminist litigators responded by winning the right to expert testimony to explain patterns of response to abuse summed up in battered woman syndrome, rather than insistently denying that exit is the appropriate focus at all. Battered woman syndrome explains the woman's failure to leave in part through the psychological theory of learned helplessness. Even when experts simultaneously emphasize objective obstacles to leaving such as economic constraints, and even when experts try to draw a complex portrait of the woman's experience, courts tend to hear "learned helplessness" as utter dysfunctionality and a complete lack of agency. This portrait of a battered woman may be difficult to reconcile with her violent act of self-defense, and some juries remain unpersuaded.[27]

By responding in terms of exceptionality, explaining the victim subtly reinforces the ideology of exit. A woman pursuing her work in the face of harassment therefore risks future disbelief. In a particularly ironic twist, once victimization is *expected,* the woman's agency can become invisible even when it takes the form of exit—a woman may be condemned for not leaving soon enough. Therefore Anita Hill could speak of herself, and the press could speak of her, both as someone who left and moved on—and simultaneously as someone who stayed.

When agency is equated with exit, failure to exit must be a sign of a positive choice or a symptom of such subjugation that agency no longer exists. In the rhetoric of victimization, battered women fail to leave because they are helpless, harassed women mysteriously "believe that they should not, or cannot, leave their jobs."[28] But helplessness and lack of agency present a picture with which most women refuse to identify. This makes it more difficult for us to understand our own lives in a context of violence and power. Denying commonality with battered women leaves our sense of agency intact—but it also leads us to deny the danger of episodes of rage or violence and to be unaware that hotlines for battered women are the appropriate place to call for help when we are attacked. A similar dynamic exists in regard to abuse at work. Virtually all of us who work outside the home have put up with some behaviors that we found ugly or hurtful in order to keep a job or protect the possibility of getting another. Yet this common ground was not recognized by many people watching the confirmation hearings.

People's sense of agency in their own lives is very strong. [T]his strong sense of agency reflects both sound self-knowledge and denial of the impact of structures of power. . . . Belief in one's own agency trumps identifying with victims. . . .

This is the terrain the conservatives capture, part of the ground upon which Senator Hatch stood when he attacked Anita Hill the day after she testified. One component of the conservative attack is to render her way of exercising agency invisible to the public and disguise its meaning. The significance of her work, her perceived success in stopping harassment, and the particular agency involved in "staying" to work on terms one has defined—all disappeared. How could all that agency become invisible. . . .

One columnist called Anita Hill a "perfect victim."[29] But victimization is not "perfect." It implies a one-way exercise of power, harm without strength, oppression without struggle.[30] People do not identify with those they pity, and this allowed the paradox: To the extent she was seen as a victim, she had not behaved in the way people thought she should; to the extent she had been strong, she had not seemed like a "victim.". . . A model of victimization had been imposed by cultural understanding and the processing of her experience through the mouths of Senate Republicans and the media, and this model took over the story she actually told.

In addition to indirectly promoting victimization, a focus on exit is directly opposed to the idea of resistance. In love and work, women build lives under conditions of inequality, and whatever we find of success, security, love and companionship is built on or against unequal ground. Exit proposes that one should leave, rather than hold on to the ground. Exit proposes that one should leave, rather than hold on to what has been gained. In battering, this stigmatizes women's efforts to make viable families out of the raw material handed them by a profoundly sexist and violent society. In sexual harassment, the secrecy surrounding the abuse and the social expectation that women will react by departing create a "death before dishonor" mentality that denies respect to the stubborn determination to keep the job. Sexual harassment is frightening, ugly, debilitating, and humiliating—staying should not be understood as negating the harm—but agency may be exercised through working. When the only recognizable act of agency is exit, this makes acts of resistance like those Anita Hill described (doing one's job and telling the perpetrator to stop) into acceptance of victimization.

Anita Hill was used to exercising agency. She is the daughter of a farmer from Oklahoma. She was the youngest of thirteen children, one of few African-American women at Yale. She was used to being able to work hard enough, and well enough, and successfully enough to take hold of the world and shape it. Her expectations of her own ability to define a work environment would be very high. She said that during each of the offensive discussions, she was able to stop the discussion for that day, though he began again another time. But the greater her sense of her own agency, the more likely that she would believe she could restrain him, and therefore that all her agency would be later rendered invisible because it was not exercised as exit.

Could Anita Hill have been insufficiently presented as a victim? . . . When Anita Hill described the will of a young woman to carry on her work under adverse conditions, the emphasis on exit and the construction of victimization helped prevent the public from hearing what she said.

An increasing emphasis on victimization could be an important mistake. Elizabeth Schneider has pointed out that although victimization has sometimes been a significant part of feminist analysis, there are inherent tensions in portraying agency and victimization in battered women's experiences.[31] Some black feminists have criticized a rhetoric of victimization or do not use it.[32] bell hooks associates privilege with claims of victimization and argues that women who face exploitation daily "cannot afford to relinquish the belief that they exercise some measure of control, however relative, over their lives."[33] If we cannot speak of both exploitation and agency, we will not be heard by the women who insist on perceiving it in themselves, and we will help stifle their voices when they speak.

Agency and Oppression

At the time, staying seemed the only reasonable choice. At that time, staying was . . . a choice that I made because I wanted to do the work. I in fact believed that I could make that choice, to do the work, and that's what I wanted to do. And I did not want to let that type of behavior control my choices. So I attempted to end the behavior. And for some time, the behavior did stop. I attempted to make that effort. So the choice to continue with the same person to another agency involved a belief that I had stopped the behavior that was offensive.[34]

Anita Hill never said she believed that Clarence Thomas had simply stopped harassing her. Throughout her testimony, she had spoken of offensive *behavior*, rather than of Thomas himself, as the problem. At the end of the day, responding to a question from Senator DeConcini about why she stayed, she said *she thought she had stopped it.* Her choices had not been controlled. She would be able to go on with her work. She believed she had won.

Most sexual harassment cases turn, as did the confirmation hearings, on the credibility of the witnesses.[35] Credibility in turn depends on the capacities of the listener to hear and understand. Anita Hill's account of the move to the EEOC was undermined by making invisible to her intelligent determination to defend herself on the job, and by completely collapsing her work into issues of sex and job loss.

If agency among the oppressed is judged only by effectuated change, it is defined almost out of existence. The acting, aware self is often realized in love and in work through resistance against oppression, survival, and partial victories—like women who "just deal with" harassment, or women who seek to hold on to marriages without violence. Or—even closer to the experience of many women—the self is realized through a *combination* of accommodation and resistance, through private resistance chosen because oppression itself simultaneously makes exit difficult and open resistance impractical. This duality may sometimes create or allow individualism: When working women say they "just deal with" harassment, this implies they have power to resist but may permit later denial commonality with a woman who publicly describes the experience of harassment.

Contemporary conservative insistence on agency treats self-realization as a question of pure will, not constrained in any serious way.[36] Conservatism equates all analysis of oppression by race or gender with individual victimization and treats it as negating agency. The conservative claim that agency may be exercised without struggle is very different from claiming agency through liberatory struggle, through resistance to oppression.[37] "Pure" victimization also denies the many ways people resist oppression. For women, the stigma and shame of being sexually assaulted creates a circumstance that will often discourage publicity (including lawsuits) and therefore tend to make resistance individual. This should not equate staying with either acceptance of victimization or claims of pure individual agency without struggle.

If we were better at articulating *both* oppression *and* resistance, at both the individual and collective level, we might be less confused. But law does not make this easy, and feminist legal scholarship has had difficulty dealing with both oppression and an insistence on agency.[38] In feminist activism, pain suffered privately became political—not *only* by being spoken to other women, but by being spoken to the world and collectively acted upon in the creation of alternative institutions. Speakouts led to political action that included personal transformation sought through the struggle for social transformation. The legal claim for sexual harassment as sex discrimination was strategically created to reveal oppression as part of political change. But even here, litigation is largely a one-on-one undertaking: this woman, this man; he said, she said; a question of credibility of this *individual woman* making an *individual claim*, subject to being discredited by her *individual traits*. Even if her actions are completely consistent with those of other assaulted women—as Anita Hill's were—her place in the world of response to assault is not visible. The challenge is to find ways to represent both oppression and agency in *law*, with its strong impetus toward individualism and victimization.

What decides whether a claim about pain is collective and transformative or heard to represent victimization without agency? The answer may be part culture and part the structure of legal argument. When experts describe normal reactions to battering and emphasize economic constraints and physical danger, but are heard as describing women as pathologically helpless, both the structure of expert testimony (dealing with matters beyond the layman's ken) and the persistence of social stereotypes are involved. . . .

So part of the struggle against oppression is more articulation, of more experience, of *more women,* learning difference as well as pain—in Angela Harris's lovely phrase, "integrity as will and idea"—and learn from women who have constructed lives under oppression their example of creativity and will.[39]

Both this articulation and the political action built on it are parts of the effort to bring law and societal perception closer to the experience of the subordinated and to counteract the persistent misrepresentation of resistance to oppression as victimization.[40] But political action, like the consciousness of oppression, should include the many forms of oppression that intersect here to authenticate acts of resistance as they happen, show the significance of "staying" at work or in a relationship as well as "leaving," and reveal the nature and mechanisms of oppression. . . .

Racism in the fear of loss of work does not need to be forced into the discussion of sexual harassment—it is already here. In the confirmation hearings, it was articulated by J. C. Alvarez: "You don't follow them to the next job—especially if you are a black, female, Yale law school graduate. Let's face it, out in the corporate sector, companies fight over women with those kinds of credentials."[41] The claim that "companies fight" over "black, female" graduates of Yale uses rhetoric that invokes contemporary white fears of being disfavored by affirmative action to argue that Anita Hill's fear of job loss was not credible. This implies there is *no* credible explanation for failure to exit—educated black women are the luckiest people in today's market! In fact, there are still very few black women attorneys in the corporate world, and given pervasive suspicions of the competence of blacks and of women, the recommendations of supervisors are crucial to status in the professional job market. To argue from this starting point, however, falls into the structure of conceding the focus on exit and raising oppression defensively to disprove exit (but racism and discrimination are real!).

In the aftermath of the confirmation hearings and in other current legal and political contests in the fields of gender and of race, we need to recover the idea of sexual harassment as simultaneous oppression in *work* as well as sex and race. It is a fundamental critical insight that the very task of law is to make the exercise of power invisible.[42] This leaves a continuing role for critique: Legal intellectuals, analyzing a reactionary court in the midst of a crisis of work, can help make power visible again in many dimensions by unpacking the background of power.

In law and politics, we need to choose terms of discussion and forms of legal challenge for their capacity to mobilize consciousness, not solely for their potential legal success. If law pursues us toward victimization rather than struggle and resistance, it also pushes us toward *only* particularity because our legal regime is founded on the fictions of formal equality and mutual free agency. If we move too far toward the norms of employment that permit abuse in the workplace, and leave behind particular injuries by race or gender, then we rapidly reach harms that are not remediable because they are the very foundation of our law—like employment at will, or the freedom of plants to close.

Yet abuse of employees—as well as acceptance of sexual abuse of women—helps make sexual harassment hard to remedy. A woman must prove very specific elements to get past the general difficulty of controlling offensive behavior.[43] If she cannot, then she loses, even if the behavior was offensive. If we only see the harm of women by men, we lose a sense of the ways sexual harassment is part of other systemic misuse of power in our society. Regina Austin has pointed out that an interest in fighting abuse on the job can span divisions between different sectors in the workforce, from unskilled labor to white collar and professional employees.[44]

bell hooks has called on women to work toward ending all violence in society, including racism and the violence of the workplace, as part of a movement to end violence against women.[45] If we focus on resistance to oppression, then ending sexual harassment means work against harassment *and* against the abuse of workers. Feminist work against sexual harassment then includes issues of more jobs and more job security. It includes resistance to current attacks on affirmative action—by rejecting the rhetoric that pretends away power, and by working for more jobs for all. In *any* contest about work, including opposition to sexual harassment, antiracism is also essential, because concepts of both employability and sexuality are deeply entwined with concepts of race. In battering, the effort to end the batterer's power and control and the social structures that reinforce it makes allies of men as well as women who oppose that exercise of power. In dealing with harms to women, shifting focus from victimization to oppression increases the possibilities for alliance.

Finally, in order to reveal both agency and oppression, we need to reject false questions that define and structure legal discourse. Exit hides both oppression and resistance. Staying at work can mean victory, stubborn persistence at a chosen goal, or nightmare and exploitation; leaving may mean going without work, or it may bring a successful turn in career path. Staying in a marriage could prove to be retaining a family without violence, or it may well be the result of death threats and custody suits; leaving may mean giving up on having both love and safety, or it can be empowerment and a loving family forged by a single mother. Any snapshot labeled "exit" or "no exit" will not show whether this woman is in this home, this job, because she is fighting for this territory or because her will to leave has been defeated. For work against subordination, her will against oppression is what she needs, and what we need to know.

Law itself funnels and shapes consciousness and resistance to oppression. There are good reasons to use law on behalf of the subordinated, and it is worth fighting within the field of law for the principle that law should do justice. In the coming months and years, antisubordination efforts including the fight to end sexual harassment will continue to move through the legal system and other political arenas. . . .

. . . To work together, to reach the very people who are hurting too, we will need to hear strength as well as pain—the articulation of experience that is an integral part of the struggle against subordination is not an appeal for pity. When we speak of oppression and resistance, we must not be told—and we must not tell others—to take things as they are or leave them. This discussion is part of a demand for the transformation of power, and it cannot be answered by showing us the door.

Notes

1. Senator Jim Exon, explaining his vote in favor of the confirmation of Clarence Thomas; Maureen Dowd, Republicans Gain Edge by Going Nasty Early, N.Y. Times, Oct. 15, 1991, at A18.

2. State v. Kelly, 478 A.2d 364, 377 (N.J. 1984).

3. A survey of judges, who are in the business of hearing testimony and weighing credibility, revealed that two-thirds of them believed Anita Hill's testimony. Scott Armstrong, Women Seeking Office Quickened by Thomas Flap, Christian Sci. Monitor, Oct. 22, 1991, U.S. section, at 1.

4. Cf. William Raspberry, Thomas's Credential: Deprivation, Wash. Post, Sept. 20, 1991, at A27 (quoting Jesse Jackson referring to Clarence Thomas as "the most sponsored black man in American history").

5. Dowd, *supra* note 1 (J. Bennett Johnston, Democratic Senator from Louisiana, explaining why he found Anita Hill's testimony implausible).

6. State v. Kelly, 478 A.2d 364, 377 (N.J. 1984).

7. See, e.g., Tamar Lewin, A Case Study of Sexual Harassment and the Law, N.Y. Times, Oct. 11, 1991, at A17 (women fear reprisals if they sue for sexual harassment; women fear that their careers and reputation will suffer even if they win; most women do not make formal complaints or leave the job); Emily Courie, Women in the Large Firms: A High Price for Admission, Nat'l L.J., Dec. 11, 1989, at 3–5 (survey found that at least 60% of women at large firms experienced unwanted sexual attention of some kind); cf. Lin Farley, Sexual Shakedown: The Sexual Harassment of Women on the Job 21–22 (1978) (only 9% of women quit immediately upon harassment; most stayed, though many of these did quit eventually when the situation escalated later).

8. Witnesses Support Account by Judge Thomas's Accuser, N.Y. Times, Oct. 13, 1991, at A1, A10.

9. See the discussion of difficulties of estimating violence in marriage in Diana E. H. Russell, Rape in Marriage 96–101 (1982). The rate of physical abuse in marriage has been estimated by Lenore Walker and other experts at about 50%, though the lowest recent estimate is 12% and the highest is 60%. . . .

10. In one study of all women seeking divorce through a Legal Aid office in a five-day period, twenty of fifty wives were identified as "battered women" and thirteen more said that their husbands had been violent with them on one occasion—making a total of 66% who had experienced violence by their husbands at least once. Barbara Parker & Dale N. Schumacher, The Battered Wife Syndrome and Violence in the Nuclear Family of Origin: A Controlled Pilot Study, 6 Am. J. Pub. Health 760–761. In another study, 37% of women who applied for divorce listed physical abuse among their complaints. Richard A. Stordeur & Richard Stille, Ending Men's Violence Against Their Partners: One Road to Peace 21 (1989) (citing G. Thorman, Family Violence (1980)); see also Russell, *supra* note 9, at 96 (21% of divorced women in study reported ex-husbands were physically violent with them).

11. 477 U.S. 57 (1986).

12. Nancy Gibbs, Office Crimes, Time, Oct. 21, 1991, at 52, 54 (quoting Catherine Broderick, a lawyer at the Securities and Exchange Commission and successful plaintiff in a sexual harassment suit against the SEC).

13. Albert O. Hirschman, Exit, Voice and Loyalty: Responses to Decline in Firms, Organizations, and States 112 (1970). For the ideology of exit in sexual harassment, see Farley, *supra* note 7, at 24 (most women are advised to quit; quitting is the prevailing social advice).

14. Hirschman, *supra* note 13, at 33–34.

15. Catherine A. MacKinnon, Feminism Unmodified 114 (1987).

16. Ellen Israel Rosen, Bitter Choices: Blue-Collar Women In and Out of Work 14–15 (1987) (noting that blue-collar women describe both the pressure of work and also expressions of pride in their trades, strong friendships, and accomplishments at work).

17. Senator Joseph Biden, in his opening remarks at the Senate Judiciary Committee Hearing on October 11, 1991. Videotape of Senate Judiciary Committee meetings on sexual harassment charged against Clarence Thomas, Oct. 11, 1991.

18. State v. Kelly, 478 A.2d 364, 377 (N.J. 1984).

19. The radical feminist project of consciousness-raising was described as "[t]he process of transforming the hidden, individual fears of women into a shared sense of the meaning of them as social problems, the release of anger, anxiety, the struggle of proclaiming the painful and transforming it into the political." New York Radical Feminists, Rape: The First Sourcebook for Women 6 (1974) (quoting Juliet Mitchell, Woman's Estate (1973)) [hereinafter NYRF]. While problems arose (at the time and later) from some of the tendencies of consciousness-raising groups to generalize the experience of their often homogeneous members as the experience of all women, with results that distorted its application as "feminist method" (see Christine Littleton, Feminist Jurisprudence: The Difference Method Makes, 41 Stan L. Rev. 751, 773 (1989)), consciousness-raising groups also served a valuable function in providing a forum focused on unlearning sexism. bell hooks, Feminist Theory from Margin to Center 48 (1984).

20. NYRF, *supra* note 19, at 27–28, 274. The first speak-out was organized by the feminist group Redstockings after women were not permitted to testify at a legislative hearing on abortion law reform in which testimony was taken from fifteen experts, fourteen of whom were men. *Id.* at 28.

21. Farley, *supra* note 7, at 74.

22. These works include Susan Brownmiller, Against Our Will (1975); Sandra Butler, Conspiracy of Silence: The Trauma of Incest (1978); Del Martin, Battered Wives (1976); Catharine A. MacKinnon, Sexual Harassment of Working Women (1979).

23. See, e.g., Susan Estrich, Sex at Work, herein, at 755, 769 (noting that superwomen who do not complain and continue competent work may not recover because their situations were not psychologically debilitating enough to constitute a hostile environment).

24. See, e.g., Linda Gordon, Heroes of Their Own Lives: The Politics and History of Family Violence in America (1988).

25. Battered woman syndrome is "a collection of specific characteristics and effects of abuse on the battered woman." While battered woman syndrome will not affect all women who experience violence from their partners, women who experience this syndrome are unable to respond effectively to violence. Mary Ann Douglas, The Battered

Woman Syndrome, in Daniel J. Sonkin ed., Domestic Violence on Trial: Psychological and Legal Dimensions of Family Violence 40 (1987). [T]he emphasis on helplessness and the implications of pathology which some courts have drawn from this testimony can contribute to stereotypical perceptions of women. Martha Mahoney, Legal Images of Battered Women: Redefining the Issue of Separation, herein, at 341; see also Elizabeth M. Schneider, Describing and Changing: Women's Self-Defense Work and the Problem of Expert Testimony, herein, at 311.

26. For example, the explanation by Ellen Wells, one of the friends whom Anita Hill told about harassment contemporaneously: "When you're confronted with something like that, you feel powerless and vulnerable. And unless you have a private income, you have no recourse. And since this is generally done in privacy, there are no witnesses. And it's your word, an underling, against that of a superior, someone who is obviously thought well of or they would have risen to the position they hold." Witnesses Support Account by Judge Thomas's Accuser, N.Y. Times, Oct. 14, 1991, at A10.

27. For a thoughtful discussion of the tension between agency and victimization in representing battered women who kill their abusers, see Schneider, Describing and Changing, herein, at 322–323.

28. Videotape of Hearings, *supra* note 17 (remarks of Senator Biden).

29. Anna Quindlen, The Perfect Victim, N.Y. Times, Oct. 16, 1991, at A25.

30. This is why the terms "survivor" has replaced "victim" in feminist vocabulary (as in "rape survivor," "domestic violence survivor"). See e.g., Edward Gondolf & Ellen Fisher, Battered Women as Survivors: An Alternative to Treating Learned Helplessness 77–78 (1988) (describing battered women as survivors).

31. Schneider, Describing and Changing, herein, at 322 (urging feminists to explore "the role of both victimization and agency in women's lives" because portraying women solely as victims or agents is not adequate to explain the complex realities of women's lives, and showing that emphasizing only victimization among battered women helps make violent self-defense hard for judges and juries to understand); see also Littleton, Women's Experience and the Problem of Transition, herein (need to emphasize victimization of women conceals questions of male power and domination).

32. Angela Harris, Race and Essentialism in D. Weisberg ed., Feminist Legal Theory 348, 354–355 (Temple Univ. Press, 1993) (criticizing the view of women as victims, and calling upon feminism to learn from the strength of black women who have constructed their lives under conditions of oppression); Kimberle Crenshaw, Demarginalizing the Intersection of Race and Sex: A Black Feminist Critique of Antidiscrimination Doctrine, Feminist Theory and Antiracist Politics, in Feminist Legal Theory: Foundations, *supra*, at 383, 394 (focusing on the need to embrace the intersection of race and gender in the struggle against oppression; arguing for placing "those who are currently marginalized in the center" to resist compartmentalizing experiences and undermining collective political action).

33. hooks, *supra* note 19, at 45.

34. Anita Hill, Videotape of Hearings, *supra* note 17 (first seven minutes of Tape #4 in answer to Sen. DeConcini).

35. Estrich, Sex at Work, herein, at 755.

36. Richard Delgado points out the importance of agency in the writings of black conservatives. Richard Delgado, Enormous Anomaly? Left-Right Parallels in Recent Writing About Race, 91 Cal. L. Rev. 1547 (1991).

37. Clarence Thomas himself may have shown that conservatism, not agency, is the essence of this position when he switched during the confirmation hearings from a

claim of agency-without-struggle (civil rights advocates whine, moan and bitch when they could be working with a Republican administration) to a claim of victimization (I am being lynched) without moving a millimeter toward liberatory struggle. See Juan Williams, EEOC Chairman Blasts Black Leaders, Wash. Post, Oct. 25, 1984, at A7 (reporting remarks on whining). A complete analysis of Clarence Thomas's testimony is beyond the scope of this article, however.

38. Within feminist theory, equating female existence with victimization has been understood as denying agency; insisting on agency has been heard as denying the inevitable situation of every woman as part of a subordinated sex. See Feminist Discourse, Moral Values, and the Law—A Conversation, 34 Buffalo L. Rev. 11, 75 (1985), in which Mary Dunlap, a feminist lawyer, responded to Catharine MacKinnon's discussion of oppression. MacKinnon emphasized harm to women: a boot is on your neck; you have no authentic voice; confront your victimization. Dunlap stood and said she was not subordinate to any man, that she frequently contested efforts at her subordination; she urged women to stand to show they did not have to be subordinated. For a thoughtful discussion of this exchange, and later development of these themes in the work of MacKinnon, see Stephanie Wildman, The Power of Women, 2 Yale J.L. & Feminism 435 (1990) (reviewing Catharine A. MacKinnon, Toward a Feminist Theory of the State (1989)).

39. Harris, Race and Essentialism, in Feminist Legal Theory: Foundations, *supra* note 32, at 348.

40. Several types of political action were proposed after the hearings, including a new national party. Ellen McGarrahan, Miami Herald, Oct. 17, 1991, at 4B. In addition, feminists placed increased energies on electing women. Kay Mills, L.A. Times, Dec. 1, 1991, at M3.

41. J. C. Alvarez, quoted in Hill, Thomas Witnesses Recount Own Experiences, Miami Herald, Oct. 14, 1991, at 14A. This remark was widely quoted and emphasized in press coverage.

42. See, e.g., Karl Klare, The Public/Private Distinction in Labor Law, 130 U. Pa. L. Rev. 1358, 1358 (1982) ("[t]he peculiarity of legal discourse is that it tends to constrain the political imagination and to induce belief that our evolving social arrangements and institutions are just and rational, or at least inevitable, and therefore legitimate.").

43. Estrich, Sex at Work, herein, at 755, 761–764 (noting that in order to prevail, a plaintiff must have expressed that the behavior was unwelcome); *id.* at 761 (hostile work environment must have been pervasive and debilitating, so significant as to substantially and adversely affect the entire work experience of female employee).

44. Regina Austin, Employer Abuse, Worker Resistance, and the Tort of Intentional Infliction of Emotional Distress, herein, at 797.

45. hooks, *supra* note 19, at 122, 130. This also involves a rejection by women of participation in violence and subordination.

❖ PART IV

REPRODUCTION

Section 6

Motherhood and
Reproductive Control

A. Motherhood

Introduction

MOTHERHOOD HAS OCCUPIED a central place in feminist practice and theory.[1] From its beginnings, the women's liberation political agenda targeted the problems faced by working mothers. At the second annual conference of the National Organization for Women in 1967, feminists advocated the establishment of daycare centers in the belief that government-subsidized childcare was necessary in the fight for equality.[2] Continuing the battle during the 1970s, feminists allied with church groups, unions, civil rights organizations, and child welfare advocates to promote legislation.

> Many believed that the right kind of child care could reshape the society. . . . Liberals and feminists believed that racially mixed centers could help put an end to racism [and] combat sex stereotypes: In feminist-run centers, girls wouldn't be relegated to the housekeeping corner. And, of course, affordable child care would free women so that they could compete in the job market.[3]

These early legislative efforts, however, were unsuccessful. Comprehensive reform would take two decades.[4]

Second wave feminists criticized women's role in the family, subscribing to the view that the transformation of social, especially familial, relationships would ameliorate the quality of life.[5] The patriarchal family was seen as a primary source of women's oppression—both creating it and perpetuating it. Feminists viewed the transformation of the family as essential because

> the family is the primary institution for organizing gender relations in society. It is where the sexual division of labor, the regulation of sexuality, and the social construction and reproduction of gender are rooted. Gender hierarchy is

created, reproduced, and maintained on a day-to-day basis through interaction among members of a household.[6]

Feminists' criticisms of the family, sociologist Evelyn Nakano Glenn suggests, were influenced by the literature of both Marxism and radical psychology.[7] Echoing Marx and Engels, Marxist feminists blamed the ills of the family (such as alienation and oppression) on changes in the modes of production.[8] The radical psychology movement highlighted the pathological nature of family relationships.[9] However, the latter school of thought, Glenn maintains, "grossly distorts" the picture by labeling women as the primary perpetrators of families' harmful effects on children.[10]

Ann Snitow identifies three stages of feminist scholarship about motherhood. The first stage was characterized, she explains, by antifamilism.[11] Snitow points to publication of Betty Friedan's *The Feminine Mystique* (which identified the malaise of the middle-class housewife) as marking the beginning of this period.[12] She terms this first period of "early feminist mother-hating," from 1963 to 1975, a stage of "demon texts."[13] Feminists were "on the defensive"[14] and "spoke skeptically about the importance of motherhood."[15] Positive descriptions of mothering were "taboo"[16] or the subject of apology. In feminists' quest to improve the status of women, they subscribed to "moving beyond, or avoiding altogether, home and motherhood."[17]

Snitow identifies 1976 as the beginning of the second period of feminist theorizing about motherhood.[18] However, Snitow here appears to overlook the importance of the transitional work by Jessie Bernard, *The Future of Motherhood*.[19] Bernard explored motherhood as a role, a symbol, and an institution. With Bernard's classic, we witness the recognition of motherhood as a social construct, influenced by social conditions such as declining fertility rates and the increasing proportion of mothers in the labor force.[20] Bernard heralded more theoretical assessment of motherhood as ideology and institution.

In this second, more focused stage of feminist theory, according to Snitow, mothers became worthy subjects of study in their own right.[21] Feminists "tried to take on the issue of motherhood seriously, to criticize the institution, explore the actual experience, theorize the social and psychological implications."[22] Glenn concurs that feminist writers in this period challenged the foundations of motherhood as a social construct.[23]

A significant benchmark is Adrienne Rich's *Of Woman Born*[24] in 1976. Like Bernard, Rich explored motherhood as an institution. However, Rich enriched the analysis with her own experience.[25] This stage of feminist inquiry is also social-psychological in focus. Two classic psychoanalytic explanations of gender differences appear: Nancy Chodorow's *The Reproduction of Mothering*[26] and Dorothy Dinnerstein's *The Mermaid and the Minotaur*.[27] In addition, we witness the cross-fertilization of American feminism and French feminism.[28] Such French writers as Julia Kristeva, Helene Cixous, and Luce Irigaray "emphasized the salient role that motherhood plays in providing access to unappreciated and previously unspoken female experiences."[29]

Feminists in the third stage, beginning in 1980, according to Snitow, continue the exploration of the implications of motherhood.[30] Scholarship now valorizes motherhood. Sara Ruddick's article "Maternal Thinking"[31] and Carol Gilligan's *In a Different Voice*[32] affirm women's uniqueness, especially their nurturing qualities. Literature in this third period "tends now to leave out the down part of the mother's story—her oppression, fury, regrets."[33]

Theory in this third stage significantly broadens the focus. Scholarship highlights the role of women of color, single women, and poor women,[34] acknowledging that mothers' experiences differ according to race, class, ethnicity, age, marital status, and sexual orientation.[35] Scholarship examines the influence of societal events (the increasing incidence of divorce, the abortion rights movement) on women's roles as mothers[36] and explores problems engendered by women's expanding employment opportunities.[37] Finally, scholarship reveals an awareness of a backlash against feminism.[38]

In this stage, although Snitow does not mention it, the focus also broadens to include scholarship about fathers. Whereas literature in the 1960s and 1970s pointed out the extent of fathers' lack of involvement with their children, the focus now changes to incorporate greater interest in fathers' distinct roles in childrearing.[39] Some scholars begin to express "annoy[ance] that we lack a history of fatherhood."[40] In response, feminists, who formerly advocated an increased childrearing role for fathers, now question whether fathers and mothers are indeed interchangeable.[41]

This third period Snitow characterizes as "a record of frustration, retrenchment, defeat and sorrow."[42] Feminists realize the limits of their earlier reform efforts, such as no-fault divorce and the evolution of child custody laws. "[O]nce-desired changes recede as imaginable possibilities."[43] Snitow tentatively suggests that, in this last stage, feminist scholarship shifts (mirroring a similar shift in politics) from motherhood to families.[44]

If Snitow's hypothesis is valid, then, it may be said that feminist theory on motherhood has evolved from an antifamily stance to a reconceptualization of the family. This reconceptualization recognizes the diversity of family life by taking into account those individuals who do not fit the traditional mold, for example, lesbian mothers, single mothers, surrogate mothers, mothers without custody, and the infertile. This view focuses on the societal implications of motherhood in the modern family. With this most recent stage, motherhood has taken on novel and complex dimensions, incorporating new "meanings, practices and ideologies."[45]

According to Glenn, contemporary feminist theorizing about motherhood explores several themes. First, feminists challenge the theory that motherhood's characteristics are a biological universal.[46] This challenge to universalism, she claims, reveals that ideology about motherhood is a social construct of the dominant class of white, middle-class women.[47] Second, feminists analyze the construction of motherhood, or the ideologies that distort our understanding of motherhood.[48] These myths include: "all women need to be mothers, that all mothers need their children and that all children need their mothers."[49] As Glenn observes, not all ideologies are equal, that is, the ideology of the dominant group prevails and yields harmful consequences for women who deviate.

A third theme of feminist theory, is the deconstruction of motherhood by recognizing and challenging the oppositional character of the elements of mothering.[50]

Among the elements Glenn identifies are the identification of woman with the role of mother; the view of mother and child as a union of identical interests; and the opposition of the public-private dimension. Yet another theme in feminist work on mothering is the exploration of motherhood in the context of power and inequality.[51] Feminists, Glenn suggests, are concerned with patriarchal control of mothering, not just by husbands and fathers, but also by male-dominated institutions. Poor women, especially women of color, experience that control in unique ways. Finally, feminist theory focuses on the difference-versus-equality debate.[52] Feminists are caught in a contradiction—whether to assert their rights based on minimization of their differences or to affirm the special qualities of women as mothers. Feminists are troubled by the realization that gender-neutral reforms have their cost.[53]

Psychologists Phoenix, Wolcott, and Lloyd highlight additional themes in feminist theory about motherhood. They emphasize that motherhood has been "professionalized."[54] That is, motherhood has been established as an area of expertise for mothers to live up to. Often, these authors add, the supporting evidence for popular ideas about motherhood is nonexistent.

The social psychological literature about motherhood encompasses a related theme which theorists have termed "the fantasy of the perfect mother."[55] Chodorow and Contratto suggest that scholars have fashioned unrealistic images of the perfect, all-powerful mother, with the consequence of contributing to blaming the mother for any ensuing failure. Jane Swigart pursues this theme further in *The Myth of the Bad Mother*,[56] by exploring psychological theories about maternal love. Feminist scholarship now explores this topic from the perspective of the French feminists.[57] The "bad mother" continues to be an important topic of exploration for feminist theorists and feminist legal theorists alike, as the essays herein reveal.

Although feminist theorists (especially sociologists and psychologists) have addressed the topic of motherhood, feminist legal theorists have neglected the subject until recently. As of 1991, a comprehensive bibliography of feminist legal literature listed no category of works on "motherhood."[58] The current *Index to Legal Periodicals* still fails to include such a category, preferring to list the few relevant entries under the general heading "Women."[59] Fineman points out that "Women have been defined in feminist legal discourse mainly as 'wives,' not as mothers."[60]

Early legal scholarship sidestepped the issue by focusing instead on the problems experienced by working women, such as maternity leave[61] or fetal protection policies.[62] Societal events such as the increase in divorce rates shifted attention to the problems that mothers experienced in custody decision making. In particular, feminists debated the virtues and costs of different custody options: maternal preference, the gender-neutral primary caregiver presumption, and joint custody.[63] Feminists highlighted the manner in which women suffer in custody determinations because of equality rhetoric.[64]

Of course, literature on many feminist issues (such as abortion and battering) concerns motherhood indirectly. But, for the most part, motherhood is relevant in much of legal literature only in a secondary sense. Mothers are studied because they are part of some larger social issue or social problem, as revealed by the use of *mother* as a noun modified by the important "problem": teen mother, lesbian mother, welfare mother. Only with the advent of interest in the new reproductive technologies do we witness the emergence of a more theoretical concern with the meaning of motherhood.[65] Scholars began questioning the implications of the new reproductive technologies for women. In the course of their discussions, they began challenging the ideology of motherhood.[66]

One legal scholar who has been influential in establishing a niche for the topic of motherhood in feminist legal theory is Professor Martha Fineman of Columbia University. Her two recently published books attempt to bring motherhood to the forefront of feminist legal theory.[67] In *The Neutered Mother,* Fineman explores the role of negative images of motherhood in law reform. She points out that our view of motherhood is tainted by ideas of the traditional nuclear family. She suggests a transformation of family law that would end marriage as a legal category. Her collection of essays *Mothers in Law* explores different aspects of the legal regulation of motherhood, especially the "deviant" mother, and mothers in special contexts.

The essays in this chapter enhance our understanding of the legal regulation of motherhood. The first essay by Carol Sanger, "M Is for the Many Things," provides an overview of the legal treatment of motherhood by feminist legal theorists.[68] After an insightful exploration of the reasons for the long neglect of the topic,[69] Sanger argues that feminists must create a new legal conceptualization of motherhood that is based in the practical experiences of mothers.

The experiences of drug-addicted mothers, the majority of whom are African American, are explored by Dorothy Roberts. Roberts asserts that these women are punished not so much for harming their unborn as for reasons of race, poverty, and substance abuse—factors that society perceives as causing these women to be unfit mothers. Roberts's essay illustrates an example in which the law treats women who deviate from the image of the perfect mother.

Nancy Ehrenreich's analysis of court-ordered Caesarean sections continues this theme. Ehrenreich theorizes that, because women of color are perceived as bad mothers, their decisions about C-sections are more often questioned than are those of middle-class white women. Her essay broadens the focus to the institutional level by delineating the contours of the mutually legitimating relationship between law and medicine to define good mothering.

Regina Austin's "Sapphire Bound!" explores the legal treatment of unwed mothers. Austin uses the case of Chambers v. Omaho Girls Club[70] (terminating the employment of a young, pregnant African American) as a vehicle to explore the consequences for some young women of deviating from the norm. Chambers's thoughtful Black feminist critique interprets the decision as an attempt to control the threat posed by young pregnant African American women to middle-class white morality. Austin's analysis demonstrates how the legal system conceptualizes the cultural and racial components of good mothers.

Marie Ashe and Naomi Cahn's essay expands on the notion of the image of the good mother in the law by exploring the legal treatment of mothers in child abuse cases.[71] Ashe and Cahn argue that two contradictory images of the bad mother (as the autonomous evildoer or the victim) influence punishment. However, Ashe and Cahn enrich the analysis with their theoretical exploration of the treatment of the bad mother by various strands of feminism. Echoing Sanger's call for a feminist re-visioning of motherhood, they suggest that postmodernist feminism, with its rejection of objectivity and essentialism, may be the most promising theory for a feminist reconceptualization of motherhood.

Notes

1. Ideology about motherhood, of course, goes back further than early second stage theory. Family historians point to the mid- to late nineteenth century when, in response to urbanization and industrialization, motherhood witnessed a deification, especially by the middle classes—sometimes referred to as "the cult of domesticity." See generally C. Degler, At Odds: Women and the Family in America from the Revolution to the Present (Oxford Univ. Press, 1980); B. Ehrenreich & D. English, For Her Own Good: 150 Years of the Experts' Advice to Women (Doubleday, 1978); Michael Grossberg, Governing the Hearth: Law and the Family in Nineteenth Century America (Univ. North Carolina Press, 1985); Richard Sennett, Families Against the City: Middle Class Homes of Industrial Chicago, 1872–1890 (Harvard Univ. Press, 1984); Hareven, Family Time and Historical Time, 106 Daedalus 57 (Spring 1977); Welter, The Cult of True Womanhood: 1820–1860, 18 Am. Q. 151 (Summer 1966).

A review of the vast sociological and psychological literature on motherhood is beyond the scope of this introduction. Rather, this introduction attempts to highlight the overarching themes, stages, and issues in the field which are relevant to an understanding of the legal essays that follow.

2. F. Davis, Moving the Mountain: The Women's Movement in America Since 1960, 66 (Simon & Schuster, 1991). NOW's Bill of Rights advocated "child care facilities . . . established by federal law on the same basis as parks, libraries and public schools." Cited in *id.* at 281.

3. Davis, *supra* note 2, at 281–282. See generally S. Kamerman & A. Kahn, Child Care Family Benefits and Working Parents: A Study in Comparative Policy (Columbia Univ. Press, 1981).

4. Davis attributes this failure to three factors: right-wing opposition to "communal child rearing," the lack of unity among childcare advocates, and the lack of public support for childcare. Davis, *supra* note 2, at 285–286. Childcare legislation was finally enacted in 1984, 1988, and 1990, when Congress authorized funds for childcare referral services, after-school programs, the establishment of additional childcare centers and the expansion of Head Start programs, and the provision of tax credits for childcare. *Id.* at 449–450.

5. Breines, Cerullo & Stacey, Social Biology, Family Studies, and Antifeminist Backlash, 4 Feminist Stud. 43 (Feb. 1978).

6. E. Glenn, Gender and the Family, in B. Hess and M. Ferree eds., Analyzing Gender: A Handbook of Social Science Research 348 (Sage, 1987).

7. *Id.* at 357.

8. *Id.* See also B. Wearing, The Ideology of Motherhood: A Study of Sydney Suburban Mothers 16–20 (George Allen & Unwin, 1984) (discussion of Marxian and Weberian views about mothering).

9. Glenn, *supra* note 6, at 357 (citing R. D. Laing, The Politics of Experience and the Bird of Paradise (Penguin, 1967); R. D. Laing, The Politics of the Family and Other Essays (Random House, 1972); R. D. Laing & A. Esterson, Sanity, Madness and the Family (Penguin, 1964)).

10. Glenn, *supra* note 6, at 357.

11. Snitow, Feminism and Motherhood: An American Reading, 40 Feminist Rev. 32, 34 (1992).

12. *Id.* at 35 (citing B. Friedan, The Feminine Mystique (W. W. Norton & Co., 1963)).

13. *Id.* at 35 ("demon texts"), 37 ("early feminist mother-hating"). Snitow amplifies on the definition of "demon texts" as follows: "books demonized, apologized for, endlessly quoted out of context, to prove that the feminism of the early seventies was, in Friedan's words of recantation, 'strangely blind.' *Id.* at 35.

14. *Id.* at 41.

15. *Id.* at 42.

16. *Id.* at 41.

17. D. Bassin, M. Honey, & M. Kaplan eds., Representations of Motherhood 6 (Yale Univ. Press, 1994).

18. Snitow, *supra* note 11, at 38. The beginning date appears to be approximate. Earlier in her article, Snitow states that the second stage lasted from 1975 to 1979. *Id.* at 34.

19. J. Bernard, The Future of Motherhood (Dial, 1974). Snitow includes Bernard's book in her "time-line," but neglects to discuss the importance of this work.

20. *Id.* at viii.

21. *Id.* at 34.

22. *Id.*

23. Glenn, Gender and the Family, in Analyzing Gender, *supra* note 6, at 357.

24. A. Rich, Of Woman Born: Motherhood as Experience and Institution (W. W. Norton, 1976).

25. For a recent empirical study of mothers' subjective experiences, see M. Kaplan, Mothers' Images of Motherhood: Case Studies of Twelve Mothers (Routledge, 1992).

26. N. Chodorow, The Reproduction of Mothering (Univ. Calif. Press, 1978).

27. D. Dinnerstein, The Mermaid and the Minotaur: Sexual Arrangements and Human Malaise (Harper & Row, 1976).

28. Snitow, *supra* note 11, at 38 (citing Helene Cixous, The Laugh of the Medusa, 1 Signs 875 (1976)).

29. Bassin, Honey & Kaplan, *supra* note 17, at 9.

30. See Snitow, *supra* note 11, at 39.

31. *Id.* at 39 (citing Ruddick, Maternal Thinking, 6 Feminist Stud. 342 (1980)).

32. *Id.* (citing C. Gilligan, In a Different Voice: Psychological Theory and Women's Development (Harvard Univ. Press, 1982)).

33. *Id.* at 42.

34. *Id.*

35. For an interesting empirical study of the influence of marital status, see S. McRae, Cohabiting Mothers: Changing Marriage and Motherhood (London: Policy Studies Institute, 1993).

36. Snitow, *supra* note 11, at 41 (citing R. Petchesky's Abortion and Women's Choice: The State, Sexuality, and Reproductive Freedom (Longman, 1984); K. Luker,

Abortion and the Politics of Motherhood (Univ. California Press, 1984); L. Weitzman, The Divorce Revolution: The Unexpected Social and Economic Consequences for Women and Children in America (Free Press, 1985)).

37. Snitow, *supra* note 11, at 41 (citing K. Gerson, Hard Choices: How Women Decide About Work, Careers and Motherhood (Univ. California Press, 1985)).

38. *Id.* at 40–41 (citing S. Miller, The Good Mother (Harper & Row, 1986); S. Hewlett, A Lesser Life: The Myth of Women's Liberation in America (William Morrow, 1986)).

39. A. Phoenix, A. Woollett & E. Lloyd eds., Motherhood: Meanings, Practices and Ideologies 4 (Sage, 1994).

40. Thomas W. Laqueur, The Facts of Fatherhood, in M. Hirsch & E. Keller eds., Conflicts in Feminism 205 (Routledge, 1990). See also S. Ruddick, Thinking about Fathers, in *id.* at 222. For a bibliography on fatherhood, see J. Snarey, How Fathers Care for the Next Generation: A Four-Decade Study 363–394 (Harvard Univ. Press, 1993).

41. Phoenix, Woollett & Lloyd, *supra* note 39, at 4. Diane Richardson, who notes the burgeoning scholarly interest in fatherhood, cynically asks whether such research reflects men's greater involvement in childcare or is an attempt by men to reaffirm their power within the family. D. Richardson, Women, Motherhood and Childrearing 58 (St. Martin's Press, 1993) (citing S. Pollock and J. Sutton, The Politics of Fatherhood (London: Women's Press, 1987)).

42. Snitow, *supra* note 11, at 40.

43. *Id.* at 34.

44. *Id.*

45. Phoenix, Woollett & Lloyd, *supra* note 39. Phoenix, Woollett, and Lloyd elaborate on these current feminist issues as follows: "the meanings that motherhood has for women (whether or not they are mothers)"; "the ways in which women actually mother within the circumstances in which they live"; and, the ideologies that "construct what motherhood is considered to be and hence circumscribe the range of practices that mothers seek to employ with their children." *Id.* at 5.

46. E. Glenn, G. Chang & L. Forcey eds., Mothering: Ideology, Experience, and Agency 4 (Routledge, 1994).

47. *Id.* at 5.

48. *Id.* at 9–12.

49. *Id.* at 9 (citing A. Oakley, Woman's Work: The Housewife, Past and Present 186 (Pantheon Books, 1974)).

50. *Id.* at 13–16.

51. *Id.* at 16–22.

52. *Id.* at 22–26.

53. Snitow, *supra* note 11, at 43.

54. Phoenix, Wolcott & Lloyd, *supra* note 39, at 7–8. See also Ehrenreich & English, *supra* note 1.

55. Chodorow & Contratto, The Fantasy of the Perfect Mother, in B. Thorne with M. Yalom eds., Rethinking the Family 54 (Longman, 1982).

56. J. Swigart, The Myth of the Bad Mother: The Emotional Realities of Mothering (Doubleday, 1991).

57. See J. Doane & D. Hodges, From Klein to Kristeva: Psychoanalytic Feminism and the Search for the "Good Enough" Mother (Univ. Mich. Press, 1992).

58. See F. DeCoste, K. Munro & L. MacPherson, Feminist Legal Literature: A Selective Annotated Bibliography (Garland, 1991).

59. See 88 Index to Legal Periodicals & Books 272 (Feb. 1995). The Index cross-references articles by means of a "see also" to such topics as: "Battered Women," "Feminist Jurisprudence," "Married Women," and "Sex Discrimination." Such an omission is illustrative of the stage of development of a new field. On the importance of classification in the "discovery" of social problems, see M. Spector & J. Kitsuse, Constructing Social Problems 8–22 (Cummings, 1977).

60. M. Fineman, The Neutered Mother, The Sexual Family and other Twentieth Century Tragedies 26 (Routledge, 1995).

61. See, e.g., the essays on The Equality Debate: Equal Treatment versus Special Treatment, in D. Weisberg ed., Feminist Legal Theory: Foundations 121–207. (Temple Univ. Press, 1993).

62. See, e.g., Becker, From Muller v. Oregon to Fetal Vulnerability Policies, 53 U. Chi. L. Rev. 1219 (1986).

63. See, e.g., Bartlett & Stack, Joint Custody, Feminism and the Dependency Dilemma, 2 Berkeley Women's L.J. 9 (1986); Erickson, The Feminist Dilemma Over Unwed Parents' Custody Rights: The Mother's Rights Must Take Priority, 2 Law & Ineq. J. 447 (1984). See also Chambers, Rethinking the Substantive Rules for Custody Disputes in Divorce, 83 Mich. L. Rev. 477 (1984); Fineman & Opie, The Uses of Social Science Data in Legal Policymaking: Custody Determination at Divorce, 1987 Wis. L. Rev. 107 (feminist rebuttal to Chambers).

64. See, e.g., M. Fineman, The Illusion of Equality: The Rhetoric and Reality of Divorce Reform (Univ. Chicago Press, 1991); Fineman, Dominant Discourse, Professional Language, and Legal Change in Child Custody Decisionmaking, 101 Harv. L. Rev. 717 (1988). See also Boyd, Child Custody, Ideologies, and Employment, 3 Can. J. Women & L. 111 (1989).

65. See, e.g., Stumpf, Redefining Mother: A Legal Matrix for New Reproductive Technologies, 96 Yale L.J. 187 (1986); Note, Rethinking (M)otherhood: Feminist Theory and State Regulation of Pregnancy, 103 Harv. L. Rev. 1325 (1990).

66. See the essays on Reproductive Technologies and Adoption, herein at 1041–1166.

67. Fineman, The Neutered Mother, *supra* note 60; M. Fineman & I. Karpin eds., Mothers in Law: Feminist Theory and the Legal Regulation of Motherhood (Routledge, 1995).

68. See also C. Sanger, Separating from Children (Univ. California Press, forthcoming), Sanger, Separating from Children, 96 Colum. L. Rev. (forthcoming 1996).

69. See also Mary Becker, Maternal Feelings: Myth, Taboo, and Child Custody, 1 S. Cal. Rev. L. & Women's Stud. 133, 159–167 (1992).

70. 629 F. Supp. 925 (D. Neb. 1986), *aff'd,* 834 F.2d 697 (8th Cir. 1987), *reh'g denied,* 840 F.2d 583 (1988).

71. See also Ashe, The "Bad Mother" in Law and Literature: A Problem of Representation, 43 Hastings L.J. 1017 (1992).

M Is for the Many Things

CAROL SANGER

. . .

Motherhood the Subject

MOTHERHOOD IS at present and at last academically fashionable. With few exceptions such as Adrienne Rich's *Of Woman Born* in 1976, motherhood's neglect in curricula and scholarship mirrored its uneasy reception by feminists in general. The identification of motherhood as a source of subordination led early feminists to direct their energies toward creating social structures less encumbered by maternal obligation. Thus, feminist politics aimed at such reforms as increasing access to abortion, child care, property, education and jobs. Distancing women from motherhood seemed the key to a better life. More recently, however, the problems of mothers themselves (or at least the problems of some mothers) have been included within feminist political agenda: mothers in the workplace, mothers seeking child custody and support, mothers and health care.

Within the academy consideration of motherhood was avoided for many of the same reasons that made women's issues in general disfavored topics of research: too soft, too unimportant, no funding, few colleagues, and who cares. The study of motherhood may have been a particularly suspicious choice for scholarship, risking confirmation in the eyes of colleagues who knew all along what women, even professional women, were really about. In areas where mothers *were* studied, like psychology, the undertaking was tinged with an assumption of pathology. The inquiry was essentially to discover why mothers made everyone crazy.[1] This was not a particularly unfeminist position. As Betty Friedan explained[2] and Anne Sexton demonstrated,[3] motherhood made mothers crazy too.

Similar constraints were at work in legal scholarship. As in other fields, writing on women's topics was a precarious career decision. And too, there is no reason why all

---

1 S. Cal. Rev. L. & Women's Stud. 15 (1992).

women, all feminists, or all mothers should want to write about motherhood. But neither personal nor professional preferences, even if politic, seem sufficient to explain the lack of attention given to motherhood, especially by feminist legal theorists. An important example is Catharine MacKinnon's omission of mothering from her many powerful descriptions and analyses of women's subordination. Child rearing takes its place among the other services MacKinnon identifies that women perform for men,[4] and of the denial of reproductive control that MacKinnon forcefully addresses. But as Stephanie Wildman has pointed out, the absence of mother's lives with children in MacKinnon's description of "women's concrete reality" "renders invisible and irrelevant to her feminism unmodified this reality of most women's lives."[5]

I want to suggest that feminism itself, inspired *and* constrained by its commitment to improving the lives of women, is in part responsible for motherhood's delayed debut in feminist legal scholarship. The two explanations I offer look to the influence of reformist strategies and to feminism's understandable insistence on working through issues of sex first. Like all theoretical disciplines inspired by the doctrine of praxis, feminism has been alert to the implicit as well as explicit relationships between theories, goals, and practical consequences. Certainly a sensitivity to political consequences has contributed to a circumscribed consideration of motherhood within legal scholarship. Consider, for example, two topics clearly related to motherhood that *have* been high on the feminist agenda: abortion and child custody. Because the law in these areas has been (and remains) actively contested, scholarship regarding both abortion and custody has had significant strategic dimensions that have necessarily obscured, or at least delayed, fuller consideration of the meaning of the work of motherhood.

Abortion first. The legal theories that secured the right to abortion developed within a framework of privacy that focused on a woman's right to control her trimestered body. That analysis necessarily diverted attention from a woman's interest in controlling her post-pregnant, child-now-out-of body life. As abortion became a reproductive rather than a maternal issue, the very idea of motherhood became antithetical to a pro-choice position instead of its essence. But deciding whether or not to have an abortion is making a decision exactly about what place motherhood will occupy in one's life. The decision necessarily encompasses hard thinking on such questions as when one should become a mother, how often, with whom, and what obligations already exist to other children, to a partner, or to oneself.

Ceding motherhood as an experience, a symbol, and a virtue to the anti-abortion camp[6] has had consequences for how we explore (or do not explore) other issues relating to mothers. For example, Maureen Sweeney argues that oversimplification of the abortion issue on a theoretical level has led to a general silence within the feminist community regarding the issue of adoption, particularly the concerns of birth mothers.[7] She suggests that the women's movement has too firmly adopted the dichotomy of adoption as the alternative to abortion so that favoring adoption is too quickly equated with opposing abortion. Much the same can be said about the hostile attitude of many feminists toward infertile women whose desires for children are often viewed as no more than "evidence for women's oppressive socialization to become mothers, and their continued subservience to institutionalized medicine. . . ."[8] The fear here seems to be that by recognizing the desire to be a mother, one may inadvertently strengthen or validate arguments that oppose abortion and women's claims to control their fertility.

Custody is a second issue where doctrinal and political priorities have diverted attention from thinking more broadly about the functions of motherhood. The principal modern reform in custody law—the shift from the tender years maternal presumption to the gender neutral "best interests of the child" test—occurred in the early 1970s when "equality" dominated the feminist stage. In those days, favoring the tender years presumption—agreeing that mothers should automatically receive custody of their children—smacked of dowdy maternalism and role inequality. "Difference" as a competing basis for reform had not yet begun to act up. As a result, the theories of custody become conceptually estranged from the business of mothering.

But custody law has evolved. Women observed and experienced the economically harsh consequences of equality, or what Martha Fineman identifies as the "illusion of inequality,"[9] in the broader context of no-fault divorce and the American labor market.[10] Different and more sophisticated notions of common sense and fairness now direct many women toward a primary caretaker rule. This standard favors women not because of their inherently sweeter natures, but because mothers tend to do the daily tasks that are the stuff of parenting. Consideration of custody now starts not from a preference for gender equality with custody rules falling in behind, but from an assessment of what having custody of a child means—in many ways a description of mothering—and the legal implications that follow from that.

Legal and political strategies offer one explanation of feminism's obscured view of motherhood. Another reason motherhood has been what I would describe as a "second stage feminist issue" is that in uncovering law's complicity with patriarchy, before one gets to motherhood one stumbles into sex. This is the necessary beginning. Sexual intercourse has preceded motherhood in almost every individual case. But the fact of motherhood itself immediately reinforces the conditions that have made oppression through sex possible. Gerda Lerner and others argue that because women were mothers, they have always been more vulnerable to sexual subordination and thus to other forms of domestic and economic oppression.[11] The assignment of child rearing to women is at the core of the sexual division of labor. Feminist theorists recognize this relationship, but until recently they have been content to describe only the function of mothering within the patriarchal scheme, rather than to explore the job itself.[12]

Another explanation for focusing the investigation on sex first is that rape, pornography, and sexual harassment are vivid issues that could not wait. In contrast to the immediacy of sexual violence, the harms of motherhood are quieter—quotidian rather than dramatic. The harms of motherhood are also less universally accepted among women themselves. We properly reject rape out of hand, but motherhood is more complicated because of an ambivalence towards the task and the idea. For some women the ambivalence is a kind of embarrassment; the decision to become a mother, especially if happily taken, seems to unravel or compromise whatever accommodation between the personal and political they had worked out.

Of course, for many women, the discovery of motherhood as a source of complicated pleasures is nothing new. As bell hooks has insisted, deciding where oppression lies has long depended on who was calling the shots:

> Some white middle class, college-educated women argued that motherhood was a serious obstacle to women's liberation. . . . Had black women voiced their views on motherhood, it would not have been named a serious obstacle to our freedom as women. Racism, availability of jobs, lack of skills or education and a number of other issues would have been at the top of the list—but not motherhood.[13]

hooks argues that motherhood has become politically important only because enough white women have finally entered an inhospitable work place and are recognizing, as black women who have always worked outside their homes have long known, that homelife can sometimes provide contrasting satisfactions.[14]

As a result of all these factors, current scholarship now recognizes that motherhood is here to stay, "as experience or as subject for research, now as controversial as it once was bland."[15] Some of the controversy is familiar. Increased attention to motherhood, even when supportive of the institution, has awakened old claims about its role in the oppression of women. New reproductive technologies have provided additional fuel for the fire as there are now more routes to motherhood, complete with their own technologically enhanced potential for oppression.[16] At the same time, revised and more positive feminist views about motherhood's virtues now find greater acceptance.[17] Michelle Stanworth describes the tension:

> On the one hand, maternal practices are increasingly acknowledged as a source of alternative values. . . . On the other hand, the material and social disadvantages that follow from childcare, the cultural associations with birth that condemn women to an inferior place in symbolic systems; the psychological effects on future adults of asymmetrical mothercare: all suggests that motherhood locks women into structures of dependency and powerlessness.[18]

The inclusion and reconsideration of motherhood in legal scholarship is due in part to work in other disciplines that has been too rich and too related to ignore. Lenore Weitzman's observations about the economic consequences of divorce for mothers,[19] Nancy Chodorow's exploration of why women mother,[20] and Susan Okin's insistence on the interrelation between family life and social justice[21] not only call for but compel consideration of law's complicity in existing arrangements. The willingness of legal scholars at last to "turn outward"[22] may be a case of not wanting to be left behind.

Recent legal attention to motherhood also results from women and mothers acting in ways that have provoked legal responses. Women contract to become mothers; pregnant women get arrested for abuse to fetuses; women aren't hired because they might become mothers and are fired because they have. In our society these activities have become legal matters, litigated, legislated, and taught in law schools, if sometimes under fancier aliases such as reproductive technologies, workplace safety, or lawyering skills.

Legal scholars are now reviewing how law conceptualizes mothers—historically,[23] comparatively,[24] and functionally[25]—in an effort to understand what social and economic values those conceptualizations represent and the uses to which they may be put. The starting point for much of this work is in the observed or self-described experiences of mothers. For example, legal biography is increasingly inundated by consideration of the ways that women lawyers,[26] law professors, and law reformers[27] have taken account of their own motherhood, personally and strategically.

My own work on mothers who choose to separate from their children is another example.[28] That project explores the ways in which law regards one particular aspect of mothering—its rejection, as seen in decisions by mothers to part from their children. Such decisions are of great interest to the law and are regulated accordingly. Some regulations prohibit decisions to separate (the case of surrogacy); others monitor them (adoptions); and still others require separation (the case of workfare). The differences among these regulations tell us something about official expectations regarding maternal duties, about the regard in which different mothers are held, and about where and under what circumstances deviations from maternal norms are permitted or required.

But the task here is something more than a cataloguing of maternal experiences. We are trying to understand both the existing and the desirable relationship between the law and women who are mothers. An immediate complexity revealed by the undertaking is the question of when a woman's status as a mother—for women are rarely *only* mothers—should signify legally. Within our culture motherhood is taken as an all-embracing status affecting almost the whole of mothers' lives, not just the parts devoted to their children. When does it matter that an accident victim, a welfare claimant, a job applicant, a battered wife, a prospective juror, an unsentenced defendant, or a prisoner is also a mother? Under what circumstances do concerns about motherhood, either in individual cases or as a social category, contribute to or control a legal or policy decision? With whom does authority reside to decide what role mothering will take? And what model of motherhood will be invoked in making these decisions?

These questions are all ways of asking where motherhood fits in the context of women's lives and in law and legal culture. Part of the work of feminist legal scholars is to develop analyses that locate sensible boundaries and transit points between women's multiple and reconfiguring identities. Consider a mother who is someone's lover, a law student, and a reservist in the National Guard. Should a custody decision be influenced by the fact that she has an intimate companion, studies law, or may be called to active service? Should her law school or the legal profession or the armed forces take account of her status as a mother? When should a woman's maternal identity prevail over the many other identities she holds simultaneously?

The issue is not easy. Identification as a mother for one purpose risks permanence or overuse of the identity for other purposes. One approach is to follow Dean Herma

Kay's sensible description of pregnancy as episodic:[29] a condition that is legally relevant when it is physically relevant. The technique is a bit harder with motherhood than with pregnancy. A woman with children is always a mother; the status does not physically come and go. Nevertheless, we have no trouble separating the parental status of fathers from their other roles. Thus the task with regard to women is not impossible but only less familiar. We must simply and repeatedly ask in each instance whether it is relevant that the lover/student/soldier is a mother?

The situation is all the more complicated because motherhood is not only one among a woman's many statuses, it is a relational status as well. That is, every mother is *somebody's* mother and her relationship with that person may also be multi-faced. Her child may at different times during her life be her darling or her assailant, her landlord or her tenant, her debtor or her source of support, her greatest comfort or her endless concern. How crucial to law are the changing natures of these maternal relationships? Motherhood is also often relational with respect to another adult, as many mothers have husbands or partners. To the extent that spousal relationships encompass legal and personal obligations, they too complicate consideration of motherhood. What, for example, is the appropriate hierarchy of loyalties—legally, personally, culturally—for a woman who puts her marital status and relationship above her maternal one?

The task for scholars is the harder for these contradictory demands. It requires an acknowledgment and a full description of the substantial room that motherhood takes up in women's lives. But it also requires that motherhood, despite its capacity to overwhelm, not be mistaken for the whole show. At the very time that scholarship becomes more located in the experiences of mothers, mothers should not be reduced to only those experiences. [A]ttempts at distilling all women into mothers and all mothers into good ones are bound to be unreliable. . . .

Notes

1. Paula Caplan & Ian Hall-McCorquodale, Mother-Blaming in Major Clinical Journals, 55 Am. J. Orthopsychiatry 345–353 (1985). The practice goes back to the early days of psychology. In 1928, a psychologist dedicated his book on child development "to the first mother who brings up a happy child." John Broadus Watson, Psychological Care of Infant and Child (1928), cited in Catherine McBride-Chang, Carol Nagy Jacklin & Chandra Reynolds, Mother-Blaming, Psychology and the Law, 1 S. Cal. Rev. L. & Women's Stud. 69 (1992). Nancy Chodorow and Susan Contratto argue that much contemporary feminist writing continues to focus on the harm that mothers do to their children. Their psychoanalytic explanation is that: "[d]rawing from and reflecting a cultural ideology and infantile sense of infantile need and maternal responsibility for the outcomes of child-rearing, feminists begin by identifying with the child and blaming the mother, or by expecting her to be more than perfect." See Nancy Chodorow & Susan Contratto, The Fantasy of the Perfect Mother, in Barrie Thorne & Marilyn Yalom eds., Rethinking the Family: Some Feminist Questions 54, 67 (1982).

2. Betty Friedan, The Feminine Mystique (1963). For a social history of the domestic life of housewives that led up to a book like *The Feminine Mystique,* see the discussion in Glenna Matthews, Just a Housewife: The Rise and Fall of Domesticity in America (1987) ("Before [Friedan] published her book, women were most often blamed personally for their unhappiness. Afterwards, there began to be an appreciation that social arrangements could receive some of the blame.") *Id.* at 219.

3. Dianne W. Middlebrook, Anne Sexton: A Biography (1991).

4. Catharine MacKinnon, Toward a Feminist Theory of the State 10, 246 (1989).

5. Stephanie M. Wildman, Review Essay: The Power of Women, 2 Yale J.L. & Feminism 435, 452 (1990) (reviewing Catharine MacKinnon, Toward a Feminist Theory of the State). Wildman points out that respect for feminist methodology requires attention to the experience of mothering—women talking about their lives with children. *Id.* at 450. . . .

6. For a discussion of how the political right has monopolized the vocabulary of the family, see Rushworth M. Kidder, Marriage in America: Staking Out High Ground in "Pro Family" Debate, Christian Sci. Monitor, Nov. 26, 1985, at 25. One mechanism has been to portray the fetus through visual imagery as a free standing (or free floating) family member, unprotected by and unconnected to its mother; see discussion of the antiabortion film "The Silent Scream," in Rosalind Petchesky, Foetal Images: The Power of Visual Culture in the Politics of Reproduction, in Michelle Stanworth ed., Reproductive Technologies 57–64 (1987).

7. Maureen Sweeney, Between Sorrow and Happy Endings: A New Paradigm of Adoption, 2 Yale J.L. & Feminism 329, 335 (1990).

8. Margarete J. Sandelowski, Failures of Volition: Female Agency and Infertility in Historical Perspective, 15 Signs 475, 498 (1990). Barbara Rothman argues that infertility treatment incorporates much that is bad for women within the American medical establishment: "it is available only to the well-to-do, it is male dominated, and it is offered in a way that is totally divorced from the context of one's life. And worse, it doesn't work. In vitro fertilization (IVF) fails 90 percent of the women who try it." Barbara K. Rothman, Recreating Motherhood: Ideology and Technology in a Patriarchal Society 148 (1989).

9. Martha Fineman, The Illusion of Equality 26–33 (1991) (urging a transition within feminism from the ideal of equality to its abdication).

10. As Victor Fuchs points out, divorce is not the only cause of women's lesser economic status. See generally Victor Fuchs, Women's Quest for Economic Equality 1988), especially ch. 3, "The More Things Change . . ." 32–52 (describing consequences for women of occupational segregation, hours of paid work, and sex-based wage gaps). But while divorce may not be the central explanation, having children *is:* "the biggest source of women's economic disadvantage [is] their greater desire for and concern about children." *Id.* at 140, 60–64.

11. Gerda Lerner, The Creation of Patriarchy 38–53 (1986). See also Judith Grant, Intimate Work: The Regulation of Female Sexuality and Reproduction, 1 S. Cal. Rev. L. & Women's Stud. 225 (1992) (examining patriarchy and the control of women's sexuality).

12. Another reason the experience of mothering may have been downplayed within legal discourse is because "until child rearing encroaches upon the male privilege of ownership or control," law isn't so very interested. Wildman, *supra* note 5, at 450. But not taking a topic seriously until law does is playing by boys' rules, and, as Wildman points out, feminists have rejected that approach in areas like pornography

and sexual harassment. Nervousness about naming, let alone claiming, the experiences of motherhood may have played a part here.

13. bell hooks, Feminist Theory: From Margin to Center 133 (1984).

14. *Id.* at 134.

15. Editor's Note, On the Reproduction of Mothering: A Methodological Debate, 6 Signs 482 (1981).

16. . . . Stanworth suggests that conflicts among feminists about motherhood play out more safely on technological turf: "The fears generated by conceptive technologies may be a way not only for women to articulate perceived threats to motherhood, but also to keep those threats at bay, by projecting them onto one particular group of women (the infertile) who aren't 'really' women anyway." Michelle Stanworth, Birth Pangs, in Marianne Hirsch & Evelyn Keller eds., Conflicts in Feminism 296–297 (1990).

17. See, e.g., Sara Ruddick, Maternal Thinking, in Rethinking the Family, *supra* note 1, at 76.

18. M. Stanworth, *supra* note 16.

19. Lenore Weitzman, The Divorce Revolution: The Unexpected Social and Economic Consequences for Women and Children in America (1985). Although Weitzman's findings have been criticized as overstating both the degree of poverty into which women fall and the role of no-fault in bringing about that reduced economic status, see e.g., Marsha Garrison, The Economics of Divorce: Changing Rules, Changing Results, in Stephen D. Sugarman & Herma Hill Kay eds., Divorce Reform at the Crossroads 75 (1990), Weitzman's central point holds: women (and children) are significantly less well off after divorce.

20. Nancy Chodorow, The Reproduction of Mothering: Psychoanalysis and the Sociology of Gender (1978).

21. Susan Okin, Justice, Gender and the Family (1989).

22. Martha Minow, Law Turning Outward, 73 Telos 79 (1987).

23. Martha Chamallas with Linda K. Kerber, Women, Mothers, and the Law of Fright: A History, 88 Mich. L. Rev. 814 (1990); Hendrik Hartog, Abigail Bailey's Coverture: Law in a Married Woman's Consciousness, in Austin Sarat ed., Law in Everyday Life (Univ. Michigan Press, 1993).

24. Mary Anne Glendon, Abortion and Divorce in Western Law (1987); Taimie Bryant, OYA-KO Shinju: Death at the Center of the Heart, 8 UCLA Pac. Basin L.J. 1 (1990).

25. Nancy Polikoff, This Child Does Have Two Mothers: Redefining Parenthood to Meet the Needs of Children in Lesbian-Mother and Other Non-Traditional Families, 78 Geo. L.J. 459 (1990).

26. Barbara Allen Babcock, Clara Shortridge Foltz: Constitution-Maker, 66 Ind. L.J. 849 (1991). Foltz, the first woman to graduate from law school in California (and inventor of the office of public defender) was exceptional in that she already had five children before she became a lawyer. . . .

27. Elizabeth B. Clark, Self-Ownership and the Political Theory of Elizabeth Cady Stanton, 21 Conn. L. Rev. 905 (1989).

28. Carol Sanger, Separating from Children (forthcoming Univ. California Press); Carol Sanger, Separating from Children, 96 Colum. L. Rev. (forthcoming 1996).

29. Herma Hill Kay, Equality and Difference: A Perspective on the Case of Pregnancy, 1 Berkeley Women's L.J. 1, 21 (1985).

Punishing Drug Addicts Who Have Babies: Women of Color, Equality, and the Right of Privacy

Dorothy E. Roberts

Prologue

A former slave named Lizzie Williams recounted the beating of pregnant slave women on a Mississippi cotton plantation: "I[']s seen nigger women dat was fixin' to be confined do somethin' de white folks didn't like. Dey [the white folks] would dig a hole in de ground just big 'nuff fo' her stomach, make her lie face down an whip her on de back to keep from hurtin' de child."[1]

In July 1989, Jennifer Clarise Johnson, a twenty-three-year-old crack addict, became the first woman in the United States to be criminally convicted for exposing her baby to drugs while pregnant.[2] Florida law enforcement officials charged Johnson with two counts of delivering a controlled substance to a minor after her two children tested positive for cocaine at birth. Because the relevant Florida drug law did not apply to fetuses, the prosecution invented a novel interpretation of the statute. The prosecution obtained Johnson's conviction for passing a cocaine metabolite from her body to her newborn infants during the sixty-second period after birth and before the umbilical cord was cut.

Introduction

A growing number of women across the country have been charged with criminal offenses after giving birth to babies who test positive for drugs.[3] The majority of these women, like Jennifer Johnson, are poor and Black.[4] Most are addicted to crack cocaine.[5] The prosecution of drug-addicted mothers is part of an alarming trend towards greater state intervention into the lives of pregnant women under the rationale of protecting the fetus from harm. This intervention has included compelled medical treatment, greater restrictions on abortion, and increased supervision of pregnant women's conduct.

---

104 Harv. L. Rev. 1419 (1991). Copyright © 1991 by the Harvard Law Review Association.

Such government intrusion is particularly harsh for poor women of color. They are the least likely to obtain adequate prenatal care, the most vulnerable to government monitoring, and the least able to conform to the white, middle-class standard of motherhood. They are therefore the primary targets of government control.

The prosecution of drug-addicted mothers implicates two fundamental tensions. First, punishing a woman for using drugs during pregnancy pits the state's interest in protecting the future health of a child against the mother's interest in autonomy over her reproductive life—interests that until recently had not been thought to be in conflict. Second, such prosecutions represent one of two possible responses to the problem of drug-exposed babies. The government may choose either to help women have healthy pregnancies or to punish women for their prenatal conduct. Although it might seem that the state could pursue both of these avenues at once, the two responses are ultimately irreconcilable. Far from deterring injurious drug use, prosecution of drug-addicted mothers in fact deters pregnant women from using available health and counseling services because it causes women to fear that, if they seek help, they could be reported to government authorities and charged with a crime. Moreover, prosecution blinds the public to the possibility of nonpunitive solutions and to the inadequacy of the nonpunitive solutions that are currently available.

The debate between those who favor protecting the rights of the fetus and those who favor protecting the rights of the mother has been extensively waged in the literature.[6] This [essay] suggests that both sides of the debate have largely overlooked a critical aspect of government prosecution of drug-addicted mothers. Can we determine the legality of the prosecutions simply by weighing the state's abstract interest in the fetus against the mother's abstract interest in autonomy? Can we determine whether the prosecutions are fair simply by deciding the duties a pregnant woman owes to her fetus and then assessing whether the defendant has met them? Can we determine the constitutionality of the government's actions without considering the race of the women being singled out for prosecution?

Before deciding whether the state's interest in preventing harm to the fetus justifies criminal sanctions against the mother, we must first understand the mother's competing perspective and the reasons for the state's choice of a punitive response. This Article seeks to illuminate the current debate by examining the experiences of the class of women who are primarily affected—poor Black women.

Providing the perspective of poor Black women offers two advantages. First, examining legal issues from the viewpoint of those whom they affect most[7] helps to uncover the real reasons for state action and to explain the real harms that it causes. It exposes the way in which the prosecutions deny poor Black women a facet of their humanity by punishing their reproductive choices. The government's choice of a punitive response perpetuates the historical devaluation of Black women as mothers. Viewing the legal issues from the experiential standpoint of the defendants enhances our understanding of the constitutional dimensions of the state's conduct.[8]

Second, examining the constraints on poor Black women's reproductive choices expands our understanding of reproductive freedom in particular and of the right of privacy in general. Much of the literature discussing reproductive freedom has adopted a white middle-class perspective, which focuses narrowly on abortion rights. The feminist critique of privacy doctrine has also neglected many of the concerns of poor women of color.

My analysis presumes that Black women experience various forms of oppression simultaneously,[9] as a complex interaction of race, gender, and class that is more than the sum of its parts. It is impossible to isolate any one of the components of this oppression or to separate the experiences that are attributable to one component from experiences attributable to the others. The prosecution of drug-addicted mothers cannot be explained as simply an issue of gender inequality. Poor Black women have been selected for punishment as a result of an inseparable combination of their gender, race, and economic status. Their devaluation as mothers, which underlies the prosecutions, has its roots in the unique experience of slavery and has been perpetuated by complex social forces. . . .

The Devaluation of Black Motherhood

The systematic, institutionalized denial of reproductive freedom has uniquely marked Black women's history in America. An important part of this denial has been the devaluation of Black women as mothers. A popular mythology that degrades Black women and portrays them as less deserving of motherhood reinforces this subordination. This mythology is one aspect of a complex set of images that deny Black humanity in order to rationalize the oppression of Blacks.[10]

In this Part, I will discuss three manifestations of the devaluation of Black motherhood: the original exploitation of Black women during slavery, the more contemporary, disproportionate removal of Black children from their mothers' custody, and sterilization abuse. . . .

A. The Slavery Experience

The essence of Black women's experience during slavery was the brutal denial of autonomy over reproduction. Female slaves were commercially valuable to their masters not only for their labor, but also for their capacity to produce more slaves.[11] Henry Louis Gates, Jr., writing about the autobiography of a slave named Harriet A. Jacobs, observes that it "charts in vivid detail precisely how the shape of her life and the choices she makes are defined by her reduction to a sexual object, an object to be raped, bred or abused."[12] Black women's childbearing during slavery was thus largely a product of oppression rather than an expression of self-definition and personhood.

The method of whipping pregnant slaves that was used throughout the South [described above] vividly illustrates the slaveowners' dual interest in Black women as both workers and childbearers. Slaveowners forced women to lie face down in a depression in the ground while they were whipped. This procedure allowed the masters to protect the fetus while abusing the mother. It serves as a powerful metaphor for the evils of a fetal protection policy that denies the humanity of the mother. It is also a forceful symbol of the convergent oppressions inflicted on slave women: they were subjugated at once both as Blacks and as females.

From slavery on, Black women have fallen outside the scope of the American ideal of womanhood. Slave owners forced slave women to perform strenuous labor that contradicted the Victorian female roles prevalent in the dominant white society. Angela Davis has observed: "judged by the evolving nineteenth-century ideology of femininity, which emphasized women's roles as nurturing mothers and gentle companions and housekeepers for their husbands, Black women were practically anomalies."[13] Black women's historical deviation from traditional female roles has engendered a mythology that denies their womanhood.

One of the most prevalent images of slave women was the character of Jezebel, a woman governed by her sexual desires. As early as 1736, the South Carolina Gazette described "African Ladies" as women "of 'strong robust constitution' who were 'not easily jaded out' but able to serve their lovers 'by Night as well as Day.' "[14] This ideological construct of the licentious Jezebel legitimated white men's sexual abuse of Black women. The stereotype of Black women as sexually promiscuous helped to perpetuate their devaluation as mothers.

The myth of the "bad" Black woman was deliberately and systematically perpetuated after slavery ended. For example, historian Philip A. Bruce's book, *The Plantation Negro as a Freeman,* published in 1889, strengthened popular views of both Black male and Black female degeneracy. Bruce traced the alleged propensity of the Black man to rape white women to the "wantonness of the women of his own race" and "the sexual laxness of plantation women as a class."[15] This image of the sexually loose, impure Black woman that originated in slavery persists in modern American culture.

Black women during slavery were also systematically denied the rights of motherhood. Slave mothers had no legal claim to their children. Slave masters owned not only Black women, but also their children. They alienated slave women from their children by selling them to other slaveowners and by controlling childrearing. In 1851, Sojourner Truth reminded the audience at a women's rights convention that society denied Black women even the limited dignity of Victorian womanhood accorded white women of the time, including the right of mothering:

> Dat man ober dar say dat women needs to be helped into carriages, and lifted ober ditches, and to have de best place every whar. Nobody eber help me into carriages, or ober mud puddles, or gives me any best place . . . and ar'n't I a woman? Look at me! Look at my arm! . . . I have plowed, and planted, and gathered into barns, and no man could head me—and ar'n't I a woman? I could work as much and eat as much as a man (when I could get it), and bear de lash as well—and ar'n't I a woman? I have borne thirteen children and seen em mos' all sold off into slavery, and when I cried out with a mother's grief, none but Jesus heard—and ar'n't I a woman?[16]

Black women struggled in many ways to resist the efforts of slave masters to control their reproductive lives. They used contraceptives and abortives, escaped from plantations, feigned illness, endured severe punishment, and fought back rather than submit to slave masters' sexual domination.[17] Free Black women with the means to do so purchased freedom for their daughters and sisters.[18] Black women, along with Black men, succeeded remarkably often in maintaining the integrity of their family life despite slavery's disrupting effects.[19]

B. The Disproportionate Removal of Black Children

The disproportionate number of Black mothers who lose custody of their children through the child welfare system is a contemporary manifestation of the devaluation of Black motherhood.[20] This disparate impact of state intervention results in part from Black families' higher rate of reliance on government welfare. Because welfare families are subject to supervision by social workers, instances of perceived neglect are more likely to be reported to governmental authorities than neglect on the part of more affluent parents. Black children are also removed from their homes in part because of the child welfare system's cultural bias and application of the nuclear family pattern to Black families. Black childrearing patterns that diverge from the norm of the nuclear family have been misinterpreted by government bureaucrats as child neglect. For example, child welfare workers have often failed to respect the longstanding cultural tradition in the Black community of shared parenting responsibility among blood-related and non-blood kin.[21] The state has thus been more willing to intrude upon the autonomy of poor Black families, and in particular of Black mothers, while protecting the integrity of white, middle-class homes.

This devaluation of Black motherhood has been reinforced by stereotypes that blame Black mothers for the problems of the Black family. This scapegoating of Black mothers dates back to slavery, when mothers were blamed for the devastating effects on their children of poverty and abuse of Black women. When a one-month-old slave girl named Harriet died in the Abbeville District of South Carolina on December 9, 1849, the census marshal reported the cause of death as "'[s]mothered by carelessness of [her] mother.' "[22] This report was typical of the United States census mortality schedules for the southern states in its attribution of a Black infant death to accidental suffocation by the mother. Census marshal Charles M. Pelot explained: "'I wish it to be distinctly understood that nearly all the accidents occur in the negro population, which goes clearly to prove their great carelessness & total inability to take care of themselves.' "[23] It now appears that the true cause of these suffocation deaths was Sudden Infant Death Syndrome.[24] Black children died at a dramatically higher rate because of the hard physical work, poor nutrition, and abuse that their slave mothers endured during pregnancy.

The scapegoating of Black mothers has manifested itself more recently in the myth of the Black matriarch, the domineering female head of the Black family. White sociologists have held Black matriarchs responsible for the disintegration of the Black family and the consequent failure of Black people to achieve success in America.[25] Daniel Patrick Moynihan popularized this theory in his 1965 report, *The Negro Family: The Case for National Action*. According to Moynihan:

> At the heart of the deterioration of the fabric of the Negro society is the deterioration of the Negro family. It is the fundamental cause of the weakness of the Negro community . . . . In essence, the Negro community has been forced into a matriarchal structure which, because it is so out of line with the rest of the American society, seriously retards the progress of the group as a whole.[26]

Thus, Moynihan attributed the cause of Black people's inability to overcome the effects of racism largely to the dominance of Black mothers.

C. The Sterilization of Women of Color

Coerced sterilization is one of the most extreme forms of control over a woman's reproductive life. By permanently denying her the right to bear children, sterilization enforces society's determination that a woman does not deserve to be a mother. Unlike white women, poor women of color have been subjected to sterilization abuse for decades.[27] The disproportionate sterilization of Black women is yet another manifestation of the dominant society's devaluation of Black women as mothers.

Sterilization abuse has taken the form both of blatant coercion and trickery and of subtle influences on women's decisions to be sterilized.[28] In the 1970s, some doctors conditioned delivering babies and performing abortions on Black women's consent to sterilization.[29] In a 1974 case brought by poor teenage Black women in Alabama, a federal district court found that an estimated 100,000 to 150,000 poor women were sterilized annually under federally-funded programs.[30] Some of these women were coerced into agreeing to sterilization under the threat that their welfare benefits would be withdrawn unless they submitted to the operation. Despite federal and state regulations intended to prevent involuntary sterilization, physicians and other health care providers continue to urge women of color to consent to sterilization because they view these women's family sizes as excessive and believe these women are incapable of effectively using other methods of birth control.

Current government funding policy perpetuates the encouragement of sterilization of poor, and thus of mainly Black, women. The federal government pays for sterilization services under the Medicaid program,[31] while it often does not make available information about and access to other contraceptive techniques and abortion.[32] In effect, sterilization is the only publicly-funded birth control method readily available to poor women of color.

Popular images of the undeserving Black mother legitimate government policy as well as the practices of health care providers. The myth of the Black Jezebel has been supplemented by the contemporary image of the lazy welfare mother who breeds children at the expense of taxpayers in order to increase the amount of her welfare check.[33] This view of Black motherhood provides the rationale for society's restrictions on Black female fertility.[34] It is this image of the undeserving Black mother that also ultimately underlies the government's choice to punish crack-addicted women. . . .

Unconstitutional Government Standards for Procreation: The Intersection of Privacy and Equality

The equal protection clause and the right of privacy provide the basis for two separate constitutional challenges to the prosecution of drug-addicted mothers. The singling out of Black mothers for punishment combines in a single government action several wrongs prohibited by both constitutional doctrines. Black mothers are denied autonomy over procreative decisions because of their race. The government's denial of Black women's fundamental right to choose to bear children serves to perpetuate the legacy of racial discrimination embodied in the devaluation of Black motherhood. The full scope of the government's violation can better be understood, then, by a constitutional theory that acknowledges the complementary and overlapping qualities of the Constitution's guarantees of equality and privacy. Viewing the prosecutions as imposing a racist government standard for procreation uses this approach.

Poor crack addicts are punished for having babies because they fail to measure up to the state's ideal of motherhood. . . . Moreover, a government policy that has the effect of punishing primarily poor Black women for having babies evokes the specter of racial eugenics, especially in light of the history of sterilization abuse of women of color. These factors make clear that these women are not punished simply because they may harm their unborn children. They are punished because the combination of their poverty, race, and drug addiction is seen to make them unworthy of procreating.

This aspect of the prosecutions implicates both equality and privacy interests. The right to bear children goes to the heart of what it means to be human. The value we place on individuals determines whether we see them as entitled to perpetuate themselves in their children. Denying someone the right to bear children—or punishing her for exercising that right—deprives her of a basic part of her humanity. When this denial is based on race, it also functions to preserve a racial hierarchy that essentially disregards Black humanity. . . .

[The] concept of privacy includes not only the negative proscription against government coercion, but also the affirmative duty of government to protect the individual's personhood from degradation and to facilitate the processes of choice and self-determination. This approach shifts the focus of privacy theory from state nonintervention to an affirmative guarantee of personhood and autonomy. Under this post-liberal doctrine, the government is not only prohibited from punishing crack-addicted women for choosing to bear children; it is also required to provide drug treatment and prenatal care. Robin West has eloquently captured this progressive understanding of the due process clause in which privacy doctrine is grounded:

> The ideal of due process, then, is an individual life free of illegitimate social coercion facilitated by hierarchies of class, gender, or race. The goal is an affir-

matively autonomous existence: a meaningfully flourishing, independent, enriched individual life.[35]

This affirmative view of privacy is enhanced by recognizing the connection between privacy and racial equality. The government's duty to guarantee personhood and autonomy stems not only from the needs of the individual, but also from the needs of the entire community. The harm caused by the prosecution of crack-addicted mothers is not simply the incursion on each individual crack addict's decisionmaking; it is the perpetuation of a degraded image that affects the status of an entire race. The devaluation of a poor Black addict's decision to bear a child is tied to the dominant society's disregard for the motherhood of all Black women. The diminished value placed on Black motherhood, in turn, is a badge of racial inferiority worn by all Black people. The affirmative view of privacy recognizes the connection between the dehumanization of the individual and the subordination of the group.

Thus, the reason that legislatures should reject laws that punish Black women's reproductive choices is not an absolute and isolated notion of individual autonomy. Rather, legislatures should reject these laws as a critical step towards eradicating a racial hierarchy that has historically demeaned Black motherhood. Respecting Black women's decision to bear children is a necessary ingredient of a community that affirms the personhood of all of its members. The right to reproductive autonomy is in this way linked to the goal of racial equality and the broader pursuit of a just society. This broader dimension of privacy's guarantees provides a stronger claim to government's affirmative responsibilities.

Feminist legal theory, with its emphasis on the law's concrete effect on the condition of women, calls for a reassessment of traditional privacy law. It may be possible, however, to reconstruct a privacy jurisprudence that retains the focus on autonomy and personhood while making privacy doctrine effective.[36] Before dismissing the right of privacy altogether, we should explore ways to give the concepts of choice and personhood more substance.[37] In this way, the continuing process of challenge and subversion—the feminist critique of liberal privacy doctrine, followed by the racial critique of the feminist analysis—will forge a finer legal tool for dismantling institutions of domination. . . .

Notes

1. Johnson, Smothered Slave Infants: Were Slave Mothers at Fault?, 47 J. Soc. Hist. 493, 513 (1981).

2. See State v. Johnson, No. E89–890-CFA, slip op. at 1 (Fla. Cir. Ct. July 13, 1989), *aff'd*, No. 89–1765, 1991 Fla. App. LEXIS 3583 (Fla. Dist. Ct. App. Apr. 18, 1991). [The case subsequently was reversed by the Florida Supreme Court, Johnson v. State, 602 So. 2d 1288 (Fla. 1992)]. . . .

3. Since 1987, at least 50 so-called "fetal abuse" cases have been brought in 19 states and the District of Columbia. See Hoffman, Pregnant, Addicted—And Guilty?, N.Y. Times, Aug. 19, 1990, §6 (Magazine), at 32, 35; see also Lewin, Drug Use in Pregnancy: New Issue for the Courts, N.Y. Times, Feb. 5, 1990, at A14, col. 1. . . .

Several courts have recently dismissed such "fetal abuse" cases. See, e.g., People v. Hardy, No. 128458, 1991 Mich. App. LEXIS 135 (Mich. Ct. App. Apr. 1, 1991); Judge Drops Charges of Delivering Drugs to an Unborn Baby, N.Y. Times, Feb. 5, 1991, at B6, col. 4.

4. According to a memorandum prepared by the ACLU Reproductive Freedom Project, of the 52 defendants, 35 are African-American, 14 are white, 2 are Latina, and 1 is Native American. See Paltrow & Shende, State by State Case Summary of Criminal Prosecutions Against Pregnant Women and Appendix of Public Health and Public Interest Groups Opposed to These Prosecutions, Oct. 29, 1990 (unpublished memorandum to ACLU Affiliates and Interested Parties); telephone interviews with Joseph Merkin, Attorney for Sharon Peters (Jan. 7, 1991), James Shields, North Carolina ACLU (Jan. 7, 1991), and Patrick Young, Attorney for Brenda Yurchak (Jan. 7, 1991); see also Kolata, Bias Seen Against Pregnant Addicts, N.Y. Times, July 20, 1990, at A13, col. 1 (indicating that of 60 women charged, 80% were minorities). . . .

5. See Hoffman, *supra* note 3, at 35 (noting that "with the exception of a few cases, prosecutors have not gone after pregnant alcoholics").

6. For arguments supporting the mother's right to autonomy, see Gallagher, Prenatal Invasions & Interventions: What's Wrong with Fetal Rights, 10 Harv. Women's L.J. 9 (1987); Goldberg, Medical Choices During Pregnancy: Whose Decision Is It Anyway?, 41 Rutgers L. Rev. 591 (1989); McNulty, Pregnancy Police: The Health Policy and Legal Implications of Punishing Pregnant Women for Harm to Their Fetuses, 16 N.Y.U. Rev. L. & Soc. Change 277, 279–290 (1988); and Note, The Creation of Fetal Rights: Conflicts with Women's Constitutional Rights to Liberty, Privacy, and Equal Protection, 95 Yale L.J. 599 (1986).

For arguments advocating protection of the fetus, see King, The Juridical Status of the Fetus: A Proposal for Legal Protection of the Unborn, 77 Mich. L. Rev. 1647, 1682–1684 (1979); Parness & Pritchard, To Be or Not to Be: Protecting the Unborn's Potentiality of Life, 51 U. Cin. L. Rev. 257, 267–286 (1982); Robertson, Procreative Liberty and the Control of Conception, Pregnancy, and Childbirth, 69 Va. L. Rev. 405, 437–443 (1983); Walker & Puzder, State Protection of the Unborn After Roe v. Wade: A Legislative Proposal, 13 Stetson L. Rev. 237, 253–263 (1984).

7. A growing body of scholarship challenges dominant-group scholars' claims to neutrality or universality. . . . Feminist legal theory is perhaps the most established example of this alternative jurisprudence. See, e.g., MacKinnon, Feminism, Marxism, Method, and the State: Toward Feminist Jurisprudence, in D. Weisberg ed., Feminist Legal Theory: Foundations 427 (Temple Univ. Press, 1993); Scales, The Emergence of Feminist Jurisprudence: An Essay, in *id.* at 40; West, Jurisprudence and Gender, in *id.*, at 75.

The scholarship of people of color is a more recent variety of alternative jurisprudence. See, e.g., D. Bell, And We Are Not Saved (1987); Cook, Beyond Critical Legal Studies: The Reconstructive Theology of Dr. Martin Luther King, Jr., 103 Harv. L. Rev. 985 (1990); Crenshaw, Race, Reform, and Retrenchment: Transformation and Legitimation in Antidiscrimination Law, 101 Harv. L. Rev. 1331 (1988). Among this latter group are scholars who, like me, are particularly concerned with the legal problems and concrete experiences of Black women. . . . See, e.g., Austin, Sapphire Bound!, herein, at 908; Harris, Race and Essentialism in Feminist Legal Theory, in Feminist Legal Theory: Foundations, *supra* note 7, at 348; Scales-Trent, Black Women and the Constitution: Finding Our Place, Asserting Our Rights, 24 Harv. C.R.-C.L. L. Rev. 9 (1989).

8. For a description and critique of feminist standpoint epistemology, see Bartlett, Feminist Legal Methods, in Feminist Legal Theory: Foundations, *supra* note 7, at 550. Bartlett criticizes feminist standpoint epistemology because it tends to standardize women's characteristics, it denies the significance of the viewpoints of non-victims, it does not explain differences of perception among women, and it engenders adversarial politics. . . . These criticisms have merit. Notwithstanding the problems inherent in adopting a general feminist standpoint epistemology, I believe there is value in the limited project of focusing on the perspective of Black women, especially because that perspective has traditionally been ignored.

9. See Harris, *supra* note 7. . . . The theme of the simultaneity of multiple forms of oppression is common in Black feminist writings. See, e.g., Combahee River Collective, A Black Feminist Statement, in C. Moraga & G. Anzaldua eds., This Bridge Called My Back: Writings By Radical Women of Color 210, 213 (1981); b. hooks, Ain't I a Woman: Black Women and Feminism 12 (1981) ("[A]t the moment of my birth, two factors determined my destiny, my having been born black and my having been born female.").

10. See, e.g., Gresham, The Politics of Family in America, Nation, July 24/31, 1989, at 120 (describing the dominant society's resistance to the concept of Black people as "vulnerable human beings"). For a discussion of the hegemonic function of racist ideology, see Crenshaw, *supra* note 7, at 1370–1381 (1988). See generally G. Frederickson, The Black Image in the White Mind 256–282 (1971) (discussing the propagation of theories of Black inferiority and degeneracy at the turn of the century); J. Williamson, The Crucible of Race: Black-White Relations in the American South Since Emancipation 111–151 (1984) (discussing the prevalence of theories near the turn of the century that Blacks, freed from slavery, were returning to their "natural state of bestiality").

11. See A. Davis, Women, Race, and Class 7 (1981); J. Jones, Labor of Love, Labor of Sorrow: Black Women, Work and the Family from Slavery to the Present 12 (1985). Legislation giving the children of Black women and white men the status of slaves left female slaves vulnerable to sexual violation as a means of financial gain. See P. Giddings, When and Where I Enter: The Impact of Black Women on Race and Sex in America 37 (1984). For a discussion of such laws in Virginia and Georgia, see A. Higginbotham, In the Matter of Color 42–45, 252 (1978).

White masters controlled their slaves' reproductive capacity by rewarding pregnancy with relief from work in the field and additions of clothing and food, punishing slave women who did not give birth, manipulating slave marital choices, forcing them to breed, and raping them. See Jones, *supra,* at 34–35; D. Sterling ed., We Are Your Sisters: Black Women in the Nineteenth Century 24–26 (1984); Clinton, Caught in the Web of the Big House: Women and Slavery, in W. Raser, R. Saunders & J. Wakelyn eds., The Web of Southern Social Relations 19, 23–28 (1985).

12. Gates, To Be Raped, Bred or Abused, N.Y. Times Book Rev., Nov. 22, 1987, at 12 (reviewing H. Jacobs, Incidents in the Life of a Slave Girl (J. Yellin ed. 1987)).

13. Davis, *supra* note 11, at 7.

14. D. White, Ar'n't I a Woman? Female Slaves in the Plantation South 30 (1985).

15. P. Bruce, The Plantation Negro as a Freeman 84–85 (1889).

16. O. Gilbert, Narrative of Sojourner Truth 133 (1878).

17. See Giddings, *supra* note 11, at 46; We Are Your Sisters, *supra* note 11, at 25–26, 58–61; White, *supra* note 14, at 76–90.

18. See Black Women in G. Lerner ed., White America 40–42 (1973). This practice is poignantly described in the words of a former slave named Anna Julia Cooper in a speech given in 1893 to the Congress of Representative Women: "Yet all through the darkest period of the colored women's oppression in this country her yet unwritten history is full of heroic struggle, a struggle against fearful and overwhelming odds, that often ended in horrible death, to maintain and protect that which woman holds dearer than life. The painful, patient, and silent toil of mothers to gain a fee simple title to the bodies of their daughters, the despairing fight, as of an entrapped tigress, to keep hallowed their own persons, would furnish material for epics." B. Loewenberg & R. Bogin eds., Black Women in Nineteenth-Century American Life 329 (1976).

19. See generally H. Gutman, The Black Family in Slavery and Freedom, 1790–1925 (1976) (describing the life of the Black family during slavery); Jones, "My Mother Was Much of a Woman": Black Women, Work, and the Family Under Slavery, 8 Feminist Stud. 235, 252–261 (1982) (describing the sexual division of labor initiated by slaves within their own communities).

20. See Gray & Nybell, Issues in African-American Family Preservation, 69 Child Welfare 513, 513 (1990) (noting that about half of the children in foster care are Black); Hogan & Sin, Minority Children and the Child Welfare System: An Historical Perspective, 33 Soc. Work 493 (1988). Once Black children enter foster care, they remain there longer and receive less desirable placements than white children; they are also less likely than white children to be returned home or adopted. See B. Mandell, Where Are the Children? A Class Analysis of Foster Care and Adoption 36 (1973); Gray & Nybell, *supra*, at 513–514; Stehno, Differential Treatment of Minority Children in Service Systems, 27 Soc. Work 39, 39–41 (1982). These realities have led some Blacks to deem foster care a system of legalized slavery. See Mandell, *supra*, at 60. Malcolm X described the state's disruption of his own family in these terms: "Soon the state people were making plans to take over all of my mother's children. . . . A Judge . . . in Lansing had authority over me and all of my brothers and sisters. We were "state children," court wards; he had the full say-so over us. A white man in charge of a black man's children! Nothing but legal, modern slavery—however kindly intentioned. . . . I truly believe that if ever a state social agency destroyed a family, it destroyed ours." M. Little, The Autobiography of Malcolm X 20–21 (1965).

21. See Stack, Cultural Perspectives on Child Welfare, 12 N.Y.U. Rev. L. & Soc. Change 539, 539–543 (1983–1984).

22. Johnson, *supra* note 1, at 493 (quoting S. Carolina Mortality Schedules, 1850, Abbeville District).

23. *Id.* at 495 (quoting S. Carolina Mortality Schedules, 1850, Abbeville District).

24. See *id.* at 496–508; Savitt, Smothering and Overlaying of Virginia Slave Children: A Suggested Explanation, 49 Bull. Hist. Med. 400, 400 (1975).

25. See Giddings, *supra* note 11, at 325–335 (1984); hooks, *supra* note 9, at 70–83; R. Staples, The Black Woman in America 10–34 (1976); Gresham, *supra* note 10, at 117–118.

26. Office of Planning & Policy Research, U.S. Dept. of Labor, The Negro Family: The Case for National Action 5 (1965).

27. See Davis, *supra* note 11, at 215–221; Nsiah-Jefferson, Reproductive Laws, Women of Color, and Low-Income Women, herein, at 1007. One study found that 43% of women sterilized in 1973 under a federally funded program were Black, although only 33% of the patients were Black. See Note, Sterilization Abuse: Current State of the

Law and Remedies for Abuse, 10 Golden Gate U.L. Rev. 1147, 1153 n.30 (1980). Spanish-speaking women are twice as likely to be sterilized as those who speak English. See Levin & Taub, Reproductive Rights, in C. Lefcourt ed., Women and the Law §10A.07 [3][b], at 10A-28 (1989). . . .

28. See Clarke, Subtle Forms of Sterilization Abuse: A Reproductive Rights Analysis, in R. Arditti, R. Klein & S. Minden eds., Test-Tube Women 120, 120–132 (1984); Nsiah-Jefferson, *supra* note 27, at 1014; Petchesky, Reproduction, Ethics, and Public Policy: The Federal Sterlization Regulations, 9 Hastings Center Rep. 29, 32 (1979).

29. See Nsiah-Jefferson, *supra* note 27, at 1014.

30. See Relf v. Weinberger, 372 F.Supp. 1196, 1199 (D.D.C. 1974), *on remand sub nom.* Relf v. Mathews, 403 F. Supp. 1235 (D.D.C. 1975), *vacated sub nom.* Relf v. Weinberger, 565 F.2d 722 (D.C. Cir. 1977).

31. Subchapters XIX and XX of the Social Security Act provide matching funds for sterilization reimbursement. See 42 U.S.C. §§1396a(10) (A), 1397a(a)(2)(1988).

32. See Petchesky, *supra* note 28, at 39; Note, *supra* note 27, at 1154.

33. See Harrington, Introduction to S. Sheehan, A Welfare Mother at x–xi (1976); Milwaukee County Welfare Rights Org., Welfare Mothers Speak Out 72–92 (1972). In a chapter entitled "Welfare Mythology," the Milwaukee County Welfare Rights Organization portrays a common image of welfare mothers: "You give those lazy, shiftless good-for-nothings an inch and they'll take a mile. You have to make it tougher on them. They're getting away with murder now. You have to catch all those cheaters and put them to work or put them in jail. Get them off the welfare rolls. I'm tired of those niggers coming to our state to get on welfare. I'm tired of paying their bills just so they can sit around home having babies, watching their color televisions, and driving Cadillacs." *Id.* at 72. Writers in the 1980s claimed that welfare induces poor Black women to have babies. See, e.g., C. Murray, Losing Ground 154–166 (1984). Other researchers have refuted this claim. See, e.g., Darity & Myers, Does Welfare Dependency Cause Female Headship? The Case of the Black Family, 46 J. Marriage & Fam. 765, 773 (1984) (concluding that "[t]he attractiveness of welfare and welfare dependency exhibit no effects on black female family heads").

34. This thinking was reflected in a recent newspaper editorial suggesting that Black women on welfare should be given incentives to use Norplant, a new contraceptive. See Poverty and Norplant: Can Contraception Reduce the Underclass?, Phila. Inquirer, Dec. 12, 1990, at A18, col. 1. On January 2, 1991, a California judge ordered a Black woman on welfare who was convicted of child abuse to use Norplant for three years as a condition of probation. See Lev, Judge Is Firm on Forced Contraception, but Welcomes an Appeal, N.Y. Times, Jan. 11, 1991, at A17, col. 1; see also Lewin, Implanted Birth Control Device Renews Debate over Forced Contraception, N.Y. Times, Jan. 10, 1991, at A20 col. 1 (reviewing the debate on forced use of Norplant). . . .

35. West, Progressive and Conservative Constitutionalism, 88 Mich. L. Rev. 641, 707 (1990).

36. The word "privacy" may be too imbued with limiting liberal interpretation to be a useful descriptive term. "Privacy" connotes shielding from intrusion and thus may be suitable to describe solely the negative proscription against government action. Moreover, the word conjures up the public-private dichotomy. "Liberty," on the other hand, has more potential to include the affirmative duty of government to ensure the conditions necessary for autonomy and self-definition. In reconstructing the constitutional guarantees I have been discussing, it may be more appropriate to rely on the

broader concept of "liberty." See A. Allen, Uneasy Access: Privacy for Women in a Free Society 98–101 (1988) (discussing the differences between the "liberty" and "privacy").

37. In answering the critical legal studies' critique of rights, Patricia Williams notes that oppression is the result not of "rights-*assertion*," but of a failure of "rights-*commitment*." Williams, Alchemical Notes: Reconstructing Ideals from Deconstructed Rights, in Feminist Legal Theory: Foundations, *supra* note 7, at 496, 503 (emphasis in original). In the same way, the concepts of choice, personhood, and autonomy that are central to privacy doctrine are not inherently oppressive, any more than is the concept of equality (which has also been interpreted in ways that perpetuate hierarchy and domination). It is the . . . liberal notions—such as negative rights, neutral principles, the public-private dichotomy, and formal equality—that have limited privacy's usefulness for attaining reproductive freedom. See Matsuda, Looking to the Bottom: Critical Legal Studies and Reparations, 22 Harv. C.R.-C.L. L. Rev. 323, 334–335 (1987) (demonstrating how women and people of color can adopt and transform constitutional text for radical objectives).

The Colonization of the Womb

NANCY EHRENREICH

[THIS ESSAY FOCUSES] on instances of forced medical treatment during pregnancy (especially Cesarean sections),[1] . . . It is impossible to fully understand why courts have been willing to coercively intervene in certain women's reproductive lives without understanding such cases as power struggles—struggles over the control of reproduction and the meaning of motherhood. . . .

DUALISTIC IMAGES AND DIFFERENTIAL TREATMENT

. . .

Good Patients and Bad Patients: The Images in the Medical Context

. . . Several studies have found that poor women of color receive different treatment at the hands of medical professionals than do privileged European-American women, and that that treatment is associated with negative stereotypes about such women.[2] Sociologist Alexandra Dundas Todd, in her study of interactions between gynecologists and women patients, found that

> the darker a woman's skin and/or the lower her place on the economic scale, the poorer the care and efforts at explanation she received. Women of color and/or an economically poor background were more apt to be seen as "difficult" patients when they asked questions, were more likely . . . to be talked down to, scolded, and patronized.[3]

Todd reports that such women were also more likely to be urged to use the Pill or the IUD—both of which are often dangerous, uncomfortable, or painful—as birth control methods, rather than the diaphragm. She attributes this differential treatment to the fact that low-income white women and women of color were generally perceived as too unintelligent, irresponsible, or unmotivated to use a method such as the diaphragm.[4]

---

43 Duke L. J. 492 (1993).

Physicians perceive minority women not only as noncompliant patients but also as litigious ones. Contrary to reality, they believe that poor patients are generally more likely to sue than other patients[5] and therefore (given the conflation of the categories) assumedly think the same of most women of color. They also are much more likely to suspect that such women are drug abusers. In a study published in the *New England Journal of Medicine*, African-American mothers were found to be ten times more likely to be screened and reported for substance abuse during pregnancy than white mothers, although the actual levels of drug use in the two populations were comparable.[6]

[I]n the Cesarean section context this pattern continues. The leading study in the area, a national survey covering forty-five states and the District of Columbia, found that of the women subjected to court-ordered Cesarean sections, 80% were women of color (47% African-American, 33% African or Asian) and only 20% were white Americans. Fifty percent were unmarried, and 27% did not speak English as their primary language.[7] All of the women either were treated in a teaching-hospital clinic or were receiving public assistance.[8] . . .

Although this study does not provide detailed accounts of the physicians' justifications for seeking intervention in these instances, the language used in case reports about forced Cesarean sections suggests that the doctors tend to see the women against whom they seek such orders as bad mothers.[9] For example, in one article on the subject, four obstetricians speculated that when a woman refuses surgical intervention in her labor, "[i]t is probable that the patient hopes to be freed in this way of [a] pregnancy . . . undesired because it is an unplanned pregnancy, the woman is divorced or widowed, the pregnancy is an extramarital one, there are inheritance problems, etc."[10] Another case report relates that the doctors and nurses attending the woman in question viewed her refusal of the surgery as evidencing "unreasonable insensitivity to the welfare of her infant," and that they were "bewildered and angered by her attitude and stubbornness."[11] The authors of this article also made a point of mentioning that the woman lost custody of her children several months after undergoing the forced Cesarean. Since, as the article states, this ruling was unrelated to the events surrounding the birth, it is difficult to avoid drawing the conclusion that the authors mention it only because they view it as confirming their negative assessment of the woman's character and thereby mean to suggest that refusing the Cesarean itself was also a neglectful act.

The dynamic operating here is more complicated, however. . . . Cesareans are provided, in general, at a much higher rate to affluent women than to poor women.[12] Since minorities are a disproportionately large share of the poor, it is therefore likely that Cesareans also are provided at a higher rate to white women than to women of color. Given that the primary reason for ordering a Cesarean is concern for the welfare of the fetus, these data make one wonder whether the difference in rates might suggest greater physician concern about affluent white fetuses than black, brown, or low-income white ones.[13] The greater rate of prescribing the surgery for privileged women also, of course, makes the prevalence of court-ordered C-sections for outsider women all the more striking.

In that respect, the Cesarean data epitomize the situation in which outsider women find themselves in the medical realm, where they are often simultaneously coerced into undergoing some procedures and deprived of access to others. A brief reference to history sheds some light on this apparently contradictory situation. At the inception of the birth control movement of the late nineteenth and early twentieth centuries, Margaret Sanger and other activists presented contraception as a woman's right. These reformers, primarily upper-class white women, saw birth control as a privilege—as part of their autonomy over their bodies. However, the movement spearheaded by the American Birth Control League eventually took on a eugenic flavor, and, by the time it became associated with the efforts of the Eugenics Society and focused its efforts on getting contraceptives to low-income women, birth control had become an obligation, rather than a right.[14]

[A] similar dynamic may be at work here. When a laboring woman is defined as a good girl, the physician is likely to have concern for the well-being of her child and to offer the surgery to her as valuable medical technology. In the event that she refuses it, however, her motivations are not as likely to be questioned, her autonomy is likely to be valued, and she is unlikely to be ordered to comply with the doctor's advice. In contrast, when the laboring woman is seen as a bad girl, reduced concern for her offspring (and, probably, less medical insurance coverage for surgeries) translates into fewer offers of C-sections. However, the concomitant lack of trust in her maternal judgment and selflessness is reflected in a perceived need to coerce her into complying with the doctor's orders. Just as Sanger trusted privileged women, but not outsider women, to make "responsible" reproductive decisions, so in this context physicians and judges are not willing to trust the judgments of those not of their kind. Furthermore, in both situations, that distrust expresses a reaction to outsider women's failure to comply with white middle-class behavioral norms, such as limiting family size or obeying doctors. In short, both Sanger's movement and modern medical practices coercively impose one group's norms on another.

Historically, outsider women have been plagued not only by medical acceptance of this bad mother image but also by physicians' belief that such women are somehow less than human. For example, female slaves were used as guinea pigs in the nineteenth century by an obstetrical surgeon who believed that they were impervious to the pain involved.[15] More recently, women of color not only have been the unknowing subjects of experimentation but also have been subjected to unnecessary procedures, such as hysterectomies, in order to train medical residents.[16] Women of color also tend to receive less pain medication during labor than privileged women, again reflecting medical presuppositions about their strength and (supposedly) animal-like imperviousness to pain.[17] The chilling dehumanization of such patients fostered by the process of medical school socialization legitimates such practices.[18]

Good and Bad Control: The Images in the Legal Context

Discussions of Cesarean section cases by both legal academicians and judges reveal that legal assessments of such cases are affected by and reflect imagery similar to that found in medical discourse. I will discuss two examples: the work of John Robertson, a law professor who writes frequently in the area of reproductive rights and reproductive technology, and the case of In re Madyun Fetus,[19] one of the few forced Cesarean section cases for which there is a published judicial opinion. Robertson is the preeminent advocate of increased interventions in the reproductive lives of women.[20] . . . The *Madyun* case more explicitly raises race and class issues because it involved a black, Muslim woman.

Distinguishing between the freedom to procreate and freedom in procreation, Robertson argues that once a woman decides to carry her pregnancy to term she has no constitutional right to make her own decisions about how her pregnancy and labor will be conducted. Rather, she has a legal duty not to put her fetus at risk and can be subject to homicide or child abuse charges for violating that duty. This obligation would not only require a pregnant woman to accede to a Cesarean section but also would preclude her refusal of "established," "safe" fetal therapy and could be grounds for prohibiting her from smoking, drinking, or otherwise failing to maintain her own health.[21]

Robertson sees the interests at stake in coercive intervention cases as grossly unequal. The risk of a Cesarean to the fetus he correctly identifies as that of bodily injury, impairment, or death. The mother's interests, however, he defines as her "wish for vaginal delivery" or even her "insistence on vaginal delivery."[22] Similarly, in discussing home birth, Robertson identifies the woman's interest as having a "satisfying [birth] experience"[23] and opines that "[a] woman's interest in an aesthetically pleasing or emotionally satisfying birth should not be satisfied at the expense of the child's safety."[24] These statements reveal that Robertson clearly has little sympathy for women who might reject the traditional medical model by refusing surgical interventions or by birthing at home. Reducing their concerns for the safety of their infants or themselves to "aesthetic" preoccupations, he treats such women as selfish and unreasonable—concerned more with their own personal tastes than with the health and safety of their babies.

The reasons that Robertson proffers for why some mothers might refuse a Cesarean section are highly suspicious of such women's motivations and concern for their offspring. . . . The least offensive of these postulated reasons for refusal is "religious beliefs," a well-established ground for personal expressions of autonomy. Robertson does not discuss this ground separately, however, leaving the reader to assume that he considers it no more significant than any of the others. The next reason, "eccentric preferences," clearly seeks to delegitimize the woman's concerns; it suggests that they are whimsical and subjective and therefore entitled to little deference. The third reason, "idiosyncratic weightings of the values at issue," again clearly constructs the objecting woman as abnormal and outside the bounds of conventional morality. Moreover, the fact that it is values that are being weighed leads to the inescapable conclusion that Robertson believes these women might actually value their own (implicitly selfish and trivial) preferences over the safety of their children. Completely absent from this formulation is the possibility that the woman might have legitimate concerns for her own safety or that of the fetus.[25] Robertson's analysis clearly evinces neither an awareness of the history of outsider women's mistreatment at the hands of the medical profession nor any recognition that they may have legitimate reason to distrust medical diagnoses as a result. "Fear of surgery," the fourth reason, evokes the traditional disparaging image of weak femininity and suggests the need for a strong court to force the woman to do the right thing. The fifth reason, "desire not to have the child," not only questions the integrity of the mother but also sounds the theme of maternal dangerousness: these women are so evil that they would kill their fetuses just to avoid taking care of them. . . .

The opinion of Judge Richard A. Levie in *Madyun*, although much less judgmental in tone, nevertheless reveals a similar skepticism about the moral worth and decision-making capacity of the mother involved in that case. The case of Ayesha Madyun, a 19-year-old black college student experiencing her first pregnancy, was brought before the judge when physicians concluded that her labor was progressing so slowly that there was a significant risk of infection to the fetus. Ms. Madyun and her husband objected to the surgery both for religious reasons and on the ground that it was unnecessary. Concluding that the "stronger basis" for the Madyuns' position was their disbelief in the need for surgery, the judge ordered the hospital "to take such steps as are medically indicated, including but not limited to a C-section, to preserve and protect the birth and safety of the fetus."[26]

Although not questioning the genuineness of the Madyuns' feelings about their situation, Judge Levie nevertheless seemed to view their position as selfish, contending that he could not "indulge the desires of the parents" when those desires put the fetus at risk: "It is one thing," he wrote, "for an adult to gamble with nature regarding his or her own life; it is quite another when the gamble involves the life or death of an unborn infant."[27] To him, the couple was gambling—taking a high-stakes risk in the hopes of having the luck to come out unscathed. They were not engaging in reasoned decisionmaking, careful weighing of risks and benefits, or responsible parenting. Rather, they were being self-indulgent, selfishly eschewing the safe path provided by the doctors. Noting that he would not allow them to make "martyrs" of their fetus, the judge clearly saw the Madyuns' efforts as not only selfish but foolish as well. To him, they were either well-meaning but misguided zealots or reckless risk-takers.[28]

It is possible, of course, that Judge Levie was absolutely correct about the Madyuns. In the face of medical testimony that there was a 50% to 75% chance of fetal infection but only a 0.25% risk to the mother from a Cesarean,[29] the couple's objections to the surgery would no doubt have seemed unreasonable to many. If one accepts Judge Levie's conclusion that the situation posed "minimal" risks to the mother and "significant" risks to the fetus, it is difficult indeed to understand why any parents would refuse the operation other than for selfish or irrational reasons.

The judge's reliance on the medical testimony seems less understandable, however, if one probes the assumptions that underlie it. . . .

As many writers have pointed out, medicine (as practiced in the United States) conceives of female reproductive processes, from menstruation to childbirth to menopause, as pathological, disease-like conditions that need to be controlled to prevent them from harming the women in whose bodies they occur (or, in the case of childbirth, the fetuses those women are carrying).[30] . . .

Childbirth itself is also seen as a dangerous, pathological, and unpredictable medical event. The role of the physician during labor is conceptualized, therefore, as imposing control and predictability on this process (and, hence, on the women through whom it is played out). Physicians "manage" the labor, performing various interventions to assure that it proceeds along the lines of "normal" births, lines that are derived by averaging the wide range of patterns that labor actually follows among different women into a standardized set of "stages" with their own prescribed durations and symptomatology. In addition, successful childbirth has increasingly become equated with only the production of a "perfect" product, a child free of infection or disabilities. The closer a physician can get to eliminating all risk of such problems, the more likely it is that he will accomplish a "successful" birth. A concern with risk elimination thus is also an integral part of the medical model of reproduction.[31] . . .

In recent years, however, the medical model of reproduction has come under sustained attack by a burgeoning (at the beginning, primarily white) women's health movement.[32] As a result of the efforts of the National Women's Health Network, the Boston Women's Health Book Collective (authors of the well-known *Our Bodies, Ourselves*), and others, the noninterventionist, woman-oriented approach to birth that characterized the midwifery practices of the nineteenth and twentieth centuries has been revitalized. More recently, the Black Women's Health Project and other organizations have added their concern with preventing coercion and with increasing outsider women's access to medical care to the attack on the medical model. These developments have begun to expose the contingency of the medical model of birthing and have set the stage for a reinterpretation of the refusal of medical advice as resistance to prevailing forms of social power. Implicit in these attacks on the medical model have been two assertions: (1) that medicine is a cultural construct, and (2) that medicine is a hegemonic discourse. . . .

The association of medicine with reason, facts, and objectivity has been challenged through efforts to show that medicine is in fact a product of culture, rather than separate and apart from it—that it is socially constructed. These efforts have followed a number of trajectories. Historians, for example, have examined the development of obstetrics as a field of specialization during the nineteenth century, noting that the rise of the medical profession in general and obstetricians in particular occurred through the exclusion of women from medical schools and the concomitant stigmatization of female health care providers, particularly midwives.[33] This development occurred even though at the time midwives were actually providing safer and more effective care than physicians.[34] Moreover, an examination of the changing rules of thumb applied to women's reproductive and parenting behavior over the years reveals that those rules have been based as much on stereotyped images of women as on physicians' "objective" assessments of their patients' needs.

In the areas of childbirth and infant health, the rules of thumb have changed with startling rapidity. Just a generation ago, numerous behaviors and procedures were recommended that are now considered harmful. To list just a few, women were told to: (1) stringently limit weight gain during pregnancy, now considered very dangerous to the fetus; (2) feed infants on rigid feeding schedules, now considered unnecessary, if not cruel; (3) use infant formula, rather than breast milk, despite the latter's natural antibodies and freedom from contamination; (4) take diethylstil-bestrol (DES) to prevent miscarriage, although it was carcinogenic and useless as a miscarriage-preventative; (5) ease labor with pain-relieving medicines that drugged their babies; and (6) accept elective induction of labor (through physician rupturing of the membranes), which can result in stronger contractions that damage infants' skulls, cut off infants' oxygen supply, and rupture women's uteri.[35] The definition of "failure to progress," one of the most common "indicators" for a Cesarean, also has changed over the years; a woman is now allowed to labor less time before she will be so labelled.[36] Similarly, the accepted medical practice of prohibiting a woman who has undergone one C-section from delivering vaginally has now been nearly universally condemned.[37]

These numerous and significant changes in conventional medical wisdom are not simply part of some inevitable, progressive process of improvement in medical knowledge. Many of the changes, including, for example, the recent increased awareness of the overuse of Cesareans, came about as the result of pressure exerted by the women's health movement and proponents of alternative birthing practices. Furthermore, analysts have tied such changes in medical "truths" to changes in societal images of women.[38]

. . . By identifying the cultural content of medical verities of a hundred, fifty, or even ten years ago, critics raise questions about the "truth" of those espoused today. In revealing that medical knowledge is socially constructed, they also draw attention to the particular ideological messages . . . that produce and legitimate that knowledge. . . .

[W]hether one focuses on outsider women's struggles for survival against open coercion and violence or on privileged women's acquiescence in a demeaning and disempowering conceptualization of their social role, refusals to accede to doctors' orders take on a new light when birthing is seen as the site of struggle and resistance. . . .

In refusing a Cesarean section, a woman is resisting a patriarchal view of herself and her role in reproduction. A high-income white woman who rejects the medical model of childbirth is resisting a vision of herself as an object to be "managed," as passive, incompetent, selfless, and emotional. Moreover, she is resisting an image of the reproductive process as a pathological, flawed undertaking fraught with danger, and of her own body as incompetent, threatening, and out of control. A low-income woman of color who refuses a C-section is rejecting not only the notion that her body is dangerous but also an image of herself as stupid, irresponsible, and selfish and as impervious to pain, discomfort, or inconvenience. . . .

Refusal of a Cesarean not only challenges applicable gender categories but also violates the prevailing norm of obedience to medical authority. . . .

Law and Medicine as Mutually Legitimating Discourses and Practices

If the refusal of a [Cesarean] section can be interpreted as resistance to the dominant ideology, a court-ordered Cesarean section is an overt repression of alternative actions and alternative ways of knowing. A court-ordered Cesarean section not only determines the authority of a particular doctor over a particular woman, it confirms medical authority in birthing.[39]

. . . Legal authorities in general pay great deference to medical expertise. The most obvious example of this deference, of course, is the retention of a custom standard to define medical malpractice. Whereas negligent behavior in the vast majority of activities is judged by a reasonable person standard, medicine (along with other professions) is allowed to be its own judge, with the standard of care for malpractice suits defined as what a reasonably prudent physician (not layperson) would do. Although the courts rejected more than sixty years ago the notion that ship captains or masons or police officers should be allowed to set their own standards,[40] physicians are still thought appropriately to do so.[41] While judges apparently feel perfectly comfortable deciding (or asking a jury to decide) what constitutes reasonable care for other holders of technical knowledge (based, of course, on expert testimony), they are apparently very uneasy doing what seems to be the second-guessing of doctors.

In the area of reproduction, this judicial deference to medical authority is particularly marked. The grandfather opinion establishing physicians as the gatekeepers of women's reproductive rights is, of course, Justice Blackmun's opinion in Roe v. Wade. Despite his obvious concern for women required to undergo forced childbirth, Justice Blackmun nevertheless "subsumed the woman's right to privacy within the ambit of the doctor-patient relationship, and ultimately subordinated her interest to the physician's."[42] Characterizing the abortion decision as primarily a medical, rather than a moral, one, Justice Blackmun articulated the *Roe* right as the right of "the attending physician, in consultation with his patient . . . to determine . . . that, in his medical judgment, the patient's pregnancy should be terminated."[43] Thus, even the foundational reproductive rights case really only gives the woman the right to have a doctor decide for her. . . .

Deference can be particularly extreme in the Cesarean section context. Susan Irwin and Brigitte Jordan, in their study of nine forced C-section cases, report that judges are much more likely to listen to medical testimony, which tends to be stated in numbers, than to the testimony of the woman herself, which tends to be stated in experiential terms.[44] More importantly, judges in the cases those authors reviewed overvalued both medical opinion and machine data, causing Irwin and Jordan to note that "if produced by the medical staff any number, reasonable or not, had legitimacy."[45] In contrast, the more "contextualized" knowledge conveyed by laboring women, such as conclusions based on accounts of their previous labors, was "easily dismissed as personal, subjective, idiosyncratic . . . in a word, unscientific."[46] Moreover, any one medical opinion was treated as authoritative, with no attempts made to obtain conflicting opinion from, for example, physicians outside the hospital involved,[47] and with no concern expressed that testimony elicited from only one or two doctors might prove unreliable.

When considered in light of the sets of associations previously described, law's great deference to medicine is perhaps not surprising. [L]aw is associated with many of the same traits as medicine. Both are thought to be neutral and objective pursuits, devoid of personal bias or subjective self-interest. Both are seen as coldly rational—as based on facts and rules, rather than opinions and values. Moreover, both are seen as controlling people: whereas medicine controls their physical bodies, law controls the body politic, providing a peaceful means for resolving disputes that otherwise might dissolve into warfare. Put another way, medicine controls physical nature, whereas law avoids a social "state of nature." Finally, both fields are populated by elite white men who enjoy very comfortable incomes and high status. Given these affinities, judicial trust in the medical profession to make dispassionate and value-free decisions in individual cases is not surprising.

Because law and medicine are thought to share these valued traits, judicial deference to medicine does not undermine the legitimacy of law but rather reinforces it. If we accept that the types of situations addressed in this Article pose justiciable issues—that is, if we accept that judges have any business deciding whether a woman can be forced to undergo Cesarean surgery in any particular instance (itself a debatable point)[48]—then the stricture that such decisions be reached neutrally, objectively, and dispassionately comes into play. Presumably believing themselves to be operating under such a stricture, judges are probably loathe to base their decisions on criteria that seem subjective, interested, or emotional. A particular party's own assessment of the situation is always suspect in law; in the birthing context, the female patient's views are paradigmatically subjective, with all the negative connotations. In contrast, by deferring to the medical professionals who testify in such a case, the court preserves its neutral image.

Deferring to medical opinion thus legitimates judicial power. Were a court to acknowledge that there is more than one effective way to give birth, it would have to acknowledge as well that birthing is a contested terrain, in which battles over social power are waged. In contrast, by perceiving and presenting its decision as based on rational medical assessment, the court obscures the possibility that the decision is instead the product of some combination of race, class, and gender assumptions or of the court's own vision of the good life. Constructing the choice as between superstition and self-interest, on the one hand, and science and disinterest, on the other, judicial deference precludes the possibility that the court's decision effectuates instead a choice between male and female control of reproduction.

Court-ordered C-sections not only legitimate the judicial system but also reinforce the cultural authority of the medical profession. By treating the physician as the only legitimate source of information about the woman's body and the birthing process, judicial decisions ordering such surgeries both rely upon and express the assumption that medical knowledge is monolithic. By devaluing other types of knowledge—whether the individual woman's or the alternative birth movement's—and by placing the power of the state behind the physician's decision, "court-ordered cesarean sections maintain medical authority by contributing to the reproduction of relations in which physicians control birthing."[49] Judicial deference to medical opinion in such cases also confirms the objectivity and neutrality of medical judgments, and thereby obscures the operation of social power in those judgments. Since courts are thought to base their decisions in such cases on facts, not values, their reliance on medical testimony gives credence to medicine's self-presentation. Indeed, the lack of attention given to the views of the women patients themselves contrasts with that given the physicians, creating the distinct impression that courts are discerning in the types of evidence they will accept and thereby redounding to the benefit of the doctors (as well as the judges). Thus, just as medicine's image as objective science provides the basis on which legal choices about who controls reproduction can be presented as distanced and objective dispute resolution, so law's image as rational and unbiased provides the basis on which medical decisions about who controls reproduction can be presented as the product of neutral scientific judgment.

In summary, court-ordered Cesarean sections can be seen, not as deserved control of dangerous women, but rather as coercive responses to acts of resistance by outsider women who seek to prevent the control of their reproductive activities by privileged men. The relationship between the medical and legal professions, however, prevents the recognition of this aspect of such interactions. By mutually reinforcing each other's objectivity and neutrality, medicine and law obscure the social power that they together exert. . . .

Notes

1. A national survey of court-ordered obstetrical procedures recently conducted revealed that of 15 court orders for Cesarean sections that had been sought in 11 states, 14 were obtained. Veronika E. B. Kolder et al., Court-Ordered Obstetrical Interventions, 316 New Eng. J. Med. 1192, 1193 (1987). . . . Moreover, there is some indication that doctors may be performing C-sections on women without obtaining either consent or a court order. Susan Irwin & Brigitte Jordan, Knowledge, Practice, and Power: Court-Ordered Cesarean Sections, 1 Med. Anthropology Q. 319, 332 n.15 (1987); Ronna Jurow & Richard H. Paul, Cesarean Delivery for Fetal Distress Without Maternal Consent, 63 Obstetrics & Gynecology 596, 596–598 (1984) (reporting that such unauthorized surgeries occur).

Probably due to the fact that the birth of the child renders any subsequent appeal moot, there are very few reported cases of court-ordered Cesareans. I have identified only three: In re A.C., 573 A.2d 1235 (D.C. 1990) (en banc); In re Madyun Fetus, 114 Daily Wash. L. Rep. 2233 (D.C. Super. Ct. 1986); and Jefferson v. Griffin Spalding County Hosp. Auth., 274 S.E.2d 457 (Ga. 1981). For discussions of unreported cases, see Irwin & Jordan, *supra*, at 321–325; Nancy K. Rhoden, The Judge in the Delivery Room: The Emergence of Court-Ordered Cesareans, 74 Cal. L. Rev. 1951, 1951 n.4 (1986). . . .

2. See, e.g., Julia A. Boyd, Ethics and Cultural Diversity in Feminist Theory: Keys to Power, in Evelyn C. White ed., The Black Women's Health Book at 226–234 (1990) (describing barriers to adequate psychiatric treatment of black women); Vida L. Jones, Lupus and Black Women: Managing a Complex Chronic Disability, in *id.* at 160, 164 (discussing the effect of racial bias on diagnoses of lupus).

3. Alexandra D. Todd, Intimate Adversaries 77 (1989).

4. See, e.g., *id.* at 73–74. . . .

5. Molly McNulty, Pregnancy Police: The Health Policy and Legal Implications of Punishing Pregnant Women for Harm to Their Fetuses, 16 N.Y.U. Rev. L. & Soc. Change 277, 298 (1987–1988).

6. Ira J. Chasnoff et al., The Prevalence of Illicit-Drug or Alchohol Use During Pregnancy and Discrepancies in Mandatory Reporting in Pinnelas County, Florida, 322 New Eng. J. Med. 1202 (1990).

7. Kolder et al., *supra* note 1, at 1192, 1193. It is striking that, apparently, none of these women were Latina.

8. *Id.* at 1193.

9. Lisa Ikemoto has similarly argued that both judges and doctors view women against whom treatment orders are sought and obtained as bad mothers. See Lisa C. Ikemoto, Furthering the Inquiry: Race, Class, and Culture in the Forced Medical Treatment of Pregnant Women, 59 Tenn. L. Rev. 487, 510–512 (1992). . . .

10. J. R. Leiberman et al., The Fetal Right to Live, 53 Obstetrics & Gynecology 515, 515 (1979).

11. Watson A. Bowes, Jr. & Brad Selgestad, Fetal Versus Maternal Rights: Medical and Legal Perspectives, 58 Obstetrics & Gynecology 209, 211 (1981). In this case, the surgery was sought for a patient who was obese, a condition that significantly raises the risks attendant to Cesareans. See George J. Annas, Forced Cesareans: The Most Unkind Cut of All, 12 Hastings Ctr. Rep., June 1982, at 16, 17.

12. Deborah A. Sullivan & Rose Weitz, Labor Pains 37 (1988); Linda R. Monroe, Affluent Women Twice as Likely as Poor to Have Cesarean Births, L.A. Times, July 27, 1989, §1, at 3.

13. The fact that affluent women have more and better insurance coverage also might explain part of the differential, but I doubt that it explains all of it. . . .

14. Angela Y. Davis, Women, Race, and Class 210–215 (1981).

15. G. J. Barker-Benfield, The Horrors of the Half-Known Life: Male Attitudes Toward Women and Sexuality in the Nineteenth-Century 101 (1976).

16. Sharon de Maehl & Linda Thurston, Crimes in the Clinic: A Report on Boston City Hospital, 2 The Second Wave 17, 17 (1973); Laurie Nsiah-Jefferson, Reproductive Laws, Women of Color, and Low-Income Women, herein, at 1014.

17. Diana Scully, Men Who Control Women's Health: The Miseducation of Obstetrician-Gynecologists 43 (1980).

18. *Id.* at 120–140. . . .

19. 114 Daily Wash. L. Rep. 2233 (D.C. Super. Ct. 1986).

20. See John A. Robertson, Embryos, Families, and Procreative Liberty: The Legal Structure of the New Reproduction, 59 S. Cal. L. Rev. 939 (1986); John A. Robertson, In the Beginning: The Legal Status of Early Embryos, 76 Va. L. Rev. 437 (1990); Robertson, Procreative Liberty and the Control of Conception, Pregnancy, and Childbirth, 69 Va. L. Rev. 405 (1983); John A. Robertson, Procreative Liberty and Human Genetics, 39 Emory L.J. 697 (1990); John A. Robertson, The Right to Procreate and In Utero Fetal Therapy, 3 J. Legal Med. 333 (1982); John A. Robertson, Surrogate Mothers: Not So Novel After All, 13 Hastings Ctr Rep., Oct. 1983, at 28.

21. A pregnant woman could even be required to undergo prenatal diagnosis, Robertson, Procreative Liberty and the Control of Conception, *supra* note 20, 449–50, and could be "excluded . . . from workplaces inimical to fetal health." *Id.* at 443.

22. *Id.* at 455.

23. *Id.* at 406. He cites this as a general concern underlying women's interests in controlling the "timing and details" of reproductive activity. *Id.*

24. *Id.* at 453.

25. *Id.* at 455 n.162. Joel Finer similarly implies that some women who refuse Cesareans are irrational. Joel J. Finer, Toward Guidelines for Compelling Cesarean

Surgery: Of Rights, Responsibility, and Decisional Authenticity, 76 Minn. L. Rev. 239, 276, 287 (1991). . . .

26. *Madyun,* 114 Daily Wash. L. Rep. 2233, 2240 (D. C. Super. Ct. 1986).

27. *Id.*

28. One can only guess what role the Madyuns' race and non-Western religion played in the judge's reaction to them. Given the statistics on forced Cesareans, it is hard to escape the conclusion that their "otherness" made it easier for him to dismiss their concerns. On the other hand, the fact that Ms. Madyun was a married woman who appeared at the hospital with her husband may very well have saved her from the dismissive treatment so often encountered by women who refuse Cesareans. See, e.g., Ikemoto, *supra* note 9, at 506 (noting that when a court has refused to order medical treatment, the woman has usually been married). . . .

29. *Madyun,* 114 Daily Wash. L. Rep. at 2239.

30. See, e.g., Emily Martin, The Woman in the Body 45 (1992) (describing how menstruation is conceived of as a dysfunctional disintegration); Barbara K. Rothman, In Labor: Women and Power in the Birthplace 36 (1991) (noting that doctors sometimes see women's reproductive processes as disease-like).

31. Nancy Rhoden, in her groundbreaking article on forced Cesarean sections, explains the "maximin" decision strategy that many obstetricians use. Rhoden, *supra* note 1, at 2017, 2021. "A maximin strategy focuses on the worst possible outcome in a situation of uncertainty (here, fetal death or damage), and takes action to prevent that outcome, regardless of the outcome's actual probability of occurrence." *Id.* at 2017. . . .

32. For a general discussion of alternative models of birthing and their criticisms of the medical model, see Raymond G. Devries, Regulating Birth: Midwives, Medicine and the Law (1985); Sullivan & Weitz, *supra* note 12; Shelly Romalis ed., Childbirth: Alternatives to Medical Control (1981).

33. See Barbara Ehrenreich & Deirdre English, For Her Own Good: 150 Years of the Experts' Advice to Women 62–88 (1978) (discussing the rise of physicians and the exclusion of midwives); Rothman, *supra* note 30.

34. Barbara Ehrenreich & Deirdre English, Witches, Midwives, and Nurses: A History of Women Healers 23–24, 34 (1973).

35. Sullivan & Weitz, *supra* note 12 at 32.

36. Rhoden, *supra* note 1, at 2017–2021.

37. See Warren E. Leary, Birth Experts Caution on Repeated Caesareans, N.Y. Times, Oct. 27, 1988, at B16. In 1985, repeat C-sections accounted for 36% of the surgeries. F. Gary Cunningham et al., Williams Obstetrics 442 (19th ed. 1993).

38. See generally Ehrenreich, *supra* note 33. As Ehrenreich points out, for example, in the nineteenth century, the rise of diagnoses of hysteria and other "female" maladies corresponded to the development of the romantic ideal of women as frail, sickly, and irrational, *id.* at 91–126, and in the mid-twentieth century, doctors' views of children as needing permissiveness directly corresponded to their perceptions of women as instinctively and ecstatically nurturing. *Id.* at 190–239.

39. Irwin & Jordan, *supra* note 1, at 331.

40. See, e.g., The T. J. Hooper, 60 F.2d 737, 740 (2d Cir.), *cert. denied,* 287 U.S. 662 (1932).

41. W. Page Keeton et al., Prosser and Keeton on the Law of Torts §32, at 189. . . .

Of course, this treatment of medicine is not unique. Lawyers and other professions also get to set their own standards. In fact, the parallels between prevailing images of, and judicial attitudes toward, law and medicine . . . may account, in part, for their similar treatment. . . .

42. Andrea Asaro, The Judicial Portrayal of the Physician in Abortion and Sterilization Decisions: The Use and Abuse of Medical Discretions, 6 Harv. Women's L.J. 51, 53 (1983) (citing *Roe,* 410 U.S. at 163).

43. 410 U.S. 113, at 163 (1973). For additional examples of judicial deference to physicians in abortion and sterilization cases, see Asaro, *supra* note 42, at 55–59, 95–98.

44. Irwin & Jordan, *supra* note 1, at 329.

45. *Id.*

46. *Id.*

47. *Id.* at 330–331. Although time constraints undoubtedly account for at least part of this failure to seek alternative medical opinions, some of the cases Irwin and Jordan describe extended over days or even weeks, *id.* at 322–323 (describing cases involving placenta previa, known well in advance of the labor), which suggests that time shortage was not the only reason for the failure.

48. See Dawn Johnsen, Shared Interests: Promoting Healthy Births Without Sacrificing Women's Liberty, 43 Hastings L.J. 569 (1991–1992); McNulty, *supra* note 5; Rhoden, *supra* note 1.

49. Irwin & Jordan, *supra* note 1, at 331.

❖ *Sapphire Bound!*

REGINA AUSTIN

. . . I GREW UP THINKING that "Sapphire" was merely a character on the Amos 'n' Andy program, a figment of a white man's racist/sexist comic imagination.[1] Little did I suspect that Sapphire was a more generally employed appellation for the stereotypical Black Bitch—tough, domineering, emasculating, strident, and shrill.[2]. . .We really cannot function effectively without coming to terms with Sapphire. . . .

A Sapphire Named Crystal

The task of articulating and advancing distinctive minority feminist jurisprudential stances will become easier as those of us interested in the status of minority women begin to analyze concrete cases and legal problems. To substantiate my point that a black feminist perspective can and must be made manifest, I have attempted to apply the rough, tentative thesis I advance above to the examination of a particular decision, Chambers v. Omaha Girls Club.[3]

The plaintiff, Crystal Chambers, was employed by the defendant Girls Club of Omaha (the Club) as an arts and crafts instructor at a facility where approximately ninety percent of the program participants were black. Two years later, Chambers, an unmarried black woman in her early twenties, was discharged from her job when she became pregnant. Her dismissal was justified by the Club's so-called "negative role model rule" which provided for the immediate discharge of staff guilty of "[n]egative role modeling for Girls Club Members," including "such things as single parent pregnancies."[4]

In her lawsuit, Crystal Chambers attacked the role model rule on several grounds. In her Title VII claims, for example, she maintained that the rule would have a disparate impact on black women because of their significantly higher fertility rate. She further asserted that her discharge constituted per se sex discrimination barred by the Pregnancy Discrimination Act of 1978. Although the soundness of these arguments

1989 Wis. L. Rev. 539. Copyright © 1989 by the Board of Regents of the University of Wisconsin System. Reprinted by permission of the Wisconsin Law Review.

was acknowledged, they were effectively countered by the business necessity and the bona fide occupational qualification defenses.

The district court ruled against Crystal Chambers because it concluded that the Club's role model rule was the product of its dedication to the goal of "helping young girls reach their fullest potential."[5] Programmatic concerns provided adequate support for the rule. According to the findings, the Club's activities were characterized by a "high staff to member ratio," "extensive contact" and "close relationships" between the staff and members, and an "open, comfortable atmosphere."[6] "Model" behavior by the staff and imitation by the members were essential to the Club's agenda:

> Those closely associated with the Girls Club contend that because of the unique nature of the Girls Club's operations, each activity, formal or informal, is premised upon the belief that the girls will or do emulate, at least in part, the behavior of staff personnel. Each staff member is trained and expected to act as a role model and is required, as a matter of policy, to be committed to the Girls Club philosophies so that the messages of the Girls Club can be conveyed with credibility.[7]

The Club's goal was to expose its members "to the greatest number of available positive options in life."[8] "[T]eenage pregnancy [was] contrary to this purpose and philosophy" because it "severely limit[s] the available opportunities for teenage girls."[9] Citing plaintiff's expert, the court stated that "[t]eenage pregnancy often deprives young women of educational, social and occupational opportunities, creating serious problems for both the family and society."[10] The Club had several programs that related to pregnancy prevention.

In the opinion of the district court, the Club "established that it honestly believed that to permit single pregnant staff members to work with the girls would convey the impression that the Girls Club condoned pregnancy for the girls in the age group it serves."[11] Furthermore, "[w]hile a single pregnant working woman may, indeed, provide a good example of hard work and independence, the same person may be a negative role model with respect to the Girls Club objective of diminishing the number of teenage pregnancies."[12] The Club pointed to the reaction of two members to the earlier pregnancies of other single staffers in accounting for the genesis of the rule. In one case, a member who stated "that she wanted to have a baby as cute" as that of a staff member became pregnant shortly thereafter. In the second, a member became upset upon hearing of the pregnancy of an unmarried staff member.

As painted by the court, there were numerous indications that the operative animus behind the role model rule was paternalistic, not racist or sexist. The North Omaha facility was "purposefully located to better serve a primarily black population."[13] Although the Club's principal administrators were white, the girls served were black, the staff was black, and Crystal Chambers' replacement was black. "[G]reat sensitivity" was shown to the problems of the staff members, including those who were black, pregnant, and unmarried.[14] Plaintiff was even offered help in finding other employment after she was fired.

The district court concluded its opinion as follows:

> This Court believes that the policy is a legitimate attempt by a private service organization to attack a significant problem within our society. The evidence has shown that the Girls Club did not intentionally discriminate against the plaintiff and that the policy is related to the Girls Club's central purpose of fostering growth and maturity of young girls. . . . The Court emphasizes, however, that this decision is based upon the *unique* mission of the Girls Club of Omaha, the age group of the young women served, the geographic locations of the Girls Club facilities, and the comprehensive and historical methods the organization has employed in addressing the problem of teenage pregnancy. . . . [15]

There were dissenting views among the Eighth Circuit judges who considered the case. In opposing the judgment in the Club's favor, Judge McMillian demanded hard evidence to support the legality of the negative role model rule:

> Neither an employer's sincere belief, without more, (nor a district court's belief), that a discriminatory employment practice is related and necessary to the accomplishments of the employer's goals is sufficient to establish a BFOQ or business necessity defense. The fact that the goals are laudable and the beliefs sincerely held does not substitute for data which demonstrate a relationship between the discriminatory practice and the goals. [16]

For those who have no understanding of the historical oppression of black women and no appreciation of the diversity of their contemporary cultural practices, the outcome of the *Chambers* case might have a certain policy appeal, one born of sympathy for poor black youngsters and desperation about stemming "the epidemic" of teenage pregnancy that plagues them. [17] According to such an assessment, the Club's hope that its members could be influenced by committed counselors who, by example, would prove that life offers more attractive alternatives than early pregnancy and single parenthood was at worst benign, if it was not benevolent.

But for better informed, more critical evaluators, the opinions are profoundly disturbing. Firing a young unmarried, pregnant black worker in the name of protecting other young black females from the limited options associated with early and unwed motherhood is ironic, to say the least. The Club managed to replicate the very economic hardships and social biases that, according to the district court, made the role model rule necessary in the first place. Crystal Chambers was not much older than some of the Club members and her financial and social status after being fired was probably not that much different from what the members would face if they became pregnant at an early age, without the benefit of a job or the assistance of a fully employed helpmate. On the other hand, she was in many respects better off than many teen mothers. She was in her early twenties and had a decent job. Chambers' condition became problematic because of the enforcement of the role model rule.

The material consequences that befell Crystal Chambers, and that plague other black women who have children despite their supposed role modeling responsibilities, are not inherent by-products of single pregnancy and motherhood. The condemnation and the economic hardships that follow in its wake are politically and socially contingent. Furthermore, they are not the product of a consensus that holds across race, sex, and class boundaries.

Judged by the values and behavior that are said to be indigenous to low-income, black communities of the sort from which the Club members came, sacking pregnant unmarried Crystal Chambers was not a "womanly" move. It was cold. The Club's actions stand in stark contrast to the tolerance pregnant teens and young single mothers report receiving from their female relatives and peers.[18] Although disapproving of teenage pregnancy, black culture in general does not support abandoning the mothers or stigmatizing their offspring. Allowing for cultural heterogeneity, it is entirely possible that the black people of Omaha approved of the Club's actions. By and large, however, excluding young mothers and their children from good standing in the community would not strike most black women as being fair, feasible, or feminine.

This perspective is informed by a broader understanding of the exaggerated hostility that is generated by the pregnancies of poor, young, unmarried black females whose customs and conventions concerning childbearing and motherhood diverge from those of the mainstream. Because essentialist notions suggest that they cannot be harmed by those who are of the same gender and/or race, these females are vulnerable to the insidiously detrimental ministrations of do-good white women and "bougie"[19] blacks. Moreover, middle-aged meddlers of every sort feel themselves entitled to heap upon these females a wisdom that has little to recommend it beyond the fact that its proponents have lived longer. If young unmarried black pregnant workers are to be adequately protected, the pregnancy discrimination law, in conjunction with provisions directed at racial and sexual oppression, must assure them working conditions that acknowledge the reproductive norms not only of females as opposed to males, but also of blacks as opposed to whites, of the young as opposed to the old, and of poor and working folks as opposed to the middle class.

Implicit in the *Chambers* decision, however, is an assumption that the actual cultural practices and articulated moral positions of the black females who know the struggles of early and single motherhood firsthand are both misguided and destructive. The older women are apparently so outrageous that they represent a grave threat to their own daughters. Yet, for some of us, their portrayal in the *Chambers* opinions is more flattering than the authors intended. Grounded in a culture that turns "bad" (pronounced "baaad") on its head and declares conduct that offends the white, male, and middle-class establishments, wily, audacious, and good, a black feminist scholar has to wonder whether the villainous black women one discerns lurking in the interstices of the opinions are not doing something right. A black feminist jurisprudential analysis of *Chambers* must seriously consider the possibility that young, single, sexually active, fertile, and nurturing black women are being viewed ominously because they have the temerity to attempt to break out of the rigid economic, social, and political categories that a racist, sexist, and the class-stratified society would impose upon them.

Although the outcome hinged upon it, the opinions are awfully vague about the adverse effect continued employment of an unmarried pregnant arts and crafts instructor would have had in promoting teenage pregnancy among the young black Club members. I want to suggest a few possible relationships whose plausibility is attributable to a deep suspicion of black women's sexuality and an intense desire to control their "excessive" promiscuity and fecundity. The first is reminiscent of a bad joke. The Club and the courts conceivably subscribe to a theory of reproduction, that can only be termed "primitive," which posits that simply seeing an unmarried pregnant woman can have such a powerful impact on adolescent females that they will be moved to imitate her by becoming pregnant themselves. If the girls are poor and they and the woman are black, such a hypothesis might be given credence in some quarters. Under it, Crystal Chambers' mere pregnant presence at the Club would be considered a corrupting influence in light of the Club's goals. Surely, the Club and the courts do not believe that black teenage pregnancy is the product of social voyeurism or a female variant of "reckless eyeballing."[20]

It is more likely that unmarried, pregnant Crystal was thought to be a problem because she functioned as an icon, a reminder of a powerful culture from which the Club members had to be rescued. The Club was supposed to be a wholesome haven where young black girls would be introduced to an alternative array of positive life choices. Crystal Chambers tainted the environment by introducing into it the messy, corrupting cultural orientations that were the target of the Club's "repress and replace" mission.

There is a widespread belief that poor black women who raise children alone in socially and economically isolated enclaves encourage teenage pregnancy by example, subsidize it through informal friendship and extended family networks, and justify it by prizing motherhood, devaluing marriage, and condoning welfare dependency. Operating on similar assumptions, the Club set about exposing (literally it seems) its young members to counterimages that would act as antidotes to the messages they absorbed at home. In a newspaper story concerning Chambers' lawsuit, the attorney for the Club stated that while there was no intent "to condemn any parent of these girls or any of the parent's life decisions," the Club did undertake to introduce the young members to alternatives that were different from those of the "girl's home life."[21] The attorney continued, "We're trying to say that at age 14, girls aren't necessarily emotionally mature enough to make the decision to voluntarily get pregnant. Their parents may have been."[22] The Omaha World-Herald ran an editorial in support of the firing that continued the theme. The editorial states:

> The absence of strong family structures among many poor blacks has long been identified as a major obstacle to blacks' entering the mainstream. A high rate of out-of-wedlock pregnancies among poor blacks contributes both to the perpetuation of the poverty cycle and to the weakness of families caught in that cycle.[23]

The editorial further argues that if, as Crystal Chambers asserted, "'half the girls at the club have mothers who aren't married,'" that is "one of the reasons the dismissal policy makes the sense."[24]

This assessment of the dangerousness of the mothers whose ranks Crystal was about to join attributes to black teenagers a level of passivity not often associated with adolescence. Looking to their parents' cultural orientations to explain teenage pregnancy may be giving the teens too little credit for attempting to shape the course of their own lives. It also attributes too much power to parents whose economic and social standing renders them impotent to control either their children's life chances or lives.

Furthermore, the Club's conduct is indicative of the way in which the battle to curb black teenage pregnancy via the use of role models has become a pretext for continuing and expanding the economic and ideological war on unwed black mothers. The stress on the impact on teenage pregnancy of single middle-class role models who opt to have children is furnishing the opportunity to add a new twist to the historical efforts to ridicule and control black women's sexuality and reproduction.

Although Crystal Chambers' firing was publicly justified on the ground that she would have an adverse impact on the young Club members, it is likely that the Club in part sacked her because she resisted its effort to model her in conformity with white and middle-class morality. In its struggles against the culture of the girls' mothers, Crystal Chambers, employee and arts and crafts instructor, was supposed to be on the Club's side. But like a treasonous recruit, Crystal turned up unmarried and pregnant. As such, she embodied the enemy. If the Club could not succeed in shaping and restraining the workers whose economic welfare it controlled, how could it expect to win over the young members and supplant their mothers' cultural legacy. The requirement that one allow one's self to be modeled in order to keep one's job is not limited to blacks who are young fertile females. To a certain extent, the trouble Crystal Chambers encountered is a generic infliction suffered by black role models on both sexes and all ages who reject the part and become rebellious renegades or traitors to the cause of black cultural containment.

In sum, then, faulty conceptions of "role modeling" lie at the heart of the policy basis of the *Chambers* decision. . . .

Role models are not an adequate response to material conditions that limit the choices of young black women, both those who get pregnant and those who do not. . . . Material conditions have to be altered in a way that gives black youngsters the hope that they can come close to being the heroines and heroes of their own lives. To the extent that material conditions remain the same, they must be the subject of a sustained and forthright critique. Role models who do not have power to affect young women's life chances and who stand between them and the means to improve their prospects might as well be the enemy.

There are conceptions of "role modeling" that are not quite so alien to the political and cultural heritage of African-American women. As far as I am concerned, Crystal Chambers became more nearly a role model when she fought back, When she became a Sapphire. Her legal protest brought the Club's contempt for the values of the population it served into the open. Her behavior and her lawsuit challenged the hegemony of the Club's white, patriarchal, and middle-class orientation. Her single motherhood represented an alternative social form that one might choose deliberately, rationally, and proudly. She made manifest the critique that is "life-as-it-is-lived" by ordinary black single mothers. Refusing to go along with the program, she joined the host of non-elite black women who everyday mount local, small-scale resistance grounded in indigenous cultural values, values whose real political potential is often hidden even from those whose lives they govern. . . .

Notes

1. . . . Amos 'n' Andy originated as a radio comedy program about two black males. B. Andrews & A. Juilliard, Holy Mackerel! The Amos 'n' Andy Story 15–16 (1986). It was first broadcast in 1928, and the characters were played by the program's white originators. *Id.* Amos 'n' Andy came to CBS television in 1951, *id.* at 60–61, with a cast of carefully chosen black actors. *Id.* at 45–59. Various black civil rights organizations condemned the television version "as insulting to blacks" and as portraying blacks "in a stereotyped and derogatory manner." The sponsor withdrew from the show, and it was dropped by the network in 1953. *Id.* at 61, 101. It lived on in syndication until 1966. *Id.* at 118, 121–122. . . .

2. b. hooks, Ain't I a Woman: Black Women and Feminism 85–86 (1981); Scott, Debunking Sapphire: Toward a Non-Racist and Non-Sexist Social Science, in G. Hull, P. Scott & B. Smith eds., All the Women Are White, All the Blacks Are Men, But Some of Us Are Brave 85 (1982).

3. 629 F. Supp. 925 (D. Neb. 1986), *aff'd,* 834 F.2d 697 (8th Cir. 1987), *reh'g denied,* 840 F.2d 583 (1988).

4. 834 F.2d at 699 n.2.

5. *Id.*

6. 629 F. Supp. at 928.

7. *Id.*

8. *Id.* at 950.

9. *Id.*

10. *Id.* at 928–929.

11. *Id.*

12. *Id.* at 951.

13. *Id.* at 934.

14. *Id.* at 934.

15. *Id.* at 951–952 (emphasis in original).

16. 834 F.2d at 708.

17. The trial court asserted, apparently based on the testimony, that "the number of teenage pregnancies among blacks is presently much higher than among whites." 629 F.Supp. at 928. It appears that in Douglas County, Nebraska, in 1981, "the fertility rate of black teenagers [was] approximately 2½ times greater than that for whites." *Id.* at 949 n.45. Blacks, however, comprised only 12.8% of the population. *Id.* Although the court's statement may have been true for Douglas County, it does not reflect the national picture. Marian Wright Edelman puts the "epidemic" in perspective: "Contrary to popular perception, the majority of teen parents (342,283 of 499,038 in 1983) are white. Poor and minority teens, however, have a disproportionate share of teen births and are disproportionately affected by the social and economic consequences of early parenthood. A black teen is twice as likely to become pregnant as a white teen. A

black teen is five times as likely as a white teen to become an unwed parent." M. Edelman, Families in Peril: An Agenda for Social Change 57 (1987).

18. I. Garfinkel & S. McLanahan, Single Mothers and Their Children: An American Dilemma 83–84 (1986); Evans, Adolescent Sexual Activity, Pregnancy, and Childbearing: Attitudes of Significant Others as Risk Factors, in S. Battle ed., The Black Adolescent Parent 75, 89, 92 (1987). The extent to which tolerance is accompanied by familial support may be decreasing. Joyce Ladner reports that the child care assistance black teenagers receive from their mothers is declining because their mothers "are more likely to be in the workforce or still in their childbearing years, and thus have less time to take care of grandchildren." Ladner, Black Teenage Pregnancy: A Challenge for Educators, 56 J. Negro Educ. 53, 61 (1987) (citation omitted). Ladner argues that the increased parenting responsibilities placed on inexperienced, poorly educated teen mothers has serious negative consequences for their children. Ladner, Teenage Pregnancy: The Implication for Black Americans, in J. Williams ed., The State of Black America 1986, at 65 (1986). See also Boone, Social and Cultural Factors in the Etiology of Low Birthweight Among Disadvantaged Blacks, 20 Soc. Sci. & Med. 1001, 1004, 1006 (1985) (friends reported to be a more reliable source of support than family).

19. The term is variously spelled. "Bougie" or "boojy" is "an adjective, derived from bourgeoisie, referring to elitist blacks whose money and position make them think they're white." G. Smitherman, Talkin and Testifyin: The Language of Black America 251 (1977).

20. I. Reed, Reckless Eyeballing (1986). In Reed's novel, the term refers to the offense committed by a black man who "stares at a white woman too long." *Id.* at 25.

In Ponton v. Newport News School Bd., 632 F. Supp. 1056 (E.D. Va. 1986), the court rejected the notion that "the mere sight of an unmarried, pregnant teacher would have a sufficiently undesirable influence on schoolchildren to justify excluding the teacher from the classroom." *Id.* at 1062. The court in Ponton, however, assumed that the plaintiff's students would not be close enough to her to know her marital status and that her single pregnancy would not interfere with her ability to teach the prescribed curriculum. *Id.* at 1062–1063.

21. Unwed Mothers Challenge Firing at Omaha Girls Club, Omaha World-Herald, Dec. 1, 1982, at 1, col. 1.

22. *Id.*

23. Dismissal of Two Girls Club Staffers Was Logical, Omaha World-Herald, Dec. 11, 1982, at 20, col. 1.

24. *Id.*

⬙ Child Abuse: A Problem for Feminist Theory

Marie Ashe and Naomi R. Cahn

A BROAD PROFESSIONAL and popular awareness of the disturbing and not uncommon reality of child abuse has developed during the past two decades. Responses in legislation and the legal process reflect this awareness. Prosecution of child abuse has greatly accelerated; children's accounts of sexual abuse and other forms of abuse are now recognized as deserving credence; and procedural accommodations have been instituted in many jurisdictions to aid child victims in telling their stories. Increased awareness of child abuse has been accompanied by popular reactions of outrage and horror and by widespread condemnation of its perpetrators.

The accounts of child abuse delivered through popular media and various types of professional literature have tended to tell the story of child abuse with a focus on the experience of child victims and have devoted only very limited attention to the realities and experiences of perpetrators of such abuse. While parents, particularly mothers, are regularly brought under the jurisdiction of trial courts in child dependency proceedings, pursuant to which children are removed temporarily or permanently from their custody, there is a surprising dearth of literature about the complexities of such parents. The developing contemporary understanding of child abuse within and without the legal system, to the degree that it focuses on perpetrators of abuse, tends to reduce to a story of "bad mothers."

This Article attempts to expand the scope of discussion regarding the "bad mother" and suggests ways in which a fuller dialogue may take place. . . .

Prevailing Cultural Interpretations of the "Bad Mother"

The "Bad Mother" in Literature

If we define the "bad mother" as the woman whose neglectful, abusive, reckless, or murderous behavior threatens or destroys her children, we can locate her powerful figure throughout the literature of Western culture. She is apparent in ancient Greek lit-

---

Originally published in full in *Texas Journal of Women and the Law*, Volume 2 (1993).

erature in the familiar figures of Medea murdering her children to the horror of the chorus; of Agave, murdering her son Pentheus, tearing apart his limbs, and bearing his head into her city; and of Jocasta, the fatefully destructive mother of Oedipus. Each of these literary figures manifests a powerfully destructive woman whose excessive and transgressive violations of law bring destruction upon herself, her household, and her community.

The "bad mother" is also prominent in Judeo-Christian mythology. She appears in the disturbing figure of the infanticidal Lilith, defined in Jewish apocrypha as the first wife of Adam. The "bad mother" also operates centrally in the biblical account of the judgment of Solomon.[1] That account, which is often cited as a paradigm of wisdom and good judgment, marks the foundation of the definition of a bad mother in Western culture in general and Western law in particular.[2] . . .

The "bad mother" has been a common character in Western fiction. In the most familiar of Western fairy tales, she often figures as a "step"-mother.[3] In European and American fiction, the "bad mother" is typically depicted as horrifying, excessive in some essential way, and worthy of great fear. She is often depicted as so split off from the normal reality of "good motherhood" that she is characterized as the bizarre and crazy persona—the "madwoman" consigned to "the attic" of deviance or marginality. The "bad mother" is depicted as the figure always threatening to exceed, to violate the norms that prescribe the boundaries and the scope of her duty. Her boundary-violations have tragic consequences for her community by inviting destruction upon all its members.

It can be argued that the "bad mother," in her literary appearances, operates as a character within a child's story. In her standard manifestations, she appears not in her own complexity and moral agency, but as an "other" defined from the perspective of a fearful and deprived child.

From perhaps unknowable origins, the "bad mother" figure operates archetypally and paradigmatically to construct her own "other"—the "good mother"—who becomes, by extension, the "good woman," a figure highly constrained and highly constraining. This "other" to the "bad mother" model is defined in our oldest literature. . . . She has continued to operate into the contemporary period. Alicia Ostriker observes that "good motherhood is selfless, cheerful, and deodorized. It does not include resentment, anger, violence, alienation, disappointment, grief, fear, exhaustion—or erotic pleasure. It is ahistorical and apolitical. It excludes the possibility of abortion."[4] Clearly, it does not include the reality of child abuse.

In recent years, women writing in fiction and poetry, as well as in other feminist works, have attempted new formulations of "motherhood" that can be characterized as attempts to escape the constraints imposed upon women by the power of competing pre-feminist models of bad and good motherhood.[5] Such work has relevance to lawyers and legal theorists to the degree that it weakens the foundations of the stereotype and invites a new and different appreciation of the complexity of the "bad mother." . . .

Discussion of the project of subjectifying motherhood has appeared in recent feminist literary theory. Manifestations of the project have been apparent in ways pointedly relevant to legal theory in the novels of, for example, Edna O'Brien, Toni Morrison, Mary Gordon, Sue Miller, and Marge Piercy—each of whom has constructed in her fiction critical and newly-imagined figures of the neglectful or abusive mother that attempt to "do justice" to the realities of women's lives.[6] These emergent figures include mothers whose apparent destructiveness is not reduced to a categorization as "evil," as "incomprehensible," or as "crazy." It may be that the richness of these efforts resides in their embodying, at one and the same time, the voices and stories of neglected children, of abused children, of murdered children, and of highly complex "bad mothers."

The "Bad Mother" in Popular Culture

Joan Williams writes of a gender war between women that "pits 'mommies versus mommies' "[7] in the context of the conflict between work and family for working mothers. Her concept of a gender war is useful to describe views of mothers prevailing in popular culture. On one hand, as Williams points out, popular media has recently focused on women leaving the workplace to spend time with their children. These mothers are depicted as selfless and as finding fulfillment in their role of caretaking. They are interpreted as acting in the ways that mothers are supposed to act. Williams contrasts this image with that of the "harried super-mom," expected to work, take care of children, act as housekeeper, and perform as a wife. A third image—one that is central to this Article, although beyond the scope of Professor Williams' examination of gender wars—is of a woman who is neither the selfless mother, nor the supermother, but rather the neglectful or abusive mother depicted either as utterly unnatural in her agency or as utterly victimized. This figure, too, becomes a focus of gender wars. Either she is blamed for her individual, autonomous choice to abuse her child, or, if she is not condemned for her choice, she is pitied for her victimization, for her utter lack of choice. A war of interpretation thus surrounds the bad mother figure and centers on the issue of agency. This struggle involves competing understandings of such women, one which defines them as fully responsible moral agents and another which defines them as victims of individual men and of patriarchal society.

Two particularly troubling pictures of "bad mothers" in popular culture have emerged over the past five years: the picture of an individual woman, Hedda Nussbaum; and the picture of a class of women, namely pregnant, drug-addicted (especially crack-addicted) women. Each has been controversial, as each has juxtaposed images of good mothers against images of bad mothers, and women as victims against women as perpetrators of abuse. The story of Hedda Nussbaum has deeply divided feminists; the question of how to respond to pregnant women who abuse drugs has created similar division.

Popular accounts of the facts of the Nussbaum case are in general agreement. Hedda Nussbaum met Joel Steinberg in 1975. Throughout their relationship, Steinberg abused Nussbaum severely, frequently causing visible bruises as well as fractured bones. In 1981, Nussbaum and Steinberg illegally adopted a two-year-old child whom they called Lisa. Six years later, Lisa died as a result of severe physical abuse, apparently perpetrated by Joel Steinberg. Although criminal charges were initially brought against

Nussbaum on the basis of Lisa's death, those charges were eventually dropped, and Nussbaum testified against Steinberg during the trial at which he was convicted of first degree manslaughter. Responses by feminists to the Nussbaum issues fell into two categories. On the one hand, Nussbaum was canonized as the archetypal victim. Three hundred prominent women signed a letter requesting that the public refocus its attention onto the men responsible for domestic violence, rather than blame women victims for staying with such men.[8] This response demonstrates an understanding of Hedda Nussbaum as a person so victimized as to be incapable of moral agency. On the other hand, there was some tendency to blame Hedda Nussbaum as a fully responsible and autonomous agent. Susan Brownmiller, a prominent feminist, suggested, for example, that "Hedda Nussbaum, far from being a passive victim, was an active participant in her own—and Lisa's—destruction."[9]

Similarly conflicting views have been expressed about pregnant crack-addicted mothers. . . .

On the other hand, some writers have urged that the problem of crack-addicted pregnant women must be put into its social context. They have further argued that a contextualized understanding should lead us away from the tendency to blame and to prosecute criminally.[10] This perspective reflects an understanding that, to the extent that these women are morally culpable, their culpability is highly diminished. It also suggests not only that there are insufficient programs for pregnant women seeking drug treatment, but also that prosecutions have a disproportionate impact on poor and minority women.[11]

The conflicting characterizations of "bad mothers" in popular culture, apparent in popular discussions of Hedda Nussbaum and in treatment of pregnant, drug-addicted women, seem inadequate. As perhaps most parents have reason to know, and as occasional feminist writings on motherhood have clearly stated, the gap between purportedly natural feelings of intimacy and nurturance and ostensibly unnatural feelings of aggression and rage has been enormously exaggerated.[12] Popular simplistic and reductive interpretations of abusive mothers may constitute attempts by parents to drive away a recognition of their own tendencies toward verbal and physical violence against children. Both the model of the bad mother as the autonomous, powerful, and fully responsible evildoer and the countervailing model of her as the helpless victim create barriers to our respectful understanding of women whom we experience as disturbing and challenging. . . .

The "Bad Mother" in Legal Proceedings

. . . All states and the District of Columbia have various methods of dealing with parents who abuse or neglect their children, including prosecution for the underlying criminal offense, and/or civil actions under abuse and neglect statutes. . . . The focus of the "child protector" system is, of course, to ensure that children are safe; quite often, this seems to result in removal of the child from her family at the earliest legally permissible opportunity.

The definition of "bad mothering" applied in prosecution of child abuse and neglect is a broad one, and few explicit standards curb the discretion of prosecutors. For example, in the District of Columbia, an abused child is defined as "a child whose parent, guardian, or custodian inflicts or fails to make reasonable efforts to prevent the infliction of physical or mental injury upon the child, including excessive corporal punishment, an act of sexual abuse, molestation, or exploitation, or an injury that results from exposure to drug-related activity in the child's home environment."[13]

Such a broad standard allows and requires prosecutors to define appropriate parental behavior according to their discretion. As a result, decisions concerning prosecutions will tend to reflect race, class, and gender biases of prosecutors who have tended to be white, middle-class, and male. Mothering is taken out of its context in abuse prosecution and is judged by a judiciary that assumes middle-class, sexist, and racist norms. Mothers—across classes and cultures—are expected to perform in ways that satisfy those norms.

Criticism of prosecutorial and judicial discretion does not resolve the problem of child abuse in legal and moral terms. It does not by itself offer guidance concerning the distinctions of blameworthiness that might properly be made among parents who abuse their children. It does not answer the question whether the civil or criminal law should, for example, treat battered women who abuse their children differently from men who abuse their children. Various commentators have begun to struggle with these questions. Consider the thoughts of Albert Alschuler:

> Imagine that a brutal man (call him Joel Steinberg) and a lover whom he has physically abused for years (call her Hedda Nussbaum) have participated in the same act of child abuse. Imagine further that the battered woman participant has no defense of insanity or duress but that she comes close. The seriousness of the crime (judged in the abstract) is the same for both offenders. Still, I think that their "dessert" differs greatly and that imposing identical sentences would offend ordinary concepts of "proportionality."[14]

The question that Alschuler does not address is why he would hold the woman less culpable than the man.

Not everyone subscribes to the same "ordinary concepts" as Alschuler. Indeed, his opinions differ from those of many judges and social service workers who, studies indicate, are likely to blame mothers for anything that happens to their children.[15] This difference appears to be caused by conflicting images of women: On the one hand it seems to be proposed by commentators such as Alschuler that because they are victims of male patriarchy, battered women should not be blamed for hurting their children when they themselves are being battered; on the other hand, many workers in the field apparently assume that because mothers are supposed to be nurturing, their culpability exceeds that of other adults when they are abusive.

Martha Minow has proposed a partial answer to this dilemma of determining responsibility and culpability. Minow has suggested that the context of "bad mothers," which includes complex family dynamics and a society unresponsive to domestic violence, is perhaps to blame for family violence.[16] This proposition provides a context for understanding the mother's actions: why she did not leave the abusive situation; why she did not—or could not—prevent her partner from abusing a child; and why she herself may have abused her child. This interpretation allows us to move beyond mere blaming of the mother herself and permits our focusing on her embeddedness within systems that foster violence. While it does not entirely resolve the issue of how to understand the "bad mother" as moral agent, it reminds us of the need for examination of context, an approach to which much feminist theory has reliably directed attention.

Feminist Theory

Accounts of good and bad mothering . . . have significant relevance to feminist theory. In exploring its relevance, it will be useful to consider certain strands of feminist work that can be loosely designated as liberal feminism, cultural feminism, radical feminism, and postmodernist feminism. . . .

1. Liberal Feminism

A strain of feminist theory, often designated as liberal feminism, emerged in the 1960s and focused largely on supporting women's access to, and equality in, the workplace. Liberal feminism typically emphasized the value of individual and autonomous personal development for both men and women. It stressed that biology should not determine destiny.[17] Because the goal was to demonstrate the ways in which sex- or gender-based classifications limit women,[18] liberal feminists de-emphasized pregnancy and motherhood, viewing them as too confining in terms of gender ideology for women.[19] The equal treatment approach of liberal feminism supports a treatment of men and women that emphasizes their sameness rather than their difference. For liberal feminists, pregnancy tends to be treated as merely one of a multitude of physical disabilities that both women and men may experience, rather than as a defining experience for women. This analysis has led liberal feminists to support, for example, parental leave from work, rather than maternity leave, on the theory that parents should be treated equally and that mothers should not receive special treatment. Legal treatment of women and men on the basis of their differences, liberal feminists urge, would support women's being marginalized and stereotyped, and would also support men's continuing failure to assume an appropriately equal share of parental responsibility.

Liberal feminists argue that women's biology does not require that they stay out of the workplace in order to provide child care any more than it limits women to nurturing occupations such as teaching or nursing. They urge that such stereotypes prevent women from achieving their potential. While liberal legal feminists acknowledge that there are differences between men and women, they believe that the appropriate focus is on differences among women and differences among men. Thus, while liberal feminists do not entirely ignore motherhood, they focus on barriers to women's equality, such as assumptions based on stereotypes about women's abilities. The focus of liberal feminism on the importance of inclusion of women in the workplace can lead its proponents to minimize the difficulties—including child neglect, and perhaps abuse—occasioned by the inability of highly stressed and exhausted working parents to provide adequate attention and nurturance to children. The focus of liberal feminism—at least in its original formulation—on the desirability of sameness may have contributed to its failure to look beyond the issues of including women in the workplace. That limited focus may also account for its failure to fully confront issues relating to women's reproductive experiences and to the reality of child neglect or abuse.

It is not surprising that few, if any, feminists focusing on equality and sameness theory have addressed the issue of child abuse perpetrated by women. Liberal feminism's de-emphasis of the differences between women and men can erase or turn attention away from significant contextual differences that attach to the biological and cultural conditions that typically differentiate the reproductive and childcaring experiences of women and men. Because the story of liberal feminism is, in general, a story of the sameness of women and men, and because the woman imagined by liberal feminism is a separate, independent, autonomous individual, liberal feminism does not appear to have reached the complexities of the moral agency of mothers-in-relationship-to-children and of the legal treatment needed to do justice to that reality. . . .

2. Cultural Feminism

Cultural feminism has generally been identified by its focus on the differences that exist between women and men and its support for the position that women and men should be treated differently by the law for some purposes. For example, cultural feminists typically assert that women invoke an ethic of care in their moral reasoning in contrast to men who are more oriented toward an ethic of rights.[20] Cultural feminism also defines women as more oriented toward relationships than are men. It characterizes women as tending to perceive morally troubling problems as situations in which people might be hurt, and as trying to resolve conflicts by strategies that maintain connection and relationship. Men, by contrast, are viewed as less connected to others, and as highly oriented toward individual autonomy and impartial rules. It is asserted by cultural feminists that men tend to see problems in terms of violations of abstract rights, rather than in terms of real and complex relationships between people.

Unlike liberal feminists, many cultural feminists have made the experience of mothering central to their theories.[21] Many cultural feminists suggest that it is because women are mothers that they are more connected to others. Their image is of a natural mother who recognizes and appreciates her interdependence with her children. Cultural feminists celebrate women's role as nurturer.[22] Indeed, they tend to celebrate women's positive values to a degree that erases certain negative aspects of women's experience and activity.

In legal theory, their valorization of motherhood has led these different feminists to advocate special protections to accommodate women's particular experiences.[23] They have challenged gender neutrality as disadvantageous to women. Thus, for example, in discussions of pregnancy benefits, cultural feminists have not hesitated to assert that maternal leave should be supported even in the absence of gender-neutral parental leave because of their belief that maternal leave provides a recognition of women's special needs that is appropriate for ensuring women's equality within the workplace.[24]

The willingness of cultural feminism to entertain the reality of some difference between women and men, as well as its focus on motherhood, might suggest that theory's greater capacity for interpretation of "bad mothers." Indeed, the cultural feminists' argument that it is important to understand the pain in women's lives as different from that in men's lives[25] could result in increased attention to why women abuse their children. However, the cultural feminist celebration of motherhood does not—at least at this point—include "bad mothers." Indeed, it is not entirely clear what a coherent cultural feminist analysis of "bad mothers" could be. The largely uncritical—and often essentialistic—emphasis by cultural feminism on caring as an attribute of women hardly leaves room for consideration of women who do not or cannot care for their children, and seems to offer no escape from the prevailing images of "bad mothers" as either utterly unnatural or utterly victimized.

3. Radical Feminism

Radical feminism has tended to concentrate on the nature of gender relationships rather than on the nature of motherhood per se. To the degree that it has considered motherhood, however, it has been characterized by a very marked devaluing of the self-sacrificing aspects of good motherhood supported by cultural feminism and, as suggested above, by prevailing psychological theory. Thus, for example, Catharine MacKinnon indicates a strong impatience with cultural feminism's high valuation of nurturing behavior.[26] MacKinnon seems to characterize the nurturance touted by the cultural feminists as merely the learned behavior of victims[27] and the positive valuation of such behaviors by cultural feminists as an instance of "false consciousness."[28] The discourse of radical feminism, of MacKinnon's "feminism unmodified," expresses a refusal to recognize positive and empowering experiences that some women report even within the limits imposed by motherhood as a cultural institution. Thus, MacKinnon speaks disparagingly of mothers who failed to engage in effective political activity because they were instead at home "wiping their babies' asses."[29] This reductionist discourse denigrates the experiences of many women who read it as denying or erasing the significance of their central relationships with their children.

Radical feminism has been sharply criticized for its devaluation of women-as-mothers.[30] While MacKinnon and other radical feminists write powerfully about issues of sexuality in ways that emphasize that the category "women" cannot and must not be reduced to the category "mothers," radical feminism remains inadequate in its treatment of motherhood. . . . For this reason, radical feminism offers limited insights with regard to feminist theory's struggle with the reality of the "bad mother" as a perpetrator of child abuse. While it suggests the role of patriarchy in creating "bad mothers," it utterly fails to explore the agency of women who abuse.

4. Postmodernist Feminism

In recent years, certain legal theory has come to be marked by features that can be identified as postmodernist. These features include a characteristic awareness of the partiality and contingency of every claim to knowledge, and an eschewing of "grand narrative" and "grand theory" in favor of smaller narratives.[31] As expressed in feminist legal theory, such features have included, specifically, an avoidance of the claim to speak for all women. Thus, the critical efficacy of much of postmodernist feminist legal theory has often been accomplished by its introduction or reintroduction of subjectivities that had been obscured or denied by dominant accounts.

Postmodernist feminism has a peculiar status that has begun to be discussed extensively in legal theory as well as in other disciplines.[32] To the degree that postmodernist feminism is postmodernist, it expresses profound and persisting skepticism; to the degree that it is feminist, it expresses—within a world in which everything is thrown into question—conviction and certainty concerning the reality of the cultural oppression of women. Postmodernist feminist theory tells certain stories that have given rise to that belief in the oppression of women; stories that support the belief; and stories that begin to suggest possibilities of escape.

Within feminist legal theory, issues of reproduction, violence toward women, and the intersections of gender and racial oppression have begun to be treated in specifically postmodernist narratives.[33] Accounts of "bad mothers" have, however, been absent from such analyses, just as they have been absent from, or reductively defined in negative terms in, most feminist theory. The reasons for this reality are both intellectual and political. As has been suggested, it has seemed impossible to adequately treat "bad mothers" within the binaristic limits of traditional theory without reducing the discussion of motherhood to simplistic accounts of power or victimization. And feminists have not found it politically desirable to emphasize the badness of any women— particularly the badness of some mothers. Feminist theory has, however, been seriously limited by its failure to address the bad mother reality.

Postmodernism has created a space within which new kinds of inquiry into the experiences and motivations of "bad mothers" can be undertaken. Postmodernist approaches support new directions in interpreting the intersections between violence against women and violence by women. Postmodernism legitimates stories of "bad mothers" as essential to theory. It both recognizes the difficulties of telling such stories and invites their tellings. . . . Postmodernism supports new imaginings not only by having opened up the possibility of various "new narratives," but also by its creation of a space within which those narratives—including, for example, narratives of children as well as those of women—can intersect.[34] Thus a specifically and explicitly postmodernist feminism may offer the greatest possibility for engagement of feminist theory with the reality of child abuse by "bad mothers."

Postmodernist directions allow for pursuits that will enable enriching interaction among liberal, cultural, and radical feminism. A recent nonlegal writing concerning "bad motherhood" that demonstrates such an interaction of liberal, cultural, and radical feminist themes is Jane Swigart's *The Myth of the Bad Mother: The Emotional Realities of Mothering.*[35] Swigart's writing manifests some postmodernist characteristics in its intermingling of narrative and its interdisciplinary treatment of both literature and psychology, and it constitutes a powerful critical account of the stereotype of bad mothering. The book does not explicitly address the question of when judicial intervention into families is justified and necessary, nor does it explicitly explore how the bad mother stereotype might be displaced within the existing legal system. Swigart's book does, however, provide a powerful commencement of the task of telling the bad mother story from the perspective of both mothers' and children's experiences. The incorporation of such complex perspectives into feminist legal theory concerning motherhood—good and bad—remains to be accomplished.

. . . Feminism is limited to the degree that it fails to give some account of aspects of women that seem ugly or undesirable. As many feminists have argued, the meaning of woman is not unitary; not only does it go beyond white, middle-class, heterosexual women, it also includes "bad mothers." In its attempt to give an account of alternative women's realities, feminist theory must explore the different forms that those realities take. If feminist theory is "outsider" criticism,[36] "bad mothers" are "outsiders" to feminist theory. A feminism that excludes or reduces any woman is clearly inadequate. What we are urging is that feminism attempts to include these outsiders. . . .

A gap exists between the experiences of oppressed people and the representation of those experiences by those who purport to understand them and to advocate on their behalf. It behooves us to be mindful of that reality as we struggle to re-present both motherhood and childhood. . . .

Notes

1. 1 Kings 3:16–28 (deciding two mothers' conflict over the right to a child in favor of the woman who would rather surrender the child than see it killed).

2. See Ann Althouse, Beyond King Solomon's Harlots: Women in Evidence, 65 S. Cal. L. Rev. 1265, 1268, 1270 (1992) (noting Solomon's perceived wisdom in judging that good mothers nurture and sacrifice and bad mothers invite ill to befall their children); Marie Ashe, Abortion of Narrative: A Reading of the Judgment of Solomon, 4 Yale J.L. & Feminism 81, 86 (1991) (presenting Solomon's judgment as the equation of good motherhood with nurturing and sacrifice and bad motherhood with violence and infanticide).

3. Examples of such nearly universally known Western fairy tales include Snow White, Cinderella, and Hansel and Gretel. . . . For one analysis of the psychological significance of such stories, see Bruno Bettelheim, The Uses of Enchantment: The Meaning and Importance of Fairy Tales (1976).

4. Alicia S. Ostriker, Stealing the Language: The Emergence of Women's Poetry in America 179 (1986).

5. See Adrienne Rich, Of Woman Born: Motherhood as Experience and as Institution (1976) (discussing different meanings of motherhood and the effect on female potentialities of motherhood as an institution); see also Audre Lorde, Man Child: A Black Lesbian Feminist's Response, in Sister Outsider 72 (1984) (exploring the experience of parenting a boy from a lesbian mother's perspective).

6. See Edna O'Brien, Time and Tide (1992); Mary Gordon, Men and Angels (1985); Sue Miller, The Good Mother (1986); Toni Morrison, Beloved (1987); Marge Piercy, Woman on the Edge of Time (1976).

7. Joan Williams, Gender Wars: Selfless Women in the Republic of Choice, 66 N.Y.U. L. Rev. 1559, 1624 (1991) (quoting Nina Darnton, Mommy v. Mommy, Newsweek, June 4, 1990, at 64).

8. See Paula Span, Women Protest "Hedda-Bashing"; 300 Sign Response to Steinberg Case, Wash. Post, Mar. 13, 1989, at B1 (quoting Lois Gould, a novelist, who said, "I began to be quite amazed at the turning of attention to this woman, to her 'culpability,' when you've never seen a clearer case of a victim.").

In a *Newsday* interview, Catharine MacKinnon explained that the case presented "a hard situation, but the person who made it hard is Joel Steinberg. When you are battered within an inch of your life, you're just trying to survive, so you do a great many horrible things to make it more likely that you will live." The New York Newsday Interview with Catharine MacKinnon; Private Acts Are Public Affairs, Newsday, June 12, 1989, at 57.

9. Susan Brownmiller, Hedda Nussbaum, Hardly a Heroine, N.Y. Times, Feb. 2, 1989, at A25. Brownmiller repeated these themes in 1989 in her novel *Waverly Place.*

10. See Tracy Higgins, Note, Rethinking (M)otherhood: Feminist Theory and State Regulation of Pregnancy, 103 Harv. L. Rev. 1325, 1341 (1990) (arguing that state regulation of pregnancy may be appropriate in cases of substance abuse, but such regulation must reflect both an understanding of a woman's position in pregnancy and the specific needs of pregnant addicts).

11. See Dorothy E. Roberts, Punishing Drug Addicts Who Have Babies: Women of Color, Equality, and the Rights of Privacy, herein, at 882.

12. See Rich, Of Woman Born, *supra* note 5, at 21 (illustrating the love-hate maternal relationship); see also Dacia Maraini, On Of Woman Born, 4 Signs 687, 688 (1979) (noting that "Rich is questioning a stereotype—a mother loves in a constant, blind, and altruistic manner—by observing her own maternal feelings," which often include frustration and anger).

13. D.C. Code Ann. §16–2301(23) (Supp. 1991). This statute was upheld against a vagueness challenge in In re J.A. & L.A., 601 A.2d 69 (D.C. 1991).

14. Albert W. Alschuler, The Failure of Sentencing Guidelines: A Plea for Less Aggregation, 58 U. Chi. L. Rev. 901, 909–910 (1991); see also Martha Minow, Words and the Door to the Land of Change: Law, Language, and Family Violence, 43 Vand. L. Rev. 1665, 1682 (1990) ("The debate over whether to blame a battered woman for her neglect or abuse of a child has a long history.").

15. See Linda Gordon, Heroes of Their Own Lives 262–263 (1988) (arguing that in the Progressive Era, child protectors believed that if mothering was not done well, "that inadequacy was not a sign of obstacles, resistance, or inadequate resources, but of character flaw"); see also State v. Tanner, 675 P.2d 539 (Utah 1983) (allowing evidence of mother's past abuse to show a pattern of behavior relevant to establish absence of mistake or accident in manslaughter prosecution of mother for killing child).

16. See Minow, *supra* note 14, at 1665, 1682–1683 (1990) (arguing that the two features missing in the debate over assessing the blame for family violence are, first, the "real possibility that violence within a family involves a system of human interactions that should all be changed, rather than [focusing on] a single, sick, and malevolent wrongdoer" and, second, "the family's embeddedness in larger social patterns—of neighbors who look the other way, police and social workers who do not respond to reports of violence, and public attitudes that tolerate or deny family violence").

17. See Rosemarie Tong, Feminist Thought 31 (1989) (discussing liberal feminist views on the relationship between biology, identity, and personality type).

18. Wendy W. Williams, Notes From a First Generation, 1989 U. Chi. Legal F. 99, 105; see also Nadine Taub & Wendy W. Williams, Will Equality Require More Than Assimilation, Accommodation, or Separation from the Existing Legal Structure? 37 Rutgers L. Rev. 825 (1985) (describing how since the 1970s feminist litigators, in order to expunge stereotypes from the law, have insisted that sex differences are not inherent and physical differences are not absolute).

19. See June Carbone & Margaret F. Brinig, Rethinking Marriage, 65 Tul. L. Rev. 983 (1991) (stating that "liberal feminism encouraged women to devalue, if not abandon" their domestic roles); Martha R. Mahoney, Legal Images of Battered Women: Redefining the Issue of Separation, 90 Mich. L. Rev. 1, 46 (1991) (stating that liberal legal feminists have tried to make motherhood less central to women's identity); see also Martha Fineman, The Neutered Mother, 46 U. Miami L. Rev. 653, 667 (1992) (asserting that liberal feminists have constructed negative images of motherhood in order to gain equality for women).

20. See Carol Gilligan, In a Different Voice 100 (1982) ("For men, the moral imperative appears rather as an injunction to respect the rights of others and thus to protect from interference the rights to life and self-fulfillment. Women's insistence on care is at first self-critical rather than self- protective, while men initially conceive obligation to others negatively in terms of noninterference.").

21. See Nancy Chodorow, The Reproduction of Mothering: Psychoanalysis and the Sociology of Gender 354 (1978) ("Women are prepared psychologically for mothering through the developmental situation in which they grew up, and in which women have mothered them."); Sara Ruddick, Maternal Thinking, 6 Feminist Stud. 342, 343 (1980) (describing the experience of mothering in conjunction with concepts of power and powerlessness); Robin West, Jurisprudence and Gender, in D. Weisberg ed., Feminist Legal Theory: Foundations 75, 79 (Temple Univ. Press, 1993) (explaining that cultural feminists believe "women have a 'sense' of existential 'connection' to other human life which men do not").

22. See, e.g., Nel Noddings, Ethics from the Standpoint of Women, in Deborah L. Rhode ed., Theoretical Perspectives on Sexual Difference 160 (1990) (defending the construction of a female ethic built on women's traditional role as nurturer and addressing the primary objections to such an ethic of caring).

23. See, e.g., Christine A. Littleton, Does It Still Make Sense to Talk About Women?, 1 UCLA Women's L.J. 15, 19 (1991) (explaining the pitfalls of not addressing women's particular experiences in sexual equity cases); Christine A. Littleton, Reconstructing Sexual Equality, in Feminist Legal Theory: Foundations, *supra* note 21, at 248 (proposing a theory of sexual equality called "equality as acceptance" and arguing that "women's biological and cultural differences from men . . . are real and significant [and] [w]omen's inequality results when society devalues women because they differ from the male norm").

24. See Linda J. Krieger & Patricia M. Cooney, The Miller-Wohl Controversy: Equal Treatment, Positive Action and the Meaning of Women's Equality, in Feminist Legal Theory: Foundations, *supra* note 21, at 156 (presenting the view that because women can become pregnant, they are subjected to a disability that men do not confront and, therefore, are disadvantaged by a no-sick-leave policy); Littleton, Does It Still Make Sense to Talk About Women?, *supra* note 23, at 26–27 (discussing the debate about the dangers of arguing for pregnancy leave under a "special" needs theory and thus diluting feminist claims of equality with men); see also Lucinda Finley, Transcending Equality Theory: A Way Out of the Maternity and Workplace Debate, in Feminist Legal Theory: Foundations, *supra* note 21, at 190 (concluding that maternity leave benefits men, women, and children).

A similar position was taken by a coalition of women's rights groups that argued in favor of pregnancy disability leave. Brief Amicus Curiae for the Coalition for Reproductive Equality in the Workplace, California Fed. Sav. & Loan Ass'n v. Guerra, 479 U.S. 272 (1980).

25. See Robin West, The Difference in Women's Hedonic Lives: A Phenomenological Critique of Feminist Legal Theory, herein at 162 (arguing that women's suffering is different from men's and, therefore, the legal system must address women's suffering directly).

26. See Catharine A. MacKinnon, Feminism Unmodified: Discourses on Life and Law 74 (1987) (arguing that such a valuation of traditionally feminine traits presents a significant risk of contributing to the cycle of male dominance); see also Ellen C. Dubois et al., Feminist Discourse, Moral Values and the Law—A Conversation, 34 Buff. L. Rev. 11, 27 (1985) (comments of Catharine A. MacKinnon from a discussion held on Oct. 19, 1984, at the law school of State University of New York at Buffalo as part of the James McCormick Mitchell Lecture Series) (suggesting that women define themselves in male-imposed terms of caring, responsibility, and relationship as a way of gaining respect in an unequal world).

27. See Dubois, Feminist Discourse, *supra* note 26, at 74 (arguing that having women identify with a positively valued feminine stereotype results in the continued victimization of women in a male-dominated society).

28. See Lucinda M. Finley, The Nature of Domination and the Nature of Women: Reflections on Feminism Unmodified, 82 Nw. U. L. Rev. 352, 383 (1988) (reviewing Catharine A. MacKinnon, Feminism Unmodified: Discourses on Life and Law (1987)) (criticizing MacKinnon's "attribution of false consciousness or cooptation [as] too glib"). Robin West also refers to the "false consciousness" of women. West, *supra* note 25, at 163 (claiming that one of the reasons feminist legal theorists neglect the "phenomenological, subjective, and hedonic distinctiveness of women's lives" is the problem of "false consciousness").

29. Catharine A. MacKinnon, Unthinking ERA Thinking, 54 U. Chi. L. Rev. 759, 759 (1987) (reviewing Jane J. Mansbridge, Why We Lost The ERA (1986)).

30. Brenda Waugh, When Did We Last Meet? Let Us Now Speak, 12 Legal Stud. F. 221 (1988) (reviewing Catharine A. MacKinnon, Feminism Unmodified: Discourses on Life and Law (1987)).

31. See generally Kathryn Abrams, Hearing the Call of the Stories, 79 Cal. L. Rev. 971, 982–1012 (1991) (examining feminist scholars' use of the narrative and discussing the work of Susan Estrich, Martha Mahoney, Patricia Williams, and Marie Ashe).

32. See, e.g., Mary Joe Frug, Postmodern Legal Feminism (1992).

33. See, e.g., Abrams, *supra* note 31, at 984–1012 (considering narratives relating to gender and racial intersections, reproduction, and violence against women).

34. Marie Ashe, The "Bad Mother" in Law and Literature: A Problem of Representation, 43 Hastings L.J. 1017, 1029–1030 (1992) (stating that the French postmodernists, such as Michel Foucault, Jacques Derrida, and Julia Kristeva, have "demonstrated the present impossibility of 'grand theory' and . . . opened up space for new narratives").

35. Jane Swigart, The Myth of the Bad Mother: The Emotional Realities of Mothering (1990).

36. See Mari Matsuda, Public Response to Racist Speech: Considering the Victim's Story, 87 Mich. L. Rev. 2320, 2322–2324 (1989) (defining feminist jurisprudence as outsider jurisprudence—"a methodology grounded in the particulars of [a given group's] social reality and experience").

B. Abortion

Introduction

SOCIAL CONTROL of women's reproductive capacity has been a central concern of the women's movement. Framing the issue as women's right "to control their own bodies,"[1] feminists today regard reproductive control as a prerequisite to personal and political empowerment.[2] In contrast, abortion rights were not a concern of nineteenth-century feminists, who worried instead about death from childbirth.[3] This distinguishes abortion from other feminist concerns (such as battering, prostitution, and employment) which are shared by historical and contemporary feminists.

By 1970 abortion was gaining prominence as a feminist issue. Feminists advocated access to safe and legal abortion and condemned the disproportionate impact of abortion restrictions on poor women and women of color.[4] Despite an initial concern with the broader range of reproductive rights (contraception and sterilization abuse, as well as abortion),[5] feminist reformers subsequently concentrated primarily on abortion.[6]

Liberal feminists in particular targeted abortion rights. At the first national conference, the National Organization for Women passed a resolution supporting "[t]he right of women to control their own reproductive lives by removing from the penal code laws limiting access to contraceptive information and devices, and by repealing penal laws governing abortion."[7] Not all feminists were supportive. Some resigned in protest, worrying that NOW's advocacy of abortion would jeopardize the organization.[8]

Nonetheless, the abortion rights movement gathered momentum. Radical feminists joined liberal feminists.[9] Early feminist theory provided a rights-based claim for the political agenda.[10] And, throughout the 1960s, grassroots organizations established abortion referral services in states where abortion was illegal as well as in those few states where it was legal.[11]

Feminists also lobbied for repeal of abortion restrictions.

The 1969 AMA Convention in New York was surrounded by picketers from the women's movement wielding signs and leaflets "demanding that doctors sign a petition for repeal." Feminists from NOW and other women's liberation groups invaded the AMA meeting, as well as courtrooms, legislative hearing rooms, district attorneys' offices, and the streets . . . and provided the most visible external pressure for change in the abortion laws.[12]

Although feminists predominated in the abortion reform movement, other influences were apparent as well.[13] A distinct reproductive rights movement formed, influenced by Lawrence Lader, author of a book advocating abortion repeal.[14] Clergy also provided support in the form of referral services.[15] Nonfeminist organizations, such as the American Medical Association, American College of Obstetricians and Gynecologists, American Medical Women's Association, American Public Health Association, Group for the Advancement of Psychiatry, and Planned Parenthood–World Population,[16] also advocated abortion reform.

Another call for reform was emerging in legal channels. The American Law Institute (ALI) proposed a Model Penal Code in 1959 with new abortion provisions,[17] liberalizing abortion for pregnancies resulting from rape or incest, for those involving a deformed fetus, and for those whose continuation would impair the mother's mental or physical health ("therapeutic abortions").[18] During the 1960s, birth defects caused by thalidomide and rubella[19] contributed to support for the ALI proposals. Colorado, North Carolina, and California enacted the first reforms in 1967 premised on the ALI provisions.[20] In 1967 "twenty-eight state legislatures considered liberalization bills; by 1970 twelve had passed them."[21] The ALI proposals, however, resulted in only limited reform.[22] Ironically, some ensuing statutory revisions served to strengthen restrictions by imposing onerous procedural requirements on abortion. Other revisions mandated residency requirements and consent by husbands or parents.[23] Such provisions significantly impeded access to abortion services.[24]

With the realization of the limited nature of reform, radical and socialist feminists instead began advocating repeal.[25] They opposed the distinction between therapeutic and elective abortions, and campaigned for abortion for *all* women.[26] Repeal was most successful in Hawaii and New York, the first states to eliminate their laws in 1970.[27] The struggle in New York was "particularly fierce" (repeal legislation passing by one vote), pitting conservatives and the religious right against feminists.[28] Other states followed.[29] With litigators challenging restrictive laws,[30] the stage was set for the famous Supreme Court decision in 1973.

Roe and Its Aftermath

The abortion law challenged in Roe v. Wade[31] had its origins in nineteenth-century Anglo-American prohibitions.[32] Parliament first enacted legislation (Lord Ellenborough's

Act)[33] in 1803 penalizing abortion before "quickening" (the moment when fetal movement became perceptible). American jurisdictions began enacting restrictive statutes somewhat later, from 1821 to 1841.[34]

Nineteenth-century physicians actively supported abortion restrictions.[35] In 1859, the fledgling American Medical Association (AMA) began an aggressive campaign opposing abortion before quickening.[36] "Between 1860 and 1880 the regular physicians' campaign against abortion in the United States produced the most important burst of anti-abortion legislation in the nation's history."[37] Forty states enacted statutes during this period.[38]

Physicians were motivated, Mohr explains, by a desire to end competition from nonmedical practitioners.[39] Additionally, Petchesky suggests that physicians desired "to establish an ideological hegemony that would give them an *exclusive* authority over their principal clientele—upper- and middle-class married women."[40] Petchesky adds that the AMA utilized moral, rather than medical, arguments.[41]

Other factors also contributed to the criminalization of abortion. The decline of the white Protestant birthrate (compared to that of Catholics, immigrants, and nonwhites) led to fears of "race suicide."[42] The codification movement of the criminal law, stemming from a desire to restrict judicial discretion, provided another impetus.[43] The Catholic church, too, opposed abortion with an 1869 papal enactment.[44]

Despite fear of criminal sanctions, women still sought abortions. Abortionists practiced a lucrative trade; 200 abortionists practiced full time in New York City in 1870 (although all states then prohibited abortion).[45] Affluent women utilized illegal services or obtained a legal abortion under a "medical necessity" exception. Women also used self-help folk methods (potions, instruments inserted into the uterus, strenuous exercise, and abdominal pressure).[46] Despite widespread violations, few criminal indictments resulted.[47]

Abortion reemerged as a public issue in the 1960s, due in large part to feminist influences. Their efforts culminated in Roe v. Wade in 1973—called "the second wave's biggest, most significant victory."[48] On the same day, the Supreme Court decided *Roe*[49] and the lesser known Doe v. Bolton.[50]

Roe examined the constitutionality of an 1850s Texas statute prohibiting abortion except to save the life of the mother.[51] The Supreme Court ruled that the state could not interfere with abortion during the first trimester; during the second trimester, the state may regulate abortion if the regulation is reasonably related to maternal health. After viability, however, the state may prohibit abortions in the interest of potential life. The Court grounded its decision on the right to privacy which inheres, according to the Court, in the Fourteenth Amendment's guarantee of personal liberty.

Doe v. Bolton challenged Georgia's ALI model statute mandating residency and procedural requirements.[52] The Court invalidated the requirements that an abortion could be performed only in an accredited hospital after approval by three physicians and a hospital review board panel.

Roe's impact was far reaching. Its effect was "to enunciate a principle under which the existing abortion legislation in at least forty-nine states and the District of Columbia was invalid."[53] Surprisingly, *Roe* engendered a spate of criticism.[54] Feminist and other critics charged the Court with judicial activism, usurping the power of the legislature, and engrafting a new right in the Constitution.[55] The trimester approach and the emphasis on viability, in particular, were criticized.[56] Some writers castigated the Court for short-circuiting legislative reform.[57] Feminists also criticized *Roe* for failing to declare unconstitutional the regulation of abortion at any stage of pregnancy.[58] Many feminists criticized the case for its doctrinal basis in the right to privacy rather than in equal protection,[59] a criticism that is explored further in the essays herein.

Conservative pro-life forces mobilized to undercut *Roe*. "For about a decade following the 1973 decision, the 'fetal personhood' campaign, spearheaded by the Catholic Church and later joined by Protestant New Right fundamentalists, held center stage."[60] Federal legislation was introduced to limit *Roe;* proposals were advanced to amend the Constitution.[61]

Pro-life advocates urged reconsideration of *Roe*. Subsequent Supreme Court decisions, although not overturning *Roe,* retreated from its holding. In Harris v. McRae,[62] the Court upheld the constitutionality of the Hyde Amendment, eliminating federal Medicaid funds for abortions, despite the use of such funds for childbirth. The Court reasoned that, although the state could not prohibit an abortion, it did not have to fund it. Subsequently, in Rust v. Sullivan,[63] the Court upheld regulations prohibiting federally funded programs from providing abortion counseling or referrals.

Abortion opponents continued efforts to limit *Roe* through statutes making abortion more burdensome. Conservative members of the Court made inroads on *Roe*. In Webster v. Reproductive Health Services,[64] the court upheld, in a plurality opinion, a Missouri statute that prohibited the use of public funds, employees, or facilities for any abortion not necessary to save the woman's life and that required viability tests on the fetus of women 20 or more weeks pregnant. The funding restriction effectively eliminated abortions at public hospitals, even for paying patients. Moreover, the court let stand the statute's preamble that defined life as beginning at conception—avoiding the issue of its constitutionality by reasoning that the language had no regulatory effect.

Webster aroused renewed expectations that the Court might overrule *Roe*. Another opportunity arose in Planned Parenthood v. Casey.[65] *Casey* upheld all but one of Pennsylvania's restrictive provisions, including a mandatory waiting period; an informed consent requirement mandating the provision of information regarding fetal description, state-funded prenatal care, and the biological father's child support obligations; and an informed consent requirement for minors who must secure consent of at least one parent. (The Court invalidated only the spousal notification requirement). Although the joint opinion reaffirms abortion as a basic right rooted in liberty and privacy, it also enunciates a new "undue burden" standard[66] for permissible state regulation. In the face of such judicial decisions, some reformers proposed the Freedom of Choice Act[67] to amend the Constitution by codifying *Roe*.

Feminist Perspectives on Abortion

A feminist perspective emerges from the voluminous literature on abortion. Political scientist Mary Seegers[68] identifies the following elements of such a perspective: an emphasis on pregnancy as involuntary in a society devaluing childbearing and childrearing; a recognition of the "asymmetrical impact" of pregnancy; abortion as an issue of autonomy in reproductive control in a patriarchal society;[69] an understanding of ethical dilemmas that are distinct from those in other contexts (such as homicide);[70] and a linkage of abortion to the objectives (justice, liberty, equality, and autonomy) of the women's movement.[71]

Rothman points to an additional element, the centrality of the fetus in the birth process, which was prompted by technological advances in prenatal screening and diagnosis, as a development with consequences for abortion.[72] Luker identifies influences brought about by ideology and social roles. Her sociological study of activists reveals that pro-life and pro-choice advocates have different attitudes about the traditional division of labor and motherhood. Pro-choice supporters want to abolish the traditional division of labor; pro-life advocates, lacking educational resources to compete in the labor market, defend it. Moreover, Luker suggests that the current controversy represents pro-life advocates' struggle to elevate motherhood in a society that devalues childrearing and homemakers.[73]

Many contemporary feminists regard abortion as an issue of gender equality.[74] Such a view, bolstered by the Canadian experience,[75] appears in the writings of many feminists, as explained below.

Liberal Feminist Perspectives

Securing the right to abortion was one of the most important victories of liberal feminism. Liberal feminist organizations (such as NOW, and the ACLU) lobbied for legislative and judicial reform. The establishment of the largest reform organization, the National Association for Repeal of Abortion Law (NARAL), was the direct result of liberal feminist efforts.[76]

Liberal values of autonomy and privacy inform the pro-choice movement, stemming from liberal feminist conceptions of privacy as well as sexuality.

> A central question for liberal political theory has always been how to define the right to privacy and so set the limits of legitimate state authority. . . . Contemporary liberal feminists offer no such direct challenge to the right to privacy. Indeed, they appeal to that right in order to justify the abolition of restrictions on abortion and on women's sexuality.[77]

Liberal feminists believe that sexual activity is a private matter in which the state should refrain from interfering.[78]

The right to privacy furnishes the rationale for the Supreme Court's removal of abortion restrictions in Roe v. Wade. Janet Benshoof of the ACLU's Reproductive Freedom Project defends the Supreme Court's emphasis on this rationale.[79] She counters the criticism that the Court fabricated a new right in *Roe*, arguing that the right to privacy follows from established legal precedents upholding the right to make personal decisions without government interference. According to Benshoof, privacy is comprised of two rights—a right of noninterference and personal autonomy—both of which, she argues, were recognized by case law prior to *Roe*.[80]

However, feminists increasingly recognize the complex meanings of privacy and the limitations of the doctrine.[81] Copelon elaborates:

> There has emerged a sharp tension between two notions of privacy: the liberal idea of privacy as the negative and qualified right to be left alone (so long as nothing too significant is at stake), and the more radical ideal of privacy as the positive liberty of self-determination and an aspect of equal personhood. Both practically and theoretically, the privacy doctrine is double-edged, having within it the tendency to constrain as well as to expand reproductive rights.[82]

Copelon notes an evolution in privacy doctrine. Early cases including *Roe*, she suggests, characterize the abortion decision as the physician's. Subsequent decisions, on the other hand, confer the right on the woman.[83] For Copelon, this signals an important reconceptualization.

> Formulating the abortion right this way is doubly significant because it places the right to make autonomous decisions about childbearing in the context of equality. That women should have the right to abortion is not an instance of special treatment; it is instead an extension to women of the traditional liberal constitutional values of liberty, possession of self, and opportunity to participate as producer and citizen. [This] reflects . . . a deeply held feminist understanding of the necessity of the abortion right to women's full personhood.[84]

However, some scholars argue that analyses of abortion from an equality perspective have been impeded by the liberal concept of equality.[85] So the argument goes, the liberal concept of treating likes alike flounders in the context of reproduction, such as pregnancy and abortion, because women and men are not similarly situated biologically.

Liberal feminists' emphasis on the relationship between reproductive freedom and equality is shared by other feminists. However, liberal feminists' views differ from others as to the optimum reform strategy. Underlying NARAL was a theoretical assumption that removing the state would result in the "right to choose."[86] Radical feminists disagreed. They believed that

> the existing medical-care system, like other capitalist markets, does not adequately meet people's needs; how and by whom abortions (or other health services) are provided is a critical dimension of whether real needs will be met. This deeper understanding was often implicit in how radical feminists conducted the abortion struggle, but it failed to be translated either into a popular feminist discourse or into public policy.[87]

Instead, the liberal position came to define the rhetoric of the abortion rights movement.[88]

Some feminists vehemently criticize liberal ideology on abortion. Socialist feminist Sandra Harding, for example, criticizes the moral and political assumptions of liberal theory. The fundamental question for liberal philosophers, according to Harding, is the personhood of the fetus. Harding accuses liberal theory's focus on personhood as contributing to conservative efforts to control female sexuality.[89] Harding also claims that the liberal concept of abortion, as the adjudication of conflicting rights, works to women's detriment. She questions the utility of claims that pit rights against others.[90] Rather than the liberal emphasis on individual rights, Harding prefers an emphasis on social needs, especially the creation of social conditions that facilitate the "fulfillment of [reproductive] responsibilities."[91]

Radical Feminist Perspectives

Radical feminists joined liberal feminists in the forefront of abortion law reform in theory and practice. As Pleck notes, "In the late 1960s, abortion was the first major issue for radical feminism."[92] Radical feminist Shulamith Firestone advanced the view that biology, especially women's reproductive role, is the source of women's oppression. For Firestone, only a biological revolution in which women seize control of the means of reproduction would bring an end to distinctions based on gender and lead to women's liberation.[93]

Radical feminists had dramatic reform strategies. Redstockings, the radical feminist organization, for example, disrupted legislative hearings in 1969 to urge repeal of abortion laws.[94] Shortly thereafter, the organization held a consciousness-raising "speak-out."[95] Another radical feminist group, The Feminists, held a demonstration at New York City's Criminal Court in support of an abortionist and to urge repeal of abortion laws.[96] Other radical feminists spearheaded repeal efforts by means of various organizations.[97] Radical feminists also joined liberal feminists to improve access to abortion services.[98]

Despite their common opposition to abortion restrictions, radical and liberal feminists' views diverge. One difference concerns their political agendas: liberal feminists favor the "right to choose" versus radical feminists' advocating access for all. In addition, radical feminism offers a more theoretical explanation for women's oppression in general and abortion law in particular. For radical feminists, male dominance is the source of inequality; the goal is to combat pervasive patriarchal relations.[99]

For radical feminists, patriarchy forces women to be mothers. Reproduction is characterized by many forms of compulsion:

> Contemporary patriarchy deprives young women of adequate contraceptive information, and the contraceptives it does make available are inconvenient, unreliable, expensive and dangerous. Patriarchy limits abortions and often seeks to deny them entirely, but at the same time it subjects women to intense and unremitting pressure to engage in sexual relations.[100]

According to some radical feminists, all sex is forced sex. A belief in the similarity between rape and "consensual" sex leads Dworkin to criticize antiabortion foes who would allow abortion for rape victims. "[I]f a woman can be forced to bear a child conceived by force in marriage, there is no logic in differentiating pregnancy as a result of rape."[101]

The relationship between reproductive freedom and male violence against women is a topic of some controversy among feminists. Some feminists criticize the radical feminist view of all sexual relations as coercive. Copelon, for example, charges: "This view is a flat and dangerous stereotype, for it precludes exploration and appreciation of women's capacity for sexual agency, power, and desire."[102] As applied to abortion, Copelon adds: "Even accepting, as I do, that many women are vulnerable to sexual coercion as a product of inequality, abortion does not increase their abuse."

Radical feminist Adrienne Rich's characterization of abortion as violence against women prompted a scholarly debate between Catharine MacKinnon and socialist feminist Rosalind Petchesky. In a famous remark, Rich points out:

> In a society where women entered sexual intercourse willingly, where adequate contraception was a genuine social priority, there would be no "abortion issue." . . . Abortion is violence. . . . It is the offspring, and will continue to be the accuser of a more pervasive and prevalent violence, the violence of rapism.[103]

MacKinnon cites Rich's remarks to preface an essay (included herein) that analyzes the significance of Roe v. Wade. Petchesky responds, charging that neither Rich nor MacKinnon adequately explains the analogy of abortion to violence.[104] Petchesky suggests several possible meanings. Perhaps, Petchesky proposes, radical feminists mean that abortion is a dangerous bodily violation.[105] Petchesky counters by pointing to the safety of early abortions and claiming that trauma arises instead from the responses of patriarchal society. Moreover, Petchesky criticizes the metaphor on historical grounds, saying that it "denies both the historical agency of women in struggling to secure safe, legal abortions and the importance of abortion as a tool of women's self-determination."[106] She also criticizes the underlying assumption that

> "compulsory heterosexuality" creates a political and social climate of which unwanted pregnancies are the characteristic expression: the heterosexual woman borne down, pitiful, "caught" in sexual domination and its unwanted fruits.[107]

Petchesky suggests that heterosexuality contributes to male irresponsibility for birth control and children (which she characterizes as a form of power). Finally, she points out that unwanted pregnancies occur "for a whole variety of reasons that may have little to do with male coercion."[108]

Disagreeing that women are victims of abortion under modern medical and legal conditions, Petchesky suggests instead that women are its agents and beneficiaries. Moreover, she criticizes MacKinnon's characterization of the state as an "instrument" of men—arguing instead that the "gate keepers" to reproductive services are often women.[109] Petchesky thereby disputes MacKinnon's emphasis on victimization in abortion and other contexts.[110]

MacKinnon, in a surrebuttal, responds that Petchesky misses the point.[111] MacKinnon characterizes the fundamental disagreement as follows: "I criticize sexuality as a sphere of inequality," whereas Petchesky "defend[s] it as if it is a sphere of equality."[112] MacKinnon lambasts her critics for labeling conditions of "constraint and necessity" as freedom and also for failing to understand the sexual basis of gender inequality.

MacKinnon's most important contribution to the abortion debate is her cogent criticism of the privacy doctrine as a rationale for abortion. The privacy doctrine, underlying the liberal defense of abortion, assumes a dichotomy between the public and the private. MacKinnon is joined by other feminists who reject this dichotomy.[113] She criticizes the assumption inherent in liberal ideology of equally autonomous individuals with regard to sexual intercourse. Since sexual intercourse "cannot simply be presumed coequally determined,"[114] state noninterference in the abortion decision perpetuates male exploitation of women. MacKinnon is skeptical of male support of abortion rights. She suggests that the abortion right conferred by the Supreme Court was prompted by male interests in preserving sexual availability.[115] Her skepticism of male advocacy of abortion rights is shared by Andrea Dworkin.[116]

MacKinnon proposes the different rationale of equality doctrine to ensure greater access to abortion. She explains:

> [C]riminal abortion statutes of the sort invalidated in *Roe* violate equal protection of the laws. They make women criminals for a medical procedure that only women need, when much of the need for this procedure as well as barriers to access to it have been created by social conditions of sex inequality. Forced motherhood is sex inequality. Because pregnancy can be experienced only by women, and because of the unequal social predicates and consequences pregnancy has for women, any forced pregnancy will always deprive and hurt one sex only as a member of her gender.[117]

MacKinnon's views have been sharply criticized by liberal theorist Ronald Dworkin,[118] who charges that MacKinnon "conflates different senses of 'privacy.'" He disagrees with MacKinnon that recognition of a right to privacy leaves women to be exploited by their husbands, or that it denies collective social responsibility for financing abortion for poor women. He criticizes MacKinnon for "disparag[ing] the motives of men who favor women's right to abortion."[119] He charges her with downplaying woman's unique contribution to and relationship with the fetus.[120] Finally, he is critical of MacKinnon's (and the radical feminist) claim that sexual subordination is at the heart of the abortion controversy.

> I do not believe, finally, that even a great and general improvement in gender equality in the United States would either undercut the argument that women have a constitutional right to abortion or obviate the need for such a right.[121]

Dworkin's criticisms, regrettably, reveal a lack of understanding of the feminist perspective—even a failure to recognize the possibility that a feminist perspective on abortion might differ from that of men.

Marxist and Socialist Feminist Perspectives

Reproduction occupies a less central place for Marxist theory. Marx and Engels devoted little attention to sexuality or reproduction, and none to abortion. In order to understand Marxist and socialist feminist perspectives on abortion, it is first necessary to explore those views on women's oppression.

Many feminists have criticized Marxism's view of women's nature and the sources of women's oppression.[122] Engels explored the sources of women's oppression in *The Origin of the Family, Private Property and the State,*[123] claiming that capitalism and the institution of private property constitute a cause of women's subordination. Many feminists, however, criticize as shortsighted the notion that capitalism's downfall will ensure women's equality. As Hartmann explains, "[S]ince capital and private property do not cause the oppression of women as *women,* their end alone will not result in the end of women's oppression."[124] Marxism's failure to regard reproduction as productive labor is a particular source of criticism.

> Marx tells us that men are shaped by their relation to the mode of production. But we have seen that women . . . are shaped by their relation to the mode of reproduction. So in the Marxian vision of freedom, realized when the means of production are collectively owned and controlled, the matter of freedom for reproducers and reproduction is ignored. Reproductive work is not regarded as work, and Marx joins the liberals in viewing the organization of this work non-political.[125]

The Marxist inattention to reproduction is addressed briefly in an early socialist feminist work by Juliet Mitchell, who compares wage labor to reproduction.[126] Other feminists, however, criticize Mitchell for the relegation of reproduction, sexuality, and childrearing to the ideological realm, and for a failure to identify a material base for patriarchy.[127]

More contemporary socialist feminists join in criticizing Marxist views of reproduction. O'Brien attempts to remedy Marxists' omission of reproduction by providing a feminist theory of the source of women's oppression.[128] She theorizes that, in reproduction, two opposites come together and synthesize a new product. In the course of this process, she remarks, the male is alienated because of his separation from sperm upon ejaculation. As a result, the nature of alienation (a fundamental Marxist concept) is different for men and women:

> The birth of the child is women's alienation of that unity to which men have no experiential access, but women's alienation from their seed is *mediated in labour.* Women do not, like men, have to take action to annul their alienation from the race, for their labour confirms their integration. Not only does this fact differentiate male and female reproductive consciousness, it differentiates male and female temporal consciousness. . . . Female temporal consciousness is continuous, whereas male temporal consciousness is discontinuous.[129]

Men resist alienation, she theorizes, by appropriation of the child and assertions of paternity. Men attempt to assert control not only over the child, but also over the woman.[130]

Socialist feminist Cossman takes the analysis further by combining O'Brien's views with those of MacKinnon to explain how abortion threatens male dominance.[131] She suggests that abortion, which represents women's rejection of the product of man's reproductive labor, exacerbates male alienation. Men thereby respond in two ways: to deny women the right to abortion, and to attempt to reassert control over abortion in the male medical profession. Cossman's theory provides an intriguing synthesis of radical and socialist feminist views to explain the male response to abortion.

Socialist feminist Sandra Harding[132] offers another critique of Marxist theory. Concurring with Cossman, Harding suggests that Marxists view reproduction, in general, and abortion, in particular, from the male perspective. Harding castigates Marxist theory for its assumption that certain aspects of the sexual division of labor (housework and reproduction) are women's sphere. In addition, according to Harding, Marxism neglects to explain how essential tasks will be accomplished "after the revolution."

Abortion, for Marxists, is a dispute involving class antagonisms.

> From the perspective of Marxism, the abortion dispute appears merely as a typical bourgeois attempt to obscure the fundamental class organization of social life. There are no *social, human* needs, perceptions, or values that women across the class spectrum can share, because class divisions drive women into antagonistic relations with each other as firmly as they separate the proletariat and the bourgeoisie to which women fundamentally "belong."[133]

This Marxist view of class struggle as a mode of conflict resolution, according to Harding, fails to serve women's interests in the context of abortion. Instead, as a solution to the failings of Marxism (and liberalism as well), Harding proposes that feminists and antifeminists unite in their common beliefs (motherhood as a socially valuable activity; the social value of children; the importance of women's life needs; and the recognition of male sexuality as posing problems for women).[134]

Mahowald adds another socialist feminist voice to the abortion debate.[135] Like some radical and liberal feminists, Mahowald emphasizes equality-based arguments.[136] Her concept of equality incorporates respect for biological and psychological differences, an attention to these differences, a definition of equality as an equal share of rewards and social services, and an emphasis on autonomy.[137] Applied to abortion, Mahowald's version of socialist feminism "insists that the fetus is morally relevant to abortion decisions, but not exclusively determinative of their morality."[138]

Socialist feminist Petchesky suggests the desirability of a synthesis of Marxist and feminist perspectives in views of reproductive freedom.[139] She proposes that Marxism has special application to the abortion debate. Conceiving of reproductive freedom as class-based and socially constructed, Petchesky recharacterizes the central feminist issue: feminists must focus not so much on choice, but rather on the need to change the "social conditions of choosing, working, and reproducing."[140]

Some socialist feminists criticize liberal, as well as Marxist, ideology as applied to the abortion debate. Brown joins other socialist feminists in criticizing the liberal reliance on the right to privacy.[141] Like MacKinnon and others, Brown suggests that a focus on reproduction as private relates women to a private sphere, to women's detriment. In addition, Brown criticizes the liberal emphasis in abortion decision making as an issue of individual rights,[142] suggesting instead that abortion is "a facet of historically shaped social relationships and processes."[143] Brown bases her views in part on the work of Carol Gilligan, whose findings stem from research conducted, in part, in the context of abortion decision making.[144]

Copelon might also be labeled a socialist feminist for her emphasis on the role of social conditions. From this vantage point, she joins criticisms of privacy as a basis for abortion rights. She suggests that the privacy rationale is flawed "because it perpetuates the myth that the right to choose is inherent in the individual, a given of private life, rather than acknowledging that choices are shaped, facilitated, or denied by social conditions."[145] Moreover, Copelon charges that conceptualizing privacy as governmental noninterference emphasizes the "negative" right of privacy which "carries no corresponding obligation on the part of the state to facilitate choice."[146] For Copelon, feminists should seek autonomy and the restructuring of the workforce and family as goals.

Socialist feminist Alison Jaggar shares a recognition of the social context of the abortion decision.[147] Jaggar concurs with Petchesky[148] that women, rather than men, should control reproduction. Jaggar reaches this conclusion based not on liberal notions of privacy or autonomy, but rather on mothers' primary responsibility for childrearing.[149] However, Jaggar's preferred solution to the abortion controversy is the transformation of the emphasis on individual rights to one of fulfillment of human needs.[150]

Feminist Legal Theory

The abortion debate lies at the intersection of philosophy and law.[151] Such a controversial subject has, not surprisingly, generated a voluminous legal and philosophical literature.[152] Philosophical examinations emphasize the relationship between law and morality;[153] the personhood of the fetus;[154] and analogies between abortion and murder (mercy killing, infanticide, and the samaritan obligation).[155] Legal literature, on the other hand, emphasizes criticisms of Roe v. Wade, the competing rights of the parties in abortion decision making, and the abortion funding cases.[156]

Both the philosophical and the legal literature reflect a serious lacuna. Few works view the gender-based nature of abortion. This gap is slowly being remedied by feminist legal theory focusing on the relationship between the state, power, gender, and sexuality; abortion and gender inequality; the significance of the abortion right from a feminist perspective; and the relationship between the right to abortion and issues of class and race.

Several of these concerns are reflected in the essays here. From a socialist feminist perspective, Linda Gordon argues that the history of birth control, especially its regulation, must be understood in terms of social conditions. Gordon illuminates the interaction between social movements and the development of sexual ideology.

Considerable opposition to abortion is based on the premise that personhood arises at conception. Judith Jarvis Thomson argues that, even conceding this premise as true, abortion is justified, nonetheless, as a means of self-defense.[157] Thomson's view appears conservative in retrospect because it was written when abortion was still illegal. Thomson reaches her conclusion deductively, based on a famous analogy: the similarity of the fetus to a renowned, unconscious violinist who needs new kidneys to cure a fatal ailment. Her essay, part of the tradition that views abortion as a conflict between rights,[158] illuminates the nature and contextuality of rights-based claims (right to life versus right to self-determination).

Thomson's essay remains controversial for abortion opponents and supporters alike. Although one legal scholar defends her analogy of samaritanism,[159] many commentators criticize her thesis.[160] Some criticize her analogy of abortion to self-defense[161] or samaritanism.[162] Still other scholars have found fault with her characterization of abortion as a balancing of rights,[163] or with her conclusion about the diminished moral rights of the fetus.[164]

Feminists, including Catharine MacKinnon, have been among Thomson's sharpest critics.[165] Here, MacKinnon elaborates on some of her criticisms of Thomson's thesis. MacKinnon also casts doubt on the liberal emphasis on privacy as the rationale for the abortion right, because, she argues, this rationale merely affirms male dominance.

Concurring with MacKinnon about the desirability of analyzing abortion from an equality perspective, Siegel applies antisubordination principles to identify how abortion restrictions contribute to women's status.[166] Siegel's socialist feminist analysis of the social framework of abortion highlights the relationship between reproductive control, the regulation of motherhood, and women's roles.

Essays by Laurie Nsiah-Jefferson and Ruth Colker, respectively, turn the focus to the disproportionate impact of abortion restrictions. Nsiah-Jefferson's essay makes an important contribution with its exploration of the interrelationship between race, class, and gender.[167] Colker broadens the focus by incorporating issues of age as well, through her concern with the problem of teenage pregnancy. Colker proposes a broad-based challenge to our reproductive health policies based on equal protection doctrine.

Lori L. Heise probes the controversial radical feminist view of the role of male violence against women in the context of reproductive control. Her essay adds breadth to the discussion by highlighting the range of reproductive health issues (sterilization, AIDS prevention, family planning, battering during pregnancy, medical treatment of pregnancy and birth). Especially valuable is her elucidation of the link between violence and reproductive freedom in the pro-life advocates' denial of access to abortion clinics.

Notes

1. L. Gordon, Woman's Body, Woman's Right: Birth Control in America 399 (Penguin Books, 1990). See also S. Abbott & B. Love, Is Women's Liberation a Lesbian Plot? in V. Gornick & B. Moran eds., Woman in Sexist Society: Studies in Power and Powerlessness 604 (Penguin, 1972).

2. See, e.g., W. Brown, Reproductive Freedom and the Right to Privacy: A Paradox for Feminists, in I. Diamond ed., Families, Politics, and Public Policy: A Feminist Dialogue on Women and the State 336 (Longman, 1983); L. Gordon, Woman's Body, *supra* note 1, at 398; Cossman, The Precarious Unity of Feminist Theory and Practice: The Praxis of Abortion, 44 U. Toronto Fac. L. Rev. 85 (1986).

3. Gordon, *supra* note 1, at 108–111; Tribe, Abortion: A Clash of Absolutes 33 (W. W. Norton, 1990). See also Mohr, Abortion in America: The Origins and Evolution of National Policy, 1800–1900 253 (Oxford Univ. Press, 1978).

4. L. Cisler, Unfinished Business: Birth Control and Women's Liberation, in R. Morgan ed., Sisterhood Is Powerful: An Anthology of Writings from the Women's Liberation Movement 278, 288–304 (Vintage, 1970).

5. Concern focused on the safety and effectiveness of contraceptives and access thereto by the unmarried. Cisler, Unfinished Business, *supra* note 4, at 280–281. Other concerns were limitations on women's right to voluntary sterilization (e.g., hospital committees requiring a patient to be over 30, have several living children and her husband's consent), as well as the practice of forced sterilization as punishment for promiscuity. *Id.* at 286, 287–288. On the movement against sterilization abuse, see Gordon, *supra* note 1, at 433–436. See also B. Rothman, Reproduction, in B. Hess & M. Ferree eds. Analyzing Gender: A Handbook of Social Science Research 154 (Sage, 1987).

6. Concern over access to contraception waned after the Supreme Court decision in Eisenstadt v. Baird, 405 U.S. 438 (1972), guaranteeing the right of the unmarried to contraceptives, and Griswold v. Connecticut, 381 U.S. 479 (1965) (guaranteeing the right for married couples). A few organizations, such as the Committee for Abortion Rights and Against Sterilization Abuse (CARASA), focused on both sterilization and abortion. Gordon, *supra* note 1, at 435. Even Gordon concedes that sterilization abuse receded in importance "because so much of the energy of reproductive rights advocates has had to go into defending abortion rights." *Id.* at 436.

7. NOW (National Organization for Women) Bill of Rights, reprinted in Morgan, *supra* note 4, at 575, 576 ("Historical Documents"). See also Tribe, *supra* note 3, at 45.

8. Tribe, *supra* note 3, at 45. Tribe also points out that some early second-wave feminists feared that support for abortion rights would taint them as immoral. *Id.* at 44.

9. *Id.* See also A. Echols, Daring to Be Bad: Radical Feminism in America 1967–1975, 140–142 (Univ. Minn. Press, 1989).

10. Tribe, *supra* note 3, at 44.

11. Cisler, Unfinished Business, in Sisterhood Is Powerful, *supra* note 4, at 312; F. Davis, Moving the Mountain: The Women's Movement in America Since 1960 232 (Simon & Schuster, 1991). On the most famous abortion collective (named "Jane" after the founder-student who provided referrals from her dormitory), see Jane, Just Call "Jane" in M. Fried ed., From Abortion to Reproductive Freedom: Transforming a Movement 93–100 (South End Press, 1990); R. Petchesky, Abortion and Woman's Choice: The State, Sexuality, and Reproductive Freedom 128–129 (Longman, 1984).

12. Petchesky, *supra* note 11, at 129.

13. L. Cisler, Abortion Law Repeal (sort of): A Warning to Women, in A. Koedt, E. Levine & A. Rapone eds., Radical Feminism 153 (Quadrangle Books, 1973).

14. Davis, *supra* note 11, at 164 ("Lader was virtually the father of the reproductive rights movement on the East Coast.") See also L. Lader, Abortion (Bobbs-Merrill, 1966).

15. Davis, *supra* note 11, at 165. See also Tribe, *supra* note 3, at 40 (21 members of the clergy in 1967 offered abortion referral service).

16. B. Sarvis & H. Rodman, The Abortion Controversy 10 (Columbia Univ. Press, 1973).

17. Tribe, *supra* note 3, at 36. See also American Law Institute, Model Penal Code §207.11 (May 1959) (Tentative Draft No. 9).

18. American Law Institute, Model Penal Code §230.3 (1962) ("justifiable abortions"). See also Cisler, Unfinished Business, in Sisterhood Is Powerful, *supra* note 4, at 307, 308; Tribe, *supra* note 3, at 36 (pointing out that ALI provisions were defenses to criminal charges).

19. On the influence of the 1962 Sherri Finkbine-thalidomide case and the 1963–1964 rubella epidemic, see Davis, *supra* note 11, at 163; Gordon, *supra* note 1, at 403; Lader, *supra* note 14, at 6, 10–16; Mohr, *supra* note 3, at 252–253; Tribe, *supra* note 3, at 37–38.

20. Davis, *supra* note 11, at 164; Sarvis & Rodman, *supra* note 16, at 43; Tribe, *supra* note 3, at 42.

21. Tribe, *supra* note 3, at 42.

22. Cisler, Abortion Law Repeal, in Radical Feminism, *supra* note 13, at 153 ("the circumstances covered by 'reform' *are* tragic but they affect very few women's lives"). *Id.*

23. On the establishment of hospital review committees, see generally Sarvis & Rodman, *supra* note 16, at 39, 42, 46 (committees were criticized as arbitrary and capricious, lacking appeal procedures, and having discriminatory impact). On residency requirements, see *id.* at 44.

24. Cisler, Abortion Law Repeal, in Radical Feminism, *supra* note 13, at 154, 157; Tribe, *supra* note 3, at 43.

25. Petchesky, *supra* note 11, at 126. See also Echols, *supra* note 9, at 140–141; Tribe, *supra* note 3, at 43–45.

26. Petchesky, *supra* note 11, at 125–126.

27. Tribe, *supra* note 3, at 46 (Hawaii), 47–48 (New York).

28. *Id.* at 47–48.

29. Sarvis & Rodman, *supra* note 16, at 47; Tribe, *supra* note 3, at 49.

30. For pre-*Roe* cases declaring abortion laws unconstitutional, see People v. Belous, 458 P.2d 194 (Cal. 1969); U.S. v. Vuitch, 305 F. Supp. 1032 (D.D.C. 1969), *rev'd,* 402 U.S. 62 (1971).

31. 410 U.S. 113 (1973).

32. Mohr, *supra* note 3, at 23–24.

33. *Id.* at 5. Ellenborough's Act, 1803, 43 Geo. 3, ch. 58 (Eng.). See also M. Grossberg, Governing the Hearth: Law and the Family in Nineteenth-Century America 160 (Univ. North Carolina, 1985).

34. Ten states and one territory passed laws in this period. Grossberg, *supra* note 33, at 161. Connecticut passed the first antiabortion statute in 1821, prohibiting (postquickening) inducement of abortion by poisoning. Tribe, *supra* note 3, at 29. See also Mohr, *supra* note 3, at 20.

35. Gordon, *supra* note 1, at 59; Mohr, *supra* note 3, at 147–170; Tribe, *supra* note 3, at 30–34; Petchesky, *supra* note 11, at 78.

36. Mohr, *supra* note 3, at 157; Tribe, *supra* note 3, at 30.

37. Mohr, *supra* note 3, at 200.

38. *Id.*

39. *Id.* at 160. Mohr cites, additionally, a desire to promote professionalism and to influence national policy making. *Id.* at 162–163.

40. Petchesky, *supra* note 11, at 82. See also Tribe, *supra* note 3, at 33 (physicians' campaign illuminated the threat that abortion posed to traditional sex roles).

41. Petchesky, *supra* note 11, at 80. Siegel is more forthright in labeling misogyny as the source of the nineteenth century physicians' campaign. See Reva Siegel, Reasoning from the Body: A Historical Perspective on Abortion Regulation and Questions of Equal Protection, 44 Stan. L. Rev. 261, 301–308 (1992) (excerpted herein).

42. Mohr, *supra* note 3, at 167. On fear of "race suicide" as contributing to the birth control movement, see Gordon, *supra* note 1, at 133–155; Tribe, *supra* note 3, at 32–33.

43. Grossberg, *supra* note 33, at 161, 168.

44. Tribe, *supra* note 3, at 31. Tribe suggests that the clergy were influenced, in large part, by the medical profession. *Id.* at 32.

45. Gordon, *supra* note 1, at 53.

46. On folk methods, see *id.* at 35–39.

47. Tribe, *supra* note 3, at 35.

48. Davis, *supra* note 11, at 158.

49. 410 U.S. 113 (1973).

50. 410 U.S. 179 (1973).

51. On the history of the statute, see Mohr, *supra* note 3, at 138–139.

52. 410 U.S. 179, 202–205 (1973).

53. Tribe, *supra* note 3, at 12.

54. *Id.* at 79 ("no judicial ruling since segregated public schools were held unconstitutional . . . has generated anything resembling the degree of criticism . . . triggered by Roe v. Wade"). For early critiques, see Ely, The Wages of Crying Wolf: A Comment on Roe v. Wade, 82 Yale L.J. 920 (1973); Heymann & Barzelay, The Forest and the Trees: Roe v. Wade and Its Critics, 53 B.U. L. Rev. 765 (1973). See also R. Dworkin, Life's Dominion: An Argument About Abortion, Euthanasia, and Individual Freedom 51 (Knopf, 1993) (feminists were among *Roe's* most "savage critics").

55. See generally Tribe, *supra* note 3, at 79–83.

56. See Mohr, *supra* note 3, at 57. For criticism of the trimester scheme, see City of Akron v. Akron Center for Reproductive Health, 462 U.S. 416, 454, 458 (1983) (O'Connor, J., dissenting) (trimester scheme "on a collision course with itself"). Some commentators point out that the trimester scheme disproportionately burdens poor women and women of color. See, e.g., Nsiah-Jefferson, Reproductive Laws, Women of Color, and Low-Income Women, herein at 1007, 1008.

57. Tribe, *supra* note 3, at 49 (citing Mary Ann Glendon, Abortion and Divorce in Western Law 21 (Harvard Univ. Press, 1987)). This view is shared by Justice Ruth Bader Ginsburg. See Ginsburg, Some Thoughts on Autonomy and Equality in Relation to Roe v. Wade, 63 N.C. L. Rev. 375, 381–382 (1985). However, Tribe disputes the idea of a legislative trend by pointing out that the repeal movement was defeated in many state legislatures in the 1970s. Tribe, *supra* note 3, at 49–50. Compare Estrich & Sullivan, Abortion Politics: Writing for an Audience of One, 138 U. Pa. L. Rev. 119, 150–155 (1989) (inappropriateness of legislative reform).

58. Mohr, *supra* note 3, at 249.

59. For feminist critiques of the privacy rationale, see W. Brown, Reproductive Freedom, in Families, Politics, and Public Policy, *supra* note 2, at 336; R. Copelon, From Privacy to Autonomy: The Conditions for Sexual and Reproductive Freedom, in From Abortion to Reproductive Freedom, *supra* note 11, at 27; C. MacKinnon, Abortion: On Public and Private, in Toward a Feminist Theory of the State (Harvard Univ.

Press, 1989), C. MacKinnon, Roe v. Wade: A Study in Male Ideology, in J. Garfield & P. Hennessey eds., Abortion: Moral and Legal Perspectives 45 (Univ. Mass. Press, 1984); Ginsburg, *supra* note 57; Olsen, Unraveling Compromise, 103 Harv. L. Rev. 105, 117 (1989) (critique of privacy rationale concluding that Court should retain it but "dismantle the false dichotomies underlying it"); Stein, Living with the Risk of Backfire: A Response to the Feminist Critiques of Privacy and Equality, 77 Minn. L. Rev. 1153 (1993). See also Tribe, *supra* note 3, at 105 ("Laws restricting abortion so drastically shape the lives of women, and only of women, that their denial of equality hardly needs detailed elaboration.").

60. Copelon, From Privacy to Autonomy, in From Abortion to Reproductive Freedom, *supra* note 11, at 28. See also Petchesky, *supra* note 11, at 241–276.

61. See, e.g., The Helms-Hyde Human Life Bill, S. 158, H.R. 900, 97th Cong., 1st Sess. (1981). See also Bopp, An Examination of Proposals for a Human Life Amendment, 15 Cap. U. L. Rev. 417 (1986); Copelon, Testimony on Constitutional Amendments to Negate Roe v. Wade Given Before the Subcommittee on the Constitution of the Senate Judiciary Committee, 8 Women's Rts. L. Rep. 179 (1985); S. Galebach, A Human Life Statute, in Abortion: Moral and Legal Perspectives, *supra* note 59, at 123.

62. 448 U.S. 197 (1980).

63. 500 U.S. 173 (1991).

64. 492 U.S. 490 (1989).

65. 112 S. Ct. 2791 (1992).

66. The test, first suggested by Justice O'Connor in City of Akron v. Akron Center for Reproductive Health, 462 U.S. 416, 453 (1983) (O'Connor, J., dissenting), was reiterated in *Webster*, 492 U.S. at 529–531 (O'Connor, J., concurring). For a discussion of the undue burden standard, see Estrich & Sullivan, *supra* note 57, at 132–140 (1989).

67. H.R. 25, 103d Cong., 1st Sess. (1993). See also Peggy S. McClard, Comment, The Freedom of Choice Act: Will the Constitution Allow It?, 30 Houston L. Rev. 2041 (1994).

68. M. Seegers, Abortion and the Culture: Toward a Feminist Perspective, in S. Callahan & D. Callahan eds., Abortion: Understanding Differences 229 (Plenum, 1984).

69. *Id.* at 239.

70. *Id.* at 240–241. Feminists use this argument to counter concerns that women will abuse reproductive freedom.

71. *Id.* at 241–242. Seegers also theorizes that the feminist perspective on abortion includes a recognition of the rights of the fetus and woman as contingent on certain conditions, rather than absolute. Many feminists, especially liberal and radical feminists, would disagree, believing that the woman's right is paramount. See, e.g., Davis, *supra* note 9, at 166; A. Dworkin, Right-Wing Women 97 (Perigee, 1983); Echols, *supra* note 9, at 141; N. Gillespie, Abortion and Human Rights, in Joel Feinberg ed., The Problem of Abortion 94, 99 (Wadsworth, 2d ed. 1984); A. Jaggar, Feminist Politics and Human Nature 198 (Rowman & Allenheld, 1983).

72. Rothman, Reproduction, in Analyzing Gender, *supra* note 5, at 164–165.

73. K. Luker, Abortion and the Politics of Motherhood 205 (Univ. Calif., 1984). Luker's essay explains that feminists are on both sides of the abortion debate. *Id.* at 113. For a discussion of abortion by a self-characterized "pro-life feminist," see S. Callahan, Abortion and the Sexual Agenda, in R. Baird & S. Rosenbaum eds., The Ethics of Abortion: Pro-Life! v. Pro-Choice! 131 (Prometheus Books, 1989) (arguing that women cannot achieve full equality in a society that condones abortion).

74. See Ginsburg, *supra* note 57; Karst, The Supreme Court, 1976 Term—Fore-

word: Equal Citizenship Under the Fourteenth Amendment, 91 Harv. L. Rev. 1, 57–59 (1977); Law, Rethinking Sex and the Constitution, 132 U. Pa. L. Rev. 955 (1984); Olsen, *supra* note 59, at 118 (citing additional commentators).

75. Proponents of this view are bolstered by the Canadian Charter of Rights and Freedoms' explicit guarantee of sex equality, which contrasts with our constitutional guarantee of "equal treatment" in the Fourteenth Amendment. On abortion under the Canadian Charter, see generally Martin, Canada's Abortion Law and the Canadian Charter of Rights and Freedoms, 1 Can. J. Women & Law. 339 (1986); Mathewson, Security of the Person, Equality and Abortion in Canada, 1989 U. Chi. Legal Forum 251; Morgentaler v. Regina, 62 CR 3d 1, 1 S.C.R. 30 (Can. 1988) (invalidating statute requiring women to obtain written approval from an accredited hospital's review committee). See also Olsen, *supra* note 59, at 119–120 n.69 ("The Women's Legal Education and Action Fund (LEAF) of Canada has submitted amicus briefs in Canadian abortion cases that carry the equality analysis further than American feminists have. While LEAF's argument may not directly apply to cases in the United States because of differences between our Bill of Rights and fourteenth amendment and the Canadian Charter of Rights and Freedoms, it can and should inform the American debate on abortion.")

76. Jaggar, *supra* note 71, at 203 n.7. See also Tribe, *supra* note 3, at 46 (formation of NARAL). NARAL was renamed the National Abortion Rights Action League after Roe v. Wade was decided.

77. Jaggar, *supra* note 71, at 198.

78. *Id.* at 180.

79. J. Benshoof, The Legacy of Roe v. Wade, in Abortion: Moral and Legal Perspectives, *supra* note 59, at 36.

80. *Id.* at 36–37. For an essay arguing that autonomy is a "fundamental right" protected by the Constitution that is violated by restrictions on women's reproductive freedom, see Ridder & Woll, Transforming the Grounds: Autonomy and Reproductive Freedom, 2 Yale J.L. & Fem. 75, 82–84 (1989).

81. Stein, *supra* note 59, at 1155.

82. Copelon, From Privacy to Autonomy, in From Abortion to Reproductive Freedom, *supra* note 11, at 33. See also Copelon, Unpacking Patriarchy: Reproduction, Sexuality, Originalism and Constitutional Change, in J. Lobel ed., A Less than Perfect Union: Alternative Perspectives on the U.S. Constitution 303, 316 (Monthly Review Press, 1988), and Copelon, Beyond the Liberal Idea of Privacy: Toward a Positive Right of Autonomy, in M. McCann & G. Houseman eds., Judging the Constitution: Critical Essays on Judicial Lawmaking 287, 297–394 (Scott, Foresman & Co., 1989).

83. Copelon, From Privacy to Autonomy, in From Abortion to Reproductive Freedom, *supra* note 11, at 35 (citing Whalen v. Roe, 429 U.S. 589 (1977), and Thornburgh v. American College of Obstetricians and Gynecologists, 476 U.S. 747 (1986)).

84. *Id.*

85. Our concept of equality, rooted in the Fourteenth Amendment equal protection clause, has been interpreted to require treating alike those persons who are similarly situated. For a discussion of this standard applied to pregnancy, see the essays on The Equality Debate: Equal Treatment versus Special Treatment, in D. Weisberg ed., Feminist Legal Theory: Foundations 121–207 (Temple Univ. Press, 1993).

86. Petchesky, *supra* note 11, at 131.

87. *Id.* For an example of this "repeal rather than reform" view, see Cisler, Abortion Law Repeal, in Radical Feminism, *supra* note 13, especially 154–160.

88. Gordon, *supra* note 1, at 406 (as reflected in the characterization of the "pro-choice" movement).

89. Sandra Harding, Beneath the Surface of the Abortion Debate: Are Women Fully Human, in Abortion: Understanding Differences, *supra* note 68, at 203, 213.

90. *Id.* at 216.

91. *Id.* at 214.

92. Pleck, Domestic Tyranny, *supra* note 3, at 184.

93. S. Firestone, The Dialectic of Sex: The Case for Feminist Revolution (Bantam Books, 1970), especially 1–12. For an excellent discussion of Firestone's views (and her critics), see R. Tong, Feminist Thought: A Comprehensive Introduction 72–84 (Westview Press, 1989).

94. Echols, *supra* note 9, at 141.

95. *Id.* at 142. See also Tribe, *supra* note 3, at 44.

96. Echols, *supra* note 9, at 171.

97. Shulamith Firestone founded Redstockings; Lucinda Cisler founded New Yorkers for Abortion Law Repeal. *Id.* at 140, 141.

98. For example, both radical feminists and NOW feminists were members of the famous Chicago collective which provided referral services from 1969 to 1973. Jane, Just Call "Jane," in From Abortion to Reproductive Freedom, *supra* note 11, at 93, 97.

99. Jaggar, *supra* note 71, at 256.

100. *Id.* at 256–257.

101. A. Dworkin, Abortion, in Right-Wing Women, *supra* note 71, at 87. See also *id.* at 87–88.

102. Copelon, From Privacy to Autonomy, in From Abortion to Reproductive Freedom, *supra* note 11, at 42 n.26.

103. A. Rich, Of Woman Born: Motherhood as Experience and Institution 267, 269 (Norton, 1976).

104. Petchesky, Abortion as "Violence Against Women": A Feminist Critique, 18 Radical America 64 (1983). MacKinnon's essay was first published as MacKinnon, The Male Ideology of Privacy: A Feminist Perspective on the Right to Abortion, 17 Radical America 23 (1983). Petchesky amplifies on her critique of abortion as a form of male violence in Abortion and Woman's Choice, *supra* note 11, at 389.

105. Petchesky, Abortion as Violence, *supra* note 104, at 65.

106. *Id.* at 64.

107. *Id.* at 66.

108. *Id.*

109. *Id.* at 64.

110. Petchesky disagrees also with MacKinnon on the issue of pornography. See *id.* at 67.

111. MacKinnon, Reply By MacKinnon, 18 Radical America 69 (1983).

112. *Id.* at 70.

113. See, e.g., Schneider, The Violence of Privacy, herein at 388, 389.

114. MacKinnon, Privacy v. Equality: Beyond Roe v. Wade, herein at 985, 986.

115. *Id.* at 990.

116. *Id.* citing Dworkin, Right-wing Women, *supra* note 71, at 95 (1983) ("Getting laid was at stake.")

117. MacKinnon, Reflections on Sex Equality Under Law, 100 Yale L.J. 1281, 1319 (1991) (this view is also expressed in the essay herein).

118. Dworkin, Life's Dominion, *supra* note 54, at 52–56. Ronald Dworkin has also criticized MacKinnon's views on pornography. See Dworkin, Women and Pornography, N.Y. Rev. Books, Oct. 21, 1993, at 36 (reviewing C. MacKinnon, Only Words (1993)); MacKinnon, Pornography: An Exchange, N.Y. Rev. Books, Mar. 3, 1994, at 47, 48; Dworkin, Reply, N.Y. Rev. Books, Mar. 3, 1994, at 48 (surreply).

119. Dworkin, Life's Dominion, *supra* note 54, at 53–54.

120. *Id.* at 55.

121. *Id.* at 56.

122. See, e.g., Catharine MacKinnon, Feminism, Marxism, Method and the State: Toward Feminist Jurisprudence in Weisberg, *supra* note 85, at 427; Feminism, Marxism, Method and the State: An Agenda for Theory, in *id.* at 437; L. Sargent ed., Women and Revolution: A Discussion of the Unhappy Marriage of Marxism and Feminism (South End Press, 1981).

123. F. Engels, The Origin of the Family, Private Property and the State (International Pub., 1973).

124. Hartmann, Unhappy Marriage, in Women and Revolution, *supra* note 122, at 4.

125. Brown, Reproductive Freedom, in Families, Politics and Public Policy, *supra* note 2, at 326.

126. See Juliet Mitchell, Woman's Estate (Vintage Books, 1973).

127. See, e.g, Hartmann, Unhappy Marriage, in Women and Revolution, *supra* note 122, at 11–12.

128. O'Brien, The Politics of Reproduction (Routledge & Kegan Paul, 1981).

129. *Id.* at 32.

130. *Id.* at 53–54, 58–59.

131. Cossman, *supra* note 2, at 93–94.

132. Harding, Beneath the Surface, in Abortion: Understanding Differences, *supra* note 68, at 216–19.

133. *Id.* at 219.

134. *Id.* at 223–224.

135. Mahowald, Abortion and Equality, in Abortion: Understanding Differences, *supra* note 68, at 195.

136. *Id.* at 177. ("[S]ome principle needs to be introduced as a criterion by which to order [the arguments]. To that end, I propose a concept of equality. . . .") *Id.* at 181.

137. *Id.* at 185.

138. Id. at 195.

139. R. Petchesky, Introduction: Beyond "A Woman's Right to Choose"—Feminist Ideas About Reproductive Rights, Abortion and Woman's Choice: The State, Sexuality, and Reproductive Freedom 2 (Northeastern Univ. Press, rev. ed. 1990) at 2.

140. *Id.* at 11. Another socialist feminist, Sheila Rowbotham, has also addressed the significance of the social relations of reproduction. Like many socialist feminists, Rowbotham is critical of the Marxist model of class struggle. For a criticism of Rowbotham's views of reproduction, see O'Brien, *supra* note 128, at 76.

141. Brown, Reproductive Freedom, in Families, Politics and Public Policy, *supra* note 2, at 332.

142. *Id.* at 330. See also Stein, *supra* note 59, at 1168, and 1168 n.55 (characterizing the neglect of the value of connection as an aspect of the privacy critique and identifying feminist adherents of this viewpoint).

143. Brown, Reproductive Freedom, in Families, Politics, and Public Policy, *supra*

note 2, at 331. (Brown is labeled here as a socialist feminist for her emphasis on the social and historical context of abortion).

144. C. Gilligan, In a Different Voice: Psychological Theory and Women's Development (Harvard Univ. Press, 1982). For a discussion of the importance of Gilligan's work for feminist legal theory (as well as criticism), see Bender, A Lawyer's Primer on Feminist Theory and Tort, in Weisberg, *supra* note 85, at 58, 63–67; MacKinnon, Difference and Dominance: On Sex Discrimination, *id.* at 276, 280–281; Scales, The Emergence of Feminist Jurisprudence: An Essay, *id.* at 40, 42–45.

145. Copelon is labeled a socialist feminist because of her emphasis on social conditions and her belief that "choices are shaped, facilitated, or denied by social conditions." Copelon, From Privacy to Autonomy, in From Abortion to Reproductive Freedom, *supra* note 11, at 38.

146. *Id.*

147. Jaggar, Abortion and a Woman's Right to Decide, in C. Gould & M. Wartofsky eds., Women and Philosophy: Toward a Theory of Liberation 348 (Putnam, 1976).

148. Petchesky, *supra* note 11, at 3–8.

149. Jaggar, Abortion and a Women's Right to Decide, in Women and Philosphy, *supra* note 147, at 354.

150. *Id.* at 358.

151. J. Garfield, Introduction: Abortion: Persons, Morality, and the Law, in Abortion: Moral and Legal Perspectives, *supra* note 59 (" . . . the issue, laying as it does on the boundary between moral philosophy and legal theory, offers a splendid opportunity for interdisciplinary cooperation between these two fields"). *Id.* at 1.

152. For bibliographies, see *id.* at 316; S. Callahan & D. Callahan, Abortion: Understanding Differences, *supra* note 68, at 211–212; M. Vetterling-Braggin, F. Elliston & J. English eds., Feminism and Philosophy 441 (Rowman & Littlefield, 1977). For an excellent review of liberal and conservative views on abortion, see L. Sumner, Abortion and Moral Theory (Princeton, 1981), especially 40–81 (liberal view), 82–123 (conservative view).

153. See, e.g., J. Noonan, Jr., ed., The Morality of Abortion: Legal and Historical Perspectives (Harvard Univ. Press, 1970); P. Ramsey, The Morality of Abortion, in J. Rachels ed., Moral Problems: A Collection of Philosophical Essays (Harper & Row, 1975).

154. This issue is a central concern in philosophical discussions of abortion. See, e.g, M. Warren, On the Moral and Legal Status of Abortion, in The Problem of Abortion, *supra* note 71, at 10; Ruth Macklin, Personhood and the Abortion Debate, in Abortion: Moral and Legal Perspectives, *supra* note 59, at 81.

155. See, e.g., Purdy & Tooley, Is Abortion Murder?, in R. Perkins ed., Abortion : Pro and Con 129 (Schenkman, 1974); Tooley, Abortion and Infanticide, 2 Phil. & Pub. Aff. 1 (1972).

156. See, e.g., Kolbert, Webster v. Reproductive Health Services: Reproductive Freedom Hanging by a Thread, 11 Women's Rts. L. Rep. 153 (1989); Tribe, The Abortion Funding Conundrum: Inalienable Rights, Affirmative Duties, and the Dilemma of Dependence, 99 Harv. L. Rev. 330 (1985), and sources cited *supra* n. 54.

157. For another essay criticizing self-defense as a justification for abortion, see Davis, Abortion and Self Defense, 13 Phil. & Pub. Aff. 175 (1984).

158. R. Langer, The Right to Privacy and the Right to Life 26 (1990) (unpublished Ph.D. dissertation, University of California, Riverside) ("The overall abortion controversy has been characterized in popular language as the conflict between the right to privacy and the right to life.").

159. Regan, Rewriting Roe v. Wade, 77 Mich. L. Rev. 1569 (1979) (pointing out its constitutional implication that requiring more of the pregnant woman than of good samaritans, in general, violates equal protection).

160. See, e.g., Brody, Thomson on Abortion, 1 Phil. & Pub. Aff. 335 (Spring 1972); Finnis, The Rights and Wrongs of Abortion, in M. Cohen, R. Nagel & T. Scanlon eds., The Rights and Wrongs of Abortion 106 (Princeton Univ. Press, 1974) (originally entitled The Rights and Wrongs of Abortion: A Reply to Judith Jarvis Thomson, 2 Phil. & Pub. Aff. 117 (1973)); Langer, *supra* note 158. See also R. Posner, The Problems of Jurisprudence 349–352 (Harvard Univ. Press, 1990) (criticizing Thomson's analogy as an illustration of the indeterminacy of moral philosophy and as a flawed application of the tort rescue doctrine).

161. See, e.g., J. English, Abortion and the Concept of a Person, in The Ethics of Abortion, *supra* note 73, at 86–89; Brody, Thomson on Abortion, 1 Phil. & Pub. Aff. 335 (1972); Davis, Abortion and Self Defense, *supra* note 157.

162. See, e.g., Finnis, Rights and Wrongs of Abortion, in The Rights and Wrongs of Abortion, *supra* note 160, at 106; H. Gensler, An Appeal for Consistency, in The Ethics of Abortion, *supra* note 73, at 93, 98.

163. Finnis, Rights and Wrongs of Abortion, in The Rights and Wrongs of Abortion, *supra* note 160, at 85 (criticizing Thomson's use of rights terminology). Thomson, in turn, challenged Finnis's analysis in her book, Rights, Restitution, and Risk 20–32 (Harvard Univ. Press, 1986). See also the criticism of Thomson's use of the various meanings of rights in R. Langer, The Right to Privacy and the Right to Life, *supra* note 158, at 26–45.

164. See, e.g., M. Warren, Moral and Legal Status of Abortion, in The Problem of Abortion, *supra* note 71, at 106–108.

165. See, e.g., Dworkin, Life's Dominion, *supra* note 54, at 54. Some feminist criticism concerns Thomson's analogy of pregnancy to the ill violinist. *Id.* In a different essay, MacKinnon criticizes Thomson's usage of gender-neutral terms, arguing that it impedes the understanding of abortion by obscuring the underlying gender-based inequality. See MacKinnon, Male Ideology of Privacy, *supra* note 104, at 29.

166. Here she differs from those feminists who criticize MacKinnon's approach. See, e.g., Law, *supra* note 74, at 1005 (claiming MacKinnon's approach adds "unnecessary complexity" to application of equality doctrine; "overestimates judges' capacities to identify and avoid socially imposed constraints on equality"; disregards the historical practice of reliance on protective laws to oppress women; and perpetuates the misleading assumption that a constitutional standard can "dismantle the deep structures" that contribute to sex discrimination).

167. For a rare early essay incorporating this perspective, see Sarvis & Rodman, *supra* note 16 (Chapter 8, "Social and Cultural Aspects of Abortion: Class and Race"). For other feminist writers who have also taken note of class, race, and reproduction, see A. Rich, Of Woman Born: Motherhood as Experience and Institution xxii (Norton, 2d ed. 1986) (linking issues of class and race with abortion rights with sterilization abuse); A. Davis, Women, Race and Class 203–221 (Random House, 1981) (abortion rights movement in the early 1970s included few women of color because of their negative experiences with forced sterilization). See also Behuniak-Long, Friendly Fire: *Amici Curiae* and Webster v. Reproductive Health Services, 74 Judicature 261, 267 (1991) (among *amici* briefs in *Webster,* the National Council of Negro Women and other groups presented data on the disproportionate impact that a reversal of *Roe* would entail for poor and minority women).

ROE v. WADE

410 U.S. 113 (1973)

Mr. Justice BLACKMUN delivered the opinion of the Court.

This Texas federal appeal and its Georgia companion, Doe v. Bolton, 410 U.S. 179, present constitutional challenges to state criminal abortion legislation. . . .

We forthwith acknowledge our awareness of the sensitive and emotional nature of the abortion controversy, of the vigorous opposing views, even among physicians, and of the deep and seemingly absolute convictions that the subject inspires. One's philosophy, one's experiences, one's exposure to the raw edges of human existence, one's religious training, one's attitudes toward life and family and their values, and the moral standards one establishes and seeks to observe, are all likely to influence and to color one's thinking and conclusions about abortion.

In addition, population growth, pollution, poverty, and racial overtones tend to complicate and not to simplify the problem.

Our task, of course, is to resolve the issue by constitutional measurement, free of emotion and of predilection. We seek earnestly to do this, and, because we do, we have inquired into, and in this opinion place some emphasis upon, medical and medical-legal history and what that history reveals about man's attitudes toward the abortion procedure over the centuries. We bear in mind, too, Mr. Justice Holmes' admonition in his now-vindicated dissent in Lochner v. New York, 198 U.S. 45, 76 (1905): "(The Constitution) is made for people of fundamentally differing views, and the accident of our finding certain opinions natural and familiar, or novel, and even shocking, ought not to conclude our judgment upon the question whether statutes embodying them conflict with the "Constitution of the United States."

The Texas statutes that concern us here are Arts. 1191–1194 and 1196 of the State's Penal Code, Vernon's Ann.P.C. These make it a crime to "procure an abortion," as therein defined, or to attempt one, except with respect to "an abortion procured or attempted by medical advice for the purpose of saving the life of the mother." Similar statutes are in existence in a majority of the States. . . .

Jane Roe [a pseudonym], a single woman who was residing in Dallas County, Texas, instituted this federal action in March 1970 against the District Attorney of the county. She sought a declaratory judgment that the Texas criminal abortion statutes were unconstitutional on their face, and an injunction restraining the defendant from enforcing the statutes.

Roe alleged that she was unmarried and pregnant; that she wished to terminate her pregnancy by an abortion "performed by a competent, licensed physician, under safe, clinical conditions"; that she was unable to get a "legal" abortion in Texas because her life did not appear to be threatened by the continuation of her pregnancy; and that she could not afford to travel to another jurisdiction in order to secure a legal abortion under safe conditions. She claimed that the Texas statutes were unconstitutionally vague and that they abridged her right of personal privacy, protected by the First, Fourth, Fifth, Ninth, and Fourteenth Amendments. By an amendment to her complaint Roe purported to sue "on behalf of herself and all other women" similarly situated. . . .

[The District Court found the Texas abortion statutes were unconstitutionally vague and an overbroad infringement of the plaintiff's Ninth Amendment rights, 314 F. Supp. 1217 (N.D. Tex. 1970). The District Court held, and the Supreme Court agreed, that the case was not rendered moot by the termination of her pregnancy prior to the decision. *Ed.*]

The principal thrust of appellant's attack on the Texas statutes is that they improperly invade a right, said to be possessed by the pregnant woman, to choose to terminate her pregnancy. Appellant would discover this right in the concept of personal "liberty" embodied in the Fourteenth Amendment's Due Process Clause; or in personal marital, familial, and sexual privacy said to be protected by the Bill of Rights or its penumbras, see Griswold v. Connecticut, 381 U.S. 479 (1965); Eisenstadt v. Baird, 405 U.S. 438 (1972); or among those rights reserved to the people by the Ninth Amendment, Griswold v. Connecticut, 381 U.S., at 486 (Goldberg, J., concurring). Before addressing this claim, we feel it desirable briefly to survey, in several aspects, the history of abortion, for such insight as that history may afford us, and then to examine the state purposes and interests behind the criminal abortion laws.

It perhaps is not generally appreciated that the restrictive criminal abortion laws in effect in a majority of States today are of relatively recent vintage. Those laws, generally proscribing abortion or its attempt at any time during pregnancy except when necessary to preserve the pregnant woman's life, are not of ancient or even of common-law origin. Instead, they derive from statutory changes effected, for the most part, in the latter half of the 19th century. . . .

Three reasons have been advanced to explain historically the enactment of criminal abortion laws in the 19th century and to justify their continued existence.

It has been argued occasionally that these laws were the product of a Victorian social concern to discourage illicit sexual conduct. Texas, however, does not advance this justification in the present case, and it appears that no court or commentator has taken the argument seriously. . . .

A second reason is concerned with abortion as a medical procedure. When most criminal abortion laws were first enacted, the procedure was a hazardous one for the woman. . . . Thus, it has been argued that a State's real concern in enacting a criminal abortion law was to protect the pregnant woman, that is, to restrain her from submitting to a procedure that placed her life in serious jeopardy.

Modern medical techniques have altered this situation. Appellants and various *amici* refer to medical data indicating that abortion in early pregnancy, that is, prior to the end of the first trimester, although not without its risk, is now relatively safe. Mortality rates for women undergoing early abortions, where the procedure is legal, appear to be as low as or lower than the rates for normal childbirth.

Consequently, any interest of the State in protecting the woman from an inherently hazardous procedure, except when it would be equally dangerous for her to forgo it, has largely disappeared. Of course, important state interests in the areas of health and medical standards do remain. The State has a legitimate interest in seeing to it that abortion, like any other medical procedure, is performed under circumstances that insure maximum safety for the patient. This interest obviously extends at least to the performing physician and his staff, to the facilities involved, to the availability of after-care, and to adequate provision for any complication or emergency that might arise. The prevalence of high mortality rates at illegal "abortion mills" strengthens, rather than weakens, the State's interest in regulating the conditions under which abortions are performed. Moreover, the risk to the woman increases as her pregnancy continues. Thus, the State retains a definite interest in protecting the woman's own health and safety when an abortion is proposed at a late stage of pregnancy,

The third reason is the State's interest—some phrase it in terms of duty—in protecting prenatal life. Some of the argument for this justification rests on the theory that a new human life is present from the moment of conception. The State's interest and general obligation to protect life then extends, it is argued, to prenatal life. Only when the life of the pregnant mother herself is at stake, balanced against the life she carries within her, should the interest of the embryo or fetus not prevail. Logically, of course, a legitimate state interest in this area need not stand or fall on acceptance of the belief that life begins at conception or at some other point prior to life birth. In assessing the State's interest, recognition may be given to the less rigid claim that as long as at least *potential* life is involved, the State may assert interests beyond the protection of the pregnant woman alone.

Parties challenging state abortion laws have sharply disputed in some courts the contention that a purpose of these laws, when enacted, was to protect prenatal life. Pointing to the absence of legislative history to support the contention, they claim that most state laws were designed solely to protect the woman. Because medical advances have lessened this concern, at least with respect to abortion in early pregnancy, they argue that with respect to such abortions the laws can no longer be justified by any state interest. There is some scholarly support for this view of original purpose. . . .

It is with these interests, and the weight to be attached to them, that this case is concerned.

The Constitution does not explicitly mention any right of privacy. In a line of decisions . . . , the Court has recognized that a right of personal privacy, or a guarantee of certain areas or zones of privacy, does exist under the Constitution. In varying contexts, the Court or individual Justices have, indeed, found at least the roots of that right in the First Amendment; in the Fourth and Fifth Amendments, in the penumbras of the Bill of Rights; in the Ninth Amendment, or in the concept of liberty guaranteed by the first section of the Fourteenth Amendment. These decisions make it clear that only personal rights that can be deemed "fundamental" or "implicit in the concept of ordered liberty," Palko v. Connecticut, 302 U.S. 319, 325 (1937), are included in this guarantee of personal privacy. They also make it clear that the right has some extension to activities relating to marriage, Loving v. Virginia, 388 U.S. 1, 12 (1967); procreation, Skinner v. Oklahoma, 316 U.S. 535, 541–542 (1942); contraception, Eisenstadt v. Baird, 405 U.S., at 453–454, oil 460, 463 (White, J., concurring in result); family relationships, Prince v. Massachusetts, 321 U.S. 158, 166 (1944); and child rearing and education, Pierce v. Society of Sisters, 268 U.S. 510, 535 (1925), Meyer v. Nebraska, *supra.*

This right of privacy, whether it be founded in the Fourteenth Amendment's concept of personal liberty and restrictions upon state action, as we feel it is, or, as the District Court determined, in the Ninth Amendment's reservation of rights to the people, is broad enough to encompass a woman's decision whether or not to terminate her pregnancy. The detriment that the State would impose upon the pregnant woman by denying this choice altogether is apparent. Specific and direct harm medically diagnosable even in early pregnancy may be involved. Maternity, or additional offspring, may force upon the woman a distressful life and future. Psychological harm may be imminent. Mental and physical health may be taxed by child care. There is also the distress, for all concerned, associated with the unwanted child, and there is the problem of bringing a child into a family already unable, psychologically and otherwise, to care for it. In other cases, as in this one, the additional difficulties and continuing stigma of unwed motherhood may be involved. All these are factors the woman and her responsible physician necessarily will consider in consultation.

On the basis of elements such as these, appellant and some *amici* argue that the woman's right is absolute and that she is entitled to terminate her pregnancy at whatever time, in whatever way, and for whatever reason she alone chooses. With this we do not agree. Appellant's arguments that Texas either has no valid interest at all in regulating the abortion decision, or no interest strong enough to support any limitation upon the woman's sole determination, are unpersuasive. The Court's decisions recognizing a right of privacy also acknowledge that some state regulation in areas protected by that right is appropriate. As noted above, a State may properly assert important interests in safeguarding health, in maintaining medical standards, and in protecting potential life. At some point in pregnancy, these respective interests become sufficiently compelling to sustain regulation of the factors that govern the abortion decision. The privacy right involved, therefore, cannot be said to be absolute. In fact, it is not clear to us that the claim asserted by some *amici* that one has an unlimited right to do with one's body as one pleases bears a close relationship to the right of privacy previously articulated in the Court's decisions. The Court has refused to recognize an unlimited right of this kind in the past. Jacobson v. Massachusetts, 197 U.S. 11 (1905) (vaccination); Buck v. Bell, 274 U.S. 200 (1927) (sterilization).

We, therefore, conclude that the right of personal privacy includes the abortion decision, but that this right is not unqualified and must be considered against important state interests in regulation. . . .

Where certain "fundamental rights" are involved, the Court has held that regulation limiting these rights may be justified only by a "compelling state interest," and that legislative enactments must be narrowly drawn to express only the legitimate state interests at stake.

The District Court held that the appellee failed to meet his burden of demonstrating that the Texas statute's infringement upon Roe's rights was necessary to support a compelling state interest, and that, although the appellee presented "several compelling justifications for state presence in the area of abortions," the statutes outstripped these justifications and swept "far beyond any areas of compelling state interest." 314 F.Supp., at 1222–1223. Appellant and appellee both contest that holding. Appellant, as has been indicated, claims an absolute right that bars any state imposition of criminal penalties in the area. Appellee argues that the State's determination to recognize and protect prenatal life from and after conception constitutes a compelling state interest. As noted above, we do not agree fully with either formulation.

The appellee and certain *amici* argue that the fetus is a "person" within the language and meaning of the Fourteenth Amendment. In support of this, they outline at length and in detail the well-known facts of fetal development. If this suggestion of personhood is established, the appellant's case, of course, collapses, for the fetus' right to life would then be guaranteed specifically by the Amendment. . . .

The Constitution does not define "person" in so many words. Section 1 of the Fourteenth Amendment contains three references to "person." The first, in defining "citizens," speaks of "persons born or naturalized in the United States." The word also appears both in the Due Process Clause and in the Equal Protection Clause. "Person" is used in other places in the Constitution: in the listing of qualifications for Representatives and Senators; in the Apportionment Clause; in the Migration and Importation provision; in the Emolument Clause, Art; in the Electors provisions; in the provision outlining qualifications for the office of President; in the Extradition provisions; and the superseded Fugitive Slave Clause 3; and in the Fifth, Twelfth, and Twenty-second Amendments, as well as in §§2 and 3 of the Fourteenth Amendment. But in nearly all these instances, the use of the word is such that it has application only postnatally. None indicates, with any assurance, that it has any possible prenatal application.[54]

---

[54]When Texas urges that a fetus is entitled to Fourteenth Amendment protection as a person, it faces a dilemma. Neither in Texas nor in any other State are all abortions prohibited. Despite broad proscription, an exception always exists. The exception contained in Art. 1196, for an abortion procured or attempted by medical advice for the purpose of saving the life of the mother, is typical. But if the fetus is a person who is not to be deprived of life without due process of law, and if the mother's condition is the sole determinant,

All this, together with our observation, *supra*, that throughout the major portion of the 19th century prevailing legal abortion practices were far freer than they are today, persuades us that the word "person," as used in the Fourteenth Amendment, does not include the unborn. . . .

This conclusion, however, does not of itself fully answer the contentions raised by Texas, and we pass on to other considerations.

The pregnant woman cannot be isolated in her privacy. She carries an embryo and, later, a fetus. . . . The situation therefore is inherently different from marital intimacy, or bedroom possession of obscene material, or marriage, or procreation, or education, with which *Eisenstadt* and *Griswold, Stanley, Loving, Skinner* and *Pierce* and *Meyer* were respectively concerned. As we have intimated above, it is reasonable and appropriate for a State to decide that at some point in time another interest, that of health of the mother or that of potential human life, becomes significantly involved. The woman's privacy is no longer sole and any right of privacy she possesses must be measured accordingly.

Texas urges that, apart from the Fourteenth Amendment, life begins at conception and is present throughout pregnancy, and that, therefore, the State has a compelling interest in protecting that life from and after conception. We need not resolve the difficult question of when life begins. When those trained in the respective disciplines of medicine, philosophy, and theology are unable to arrive at any consensus, the judiciary, at this point in the development of man's knowledge, is not in a position to speculate as to the answer.

It should be sufficient to note briefly the wide divergence of thinking on this most sensitive and difficult question. There has always been strong support for the view that life does not begin until live birth. This was the belief of the Stoics. It appears to be the predominant, though not the unanimous, attitude of the Jewish faith. It may be taken to represent also the position of a large segment of the Protestant community, insofar as that can be ascertained; organized groups that have taken a formal position on the abortion issue have generally regarded abortion as a matter for the conscience of the individual and her family. As we have noted, the common law found greater significance in quickening. Physicians and their scientific colleagues have regarded that event with less interest and have tended to focus either upon conception, upon live birth, or upon the interim point at which the fetus becomes "viable," that is, potentially able to live outside the mother's womb, albeit with artificial aid. Viability is usually placed at about seven months (28 weeks) but may occur earlier, even at 24 weeks. The Aristotelian theory of "mediate animation," that held sway throughout the Middle Ages and the Renaissance in Europe, continued to be official Roman Catholic dogma until

does not the Texas exception appear to be out of line with the Amendment's command? There are other inconsistencies between Fourteenth Amendment status and the typical abortion statute. [I]n Texas the woman is not a principal or an accomplice with respect to an abortion upon her. If the fetus is a person, why is the woman not a principal or an accomplice? Further, the penalty for criminal abortion specified by Art. 1195 is significantly less than the maximum penalty for murder prescribed by Art. 1257 of the Texas Penal Code. If the fetus is a person, may the penalties be different?

the 19th century, despite opposition to this "ensoulment" theory from those in the Church who would recognize the existence of life from the moment of conception. The latter is now, of course, the official belief of the Catholic Church. [T]his is a view strongly held by many non-Catholics as well, and by many physicians. Substantial problems for precise definition of this view are posed, however, by new embryological data that purport to indicate that conception is a "process" over time, rather than an event, and by new medical techniques such as menstrual extraction, the "morning-after" pill, implantation of embryos, artificial insemination, and even artificial wombs.

In areas other than criminal abortion, the law has been reluctant to endorse any theory that life, as we recognize it, begins before life birth or to accord legal rights to the unborn except in narrowly defined situations and except when the rights are contingent upon life birth. For example, the traditional rule of tort law denied recovery for prenatal injuries even though the child was born alive. That rule has been changed in almost every jurisdiction. In most States, recovery is said to be permitted only if the fetus was viable, or at least quick, when the injuries were sustained, though few courts have squarely so held. In a recent development, generally opposed by the commentators, some States permit the parents of a stillborn child to maintain an action for wrongful death because of prenatal injuries. Such an action, however, would appear to be one to vindicate the parents' interest and is thus consistent with the view that the fetus, at most, represents only the potentiality of life. Similarly, unborn children have been recognized as acquiring rights or interests by way of inheritance or other devolution of property, and have been represented by guardians ad litem. Perfection of the interests involved, again, has generally been contingent upon live birth. In short, the unborn have never been recognized in the law as persons in the whole sense.

In view of all this, we do not agree that, by adopting one theory of life, Texas may override the rights of the pregnant woman that are at stake. We repeat, however, that the State does have an important and legitimate interest in preserving and protecting the health of the pregnant woman, whether she be a resident of the State or a non-resident who seeks medical consultation and treatment there, and that it has still another important and legitimate interest in protecting the potentiality of human life. These interests are separate and distinct. Each grows in substantiality as the woman approaches term and, at a point during pregnancy, each becomes "compelling."

With respect to the State's important and legitimate interest in the health of the mother, the "compelling" point, in the light of present medical knowledge, is at approximately the end of the first trimester. This is so because of the now-established medical fact . . . that until the end of the first trimester mortality in abortion may be less than mortality in normal childbirth. It follows that, from and after this point, a State may regulate the abortion procedure to the extent that the regulation reasonably relates to the preservation and protection of maternal health. Examples of permissible state regulation in this area are requirements as to the qualifications of the person who is to perform the abortion; as to the licensure of that person; as to the facility in which the procedure is to be performed, that is, whether it must be a hospital or may be a clinic or some other place of less-than-hospital status; as to the licensing of the facility; and the like.

This means, on the other hand, that, for the period of pregnancy prior to this "compelling" point, the attending physician, in consultation with his patient, is free to determine, without regulation by the State, that, in his medical judgment, the patient's pregnancy should be terminated. If that decision is reached, the judgment may be effectuated by an abortion free of interference by the State.

With respect to the State's important and legitimate interest in potential life, the "compelling" point is at viability. This is so because the fetus then presumably has the capability of meaningful life outside the mother's womb. State regulation protective of fetal life after viability thus has both logical and biological justifications. If the State is interested in protecting fetal life after viability, it may go so far as to proscribe abortion during that period, except when it is necessary to preserve the life or health of the mother. Measured against these standards, Art. 1196 of the Texas Penal Code, in restricting legal abortions to those "procured or attempted by medical advice for the purpose of saving the life of the mother," sweeps too broadly. The statute makes no distinction between abortions performed early in pregnancy and those performed later, and it limits to a single reason, "saving" the mother's life, the legal justification for the procedure. The statute, therefore, cannot survive the constitutional attack made upon it here.

This conclusion makes it unnecessary for us to consider the additional challenge to the Texas statute asserted on grounds of vagueness.

To summarize and to repeat:

1. A state criminal abortion statute of the current Texas type, that excepts from criminality only a life-saving procedure on behalf of the mother, without regard to pregnancy stage and without recognition of the other interests involved, is violative of the Due Process Clause of the Fourteenth Amendment.

(a) For the stage prior to approximately the end of the first trimester, the abortion decision and its effectuation must be left to the medical judgment of the pregnant woman's attending physician.

(b) For the stage subsequent to approximately the end of the first trimester, the State, in promoting its interest in the health of the mother, may, if it chooses, regulate the abortion procedure in ways that are reasonably related to maternal health.

(c) For the stage subsequent to viability, the State in promoting its interest in the potentiality of human life may, if it chooses, regulate, and even proscribe, abortion except where it is necessary, in appropriate medical judgment, for the preservation of the life or health of the mother.

2. The State may define the term "physician," as it has been employed in the preceding paragraphs of this Part XI of this opinion, to mean only a physician currently licensed by the State, and may proscribe any abortion by a person who is not a physician as so defined.

This holding, we feel, is consistent with the relative weights of the respective interests involved, with the lessons and examples of medical and legal history, with the lenity of the common law, and with the demands of the profound problems of the present day. The decision leaves the State free to place increasing restrictions on abortion as the period of pregnancy lengthens, so long as those restrictions are tailored to the recognized state interests. The decision vindicates the right of the physician to administer medical treatment according to his professional judgment up to the points where important state interests provide compelling justifications for intervention. Up to those points, the abortion decision in all its aspects is inherently, and primarily, a medical decision, and basic responsibility for it must rest with the physician. . . .

[The concurring opinion of Justice Stewart, and the dissenting opinions of Justices Rehnquist and White, are omitted.]

Editor's Note:

In Planned Parenthood of Southeastern Pennsylvania v. Casey, 112 S. Ct. 2791 (1992), the Supreme Court (1) reaffirmed *Roe's* constitutional protection for abortion as a right rooted in liberty and privacy; (2) but rejected *Roe's* trimester scheme in favor of a recognition that "there is a substantial state interest in potential life throughout pregnancy" (*id.* at 2820), thereby permitting the state to impose regulations throughout pregnancy so long as the regulations met a newly announced standard; (3) enunciated a new "undue burden" standard for evaluating the permissibility of state regulation of abortion.

The Struggle for Reproductive Freedom: Three Stages of Feminism

LINDA GORDON

. . . THE STRUGGLE FOR birth control which emerged in the nineteenth century . . . was part of a feminist movement, challenging the subordination of women in sexuality particularly and in the family and society generally. From then on, the birth control movement, even when organizationally autonomous, has always reflected the historical strength and development of feminism.

In the last hundred years there have been three stages in the sexual ideology of the feminists, each of which strongly affected the struggle for reproductive freedom. First, from the mid-nineteenth century to the 1890s, the feminists of the suffrage movement adhered to a sexual ideal which I shall call domesticity; briefly, they believed that sexual activity belonged only within marriage and they were skeptical of its importance in women's lives. Second, in the period near World War I, a new group of feminists, including many men, rejected the antisexual attitudes of the suffragists and associated women's interests with sexual liberation—endorsing amarital sexual activity and, even more important, emphasizing and romanticizing the importance of sexual pleasure. Third, in the 1970s, feminists [criticized] the earlier positions by analyzing the nature of sexual intercourse itself, suggesting that our norms of sexual behavior are distorted by male supremacy, opening to consideration the requirements of women's own sexual pleasure. In each of these stages the questions of reproductive freedom and sexual freedom were hardly separable. Since we cannot separate these issues nor divide reproductive *goals* from the *process* of their transformation, we must regard this as a history of conflict between social radicals and social conservatives, both sets of views historically specific.

1. Let us begin about the year 1870 and look at what I will call the Victorian sexual system. It is useful to think of it as a system because it was composed of many related parts; it had a fundamental coherence, although, like all such cultural systems, it contained dissidence and contradictions. The feminist reformers who took up the birth control issue shared many convictions with their conservative opponents.

Victorian conservative moralists agreed that the purpose of sexual activity for women should be reproduction, and many denied that women had a sex drive independent of a desire for motherhood. Those who recognized the existence of female sexuality assumed it to be entirely consonant with the satisfaction of men. The relationships that women had with other women, though often passionate, were virtually defined as asexual, making lesbianism practically invisible except as a rare aberration. Enjoying a sharply double standard, rationalized through a notion of separate spheres for the sexes, men simultaneously celebrated (and possibly resented) the chastity of their wives and indulged themselves with prostitutes and other low status women.

By the mid-nineteenth century the same social changes that had created this system threatened its stability. The industrialization of production that had created the separation between men's and women's lives and work, made women's traditional labor degraded, unrewarding, and unappreciated. But while the content of women's work changed, its form remained the same. The changes were not well understood, but were sharply felt. Even today few recognize that housework as we know it was born in advanced industrial society, reflecting the transformation of women who had been manufacturers, farmers, skilled teachers, and healers into small-scale janitors. At the same time, urban life increasingly detached men of all classes from their families and homes into other workplaces. Responding to these changes, two directly antagonistic social movements developed around the issue of reproduction. On the conservative side, fears of underpopulation, the decline of the family, and the increasing independence of women coalesced into a series of pressures for more rigorous bans on birth control, sex education, and extra-domestic activities among women. In the United States these groups succeeded in enacting the "Comstock" law which prohibited the mailing of obscene material and in then classifying birth control information as obscene; they also secured federal prosecution of several cases under this law. They conducted a propaganda campaign, deliberately confounding contraception with abortion and branding as murder and licentiousness the whole project of birth control.

Contesting the conservative view of reproductive and sexual morality was a powerful feminist movement. It produced a birth control demand, "Voluntary Motherhood," which expressed its principles exactly. The main issue was a woman's right to dignity and autonomy, but it was also implied that willing mothers would be better parents, wanted children better people. The cult of motherhood was thus argued as passionately by feminists as by antifeminists: conservatives argued that motherhood was the basic reason women should stay at home; feminists argued that motherhood was the main reason women needed more power, independence, and respect. These feminists did not urge that women should desert the home, and certainly did not contemplate—as few feminists did until the 1930s—that men should share in domestic work.[1] Furthermore, by the explicitly sexual content of their birth control ideas, the feminists also endorsed a kind of domesticity. They believed that abstinence, not contraception, was the only proper form of birth control. They shared the general religious and moral view that sex should be only for reproduction and only within marriage. They were partly motivated by religious and antitechnological feelings, a response to the apparent degradation of women in industrial society. But they also understood contraception not as a tool for a woman's own self-assertion but as a weapon used by men against women: nonreproductive sex appeared to them to be a means for men to escape their responsibility to women.[2] They saw contraception as a tool of prostitutes and as a potential tool of men in turning women into prostitutes.

The feminists wanted not only voluntary motherhood but also voluntary sex. The nineteenth-century marital system rested, legally as well as in custom, on women's sexual submission to their husbands; refusal of sexual services was grounds for divorce in many states. Feminist insistence on women's right to say no and to justify this on birth control grounds was a fundamental rejection of male dominance in sex. They wanted to end the double standard by imposing chastity on men. Their strong emphasis on women's sisterhood had, at least for us today, sexual implications as well, for they created lasting bonds and passionate loves among women. Interestingly, it was often these voluntary motherhood advocates who simultaneously asserted the existence of female sexual drives. They understood, however, that the discovery of women's own sexual preferences and sensations could not even begin while women were subordinate to men's every sexual whim. Feminist ideas were thus at once antisex and prosex, and feminists were not able to resolve this tension because they did not (or perhaps did not dare) follow women's sexual feelings where they led—to woman-defined kinds of sexual activity not necessarily compatible with conventional heterosexual intercourse.

In their sexual attitudes the nineteenth-century feminists were mainly anti-male. In this respect they were the predecessors of today's radical feminists, not of socialist feminists or liberal feminists. Their critique of the family was a critique of male dominance within it. They did not analyze the family or the sexual division of labor as formations which had become assimilated to capitalism, nor did they perceive that men were not always free agents themselves in these formations. On the other hand, in other aspects of their feminism these activists were often pro-male. Seeing women as victims who had been deprived of the opportunity to realize their full human potential, they saw the male as the human type. This was explicit in the work of a few theorists, especially Charlotte Perkins Gilman, and was implicit in the demands of many other feminists for education and professional work. Feminist thought reflected rapid social changes which were sending women out of their homes into the man's world—into schools, offices, factories, restaurants, theaters, etc. The pro-male point of view made it seem inconceivable that men should do housework and parenting.

In their sexual attitudes, in short, the feminists were defending domesticity, yet their agitation on other questions was encouraging a rejection of domestic life. But celibacy was not a stable alternative for the thousands of single career women at the turn of the twentieth century.

Partly due to the large numbers of non-marrying women, but also because of extensive use of birth control, by the turn of the century birthrate declines in the United States had become highly visible. Between 1905 and 1910 there arose a campaign against "race suicide," whose propagandists protested population decline (having been reared with the mercantilist notion that a healthy nation had to have a growing population), fearing the decline of WASP ruling-class hegemony due to the higher birth rate among Catholic working-class immigrants. Underlying it was an antifeminist backlash, an attack on women's "selfishness," or rejection of domesticity and mothering. (Ironically, the race suicide propaganda let a great many people know of the existence of birth control methods and probably promoted the use of contraception.)

2. Starting in the 1890s a group of feminists, at first mainly European, began to espouse different sexual ideas critical of domesticity. Many were men, such as Havelock Ellis, Edward Carpenter, later Wilhelm Reich. Men and women alike tended to consider sexual repression as a problem of equal weight for both sexes, though different in nature; and they usually argued that women's liberation would be good for both sexes, that men as well as women suffered from the false sex-gender system, the polarization of sex roles.

In many ways this turn-of-the-century group of feminists took the focus off women and placed it on sex; they tended to view women's subordination as a function of sexual repression, whereas the suffrage movement by and large thought that the distortion of sexual needs and practices was a product of male supremacy.

Certain implications of this sexual-liberation emphasis should be noticed. First, the concern with men's sexual repression tended to mask the fact that men remained the dominant sex, the beneficiaries of the exploitation of women,[3] and to present men and women as equal victims of a system so abstract that its persistence was inexplicable. In this respect the sexual liberation theorists did not encourage a women's movement. Second, the attack on sexual repression tended inevitably to spotlight the family as the central structure for the perpetuation of repression and to endorse nonmarital sex. Inasmuch as the family was undoubtedly still the main prop of male supremacy in the early twentieth century (and possibly still is), sexual liberation theory was extremely encouraging to the development of a more fundamental challenge to the sex-gender system from a feminist perspective.

Birth control was a very important issue for the sexual-liberation feminists because without it sex could not be separated from the family. They therefore enthusiastically supported and built the birth control movement when it revived in the World War I era. Its reemergence was a response both to the publicity of the race suicide proponents and partly because of the new demographic and sexual situation of women. The urban economy was making smaller families economically possible for professional, business, and working-class women; women were more in the world—working-class women often in the labor force, more privileged women in higher education, the professions, and volunteerism; the requirements of female chastity were weakening for all classes. These developments were all part of the decline of patriarchal power, which had been founded not only on control of women but also on control of families. The entire family structure was being altered by industrial capitalism. The employment of sons and daughters weakened fatherly authority, while the wage labor of the fathers removed them from the home, where they had traditionally exercised authority, and deprived them of the economic and psychic ability to enjoy large families. The uprooting experience of immigration and the impact of individualist liberal ideology also weakened the legitimacy of the patriarchal organization of society. And feminism was itself a product of the frustrations and opportunities presented to women, middle-class women first and most prominently, by the decline of patriarchy.

The organizational impetus for the revived birth control movement came primarily from feminists in the Socialist Party. Their energy was available because so many women were repelled by the conservatism of the suffrage organizations and because socialism was not dealing energetically with any women's issues. They learned the political importance of the birth control issue from the masses, and I use that word advisedly. The experiences of Margaret Sanger and many other birth control organizers show that enormous popular demand virtually forced the issue upon them. Once they began to organize around it, birth control information reached thousands of women previously unexcited by suffrage or other women's rights issues; birth control seemed to them more immediate, more personal, and more tied to class struggle.

The birth control movement of 1914–1920 was a mass movement with leagues in all big cities and many towns. It was a grassroots movement: a few speakers toured nationally, and in the 1920s national organizations arose, but most leagues sprang up locally and autonomously, often initiated by women socialists. People distributed illegal birth control leaflets on the streets, opened illegal clinics, courted arrest in order to use their trials as political forums, and even served time in jail.

This movement should not be seen as some kind of spontaneous revolt of prepolitical women. Underlying it was a new radicalism in sexual behavior among many young urban women, influenced by and participating in the feminist sexual-liberation ideology. Their work in birth control was part of an attempt to resolve the contradictions of nineteenth-century feminism which had criticized the family but remained faithful to ideas of permanent monogamy, sex only for reproduction and within marriage.

World War I–era feminist socialists began a critique of the family itself, calling it a prop of bourgeois, male supremacist society, morality, and character structure. In differing degrees these feminists accepted the "sexual revolution"—the normality of divorce; sexual relations before marriage, without ruining a woman's reputation; numerous sexual partners; contraception; and a host of activities previously considered improper, including dating. They thought that enjoyment was a good enough reason for sex and most other activities. They despised so-called bourgeois hypocrisy and paid at least lip service to a single standard of sexual freedom.

In this rejection of domesticity and family-centered sex these early-twentieth-century feminists became, despite their intentions, more pro-male than their predecessors. Their characteristic solution to problems of child care and housework was to propose that women be hired to do those tasks. They were socialists but their proposals, like those of most socialists of their era, were in line with the development of capitalism. And the male was still for them the human type, male culture in most respects human culture. This group of radicals did not fully challenge the sex-gender system either. Redefining the possibilities of the feminine somewhat, they continued to accept a certain view of male gender as permanent.

No feminism prior to the mid-twentieth century analyzed the full complexities of women's reproductive and sexual imprisonment. But, without bemoaning the loss of something doomed by historical change, we should recognize that nineteenth century feminist ideas had certain important realizations about women that were lost in the early twentieth century. Feminist thinkers like Elizabeth Cady Stanton, Elizabeth Blackwell, and Charlotte Perkins Gilman understood that women needed a space—physical, psychological, and intellectual—where they were separated from men and insulated from men's demands before they could develop their own sexual feelings, hopes, and theories. Their emphasis on sisterhood and women's solidarity put them in a position of greater fidelity to the masses of women and gave them a strategic sense of the power of women as a collectivity. By contrast, many early-twentieth-century feminists, including birth control leaders like Margaret Sanger and Emma Goldman, had uncritically bought a "sexual" revolution that was really a heterosexual revolution. It drew women out of protected areas, out of women's spaces, into a man's world. It ignored the fact that it is dangerous—physically, emotionally, socially, and economically—for women to indulge in nonmarital sex. Although their sex manuals contributed to sex education and to breaking the chains of prudish ignorance, they steadfastly encouraged women to get sexual pleasure and orgasms from male-oriented intercourse and, by implication, blamed them for frigidity if they could not. Most of them did not believe in the need for an autonomous women's movement. In sexual relations, education, and work they accepted a set-up that placed women *individually* in a man's world, isolated in their danger. Although it was progressive that they urged women to dare, to find the confidence—they didn't say where—to take on men's burdens, their strategy in effect denied women solidarity with other women. Nor did they offer a way to reject women's traditional burdens while assuming men's.

Nevertheless, the birth control movement of the World War I period was a big advance for women. It promoted and finally legalized contraception, and it encouraged partial emergence from sexual constriction. But as part of the heterosexual "sexual revolution," it also created pain, confusion, and loneliness for many women; the transformation out of millennia of subordination cannot be expected to be easy.

The Commoditization of Birth Control, Sex, and Women's Labor

Before we can examine the third stage of feminist sexual ideas we must look briefly at a less optimistic period, from about 1920 to 1965. The decline of the entire left, feminist and nonfeminist, after World War I enervated the birth control movement. Oddly, the power of the Communist Party in the 1930s and early 1940s did not stimulate a feminist revival. But although birth control as a social movement was weakened, birth control as a commodity became legal and widespread. This process occurred in two major stages. First, between 1920 and 1945, the birth control campaign became a professional, male-dominated, centralized, and respectable service project, primarily influenced by elitist and eugenical convictions that the poor should be helped and pacified by having their birth rates lowered. Then, between 1945 and 1960, it became an international population control campaign, ultimately controlled by the United States ruling class through its corporate foundations. These transformations were paralleled by the commercial production and mass marketing of contraceptives and by medical research and development keyed to fertility reduction at all costs, including disregard for health and civil liberties. Birth control is today a commodity and, like all commodities in advanced capitalist society, it is offered to us in such a way that we cannot always distinguish our personal need for the product from the "needs" defined for us by social policy.

With the decline of mass participation, the forward motion the birth control movement had created for women ceased. It is not clear that the increased dissemination of contraception in the United States between 1920 and 1960 created any significant improvement in the lives of most working-class women. The difference between two and ten pregnancies, births, and children is enormous in terms of time and energy. But time and energy are in themselves empty quantities; it is not that the labor of producing children was so unrewarding that reducing it was an automatic gain, and the value of what has replaced this childrearing labor is questionable. Despite smaller families, women seem to spend as many hours on housework and mothering as a century ago. Partly due to smaller families, many more women have entered the labor force and gained at least the promise of independent incomes, but these incomes have been quickly eaten up by family needs, as the inadequecy of men's real wages makes the two-income family increasingly the norm. Employment certainly has not meant intellectual growth for women, as women's jobs are still the worst in pay and working conditions. There are proportionately fewer women in the professions today than in 1920. Furthermore, employment has not relieved most women from exclusive responsibility for reproductive labor and family maintenance. And women as a group—as a gender—continue to be defined mainly by their work in the family.

Despite women's continued social identity with the family, families are in fact dissolving with the rapid increase of divorce and more individualist behavior on the part of all family members. These changes, while perhaps liberating in potential, have in fact rendered people more susceptible to manipulation and have encouraged self-destructive behavior. Sexual health, measured either physically or psychologically, is in some respects deteriorating, as evidenced in spreading venereal disease, rape, and sexual encounters stripped of obligations between people as subjects. The balance between helpful practicality about sex and its dehumanization is a delicate one. Frank discussion of sexual techniques is a needed extension of sex education, a continuation of the best traditions of feminism; but the marketing of sex cookbooks for the "connoisseur" is moving, as commoditization always does, in an antihuman direction by carving up the human experience. Sex thus becomes severed from economic, social, political, and emotional life. Prostitution is providing more sexual services for cash, as in massage parlors and modeling, or even for barter, as in swinging and in "personal" advertisements for companionship. At the same time, the commercialization of sexual pleasure and the new norms that make celibacy or sexual restraint seem deviant provide new tools for male chauvinism and the sexist exploitation of women.

3. In the 1970s a revised feminist movement reexamined sex and reproduction politically and reintroduced a libertarian view of both. Women's liberation began where the World War I sex radicals had left off—with a denunciation of the family's role in sexual repression and women's suppression. This denunciation has since been tempered, as we understand how difficult it is to replace the family's supportive functions. But the demystification of the family has allowed a new look at sex and sexual relationships. The romanticism of the sexual-liberation theorists about love and orgasm has been criticized along with the antigenital bias of the suffragists. Contemporary feminists have not only explored new forms of emotional commitments, both long and short term, but have defetishized the sex act itself for the first time in modern history.

The separation of sex from reproduction was not possible, even in imagination, as long as heterosexual intercourse was the definition of the sex act. Changing our view of what constituted proper sexual satisfaction for women has been one of the major historical contributions of the women's liberation movement, its implications most fully expressed in lesbian feminism.

The debunking of the myth of vaginal orgasm was not a sudden breakthrough but a product of a century of agitation that well illustrates a fundamental unity among several waves of feminism. Sex education has been a principal demand of feminists in the United States since the 1840s. The cultural values and physiological information to be offered have changed radically, but all the feminists sought to throw off the blanket of suppression and lies about women's psychological and physiological sexuality. Their goal was the restoration of the legitimacy of female sexual pleasure, though the definition of its proper form changed historically. Since at least the 1870s, feminist groups used forms of "consciousness-raising," discussions among women which revealed the interface between "personal" and "political" problems, sexual problems always looming large among them. Feminist groups have continually attacked, for example, conventional fashions in dress, realizing that the transformation of women into decorations helped to lower their self-esteem and, ironically, stunt their sexual development, keeping them eternally objects and never subjects. Feminists in all periods have emphasized the strength and flexibility of women's bodies as against their beauty, attempting to break the exclusive association of the female body with sexuality; simultaneously, feminists have tried to reintegrate sexuality into full human relationships and fought the commoditization of sex, which required the sacrifice of women as prostitutes to men's distorted sexuality.

There is unity in the feminist tradition, and it is important to see our own historical debts. It is also important to see where we have transcended previous feminism. One vital respect in which mid-twentieth-century feminists have gone further is in avoiding both "blaming-the-victim" analyses (whose action implications are personal struggles to overcome inner obstacles to sexual or other satisfaction) and economic-determinist analyses (whose action implications deny the importance of "personal life" and women's ego structures). The socialist feminist approach of the 1970s has, at its best, encouraged both personal and collective struggle for change. The strategy is to ask for everything, demanding that the society should be structured to allow women to do a little of everything, or at least to have a choice, without faulting women for not being able to do everything.

Contemporary feminism has already significantly improved women's situation, but these improvements have been mainly the result of the process of the struggle itself rather than of specific reforms. Our major gains have been in women's aspirations, self-esteem, and political awareness.

These gains are particularly evident in the structure of family and sexual life. In every historical period one effect of feminism was to raise the status and the opportunities of single women; today the improved position of single women is noticeable. In accomplishing this, feminism's influence has helped married women to challenge their husbands' privileges partly because they had seen the possibility of a life outside marriage. In this respect again the lesbian liberation movement has made possibly the most important contribution to a future sexual liberation. It is not that feminism produced more lesbians. There have always been many lesbians, despite high levels of repression; and most lesbians experience their sexual preference as innate and nonvoluntary. What the women's liberation movement did create was a homosexual liberation movement that politically challenged male supremacy in one of its most deeply institutionalized aspects—the tyranny of heterosexuality. The political power of lesbianism is a power that can be shared by all women who choose to recognize and use it: the power of an alternative, a possibility that makes male sexual tyranny escapable, rejectable—possibly even doomed. . . .

Notes

1. The popularity of matriarchy theory among nineteenth-century feminists suggests a longing for preexisting models of a good society rather than acceptance of the need to define and invent a good society anew. Their exclusive emphasis on suffrage (like the emphasis of later feminists on sexual liberation and birth control) suggests that they were mistaking symptoms and aspects of male supremacy for the whole, that they were unable to comprehend its systematic, coherent, and pervasive forms.

2. The fact that contraception then was not a commodity but a "home-made" procedure or invention made it less fetishized, its social meaning clear.

3. I am purposefully using this word not only in its Marxist sense, referring to the production of surplus value, but also in the common sense usage of being used, ripped off. I do this because I think feminists are correct in perceiving a fundamental similarity between the two forms of exploitation and the alienation from one's labor and one's self that they produce.

A Defense of Abortion

JUDITH JARVIS THOMSON

MOST OPPOSITION to abortion relies on the premise that the fetus is a human being, a person, from the moment of conception. The premise is argued for; but, as I think, not well. Take, for example, the most common argument. We are asked to notice that the development of a human being from conception through birth into childhood is continuous; then it is said that to draw a line, to choose a point in this development and say "before this point the thing is not a person, after this point it is a person" is to make an arbitrary choice, a choice for which in the nature of things no good reason can be given. It is concluded that the fetus is, or anyway that we had better say it is, a person from the moment of conception. But this conclusion does not follow. Similar things might be said about the development of an acorn into an oak tree, and it does not follow that acorns are oak trees, or that we had better say they are. Arguments of this form are sometimes called "slippery slope arguments"—the phrase is perhaps self-explanatory—and it is dismaying that opponents of abortion rely on them so heavily and uncritically.

I am inclined to agree, however, that the prospects for "drawing a line" in the development of the fetus look dim. I am inclined to think also that we shall probably have to agree that the fetus has already become a human person well before birth. Indeed, it comes as a surprise when one first learns how early in its life it begins to acquire human characteristics. By the tenth week, for example, it already has a face, arms and legs, fingers and toes; it has internal organs, and brain activity is detectable.[1] On the other hand, I think that the premise is false, that the fetus is not a person from the moment of conception. A newly fertilized ovum, a newly implanted clump of cells, is no more a person than an acorn is an oak tree. But I shall not discuss any of this. For it seems to me to be of great interest to ask what happens if, for the sake of argument, we allow the premise. How, precisely, are we supposed to get from there to the conclusion that abortion is morally impermissible? Opponents of abortion commonly spend most of their time establishing that the fetus is a person, and hardly any time explaining the step from there to the impermissibility of abortion. Perhaps they think the step too simple and obvious to require much comment. Or perhaps instead they are simply being economical in argument. Many of those who defend abortion rely on the premise that the fetus is not a person, but only a bit of tissue that will become a person at birth; and

Thomson, Judith Jarvis, A Defense of Abortion, 1 Phil & Pub. Aff. 47 (1971). Copyright © 1971 by Princeton University Press. Reprinted by permission of Princeton University Press.

why pay out more arguments than you have to? Whatever the explanation, I suggest that the step they take is neither easy nor obvious, that it calls for closer examination than it is commonly given, and then when we do give it this closer examination we shall feel inclined to reject it.

I propose, then, that we grant that the fetus is person from the moment of conception. How does the argument go from here? Something like this, I take it. Every person has a right to life. So the fetus has a right to life. No doubt the mother has a right to decide what shall happen in and to her body; everyone would grant that. But surely a person's right to life is stronger and more stringent than the mother's right to decide what happens in and to her body, and so outweighs it. So the fetus may not be killed; an abortion may not be performed.

It sounds plausible. But now let me ask you to imagine this. You wake up in the morning and find yourself back to back in bed with an unconscious violinist. A famous unconscious violinist. He has been found to have a fatal kidney ailment, and the Society of Music Lovers has canvassed all the available medical records and found that you alone have the right blood type to help. They have thereby kidnapped you, and last night the violinist's circulatory system was plugged into yours, so that your kidneys can be used to extract poisons from his blood as well as your own. The director of the hospital now tells you, "Look, we're sorry the Society of Music Lovers did this to you—we would never have permitted it if we had known. But still, they did it, and the violinist now is plugged into you. To unplug you would be to kill him. But never mind, it's only for nine months. By then he will have recovered from his ailment, and can safely be unplugged from you." Is it morally incumbent on you to accede to this situation? No doubt it would be very nice of you if you did, a great kindness. But do you *have* to accede to it? What if it were not nine months, but nine years? Or longer still? What if the director of the hospital says, "Tough luck, I agree, but you've now got to stay in bed, with the violinist plugged into you, for the rest of your life. Because remember this. All persons have a right to life, and violinists are persons. Granted you have a right to decide what happens in and to your body, but a person's right to life outweighs your right to decide what happens in and to your body. So you cannot ever be unplugged from him." I imagine you would regard this as outrageous, which suggests that something really is wrong with that plausible-sounding argument I mentioned a moment ago.

In this case, of course, you were kidnapped; you didn't volunteer for the operation that plugged the violinist into your kidneys. Can those who oppose abortion on the ground I mentioned make an exception for a pregnancy due to rape? Certainly. They can say that persons have a right to life only if they didn't come into existence because of rape; or they can say that all persons have a right to life, but that some have less of a right to life than others, in particular, that those who came into existence because of rape have less. But these statements have a rather unpleasant sound. Surely the question of whether you have a right to life at all, or how much of it you have, shouldn't turn on the question of whether or not you are the product of a rape. And in fact the people who oppose abortion on the ground I mentioned do not make this distinction, and hence do not make an exception in case of rape.

Nor do they make an exception for a case in which the mother has to spend the nine months of her pregnancy in bed. They would agree that would be a great pity, and hard on the mother; but all the same, all persons have a right to life, the fetus is a person, and so on. I suspect, in fact, that they would not make an exception for a case in which, miraculously enough, the pregnancy went on for nine years, or even the rest of the mother's life.

Some won't even make an exception for a case in which continuation of the pregnancy is likely to shorten the mother's life; they regard abortion as impermissible even to save the mother's life. Such cases are nowadays very rare, and many opponents of abortion do not accept this extreme view. All the same, it is a good place to begin: a number of points of interest come out in respect to it.

1. Let us call the view that abortion is impermissible even to save the mother's life "the extreme view." I want to suggest first that it does not issue from the argument I mentioned earlier without the addition of some fairly powerful premises. Suppose a woman has become pregnant, and now learns that she has a cardiac condition such that she will die if she carries the baby to term. What may be done for her? The fetus, being a person, has a right to life, but as the mother is a person too, so has she a right to life. Presumably they have an equal right to life. How is it supposed to come out that an abortion may not be performed? If mother and child have an equal right to life, shouldn't we perhaps flip a coin? Or should we add to the mother's right to life her right to decide what happens in and to her body, which everybody seems to be ready to grant—the sum of her rights now outweighing the fetus' right to life?

The most familiar argument here is the following. We are told that performing the abortion would be directly killing[2] the child, whereas doing nothing would not be killing the mother, but only letting her die. Moreover, in killing the child, one would be killing an innocent person, for the child has committed no crime, and is not aiming at his mother's death. And then there are a variety of ways in which this might be continued. (1) But as directly killing an innocent person is always and absolutely impermissible, an abortion, may not be performed. Or, (2) as directly killing an innocent person is murder, and murder is always an absolutely impermissible, an abortion may not be performed. Or, (3) as one's duty to refrain from directly killing an innocent person is more stringent than one's duty to keep a person from dying, an abortion may not be performed. Or, (4) if one's only options are directly killing an innocent person or letting a person die, one must prefer letting the person die, and thus an abortion may not be performed.

Some people seem to have thought that these are not further premises which must be added if the conclusion is to be reached, but that they follow from the very fact that an innocent person has a right to life. But this seems to me to be a mistake, and perhaps the simplest way to show this is to bring out that while we must certainly grant that innocent persons have a right to life, the theses in (1) through (4) are all false. Take (2), for example. If directly killing an innocent person is murder, and thus is impermissible, then the mother's directly killing the innocent person inside her is murder, and thus is impermissible. But it cannot seriously be thought to be murder if the mother performs an abortion on herself to save her life. It cannot seriously be said that she *must* refrain, that she *must* sit passively by and wait for her death. Let us look again at the case of you and the violinist. There you are, in bed with the violinist, and the director of the hospital says to you, "It's all most distressing, and I deeply sympathize, but you see this is putting an additional strain on your kidneys, and you'll be dead within the month. But you *have* to stay where you are all the same. Because unplugging you would be directly killing an innocent violinist, and that's murder, and that's impermissible." If anything in the world is true, it is that you do not commit murder, you do not do what is impermissible, if you reach around to your back and unplug yourself from that violinist to save your life.

The main focus of attention in writings on abortion has been on what a third party may or may not do in answer to a request from a woman for an abortion. This is in a way understandable. Things being as they are, there isn't much a woman can safely do to abort herself. So the question asked is what a third party may do, and what the mother may do, if it is mentioned at all, is deduced, almost as an afterthought, from what it is concluded that third parties may do. But it seems to me that to treat the matter in this way is to refuse to grant to the mother that very status of person which is so firmly insisted on for the fetus. For we cannot simply read off what a person may do from what a third party may do. Suppose you find yourself trapped in a tiny house with a growing child. I mean a very tiny house, and a rapidly growing child—you are already up against the wall of the house and in a few minutes you'll be crushed to death. The child on the other hand won't be crushed to death; if nothing is done to stop him from growing he'll be hurt, but in the end he'll simply burst open the house and walk out a free man. Now I could well understand it if a bystander were to say, "There's nothing we can do for you. We cannot choose between your life and his, we cannot be the ones to decide who is to live, we cannot intervene." But it cannot be concluded that you too can do nothing, that you cannot attack it to save your life. However innocent the child may be, you do not have to wait passively while it crushes you to death. Perhaps a pregnant woman is vaguely felt to have the status of house, to which we don't allow the right of self-defense. But if the woman houses the child, it should be remembered that she is a person who houses it.

I should perhaps stop to say explicitly that I am not claiming that people have a right to do anything whatever to save their lives. I think, rather, that there are drastic limits to the right of self-defense. If someone threatens you with death unless you torture someone else to death, I think you have not the right, even to save your life, to do so. But the case under consideration here is very different. In our case there are only two people involved, one whose life is threatened, and one who threatens it. Both are innocent: the one who is threatened is not threatened because of any fault, the one who threatens does not threaten because of any fault. For this reason we may feel that we bystanders cannot intervene. But the person threatened can.

In sum, a woman surely can defend her life against the threat to it posed by the unborn child, even if doing so involves its death. And this shows not merely that the theses in (1) through (4) are false; it shows also that the extreme view of abortion is false, and so we need not canvass any other possible ways of arriving at it from the argument I mentioned at the outset.

2. The extreme view could of course be weakened to say that while abortion is permissible to save the mother's life, it may not be performed by a third party, but only by the mother herself. But this cannot be right either. For what we have to keep in mind is that the mother and the unborn child are not like two tenants in a small house which has, by an unfortunate mistake, been rented to both: the mother *owns* the house. The fact that she does adds to the offensiveness of deducing that the mother can do nothing from the supposition that third parties can do nothing. But it does more than this: it casts a bright light on the supposition that third parties can do nothing. Certainly it lets us see that a third party who says "I cannot choose between you" is fooling himself if he thinks this is impartiality. If Jones has found and fastened on a certain coat, which he needs to keep him from freezing, but which Smith also needs to keep him from freezing, then it is not impartiality that says "I cannot choose between you" when Smith owns the coat. Women have said again and again "This body is *my* body!" and they have reason to feel angry, reason to feel that it has been like shouting into the wind. Smith, after all, is hardly likely to bless us if we say to him, "Of course, it is your coat, anybody would grant that it is. But no one may choose between you and Jones who is to have it."

We should really ask what it is that says "no one may choose" in the face of the fact that the body that houses the child is the mother's body. It may be simply a failure to appreciate this fact. But it may be something more interesting, namely the sense that one has a right to refuse to lay hands on people, even where it would be just and fair to do so, even where justice seems to require that somebody do so. Thus justice might call for somebody to get Smith's coat back from Jones, and yet you have a right to refuse to be the one to lay hands on Jones, a right to refuse to do physical violence to him. This, I think, must be granted. But then what should be said is not "no one may choose," but only "*I* cannot choose," and indeed not even this, but "*I* will not *act*," leaving it open that somebody else can or should, and in particular that anyone in a position of authority, with the job of securing people's rights, both can and should. So this is no difficulty. I have not been arguing that any given third party must accede to the mother's request that he perform an abortion to save her life, but only that he may.

I suppose that in some views of human life the mother's body is only on loan to her, the loan not being one which gives her any prior claim to it. One who held this view might well think it impartiality to say "I cannot choose." But I shall simply ignore this possibility. My own view is that if a human being has any just, prior claim to anything at all, he has a just, prior claim to his own body. And perhaps this needn't be argued for here anyway since, as I mentioned, the arguments against abortion we are looking at do grant that the woman has a right to decide what happens in and to her body.

But although they do grant it, I have tried to show that they do not take seriously what is done in granting it. I suggest the same thing will reappear even more clearly when we turn away from cases in which the mother's life is at stake, and attend, as I propose we now do, to the vastly more common cases in which a woman wants an abortion for some less weighty reason than preserving her own life.

3. Where the mother's life is not at stake, the argument I mentioned at the outset seems to have a much stronger pull. "Everyone has a right to life, so the unborn person has a right to life." And isn't the child's right to life weightier than anything other than the mother's own right to life, which she might put forward as ground for an abortion?

This argument treats the right to life as if it were unproblematic. It is not, and this seems to me to be precisely the source of the mistake.

For we should now, at long last, ask what it comes to, to have a right to life. In some views having a right to life includes having a right to be given at least the bare minimum one needs for continued life. But suppose that what in fact *is* the bare minimum a man needs for continued life is something he has no right at all to be given? If I am sick unto death, and the only thing that will save my life is the touch of Henry Fonda's cool hand on my fevered brow, then all the same, I have no right to be given the touch of Henry Fonda's cool hand on my fevered brow. It would be frightfully nice of him to fly in from the West Coast to provide it. It would be less nice, though no doubt well meant, if my friends flew out to the West Coast and carried Henry Fonda back with them. But I have no right at all against anybody that he should do this for me. Or again, to return to the story I told earlier, the fact that for continued life that violinist needs the continued use of your kidneys does not establish that he has a right to be given the continued use of your kidneys. He certainly has no right against you that *you* should give him continued use of your kidneys. For nobody has any right to use your kidneys unless you give him such a right; and nobody has the right against you that you shall give him this right—if you do allow him to go on using your kidneys, this is a kindness on your part, and not something he can claim from you as his due. Nor has he any right against anybody else that *they* should give him continued use of your kidneys. Certainly he had no right against the Society of Music Lovers that they should plug him into you in the first place. And if you now start to unplug yourself, having learned that you will otherwise have to spend nine years in bed with him, there is nobody in the world who must try to prevent you, in order to see to it that he is given something he has a right to be given.

Some people are rather stricter about the right to life. In their view, it does not include the right to be given anything, but amounts to, and only to, the right not to be killed by anybody. But here a related difficulty arises. If everybody is to refrain from killing that violinist, then everybody must refrain from doing a great many different sorts of things. Everybody must refrain from slitting his throat, everybody must refrain from shooting him—and everybody must refrain from unplugging you from him. But does he have a right against everybody that they shall refrain from unplugging you from him? To refrain from doing this is to allow him to continue to use your kidneys. It could be argued that he has a right against us that *we* should allow him to continue to use your kidneys. That is, while he had no right against us that we should give him the use of your kidneys, it might be argued that he anyway has a right against us that we shall not now intervene and deprive him of the use of your kidneys. I shall come back to third-party interventions later. But certainly the violinist has no right against you that *you* shall allow him to continue to use your kidneys. As I said, if you do allow him to use them, it is a kindness on your part, and not something you owe him.

The difficulty I point to here is not peculiar to the right to life. It reappears in connection with all the other natural rights; and it is something which an adequate account of rights must deal with. For present purposes it is enough just to draw attention to it. But I would stress that I am not arguing that people do not have a right to life—quite to the contrary, it seems to me that the primary control we must place on the acceptability of an account of rights is that it should turn out in that account to be a truth that all persons have a right to life. I am arguing only that having a right to life does not guarantee having either a right to be given the use of or a right to be allowed continued use of another person's body—even if one needs it for life itself. So the right to life will not serve the opponents of abortion in the very simple and clear way in which they seem to have thought it would.

4. There is another way to bring out the difficulty. In the most ordinary sort of case, to deprive someone of what he has a right to is to treat him unjustly. Suppose a boy and his small brother are jointly given a box of chocolates for Christmas. If the older boy takes the box and refuses to give his brother any of the chocolates, he is unjust to him, for the brother has been given a right to half of them. But suppose that, having learned that otherwise it means nine years in bed with that violinist, you unplug yourself from him. You surely are not being unjust to him, for you gave him no right to use your kidneys, and no one else can have given him any such right. But we have to notice that in unplugging yourself, you are killing him; and violinists, like everybody else, have a right to life, and thus in the view we were considering just now, the right not to be killed. So here you do what he supposedly has a right you shall not do, but you do not act unjustly to him in doing it.

The emendation which may be made at this point is this: the right to life consists not in the right not to be killed, but rather the right not to be killed unjustly. This runs a risk of circularity, but never mind: it would enable us to square the fact that the violinist has a right to life with the fact that you do not act unjustly toward him in unplugging yourself, thereby killing him. For if you do not kill him unjustly, you do not violate his right to life, and so it is no wonder you do him no injustice.

But if this emendation is accepted, the gap in the argument against abortion stares us plainly in the face: it is by no means enough to show that the fetus is a person, and to remind us that all persons have a right to life—we need to be shown also that killing the fetus violates its right to life, i.e., that abortion is unjust killing. And is it?

I suppose we may take it as a datum that in a case of pregnancy due to rape the mother has not given the unborn person a right to the use of her body for food and shelter. Indeed, in what pregnancy could it be supposed that the mother has given the unborn person such a right? It is not as if there were unborn persons drifting about the world, to whom a woman who wants a child says "I invite you in."

But it might be argued that there are other ways one can have acquired a right to the use of another person's body than by having been invited to use it by that person. Suppose a woman voluntarily indulges in intercourse, knowing of the chance it will issue in pregnancy, and then she does become pregnant; is she not in part responsible for the presence, in fact the very existence, of the unborn person inside her? No doubt she did not invite it in. But doesn't her partial responsibility for its being there itself give it a right to the use of her body. If so, then her aborting it would be more like the boy's taking away the chocolates, and less like your unplugging yourself from the violinist—doing so would be depriving it of what it does have a right to, and thus would be doing it an injustice.

And then, too, it might be asked whether or not she can kill it even to save her own life: If she voluntarily called it into existence, how can she now kill it, even in self-defense?

The first thing to be said about this is that it is something new. Opponents of abortion have been so concerned to make out the independence of the fetus, in order to establish that it has a right to life, just as its mother does, that they have tended to over-look the possible support they might gain from making out that the fetus is *dependent* on the mother, in order to establish that she has a special kind of responsibility for it, a responsibility that gives it rights against her which are not possessed by any independent person—such as an ailing violinist who is a stranger to her.

On the other hand, this argument would give the unborn person a right to its mother's body only if her pregnancy resulted from a voluntary act, undertaken in full knowledge of the chance a pregnancy might result from it. It would leave out entirely the unborn person whose existence is due to rape. Pending the availability of some further argument, then, we would be left with the conclusion that unborn persons whose existence is due to rape have no right to the use of their mothers' bodies, and thus that aborting them is not depriving them of anything they have a right to and hence is not unjust killing.

And we should also notice that it is not at all plain that this argument really does go even as far as it purports to. For there are cases and cases, and the details make a difference. If the room is stuffy, and I therefore open a window to air it, and a burglar climbs in, it would be absurd to say, "Ah, now he can stay, she's given him a right to the use of her house—for she is partially responsible for his presence there, having voluntarily done what enabled him to get in, in full knowledge that there are such things as burglars, and that burglars burgle." It would be still more absurd to say this if I had had bars installed outside my windows, precisely to prevent burglars from getting in, and a burglar got in only because of a defect in the bars. It remains equally absurd if we imagine it is not a burglar who climbs in, but an innocent person who blunders or falls in. Again, suppose it were like this: people-seeds drift about in the air like pollen, and if you open your windows, one may drift in and take root in your carpets or up-holstery. You don't want children, so you fix up your windows with fine mesh screens, the very best you can buy. As can happen, however, and on very, very rare occasions does happen, one of the screens is defective; and a seed drafts in and takes root. Does the person-plant who now develops have a right to the use of your house? Surely not—despite the fact that you voluntarily opened your windows, you knowingly kept carpets and upholstered furniture, you knew that screens were sometimes defective. Someone may argue that you are responsible for its rooting, that it does have a right to your house, because after all you *could* have lived out your life with bare floors and furniture, or with sealed windows and doors. But this won't do—for by the same token anyone can avoid a pregnancy due to rape by having a hysterectomy, or anyway by never leaving home without a (reliable!) army.

It seems to me that the argument we are looking at can establish at most that there are some *cases* in which the unborn person has a right to the use of its mother's body, and therefore *some* cases in which abortion is unjust killing. There is room for much discussion and argument as to precisely which, if any. But I think we should side-step this issue and leave it open, for at any rate the argument certainly does not establish that all abortion is unjust killing.

5. There is room for yet another argument here, however. We surely must all grant that there may be cases in which it would be morally indecent to detach a person from your body at the cost of his life. Suppose you learn that what the violinist needs is not nine years of your life, but only one hour: all you need to do to save his life is to spend one hour in that bed with him. Suppose also that letting him use your kidneys for that one hour would not affect your health in the slightest. Admittedly you were kidnapped. Admittedly you did not give anyone permission to plug him into you. Nevertheless it seems to me plain you *ought* to allow him to use your kidneys for that hour—it would be indecent to refuse.

Again, suppose pregnancy lasted only an hour, and constituted no threat to life or health. And suppose that a woman becomes pregnant as a result of rape. Admittedly she did not voluntarily do anything to bring about the existence of a child. Admittedly she did nothing at all which would give the unborn person a right to the use of her body. All the same it might well be said, as in the newly emended violinist story, that she *ought* to allow it to remain for that hour—that it would be indecent in her to refuse.

Now some people are inclined to use the term "right" in such a way that it follows from the fact that you ought to allow a person to use your body for the hour he needs, that he has a right to use your body for the hour he needs, even though he has not been given that right by any person or act. They may say that it follows also that if you refuse, you act unjustly toward him. This use of the term is perhaps so common that it cannot be called wrong; nevertheless it seems to me to be an unfortunate loosening of what we would do better to keep a tight rein on. Suppose that box of chocolates I mentioned earlier had not been given to both boys jointly, but was given only to the older boy. There he sits, stolidly eating his way through the box, his small brother watching enviously. Here we are likely to say "You ought not to be so mean. You ought to give your brother some of those chocolates." My own view is that it just does not follow from the truth of this that the brother has any right to any of the chocolates. If the boy refuses to give his brother any, he is greedy, stingy, callous—but not unjust. I suppose that the people I have in mind will say it does follow that the brother has a right to some of the chocolates, and thus that the boy does act unjustly if he refuses to give his brother any. But the effect of saying this is to obscure what we should keep distinct, namely the difference between the boy's refusal in this case and the boy's refusal in the earlier case, in which the box was given to both boys jointly, and in which the small brother thus had what was from any point of view clear title to half.

A further objection to so using the term "right" that from the fact that A ought to do a thing for B, it follows that B has a right against A that A do it for him, is that it is going to make the question of whether or not a man has a right to a thing turn on how easy it is to provide him with it; and this seems not merely unfortunate, but morally unacceptable. Take the case of Henry Fonda again. I said earlier that I had no right to the touch of his cool hand on my fevered brow, even though I needed it to save my life. I said it would be frightfully nice of him to fly in from the West Coast to provide me with it, but that I had no right against him that he should do so. But suppose he isn't on the West Coast. Suppose he has only to walk across the room, place a hand briefly on my brow—and lo, my life is saved. Then surely he ought to do it, it would be indecent to refuse. Is it to be said "Ah, well, it follows that in this case she has a right to the touch of his hand on her brow, and so it would be an injustice in him to refuse"? So that I have a right to it when it is easy for him to provide it, though no right when it's hard? It's rather a shocking idea that anyone's rights should fade away and disappear as it gets harder and harder to accord them to him.

So my own view is that even though you ought to let the violinist use your kidneys for the one hour he needs, we should not conclude that he has a right to do so—we should say that if you refuse, you are, self-centered and callous, indecent in fact, but not unjust. And similarly, that even supposing a case in which a woman pregnant due to rape ought to allow the unborn person to use her body for the hour he needs, we should not conclude that he has a right to do so; we should conclude she is self-centered, callous, indecent, but not unjust, if she refuses. The complaints are no less grave; they are just different. However, there is no need to insist on this point. If anyone does wish to deduce "he has a right" from "you ought," then all the same he must surely grant that there are cases in which it is not morally required of you that you allow that violinist to use your kidneys, and in which he does not have a right to use them, and in which you do not do him an injustice if you refuse. And so also for mother and unborn child. Except in such cases as the unborn person has a right to demand it—and we were leaving open the possibility that there may be such cases—nobody is morally *required* to make large sacrifices, of health, of all other interests and concerns, of all other duties and commitments, for nine years, or even for nine months, in order to keep another person alive.

6. We have in fact to distinguish between two kinds of Samaritan: the Good Samaritan and what we might call the Minimally Decent Samaritan. The story of the Good Samaritan, you will remember, goes like this:

A certain man went down from Jerusalem to Jericho, and fell among thieves, which stripped him of his raiment, and wounded him, and departed, leaving him half dead.

And by chance there came down a certain priest that way; and when he saw him, he passed by on the other side.

And likewise a Levite, when he was at the place, came and looked on him, and passed by on the other side.

But a certain Samaritan, as he journeyed, came where he was; and when he saw him he had compassion on him.

And went to him, and bound up his wounds, pouring in oil and wine, and set him on his own beast, and brought him to an inn, and took care of him.

And on the morrow, when he departed, he took out two pence, and gave him to the host, and said unto him, "Take care of him; and whatsoever thou spendest more, when I come again, I will repay thee." (Luke 10:30–35)

The Good Samaritan went out of his way, at some cost to himself, to help one in need of it. We are not told what the options were, that is, whether or not the priest and the Levite could have helped by doing less than the Good Samaritan did, but assuming they could have, then the fact they did nothing at all shows they were not even Minimally Decent Samaritans, not because they were not Samaritans, but because they were not even minimally decent.

These things are a matter of degree, of course, but there is a difference, and it comes out perhaps most clearly in the story of Kitty Genovese, who, as you will remember, was murdered while thirty-eight people watched or listened, and did nothing at all to help her. A Good Samaritan would have rushed out to give direct assistance against the murderer. Or perhaps we had better allow that it would have been a Splendid Samaritan who did this, on the ground that it would have involved a risk of death for himself. But the thirty-eight not only did not do this, they did not even trouble to pick up a phone to call the police. Minimally Decent Samaritanism would call for doing at least that, and their not having done it was monstrous.

After telling the story of the Good Samaritan, Jesus said, "Go, and do thou likewise." Perhaps he meant that we are morally required to act as the Good Samaritan did. Perhaps he was urging people to do more than is morally required of them. At all events it seems plain that it was not morally required of any of the thirty-eight that he rush out to give direct assistance at the risk of his own life, and that it is not morally required of anyone that he give long stretches of his life—nine years or nine months—to sustaining the life of a person who has no special right (we were leaving open the possibility of this) to demand it.

Indeed, with one rather striking class of exceptions, no one in any country in the world is *legally* required to do anywhere near as much as this for anyone else. The class of exceptions is obvious. My main concern here is not the state of the law in respect to abortion, but it is worth drawing attention to the fact that in no state in this country is any man compelled by law to be even a Minimally Decent Samaritan to any person; there is no law under which charges could be brought against the thirty-eight who stood by while Kitty Genovese died. By contrast, in most states in this country women are compelled by law to be not merely Minimally Decent Samaritans, but Good Samaritans to unborn persons inside them. This doesn't by itself settle anything one way or the other, because it may well be argued that there should be laws in this country—as there are in many European countries—compelling at least Minimally Decent Samaritanism.[3] But it does show that there is a gross injustice in the existing state of the law. And it shows also that the groups currently working against liberalization of abortion laws, in fact working toward having it declared unconstitutional for a state to permit abortion, had better start working for the adoption of Good Samaritan laws generally, or earn the charge that they are acting in bad faith.

I should think, myself, that Minimally Decent Samaritan laws would be one thing, Good Samaritan laws quite another, and in fact highly improper. But we are not here concerned with the law. What we should ask is not whether anybody should be compelled by law to be a Good Samaritan, but whether we must accede to a situation in which somebody is being compelled—by nature, perhaps—to be a Good Samaritan. We have, in other words, to look now at third-party interventions. I have been arguing that no person is morally required to make large sacrifices to attain the life of another who has no right to demand them, and this even where the sacrifices do not include life itself; we are not morally required to be Good Samaritans or anyway Very Good Samaritans to one another. But what if a man cannot extricate himself from such a situation? What if he appeals to us to extricate him? It seems to me plain that there are cases in which we can, cases in which a Good Samaritan would extricate him. There you are, you were kidnapped, and nine years in bed with that violinist lie ahead of you. You have your own life to lead. You are sorry, but you simply cannot see giving up so much of your life to the sustaining of his. You cannot extricate yourself, and ask us to do so. I should have thought that—in light of his having no right to the use of your body—it was obvious that we do not have to accede to your being forced to give up so much. We can do what you ask. There is no injustice to the violinist in our doing so.

7. Following the lead of the opponents of abortion, I have throughout been speaking of the fetus merely as a person, and what I have been asking is whether or not the argument we began with, which proceeds only from the fetus' being a person, really does establish its conclusion. I have argued that it does not.

But of course there are arguments and arguments, and it may be said that I have simply fastened on the wrong one. It may be said that what is important is not merely the fact that the fetus is a person, but that it is a person for whom the woman has a special kind of responsibility issuing from the fact that she is its mother. And it might be argued that all my analogies are therefore irrelevant—for you do not have that special kind of responsibility for that violinist, Henry Fonda does not have that special kind of responsibility for me. And our attention might be drawn to the fact that men and women both are compelled by law to provide support for their children.

I have in effect dealt (briefly) with this argument in section 4 above; but a (still briefer) recapitulation now may be in order. Surely we do not have any such "special responsibility" for a person unless we have assumed it, explicitly or implicitly. If a set of parents do not try to prevent pregnancy, do not obtain an abortion, and then at the time of birth of the child do not put it out for adoption, but rather take it home with them, then they have assumed responsibility for it, they have given it rights, and they cannot *now* withdraw support from it at the cost of its life because they now find it difficult to go on providing for it. But if they have taken all reasonable precautions against having a child, they do not simply by virtue of their biological relationship to the child who comes into existence have a special responsibility for it. They may wish to assume responsibility for it, or they may not wish to. And I am suggesting that if assuming responsibility for it would require large sacrifices, then they may refuse. A Good Samaritan would not refuse—or anyway, a Splendid Samaritan, if the sacrifices that had to be made were enormous. But then so would a Good Samaritan assume responsibility for that violinist; so would Henry Fonda, if he is a Good Samaritan, fly in from the West Coast and assume responsibility for me.

8. My argument will be found unsatisfactory on two counts by many of those who want to regard abortion as morally permissible. First, while I do argue that abortion is not impermissible, I do not argue that it is always permissible. There may well be cases in which carrying the child to term requires only Minimally Decent Samaritanism of the mother, and this is a standard we must not fall below. I am inclined to think it a merit of my account precisely that it does *not* give a general yes or a general no. It allows for and supports our sense that, for example, a sick and desperately frightened fourteen-year-old schoolgirl, pregnant due to rape, may *of course* choose abortion, and that any law which rules this out is an insane law. And it also allows for and supports our sense that in other cases resort to abortion is even positively indecent. It would be indecent in the woman to request an abortion, and indecent in a doctor to perform it, if she is in her seventh month, and wants the abortion just to avoid the nuisance of postponing a trip abroad. The very fact that the arguments I have been drawing attention to treat all cases of abortion, or even all cases of abortion in which the mother's life is not at stake, as morally on a par ought to have made them suspect at the outset.

Secondly, while I am arguing for the permissibility of abortion in some cases, I am not arguing for the right to secure the death of the unborn child. It is easy to confuse these two things in that up to a certain point in the life of the fetus it is not able to survive outside the mother's body; hence removing it from her body guarantees its death. But they are importantly different. I have argued that you are not morally required to spend nine months in bed, sustaining the life of that violinist; but to say this is by no means to say that if, when you unplug yourself, there is a miracle and he survives, you then have a right to turn around and slit his throat. You may detach yourself even if this costs him his life; you have no right to be guaranteed his death, by some other means, if unplugging yourself does not kill him. There are some people who will feel dissatisfied by this feature of my argument. A woman may be utterly devastated by the thought of a child, a bit of herself, put out for adoption and never seen or heard of again. She may therefore want not merely that the child be detached from her, but more, that it die. Some opponents of abortion are inclined to regard this as beneath contempt—thereby showing insensitivity to what is surely a powerful source of despair. All the same, I agree that the desire for the child's death is not one which anybody may gratify, should it turn out to be possible to detach the child alive.

At this place, however, it should be remembered that we have only been pretending throughout that the fetus is a human being from the moment of conception. A very early abortion is surely not the killing of a person, and so is not dealt with by anything I have said here.

Notes

1. Daniel Callahan, Abortion: Law, Choice and Morality 373 (New York, 1970). This book gives a fascinating survey of the available information on abortion. The Jewish tradition is surveyed in David M. Feldman, Birth Control in Jewish Law, Part 5 (New York, 1968); the Catholic tradition in John T. Noonan, Jr., An Almost Absolute Value in History, in John T. Noonan Jr., ed., The Morality of Abortion (Cambridge, Mass., 1970).

2. The term "direct" in the arguments I refer to is a technical one. Roughly, what is meant by "direct killing" is either killing as an end in itself, or killing as a means to some end, for example, the end of saving someone else's life. . . .

3. For a discussion of the difficulties involved, and a survey of the European experience with such laws, see James M. Ratcliffe ed., The Good Samaritan and the Law (New York, 1966).

Privacy v. Equality: Beyond Roe v. Wade

CATHARINE A. MACKINNON

> In a society where women entered sexual intercourse willingly, where adequate contraception was a genuine social priority, there would be no "abortion issue.". . . Abortion is violence. . . . It is the offspring, and will continue to be the accuser of a more pervasive and prevalent violence, the violence of rapism.
>
> —*Adrienne Rich*, Of Woman Born *(1976)*

ROE V. WADE[1] guaranteed the right to choose abortion, subject to some countervailing considerations, by conceiving it as a private choice, included in the constitutional right to privacy. In this critique of that decision, I first situate abortion and the abortion right in the experience of women. The argument is that abortion is inextricable from sexuality, assuming that the feminist analysis of sexuality is our analysis of gender inequality. I then criticize the doctrinal choice to pursue the abortion right under the law of privacy. The argument is that privacy doctrine reaffirms and reinforces what the feminist critique of sexuality criticizes: the public/private split. The political and ideological meaning of privacy as a legal doctrine is connected with the concrete consequences of the public/private split for the lives of women. This analysis makes Harris v. McRae,[2] in which public funding for abortions was held not to be required, appear consistent with the larger meaning of *Roe*.

I will neglect two important explorations, which I bracket now. The first is: what are babies to men? On one level, men respond to women's rights to abort as if confronting the possibility of their own potential nonexistence—at *women's* hands, no less. On another level, men's issues of potency, of continuity as a compensation for mortality, of the thrust to embody themselves or their own image in the world, underlie their relation to babies (as well as to most else). To overlook these meanings of abortion to men as men is to overlook political and strategic as well as fundamental theoretical issues and to misassess where much of the opposition to abortion is coming from. The sec-

The author discussed these ideas at the Conference on Persons, Morality, and Abortion, Hampshire College, Amherst, Massachusetts, Jan. 21, 1983, and at the Planned Parenthood Conference, "Who Governs Reproduction?" New Haven, Connecticut, Nov. 2, 1985.

Reprinted by permission of the publishers from *Feminism Unmodified* by Catharine A. MacKinnon, Cambridge, Mass.: Harvard University Press. Copyright © 1987 by the President and Fellows of Harvard College.

ond issue I bracket is one that, unlike the first, has been discussed extensively in the abortion debate: the moral rightness of abortion itself. My stance is that the abortion choice must be legally available and must be *women's,* but not because the fetus is not a form of life. In the usual argument, the abortion decision is made contingent on whether the fetus is a form of life. I cannot follow that. Why should women not make life or death decisions? This returns us to the first bracketed issue.

The issues I will explore have largely not been discussed in the terms I will use. Instead, I think, women's embattled need to survive in a world hostile to our survival has precluded our exploring these issues as I am about to. That is, the perspective from which we have addressed abortion has been shaped and constrained by the very situation that the abortion issue puts us in and requires us to address. We have not been able to risk thinking about these issues on our own terms because the terms have not been ours. The attempt to grasp women's situation on our own terms, from our own point of view, defines the feminist impulse. If doing that is risky, our situation also makes it risky not to. So, first feminism, then law.

Most women who seek abortions became pregnant while having sexual intercourse with men. Most did not mean or wish to conceive. In contrast to this fact of women's experience, which converges sexuality with reproduction with gender, the abortion debate has centered on separating control over sexuality from control over reproduction, and on separating both from gender and the life options of the sexes. Liberals have supported the availability of the abortion choice as if the woman just happened on the fetus.[3] The political right, imagining that the intercourse preceding conception is usually voluntary, urges abstinence, as if sex were up to women, while defending male authority, specifically including a wife's duty to submit to sex. Continuing with this logic, many opponents of state funding of abortions, such as supporters of some versions of the Hyde Amendment, would permit funding of abortions when pregnancy results from rape or incest.[4] They make *exceptions* for those special occasions during which they presume women did *not* control sex. From all this I deduce that abortion's proponents and opponents share a tacit assumption that women significantly do control sex.

Feminist investigations suggest otherwise. Sexual intercourse, still the most common cause of pregnancy, cannot simply be presumed coequally determined. Feminism has found that women feel compelled to preserve the appearance—which, acted upon, becomes the reality—of male direction of sexual expression, as if male initiative itself were what we want, as if it were that which turns us on. Men enforce this. It is much of what men want in a woman. It is what pornography eroticizes and prostitutes provide. Rape—that is, intercourse with force that is recognized as force—is adjudicated not according to the power or force that the man wields, but according to indices of intimacy between the parties. The more intimate you are with your accused rapist, the less likely a court is to find that what happened to you was rape. Other indices of intimacy include intercourse itself. If "no" can be taken as "yes," how free can "yes" be?

Under these conditions, women often do not use birth control because of its social meaning, a meaning we did not create. Using contraception means acknowledging and planning the possibility of intercourse, accepting one's sexual availability, and appearing non-spontaneous. It means appearing available to male incursions. A good user of contraception can be presumed sexually available and, among other consequences, raped with relative impunity. (If you think this isn't true, you should consider rape cases in which the fact that a woman had a diaphragm in is taken as an indication that what happened to her was intercourse, not rape. "Why did you have your diaphragm in?") From studies of abortion clinics, women who repeatedly seek abortions (and now I'm looking at the repeat offenders high on the list of the right's villains, their best case for opposing abortion as female irresponsibility), when asked why, say something like, "The sex just happened." Like every night for two and a half years.[5] I wonder if a woman can be presumed to control access to her sexuality if she feels unable to interrupt intercourse to insert a diaphragm; or worse, cannot even want to, aware that she risks a pregnancy she knows she does not want. Do you think she would stop the man for any other reason, such as, for instance, the real taboo—lack of desire? If she would not, how is sex, hence its consequences, meaningfully voluntary for women? Norms of sexual rhythm and romance that are felt interrupted by women's needs are constructed against women's interests. Sex doesn't look a whole lot like freedom when it appears normatively less costly for women to risk an undesired, often painful, traumatic, dangerous, sometimes illegal, and potentially life-threatening procedure than to protect themselves in advance. Yet abortion policy has never been explicitly approached in the context of how women get pregnant, that is, as a consequence of intercourse under conditions of gender inequality; that is, as an issue of forced sex.

Now, law. In 1973 Roe v. Wade found that a statute that made criminal all abortions except those to save the life of the mother violated the constitutional right to privacy.[6] The privacy right had been previously created as a constitutional principle in a case that decriminalized the prescription and use of contraceptives.[7] Note that courts use the privacy rubric to connect contraception with abortion through privacy in the same way that I just did through sexuality. In *Roe* that right to privacy was found "broad enough to encompass a woman's decision whether or not to terminate her pregnancy." In 1977 three justices observed, "In the abortion context, we have held that the right to privacy shields the woman from undue state intrusion in and external scrutiny of her very personal choice."[8]

In 1981 the Supreme Court in Harris v. McRae decided that this right to privacy did not mean that federal Medicaid programs had to fund medically necessary abortions. Privacy, the Court had said, was guaranteed for "a woman's *decision* whether or not to terminate her pregnancy." The Court then permitted the government to support one decision and not another: to fund continuing conceptions and not to fund discontinuing them. Asserting that decisional privacy was nevertheless constitutionally intact, the Court stated that "although the government may not place obstacles in the path of a woman's exercise of her freedom of choice, it need not remove those not of its own creation."[9] It is apparently a short step from that which the government has a duty *not* to intervene in to that which it has *no* duty to intervene in.

The idea of privacy, if regarded as the outer edge of the limitations on government, embodies, I think, a tension between the preclusion of public exposure or governmental intrusion, on the one hand, and autonomy in the sense of protecting personal self-action on the other. This is a tension, not just two facets of one whole right. In the liberal state this tension is resolved by demarking the threshold of the state at its permissible extent of penetration into a domain that is considered free by definition: the private sphere. It is by this move that the state secures to individuals what has been termed "an inviolable personality" by ensuring what has been called "autonomy or control over the intimacies of personal identity."[10] The state does this by centering its self-restraint on body and home, especially bedroom. By staying out of marriage and the family, prominently meaning sexuality—that is to say, heterosexuality—from contraception through pornography to the abortion decision, the law of privacy proposes to guarantee individual bodily integrity, personal exercise of moral intelligence, and freedom of intimacy.[11] But if one asks whether *women's* rights to these values have been guaranteed, it appears that the law of privacy works to translate traditional social values into the rhetoric of individual rights as a means of subordinating those rights to specific social imperatives.[12] In feminist terms, I am arguing that the logic of *Roe* consummated in *Harris* translates the ideology of the public sphere into the individual woman's legal right to privacy as a means of subordinating women's collective needs to the imperatives of male supremacy.

This is my retrospective on Roe v. Wade. Reproduction is sexual, men control sexuality, and the state supports the interest of men as a group. *Roe* does not contradict this. So why was abortion legalized? Why were women even imagined to have such a right as privacy? It is not an accusation of bad faith to answer that the interests of men as a social group converged with the definition of justice embodied in law in what I call the male point of view. The way the male point of view constructs a social event or legal need will be the way that social event or legal need is framed by state policy. For example, to the extent that possession is the point of sex, illegal rape will be sex with a woman who is not yours unless the act makes her yours. If part of the kick of pornography involves eroticizing the putatively prohibited, illegal pornography—obscenity—will be prohibited enough to keep pornography desirable without ever making it truly illegitimate or unavailable. If, from the male standpoint, male is the implicit definition of human, maleness will be the implicit standard by which sex equality is measured in discrimination law. In parallel terms, abortion's availability frames, and is framed by, the conditions men work out among themselves to grant legitimacy to women to control the reproductive consequences of intercourse.

Since Freud, the social problem posed by sexuality has been perceived as the problem of the innate desire for sexual pleasure being repressed by the constraints of civilization. In this context, the inequality of the sexes arises as an issue only in women's repressive socialization to passivity and coolness (so-called frigidity), in women's so-called desexualization, and in the disparate consequences of biology, that is, pregnancy. Who defines what is sexual, what sexuality therefore is, to whom what stimuli are erotic and why, and who defines the conditions under which sexuality is expressed—these issues are not even available to be considered. "Civilization's" answer to these questions fuses women's reproductivity with our attributed sexuality in its definition of what a woman is. We are defined as women by the uses to which men put us. In this context it becomes clear why the struggle for reproductive freedom has never included a woman's right to refuse sex. In this notion of sexual liberation, the equality issue has been framed as a struggle for women to have sex with men on the same terms as men: "without consequences." In this sense the abortion right has been sought as freedom from the reproductive consequences of sexual expression, with sexuality defined as centered on heterosexual genital intercourse. It is as if biological organisms, rather than social relations, reproduced the species. But if your concern is not how more people can get more sex, but who defines sexuality—pleasure and violation both—then the abortion right is situated within a very different problematic: the social and political problematic of the inequality of the sexes. As Susan Sontag said, "Sex itself is not liberating for women. Neither is more sex. . . . The question is, what sexuality shall women be liberated to enjoy?"[13] To address this requires reformulating the problem of sexuality from the repression of drives by civilization to the oppression of women by men.

Arguments for abortion under the rubric of feminism have rested upon the right to control one's own body—gender neutral. I think that argument has been appealing for the same reasons it is inadequate: socially, women's bodies have not been ours; we have not controlled their meanings and destinies. Feminists tried to assert that control without risking pursuit of the idea that something more might be at stake than our bodies, something closer to a net of relations in which we are (at present unescapably) gendered.[14] Some feminists have noticed that our right to decide has become merged with the right of an overwhelmingly male profession's right not to have its professional judgment second-guessed by the government.[15] But most abortion advocates argue in rigidly and rigorously gender-neutral terms.

Thus, for instance, Judith Jarvis Thomson's argument that an abducted woman has no obligation to be a celebrated violinist's life support system meant that women have no obligation to support a fetus.[16] The parallel seems misframed. No woman who needs an abortion—no woman, period—is valued, no potential a woman's life might hold is cherished, like a gender-neutral famous violinist's unencumbered possibilities. The problems of gender are thus underlined here rather than solved, or even addressed. Too, the underlying recognition in the parallel of the origin of the problem in rape—the origin in force, in abduction, that gives the hypothetical much of its moral weight—would confine abortions to instances in which force is recognized as force, like rape or incest. The applicability of this to the normal case of abortion is neither embraced nor disavowed, although the parallel was meant to apply to the normal case, as is abortion policy, usually. This parable is constructed precisely to begin the debate after sex occurred, yet even it requires discussion of intercourse in relation to rape in relation to conception, in order to make sense. Because this issue has been studiously avoided in the abortion context, the unequal basis on which woman's personhood is being constructed is obscured.

In the context of a sexual critique of gender inequality, abortion promises to women sex with men on the same reproductive terms as men have sex with women. So long as women do not control access to our sexuality, abortion facilitates women's heterosexual availability. In other words, under conditions of gender inequality, sexual liberation in this sense does not free women; it frees male sexual aggression. The availability of abortion removes the one remaining legitimized reason that women have had for refusing sex besides the headache. As Andrea Dworkin puts it, analyzing male ideology on abortion, "Getting laid was at stake."[17] The Playboy Foundation has supported abortion rights from day one; it continues to, even with shrinking disposable funds, on a level of priority comparable to that of its opposition to censorship.

Privacy doctrine is an ideal vehicle for this process. The liberal ideal of the private—and privacy as an ideal has been formulated in liberal terms—holds that, so long as the public does not interfere, autonomous individuals interact freely and equally. Conceptually, this private is hermetic. It *means* that which is inaccessible to, unaccountable to, unconstructed by anything beyond itself. By definition, it is not part of or conditioned by anything systematic or outside of it. It is personal, intimate, autonomous, particular, individual, the original source and final outpost of the self, gender neutral. It is, in short, defined by everything that feminism reveals women have never been allowed to be or to have, and everything that women have been equated with and defined in terms of *men's* ability to have. To complain in public of inequality within it contradicts the liberal definition of the private. In this view, no act of the state contributes to—hence should properly participate in—shaping the internal alignments of the private or distributing its internal forces. Its inviolability by the state, framed as an individual right, presupposes that the private is not already an arm of the state. In this scheme, intimacy is implicitly thought to guarantee symmetry of power. Injuries arise in violating the private sphere, not within and by and because of it.

In private, consent tends to be presumed. It is true that a showing of coercion voids this presumption. But the problem is getting anything private to be perceived as coercive. Why one would allow force in private—the "why doesn't she leave" question asked of battered women—is a question given its urgency by the social meaning of the private as a sphere of choice. But for women the measure of the intimacy has been the measure of the oppression. This is why feminism has had to explode the private. This is why feminism has seen the personal as the political. The private is the public for those for whom the personal is the political. In this sense, there is no private, either normatively or empirically. Feminism confronts the fact that women have no privacy to lose or to guarantee. We are not inviolable. Our sexuality is not only violable, it is—hence, we are—seen *in* and *as* our violation. To confront the fact that we have no privacy is to confront the intimate degradation of women as the public order.

In this light, a right to privacy looks like an injury got up as a gift. Freedom from public intervention coexists uneasily with any right that requires social preconditions to be meaningfully delivered. For example, if inequality is socially pervasive and enforced, equality will require intervention, not abdication, to be meaningful. But the right to privacy is not thought to require social change. It is not even thought to require any social preconditions, other than nonintervention by the public. The point of this for the abortion cases is not that indigency—which was the specific barrier to effective choice in *Harris*—is well within the public power to remedy, nor that the state is exempt in issues of the distribution of wealth. The point is rather that Roe v. Wade presumes that government intervention into the private sphere promotes a woman's freedom of choice. When the alternative is jail, there is much to be said for this argument. But the *Harris* result sustains the ultimate meaning of privacy in *Roe:* women are guaranteed by the public no more than what we can get in private—that is, what we can extract through our intimate associations with men. Women with privileges get rights.

So women got abortion as a private privilege, not as a public right. We got control over reproduction that is controlled by "a man or The Man," an individual man or the doctors or the government. Abortion was not decriminalized; it was legalized. In *Roe* the government set the stage for the conditions under which women gain access to this right. Virtually every ounce of control that women won out of this legalization has gone directly into the hands of men—husbands, doctors, or fathers—or is now in the process of attempts to reclaim it through regulation.[18] This, surely, must be what is meant by reform.

It is not inconsistent, then, that framed as a privacy right, a woman's decision to abort would have no claim on public support and would genuinely not be seen as burdened by that deprivation. Privacy conceived as a right against public intervention and disclosure is the opposite of the relief that *Harris* sought for welfare women. State intervention would have provided a choice women did *not* have in private. The women in *Harris,* women whose sexual refusal has counted for particularly little, needed something to make their privacy effective.[19] The logic of the Court's response resembles the logic by which women are supposed to consent to sex. Preclude the alternatives, then call the sole remaining option "her choice." The point is that the alternatives are precluded *prior to* the reach of the chosen legal doctrine. They are precluded by conditions of sex, race, and class—the very conditions the privacy frame not only leaves tacit but exists to *guarantee.*

When the law of privacy restricts intrusions into intimacy, it bars change in control over that intimacy. The existing distribution of power and resources within the private sphere will be precisely what the law of privacy exists to protect. It is probably not coincidence that the very things feminism regards as central to the subjection of women—the very place, the body; the very relations, heterosexual; the very activities, intercourse and reproduction; and the very feelings, intimate—form the core of what is covered by privacy doctrine. From this perspective, the legal concept of privacy can and has shielded the place of battery, marital rape, and women's exploited labor; has preserved the central institutions whereby women are *deprived* of identity, autonomy, control and self-definition; and has protected the primary activity through which male supremacy is expressed and enforced. Just as pornography is legally protected as individual freedom of expression—without questioning whose freedom and whose expression and at whose expense—abstract privacy protects abstract autonomy, without inquiring into whose freedom of action is being sanctioned at whose expense.

To fail to recognize the meaning of the private in the ideology and reality of women's subordination by seeking protection behind a right *to* that privacy is to cut women off from collective verification and state support in the same act. I think this has a lot to do with why we can't organize women on the abortion issue. When women are segregated in private, separated from each other, one at a time, a right to that privacy isolates us at once from each other and from public recourse. This right to privacy is a right of men "to be let alone"[20] to oppress women one at a time. It embodies and reflects the private sphere's existing definition of womanhood. This is an instance of liberalism called feminism, liberalism applied to women as if we *are* persons, gender neutral. It reinforces the division between public and private that is *not* gender neutral. It is at once an ideological division that lies about women's shared experience and that mystifies the unity among the spheres of women's violation. It is a very material division that keeps the private beyond public redress and politicizes women's subjection within it. It keeps some men out of the bedrooms of other men.[21]

Notes

1. Roe v. Wade, 410 U.S. 113 (1973).
2. Harris v. McRae, 448 U.S. 297 (1980). This is not to support the *Harris* ruling or to propose individual hearings to determine coercion prior to allowing abortions. Nor is it to criticize Justice Blackmun, author of the majority opinion in *Roe,* who undoubtedly saw legalizing abortion as a way to help women out of a desperate situation, which it has done.
3. D. H. Regan, Rewriting Roe v. Wade, 77 Mich. L. Rev. 1569 (1979), in which the Good Samaritan happens upon the fetus.
4. As of 1973, ten states that had made abortion a crime had exceptions for rape and incest; at least three had exceptions for rape only. Many of these exceptions were based on Model Penal Code §230.3 (Proposed Official Draft 1962), quoted in Doe v. Bolton, 410 U.S. 179, 205–207, App. B (1973), permitting abortion, inter alia, in cases of "rape, incest, or other felonious intercourse." References to states with incest and rape exceptions can be found Roe v. Wade, 410 U.S. 113 n.37 (1973). Some versions of the Hyde Amendment, which prohibits use of public money to fund abortion, have contained exceptions for cases of rape or incest. All require immediate reporting of the incident.
5. Kristin Luker, Taking Chances: Abortion and the Decision Not to Contracept (1976).
6. Roe v. Wade, 410 U.S. 113 (1973).
7. Griswold v. Connecticut, 381 U.S. 479 (1965).
8. Eisenstadt v. Baird, 405 U.S. 438 (1972).
9. Harris v. McRae, 448 U.S. 297 (1980).
10. T. Gerety, Redefining Privacy, 12 Harv. C.R.-C.L. L. Rev. 233, 236 (1977).
11. Kenneth I. Karst, The Freedom of Intimate Association, 89 Yale L.J. 624 (1980); Developments—The Family, 93 Harv. L. Rev. 1157 (1980); Doe v. Commonwealth Atty, 403 F. Supp. 1199 (E.D. Va. 1975), *aff'd without opinion,* 425 U.S. 901 (1976), but cf. People v. Onofre, 51 N.Y.2d 476 (1980), *cert. denied,* 451 U.S. 987 (1981).

The issue was finally decided, for the time, in Bowers v. Hardwick, 478 U.S. 186 (1986) (statute criminalizing consensual sodomy does not violate right to privacy).

12. Tom Grey, Eros, Civilization and the Burger Court, 43 Law & Contemp. Probs. 83 (1980).

13. Susan Sontag, The Third World of Women, 40 Partisan Rev. 188 (1973).

14. See Adrienne Rich, Of Woman Born: Motherhood as Experience and Institution chap. 3 (1977), esp. 47, 48: "The child that I carry for nine months can be defined *neither* as me or as not-me" (emphasis in the original).

15. Kristin Booth Glen, Abortion in the Courts: A Lay Woman's Historical Guide to the New Disaster Area, 4 Feminist Stud. 1 (1978).

16. Judith Jarvis Thomson, A Defense of Abortion, herein at 971.

17. Andrea Dworkin, Right Wing Women 95 (1983). You must read this book. See also Friedrich Engels arguing on removing private housekeeping into social industry, Origin of the Family, Private Property and the State (1884).

18. H. L. v. Matheson, 450 U.S. 398 (1981); Bellotti v. Baird, 443 U.S. 622 (1979); but cf. Planned Parenthood of Central Missouri v. Danforth, 428 U.S. 52 (1976). See also Introduction, *supra* note 1.

19. See Dworkin, *supra* note 17, at 98–99.

20. S. Warren and L. Brandeis, The Right to Privacy, 4 Harv. L. Rev. 190, 205 (1890); but note that the right of privacy under some state constitutions has been held to include funding for abortions: Committee to Defend Reproductive Rights v. Meyers, 29 Cal. 3d 252 (1981); Moe v. Secretary of Admin. and Finance, 417 N.E. 2d 387 (Mass. 1981).

21. As Andrea Dworkin once said to me, women may identify with the fetus not only because what happens to it, happens to them, but also because, like them, it is powerless and invisible. The vicissitudes of abortion law and policy have vividly expressed that commonality while purporting to relieve it. The discussion in this speech is a beginning attempt to recast the abortion issue toward a new legal approach and political strategy: sex equality.

Examination of the legal record in these two cases reveals little attempt other than in one amicus brief to argue that state action against abortions is a practice of sex discrimination. The original complaint in Roe v. Wade contained a cause of action for denial of equal protection of the laws, First Amended Complaint CA-3-3690-B (N.D. Tex., Apr. 22, 1970) IV, 5. But the inequality complained of did not, as it developed, refer to inequality on the basis of sex, and oral argument in the district court appears to have been confined largely to the right to privacy. "Aside from their Ninth Amendment and vagueness arguments, plaintiffs have presented an array of constitutional arguments. However, as plaintiffs conceded in oral argument, these additional arguments *are peripheral to the main issues.* Consequently, they will not be passed upon." Opinion of the District Court, Civil Action No. CA-3-3690-B and 3-3691-C (June 17, 1970), 116 n.7 (emphasis added). In the U.S. Supreme Court, the Center for Constitutional Rights filed an amicus brief arguing that criminal abortion statutes like those of Texas and Georgia "violate the most basic Constitutional rights of women." "[I]t is the woman who bears the disproportionate share of the de jure and de facto burdens and penalties of pregnancy, child birth and child rearing. Thus, any statute which denies a woman the right to determine whether she will bear those denies her the equal protection of the laws." Brief *Amicus Curiae* on behalf of New Women Lawyers, Women's Health and Abortion Project, Inc., National Abortion Action Coalition 6

(Aug. 2, 1971). However, the brief assumes that sex is equal and voluntary, even if pregnancy is not: "Man and woman have equal responsibility for the act of sexual intercourse. Should the woman accidentally become pregnant, against her will, however, she endures in many instances the entire burden or 'punishment.'" *Id.* at 26. "And it is not sufficient to say that the woman 'chose' to have sexual intercourse, for she did not choose to become pregnant." *Id.* at 31.

A brief to the Supreme Court for Planned Parenthood by Harriet Pilpel, now general counsel for the American Civil Liberties Union, argued *amicus curiae* that the same privacy that protected the possession of pornography in the home should protect the abortion right. In so doing she suggested that abortion may, indeed, be an issue of sexuality: "A wide range of private individual activity in the areas of marriage, the family and sex has thus been safeguarded against governmental interference. The right to procreate, described by this Court as 'one of the basic civil rights of man' led the Court to invalidate as a violation of equal protection an Oklahoma statute which imposed sterilization upon persons convicted of embezzlement. . . . Similarly, the right to marry, the right to direct the education of one's children, the right to have possession of pornography in the privacy of one's own home, have all been held to be fundamental rights under the Constitution." Brief for Planned Parenthood Federation of America, Inc. and American Association of Planned Parenthood Physicians as *amici curiae,* Sept. 15, 1972, at 33. Other vigorous briefs argued that the criminal abortion statutes discriminated against poor and nonwhite women—never women, period. In a brief of Women for the Unborn et al. in support of opponents of the abortion right, the unborn are argued to be a class deserving of equal protection. Thus, proponents of the abortion right failed to make an equality claim for women—other than the lone amicus brief which argued women's rights and equal protection but based it on gender not sexual inequality—while opponents of the abortion right made equality claims for the fetuses the women were carrying.

The complaint in Harris v. McRae alleged discrimination "based on poverty, race and minority status, which deprives and punishes the plaintiff class of women in violation of due process and equal protection of the law." Plaintiffs' and Proposed Intervenors' Amended Complaint, McRae v. Califano, 74 Civ. 1804 (JFD) Jan. 5, 1977, para. 74. No discrimination on the basis of sex. Only one brief argues sex discrimination, and that is not to make the legal argument not paying for abortions, a state act that hurts only women, is sex discrimination. It is to argue that since women are socially discriminated against on the basis of sex, denying them abortions is an additional hardship: "The plight of indigent women denied medically necessary abortions is exacerbated by the pervasive sex discrimination that impacts especially hard on women in poverty." Brief *Amici Curiae* for NOW et al., No. 79–1268 (U.S. Supreme Court, filed Mar. 18, 1980), 44.

As a whole, virtually every kind of social discrimination against women other than sexual, and every illegal discrimination against women other than gender, has been used to try to support the abortion right. With the partial exception of the CCR brief— an effort both made audacious and weakened by the fact that sex discrimination as a constitutional doctrine had just been recognized—burdens on abortion have never been legally argued as simple sex discrimination.

Reasoning from the Body: A Historical Perspective on Abortion Regulation and Questions of Equal Protection

REVA SIEGEL

[T]HERE ARE SERIOUS constitutional concerns presented by abortion-restrictive regulation that [Roe v. Wade] does not address. Restricting women's access to abortion implicates constitutional values of equality as well as privacy. . . . A growing number of commentators have begun to address abortion regulation as an issue of sexual equality,[1] articulating concerns scarcely recognized in prevailing accounts of abortion as a right of privacy. Properly understood, constitutional limitations on antiabortion laws, like constitutional limitations on antimiscegenation laws, have moorings in both privacy and equal protection.

There are, however, substantial impediments to analyzing abortion-restrictive regulation in an equal protection framework, which few proponents of the claim have confronted. The Court has yet to characterize laws governing pregnancy as sex-based state action for purposes of equal protection review;[2] but, even if it did so, a deeper jurisprudential problem remains. The Court typically reasons about reproductive regulation in physiological paradigms, as a form of state action that concerns physical facts of sex rather than social questions of gender. It has often observed that the reality of reproductive differences between the sexes justifies their differential regulatory treatment. This mode of reasoning about reproductive regulation obscures the possibility that such regulation may be animated by constitutionally illicit judgments about women. Thus, while sex-based state action is generally scrutinized to ensure it is free of "old notions of role typing" or other vestiges of the separate spheres tradition—such as the assumption that women are "child-rearers" or the assumption that "the female [is] destined solely for the home and the rearing of the family"[3]—regulation which directly concerns women's role in reproduction has yet to receive similar scrutiny.

Like any other form of sex-based state action, regulation directed at women's role in reproduction demands exacting scrutiny to ensure it does not reflect or enforce traditional gender role assumptions. Equal protection jurisprudence has repeatedly articulated principles that would support such an inquiry. But current doctrine lacks the critical capacity to discern gender bias in reproductive regulation, a grasp of how

44 Stan. L. Rev. 261 (1992). Copyright 1992 by the Board of Trustees of the Leland Stanford Junior University.

regulation respecting pregnancy—a "real" physical difference between the sexes—can nevertheless be sexually discriminatory. Without this understanding, analysis of abortion-restrictive regulation cannot be fully assimilated into an equal protection framework.

Abortion-restrictive regulation can be analyzed as an expression of sex discrimination: as legislation that reflects traditional sex-role assumptions about women and presents problems of gender bias discernible in other forms of sex-based state action. But to perform this analysis, it is necessary to break out of the physiological paradigms in which the Court reasons about reproductive regulation in both privacy and equal protection law. More than any doctrinal factor, it is the physiological framework in which the Court reasons about reproductive regulation that obscures the gender-based judgments that may animate such regulations and the gender-based injuries they can inflict on women. When abortion-restrictive regulation is analyzed in physiological paradigms, as past cases have shown, the inquiry focuses on questions concerning gestation. By contrast, if restrictions on abortion are analyzed in a social framework, they present questions concerning the regulation of motherhood, and, thus, value judgments concerning women's roles.

[This article analyzes] abortion-restrictive regulation in an equal protection framework. [A]bortion-restrictive regulation can violate the antidiscrimination and antisubordination principles which give the constitutional guarantee of equal protection its meaning. . . .

The Antisubordination Inquiry

. . . Today, equal protection doctrine is largely elaborated from an antidiscrimination perspective, whose dominant focus is the judgment and justifications of the state actors deploying public power, rather than the impact of a particular exercise of power on the citizens subject to it.[4] A growing number of constitutional commentators would reorient the focus of equal protection analysis so that it directly considered the impact of state action on the citizens affected by it, a paradigm shift of consequence to numerous areas of constitutional debate.[5]. . .

. . . Abortion-restrictive regulation has several characteristics that make it particularly suitable for analysis under . . . antisubordination principles. First, abortion-restrictive regulation is sex-based state action: It is regulation directed at women as a class, and not dispersed across the citizenry at large. Second, the most dramatic and visible of its effects—the continuation of an unwanted pregnancy—is an intended consequence of social policy. Indeed, as I have already argued, it is fair to characterize forced childbearing as the principal purpose of abortion-restrictive regulation. Third, abortion-restrictive regulation has historically functioned as caste legislation. Finally, today, as in the past, the injury inflicted on women by compelling them to bear children is a specific form of status harm, one that plays a central role in women's subordination.

These factors together provide for a highly focused application of antisubordination principles. Because a state adopting restrictions on abortion intentionally inflicts a traditional form of status harm on a constitutionally suspect class, courts evaluating the constitutionality of the state's action should examine what the state is doing to women, and not simply why it does it. Examining how restrictions on abortion harm women supplies an independent and sufficient basis for evaluating the constitutionality of abortion-restrictive regulation. It also supplies evidence relevant to more conventional forms of equal protection analysis: If one wants to determine whether a state's decision to adopt abortion-restrictive regulation rests on constitutionally offensive sex-role assumptions about women, it is crucial to examine what a state adopting restrictions on abortion does to women.

This section considers how state action restricting abortion injures women, addressing several points which bear on this question. . . .

1. Abortion Restrictions Coerce Childbearing and Childrearing

Laws that forbid or impair women's access to abortion[6] in fact have many effects on women's lives. Restrictions on abortion affect not only pregnant women, but all women who believe they are capable of conceiving, whether or not they are presently sexually active, whether or not they engage in some form of contraceptive practice. Because such laws deprive women of means to determine whether or not they will become mothers should they become pregnant, they impair the possibility of sexual pleasure for women, and aggravate the force of sexual fear.[7] Abortion-restrictive regulation does not of course prevent all pregnant women who seek abortions from obtaining them; rather, it subjects all pregnant women seeking abortions to social indignity, some to illicit procedures fraught with fear and physical hazard, and the rest to the burden of state-coerced pregnancy.

Laws restricting women's access to abortion are only intermittently discussed in their compulsive aspect. Even then, discussion often seems to assume that such regulation coerces women into performing only the work of child bearing. But if abortion-restrictive regulation is evaluated in light of actual social practice, it is clear that such regulation coerces women to perform, not only the work of childbearing, but the work of childrearing as well.

Hypothetically, a woman compelled to bear a child she does not want could give it up for adoption, abandon it, or pay someone to care for the child until maturity. In this society, however, these are not options that women avail themselves of with great frequency for the simple reason that few women are able to abandon a child born of their body.[8] That society as a whole, or some women in particular, may judge it morally preferable to give a child up to adoption rather than abort a pregnancy is beside the point. Once compelled to bear a child against their wishes, most women will feel obligated to raise it. A woman is likely to form emotional bonds with a child during pregnancy; she is likely to believe that she has moral obligations to a born child that are far greater than any she might have to an embryo/fetus; and she is likely to experience intense familial and social pressure to raise a child she has borne. The pressure on women to raise children they have borne will intensify dramatically if they are married and/or have other children. . . .

Thus, while discussions of abortion-restrictive regulation often assume that women who are forced to bear children can simply abandon them at will, the premise is wholly at odds with the norms of the society that would compel women to bear children. Many women will simply assume they must raise children which the state forces them to bear; others may well choose to raise the child, but they will exercise this choice under social conditions that virtually dictate the outcome of their decision. Legislatures that enact restrictions on abortion understand this. They both desire and expect that most women will raise the child they are forced to bear, and in the vast majority of cases, women will.

Of course, a state can deny responsibility for imposing motherhood on women simply by emphasizing that the pregnant woman has chosen to raise the child that the state forced her to bear. Arguments about women's choices offer a familiar way to rationalize state action enforcing gender status roles. But, if one considers the powerful norms governing women's choices about whether to raise their children, it is clear that such formalistic arguments do not relieve the state of responsibility for dictating the pregnant woman's social fate. In twentieth century America, when a legislature restricts women's access to abortion, it is forcing women to bear and rear children.

2. The Work of Bearing and Rearing Children

What then does the state do to women by forcing them to bear children? To answer this question, it is necessary to consider what is entailed for women in performing the work of motherhood. While the burdens of motherhood are to a significant extent a matter of common knowledge, it is nonetheless important to consider certain aspects of the work that are regularly omitted from discussions of abortion. Too often, analysis of abortion-restrictive regulation is dominated by physiological paradigms, with the result that the injuries such regulation inflicts tend to be attributed to and described in terms of the female body. If the decision whether to terminate a pregnancy has special significance in women's lives, it is in part, but only in part, because of the physiology of reproduction. From the point of gestation onwards, a woman performing the work of parenting assumes the social role of motherhood, a role and status that defines her identity, relations, and life prospects in diverse social arenas.

For women, the work of parenting begins in a lengthy period of bodily labor. Because the work of making life does proceed within a woman's body, it can subject her to physical discomfort, pain, disability, and risk throughout the term of pregnancy, and after. These physical burdens alone are sufficient grounds for many to hesitate before assuming the work. Yet, because gestation is not simply a reflex process, its impositions are not solely physiological. Childbearing, like childrearing, involves work to be performed in accordance with detailed prescriptive norms.[9] A woman who attempts to conduct her pregnancy in conformity with such norms will find herself making daily judgments as she attempts to accommodate her life to the process of making life:

choices about what to eat and drink, about how to exercise, about securing appropriate medical care, and about negotiating quotidian forms of risk associated with travel, leisure activities, and the work she performs on the job and at home.[10] The work of gestation thus involves on-going calculations and compromises that can have a pervasive impact on women's lives; its impositions are simultaneously physical and social.

Because gestation is a social as well as a physiological act, it implicates women in relationships and defines their identity in many ways. A woman may experience pregnancy as a bond tying her to a man with whom she may or may not wish to be involved, or, alternately, it may signify the brute fact of his absence or abandonment. During the course of gestation, a pregnant woman often bonds to the unborn life she bears, so that over time a maternal relation is formed that she may feel herself incapable of severing. Nor is this relational aspect of pregnancy a matter of intimate experience alone. A woman may find that pregnancy comes to embody her social identity to others, who may treat her with love and respect or, alternatively, abuse her as a burden, scorn her as unwed, or judge her as unfit for employment.[11] Or, precisely because the work of pregnancy is believed to involve intellectual and moral judgments, they may brand her, socially or legally, as an irresponsible mother.[12] Pregnancy, and the period of lactation that follows it,[13] are not merely burdensome, disruptive, or even consuming forms of work. They amplify the gendered judgments and constraints to which women are already subject, exposing them to material and dignitary injuries having nothing to do with the physiology of reproduction, and entangling them in relationships that profoundly define their identity and life prospects.

Finally, notwithstanding changing norms of family life, it remains the case that it is women who perform the vast majority of the labor necessary to make infants into adults.[14] Mothers are expected to subordinate their personal interests to children in a way that men are not; most women give themselves over to the nurturance of life in a way that men do not—and face stigmatization, unlike men, if they will not. Consequently, a woman's identity, relations, and prospects are defined by becoming a parent in a way that a man's are not.[15]

While this society celebrates the work of childcare, it continues to view the work of raising children as "women's work." Childcare remains status work, organized and valued in ways that limit the life prospects of those who perform it. Most prominently, childcare is uncompensated labor, traditionally performed under conditions of economic dependency[16]; consequently, it remains a form of undercompensated labor for those who are paid to assist in the work. It is not merely the uncompensated character of childcare that betrays its peculiar social valuation. Those who devote their personal energies to raising children are likely to find their freedom to participate in so-called public sphere activities impaired for years on end, for the evident reason that most activities in the realms of education, employment, and politics are defined and structured as incommensurate with that work.[17] Thus, a woman who becomes a parent will likely find that the energy she invests in childrearing will compromise her already constrained opportunities and impair her already unequal compensation in the work force[18]—all the more so if she raises the child alone, whether by choice, divorce, or abandonment. Considered in cold dollar terms, it is the institution of motherhood that gives a gendered structure to the economics of family life, and a gendered face to poverty in the nation's life.[19]

3. Abortion Restrictions as Status-Enforcing State Action

In assessing the social effects of restrictions on abortion, it is important to observe not only that such regulation compels women to perform the work of bearing and rearing children, but that it lacks any provision that would mitigate or offset the social consequences of enforced motherhood for women. No modern legislature interested in adopting restrictions on abortion has, to my knowledge, offered to compensate women for this work; to protect women's employment and education opportunities while they perform the work of motherhood; or to provide women adequate childcare so that they are not pushed into dependency upon men or the state. Nor has a legislature required that men fathering the children women are forced to bear assume primary responsibility for the work of nurturance and maintenance women typically provide. Thus, when the state enacts restrictions on abortion, it coerces women to perform the work of motherhood without altering the conditions that continue to make such work a principal cause of their secondary social status.

For this reason, state action compelling motherhood injures women in predictable ways. Both the work of childbearing and the work of childrearing compromise women's opportunities in education and employment; neither the work of childbearing nor the work of childrearing produces any material compensation for women; most often the work of childbearing and the work of childrearing entangle women in relations of emotional and economic dependency—to men, extended family, or the state. None of these consequences is inherent in the physiology of reproduction; all are socially produced, reflecting communal designation of the work of mothering as "women's work." There is no other form of socially essential labor in this society similarly organized or valued: The more effort a woman personally invests in it, the more time she devotes to it, the more inexorably economically dependent she becomes. From this perspective, it is apparent that compelled pregnancy will injure women in context-dependent ways. It may be endured by women who have ordered their lives in conformity with traditional norms of motherhood, but it will profoundly threaten the material and psychic welfare of any woman whose life deviates from this traditional norm, whether by choice or socio-economic circumstance.[20] When the state deprives women of choice in matters of motherhood, it deprives women of the ability to lead their lives with some rudimentary control over the sex-role constraints this society imposes on those who bear and rear children. It makes the social reality of women's lives more nearly conform with social stereotypes of women's lives. Considered from this perspective, choice in matters of motherhood implicates constitutional values of equality and liberty both.

Women are centuries-versed in negotiating the conditions of motherhood, and deriving meaning, value, pleasure, and purpose from work that this society all too frequently disparages. Under such conditions, mothering is work that for a woman, and amongst women, variously promises joy, rage, identity, and entrapment.[21] But the fact that most women will give themselves to children in ways that belie what is taken from them, does not alter the fact that coercing motherhood is an act of violence against women,[22] one that devalues what women give, and give up, in parenting and who they might be apart from that work.

Restrictions on abortion thus offend constitutional guarantees of equal protection, not simply because of the status-based injuries they inflict on women, but also because of the status-based attitudes about women they reflect. For centuries, this society has defined women as mothers and defined the work of motherhood as women's work. These are the assumptions which make it "reasonable" to force women to become mothers. Absent these deep-rooted assumptions about women, it is impossible to explain why this society insists that restrictions on abortion are intended to protect the unborn, and yet has never even considered taking action that would alleviate the burdens forced motherhood imposes on women.

Restrictions on abortion reflect the kind of bias that is at the root of the most invidious forms of stereotyping: a failure to consider, in a society always at risk of forgetting, that women are persons, too. It is a bias that manifests itself in this society's unreflective expectation that women should assume the burdens of bearing and rearing future generations, its tendency to denigrate the work of motherhood, and its readiness to castigate women who seek to avoid maternity as lacking in humanity, proof of which consists in a woman's failure perfectly to subordinate her energies, resources, and prospects to the task of making life—to a degree that men, employers, and the community as a whole most often will not.

This society has "unclean hands" in matters respecting motherhood. While it may possess the power, it sorely lacks the moral grounds to "balance" the rights of women and the unborn as if it were a disinterested bystander to a conflict thrust upon women by nature. We may stand a century away from the attitudes expressed in the nineteenth century campaign, but we are still generations away from any prospect of transcending their ideological or institutional legacy. In a society that viewed women as full and equal citizens—as something more than particularly valuable means to an important social end—the test for determining the constitutionality of abortion-restrictive regulation might be: Has the state asserted its interest in promoting the welfare of the unborn in a fashion consistent with promoting the welfare of women?

In an inchoate fashion, *Roe* embodied this understanding. The Court understood that regulation of women's conduct premised on a theory of fetal personhood would deeply conflict with public recognition of women's personhood. *Roe's* trimester framework accommodated this conflict practically, but gave only a partial account of its sense. By allowing states to prohibit abortions at the point of fetal viability, the Court hoped to craft a constitutional compromise. But *Roe's* viability rule can function as a legitimate constitutional compromise only if it provides women reasonable access to abortion in the early months of pregnancy, the period they normally seek abortions; and if it is understood, not simply as an ambiguous recognition of fetal personhood, but as an explicit constitutional affirmation of women's personhood. The Constitution requires government to respect women's freedom to refuse motherhood because decisions about abortion are both deeply personal and profoundly social: When a pregnant woman decides whether to become a mother, she faces dilemmas in which the community itself is inextricably complicit.

State action on behalf of the fetus in utero must find its constitutional bearings, and constraints, in the community's relation to the citizen in whom unborn life resides. In this sense, the common law criterion of quickening gave surer moral guidance to the regulation of abortion than the "scientific" concept of viability with which *Roe* replaced it. At least the common law criterion of quickening located the unborn internal to a born, sentient being, rather than presenting the unborn as an autonomous life form—an illusion sustained for more than a century now by medical rhetoric. If *Roe* survives in some form, it will be because those charged with expounding federal and state constitutions do not, in their hearts, credit this dehumanizing myth of human genesis. It will be because they recognize that women's lives are required to make potential life recognizable as a person, and recognize that because women are equal citizens too, their labor in bearing life is a gift with which they can endow the community, not a resource the community can expropriate to its use.

Conclusion

For too long this nation has regulated women's status through the institution of motherhood. Its judgments about the ways in which it is reasonable to impose on women as mothers are deeply distorted by a long history of denigrating, controlling, and using women as mothers. For this reason, the physiological paradigms that currently dominate review of reproductive regulation are deeply pernicious. They invite public actors to use state power against women without the minimal forms of self-scrutiny that requirements of equal protection normally impose. They invite abusive exercise of public power against women because they suspend rudimentary safeguards on the exercise of such power in precisely those circumstances where safeguards are most needed. Before this society rushes to judge women's conduct toward the unborn, it ought to reflect upon its own conduct toward women. Instead of devising new ways to control women as mothers, it needs to promote the welfare of future generations by means that respect and support women in their work as mothers. Only then will the story of the nineteenth century criminal abortion campaign be a closed chapter in American history—and not a continuing part of American life.

Notes

1. See Guido Calabresi, Ideals, Beliefs, Attitudes, and the Law: Private Law Perspectives on a Public Law Problem 101–106 (1985); Catharine A. MacKinnon, Feminism Unmodified: Discourses on Life and Law 93–102 (1987); Laurence H. Tribe, American Constitutional Law §15–10, at 1353–1359 (2d ed. 1988); Ruth Bader Gins-

burg, Some Thoughts on Autonomy and Equality in Relation to Roe v. Wade, 63 N.C. L. Rev. 375 (1985); Kenneth L. Karst, Foreword: Equal Citizenship Under the Fourteenth Amendment, 91 Harv. L. Rev. 1, 53–59 (1977); Kenneth L. Karst, Woman's Constitution, 1984 Duke L.J. 447, 472–475; Sylvia A. Law, Rethinking Sex and the Constitution, 132 U. Pa. L. Rev. 955 (1984); Catharine A. MacKinnon, Reflections on Sex Equality Under Law, 100 Yale L.J. 1281, 1308–1324 (1991); Frances Olsen, Unraveling Compromise, 103 Harv. L. Rev. 105, 117–135 (1989); Donald H. Regan, Rewriting Roe v. Wade, 77 Mich. L. Rev. 1569, 1621–1645 (1979); Ellen Relkin & Sudi Solomon, Using State Constitutions to Expand Public Funding for Abortions: Throwing away the Carrot with the Stick, 9 Women's Rts. L. Rep. 27 (1986) (privacy and equal protection); Cass Sunstein, Neutrality in Constitutional Law (With Special Reference to Pornography, Abortion, and Surrogacy), 92 Colum. L. Rev. 1 (1992).

2. See Geduldig v. Aiello, 417 U.S. 484 (1974)....

3. Stanton v. Stanton, 421 U.S. 7, 14 (1975).

4. The clearest illustration of this orientation is the requirement that plaintiffs challenging the discriminatory impact of facially neutral state action must show that state actors adopted the challenged policy with discriminatory purpose. See Personnel Adm'r of Mass. v. Feeney, 442 U.S. 256, 274, 279 (1979). Doctrines governing the review of explicitly race- and sex-based state action are informed by this antidiscrimination perspective in less apparent ways. The fact that such action triggers heightened scrutiny reflects concern that the state will inflict or perpetuate forms of status injury by legislating in race- and sex-based terms. Yet, doctrinal standards for determining the constitutionality of such action scrutinize the character of a legislature's judgments, without directly putting in issue the actual impact of its actions on members of protected classes. The results in many of the Court's gender discrimination cases might well be different if the Court inquired, not whether the state's decision to regulate on the basis of sex was substantially related to important governmental ends, but instead: Has the challenged action harmed women in ways that enforce, perpetuate, or aggravate their subordinate social status?

5. Commentators have employed antisubordination values to distinguish between benign and invidious race- and sex-based state action, as well as to criticize doctrines requiring a showing of discriminatory purpose to challenge facially neutral state action. See, e.g., C. MacKinnon, *supra* note 1, at 32–45; Catharine A. MacKinnon, Sexual Harassment of Working Women 117 (1979) (arguing that courts examining state action for sex discrimination should inquire "whether the policy or practice in question integrally contributes to the maintenance of an underclass or a deprived position because of gender status"); L. Tribe, *supra* note 1, §16–21, at 1514–1521; Owen M. Fiss, Groups and the Equal Protection Clause, 5 Phil. & Pub. Aff. 107, 157 (1976) (proposing to substitute for the equal treatment principle a group-disadvantaging principle premised on a theory of "status harm" that would inquire whether a challenged practice would "impair or threaten or aggravate the status or position of the group")....

6. Here I address laws that prohibit or restrict the performance of abortion in ways that signify social condemnation of the practice, including laws that attempt to deter women from obtaining abortions by interposing procedural obstacles, financial barriers, or other practical impediments to access to the procedure. Depending on a woman's age, financial means, family situation, and sophistication, she may or may not be deterred by them. Some women will be able to evade laws prohibiting abortions; others will be prevented from obtaining abortions by laws that merely interpose practical impediments to abortion.

7. Cf. G. Calabresi, *supra* note 1; C. MacKinnon, *supra* note 1, at 93–102; Law, *supra* note 1, at 1019–1020.

8. [W]hile premarital births account for the preponderance of adoption placements, only 6% of all babies born premaritally to women 15 to 44 years of age in 1982 were placed for adoption. . . . Christine A. Bachrach, Adoption Plans, Adopted Children, and Adoptive Mothers, 48 J. Marriage & Fam. 243, 249–250 (1986).

9. In the nineteenth century, physicians advanced a theory of "prenatal impressions," which required a pregnant woman to avoid all shocking sights, intellectual stimulation, or powerful emotions, such as anger or lust, lest the baby be deformed in the womb. As they understood it, during pregnancy the brain and uterus competed for phosphates, such that every mental effort of the mother could deprive her unborn of substances required for proper development. See Barbara Ehrenreich & Deidre English, For Her Own Good: 150 Years of the Experts' Advice to Women 111, 127 (1978); see also Carl N. Degler, At Odds: Women and the Family in America from the Revolution to the Present 79–82 (1980) (gestation and breast-feeding); Charles E. Rosenberg, No Other Gods: On Science and American Social Thought 26–29, 58, 68 (1961).

10. Today, as in the nineteenth century, the pregnant woman is advised to conduct the work of gestation with attention to a complex set of factors that may affect the development of the unborn in utero. Common conditions and activities of the pregnant woman that are currently believed to have some bearing on fetal development include: "being overweight or underweight, working or even living in certain environments, rejecting or undergoing specific medical treatments, exercising, failing to eat 'well,' failing to 'stay off of her feet,' smoking, drinking alcohol, ingesting caffeine, taking nonprescription, prescription, or illegal drugs, and suffering physical harm through accident or illness." Dawn Johnsen, From Driving to Drugs: Governmental Regulation of Pregnant Women's Lives After *Webster,* 138 U. Pa. L. Rev. 179, 192 (1989). Conducting a pregnancy with attention to such concerns produces a daily regimen of calculations and compromises, not unlike that urged upon pregnant women a century ago. See Rosenberg, *supra* note 9, at 58 (discussing nineteenth century medical advice) ("A woman who lived 'unphysiologically'—and she could do so by reading or studying in excess, by wearing improper clothing, by long hours of factory work, or by a sedentary, luxurious life—could produce only weak and degenerate offspring.").

11. On pregnancy discrimination in employment before enactment of the Pregnancy Discrimination Act, see Lucinda M. Finley, Transcending Equality Theory: A Way Out of the Maternity and the Workplace Debate, 86 Colum. L. Rev. 1118, 1123–1125 (1986). . . .

12. Public outrage directed at pregnant, drug-dependent women is but one manifestation of this response. Advocates for providing state protection to the fetus in utero believe the pregnant woman has a duty of care to the unborn implicating choices in all aspects of her life, breach of which warrants state intervention, whether in the form of civil liability, criminal prosecution, forcible surgical treatment, "protective" incarceration, or deprivation of child custody.

13. The same compound of physiological and social forces that shape the work of gestation governs the work of breast-feeding an infant once it is born. Women are alone physiologically capable of engaging in the work, but the choice to engage in it and the conditions under which it is performed are fundamentally social. Like gestation, breast-feeding an infant is a practice subject to a diverse array of prescriptive norms; women are pressured to perform the work and stigmatized for performing it in highly context-bound ways. Suffice it to observe that a woman nursing a baby will likely

meet with approval if she is sitting in her bedroom, and scorn if sitting in a corporate board room.

14. Presently, 45% of women with pre-school age children withdraw from the labor force to care for them personally, while 55% continue to engage in some form of paid employment. Felicity Barringer, Census Report Shows a Rise in Child Care and its Costs, N.Y. Times, Aug. 16, 1990, at A12; see also Ruth Sidel, On Her Own (1990) (in 1987, 63% of women with college degrees remained in the work force after bearing a child, as compared with 38% of high school graduates).

Even when mothers are employed, they continue to perform a larger share of the work of family maintenance than do men. For example, a 1986 study of a Boston-based firm found that employed women work twice as many hours on childcare and home-making as men, even when the woman's income is greater than the man's, and that married female parents spend a total of 85 hours a week on work, in and out of the home, while married male parents spend 65 hours. Other studies suggest that even where parents share child care, fathers are more likely to "play" with children, and mothers to carry out most of the caretaking activities. *Id.* at 202–204; see also Arlie Hochschild, The Second Shift: Working Parents and the Revolution at Home 271–279 (1989) (research on who does the housework and childcare in two-income households).

15. For these reasons, women as a group more frequently compromise employment opportunities to accommodate family needs than do men. Cf. Deborah L. Rhode, Perspectives on Professional Women, 40 Stan. L. Rev. 1163, 1183–1187 (1988) (examining accommodations of familial and occupational commitments among professionals).

16. On the uncompensated character of the work of family maintenance, see Catharine A. MacKinnon, Toward a Feminist Theory of the State 60–80 (1989); Ellen Malos ed., The Politics of Housework (1980); Joan Acker, Class, Gender, and the Relations of Distribution, 13 Signs 473 (1988); Heidi I. Hartmann, The Family as the Locus of Gender, Class, and Political Struggle: The Example of Housework, in Sandra Harding ed., Feminism and Methodology 109 (1987).

17. For example, an article in the American Bar Association Journal offered women entering the practice of law the following tips for success: "Don't 'shirk late hours or weekend projects.' Don't cook and tell, i.e., avoid going home to cook dinner—or if you do, don't let any one know. Keep your 'personal life in the background. . . . Never make excuses based on the needs of a spouse or children. . . .'" Rhode, *supra* note 15, at 1186, quoting Nell B. Strachan, A Map for Women on the Road to Success, A.B.A. J., May 1984, at 94, 94–95; see also R. Sidel, *supra* note 14, at 200–201 (in medical profession, it may be acceptable for doctors to take time off for traditionally male responsibilities, but not for traditionally female responsibilities associated with family care). Those women who do attempt to accommodate work and family commitments are often penalized for it. See Leslie Bender, Sex Discrimination or Gender Inequality?, 57 Fordham L. Rev. 941, 943 n.10 (1989); Claudia Deutsch, Saying No to the "Mommy Track," N.Y. Times, Jan. 28, 1990, at 29 (describing "Mommy Track" as a "devil's bargain"); Women in the Work Force: The Mommy Track v. the Fast Track, N.Y. Times, May 21, 1989, at 2 (positive and negative responses to "Mommy Track").

18. In analyzing the size of a gender-based "wage gap," it is conventional practice to exclude variables that may contribute to such a gap but that do not reflect the operations of sex discrimination in employment, at least as conventionally understood. It should be noted that such variables—for example, whether individuals work full-time

or part-time, their general experience in the labor force, and their tenure with their employer—are all crude biographical proxies for time women devote to care of home and children. Cf. Paul Weiler, The Wages of Sex: The Uses and Limits of Comparable Worth, 99 Harv. L. Rev. 1728, 1780–1784 (1986) (noting the role of these factors in wage disparities); see also *id.* at 1786 (citing econometric study suggesting that the "addition of each child enhances the man's earnings by another three percent while depressing that of the woman's by fully ten percent").

19. Almost all single-parent households are headed by women, and these households are disproportionately represented amongst the ranks of the nation's poor. In 1988, nearly a quarter of the nation's children were living in single-parent households; 21.4% living with their mother only, and 2.9% with their father only. U.S. Bureau of the Census, Current Population Reports: Special Studies, Series P-23, No. 162, Studies in Marriage and the Family, at 18. In 1989, more than half of the children who lived in households headed by women lived in poverty, while only 20.3% of children who lived in single-parent households headed by their father lived below the poverty level. U.S. Bureau of the Census, Current Population Reports, Series P-20, No. 445, Marital Status and Living Arrangements: March 1989, at 37, tbl. 6. . . .

20. . . . In 1987, when a group of abortion patients was asked about their reasons for seeking an abortion, three-quarters said that having a baby would interfere with work, school, or other responsibilities, two-thirds said they could not afford to have a child, and half said that they did not want to be a single parent or had relationship problems. Aida Torres & Jacqueline Darroch Forrest, Why Do Women Have Abortions?, 20 Fam. Plan. Persp. 169, 169 (1988).

21. See, e.g., Adrienne Rich, Of Woman Born: Motherhood as Experience and Institution (1986); Alice Walker, In Search of Our Mothers' Gardens (1983); Regina Austin, Sapphire Bound!, 1989 Wis. L. Rev. 539, 558–574; Eileen Boris, Looking at Women's Historians Looking At "Difference," 3 Wis. Women's L.J. 213, 218–222 (1987); Robin West, Jurisprudence and Gender, 55 U. Chi. L. Rev. 1, 28–36 (1988).

22. Cf. West, *supra* note 21, at 28–36 (considering wanted, and especially, unwanted, pregnancy and motherhood as invasive experiences for women, which can constitute an assault upon body and identity in a fashion analogous to intercourse or rape); *id.* at 29 ("[i]nvasion and intrusion, rather than intimacy, nurturance and care, is the 'unofficial' story of women's subjective experience of connection" to others); Ellen Willis, Abortion: Is a Woman a Person?, in Ann Snitow, Christine Stansell & Sharon Thompson eds., Powers of Desire: The Policits of Sexuality 471, 473 (1983) ("However gratifying pregnancy may be to a woman who desires it, for the unwilling it is literally an invasion—the closest analogy is the difference between lovemaking and rape.").

Reproductive Laws, Women of Color, and Low-Income Women

Laurie Nsiah-Jefferson

REPRODUCTIVE RIGHTS, like other rights, are not just a matter of abstract theory. How these rights can be exercised and which segments of the population will be allowed to exercise them must be considered in light of existing social and economic conditions. Therefore, concerns about the effects of race, sex, and poverty, as well as law and technology must be actively integrated into all work and discussions addressing reproductive health policy.

. . . Many, though not all, women of color are poor. Women of color are not all one group, just as women of color and poor women are not one group. They have different needs, behaviors, and cultural and social norms. One thing they do share is having been left out of the decision-making process concerning reproductive rights. Although my experience is as a black woman, I will attempt to identify issues that appear to be nearly universal to both women of color and poor women, and point out instances where their perspectives might differ.

There is little information available about the reproductive needs of women of color. In general, the demographic data about non-Caucasian women are clustered together under the heading "nonwhite" as if there were only two racial groups, white and nonwhite. For example, published abortion statistics are broken down only into two ethnic categories—white and black. As a result of this dichotomization, understanding of the experience of specific groups such as Native American, Asian/Pacific Islander, and Latina women is inadequate. This dichotomization is itself evidence of the pressing need for more precise data gathering on issues concerning women of color. The information that is available generally fails to consider the obvious cultural and social differences related to differences in ethnicity and national heritage. In many cases, this has made it difficult to define and address particular problems and to make recommendations about their solutions.

For many women of color, taking control over their reproduction is a new step, and involves issues never before considered. One reason for this is that women of color have not always had access to the pro-choice movement. In the past, it has been diffi-

In Sherrill Cohen & Nadine Taub eds., Reproductive Laws for the 1990s, pp. 15–38 (1988). Totowa, N.J.: The Humana Press.

cult for many middle-class white feminists to understand and include the different perspectives and experiences of poor and minority women. Thus, it is particularly important that adequate information on the needs and experiences of all women be made
available now.

The broader economic and political structures of society impose objective limitations on reproductive choice, that is, decisions as to when, whether, and under what
conditions to have a child. Very simply, women of color and poor women have fewer
choices than other women. Basic health needs often go unmet in these communities.
Poor women and women of color have a continuing history of negative experiences concerning reproduction, including their use of birth control pills, the IUD, and contraceptive injections of Depo-Provera;[1] sterilization abuse;[2] impeded access to abortion;[3]
coercive birthing procedures and hysterectomy;[4] and exposure to workplace hazards.[5]

. . . Given the history and circumstances of these groups, there are two overarching
concerns. One is the desire to make reproductive services, including new technologies,
broadly accessible. The other is the need to safeguard against abuse. . . .

Time Limits on Abortion

Poor women and women of color often live under circumstances that make it difficult
for them to obtain early abortions. . . . Thus, it is important to understand the laws restricting late abortions will continue to have a particular impact on poor women and
women of color.

The Disproportionate Need for Post-First-Trimester Abortions

A significantly higher percentage of nonwhite women who get abortions do so after
the first trimester, or first 12 weeks, of pregnancy. Of all abortions obtained by white
women in 1983, 8.6 percent took place in the 13th week or later, but 12.0 percent of
nonwhite women having abortions obtained them in that period.[6] These figures represent the numbers of women who actually succeed in obtaining post-first-trimester
procedures, and they may seriously understate actual demand. Financial, geographical, and other barriers to access are likely to have a greater impact on nonwhite women,
whose overall abortion rate is more than twice that of whites.[7]

There is little information directly concerning very late abortions. Available data
on women who obtain abortions after the first trimester, however demonstrate that financial factors are very important. The enactment and implementation of the Hyde
Amendment terminating federal Medicaid funding for abortions has caused many
poor women to delay having abortions while they raise the necessary funds. A study of
a St. Louis clinic, for example, showed that, in 1982, 38 persons of the Medicaid-
eligible women interviewed who sought abortions after the 10th week attributed the
delay between receiving the results of their pregnancy tests and obtaining their abortions to financial problems.[8]. . . Even where state Medicaid funding is in theory still

available for abortions, it is often not available in practice. Welfare workers and other state officials do not always inform Medicaid recipients of their right to obtain Medicaid-funded abortions.[9] Not all abortion providers are aware that reimbursement is available from Medicaid. Some providers are unwilling to accept Medicaid. . . . in part because Medicaid reimbursement rates are so low.

Difficulty in locating abortion services also causes delay. . . . The availability of abortion services . . . varies considerably by state.[10] Because abortion facilities are concentrated in metropolitan areas, access to abortion services is particularly difficult for rural women. . . . Although geographic access may not pose a significant problem for women of color from northern states who are concentrated in inner cities, it is a concern for women of color in southern states.

Not only are Native American women who live on reservations denied federal funding for abortions, but no Indian Health Service clinics or hospitals may perform abortions even when payment for those procedures is made privately.[11] The Indian Health Service may be the only health care provider within hundreds of miles of the reservation, and as a result the impact of the regulations can be quite severe.

Women in prison, who are disproportionately poor and of color, may also have great difficulty in gaining access to abortion facilities. Abortion services are rarely available at the prison, and prison authorities are unwilling to release inmates for treatment.[12] Recently adopted federal regulations specifically deny abortion services to federal prisoners.[13]

Even where abortion services exist, lack of information about them deters early abortion. Language barriers and the absence of culturally sensitive bilingual counselors and educational materials make gaining information about abortion services a special problem for Asian/Pacific and Hispanic women. . . .

[Another factor has] been identified as especially important in accounting for very late abortions: youth. . . .

In 1981 . . . 43 percent of all abortions performed after the 20th week of pregnancy were performed on teenagers.[14] Women under 15 years of age are most likely to obtain the latest abortions (those at 21 weeks or more gestation). . . . Teenagers of color often have particular difficulty in obtaining an abortion. One study found that 4 out of 10 black teenagers were unable to obtain a desired abortion, as compared to 2 out of 10 white teenagers.[15] . . .

Time limits on abortion may be imposed by various laws. Currently, there is concern about statutes that impose prohibitions on post-viability abortions or seek to compel the use of the method most likely to preserve fetal life unless the woman's health would be jeopardized. Poor women and women of color bear the brunt of such laws because women with money and power can find ways to circumvent the law, just as they did prior to the legalization of abortion. Affluent women can either travel to a place where a procedure is legal or find a doctor who will certify that their health is at stake. Poor women who do not have such options are denied autonomy because, as the experience with Medicaid provisions allowing reimbursement only for health-threatening situations suggests, few doctors are willing to risk prosecution under these statutes.

Time limits on abortion may result from a provider's decision not to perform procedures past a certain point in pregnancy. Poor women and women of color today have limited access to facilities that provide abortions after the first trimester.[16] Public hospitals are a major source of health care for poor women, yet only 17 percent of all public hospitals report performing abortions in 1985.[17] . . .

The number of abortions needed can be drastically reduced by teaching men and women how to prevent unintended pregnancy. . . . To be effective, family planning services must present information and services in culturally appropriate ways, involving bilingual materials and personnel. Family planning programs must also take account of cultural attitudes and biases about birth control. [S]uch programs must make women of color aware of how the ability to take control of reproductive decisions will benefit their lives.

Prenatal Screening

Prenatal screening offers women the opportunity to obtain limited information about the status of the fetus they are carrying. . . . Of the many social, economic, and political issues that the use of this technology poses, questions of access, cultural and class differences, informed consent, confidentiality, and eugenics are of particular concern to poor women and women of color. . . .

Financial, cultural, social, and geographic factors all affect access to services. A particularly important factor for women of color and poor women is the cost of many prenatal screening procedures. For example, estimates on the cost of amniocentesis range from $400 to $1000. Amniocentesis for genetic purposes should be performed between the 16th and 20th weeks of pregnancy. The federal government directly supports providers of genetic services on a very limited basis.[18] A woman dependent upon Medicaid or the MCHP [Maternal and Child Health Program] may be able to learn the physical condition of her fetus but be unable to afford an abortion, the only "treatment" alternative in almost every case. . . .

[In addition,] [m]any low-income women are unable to avail themselves of prenatal screening because they begin prenatal care too late or receive none at all. Some poor women and women of color request screening as late as 20 weeks into their pregnancies—too late to schedule counseling, undergo the procedure, obtain the results, and have further counseling on the decision of whether to continue the pregnancy. . . . Increased outreach and education can encourage such women to seek out prenatal care earlier in their pregnancies. . . .

Confidentiality in the prenatal screening process is an extremely important issue for people of color who have experienced adverse consequences when intimate information is revealed to third parties. For example, when employers have been given access to information concerning individuals who have the sickle cell trait, they have used it to justify refusals to hire, promote, or retain the employees.[19] Likewise, some insurance companies have refused sickle cell carriers health and life insurance or inflated the cost of their premiums, although there is no evidence that the carriers have a higher risk of disease or a shorter life span.

AIDS screening presents special problems. The Centers for Disease Control have suggested that all fertile women at high risk for contracting AIDS or AIDS-Related-Complex be tested for HIV antibodies. This would include prostitutes, hemophiliacs, intravenous drug users, Haitians, and sex partners of men in high risk groups.[20] To date, such testing has not been made mandatory. Although some pregnant women are anxious to find out whether they test positively or negatively for the disease, fear of job loss and ostracism as well as fear of the deadly consequences of the disease itself may prevent other women from seeking needed prenatal care if they know that AIDS screening is part of the treatment. Assurances that test results will be kept confidential should help address the first fear.

A related problem involves the need to assure confidentiality in the identification and testing of prospective parents required for prenatal screening. Where children are conceived outside the bonds of matrimony, it may be harder to get both parties tested. The woman may be unable or unwilling to contact the male partner. Moreover, the possibility that the male partner's identity will be revealed to social workers and other public officials mandated to collect child support from fathers often makes the male unwilling to come forward. In addition, teenage prospective parents may be fearful that their parents will learn of their sexual activity as a result of testing. . . .

Fetus as Patient

The topic of fetus as patient involves attempts by medical and legal authorities to compel women to follow doctors' orders, and accept particular medical procedures while pregnant and when they give birth. For example, doctors and hospitals may seek court orders forcing women to undergo surgery on the fetus or to submit to cesarean sections rather than to give birth vaginally. Women may also be subject to criminal prosecution for "fetal abuse" or to civil suit by their children for their behavior while pregnant.

Medical and legal actions in the name of fetal rights raise many issues for poor women and women of color. A basic question is whether it is right to hold individual women responsible for poor outcomes at birth when many women are not able to live under healthful conditions. This topic thus implicates the general socioeconomic conditions poor women and women of color experience that result in their lack of access to basic prenatal care and advanced prenatal, perinatal, and neonatal technologies. Holding individual women responsible under present circumstances is morally unjust, and it diverts attention from the need to correct the serious inequities that permeate today's society.

There is good reason to believe that poor women and women of color will be especially vulnerable to prosecutors' attempts to hold mothers responsible for bad reproductive outcomes. As a general matter, their children experience greater rates of infant mortality and low birth weight, which can result in physical and neurological illness. Infant mortality and morbidity among mothers who live below the poverty line are greatly increased, sometimes to as much as twice the rate experienced by other women. . . .

Socioeconomic conditions are an important element in these poor reproductive outcomes. Low-income women and women of color lack access to prenatal and neonatal care. In addition, many suffer from general ill health, broken families, and lack of social supports. . . .

Recent evidence suggests that hospital authorities' efforts to force pregnant women to accept high-tech procedures will be aimed disproportionately at low-income women and women of color. In 1987, the New England Journal of Medicine published a report on the incidence of court-ordered obstetrical interventions, including forced cesarean sections and intrauterine transfusions. The report revealed that 81 percent of the women subjected to such court orders were black, Hispanic, or Asian; 44 percent were not married; 24 percent were not native English speakers; and none were private patients.[21] Attempts to compel submission to procedures such as cesarean section, fetal monitoring, and other technologies presuppose that they have been adequately explained and that the pregnant woman has no good reason for refusing the procedure. Neither assumption may be warranted. . . .

Reproductive Hazards in the Workplace

The reproductive health of minority and poor women may be impaired directly, through job-related hazards, or indirectly, as a consequence of having low-paying jobs without benefits. Thus their reproductive health, like their general health, is affected by their status as workers, as members of a minority group, and as women. Women of color and poor women often have the most hazardous jobs, risking physical, chemical, and psychological injury.[22] Their low income may restrict their access to health care, and force them to live in neighborhoods contaminated by environmental pollutants and to exist on inadequate diets. Many work in positions with low pay and long hours, without benefits such as health insurance, maternity leave, vacation time, or sick pay.[23] Moreover, poverty and discrimination increase stress. Women who are heads of households are particularly likely to suffer hardships.[24]

Poor women and women of color generally have limited recourse when their rights are violated. They have been excluded from trade unions that could have improved their circumstances in the past, and they are afraid to unionize now for fear of losing their jobs. . . .

[For example], [w]omen working in low-income jobs in the health field are exposed to heavy lifting and to chemical hazards such as sterilizing gases, anesthetic gases, X-rays, and drugs.[25] As a result, black hospital workers suffer an even higher rate of primary and secondary infertility than black people generally. Similarly, although little research has been done specifically on reproductive hazards encountered by minority or other hospital workers, nonprofessional hospital workers may be at elevated risk for certain types of cancers (especially breast cancer) because of exposure to radiation and various chemical agents. Cancer-causing agents usually also cause spontaneous abortion.

The textile industry is another source of danger to poor women of color. . . . Most women who work in such jobs are afraid to complain for fear of being fired or reported to immigration authorities as illegal aliens.

Women of color are also found in laundry and cleaning establishments. In 1980, 40 percent of all clothing ironers and pressers, and 23 percent of all laundry and dry cleaning operatives were black.[26] Jobs in this sector also pose serious health risks.

Many minorities, especially blacks and Chicanos, work in agriculture. Of the estimated five million migrant and seasonal workers, 75 percent are Chicano, and 20 percent are black.[27] These workers are exposed to pesticides that cause liver, renal, and reproductive damage.[28]

For some poor women and women of color, the financial precariousness of their work poses the greatest hazard. Women in low-paying positions, whether in agriculture or as domestics, in private homes, tend to have no health or other benefits, such as sick leave or vacation. As a result, many women are forced to work throughout their pregnancies and to return to work immediately after giving birth irrespective of the risks to their health. For example, some jobs require women to stand on their feet all day, although continuous standing can cause complications during pregnancy. Moreover, many of these jobs pay just enough to prevent women from being eligible for Medicaid and the prenatal care services it covers.

Although there is a definite need to protect women from reproductive and other health hazards in the workplace, there is also a danger that protection will take the form of denying them their jobs. Some companies will exclude women of reproductive age from the workplace rather than make working conditions safe. Others may offer a woman another job, usually at reduced pay. Employer policies of this type have a severe impact on poor women and women of color. . . .

Laws and regulations now on the books at the federal and state level are supposed to protect workers from hazards and discrimination in the workplace. These laws theoretically guarantee workers the right to know about their working environment and protect those who speak out against hazards.[29] Unfortunately, these laws are rarely enforced adequately.[30] In addition, domestic and agricultural workers, who are disproportionately poor and minority, are excluded from their coverage. . . .

Interference and Reproductive Choice

. . . The problem of sterilization abuse illustrates the range of ways poor women and women of color experience interference with their reproductive choice. At times, poor women and women of color have been subjected to blatant coercion; at other times, their "choice" of sterilization has been based on inadequate or no informed consent, the effects of poverty, differential government funding schemes, and lack of birth control information.

Blatant sterilization abuse was exposed in the 1970s. Public assistance officials tricked illiterate black welfare recipients into consenting to the sterilization of their teenage daughters.[31] Native American women under 21 years of age were subjected to radical hysterectomies, and informed consent procedures were ignored.[32] Doctors agreed to deliver the babies of black Medicaid patients on the condition that the women would be sterilized.[33] Doctors have also conditioned the performance of abortions on "consent" to sterilization.[34]

But one must question how voluntary the choice of sterilization is in other cases as well. Complete information is crucial to voluntary choice, yet many women elect sterilization under the mistaken belief that the procedure is reversible. Medical personnel often encourage that belief by referring to the procedure as "tying the tubes"; many women assume that what can be tied, can be untied later.[35] . . .

Physicians' attitudes are one reason why some poor women and women of color may still be subject to involuntary sterilization. Some doctors, oblivious to their patients' preferences and cultural differences in attitudes towards family size and legitimacy, regard "excessive" childbearing by poor women and women of color as deviant or inappropriate. Doctors convey these attitudes to their patients, who come to believe that they will not be accepted as patients unless they conform to the medical profession's analysis of their behavior and problems.[36] Classism and racism lead physicians and other health care providers to urge sterilization on patients they believe incapable of using other methods effectively. For example, a Boston clinic serving primarily black clients reported that 45 percent of its black clients "chose" tubal ligation as a method of birth control after their first child was born.[37] . . .

Sterilization rates as high as 65 percent of Hispanic women have been reported in the northeast United States.[38] . . . Native American women fare no better. It is estimated that between 30 percent and 42 percent of all Native Americans have been sterilized, resulting in a steadily declining birth rate.[39]

Unnecessary surgery is another form of sterilization abuse. The number of conditions that require removal of female reproductive organs are relatively few, and fibroid tumors are not generally considered in that category. However, many women have gone to a physician for treatment of fibroids—a condition especially common among black women—and been told that a hysterectomy was the only cure.[40] In other cases, doctors have advocated hysterectomy for women they perceive as having too many children,[41] or to provide interns and residents with experience.[42] Unfortunately, such practices appear to persist despite the restrictions on Medicaid reimbursement of hysterectomies for these purposes in effect since 1975.[43] . . .

High unemployment and profound economic insecurity have likewise led to the "choice" of sterilization as a method of contraception. Women who feel they must forgo permanently the possibility of having children they would like to have because they cannot afford a child or even the cost of delivery have been deprived of their reproductive choice. . . .

Access to New Reproductive Technologies

Because the health care in the United States is organized on a for-profit basis, the needs of poor and minority women receive little attention generally. Access to reproductive technologies is particularly problematic. For example, each in vitro fertilization procedure costs from $3500 to $5000 per attempt, and most couples make several attempts at achieving pregnancy. Private insurers rarely cover such procedures, so the new technologies are often beyond the reach of even middle-class women. In regard to poor and minority women, governmental concern appears to be focused primarily on reducing fertility rather than improving it. . . .

Social criteria for services impose additional barriers to access. Most in vitro clinics are highly selective, accepting only married, heterosexual women with adequate resources.[44] This is a problem for many potential clients since, for example, in 1985, 57.3 percent of black women were not married.[45] . . .

Childlessness is a very serious concern in communities of color. As a result of cultural norms and restricted opportunities for women to have a profession or a career, motherhood and family life are generally valued very highly. Therefore, losing the option of procreating and parenting can be devastating to a poor woman or a woman of color.[46]

Sociocultural factors make it difficult for some poor women and women of color to obtain treatment for infertility. Shame and fear may make it hard for them to discuss their reproductive difficulties. Moreover, physicians and other health personnel may want to involve the woman's partner in the treatment process and expect him to be knowledgeable about her menstrual cycle, and other aspects of her physical condition. This may present particular problems for some poor women and women of color, who live in cultures in which certain subjects are essentially taboo and in which distinct roles are assigned to men and women. Some women fear losing their mate if they prove infertile. At the same time, infertility testing may be problematic for men in such cultures, especially when their feelings of masculinity are at least partially based on their ability to father children.

Sociocultural factors also shape alternatives to reproductive technologies as the response to unwanted childlessness. Adoption in poor or minority communities is not always the same as the adoption referred to by the agencies serving the primarily white middle class. In many instances, poor or minority women have not formally adopted children, but have raised the children of other family members who, for a variety of reasons, were unable to care for them. This extended family concept is prevalent in many cultures of color and in some white ethnic communities.

Formal adoption is less common, primarily because, until recently, adoption agencies excluded people of color from the adoption process and imposed other socioeconomic barriers. Minorities believe in the concept of adoption, but may be wary of the bureaucracy of adoption administrators.[47] In the past 10 years, more adoption officials have attempted to recruit minority families to adopt children, and formal adoption is becoming a more viable alternative to childlessness.[48]. . . .

Conclusion

Poor women and women of color have pressing needs for health services, including reproductive health services. They also have a history of maltreatment by the health care delivery system. For such women, making existing rights a reality and meeting the challenges posed by new modes of reproduction and reported advances in prenatal and perinatal technology are crucially related to these needs and history. Reproductive laws and policies for the 1990s must respond to the concerns of all women. . . .

Notes

1. Clarke, Subtle Forms of Sterilization Abuse: A Reproductive Rights Analysis, in R. Arditti, R. Klein & S. Minden eds., Test Tube Women 188, 199 (1984); Birth Control Blamed For Health Problems, Intern Extra, Apr. 7, 1984, at 60; Native Americans Given Depo-Provera, 8:1 Listen Real Loud A-7 (1987).

2. Levin & Taub, Reproductive Rights, in C. Lefcourt ed., Women and the Law 10A-27–28 (1987).

3. E. Blaine, Testimony presented to the National Women's Health Network entitled The Impact on Women of Color of Restricting Medicaid Funding for Abortion (1985).

4. See generally Arnold, Public Health Aspects of Contraceptive Sterilization, in S. Newman & Z. Klein eds., Behavioral-Social Aspects of Contraceptive Sterilization (1978).

5. See generally Mullings, Women Of Color and Occupational Health, in W. Chavkin ed., Double Exposure (1984).

6. Telephone interview with spokesperson, Alan Guttmacher Inst. (Sept. 23, 1987).

7. Henshaw, Characteristics of U.S. Women Having Abortions 1982–1983, 19:1 Fam. Plan. Persps. 5, 6 (1986). Abortion rate data must be understood in the context of nonwhite women's significantly higher fertility rate, a rate that was, for example, 35 percent higher than that for white women in 1981. Centers for Disease Control, Abortion Surveillance 1981, Table 14 at 37 (Nov. 1985).

8. In 1982, 50 percent of all Medicaid-eligible women at the clinic had abortions at 10 weeks or later. The abortion rate at 10 weeks or later for women not eligible for (or not needing) Medicaid was only 37 percent. Post 13-week abortions were excluded from this portion of the study. Characteristics of U.S. Women, *supra* note 7, at 172.

9. An unpublished survey of welfare caseworkers in the northern counties of New Jersey indicated that, out of the 42 caseworkers interviewed, only six demonstrated adequate knowledge of the availability of state-funded Medicaid reimbursement for abortion. S. Cohen, Welfare Caseworkers and Information About Restored State Medicaid Funding For Abortion: Summary of Sample Survey (A.C.L.U. of N.J. May 1984).

10. "In 17 states, fewer than half of all women of reproductive age live in counties with identified abortion providers. In four States—Kentucky, Mississippi, South Dakota, and West Virginia—less than 30 percent of such women live in counties with any abortion provider." Kentucky and West Virginia, of course, have significant poor populations, and Mississippi has both a large poor and a large black population. Henshaw,

Forrest & Blaine, Abortion Services in the United States 1981 and 1982, 16:3 Fam. Plan. Persps. 119, 122 (1984).

11. In 1982, the U.S. Department of Health and Human Services (DHHS) promulgated and implemented regulations designed to bring abortion policy in the Indian Health Service in line with that in other DHHS-administered health programs. Under these regulations, abortions may be performed only when the woman's life is endangered. Alan Guttmacher Inst., 5:6 Issues in Brief 1, 2 (1985).

12. See generally Monmouth County Correctional Inst. Inmates v. Lanzaro, 834 F.2d 326 (3d Cir. 1987).

13. See 28 C.F.R. 551.23 (during fiscal year 1987 the Bureau of Prisons may pay for an abortion only where the life of the mother would be endangered if the fetus were carried to term or if the pregnancy is the result of rape).

14. Centers for Disease Control, Abortion Surveillance 1981, *supra* note 7, Table 14 at 37.

15. Alan Guttmacher Inst., Teenage Pregnancy: The Problem That Hasn't Gone Away (1981).

16. Henshaw, Forrest & Van Vort, Abortion Services in the United States, 1984 and 1985, 19:2 Fam. Plan. Persps. (1987) [hereinafter Abortion Services 1984 and 1985].

17. *Id.*

18. Title 11 of the Public Health Service Act (the Genetic Diseases Act) provided for direct federal support until the Reagan administration altered the regulations. The state governments now receive these funds through the categorical block grants (Maternal and Child Health Program). Disbursement of funds is discretionary within a range of services. Telephone interview with spokesperson, Alan Guttmacher Inst. (Jan. 16, 1988).

19. Hubbard & Henifin, Genetic Screening of Prospective Parents and of Workers, in Humber & Almeder ed., Biomedical Ethics Reviews 92, 100 (1984).

20. Recommendations for Assisting in the Prevention of Perinatal Transmission of Human T-Lymphotropic Virus Type III Lymphadenopathy-Associated Virus and Acquired Immune Deficiency Syndrome, 34:48 Morbidity & Mortality Weekly Rep. 721, 724 (1985).

21. Kolder, Gallagher & Parsons, Court-Ordered Obstetrical Interventions, 316 New Eng. J. Med. 1192, 1192–1196 (1987). . . .

22. One indication of the general health problems people of color face is that black workers are almost one and one-half times more likely than white workers to be severely disabled by job-related injuries and illnesses. 10:3 Chicago Rep. 1, 2 (1981).

23. See generally U.S. Comm'n on Civ. Rts., Health Insurance Coverage & Employment Opportunities for Minorities & Women, Clearinghouse Publication No. 72 (Sept. 1982).

24. See Mullings, Women of Color, *supra* note 5, at 125 (Mullings points out, even in two-parent households, a black woman often bears greater responsibility for providing sustenance to her family than the average white woman).

25. Mass. Coalition for Occupational Health & the Boston Women's Health Book Collective, Our Jobs, Our Health 15, 40–42 (1983).

26. Westcott, Blacks in the 1970's: Did They Scale the Job Ladder, 105:6 Monthly Lab. Rev. 29, 32 (1982).

27. See 3:5 Women's Occupational Health Resource Center News 4 (1981).

28. Kutz, Yobs & Strassman, Stratification of Organochlorine Insect Residues in Human Adipose Tissue, 19:9 J. Occupational Med. 619, 619–622 (1977); Davis, The

Impact of Workplace Health and Safety on Black Workers: Assessment and Prognosis, 31:12 Lab. L.J. 723, 729 (1980).

29. See generally Bertin, Reproductive Hazards in the Workplace, in Humber & Almeder eds., Biomedical Ethics Reviews (1984).

30. *Id.*

31. See Levin & Taub, *supra* note 2, at 10A-27–28.

32. Alliance Against Women's Oppression, "Caught in the Crossfire: Minority Women and Reproductive Rights," p. 1, 5 (Jan. 1983).

33. Walker v. Price, 560 F.2d 609 (4th Cir. 1977).

34. Clarke, *supra* note 1, at 197.

35. One study reported that 45 percent of the sterilized black women interviewed did not know the procedure was irreversible. Forty percent of the sample said they regretted being sterilized. *Id.* at 195.

36. *Id.*

37. Martha Eliot Health Center, Reproductive Health Report 1–2 (1985).

38. In 1981, a psychologist found that 65 percent of the Puerto Rican women in Hartford and 55 percent of all Latin women in Springfield, Mass. had been sterilized. Personal communication from Dr. Vickie Barres, Brookside Family Health center, Jamaica Plain, Boston, Apr. 1985.

39. Caught in the Crossfire, *supra* note 32, at 1.

40. D. Scully, Men Who Control Women's Health: The Miseducation of Obstetrician-Gynecologists 120–140 (1980).

41. Clarke, *supra* note 1, at 193–194.

42. Scully, *supra* note 40, at 120–140.

43. Clarke, *supra* note 1, at 205 n.12.

44. G. Corea, The Mother Machine: Reproductive Technologies from Artificial Insemination to Antisocial Wombs 145 (1985).

45. Bureau of the Census, U.S. Dept. of Com., Statistical Abstract of the U.S., No. 49, Marital Status of Black and Spanish Origin Population: 1970–85, 40 (1987). In 1985, 32 percent of black women were never married, 11 percent were divorced and 14.3 percent were widowed.

46. Corea, *supra* note 44, at 169–172.

47. Telephone interview with Devera Foreman, Philadelphia Chapter-Association of Black Psychologists (1986).

48. *Id.*

An Equal Protection Analysis of
U.S. Reproductive Health Policy:
Gender, Race, Age, and Class

RUTH COLKER

THE PURPOSE OF THIS essay is to bring an "anti-essentialist" and "reproductive health" perspective to the public policy debate concerning pregnancy-related regulations, including, but not limited to, abortion regulations. . . .

[T]he abortion debate, as reflected in both pro-choice and pro-life writings, has often been overly superficial and general in its description of how women are affected by various reproductive choices,[1] thereby suffering from a problem of essentialism. The variables of race, age, sexual orientation, handicap, religion, and social class affect how various reproductive decisions influence women's lives. Nevertheless, the abortion debate tends to focus on all "women" as if they are a monolithic category. Recently, it has become fashionable to discuss the "problem of teenage pregnancy," but even this more focused discussion is unsatisfactory because it fails to reflect that pregnancy does not affect all adolescents in the same way. Finally, the popularity of the abortion debate is a reflection of the problem of essentialism because this debate chooses one issue for debate—abortion—and generally ignores the larger and more complex problems relating to reproductive health issues, of which pregnancy is only one part. . . .

In the analysis that follows, I try to document quantitatively and qualitatively the various ways that pregnancies disadvantage the lives of adolescents. . . .

The Magnitude of the Problem of Unintended Pregnancies and Early Childbirth . . .

"One out of every ten women 15–19 years old becomes pregnant each year in the United States, a proportion that has changed little in the last fifteen years."[2] It was estimated in 1981 that more than five million women fifteen to nineteen years old were at risk of unintended pregnancy.[3] Although forty-three percent of unintended preg-

1991 Duke L.J. 324.

nancies occur among women using contraceptives, three-fourths of all unintended adolescent pregnancies occur to those who do not practice contraception.[4]

The U.S. teenage birthrate is much higher than that of other developed countries, with the maximum relative difference occurring for adolescents under the age of fifteen. Moreover, this disparity continues to grow.[5] Since 1973, although the proportion of wanted births has risen for women age twenty-five to thirty-nine, the proportion of births that were considered "mistimed" for never-married adolescents increased by thirty-seven percent.[6] Unwanted childbearing is more common among unmarried African-Americans than among their white counterparts (thirty percent versus eighteen percent), but varies little among unmarried African-American women according to the mother's current age. By contrast, the rate of unwanted childbearing among single white women is almost cut in half after the age of twenty-four. . . .[7] Hispanic women, age fifteen to nineteen, are about as likely as non-white women to give birth but less likely to have an abortion.[8]

. . . Although African-American adolescents are more likely to be sexually active than white adolescents, they also are less likely to use contraceptives. Forty percent of African-American adolescents, as contrasted with twenty-four percent of whites, reported never having used a contraceptive during intercourse.[9] These statistics yield the not-surprising result that, in 1979, thirty percent of African-American teenage women in metropolitan areas had had a premarital pregnancy, as compared to fourteen percent of whites.

In understanding these statistics, however, it is important to control for social class. Within the group of African-American teenage women, for example, dramatic differences in contraceptive use exist depending upon social class. One study found that forty-four percent of African-American teenage women who were of high social class, had intact families, and resided in a non-ghetto neighborhood, used a contraceptive at first intercourse, as compared with only twelve percent of those who were of low social class, did not have intact families, and resided in a ghetto neighborhood.[10] The statistics for these "higher class" African-American women appear to be similar to a comparable group of white women. . . . This finding about contraceptive use at first intercourse is important because other studies demonstrate that those who use contraceptives at first intercourse are more consistent users thereafter.[11] . . .

To understand the magnitude of the problem of unintended pregnancies for adolescents, we need to understand the impact on the physical health of the mother, as well as the socioeconomic consequences stemming from early childbirth. . . .

1. *Physical Health.* "[A]dolescent mothers between the ages of fifteen and nineteen years are twice as likely to die from hemorrhage and miscarriage than mothers over twenty years of age."[12] The maternal mortality and morbidity rate is sixty percent higher for this group than for older women.[13] Adolescent mothers are "23 percent more likely to experience a premature birth with complications such as anemia, prolonged labor and nutritional deficiency," and ninety-two percent more likely to experience anemia than older mothers.[14] The risk of health problems and medical complications are even higher for African-American adolescents because of the inequitable distribution of resources in society.[15]

Socioeconomic factors, rather than age, seem to contribute substantially to adverse health consequences from teenage pregnancy.[16]. . . Several studies suggest that pregnancy outcomes among adolescents who receive good prenatal care are no different from, or are better than, those of older women.[17] Thus, the underlying problem is one of poverty. . . .

In countries where adverse health consequences were not found for adolescents, an excellent prenatal care system was in place.[18] Thus, it is not the age or race of the adolescents that cause their pregnancy to coincide with adverse health consequences, but it is the lack of access to adequate prenatal care that causes these adverse health consequences. . . .

2. *Education*. . . . High school graduation rates are affected markedly for women age twenty-one to twenty-nine, by age at first birth. As of 1986, African-American women who delay their first birth until age twenty have a better than ninety-two percent chance of graduating from high school.[19] By contrast, African-American women who have their first child under the age of seventeen have only a sixty percent chance of high school graduation, and African-American women who have their first birth at the age of eighteen to nineteen have only a seventy-five percent chance of high school graduation.[20] For white women the statistics are comparable. . . .

. . . Hispanic women, however, had only a thirty-three percent chance of completing school if they conceived a child while in high school but gave birth after leaving school, and had a fifty-nine percent chance of completing high school if they both conceived and gave birth before leaving school.[21] The latter statistic is about ten percentage points lower than the comparable group of African-American and white women; however, the former statistic is more than twenty percentage points lower than the comparable group of African-American and white women. Thus, early childbearing has a dramatic influence in the educational lives of Hispanic women, and a very significant influence in the educational lives of white and African-American women.

Although the impact of early childbearing may be more significant for Hispanic women than for African-American or white women, it is interesting to note that Hispanic women are much less likely to bear children before leaving school than are African-American women. Nineteen percent of African-American women gave birth before leaving school in 1983, whereas only seven percent of Hispanic women gave birth before leaving school.[22] (The figure for white women was four percent.) Thus, if we encourage African-American and Hispanic women to use contraception during high school if they are sexually active, their pregnancies more likely will be intentional rather than unwanted or mistimed. The reasons for targeting them are somewhat different. African-American women are at a greater risk of giving birth before leaving school than Hispanic women, but Hispanic women are more likely to face serious consequences when they do give birth before leaving school. . . .

[W]e need to modify our strategy for adolescents to encourage them to stay in school during and after their pregnancies. Federal law that prohibits pregnancy-related discrimination in education does not appear to help. . . .

Contraception and Sex Education

One way to avoid the problems of early childbirth is to use contraception to avoid pregnancy. Nevertheless, as compared with other western countries, U.S. social policy is entirely ineffectual in preventing early childbirth for poor adolescents through contraception. In 1978, the United States Congress passed the Adolescent Health, Services, and Pregnancy Prevention and Care Act,[23] which promoted the distribution of contraceptives and abortion counseling or referral. In 1981, Congress folded the Adolescent Health Services and Pregnancy Prevention and Care Act into the Maternal and Child Health block grant to the states, and enacted the Adolescent Family Life Act (AFLA).[24] The AFLA is fundamentally different from the 1978 Adolescent Pregnancy Prevention Act in that it supports "chastity" and adoption, but not contraception or abortion. Although the 1978 Act required grantees to offer counseling and referral about abortion, the 1981 Act forbids such counseling or referral.

The rationale behind this approach is the assumption that sex education and the availability of contraceptives and abortions promotes sexual behavior and unintended pregnancies. Proponents consider the message of abstinence to be the most effective way to limit teenage sexual activity and thus unintended pregnancies. However, empirical surveys suggest the opposite. Studies of teenage pregnancy in developed countries show that countries with more liberal attitudes toward talking about sex have the lowest birthrates.[25] In addition, one study found that exposure to contraceptive education had no consistent effect on the probability that a woman, who had not previously experienced intercourse, would subsequently initiate intercourse.[26] . . . Thus, increased sex education may actually delay the onset of sexual activity as well as reduce the pregnancy rate.[27]

The U.S. policy on family planning, as compared to other developed countries, differs in one important respect. In the United States, policy analysts are not sure whether they should advocate the prevention of teenage sexual activity or unwanted teenage pregnancy; in other developed countries, national policy is squarely behind preventing unwanted teenage pregnancy irrespective of the prevalence of sexual activity among adolescents.[28] Thus, easily accessible and relatively free contraceptives, which are made available in most developed countries and which substantially help to lower the rate of unintended teenage pregnancy, are not part of the U.S. national family planning policy. . . .

Another important aspect of an effective contraceptive policy would be to have a wide range of inexpensive contraceptive services available to adolescents. American adolescents, however, do not have many services readily available to them. Most adolescents obtain contraceptives (if they obtain them at all) at family planning clinics rather than from private physicians.[29] Only seven out of ten clinics, and five out of ten private physicians, accept Medicaid payment for contraceptive services. Thus, poor adolescents may have no affordable way to obtain the contraceptive pill, which is generally considered to be the most appropriate birth control option for adolescent females. In addition, many private physicians will not serve an unmarried minor without parental consent.[30] We know the difficulties of parental consent and notification statutes from the abortion cases. . . .

The only good news in the family planning area is that the United States Congress has modified Medicaid so that women who do not meet the income and family structure criteria for cash assistance are eligible for Medicaid as long as they meet certain income criteria. By July 1990, states had to extend Medicaid coverage to infants and pregnant women with incomes up to the federal poverty level, and had the option of covering infants and pregnant women with incomes up to 185% of the poverty level. As of July 1988, forty states have opted to expand their Medicaid programs to cover infants and pregnant women with incomes of 100% of the poverty level.[31] It is too soon to assess whether that money is actually reaching poor, pregnant adolescents. . . .

Prenatal Care

Another way to avoid some of the negative consequences of early childbirth, especially for the child, is to have available an excellent system of prenatal care. The importance of adequate prenatal care cannot be overstated. . . . Women who do not obtain adequate prenatal care are much more likely than those who do to have a low birth-weight baby, to gain too little weight during pregnancy, or to have a premature birth.[32] Because nearly half of all women under the age of twenty receive inadequate prenatal care,[33] these women are at high risk of having pregnancy-related complications. By not preventing these complications early in the pregnancy, we raise the ultimate cost of the medical complications associated with the pregnancy and place the mother's and child's health at risk.

Despite the importance of effective and accessible prenatal care, it is no more available to poor adolescents after pregnancy than were contraceptives and sex education prior to pregnancy. . . . Females under the age of eighteen, . . . receive the least amount of prenatal care; 48.5% receive first-trimester prenatal care; 12.7% receive third-trimester care only; and some receive no care.[34] In addition, the percentage of female adolescents who receive third-trimester only or no care is substantially higher for African-American and Hispanic adolescents than for white adolescents.[35]

The structure of the federal Medicaid program explains the unavailability of prenatal care for certain groups in society. Eligibility for Medicaid is based on poverty and family structure. As of 1985, only one state, Vermont, had an eligibility level that exceeded the federal poverty level and twenty-three states had income limits that were less than half of the federal poverty level.[36] If the new Medicaid rules are successful, these figures should improve. In addition, prenatal care, delivery, and postpartum care are not mandated under the Medicaid program. . . . Only twelve states provide all of the services under Medicaid that are considered part of an "adequate" prenatal health care system.[37] Pregnant adolescents can have special problems receiving Medicaid coverage because they often need to present their parent's Medicaid card at the doctor's office to receive treatment.[38] Finally, it can be difficult to find a doctor who will accept Medicaid payment. . . .[39] . . .

Abortion

Another way to avoid early childbirth stemming from unwanted pregnancies is to have accessible abortion—especially at the early stages of pregnancy when it is safest. But the Supreme Court has long supported restraints on abortions for adolescents. Moreover, the restrictions approved in Webster v. Reproductive Health Services[40] that increased the costs of second trimester abortion and that made abortions unavailable in hospitals on public property will have a dramatic effect on adolescents, because they are disproportionately affected by these measures. Although adolescents manage to have abortions in relatively large numbers, they do so by overcoming substantial burdens that are placed in their way. The consequence is that adolescents have disproportionately late-term abortions, thereby increasing the health risks of the procedure and raising its cost.

Despite parental consent laws and the unavailability of Medicaid for abortions, about six percent of eighteen- to nineteen-year-olds had abortions in 1981, the highest rate of any age group.[41] Female adolescents are the second most likely group to face a pregnancy, and the most likely group to terminate it by abortion, despite the relative difficulty for many of them to obtain an abortion.[42]

The rate of abortions per 1000 women was much higher in 1981 for non-white adolescents as compared to white adolescents (59.7 compared with 33.5). However, the ratio of abortions per 100 abortions plus live births was higher for white adolescents than non-white adolescents (41.8 compared with 39.6). These statistics reflect a much higher pregnancy rate in the non-white community than the white community. Thus, in absolute terms, non-white adolescents experienced many more abortions *and* births than white adolescents, and were, overall, less likely to terminate a pregnancy through abortion. Non-white adolescents are therefore in much greater need of all reproductive health services than white adolescents.

Adolescent females are disproportionately likely to have abortions in the second trimester. In 1981, between six and eight percent of the abortions performed on women over the age of twenty-five took place at thirteen or more weeks gestation.[43] In the same year for women under the age of twenty, between ten and twenty-three percent of the abortions performed took place at thirteen or more weeks' gestation, with the highest statistic for women under the age of fourteen.[44] There appears to be an inverse, geometric relationship between age and second trimester abortions for women under the age of twenty. Thus, when adolescent females do face unintended pregnancies and decide to have an abortion, they disproportionately face the high health risks of second trimester abortions. . . .

More recent statistics depict a similar trend, although the overall number of abortions may be declining. . . .

. . . Only one study that I have found . . . analyzes the short-term and long-term consequences for adolescents who procure abortions as compared with pregnant adolescents who bear the child and care for it or relinquish it for adoption. [That] study sought to determine if the young women (360 African-American teenage women of similar socioeconomic backgrounds who sought pregnancy tests from two Baltimore reproductive health providers) who terminated their pregnancies fared differently than the women who carried their pregnancies to term. In terms of educational status, the study found that the women who carried their pregnancies to term attained significantly less education. Interestingly, the difference became more significant over the two year period of the study.[45] This negative change in their educational experience was not consistent with their educational expectations, as expressed during interviews. As for economic well-being, the abortion group's economic status improved over the two year period, while at the same time the child bearer's economic well-being deteriorated. Even when the effect of the presence of the baby was removed from the calculation of household income, the abortion group performed significantly better than the child bearing group. . . .

This study confirms my initial thesis: Pregnancy, in itself, need not be a problem for adolescents. The pregnancy becomes problematic due to the socially created, negative life consequences of carrying the pregnancy to term and the high possibility of another unintended pregnancy, which also may be carried to term. Adolescent women who procure an abortion will, on average, fare better than their peers who bear the child. However, both sets of adolescents remain at high risk of undergoing another unintended pregnancy with subsequent child care responsibilities. By putting substantial obstacles in the path of adolescents who want abortions, we cause them to delay their abortion and thereby undergo significant health risks. In contrast, by facilitating their ability to procure an abortion, we may improve the quality of their lives as well as the lives of their future children. . . .

Equal Protection Framework . . .

The recent case of Hodgson v. Minnesota[46] highlights the need to protect female adolescents from coercive state policies, as well as the difficulty of obtaining such protection under contemporary legal doctrine. In that case, Minnesota largely succeeded in creating a public policy that favors childbirth over abortion through a two-parent notification requirement with judicial bypass, ignoring entirely the dramatic negative consequences of such a policy on the lives of female adolescents and their future offspring.[47] The primary interests that Minnesota claimed to be considering by enacting the law were the interests of the parents of the pregnant adolescent and the family unit comprised of the pregnant adolescent and her parents—Minnesota did not maintain that the adolescent's self-perceived best interests should control. Although the federal district court had concluded that one major motivation behind the parental notification statute had been to favor childbirth over abortion, the state did not even attempt to argue in favor of this policy before the Supreme Court because it understood that such a policy choice did not further the well-being of the pregnant adolescent.[48] . . .

[Justice Stevens, speaking for the majority in *Hodgson*, reached the decision] without serious consideration of the impact of coerced pregnancies on the lives of pregnant adolescents and the children born to them. He simply refuted the state's assertions about the parents' interests being served by the forced two-parent notification procedure. He did not find fault with the state for admittedly not making the well-being of adolescents a prime consideration. Under my proposed analysis, the impact on the pregnant adolescents would be the focus of the analysis under heightened scrutiny rather than a side issue that is easily ignored while "parents rights" (without responsibilities) are discussed.[49] . . .

Doctrinal Advantages of Equal Protection Doctrine

Traditionally, the courts have used a privacy framework to resolve abortion cases. (That is the framework used in *Hodgson*.) . . . In the fifteen years [after Roe v. Wade], the Court applied this framework to invalidate nearly all restrictions against abortion except: (1) Congressional and state limitations on Medicaid that made it very difficult for poor people to obtain government-funded abortions,[50] and (2) parental consent and notification statutes that made it difficult for adolescents to preserve their privacy and obtain expeditious abortions.[51] Many feminists criticized the Court's privacy approach, because it could not protect the most disadvantaged women from coercive anti-abortion regulations. . . .

In addition, feminist pro-choice litigators have continued to use the privacy approach because of doctrinal problems with the equal protection approach. . . .

There are two major doctrinal difficulties in trying to apply current equal protection doctrine to reproductive health issues: (1) the Geduldig v. Aiello[52] holding that pregnancy is not a sex-based condition, and (2) the Personnel Administrator v. Feeney[53] holding that purposeful discrimination must be established by proving that a legislature acted "because of" its desire to harm women rather than "in spite of" this desire. Although these doctrinal difficulties are enormous, they can be overcome without revolutionizing equal protection doctrine. [W]hen a female plaintiff desires to challenge a state's reproductive health policies, she has the option of (1) establishing that the policy is explicitly sex-based and therefore is a presumptive example of intentional sex-based discrimination, or (2) that the policy is gender-neutral but creates a disparate impact on the basis of sex that can be categorized as "intentional."

The stumbling block to the first strategy is *Geduldig*. In *Geduldig*, the Court found that pregnancy is not a sex-based condition and therefore did not apply heightened scrutiny to a case involving a pregnancy-based exclusion from disability insurance. Because, in the Court's opinion, the case did not present an example of sex discrimination (or any other suspect class of discrimination), it considered minimal rational basis scrutiny to be appropriate. Under this lenient standard, the Court held that the state's economic arguments for excluding pregnancy from its disability insurance were a sufficient justification.

The stumbling block for the second strategy is *Feeney*. In *Feeney*, the Court clarified that the intent standard could only be met with evidence that the legislature enacted its policy because it desired to harm women rather than in spite of such a desire. Thus, the fact that the Massachusetts Legislature precluded ninety-eight percent of women from obtaining civil service jobs through its veteran's preference statute was not sufficient evidence to warrant heightened scrutiny because that action was not instituted for the purpose of harming women; the legislature did not seriously contemplate the impact on women when it passed and maintained its veteran's preference.

Feminist critiques of the Court's decisions concerning reproductive health have largely focused on *Geduldig* rather than *Feeney*. They have criticized *Geduldig* by focusing on the absurdity of the Court's conclusion that pregnancy is not a sex-based condition.[54] They have argued that it is ridiculous to suggest that a legislature is unaware that pregnancy-related restrictions adversely affect women, and not men, because everyone knows that only women can become pregnant.

These critiques of *Geduldig* have been unsuccessful, in part, because they misunderstand the Court's reluctance to extend heightened scrutiny to pregnancy-related distinctions. I understand the Court to be saying that pregnancy-related restrictions are not first-order sex-based equal protection problems because they are based on a real physical difference between men and women. . . . The Court simply does not see those biologically-based restrictions as, in Justice O'Connor's words, "unduly burden[ing]" women's lives.[55]

I propose two strategies to overcome this trend. First, feminists should attack the *Feeney* test for how to prove purposeful discrimination rather than the *Geduldig* holding itself. If we can meet the standard set forth in *Feeney* (or a modified version of it), we would not have to win under *Geduldig*. Second, feminists should present the record of the systematic disadvantage of women through increased use of the reproductive health literature. We may not ultimately persuade the Court that all pregnancy-related restrictions disadvantage women's lives in a dramatic way; however, by focusing on the literature concerning female adolescents, we may be able to make the Court see that many of these restrictions dramatically disadvantage female adolescents. Under privacy doctrine, female adolescents have received a lower level of scrutiny than adult women because of the courts' deference to parents under privacy doctrine.[56] I believe that an equal protection approach can demonstrate that pregnant female adolescents are, in fact, the group most in need of heightened scrutiny because the sphere of family-related privacy, coupled with legislative insensitivity, has caused them to be a highly disadvantaged and politically powerless group. . . .

Thus, I suggest that the Court continue to insist that discriminatory intent be established when a state develops a facially neutral statute that disproportionately impacts women. However, the definition of "intent" does not have to be the narrow definition utilized in *Feeney*. A legislature, for example, could be considered to have an unconstitutional state of mind (or "intent") when it entirely ignores a statute's impact on women, and imposes burdens on women that it would not be willing to impose on men. . . .

Returning to the thesis of this essay—the example of female adolescents—I believe that it should be sufficient to present the following two-step analysis in order to show a gender-based violation of equal protection. First, using the empirical evidence that I have described above, we would show that our current reproductive health policies have a disparate impact against female adolescents. Because all of the individuals in that category are female, we would argue that we had shown that a facially neutral policy produced a gender-based disparate impact. Second, using my modified *Feeney* test, we would argue that a legislature that respected the well-being of female adolescents would not have passed the legislation in question. Because female adolescents are often poor and do not necessarily have the right to vote, they are especially deserving of the Court's protection. It is difficult to imagine that legislatures would deliberately want to harm female adolescents; however, if their blindness to the effects of their policies on this group is causing enormous disadvantages for this group, then the equal protection clause mandates that the Court intercede.[57] . . .

Notes

1. See, e.g., Mary Ann Glendon, Abortion and Divorce in Western Law (1987) (disagreeing with *Roe* decision); Christine Overall, Ethics and Human Reproduction (1987) (pro-choice); John Hart Ely, The Wages of Crying Wolf: A Comment on Roe v. Wade, 82 Yale L.J. 920 (1973) (disagreeing with *Roe* decision). A somewhat more sensitive account of the abortion issue is provided by Rosalind Petchesky. See Rosalind Pollack Petchesky, Abortion and Woman's Choice: The State, Sexuality, and Reproductive Freedom (1984) (discussing history, practice, and politics). However, Petchesky does not discuss adolescents until page 200, and then does so only in universal terms—describing teenagers as if they are a monolithic group.

2. James Trussell, Teenage Pregnancy in the United States, 20 Fam. Plan. Persp. 262 (1988).

3. Margaret Terry Orr, Private Physicians and the Provision of Contraceptives to Adolescents, 16 Fam. Plan. Persp. 83 (1984).

4. Trussell, *supra* note 2, at 262.

5. Elise Jones, Jacqueline Darroch Forrest, Noreen Goldman, Stanley Henshaw, Richard Lincoln, Jeannie Rosoff, Charles Westoff & Deirdre Wulf, Teenage Pregnancy in Developed Countries: Determinants and Policy Implications, 17 Fam. Plan. Persp. 53, 55 (1985).

6. Unwanted Childbearing in United States Declines, But Levels Still High Among Blacks, Singles, 17 Fam. Plan. Persp. 274 (1985) (digest section reporting on recent study).

7. *Id.* (citing W. C. Pratt and M. C. Horn, Wanted and Unwanted Childbearing United States, 1973–1982, Advance Data from Vital and Health Statistics, No. 108 (1985)).

The 1985 statistics confirm the relatively high fertility rate for teenagers. Per 1000 women, the pregnancy rate for females was 16.6 for females under age 15 and 109.8 for females age 15 to 19. (For older women, the comparable statistics are around 10%.) For non-white females, these figures are much higher: 50.8 for females under age 15 and 185.8 for females age 15 to 19. Stanley Henshaw & Jennifer Van Vort, Teenage Abortion, Birth and Pregnancy Statistics: An Update, 21 Fam. Plan. Persp. 85 (1989).

8. Henshaw & Van Vort, *supra* note 7, at 86.

9. Dennis Hogan, Nan Marie Astone & Evelyn Kitagawa, Social and Environmental

Factors Influencing Contraceptive Use Among Black Adolescents, 17 Fam. Plan. Persp. 165 (1985).

10. *Id.* at 168.

11. *Id.* at 168–169.

12. Alva Barnett, Factors that Adversely Affect the Health and Well-Being of African-American Adolescent Mothers and Their Infants, in Dionne Jones & Stanley Battle eds., Teenage Pregnancy: Developing Strategies for Change in the Twenty-First Century 101, 105 (1990) (citing Klerman, Adolescent Pregnancy: A New Look at a Continuing Problem, 70 Am. J. Pub. Health 776, 776–778 (1980)).

13. *Id.*

14. *Id.* at 106. . . .

15. *Id.*

16. Carolyn Makinson, The Health Consequences of Teenage Fertility, 17 Fam. Plan. Persp. 132 (1985). For example, one U.S. study found that African-American teenagers in urban clinics had a high rate of pregnancy-induced hypertension, anemia, prematurity and perinatal mortality, but that teenagers from more economically advantaged backgrounds did not have more health complications than older women. *Id.* at 133.

17. Trussell, *supra* note 2, at 268.

18. Makinson, *supra* note 16, at 133 (reporting Swedish experience).

19. Dawn Upchurch & James McCarthy, Adolescent Childbearing and High School Completion in the 1980s: Have Things Changed?, 21 Fam. Plan. Persp. 199, 200 (1989).

20. *Id.*

21. Frank Mott & William Marsiglio, Early Childbearing and Completion of High School, 17 Fam. Plan. Persp. 234, 235 (1985).

22. *Id.* at 237.

23. Health Services and Centers Amendments of 1978, Pub. L. No. 95–626, §§601–608, 92 Stat. 3551, 3595–3601 (codified as amended at 42 U.S.C. §300a-21 to -28; repealed by Omnibus Budget Reconciliation Act of 1981, Pub. L. No. 97–35, §955, 95 Stat. 357, 578–592 (codified as amended at 42 U.S.C. §300z (1988)).

24. 42 U.S.C. §300z (1988).

25. Jones et al., *supra* note 5, at 54.

26. Trussell, *supra* note 2, at 267.

27. One assumption that often seems to accompany discussions of the usefulness of sex education programs is that it is necessarily bad if such programs serve to encourage sexual activity among adolescents. James Trussell observes that the prevalence of sexual activity should not be so relevant to the discussion about these programs. Instead, he argues that preventing pregnancy should be judged the most important factor, irrespective of the rates of teenage sexual activity. *Id.* at 269. As long as sexual activity is consensual, our primary focus should be on the prevention of unintended pregnancies. In fact, I would even go further and say that our focus should be on preventing unintended childbirth and childcare rather than pregnancy, unless studies demonstrate that abortion or adoption have negative consequences for pregnant adolescents.

28. Jones et al., *supra* note 5, at 60–61.

29. Orr, *supra* note 3, at 86; see also William Mosher, Use of Family Planning Services in the United States: 1982 and 1988, 184 Advance Data 1 (April 11, 1990) (reporting that black women, poor women, and teenagers were more likely to rely on clinics for their reproductive health services than were white, higher-income, and older women).

30. Orr, *supra* note 3, at 86.

31. Rachel Benson Gold & Sandra Guardado, Public Funding of Family Planning, Sterilization and Abortion Services, 1987, 20 Fam. Plan. Persp. 228, 228 (1988).

32. Rachel Benson Gold, Asta Kenney & Susheela Singh, Paying for Maternity Care in the United States, 19 Fam. Plan. Persp. 190, 193 (1987).

33. *Id.* at 192.

34. Susheela Singh, Aida Torres & Jacqueline Darroch Forrest, The Need for Prenatal Care in the United States: Evidence from the 1980 National Natality Survey, 17 Fam. Plan. Persp. 118, 118 (1985).

35. *Id.* at 121. One study estimates that 8.3% of white mothers receive third trimester-only care or none whatsoever, whereas the statistic is 12.8% for African-American mothers and 11.9% for Hispanic mothers. *Id.*

Nevertheless, it is important not to overstate the significance of age for Hispanic women. Among Hispanic mothers, the incidence of inadequate care is nearly as high among 20–24-year-olds (11%) as among adolescents (12%). (Inadequate care is defined as third trimester-only care, or none at all.) For African-American women, however, there was a more marked difference between inadequate prenatal care for adolescents (12.8%) as compared with 20–24-year-olds (6.4%). For Hispanic mothers, then, the problem of inadequate prenatal care is prevalent irrespective of whether they bear a child as adolescents or in their early 20s. There is no reason to single out pregnant, Hispanic adolescents for special attention in terms of prenatal care; all pregnant, Hispanic women under the age of 25 need to be targeted. . . .

36. Rachel Benson Gold & Asta Kenney, Paying for Maternity Care, 17 Fam. Plan. Persp. 103, 107 (1985).

37. *Id.* at 108–109.

38. *Id.*

39. [1983 study indicated only 46 percent of obstetricians in private practice accept Medicaid for delivery.] *Id.* . . .

40. 492 U.S. 490 (1989). For further discussion of the impact of this decision on female adolescents, see Ruth Colker, Feminist Litigation: An Oxymoron?—A Study of the Briefs Filed in William L. Webster v. Reproductive Health Services, 13 Harv. Women's L.J. 137, 175–178 (1990).

41. Stanley Henshaw, Nancy Binkin, Ellen Blaine & Jack Smith, A Portrait of American Women Who Obtain Abortions, 17 Fam. Plan. Persp. 90 (1985).

42. *Id.*

43. David Grimes, Second-Trimester Abortions in the United States, 16 Fam. Plan. Persp. 260, 262 (1984).

44. *Id.*

45. Laurie Schwab Zabin, Marilyn Hirsch & Mark Emerson, When Urban Adolescents Choose Abortion: Effects on Education, Psychological Status and Subsequent Pregnancy, 21 Fam. Plan. Persp. 248, 250 (1989).

46. 110 S.Ct. 2926 (1990).

47. The Supreme Court held that the two-parent notification requirement was constitutional as long as a judicial bypass procedure existed. *Id.* at 2950–2951, 2969–2971. Female adolescents are therefore burdened by notifying both parents or undergoing a court procedure—both forms of intrusion will cause many adolescents to delay or to refrain from obtaining an abortion, despite the fact that the pregnancy is unintended and unwanted. What I find puzzling about the Court's ruling is that the Court apparently ruled that a judicial bypass—which itself is burdensome, stressful, and not guaranteed to

yield a positive result for the petitioner—can undo the unconstitutionality of the two-parent notification requirement. . . .

48. *Id.* at 2937 (noting that the state "affirmatively disavow[ed] . . . state interest as a basis for upholding the law").

49. Ironically, pregnant adolescents are themselves potential parents but receive no respect by the state for that potential parenthood (although the state does prefer to refer to the pregnant adolescent as a "mother" during the course of her pregnancy). If the state really viewed the fetus inside the pregnant woman as a child then it would have had to give the pregnant adolescent as much respect, as a parent, as it gave the parents of the pregnant adolescent.

50. See Harris v. McRae, 448 U.S. 297 (1980). . . .

51. See Bellotti v. Baird, 443 U.S. 622, 640 (1979). . . .

52. See Geduldig v. Aiello, 417 U.S. 484, 494–95 (1974). . . .

53. [442 U.S. 256 (1979)].

54. See generally Sylvia Law, Rethinking Sex and the Constitution, 132 U. Pa. L. Rev. 955, 983 (1984) (describing the numerous criticisms of *Geduldig* as a "cottage industry").

55. Akron v. Akron Center for Reproductive Health, Inc., 462 U.S. 416, 453 (1983) (O'Connor, J., dissenting).

56. See Bellotti v. Baird, 443 U.S. 622, 640–641 (1979) (permitting state to require parental consultation in the abortion decision). As Justice O'Connor has explained, the Court has extended the liberty interest to choose an abortion to adolescents but with some "important limitations." Hodgson v. Minnesota, 110 S.Ct. 2926, 2949 (O'Connor, J. concurring).

57. This view is similar to the general perspective articulated by John Hart Ely. See John Hart Ely, Democracy and Distrust: A Theory of Judicial Review 135–170 (1980) (courts should protect constitutional rights irrespective of why they are denied, and should also strive to protect politically weak minorities where legislative action is harmful to such minorities).

Unfortunately, even if I could persuade the Court to modify the *Feeney* test, as I have suggested, one major doctrinal problem might remain. In equal protection analysis, we are accustomed to talking about the impact of a policy on one particular subgroup that receives close scrutiny by the courts such as African-Americans or women. The Supreme Court has refused to use close scrutiny in analyzing the impact of restrictive abortion policies on a subgroup of women—poor, minority women. See Harris v. McRae, 448 U.S. 297, 322–326 (1980) (applying a rational relationship test, as there was no suspect classification, and rejecting an equal protection claim by poor, minority women). In the Title VII context, some courts have recognized that it is unlawful to have combined categories, such as African-American women, face different treatment; nevertheless, the courts have never defined a subclass on the basis of class, race, and sex terms. See, e.g., Jefferies v. Harris County Community Action Ass'n, 615 F.2d 1025, 1032 (5th Cir.1980) (recognizing the Title VII forbids race or sex discrimination, which includes discrimination based on a combination of those categories). Moreover, the recognition that African-American women constitute a protected class has not been broadly utilized under Title VII, nor has it been introduced into equal protection doctrine. It is important for this concept of combined categories to be introduced into equal protection doctrine in order for legal doctrine to be sensitive to the essentialism critique. . . .

Reproductive Freedom and Violence Against Women: Where Are the Intersections?

LORI L. HEISE

. . . GENDER VIOLENCE is a major yet often underrecognized obstacle to reproductive choice. In both the abortion rights movement in the United States and the reproductive health movement globally, the "enemy" of self-determination and choice is usually seen as imposing from the top down. In industrial countries, it is the government—through the courts, the legislature, and bureaucratic rulemaking—that threatens to "take away" women's reproductive autonomy. The image is one of the public sphere invading that which is private—of the state interfering with a woman's right to control her own body.

In developing countries, activism has focused on resisting what are considered programs and technologies imported from industrialized countries that emphasize population control and contraceptive efficacy over the health and autonomy of women. Instead, women's health advocates have argued for a women-centered approach to reproductive care that emphasizes choice, safety, and services to address the full range of women's reproductive health needs.

Nonetheless, there is an enemy of choice that exists at the level of our most personal relationships—one that does not often enter into official discussions on reproductive choice: male violence. Violence, in the form of rape, sexual abuse or battering affects women's ability to protect themselves from unwanted pregnancy and sexually transmitted diseases (STDs), including AIDS. Even where violence is not used to control women's behavior, the possibility of violence helps create an atmosphere of female deference to male decision-making regarding sexual behavior and contraceptive use. These interpersonal barriers to women's reproductive autonomy can be as significant as government policy, if not more so. . . .

It is generally assumed that women in consensual unions have greater say over their sexual lives than victims of rape. But here too gender power relations—often enforced through violence—greatly shape women's sexual and reproductive decision-making.

Women's decisions regarding family planning use are a case in point. The family planning literature documents that for many women, fear of male reprisal greatly lim-

Lori L. Heise, "Reproductive Freedom and Violence Against Women: Where Are the Intersections?," *Journal of Law, Medicine & Ethics*, 21, no. 2 (1993):206–16. Reprinted with permission of the Society of Law, Medicine & Ethics and Lori L. Heise.

its their ability to use contraception.[1] Men in many cultures react negatively to birth control because they think it signals a woman's intentions to be unfaithful (the logic is that protection against pregnancy allows a woman to be promiscuous). Where children are a sign of male virility, a woman's attempt to use contraception may also be interpreted as an affront to her partner's masculinity.[2] While male attitudes are not always defining, studies from countries as diverse as Mexico, South Africa, and Bangladesh have found that partner approval is the single greatest predictor of women's contraceptive use.[3] When partners disapprove, women either forgo contraception, leaving themselves open to the risks of incessant childbearing, or they resort to family planning methods they can use without their partners' knowledge.

The unspoken reality behind this subterfuge is that women can be beaten if they do not comply with men's sexual and childbearing demands. . . .

In other countries, legal provisions requiring spousal permission before dispensing birth control can actually put women at increased risk of violence. According to Pamela Onyango of Family Planning International Assistance, women in Kenya have been known to forge their partner's signature rather than open themselves to violence or abandonment by requesting permission to use family planning services.[4] Nor are Kenyan women alone in their fear of such consequences. Researchers conducting focus groups on sexuality in Mexico and Peru found that women held similar concerns—fear of violence, desertion, or accusations of infidelity—if they brought up birth control.[5] Not surprisingly, when family planning clinics in Ethiopia removed their requirement for spousal consent, clinic use rose 26 percent in just a few months.[6] . . .

Often women who are married have even less to say over their sexual lives than they have over birth control. Far from an act of mutual love and respect, sexual intercourse for many women is an unpleasant duty that they tolerate rather than enjoy. In focus group discussions with Mexican women about men, sex and marriage, many women expressed deep resentment about how men treated them in sexual relationships.[7] Women in particular mentioned:

- physical abuse by husbands to coerce the wife's sexual compliance;
- widespread male infidelity;
- men's authoritarian attitudes toward their wives;
- threats of abandonment if wives failed to meet their husbands' sexual demands or their demands for more children; and
- an abiding sense of depersonalization, humiliation and physical dissatisfaction during sex.

Perhaps more than anything, the Spanish phrase women commonly use for sex captures their sentiment: "el me use" (he uses me). Fortunately, the women of this study did not appear resigned to their fate. Most felt it was both appropriate and necessary for women to struggle for fairer and more considerate treatment.

Men's superior strength and their control over economic resources make women's struggle for dignity and sexual self determination difficult. . . . Studies evaluating natural family planning in the Philippines and sexual attitudes among the women in

Guatemala also emphasize forced sex by partners, especially when the men arrive home drunk.[8] The summary document of the Guatemalan focus groups observes, "It is clear from the replies the women gave . . . that being forced through violence to have sex by their partner is not an uncommon experience for Guatemalan women." When asked if a wife could refuse her husband, most women said no because of their husbands' superior strength. . . .[9]

[T]he price of self-defense is high. An analysis of news articles published on wife abuse in Thailand observes, "It is noteworthy that some wives were killed just because they refused sexual intercourse with their husbands."[10] This observation shows well the impact that violence or terroristic threats can have on women's sexual autonomy and reproductive freedom.

The specter of AIDS adds a new critical dimension to gender power relations and reproductive rights. So far, most AIDS prevention programs have recommended partner reduction, condom promotion, and STD treatment as ways to prevent transmission of HIV. But men's physical strength and women's economic dependence on men greatly limit women's ability to protect themselves.

Strategies based on "negotiating" condom use, for example, assume an equity of power between women and men that simply does not exist in many relationships. . . . The problem is that given today's options, "negotiating condom use" is the only self preservation strategy available to women. Clearly things can and should be done to help empower women and strengthen their negotiating position. Women need independent sources of income and training in how best to broach the subject of condom use. And AIDS programs must begin drawing on women's demonstrated capacity for collective action. But women desperately need a new option for protecting themselves against sexually transmitted diseases—one that puts control of the technology into women's hands.

In this regard, women are uniquely vulnerable. AIDS activists are empowering men by giving them information, and men have a technology—condoms—to use on their own behalf. Advocates are reaching IV drug users as well, and they have protective technologies, namely clean needles and bleach, that are within their power. Only women, who are up against centuries of social conditioning that grants sexual license to men, are being asked to defend themselves without a method that they control.

Recently, after pressure from women's organizations and other health nonprofits, there has been increasing interest in exploring female controlled options of HIV prevention. In March, the Population Council in New York published, "The Development of Microbicide: A New Method of HIV Prevention for Women," a paper that argues that it is indeed possible to develop a vaginal product women could use to protect themselves from HIV without their partner's knowledge. (The paper also evaluates the potential of other female controlled methods such as the female condom.) As the paper concludes: "Only a persistent and conscious neglect of women's needs will explain continued inattention to this important area of research."[11] . . .

If one looks at the broader issue of reproductive health rather than the more narrow question of reproductive rights, there are . . . additional links that can be drawn between violence and health. The first involves the impact of battering during pregnancy. . . . While pregnancy should be a time when the health and well-being of women are especially protected, surveys suggest that pregnant women are prime targets for abuse. Results from a large prospective study of battery during pregnancy among low-income in Baltimore and Houston, for example, indicate that one out of *every six* pregnant women is battered during her pregnancy. (The study, published in the Journal of the American Medical Association, followed a stratified cohort of 691 white, African-American and Hispanic women for three years.)[12] Sixty percent of the abused women in this study reported two or more episodes of violence, and they were twice as likely as non-abused women to begin prenatal care in the third trimester. Other studies indicate that women battered during pregnancy run twice the risk of miscarriage and four times the risk of having a low birth weight baby compared with women who are not beaten.[13] Low birth weight is a powerful predictor of a child's survival prospects in the first year of life.

Battering during pregnancy is likely to have an even greater impact on Third World mothers who are already malnourished and overworked. A survey of 342 randomly sampled women in Mexico City revealed that 20 percent of those battered reported blows to the stomach during pregnancy.[14] In another study of 80 battered women who sought judicial intervention against their partners in San Jose, Costa Rica, 49 percent report being beaten during pregnancy. Of these, 7.5 percent reported miscarriages due to the abuse.[15] . . .

Reproductive health activists, especially women from developing countries, have also been instrumental in identifying and challenging violence within the reproductive health system itself. Contrary to the organizing ethic of all medical care—first do no harm—there is ample evidence that "health care" as practiced in some parts of the world, exposes women to increased risk instead of improving their health and well being.

Perhaps the most notorious example of this type of "medical violence" is forced sterilization. During the 1970s, a series of scandals involving sterilization came to light in places as diverse as the United States, Puerto Rico and India.[16] In the United States, for example, instances of involuntary sterilization of poor, minority, and mentally retarded young women during the early 1970s led to the enactment of more stringent sterilization regulations in 1978. The incident that galvanized attention around the issue was the now infamous *Relf* case in which two black teenagers in Alabama were sterilized without their consent or knowledge. Ruling against the government, a federal district court judge found:

> . . . uncontroverted evidence in the record that minors and other incompetents have been sterilized with federal funds and that an indefinite number of poor people have been improperly coerced into accepting a sterilization operation under the threat that various federally supported welfare benefits would be withdrawn unless they submitted to irreversible sterilization.[17]

Recent talk in state legislatures of linking certain welfare benefits to a woman's willingness to submit to surgical implantation of Norplant harkens back to the logic and rationale of this early sterilization abuse.

While today there are few instances of direct coercion in cases of sterilization, women's health advocates still worry that various forms of "structural coercion" lead women to choose sterilization when some other form of birth control may better suit their needs. In Brazil and Puerto Rico, for example, government policies severely limit access to reversible contraceptives, such as condoms, diaphragms, and IUDs. As a result, 60 percent of Puerto Rican female contraceptive users and 41 percent of those from Brazil, are sterilized.[18] According to a World Bank report on women's reproductive health in Brazil, "many women resort to sterilization despite its irreversibility because of the lack of alternative methods."[19]

Clearly, sterilization as a method is not inherently bad. Many women who have completed their childbearing welcome sterilization as a way to put aside permanently concerns of unwanted pregnancy. But sterilization must be offered without pressure or incentives, and with the full knowledge and consent of the woman. As reproductive rights activist Betsy Hartman observes, "In the right hands [sterilization] can be a powerful tool of reproductive freedom. In the wrong hands it is an intrusive act of physical violence, no matter how clean the surgeon's gloves. . . ."[20]

Elsewhere, women's health activists have begun to challenge the brutish, humiliating treatment that women sometimes endure at the hands of the professional health care system. Women's treatment during pregnancy and birth are areas of particular concern. In Sao Paulo, Brazil, for example, the hospital system has so few beds reserved for poor people that pregnant women in labor often have to go from hospital to hospital to find an institution willing to accept them. A recent maternal mortality survey documents a case in which a low-income woman in labor had to go to 11 different hospitals before one agreed to admit her.[21]

Once there, a woman's treatment does not necessarily improve. According to Dr. Simone Grilo Dinez of the Sexuality and Health Collective of Sao Paulo, a woman in labor is not allowed contact with anyone she knows, she has a 50 percent chance of having a caesarean section, and a 15–40 percent chance of contracting a hospital infection. Childbirth is largely orchestrated for the convenience of doctors, which explains in part why Sao Paulo's caesarean rate is more than three times what is considered medically necessary.[22] Women in Brazil and elsewhere recount stories of being ridiculed for crying out during childbirth, with degrading comments like, "I wonder how loud you were screaming when you were lying with your husband." One Mexican women recalls, "It all resembled torture . . . it seemed they were punishing us all the way, for a great sin, the sin of having enjoyed some past moment of pleasure."[23] Dr. Grilo Dinez says that Brazilian doctors withhold anaesthesia when performing D & Cs after illegal abortions for the same reason—to make women pay. Similar accusations have been made against physicians operating on native women in Canada.[24]

Many activists have come to see such treatment as violence perpetrated by the medical system itself. [P]rogressive policy-makers have come to realize that the success or failure of different health programs hinges in part on how clients are treated by service providers.[25]

A final link between violence and the reproductive health care system itself is the growing use of violence by anti-abortion forces in the United States. Between 1984 and 1991 there were 47 reported arson attacks on abortion clinics, 24 bombings, 39 attempted bombings or arson attacks, 76 death threats to providers, 20 burglaries, and 497 instances of invasion or vandalism.[26] More recently, the anti-choice, fundamentalist group, "Operation Rescue," has taken to blocking women's access to clinics by physically barring their way. Since 1988, at least 286 clinics have been blockaded by pro-life demonstrators and more than 28,943 arrests have been made for assault, trespass and invasion.[27] Perhaps no other example better illustrates the implications of violence for reproductive freedom than the use of physical force to prevent women from exercising their constitutional right to abortion.

Even this cursory review of violence and reproductive health suggests a broad area of overlap between the concerns of the reproductive rights movement and the issue of violence against women. The question then becomes how can this intersection be translated into policy suggestions useful for those working on reproductive health issues and gender violence.

Clearly the most important recommendation is that the two movements better exploit their potential to serve as natural allies. Legal changes related to domestic violence or rape, for example, are centrally important to many women's reproductive freedom. The women's health movement can help mobilize its constituency to provide crucial political support on important initiatives regarding violence. Likewise, on issues of reproductive rights and health, advocates working in the field of violence should recognize that the ability to control one's own body is often a prerequisite to taking control of one's life. Unwanted children make it more difficult for women to leave abusive relationships and powerlessness in the reproductive sphere reinforces women's sense of powerlessness over their lives in general.

On a programmatic level there is much the reproductive health/rights community can do to reflect the reality of violence in many women's lives. First, the existence of forced sex and violence should be openly acknowledged in the rhetoric and demands of the reproductive health movement. Calls for reproductive autonomy should condemn negation of choice at the individual level (e.g., through marital rape) as well as at the level of the state.

Further, advocates' positions on various reproductive technologies should acknowledge that some women need methods that they can use without their partner's cooperation or consent. In their zeal to protect women from potentially harmful methods—such as Depo-Provera and other injectables—reproductive rights activists have at times found themselves at odds with the very women they are attempting to serve. Experience has shown that for women living with partners who object to contraceptive use (especially violent partners), the ability to use a method surreptitiously may override other long term safety concerns in the minds of some women. . . . This it not to say that dangerous methods should be approved just because they are convenient. Rather, it is a plea that health activists respect the primacy of "safety from violence" in some women's sexual and reproductive decision-making.

Reproductive health care providers can also play an important role in identifying and referring survivors of sexual assault, child sexual abuse and battering. By virtue of their on-going contact with women throughout their lives, family planning providers, nurses, and prenatal care clinicians are especially well positioned to identify and counsel victims of abuse. . . .

The cooperation of reproductive health workers is especially important in politically repressive countries where women are unlikely to seek help from the police or other governmental authorities. These same women may admit abuse, however, when questioned gently in private by a supportive health care provider. . . .

At the same time, advocates working to combat violence must fight for alternatives that grant women as much reproductive autonomy as possible, given the presence of violence in many women's lives. The top priority on this front would be to join forces with women's health advocates and AIDS activists to demand the development of a safe, effective female-controlled virucide that women could use vaginally to protect themselves from HIV and other STDs. Even though two expert groups of scientists—one sponsored by the Population Council and another convened in Great Britain by the Medical Research Council—have agreed that such a product could feasibly be developed, there has been little serious effort to pursue this line of research.[28] Both the reproductive health movement and battered women's advocates should marshall their constituencies to lobby for more research on female-controlled methods.

Finally, we need more and better research into the impact that sexual victimization appears to have on individuals' sexual risk-taking behavior as adults. This new line of research suggests that some of the most intractable reproductive health issues of our time—teenage pregnancy, STDs, drug use during pregnancy—may be linked to unresolved issues around sexual victimization. Like it or not, the intersection of violence and reproductive decision-making is showing up in the realities of women's lives. Both movements had better organize to confront it.

Notes

1. Ruth Dixon-Mueller, Sexuality, Gender, and Reproductive Health, draft paper prepared for the International Women's Health Coalition, New York (1992).

2. Chris Elias & Lori Heise, The Development of Microbicide: A New Method of HIV Prevention for Women, Working Paper No. 6 (New York: The Population Council, 1993).

3. By no means is male approval always the greatest determinant of contraceptive use. For studies indicating where it is, see Men—New Focus for Family Planning Programs, Population Reports Series J, no. 33 (1986). Bangladesh data from D. Lawrence Kincaid et al., Family Planning and the Empowerment of Women in Bangladesh, paper presented at the 199th Annual Meeting of the American Public Health Association, Atlanta, Nov. 13, 1991.

4. Suzanna Stout Banwell, Law, Status of Women and Family Planning in Sub-Saharan Africa: A Suggestion for Action 14 (Nairobi: The Pathfinder Fund, 1990).

5. Mexico example from Evelyn Folch-Lyon, Luis Macorra & S. Bruce Schearer, Focus Group and Survey Research on Family Planning in Mexico, 12 Stud. Fam. Plan.

409–432 (1981). Peru example from Alfredo Fort, Investigating the Social Context of Fertility and Family Planning: A Qualitative Study in Peru, 15 Int'l Fam. Plan. Persp. 88–94 (1989).

6. Rebecca Cook & Deborah Maine, Spousal Veto over Family Planning Services, 77 Am. J. Pub. Health 339 (1987).

7. Folch-Lyon et al., *supra* note 5.

8. Philippines data cited in Laurie Liskin, Periodic Abstinence: How Well Do New Approaches Work? Population Reports, Population Information Program, Johns Hopkins Univ. (1981).

9. Preliminary Report, Guatemala City Women: Empowering a Vulnerable Group for HIV Prevention, (Guatemala City: DataPro SA and the Asociacion Guatemalteca para la Prevencion y Control del SIDA, 1991).

10. Siriporn Skrobanek, Violence Against Women in the Family: The Case of Thailand, cited in Archavanitkul and Pramualratana, Factors Affecting Women's Health in Thailand (Bangkok: Foundation for Women).

11. Elias & Heise, *supra* note 2.

12. Judith McFarlane et al., Assessing for Abuse During Pregnancy: Severity and Frequency of Injuries and Associated Entry into Prenatal Care, 267 J. Am. Med. Soc'y 3176 (1992).

13. Evan Stark et al., Wife Abuse in the Medical Setting: An Introduction for Health Personnel. Monograph #7, (Washington, D.C.: Office of Domestic Violence, 1981): Linda F. Bullock & Judith McFarlane, The Birth-Weight Battering Connection, Am. J. Nursing 1153 (1989).

14. Rosario Valdez Santiago & Elizabeth Shrader Cox, Violencia Domestica: Caracteristicas y Alternativas de Solucion en Mexico, paper presented at "Leading the Way Out," an international conference on violence against women sponsored by the Global Fund for Women, Menlo Park, California, 1991.

15. Juan Gerardo Ugalde, Sindrome de la Mujer Agredida, In Mujer 5 (San Jose, Costa Rica: Cefemima, 1988).

16. Rosalind Petchesky, Abortion and Woman's Choice: The State, Sexuality, and Reproductive Freedom (Northeastern Univ. Press, 1990).

17. Quoted in Rosalind Petchesky, Reproduction, Ethics, and Public Policy: The Federal Sterilization Regulations, Hastings Center Report, Oct. 1979.

18. Jodi Jacobson, Women's Reproductive Health: The Silent Emergency (Washington, D.C.: Worldwatch Institute, 1991).

19. Helen Saxenian, Brazil: Women's Reproductive Health, unpublished draft, World Bank, Dec. 29, 1989.

20. Betsy Hartmann, Reproductive Rights and Wrongs 242 (South End Press, 1995).

21. Dr. Simone Grilo Dinez, personal communication, June 7, 1991.

22. Brazil has the highest rate of caesarean section deliveries in the world. In 1981 an estimated 31 percent of all births were by caesarean compared with under 10 percent in the Netherlands, 15 percent in England and Wales, 20 percent in Canada, and 25 percent in the United States. . . . See Helen Saxenian, Brazil: Women's Reproductive Health (draft) (Washington, D.C.: World Bank, 1989).

23. Health Services and Maternity in Mexico, Women's Global Network for Reproductive Rights, Newsletter 36, July–September 1991.

24. Mary Eberts, Emerging Legal Issues in Health Care, paper presented at the 3rd International Conference of the American Society of Law and Medicine, Toronto, Ontario, July 1992.

25. Barbara Mensch, Quality of Care: A Neglected Dimension," in Marge Koblinsky, Judith Timyan & Jill Gay eds., Women's Health: A Global Perspective (Westview Press, 1993).

26. Incidents of Violence and Disruption Against Abortion Providers (Washington, D.C.: National Abortion Federation, 1991).

27. *Id.*

28. Report of the Virucide Meeting, sponsored by the Medical Research Council, Margaret Pyke Center, London, Apr. 12, 1991.

C. Reproductive Technology and Adoption

Introduction

THE ISSUE OF WOMEN'S reproductive freedom currently centers on the new reproductive technologies.[1] Primary among these are *in vitro* fertilization (IVF), embryo transplants, and surrogate motherhood. Several social conditions contributed to the development and use of these technologies: an increase in infertility resulting from delayed childbearing, harmful contraceptive methods, and pelvic inflammatory disease; and the shortage of infants for adoption.[2] Whereas feminist concern with reproductive control formerly focused on the means to prevent reproduction (contraception and abortion), contemporary concerns address the means to facilitate reproduction.[3]

Many feminists oppose such technology. The vehemence of their opposition is all the more surprising in the face of widespread feminist support for reproductive freedom in contraception and abortion.[4] Foremost among the issues raised by the new reproductive technologies are the implications of the technology for the subordination of women. A controversial subject of debate is whether the new technologies enhance or impede women's equality.

The controversy raises the equality versus difference debate, which has figured prominently in maternity policies and occupational segregation, in yet another context. Its reemergence is not surprising, because the reproductive technologies lie at the intersection of motherhood and employment.[5] Flora Davis characterizes the controversy thus:

> [T]he feminist divide surfaces once again. Equality feminists argued that a woman had a right to try test-tube fertilization or surrogate motherhood if she wanted to; the choice should be hers. Difference feminists, convinced that women needed special treatment (in this case, protection), insisted that some of the new

technologies should be banned or at least recognized for what they were—men's latest attempts to control female fertility and make use of women's bodies.[6]

Surrogacy, despite the small number of surrogate mothers,[7] has provoked the most heated debate. The practice first came to public attention in 1976, when a woman advertised for a "healthy, blue-eyed woman who is willing to carry my husband's child."[8] Articles slowly began appearing in the legal literature, culminating in a vast body of literature.[9] Legal professionals were influential in the practice from its beginning, many establishing commercial surrogacy organizations.[10]

Feminist battle lines were drawn in the case of In the Matter of Baby M.[11] Feminists submitted *amici curiae* briefs to the New Jersey Supreme Court on both sides of the issue. The National Association of Surrogate Mothers argued that surrogacy enhanced women's control of reproduction; opponents argued that reproductive technologies commercialized reproduction and inhibited women's freedom and opportunities.[12] In the case, a married couple entered into a contract with Mary Beth Whitehead for her to be inseminated with the husband's sperm. When Whitehead gave birth, she was unable to relinquish the child and revoked the contract. The parties sought judicial resolution. Upholding the contract, the trial court awarded custody to the couple based on the best-interests-of-the-child standard and recognized a constitutional right of privacy to make procreative choices that included surrogacy. Reversing, the New Jersey Supreme Court held the surrogacy contract violative of public policy and rejected the couple's constitutional claims. Nonetheless, the court awarded custody to the couple (conferring visitation on Whitehead) based on the best-interests standard.

The case prompted considerable legislative activity. In its aftermath, 27 states introduced 76 bills; 10 state commissions studied the issue; and 4 states made surrogacy contracts unenforceable.[13] By the end of 1990, 13 states had legislation.[14] Although most statutes make surrogacy agreements void, a few permit such arrangements subject to state regulation.[15] The National Conference of Commissioners on Uniform State Laws, as well as the Family Law Section of the American Bar Association, have promulgated model legislation.[16] In addition, a number of countries established commissions to recommend legislation,[17] the most renowned of which was the British Warnock Committee.

As in the pornography campaign, feminist forces quickly coalesced around the surrogacy issue. Both liberal and radical feminists opposed surrogacy in legislative hearings.[18] On this battleground, as in the pornography campaign, antisurrogacy feminists aligned with conservative groups normally thought of as antifeminist.[19]

Feminist Perspectives

Commentators date the origins of feminist responses to the new reproductive technology to the mid-1960s.[20] Women first hailed the liberating effects of oral contraceptives but later became disillusioned with medicalization of childbirth, the health risks of contraceptives, the prioritization of the fetus, and the limitation of access to technology based on age, ethnicity, social class, sexual orientation, and disability.[21]

Several features characterize a feminist perspective on reproductive technologies. According to Christine Overall, such a perspective (1) reflects the broad range of issues pertaining to women's role in reproduction; (2) is critical of taken-for-granted assumptions about reproduction; and (3) explores the implications of the technologies, especially their effects on women and children.[22] Other feminists identify feminist values in the feminist perspective. These include respect for the individual; the incorporation of personal experience into political and ethical judgments; a concern with autonomy and choice; a focus on the wholeness of the individual, the human community, and the community of women; and a belief in connectedness and nonhierarchism.[23] Lori Andrews identifies additional feminist concerns: the social context of infertility; exploitation; medicalization resulting in women's loss of control over their bodies; and financial and social restrictions on access.[24]

Liberal Feminist Perspectives

Liberal feminists are the staunchest advocates of the new reproductive technology. With their emphasis on free choice, they believe that surrogacy contracts should be valid if entered into voluntarily. Their support is consistent with liberal ideology affirming the realization of self-fulfillment with minimal state intervention.

Some liberal feminist advocates of the contractual model, (including Lori Andrews, Marjorie Shultz, Nadine Taub, and Carmel Shalev),[25] recognize the relationship between reproductive rights and equality. Andrews fears that a ban on surrogacy would impede equality.[26] She reminds feminists that, in the past, protective legislation foreclosed economic opportunities.[27] Moreover, she worries that government regulation of surrogacy may lead to increasing restrictions on contraceptive choice and abortion.[28]

Marge Shultz, who shares Andrews's concern with gender equality, advocates a contract approach of "intent-based parenthood."[29] This gender-neutral approach would "recognize the importance and the legitimacy of individual efforts to project intentions and decisions into the future."[30] Shultz's influence on subsequent case law is discussed in an essay herein by Anita Allen. Nadine Taub, sharing the concern with equality, also supports surrogacy. For her, legal recognition would respect woman's decision making,[31] and expand employment opportunities.[32]

Some liberal feminists support surrogacy based on other feminist concerns. Sistare, for example, bases her support on autonomy in reproductive decision making, which she defines as women's "freedom to control their bodies, their lives, their reproductive powers, and to determine the social use of those reproductive capacities."[33] Hall defines this interest similarly.[34]

Some liberal feminists point to the benefits of surrogacy. Purdy, for example, highlights the transfer of pregnancy burdens to women at lower risk; the creation of opportunities for single women and lesbians to form families; and creation of a means of reproduction that can be controlled by women.[35]

Many liberal feminists rebut the charge that surrogacy exploits women. Some question whether surrogacy poses more serious occupational hazards than other occupations.[36] Ruth Macklin labels the exploitation argument paternalistic.[37] Other liberal feminists discount the likelihood of exploitation.[38] Advocates of surrogacy argue that surrogacy, rather than devaluing motherhood, promotes respect for it.

> It would do so in the capitalist mode of paying well for what is deemed rare and precious. It would also encourage recognition that women—many women—really do enjoy the experiences of pregnancy and giving birth. . . . Those who fear that maternity and women's reproductive role will be devalued by surrogacy ought to reconsider in light of this possibility.[39]

Liberal feminists deplore critics' attempt to prohibit women from benefiting from their reproductive capacities. Therein Sistare notes an irony:

> [Why is there] this new fear of capitalist exploitation just when women have attained special access to the capitalist game—access not open to men and largely independent of traditional social controls[?][40]

Sistare hypothesizes that critics fear that "women's reproductive services will no longer be cheap or available on demand."[41] Andrews concurs, charging that a concern with exploitation masks the real issue: "[I]t is the underlying activity, not just its potentially exploitative nature that is horrifying to many."[42]

Some liberal feminists offer only qualified support of surrogacy. However, no consensus emerges from this middle ground. Field, for example, argues that surrogacy contracts should be permitted but subject to regulation, enabling the biological mother to revoke her consent until the child is given to the contracting couple. If the birth mother revokes consent, Field suggests that the father still may choose "to develop and maintain a relationship with the biological child,"[43] in which case he incurs liability for child support. Like Field, Taub urges recognition of surrogacy subject to the biological mother's postbirth consent. However, Taub does not define the period for revocation.[44] Although uncertainty and litigation may result, Taub believes such costs must be accepted.[45]

A few scholars support surrogacy based on liberal, but not particularly feminist, values. Richard Posner in an essay herein, for example, supports surrogacy based on the laissez-faire principle that individuals should pursue their self-interest in contractual arrangements with minimal state interference. John Robertson defends surrogacy based on the procreative right of the infertile couple,[46] pointing out that prohibition constitutes "unjustified paternalism,"[47] since the surrogate made a free and informed choice.

Another advocate, Peter Schuck, defends surrogacy on economic and moral grounds.[48] Schuck counters the charge that surrogacy is alienating by analogizing it to the "venerable practice" of wet nurse.[49] He also disagrees that economic coercion undercuts the surrogate's autonomy,[50] arguing that the surrogate's economic status should not vitiate consent.[51] Feminists criticize such liberal, but nonfeminist, views in the essays herein.

It is important to add that not all liberal feminists support surrogacy. Some charge that it violates public policy;[52] infringes on the biological mother's right to privacy and autonomy;[53] violates the Thirteenth Amendment ban on slavery;[54] poses harmful consequences for children;[55] and, dehumanizes women.[56] Their concerns mirror those of adherents of other feminist schools of thought.

Radical Feminist Perspectives

Radical feminists are the most outspoken opponents of the new reproductive technology. Paradoxically, early radical feminist Shulamith Firestone hailed the new technology.[57] Viewing reproduction as the source of women's oppression, Firestone envisioned a feminist revolution, analogous to a Marxist socialist revolution, that would enable women to acquire control of fertility, thereby eliminate their dependence on man, and ultimately end the patriarchal family.[58]

Contemporary radical feminists almost universally reject Firestone's views on reproductive technology.[59] Radical feminist opposition has taken the form of testimony at national and international legislative hearings, panels at international conferences, and the establishment of an international feminist organization (Feminist International Network of Resistance to Reproductive and Genetic Engineering, or FINRRAGE).[60] At one international hearing, a radical feminist proposed adoption of the MacKinnon-Dworkin civil rights approach (from the pornography campaign) to enable women to file malpractice complaints against physicians because reproductive technology is a "'violation against the human rights of women.' "[61]

Issues of consent and choice figure prominently in radical feminist discourse. Radical feminists criticize the liberal framework that defends reproductive technologies as the exercise of free choice.[62] They also criticize the notion of choice as a private right. They charge that recognition of a public-private distinction reinforces women's oppression by minimizing the importance of social context in reproductive decision making.[63]

Many radical feminists question the meaning of a woman's consent.[64] Arditti, Klein, and Minden query: "[H]ow can women choose freely in a society where the right to choose must be bought?"[65] Pateman scoffs at the view that surrogacy rests on freedom of contract: "Ironies never cease in the matter of women and contract. After the long history of exclusion of women from contract, the surrogacy contract is presented as a woman's contract."[66] Both Dworkin and Corea criticize the surrogate's freedom of choice as socially constructed—so conditioned by societal views of infertility and maternity as not to permit choice.[67]

Radical feminists also highlight factors that undermine women's consent, such as issues of race, class, age, marital status, and sexual orientation.[68] They attribute women's free choice to false consciousness, deluding themselves into believing that their choice is genuine.[69] Further, they charge that the resources spent to ensure the choice of a few will backfire by resulting in fewer medical resources for others.[70]

Radical feminists distinguish issues of abortion from those of reproductive technology. Some argue that the meaning of reproductive freedom now must be reassessed.

> For feminists the issue then becomes one of choice versus control. Within the area of abortion, we claimed the "right to choose," but I argue that we mean, the "right to control" our own bodies. We have then to ask whether the new reproductive technologies give women greater control over our lives. The evidence . . . shows that they patently do not.[71]

Scutt, concurring that the terminology of "choice" is no longer appropriate, suggests that choice is now "being used against women and women's rights."[72]

Radical feminists express alarm about the consequences of exercising reproductive choice. They fear that women and motherhood will be threatened; dehumanization will result from becoming "test-tube women,"[73] "living laboratories,"[74] or a "mother machine."[75] They worry that women will be rendered "obsolete as childbearers";[76] the medical profession will usurp greater control over reproduction;[77] the new reproductive technologies infringe women's self-determination,[78] and "brainwash" women into believing that they are inferior to "artificial wombs."[79] Whereas some radical feminists suggest woman-control of the technology as the solution, others disagree.[80]

Victimization imagery is prominent in radical feminist views. As one radical feminist graphically describes:

> [W]omen are dismembered for science's sake in labs, and embryos are transferred, replaced, divided, frozen, flushed out. . . . "real" life violence against women increases daily.[81]

Radical feminists also fear that the new reproductive technologies, by fostering divisiveness, constitute a war against women.[82]

Their focus on victimization leads many radical feminists to analogize surrogacy to prostitution. Scutt points out that in both practices, others control women's bodies.[83] Pateman, although finding contracts in both surrogacy and prostitution to be the products of capitalism,[84] believes surrogacy is more objectionable because the self is more intimately involved.[85]

Perhaps the most famous analogy of surrogacy and prostitution is found in Dworkin's formulation of "the brothel model" and "the farming model."[86] The farming model characterizes motherhood. Surrogacy is characterized by the brothel model. In the latter, women sell body parts and acts. The woman is "inferior, subservient, and used. . . . Her function is limited, specialized, sex-specific, and intensely and intrinsically dehumanizing."[87]

Radical feminists also explore the patriarchal implications of surrogacy. They believe that surrogacy reaffirms patriarchy by its recognition of father's rights.[88] For Pateman, surrogacy transforms contract doctrine, representing a new version of patriarchy.[89] Before the advent of surrogacy, she theorizes, maternity was certain; paternity was dependent on woman's testimony. Surrogacy alters this biological and social fact because men now can be certain of paternity, thereby changing the traditional meaning of fatherhood.[90] The characterization of surrogacy as an aid for infertile women only serves to obscure these patriarchal implications, Pateman charges. She advocates a reconceptualization, treating surrogacy not as a gift from one woman to another, but rather as a recognition of men's demand for a service.[91]

Janice Raymond's analysis of *Baby M.* leads her to conclude that legal recognition of surrogacy affirms "a spermatic market in which liquid assets wield control. The sperm donor has both money and vital fluids. [T]he Rule of Sperm appropriates both woman and child."[92] Raymond redefines surrogacy as "a reproductive *menage à trois,* again with the man at the center."[93]

Radical feminists fear that technology is altering the terms by which men control reproduction.

> Artificial insemination, in vitro fertilization, sex selection, genetic engineering, fetal monitoring, artificial wombs that keep the fetus alive outside the mother's body, fetal surgery, embryo transplants, and eventual cloning . . . make the womb the province of the doctor, not the woman; . . . all make reproduction controllable by men on a scale heretofore unimaginable.[94]

The concern with increased control of reproduction by men and by a male medical establishment is shared by other radical feminists.[95] Such views contribute to profound pessimism on the part of radical feminists.[96]

Prominent radical feminist Catharine MacKinnon has had little to say about the new reproductive technologies.[97] Her discussions of reproductive control focus instead on contraception, pregnancy, and abortion.[98] Notwithstanding her silence, some legal scholars theorize applications of MacKinnon's "antisubordination" approach. Both Mahoney and Becker conclude that such an application to surrogacy yields unclear results.[99] If surrogacy exploits women and maintains patriarchy, then MacKinnon's approach should lead to prohibition, Mahoney suggests. On the other hand, she adds, one could argue "that a law prohibiting women from doing what they wish with their bodies is also demeaning [and] the enforcement of contracts may be seen as empowering women, in that it allow them to determine their own fate."[100] Concurring, Becker points out that, although surrogacy might increase the commodification of women, it might also provide economic opportunities.[101]

Some feminist scholars criticize radical feminist views of reproductive technology. Liberal feminist Lynn Paltrow questions the imagery of victimization.[102] Paltrow scoffs at the underlying biological determinism that denigrates women's capabilities. Paltrow also disagrees with the belief that women are passive in the face of technology, because it minimizes women's role in securing reproductive rights.[103]

Paltrow criticizes radical feminists' alarmist vision. Citing the work of Gena Corea ("my writing on the new reproductive technologies [is] a scream of warning to other women")[104] and Viola Roggencamp ("Feminists worldwide need to organize and to expose—and resist—the systematic eradication of women"),[105] Paltrow warns: "[T]he danger is that they leave us in shock, too overwhelmed to act."[106]

Instead, she urges women to be vigilant about their rights.[107] Paltrow refocuses the debate:

> [W]e need to be concerned also about the dangers posed by feminist prescriptions which can divide us and feminist visions which deny our power and our ability to make choices even within the constraints of patriarchy.[108]

Radical feminist views, she believes, endanger victories in the area of reproductive rights generally.[109] For Paltrow, the radical feminist solution of separatism and women-dominated control of reproduction merely poses new problems.[110]

Other feminists add criticisms of radical feminist views. Purdy joins Paltrow in rejecting biological determinism.[111] Purdy labels radical feminist views as "sexist" for characterizing the infertile woman's desire for a child as "unreasonable or immoral."[112] Stanworth points out that the threat to motherhood foreseen by radical feminists actually stems from many other societal conditions (such as increasing materialism and the rising rate of divorce).[113]

Liberals and liberal feminists alike criticize the radical feminist analogy of prostitution to surrogacy. Schuck, for example, distinguishes the phenomena:

> Prostitution, unlike surrogacy, does not advance society's fundamental interest in sustaining family values and creating new, wanted life. Nor is the integrity of the prostitute's choice protected by regulation. Prostitution's close link to violence, substance abuse, degrading behavior, and sexually transmitted diseases such as AIDS are additional distinguishing features.[114]

Purdy, too, rejects the analogy, conceding that, whereas it might have emotional appeal, it rests on a condemnation of "a lazy person's way of exploiting their own 'natural resources'".[115] She terms this a "naive view" of the necessary attributes to success of either a prostitute or a pregnancy.[116]

Theorists also rebut the characterization of surrogacy as exploitation. Like Posner, Purdy finds surrogacy indistinguishable from other services the rich purchase from those less wealthy.[117] She rejects, too, that surrogacy reaffirms patriarchal power, doubting that men want to control reproduction.[118] Stanworth charges that feminists should not join the radical feminists' rejection of reproductive technology, but rather address the problem of infertility through improved research and enhanced access to reproductive technologies.[119]

Marxist Feminist Perspectives

In Marxist feminist writings (less numerous than those of other perspectives), Kelly Oliver criticizes the liberal emphasis on rights and autonomy.[120] Incorporating a Marxist sensitivity to class, she argues that pitting the rights of the biological mother against those of the biological father "conceals social and class interests behind the illusion of formal equality in contract."[121] She refutes the idea that the surrogate is an equal party to the contract. Like radical feminists, Oliver questions the "voluntariness" of surrogates' consent.[122]

Moreover, Oliver criticizes the liberal argument that surrogacy promotes equality. Relying on Dworkin for support, she rejects the analogy equating the surrogate mother with the sperm donor.[123] Oliver also points out that the liberal emphasis on rights obscures the fact that surrogacy benefits men.[124] She charges that class issues in *Baby M.* influenced the custody outcome.[125]

Focusing on the Marxist distinction between alienated and estranged labor leads Oliver to conclude that the surrogate is "doubly estranged." She is estranged from her body and the product of her labor (the child); from the process of production (by being regarded as a machine); from her existence as a social being (by being valued only for reproductive services); and from others (as a result of viewing children as commodities and women as producers of children).[126]

In contrast to Oliver's focus on surrogacy, Gimenez analyzes the significance of reproductive technologies generally.[127] For Gimenez, reproductive technologies constitute a step in the development of science under capitalism.[128] She points out that capitalism relegates women to the private realm of reproduction. However, changes in reproduction and production alter the material conditions of life, which in turn effect changes in consciousness.[129] By separating procreation from sexuality, Gimenez suggests, reproductive technologies will generate new forms of consciousness—"new objects for sale and lease" and "new historical subjects willing to enter in these relations."[130] By clashing with accepted ideas, these technologies will have considerable impact by yielding new conceptualizations about womanhood and motherhood.

Socialist Feminist Perspectives

Socialist feminists have addressed surrogacy by drawing insights from both radical and Marxist perspectives. Socialist feminists share a view with radical feminists: that procreation is historically and socially determined.[131]

Most socialist feminists vehemently oppose surrogacy.[132] They believe that both patriarchy and capitalism contribute to surrogacy. Concurring with radical feminists, they assert that surrogacy reflects a new manifestation of patriarchy in the form of male control over women's reproductive capacities. Surrogacy is "motherhood under capitalism"[133] and reflects "the commodification of children and the proletarianization of motherhood"[134] and the conception "of our bodies and our physical capacities as property, appropriate for sale or rental in the market."[135]

Socialist feminists believe that surrogacy should not be viewed as a private transaction or a matter of individual rights. They insist that individual interests in reproductive freedom are entwined with social concerns.[136]

Socialist feminists also disagree that surrogacy promotes liberal values of equality. For example, socialist feminists criticize *Baby M.* for its reaffirmation of gender inequality. Eisenstein, who believes that a distinction between pregnancy and motherhood would promote equality, argues that *Baby M.* severs the connection, thereby resulting in inequality.[137] For Eisenstein, the trial court adopts the "illusion" of equality by awarding custody to the biological father.[138]

Further, some socialist feminists disagree that surrogacy expands employment opportunities. Gibson suggests that surrogacy will "reinforce existing roles for and attitudes toward women"[139] and "reduce pressures" to expand opportunities for working class women.[140]

Socialist feminists also disagree that surrogacy promotes autonomy in reproductive decisionmaking. They argue instead that it threatens autonomy. Regulation of behavior (for instance, diet) during pregnancy interferes with bodily integrity. Restrictions on the surrogate's right to abortion also violate autonomy.[141] Socialist feminists believe that state regulation would exacerbate rather than cure the infringement.[142]

In addition, socialist feminists criticize liberal assumptions about choice. Some socialist feminists, like radical feminists, disagree that the surrogate is an equal and autonomous party.[143] In addition, Overall criticizes the liberal "free market model" for framing the issue as the existence of reproductive choice.[144]

Overall and Rothman also mourn the loss of choice which surrogacy entails. Overall characterizes these "losses" thus:

> If surrogate motherhood becomes a socially approved "choice", it will affect how women see both their Marxist relationships to their children and the use of their reproductive capacities, and it will further distort the social construction of women's reproductive roles.[145]

Rothman suggests that, in gaining the choice to "control the quality of our children, we may be losing the choice not to control the quality, the choice of simply accepting them as they are."[146] In addition, the expansion of choice for the infertile creates a burden—"of not trying hard enough."[147]

Socialist feminists criticize other features of the liberal perspective, such as the treatment of surrogacy as reproductive labor. For Overall, analogizing surrogacy to reproductive labor serves to expand the commodification of reproduction from merely the sale of reproductive products (sperm) to reproductive services (gestation).[148] She contends that this assumption ignores underlying power relations.[149] Satz has termed socialist feminists who adhere to this view as subscribing to an "asymmetry thesis"[150]—the belief that the treatment of reproductive labor should differ from that of other labor.

These socialist feminist views have been the subject of criticism. Despreaux rejects Rothman's view that reproductive technologies restrict, rather than respect, women's right to choose.[151] Despreaux charges that Rothman frames her argument by reference to the same liberal terminology Rothman discounts. Such a characterization, according to Despreaux, neglects important values of "relationality and connection"[152] which enable women to make reproductive decisions in a socially responsible manner. Socialist feminists, like radical feminists, also have been criticized for their emphasis on victimization. For example, Despreaux criticizes the victimization imagery inherent in Rothman's suggestion that reproductive technology forecloses choice.[153]

Like Marxist feminists, socialist feminists recognize the racial and class issues presented by the new reproductive technologies.[154] Socialist feminists worry about the exploitation of women of color.[155] Some commentators criticize the role of social class in *Baby M.*[156] Socialist feminists note also the element of discriminatory access to reproductive technologies.[157] Many doubt that state regulation would prevent these features.[158]

Some socialist feminists take the Marxist analysis one step further by focusing on the alienation inherent in surrogacy.[159] For Rothman, reproductive technology accelerates a trend in reproductive control: the increasing alienation of the woman, both from labor as well as from the infant.[160] Overall points to several manifestations of alienation: the surrogate "surrenders her individuality"[161] by yielding the use of her body as well as the product of her labor in return for a fee. The requirement of surrender of the infant entails the "extreme" form of alienated labor.[162] The surrogate becomes interchangeable, an incubator without unique attributes.[163]

Socialist feminists, sharing radical feminist concerns, believe that surrogacy, and the new reproductive technologies in general, pose a threat to women.[164] By constraining reproductive freedom, technology increases male control over women's procreative choices.[165] They also believe that the surrogate's exploitation is a given in our class-based society.[166] Gibson suggests that exploitation is economic, social, and psychological:[167] being taken advantage of because of "her limited financial resources and security," "the restricted social roles and resources available to one in her combined gender and economic status," and the impact on the surrogate's self-esteem.[168]

Moreover, socialist feminists echo radical feminist concerns about commodification (that technology leads to the treatment of women and children as commodities).[169] Commodification leads to another criticism—the reemergence of a concern with eugenics. For Rothman, this concern with "quality control" signifies that the pregnant women will be subject to increasing dietary and behavioral restrictions so as not to produce "flawed products."[170] Quality control will also affect any ensuing children.[171] The commodification argument is explored more fully in the essay herein by Radin.

The value of the socialist feminist critique is its theoretical exploration of the implications of reproductive technology for the family. Barrett and McIntosh maintain that the controversy about reproductive technology underscores that the family is constructed by social conditions.[172] These authors suggest that the development of reproductive technology reflects the continuation of a trend in the evolution of family forms that emphasize voluntary and social, more than biological, parenthood.

Many socialist feminists concur that the reproductive technologies contribute to evolving conceptions of motherhood.[173] Stanworth suggests that the technologies "deconstruct" motherhood.[174] Some socialist feminists agree with radical feminists that surrogacy devalues motherhood.[175] Another socialist feminist suggests that surrogacy "pluralize[s] the notion of motherhood"[176]—expanding the definition of mother by differentiating biological and social aspects. Although Eisenstein lauds this objective, she also worries about the consequences.

Socialist feminists situate the new reproductive technologies in the larger social context of the reproductive control movement. One commentator suggests that many of the same foci are involved, including the role of women in the family, the role of medical technology and the medical profession, the needs of society, the relations between men and women, and the function of law.[177] Gordon, similarly, identifies parallels. She notes an increasing determination to exercise reproductive choice, as well as a concern with the implications of separating reproduction from sexuality and marriage.[178]

The essays in this Part enhance our understanding of reproductive technology and the status of women. They reflect a concern with the relationship between gender, family formation, law, and equality. In the first essay, Norma Jean Wikler provides an excellent overview and critique of feminist concerns. She views the legacy of the reproductive technologies as a reconsideration of the meaning of equality.

The next two essays concentrate on surrogacy, presenting a defense of surrogacy from a liberal perspective. For Lori Andrews, feminist principles underlie the debate. Her essay contributes a cogent criticism of radical feminist perspectives. Richard Posner, presenting the case for surrogacy from a legal and economic perspective, subjects surrogacy to the same market analysis as other commercial transactions in which equal, autonomous parties pursue their self-interest. Like Andrews, Posner examines and criticizes radical feminist views.

Gena Corea, a staunch opponent of reproductive technologies, provides the radical feminist rebuttal. In testimony before the California Assembly Judiciary Committee, a portion of which is included here, she criticizes the liberal perspective by analogizing the liberty to procreate noncoitally ("junk liberty") to junk food. She calls attention to the experiences of actual surrogates to buttress her opposition.

Anita Allen, in "The Socio-economic Struggle for Equality: The Black Surrogate Mother," revisits the theme of surrogacy as exploitation. Analogizing surrogacy to the American slave experience, Allen analyzes the case of Johnson v. Calvert,[179] in which an African-American woman served as a surrogate for a white couple. Her essay is an important addition to the small but growing literature exploring the African-American perspective.[180]

Margaret Radin addresses the objection that surrogacy treats women as commodities. Using terminology derived from property law, Radin analyzes surrogacy by means of the concept of "market-inalienability." By this she signifies those items, such as body organs, which are nonsalable although transferable by gift. Contrary to the liberal view in which nearly all objects are commodifiable, Radin concludes that surrogacy is socially undesirable and should not be permitted.[181] Her essay is valuable for its provocative analysis of the analogy between prostitution and surrogacy.

The divergence of thought that these essays represent illustrates a conflict not only in feminist legal theory but also in feminism, itself. Perhaps such a tension may restrict the development of feminist legal theory, for, as one feminist suggests, "it is doubtful whether feminist analysis will develop any further when it remains caught in an opposition between liberation and oppression."[182] Alternatively, it is hoped, the conflict may present an opportunity for greater understanding of the sources of women's subordination and thereby contribute to equality.

Notes

1. For feminist criticism of the nomenclature associated with the new reproductive technologies, see L. Andrews, Alternative Modes of Reproduction, in S. Cohen & N. Taub eds., Reproductive Laws for the 1990s 362 (Humana Press, 1989); B. Roth-

man, Recreating Motherhood: Ideology and Technology in a Patriarchal Society 261 n.3 (W. W. Norton, 1989); R. Tong, Feminist Thought: A Comprehensive Introduction 250 n.65 (Westview Press, 1989). Compare R. Posner, Sex and Reason 420 (Harvard Univ. Press, 1992) (criticizing feminists).

Although the phrase "new reproductive technologies" is utilized here, such technology is not new. See J. Lorber, In Vitro Fertilization and Gender Politics, in E. Baruch, A. d'Adamo & J. Seager eds., Embryos, Ethics and Women's Rights: Exploring the New Reproductive Technologies 119 (Haworth, 1988) (human in vitro fertilization was successful in the United States in 1940s).

2. Capron, Alternative Birth Technologies: Legal Challenges, 29 U.C. Davis L. Rev. 679, 683 (1987). See also L. Gordon, Woman's Body, Woman's Right: A History of Birth Control in America 464 (Penguin, rev. ed. 1990).

3. Gordon, *supra* note 2, at 457.

4. J. Murphy, Is Pregnancy Necessary? Feminist Concerns About Ectogenesis, in H. Holmes & L. Purdy eds., Feminist Perspectives in Medical Ethics 181 (Indiana Univ. Press, 1992).

5. Some feminists characterize the controversy as the intersection of the family and the market. See, e.g., Areen, *Baby M* Reconsidered, 76 Geo. L.J. 1741, 1741 (1988). See generally Olsen, The Family and the Market: A Study of Ideology and Legal Reform, 96 Harv. L. Rev. 1497 (1983).

6. F. Davis, Moving the Mountain: The Women's Movement in America Since 1960, 255–256 (Simon & Schuster, 1991). See also J. Mahoney, An Essay on Surrogacy and Feminist Thought, in L. Gostin ed., Surrogate Motherhood: Politics and Privacy 183, 188 (Indiana Univ. Press, 1990); Gibson, Contract Motherhood: Social Practice in Social Context, 3 Women & Crim. Just. 55, 55–57 (1992) (both recognizing that surrogacy raises the equal treatment/special treatment debate).

7. Approximately 4,000 children were born to surrogates by the end of the 1980s. H. Nelson, Scrutinizing Surrogacy, in H. Holmes ed., Issues in Reproductive Technology I: An Anthology 298 (Garland Press, 1992) (citing Kasindorf, And Baby Makes Four, L.A. Times Mag., Jan. 20, 1991, at 10, which in turn cites Bill Handel of the Center for Surrogate Parenting, Inc.); Singer, The Privatization of Family Law, 1992 Wis. L. Rev. 1443, 1489 (citing Mathews, California Surrogate Stirs Dispute, Wash. Post, Sept. 21, 1990, at A8). Few women breach the contract. See M. Field, Surrogate Motherhood: The Legal and Human Issues 162 n.16 (Harvard Univ. Press, 1988) (of 500 contracts, 495 "have been fulfilled without incident").

8. For sources dating the interest in surrogacy to 1976, see G. Corea, The Mother Machine: Reproductive Technologies from Artificial Insemination to Artificial Wombs 213 (Harper & Row, 1985); Field, *supra* note 7, at 5; N. Keane & D. Breo, The Surrogate Mother 33 (Everest House, 1981). The advertisement is cited in Note, Contracts to Bear a Child, 66 Calif. L. Rev. 611, 611 (1978).

9. For early articles, see Black, Legal Problems of Surrogate Motherhood, 16 New Eng. L. Rev. 373 (1981); Keane, Legal Problems of Surrogate Motherhood, 1980 S. Ill. U. L.J. 147. See also D. Cirasole & J. Seager, Women and Reproductive Technologies: A Partially Annotated Bibliography, in Embryos, Ethics and Women's Rights, *supra* note 1, at 237–259; Field, *supra* note 7, at 201–210; H. Holmes, Contract Pregnancy: An'Annotated Bibliography, in Issues in Reproductive Technology, *supra* note 7, at 381; L. Gostin, Bibliography, in Surrogate Motherhood: Politics and Privacy, *supra* note 6, at 338; P. Spallone & D. Steinberg eds., Made to Order: The Myth of Reproductive and Genetic Progress 231–236 (Pergamon, 1987); M. Stanworth ed., Re-

productive Technologies: Gender, Motherhood and Medicine 201–218 (Univ. Minn. Press, 1987).

10. By 1988, approximately twenty such commercial ventures existed. Gordon, *supra* note 2, at 463. Noel Keane catapulted to fame as the most famous "baby broker." See Gladwell & Sharpe, Meet the Surrogacy Entrepreneur: *Baby M.* Winner, New Republic, May 4, 1987, at 16. Kentucky attorney Katie Brophy and a physician established Surrogate Parenting Associates. California attorney William Handel, another lawyer and a physician, established the Center for Surrogate Parenting, Inc. Philadelphia lawyer Burton Satzberg established Surrogate Mothering, Ltd., with a gynecologist and psychologist. L. Andrews, New Conceptions: A Consumer's Guide to the Newest Fertility Treatments 205 (St. Martin's Press, 1984). See also Nakamura, Behind the "*Baby M.*" Decision: Surrogacy Lawyering Reviewed, 13 Fam. L. Rep. 3019 (June 2, 1987).

11. 525 A.2d 1128 (N.J. Ch. Div. 1987), *aff'd in part, rev'd in part, remanded,* 537 A.2d 1227 (N.J. 1988).

12. For background on these *amici,* see L. Andrews, Between Strangers: Surrogate Mothers, Expectant Fathers, and Brave New Babies 171–182 (Harper & Row, 1989). Nineteen *amici* briefs were filed. Rothenberg, Gestational Surrogacy and the Health Care Professional: *Baby M* and Beyond, in Surrogate Motherhood: Politics and Privacy, *supra* note 6, at 205.

13. Andrews, *supra* note 12, at 229. For a review of legislation pending in 1988, see Taub, Surrogacy, Sorting Through the Alternatives, 4 Berkeley Women's L.J. 285, 286, 287 n.8 (1989–1990).

14. Singer, *supra* note 7, at 1494.

15. Singer cites statutes in Florida, New Hampshire, and Nevada that authorize noncommercial surrogacy agreements permitting the surrogate to revoke consent until a designated time after birth. *Id.* at 1495.

16. Unable to agree, the commissioners drafted alternative approaches. See Unif. Status of Children of Assisted Conception Act (USCACA), §5, 9B U.L.A. 165 (Supp. 1994) ("Alternative B" making such agreements void); Unif. Status of Children of Assisted Conception Act, §§5–9, 9B U.L.A. 158–165 (Supp. 1994) ("Alternative A" permitting surrogacy but subject to regulation). See generally Singer, *supra* note 7, at 1495, n.243. See also American Bar Association Summary of Action on the Delegates 1989 Midyear Meeting 52 (Feb. 6–7, 1989) (House of Delegates adopted USCACA instead of their Model Act).

17. Feinerman, A Comparative Look at Surrogacy, 76 Geo. L.J. 1837, 1837 (1988) (24 countries appointed commissions). See also Field, *supra* note 7, at 22 (discussing Warnock Committee recommendation prohibiting commercial surrogacy); J. Zipper & S. Sevenhuijsen, Surrogacy: Feminist Notions of Motherhood Reconsidered, in Reproductive Technologies: Gender, Motherhood and Medicine, *supra* note 9, at 118, 134 (discussing West German Benda Committee and Dutch Gezondheidsraad Committee).

See also J. Gallagher, Eggs, Embryos and Foetuses: Anxiety and the Law, in Reproductive Technologies: Gender, Motherhood and Medicine, *supra* note 9, at 143–144; Note, Surrogate Parenting: What We Can Learn from Our British Counterparts, 39 Case W. Res. L. Rev. 217 (1988–1989).

18. Two New York women's groups (a NOW chapter and the State Coalition on Women's Legislative Issues) voiced their opposition. Andrews, *supra* note 12, at 222. See also the policy statement from the New York State Task Force on Life and the Law, reprinted in Surrogate Motherhood: Politics and Privacy, *supra* note 6, at 315, and Gena Corea's testimony, herein, at California legislative hearings.

19. See Andrews, *supra* note 12, at 176; Gordon, *supra* note 2, at 457; Zipper & Sevenhuijsen, Surrogacy, in Reproductive Technologies, *supra* note 9, at 136. On the differences between these opponents, see J. Raymond, Fetalists and Feminists: They Are Not the Same, in Made to Order, *supra* note 9, at 58.

20. See Andrews, *supra* note 12, at xiii; M. Stanworth, Birth Pangs: Conceptive Technologies and the Threat to Motherhood, in M. Hirsch & E. Keller eds., Conflicts in Feminism 289 (Routledge, 1990).

21. Stanworth, Reproductive Technologies, *supra* note 9, at 289–290 (characterizing the early period "the honeymoon with technology").

22. C. Overall, Ethics and Human Reproduction: A Feminist Analysis 10–11 (Allen & Unwin, 1987); Overall, Reproductive Ethics: Feminist and Non-Feminist Approaches, 1 Can. J. Women & Law 271, 276–277 (1986). Overall attributes feminist approaches to the emerging field of feminist ethics. Overall, Ethics and Human Reproduction, *supra,* at 2–4.

See also S. Sherwin, Feminist Ethics and In Vitro Fertilization, in M. Hanen & K. Nielsen eds., Science, Morality and Feminist Theory 265 (Univ. of Calgary Press, 1987); S. Sherwin, Feminist and Medical Ethics: Two Different Approaches to Contextual Ethics, in Feminist Perspectives in Medical Ethics, *supra* note 4, at 17, 24–27 (advocating feminist ethics to understand the new reproductive technology).

On the argument that the children of surrogates will be harmed by knowledge of their conception, see Sistare, Reproductive Freedom and Women's Freedom: Surrogacy and Autonomy, 19 Phil. F. 227, 232 (1988). Compare Posner's rebuttal in his essay herein, at 1107.

23. H. Holmes, Reproductive Technologies: The Birth of a Woman-Centered Analysis, in H. Holmes, Beth B. Hoskins & Michael Gross eds., The Custom-Made Child? Woman-Centered Perspectives 8–11 (Humana, 1981).

24. Andrews, Alternative Modes of Reproduction, in Reproduction Laws for the 1990s, *supra* note 1, at 374, 380, 387.

25. See, e.g., Andrews, *supra* note 12; C. Shalev, Birth Power: The Case for Surrogacy (Yale Univ. Press, 1989); Shultz, Reproductive Technology and Intent-Based Parenthood: An Opportunity for Gender Neutrality, 1990 Wis. L. Rev. 297; Taub, *supra* note 13.

26. See generally Andrews, *supra* note 12; Andrews, Alternative Modes of Reproduction, in Reproductive Laws for the 1990s, *supra* note 1; Andrews, Surrogate Motherhood: The Challenge for Feminists, herein, at 1092; Andrews, Prohibiting New Reproductive Technologies: The Counterpoint, in G. McCuen ed., Hi-tech Babies: Alternative Reproductive Technologies (Hudson, Wis: G.E. McCuen Pub., 1990) (testimony before the House Select Committee on Children, Youth and Families, May 21, 1987). Andrews testified at two New York legislative hearings and served as a member of the Michigan Task Force on Reproductive Technologies vs. Best Interests of the Child.

27. Andrews, Alternative Modes of Reproduction, in Reproductive Laws for the 1990s, *supra* note 1, at 371.

28. *Id.* at 390.

29. Shultz, *supra* note 25, at 321–340.

30. *Id.* at 302. For another prosurrogacy essay based on this theory, see Hill, The Case for Enforcement of the Surrogate Contract, 8 Pol. & Life Sci. 147 (1990).

31. Taub, *supra* note 13, at 294.

32. *Id.* See also Purdy, Surrogate Mothering: Exploitation or Empowerment?, 3

Bioethics 18, 34 (1989) (surrogacy, being part time, "less risky and more enjoyable than other jobs," could enable some women—especially "students, aspiring writers, and social activists"—to enjoy career opportunities).

33. Sistare, *supra* note 22, at 228.

34. Hall, Rights and the Problem of Surrogate Parenting, 35 Phil. Q. 414, 423 (1985). For other feminists who support surrogacy based on a concern with autonomy in reproductive decision, see Shalev, *supra* note 25; Purdy, Surrogate Mothering, *supra* note 32, at 24; Purdy, A Response to Dodds & Jones, 3 Bioethics 40 (1989).

35. L. Purdy, Another Look at Contract Pregnancy, in Issues in Reproductive Technology, *supra* note 7, at 303, 304; Purdy, Surrogate Mothering, *supra* note 32, at 21. But cf. Dodds & Jones, A Response to Purdy, 3 Bioethics 35 (1990) (rejecting benefits cited by Purdy).

36. See, e.g., P. Davis, Alternative Modes of Reproduction: The Locus and Determinants of Choice, in Reproductive Laws for the 1990s, *supra* note 1, at 421, 416 (citing Law, Embryos and Ethics, 17 Fam. Planning Persp. 140, 144 (1985)); Purdy, Surrogate Motherhood, *supra* note 32, at 32–33.

37. R. Macklin, Is There Anything Wrong with Surrogate Motherhood? An Ethical Analysis, in Surrogate Motherhood: Politics and Privacy, *supra* note 6, at 141.

38. Sistare, *supra* note 22, at 233–234.

39. *Id.* at 238–239. See also Purdy, Surrogate Mothering, *supra* note 32, at 34.

40. Sistare, *supra* note 22, at 235.

41. *Id.* at 237.

42. Andrews, Alternative Modes of Reproduction, in Reproductive Laws of the 1990's, *supra* note 1, at 371.

43. Field, *supra* note 7, at 151.

44. Taub, *supra* note 13, at 296. Taub, a litigator in the area of reproductive rights and Director of the Women's Rights Litigation Clinic at Rutgers Law School, filed *amicus* briefs in *Baby M.* See also Taub, Feminist Tensions and the Concept of Motherhood, in J. Offerman-Zuckerberg ed., Gender in Transition 217 (Plenum Medical, 1989); Taub, Surrogacy: A Preferred Treatment for Infertility?, 16 Law, Med. & Health Care 89 (1988).

45. Taub, *supra* note 13, at 299. For other liberal feminists who adopt a middle ground, see Davis, Alternative Modes of Reproduction, in Reproductive Laws for the 1990s, *supra* note 1, at 421; R. Macklin, Is There Anything Wrong with Surrogate Motherhood?, in Surrogate Motherhood: Politics and Privacy, *supra* note 6, at 136; B. Steinbock, Surrogate Motherhood as Prenatal Adoption, in *id.* at 123.

46. Robertson, Decisional Authority, Decisional Authority Over Embryos and Control of IVF Technology, 28 Jurimetrics J. 285, 290 (1988). See also J. Robertson, Children of Choice: Freedom and the New Reproductive Technologies (Princeton Univ. Press, 1994); J. Robertson, Procreative Liberty and the State's Burden of Proof in Regulating Noncoital Reproduction, in Surrogate Motherhood: Politics and Privacy, *supra* note 6, at 24; Robertson, Procreative Liberty and the Control of Conception, Pregnancy and Childbirth, 69 Va. L. Rev. 405 (1983). The *Baby M.* trial court, although not the appellate court, adopted Robertson's interpretation. In re Baby M., 525 A.2d 1128, 1164 (N.J. Ch. Div. 1987).

47. Robertson, Decisional Authority, *supra* note 46, at 298.

48. Schuck, Some Reflections on the *Baby M* Case, 76 Geo. L.J. 1793 (1988). See also L. Gostin, A Civil Liberties Analysis of Surrogacy Arrangements, in Surrogate Motherhood: Politics and Privacy, *supra* note 6, at 3 (liberal defense of surrogacy).

49. Schuck, *supra* note 48, at 1798. See also Glenn, From Servitude to Service Work: Historical Continuities in the Racial Division of Paid Reproductive Labor, 18 Signs 1 (1992).

50. Schuck, *supra* note 48, at 1799.

51. *Id.* at 1800.

52. Areen, *Baby M* Reconsidered, *supra* note 5.

53. Allen, Privacy, Surrogacy, and the *Baby M* Case, 76 Geo. L.J. 1759, 1762 (1988); Anderson, Is Women's Labor a Commodity?, 19 Phil. & Pub. Aff. 71, 80–87 (1990); Dodds & Jones, Surrogacy and Autonomy, Surrogacy and Autonomy, 3 Bioethics 1, 6–7 (1989).

54. A. Holder, Surrogate Motherhood and the Best Interests of Children, in Surrogate Motherhood: Politics and Privacy, *supra* note 6 at 77, 82–83; Allen, Surrogacy, Slavery and the Ownership of Life, 13 Harv. J.L. & Pub. Pol'y 139 (1990).

55. Okin, A Critique of Pregnancy Contracts: Comments on Articles by Hill, Merrick, Shevory and Woliver, 8 Pol. & Life Sci. 205, 208 (1990).

56. See, e.g., Anderson, *supra* note 53; Ketchum, Selling Babies and Selling Bodies, 4 Hypatia 116 (Fall 1989).

57. Shulamith Firestone, The Dialectic of Sex: The Case for Feminist Revolution 219–231 (William Morrow & Co., 1970).

58. *Id.* at 11.

59. See Tong, *supra* note 1, at 79, 81 (citing radical feminists Adrienne Rich, Andrea Dworkin, novelist Margaret Atwood, Gena Corea, and Robyn Rowland). Although Firestone is cited for her early support of technology, commentators often fail to mention that she acknowledged the double-edged sword of reproductive developments. See Firestone, *supra* note 57, at 10, 224.

60. On radical feminists' activities, see R. Klein, Genetic and Reproductive Engineering—the Global View, in J. Scutt ed., The Baby Machine: Reproductive Technology and the Commercialisation of Motherhood 235, 252 (Merlin Press, 1990); J. Raymond, Preface, in G. Corea & D. Steinberg eds., Man-Made Women, How New Reproductive Technologies Affect Women 9 (Indiana Univ. Press, 1987); Zipper & Sevenhuijsen, Surrogacy, in Reproductive Technologies, *supra* note 9, at 136.

FINNRAGE was organized by Gena Corea, Renate Klein, Janice Raymond, Jalna Hanmer, and Robyn Rowland. See Baruch, d'Adamo & Seager, Embryos, Ethics & Women's Rights, *supra* note 1, at xiii; R. Rowland, Living Laboratories: Women and Reproductive Technologies ix (Indiana Univ. Press, 1992); Stallone & Steinberg, Made to Order, *supra* note 9, at 2–3.

61. Renate Duelli Klein made the statement in hearings before the European Parliament. Cited in Zipper & Sevenhuijsen, Surrogacy, in Reproductive Technologies, *supra* note 9, at 136.

62. Jalna Hanmer, Transforming Consciousness: Women and the New Reproductive Technologies, in Man-Made Women, *supra* note 60, at 88, 104; J. Hanmer, A Womb of One's Own, in R. Arditti, R. Klein & S. Minden eds., Test-Tube Women: What Future for Motherhood? 438, 441 (Pandora Press, 1984); Tong, *supra* note 1, at 90.

63. G. Corea, J. Hanmer, R. Klein, J. Raymond & R. Rowland, Prologue, in Made to Order, *supra* note 9, at 1, 7.

64. A. Dworkin, Right-Wing Women 174–187 (Perigee, 1983; orig. published by Putnam, 1978).

65. Arditti, Klein & Minden, Introduction, in Test-Tube Women, *supra* note 62, at 2.

66. C. Pateman, The Sexual Contract 213–214 (Stanford Univ. Press, 1988).

67. See, e.g., Corea, Mother Machine, *supra* note 8, at 3. See also *id.* at 5 (citing personal remarks of Dworkin); J. Gallagher, Eggs, Embryos and Foetuses: Anxiety and the Law, in Reproductive Technologies, *supra* note 9, at 146 (citing Corea, Mother Machine, *supra* note 10, at 166–185). Some socialist feminists also share this view. See Gallagher, *supra* this note, at 146 (citing B. Rothman, The Meanings of Choice in Reproductive Technology, in Test-Tube Women, *supra* note 62, at 23–34).

68. See, e.g., Corea et al., Prologue, in Made to Order, *supra* note 9, at 8; Scutt, Disturbing Connections: Artificial and Natural Conception and the Right to Choose, in The Baby Machine, *supra* note 60, at 178.

69. Rowland, Motherhood, Patriarchal Power, in Man-Made Women, *supra* note 60, at 74, 86.

70. Corea et al., Prologue, in Made to Order, *supra* note 9, at 7.

71. R. Rowland, Of Women Born, But for How Long? The Relationship of Women to the New Reproductive Technologies and the Issue of Choice, in Made to Order, *supra* note 9, at 72. See also R. Klein, What's "New" About the "New" Reproductive Technologies?, in Man-Made Women, *supra* note 60, at 64, 69.

72. Scutt, Disturbing Connections: Artificial and Natural Conception and the Right to Choose, in The Baby Machine, *supra* note 60, at 180.

73. Hence the title of the work by Arditti, Klein & Minden, Test-Tube Women, *supra* note 62.

74. Hence the title of Rowland, Living Laboratories, *supra* note 64.

75. Hence the title of G. Corea, Mother Machine, *supra* note 8.

76. Klein, What's "New" About the "New" Reproductive Technologies? in Man-Made Women, *supra* note 60, at 65 ("test-tube women"), 70 ("obsolete").

77. *Id.* at 65; J. Raymond, Feminist Ethics, Ecology, and Vision, in Test-Tube Women, *supra* note 62, at 427, 429; Rowland, Motherhood, Patriarchal Power, Alienation and the Issue of Choice in Sex Preselection, in Man-Made Woman, *supra* note 60, at 84.

78. J. Scutt, Disturbing Connection, in The Baby Machine, *supra* note 60, at 182.

79. Hanmer, Transforming Consciousness, in Man-Made Women, *supra* note 60, at 96; Klein, What's New About the New Reproductive Technology, in *id.* at 69.

80. Compare Hanmer, Transforming Consciousness, in Man-Made Women, *supra* note 60, at 96; Klein, What's "New" About the "New" Reproductive Technologies? in *id.* at 69; Rowland, Motherhood, Patriarchal Power, in *id.* at 80 (new technology should be controlled by women); with Arditti, Klein & Minden, Introduction, in Test-Tube Women, *supra* note 62, at 4; M. Mies, "Why Do We Need All This?" A Call Against Genetic Engineering and Reproductive Technology, in Made to Order, *supra* note 9, at 41 (woman-controlled technology nonetheless "an instrument of domination").

81. Klein, What's "New" about the "New" Reproductive Technologies? in Man-Made Women, *supra* note 60, at 70.

82. See Corea et al., Prologue, in Made to Order, *supra* note 9, at 10; Raymond, Fetalists and Feminists, in Made to Order, *supra* note 9, at 62.

83. J. Scutt, Disturbing Connections, in The Baby Machine, *supra* note 60, at 214–215.

84. Pateman, *supra* note 66, at 143.

85. *Id.* at 215. For a criticism of Pateman's views, see Satz, Markets in Women's Reproductive Labor, 21 Phil. & Pub. Aff. 107, 113–114 (1992).

86. Dworkin, *supra* note 64, at 174–187.

87. *Id.* at 177–178.

88. Tong, *supra* note 1, at 93.

89. Pateman, *supra* note 66, at 216.

90. *Id.* at 217.

91. *Id.* at 211.

92. Raymond, The Spermatic Market: Surrogate Stock and Liquid Assets, 1 Reproductive & Genetic Engineering 66 (1988).

93. *Id.* at 68.

94. Dworkin, *supra* note 64, at 187.

95. See also Raymond, Preface, in Man-Made Women, *supra* note 60, at 12. Dworkin adds: "Motherhood is becoming a new branch of female prostitution with the help of scientists who want access to the womb for experimentation and for power." Dworkin, *supra* note 64, at 187.

96. See Arditti, Klein & Minden, Test-Tube Women, *supra* note 62, at 2; Corea, Mother Machine, *supra* note 8, at 221; Dworkin, *supra* note 64, at 187–188; Klein, What's "New" About the "New" Reproductive Technologies?, in Man-Made Women, *supra* note 60, at 65; Raymond, Fetalists and Feminists, in Made to Order, *supra* note 9, at 62; Rowland, Of Women Born, But for How Long?, in Made to Order, *supra* note 9, at 77.

97. Terming surrogacy another "form of social discrimination and exploitation," MacKinnon refers to it only occasionally in terms of the consequences that would flow from adoption of her approach to equality. See MacKinnon, Toward a Feminist Theory of the State 248 (Harvard Univ. Press, 1989). A possible explanation for this shortsightedness stems from MacKinnon's neglect of topics regarding motherhood and children. See Wildman, Review Essay: The Power of Women, 2 Yale J.L. & Fem. 435, 447 (1990) (criticizing MacKinnon on this basis).

98. See, e.g., MacKinnon, Reflections on Sex Equality Under Law, 100 Yale L.J. 1281, 1308–1324 (1991). Ultrasound merits a brief mention as a technology that is "controlled by men" and that distances the woman from the fetus. *Id.* at 1310–1311.

99. Mary Becker, Four Feminist Theoretical Approaches and the Double Bind of Surrogacy, 69 Chi.-Kent L. Rev. 303, 304 (1993); J. Mahoney, An Essay on Surrogacy and Feminist Thought, in Surrogate Motherhood: Politics and Privacy, *supra* note 6, at 189.

100. Mahoney, An Essay on Surrogacy and Feminist Thought, in Surrogate Motherhood: Politics and Privacy, *supra* note 6, at 189.

101. Becker, *supra* note 99, at 307.

102. Paltrow's criticism is in the form of a book review of a radical feminist collection of essays. Paltrow, Test-Tube Women: What Future for Motherhood, 8 Women's Rts L. Rep. 303 (1985) (reviewing Arditti, Klein & Minden, Test-Tube Women, *supra* note 62).

103. *Id.* at 304.

104. *Id.* (citing G. Corea, Egg Snatchers, in Test-Tube Women, *supra* note 62, at 48).

105. *Id.* (citing V. Roggencamp, Abortion of a Special Kind: Male Sex Selection in India, in Test-Tube Women, *supra* note 62, at 276).

106. *Id.* at 305.

107. *Id.*

108. *Id.* at 307.

109. *Id.* at 306.

110. *Id.* at 307.

111. See, e.g., Purdy, Another Look at Contract Pregnancy, in Issues in Reproductive Technology, *supra* note 7, at 307.

112. *Id.* at 310.

113. Stanworth, Birth Pangs, in Conflicts in Feminism, *supra* note 20, at 298.

114. Schuck, *supra* note 48, at 1800 n.25.

115. Purdy, Surrogate Motherhood, *supra* note 32, at 24.

116. *Id.*

117. Purdy, Another Look at Contract Pregnancy, in Issues in Reproductive Technology, *supra* note 7, at 315.

118. *Id.* at 313.

119. Stanworth, Birth Pangs, in Conflicts in Feminism, *supra* note 20, at 295–296. See also N. Taub, A Preferred Treatment for Infertility?, in Surrogate Motherhood: Politics and Privacy, *supra* note 6, at 221.

120. K. Oliver, The Matter of *Baby M:* Surrogacy and the Courts, in Issues in Reproductive Technology, *supra* note 7, at 321, 322.

121. Oliver, Marxism and Surrogacy, 4 Hypatia 95, 96 (Fall 1989). For a liberal feminist who also notices the class implications of the new reproductive technologies, see Taub, *supra* note 13, at 288.

122. Oliver, Marxism and Surrogacy, *supra* note 121, at 97.

123. *Id.* (citing Corea, Mother Machine, *supra* note 8, at 226, who in turn cites Dworkin).

124. Here she concurs with radical feminist Gena Corea: "as Gena Corea points out in *The Mother Machine,* it is the man's right to procreate that is protected: 'The overriding ethic is that the man's issue be reproduced in the world.' " Oliver, Matter of *Baby M., supra* note 120, at 328 (citing Corea, Mother Machine, *supra* note 8, at 223).

125. Oliver, Matter of *Baby M., supra* note 120, at 327–328. For a similar discussion, see Harrison, Social Construction of Mary Beth Whitehead, 1 Gender & Soc'y 300, 301 (1987).

126. Oliver, Marxism and Surrogacy, *supra* note 121, at 105.

127. Gimenez, The Mode of Reproduction in Transition: A Marxist-Feminist Analysis of the Effects of Reproductive Technologies, 5 Gender & Soc'y 334 (1991). See also M. Gimenez, Feminism, Pronatalism, and Motherhood, in J. Trebilcot ed., Mothering: Essays in Feminist Theory 287 (Rowman & Allanheld, 1983) (linking capitalism, pronatalism, and sexism).

128. Gimenez, Mode of Reproduction, *supra* note 127, at 335.

129. *Id.* at 344 (citing Marx, A Contribution to the Critique of Political Economy 21 (Int'l Pub. Co., 1970, orig. published 1859)).

130. *Id.* at 347–348.

131. A. Jaggar, Feminist Politics and Human Nature 128 (Rowman & Littlefield, 1988).

132. See, e.g., Overall, Ethics and Human Reproduction, *supra* note 22; Rothman, Recreating Motherhood, *supra* note 1; Z. Eisenstein, The Female Body and the Law (Univ. California Press, 1988); W. Chavkin, B. Rothman & R. Rapp, Alternative Modes of Reproduction: Other Views and Questions, in Reproductive Laws for the 1990s, *supra* note 1, at 405. But cf. J. Ollenburger & J. Hamlin, All Birthing Should Be Paid Labor—A Marxist Analysis of the Commodification of Motherhood, in H. Richardson ed., On the Problem of Surrogate Motherhood: Analyzing the *Baby M* Case (Edwin Mellen Press, 1987) (supporting surrogacy).

133. Rothman, Recreating Motherhood, *supra* note 1, at 65.

134. *Id.* at 66.

135. Gibson, *supra* note 6, at 69.

136. *Id.* at 57.

137. Eisenstein, *supra* note 132, at 192.

138. *Id.* at 194.

139. Gibson, *supra* note 6, at 72.

140. *Id.* at 63.

141. *Id.* at 63, 83.

142. See *id.* at 85 (such regulations as mandatory screening and counseling for potential surrogates would violate women's autonomy).

143. See, e.g., Overall, Ethics and Human Reproduction, *supra* note 22, at 127; Eisenstein, *supra* note 132, at 193.

144. Overall, Ethics and Human Reproduction, *supra* note 22, at 124. She also criticizes the radical feminist "prostitution model" on the same basis.

145. *Id.*

146. Rothman, Meanings of Choice in Reproductive Technology, in Test-Tube Women, *supra* note 62, at 30.

147. *Id.* at 31.

148. Overall, Ethics and Human Reproduction, *supra* note 22, at 121.

149. *Id.* at 122.

150. Satz, *supra* note 85. Radical feminists, such as Gena Corea and Carole Pateman, also adhere to the "asymmetry thesis." See *id.* at 108 n.3. Compare Ollenburger & Hamlin, *supra* note 132, at 66 (socialist feminist rejection of asymmetry thesis).

151. Despreaux, Surrogate Motherhood: A Feminist Perspective, 9 Res. Soc. Health Care 99 (1989).

152. *Id.* at 110.

153. *Id.*

154. See, e.g., Rothman, Recreating Motherhood, *supra* note 1, at 24; Rothman, Cheap Labor: Sex, Class, Race—and "Surrogacy," 25 Soc'y 21, 23 (1988).

155. See, e.g., Chavkin, Rothman & Rapp, Alternative Modes of Reproduction: Other Views and Questions, in Reproductive Laws for the 1990s, *supra* note 1, at 405, 406; Gibson, *supra* note 6, at 67–68, 90 n.35. But cf. Ollenburger & Hamlin, *supra* note 132, at 62 (women of color are not likely to be sought-after surrogates because of the desire for white infants).

156. Rothman, Recreating Motherhood, *supra* note 1, at 24. See also Rothman, Cheap Labor, *supra* note 154.

157. Davis, Alternative Modes of Reproduction, in Reproductive Laws for the 1990s, *supra* note 1, at 254 (referring to a criticism by Barbara Katz Rothman).

158. Chavkin, Rothman & Rapp, Alternative Modes of Reproduction: Other Views and Questions, in Reproductive Laws for the 1990s, *supra* note 1, at 406.

159. See, e.g., Overall, Ethics and Human Reproduction, *supra* note 22, at 126; Gibson, *supra* note 6, at 78–81. Socialist feminists here echo the refrain voiced by Marxist feminist Oliver.

160. B. Rothman, Reproduction, in B. Hess & M. Ferree eds., Analyzing Gender: A Handbook of Social Science Research 154, 167 (Sage, 1987). Compare Jaggar, *supra* note 131, at 310 (mothers' loss of control in birthing).

161. Overall, Ethics and Human Reproduction, *supra* note 22, at 126.

162. *Id.*

163. *Id.* at 127.

164. See, e.g., Chavkin, Rothman & Rapp, Alternative Modes of Reproduction: Other Views and Questions, in Reproductive Laws for the 1990s, *supra* note 1, at 405; Gibson, *supra* note 6, at 59; Stanworth, Reproductive Technologies, *supra* note 9, at 13.

165. However, at least one socialist feminist counters that this argument ignores the fact that "[w]omen have in fact gained substantially, certainly more than have men, from medical advances in reproductive care. . . . " Gordon, *supra* note 2, at 467.

166. Chavkin, Rothman & Rapp, Alternative Modes of Reproduction: Other Views and Questions, in Reproductive Laws for the 1990s, *supra* note 1, at 405.

167. Gibson, *supra* note 6, at 70–71.

168. *Id.* at 70. Gibson adds that all parties exploit the child, treating it merely as a means to their own ends. *Id.* at 71.

169. See, e.g., Rothman, Recreating Motherhood, *supra* note 1, at 20.

170. *Id.* at 21.

171. *Id.* at 21–22.

172. M. Barrett & M. McIntosh, The Anti-Social Family 168 (Verso, 2d ed. 1991).

173. Stanworth, Reproductive Technologies, *supra* note 9, at 16–17; Rothman, Reproduction, in Analyzing Gender, *supra* note 160, at 169. See also Rothman, Recreating Motherhood, *supra* note 1.

174. Stanworth, Reproductive Technologies, *supra* note 9, at 16.

175. See, e.g., Chavkin, Rothman & Rapp, Alternative Modes of Reproduction: Other Views and Questions, in Reproductive Laws for the 1990s, *supra* note 1, at 406 (reducing women to reproductive vessels); Rothman, Recreating Motherhood, *supra* note 1, at 20–22. As explained in the text, this view is shared by Corea and Dworkin, among other radical feminists.

176. Eisenstein, *supra* note 132, at 194.

177. R. Albury, Who Owns the Embryo? in Test-Tube Women, *supra* note 62, at 54.

178. Gordon, *supra* note 2, at 457–458.

179. 851 P.2d 776 (Cal. 1993), *cert. denied,* 114 S. Ct. 206 (1993).

180. See also Horsburgh, Jewish Women, Black Women: Guarding Against the Oppression of Surrogacy, 8 Berkeley Women's L.J. 29 (1993); Sanders, Surrogate Motherhood and Reproductive Technologies: An African-American Perspective, 25 Creighton L. Rev. 1707 (1992).

181. For criticisms of Radin's arguments, see Jeanne Schroeder, Virgin Territory: Margaret Radin's Imagery of Personal Property as the Inviolate Feminine Body, 79 Minn. L. Rev. 55 (1994) (Radin ignores the subjective aspects of property law); Stephen J. Schnably, Property and Pragmatism: A Critique of Radin's Theory of Property and Personhood, 45 Stan. L. Rev. 347 (1993) (criticizing Radin's women-as-victim paradigm).

182. Despreaux, *supra* note 151, at 102 (citing Zipper & Sevenhuijsen, Surrogacy, in Reproductive Technologies, *supra* note 9, at 120).

IN THE MATTER OF BABY M.

537 A.2d 1227 (N.J. 1988)

WILENTZ, Chief Justice.

In this matter the Court is asked to determine the validity of a contract that purports to provide a new way of bringing children into a family. For a fee of $10,000, a woman agrees to be artificially inseminated with the semen of another woman's husband; she is to conceive a child, carry it to term, and after its birth surrender it to the natural father and his wife. The intent of the contract is that the child's natural mother will thereafter be forever separated from her child. The wife is to adopt the child, and she and the natural father are to be regarded as its parents for all purposes. The contract providing for this is called a "surrogacy contract," the natural mother inappropriately called the "surrogate mother." . . .

In February 1985, William Stern and Mary Beth Whitehead entered into a surrogacy contract. It recited that Stern's wife, Elizabeth, was infertile, that they wanted a child, and that Mrs. Whitehead was willing to provide that child as the mother with Mr. Stern as the father.

The contract provided that through artificial insemination using Mr. Stern's sperm, Mrs. Whitehead would become pregnant, carry the child to term, bear it, deliver it to the Sterns, and thereafter do whatever was necessary to terminate her maternal rights so that Mrs. Stern could thereafter adopt the child. Mrs. Whitehead's husband, Richard, was also a party to the contract; Mrs. Stern was not. Mr. Whitehead promised to do all acts necessary to rebut the presumption of paternity under the Parentage Act. N.J.S.A. 9:17–43a(1), -44a. Although Mrs. Stern was not a party to the surrogacy agreement, the contract gave her sole custody of the child in the event of Mr. Stern's death. Mrs. Stern's status as a nonparty to the surrogate parenting agreement presumably was to avoid the application of the baby-selling statute to this arrangement. N.J.S.A. 9:3–54.

Mr. Stern, on his part, agreed to attempt the artificial insemination and to pay Mrs. Whitehead $10,000 after the child's birth, on its delivery to him. In a separate contract,

Mr. Stern agreed to pay $7,500 to the Infertility Center of New York ("ICNY"). The Center's advertising campaigns solicit surrogate mothers and encourage infertile couples to consider surrogacy. ICNY arranged for the surrogacy contract by bringing the parties together, explaining the process to them, furnishing the contractual form, and providing legal counsel.

The history of the parties' involvement in this arrangement suggests their good faith. William and Elizabeth Stern were married in July 1974, having met at the University of Michigan, where both were Ph.D candidates. Due to financial considerations and Mrs. Stern's pursuit of a medical degree and residency, they decided to defer starting a family until 1981. Before then, however, Mrs. Stern learned that she might have multiple sclerosis and that the disease in some cases renders pregnancy a serious health risk. Her anxiety appears to have exceeded the actual risk, which current medical authorities assess as minimal. Nonetheless that anxiety was evidently quite real, Mrs. Stern fearing that pregnancy might precipitate blindness, paraplegia, or other forms of debilitation. Based on the perceived risk, the Sterns decided to forgo having their own children. The decision had a special significance for Mr. Stern. Most of his family had been destroyed in the Holocaust. As the family's only survivor, he very much wanted to continue his bloodline. Initially the Sterns considered adoption, but were discouraged by the substantial delay apparently involved and by the potential problem they saw arising from their age and their differing religious backgrounds. They were most eager for some other means to start a family. The paths of Mrs. Whitehead and the Sterns to surrogacy were similar. Both responded to advertising by ICNY. The Sterns' response, following their inquiries into adoption, was the result of their long-standing decision to have a child. Mrs. Whitehead's response apparently resulted from her sympathy with family members and others who could have no children (she stated that she wanted to give another couple the "gift of life"); she also wanted the $10,000 to help her family. . . .

. . . On February 6, 1985, Mr. Stern and Mr. and Mrs. Whitehead executed the surrogate parenting agreement. After several artificial inseminations over a period of months, Mrs. Whitehead became pregnant. The pregnancy was uneventful and on March 27, 1986, Baby M was born. . . .

Mrs. Whitehead realized, almost from the moment of birth, that she could not part with this child. . . . Nonetheless, Mrs. Whitehead was, for the moment, true to her word. Despite powerful inclinations to the contrary, she turned her child over to the Sterns on March 30 at the Whiteheads' home.

The Sterns were thrilled with their new child. . . . The Sterns looked forward to raising their daughter, whom they named Melissa. While aware by then that Mrs. Whitehead was undergoing an emotional crisis, they were as yet not cognizant of the depth of that crisis and its implications for their newly-enlarged family.

Later in the evening of March 30, Mrs. Whitehead became deeply disturbed, disconsolate, stricken with unbearable sadness. . . . The next day she went to the Sterns' home and told them how much she was suffering. . . . She told them that she could not live without her baby, that she must have her, even if only for one week, that thereafter she would surrender her child. The Sterns, concerned that Mrs. Whitehead might indeed commit suicide, not wanting under any circumstances to risk that, and in any event believing that Mrs. Whitehead would keep her word, turned the child over to her. It was not until four months later, after a series of attempts to regain possession of the child, that Melissa was returned to the Sterns, having been forcibly removed from the home where she was then living with Mr. and Mrs. Whitehead, the home in Florida owned by Mary Beth Whitehead's parents.

The struggle over Baby M began when it became apparent that Mrs. Whitehead could not return the child to Mr. Stern. Due to Mrs. Whitehead's refusal to relinquish the baby, Mr. Stern filed a complaint seeking enforcement of the surrogacy contract. He alleged, accurately, that Mrs. Whitehead had not only refused to comply with the surrogacy contract but had threatened to flee from New Jersey with the child in order to avoid even the possibility of his obtaining custody. The court papers asserted that if Mrs. Whitehead were to be given notice of the application for an order requiring her to relinquish custody, she would, prior to the hearing, leave the state with the baby. And that is precisely what she did. After the order was entered, ex parte, the process server, aided by the police, in the presence of the Sterns, entered Mrs. Whitehead's home to execute the order. Mr. Whitehead fled with the child, who had been handed to him through a window while those who came to enforce the order were thrown off balance by a dispute over the child's current name.

The Whiteheads immediately fled to Florida with Baby M. They stayed initially with Mrs. Whitehead's parents, [later] at roughly twenty different hotels, motels, and homes in order to avoid apprehension. From time to time Mrs. Whitehead would call Mr. Stern to discuss the matter; the conversations, recorded by Mr. Stern on advice of counsel, show an escalating dispute about rights, morality, and power, accompanied by threats of Mrs. Whitehead to kill herself, to kill the child, and falsely to accuse Mr. Stern of sexually molesting Mrs. Whitehead's other daughter.

Eventually the Sterns discovered where the Whiteheads were staying, commenced supplementary proceedings in Florida, and obtained an order requiring the Whiteheads to turn over the child. Police in Florida enforced the order, forcibly removing the child from her grandparents' home. She was soon thereafter brought to New Jersey and turned over to the Sterns. The prior order of the court, issued ex parte, awarding custody of the child to the Sterns pendente lite, was reaffirmed. . . . Pending final judgment, Mrs. Whitehead was awarded limited visitation with Baby M.

The Sterns' complaint, in addition to seeking possession and ultimately custody of the child, sought enforcement of the surrogacy contract. Pursuant to the contract, it asked that the child be permanently placed in their custody, that Mrs. Whitehead's parental rights be terminated, and that Mrs. Stern be allowed to adopt the child, i.e., that, for all purposes, Melissa become the Sterns' child.

The trial took thirty-two days over a period of more than two months. It included numerous interlocutory appeals and attempted interlocutory appeals. There were twenty-three witnesses to the facts recited above and fifteen expert witnesses, eleven testifying on the issue of custody and four on the subject of Mrs. Stern's multiple sclerosis; the bulk of the testimony was devoted to determining the parenting arrangement most compatible with the child's best interests. Soon after the conclusion of the trial, the trial court announced its opinion from the bench. It held that the surrogacy contract was valid; ordered that Mrs. Whitehead's parental rights be terminated and that sole custody of the child be granted to Mr. Stern; and, after hearing brief testimony from Mrs. Stern, immediately entered an order allowing the adoption of Melissa by Mrs. Stern, all in accordance with the surrogacy contract. Pending the outcome of the appeal, we granted a continuation of visitation to Mrs. Whitehead, although slightly more limited than the visitation allowed during the trial.

Although clearly expressing its view that the surrogacy contract was valid, the trial court devoted the major portion of its opinion to the question of the baby's best interests. . . . We agree substantially with both its analysis and conclusions on the matter of custody.

The court's review and analysis of the surrogacy contract, however, is not at all in accord with ours. The trial court concluded that the various statutes governing this matter, including those concerning adoption, termination of parental rights, and payment of money in connection with adoptions, do not apply to surrogacy contracts. 217 N.J. Super. at 372–373. It reasoned that because the Legislature did not have surrogacy contracts in mind when it passed those laws, those laws were therefore irrelevant. . . . It then held that surrogacy contracts are valid and should be enforced, *id.* at 388, and furthermore that Mr. Stern's rights under the surrogacy contract were constitutionally protected.

Mrs. Whitehead appealed [contending] that the surrogacy contract, for a variety of reasons, is invalid. She contends that it conflicts with public policy since it guarantees that the child will not have the nurturing of both natural parents—presumably New Jersey's goal for families. She further argues that it deprives the mother of her constitutional right to the companionship of her child, and that it conflicts with statutes concerning termination of parental rights and adoption. With the contract thus void, Mrs. Whitehead claims primary custody (with visitation rights in Mr. Stern) both on a best interests basis (stressing the "tender years" doctrine) as well as on the policy basis of discouraging surrogacy contracts. She maintains that even if custody would ordinarily go to Mr. Stern, here it should be awarded to Mrs. Whitehead to deter future surrogacy arrangements.

In a brief filed after oral argument, counsel for Mrs. Whitehead suggests that the standard for determining best interests where the infant resulted from a surrogacy contract is that the child should be placed with the mother absent a showing of unfitness. All parties agree that no expert testified that Mary Beth Whitehead was unfit as a mother; the trial court expressly found that she was not "unfit," that, on the contrary, "she is a good mother for and to her older children," 217 N.J. Super. at 397; and no one now claims anything to the contrary.

One of the repeated themes put forth by Mrs. Whitehead is that the court's initial ex parte order granting custody to the Sterns during the trial was a substantial factor in the ultimate "best interests" determination. That initial order, claimed to be erroneous by Mrs. Whitehead, not only established Melissa as part of the Stern family, but brought enormous pressure on Mrs. Whitehead [which caused her] to act in ways that were thought to be inimical to the child's best interests in that they demonstrated a failure of character, maturity, and consistency. . . .

The Sterns claim that the surrogacy contract is valid and should be enforced, largely for the reasons given by the trial court. They claim a constitutional right of privacy, which includes the right of procreation, and the right of consenting adults to deal with matters of reproduction as they see fit. As for the child's best interests, their position is factual: given all of the circumstances, the child is better off in their custody with no residual parental rights reserved for Mrs. Whitehead.

Of considerable interest in this clash of views is the position of the child's guardian ad litem, wisely appointed by the court at the outset of the litigation. As the child's representative, her role in the litigation, as she viewed it, was solely to protect the child's best interests. She therefore took no position on the validity of the surrogacy contract, and instead devoted her energies to obtaining expert testimony uninfluenced by any interest other than the child's. . . . She first took the position, based on that testimony, that the Sterns should have primary custody, and that while Mrs. Whitehead's parental rights should not be terminated, no visitation should be allowed for five years. As a result of subsequent developments, mentioned *infra*, her view has changed. She now recommends that no visitation be allowed at least until Baby M reaches maturity. . . .

Invalidity and Unenforceability of Surrogacy Contract

We have concluded that this surrogacy contract is invalid. . . . The surrogacy contract conflicts with: (1) laws prohibiting the use of money in connection with adoptions; (2) laws requiring proof of parental unfitness or abandonment before termination of parental rights is ordered or an adoption is granted; and (3) laws that make surrender of custody and consent to adoption revocable in private placement adoptions.

Our law prohibits paying or accepting money in connection with any placement of a child for adoption. N.J.S.A. 9:3–54a. . . . Considerable care was taken in this case to structure the surrogacy arrangement so as not to violate this prohibition. The arrangement was structured as follows: the adopting parent, Mrs. Stern, was not a party to the surrogacy contract; the money paid to Mrs. Whitehead was stated to be for her services—not for the adoption; the sole purpose of the contract was stated as being that "of giving a child to William Stern, its natural and biological father"; the money was purported to be "compensation for services and expenses and in no way . . . a fee for termination of parental rights or a payment in exchange for consent to surrender a child for adoption"; the fee to the Infertility Center ($7,500) was stated to be for legal representation, advice, administrative work, and other "services." Nevertheless, it seems clear that the money was paid and accepted in connection with an adoption. . . .

. . . The surrogacy agreement requires Mrs. Whitehead to surrender Baby M for the purposes of adoption. The agreement notes that Mr. and Mrs. Stern wanted to have a child, and provides that the child be "placed" with Mrs. Stern in the event Mr. Stern dies before the child is born. The payment of the $10,000 occurs only on surrender of custody of the child and "completion of the duties and obligations" of Mrs. Whitehead, including termination of her parental rights to facilitate adoption by Mrs. Stern. As for the contention that the Sterns are paying only for services and not for an adoption, we need note only that they would pay nothing in the event the child died before the fourth month of pregnancy, and only $1,000 if the child were stillborn, even though the "services" had been fully rendered. Additionally, one of Mrs. Whitehead's estimated costs, to be assumed by Mr. Stern, was an "Adoption Fee," presumably for Mrs. Whitehead's incidental costs in connection with the adoption.

Mr. Stern knew he was paying for the adoption of a child; Mrs. Whitehead knew she was accepting money so that a child might be adopted; the Infertility Center knew that it was being paid for assisting in the adoption of a child. The actions of all three worked to frustrate the goals of the statute. It strains credulity to claim that these arrangements, touted by those in the surrogacy business as an attractive alternative to the usual route leading to an adoption, really amount to something other than a private placement adoption for money.

The prohibition of our statute is strong. Violation constitutes a high misdemeanor, N.J.S.A. 9:3–54c, a third-degree crime, N.J.S.A. 2C:43-lb, carrying a penalty of three to five years imprisonment. N.J.S.A. 2C:43–6a(3). The evils inherent in baby bartering are loathsome for a myriad of reasons. The child is sold without regard for whether the purchasers will be suitable parents. N. Baker, Baby Selling: The Scandal of Black Market Adoption 7 (1978). The natural mother does not receive the benefit of counseling and guidance to assist her in making a decision that may affect her for a lifetime. In fact, the monetary incentive to sell her child may, depending on her financial circumstances, make her decision less voluntary. *Id.* at 44.
. . .

Baby-selling potentially results in the exploitation of all parties involved. *Id.* Conversely, adoption statutes seek to further humanitarian goals, foremost among them the best interests of the child. The negative consequences of baby buying are potentially present in the surrogacy context, especially the potential for placing and adopting a child without regard to the interest of the child or the natural mother.

(2) The termination of Mrs. Whitehead's parental rights, called for by the surrogacy contract and actually ordered by the court, 217 N.J. Super. at 399–400, fails to comply with the stringent requirements of New Jersey law. . . .

Our statutes, and the cases interpreting them, leave no doubt that where there has been no written surrender to an approved agency or to DYFS [Division of Youth and Family Services], termination of parental rights will not be granted in this state absent a very strong showing of abandonment or neglect. [citations omitted] That showing is required in every context in which termination of parental rights is sought, be it an action by an approved agency, an action by DYFS, or a private placement adoption proceeding, even where the petitioning adoptive parent is, as here, a stepparent. . . . It is clear that a "best interests" determination is never sufficient to terminate parental rights; the statutory criteria must be proved.

In this case a termination of parental rights was obtained not by proving the statutory prerequisites but by claiming the benefit of contractual provisions. From all that has been stated above, it is clear that a contractual agreement to abandon one's parental rights, or not to contest a termination action, will not be enforced in our courts. The Legislature would not have so carefully, so consistently, and so substantially restricted termination of parental rights if it had intended to allow termination to be achieved by one short sentence in a contract.

Since the termination was invalid, it follows, as noted above, that adoption of Melissa by Mrs. Stern could not properly be granted.

(3) The provision in the surrogacy contract stating that Mary Beth Whitehead agrees to "surrender custody . . . and terminate all parental rights" contains no clause giving her a right to rescind. It is intended to be an irrevocable consent to surrender the child for adoption—in other words, an irrevocable commitment by Mrs. Whitehead to turn Baby M over to the Sterns and thereafter to allow termination of her parental rights. . . .

Such a provision, however, making irrevocable the natural mother's consent to surrender custody of her child in a private placement adoption, clearly conflicts with New Jersey law.

Our analysis commences with the statute providing for surrender of custody to an approved agency and termination of parental rights on the suit of that agency. . . . The statute speaks of such surrender as constituting "relinquishment of such person's parental rights in or guardianship or custody of the child named therein and consent by such person to adoption of the child." *Id.* We emphasize "named therein," for we construe the statute to allow a surrender only after the birth of the child. The formal consent to surrender enables the approved agency to terminate parental rights. . . .

It is clear that the Legislature so carefully circumscribed all aspects of a consent to surrender custody—its form and substance, its manner of execution, and the agency or agencies to which it may be made—in order to provide the basis for irrevocability. It seems most unlikely that the Legislature intended that a consent not complying with these requirements would also be irrevocable, especially where, as here, that consent falls radically short of compliance. Not only do the form and substance of the consent in the surrogacy contract fail to meet statutory requirements, but the surrender of custody is made to a private party. . . .

. . . There is only one irrevocable consent, and that is the one explicitly provided for by statute: a consent to surrender of custody and a placement with an approved agency or with DYFS. The provision in the surrogacy contract, agreed to before conception, requiring the natural mother to surrender custody of the child without any right of revocation is one more indication of the essential nature of this transaction: the creation of a contractual system of termination and adoption designed to circumvent our statutes.

Public Policy Considerations

The surrogacy contract's invalidity, resulting from its direct conflict with the above statutory provisions, is further underlined when its goals and means are measured against New Jersey's public policy. The contract's basic premise, that the natural parents can decide in advance of birth which one is to have custody of the child, bears no relationship to the settled law that the child's best interests shall determine custody. . . .

The surrogacy contract [also] violates the policy of this State that the rights of natural parents are equal concerning their child, the father's right no greater than the mother's. . . . The whole purpose and effect of the surrogacy contract was to give the father the exclusive right to the child by destroying the rights of the mother.

The policies expressed in our comprehensive laws governing consent to the surrender of a child . . . stand in stark contrast to the surrogacy contract and what it implies. Here there is no counseling, independent or otherwise, of the natural mother, no evaluation, no warning. . . .

Mrs. Whitehead was examined and psychologically evaluated, but if it was for her benefit, the record does not disclose that fact. The Sterns regarded the evaluation as important. . . . Yet they never asked to see it, and were content with the assumption that the Infertility Center had made an evaluation and had concluded that there was no danger that the surrogate mother would change her mind. . . . It is apparent that the profit motive got the better of the Infertility Center. Although the evaluation was made, it was not put to any use, and understandably so, for the psychologist warned that Mrs. Whitehead demonstrated certain traits that might make surrender of the child difficult and that there should be further inquiry into this issue in connection with her surrogacy. . . .

Under the contract, the natural mother is irrevocably committed before she knows the strength of her bond with her child. She never makes a totally voluntary, informed decision, for quite clearly any decision prior to the baby's birth is, in the most important sense, uninformed, and any decision after that, compelled by a pre-existing contractual commitment, the threat of a lawsuit, and the inducement of a $10,000 payment, is less than totally voluntary. Her interests are of little concern to those who controlled this transaction. . . .

Worst of all, however, is the contract's total disregard of the best interests of the child. There is not the slightest suggestion that any inquiry will be made at any time to determine the fitness of the Sterns as custodial parents, of Mrs. Stern as an adoptive parent, their superiority to Mrs. Whitehead, or the effect on the child of not living with her natural mother.

This is the sale of a child, or, at the very least, the sale of a mother's right to her child, the only mitigating factor being that one of the purchasers is the father. Almost every evil that prompted the prohibition of the payment of money in connection with adoptions exists here.

The differences between an adoption and a surrogacy contract should be noted, since it is asserted that the use of money in connection with surrogacy does not pose the risks found where money buys an adoption. Katz, Surrogate Motherhood and the Baby-Selling Laws, 20 Colum. J.L. & Soc. Probs. 1 (1986).

First, and perhaps most important, all parties concede that it is unlikely that surrogacy will survive without money. Despite the alleged selfless motivation of surrogate mothers, if there is no payment, there will be no surrogates, or very few. That conclusion contrasts with adoption; for obvious reasons, there remains a steady supply, albeit insufficient, despite the prohibitions against payment. The adoption itself, relieving the natural mother of the financial burden of supporting an infant, is the equivalent of payment.

Second, the use of money in adoptions does not produce the problem—conception occurs, and usually the birth itself, before illicit funds are offered. With surrogacy, the "problem," if one views it as such, consisting of the purchase of a woman's procreative capacity, at the risk of her life, is caused by and originates with the offer of money.

Third, with the law prohibiting the use of money in connection with adoptions, the built-in financial pressure of the unwanted pregnancy and the consequent support obligation do not lead the mother to the highest paying, ill-suited, adoptive parents. She is just as well off surrendering the child to an approved agency. In surrogacy, the highest bidders will presumably become the adoptive parents regardless of suitability, so long as payment of money is permitted.

Fourth, the mother's consent to surrender her child in adoptions is revocable, even after surrender of the child, unless it be to an approved agency, where by regulation there are protections against an ill-advised surrender. In surrogacy, consent occurs so early that no amount of advice would satisfy the potential mother's need, yet the consent is irrevocable.

The main difference, that the plight of the unwanted pregnancy is unintended while the situation of the surrogate mother is voluntary and intended, is really not significant. [T]he essential evil is the same, taking advantage of a woman's circumstances (the unwanted pregnancy or the need for money) in order to take away her child, the difference being one of degree.

In the scheme contemplated by the surrogacy contract in this case, a middle man, propelled by profit, promotes the sale. Whatever idealism may have motivated any of the participants, the profit motive predominates, permeates, and ultimately governs the transaction. . . .

Intimated, but disputed, is the assertion that surrogacy will be used for the benefit of the rich at the expense of the poor. See, e.g., Radin, "Market Inalienability," 100 Harv. L. Rev. 1849, 1930 (1987). In response it is noted that the Sterns are not rich and the Whiteheads not poor. Nevertheless, it is clear to us that it is unlikely that surrogate mothers will be as proportionately numerous among those women in the top twenty percent income bracket as among those in the bottom twenty percent. Put differently, we doubt that infertile couples in the low-income bracket will find upper income surrogates.

In any event, even in this case one should not pretend that disparate wealth does not play a part simply because the contrast is not the dramatic "rich versus poor." At the time of trial, the Whiteheads' net assets were probably negative—Mrs. Whitehead's own sister was foreclosing on a second mortgage. . . . The Sterns are both professionals, she a medical doctor, he a biochemist. Their combined income when both were working was about $89,500 a year and their assets sufficient to pay for the surrogacy contract arrangements.

The point is made that Mrs. Whitehead agreed to the surrogacy arrangement, supposedly fully understanding the consequences. Putting aside the issue of how compelling her need for money may have been, and how significant her understanding of the consequences, we suggest that her consent is irrelevant. There are, in a civilized society, some things that money cannot buy. . . . There are, in short, values that society deems more important than granting to wealth whatever it can buy, be it labor, love, or life. Whether this principle recommends prohibition of surrogacy, which presumably sometimes results in great satisfaction to all of the parties, is not for us to say. We note here only that, under existing law, the fact that Mrs. Whitehead "agreed" to the arrangement is not dispositive.

The long-term effects of surrogacy contracts are not known, but feared—the impact on the child who learns her life was bought, that she is the offspring of someone who gave birth to her only to obtain money; the impact on the natural mother as the full weight of her isolation is felt along with the full reality of the sale of her body and her child; the impact on the natural father and adoptive mother once they realize the consequences of their conduct. . . .

The surrogacy contract creates, it is based upon, principles that are directly contrary to the objectives of our laws. It guarantees the separation of a child from its mother; it looks to adoption regardless of suitability; it totally ignores the child; it takes the child from the mother regardless of her wishes and her maternal fitness; and it does all of this, it accomplishes all of its goals, through the use of money.

Beyond that is the potential degradation of some women that may result from this arrangement. In many cases, of course, surrogacy may bring satisfaction, not only to the infertile couple, but to the surrogate mother herself. The fact, however, that many women may not perceive surrogacy negatively but rather see it as an opportunity does not diminish its potential for devastation to other women.

In sum, the harmful consequences of this surrogacy arrangement appear to us all too palpable. In New Jersey the surrogate mother's agreement to sell her child is void. Its irrevocability infects the entire contract, as does the money that purports to buy it.

Termination

We have already noted that under our laws termination of parental rights cannot be based on contract, but may be granted only on proof of the statutory requirements. . . .

Nothing in this record justifies a finding that would allow a court to terminate Mary Beth Whitehead's parental rights under the statutory standard. It is not simply that obviously there was no "intentional abandonment or very substantial neglect of parental duties without a reasonable expectation of reversal of that conduct in the future," N.J. S.A. 9:3–48c(1), quite the contrary, . . . trial court never found Mrs. Whitehead an unfit mother and indeed affirmatively stated that Mary Beth Whitehead had been a good mother to her other children.

Although the best interests of the child is dispositive of the custody issue in a dispute between natural parents, it does not govern the question of termination. It has long been decided that the mere fact that a child would be better off with one set of parents than with another is an insufficient basis for terminating the natural parent's rights [citations omitted]. Furthermore, it is equally well settled that surrender of a child and a consent to adoption through private placement do not alone warrant termination. . . .

Although the statutes are clear, they are not applied rigidly on all occasions. The statutory standard, strictly construed, appears harsh where the natural parents, having surrendered their child for adoption through private placement, change their minds and seek the return of their child and where the issue comes before the court with the adoptive parents having had custody for years, and having assumed it quite innocently. . . .

The present case is distinguishable. . . . Mary Beth Whitehead had custody of Baby M for four months before the child was taken away. Her initial surrender of Baby M was pursuant to a contract that we have declared illegal and unenforceable. . . .

There is simply no basis, either in the statute or in the peculiar facts . . . to warrant termination of Mrs Whithead's parental rights. We therefore conclude that the natural mother is entitled to retain her rights as a mother.

Constitutional Issues

Both parties argue that the Constitutions—state and federal—mandate approval of their basic claims. . . . The right asserted by the Sterns is the right of procreation; that asserted by Mary Beth Whitehead is the right to the companionship of her child. . . .

The right to procreate, as protected by the Constitution, has been ruled on directly only once by the United States Supreme Court. See Skinner v. Oklahoma, 316 U.S. 535 (1942) (forced sterilization of habitual criminals violates equal protection clause of Fourteenth Amendment). . . . The right to procreate very simply is the right to have natural children, whether through sexual intercourse or artificial insemination. It is no more than that. Mr. Stern has not been deprived of that right. Through artificial insemination of Mrs. Whitehead, Baby M is his child. The custody, care, companionship, and nurturing that follow birth are not parts of the right to procreation; they are rights that may also be constitutionally protected, but that involve many considerations other than the right of procreation. To assert that Mr. Stern's right of procreation gives him the right to the custody of Baby M would be to assert that Mrs. Whitehead's right of procreation does not give her the right to the custody of Baby M; it would be to assert that the constitutional right of procreation includes within it a constitutionally protected contractual right to destroy someone else's right of procreation. We conclude that the right of procreation is best understood and protected if confined to its essentials, and that when dealing with rights concerning the resulting child, different interests come into play. There is nothing in our culture or society that even begins to suggest a fundamental right on the part of the father to the custody of the child as part of his right to procreate when opposed by the claim of the mother to the same child. We therefore disagree with the trial court: there is no constitutional basis whatsoever requiring that Mr. Stern's claim to the custody of Baby M be sustained. . . .

Mr. Stern also contends that he has been denied equal protection of the laws by the State's statute granting full parental rights to a husband in relation to the child produced, with his consent, by the union of his wife with a sperm donor. N.J.S.A. 9:17–44. The claim really is that of Mrs. Stern. It is that she is in precisely the same position as the husband in the statute: she is presumably infertile, as is the husband in the statute; her spouse by agreement with a third party procreates with the understanding that the child will be the couple's child. The alleged unequal protection is that the understanding is honored in the statute when the husband is the infertile party, but no similar understanding is honored when it is the wife who is infertile.

It is quite obvious that the situations are not parallel. A sperm donor simply cannot be equated with a surrogate mother. The State has more than a sufficient basis to distinguish the two situations—even if the only difference is between the time it takes to provide sperm for artificial insemination and the time invested in a nine-month pregnancy—so as to justify automatically divesting the sperm donor of his parental rights without automatically divesting a surrogate mother. Some basis for an equal protection argument might exist if Mary Beth Whitehead had contributed her egg to be implanted, fertilized or otherwise, in Mrs. Stern, resulting in the latter's pregnancy. That is not the case here, however.

Mrs. Whitehead, on the other hand, asserts a claim that falls within the scope of a recognized fundamental interest protected by the Constitution. As a mother, she claims the right to the companionship of her child. This is a fundamental interest, constitutionally protected. . . . We have decided that both the statutes and public policy of this state require that that termination be voided and that her parental rights be restored. It therefore becomes unnecessary to decide whether that same result would be required by virtue of the federal or state Constitutions. . . .

Custody

Having decided that the surrogacy contract is illegal and unenforceable, we now must decide the custody question without regard to the provisions of the surrogacy contract. . . . Under the Parentage Act the claims of the natural father and the natural mother are entitled to equal weight, i.e., one is not preferred over the other solely because it is the father or the mother. N.J.S.A. 9:17–40. The applicable rule given these circumstances is clear: the child's best interests determine custody. . . .

. . . The question of custody in this case, as in practically all cases, assumes the fitness of both parents, and no serious contention is made in this case that either is unfit. The issue here is which life would be better for Baby M, one with primary custody in the Whiteheads or one with primary custody in the Sterns.

The circumstances of this custody dispute are unusual and they have provoked some unusual contentions. The Whiteheads claim that even if the child's best interests would be served by our awarding custody to the Sterns, we should not do so. . . . Their position is that in order that surrogacy contracts be deterred, custody should remain in the surrogate mother unless she is unfit, regardless of the best interests of the child. We disagree. Our declaration that this surrogacy contract is unenforceable and illegal is sufficient to deter similar agreements. We need not sacrifice the child's interests in order to make that point sharper. . . .

The Whiteheads also contend that the award of custody to the Sterns pendente lite was erroneous and that the error should not be allowed to affect the final custody decision. As noted above, at the very commencement of this action the court issued an ex parte order requiring Mrs. Whitehead to turn over the baby to the Sterns. . . . The Sterns retained custody of the child throughout the [one and one-half years of] litigation. The Whiteheads' point, assuming the pendente award of custody was erroneous, is that most of the factors arguing for awarding permanent custody to the Sterns resulted from that initial pendente lite order. Some of Mrs. Whitehead's alleged character failings, as testified to by experts and concurred in by the trial court, were demonstrated by her actions brought on by the custody crisis. For instance, in order to demonstrate her impulsiveness, those experts stressed the Whiteheads' flight to Florida with Baby M; to show her willingness to use her children for her own aims, they noted the telephone threats to kill Baby M and to accuse Mr. Stern of sexual abuse of her daughter; in order to show Mrs. Whitehead's manipulativeness, they pointed to her threat to kill herself; and in order to show her unsettled family life, they noted the innumerable moves from one hotel or motel to another in Florida. . . . The Whiteheads' conclusion is that had the trial court not given initial custody to the Sterns during the litigation, Mrs. Whitehead not only would have demonstrated her perfectly acceptable personality—the general tenor of the opinion of experts was that her personality problems surfaced primarily in crises—but would also have been able to prove better her parental skills along with an even stronger bond than may now exist between her and Baby M. Had she not been limited to custody for four months, she could have proved all of these things much more persuasively through almost two years of custody.

The argument has considerable force. It is of course possible that the trial court was wrong in its initial award of custody. It is also possible that such error, if that is what it was, may have affected the outcome. We disagree with the premise, however, that in determining custody a court should decide what the child's best interests would be if some hypothetical state of facts had existed. Rather, we must look to what those best interests are, today, even if some of the facts may have resulted in part from legal error. The child's interests come first: we will not punish it for judicial errors, assuming any were made. . . . The custody decision must be based on all circumstances, on everything that actually has occurred, on everything that is relevant to the child's best interests. . . .

There were eleven experts who testified concerning the child's best interests, either directly or in connection with matters related to that issue. Our reading of the record persuades us that the trial court's decision awarding custody to the Sterns (technically to Mr. Stern) should be affirmed. . . .

Our custody conclusion is based on strongly persuasive testimony contrasting both the family life of the Whiteheads and the Sterns and the personalities and characters of the individuals. The stability of the Whitehead family life was doubtful at the time of trial. Their finances were in serious trouble (foreclosure by Mrs. Whitehead's sister on a second mortgage was in process). Mr. Whitehead's employment, though relatively steady, was always at risk because of his alcoholism, a condition that he seems not to have been able to confront effectively. Mrs. Whitehead had not worked for quite some time, her last two employments having been part-time. One of the Whiteheads' positive attributes was their ability to bring up two children, and apparently well, even in so vulnerable a household. Yet substantial question was raised even about that aspect of their home life. The expert testimony contained criticism of Mrs. Whitehead's handling of her son's educational difficulties. Certain of the experts noted that Mrs. Whitehead perceived herself as omnipotent and omniscient concerning her children. She knew what they were thinking, what they wanted, and she spoke for them. As to Melissa, Mrs. Whitehead expressed the view that she alone knew what that child's cries and sounds meant. Her inconsistent stories about various things engendered grave doubts about her ability to explain honestly and sensitively to Baby M—and at the right time—the nature of her origin. Although faith in professional counseling is not a sine qua non of parenting, several experts believed that Mrs. Whitehead's contempt for professional help, especially professional psychological help, coincided with her feelings of omnipotence in a way that could be devastating to a child who most likely will need such help. In short, while love and affection there would be, Baby M's life with the Whiteheads promised to be too closely controlled by Mrs. Whitehead. The prospects for a wholesome independent psychological growth and development would be at serious risk.

The Sterns have no other children, but all indications are that their household and their personalities promise a much more likely foundation for Melissa to grow and thrive. There is a track record of sorts—during the one and a-half years of custody Baby M has done very well, and the relationship between both Mr. and Mrs. Stern and the baby has become very strong. The household is stable, and likely to remain so. Their finances are more than adequate, their circle of friends supportive, and their marriage happy. Most important, they are loving, giving, nurturing, and open-minded people. They have demonstrated the wish and ability to nurture and protect Melissa, yet at the same time to encourage her independence. Their lack of experience is more than made up for by a willingness to learn and to listen, a willingness that is enhanced by their professional training, especially Mrs. Stern's experience as a pediatrician. They are honest; they can recognize error, deal with it, and learn from it. They will try to determine rationally the best way to cope with problems in their relationship with Melissa. When the time comes to tell her about her origins, they will probably have found a means of doing so that accords with the best interests of Baby M. All in all, Melissa's future appears solid, happy, and promising with them.

Based on all of this we have concluded, independent of the trial court's identical conclusion, that Melissa's best interests call for custody in the Sterns. Our above-mentioned disagreements with the trial court do not, as we have noted, in any way diminish our concurrence with its conclusions. We feel, however, that those disagreements are important enough to be stated. They are disagreements about the evaluation of conduct. They also may provide some insight about the potential consequences of surrogacy.

It seems to us that given her predicament, Mrs. Whitehead was rather harshly judged—both by the trial court and by some of the experts. She was guilty of a breach of contract, and indeed, she did break a very important promise, but we think it is expecting something well beyond normal human capabilities to suggest that this mother should have parted with her newly born infant without a struggle. . . . We do not countenance, and would never countenance, violating a court order as Mrs. Whitehead did, even a court order that is wrong; but her resistance to an order that she surrender her infant, possibly forever, merits a measure of understanding. We do not find it so clear that her efforts to keep her infant, when measured against the Sterns' efforts to take her away, make one, rather than the other, the wrongdoer. The Sterns suffered, but so did she. And if we go beyond suffering to an evaluation of the human stakes involved in the struggle, how much weight should be given to her nine months of pregnancy, the labor of childbirth, the risk to her life, compared to the payment of money, the anticipation of a child and the donation of sperm?

There has emerged a portrait of Mrs. Whitehead, exposing her children to the media, engaging in negotiations to sell a book, granting interviews that seemed helpful to her, whether hurtful to Baby M or not, that suggests a selfish, grasping woman ready to sacrifice the interests of Baby M and her other children for fame and wealth. That portrait is a half-truth, for while it may accurately reflect what ultimately occurred, its implication, that this is what Mary Beth Whitehead wanted, is totally inaccurate, at least insofar as the record before us is concerned. There is not one word in that record [which] suggests that her change of mind and her subsequent fight for her child was motivated by anything other than love—whatever complex underlying psychological motivations may have existed. . . .

. . . Although there is no substitute for reading the entire record, including the review of every word of each expert's testimony and reports, a summary of their conclusions is revealing. Six experts testified for Mrs. Whitehead: one favored joint custody, clearly unwarranted in this case; one simply rebutted an opposing expert's claim that Mary Beth Whitehead had a recognized personality disorder; one testified to the adverse impact of separation on Mrs. Whitehead; one testified about the evils of adoption and, to him, the probable analogous evils of surrogacy; one spoke only on the question of whether Mrs. Whitehead's consent in the surrogacy agreement was "informed consent"; and one spelled out the strong bond between mother and child. None of them unequivocally stated, or even necessarily implied, an opinion that custody in the Whiteheads was in the best interests of Melissa—the ultimate issue. The

Sterns' experts, both well qualified—as were the Whiteheads'—concluded that the best interests of Melissa required custody in Mr. Stern. Most convincingly, the three experts chosen by the court-appointed guardian ad litem of Baby M, each clearly free of all bias and interest, unanimously and persuasively recommended custody in the Sterns.

Some comment is required on the initial ex parte order awarding custody pendente lite to the Sterns. The issue, although irrelevant to our disposition of this case, may recur; and when it does, it can be of crucial importance. When father and mother are separated and disagree, at birth, on custody, only in an extreme, truly rare, case should the child be taken from its mother pendente lite, i.e., only in the most unusual case should the child be taken from its mother before the dispute is finally determined by the court on its merits. The probable bond between mother and child, and the child's need, not just the mother's, to strengthen that bond, along with the likelihood, in most cases, of a significantly lesser, if any, bond with the father—all counsel against temporary custody in the father. A substantial showing that the mother's continued custody would threaten the child's health or welfare would seem to be required.

. . . Any application by the natural father in a surrogacy dispute for custody pending the outcome of the litigation will henceforth require proof of unfitness, of danger to the child, or the like, of so high a quality and persuasiveness as to make it unlikely that such application will succeed. [Even the mother's] threats to flee should not suffice to warrant any other relief unless her unfitness is clearly shown. At most, it should result in an order enjoining such flight. The erroneous transfer of custody, as we view it, represents a greater risk to the child than removal to a foreign jurisdiction, unless parental unfitness is clearly proved. . . .

Visitation

The trial court's decision to terminate Mrs. Whitehead's parental rights precluded it from making any determination on visitation. Our reversal of the trial court's order, however, requires delineation of Mrs. Whitehead's rights to visitation. It is apparent to us that this factually sensitive issue, which was never addressed below, should not be determined de novo by this Court. We therefore remand the visitation issue to the trial court for an abbreviated hearing and determination as set forth below. . . .

When we examine the record on visitation, the only testimony explicitly dealing with the issue came from the guardian ad litem's experts. Examination of this testimony in light of the complete record, however, reveals that it was an insignificant part of their opinions. The parties, those with a real stake in the dispute, offered no testimony on the issue. The cause for this insufficiency of guidance on the visitation issue was unquestionably the parties' concentration on other, then seemingly much more important, questions. . . .

We also note the following for the trial court's consideration: First, this is not a divorce case where visitation is almost invariably granted to the non-custodial spouse. To some extent the facts here resemble cases where the non-custodial spouse has had practically no relationship with the child; but it only "resembles" those cases. In the instant case, Mrs. Whitehead spent the first four months of this child's life as her mother and has regularly visited the child since then. Second, she is not only the natural mother, but also the legal mother, and is not to be penalized one iota because of the surrogacy contract. . . .

In all of this, the trial court should recall the touchstones of visitation: that it is desirable for the child to have contact with both parents; that besides the child's interests, the parents' interests also must be considered; but that when all is said and done, the best interests of the child are paramount.

We have decided that Mrs. Whitehead is entitled to visitation at some point, and that question is not open to the trial court on this remand. The trial court will determine what kind of visitation shall be granted to her, with or without conditions, and when and under what circumstances it should commence. It also should be noted that the guardian's recommendation of a five-year delay is most unusual—one might argue that it begins to border on termination. Nevertheless, if the circumstances as further developed by appropriate proofs or as reconsidered on remand clearly call for that suspension under applicable legal principles of visitation, it should be so ordered. . . .

Conclusion

This case affords some insight into a new reproductive arrangement: the artificial insemination of a surrogate mother. The unfortunate events that have unfolded illustrate that its unregulated use can bring suffering to all involved. Potential victims include the surrogate mother and her family, the natural father and his wife, and most importantly, the child. Although surrogacy has apparently provided positive results for some infertile couples, it can also, as this case demonstrates, cause suffering to participants, here essentially innocent and well-intended.

We have found that our present laws do not permit the surrogacy contract used in this case. Nowhere, however, do we find any legal prohibition against surrogacy when the surrogate mother volunteers, without any payment, to act as a surrogate and is given the right to change her mind and to assert her parental rights. Moreover, the Legislature remains free to deal with this most sensitive issue as it sees fit, subject only to constitutional constraints.

If the Legislature decides to address surrogacy, consideration of this case will highlight many of its potential harms. We do not underestimate the difficulties of legislating on this subject. In addition to the inevitable confrontation with the ethical and moral issues involved, there is the question of the wisdom and effectiveness of regulating a matter so private, yet of such public interest. Legislative consideration of surrogacy may also provide the opportunity to begin to focus on the overall implications of the new reproductive biotechnology—in vitro fertilization, preservation of sperm and eggs, embryo implantation and the like. The problem is how to enjoy the benefits of the technology—especially for infertile couples—while minimizing the risk of abuse. The problem can be addressed only when society decides what its values and objectives are in this troubling, yet promising, area.

Society's Response to the New Reproductive Technologies: The Feminist Perspective

NORMA JULIET WIKLER

THE SOCIAL ROLE of women has been and continues to be primarily defined by the biological fact that only the female of our species can become pregnant. Although both men and women participate in human reproduction, the tasks of bearing and raising children are commonly considered women's jobs. Thus, when there are changes on the horizon in the area of reproductive technology, women are bound to be interested. Feminists, who base much of their critique of existing institutions on the claim that the social context of reproduction has been disadvantageous to women, are understandably concerned that the new developments will similarly operate against the interests of women.

As advances in the laboratory become publicly known, feminists begin to fashion a political response. However, the technological developments are still too new, and the social consequences of them too uncertain, to have fostered a comprehensive and unified critique. Indeed, the diversity of feminist thought may preclude such a response. Nevertheless, feminists around the world have been increasingly interested in the changes in reproductive technology and the ideological dilemmas arising from them. The emerging feminist literature on new reproductive technologies emphasizes two themes. First, social changes likely to result from these scientific developments will reflect the existing imbalance of power between males and females.[1] Benefits will more likely accrue to men and costs to women. Any inherent capacity of the technologies to free women from male domination will tend to be suppressed. From this perspective, projections of social consequences produced by advances in reproductive technologies which ignore the impact of this power imbalance will be seriously misleading.

Second, the primary focus of societal control and exploitation of women is on their sexual and reproductive capacities, that is, their roles as sex object and child bearer. Accordingly, feminists fear that the application of the new reproductive technologies will be manipulated so as to limit women's autonomy, ensuring that these female capacities will be used in the interest of the male-dominated social order.[2] Central to this

Norma Juliet Wikler, Society's Response to the New Reproductive Technologies: The Feminist Perspectives, 59 S. Cal. L. Rev. 1043–1057 (1986), reprinted with the permission of the Southern California Law Review.

theme is the conflict between social control over reproduction and a woman's right to control her body.

This essay reports on the emerging feminist literature and briefly compares feminist thought to the "consumer" perspective. The consumer perspective, though often classed with the feminist views, offers a distinct position on many of these issues.

I. Feminist Perspectives on the New Reproductive Technologies

Technological developments in human reproduction range from the space-age to the homespun. The first artificial womb is bound to be a million-dollar apparatus, tightly tethered to the laboratory during its first year of development. Yet one potent technology of potentially enormous social importance—the turkey baster, used for self-insemination with donated sperm—can be bought for under a dollar at any grocery store. There is, similarly, a broad continuum in terms of the immediacy of social impact of this new technology: at one end is the unlikely possibility of human-age hybrids, while at the other end lies the more pressing issue of sex preselection.

A. The Impact of New Reproductive Technologies: The Example of Sex Preselection

A recent international conference which drew feminist scholars and activists from thirty-five countries included a session on sex preselection technology.[3] The panelists highlighted the feminist concern that those who preselect their child's gender will choose to have males, and predicted the worst for the interests of women. As one panelist asserted:

> Given the well-documented societal preference for male children—and the fact that millions of women, as well as men, in the western world, not just third world countries, still react to the birth of daughters with disappointment, sorrow, and even economic and social penalties—the potential widespread commercial availability of sex preselection techniques opens up ominous possibilities.[4]

Panelists from India elevated this concern from the level of speculation to the level of fact in their discussion of the practice of selective abortion of female fetuses in Punjab, India. One abortion clinic allegedly uses amniocentesis primarily for sex selection and advertises that fact on billboards. Advertisements for the clinic were reported to have appeared in buses and as commercials at the cinema.[5] Though the government bans the use of amniocentesis for sex selection, these Indian scholars believe that the practice continues.

The widespread use of sex preselection could reduce the size of the female population. Despite hypothetical gains for women in such a situation, such as increased value in the dating and marriage markets, historical evidence leads to contrary empirical conclusions. Two American researchers reported on studies of several modern and ancient populations with sex ratio imbalances.[6] They found that most societies with a preponderance of males are characterized by "bride-price and bride-service, great importance attached to virginity, emphasis on the sanctity of the family . . . proscriptions against adultery . . . marriage at an early age, and [prejudice against] women . . . regarded as inferior to men . . . [in] reasoned judgment, scholarship and political affairs."[7]

Feminist theory suggests that in a male favored social order women will be oppressed whether they comprise a minority or majority. Nevertheless panelists held the view that women do worse as a group if they are greatly outnumbered. One Australian psychologist concluded:

> Women are the most exploited, manipulated, oppressed and brutalized group in the world, yet we have the numbers. What would our status be as a vastly outnumbered group? And how many women would be prepared to accept a world where their value as breeders or sexual objects only would be recognized?[8]

Feminists fear that sex preselection technology may also become a tool to engineer social policies which would further diminish the female population. There is evidence justifying this apprehension. Some observers have reported that population control experts endorse sex selection as a means of population control in third world countries. These experts assume that couples who have the option will satisfy their desire for a son through a first child and then will be more willing to limit family size.[9]

B. Attitudes Towards Experts and Practitioners

Apprehension about the impact the new reproductive technologies will have on the welfare of women has been accompanied by a frequently-voiced distrust of researchers and clinicians. The current feminist alienation from the technological and medical establishment is rooted in the women's health movement of the 1970's. Indeed, the latter was necessitated, in the feminist view, by the failings of the former. Experience has caused feminist health activists to view developments in reproductive technology with caution because of its known hazards to women and children.[10]

Feminist writers have linked social freedom with the practice of obstetrics and gynecology because the intersection of the two occurs over the issue of a woman's control over her body. Control of fertility was essential for the recent empowerment of women. While feminists valued the contributions of physicians and medical researchers which made this possible, they also felt victimized by the dangers of these contraceptive techniques.

Accordingly, feminists distrust the new reproductive technologies partly on the grounds that they are unlikely to be more safe or more beneficial than the older ones. As one commentator wrote:

> The pill was hailed once as the true liberator of women, yet its resulting "freedom" is now viewed with suspicion and scepticism by feminists. It ensured that

most women users had control over their fertility; [sic] but also that they were then "at fault" if they became pregnant. . . . In addition, it led to higher rates of cancer and thrombosis, and continues to be a drug which is taken on the basis of little and poor research into its side effects. . . . Can we assume that sex pres-election will be an equivalent advance in women's reproduction [sic] freedom?[11]

Further distrust is engendered by the view of some that the interests of women count for little, and that the centers of power and wealth operate for the benefit of men. Physicians and medical researchers are portrayed as acting out of self-interest and are put in the same class as industrial polluters:

[The] reproductive technologies are controlled by the same people—the same multinational corporations, the same medical establishment, and the same pa-triarchal values—who brought us DES and thalidomide, who encourage steril-ization while denying abortion, who perform thousands of unnecessary hys-terectomies, and who are poisoning our air, water, land and bodies. Their control of reproductive technology is not likely to benefit women.[12]

From this perspective, the best solution would be to exclude the "experts" alto-gether, as the women's health movement has attempted to do in areas such as child-birth. However, since many of the new prenatal and reproductive technologies require the intervention of experts, feminists fear that recent gains in women's reproductive autonomy may be lost to the medical establishment.

C. Distributive Concerns

The risks notwithstanding, access to the new reproductive technologies will be valuable to women with reproductive problems. However, some feminists have voiced concern that not all women who desire and could benefit from the new technologies will have access to them; those who are generally deprived of goods and services will likely be de-nied these services as well. In making this critique, these feminists incorporate a wider critique of social stratification based on race and class. Although white married women who can afford the new technologies are regarded by feminist writers as a highly vul-nerable group easily exploited because of their desperation, the most disadvantaged women are likely to be poor, black, single, or lesbian. Historical experience supports this view. In the nineteenth century, poor and mostly non-white women acted as wet nurses, selling their milk to mothers of the upper classes, sometimes depriving their own children in the process. No sophisticated analysis is needed to see the parallel in surrogate motherhood and the sale of human eggs.

According to these feminists, the same phenomenon could spread across national boundaries. Disadvantaged women could be victimized by an overselling of the bene-fits of advanced reproductive technology. The effort to persuade women of third world countries to use baby formula in place of nutritionally and economically superior mother's milk may forecast the impact of the new reproductive technologies on women in the poorer nations.

II. Feminist Dilemmas Regarding Reproductive Technology

The new reproductive technologies pose dilemmas for feminists and for feminist theory. In fact, the new developments pose a challenge to some important planks in the feminist platform, encouraging feminists to develop a coherent theoretical analysis and a coherent program for public policy.

Historically, the principal aim of feminism has been equality between the sexes. In each era, this principle has involved different interpretations and given rise to political programs most appropriate to feminists of the time. Thus, while feminists of an earlier era argued for equal political rights on the grounds that these rights would make them better housewives, later feminists insisted on winning for women the option to be freed from the domestic role. Thus, the basic, unchanging goal of equality has always dictated, in concert with the culture of the era, the stand of the women's movement on motherhood, reproductive choice, and other issues.

The present may mark one of those watersheds in which the interpretation of the basic goal of equality is reconsidered and in which its meaning for feminism's political and social program is altered. The rise of the new reproductive technologies is prompting feminists to ask whether the movement's current positions on motherhood, choice, and other issues of primary concern to women remain expressive of the egalitarian ideal.

A. Choice and Technology

The notion of "choice" has served as an ideological cornerstone of the political program of the movements for reproductive rights and women's health. Feminists have been unequivocally "pro-choice" in their support of a woman's right to choose abortion and contraception over pregnancy (and vice-versa), to choose alternatives to orthodox medical treatment, and to decide for themselves the manner and the circumstances of childbirth.

Feminists agree that reproductive technology can extend the range of choices available to women. Still, there is concern that what increases choice in the short run may result in a loss of choice in the long run, and that what increases the number of options for some women narrows the range available to others. Additionally, there is concern over the quality, rather than the mere quantity of the choices which the new technologies may make available.

The acceptance by some earlier writers in the contemporary feminist movement of anticipated advances in reproductive technology was quite remarkable. Shulamith Firestone, whose book, *The Dialectic of Sex*,[13] was a powerful stimulant to feminist theory, virtually anointed high-tech as the savior of women. Firestone regarded pregnancy as a burden imposed upon women for the sake of the species. She saw the liberation of women as depending initially on the liberation from childbearing; her solution was test-tube reproduction.[14]

In recent years, there has been a definite, though not uniform, change in the attitudes toward childbearing and maternity expressed in feminist writing. Adrienne Rich, for example, has drawn a distinction between the experience of motherhood, which may be desirable for many women, and the institution of motherhood, which has been oppressive for many.[15] This view retains the main thrust of earlier feminist writings while rendering feminism compatible with the positive attitudes toward motherhood which many feminists have developed as a part of their personal experience.

The view expressed by Firestone and others endorses medical technology for its promised ability to help fertile women avoid pregnancy. The alternative views such as Rich's would welcome, by implication, technology which helps infertile women become pregnant. These two attitudes, however, do not lead to an unqualified endorsement of reproductive technology by feminists. Feminists fear the consequences of these technologies if they are not controlled by women for the interests of women. As the age of artificial reproduction draws near, feminists see control going to the medical profession, dominated by males and serving male-oriented social ends.

Thus, the new reproductive technologies are the source of a profound ambivalence on the part of many feminists. Feminist theory points to the conclusion that women will be the losers when reproductive power is controlled in important ways by a cadre of experts working in a patriarchal system. At the same time, many individual feminists, particularly those who deferred childbearing for career building, have benefited from these technologies as used by these same experts. Feminist social scientists demonstrated that a crucial barrier to the career ladder for many women was early motherhood, and many career women owe some of their success to their ability to spend their younger years in specialized training and full-time career building. The choice to defer childbearing would be much less attractive for women wanting to have children eventually if they could not count on the benefits of the new reproductive technology, including amniocentesis to guard against age-related birth defects and fertility drugs to deal with the natural decrease in fertility in women attempting to conceive in the last of their child-bearing years.

B. Government Intervention

In the area of reproductive decisionmaking, feminists have demanded that individuals have unrestricted freedom and that the government not intervene. Currently, feminist writing is beginning to appear which calls for reconsideration of both positions. Robyn Rowland writes:

> Past choices *opened* opportunities for women *as a social group*. But what of a "choice" which *closes* opportunities as a social group? Does the desire, the need, the wanting of choice have *no* boundaries[?] There must be a time at which the rights of one group impinge so strongly on those of the majority that social control is needed. . . . The "right" to choose the sex of your child . . . the "right" of the medical profession to *service* these rights, have been used to ensure a lack of

government and social intervention. And that *is* what we wanted with abortion and contraception and in sexuality. But is it what we want with reproductive technology that changes the sex ratio or clones human beings or changes genetic structure? . . . What is "the right to choose" in this context?[16]

In Rowland's view, government intervention in reproductive decision-making may be necessary to protect the interests of women as a group:

Policy decisions may have to be made in the reproductive area which will contradict or expand in a new direction, current feminist ideology on reproductive freedom. We have a responsibility, not just to women who want children and may be infertile, but to the generations of people who will be the results of the use of new technology. To retain control over human experimentation, women may have to consider state intervention of some kind in the areas of research funding, research application and reproductive rights—with all its inherent dangers. We may have to call for an end to research which would have helped infertile women to conceive, in consideration of the danger to women as a social group of loss of control over "natural" childbearing (e.g., the right *not* to choose the sex of your child).[17]

This view represents an almost complete reversal of the concept of the right to privacy in reproductive decisionmaking, which the Supreme Court advanced in Roe v. Wade[18] and which has been adopted as a kind of natural right by feminists. The danger to the feminist program, of course, is that once the right to privacy in reproductive decisionmaking loses its status as a natural or constitutional right, women risk losing choices that they now have. If one accepts that the government would not be violating the fundamental right to privacy by intervening in ways which Rowland and others now advocate, it is difficult to argue that it would be a violation of that right for the government to intervene in another reproductive practice, namely, abortion. Helen Holmes and Betty Hoskins are among the feminist writers who insist that inviting government intervention will jeopardize the freedoms now enjoyed: "Thus, while standing in strong opposition to these technologies, we cannot urge laws against them."[19]

The call for governmental regulation stems from a genuine and palpable fear over the ultimate consequences. Feminist theory provides general warning about the implications for women of any new and powerful technology requiring expert application and corporate or large-scale institutional funding. As Genoveffa Corca states:

Through the years, with widespread use of the technologies, social institutions will be restructured to reflect a new reality—tightened male control over female reproductive processes. We do not know exactly how this new reality will be expressed but, as sociologist Jalna Hanmer has observed, "we do know that in a system characterized by power imbalance, the greater the assymetry, [sic] the greater the potential abuse of the less powerful group."[20]

The specific fear, however, is that the new reproductive technology will empower society in its effort to attain complete control over women's reproductive capacity. Corea identifies the following, potentially useful techniques available to reproductive engineers:

- Artificial insemination
- Superovulation by hormone injection
- Estrus synchronization (to facilitate transfer of embryos between donor and recipients)
- Ova Recovery (surgical intervention or lavage)
- Twinning (multiple individuals from one fertilized egg)
- Embryo transfer from donor to recipient
- Cesarean Section[21]

Each technique could be employed without the willing cooperation of the women on whom they are performed and they are all currently being used on animals. This animal analogy haunts the writing of some authors who are fashioning a feminist response to the new developments. Corea notes that the techniques are taken from animal breeders and warns that, though "[i]t is easy to dismiss the fate of animals as one entirely different from that of women," it would be foolhardy to do so.[22] There are ways in which women's reproductive capacity could be controlled and used; women could become professional breeders. Andrea Dworkin observed that "[w]omen can sell reproductive capacities the same way old-time prostitutes sold sexual ones."[23]

The use of disadvantaged women as professional breeders has been raised as a possibility. Corea quotes a bioethicist who maintains that there are enough women available to form a caste of childbearers.[24] An unemployed nurse, for example, recently offered to bear a child for a California couple so that she could take herself and her young daughter off welfare.[25] Corea notes that leaders of the budding surrogate motherhood industry estimate that once embryo transfers become common, $1,000 will be enough to buy the services of most mothers, especially if women in poorer countries are employed.[26] One firm views Central America as a good source of low-cost surrogate mothers. This same firm publishes a quarterly directory with pictures of North America women willing to serve as breeders.[27]

In a feminist's nightmare version of *Brave New World*,[28] Corea imagines women being routinely sterilized with technology being used to facilitate reproduction if this is desired later. In this "breeding brothel" approach to reproduction, white women who are judged superior would be selected as egg donors and turned into machines for producing embryos; women of color would be used as breeders, with artificial synchronization of menstrual cycles perfecting the assembly line. This would continue until the development of the artificial womb, after which the breeder would no longer be of value.[29]

What is striking in this scenario is not so much that a woman might use her womb to nourish another's egg, but the involuntariness of it. The conflict in attitudes toward the new reproductive technologies, which is evident in recent feminist writing, is in part the result of uncertainty over how to regard surrogate mothers, subjects of experimentation, and others offering themselves up to the new technology. Should they be perceived as active agents freely pursuing their own ends, or as victims whose lack of free choice is exploited in ways not fundamentally different from the older modes of social control of reproductive capacity? This uncertainty, together with the ambivalence shown to the new technology because it is at once personally empowering while not controlled by women, presents dilemmas for feminist theoreticians which impede the development of a consistent, and therefore realizable, program for responding to the developments in reproductive technology.

III. The Consumer Perspective

Feminist perspectives on the new technologies take as their starting point the perceived interests of women as a group. In contrast, the consumer perspective voices similar concerns but has a different, though overlapping, constituency, and ultimately supports a different set of policies. This perspective focuses on the interests of infertile women and couples who desire to have children.[30]

However, feminists and consumer advocates agree on a number of points. For example, both are appalled at the number of cases of iatrogenic infertility caused by incompetent abdominal surgery, undetected pelvic inflammatory disease (P.I.D.), and inadequately tested drugs and contraceptive devices. Both seek to stop the use of untested chemicals in the workplace which causes male and female infertility, and both recognize the potential for abuse and exploitation of women with reproductive problems for financial gain and medical careerism.

Their responses to these problems, however, differ. While some feminist writers contemplate a call for a halt to all research on certain technologies,[31] the consumer advocates typically are more cautious. They demand closer scrutiny of technological development in the form of public debate, procedural guidelines, mechanisms for accountability, and research on the consequences of clinical applications.[32]

Some of these consumer advocates are tentative, for they worry that even these limited demands could lead to a shutdown of the whole enterprise. They believe that with education and support, infertile couples can hold their own with doctors and make informed, autonomous choices about treatment.

Consumer advocates have greater faith and interest in the power of individuals to use the new reproductive technologies to their own personal advantage. The feminists, on the other hand, tend to regard the individual female patient's autonomy in this area as illusory and thus are open to the possibility of interfering with an individual's freedom of choice, if so doing would protect women as a group.

IV. Critique of Feminist Analyses

The validity of the feminist perspectives necessarily depends on the truth of the feminist principles and premises. If our society is indeed structured so as to render the benefits of new technologies and advancements principally to men, certainly the same will be true of new reproductive technologies. Whether or not one is sympathetic to this view of society, some lessons can be taken from recent feminist writing.

First, feminists contend that while the new technologies can and do provide immediate and important benefits for women, they may simultaneously have the ability to inflict great harm. Hence, protecting the interests of women requires at the very least a close watch on the research and development of these technologies.

Second, feminists point out that the existing legal structure is inadequate to protect women's interests in the new technologies. Specifically, the feminist critiques suggest that the right to reproductive privacy enunciated in Roe v. Wade may not provide a sturdy foundation upon which to erect a lattice of rules, regulations, and procedures sufficient to safeguard women in their desire to control fertility. Some of the protected choices may not be free ones, and other choices may adversely affect the interests of women in particular and society in general.

The feminist critique, then, emphasizes that the capacity of the new technology for good or evil depends on the social context surrounding its use and application. Indeed, feminists, among others, note that the direction of technological innovation is not self-determining and that the kinds of reproductive technologies which would emerge in a truly gender-equal society might be quite different from those which the present system produces. This analysis has great merit, but it must be extended in order to develop a sufficiently insightful and coherent evaluation of the new reproductive developments. Literature (feminist writings included) presents reproductive technologies as if they have emerged only recently. While there is much that is new—in vitro fertilization could not have been done any time before the last few years—we have possessed the capability of restructuring the conditions and modes of human reproduction throughout history.

Reproductive brothels, for examples, could have been instituted without any new technology. Perhaps the old Southern plantations practiced some of this, but for the most part this was unheard of. One "technology" available for centuries is artificial insemination, easily accomplished with the household turkey baster or similar objects which have long been available. Such a device allows women to become pregnant with only minimal cooperation from men, and under conditions almost totally under women's control. In vitro fertilization is arguably a much less powerful force for change in social structure than artificial insemination at home.

The key to understanding the import of the new technologies is to understand why the old ones were not used. The tools were there, in some cases sitting in the kitchen cupboard. Yet, for centuries, no one thought to pick them up and use them. A critical line of inquiry for feminist social science is to explore why, given the rules of courtship, family structure, and sex role differentiation (and, on a deeper level, the determinants of these structures), those who might have been in a position to use these "technologies" did not even consider doing so.

Such an analysis will show that the most important link leads not from the laboratory to changes in the social structure, but the other way around. The sudden burst of research and development in human reproduction followed closely the recent changes in male-female relations, sexual morality, and the role and status of women, as well as the increasing number of infertile people who want children and the diminished availability of adoptable babies. There will be reciprocal causation; but if the new reproductive technologies are to drastically alter society, the root cause will be the events which prompted society to refashion its potential for using the technologies—both those technologies which have long been available and the technologies still to come.

Conclusion

The potential social consequences of the new reproductive technologies are both desirable and abhorrent. Since the primary recipients of the technologies are women, the future course of research and deployment in this area should be fully informed by women's diverse views. Feminists will have much more to say on this subject. An international network has recently been organized to monitor the reproductive technologies and to develop feminist policy positions and strategies for action with regard to their use.[33]

Thus far, however, the concerns being voiced by feminist scholars and critics are rarely heard in the discussion and debates on the reproductive technologies within medical and legal communities. Inclusion of feminist perspectives is essential if we are to achieve a responsible balance between control and freedom of inquiry, and a proper direction for that control. These are the difficult tasks that lie ahead.

Notes

1. See Rothman, The Meanings of Choice in Reproductive Technology, in R. Arditti, R. Klein & S. Minder eds., Test-Tube Women: What Future for Motherhood? 23, 23, 27 (Pandora Press, 1984).

2. See H. Holmes, B. Hoskins & M. Gross eds., The Custom-Made Child? Women-Centered Perspectives (Humana Press, 1981).

3. Proceedings of the Second International Interdisciplinary Congress on Women, Women's Worlds: Strategies for Empowerment, in Gronigen, Netherlands (Apr. 17–21, 1984). The panel was called "Death of the Female."

4. R. Steinbacher, Sex Choice: Survival and Sisterhood 5–6 (Apr. 1984) (paper presented at the Second International Interdisciplinary Congress on Women, Women's Worlds: Strategies for Empowerment, in Gronigen, Netherlands).

5. Roggencamp, Abortion of a Special Kind: Male Sex Selection in India, in Test-Tube Women, *supra* note 1, at 266, 266.

6. See H. Holmes & B. Hoskins, Prenatal and Preconception Sex Choice Technologies: A Path to Femicide? (Apr. 1984) (paper presented at the Second International Interdisciplinary Congress on Women, Women's Worlds: Strategies for Empowerment, in Gronigen, Netherlands).

7. *Id.* at 9 (quoting M. Guttentag & P. Secord, Too Many Women? The Sex Ratio Question 79 (1983)).

8. R. Rowland, Motherhood, Patriarchal Power, Alienation and the Issue of "Choice" in Sex Preselection 14 (Apr. 1984) (paper presented at the Second International Interdisciplinary Congress on Women, Women's Worlds: Strategies for Empowerment, in Gronigen, Netherlands); see Rowland, Social Implications of Reproductive Technology, 8 Int'l Rev. Nat. Plan. 189, 200 (1984).

9. Holmes & Hoskins, *supra* note 6, at 8.

10. See, e.g., F. Hornstein, Lesbians and Donor Insemination (Apr. 1980) (paper presented at the Women and the Law Conference, in Boston).

11. Rowland, Motherhood, *supra* note 8, at 11; see Rowland, Social Implications, *supra* note 8, at 194–195.

12. Logan, Ectogenesis and Ideology, in The Custom-Made Child?, *supra* note 2, at 291, 193.

13. S. Firestone, The Dialectic of Sex (1970).

14. *Id.* at 233.

15. A. Rich, Of Women Born: Motherhood as Experience and Institution (W. W. Norton, 1976).

16. Rowland, Motherhood, *supra* note 8, at 15–16 (emphasis in original); see Rowland, Social Implications, *supra* note 8, at 202–203.

17. Rowland, Motherhood, *supra* note 8, at 17.

18. 410 U.S. 113 (1973).

19. Holmes & Hoskins, *supra* note 6, at 11.

20. G. Corea, How the New Reproductive Technologies Could Be Used to Apply to Reproduction the Brothel Model of Social Control Over Women 11 (Apr. 1984) (paper presented at Second International Interdisciplinary Congress on Women, Women's Worlds: Strategies for Empowerment, in Gronigen, The Netherlands); see also G. Corea, The Mother Machine: Reproductive Technologies from Artificial Insemination to Artificial Wombs (1985).

21. Corea, New Reproductive Technologies, *supra* note 20, at 3–4.

22. *Id.* at 6.

23. *Id.* at 2 (quoting A. Dworkin, Right-wing Woman (Perigee, G.P. Putnam, 1983)).

24. *Id.* at 7.

25. *Id.*

26. *Id.* at 8.

27. *Id.* at 8–9.

28. A. Huxley, Brave New World (1932).

29. Corea, New Reproductive Technologies, *supra* note 20, at 9–15.

30. For a detailed discussion of the new reproductive technologies from the consumer perspective see L. Andrews, New Conceptions: A Consumer's Guide to the Newest Infertility Treatments, Including in Vitro Fertilization, Artificial Insemination and Surrogate Motherhood (1984).

31. See, e.g., Corea, The Mother Machine, *supra* note 20, at 318–324; Rowland, Motherhood, *supra* note 8, at 17.

32. See, e.g., S. Ruzek, The Women's Health Movement: Feminist Alternatives to Medical Control 209–235 (1978).

33. The network is called FINRRAGE (Feminist International Network of Resistance to Reproductive and Genetic Engineering). This group sponsored its first conference, Emergency Conference on The New Reproductive Technology, in Lund, Sweden (July 3–8, 1985).

Surrogate Motherhood:
The Challenge for Feminists

Lori B. Andrews

SURROGATE MOTHERHOOD presents an enormous challenge for feminists. During the course of the *Baby M* trial, the New Jersey chapter of the National Organization of Women met and could not reach consensus on the issue. "The feelings ranged the gamut," the head of the chapter, Linda Bowker, told the *New York Times*. "We did feel that it should not be made illegal, because we don't want to turn women into criminals. But other than that, what you may feel about the *Baby M* case may not be what you feel about another."

"We do believe that women ought to control their own bodies, and we don't want to play big brother or big sister and tell them what to do," Ms. Bowker continued. "But on the other hand, we don't want to see the day when women are turned into breeding machines."[1]

Other feminist groups have likewise been split on the issue, but a vocal group of feminists came to the support of Mary Beth Whitehead with demonstrations and an *amicus* brief[2]; they are now seeking laws that would ban surrogate motherhood altogether. However, the rationales that they and others are using to justify this governmental intrusion into reproductive choice may come back to haunt feminists in other areas of procreative policy and family law. . . .

The Feminist Legacy

In the past two decades, feminist policy arguments have refashioned legal policies on reproduction and the family. A cornerstone of this development has been the idea that women have a right to reproductive choice—to be able to contracept, abort, or get pregnant. They have the right to control their bodies during pregnancy, such as by refusing Cesarean sections. They have a right to create non-traditional family structures such as lesbian households or single-parent families facilitated by artificial insemination by donor. According to feminist arguments, these rights should not be overridden by possible symbolic harms or speculative risks to potential children.

16 Law, Med. & Health Care 72 (1988).

Another hallmark of feminism has been that biology should not be destiny. The equal treatment of the sexes requires that decisions about men and women be made on other than biological grounds. Women police officers can be as good as men, despite their lesser strength on average. Women's larger role in bearing children does not mean they should have the larger responsibility in rearing children. And biological fathers, as well as non-biological mothers or fathers, can be as good parents as biological mothers.

The legal doctrine upon which feminists have pinned much of their policy has been the constitutional protection of autonomy in decisions to bear and rear one's biological children.[3] Once this protection of the biologically related family was acknowledged, feminists and others could argue for the protection of non-traditional, non-biological families on the grounds that they provide many of the same emotional, physical, and financial benefits that biological families do.

In many ways, the very existence of surrogacy is a predictable outgrowth of the feminist movement. Feminist gains allowed women to pursue educational and career opportunities once reserved for men. . . . But this also meant that more women were postponing childbearing, and suffering the natural decline in fertility that occurs with age. Women who exercised their right to contraception, such as by using the Dalkon Shield, sometimes found that their fertility was permanently compromised. Some women found that the chance for a child had slipped by them entirely and decided to turn to a surrogate mother.

Feminism also made it more likely for other women to feel comfortable being surrogates. Feminism taught that not all women relate to all pregnancies in the same way. A woman could choose not to be a rearing mother at all. She could choose to lead a child-free life by not getting pregnant. If she got pregnant, she could choose to abort. Reproduction was a condition of her body over which she, and no one else, should have control. For some women, those developments added up to the freedom to be a surrogate.

In the surrogacy context, feminist principles have provided the basis for a broadly held position that contracts and legislation should not restrict the surrogate's control over her body during pregnancy (such as by a requirement that the surrogate undergo amniocentesis or abort a fetus with a genetic defect). The argument against enforcing such contractual provisions resounds with the notion of gender equality, since it is in keeping with common law principles that protect the bodily integrity of both men and women, as well as with basic contract principles rejecting specific performance of personal-services provisions. It is also in keeping with constitutional principles giving the pregnant woman, rather than the male progenitor, the right to make abortion decisions. . . .

Now a growing feminist contingent is moving beyond the issue of bodily control during pregnancy and is seeking to ban surrogacy altogether. But the rationales for such a ban are often the very rationales that feminists have fought against in the contexts of abortion, contraception, non-traditional families, and employment. The adoption of these rationales as the reasons to regulate surrogacy could severely undercut the gains previously made in these other areas. These rationales fall into three general categories: the symbolic harm to society of allowing paid surrogacy, the potential risks to the woman of allowing paid surrogacy, and the potential risks to the potential child of allowing paid surrogacy.

The Symbolic Harm to Society

For some feminists, the argument against surrogacy is a simple one: it demeans us all as a society to sell babies. And put that way, the argument is persuasive, at least on its face. But as a justification for policy, the argument is reminiscent of the argument that feminists roundly reject in the abortion context: that it demeans us as a society to kill babies.

Both arguments, equally heartfelt, need closer scrutiny if they are to serve as a basis for policy. In the abortion context, pro-choice people criticize the terms, saying we are not talking about "babies" when the abortion is done on an embryo or fetus still within the woman's womb. In the surrogacy context, a similar assault can be made on the term "sale." The baby is not being transferred for money to a stranger who can then treat the child like a commodity, doing anything he or she wants with the child. The money is being paid to enable a man to procreate his biological child; this hardly seems to fit the characterization of a sale. Am I buying a child when I pay a physician to be my surrogate fallopian tubes through in vitro fertilization (when, without her aid, I would remain childless)? Am I buying a child when I pay a physician to perform a needed Cesarean section, without which my child would never be born alive?

At most, in the surrogacy context, I am buying not a child but the pre-conception termination of the mother's parental rights. For decades, the pre-conception sale of a father's parental rights have been allowed with artificial insemination by donor. This practice, currently facilitated by statutes in at least thirty states, has received strong feminist support. In fact, when, on occasion, such sperm donors have later felt a bond to the child and wanted to be considered legal fathers, feminist groups have litigated to hold them to their pre-conception contract.[4]

Rather than focusing on the symbolic aspects of a sale, the policy discussion should instead analyze the advisability of pre-conception terminations for both women and men. For example, biological parenting may be so important to both the parent and the child that either parent should be able to assert these rights after birth (or even later in the child's life). This would provide sperm donors in artificial insemination with a chance to have a relationship with the child.

Symbolic arguments and pejorative language seem to make up the bulk of the policy arguments and media commentary against surrogacy. Surrogate motherhood has been described by its opponents not only as the buying and selling of children but as reproductive prostitution,[5] reproductive slavery,[6] the renting of a womb,[7] incubatory servitude,[8] the factory method of childbearing,[9] and cutting up women into genitalia.[10] The women who are surrogates are labeled paid breeders,[11] biological entrepreneurs,[12] breeder women,[13] reproductive meat,[14] interchangeable parts in the birth machinery,[15] manufacturing plants,[16] human incubators,[17] incubators for men's sperm,[18] a commodity in the reproductive marketplace,[19] and prostitutes.[20] Their husbands are seen, alternatively, as pimps[21] or cuckolds.[22] The children conceived pursuant to a surrogacy agreement have been called chattel[23] or merchandise to be expected in perfect condition.[24]

Feminists opposing surrogacy have also relied heavily on a visual element in the debate over *Baby M.* They have been understandably upset at the vision of a baby being wrenched from its nursing mother or being slipped out a back window in a flight from governmental authorities. But relying on the visceral and visual, a longstanding tactic of the right-to-life groups, is not the way to make policy. Conceding the value of symbolic arguments for the procreative choice of surrogacy makes it hard to reject them for other procreative choices.

One of the greatest feminism contributions to policy debates on reproduction and the family has been the rejection of arguments relying on tradition and symbolism and an insistence on an understanding of the nature and effects of an actual practice in determining how it should be regulated. For example, the idea that it is necessary for children to grow up in two-parent, heterosexual families has been contested by empirical evidence that such traditional structures are not necessary for children to flourish.[25] This type of analysis should not be overlooked in favor of symbolism in discussions of surrogacy.

The Potential Harm to Women

A second line of argument opposes surrogacy because of the potential psychological and physical risks that it presents for women. Many aspects of this argument, however, seem ill founded and potentially demeaning to women. They focus on protecting women against their own decisions because those decisions might later cause them regret, be unduly influenced by others, or be forced by financial motivations.

Reproductive choices are tough choices, and any decisions about reproduction—such as abortion, sterilization, sperm donation, or surrogacy—might later be regretted. The potential for later regrets, however, is usually not thought to be a valid reason to ban the right to choose the procedure in the first place.

With surrogacy, the potential for regret is thought by some to be enormously high. This is because it is argued (in biology-is-destiny terms) that it is unnatural for a mother to give up a child. It is assumed that because birth mothers in traditional adoption situations often regret relinquishing their children, surrogate mothers will feel the same way. But surrogate mothers are making their decisions about relinquishment under much different circumstances. The biological mother in the traditional adoption situation is already pregnant as part of a personal relationship of her own. In many, many instances, she would like to keep the child but cannot because the relationship is not supportive or she cannot afford to raise the child. She generally feels that the relinquishment was forced upon her (for example, by her parents, a counselor, or her lover).

The biological mother in the surrogacy situation seeks out the opportunity to carry a child that would not exist were it not for the couple's desire to create a child as a part of their relationship. She makes her decision in advance of pregnancy for internal, not externally enforced reasons. While 75 percent of the biological mothers who give up a child for adoption later change their minds,[26] only around 1 percent of the surrogates have similar changes of heart.

Entering into a surrogacy arrangement does present potential psychological risks to women. But arguing for a ban on surrogacy seems to concede that the government, rather than the individual woman, should determine what risks a woman should be allowed to face. This conflicts with the general legal policy allowing competent individuals to engage in potentially risky behavior so long as they have given their voluntary, informed consent.

Perhaps recognizing the dangers of giving the government widespread powers to "protect" women, some feminists do acknowledge the validity of a general consent to assume risks. They argue, however, that the consent model is not appropriate to surrogacy since the surrogate's consent is neither informed nor voluntary.

It strikes me as odd to assume that the surrogate's consent is not informed. The surrogacy contracts contain lengthy riders detailing the myriad risks of pregnancy, so potential surrogates are much better informed on that topic than are most women who get pregnant in a more traditional fashion. In addition, with volumes of publicity given to the plight of Mary Beth Whitehead, all potential surrogates are now aware of the possibility that they may later regret their decisions. So, at that level, the decision is informed.

Yet a strong element of the feminist argument against surrogacy is that women cannot give an informed consent until they have had the experience of giving birth. Robert Arenstein, an attorney for Mary Beth Whitehead, argued in congressional testimony that a "pre-birth or at-birth termination, is a termination without informed consent. I use the words informed consent to mean full understanding of the personal psychological consequences at the time of surrender of the child."[27] The feminist *amicus* brief in *Baby M* made a similar argument.

The New Jersey Supreme Court picked up this characterization of informed consent, writing that "quite clearly any decision prior to the baby's birth is, in the most important sense, uninformed."[28] But such an approach is at odds with the legal doctrine of informed consent. Nowhere is it expected that one must have the experience before one can make an informed judgment about whether to agree to the experience. Such a requirement would preclude people from ever giving informed consent to sterilizations, abortions, sex change operations, heart surgery, and so forth. The legal doctrine of informed consent presupposes that people will predict in advance of the experience whether a particular course will be beneficial to them.

A variation of the informed consent argument is that while most competent adults can make such predictions, hormonal changes during pregnancy may cause a woman to change her mind. Virtually a whole *amicus* brief in the *Baby M* appeal was devoted to arguing that a woman's hormonal changes during pregnancy make it impossible for her to predict in advance the consequences of her relinquishment.[29] Along those lines, adoption worker Elaine Rosenfeld argues that

> [t]he consent that the birth mother gives prior to conception is not the consent of . . . a woman who has gone through the chemical, biological, endocrinological changes that have taken place during pregnancy and birth, and no matter how well prepared or well intentioned she is in her decision prior to conception, it is impossible for her to predict how she will feel after she gives birth.[30]

In contrast, psychologist Joan Einwohner, who works with a surrogate mother program, points out that

> women are fully capable of entering into agreements in this area and of fulfilling the obligations of a contract. Women's hormonal changes have been utilized too frequently over the centuries to enable male-dominated society to make decisions for them. The Victorian era allowed women no legal rights to enter into contracts. The Victorian era relegated them to the status of dependent children. Victorian ideas are being given renewed life in the conviction of some people that women are so overwhelmed by their feelings at the time of birth that they must be protected from themselves.[31]

. . . In any case, feminists should be wary of a hormone-based argument, just as they have been wary of the hormone-related criminal defense of premenstrual syndrome.

The consent given by surrogates is also challenged as not being voluntary. Feminist Gena Corea, for example, in writing about another reproduction arrangement, in vitro fertilization, asks, "What is the real meaning of a woman's 'consent' . . . in a society in which men as a social group control not just the choices open to women but also women's *motivation* to choose?"[32]

Such an argument is a dangerous one for feminists to make. It would seem to be a step backward for women to argue that they are incapable of making decisions. That, after all, was the rationale for so many legal principles oppressing women for so long, such as the rationale behind the laws not allowing women to hold property. Clearly, any person's choices are motivated by a range of influences—economic, social, religious.

At a recent conference of law professors, it was suggested that surrogacy was wrong because women's boyfriends might talk them into being surrogates and because women might be surrogates for financial reasons. But women's boyfriends might talk them into having abortions or women might have abortions for financial reasons; nevertheless, feminists do not consider those to be adequate reasons to ban abortions. The fact that a woman's decision could be influenced by the individual men in her life or by male-dominated society does not by itself provide an adequate reason to ban surrogacy.

Various feminists have made the argument that the financial inducement to a surrogate vitiates the voluntariness of her consent. Many feminists have said that women are exploited by surrogacy.[33] They point out that in our society's social and economic conditions, some women—such as those on welfare or in dire financial need—will turn to surrogacy out of necessity, rather than true choice. In my view, this is a harsh reality that must be guarded against by vigilant efforts to assure that women have equal access to the labor market and that there are sufficient social services so that poor women with children do not feel they must enter into a surrogacy arrangement in order to obtain money to provide care for their existing children.

However, the vast majority of women who have been surrogates do not allege that they have been tricked into surrogacy, nor have they done it because they needed to obtain a basic of life such as food or health care. Mary Beth Whitehead wanted to pay for her children's education. Kim Cotton wanted money to redecorate her house.[34] Another surrogate wanted money to buy a car. These do not seem to be cases of economic exploitation; there is no consensus, for example, that private education, interior decoration, and an automobile are basic needs, nor that society has an obligation to provide those items. Moreover, some surrogate mother programs specifically reject women who are below a certain income level to avoid the possibility of exploitation.

There is a sexist undertone to an argument that Mary Beth Whitehead was exploited by the paid surrogacy agreement into which she entered to get money for her children's education. If Mary Beth's husband, Rick, had taken a second job to pay for their children's education (or even to pay for their mortgage), he would not have been viewed as exploited. He would have been lauded as a responsible parent.

It undercuts the legitimacy of women's role in the workforce to assume that they are being exploited if they plan to use their money for serious purchases. It seems to harken back to a notion that women work (and should work) only for pin money (a stereotype that is the basis for justifying the firing of women in times of economic crisis). It is also disturbing that in most instances, when society suggests that a certain activity should be done for altruism, rather than money, it is generally a woman's activity.

Some people suggest that since there is a ban on payment for organs, there should be a ban on payment to a surrogate.[35] But the payment for organs is different from the payment to a surrogate. . . . An organ is not meant to be removed from the body; it endangers the life of the donor to live without the organ. In contrast, babies are conceived to leave the body and the life of the surrogate is not endangered by living without the child.

At various legislative hearings, women's groups have virtually begged that women be protected against themselves, against their own decisions. Adria Hillman testified against a New York surrogacy bill on behalf of the New York State Coalition on Women's Legislative Issues. One would think that a women's group would criticize the bill as unduly intruding into women's decisions—it requires a double-check by a court on a contract made by a woman (the surrogate mother) to assure that she gave voluntary, informed consent and does not require oversight of contracts made by men. But the testimony was just the opposite. The bill was criticized as empowering the court to assess whether a surrogacy agreement protects the health and welfare of the potential child, without specifying that the judge should look into the agreement's potential effect on the natural mother.[36] What next? Will women have to go before a court when they are considering having an affair—to have a judge discern whether they will be psychologically harmed by, or later regret, the relationship?

Washington Post writer Jane Leavy has written:

I have read volumes in defense of Mary Beth, her courage in taking on a lonely battle against the upper classes, the exploited wife of a sanitation man versus the wife of a biochemist, a woman with a 9th grade education versus a pediatrician. It all strikes me as a bit patronizing. Since when do we assume that a 29-year-old mother is incapable of making an adult decision and accepting the consequences of it?[37]

Surrogate mother Donna Regan similarly testified in New York that her will was not overborne in the surrogacy context: "No one came to ask me to be a surrogate mother. I went to them and asked them to allow me to be a surrogate mother."

"I find it extremely insulting that there are people saying that, as a woman, I cannot make an informed choice about a pregnancy that I carry," she continued, pointing out that she, like everyone, "makes other difficult choices in her life."[38]

Potential Harm to Potential Children

The third line of argument opposes surrogacy because of the potential harm it represents to potential children. Feminists have had a long-standing concern for the welfare of children. But much feminist policy in the area has been based on the idea that mothers (and family) are more appropriate decision-makers about the best interests of children than the government. Feminists have also fought against using traditions, stereotypes, and societal tolerance or intolerance as a driving force for determining what is in a child's best interest. In that respect, it is understandable that feminists rallied to the aid of Mary Beth Whitehead in order to expose and oppose the faulty grounds on which custody was being determined.[39]

However, the opposition to stereotypes being used to determine custody in a best-interests analysis is not a valid argument against surrogacy itself (which is premised not on stereotypes about the child's best interest being used to determine custody, but on a pre-conception agreement being used to determine custody). And when the larger issue of the advisability of surrogacy itself comes up, feminists risk falling into the trap of using arguments about potential harm to the child that have as faulty a basis as those they oppose in other areas of family law.

For example, one line of argument against surrogacy is that it is like adoption and adoption harms children. However, such an argument is not sufficiently borne out in fact. There is evidence that adopted children do as well as non-adopted children in terms of adjustment and achievement.[40] A family of two biological parents is not necessary to assure the child's well-being.

Surrogacy has also been analogized to baby-selling. Baby-selling is prohibited in our society, in part because children need a secure family life and should not have to worry that they will be sold and wrenched from their existing family. Surrogacy is distinguishable from baby-selling since the resulting child is never in a state of insecurity.

From the moment of birth, he or she is under the care of the biological father and his wife, who cannot sell the child. There is thus no psychological stress to that child or to *any other existing child* that he or she may someday be sold. Moreover, no matter how much money is paid through the surrogacy arrangement, the child, upon birth, cannot be treated like a commodity—a car or a television set. Laws against child abuse and neglect come into play.

Paying a biological mother to give her child up for traditional adoption is criticized since the child may go to an "undeserving" stranger, whose mere ability to pay does not signify sufficient merit for rearing a child. In paid surrogacy, by contract, the child is turned over to the biological father. This biological bond has traditionally been considered to be a sufficient indicator of parental merit.

Another argument about potential harm to the resulting children is that parents will expect more of a surrogate child because of the $10,000 they have spent on her creation. But many couples spend more than that on infertility treatments without evidence that they expect more of the child. A Cesarean section costs twice as much as natural childbirth, yet the parents don't expect twice as much of the children. Certainly, the $10,000 is a modest amount compared to what parents will spend on their child over her lifespan.

Surrogacy has also been opposed because of its potential effect on the surrogate's other children. Traditionally, except in clear cases of clear abuse, parents have been held to be the best decision-makers about their children's best interests. Applying this to surrogacy, the surrogate (and not society) would be the best judge of whether or not her participation in a surrogacy program will harm her children. Not only are parents thought best able to judge their child's needs, but parents can profoundly influence the effects of surrogacy on the child. Children take their cues about things from the people around them. There is no reason to believe that the other children of the surrogate will necessarily feel threatened by their mother's contractual pregnancy. If the children are told from the beginning that this is the contracting couple's child—not a part of their own family—they will realize that they themselves are not in danger of being relinquished.

Surrogate Donna Regan told her children that "the reason we did this was because they [the contracting couple] wanted a child to love as much as we love him." Regan contrasted her case to the Whitehead case: "In the Mary Beth Whitehead case, the child did not see this as something her mother was doing for someone else, so, of course, the attitude that she got from that was that something was being taken away rather than something being given."[41]

It seems ironic for feminists to embrace the argument that certain activities might inherently lead their children to fear abandonment, and that consequently such activities should be banned. Feminists have fought hard to gain access for women to amniocentesis and late-stage abortions of fetuses with a genetic defect—even in light of similarly anecdotal evidence that when the woman aborts, her *other* children will feel that they too, might "be sent to heaven" by their mother. Indeed, it could be argued that therapeutic abortion is more devastating to the remaining children than is surrogacy. After all, the brother or sister who is aborted was intended to be part of the family; moreover, he or she is dead, not just living with other people. I personally do not feel that the potential effect of either therapeutic abortion or surrogacy on the pregnant woman's other children is a sufficient reason to ban the procedures, particularly in light of the fact that parents can mediate how their children perceive and handle the experiences.

The reactions of outsiders to surrogacy may, however, be beyond the control of parents and may upset the children. But is this a sufficient reason to ban surrogacy? William Pierce seems to think so. He says that the children of surrogates "are being made fun of. Their lives are going to be ruined."[42] It would seem odd to let societal intolerance guide what relationships are permissible. Along these lines, a judge in a lesbian custody case replied to the argument that children could be harmed by stigma by stating:

> It is just as reasonable to expect that they will emerge better equipped to search out their own standards of right and wrong, better able to perceive that the majority is not always correct in its moral judgments, and better able to understand the importance of conforming their beliefs to the requirements of reasons and tested knowledge, not the constraints of currently popular sentiment or prejudice.[43]

Feminism Revisited

Feminists are taking great pride that they have mobilized public debate against surrogacy. But the precedent they are setting in their alliance with politicians like Henry Hyde and groups like the Catholic church is one whose policy is "protect women, even against their own decisions" and "protect children at all costs" (presumably, in latter applications, even against the needs and desires of women). . . .

In fact, [this rationale] is reminiscent of earlier decisions "protecting" women that have been roundly criticized by feminists. The U.S. Supreme Court in 1872 felt it was necessary to prevent Myra Bradwell and all other women from practicing law—in order to protect women and their children. And when courts upheld sexist employment laws that kept women out of employment that men were allowed to take, they used language that might have come right out of the New Jersey Supreme Court's decision in the *Baby M* case. A woman's

> physical structure and a proper discharge of her maternal functions—having in view not merely her health, but the well-being of the race—justify legislation to protect her from the greed as well as the passion of man. The limitations which this statute place upon her contractual powers, upon her right to agree with her employer as to the time she shall labor, are not imposed solely for her benefit, but also largely for the benefit of all.[44]

The New Jersey Supreme Court rightly pointed out that not everything should be for sale in our society. But the examples given by the court, such as occupational safety and health laws prohibiting workers from voluntarily accepting money to work in an unsafe job, apply to both men and women. In addition, an unsafe job presents risks that we would not want people to undertake, whether or not they received pay. In contrast, a policy against paid surrogacy prevents women from taking risks (pregnancy and relinquishment) that they are allowed to take for free. It applies disparately—men are still allowed to relinquish their parental rights in advance of conception and to receive money for their role in providing the missing male factor for procreation.

Some feminists are comfortable with advocating disparate treatment on the grounds that gestation is such a unique experience that it has no male counterpart at law and so deserves a unique legal status.[45] The special nature of gestation, according to this argument, gives rise to special rights—such as the right for the surrogate to change her mind and assert her legal parenthood after the child is born.

The other side of the gestational coin, which has not been sufficiently addressed by these feminists, is that with special rights come special responsibilities. If gestation can be viewed as unique in surrogacy, then it can be viewed as unique in other areas. Pregnant women could be held to have responsibilities that other members of society do not have—such as the responsibility to have a Cesarean section against their wishes in order to protect the health of a child (since only pregnant women are in the unique position of being able to influence the health of the child).

Some feminists have criticized surrogacy as turning participating women, albeit with their consent, into reproductive vessels. I see the danger of the anti-surrogacy arguments as potentially turning *all* women into reproductive vessels, without their consent, by providing government oversight for women's decisions and creating a disparate legal category for gestation. Moreover, by breathing life into arguments that feminists have put to rest in other contexts, the current rationales opposing surrogacy could undermine a larger feminist agenda.

Notes

1. Iver Peterson, *Baby M* Custody Trial Splits Ranks of Feminists over Issue of Exploitation, New York Times, Feb. 24, 1987 (quoting Linda Bowker).

2. Brief filed on behalf of Amici Curiae, the Foundation on Economic Trends et al., In the Matter of Baby M, New Jersey Supreme Court, Docket No FM-25314–86E (hereafter cited as "Brief"). (The feminists joining in the brief included Betty Friedan, Gloria Steinem, Gena Corea, Barbara Katz Rothman, Lois Gould, Michelle Harrison, Kathleen Lahey, Phyllis Chesler, and Letty Cottin Pogrebin.)

3. See, e.g., Roe v. Wade, 410 U.S. 113 (1973); Griswold v. Connecticut, 381 U.S. 479 (1965); Meyer v. Nebraska, 262 U.S. 390 (1923); Pierce v. Society of Sisters, 268 U.S. 510 (1928).

4. Jhordan C. v. Mary K., 179 Cal. App. 3d 386, 224 Cal. Rptr. 530 (1986)

5. Surrogate Parenthood and New Reproductive Technologies, A Joint Public Hearing, before the N.Y. State Assembly, N.Y. State Senate, Judiciary Committees (Oct. 16, 1986) (statement of Bob Arenstein at 103–104, 125) [hereinafter N.Y. Testimony]; In the Matter of a Hearing on Surrogate Parenting before the N.Y. Standing Commit-

tee on Child Care (May 8, 1987) (statement of Adria Hillman at 174, statement of Mary Ann Dibari at 212 ["the prostitution of motherhood"].

6. Surrogacy Arrangements Act of 1987: Hearing on H.R. 2433, before the Subcomm. on Transportation, Tourism, and Hazardous Materials, 100th Cong., 1st Sess. (Oct. 15, 1987) (statement of Gena Corea at 3, 5) [hereafter, U.S. Testimony]; Robert Gould, N.Y. Testimony (May 8, 1987), *supra* note 5, at 233 (slavery).

7. Arthur Morrell, U.S. Testimony (Oct. 15, 1987), *supra* note 6, at 1.

8. William Pierce, U.S. Testimony (Oct. 15, 1987), *supra* note 6, citing Harvard Law Professor Lawrence Tribe.

9. Brief, *supra* note 2, at 19.

10. Bob Port, Feminists Come to the Aid of Whitehead's Case, St. Petersburg Times, Feb. 23, 1987, at 7A, quoting Phyllis Chesler.

11. Gena Corea, U.S. Testimony (Oct. 15, 1987), *supra* note 6, at 3; Hillman, N.Y. Testimony (May 8, 1987), *supra* note 5, at 174.

12. Ellen Goodman, Checking the Baby M Contract, Boston Globe, March 24, 1987, at 15.

13. Gena Corea, U.S. Testimony (Oct. 15, 1987), *supra* note 6, at 5; Hillman, N.Y. Testimony (May 8, 1987), *supra* note 5, at 174.

14. Gena Corea, U.S. Testimony (Oct. 15, 1987), *supra* note 6, at 5.

15. *Id.*

16. *Id.* at 2.

17. Elizabeth Kane, U.S. Testimony (Oct. 15, 1987), *supra* note 6, at 1.

18. Kay Longcope, Standing up for Mary Beth, Boston Globe, March 5, 1987, at 81, 83 (quoting Janice Raymond).

19. Brief, *supra* note 2, at 14.

20. Robert Gould, N.Y. Testimony (May 8, 1987), *supra* note 5, at 232.

21. Judianne Densen-Gerber, N.Y. Testimony (May 8, 1987), *supra* note 5, at 253; Robert Gould, N.Y. Testimony (May 8, 1987), *supra* note 5, at 232.

22. Robert Gould, N.Y. Testimony (May 8, 1987), *supra* note 5, at 232.

23. Henry Hyde, U.S. Testimony (Oct. 15, 1987), *supra* note 6, at 1 ("Commercial surrogacy arrangements, by rendering children into chattel, are in my opinion, immoral."); Dibari, N.Y. Testimony (May 8, 1987), *supra* note 5, at 212.

24. John Ray, U.S. Testimony (Oct. 15, 1987), *supra* note 6, at 7.

25. See, e.g., Maureen McGuire & Nancy J. Alexander, Artificial Insemination of Single Women, 43 Fertility and Sterility, 182–184 (Feb. 1985); Raschke & Raschke, Family Conflict and Children's Self-Concept: A Comparison of Intact and Single Parent Families, 41 J. Marriage & Fam., 367 (1979); Weiss, Growing up a Little Faster, 35 Journal of Social Issues, 97 (1979).

26. Betsy Aigen, N.Y. Testimony (May 8, 1987), *supra* note 5, at 18.

27. Robert Arenstein, U.S. Testimony (Oct. 15, 1987), *supra* note 6, at 9.

28. In re Baby M, 109 N.J. 396; 537 A.2d 1227, 1248 (1988).

29. See Brief filed on behalf of Amicus Curiae by the Gruter Institute, In the Matter of Baby M, New Jersey Supreme Court, Docket No. FM-25314–86E.

30. Hearing in re Surrogate Parenting: Hearing on S.B. 1429, before Senators Goodhue, Dunne, Misters Balboni, Abramson, and Amgott (April 10, 1987) (statement of Elaine Rosenfeld at 187). A similar argument made by Adria Hillman, N.Y. Testimony (May 8, 1987), *supra* note 5, at 175.

31. Joan Einwohner, N.Y. Testimony (April 10, 1987), *supra* note 5, at 110–111.

32. Gena Corea, The Mother Machine 3 (Harper & Row, 1985).

33. Brief, *supra* note 2, at 10, 13; Judy Breidbart, N.Y. Testimony (May 8, 1987), *supra* note 5, at 168.

34. K. Cotton and D. Winn, Baby Cotton: For Love and Money (1985).

35. Karen Peters, N.Y. Testimony (May 8, 1987), *supra* note 5, at 121.

36. Adria Hillman, N.Y. Testimony (May 8, 1987), *supra* note 5, 177–178.

37. Jane Leavy, It Doesn't Take Labor Pains to Make a Real Mom, Washington Post, April 4, 1987.

38. Donna Regan, N.Y. Testimony (May 8, 1987), *supra* note 5, at 157.

39. Michelle Harrison, Social Construction of Mary Beth Whitehead, 1 Gender & Soc'y 300 (S. 1987).

40. Teasdale and Owens, Influence of Paternal Social Class on Intelligence Level in Male Adoptees and Non-Adoptees, 56 Brit. J. Educ. Psychol. 3 (1986).

41. Donna Regan, N.Y. Testimony (May 8, 1987), *supra* note 5, at 156.

42. William Pierce, N.Y. Testimony (May 8, 1987), *supra* note 5, at 86. It should be pointed out that kids hassle other kids for a wide range of reasons. A child might equally be made fun of for being the recipient of a kidney transplant or being the child of a garbage man.

43. M.P. v. S.P., 169 N.J. Super. 425,438, 404 A.2d 1256, 1263 (Super. Ct. App. Div. 1979).

44. Muller v. Oregon, 208 U.S. 412, 422 (1907).

45. See Brief, *supra* note 2, at 11.

The Ethics and Economics
of Enforcing Contracts
of Surrogate Motherhood

RICHARD A. POSNER

MY TOPIC IS surrogate motherhood,[1] and specifically the issue—the central issue in the controversy over surrogacy—whether contracts of surrogate motherhood, that is contracts whereby a woman agrees, in exchange for money, to become impregnated through artificial insemination and to give up the newly born child to the father, should be legally enforceable, whether by damages or specific performance. I shall not consider whether such contracts *are* enforceable under existing law, nor the intricate legal questions that such contracts even when enforceable could be expected to raise,[2] but whether they *should* be enforceable. To this question of policy, issues of economics and ethics are central, and are the focus of this paper. . . .

The question of the enforceability of contracts of surrogate motherhood became front-page news with the *Baby M* case, to which I shall return. The case and the controversy it aroused are a byproduct of the increasing frequency of contracts of surrogate motherhood. Although statistics are hard to come by, it appears that by the end of 1986 at least 500 surrogate contracts had been made;[3] the number may be much greater today, despite efforts in a number of states to make such contracts unenforceable, and the resulting uncertainty that surrounds the practice of surrogate motherhood.

I conjecture that three factors are key in explaining the growing popularity of the practice. The first is scientific advances in the field of reproduction, which make infertile couples less prone to resign themselves to their infertility. The second (and I think related) factor is the decline in conventional attitudes toward sex and the family. The third, and perhaps most important factor is the acute shortage of babies for adoption. (I mean of healthy, white infants—there is no shortage of black, or handicapped, or older children for adoption, but this is because there is, unfortunately, very little demand for such children.) The extent, character, and causes of the shortage of babies for adoption are the subject of my writings on the gray and black markets in adoption, in other words, on "baby-selling," a practice that, contrary to the impression fostered by the media and others, I have not advocated but have merely tried to ex-

---

5 J. Contemp. Health L. & Pol'y 21 (1989).

plain.[4] The irony is that those who attack surrogate motherhood out of a general hostility to free markets do not realize that surrogate motherhood is itself a product, in part, of the interference with a market—the market in adoption. Yet even if there were no shortage of babies for adoption, there would be a demand for surrogate motherhood. People (a biologist would say their genes) desire genetic continuity, and surrogacy enables the man (although not his wife) to satisfy this desire.

The case for allowing people to make legally enforceable contracts of surrogate motherhood is straightforward. Such contracts would not be made unless the parties to them believed that surrogacy would be mutually beneficial. Suppose the contract requires the father and his wife to pay the surrogate mother $10,000 (apparently this is the most common price in contracts of surrogate motherhood[5]). The father and wife must believe that they will derive a benefit from having the baby that is greater than $10,000, or else they would not sign the contract. The surrogate must believe that she will derive a benefit from the $10,000 (more precisely, from what she will use the money for) that is greater than the cost to her of being pregnant and giving birth and then surrendering the baby. So *ex ante*, as an economist would say (i.e., before the fact), all the parties to the contract are made better off. The mutual benefits, moreover, depend critically on the contract's being enforceable. If it is unenforceable, the father and his wife will have no assurance that they will actually obtain a baby as a result of the contract even if the surrogate becomes pregnant. For if the surrogate, having become pregnant and given birth, changes her mind about giving up the baby, the father and wife will have lost almost a year in their quest for a baby (the period necessary for the surrogate to become pregnant plus the period of gestation); they will also be intensely disappointed. Because surrogacy is so much less attractive to the father and wife when it is not enforceable, they will not be willing to pay nearly as much as they would if it were enforceable—so the surrogate is hurt. After all, the surrogate always has the option of offering to accept a lower price in return for retaining the right to keep the baby if she wants. If she surrenders that right in exchange for a higher price, it is, at least presumptively, because she prefers the extra money to the extra freedom of choice. Her preference is thwarted if the contract is unenforceable.

There are various objections to this simple economic analysis. The one that fits the framework of economic theory most comfortably is that the analysis fails to consider that a contract of surrogate motherhood has effects on nonparties, in particular on the baby that the surrogate gives birth to. The presence of an affected but nonconsenting third party makes it difficult to say that the transaction is Pareto superior (i.e., that at least one person is made better off by the transaction and no one is made worse off)— the strongest normative concept of efficiency. In fact, however, it is very likely that the baby is made better off by the contract of surrogate motherhood, and certainly not worse off. For without the contract the baby probably wouldn't be born at all. With the contract, he (or she) becomes a member of a family consisting of the biological father and his wife. The baby's position is much like that of a baby whose mother dies during the baby's infancy and whose father then remarries. If there is any evidence that such babies, when they become adults, decide they'd rather not have been born, I am not aware of it. The surrogate baby's position is also much like that of a baby whose mother was inseminated artificially with the sperm of a man other than her husband, because he was infertile. Do such babies grow up to be miserable? So miserable that they derive a net disutility from life—would rather never have been born? Again, I am not aware of any evidence they do, and it seems unlikely they do. Although there is some evidence that adopted children are occasionally maladjusted, the best evidence seems to be that, on average, adopted children are no more unhappy or unstable than natural children.[6] And the child of a surrogate mother is only half-adopted. He is the natural son of his father, and, in effect, the adopted son of his mother (that is, the father's wife).

The remaining possibility is that knowledge that surrogate mothers are paid will blight the child's life. The child will know that his natural mother gave him up for money. But this knowledge will surely be less wrenching than knowledge that one's mother had *sold* one (as in baby selling). For the mother had agreed from the outset to bear the child for the father and the father's wife. Are children conceived after artificial insemination with sperm obtained from a sperm donor devastated to learn that their parents had *bought* the sperm? Are children embarrassed or distressed to discover that they are the product of in vitro fertilization which may have cost their parents thousands of dollars? The world is changing, and practices that seem weird and unnatural to members of the current adult generation will seem much less so, I predict, to the next generation.

A subtler third-party effect of surrogacy is on those unfortunate children who are available for adoption but whom very few people want to adopt. If surrogacy were unavailable, the comfortable white middle-class couple that turns to surrogacy because there are so few healthy white infants available for adoption might turn back to the adoption market and adopt a black or handicapped or older child. This is not likely to happen very often; an alternative of course is that the husband will abandon his wife for a woman who is fertile. Even if forbidding the enforcement of surrogacy contracts would drive a few couples into the market for adopting unwanted children (and no doubt it would), one could well question the appropriateness of placing what amounts to a heavy tax on the infertile to correct a social problem—that of unwanted children— that is emphatically not of their creation. Are the *infertile* to be blamed for a glut of unwanted children? If not, should they be taxed disproportionately in order to alleviate the glut?

The most frequent argument one hears against contracts of surrogate motherhood is that they are not truly voluntary, because the surrogate mother doesn't know what she is getting into and would not sign such a contract unless she was desperate. The first point has a more secure foundation in economics than the second. Information costs provide a traditional reason for doubting whether a particular contract is actually value-maximizing *ex ante*. If women who agree to make surrogate contracts don't know how distressed they will be when it comes time to surrender the baby, then the contracts may not result in a net increase in welfare. To put this differently, the tendency in economics to evaluate welfare on an *ex ante* rather than ex post basis depends on an assumption that expectations are not systematically biased. Contracts cannot be depended on to maximize welfare if parties signing them don't know what they're committing themselves to.

However, there is no persuasive evidence or convincing reason to believe that, on average, women who agree to become surrogate mothers underestimate the distress they will feel at having to give up the baby. Granted, Mrs. Whitehead, the surrogate mother in the *Baby M* case, underestimated that distress. But we must be wary of generalizing from a single case. There is no indication that Mrs. Whitehead's experience is typical of surrogate mothers. Hundreds of babies have been born to surrogate mothers, and since very few of these arrangements have been drawn into litigation one's guess is that most surrogate mothers do *not* balk when it comes time to surrender the baby. Newspaper and magazine interviews with surrogate mothers confirm this impression. Oblique but important corroborative evidence is that most surrogate mothers already have children and that few are under 20 years of age.[7] A mature woman who has borne children should be able to estimate the psychic cost to her of giving up her next baby. Finally, the enormous publicity that the *Baby M* case has received should provide additional warning of the perils of surrogacy, if any is needed, to women contemplating it.

Are these *desperate* women—women who value $10,000 more than a baby only because society has failed to spread a safety net under them? Even if they were, this might not justify a ban on the enforcement of surrogate contracts. To someone who is desperately in need of $10,000, a court's refusal to allow her to obtain it will seem a hypocritical token of concern for her plight, especially since the court has no power to alleviate that plight in some other way. At all events, there is no evidence that surrogate mothers are drawn from the ranks of the desperately poor, and it seems unlikely they would be. Mrs. Whitehead was not poor. A couple would be unlikely to want the baby of a *desperately* poor woman; they would be concerned about her health, and therefore the baby's. Interviews with surrogate mothers indicate not only that they are not poor, but that they have made a careful tradeoff between the use they can make of $10,000 (or whatever the contract price is) and the costs (including regret) of bearing a child for another couple.[8] When asked what they plan to do with the $10,000, they give standard middle-class answers (home improvement, a new car, a better education for their children). For many surrogate mothers, moreover, regret at giving up the child is balanced by empathy for the father's infertile wife. This is particularly likely where the surrogate mother has already had children—but that is, as I have noted, usually the case with surrogate arrangements.

There is, in short, no persuasive evidence that contracts of surrogate motherhood are less likely to maximize value than the classes of contracts that the law routinely enforces. However, other arguments are also made against the enforcement of surrogacy contracts. One is that much enforcement is inequitable because only middle-class couples can afford the price of a surrogate contract and because invariably the surrogate mother comes from a lower income class than the father and his wife. But society does not forbid contracts for luxury goods or contracts that involve the purchase of services from persons lower on the income ladder. Only wealthy people employ butlers, and butlers are invariably less well off than their employers. Nevertheless employment contracts with butlers are enforceable. Moreover, while probably no truly poor person could afford the price of a surrogate contract, it is hardly the case that only wealthy people can pay $10,000 for a good or service. Most Americans can afford a new car, and most new cars cost more than $10,000. In any event, unless envy is very intense and widespread, it is very difficult to see how people who can't afford to pay for surrogate arrangements are helped by a law that forbids those who can afford to pay to enter into enforceable contracts of surrogacy.

Next it is argued—and not only by Marxists as one might have expected—that to enforce surrogacy contracts is to endorse the "commodification" of motherhood. It is true that our society does not permit every good or service to be bought and sold, even where there are no palpable or demonstrable third-party effects. People are not permitted to make contracts of self-enslavement, to enter into suicide pacts, to agree to enter gladiatorial contests (or even to box without gloves), or to sign loan agreements enforceable by breaking the borrower's knees in the event of default. And some forms of "commodification" that are permitted, such as the sale of blood to blood banks, are heavily criticized. Apart from objections, based on a variety of grounds unrelated to surrogate motherhood, to specific forms of "commodification," there is a widespread aversion, particularly but not only among intellectuals, to placing all relations and interactions in society on a strictly pecuniary basis. It is feared that pervasive reliance on the "cash nexus" would extinguish altruism and foster anomie, anxious privatism, and other alleged ills of a capitalist system.

I am skeptical. People are what they are, and what they are is the result of millions of years of evolution rather than of such minor cultural details as the precise scope of the market principle in a particular society. I don't think we would be more selfish than we are if the market sector in this country were larger than it is, or less selfish if it were smaller. People in countries that have less "commodification" than we—countries ranging from Sweden to Ethiopia—do not appear to be less selfish than Americans. Anyway, allowing the enforcement of contracts of surrogate motherhood isn't going to have any significant effect on underlying norms and attitudes in our society. Very few fertile couples will be interested in surrogate motherhood; most couples are fertile; and the fraction of infertile couples is bound to decline with continued advances in medical technology, even as women marry later (fertility problems increase with age).

The last ethical argument that I will consider against the enforcement of surrogacy contracts is mounted by feminists. They argue that surrogacy is akin to prostitution in that it also involves the sale of female sexuality; and just as prostitution is widely regarded as exploitative of women, so surrogacy is (these feminists argue) inevitably exploitative of the deluded women who agree to market their reproductive capacity. Moreover, there is a small but irreducible risk of death or serious illness to the surrogate mother.

The argument is unconvincing. It overlooks, to begin with, the fact that the surrogates are not the only women in the picture. There are also the infertile wives to be considered. Not only are they hurt if their ability to obtain a baby (necessarily not borne by them) is impeded by a ban on the enforcement of contracts of surrogate motherhood, but their already weak bargaining position in a marriage to a fertile husband is further weakened, for under modern permissive divorce law he is always free to "walk," and seek a fertile woman to marry.[9] Beyond this, the idea that women who "sell" (really, rent) their reproductive capacity, like women who sell sexual favors, are "exploited" patronizes women. Few would argue that a gigolo or a sperm donor or a man who marries for money or a male prostitute is "exploited." These men might not be admirable, but they are not victims. The idea that women are particularly prone to be exploited in the marketplace hearkens back to the time (not so long ago) when married women were deemed legally incompetent to make enforceable contracts. I am surprised that feminists—not all of them, however[10]—should want to resurrect the idea in the surrogacy context. It is only worse when the argument is bolstered by pointing out that hormonal changes incident to pregnancy may induce a regret at parting with the baby that the surrogate mother could not have foreseen when she signed the contract. The idea that women are peculiarly dominated by their hormones (and not men by their testosterone?) is a traditional rationalization for limiting women's access to responsible employment.

The feminist criticisms of surrogacy are inconsistent with mainstream feminist thought. They reinforce the anti-feminist stereotype summed up in the slogan, "biology is destiny." The unintended implication of the feminist position on surrogate motherhood (but I emphasize that this is the position of some, not all, feminists) is, if you're infertile, you shouldn't have a baby; and if you are fertile, and have a baby, you should keep it. A main thrust of modern feminism has been to deny that biology is destiny, that it is woman's predestined lot to be a bearer and raiser of children. Some women don't want to have children; some want to have children but not in the traditional setting of heterosexual marriage; some want to have but not bear children and some, finally, want to bear but not have children (or more children)—they are the surrogate mothers. Feminism seeks to expand the opportunities of women beyond the traditional role, felt as stifling by many, of being a housewife and mother who makes a career of bearing and raising children. The opportunity to hire a surrogate mother and the opportunity to be a surrogate mother are two unconventional opportunities now open to women. It is curious that feminists, of all people, should want to close the door on these opportunities.

The last and least argument against surrogate motherhood is that it is just another form of "baby selling." This is argumentation by epithet. The surrogate mother no more "owns" the baby than the father does. What she sells is not the baby but her parental rights, and in this respect she is no different from a woman who agrees in a divorce proceeding to surrender her claim to custody of the children of the marriage in exchange for some other concession from her husband—or from a sperm donor who receives cash, but no parental rights, in exchange for his donation.

I have reviewed the arguments pro and con for the enforceability of surrogate contracts and have made no secret of how I believe the balance inclines. But in a matter that has aroused such strong emotions, argumentation *a priori* will not provide a fully convincing resolution. Evidence is more important than argument. I have mentioned evidence that surrogacy is not exploitative in the sense of making the surrogate mothers worse off, but the evidence is casual and anecdotal and a more systematic study is necessary and indeed urgent. Efforts should be made by scholars to identify and randomly sample surrogate mothers for purposes of determining the demographic and other relevant characteristics of the parties to the contracts and the experience with surrogate contracts. Are the surrogates responsible adults making apparently rational decisions? Are parties to surrogacy contracts generally satisfied? Do the contracts contain adequate safeguards of the surrogate mother's interests? What is the average price and the range of prices? How many surrogate mothers experience profound distress at giving up the baby? How many balk and have to be dragged into court? Are the children healthy and happy? These questions are answerable. Until they are answered, with greater confidence than is possible at present, the public policy issue examined [here] will not be resolved. It would, though, be a tragedy if the states or Congress sought to extirpate the practice before a rational judgment of its pros and cons could be made. . . .

Notes

1. I realize that the term "surrogate motherhood" might be thought to belittle the surrogate mother, who is, after all, the biological mother—not just a stand-in or incubator. But I shall stick with what has become the accepted term.

2. See, e.g., Smith, The Razor's Edge of Human Bonding: Artificial Fathers and Surrogate Mothers, 5 W. New. Eng. L. Rev. 639, 652–664 (1983).

3. See M. Field, Surrogate Motherhood 5 (1988).

4. See Posner, The Regulation of the Market in Adoptions, 67 B.U. L. Rev. 59 (1987); Landes & Posner, The Economics of the Baby Shortage, 7 J. Legal Stud. 323 (1978); R. Posner, Economic Analysis of Law §5.4 at 139–143 (3d ed. 1986).

5. See Field, *supra* note 3, at 25–26.

6. See, e.g., Andrews, Surrogate Motherhood: The Challenge for Feminists, herein, at 1092.

7. See Field, *supra* note 3, at 6.

8. See, e.g., Chapman, Surrogacy Successes Make New Laws All the More Ill-Advised, Chic. Trib., July 31, 1988 at 3, col. 1.

9. I realize that not all wives who want to hire surrogate mothers are infertile. Some may be fertile but endangered by pregnancy; others may simply not want to take time off from work to bear a child. The latter reason will strike many as frivolous; it is in any event rare.

10. Andrews, *supra* note 6, presents a powerful feminist defense of surrogate motherhood.

◈ *Junk Liberty*

GENA COREA

WE HEAR LOTS OF high-minded talk about "rights" and "liberty" from the defenders of the human breeding industry. It's a man's right to exercise his constitutionally protected and newly invented "procreative liberty" to hire a woman to bear a child for him. It's a woman's right to sell her body if she so chooses.

We are repeatedly told that legalizing the sale of women protects the freedom our forefathers died for.

Gary Skoloff, attorney to William Stern in the *Baby M.*[1] surrogacy case, is one of the many new single-issue defenders of women's liberation.

"If you prevent women from becoming surrogate mothers and deny them the freedom to decide . . . ," he says, "you are saying that they do not have the ability to make their own decisions."[2]

[Professor John Robertson, of the School of Law, University of Texas, is another supporter of surrogacy.]

"Since hiring a surrogate gestator is an exercise of procreative liberty on the part of the couple," he writes, "there is a strong case for a constitutional right to employ a surrogate."[3]

He argues: "Prohibition of such arrangements would interfere with the woman's and couple's right to procreate, for there is no other way for them to have offspring of their genes. Harm to the offspring or the surrogate does not appear great enough to justify limitation of the arrangement."[4]

The notion that hiring a breeder is an exercise in liberty is repeated in a host of official reports on surrogacy.

Attorney Lori Andrews, who wrote the new reproductive technologies report for a women's rights law project based at Rutgers University and also served on the ethics committee of the American Fertility Society, has been a major disseminator of the liberty line.[5]

This liberty line has been eagerly grabbed by the surrogacy industry. For example, in his testimony before the Pennsylvania House Judiciary Committee hearing on surrogacy in 1987, William Handel, director of the Center for Surrogate Parenting in Los

---

Testimony of Gena Corea, Associate Director of the Institute on Women and Technology, before the California Assembly Judiciary Committee, April 5, 1988.

Angeles, stated: ". . . The right to procreate, which encompasses the right to conceive, bear and rear children, is one of society's most highly cherished and constitutionally protected rights. . . . Surrogate parenting . . . is an alternative that should be protected as vehemently as normal reproduction. After all, the First Amendment right of procreation does not protect the *act* of procreation, but rather the fundamental nature and importance of having a child."[6]

Various legislatures and courts, including the New Jersey lower court that ruled in the Mary Beth Whitehead case, have also embraced "protective liberty" as a rationale for male use of a female breeder caste. Judge Harvey Sorkow, citing John Robertson and quoting him at length, wrote in his *Baby M.* decision:

> It must be reasoned that if one has a right to procreate coitally, then one has the right to reproduce non-coitally. . . . This court holds that the protected [reproductive] means extends to the use of surrogates. . . . It is reasoned that the donor or surrogate aids the childless couple by contributing a factor of conception and for gestation that the couple lacks.[7]

In its 1986 ethics report on the new reproductive technologies, the American Fertility Service, a professional association of some 10,000 U.S. physicians and scientists who work in reproductive biology, reveals itself as another defender of "procreative liberty."

"Couples" have a right to hire breeders, the American Fertility Society tells us.

Building on the work of feminist author Kathleen Barry, Janice Raymond, associate director at the Institute of Women and Technology, challenges the "rights" justification for surrogacy: "It is a fundamental postulate of international law that human rights must be based on human dignity. A surrogate arrangement offers no dignity to women and therefore cannot be called a real right. It violates the core of human dignity to hire a woman's body for the breeding of a child so that someone else's genes can be perpetuated."[8]

Raymond, a professor of women's studies at the University of Massachusetts, has further written in regard to the surrogacy promoters: "Give the female creature abstract rights—rights that don't really benefit women politically as a class—but don't give her dignity."[9]

Human dignity. Alejandra Munoz, the Mexican woman brought across the border illegally to serve as a so-called surrogate, inseminated and, once pregnant, kept confined in the home of the buying couple, Mario and Nattie Haro, knows her dignity was violated. So does Mary Beth Whitehead, protagonist in the *Baby M.* case. And Nancy Barrass, the so-called surrogate now fighting in California to see her child. And Patty Foster, fighting in Michigan for her child. And Elizabeth Kane, billed as America's first legal surrogate. And Laurie Yates, the young woman in Michigan who struggled long, hard, and in vain to keep the twins she bore after having been superovulated like a cow. That is, the surrogate company's doctor gave her fertility drugs because she apparently didn't get pregnant fast enough (whether for the doctor or the man hiring her is not clear).

There are many issues to discuss surrounding surrogacy: the opening up of the reproductive supermarket that the burgeoning surrogate industry is a part of; the use of so-called surrogates as "living laboratories" for the development of various new reproductive technologies; the eugenic implications of surrogacy—the search for "perfect" children of the right race, genetic material, and degree of physical perfection; the coming expansion in the traffic in women internationally when, with the use of embryo transfer technology, Third World women are used as cheap breeders for white, Western men (and at least one surrogate entrepreneur has concrete plans now for this international traffic); the expansion of father rights that surrogacy represents, and the curtailment of mother rights; the new polygamy—two women doing for one man; the erosion of self-esteem in future female children who—if the surrogate industry is not stopped—will be born into a world where there is a class of breeder women. But now I am making one point only: Human rights must be based on human dignity, and surrogacy, which violates human dignity, is no "right.". . .

Selling women as breeders, setting up a class of breeder women, violates human dignity. When the mechanisms of violating human dignity are so firmly established that no one objects to them or even finds them remarkable, which is the case in the "successful" surrogacy cases, then we are living in a society in which a woman's life is held in utter contempt.

But no. We are told that we are living in a country that protects liberty—"procreative liberty."

It is junk liberty.

We know what junk food is. It's made of junk ingredients. Nutrients have been processed out of it, leaving it with little substance, bulk. It does not nourish. Sometimes it looks and tastes good. But it can make you sick. It can leave you hungering for something real, something that can sustain your life, something that can strengthen you. Junk food has the appearance of food without the reality.

Junk liberty looks and sounds good. Even noble. But human dignity has been processed out of it. Anything of real substance, anything that can nourish and sustain a woman's Self, her soul, her life, has been processed out, leaving behind only the appearance of liberty.

Junk liberty is full of artificial preservatives, "junk rights." Women have the right to be treated as commodities. We have the right to subject our most intimate feelings and relationships to contract law. We have the right to be sold.

Junk liberty is for the people the patriarchy would like us to be: junk people, junk women. Women without dignity or substance. Women who can't feel joy or pain or love or hate or anger. Women who act like machines. Women who let themselves be used and then quietly throw themselves on the junk heap.

Junk liberty is a key concept in the marketing strategy of the surrogate industry. It is a concept used to cover up a crime against humanity.

Junk liberty. ("The triple dose of the drug had serious side effects for me [including] . . . intense pain in my left ovary. I was unable to walk because of the pain.")[10]

Junk liberty. (A surrogate mother would be required to carry with her, at all times, after the sixth month of pregnancy, a court order ordering the hospital to give her baby only to the people who paid for it.)[11]

Junk liberty. ("When I refused to give Sarah up, five cops stormtrooped my house to get her . . . . They put me in handcuffs and threw me in the police car. . . .")[12]

Junk liberty. (". . . I told the sperm donor and his wife of my need not to have them present in the delivery room. . . . They responded that their presence at the birth was part of what they paid for.")[13]

Junk liberty. ("You could devastate them [poor Mexican women] with money and things—you know, whatever they need.")[14]

The real question is not whether women have the "right," the "liberty" to sell our bodies or not. The question is not whether surrogacy is forced or voluntary. The question is this: What is surrogacy? As Janice Raymond writes, it is "an inherently unequal relationship involving the objectification, sale, and commodification of a woman's body."[15]

Kathleen Barry, author of *Female Sexual Slavery*,[16] demonstrates that prostitution is a crime against women. Following her argumentation, surrogacy—reproduction prostitution—is also a crime against women. The crime is turning a whole class of people—women—into a commodity exchange and, in so doing, violating our human dignity. The customers and the surrogacy brokers are those who commit this crime against women. The customer is buying time on a woman's body, and the broker is enabling it.

Surrogacy is not liberty. It is crime.

Women will not settle for junk liberty. We want real freedom—the substance, not just the appearance. We want real nourishment for our spirits. We want human dignity. We want it for *all* of us. We want it for women in Thailand and Bangladesh and Mexico as well as for the women who have not yet been born. We want human dignity. We will not stop fighting until we have it.

Notes

1. In the Matter of Baby M, 217 N.J. Super. 313, 525 A.2d 1128 (ch. Div. 1987), *aff'd in part, rev'd in part, remanded,* 109 N.J. 396, 537 A.2d 1227 (1988).

2. Cited in Snyder, Baby M Trial Hears Closing Arguments, Boston Globe, March 13, 1987.

3. [Gena Corea does not provide a complete citation to the particular work of John Robertson where this quotation appears. However, a similar statement of Robertson's may be found in his article, Liberalism and the Limits of Procreative Liberty: A Response to My Critics, 52 Wash. & L. L. Rev. 233, 267 n.22 (1995) (his theory of procreative liberty would confer on a married couple the right to hire a surrogate). See also John A. Robertson, Embryos, Families, and Procreative Liberty: The Legal Structure of the New Reproduction, 59 S. Cal. 939, 957–962 (1986) (discussion of a constitutional right to engage in noncoital reproduction). See generally John A. Robertson, Children of Choice: Freedom and the New Reproductive Technologies (Princeton Univ. Press, 1994). *Ed.*]

4. [Again, Gena Corea does not provide a complete citation to the particular work of Robertson. A similar statement of Robertson's, however, may be found in Robertson, Liberalism and the Limits of Procreative Liberty, *supra* note 3, at 966 (noncoital reproduction poses no direct, tangible harm to others). *Ed.*]

5. Andrews, Feminist Perspectives on Reproductive Technologies, in Reproductive Laws for the 1990s, Briefing Handbook, Women's Rights Litigation Clinic, Rutgers Law School, Newark, N.J. 07102.

6. Handel, Testimony Before the Pennsylvania House Judiciary Committee, chaired by the Hon. H. William DeWeese, Pittsburgh, Pennsylvania, Sept. 3, 1987.

7. 525 A.2d at 1164.

8. Raymond, Testimony on House Bill Number 4753 before the House Judiciary Committee, State of Michigan, Lansing Michigan, Oct. 1987.

9. Raymond, Making International Connections: Surrogacy, the Traffic in Women and De-Mythologizing Motherhood, in Therese Mailloux, Marie Rinfret, Jocelyn Olivier & Lucie Desrochers eds., Sortir la Maternité du Laboratoire (Conseil du Statut de la Femme, Quebec, 1987).

10. Barrass, Testimony submitted to the U.S. House of Representatives, Committee on Energy and Commerce, Subcommittee on Transportation, Tourism and Hazardous Materials, Oct. 12, 1987.

11. The Model Reproductive Services Act . . . drafted by the Executive Adoption Committee of the Family Law Section of the American Bar Association for approval by the Family Law Section Council at its 1987 annual meeting in San Francisco. . . . The draft states, on page 8, that the reproductive services agreement shall "State that the surrogate shall arrange to give birth to the child in a health facility that previously has been given a certified copy of the order provided for in Section 9 below and that the surrogate shall arrange to keep a certified copy of the order with her at all times after the sixth month of pregnancy." According to Robert Arenstein, a member of the Ad Hoc Surrogacy Committee, that provision of the draft has now been removed.

12. Whitehead, Testimony Before the U.S. House of Representatives, Committee on Energy and Commerce, Subcommittee on Transportation, Tourism and Hazardous Materials, Oct. 15, 1987.

13. Barrass, Testimony, *supra* note 10.

14. Corea, Tape-recorded interviews with John Stehura (president of the commercial surrogacy organization, Bionetics Foundation, Inc.), Dec. 15, 22, 1987.

15. Raymond, Testimony, *supra* note 8.

16. K. Barry, Female Sexual Slavery (Prentice-Hall, 1979).

The Socio-Economic Struggle for Equality: The Black Surrogate Mother

Anita L. Allen

. . . The American slave experience, while not equivalent to surrogacy, can help illuminate why many people find the practice of commercial surrogacy disturbing. Before the American Civil War, virtually all southern Black mothers were, in a sense, surrogate mothers. Slave women knowingly gave birth to children with the understanding that those children would be owned by others.[1] Occasionally, however, a Black woman was able to get back her child. Previously,[2] I related the true story of Polly, a Black woman who was kidnapped from her home in Illinois and sold into slavery in Missouri.[3] Polly brought and prevailed in two remarkable lawsuits, one for her own freedom and a second to obtain custody of her teenage daughter, Lucy. Polly's successful custody battle against her child's white owners is reminiscent of Mary Beth Whitehead Gould's battle against the Sterns in the *Baby M* case.

Johnson v. Calvert[4] has sparked a new wave of concern that surrogate motherhood turns women into "commercial slaves 24 hours a day for 270 days."[5] The *Johnson* case highlights a troubling truth underlying the rhetoric that contemporary surrogacy is slavery. Affluent white women's infertility, sterility, preferences and power threaten to turn poor Black women, already understood to be a servant class, into a "surrogate class." . . .

I. Anna Had a Baby

On September 19, 1990, in Orange County, California, a twenty-nine-year-old Black woman named Anna L. Johnson gave birth to a six-pound, ten-ounce baby boy. A casual observer visiting the maternity ward at St. Joseph's Hospital would have found nothing unusual in the sight of Anna Johnson breastfeeding the tiny newborn. However, as the journalists who swarmed into the hospital to report the birth knew, Johnson and the infant she delivered had an unusual relationship. They were not genetically related. They were not even of the same race. For the first time in history, an

8 Harv. BlackLetter J. 17 (1991). Reprinted by permission of the President and Fellows of Harvard College. © 1991.

African-American woman had given birth to a child exclusively of European and Philippine ancestry.[6]

Anna Johnson's pregnancy was the result of in vitro fertilization and preembryo transplant. Physicians had surgically implanted into Johnson's uterus a preembryo formed in vitro from donated gametes. Already the single mother of a preschool-aged daughter named Erica, Johnson underwent the procedure as a service to Mark and Crispina Calvert. Mark Calvert was a thirty-four-year-old insurance adjuster and Crispina Calvert, who had lost her uterus to cancer, was a thirty-six-year-old registered nurse. Crispina Calvert worked at the hospital where Anna Johnson worked as a licensed vocational nurse. The Calverts promised to pay Johnson $10,000 for her trouble.

Anna Johnson was a new kind of "surrogate mother," a surrogate gestational mother. But the human interest in Anna Johnson's miracle was not just that she was a surrogate gestational mother; Anna Johnson was, in addition, a surrogate gestator who had changed her mind about giving up a child to whom she was not genetically related. Commercial surrogate mothers had been known to change their minds before, but this was the first publicized instance in which a "surrogate carrier, gestator, womb mother, or placental mother"[7] had done so.

Johnson filed a lawsuit on August 13, 1990, when she was seven and a half months pregnant. Alleging that the Calverts had neglected her during the pregnancy and failed to make payments, and that she had developed a bond with the unborn child, Johnson sued for parental rights and child custody.

The Calverts answered that the baby was theirs alone: "He looks like an oriental baby with my husband's nose," Crispina Calvert said.[8] Although Johnson was willing to accept a court-ordered joint-custody arrangement, the Calverts were not. They announced to the news media that they would rather see the baby they would name "Christopher" in a foster home than to share parenting with their hand-picked gestator. Johnson's lawyer, Richard C. Gilbert, countered that he could not comprehend the Calverts' belief that it would be "in the baby's best interest to be taken from the breasts of its birth mother."[9]

In September 1990, Orange County Superior Court Judge Richard N. Parslow, Jr. awarded temporary custody to the Calverts and granted Johnson visitation rights.[10] In an October hearing, the court heard legal argument and expert testimony on the question of permanent custody. Some expert testimony favored the Calverts. However, medical and psychological experts testified on behalf of Anna Johnson's claim to be the "true" mother. Johnson also had other authority on her side. A California statute expressly provided that birth mothers are the natural and legal parents of their offspring.[11] In addition, a 1989 Supreme Court case had denied parental rights to a sperm donor claiming only a genetic link to a child.[12]

Anna Johnson testified at the October hearing that she did not initially plan to keep the child. Johnson said that she first changed her mind when Mark Calvert refused to take her to the hospital. She was forced to take a cab for what proved to be false labor pains. While Johnson was a patient, Crispina Calvert, who worked in the same hospital, refused to visit. Even after she began to want the child, Johnson said that she was "in a state of denial" and she kept "trying to tell myself that I am not supposed to have any emotion toward my child, but there is no way that you can prevent those emotions from taking over, and those instincts came out naturally."[13] Describing her state of mind at the time as confused, anxious and desperate, Johnson admitted sending the Calverts a letter on July 23, 1990, threatening to withhold the baby unless they paid her $5,000 immediately. She also acknowledged that the Calverts had sent her two periodic payments early.

After her testimony, Johnson told reporters she was confident of obtaining at least joint custody and visitation rights: "I know he's there . . . I know he won't forget me."[14] However, on October 22, 1990, Judge Parslow ruled that Anna Johnson had no parental rights whatsoever in the child she bore. By way of consolation, the judge offered that Crispina Calvert might elect to provide Anna Johnson with "a picture now and then, a note as to how this child is doing in life."[15]

II. Anna's "Mistakes and Weaknesses"

A. She Could Not Win

Public reaction to the final decision in the *Johnson* case was mixed.[16] . . .

As soon as Johnson's suit became public, legal policy analysts discussed Johnson v. Calvert as the next chapter in the history of a reproductive revolution of which *Baby M* was but a dramatic early scene.[17] Many observers viewed the cases as closely analogous. In both cases women became pregnant for a cash payment of $10,000 and a desire to help a childless married couple have a child of their own. In both cases the surrogate said she had developed a bond during pregnancy that made it difficult to part with the newborn as agreed. In both cases the contract to exchange reproductive services for cash raised concerns about gender inequality and "baby selling." In both cases the presumption that a woman who gives birth to a child is its legal mother seemed to implicate adoption policies. Yet, contrary to these views, Judge Parslow tried to rapidly distinguish the case before him from *Baby M*. Judge Parslow's sense of the case was that neither adoption laws, proscriptions against commercial trafficking in human beings, gender inequality, nor the developing law of genetic surrogate motherhood was relevant to his decision.[18] . . .

The race issue, Anna Johnson's race, also made Judge Parslow's ultimate decision predictable. Throughout history, Black women and mulatto women have been hired or enslaved to play a number of important de facto "mothering" roles in American families. Moreover, Black women who marry white men have sometimes wound up "mothering" white step-children. However, I suspect that few regard Black women as the appropriate legal mothers of children who are not at least part Black. Blacks are not supposed to have white children. Blacks are not supposed to want to have white children of their own—not in the adoption context[19] and not, therefore, in the surrogacy context.

For better or for worse, race is a factor in adoption, and it will also be a factor in surrogate gestation. Against this background, it was unimaginable that Anna Johnson would win custody of the child she bore from the Calverts' genetic material. Arguably, a lawsuit against the Calverts brought by a white or Asian surrogate gestator would have the same outcome. A judge deciding such a case would foresee the possibility that a Black or brown or yellow gestator might someday wind up with a white couple's genetic child unless it set a firm precedent favoring genetic parents. . . .

Judge Parslow resorted to two analogies which are indicative of how courts may come to characterize the unique role of the surrogate gestator. He analogized Johnson to a "foster parent providing care, protection and nurture during the period of time that the natural mother, Crispina Calvert, was unable to care for the child."[20] Judge Parslow admitted that "there is [sic] a lot of differences" between a gestator and foster parent, but concluded that "there is [sic] a lot of similarities."[21]

His second analogy compared surrogate gestators to "wet-nurses."[22] As recently as the last century it was common for affluent European and American families to pay women to breast-feed and tend their infants and small children. Judge Parslow thought it was plain enough that wet-nurses lack parental rights: "I'm not sure anyone would argue that the person that nursed the child . . . from seven pounds to thirty pounds got parental rights and became the mother."[23] In the judge's view, surrogate gestators are just as plainly without parental rights. One might have expected the court to resist an analogy to the medically and socially discredited practice of wet-nursing. If surrogate gestation is like wet-nursing, perhaps it, too, should be relegated to history.

To counter the impression that he endorsed the use of surrogacy by women who are neither infertile nor sterile, Judge Parslow underscored the Calverts' medical need. "This is not a vanity situation, somebody looking to avoid stretch marks," he said.[24] For medical reasons, Crispina Calvert "has no place to carry the child."[25] . . .

These rationales raise serious questions. Why does a person who is like a foster mother or a wet-nurse have no parental rights? Why does a surrogate gestator have no parental rights against those who seek out her services for "medical" reasons? To answer these questions Judge Parslow focussed on what gestators and genetic parents provide their offspring. The genes we get from our genetic parents determine "who we are, what we become."[26] By comparison to what we get through our genes, we get little in the uterine environment, not even a clear-cut reciprocal bond with our gestators.[27] The limited comparative impact of the gestator on the child's future self, and Judge Parslow's doubt of the reality of a mother-child bond during pregnancy, were the core of a larger set of arguments he offered against parental rights for gestators.

Writing [previously] about the *Baby M* case, I stressed the importance of the genetic ties that Mary Beth Whitehead Gould had to her child.[28] I argued that the parity of the surrogate's genetic ties with the biological father's was one reason to accord her equal parental rights. But to say that genetic heritage is a factor to consider in surrogate mother cases involving disputes between genetic parents, is not to say that in a battle between genetic and gestational parents, genetic parents should always win out. Like the knowledge of genetic linkage, the experiences of pregnancy and childbirth can also have an important role in shaping women's sense of their identities and responsibilities. . . .

III. Beyond Anna's Story

A. Rejecting Intent Rule

What norms should govern modern procreative arrangements and parental status? In a recent article Professor Marjorie Shultz defended a principle of intent as the optimal norm.[29] She urged that the inevitable disputes that arise in the context of collaborative procreation made increasingly possible through new reproductive technologies should be resolved, in the first instance, by reference to the intentions of the parties. The standard of intent presumably respects the autonomous plans and expectations created through voluntary exchanges. It assumes women's competence. It avoids judicial paternalism by giving effect to women's efforts to make choices concerning the use of their reproductive capacities. It assures men secure, responsible roles in procreation. The norm of intent entails legal respect for individual autonomy, including female autonomy, and legal minimalization of the impact of knowing or purposeful harm. Yet the norm of intent is problematic. It is inconsistently applied and it is based on an assumption of greater equality of opportunity than actually exists.

On the surface, the standard of intent appears morally well-founded. Its "morality" justifies the pain it causes those who change their minds and renege on prior agreements. Courts that enforce surrogacy agreements of the sort at issue in *Baby M* and *Johnson* inflict pain on the losing surrogate. A losing surrogate not only suffers grievous emotional loss, but she must also confront a fate she once chose in ignorance of its true character but no longer chooses. From the point of view embraced when the standard of intent is accepted, the evils that the losing surrogate suffers are not evils at all; they are voluntary choices. Or, if they are evils, they are justly imposed.

One problem with the standard of intent is that it is and would be inconsistently applied. Already it is not applied across the board in cases involving non-traditional parenting arrangements, such as homosexual relationships.[30] Moreover, if courts can justify enforcing surrogacy contracts by appeal to intent, they can, by the same token, justify enforcing betrothals, marital vows and other personal undertakings. Yet, the latter contracts are no longer enforced. I believe surrogacy arrangements should be treated in the same manner as other personal agreements, that is, as unenforceable commitments, rather than as enforceable commercial contracts. In those instances where custody battles arise out of failed surrogacy agreements, courts should be ready to intervene in the "best interest of the child," just as they currently intervene when custody battles arise out of failed marriages or love affairs.

In practice, the "best interest of the child" interventions might still turn out to favor genetic parents more often than gestators. But the explicit reason would not be the backward-looking reason that parties once intended that result. It would be the forward-looking reason that the court is persuaded of the genetic parents' superior abilities to provide a home for the child. Conceivably, genetic parents would always win under a "best interest of the child" analysis when they were white and more affluent than the child's minority gestator.

Another problem with the standard of intent is that it presupposes a backdrop of greater equality of opportunity than presently exists. Ceteris paribus, a woman with practical nursing skills has more opportunity and a wider foundation for self-determination than a woman without skills and no high school diploma. Yet, opportunity is a matter of degree. The United States has a recent history of legally enforced race and gender inequality. . . . Habitually low social expectations concerning appropriate vocations for white women and certain minority groups limit the horizons of individuals in these groups faced with "free" choices. Moreover, some forms of liberty and contractual voluntarism impinge upon other, equally important values. If liberty must be tempered by fairness, equality and dignity, it is doubtful that the standard of intent can do all of the normative work that must be done in the wide field of procreative arrangements and parental status.

B. New Face, Old Problem

What can the white man say to the Black woman? For four hundred years he ruled over the Black woman's womb. . . . It was he who placed our children on the auction block. . . . We see him . . . make the Black mother, who must sell her body to feed her children, go down on her knees to him.[31]

Minority women increasingly will be sought to serve as "mother machines" for embryos of middle and upper-class clients. It's a new, virulent form of racial and class discrimination. Within a decade, thousands of poor and minority women will likely be used as a "breeder class" for those who can afford $30,000 to $40,000 to avoid the inconvenience and danger of pregnancy.

It has been said many times before, but it bears repeating: tolerating practices that convert women's wombs and children into valuable market commodities threatens to deny them respect as equals. Commercial surrogacy encourages society to think of economically and socially vulnerable women as at its disposal for a price. Segments of the public will draw the obvious parallels to slavery and prostitution.[32] Their reaction may seem melodramatic. But it is a telling reminder of social attitudes and history. Genetic heritage, while a factor, should not be dispositive in a battle between genetic and gestational parents. The experience of pregancy and childbirth, like the knowledge of genetic linkage, can play an important role in shaping women's sense of themselves and their responsibilities.

I believe that policymakers should discourage surrogacy, chiefly by (1) refusing to legally enforce commercial surrogacy agreements; (2) ascribing to surrogates parental rights that they may voluntarily relinquish only after the birth of a child they are paid to carry;[33] and by (3) making no distinction between genetic and gestational surrogates when it comes to the assignment of parental rights. Legislation shaped around points (1) and (3) would increase the risks of entering into surrogacy arrangements for the economically more powerful parties (the consumers and brokers of surrogacy) and decrease the risk of surrogacy arrangements for the less economically powerful (the surrogates).

Black gestators would remain vulnerable to emotional devastation even if surrogacy policies were in line with points (1), (2) and (3), and if race were not a factor for the court in awarding child custody under the "best interest" standard. A Black gestator who wanted to keep her white offspring, as Anna Johnson did, would likely be pressured by family, friends, and experts to do otherwise. She would know that racism could add special stresses on individual members of her multiracial family, leading to acrimony and rejection.

Limitations on the alienability of parental rights, point (2) above, can greatly benefit some surrogate mothers. Inalienable post-delivery parental rights as limitations on surrogacy would clearly benefit white surrogates who, like Mary Beth Whitehead Gould, want to keep their genetically-related children. The benefit of point (2) to gestational surrogates, especially Black gestational surrogates, is less clear. First, genetic ties have special meaning in American culture. In deciding child custody under the "best interest of the child" standard, I predict courts would be reluctant to award children to gestational, as opposed to similarly situated genetic, parents. Second, since genetic parents will probably be better educated and more affluent than gestational surrogates, courts are likely to view them as better equipped to provide good homes. Third, most consumers of surrogacy are whites who want white children. Although Black women's infertility and sterility rate is higher than white women's,[34] few Black women utilize surrogate mothers.[35] It follows that most Blacks who are surrogates will be surrogate gestators for whites. The children born to Black gestational surrogates will be of another race. Racial difference between mother and child may incline courts against awarding custody to the Black surrogate gestator.

The number of Black gestators who could master their rational fears and overcome judicial resistance to go with their hearts would likely be small compared to the number who, with tragic emotional consequences, would feel compelled to give up their offspring. We can only imagine what Anna Johnson's life would have been like had she prevailed in her custody bid. Perhaps her own bi-racial heritage steeled her for the battles she would have faced as head of a multiracial family. Her willingness to fight to parent her gestational child was virtually as remarkable as the biotechnology that made it possible. Like Polly, the slave who sued for her own freedom and then for the right to own her own child, Anna Johnson was exceptionally courageous.

According to my analysis, few Black surrogates who desire to keep their gestational children could easily decide to do so. Surrogacy laws, even surrogacy laws that equally favor genetic and gestational surrogates over genetic parents, offer Black gestational surrogates little protection. As an ironic consequence, Black gestators could be the safest surrogate mothers for white women who want white children. In light of these inequities, the *Johnson* case may force the conclusion on behalf of Black women that a per se ban on commercial surrogacy is the safest—the wisest—course.

Notes

1. In some aspects, American slavery was analogous to a de facto system of surrogacy. Slave owners were recognized not only as the owners of the slaves but they were also owners of the natural children to which the slaves gave birth. These ownership rights allowed the children to be bought or sold to third parties, regardless of the wishes of the natural mother.

2. Anita L. Allen, Surrogacy, Slavery and the Ownership of Life, 13 Harv. J.L. & Pub. Pol'y 139 (Winter 1990).

3. Lucy Delaney, Struggles for Freedom, in Six Women's Slave Narratives 9 (1988) (woman held wrongly in slavery later sues for her own release and "the right to own her own child").

4. [Johnson v. Calvert, 851 P.2d 776 (Cal. 1993). The author relies on the transcript of the trial court. Reporter's Transcript, Johnson v. Calvert (No. X 63 31 90 Consolidated with AD 57638 (Cal. Super. Ct. Oct. 22, 1990). The trial court ruling, discussed here, which declared the Calverts the legal parents, was affirmed by the Court of Appeal and subsequently by the California Supreme Court.]

5. Jeremy Rifkin & Andrew Kimbrell, Put a Stop to Surrogate Parenting Now, USA Today, Aug. 20, 1990, §A, at 8 (final ed.).

6. This is the first case in which a surrogate mother without genetic links to the child sought custody of the child. See Martin Kasindorf, Birth Mother Is True Parent, Doctor Testifies, Newsday, Oct. 10, 1990, at 15 (News). Anna Johnson, described in the media as Black or as an African-American, described herself at the evidentiary hearing in the case as "half-white." See Martin Kasindorf, Overwhelming Maternal Instincts; Surrogate Mom Explains Decision, Newsday, Oct. 11, 1990, at 15 (News). Mark Calvert, the father, was described as Caucasian. Crispina Calvert, the genetic mother, was described in news reports both as a "Filipina" and as of "mixed Asian ancestry." See Charles Bremner, Surrogate Mother Loses Claim to Baby, The Times, Oct. 23, 1990, at 11, col. 4 (Overseas).

7. See Ethics Committee of the American Fertility Society, 46 (3), Ethical Considerations, of the New Reproductive Technologies 585 (Supp. 1, 1986).

8. Custody Battle Begins Over Surrogate's Baby, L.A. Times, Sept. 21, 1990, §A, at 1, col. 3 (Orange Cty. ed., Metro Desk).

9. *Id.*

10. See Who's Mommy? Without a Law Its Hard to Know, Newsday, Sept. 24, 1990, at 48 (Viewpoints) (Nassau and Suffolk ed.). See also Genetic Parents Given Sole Custody of Child, L.A. Times, Oct. 23, 1990, §A, at 1, col. 2 (Metro).

11. Calif. Civil Code §7003 (1983) reads in part:

§7003. Method of establishment
The parent and child relationship may be established as follows:
(1) Between a child and the natural mother it may be established by proof of her giving birth to the child, or under this part. . . .

See also Calif. Civil Code §7001 (1983):

§7001. Parent and child relationship; defined
As used in this part, "parent and child relationship" means the legal relationship between a child and his natural or adoptive parents incident to which the law confers or imposes rights, privileges, duties, and obligations. It includes the mother and child relationship and the father and child relationship.

12. Michael H. and Victoria D. v. Gerald D., 491 U.S. 110 (1989).

13. Kasindorf, *supra* note 6.

14. *Id.*

15. See Transcript, *supra* note 4, at 20.

16. Sonni Efron & Kevin Johnson, Decision Hailed as Proper, Criticized as Outrageous, L.A. Times, Oct. 23, 1990, §A, at 1, col. 5 (Orange Cty ed., Metro Desk). See also Voices, L.A. Times, Oct. 23, 1990, §A, at 12, col. 1 (Orange Cty ed., Foreign).

17. See California Surrogacy Case Raises New Questions About Parenthood, Christian Science Monitor, Sept. 25, 1990, at 1, col. 1 (U.S.).

18. Transcript, *supra* note 4, at 3.

19. Official bans on transracial adoptions have been held unconstitutional. See, e.g., Compos v. McKeithen, 341 F.Supp. 264 (E.D. La. 1972) (three-judge court) (invalidating Louisiana statute prohibiting interracial adoption as a violation of the Equal Protection Clause). However, while whites are sometimes permitted to adopt Black or bi-racial children, it is virtually unheard of for an adoption agency to offer a healthy, able-bodied white child to Black parents for adoption. Cf. Patricia Ballard, Racial Matching and the Adoption Dilemma, 17 J. Fam. Law 333 (1978–1979); Susan Grossman, A Child of a Different Color, 17 Buff. L. Rev. 303 (1968); Shari O'Brien, Race in Adoption Proceedings, 21 Tulsa L.J. 485 (1986). Cf. Richard Posner, The Regulation of the Market in Adoptions, 67 B.U. L. Rev. 59 (1987).

20. Transcript, *supra* note 4, at 5.

21. *Id.* at 6.

22. *Id.* at 17.

23. *Id.*

24. *Id.* at 6.

25. *Id.*

26. *Id.* at 8.

27. *Id.*

28. See Allen, Privacy, Surrogacy and the *Baby M* Case, 76 Geo. L.J. 1759, 1790 (1988).

29. Marjorie Shultz, Reproductive Technology and Intent-Based Parenthood: An Opportunity for Gender Neutrality, 1990 Wis. L. Rev. 297, 302.

30. In a recent case involving a lesbian couple who had intentionally utilized artificial insemination to become the parents of two children, the court refused to endorse either woman's proposed child-custody plan, and denied parental and visitation rights to the non-biological mother. The court deemed the intentions of the lesbian parents irrelevant. See Lesbian Is Denied Custody After Breakup, N.Y. Times, Mar. 24, 1991, at 22, col. 1.

31. Alice Walker, What Can the White Man . . . Say to the Black Woman 248 (20) The Nation 691 (1989).

32. Ruth Baum, Letter to the Editor, San Francisco Chronicle, Nov. 6, 1990, §A, at 20. ("I've got just one question concerning the Anna Johnson surrogate mother case: If a woman can legally rent her uterus for nine months, why should the law prevent her from renting her vagina for an hour or two? . . . [Prostitution and surrogacy involve] . . . commercial use of one's body for someone else's convenience or pleasure.")

33. See Allen, Privacy, Surrogacy, *supra* note 28.

34. Laurie Nsiah-Jefferson, Reproductive Laws, Women of Color, and Low-Income Women, herein, at 1007, 1015.

35. *Id.*

Market-Inalienability

MARGARET JANE RADIN

SINCE THE DECLARATION of "unalienable rights" of persons at the founding of our republic,[1] inalienability has had a central place in our legal and moral culture. Yet there is no one sharp meaning for the term "inalienable." Sometimes inalienable means nontransferable; sometimes only nonsalable. Sometimes inalienable means nonrelinquishable by a rightholder; sometimes it refers to rights that cannot be lost at all. In this essay I explore nonsalability, a species of inalienability I call market-inalienability. Something that is market-inalienable is not to be sold, which in our economic system means it is not to be traded in the market. . . .

The most familiar context of inalienability is the traditional liberal triad: the rights to life, liberty, and property. To this triad, liberalism juxtaposes the most familiar context of alienability: traditional property rights. Although the right to hold property is considered inalienable in traditional liberalism, property rights themselves are presumed fully alienable, and inalienable property rights are exceptional and problematic.

Economic analysis, growing out of the liberal tradition, tends to view all inalienabilities in the way traditional liberalism views inalienable property rights. When it does this, economic analysis holds fast to one strand of traditional liberalism, but it implicitly rejects—or at least challenges—another: the traditional distinction between inalienable and alienable kinds of rights. In conceiving of all rights as property rights that can (at least theoretically) be alienated in markets, economic analysis has (at least in principle) invited markets to fill the social universe. It has invited us to view all inalienabilities as problematic.

In seeking to develop a theory of market-inalienability, I argue that inalienabilities should not always be conceived of as anomalies, regardless of whether they attach to things traditionally thought of as property. Indeed, I try to show that the characteristic rhetoric of economic analysis is morally wrong when it is put forward as the sole discourse of human life. My general view deviates not only from the traditional conception of the divide between inalienable and alienable kinds of rights, but also from the traditional conception of alienable property. Instead of using the categories of eco-

100 Harv. L. Rev. 1849 (1987). Copyright © 1987 by the Harvard Law Review Association.

nomics or those of traditional liberalism, I think that we should evaluate inalienabilities in connection with our best current understanding of the concept of human flourishing. . . .

I. Market-Inalienability and Noncommodification

[T]he traditional meanings of inalienability share a common core: the notion of alienation as a separation of something—an entitlement, right, or attribute—from its holder. Inalienability negates the possibility of separation. . . . Any particular entitlement, right, or attribute may be subject to one or more forms of inalienability. . . .

[N]onsalability is what I refer to as market-inalienability. In precluding sales but not gifts, market-inalienability places some things outside the marketplace but not outside the realm of social intercourse. . . .

Market-inalienability often expresses an aspiration for noncommodification. By making something nonsalable we proclaim that it should not be conceived of or treated as a commodity. When something is noncommodifiable, market trading is a disallowed form of social organization and allocation. We place that thing beyond supply and demand pricing, brokerage and arbitrage, advertising and marketing, stockpiling, speculation, and valuation in terms of the opportunity cost of production.

Market-inalienability poses for us more than the binary choice of whether something should be wholly inside or outside the market, completely commodified or completely noncommodified. Some things are completely commodified—deemed suitable for trade in a laissez-faire market. Others are completely noncommodified—removed from the market altogether. But many things can be described as incompletely commodified—neither fully commodified nor fully removed from the market.[2] Thus, we may decide that some things should be market-inalienable only to a degree, or only in some aspects.

To appreciate the need to develop a satisfactory analysis of market-inalienability, consider the deeply contested issues of commodification that confront us. Infants and children, fetal gestational services, blood, human organs, sexual services, and services of college athletes are some salient things whose commodification is contested. . . .

How are we to determine the extent to which something ought to be noncommodified, so that we can determine to what extent market-inalienability is justified? Because the question asks about the appropriate relationship of particular things to the market, normative theories about the appropriate social role of the market should be helpful in trying to answer it. We can think of such theories as ordered on a continuum stretching from universal noncommodification (nothing in markets) to universal commodification (everything in markets). . . . Distributed along the continuum are theorists we may call pluralists[3]—those who see a normatively appropriate but limited realm for commodification coexisting with one or more nonmarket realms. . . . For a pluralist, the crucial question is how to conceive of the permissible scope of the market. An acceptable answer would solve problems of contested commodification. . . .

II. Universal Commodification

Universal commodification means that anything some people are willing to sell and others are willing to buy in principle can and should be the subject of free market exchange. Moreover, universal commodification means that everything people need or desire, either individually or in groups, is conceived of as a commodity. "Everything" includes not only those things usually considered goods, but also personal attributes, relationships, and states of affairs. Under universal commodification, the functions of government, wisdom, a healthful environment, and the right to bear children are all commodities.

Universal commodification is characterized by universal market rhetoric and universal market methodology. In universal market rhetoric—the discourse of complete commodification—everything that is desired or valued is conceived of and spoken of as a "good." Everything that is desired or valued is an object that can be possessed, that can be thought of as equivalent to a sum of money, and that can be alienated. The person is conceived of and spoken of as the possessor and trader of these goods, and hence all human interactions are sales.

Market methodology includes a cost-benefit analysis, evaluating human actions and social outcomes in terms of actual or hypothetical gains from trade measured in money. Under universal commodification, market trading and its outcomes represent individual freedom and the ideal for individuals and society. Unrestricted choice about what goods to trade represents individual freedom, and maximizing individual gains from trade represents the individual's ideal. All social and political interactions are conceived of as exchanges for monetizable gains. Politics reduces to "rent seeking" by log-rolling selfish individuals or groups, and the social ideal reduces to efficiency.[4]

In seeking efficiency through market methodology, universal commodification posits the laissez-faire market as the rule. Laissez-faire is presumptively efficient because, under universal commodification, voluntary transfers are presumed to maximize gains from trade, and all human interactions are characterizable as trades. Laissez-faire also presumptively expresses freedom, because freedom is defined as free choices of the person seen as trader.[5]

III. The Critique of Universal Commodification

A traditional critical response to universal commodification, at least since Marx, has been a global rejection of commodification. Universal decommodification or noncommodification maintains that the market ought not to exist and that social interactions involving production and consumption should be reconceived in a nonmarket way. Even if one rejects that ideal, however, as I do because of a problem of transition, the critique of universal commodification offers a crucial insight: a world in which human interactions are conceived of as market trades is different from one in which they are not. Rhetoric is not just shaped by, but shapes, reality.

A. Universal Noncommodification

Universal noncommodification holds that the hegemony of profit-maximizing buying and selling stifles the individual and social potential of human beings through its organization of production, distribution, and consumption, and through its concomitant creation and maintenance of the person as a self-aggrandizing profit- and preference-maximizer. Anticommodifiers tend to assume that we are living under a regime of universal commodification, with its attendant full-blown market methodology and market rhetoric. They also tend to assume that universal commodification is a necessary concomitant of commodification in the narrower sense—the existence of market transactions under capitalism. Anticommodifiers link rhetoric and reality in their assumption that our material relationships of production and exchange are interwoven with our discourse and our understanding of ourselves and the world.

1. ALIENABILITY AND ALIENATION: THE PROBLEM OF FETISHISM

For critics of the market society, commodification simultaneously expresses and creates alienation. The word "alienation" thus harbors an ironic double meaning. Freedom of alienation is the paramount characteristic of liberal property rights, yet Marx saw a necessary connection between this market alienability and human alienation. In his early writings, Marx analyzed the connection between alienation and commodity production in terms of estranged labor; later he introduced the notion of commodity fetishism.[6] In his treatment of estranged labor, Marx portrayed workers' alienation from their own human self-activity as the result of producing objects that became market commodities. By objectifying the labor of the worker, commodities create object-bondage and alienate workers from the natural world in and with which they should constitute themselves by creative interaction. Ultimately, laboring to produce commodities turns the worker from a human being into a commodity, "indeed the most wretched of commodities."[7] Marx continued:

> The worker becomes an ever cheaper commodity the more commodities he creates. With the increasing value of the world of things proceeds in direct proportion the devaluation of the world of men. Labour produces not only commodities; it produces itself and the worker as a commodity—and does so in the proportion in which it produces commodities generally.[8]

Commodification brings about an inferior form of human life. As a result of this debasement, Marx concluded that people themselves, not just their institutions, must change in order to live without the market. To reach the post-capitalist stage, "the alteration of men on a mass scale is necessary."[9]

The fetishism of commodities represents a different kind of human subjection to commodities (or a different way of looking at human subjection to commodities).[10] By "fetishism" Marx meant a kind of projection of power and action onto commodities. This projection reflects—but disguises—human social interactions. Relationships between people are disguised as relationships between commodities, which appear to be governed by abstract market forces. I do not decide what objects to produce, rather "the market" does. . . . Thus, the market value[11] of my commodity dictates my actions, or so it seems. As Marx put it, "[producers'] own social action takes the form of the action of objects, which rule the producers instead of being ruled by them."[12] . . .

2. Inalienability and Noncommodification: The Problem of Transition

[M]arket-inalienability does not exist as a separate category for universal commodifiers, because nonsalability by definition encompasses the universe of inalienabilities. Likewise, universal noncommodifiers do not distinguish market-inalienability as an analytical category. Market-inalienability posits a nonmarket realm that appropriately coexists with a market realm, and this implicitly grants some legitimacy to market transactions, contrary to the noncommodifier's premise. Thus, only those who think that market and nonmarket realms legitimately coexist—pluralists—readily recognize market-inalienability.

Nevertheless, some who espouse universal noncommodification for the long run might espouse pluralism in the short run, if they think that introducing piecemeal market-inalienabilities is a way of making progress toward universal noncommodification. True utopian noncommodifiers, however, would oppose even this interim pluralism; for them, inalienability should be eschewed because it recognizes the legitimacy of alienability, the heart of capitalist property relationships.

I shall call these two approaches to noncommodification evolutionary and revolutionary. The revolutionary approach criticizes, as misguided and as an artifact of capitalism, the entire world view that posits a structure of persons versus objects, and alienable versus inalienable objects. It holds that the capitalist structure permeates not only our world of social interaction and allocation of resources but also our discourse, vocabulary, and conception of human flourishing. By contrast, the evolutionary approach, interim pluralism, recognizes the necessity of working within existing market structures of capitalism to achieve universal noncommodification. It differs from the other pluralist views that seek to curtail the scope of the market only in that it does not condone the remaining market order after piecemeal inalienabilities are in place. These two approaches exemplify a pervasive dilemma for social progress: whether and how existing conceptions and structures, such as commodification, can be used now to ensure they will no longer be used in some better future. This is the problem of transition. . . .

B. The Moral and Political Role of Rhetoric

3. The "Texture of the Human World"

. . . One way to see how universal market rhetoric does violence to our conception of human flourishing is to consider its view of personhood. In our understanding of personhood we are committed to an ideal of individual uniqueness that does not cohere with the idea that each person's attributes are fungible, that they have a monetary equivalent, and that they can be traded off against those of other people. Universal market rhetoric transforms our world of concrete persons, whose uniqueness and individuality is expressed in specific personal attributes, into a world of disembodied, fungible, attribute-less entities possessing a wealth of alienable, severable "objects." This rhetoric reduces the conception of a person to an abstract, fungible unit with no individuating characteristics.

Another way to see how universal market rhetoric does violence to our conception of human flourishing is to consider its view of freedom. Market rhetoric invites us to see the person as a self-interested maximizer in all respects. Freedom or autonomy, therefore, is seen as individual control over how to maximize one's overall gains. In the extreme, the ideal of freedom is achieved through buying and selling commodified objects in order to maximize monetizable wealth. As we have seen, Marx argued with respect to those who produce and sell commodities that this is not freedom but fetishism; what and how much is salable is not autonomously determined. Whether or not we agree with him, it is not satisfactory to think that marketing whatever one wishes defines freedom. Nor is it satisfactory to think that a theoretical license to acquire all objects one may desire defines freedom. . . .

IV. Pluralism: The Liberal Heritage

[P]luralism has been a prominent tenet of traditional liberalism. Nevertheless, . . . liberal pluralism has borne within it the seeds of universal commodification; indeed, universal commodification is a more coherent liberal position than pluralism. Thus, I ultimately argue that pluralism should now be reconceived. . . .

Prominent principles in liberal pluralism include negative liberty, the person as abstract subject, and a conceptual notion of property. These principles are basic to the free market and its institutions, private property and free contract. Negative liberty and the subjectivity of personhood underlie convictions that inalienable things are internal to the person, and that inalienabilities are paternalistic. Conceptualism finds alienability to be inherent in the concept of property. These convictions make the case for liberal pluralism uneasy, always threatening to assimilate to universal commodification.

The legal infrastructure of capitalism—what is required for a functioning laissez-faire market system—includes not merely private property, but private property plus free contract. In order for the exchange system to allocate resources, there must be both private entitlement to resources and permission to transfer entitlements at will to other private owners. . . .

Two theories about freedom are central to the ideological framework in which we view inalienability: the notion that freedom means negative liberty, and the notion that (negative) liberty is identical with, or necessarily connected to, free alienability of everything in markets. The conception of freedom as negative liberty gives rise to the view that all inalienabilities are paternalistic limitations on freedom. The idea that liberty consists in alienability of everything in markets clashes with substantive requirements of personhood, making it difficult, for example, to argue against human commodification. In general, the commitment to negative liberty . . . has caused confusion in liberal pluralism and has exerted a pull toward universal commodification.

Inalienabilities are often said to be paternalistic. Paternalism usually means to substitute the judgment of a third party or the government for that of a person on the ground that to do so is in that person's best interests. For advocates of negative liberty, to substitute someone else's choice for my own is a naked infringement of my liberty. Freedom means doing (or not doing) whatever I as an individual prefer at the moment, as long as I am not harming other people. To think of inalienability as paternalism assumes that freedom is negative liberty—that people would choose to alienate certain things if they could, but are restrained from doing so by moral or legal rules saying, in effect, that they are mistaken about what is good for them.

To say that inalienabilities involve a loss of freedom also assumes that alienation itself is an act of freedom, or is freedom-enhancing. Someone who holds this view and conceives of alienation as sale through free contract is deeply committed to commodification as expressive of—perhaps necessary for—human freedom. Insofar as theories of negative freedom are allied to universal commodification, so are traditional discussions of inalienability in terms of paternalism. If we reject the notion that freedom means negative liberty, and the notion that liberty and alienation in markets are identical or necessarily connected, then inalienability will cease to seem inherently paternalistic. If we adopt a positive view of liberty that includes proper self-development as necessary for freedom, then inalienabilities needed to foster that development will be seen as freedom-enhancing rather than as impositions of unwanted restraints on our desires to transact in markets. . . .

V. Toward an Evolutionary Pluralism

. . .

A. Noncommodification and the Ideal of Human Flourishing

Universal commodification conceives of freedom as negative liberty, indeed as negative liberty in a narrow sense, construing freedom as the ability to trade everything in free markets. . . .

A more positive meaning of freedom starts to emerge if one accepts the contextuality aspect of personhood. Contextuality means that physical and social contexts are integral to personal individuation, to self-development. Even under the narrowest conception of negative liberty, we would have to bring about the social environment that makes trade possible in order to become the persons whose freedom consists in unfettered trades of commodified objects. Under a broader negative view that conceives of freedom as the ability to make oneself what one will, contextuality implies that self-development in accordance with one's own will requires one to will certain interactions with the physical and social context because context can be integral to self-development. The relationship between personhood and context requires a positive commitment to act so as to create and maintain particular contexts of environment and community. Recognition of the need for such a commitment turns toward a positive view of freedom, in which the self-development of the individual is linked to pursuit of proper social development, and in which proper self-development, as a requirement of personhood, could in principle sometimes take precedence over one's momentary desires or preferences.

Universal commodification undermines personal identity by conceiving of personal attributes, relationships, and philosophical and moral commitments as monetizable and alienable from the self. A better view of personhood should understand many kinds of particulars—one's politics, work, religion, family, love, sexuality, friendships, altruism, experiences, wisdom, moral commitments, character, and personal attributes—as integral to the self. To understand any of these as monetizable or completely detachable from the person—to think, for example, that the value of one person's moral commitments is commensurate or fungible with those of another, or that the "same" person remains when her moral commitments are subtracted—is to do violence to our deepest understanding of what it is to be human. . . .

B. Methods of Justifying Market-Inalienabilities

If some people wish to sell something that is identifiably personal, why not let them? In a market society, whatever some people wish to buy and others wish to sell is deemed alienable. Under these circumstances, we must formulate an affirmative case for market-inalienability, so that no one may choose to make fungible—commodify—a personal attribute, right, or thing. In this Section, I propose and evaluate three possible methods of justifying market-inalienability based on personhood: a prophylactic argument, assimilation to prohibition, and a domino theory.

The method of justification that correlates most readily with traditional liberal pluralism is a prophylactic argument. For the liberal it makes sense to countenance both selling and sharing of personal things as the holder freely chooses. If an item of property is personal, however, sometimes the circumstances under which the holder places it on the market might arouse suspicion that her act is coerced. Given that we cannot know whether anyone really intends to cut herself off from something personal by commodifying it, our suspicions might sometimes justify banning sales. The risk of harm to the seller's personhood in cases in which coerced transactions are permitted (especially if the thing sought to be commodified is normally very important to personhood), and the great difficulties involved in trying to scrutinize every transaction closely, may sometimes outweigh the harm that a ban would impose on would-be sellers who are in fact uncoerced. A prophylactic rule aims to ensure free choice—negative liberty—by the best possible coercion-avoidance mechanism under conditions of uncertainty. This prophylactic argument is one way for a liberal to justify, for example, the ban on selling oneself into slavery. We normally view such commodification as so destructive of personhood that we would readily presume all instances of it to be coerced. We would not wish, therefore, to have a rule creating a rebuttable presumption that such transactions are uncoerced (as with ordinary contracts), nor even a rule that would scrutinize such transactions case-by-case for voluntariness, because the risk of harm to personhood in the coerced transactions we might mistakenly see as voluntary is so great that we would rather risk constraining the exercise of choice by those (if any) who really wish to enslave themselves.

A liberal pluralist might use a prophylactic justification to prevent poor people from selling their children, sexual services, or body parts. The liberal would argue that an appropriate conception of coercion should, with respect to selling these things, include the desperation of poverty. Poor people should not be forced to give up personal things because the relinquishment diminishes them as persons, contrary to the liberal regime of respect for persons. We should presume that such transactions are not the result of free choice.

When thus applied to coercion by poverty, the prophylactic argument is deeply troubling. If poverty can make some things nonsalable because we must prophylactically presume such sales are coerced, we would add insult to injury if we then do not provide the would-be seller with the goods she needs or the money she would have received. If we think respect for persons warrants prohibiting a mother from selling something personal to obtain food for her starving children, we do not respect her personhood more by forcing her to let them starve instead. To the extent it equates poverty with coercion, the prophylactic argument requires a corollary in welfare rights. . . .

A second method of justifying market-inalienability assimilates it to prohibition. If we accept that the commodified object is different from the "same" thing noncommodified and embedded in personal relationships, then market-inalienability is a prohibition of the commodified version, resting on some moral requirement that it not exist. What might be the basis of such a moral requirement? Something might be prohibited in its market form because it both creates and exposes wealth- and class-based contingencies for obtaining things that are critical to life itself—for example, health care—and thus undermines a commitment to the sanctity of life. Another reason for prohibition might be that the use of market rhetoric, in conceiving of the "good" and understanding the interactions of people respecting it, creates and fosters an inferior conception of human flourishing. For example, we accept an inferior conception of personhood (one allied to the extreme view of negative freedom) if we suppose people may freely choose to commodify themselves.

The prohibition argument—that commodification of things is bad in itself, or because these things are not the "same" things that would be available to people in nonmarket relationships—leads to universal noncommodification. If commodification is bad in itself it is bad for everything. Any social good is arguably "different" if not embedded in a market society. To restrict the argument in order to permit pluralism, we have to accept either that certain things are the "same" whether or not they are bought and sold, and others are "different," or that prohibiting the commodified version morally matters only for certain things, but not for all of them. At present we tend to think that nuts and bolts are pretty much the "same" whether commodified or not, whereas love, friendship, and sexuality are very "different"; we also tend to think that trying to keep society free of commodified love, friendship, and sexuality morally matters more than trying to keep it free of commodified nuts and bolts.

A third method of justifying market-inalienability, the domino theory, envisions a slippery slope leading to market domination. The domino theory assumes that for some things, the noncommodified version is morally preferable; it also assumes that the commodified and noncommodified versions of some interactions cannot coexist. To commodify some things is simply to preclude their noncommodified analogues from existing. Under this theory, the existence of some commodified sexual interactions will contaminate or infiltrate everyone's sexuality so that all sexual relationships will become commodified. If it is morally required that noncommodified sex be possible, market-inalienability of sexuality would be justified. This result can be conceived of as the opposite of a prohibition: there is assumed to exist some moral requirement that a certain "good" be socially available. The domino theory thus supplies an answer (as the prohibition theory does not) to the liberal question why people should not be permitted to choose both market and nonmarket interactions: the noncommodified version is morally preferable when we cannot have both.

We can now see how the prohibition and domino theories are connected. The prohibition theory focuses on the importance of excluding from social life commodified versions of certain "goods"—such as love, friendship, and sexuality—whereas the domino theory focuses on the importance for social life of maintaining the noncommodified versions. The prohibition theory stresses the wrongness of commodification—its alienation and degradation of the person—and the domino theory stresses the rightness of noncommodification in creating the social context for the proper expression and fostering of personhood. If one explicitly adopts both prongs of this commitment to personhood, the prohibition and domino theories merge.

C. The Problem of Non-ideal Evaluation

One ideal world would countenance no commodification; another would insist that all harms to personhood are unjust; still another would permit no relationships of oppression or disempowerment. But we are situated in a nonideal world of ignorance, greed, and violence; of poverty, racism, and sexism. In spite of our ideals, justice under nonideal circumstances, pragmatic justice, consists in choosing the best alternative now available to us. In doing so we may have to tolerate some things that would count as harms in our ideal world. Whatever harms to our ideals we decide we must now tolerate in the name of justice may push our ideals that much farther away. How are we to decide, now, what is the best transition toward our ideals, knowing that our choices now will help to reconstitute those ideals?

1. THE DOUBLE BIND

Often commodification is put forward as a solution to powerlessness or oppression, as in the suggestion that women be permitted to sell sexual and reproductive services.[13] But is women's personhood injured by allowing or by disallowing commodification of sex and reproduction? The argument that commodification empowers women is that recognition of these alienable entitlements will enable a needy group—poor women—to improve their relatively powerless, oppressed condition, an improvement that would be beneficial to personhood. If the law denies women the opportunity to be comfortable sex workers and baby producers instead of subsistence domestics, assemblers, clerks, and waitresses—or pariahs (welfare recipients) and criminals (prostitutes)—it keeps them out of the economic mainstream and hence the mainstream of American life.

The rejoinder is that, on the contrary, commodification will harm personhood by powerfully symbolizing, legitimating, and enforcing class division and gender oppression. It will create the two forms of alienation that correlate with commodification of personal things. Women will partly internalize the notion that their persons and their attributes are separate, thus creating the pain of a divided self. To the extent that this self-conception is not internalized, women will be alienated from the dominant order that, by allowing commodification, sees them in this light. Moreover, commodification will exacerbate, not ameliorate, oppression and powerlessness, because of the social disapproval connected with marketing one's body.

But the surrejoinder is that noncommodification of women's capabilities under current circumstances represents not a brave new world of human flourishing, but rather a perpetuation of the old order that submerges women in oppressive status relationships, in which personal identity as market-traders is the prerogative of males. We cannot make progress toward the noncommodification that might exist under ideal conditions of equality and freedom by trying to maintain noncommodification now under historically determined conditions of inequality and bondage.

These conflicting arguments illuminate the problem with the prophylactic argument for market-inalienability. If we now permit commodification, we may exacerbate the oppression of women—the suppliers. If we now disallow commodification—without what I have called the welfare-rights corollary, or large-scale redistribution of social wealth and power—we force women to remain in circumstances that they themselves believe are worse than becoming sexual commodity-suppliers. Thus, the alternatives seem subsumed by a need for social progress, yet we must choose some regime now in order to make progress. This dilemma of transition is the double bind.

The double bind has two main consequences. First, if we cannot respect personhood either by permitting sales or by banning sales, justice requires that we consider changing the circumstances that create the dilemma. We must consider wealth and power redistribution. Second, we still must choose a regime for the meantime, the transition, in nonideal circumstances. To resolve the double bind, we have to investigate particular problems separately; decisions must be made (and remade) for each thing that some people desire to sell.

If we have reason to believe with respect to a particular thing that the domino theory might hold—commodification for some means commodification for all—we would have reason to choose market-inalienability. But the double bind means that if we choose market-inalienability, we might deprive a class of poor and oppressed people of the opportunity to have more money with which to buy adequate food, shelter, and health care in the market, and hence deprive them of a better chance to lead a humane life. Those who gain from the market-inalienability, on the other hand, might be primarily people whose wealth and power make them comfortable enough to be concerned about the inroads on the general quality of life that commodification would make. Yet, taking a slightly longer view, commodification threatens the personhood of everyone, not just those who can now afford to concern themselves about it. Whether this elitism in market-inalienability should make us risk the dangers of commodification will depend upon the dangers of each case.

2. INCOMPLETE COMMODIFICATION

One way to mediate the dilemma is through what I shall call incomplete commodification. Under nonideal circumstances the question whether market-inalienability can be justified is more complicated than a binary decision between complete commodification and complete noncommodification. Rather, we should understand there to be a continuum reflecting degrees of commodification that will be appropriate in a given context. An incomplete commodification—a partial market-inalienability[14]—can sometimes substitute for a complete noncommodification that might accord with our ideals but cause too much harm in our nonideal world.

D. Evolutionary Pluralism Applied: Problems of Sexuality and Reproductive Capacity

I now offer thoughts on how the analysis that I recommend might be brought to bear on a set of controversial market-inalienabilities. . . . The example I shall pursue is the contested commodification of aspects of sexuality and reproductive capacity: the issues of prostitution, baby-selling, and surrogacy. I conclude that market-inalienability is justified for baby-selling and also—provisionally—for surrogacy, but that prostitution should be governed by a regime of incomplete commodification.

Assuming that our ideal of personhood includes the ideal of sexual interaction as equal nonmonetized sharing, we might imagine that the "good" commodified sexuality ought not to exist: that sexual activity should be market-inalienable.[15] But perhaps prohibition of the sale of sexual services, if it aims to preserve sexuality as nonmonetized sharing, is not justified under current circumstances, because sex is already commodified.[16] Moreover, in our nonideal world, market-inalienability—especially if enforced through criminalization of sales—may cause harm to ideals of personhood instead of maintaining and fostering them, primarily because it exacerbates the double bind. Poor women who believe that they must sell their sexual services to survive are subject to moral opprobrium, disease, arrest, and violence. The ideal of sexual sharing is related to identity and contextuality, but the identity of those who sell is undermined by criminalization and powerlessness, and their ability to develop and maintain relationships is hurt by these circumstances.

Nevertheless, despite the double bind and the harms of the black market to prostitutes, fear of a domino effect could perhaps warrant market-inalienability as an effort to ward off conceiving of all sexuality as fungible. Many people would say, however, that the known availability of commodified sex by itself does not render nonfungible sexual interactions impossible or even more difficult, and that the prevalence of ideals of interpersonal sexual sharing in spite of the widespread association of sex and money is proof that the domino effect in rhetoric is not to be feared. But we must evaluate the seriousness of the risk if commodification proceeds. What if sex were fully and openly commodified? Suppose newspapers, radio, TV, and billboards advertised sexual services as imaginatively and vividly as they advertise computer services, health clubs, or soft drinks. Suppose the sexual partner of your choice could be ordered through a catalog, or through a large brokerage firm that has an "800" number, or at a trade show, or in a local showroom. Suppose the business of recruiting suppliers of sexual services was carried on in the same way as corporate headhunting or training of word-processing operators. A change would occur in everyone's discourse about sex, and in particular about women's sexuality. New terms would emerge for particular gradations of market value, and new discussions would be heard of particular abilities or qualities in terms of their market value. With this change in discourse would come a change in everyone's experience. The open market might render subconscious valuation of women (and perhaps everyone) in sexual dollar value impossible to avoid. It might make the ideal of nonmonetized sharing impossible. Thus, the argument for noncommodification of sexuality based on the domino effect, in its strongest form, is that we do not wish to unleash market forces onto the shaping of our discourse regarding sexuality and hence onto our very conception of sexuality and our sexual feelings.

This domino argument assumes that nonmonetized equal sharing relationships are the norm or are at least attainable. That assumption is now contested. Some feminists argue that male-female sexual relationships that actually instantiate the ideal of equal sharing are under current social circumstances rare or even impossible.[17] According to this view, moreover, women are oppressed by this ideal because they try to understand their relationships with men in light of it, and conceal from themselves the truth about their own condition. They try to understand what they are doing as giving, as equal sharing, while their sexuality is actually being taken from them. If we believe that women are deceived (and deceiving themselves) in this way, attempted noncommodification in the name of the ideal may be futile or even counterproductive. Noncommodification under current circumstances is part of the social structure that perpetuates false consciousness about the current role of the ideal. Some feminists also argue that many male-female sexual relationships are (unequal) economic bargains, not a context in which equal sharing occurs.[18] If that is true, attempted noncommodification means that prostitutes are being singled out for punishment for something pervasive in women's condition, and that they are being singled out because their class or race forecloses more socially accepted forms of sexual bargaining. This returns us to the double bind.

Perhaps the best way to characterize the present situation is to say that women's sexuality is incompletely commodified. Many sexual relationships may have both market and nonmarket aspects: relationships may be entered into and sustained partly for economic reasons and partly for the interpersonal sharing that is part of our ideal of human flourishing. Even if under current circumstances the ideal misleads us into thinking that unequal relationships are really equal, it seems that the way out of such ideological bondage is not to abandon the ideal, but rather to pursue it in ways that are not harmful under these nonideal circumstances. Market-inalienability seems harmful, not only because it might be ideologically two-edged, but also because of the double bind. Yet complete commodification, if any credence is given to the feared domino effect, may relinquish our conception of sexuality entirely.

The issue thus becomes how to structure an incomplete commodification that takes account of our nonideal world, yet does not foreclose progress to a better world of more equal power (and less susceptibility to the domino effect of market rhetoric). I think we should now decriminalize the sale of sexual services in order to protect poor women from the degradation and danger either of the black market or of other occupations that seem to them less desirable. At the same time, in order to check the domino effect, we should prohibit the capitalist entrepreneurship that would operate to create an organized market in sexual services even though this step would pose enforcement difficulties. It would include, for example, banning brokerage (pimping) and recruitment. It might also include banning advertising. Trying to keep commodification of sexuality out of our discourse by banning advertising does have the double bind effect of failing to legitimate the sales we allow, and hence it may fail to alleviate significantly the social disapproval suffered by those who sell sexual services. It also adds "information costs" to their "product," and thus fails to yield them as great a "return" as would the full-blown market. But these nonideal effects must be borne if we really accept that extensive permeation of our discourse by commodification-talk would alter sexuality in a way that we are unwilling to countenance.

A different analysis is warranted for baby-selling. Like relationships of sexual sharing, parent-child relationships are closely connected with personhood, particularly with personal identity and contextuality. Moreover, poor women caught in the double bind raise the issue of freedom: they may wish to sell a baby on the black market, as they may wish to sell sexual services, perhaps to try to provide adequately for other children or family members. But the double bind is not the only problem of freedom implicated in baby-selling. Under a market regime, prostitutes may be choosing to sell their sexuality, but babies are not choosing for themselves that under current nonideal circumstances they are better off as commodities. If we permit babies to be sold, we commodify not only the mother's (and father's) baby-making capacities—which might be analogous to commodifying sexuality—but we also conceive of the baby itself in market rhetoric. When the baby becomes a commodity, all of its personal attributes— sex, eye color, predicted I.Q., predicted height, and the like—become commodified as well. This is to conceive of potentially all personal attributes in market rhetoric, not merely those of sexuality. Moreover, to conceive of infants in market rhetoric is likewise to conceive of the people they will become in market rhetoric, and to create in those people a commodified self-conception.

Hence, the domino theory has a deep intuitive appeal when we think about the sale of babies. An idealist might suggest, however, that the fact that we do not now value babies in money suggests that we would not do so even if babies were sold. Perhaps babies could be incompletely commodified, valued by the participants to the interaction in a nonmarket way, even though money changed hands. Although this is theoretically possible, it seems too risky in our nonideal world. If a capitalist baby industry were to come into being, with all of its accompanying paraphernalia, how could any of us, even those who did not produce infants for sale, avoid subconsciously measuring the dollar value of our children? How could our children avoid being preoccupied with measuring their own dollar value? This makes our discourse about ourselves (when we are children) and about our children (when we are parents) like our discourse about cars. Seeing commodification of babies as an inevitable and grave injury to personhood appears rather easy. In the worst case, market rhetoric could create a commodified self-conception in everyone, as the result of commodifying every attribute that differentiates us and that other people value in us, and could destroy personhood as we know it.

I suspect that an intuitive grasp of the injury to personhood involved in commodification of human beings is the reason many people lump baby-selling together with slavery.[19] But this intuition can be misleading. Selling a baby, whose personal development requires caretaking, to people who want to act as the caretakers is not the same thing as selling a baby or an adult to people who want to act only as users of her capacities. Moreover, if the reason for our aversion to baby-selling is that we believe it is like slavery, then it is unclear why we do not prohibit baby-giving (release of a child for adoption) on the ground that enslavement is not permitted even without consideration. We might say that respect for persons prohibits slavery but may require adoption in cases in which only adoptive parents will treat the child as a person, or in the manner appropriate to becoming a person. But this answer is still somewhat unsatisfactory. It does not tell us whether parents who are financially and psychologically capable of raising a child in a manner we deem proper nevertheless may give up the child for adoption, for what we would consider less than compelling reasons. If parents are morally entitled to give up a child even if the child could have (in some sense) been raised properly by them, our aversion to slavery does not explain why infants are subject only to market-inalienability. There must be another reason why baby-giving is unobjectionable.

The reason, I think, is that we do not fear relinquishment of children unless it is accompanied by market rhetoric. The objection to market rhetoric may be part of a moral prohibition on market treatment of any babies, regardless of whether nonmonetized treatment of other children would remain possible. To the extent that we condemn baby-selling even in the absence of any domino effect, we are saying that this "good" simply should not exist. Conceiving of any child in market rhetoric wrongs personhood. In addition, we fear, based on our assessment of current social norms, that the market value of babies would be decided in ways injurious to their personhood and to the personhood of those who buy and sell on this basis, exacerbating class, race, and gender divisions. To the extent the objection to baby-selling is not (or is not only) to the very idea of this "good" (marketed children), it stems from a fear that the non-market version of human beings themselves will become impossible. Conceiving of children in market rhetoric would foster an inferior conception of human flourishing, one that commodifies every personal attribute that might be valued by people in other people. In spite of the double bind, our aversion to commodification of babies has a basis strong enough to recommend that market-inalienability be maintained.

The question of surrogate mothering seems more difficult. I shall consider the surrogacy situation in which a couple desiring a child consists of a fertile male and an infertile female. They find a fertile female to become impregnated with the sperm of the would-be father, to carry the fetus to term, to give birth to the child, and to relinquish it to them for adoption. This interaction may be paid, in which case surrogacy becomes a good sold on the market, or unpaid, in which case it remains a gift.

Those who view paid surrogacy as tantamount to permitting the sale of babies point out that a surrogate is paid for the same reasons that an ordinary adoption is commissioned: to conceive, carry, and deliver a baby. Moreover, even if an ordinary adoption is not commissioned, there seems to be no substantive difference between paying a woman for carrying a child she then delivers to the employers, who have found her through a brokerage mechanism, and paying her for an already "produced" child whose buyer is found through a brokerage mechanism (perhaps called an "adoption agency") after she has paid her own costs of "production." Both are adoptions for which consideration is paid. Others view paid surrogacy as better analogized to prostitution (sale of sexual services) than to baby-selling. They would say that the commodity being sold in the surrogacy interaction is not the baby itself, but rather "womb services."

The different conceptions of the good being sold in paid surrogacy can be related to the primary difference between this interaction and (other) baby-selling: the genetic father is more closely involved in the surrogacy interaction than in a standard adoption. The disagreement about how we might conceive of the "good" reflects a deeper ambiguity about the degree of commodification of mothers and children. If we think that ordinarily a mother paid to relinquish a baby for adoption is selling a baby, but that if she is a surrogate, she is merely selling gestational services, it seems we are assuming that the baby cannot be considered the surrogate's property, so as to become alienable by her, but that her gestational services can be considered property and therefore become alienable. If this conception reflects a decision that the baby cannot be property at all—cannot be objectified—then the decision reflects a lesser level of commodification in rhetoric. But this interpretation is implausible because of our willingness to refer to the ordinary paid adoption as baby-selling. A more plausible interpretation of conceiving of the "good" as gestational services is that this conception reflects an understanding that the baby is already someone else's property—the father's.

This characterization of the interaction can be understood as both complete commodification in rhetoric and an expression of gender hierarchy. The would-be father is "producing" a baby of his "own," but in order to do so he must purchase these "services" as a necessary input. Surrogacy raises the issue of commodification and gender politics in how we understand even the description of the problem. An oppressive understanding of the interaction is the more plausible one: women—their reproductive capacities, attributes, and genes—are fungible in carrying on the male genetic line.[20]

Whether one analogizes paid surrogacy to sale of sexual services or to baby-selling, the underlying concerns are the same. First, there is the possibility of even further oppression of poor or ignorant women, which must be weighed against a possible step toward their liberation through economic gain from a new alienable entitlement—the double bind. Second, there is the possibility that paid surrogacy should be completely prohibited because it expresses an inferior conception of human flourishing. Third, there is the possibility of a domino effect of commodification in rhetoric that leaves us all inferior human beings.

Paid surrogacy involves a potential double bind. The availability of the surrogacy option could create hard choices for poor women. In the worst case, rich women, even those who are not infertile, might employ poor women to bear children for them. It might be degrading for the surrogate to commodify her gestational services or her baby, but she might find this preferable to her other choices in life. But although surrogates have not tended to be rich women, nor middle-class career women, neither have they (so far) seemed to be the poorest women, the ones most caught in the double bind.[21]

Whether surrogacy is paid or unpaid, there may be a transition problem: an ironic self-deception. Acting in ways that current gender ideology characterizes as empowering might actually be disempowering. Surrogates may feel they are fulfilling their womanhood by producing a baby for someone else, although they may actually be reinforcing oppressive gender roles. It is also possible to view would-be fathers as (perhaps unknowing) oppressors of their own partners. Infertile mothers, believing it to be their duty to raise their partners' genetic children, could be caught in the same kind of false consciousness and relative powerlessness as surrogates who feel called upon to produce children for others. Some women might have conflicts with their partners that they cannot acknowledge, either about raising children under these circumstances instead of adopting unrelated children, or about having children at all. These considerations suggest that to avoid reinforcing gender ideology, both paid and unpaid surrogacy must be prohibited.

Another reason we might choose prohibition of all surrogacy, paid or unpaid, is that allowing surrogacy in our nonideal world would injure the chances of proper personal development for children awaiting adoption. Unlike a mother relinquishing a baby for adoption, the surrogate mother bears a baby only in response to the demand of the would-be parents: their demand is the reason for its being born. There is a danger that unwanted children might remain parentless even if only unpaid surrogacy is allowed, because those seeking children will turn less frequently to adoption. Would-be fathers may strongly prefer adopted children bearing their own genetic codes to adopted children genetically strange to them; perhaps women prefer adopted children bearing their partners' genetic codes. Thus, prohibition of all surrogacy might be grounded on concern for unwanted children and their chances in life.

Perhaps a more visionary reason to consider prohibiting all surrogacy is that the demand for it expresses a limited view of parent-child bonding; in a better view of personal contextuality, bonding should be reconceived. Although allowing surrogacy might be thought to foster ideals of interrelationships between men and their children, it is unclear why we should assume that the ideal of bonding depends especially on genetic connection. Many people who adopt children feel no less bonded to their children than responsible genetic parents; they understand that relational bonds are created in shared life more than in genetic codes. We might make better progress toward ideals of interpersonal sharing—toward a better view of contextual personhood—by breaking down the notion that children are fathers'—or parents'—genetic property.[22]

In spite of these concerns, attempting to prohibit surrogacy now seems too utopian, because it ignores a transition problem. At present, people seem to believe that they need genetic offspring in order to fulfill themselves; at present, some surrogates believe their actions to be altruistic. To try to create an ideal world all at once would do violence to things people make central to themselves. This problem suggests that surrogacy should not be altogether prohibited.

Concerns about commodification of women and children, however, might counsel permitting only unpaid surrogacy (market-inalienability). Market-inalienability might be grounded in a judgment that commodification of women's reproductive capacity is harmful for the identity aspect of their personhood and in a judgment that the closeness of paid surrogacy to baby-selling harms our self-conception too deeply. There is certainly the danger that women's attributes, such as height, eye color, race, intelligence, and athletic ability, will be monetized. Surrogates with "better" qualities will command higher prices in virtue of those qualities. This monetization commodifies women more broadly than merely with respect to their sexual services or reproductive capacity. Hence, if we wish to avoid the dangers of commodification and, at the same time, recognize that there are some situations in which a surrogate can be understood to be proceeding out of love or altruism and not out of economic necessity or desire for monetary gain,[23] we could prohibit sales but allow surrogates to give their services. We might allow them to accept payment of their reasonable out-of-pocket expenses— a form of market-inalienability similar to that governing ordinary adoption.

Fear of a domino effect might also counsel market-inalienability. At the moment, it does not seem that women's reproductive capabilities are as commodified as their sexuality. Of course, we cannot tell whether this means that reproductive capabilities are more resistant to commodification or whether the trend toward commodification is still at an early stage. Reproductive capacity, however, is not the only thing in danger of commodification. We must also consider the commodification of children. The risk is serious indeed, because, if there is a significant domino effect, commodification of some children means commodification of everyone. Yet, as long as fathers do have an unmonetized attachment to their genes (and as long as their partners tend to share it), even though the attachment may be nonideal, we need not see children born in a paid surrogacy arrangement—and they need not see themselves—as fully commodified. Hence, there may be less reason to fear the domino effect with paid surrogacy than with baby-selling. The most credible fear of a domino effect—one that paid surrogacy does share with commissioned adoption—is that all women's personal attributes will be commodified. The pricing of surrogates' services will not immediately transform the rhetoric in which women conceive of themselves and in which they are conceived, but that is its tendency. This fear, even though remote, seems grave enough to take steps to ensure that paid surrogacy does not become the kind of institution that could permeate our discourse.

Thus, for several reasons market-inalienability seems an attractive solution. But, in choosing this regime, we would have to recognize the danger that the double bind might force simulations of altruism by those who would find living on an expense allowance preferable to their current circumstances. Furthermore, the fact that they are not being paid "full" price exacerbates the double bind and is not really helpful in preventing a domino effect. We would also have to recognize that there would probably not be enough altruistic surrogates available to alleviate the frustration and suffering of those who desire children genetically related to fathers,[24] if this desire is widespread.

The other possible choice is to create an incomplete commodification similar to the one suggested for sale of sexual services. The problem of surrogacy is more difficult, however, primarily because the interaction produces a new person whose interests must be respected. In such an incomplete commodification, performance of surrogacy agreements by willing parties should be permitted, but women who change their minds should not be forced to perform. The surrogate who changes her mind before birth can choose abortion; at birth, she can decide to keep the baby.[25] Neither should those who hire a surrogate and then change their minds be forced to keep and raise a child they do not want. But if a baby is brought into the world and nobody wants it, the surrogate who intended to relinquish the child should not be forced to keep and raise it. Instead, those who, out of a desire for genetically related offspring, initiated the interaction should bear the responsibility for providing for the child's future in a manner that can respect the child's personhood and not create the impression that children are commodities that can be abandoned as well as alienated.

We should be aware that the case for incomplete commodification is much more uneasy for surrogacy than for prostitution. The potential for commodification of women is deeper, because, as with commissioned adoption, we risk conceiving of all of women's personal attributes in market rhetoric, and because paid surrogacy within the current gender structure may symbolize that women are fungible baby-makers for men whose seed must be carried on. Moreover, as with commissioned adoption, the interaction brings forth a new person who did not choose commodification and whose potential personal identity and contextuality must be respected even if the parties to the interaction fail to do so.

Because the double bind has similar force whether a woman wishes to be a paid surrogate or simply to create a baby for sale on demand, the magnitude of the difference between paid surrogacy and commissioned adoption is largely dependent on the weight we give to the father's genetic link to the baby. If we place enough weight on this distinction, then incomplete commodification for surrogacy, but not for baby-selling, will be justified. But we should be aware, if we choose incomplete commodification for surrogacy, that this choice might seriously weaken the general market-inalienability of babies, which prohibits commissioned adoptions. If, on balance, incomplete commodification rather than market-inalienability comes to seem right for now, it will appear so for these reasons: because we judge the double bind to suggest that we should not completely foreclose women's choice of paid surrogacy, even though we foreclose commissioned adoptions; because we judge that people's (including women's) strong commitment to maintaining men's genetic lineage will ward off commodification and the domino effect, distinguishing paid surrogacy adequately from commissioned adoptions; and because we judge that that commitment cannot be overridden without harm to central aspects of people's self-conception. If we choose market-inalienability, it will be because we judge the double bind to suggest that poor women will be further disempowered if paid surrogacy becomes a middle-class option, and because we judge that people's commitment to men's genetic lineage is an artifact of gender ideology that can neither save us from commodification nor result in less harm to personhood than its reinforcement would now create. In my view, a form of market-inalienability similar to our regime for ordinary adoption will probably be the better nonideal solution.

VI. Conclusion

Market-inalienability is an important normative category for our society. Economic analysis and traditional liberal pluralism have failed to recognize and correctly understand its significance because of the market orientation of their premises. In attempting to free our conceptions from these premises in order to see market-inalienability as an important countercurrent to our market orientation, I have created an archetype, universal commodification, and tried to show how it underlies both economic analysis and more traditional liberal thinking about inalienability. . . . The rhetoric of commodification has led us into an unreflective use of market characterizations and comparisons for almost everything people may value, and hence into an inferior conception of personhood.

I have created a contrasting archetype, universal noncommodification, to characterize the utopian vision—expressed by Marxists and other social critics of the market order—of a social world free of market relationships and market conceptions. Although this archetype, too, is an oversimplification, I believe it enables us to focus on the transition problem that always lies between us and our utopias. If decommodification of things important to personhood is provisionally the ideal of justice we should strive for, trying to bring it to pass now may sometimes be unjust. In attempting to make the hard choices in which both commodification and decommodification seem harmful—the transition problem of the double bind—we must evaluate each contested commodification in its temporal and social context, and we must learn to see in the commodification issue the same interconnection between rhetoric and reality that we have come to accept between physical reality and our paradigms of thought.

To the extent that we must not assimilate our conception of personhood to the market, market-inalienabilities are justified. But market-inalienabilities are unjust when they are too harmful to personhood in our nonideal world. Incomplete commodification can help us mediate this kind of injustice. To see the world of exchange as shot through with incomplete commodification can also show us that inalienability is not the anomaly that economics and more traditional liberalism conceive it to be. This perspective can also help us begin to decommodify things important to personhood—like work and housing—that are now wrongly conceived of in market rhetoric.

Market-inalienability ultimately rests on our best conception of human flourishing, which must evolve as we continue to learn and debate. Likewise, market-inalienabilities must evolve as we continue to learn and debate; there is no magic formula that will delineate them with utter certainty, or once and for all. In our debate, there is no such thing as two radically different normative discourses reaching the "same" result. The terms of our debate will matter to who we are.

Notes

[The thesis of this article has been expanded and further developed by the author in *Contested Commodities* (Harvard Univ. Press, 1996). *Ed.*]

1. The Declaration of Independence para. 2 (U.S. 1776).

2. Things that are incompletely commodified do not fully exhibit the typical indicia of traditional property and contract. For example, things that are subject to price controls are incompletely commodified because freedom to set prices is part of the traditional understanding of property and contract.

3. [By "pluralist" Professor Radin means people who believe that there are separate and self-contained spheres of social life, such as markets, politics, the family, etc. In her book *Contested Commodities*, she refers to these theorists as "compartmentalizers." *Ed.*]

4. Proponents of law and economics often note that they do not endorse the view that efficiency equals justice, because an efficient state (however efficiency is defined) is always efficient relative to an initial wealth distribution, and the initial distribution may be unjust. See, e.g., R. Posner, Economic Analysis of Law 13 (3d ed. 1986). But many of them ignore their caveat. See, e.g., *id.* at 25 (stating that efficiency is "perhaps the most common" meaning of "justice").

5. The presumptive efficiency and presumptive freedom of laissez-faire suggest that the philosophical premises of theorists whose views tend toward universal commodification may be either utilitarian or libertarian. Many law-and-economics theorists are utilitarians.

6. For discussion of Marx's early and later treatment of alienation and its rela-

tionship to commodification, see S. Avineri, The Social and Political Thought of Karl Marx 96–123 (1968), and A. Gouldner, The Two Marxisms 177–220 (1980).

7. Marx, Economic and Philosophic Manuscripts of 1844, in The Marx-Engels Reader 70 (R. Tucker, 2d ed. 1984) [hereinafter the Marx-Engels Reader].

8. *Id.* at 71 (emphasis in original).

9. Marx, The German Ideology: Part I, in The Marx-Engels Reader, *supra* note 7, at 193. . . .

10. See 1 K. Marx, Capital 71–83 (F. Engels ed. 1894, S. Moore & E. Aveling trans. 1984); cf. Balbus, Commodity Form and Legal Form: An Essay on the "Relative Autonomy of the Law," 11 Law & Soc'y Rev. 571, 573–575 (1977) (expounding Marx's theory of the fetishism of commodities).

11. What we now call market value, Marx thought of as "exchange value," which he contrasted with "use value" (the worth of something to consumers) and "value" (the amount of labor socially necessary to produce something). . . .

12. 1 K. Marx, Capital, *supra* note 10, at 79.

13. Although in the text I pursue its application to poor women, it should be evident that the double bind is broader in scope. For example, it also complicates the problem of whether people should be allowed to sell their organs.

14. The conventional term for incomplete commodification (partial market-inalienability) is, of course, restraint upon alienation.

15. I am confining the present discussion to traditional male-female prostitution because I am considering a set of would-be commodities that women would control. A different nonideal moral analysis will no doubt be required for other forms.

16. Legalized prostitution has existed in many places, and there has always been a large black market of which everyone is well aware. That those who purchase prostitutes' services are often not prosecuted seems to indicate that commodification of sexuality, at least by the purchasers, is tolerated.

17. See, e.g., C. MacKinnon, Feminism Unmodified: Discourses on Life and Law (1987); Gottlieb, The Political Economy of Sexuality, 16 Rev. Radical Pol. Econ. 143 (1984); Hantzis, Is Gender Justice a Completed Agenda? (book review), 100 Harv. L. Rev. 690 (1987); MacKinnon, Feminism, Marxism, Method and the State: Toward Feminist Jurisprudence, in D. Weisberg ed., Feminist Legal Theory: Foundations 427 (Temple Univ. Press, 1993); MacKinnon, Feminism, Marxism, Method, and the State: An Agenda for Theory, in *id.* at 437.

18. See, e.g., A. Jaggar, Feminist Politics and Human Nature (1983); P. Roos, Gender and Work 119–154 (1985); Rubin, The Traffic in Women, in R. Reiter ed., Toward an Anthropology of Women 157 (1975).

19. It is sometimes said that baby-selling violates the thirteenth amendment. See, e.g., Holder, Surrogate Motherhood: Babies for Fun and Profit, 12 Law, Med. & Health Care 115 (1984).

20. Biblical "surrogate" interactions may be seen in this way. See Genesis 16 (Abraham, Sarah, and Hagar); Genesis 30 (Jacob, Rachel, and Bilhah). Perhaps some would see artificial insemination as analogously oppressive to men, but the situations are asymmetrical because of the present gender structure.

21. See, e.g., Surrogate Motherhood: A Practice That's Still Undergoing Birth Pangs, L.A. Times, Mar. 22, 1987, 6, at 12, col. 2 (citing research finding that "[t]he average surrogate mother is white, attended two years of college, married young and has all the children she and her husband want"). Perhaps allowing surrogacy but not permitting adoption for a price would worsen the double bind for poor women, who are

less likely to be chosen as surrogates by the couples who seek this arrangement. To underscore the irony of the double bind, consider the testimony of an adopting mother who fears that surrogacy "can exploit the lower classes and the women of the Third World," and thus finds it "unconscionable" to choose as surrogates women who are poverty-stricken and need the money. *Id.* §6, at 12, col. 1.

22. See Smith, Parenting and Property, in J. Trebilcot ed., Mothering: Essays in Feminist Theory 199 (1983). Artificial insemination—and for that matter traditional procreation—poses a similar issue of genetic property. It is just as inappropriate to conceive of parent-child bonding in terms of women's genetic "property" as in terms of men's. But in the context of the present gender structure, the desire to carry on the woman's genetic line is less likely to make men fungible. Moreover, the interests of women and men are asymmetrical because the carrying of the child in the woman's body (whether or not it is hers genetically) is a stronger factor in interrelationships with a child than an abstract genetic relationship.

23. One such example occurs when a woman bears a child for her childless sister.

24. In light of the apparent strength of people's desires for fathers' genetic offspring, the ban on profit would also be difficult to enforce. As with adoption, we would see a black market develop in surrogacy.

25. Of course, we should decide upon a reasonable time limit during which she must make up her mind, for it would be injurious to the child if her life were in limbo for very long. This could be done analogously with statutory waiting periods for adoption to become final after birth.

A Feminist Analysis of Adoption

Nancy E. Dowd

. . . Adoption has received relatively little attention from feminists.[1] Yet it touches many areas of feminist concern: reproductive choice and reproductive technologies, including abortion and surrogacy; definitions and concepts of family; parental rights and roles; gay and lesbian rights; the intersection of gender, race, and class; gender roles (even though criticized as essentialist); issues of sameness and difference; choice and the contexts in which women's choices are made; and the valuing and devaluing of mothering and nurturance. There may well be, then, not simply "a" feminist analysis of adoption, but multiple analyses of adoption from the range of feminist thought.

In this review I first set out the methodology and structure of Elizabeth Bartholet's argument in *Family Bonds*. I evaluate Bartholet's thesis from a feminist perspective and present a potential feminist construction of adoption. . . .

I. Bartholet's Critique and Proposed Reform of the Adoption System

Bartholet presents her thesis within a powerful drama—the story of her own decade-long battle with infertility after the birth of her son, and her subsequent adoption of two children from Peru. It is an extraordinary yet ordinary tale, as is the story of every family's creation. Her description of her personal experience is stunning and unforgettable, because she confronts the core issue of the biologic model: how will I feel about this child who is not "mine"? But most significantly, she captures the special magic, the unique insights of adoption: that what we long for and what matters is to parent, and that the children with whom we connect, by whatever means, create the family that was meant to be. Her personal story serves as a connecting thread throughout the book and brings her discussion of policy, structure, and rules into clear focus.

In her critique, Bartholet exposes the biologic bias in the structure of infertility treatment and adoption. She compares the resources devoted to infertility treatment with the constraints imposed upon adoption.[2] What is distressing about this structure, she argues, is not only that it supports reproduction over adoption, but also that it discourages many of those who ultimately fail to reproduce from becoming parents at all. The biologic bias makes adoption a last resort obstructed by the hurdles of extensive regulation and significant expense. Although purportedly designed to further the best interests of children, the adoption system leaves many children without parents or in the limbo of the foster care system.[3]

By connecting and comparing infertility treatment and adoption, Bartholet locates adoption on a continuum of preferred means to create family, with biology first, reproductive technologies second, and adoption a distant third. This continuum is reflected in her own experience of coming to adoption reluctantly and sadly, and feeling betrayed by her body. Bartholet argues that this unavoidable sadness and pain is unnecessarily reinforced by the overvaluing of the biologic family and the stigmatization of adoption. Instead, she asserts, adoption should be facilitated and valued as an alternative family form. She envisions an adoption system that builds upon the transformative, positive promise of adoption and minimizes the sorrow and tragedy with which it is inextricably intertwined. This vision is far from the ideology and reality of the current adoption structure, which, as Bartholet demonstrates, reconstructs family in the image of the biologic family. In this structure, children's physical traits and mental characteristics ideally are matched with those of their adoptive parents, so that they may appear to be biologically connected. Indeed, the central event, the reissuance of the birth certificate, imitates biology by inserting the names of the adoptive parents on the certificate as if they were biologic parents. This symbolic event has a startling consequence—it erases the biologic parents, as if they never existed.

Because it is only an imitation of the biologic family, the adoptive family is, by definition, inferior. Bartholet captures the cultural stigma attached to adoption by pointing out the insidious connotations of the familiar reference to birthparents as the "real" or "natural" parents and the intended compliment that one's adopted children look like they are "yours". Society views adoption, she concludes, as a "debased form of parenting" and treats adopted children as "inherently inferior".

Yet as Bartholet demonstrates, available studies indicate that adoption works well for everyone involved.[4] It gives birthparents control over their lives, grants the infertile an opportunity to parent, and affords children love and nurturance. The success of adoptive families suggests that this family form demonstrates the value of nurturing and celebrates the deliberateness of the decision to parent. It also teaches that the absence of a genetic link can be liberating, because it encourages us to see children not as property or as mirrors of adults, but instead as independent, unique beings.

Furthermore, parenting across racial, ethnic, or national lines in adoptive families affirms difference rather than cultural loss. Out of its unique characteristics and challenges, Bartholet suggests, the adoptive family creates connections that shape a different concept of family:

Adoption creates a family that in important ways is not "nuclear." It creates a family that is *connected* to another family, the birth family, and often to different cultures and to different racial, ethnic, and national groups as well. Adoptive families might teach us something about the value for families of connection with the larger community (p. 186).

In order to construct the new adoption system she envisions, and better to value the adoptive family, Bartholet evaluates several aspects of the existing system in detail. They include the sealed records system; the parental screening system; racial matching in adoption; and the requirements of international adoption. Her proposals for reform in these areas are controversial; they attack aspects of the system over which there is little agreement except on the need for change.

In the chapter on sealed records, Bartholet points out that the traditional model of adoption has been to sever all links with the birth family by sealing all information on the birth family and denying access unless there is an overwhelming necessity to open the records. Recent statutory reforms in many states make it easier to open records and/or to connect adult adoptees with their biologic parents. The growth of private adoptions also has facilitated more openness; it is often a condition of the adoption.

Bartholet's response to the issue of more openness is mixed. She sees the value of openness, but she is troubled by the biologic arguments of the search movement, a grass-roots movement of birthparents and adult adoptees. The most extreme supporters of the search movement argue that adoption should be outlawed or minimized to preserve biologic family, even if that requires long-term foster care for children. On the other hand, Bartholet notes that, although supporters of closed records talk in terms of privacy, their arguments sound suspiciously like condemnations of those who place a child for adoption, and they play on a sense of threat from birthparents.

Bartholet's recommendations regarding sealed records reflect her mixed response. She argues that ideally, the presumption of sealed records should be reversed, and records should be open absent a showing of good cause to close them. However, she sees the search movement, with its profound hostility toward adoption, as a real threat to more open policies. Openness, she says, may need to be deferred to some future date when society places a higher value on adoption. Finally, Bartholet questions what openness means and notes specifically that openness concerning information, and even meeting or ongoing contact, is different from openness for purposes of shared control.

Bartholet is far more critical of parental screening. Screening, in the form of a home study report, has two purposes: to determine eligibility to adopt and to rank parents for matching with prospective children. Screening for eligibility is extremely intrusive, an unrestricted inquiry into virtually every aspect of the potential adopter's life. But Bartholet's strongest criticism is reserved for the matching process. The ranking and matching process is filled with biologic bias and blatant discrimination on the basis of race, religion, national origin, disability, marital status, and sexual orientation. Furthermore, she notes, it is a system that those with more money can avoid. . . .

Bartholet frames the screening issue as a battle between advocates of traditional screening and advocates of independent adoption, with each arguing that the adoption structure should emulate its own strict or relaxed screening requirements. She challenges the underlying premises of the debate between these two camps by advocating a system that values the child's interest in a nurturing relationship. Under her system, the role of the adoption agency would be to facilitate adoption. Bartholet would eliminate screening both for eligibility and matching, or, in the alternative, impose a heavy burden on the state to justify it. She argues that no screening exists for biologic parents, or for those who use reproductive technologies or other means to have children. Rather than require proof of fitness, Bartholet would presume fitness. Screening would be universally required but would be used only to eliminate parents who are unfit. . . . Matching of adoptive parents with children under Bartholet's reformed system would be based on the choices of adoptive parents, who would be served on a first-come, first-served basis.

Bartholet justifies this reform from the perspective of potential adoptive children. She argues that the presence of so many children in foster care demonstrates the negative effect of the matching process. Children suffer serious and often tragic damage from long-term foster care. Reforms would give children a better opportunity to connect with parents and a home.

Bartholet is especially critical of racial matching in domestic and international adoption.[5] She argues that the explicit consideration of race and the preference for or requirement of racial-matching conflicts with our articulated social and legal consensus, at least in theory, on the place of race elsewhere in our society. Bartholet opposes racial matching on the grounds that because most adopters are white, these policies deprive black children of permanent homes and consign them to lengthy or permanent stays in foster care. Although expanding the pool of black adopters would seem to be the solution, Bartholet doubts that adequate resources would be devoted to this goal. Moreover, she claims that empirical studies on transracial adoption fail to support the claim of its harmful effects, in contrast to the powerful evidence of harm from delays in permanent placement. Bartholet rejects what she characterizes as a separatist argument—that the black community is harmed by transracial adoption—and counters that the elimination of racial hostility is more important than the promotion of cultural difference.

Bartholet would end state-imposed racial matching, but she rejects a system whereby no racial preference could be expressed by the adoptive parents or by children old enough to express a preference. . . .

Having made the case for adoption reform, Bartholet returns in the last two chapters to infertility treatment. The concerns that led her to urge less regulation of adoption move her to advocate greater regulation in this area. In one chapter she lays out the parameters of in-vitro fertilization (IVF) and argues for regulation that would put the brakes on the expansion of IVF.[6] She outlines the need for regulations to inform consumers about costs, benefits, and risks of IVF; mandatory standards for the procedure; and extensive counseling for infertility that includes information, support, and a range of alternatives including adoption.

In the final chapter, she underscores her critique of infertility treatment by exploring issues that arise when surrogacy, egg and sperm donation, and IVF are combined. Using such a procedure, we can identify genetic, gestational, and social parents. The child created and given birth by these means is adopted by adults whose only connection to the child is that they planned her "creation" and want to be parents. . . . Yet the law subjects these adopters to none of the legal hurdles placed in the way of conventional adopters; reproductive technologies are virtually unregulated, with access limited primarily by the ability to pay.

Bartholet's challenging and intriguing comparison exposes the extent to which legal rules favor reproduction—albeit through third parties and sometimes with no genetic connection—over adoption. She argues that we must rethink adoption within this context consistent with our perspective of a reformed adoption system in a more conventional context. She also returns to her fundamental argument that we must reallocate resources and priorities away from infertility treatment and toward adoption.

II. Feminist Analysis: Issues and Perspectives

A. Multiple Strands of Analysis

How might a feminist view the reforms Bartholet suggests? The range of feminist theory suggests that there is no single answer to this question, but rather a rich and useful set of perspectives that provide critical insights, and sometimes conflicting analyses. . . . In this section I simply mean to suggest, without fully exploring, some of the multiple perspectives that feminists might bring to adoption, and in particular the ways feminists might evaluate Bartholet's proposals.

Bartholet's core critique of the biologic bias, and her goal of valuing adoptive families, are consistent with many feminist goals. Feminists have struggled for real, empowered choices for women; for valuing relational ties and connections typical of women; and for celebrating and valuing women's differences with each other and as compared to men. All of these goals, particularly focused on but not only relevant to women, are reflected in Bartholet's reform proposals. Furthermore, Bartholet's position is consistent with feminists' efforts to redefine families and parenting toward a recognition and understanding of nurturance, and away from rigid traditional models. Finally, her position is consistent with feminists' concerns for children, including the need for issues to be viewed from children's perspectives, or at least for children's voices to be heard.

On the other hand, some feminists might reject, or be cautious about, Bartholet's views. Feminists critical of society's limited construction of gender roles might be concerned that valuing adoption, like pouring resources into reproductive technologies, might simply reify the primary role of women as mothers. Women's childbearing and childrearing role has been the cornerstone for legal justification of their inferior status and subordination as well as the condemnation of homosexuality. From this perspective, the goal ought not to be to shift resources from infertility treatment to adoption, as Bartholet suggests, but rather to challenge the essentialism of motherhood to the cultural construction of "woman." Any reform of adoption, then, implicates the meaning and valuing of motherhood.

Feminists concerned with the discourse and images of law reform might react in different ways to Bartholet's proposed reform of the traditional screening process to require only minimal screening for adoptive parents. Feminists have pointed out that family definitions have usually been controlled and defined by patriarchal norms. The screening process reflects a particular value structure and definition of parenting and the family. Feminist analysis would suggest that one should carefully examine the underlying value structure of a new screening system, and the beneficiaries of that reform. Feminists who have critiqued traditional family norms might strongly support Bartholet's reform because it might enable nontraditional families to adopt. But other feminists might be uncomfortable with presuming fitness to parent based on the minimal abuse or neglect standard as inconsistent with prioritizing the interests of children.[7]

Bartholet's attack on racial matching in the screening process also might provoke serious disagreement from feminists. Some feminists have focused on race as a parallel yet different system of domination and discrimination, borrowing the equality, rights, and justice rhetoric of liberal jurisprudence used in the civil rights movement. Liberal feminists might agree with Bartholet's underlying argument about the inconsistency of race matching with civil rights policy but charge that, by failing to reject absolutely any consideration of race, she is trying to have it both ways. Why should adoptive parents be permitted to use the structure of the state to enforce choices based on explicit racial criteria? If, as Bartholet argues, classic strict scrutiny analysis militates against current racial matching, race should be entirely eliminated from matching parents and children.[8] The adoption structure, on this view, should incorporate the principle that race cannot be used as a factor by any of the participants.[9]

Other feminists have considered the differences as well as the connections among women, and have critiqued feminism for its implicit race (white) and class (middle class) stance.[10] And still others have challenged us to consider the intersections of gender, race, and class not as separate categories of being but rather as multiple, interacting, connected layers of consciousness.[11] Feminists who insist that race and class must always be taken into account along with gender might argue that the failure to do so is a serious drawback in Bartholet's overall analytical approach. And they might argue, as might feminists coming from other perspectives, that, in the particular instance of transracial adoption, race should be taken into account in placing racial minorities, based on evidence that same-race placement benefits children even if cross-race placements do not hurt them, and that such placement is vital to the group interests of racial minorities.

Furthermore, feminists concerned with women's choices and the construction of choice might question whether adoptive parents should be the sole parties to exercise choice in the matching process in the traditional adoption structure. Feminists have looked at choice-making in terms of both rights and context. The rights perspective has been the basis for advocating women's unilateral right of choice in abortion. No parallel exists to confer unilateral or superior rights of choice on adoptive parents to connect them with children. Or perhaps birth parents should have an equal or determinative choice. And if children have an opinion that can be articulated, how can their choices be honored? Moreover, a feminist concerned with the context of choices might question the actual process of choice-making apart from formal rights or freedom to choose. In adoption the choices of all parties are strongly influenced by innumerable factors, and interwoven among them are the roles, boundaries, and constructions of women's lives for both adoptive mothers and birthmothers. It might be equally logical to construct adoption as a first-come, first-served system for both parents and children: as parents and children come to the front of the line (with their place in line determined solely by timing), they simply should be matched.

These perspectives by no means exhaust the range of feminist analysis; this brief exploration of feminist analysis suggests, however, the multiplicity and complexity of such analysis and the way it might contribute to a thorough evaluation of traditional adoption and proposed adoption reform. . . . The question to which I now turn is whether women or others traditionally devalued or marginalized are silenced in the existing adoption structure or in Bartholet's reform proposals.

B. Feminist Analysis and Birthparents

Feminist analysis has insistently asked which voices are heard and which voices are silent in particular legal structures. Feminists have attacked the law's claim to objectivity and neutrality and have exposed the point of view or voice of particular legal rules, arguing that they tend to reflect the perspectives of those who have made up the rules—predominantly, privileged white males. Feminists' focus on the perspective of legal rules demonstrated the absence of women's perspectives, concerns, priorities, and understandings in law. Either the subjects of women's concerns go entirely unaddressed, or those who purport to speak for women do so without ever listening to them. Finally, feminists have demonstrated how purportedly neutral rules can disproportionately affect women in a gendered, *un*equal world. This insight has led feminists to insist that existing rules or law reform must be considered in view of their actual impact on women.

Bartholet's voice in this book is the voice of the adoptive mother. This point of view is made clear both by the inclusion of Bartholet's own adoption story and by the aspects of the adoption structure she chooses to write about.[12] The voices that are heard least in this book are those of birthparents. That is not to say that Bartholet does not empathize with birthparents, nor that she excludes them from her vision of a reconstructed adoption structure and a valued adoptive family.[13] It is rather to suggest that, among the many insights feminism could offer to the analysis of adoption, the analysis that adds most to this book considers the role of birthparents in adoption.

In many respects the traditional adoption model strongly disfavors birthparents. Adoption for birthparents means sending a child into a black hole from which no further information or confirmation of the well-being of the child can be gleaned. Birth-parents can be asked to finalize the nearly irrevocable termination of their rights within hours or days of the birth of their child.[14] Historically, the mother's consent was suffi-cient if she was unmarried. Even with the contemporary expansion of paternal rights, the rights of fathers are not equal to those of mothers.[15] Men must claim and establish their fatherhood. When fatherhood is undisputed or established, it still does not grant fathers equal power to decide whether to raise their child or consent to an adoption.[16]

The justification for the traditional construction of adoption was the moral con-demnation of unwed motherhood.[17] Adoption was viewed as the sole answer to an un-desirable situation. Moral fault justified the control of adoption by the state and the absolute denial of any role for the birthparents in the placement or future life of the child. The development of the independent adoption system has significantly shifted the balance of control toward the birthparents both in the placement of children and in the long-term relationship of birthparents with children. Even outside independent adoption, the trend toward openness has recast the position of birthparents.

Birthparents have always had enormous power, nonetheless, in certain aspects of the adoption structure. If an adoption is contested, all of the power of the biologic bias that Bartholet has documented so well weighs in their favor.[18] The legal rules render the adoption void if there is some error in the consent process, regardless of the du-ration or quality of the bond that has developed between the child and adoptive par-ents. The notion of children's rights has not made a dent in this approach.[19] The fo-cus is on the parents, and the interests of the biologic parents are paramount; the rights of the child and the adoptive parents are not even weighed in the decision. . . .

Where might feminist analysis lead? First, it might expose the context within which birthparents operate, particularly to the extent that it limits their choices. . . .

1. CHOOSING ADOPTION AND THE STRUCTURE OF SURRENDER: ISSUES OF CLASS, CHOICE, AND CONTROL

The feminist concern with the role of power and class, especially in connection with the control of reproductive decisions, weighs in favor of enhancing the control and range of options that birthparents exercise in the adoption process. Many birthparents operate within a context suffused with racial and class inequality. Those inequalities se-riously constrain already limited choices in the event of an unplanned or unwanted pregnancy. Bartholet acknowledges the argument that consent to adoption may rest on misery and exploitation. But she argues that we must deal with the world as it is, even if ideally we might want to eliminate many of the factors that lead people to sur-render their children.

Yet the class issues in adoption cannot be ignored. To do so ignores why many birth-parents surrender children, who can realistically consider adoption,[20] and who con-tests adoptions.[21] To ignore class issues is to ignore issues of both power and gender, because women are frequently the sole birthparent in adoption, and their disadvan-taged economic status significantly affects their choices. Money pervades adoption, and it does so in all the wrong ways.

The limits within which birthparents operate sharply contrast with choice for adoptive parents. As Bartholet points out, becoming an adoptive parent makes choice central: "Adoption involves choice on a scale most of us don't generally experience. You can't fall accidentally into adoption, as you can into pregnancy. You exercise choice down to the wire" (pp. xviii–xix). It is a choice that enables one to become a parent; unlike infertility treatment, adoption is an achievable goal. It permits the adoptive parent to take control in contrast to the loss of control involved in infertility. Bartholet's goal of reconfiguring the adoption choice is consistent with the rhetoric of choice and is sensitive to the constructions of motherhood that insure responsibility and freedom rather than dictate gender roles grounded in patriarchal patterns.

Yet I question whether the reconstruction of the choice to adopt as a truly valued one is merely another form of exploitation if the choice is made within a context in which other options are not realistically available for birthparents. Even if we accept Bartholet's argument that we cannot resolve the huge issues that constrain birthparents' decisionmaking, we should still examine how much choice and control birthparents exercise in the legal surrender of their parental rights, and in the placement and post-placement processes. A feminist approach would require empowerment, support, and counseling. It would construct the process and choice of adoption as a positive act of parenting, rather than as a stigmatized rejection of parenting, sanctioned by loss of choice and control. It is essential to that reconstruction that, at a minimum, reproductive choice be assured to *all* women. Support for adoption must not become coercion to prohibit or discourage abortion or to withhold birth control. The meager support, economic and otherwise, of single-parent families is yet another not-so-subtle form of coercion that ideally should be reformed to support the freedom of birthparents' choice-making, but is far less likely to occur.

Much can be learned toward rethinking the context within which birthparents choose adoption from independent, or private, adoption. Independent adoption accounts for an increasing number of adoptions—currently one third of nonrelated adoptions. In an independent adoption the connection between birthparents and adoptive parents is made either directly or through an intermediary, commonly a physician, attorney, minister, or friend. In the states that most heavily regulate private adoption, the state remains involved in the surrender and placement process by requiring a homestudy and support and counselling for the birthparents, and by monitoring the surrender and finalization.[22] The greatest benefit of the private adoption system for birthparents over the long term is that it allows birthparents to decide the placement of their children. This allows them both to choose the adoptive family and to negotiate post-placement information flow and contact, which can include the birthparents in the construction of the adoptive family and the long-term structure of their children's lives.

The private adoption system looks remarkably similar to Bartholet's reform model of a deregulated adoption system. The most significant difference is that Bartholet argues for a uniform system that does not permit adopters with money to buy the right to be treated differently. To be sure, that aspect of the blatant class bias of the current adoption structure should be eliminated. In addition, both the independent and the traditional adoption systems should be evaluated to determine whether they provide adequate support for birthparents, including financial support, pre- and post-natal care, and psychological counselling. Furthermore, the delivery of those resources must insure that the process of selecting adoptive parents is not affected by who can best provide support for the birthparents. Finally, private adoption, or any other adoption structure, must protect the child's interests and the presumed validity of the birthparents' choice by limiting the time for revocation or challenges, and yet insuring that all parties are represented in a challenge.

2. DEFINING THE ADOPTIVE FAMILY AND THE POST-PLACEMENT ROLE OF BIRTHPARENTS: DEFINITIONS OF FAMILY AND PARENT

Consistent with feminist scrutiny of traditional concepts of family, feminist analysis might also challenge the definition and boundaries of the adoptive family. Bartholet argues that the adoptive family should be valued instead of stigmatized, not only because adoption works for both parents and children, but also because the experience of adoptive families has valuable insights for all families. I would argue further that the definition or concept of the adoptive family should include the birthparents. Clearly, they remain a part of the family from the child's perspective, as they are part of the child's understanding of being adopted. The inclusion of the birthparents within the adoptive family makes sense, then, because the child needs to know who they are, and may want to establish a relationship with their birthparents as a child or later as an adult. Within the adoptive family—defined to include the birthparents—decisionmaking concerning the child's relationship with the birthparents ultimately should rest with the adoptive child when she or he is capable of making a reasoned, mature decision. Prior to that it should be presumed that the adoptive parents will exercise that power on behalf of the child with the child's best interests in mind.[23] A presumption or acceptance of connection and the provision of essential information may be sufficient for most adoptees. But for the child who wishes for more, a connection or relationship may be made or attempted at some point in their lives. The ultimate justification for inclusion of the birthparents is not recognition of this practical reality, however, but a vision of family for the child that maximizes the potential for a positive view of the adoption.

The role birthparents should play in the adoptive family, and the role the child should play in the birthparents' family or families, is less easy to define. Inclusion of the birthparents within the definition of family does not presume shared control in the parenting of the adopted children; the autonomy of the adoptive parents should be respected. But the issue of control is temporary. The control that adoptive parents, or any parents, can exercise in the lives of their children lasts only for a limited time. Because family relationships change over time, any definition of family must avoid locking the child, the birthparents, and the adoptive parents into a rigid structure. Flexibility is necessary, and that suggests avoiding a rights analysis that presumes potential conflict within a static set of relationships between adoptive and birthparents, or between the child and one or both sets of parents.

The characteristic response to all of this is fear. But if feminism has taught us nothing else, it has taught us that our view of reality may be constructed by cultural traditions and myths grounded only in fictions to benefit the powerful. The biologic bias that Bartholet so clearly exposes generates the myth of the threat posed by birthparents to the very parenthood of adoptive parents. It also reinforces, as Bartholet points out, the construction of adoption as a stigmatized, devalued choice that labels the woman who surrenders her child a "bad mother" who has denied her biological role. If we believe in the power and value of the bonds of the adoptive family, those bonds need not exclude the birthparents. And if we value the choice of adoption as a loving, selfless, responsible choice, that act should be supported by permitting the birthparents to remain connected to the adopted child.

In addition, open adoption should be more clearly and strongly supported in a reformed adoption system.[24] Open adoption has evolved within the independent adoption system along with a different system of screening and matching. It is an example of private decisionmaking and structuring that has evolved outside of, and in contradiction to, the traditional adoption structure. Open adoption is based on communication or "openness" between biological and adoptive parents that ranges from the exchange of life history and medical information directly or through an intermediary, to completely open arrangements between the birthparents and the adoptive parents in which all parents meet and the birthparents maintain access to the child throughout the child's life.

Open adoption is consistent with the definition of the adoptive family that I have proposed. As Bartholet notes, the trend toward more openness has allowed for greater flow of information. I argue for moving farther in that direction. The most notable drawback of open adoption at present is the unenforceability of open adoption arrangements after the adoption is finalized.[25] The law shifts power from the birthparents to the adoptive parents and preserves the rights of adoptive parents even in the face of their voluntary waiver of those rights.[26] These arrangements should be enforced unless to do so would harm the child. With or without an express agreement, whether the power to parent can be shared is a challenging and difficult question yet to be explored, but one that must be addressed with the perspective and interests of the child as primary.[27]

3. BIRTHMOTHERS AND BIRTHFATHERS: DIFFERENCE, EQUALITY, AND PARENTING

The feminist challenge to gender neutrality suggests that a reconsideration and reconstruction of the role of birthparents in adoption also requires separate examination of the roles of birthmothers and birthfathers. For birthmothers, the weight of the tradition of motherhood affects the way they experience adoption and often stigmatizes them for surrendering their child. Many birthmothers also make their decisions within the context of low income or poverty, and the confounding dilemmas posed by race. But all make their decisions within a structure that disadvantages women as a class and that provides little support for working parents.[28]

Feminists' long-range goal is to remove from the context of women's decision-making the unique disadvantages of the intersectionalities of gender, race, and class, and to maximize responsible decisions of reproductive and family choice. More immediately, feminists would reconfigure the time frame and circumstances under which birthmothers consent to surrender their children. Birthmothers make this critical decision within physical circumstances that fathers do not experience—pregnancy and childbirth. In considering the consequences of pregnancy and childbirth, one must strike a balance between reinforcing old stereotypes about pregnancy on one hand and acknowledging, on the other, the physical changes, stresses, and the mindbody connections that make a decision to surrender a child especially difficult immediately after childbirth. That balance ought to be resolved in favor of insuring that the birthmother has sufficient time to make a considered decision and that she has a sufficient time for revocation, with or without cause. The discretion to decide within a shorter time period should rest entirely with the birthmother. Short-term foster care could insure that the birthmother would have the option of either caring for the child or having the child cared for during the decisionmaking process.

For birthfathers the issues are quite different. Feminists might want to expose and analyze factors that discourage responsible fatherhood, but at the same time work to redefine the concept of being a father. This redefinition would be particularly sensitive to class issues, which substantially affect the behavior of men by virtue of the traditional economic definition of fatherhood. Feminists also would support birthfathers' ability to parent as a single parent or within a couple.

One of the most pressing questions in the existing adoption structure is where birthfathers should fit into the decisionmaking process.[29] Formal equality doctrine would dictate that fathers have equal rights with mothers, but that presumes that fathers and mothers are equally situated. Not only are men unequally situated in childbearing, but they also more often claim parental rights without exercising parental responsibilities or care after the child is born.[30]

The birthmother should be supported in her decision to place the child if that decision conflicts with the choice of the birthfather. The fundamental premise here is that the relevant family unit at the time of the surrender decision is the mother-child unit. Martha Fineman has argued that the mother-child unit is the core familial unit—that the parental relationship should be privileged over the adult sexual relationship, which would affirm the primary caretaking role of women.[31] Especially in the case of unmarried, separated, or divorced women, this makes sense in terms of what we know about the general patterns of fathers' frequently marginal involvement with their children. One could also argue, based on caretaking patterns within two-parent, married, heterosexual families, that recognition of the mother-child relationship rather than a gender-neutral parent-child relationship reflects current caretaking realities. The most significant barrier to the recognition of the mother-child unit is, Fineman argues, the widespread cultural view of single-mother families as deviant and dysfunctional, despite the social reality of increasing numbers of such families.[32]

Because it largely avoids cultural constructs of gender roles, this view of family seems to make the most sense in adoption scenarios in which the birthmother and birthfather are not in a committed relationship, and in which the burden of the pregnancy and of planning for the life of the child falls entirely or disproportionately on the mother. One could argue that that scenario is itself culturally constructed to some degree, but the biologically unavoidable relationship during pregnancy creates a parental relationship that makes the child uniquely the concern of the birthmother. This should justify a presumption that the decisions regarding placement for adoption, like the decision whether to have the child or choose an abortion, should be hers alone.[33]

What I propose is that the mother-child unit be deemed primary, and that in the absence of the father's demonstrated commitment to that family, the mother should have legal control over the decision to place the child for adoption. The inclusion of the father in the decisionmaking process should be at the option of the mother, but should not be legally required. The father's consent would not be necessary. If the father and mother are married, or if the father is in a long-term committed relationship with the mother that is functionally equivalent to marriage, then he should be entitled to defeat the presumption of sole decisionmaking by demonstrating past parenting skill or present ability and commitment to parent, defined in economic *and* noneconomic terms. In a potential conflict between the birthmother and the birthfather, however, the conflict between supporting the mother's power to determine the child's best interests over the father's opportunity to parent and his desire and ability to parent should be resolved in favor of the mother-child unit. The capability of the mother should only be questioned under circumstances in which she lacks the capacity to make the decision as currently defined in abuse and neglect proceedings. The birthmother should be able to defeat the relationship presumption raised by marriage or a marriage equivalent if she can demonstrate either that the father has no commitment to parenting, based either on past experience or current feelings, or that the relationship has dissolved, even if the legal shell of the marriage remains intact. This view of adoption is closer to the decisionmaking in exercising reproductive choice than to decisionmaking in the post-divorce family. It would confer unilateral decisionmaking rather than shared responsibility or joint custody. In the not-uncommon adoption scenario of unmarried birthparents with no committed relationship, the risks and responsibilities of the child rest on the mother; the father remains free to exercise choices in an entirely different way. The power of decisionmaking should follow where responsibility lies. With infants, that can only be measured by the mother-child relationship during the pregnancy, and the nature of the relationship of the birthfather with the birthmother for the benefit of the child.

Feminists have long criticized the limitation of the traditional father role to that of an economic provider, and have pointed to the continuing predominance of unequal gender roles in the home despite some increased formal equality and new notions of masculinity.[34] They have argued for a model of parenthood based on the role of mothers, which emphasizes nurturing and caretaking.[35] Men's physical differences in their connections to newborns might justify differences in the treatment of birthmothers and birthfathers; widespread social patterns of fathering might also justify differences in treatment.

Several questions arise in response to this argument. First, does this fly in the face of efforts to reconfigure fatherhood? By recognizing the difference in gender roles, do we reconfirm those roles? Second, does this offend formal equality principles? But perhaps most significantly, does this inadvertently undercut the claim by adoptive families that they have developed different, valuable relational ties that embody an alternative model of family? That is, not to value the bond that could exist between men and their children prior to birth and after birth is to revive the notion of a physical concept of bonding, and arguably to play into the strong biologic bias that Bartholet sees at the heart of a misguided adoption structure. The parent-child bond of an adoptive parent is most like the father-child bond—a bond created from the moment of connection, not from the moment of conception or in utero.[36] Women who bear children connect with their children in a unique way because of the experience of pregnancy. But men can bond just as powerfully, and we know they can be as nurturing as women if placed within circumstances that demand it or if they choose.[37]

But, in the final analysis, men must be responsible for their sexual acts and conscious about their decisions to parent. If a father maintains no relationship with the mother, and avoids or ignores knowledge of the pregnancy and provides no support to the mother or child, then the choice whether to involve him in the decisionmaking process should rest with the mother. The mother should not be obligated to give him notice (after all, he has notice if he can count), and she should not have her adoption decision threatened by an unknown, unlocatable, or uninterested father.

. . . There is no doubt that Bartholet's is a voice that will be heard in the discourse of adoption reform. . . . Feminist analysis can add other voices to the discourse, and may help expose key parts of the process by listening to voices silenced or subdued and by preserving multiple relationships for the benefit of the child. Feminist analysis and adoption hold in common transformative power moving beyond traditional norms that can enrich each other. The promise of their synergy is for empowerment, inclusion, and diversity of families.

Notes

This essay is a book review of Family Bonds: Adoption and the Politics of Parenting by Elizabeth Bartholet (Houghton Mifflin 1993). (Page references are to Bartholet's book.)

1. For an excellent overview of scholarship on adoption, including commentary by feminist scholars, see Janet H. Dickson, Comment, The Emerging Rights of Adoptive Parents: Substance or Specter?, 38 UCLA L. Rev. 917 *passim* (1991). For examples of feminist scholarship on adoption, see Katharine T. Bartlett, Rethinking Parenthood as an Exclusive Status: The Need for Legal Alternatives When the Premise of the Nuclear Family Has Failed, 70 Va. L. Rev. 879, 893–899 (1984); Jana B. Singer, The Privatization of Family Law, 1992 Wis. L. Rev. 1443, 1478–1488; and Maureen A. Sweeney, Between Sorrow and Happy Endings: A New Paradigm of Adoption, 2 Yale J.L. & Feminism 329, 343–353 (1990).

Feminist analysis in the area of adoption has often been peripheral to a focus on reproductive technology and surrogacy. Legal scholars in general have not given significant attention to adoption. . . .

2. Infertility treatment is geared toward solving this "problem" without consideration of the alternative of adoption (pp. 28, 30–31). Indeed, it is expected and demanded that infertility be fully explored and "resolved" before consideration of adoption (p. 31).

3. Bartholet does not examine the problems of placing older children or other hard-to-adopt children, including the physically or mentally disabled, or victims of sexual or other abuse. Rather, she focuses on removing barriers to the adoption of children who could easily be placed, which might ultimately benefit hard-to-adopt children as well. Any significant delay in declaring a child legally free for adoption makes the child much more difficult to place.

4. Bartholet discounts the presence of identity and other psychological problems as poorly supported in the literature (pp. 176–177).

5. Bartholet has previously discussed race policies in adoption in Elizabeth Bartholet, Where Do Black Children Belong? The Politics of Race Matching in Adoption, 139 U. Pa. L. Rev. 1163 *passim* (1991).

Her critique of the role of race in adoption could also be applied to disability and religious matching. . . .

6. Bartholet compares the financial, physical, emotional, and other costs of IVF with the remote possibility for a few of producing a child (pp. 201–209). This is one of few areas in which Bartholet makes explicit reference to feminist analysis, which has questioned the insensitivity of IVF programs to women's feelings about infertility (p. 206). But Bartholet also notes that feminists have been divided on IVF, because some see it as a liberating choice rather than as oppressive and harmful (p. 212).

7. One might demand a showing, even a significant showing, that a criteria be related to the ability to parent before the state may screen for it, without shifting to minimal screening. If a further objection is that the high financial cost of screening deters potential adoptive parents, then subsidizing that cost—for example, by covering it under universal health insurance—seems more logical. Indeed, many of the problems associated with the cost of adoption could be alleviated by a public commitment to subsidize these costs, just as the public currently subsidizes biologic reproduction.

The strongest argument for minimal screening, or more meaningful screening, could be made by less conventional adoptive parents, who frequently have to scale the added hurdle presented by entrenched definitions of family that include only traditional nuclear, two-parent, heterosexual, married couples.

I do not mean to suggest here that only feminists value children. Feminism's focus on women and women's concerns has led to a significant concern with children because of the central role that children play in many women's lives and the primary role that women play as caretakers in most children's lives. Women's relationship with their children, the priority of children in their lives, is a unique focus. Yet the valuing of children is not unique to feminism. . . .

8. Of course, one might argue that the benefits of having parents of the same race in the rearing of a child provide the compelling state interest to satisfy a strict scrutiny analysis.

9. Another alternative to promote the adoption of children available in the U.S. would be to disfavor international adoption and promote domestic adoption. It seems a strange irony to advocate adoption of children born in other countries, frequently across racial lines, while children in the United States are unadopted or difficult to place.

10. See, e.g., Kimberlé Crenshaw, Demarginalizing the Intersection of Race and Sex: A Black Feminist Critique of Antidiscrimination Doctrine, Feminist Theory, and

Antiracist Politics, in D. Weisberg ed., Feminist Legal Theory: Foundations 383 (Temple Univ. Press, 1993); Angela P. Harris, Race and Essentialism in Feminist Legal Theory, in *id.* at 348.

11. See, e.g., Paulette M. Caldwell, A Hair Piece: Perspectives on the Intersection of Race and Gender, 1991 Duke L.J. 365, 371–372; Mari Matsuda, When the First Quail Calls: Multiple Consciousness as Jurisprudential Method, 11 Women's Rts. L. Rep. 7, 9 (1989).

12. The fact that her own two adoptions are transracial and transnational has profoundly influenced, and continues to influence, her experience of adoption and parenting (pp. 234–235).

13. Bartholet hints at a reconception of family that includes birthparents: "My postadoption self wonders whether children in our society might not be better off if parenting relationships here were more qualified by choice and subject to change, with children encouraged to form a broader range of intimate connections and empowered to opt out of bad relationships" (p. 46).

14. See, e.g., Ariz. Rev. Stat. Ann. §§8–106(E), 8- 107(B) (1989) (establishing that consent cannot be given before 72 hours after the birth of the child); Fla. Stat. chs. 63.082(4), 63.085(1)(c) (1993) (establishing that consent may be executed immediately after the birth of the child). See generally Dickson, *supra* note 1, at 969 (noting that the timing and binding quality of birthparents' consent varies widely from state to state).

15. See Dickson, *supra* note 1, at 970 n.274; see also Katharine T. Bartlett, Re-Expressing Parenthood, 98 Yale L.J. 293, 319 (1988) (noting cases in which an expression of will by the mother trumps a contrary expression by the father).

16. See Bartlett, *supra* note 15, at 316–319; Daniel C. Zinman, Note, Father Knows Best: The Unwed Father's Right to Raise His Infant Surrendered for Adoption, 60 Fordham L. Rev. 971, 981 (1992).

17. See Dickson, *supra* note 1, at 919–927. Until the last decade or so, the social stigma placed on all members of the adoption triangle was negative. "[T]he birthmother was 'promiscuous,' the child a 'bastard,' and the adoptive parents 'barren.'" *Id.* at 926.

18. See, e.g., DeBoer v. Schmidt (In re Clausen), 502 N.W.2d 649 (Mich), *stay denied sub nom.* DeBoer v. DeBoer v. Schmidt, 114 S. Ct. 1 (1993). In *DeBoer* a baby girl born in Iowa on February 8, 1991, was relinquished two days later by her birthmother, Cara Clausen. At that time, Clausen named the child's father as Scott Seefeldt, who executed a release of custody form on February 14, 1991. The DeBoers, Michigan residents, filed a petition for adoption of the baby with an Iowa court on February 25, 1991, were granted custody during the pendency of the proceeding, and returned to Michigan with the child. See *DeBoer,* 502 N.W.2d at 652.

On March 6, 1991, Clausen filed a motion to revoke her release in which she admitted that she had lied about the child's paternity and named Daniel Schmidt as the father of the child. A week later Schmidt filed an affidavit of paternity and moved to block the adoption. The DeBoers resisted both actions, arguing that Clausen's consent was valid and that Schmidt had a prior history as an absentee parent to his previous children. See *id.* at 652–653. The parties battled through Iowa and Michigan courts over Schmidt's rights; the validity of Clausen's consent was never seriously questioned. The courts ultimately held that absent a finding of unfitness, Schmidt was entitled to block the adoption. See *id.* at 667–668. Some two-and-a-half years after placement with the DeBoers, the child was transferred to the custody of Clausen and Schmidt, now married, on August 2, 1993. . . .

For Bartholet's commentary on *DeBoer,* see Elizabeth Bartolet, Blood Parents vs. Real Parents, N.Y. Times, July 13, 1993, at A19 (arguing that the child should remain with her adoptive parents and calling for reforms in the laws that govern consent and relinquishment).

19. See generally Wendy A. Fitzgerald, Maturity, Difference, and Mystery: Children's Perspectives and the Law, 36 Ariz. L. Rev. 11 (1994) (proposing that the law should "validate children's personhood by recognizing their perspectives"); Martha Minow, Rights for the Next Generation: A Feminist Approach to Children's Rights, 9 Harv. Women's L.J. 1, 1–24 (1986) (asserting that the law should refrain from comparing the abilities of children and of adults to address their needs); Barbara B. Woodhouse, Hatching the Egg: A Child-Centered Perspective on Parents' Rights, 14 Cardozo L. Rev. 1746, 1748–1754 (1993) (arguing that "it is parents' rights, as currently understood, that undermine those values . . . necessary to children's welfare").

20. Statistics indicate that as family income decreases, the number of women who adopt children correspondingly drops, except in adoptions of related children. See Christine A. Bachrach, Patricia F. Adams, Soledad Sambrano & Kathryn A. London, Adoption in the 1980's, Advance Data (Nat'l Ctr. for Health Statistics, U.S. Dept. of Health & Human Servs.), Jan. 5, 1990, at 4.

21. Legal costs in a disputed adoption can range between $12,000 and $50,000. See Telephone Interview with Arthur Ginsburg, Attorney at Icard, Merrill, Cullis, Timm, Furen & Ginsburg, P.A., Sarasota, Fla. (Oct. 6, 1993).

22. See National Committee for Adoption, Adoption Factbook: United States Data, Issues Regulations and Resources 22–23 (1989) (showing that, of states permitting independent adoption, all but Hawaii either require or may order a homestudy before finalization of adoption).

23. The decision about the presence of the birthfamily in the life of the adoptive child and adoptive parents should be aided by unbiased input from child development specialists and others who will be guided by the best interests of the child. Although "best interests" is a standard strongly criticized in other aspects of family law, particularly because it permits the infusion of judicial bias, here I presume the ability of the adoptive parents to act in their child's best interest. Whether this presumption is any less problematic is debatable.

24. "Open adoption" has been defined as an adoption in which "the birth parents meet the adoptive parents . . . [and] relinquish all legal, moral, and nurturing rights to the child, but retain the right to continuing contact and to knowledge of the child's whereabouts and welfare." Annette Baran, Reuben Pannor & Arthur D. Sorosky, Open Adoption, 21 Soc. Work 97, 97 (1976). See generally Lincoln Caplan, An Open Adoption 85 (1990) (giving an historical account of open adoption in the United States).

25. Cf. In re Adoption of N., 355 N.Y.S.2d 956, 960 (Sur. Ct. 1974) ("[S]eparation agreements between parents do not . . . prevent a court from departing from provisions of such an agreement."). But cf. Michaud v. Wawruck, 551 A.2d 738, 741–742 (Conn. 1988) (finding that public policy does not forbid agreements between genetic and adoptive parents). See generally Annotation, Postadoption Visitation by Natural Parent, 78 A.L.R. 4th 218, 230–237 (1990) (outlining various strains of case law). The courts have been somewhat more willing to enforce visitation agreements in stepparent adoptions, or with grandparents, whose rights of visitation have some statutory support. See Karen Czapanskiy, Babies, Parents, and Grandparents: A Story in Two Cases, 1 J. Gender & L. 85, 87 n.11 (1993); Margaret M. Mahoney, Support and Custody Aspects of the Stepparent-Child Relationship, 70 Cornell L. Rev. 38, 61–78 (1984).

26. There are many power issues here, all difficult ones. Prior to adoption, power lies with the birthparents, although much in the way the system operates sometimes seems designed to prevent them from knowing this. After adoption, the power shifts entirely to the adoptive parents. How can we prevent either side from taking advantage of the other? I do not advocate equal parenting, but I do advocate that each party acknowledge the existence of the other. Furthermore, the adoptive parents should, at minimum, provide ongoing information about the child and enough contact to facilitate a meeting at some point in time, if desired, between the birthparents and the child.

27. It seems to me essential that the child's interest must be determinative, but I would be the first to admit that it is not clear how this would be done. The "best interest of the child" standard is notoriously indeterminate and often subordinates the very interests of the children it purportedly protects. See Fitzgerald, *supra* note 19, at 115, 120.

28. See Nancy E. Dowd, Work and Family: Restructuring the Workplace, 32 Ariz. L. Rev. 431, 442–468 (1990).

29. See Daniel Callahan, Bioethics and Fatherhood, 1992 Utah L. Rev. 735, 735–746; Mary Kay Kisthardt, Of Fatherhood, Families and Fantasy: The Legacy of Michael H. v. Gerald D., 65 Tul. L. Rev. 585 *passim* (1991); Zinman, *supra* note 16, at 981–992.

30. See Karen Czapanskiy, Volunteers and Draftees: The Struggle for Parental Equality, 38 UCLA L. Rev. 1415, 1415–1416 (1991).

31. See Martha Fineman, Intimacy Outside of the Natural Family: The Limits of Privacy, 23 Conn. L. Rev. 955, 970–972 (1991).

32. See *id.* at 971.

33. I do not mean to suggest that pregnancy is solely a biological function. Up to birth the mother has invested nine months of "something more than biology." Quilloin v. Walcott, 434 U.S. 246, 255–256 (1978). It hardly seems a disparate treatment of fathers to require that they make some contribution besides semen in order to have equal say in decisions regarding the child.

34. See, e.g., Nancy E. Dowd, Family Values and Valuing Family: A Blueprint for Family Leave, 30 Harv. J. on Legis. 335, 341–344 (1993).

35. See, e.g., Woodhouse, *supra* note 19, at 1844–1851 (1993) (arguing for a "generist" notion of fatherhood).

36. For a general discussion of bonding, see John Bowlby, A Secure Base: Parent-Child Attachment and Healthy Human Development 3–15 (1988).

37. See Kara L. Boucher & Ruthann M. Macolini, The Prenatal Rights of Unwed Fathers: A Developmental Perspective, 20 N.C. Cent. L.J. 45, 56–61 (1992).

TABLE OF CASES

A case is included here if it is a principal case or one that is the subject of discussion in the text or notes. Italic numbers indicate principal cases.

INDEX

CONTRIBUTORS

ANITA L. ALLEN is Professor of Law, Georgetown University Law Center.

LORI B. ANDREWS is Professor of Law, Chicago-Kent College of Law of the Illinois Institute of Technology.

ELVIA R. ARRIOLA is Professor of Law, University of Texas School of Law.

MARIE ASHE is Professor of Law, Suffolk University Law School.

REGINA AUSTIN is Professor of Law, University of Pennsylvania School of Law.

MARGARET A. BALDWIN is Professor of Law, Florida State University College of Law.

MARY E. BECKER is Professor of Law, University of Chicago School of Law.

NAOMI R. CAHN is Associate Professor of Law, George Washington University National Law Center.

MARTHA CHAMALLAS is Professor of Law, University of Pittsburgh School of Law.

RUTH COLKER is Professor of Law, University of Pittsburgh School of Law.

GENA COREA is an author, reporter, and Associate Director, Institute on Women and Technology.

MARION G. CRAIN is Professor of Law, University of North Carolina School of Law.

KIMBERLÉ CRENSHAW is Professor of Law, Columbia University School of Law.

NANCY E. DOWD is Professor of Law, University of Florida College of Law.

ANDREA DWORKIN is an author and orator.

NANCY EHRENREICH is Professor of Law, University of Denver College of Law.

THOMAS I. EMERSON (died 1991) was Augustus E. Lines Professor Emeritus of Law, Yale University School of Law.

LARS O. ERICSSON is Associate Professor of Philosophy, University of Stockholm.

SUSAN ESTRICH is Robert Kingsley Professor of Law and Political Science, University of Southern California Law Center.

JODY FREEMAN is Visiting Professor, University of California at Los Angeles School of Law.

MARY JOE FRUG (died 1991) was Professor of Law, New England School of Law.

LINDA GORDON is Professor of History, University of Wisconsin, Madison.

SUSAN GRIFFIN is a writer and poet.

LORI L. HEISE is associated with the Health and Development Policy Project.

NAN D. HUNTER is Associate Professor of Law, Brooklyn Law School.

ALICE KESSLER-HARRIS is Professor of History, Rutgers, State University of New Jersey, New Brunswick.

RAE LANGTON is Lecturer, Department of Philosophy, Monash University, Clayton, Victoria, Australia.

SYLVIA A. LAW is Professor of Law and Co-Director, Arthur Garfield Hays Civil Liberties Memorial Program, New York University School of Law.

CHRISTINE A. LITTLETON is Professor of Law, University of California at Los Angeles School of Law.

CATHARINE A. MACKINNON is Professor of Law, University of Michigan Law School.

MARTHA R. MAHONEY is Professor of Law, University of Miami School of Law.

JULIANNE MALVEAUX is an economist and syndicated columnist in San Francisco.

CARLIN MEYER is Professor of Law, New York Law School.

LAURIE NSIAH-JEFFERSON is Research Scientist, New Jersey State Department of Health.

FRANCES OLSEN is Professor of Law, University of California at Los Angeles School of Law.

CAROLE PATEMAN is Professor of Political Science, University of California at Los Angeles.

LOIS PINEAU was formerly Professor of Philosophy, Kansas State University.

RICHARD A. POSNER is Justice, U.S. Court of Appeals, Chicago, and Senior Lecturer, University of Chicago School of Law.

MARGARET JANE RADIN is Professor of Law, Stanford University School of Law.

DOROTHY E. ROBERTS is Professor of Law, Rutgers, State University of New Jersey, School of Law, Newark.

RUTHANN ROBSON is Professor of Law, City University of New York Law School at Queen's College.

CAROL SANGER is Professor of Law, Columbia University School of Law.

SUSAN SCHECHTER is Coordinator, Women's Education Project, Center for Democratic Alternatives, New York.

ELIZABETH M. SCHNEIDER is Professor of Law, Brooklyn Law School.

VICKI SCHULTZ is Professor of Law, Yale University School of Law.

JOAN W. SCOTT is Professor of Social Science, Institute for Advanced Study, Princeton.

RIVA SIEGEL is Professor of Law, Yale University School of Law.

RONNIE J. STEINBERG is Professor of Sociology, Temple University.

NADINE STROSSEN is Professor of Law, New York Law School.

JUDITH JARVIS THOMSON is Professor of Philosophy, Massachusetts Institute of Technology.

JUDITH R. WALKOWITZ is Professor of History, Johns Hopkins University.

ROBIN L. WEST is Professor of Law, Georgetown University Law Center.

NORMA JULIET WIKLER was formerly Professor of Sociology, University of California at Santa Cruz; and Research Associate, Institute for the Study of Social Change, University of California at Berkeley.

JOAN C. WILLIAMS is Professor of Law, Washington College of Law, American University.

JENNIFER WRIGGINS is Associate Professor of Law, University of Maine School of Law.